The Impact of COVID-19 on Prison Conditions and Penal Policy

The Impact of COVID-19 on Prison Conditions and Penal Policy presents the results of a worldwide exchange of information on the impact of COVID-19 in prisons. It also focuses on the human rights questions that have been raised during the pandemic, relating to the treatment of prisoners in institutions for both juveniles and adults worldwide.

The first part brings together the findings and conclusions of leading prison academics and practitioners, presenting national reports with information on the prison system, prison population rates, how COVID-19 was and is managed in prisons, and its impact on living conditions inside prisons and on reintegration programmes. Forty-four countries are covered – many in Europe, but also Argentina, Brazil, Chile, Colombia, Perú, Costa Rica, Canada, the USA, Kenya, South Africa, China, India, Japan, Australia and New Zealand. In the second part, thematic chapters concentrate explicitly on the impact of the pandemic on the application of international human rights standards in prisons and on worldwide prison population rates. The book concludes by drawing out the commonalities and diverging practices between jurisdictions, discussing the impact of measures introduced and reflecting on what could be learnt from policies that emerged during the pandemic. Particular attention is paid to whether "reductionist" strategies that emerged during the pandemic can be used to counteract mass incarceration and prison overcrowding in the future.

Although the book reflects the situation until mid 2021, after the second and during the third wave of the pandemic, it is highly relevant to the current situation, as the living conditions in prisons did not change significantly during the following waves, which showed high infection rates (in particular in the general population), but increased vaccination rates, too. In prisons, problems the pandemic raises have an even greater impact than for the general society.

Revealing many notable and interesting changes in prison life and in release programmes, this book is essential reading for students and scholars of penology, criminology, law, sociology and public health. It will also appeal to criminal justice practitioners and policy makers.

Frieder Dünkel is Professor Emeritus at the Department of Criminology at the University of Greifswald, Germany.

Stefan Harrendorf is Professor of Criminology, Criminal Law, Criminal Procedure and Comparative Criminal Law and Justice at the University of Greifswald, Germany.

Dirk van Zyl Smit is Professor Emeritus of Comparative and International Penal Law at the University of Nottingham, UK, and Professor Emeritus of Criminology at the University of Cape Town, South Africa.

Routledge Frontiers of Criminal Justice

Diversion in Youth Justice

What Can We Learn from Historical and Contemporary Practices?

Roger Smith

Policing Child Sexual Abuse
Failure, Corruption and Reform in Queensland
Paul Bleakley

Collaboration and Innovation in Criminal Justice
An Activity Theory Alternative to Offender Rehabilitation
Paulo Rocha

Genetic Surveillance and Crime Control
Social, Cultural and Political Perspectives
Helen Machado & Rafaela Granja

Impending Challenges to Penal Moderation in Germany and France
A Strained Restraint
Edited by Kirstin Drenkhahn, Fabien Jobard and Tobias Singelnstein

Policing and Boundaries in a Violent Society
A South African Case Study
Guy Lamb

Consent, Stealthing and Desire-Based Contracting in the Criminal Law
Brianna Chesser & David Nader and April Zahra

The Impact of COVID-19 on Prison Conditions and Penal Policy
Edited by Frieder Dünkel, Stefan Harrendorf and Dirk van Zyl Smit

The Virtual Reality of Imprisonment in Russia
"Preparing myself for Prison" in a Contested Human Rights Landscape
Laura Piacentini and Elena Katz

For more information about this series, please visit: www.routledge.com/Routledge-Frontiers-of-Criminal-Justice/book-series/RFCJ

The Impact of COVID-19 on Prison Conditions and Penal Policy

Edited by
Frieder Dünkel, Stefan Harrendorf
and Dirk van Zyl Smit

Routledge
Taylor & Francis Group
LONDON AND NEW YORK

First published 2022
by Routledge
2 Park Square, Milton Park, Abingdon, Oxon OX14 4RN

and by Routledge
605 Third Avenue, New York, NY 10158

Routledge is an imprint of the Taylor & Francis Group, an informa business

British Library Cataloguing-in-Publication Data
A catalogue record for this book is available from the British Library

Library of Congress Cataloging-in-Publication Data
Names: Dünkel, Frieder, editor. | Harrendorf, Stefan, editor. | Van Zyl Smit, Dirk, editor.
Title: The impact of COVID-19 on prison conditions and penal policy / edited by Frieder Dünkel, Stefan Harrendorf and Dirk van Zyl Smit.
Description: Abingdon, Oxon; New York, NY: Routledge, 2022. | Series: Routledge frontiers of criminal justice | Includes bibliographical references.
Identifiers: LCCN 2021047567 (print) | LCCN 2021047568 (ebook) | ISBN 9780367769727 (hardback) | ISBN 9780367769734 (paperback) | ISBN 9781003169178 (ebook)
Subjects: LCSH: Prisons. | Corrections. | COVID-19 Pandemic, 2020—Social aspects.
Classification: LCC HV8665 .I565 2022 (print) | LCC HV8665 (ebook) | DDC 365/.667—dc23/eng/20220103
LC record available at https://lccn.loc.gov/2021047567
LC ebook record available at https://lccn.loc.gov/2021047568

ISBN: 9780367769727 (hbk)
ISBN: 9780367769734 (pbk)
ISBN: 9781003169178 (ebk)

DOI: 10.4324/9781003169178

Typeset in Times New Roman MT Std
by codeMantra

Contents

List of contributors x
Acknowledgements xviii

1 **Introduction** 1
FRIEDER DÜNKEL, STEFAN HARRENDORF AND DIRK VAN ZYL SMIT

2 **Australia** 7
THALIA ANTHONY, LORANA BARTELS, ANDREEA LACHSZ, STEVEN CARUANA AND FELICITY GERRY

3 **Austria** 26
KARIN BRUCKMÜLLER, WALTER HAMMERSCHICK AND LUKAS LINSER

4 **Belgium** 39
OLIVIA NEDERLANDT, AN-SOFIE VANHOUCHE AND KRISTEL BEYENS

5 **Brazil** 52
ELLEN RODRIGUES AND EDUARDO KHOURY

6 **Canada** 66
SANDRA BUCERIUS, ROSEMARY RICCIARDELLI AND LUCA BERARDI

7 **Chile** 79
ÁLVARO CASTRO-MORALES, JULIO CORTÉS-OLMEDO, VIOLETA PURÁN-ROSAS AND GUILLERMO E. SANHUEZA

8 **China** 91
SPENCER D. LI

9 **Latin American prisons during the COVID-19 pandemic: the cases of Colombia, Bolivia, Perú and Argentina** 102
JUAN SEBASTIÁN HERNÁNDEZ AND CÉSAR VALDERRAMA

10 **Costa Rica** 121
CARLOS TIFFER SOTOMAYOR AND PAOLA TIFFER HANGEN

11 **Croatia** 134
MAJA MUNIVRANA AND ELIZABETA IVIČVIĆ KARAS

12 **Czech Republic** 145
HELENA VÁLKOVÁ AND JANA HULMÁKOVÁ

13 **Denmark** 158
ANETTE STORGAARD AND LINDA KJÆR MINKE

14 **England and Wales** 169
CATHERINE HEARD AND NICOLA PADFIELD

15 **Estonia** 181
ANNELI SOO AND PRIIT KAMA

16 **Finland** 192
TAPIO LAPPI-SEPPÄLÄ AND SASU TYNI

17 **France** 209
MARTINE HERZOG-EVANS

18 **Germany** 224
FRIEDER DÜNKEL AND CHRISTINE MORGENSTERN

19 **Greece** 243
MARIA ANAGNOSTAKI

20 **Hungary** 255
ZSUZSANNA JUHÁSZ

21 **India** 265
MADHURIMA DHANUKA

22 Ireland North and South 278
CIARA O'CONNELL, MARY ROGAN, MICHELLE MARTYN AND SHADD MARUNA

23 Italy 295
LORENZO PICOTTI AND LUISA RAVAGNANI

24 Japan 306
KENJI TAKEUCHI AND AKINORI OTANI

25 Kenya 316
MERCY DECHE, SARAH KINYANJUI AND CONRAD BOSIRE

26 Latvia 326
ILONA KRONBERGA

27 Lithuania 337
GINTAUTAS SAKALAUSKAS

28 The Netherlands 348
JOLANDE UIT BEIJERSE AND MIRANDA BOONE

29 New Zealand 360
ALICE MILLS

30 North Macedonia 372
GORDANA LAŽETIĆ AND ELENA MUJOSKA TRPEVSKA

31 Norway 385
BERIT JOHNSEN

32 Poland 396
BARBARA STAŃDO-KAWECKA

33 Portugal 411
ANABELA MIRANDA RODRIGUES AND INÊS HORTA PINTO

34 Romania 424
IOAN DURNESCU AND IOANA MIHAELA MORAR

35 Russia 434
SERGEI OVCHINNIKOV

36 Scotland 443
KATRINA MORRISON AND HANNAH GRAHAM

37 Serbia 455
MILAN ŠKULIĆ

38 Slovakia 465
MIROSLAVA VRÁBLOVÁ

39 Slovenia 477
DANIJELA MRHAR PRELIĆ AND ROBERT FRIŠKOVEC

40 South Africa 487
LUKAS M. MUNTINGH

41 Spain 505
JOSÉ CID, LAURA NEGREDO LÓPEZ AND CARLES SOLER

42 Sweden 521
LARS HÅKAN NILSSON AND JENNY KÄRRHOLM

43 Switzerland 529
MELANIE WEGEL AND JONAS WEBER

44 Turkey 541
GALMA AKDENIZ AND IDIL AYDINOGLU

45 The US government's response to COVID-19 outbreaks in federal, state, and local corrections 557
JAMES BYRNE, DON HUMMER, SABRINA S. RAPISARDA, AND KIMBERLY R. KRAS

46 International prisoners and the pandemic – seeking release, improved conditions and family contact before international criminal courts 581
RÓISÍN MULGREW

47 International human rights and COVID-19 in prisons: medical isolation and independent oversight 596

RÓISÍN MULGREW AND DIRK VAN ZYL SMIT

48 Prison populations before and during the pandemic: lessons from COVID-19 about over-incarceration and its consequences for health 607

CATHERINE HEARD

49 Summary analysis of the state of prisons and penal policies before, during and after the COVID-19 pandemic 634

FRIEDER DÜNKEL, STEFAN HARRENDORF AND DIRK VAN ZYL SMIT

50 What could we learn from COVID-19? – A reductionist and penal moderation approach 665

FRIEDER DÜNKEL AND SONJA SNACKEN

Index 693

Contributors

Galma Akdeniz is Assistant Professor at the Faculty of Law, Istanbul Bilgi University, Istanbul, Turkey (ORCID: 0000-0002-7255-8260) (Chapter 44, Turkey).

Idil Aydinoglu is Researcher and Attorney at Law, Member of the Istanbul Bar Association, Istanbul, Turkey (ORCID: 0000-0002-8993-1260) (Chapter 44, Turkey).

Maria Anagnostaki is Criminologist and PhD Candidate at the Faculty of Law, Department of Penal Sciences, of the National & Kapodistrian University of Athens, Greece (ORCID: 0000-0002-6253-6287) (Chapter 19, Greece).

Thalia Anthony is Professor, Faculty of Law, University of Technology, Sydney, Australia (ORCID: 0000-0002-0652-0731) (Chapter 2, Australia).

Lorana Bartels is Professor and Program Leader of Criminology, Australian National University; Adjunct Professor of Law, University of Canberra and University of Tasmania (ORCID: 0000-0002-2037-884X) (Chapter 2, Australia).

Luca Berardi is Assistant Professor of Sociology and Social Psychology, Department of Sociology, McMaster University, Hamilton, Ontario, Canada (ORCID: 0000-0002-4734-9168) (Chapter 6, Canada).

Kristel Beyens is Professor of Penology and Criminology, Criminology Department, Research group Crime and Society, Vrije Universiteit Brussels, Belgium (ORCID: 0000-0001-7073-637X) (Chapter 4, Belgium).

Miranda Boone is Professor of Penology and Penitentiary Law, Leiden University, The Netherlands (ORCID: 0000-0002-5333-4587) (Chapter 28, Netherlands).

Conrad Bosire is the former Chief Executive Officer at the National Council on Adminstration of Justice, Nairobi, Kenya (ORCID: 0000-0002-4889-6091) (Chapter 25, Kenya).

Karin Bruckmüller is Professor of Criminal Law and Criminal Procedure Law, Sigmund-Freud-University, Vienna, Austria (Chapter 3, Austria)

Sandra Bucerius is Professor of Sociology and Criminology, Director of the Centre for Criminological Research, Director University of Alberta Prison Project (UAPP), University of Alberta, Canada (ORCID: 0000-0002-7742-3103) (Chapter 6, Canada).

James Byrne is Professor at the College of Fine Arts, Humanities and Social Sciences, School of Criminology and Justice Studies, University of Massachusetts Lowell, Boston, USA (ORCID: 0000-0001-9216-9871) (Chapter 45, USA).

Steven Caruana is Coordinator of the Australia OPCAT Network and Winston Churchill Memorial Trust Fellow, Prestons, NSW, Australia (Chapter 2, Australia).

Alvaro Castro-Morales is Professor of Criminology and Penology, Universidad de Chile, Santiago de Chile, Chile (ORCID: 0000-0003-3325-4034) (Chapter 7, Chile).

José Cid is Professor of Criminology and Criminal Law. Department of Political Science and Public Law. Universidad Autónoma de Barcelona, Spain (ORCID: 0000-0001-6522-4329) (Chapter 41, Spain).

Julio Cortés-Olmedo is Lawyer and Research Assistant at the Faculty of Law, Universidad de Chile, Santiago de Chile, Chile (ORCID: 0000-0002-6832-8462) (Chapter 7, Chile).

Mercy Deche is Lecturer at the School of Law, University of Nairobi, Mombasa, Kenya (Chapter 25, Kenya).

Madhurima Dhanuka is Programme Head of the Prison Reforms Programme at the Commonwealth Human Rights Initiative, New Delhi, India (ORCID: 0000-0001-9633-5734) (Chapter 21, India).

Frieder Dünkel is Professor of Criminology, University of Greifswald, Germany. (ORCID: 0000-0002-0544-3586) (Chapters 1, Introduction, 18, Germany, 49, Summary Analysis, 50, What could we learn from COVID-19? A Reductionist and Penal Moderation Approach).

Ioan Durnescu is Professor at the Faculty of Sociology and Social Work, University of Bucharest, Bucharest, Romania (ORCID: 0000-0002-5631-7926) (Chapter 34, Romania).

Robert Friškovec is Secretary of the International Cooperation, Uprava RS za izvrševanje kazenskih sankcij (The Prison Administration of the Republic of Slovenia), Ministrstvo za pravosodje (Ministry of Justice), Ljubljana, Slovenia (ORCID: 0000-0001-9508-8671) (Chapter 39, Slovenia).

Felicity Gerry is Queen's Counsel at Crockett Chambers, Melbourne, and Carmelite Chambers, London and Professor of Legal Practice at Deakin University, Melbourne, Australia (ORCID: 0000-0003-0431-9492) (Chapter 2, Australia).

Hannah Graham is Senior Lecturer, University of Stirling, Scotland (ORCID: 0000-0003-0176-6350) (Chapter 36, Scotland).

Walter Hammerschick is Executive Director and Senior Researcher at the Institute for the Sociology of Law and Criminology, Vienna, Austria (Chapter 3, Austria).

Stefan Harrendorf is Professor of Criminology, Criminal Law, Criminal Procedure and Comparative Criminal Law and Justice, University of Greifswald, Faculty of Law and Economics, Germany (ORCID: 0000-0003-2823-7205) (Chapters 1, Introduction, and 49, Summary Analysis).

Catherine Heard is Senior Research Fellow, and Director of the World Prison Research Programme at the Institute for Crime & Justice Policy Research, Birkbeck, University of London (ORCID: 0000-0002-1736-5730) (Chapters 14, England & Wales, and 48, Prison Population Rates before and during the Pandemic).

Juan Sebastián Hernández is Researcher of the Judicial System at the Center for the Study of Law, Justice and Society – Dejusticia. (Centro de Estudios de Derecho, Justicia y Sociedad – Dejusticia), Bogotá, Colombia (ORCID: 0000-0003-3713-3694) (Chapter 9, Colombia, Bolivia, Perú and Argentina).

Martine Herzog-Evans is Professor of Criminal Law, Prison Law, Prisoner Release, Offender Supervision Law, and Criminology at the Faculty of Law, University of Reims, France (ORCID: 0000-0002-2437-6753) (Chapter 17, France).

Inês Horta Pinto is PhD Candidate at the Law Faculty, University of Coimbra, Coimbra, Portugal (ORCID: 0000-0002-4904-9476) (Chapter 33, Portugal).

Jana Hulmáková is Researcher in Criminology, Institute of Criminology and Social Prevention and Assistant Professor, Charles University, Prague, Czech Republic (ORCID: 0000-0002-2339-7480) (Chapter 12, Czech Republic).

Don Hummer is Associate Professor at the School of Public Affairs, Penn State Harrisburg, USA (ORCID: 0000-0003-3026-0287) (Chapter 45, USA)

Elizabeta Ivičević Karas is Professor of Criminal Procedural Law and Penitentiary Law at the Faculty of Law, University of Zagreb, Croatia (ORCID: 0000-0001-5279-3709) (Chapter 11, Croatia).

Berit Johnsen is Research Professor of Penology, University College of the Norwegian Correctional Service, Oslo, Lillestrøm, Norway (ORCID: 0000-0002-0041-3070) (Chapter 31, Norway).

Zsuzsanna Juhász is Associate Professor at the Institute of Criminal Law and Criminal Science, University of Szeged, Szeged, Hungary (ORCID: 0000-0002-0679-3449) (Chapter 20, Hungary)

Priit Kama was Head of the Prison Service, Ministry of Justice, Estonia (Chapter 15, Estonia).

Jenny Kärrholm is Head of the Research and Evaluation Unit of the Swedish Prison and Probation Service, Norrköping, Sweden (Chapter 42, Sweden).

Sarah Kinyanjui is Associate Dean of the School of Law, University of Nairobi, Mombasa, Kenya (Chapter 25, Kenya).

Eduardo Khoury is Researcher in Criminology, Law and Technology, Juiz de Fora Federal University, Juiz de Fora, Minas Gerais, Brazil (Chapter 5, Brazil).

Kimberly R. Kras is Assistant Professor at the Department of Criminal Justice, School of Public Affairs, San Diego State University, San Diego, USA (ORCID: 0000-0002-0592-0418) (Chapter 45, USA).

Ilona Kronberga is Adviser to the Minister of Justice, Ministry of Justice of the Republic of Latvia as well as Associate policy analyst in prisons and juvenile justice at Centre for Public Policy PROVIDUS, Riga, Latvia (Chapter 26, Latvia).

Andreea Lachsz is PhD Candidate at the Faculty of Law, University of Technology, Sydney, Australia (Chapter 2, Australia).

Tapio Lappi-Seppälä was Director of the Institute of Criminology and Legal Policy, University of Helsinki, Finland (Chapter 16, Finland).

Gordana Lažetić is Professor of Criminal Procedural Law and Penitentiary Law at the Faculty of Law "Iustinianus Primus", Skopje, North Macedonia (ORCID: 0000-0002-0719-3293) (Chapter 30, North Macedonia).

Spencer D. Li is Professor at the University of Macau, China (ORCID: 0000-0003-3424-2246) (Chapter 8, China).

Lukas Linser was Research Assistant at Sigmund-Freud-University of Vienna, Vienna, Austria (Chapter 3, Austria).

Michelle Martyn is Inspector at the Office of the Inspector of Prisons, Dublin (Chapter 22, Ireland)

Shadd Maruna is Professor at the School of Social Sciences, Education and Social Work, Belfast, Northern Ireland (ORCID: 0000-0002-4978-7073) (Chapter 22, Ireland and Northern Ireland).

Alice Mills is Senior Lecturer in Criminology at the School of Social Sciences, University of Auckland, New Zealand (ORCID: 0000 0002 6893 3857) (Chapter 29, New Zealand).

Linda Kjær Minke is Professor of Criminology, Department of Law, University of Southern Denmark, Odense, Denmark (ORCID: 0000-0001-7439-1639) (Chapter 13, Denmark).

Ioana Mihaela Morar is Associate Professor at the Faculty of Sociology and Social Work of the University of Bucharest, and Deputy General Director of the National Administration of Penitentiaries, Bucharest, Romania (ORCID: 0000-0003-0207-5092) (Chapter 34, Romania).

Christine Morgenstern is Professor of Criminal Law and Criminology, University of Greifswald, Germany and Research Fellow, Trinity College Dublin, The University of Dublin, Germany (ORCID: 0000-0002-6478-3206) (Chapter 18, Germany).

Katrina Morrison is Lecturer at the Edinburgh Napier University, Edinburgh, Scotland (ORCID: 0000-0001-9425-5933) (Chapter 36, Scotland).

Danijela Mrhar Prelić is Director General of the Slovenian Probation Administration, Ministry of Justice, Ljubljana, Slovenia (ORCID: 0000-0001-8442-940X) (Chapter 39, Slovenia).

Róisín Mulgrew is Associate Professor in Law, University of Nottingham and Lecturer above the Bar, National University of Ireland, Galway (from mid Sept 2020), Ireland (ORCID: 0000-0002-5428-8981) (Chapters 46, International Prisoners, and 47, International Human Rights and COVID-19 in Prisons).

Elena Mujoska Trpevska is Research fellow, Centre for Strategic Research, Macedonian Academy of Sciences and Arts, MASA, Skopje, North Macedonia (ORCID: 0000-0003-2309-9456) (Chapter 30, North Macedonia).

Maja Munivrana is Associate Professor of Criminal Law and International Criminal Law at the Faculty of Law, University of Zagreb, Zagreb, Croatia (ORCID: 0000-0001-9496-6102) (Chapter 11, Croatia).

Lukas M. Muntingh is Associate Professor at the Dullah Omar Institute (Africa Criminal Justice Reform), University of the Western Cape, Bellville, South Africa (ORCID: 0000-0003-4447-9538) (Chapter 40, South Africa).

Olivia Nederlandt is Professor of Criminal Law, Université Libre de Bruxelles and Université Saint-Louis Bruxelles, Brussels, Belgium (ORCID: 0000-0003-4928-3526) (Chapter 4, Belgium).

Laura Negredo López is Deputy Assistant Director-General for Open Regime and Alternative Sentences and Measures, Ministry of Interior, Madrid, Spain (Chapter 41, Spain).

Lars Håkan Nilsson is Senior medical adviser at the Research and Evaluation Unit, Swedish Prison and Probation Service, Head office in Norrköping, Sweden (Chapter 42, Sweden).

Ciara O'Connell is a Visiting Research Fellow at the School of Law, Trinity College Dublin, Dublin, Ireland (ORCID: 0000-0002-5925-0587) (Chapter 22, Ireland).

Akinori Otani is a PhD student at the Japan Society for the Promotion of Science (JSPS) with a Research Fellowship for Young Scientists at the Faculty of Law, Ryukoku University, Kyoto, Japan (ORCID: 0000-0003-3304-0052) (Chapter 24, Japan).

Sergei Ovchinnikov is a Deputy Head of the Research Institute of the FSP of Russia, Moscow, Russia (ORCID: 0000-0001-8942-0244) (Chapter 35, Russia).

Nicola Padfield is Reader in Criminal and Penal Justice, University of Cambridge and Master of Fitzwilliam College, Cambridge, England (Chapter 14, England & Wales).

Lorenzo Picotti is Professor of Criminal Law, Department of Law, University of Verona, Verona, Italy (ORCID: 0000-0003-2049-8718) (Chapter 23, Italy).

Violeta Purán-Rosas is Lawyer and Research Assistant at the Faculty of Law, University of Chile, Chile (ORCID: 0000-0003-3118-5493) (Chapter 7, Chile).

Anabela Miranda Rodrigues is Professor of Criminal Law at the Faculty of Law, University of Coimbra, Coimbra, Portugal (Chapter 33, Portugal).

Sabrina S. Rapisarda is Doctoral Research Assistant at the School of Criminology & Justice Studies, University of Massachusetts Lowell, Lowell, MA, USA (Chapter 45, USA).

Luisa Ravagnani is Researcher in Criminology, University of Brescia and the Prisoners' Ombusdman for the city of Brescia, Brescia, Italy (ORCID: 0000-0002-0900-8354) (Chapter 23, Italy).

Rosemary Ricciardelli is Professor of Criminology and Sociology at the Department of Sociology, Memorial University of Newfoundland, St. John's, Canada (ORCID: 0000-0002-0905-8968) (Chapter 6, Canada).

Ellen Rodrigues is Professor of Criminal Law and Criminology at the Faculty of Law, Juiz de Fora Federal University, Brazil (ORCID: 0000-0001-6952-7765) (Chapter 5, Brazil).

Mary Rogan is Associate Professor at the School of Law, Trinity College Dublin, The University of Dublin, Ireland (ORCID: 0000-0002-2279-9891) (Chapter 22, Ireland).

Gintautas Sakalauskas is Associate Professor at the Faculty of Law, Department of Criminal Justice, University of Vilnius, Vilnius, Lithuania (ORCID: 0000-0003-0203-5496) (Chapter 27, Lithuania).

Guillermo E. Sanhueza is Associate Professor at the Social Work Department, University of Chile, Chile (ORCID: 0000-0003-1971-7362) (Chapter 7, Chile).

Milan Škulić is Professor at the Faculty of Law, University of Belgrade and judge at the Constitutional Court of Serbia, Belgrade, Serbia (Chapter 37, Serbia).

Sonja Snacken is Professor of Criminology, Vrije Universiteit Brussel, Brussels, Belgium (ORCID: 0000-0001-8538-424X) (Chapter 50, What could we learn from COVID-19? A Reductionist and Penal Moderation Approach).

Carles Soler is Deputy Director of the Rehabilitation and Resettlement Services of the Catalan Prison Service, Barcelona, Spain (Chapter 41, Spain).

Anneli Soo is Head of Office, Department of Penal Law, University of Tartu, Tartu, Estonia (ORCID: 0000-0003-4300-5437) (Chapter 15, Estonia).

Barbara Stańdo-Kawecka is Professor at the Department of Penal Executive Law of the Jagiellonian University, Kraków, Poland (ORCID: 0000-0002-7296-1260) (Chapter 32, Poland).

Anette Storgaard is Professor in Criminology and Penology, Department of Law, University of Aarhus, Aarhus, Denmark (ORCID: 0000-0001-5375-7830) (Chapter 13, Denmark).

Kenji Takeuchi is Professor of Criminology and Criminal Policy, Kyushu University, Fukuoka, Japan (ORCID: 0000-0003-0516-6272) (Chapter 24, Japan).

Carlos Tiffer Sotomayor is Prof. Dr. Postgrado en Ciencias Penales, Facultad de Derecho, Universidad de Costa Rica. Director Programa Justicia Penal Juvenil, ILANUD, San José, Costa Rica (Chapter 10, Costa Rica).

Paola Tiffer Hangen is Associate Attorney in Criminal Law, Tiffer Legal Office, San José, Costa Rica (Chapter 10, Costa Rica).

Sasu Tyni is Senior Researcher, Institute of Criminology and Legal Policy, University of Helsinki, Helsinki, Finland (ORCID: 0000-0003-0723-331X) (Chapter 16, Finland).

Jolande uit Beijerse is Associate Professor of Criminal Law and Criminal Procedure, Erasmus University Rotterdam, Rotterdam, the Netherlands (ORCID: 0000-0001-9522-5365) (Chapter 28, Netherlands).

César Valderrama is Director of the Judicial System Line at the Center for the Study of Law, Justice and Society – Dejusticia, Bogotá, Colombia (ORCID: 0000-0003-3715-177X) (Chapter 9, Colombia, Bolivia, Perú and Argentina).

Helena Válková is Professor of Penal Law at the School of Law and Business, Prague, and Government Commissioner for Human Rights in the Czech Republic, Czech Republic (Chapter 12, Czech Republic).

An-Sofie Vanhouche is Associate Professor of Penology (Tenure track) at the Department of Criminology, Research group Crime and Society, Vrije Universiteit Brussel, Brussels, Belgium (ORCID: 0000-0002-6617-4754) (Chapter 4, Belgium).

Dirk van Zyl Smit is Professor of Comparative and International Penal Law, University of Nottingham, United Kingdom, (ORCID: 0000-0002-5540-2897)

(Chapters 1, Introduction, 47, International Human Rights and COVID-19 in Prisons, and 49, Summary Analysis).

Miroslava Vráblová is Associate Professor of Criminal Law at the Faculty of Law, Department of Criminal Law and Criminology, Trnava University, Trnava, Slovakia (ORCID: 0000-0003-0005-6592) (Chapter 38, Slovakia).

Jonas Weber is Professor of Criminology and Criminal Law, University of Berne, Berne, Switzerland (ORCID: 0000-0002-5528-6849) (Chapter 43, Switzerland).

Melanie Wegel is Professor of Delinquency and Crime Prevention at the Institute of Delinquency and Crime Prevention, University of Applied Sciences, Zurich, Switzerland (ORCID: 0000-0002-2361-7076) (Chapter 43, Switzerland).

Acknowledgements

We would like to express our deep gratitude to the publisher Routledge, in particular to Arunima Aditya and Lydia da Cruz, who supported us in many ways, further to Alexandra Fusch of the Department of Criminology, Criminal Law, Criminal Procedure and Comparative Criminal Law and Justice at Greifswald University, and to Betine van Zyl Smit for assisting with the editorial work.

Frieder Dünkel, Stefan Harrendorf and Dirk van Zyl Smit
Greifswald and Nottingham,
18 July 2021.

1 Introduction

Frieder Dünkel, Stefan Harrendorf and Dirk van Zyl Smit

1 Aims and history of the book project

The pandemic caused by COVID-19 has had a major impact on prisoners, one of the most vulnerable groups in all societies. This timely book presents the results of a worldwide exchange of information on the situation in prisons in 48 countries or jurisdictions since the beginning of the pandemic in February/March 2020. It focusses on the human rights questions that have been raised during the pandemic, relating to the living conditions of inmates in prisons worldwide.

The main goals of the book are to:

- Create new legal and penological knowledge about the measures introduced to reduce prison population rates and manage persons in custody during the pandemic;
- Provide accurate and contextualised information by authors from and with expertise in specific penal systems;
- Generate knowledge about the different approaches of jurisdictions across the globe;
- Analyse the role of human rights law and standards in the response to COVID-19 by national, regional and international authorities and bodies; and
- Explore the potential for reductionist penal reform post-COVID-19, built on expanded diversionary measures, non-custodial alternative sanctions and early release mechanisms that emerged during the pandemic.

The information presented follows from an initiative taken by Frieder Dünkel at the University of Greifswald in April 2020. At that time, dramatic changes to prison policy were becoming visible, as prison authorities throughout the world struggled to deal with the impact of COVID-19 on their institutions. Many countries had ceased executing short sentences of imprisonment, as they recognised that they create a huge influx of new inmates, thus increasing the danger of infection inside prisons. Furthermore,

DOI: 10.4324/9781003169178-1

contacts with the outside world through visits and short-term prison leave were suspended or restricted, which had a major impact on the resettlement process based on a gradual transfer from prisons into society (Dünkel et al., 2019).

From mid-April 2020, the initiators of the present study started to circulate a questionnaire to an international network of prison researchers and practitioners. Early questions about reactions to the COVID-19 pandemic were as follows:

"Is consideration being given to, or are practices being introduced in your country of:

a not executing certain prison sentences (probably short-term sentences);
b releasing certain groups of offenders (short-term prisoners such as fine defaulters, elderly prisoners, female prisoners with children, etc.) and bringing forward early release (with or without home detention);
c restricting contacts with the outside world (visits, prison leave);
d expanding internet or mobile phone communication;
e making other changes due to the COVID-19 pandemic in prison regimes (living conditions in general, solitary confinement, quarantine for incoming prisoners, reduced working or recreational activities, therapies, etc.); and
f introducing changes in prison or penal law with regard to the issues mentioned above?"

As Mulgrew and van Zyl Smit point out in Chapter 47, the "WHO, UN Office for Drugs and Crime, the SPT, CPT and UN High Commissioner for Human Rights have all stressed the human rights principles that should guide the review of restrictions on prison regimes: restrictions implemented in response to COVID-19 must be necessary, evidence-based, proportionate to the health emergency, non-arbitrary, respectful of human dignity, have a legal basis and be restricted in time." The pandemic has led to major restrictions on prisoners' rights, and it is evident from the perspective of international human rights that these restrictions must be proportionate and limited in time. This book provides the basis for an evaluation of the recommendations of human rights organisations during the pandemic.

As summarised in Chapter 49 of this book, many countries drastically reduced activities in prison. Some countries closed down their prison work facilities and restricted communication of prisoners by locking them in their cells, sometimes for 23 hours a day. This can be seen as inhuman and degrading treatment according to international human rights standards and the standards set by the CPT (see also for the jurisprudence of the European Court of Human Rights, van Zyl Smit and Snacken, 2009). Other countries found ways of limiting contacts between prisoners, by requiring them to wear masks and to keep a fixed distance from other inmates. However, some countries reported that they did not have enough masks, neither for prisoners nor for staff members. As a result, in some cases, staff members refused to go to work as they did not feel safe.

Restrictions did not become more severe everywhere. From the beginning of the pandemic, some German prisons with open regimes started to use prison leave of from two weeks up to six months to send prisoners home for a time. There had been provision for such prison leave in Federal state prison laws for some years, but the regulations had almost never been applied in practice. Turkey, the country with the highest prison population in Europe, moderated the Law on the Enforcement of Sentences in April 2020 already, expanding early release, the transfer to open prisons and the execution of sentences under home detention. About one third of the prison population was sent "on leave" to home detention (see Akdeniz and Aydinoglu, Chapter 44). These examples demonstrate that COVID-19 made things possible that were unthinkable before. The same happened with allowing video calls through internet platforms or with mobile phones handed out to prisoners, which had been taboo before the pandemic.

In sum, we found many interesting changes in prison life and in resettlement programmes, both in a good and in a bad direction. Many of these need to be explored further, in a comprehensive but critical way.

2 Outline and methodology of the present study

The book does not only focus on changes inside prisons and of prison policy, but also explores the possibilities for a wider change in penal policy from a reductionist perspective – the aim to reduce prison population rates and, especially, the influx of prisoners who face short-term imprisonment (pre-trial as well as sentenced prisoners). The COVID-19-induced pandemic has illustrated that many countries overuse imprisonment. It is not always a measure of last resort, but also used for persons sentenced for minor or petty offences, such as shoplifting, fare evasion, drug possession for personal use and traffic offences. The German practice of incarcerating fine defaulters is an extreme and much debated example (see Dünkel and Morgenstern in Chapter 18). The pandemic has demonstrated that the non-execution of such sentences can be managed without losing trust in the legitimacy of penal law. One of the aims of the book is to illustrate that imposing and executing such prison sentences is unnecessary. The so-called back-door strategies to reduce prison populations by extending early release schemes and the use of home detention (not necessarily coupled with electronic monitoring (EM)) may be seen as a way out of unjustified mass incarceration, too (see Padfield, van Zyl Smit and Dünkel, 2010; Herzog-Evans, 2014; Dünkel et al., 2019). However, mass supervision by the overuse of probationary supervision or EM should also be a matter of concern (see the "COVID-19 related statement" released by the Council for Penological Co-operation (PC-CP) of the Council of Europe on 17 April 2020; as to EM, see Dünkel, Thiele and Treig, 2017).

The methodology used for this comparative study is a classical one, relying on individual country reports on the one hand and overarching, comparative chapters on the other (for a discussion of the advantages and disadvantages of such a methodology, see Chapter 49). In its first part, this book brings together the results and ideas of leading prison academics and practitioners (see Chapters 2–45). The book presents national reports about the impact of the COVID-19 pandemic on prisons and penal policy in 48 countries/jurisdictions, most of them in Europe. But the important non-European jurisdictions of Argentina, Brazil, Chile, Colombia, Perú and Costa Rica (South and Central America), Canada and the USA (North America), Kenya and South Africa (Africa), China, India and Japan (Asia), as well as Australia and New Zealand (Australasia), are also represented. Together, they cover a large majority of the worldwide prison population. The reports by leading scholars and practitioners in prison research in their countries reveal the dynamics of the COVID-19-induced crisis and discuss how it was and is managed inside prisons and in penal and penitentiary policy.

The national book chapters in the first part (Chapters 2–45) of the book follow broadly the same outline:

1 Introduction – general situation of the prison system
(Prison population rates and the general penal climate; expansionist or reductionist policies before COVID-19; prison overcrowding; general assessment of living conditions; developments after the emergence of COVID-19; COVID-19 infections and deaths of prisoners and prison staff members with reference to the development of the pandemic in the general society)
2 Prison and penal policy concerning the execution of prison sentences during the COVID-19-induced crisis
(Non-execution of certain prison sentences [short-term sentences, sentences for fine defaulters]; early release schemes; release of certain groups of offenders such as elderly or female prisoners; penal law reforms in this context, e.g. expanding alternative "community sanctions" or early release; in addition, reforms in administrative and penal law: Criminalisation of non-compliance to COVID-19-induced contact restrictions inside and outside prisons)
3 Restrictions of contact with the outside world
(Visits; prison leave; transfers to open prisons and prison regimes; etc.)
4 Restrictions inside prisons
(Work; recreational activities; time spent outside cells; lock-up times in cells; isolation of certain prisoners)
5 Compensatory measures
(Including more frequent and longer telephone calls; use of mobile phones; internet communication; etc.)

6 Legal basis for restrictions and relaxations of the prison regime
(Prison law regulations and legal changes; accountability of prisons; involvement of judges, ombudspersons, inspectors; role of international human rights standards; jurisprudence of courts controlling restrictions and/or granting compensatory measures)
7 Returning to normal
(Possible long-term effects of COVID-19 on the prison regime and on penal and prison policies; lessons learned)

In the second part of the book, thematic chapters concentrate explicitly on several aspects of the impact of the pandemic in prisons and in penal and penitentiary policy. The treatment of prisoners of the international courts by the different "host" countries and international detention facilities is addressed by Roisin Mulgrew in Chapter 46. In Chapter 47, Roisin Mulgrew and Dirk van Zyl Smit explore whether the COVID-19-related restrictions conform to international human rights standards (and how ways can be found of limiting the interaction of prisoners by means other than strict isolation or lockdown in solitary confinement. In Chapter 48, Catherine Heard considers the worldwide prison population rates before and during the pandemic and lessons to be learnt about over-incarceration and its consequences for prison health. Frieder Dünkel, Stefan Harrendorf and Dirk van Zyl Smit summarise the national reports and draw out the commonalities and diverging practices between jurisdictions (and some suggested reasons for these), the impacts of measures introduced and also differences between what was proposed and what actually transpired. They also explore positive changes of prison life that should be preserved such as expanded forms of contact with the outside world through digital devices and internet communication (Chapter 49). Finally, in Chapter 50, Frieder Dünkel and Sonja Snacken raise the question of what can be learnt from the experience with reducing the prison population in order to prevent the spreading of COVID-19 in prisons. They reflect on general issues of prison and penal policy, proposing a reductionist approach of penal moderation to counteract mass incarceration and prison overcrowding beyond the pandemic crisis in the future.

Researching the impact of a major international pandemic on prisons while it is happening is not without its challenges. Initially, when drafting the book proposal and while our contributors were writing the substantive chapters, we thought that by the end of December 2020, the pandemic would have been overcome and that we would be returning to "normal." However, before the book was finalised, the world experienced a second and, in many countries, also a third wave of COVID-19. When we completed this introduction in July 2021, infection rates had decreased in many parts of the world, especially in the northern hemisphere, while vaccination rates were on the rise. At the time of correcting the proofs for this introduction in January 2022, however, the world has seen several more waves of COVID-19. A third round of (booster) vaccination is currently being administered, and it is still unknown when this global crisis will be truly over. Therefore, some of the conclusions might be preliminary. However, we tried to bring the accounts up to date as far as possible, for most country chapters until the end of March 2021. For some chapters, it was possible to update data partially up to January 2022.

References

Dünkel, F., Pruin, I., Storgaard, A., and Weber, J. (2019) (Eds.): *Prisoner Resettlement in Europe*. Abington, Oxon: Routledge.

Dünkel, F., Thiele, C., and Treig, J. (2017) (Eds.): *Elektronische Überwachung von Straffälligen im europäischen Vergleich*. Mönchengladbach: Forum Verlag Godesberg.

Herzog-Evans, M. (2014) (Ed.): *Offender-release and Supervision: The Role of Courts and the Use of Discretion*. AH Oisterwijk: Wolf Legal Publishers.

Padfield, N., van Zyl Smit, D., and Dünkel, F. (2010) (Eds.): *Release from Prison. European Policy and Practice*. Cullompton: Willan Publishing.

van Zyl Smit, D., and Snacken, S. (2009): *Principles of European Prison Law and Policy. Penology and Human Rights*. Oxford: Oxford University Press.

2 Australia

Thalia Anthony, Lorana Bartels, Andreea Lachsz, Steven Caruana and Felicity Gerry

1 Introduction

In the general Australian population, COVID-19 has been contained to a greater degree than in many other parts of the world. As of 10 January 2022, there have been a total of 977,444 cases, averaging at 37,668 per 1 million population. There have been 2,367 COVID-related deaths, averaging 91 per 1 million population (Worldometer, 2022). According to Worldometer (2022), Australia is ranked 46th for COVID-19 infections per 1 million population out of a total of 224 countries.

Australia is a federation, with six states (New South Wales (NSW), Victoria, Queensland, Western Australia, Tasmania and South Australia) and two territories (Northern Territory and Australian Capital Territory (ACT)). To minimise the spread of the virus across Australia, there have been border closures between these states and territories at various times since 2020. The impact of COVID-19 infections has fallen primarily on the second most populous state, Victoria, which has accounted for 40% of cases and 69% of deaths, and the most populous state, NSW, which has seen 47% of the cases and 32% of the deaths (Australian Government, 2022). The virus has also been concentrated in these two states' capital cities. Although the remainder of Australia had relatively few infections and deaths for most of the pandemic, there was a surge in cases across most of the country at the end of 2021, jumping from under 5,000 new cases a day on 22 December 2021, to 100,000 less than three weeks later.

Until recently, the infection rate of COVID-19 in prisons has also been significantly lower in Australia than in most other countries (Rapisarda and Byrne, 2020). There were few COVID-19 infections reported in adult prisons and/or youth detention centres, in NSW, Victoria, Queensland and South Australia in 2020. Many of these infections involved staff. In 2021, many prisons saw COVID outbreaks, with over 550 incarcerated people in NSW infected (AAP, 2021). This was higher than NSW community transmission in August / September 2021 and resulted in at least one death of an inmate. In response, the NSW Inspector of Custodial Services (2021) initiated an inquiry on the response to COVID in both adult and youth custodial centres,

DOI: 10.4324/9781003169178-2

since the start of the pandemic. In early 2022, it was reported that there were 128 cases in South Australia's prison system (ABC News, 2022), 37 in NSW prisons (Bruno, 2022) and 14 in Queensland youth detention (Gramenz, McKenna and Doneman, 2022).

As has been the case internationally, however, prisons in Australia are at risk of rapid spread of COVID-19 and consequent fatalities if there is an outbreak. Prisons have severe overcrowding, often operating at over 100% of design capacity (Productivity Commission, 2020). There are increasingly dormitory prisons in Australia (Justice Action, 2017), of the style commonly seen in the United States, where the potential for any virus to spread is heightened.

In relation to other diseases, such as Hepatitis C, there is evidence that the spread of infection in Australian prisons is significantly higher than in the general population (see, for example, Hepatitis Australia, 2017); 25% of people in prisons have Hepatitis C, compared with a prevalence of less than 1% in the general Australian population (Australian Institute of Health and Welfare (AIHW), 2019). There is also inadequate access to healthcare in prisons (Public Health Association of Australia, 2017).

The risk of contracting COVID-19 in prisons is especially high for First Nations people. Despite accounting for only 3% of the general Australian population, First Nations people constitute 28% of the prison population, have higher levels of chronic health conditions, are less likely to receive access to healthcare and more likely to experience neglect (Australian Law Reform Commission, 2017). These factors can be traced to historic and systemic racism in the health and law enforcement systems. First Nations organisations in Australia and families who have lost loved ones due to deaths in custody have highlighted the disproportionate impact that COVID-19 would have on First Nations people if there were major outbreaks in prisons (National Aboriginal and Torres Strait Islander Legal Services, NATSILS, 2020a, 2020b).

1.1 Legal rights and responsibilities for the health of people in prisons

International bodies have identified the need to protect the health of people in prisons. The World Health Organization (WHO) (2020b: 1) warned that incarcerated people and detainees are likely to be "more vulnerable" to COVID-19 than the general population. It recommended the release of people from prisons as a COVID-19 control measure. The United Nations (UN) High Commissioner for Human Rights has called on governments to take urgent action to protect the health and safety of people in detention (Bachelet, 2020).

The UN Committee on Economic, Social and Cultural Rights (CESCR) has long recognised that "[h]ealth is a fundamental human right indispensable for the exercise of other human rights" (2000: 1); in other words, that health *is* life. A population's health is central to its survival and makes the enjoyment of all other rights possible. Australia is a signatory to the *International Covenant on Economic, Social and Cultural Rights 1966* (*ICESCR*).

In relation to the COVID-19 outbreak, the right to health obligates the state to take positive measures "to prevent, treat and control epidemic and endemic diseases" (CESCR, 2000: 44). Accordingly, a state is in violation of its obligations under the *ICESCR* if it fails to "take all necessary steps" to provide conditions for health (2000: 52). It follows that Australia's responses to controlling COVID-19 in the community were necessary for protecting good health. However, maintaining people in restrictive and unhealthy prison environments is arguably at odds with the general tenor of Australia's COVID-19 management strategies.

Australia has acceded to treaties which incorporate explicit references to a "right to health" (for example, *International Convention on the Elimination of All Forms of Racial Discrimination 1965*: Art 5(e)(iv); *ICESCR:* Art 12.1; 12.2; *Convention on the Elimination of All Forms of Discrimination against Women 1979*: Art 12; *Convention on the Rights of the Child 1989:* Art 24). However, there is no explicit right to life or health in the Australian Constitution (*Commonwealth of Australia Constitution Act 1900* (Cth)). In the absence of a national Bill of Rights, three jurisdictions have enacted state or territory human rights legislation (*Human Rights Act 2004* (ACT); *Charter of Human Rights and Responsibilities Act 2006* (Vic); *Human Rights Act 2019* (Qld)), requiring that all statutory provisions are interpreted in a way that is compatible with human rights and imposing an obligation on public authorities to act in a way that is compatible with human rights. If we take the Victorian Charter as an example, it does not give rise to a cause of action in and of itself. However, a breach of the Charter can be litigated alongside an existing cause of action. The main power of the Charter is to exert normative influence on public authorities to consider human rights (*Bare v Independent Broad-Based Anti-Corruption Commission* (2015) 48 VR 129).

Under its federated structure of government, all Australian states and territories are signatories to the *National Health Security Agreement* (2011: cl 21(b)), which recognises that state and territory governments have "primary responsibility for the public health response, and other emergency situations, within their jurisdictions in accordance with their own public health and emergency legislation and plans". Further, state emergency legislation in Australia generally contains specific provisions in relation to proportionality (for example, *Public Health and Well Being Act* (Vic) s 9).

In the context of COVID-19, accepting that some rights are not absolute (International Covenant on Civil and Political Rights 1966, Art 4(1)), rights are restricted to protect public health, including those of incarcerated people. However, restrictive measures must be necessary, proportionate and non-discriminatory. According to the UN Human Rights Committee, "necessity" relates to the relationship between the limitation of the right and addressing the emergency (2001: [3]); "proportionality" relates to the duration and scope of the measures taken (2001: [4); and non-discrimination relates both to how the measures are crafted and to how they affect sections of society (2001: [8]). In prisons, this means that quarantine, isolation, dispersal and lockdown, which can have significant effects on mental and physical health, must be thought through, not a knee-jerk response, particularly as prisons commonly have high levels of people from minority groups, individuals with disabilities and individuals with specific vulnerabilities (AIHW, 2019).

Aside from human rights obligations, there is a general acceptance that States, in their control of detention facilities, have a duty of care to incarcerated people. This was seen in the case of Mark Rowson, an incarcerated person who sought orders to be released from Port Phillip Prison in Victoria, on the basis of the risk of COVID-19, in light of his pre-existing health issues. In *Rowson v Department of Justice and Community Safety* [2020] VSC 236, Ginnane J reaffirmed the State's duty to take reasonable care for incarcerated people's health and ordered an independent COVID-19 risk assessment, the recommendations of which were to be implemented by the government. However, Judge Ginnane's judgment was only a preliminary order, and there was no final finding as to whether the state had breached the National Guidelines promulgated by the Communicable Diseases Network Australia (2020) for controlling COVID-19. This is despite it being widely accepted that places of detention in Australia are chronically overcrowded, inadequately serviced with healthcare personnel and facilities, and contain people with unique vulnerabilities that make them susceptible to COVID-19 and more serious consequences if they become infected.

The controlled release of incarcerated people, as recommended by the WHO, took second place to the maintenance of "law and order" in Australia. State and territory governments and their agencies were more concerned to restrict the rights of people in prisons and facilitate the entry of new people into prisons. In most jurisdictions, prison penalties attached to specific breaches of COVID-19 lockdown measures. Within prisons, isolation and lockdown have been key tools for managing COVID-19.

Essentially, the effort seems to have been directed at keeping COVID-19 out of prison, rather than preparing for contagion or committing to healthcare.

The fact that there have not been more cases of COVID-19 in prisons is doubtless due in large part to national lockdowns in 2021 and early 2022 and some good luck. Yet, with many new COVID-19 outbreaks in states, prisons have been among the first sites to report cases. Therefore, we know that as Australian governments lose control of the management of COVID-19, disease in prisons is an inevitable consequence where overcrowding and vulnerability are the norm. In the event of wide community spread in Australia, the risk of uncontrolled prison outbreaks remains.

The fact that there have been relatively few cases of COVID-19 in Australian prisons does not mean that people incarcerated have escaped unscathed. Lockdowns in prison have included the isolation of vulnerable adults and children. This is highly likely to have compromised their health and well-being and to exacerbate existing vulnerabilities (Anthony, 2020c citing Deadly Connections mental health survey). Access to evidence and resources to challenge these conditions are limited. For First Nations people, the harm is exacerbated by a colonial history of trauma arising from imprisonment and a lack of community and cultural input or contact (Australian Law Reform Commission, 2017).

As our analysis in this section highlights, in the context of health, even in a pandemic, there is a rights-based framework that continues to be legally enforceable. However, Australian policy and operational responses to COVID-19 risks to prisons were issued in an ad hoc fashion without a holistic plan for the health and well-being of people inside, accountability or transparency. Following the imposition of restrictions on prisons in March 2020, the Australian Government in April 2020 endorsed adherence to the Communicable Diseases Network Australia (CDNA) (2020) guidelines for prisons. Although the CDNA guidelines were subsequently updated, including with reference to releasing people from prison to mitigate against COVID-19 risks, the Federal Government has not updated its guidelines accordingly.

To date, there has not been a systematic audit of the effects of restrictions on incarcerated people, despite state responsibilities for already overcrowded prisons and the health of vulnerable people in prisons, nor has there been robust human rights analysis of necessity and proportionality of ongoing use of restrictions by detaining authorities or governments. The long-term implications on the well-being of people who have been incarcerated during this period, with the effects of lockdown, dispersal and isolation, remain to be seen, but are likely to be significant and may last far beyond their time in custody. Indeed, the Deadly Connections survey cited below demonstrates the emerging deterioration of mental and emotional well-being for First Nations people inside.

2 Penal policy during COVID-19

In Australia, the COVID-19 response has been coordinated by a National Cabinet. This is a body comprising Federal, state and territory political leaders who, in the main, have agreed upon the COVID-19 policies and practices in each jurisdiction, which are proportionate to the COVID-19 risks in each state and territory at any given time. This has been necessary, given that health policy is primarily in the domain of the states and territories. As mentioned above, the Federal commitment to the first iteration of CDNA guidelines on prisons reflects this unified response in April

2020. Even before then, however, there was substantial consistency across Australia to the COVID-19 restrictions imposed on prison environments.

A critical aspect of the COVID-19 government response in Australia has been law enforcement. The use of policing and penalties to assure public health compliance during COVID-19 has been a "pivotal" enforcement tool (Goldworthy and Lincoln, 2020). This has included enforcement of lockdowns, social distancing and state/territory border controls. A notable exception is the ACT, which has refrained from prescribing criminal sanctions for COVID-19 breaches (Jervis-Brady, 2020). Generally speaking, the responses have constrained procedural fairness within the justice system. In Victoria, the *Emergency Measures Act 2020* (Vic) (*Omnibus Act*), enacted on 23 April 2020, increased punitive powers and suspended jury trials until November 2020. There have also been tough measures for regulating COVID-19 quarantine, with facilities overseen by police, military officers and private security.

Although the National Cabinet has provided leadership on health policies and practices, enforcement has been a matter for the states and territories. Australia's six state and two territory governments have plenary power over criminal justice. The Federal Government determines a small range of Federal offences and penalties (e.g. relating to human trafficking and terrorism). Consequently, people incarcerated in Federal prisons only account for about 2% of all people in prisons (Australian Bureau of Statistics, 2019). The overwhelming majority are locked up in prisons for state and territory offences on remand and sentence. State and territory differences in law enforcement and the management of prisons under the pandemic have largely been a matter of degree.

Prior to the pandemic, all Australian states and territories had seen increases in the imprisonment rates over the past decade. However, there is a vast discrepancy in imprisonment rates, varying from 122 per 100,000 population in the ACT, to 967 per 100,000 population in the Northern Territory (Australian Bureau of Statistics, 2021). It should also be noted that, with a pre-COVID-19 adult incarceration rate of 223 per 100,000 (Australian Bureau of Statistics, 2020) and an incarceration rate of 172 per 100,000 during the first year of the pandemic (Institute for Crime & Justice Policy Research, 2020), Australia is a comparatively high incarcerating country, relative to other Western nations. These rates are more than ten-fold for the First Nations peoples, who are the most incarcerated people on Earth (Anthony, 2017).

With an increasing prison population, prison crowding increases, as does the level of health vulnerability. As set out above, this poses particular challenges for First Nations people to retain good health, and indeed life, in such circumstances. An open letter by First Nations families (2020) whose loved ones died in prison stated:

> We know that our people are more vulnerable to contracting and dying from COVID-19. We fear that a Black COVID-19 death in custody is only a matter of time: the risk is compounded by the mass incarceration of our people and the high rates of Aboriginal deaths in custody.

> Far too often, our people have died in custody because their health issues have not been taken seriously due to racism. Prisons are not safe. Consequently, our people are 'at risk' during this pandemic and must be released.

Australia's pandemic response for prisons has emphasised isolation and lockdown (ACT Inspector of Correctional Services, 2020b). This concern adds to existing grievances relating to the isolation of children in detention centres (Victorian Ombudsman, 2019). At the same time, governments recognised the problems of a large prison population for the spread of COVID-19, following advocacy for the rights of people in prisons. Early in the pandemic, hundreds of academics, legal practitioners and justice advocates signed open letters, calling for a rights-based approach to prison arrangements, including the release of vulnerable incarcerated people (Bartels, Anthony and Fletcher, 2020), released on 20 March. This was followed by a second open letter (Gerry, Anthony and Bartels, 2020) on 9 April and third open letter (NATSILS, Anthony and Gerry, 2020) on 13 August 2020. Open letters were supplemented by the individual and combined lobbying of community legal services, law societies and institutes, First Nations organisations (e.g. Aboriginal legal services and Change the Record), First Nations families, non-government organisations and other professionals. They advocated for the rights of people in prison and decarceration (Federation of Community Legal Centres Vic and Law Institute Victoria, 2020).

One significant policy shift was the passage in March 2020 of the NSW emergency laws to release people convicted of minor offences from prisons (*COVID-19 Legislation Amendment (Emergency Measures) Act 2020* (NSW); for comment, see Anthony, 2020b; Rapisarda and Byrne, 2020). To similar effect, the ACT also passed legislation to provide for the early release of certain incarcerated people in limited circumstances (*COVID-19 Emergency Response Act 2020* (ACT) and *COVID-19 Emergency Response Legislation Amendment Act 2020* (ACT)). However, neither jurisdiction has used the legislation and it quickly emerged that it would only be used reactively, rather than as a proactive decarceration measure, as part of a responsible preventive health response to a pandemic. For example, the NSW Corrections Commissioner stated that:

> although he had special powers to release low-risk, vulnerable prisoners in the event of a coronavirus outbreak, he had not seen any need to use them as yet. "I am very pleased that the opportunity is there if I ever need to use it – I hope I won't have to".
>
> (Farquhar and Scully, 2020)

The inference is that the "need" would only arise once the contagion had breached the prison estate, which defies the logic that decarceration should be directed to preventing outbreaks.

Beyond the policy realm, the judiciary and parole boards have been more proactive during the pandemic with respect to using their existing powers to bail, order community-based sentences and release people on parole to reduce prison populations (Anthony, 2020c). Across Australia, the prison population declined by between 3% and 8% between March and June 2020 (Australian Bureau of Statistics, 2020), with a 17% decline in the number of new prisoners. More recent data from NSW indicate that the size of the population in prisons remained steady in the following quarter (Bartels, 2020; NSW Bureau of Crime Statistics and Research, 2020; Rapisarda and Byrne, 2020). The decline has been marked for First Nations people, at 5% of the total population and a 19% reduction in the number of people received into custody, compared with the previous quarter (Australian Bureau of Statistics, 2020). Reductions have been especially significant in the remand (unsentenced or untried) population, which comprises over one-third of the Australian prison population (Australian Bureau of Statistics, 2020; Sarre, Bartels and Makkai, 2020). Community corrections orders have also declined, with 78,843 people subject to community-based corrections in June 2020, compared with 83,377 in the March 2020 quarter (Australian Bureau of Statistics, 2020). According to the most recent data (September 2021), five out of eight jurisdictions had lower prison populations that in March 2020 (decreases of 5 to 14%), while three had experienced increases (between 2% and 11%). Nationally, the prison population was down 4% over this period, while the number of people on community-based correction orders was down by 5%.

Perhaps the most significant issue is that most correctional officers are not medically qualified and, outside of a pandemic, health treatment and management in prisons are reactive, rather than proactive. Aside from an argument that justice systems and corrections facilities should more generally take an evidence-based healthcare approach to incarceration/decarceration, in a pandemic, it is necessary to ensure that people are assured the highest attainable standard of physical and mental healthcare. This must necessarily include reducing the risk of contagion, through reducing the numbers of people in prison, so that those remaining can, for example, be socially distanced but also able to interact, work and exercise safely within prison and to maintain relationships with those outside. Queensland has come under the spotlight for not allowing quarantined incarcerated people any, or insufficient, out-of-cell time, both in its youth (Hurley, 2020) and adult (Smee, 2020b) facilities.

3 Restrictions of contact with the outside world

At various times, including March and June 2020, prisons across Australia restricted personal visits and other support programmes. NSW and Victoria reinstituted visits in prisons and youth detention facilities from 23 November and 11 December 2020, respectively, with options for virtual visits continuing. Visits have continued to be suspended during periods of community transmission in 2021 and early 2022. Contact with people outside is vital to the well-being of people in prisons, for emotional comfort and for material support (Penal Reform International, 2016: 1). It is also critical for the well-being of family members in the community, such as young children whose mothers are in custody.

4 Restrictions inside prisons

4.1 Restrictions for people arriving in prison

In most Australian prisons, there is a mandatory 14-day quarantine period for people arriving at prisons, including children accompanying sentenced parents. In April 2020, following a correctional centre officer testing positive to COVID-19 while off-duty, Queensland Corrective Services (2020) introduced isolation protocols to all its facilities. The protocols required all newly incarcerated people entering high-security centres to be placed into isolation for 14 days with no time out of cell. Commissioner Peter Martin APM acknowledged the move as "a significant departure" from usual procedures, but justified it by highlighting that "overseas prisons are seeing the terrible impact this pandemic can have within a prison environment" (Queensland Corrective Services, 2020). Such a general response is not based on the particular needs of individuals in prisons or the capacities of specific institutions.

On 28 March 2020, quarantine measures were also adopted by Corrections Victoria, with the establishment of "protective quarantine units" at five prisons (out of 16 prisons) in Victoria (Corrections Victoria, 2020). Comparable measures were also put in place by Corrective Services NSW (2020) and Tasmania (Elise Archer, Minister for Corrections, 2020) Tasmanian Prison Service (2020).

The CDNA (2020) guidance on routine intake quarantine for new admissions remained silent on the topic until its third iteration, on 24 July 2020. The CDNA guidance is that:

> new inmates/detainees to the facility, who have been in geographic areas with elevated risk of community transmission within the past 14 days, should be quarantined until 14 days from when they were last in the area with community transmission, prior to being allowed to mix with other inmates/detainees.
>
> (2020: 15)

The WHO (2020a) has issued guidance discouraging the use of "routine intake quarantine", noting that unnecessary medical isolation has negative impacts on mental health. The WHO Regional Office for Europe (2020: 21) has recommended that "[a]ny detainee who has (a) travelled from or lived in an identified high-risk area, or (b) had contact with a known case of COVID-19, should be placed in quarantine, in single accommodation, for 14 days from the date of travel or last possible day of contact". Governments have not been regularly reviewing the need for protective quarantine to exclude COVID-19 from places of detention, and whether it is a proportionate response, in line with developments in the community. The UN Subcommittee on Prevention of Torture and other Cruel, Inhuman or

Degrading Treatment or Punishment (2020: 3) has also suggested that, if such restrictive measures are used, they must be "on the basis of an independent medical evaluation, proportionate, limited in time and subject to procedural safeguards".

Justice advocates have continued to protest the practice as disproportionately harsh and more recently, emails obtained under Freedom of Information have demonstrated these arrangements to seemingly be based on publicly available advice from the United States Centers for Disease Control and Prevention website, rather than being informed by health expertise (Mills, 2021).

4.2 Restrictions to employment and programmes

In many prisons, opportunities to undertake work have been significantly curtailed due to COVID-19. There have been some new roles relating to COVID-19 cleaning that have raised concerns about health risk and exploitation among First Nations legal services (Victorian Aboriginal Legal Service, 2020a). There are also restrictions to programmes, due to the lack of capacity or unwillingness of providers to enter prisons.

5 Compensatory measures: Access to AVL with families

Many prisons have for the first time introduced audio-visual link (AVL) contacts between people in prisons and their families. Technology to link people in prison with their family has been a long-standing demand of advocates for people in prisons, such as Justice Action (2012) since 1998. A survey conducted by Corrective Services NSW indicated that people in prison valued the opportunity to communicate with their families through this medium; 90% of respondents were reportedly satisfied with the family video visit experience and 85% wanted family video visits to continue once COVID-19 restrictions are lifted (Anonymous, 2020). However, an independent survey of 63 First Nations people in NSW prisons and their families by Deadly Connections found that they were suffering from the lack of in-personal contact under COVID-19 restrictions (Anthony, 2020c).

A study commissioned for SHINE for Kids, a non-government organisation that supports the families of people in prison, surveyed 84 carers of children with a family member (usually a father) in prison (Flynn et al., 2020). It revealed that video conferencing and phone calls were not seen as particularly suitable for young children at home, as they were too short or were offered at times which were not appropriate for children. However, there were a number of positives, including the opportunity for parents to read a story to their child and participate in the bedtime routine. Nevertheless, respondents described the negative impact of visiting restrictions on the emotional well-being of both the person in prison and their child(ren).

6 Legal basis for restrictions and relaxations of the prison regime

6.1 An absence of safeguards

The implementation of restrictive regimes, including quarantine and lockdowns in prisons, has not been matched with the legislated safeguards, policies, procedures and practices crucial to ensuring that people in prison are not subjected to conditions or treatment that amount to a health risk, including through cruel, inhuman or degrading treatment. For example, the Victorian Aboriginal Legal Service (VALS) has raised concerns that, under the *Omnibus Act*, "there is a broad discretion to place a young person in isolation, which may be abused. There does not appear to be additional guidance, directives or training for staff on when and how to exercise their discretion under the Act", that "children who are placed in isolation for 14 consecutive days may not be allowed time out of isolation on the basis of security concerns", and that the Act permits "effectively extending isolation [of children] beyond the 14 days by having back-to-back periods of isolation" (VALS, 2020b: 20).

6.2 A lack of transparency by governments and detaining authorities

Similarly, there has consistently been a lack of transparency in relation to the treatment and conditions of people detained in prisons and youth detention facilities, as highlighted by NGOs such as VALS. It highlighted concerns in relation to "protective quarantine" and a lack of safeguards (VALS, 2020b: 5, 7, 8). There are difficulties with publicising private health data, but this does not prevent an audit of the health of people in prisons and transparency of arrangements for people in categories of health vulnerability.

6.3 External visits and monitoring: Legal basis and realities

COVID-19 has limited, but not wholly prevented, external oversight of Australian correctional facilities. In NSW, for example, the importance of maintaining oversight was enshrined in the emergency powers legislation, ensuring that the NSW Inspector of Custodial Services and Ombudsman were exempt from any visitor restrictions (*Crimes (Administration of Sentences) Act 1999* (NSW) s 275(3)). In August, the ACT Inspector of Correctional Services (2020a) indicated that it would visit both the adult and youth facilities during the pandemic and was "very conscious of the further restrictions that are being placed on those who are deprived of their liberty in response to COVID-19". In Victoria, however, there was less certainty, with emergency measures legislation granting the Secretary or the Governor the ability to prevent any "visitor" (as defined by s 33 of the *Corrections Act 1986* and including "an independent prison visitor" or "an Ombudsman officer" from entering a prison, see *Corrections Act 1986* (Vic) s 112G).

Legal uncertainty aside, as an early response to COVID-19, most external monitoring bodies across all Australian jurisdictions made the decision themselves to cease their visits, to mitigate the risk of staff introducing the virus into centres (Caruana, 2020). South Australia's Training Centre Visitor, appointed under *Youth Justice Administration Act 2016* (SA), was a notable exception, continuing to undertake a programme of regular fortnightly face-to-face visits to all units in the Adelaide Youth Training Centre by one or two staff members.

Inspectorates adjusted to a "virtual/remote" visiting model. These adjustments included daily briefings from departmental leaders, telephone briefings from centre managers, monitoring prison databases remotely and/or contacting incarcerated people and their representative organisations. In the face of strict travel restrictions to regional Western Australia, the Western Australian Inspector of Custodial Services (2020), for example, inspected a regional prison through an assessment of documentation, surveying staff and incarcerated people, conducting telephone interviews with prison staff and managers, interviewing community groups and contractors, and analysing its own information from over a dozen monitoring and liaison visits to the facility in the preceding three years.

The NSW Inspector of Custodial Services (2020) has stated that "[p]hysical visits and inspections of custodial centres will only take place at the direction of the Inspector", the ACT Inspector of Custodial Services (2020) affirmed on 25 August 2020 that "during the COVID-19 pandemic where it is safe to do so consistent with ACT Chief Health Officer advice", and the WA Inspector of Correctional Services returned to normal operations in October 2020.

In contrast, in Queensland, where there have been prison disturbances (Richardson, 2020), and conditions akin to solitary confinement (Smee, 2020b), the government has been severely criticised for its inaction in establishing an independent external monitoring body (Smee, 2020a). In the NT, no changes were made to the location of detained children, already locked in a prison condemned for adult occupation.

In Tasmania, the Custodial Inspector postponed all scheduled inspection between March and June 2020; however, no public information was made available on how COVID-19 has impacted its operations. Incarcerated people are still able to write or phone the Inspector and the Official Visitor programme. In the NT, where a regular programme of independent monitoring does not exist, the Office of the Children's Commissioner (OCC) of the Northern Territory (2020) published inspection reports for pre-COVID-19 visits to NT's youth detention facilities in June. Neither the OCC nor the NT Ombudsman has made public comment about correctional or youth detention facilities since restrictions came into force.

Reflecting on the impact of COVID-19 on external oversight and complaints handling through 2020, the NSW Ombudsman (2021) reported that it is critical that oversight and complaint handling be consciously considered, and if necessary, designed at the outset and alongside other crisis response planning activities. The Ombudsman further noted that, if a National Preventive Mechanism (NPM) had been operating in NSW in accordance with OPCAT during the COVID-19 pandemic, this would likely have had significant implications for oversight. As noted above, the NSW Inspector of Custodial Services is currently undertaking an inquiry on the response to COVID across NSW correctional facilities.

6.4 Judicial measures to manage prison environments: COVID and human rights risks

While policymakers have been reluctant to enact and implement prison release programmes, courts and parole boards have been increasingly cognisant of the health risks in prison. Generally, courts have recognised that prisons are susceptible to the spread of COVID-19, people in prisons are adversely impacted by onerous restrictions and that First Nations people are especially vulnerable (Public Defenders, 2020). This probably accounts for the statistical reduction in prisoner numbers, due to courts recognising the consequent harm, but must be seen against a background of significant case delays in some states, while there was a moratorium on jury trials in the pandemic.

7 Returning to normal – delayed and short-term

Although Australian governments eased COVID-19 community restrictions in most states and territories by mid-2020, corrective services agencies responded more slowly. In NSW, personal visits did not resume until up to nine months later. By mid-2021, prison visits were once again suspended in response to community transmission and these remained in place at least until late 2021.

In Victoria and NSW, prisons continue to use 14-day protective quarantine. This is highly concerning in the detention context, as there is no certainty when COVID-19 will cease to be a threat to health in Australia. Governments and detaining authorities cannot and should not persist with the strategies currently being employed to exclude and contain COVID-19, given the significant and potentially permanent deleterious health effects on individuals and the ever-increasing risk of current restrictive practices, which breach human rights, becoming normalised. There must be short-, medium- and long-term plans developed and executed, to ensure that Australia, at this crucial juncture, improves the justice and penal systems to ensure the highest attainable standards of health via significant reforms (Federation of Community Legal Centres Victoria and Law Institute Victoria, 2020), to include a decarceration policy.

There should be benchmarks for lifting restrictions on people in prisons, guided by human rights and evidence-based health advice, which can contribute to improved health and well-being outcomes for detained people in the long term. This includes reform to reduce high levels of anxiety, despair and feelings of powerlessness, which may precipitate protests in Australian prisons (and the accompanying, often violent, put-down responses). Overall, a rights-based approach requires short-term and long-term evidence-based healthcare. It must be coupled with a human rights model that moves us in the direction of prison abolition and cultures of social inclusion.

7.1 What can be learned

Lessons from Australia relate primarily to the need for decarceration, to enable people to acquire physical and mental health support and treatment in the community. Prisons, by contrast, are not structurally poised to cope with the health needs of people inside, nor equipped with services and an ethical framework to enable appropriate healthcare. While it is difficult to draw conclusions about the effectiveness of COVID-19 prison restrictions, as Australian prison environments have not been systematically tested for COVID-19 and community transmission rates in Australia have remained relatively low, there have been deleterious impacts on the human rights and mental well-being of the people inside prisons and youth detention centres. The crucial lesson, we suggest, is that diminishing prison populations can be highly effective in protecting rights and prioritising the human needs of individuals over punitive policies not just during a pandemic but for the realisation of commitments to rights to health and life for people in prisons. These lessons should inform a decarceration agenda that promotes a society, based on the provision of services and supports, rather than silos of exclusion from social relationships, healthcare and human rights.

References

AAP (2021, November 5): NSW prisons COVID-19 outbreak infected hundreds. Canberra Weekly. https://canberraweekly.com.au/nsw-prisons-covid-19-outbreak-infected-hundreds/

ABC News (2022, January 4): SA records 3,246 new COVID-19 cases, 102 in hospital with the disease. https://www.abc.net.au/news/2022-01-04/sa-reports-3246-covid-19-cases-102-in-hospital-with-the-disease/10073703

ACT Inspector of Custodial Services, COVID-19, https://www.ics.act.gov.au/latest-news/articles/covid-19, 25 August 2020.

Anonymous (2020): CSNSW officers enable 100,000 family video visits for inmates. *Mirage News*, 10 September, https://www.miragenews.com/csnsw-officers-enable-100-000-family-video-visits-for-inmates.

Anthony, T. (2017): Are Indigenous Australians the most incarcerated people on Earth? *The Conversation*, 6 June, https://theconversation.com/factcheck-qanda-are-indigenous-australians-the-most-incarcerated-people-on-earth-78528
Anthony, T. (2020a): Why releasing some prisoners is essential to stop the spread of coronavirus. *The Conversation*, 17 March, https://theconversation.com/why-releasing-some-prisoners-is-essential-to-stop-the-spread-of-coronavirus-133516
Anthony, T. (2020b): Explainer: How will the emergency release of NSW prisoners due to coronavirus work? *The Conversation*, 25 March.
Anthony, T. (2020c): Indigenous prison rates can fall fast: Here's the proof. *Sydney Morning Herald*, 7 August, https://www.smh.com.au/national/indigenous-prison-rates-can-fall-fast-here-s-the-proof-20200805-p55in2.html
Archer, E. (Minister for Corrections) (2020) Tasmania Prison Service COVID-19 Preparedness. *Media Release*, Tasmanian Government, 29 April, https://www.premier.tas.gov.au/releases/tasmania_prison_service_covid-19_preparedness
Australian Bureau of Statistics (2019): *Prisoners in Australia.* 2019.
Australian Bureau of Statistics (2021): *Corrective services, Australia* – September 2021.
Australian Institute of Health and Welfare (2019): *The health of Australia's prisoners: At a glance*, https://www.aihw.gov.au/getmedia/f4c958c3-98e9-46dd-8176-5da15cc2141e/prisoner_facts_infographic.pdf.aspx.
Australian Capital Territory Inspector of Correctional Services (2020a): *COVID-19.* Media release. 25 August.
Australian Capital Territory Inspector of Correctional Services (2020b): *Australian responses to COVID-19 in prisons*, https://www.ics.act.gov.au/__data/assets/pdf_file/0004/1618429/Australian-responses_web-version11.pdf.
Australian Government (2022): *Coronavirus (COVID-19) current situation and case numbers*, viewed 10 January, https://www.health.gov.au/news/health-alerts/novel-coronavirus-2019-ncov-health-alert/coronavirus-covid-19-current-situation-and-case-numbers.
Australian Institute of Health and Welfare (2019): *The health of Australia's prisoners, 2018.*
Australian Law Reform Commission (2017): *Pathways to justice – An inquiry into the incarceration rate of aboriginal and Torres Strait islander peoples.* Report 133.
Bachelet, M. (2020): *Urgent action needed to prevent COVID-19 "rampaging through places of detention.* United Nations Office of the High Commissioner for Human Rights.
Bartels, L. (2020): Sentencing review 2019–20. *Criminal Law Journal*, 44: 328–347.
Bartels, L., Anthony T., and Fletcher, K. (2020): *Open letter to Australian governments on COVID-19 and the criminal justice system*, https://alhr.org.au/wp/wp-content/uploads/2020/03/Open-letter-to-Australian-governments-on-COVID-19-and-the-criminal-justice-system-final-with-signatures.pdf.
Bruno, G. (2022, 8 January): Analysts predict one million Aussies will be living with a COVID-19 diagnosis within days. *AAP/7 News.* https://7news.com.au/lifestyle/health-wellbeing/analysts-predict-one-million-aussies-will-be-living-with-a-covid-19-diagnosis-within-days-c-5231402.
Caruana, S. (2020): COVID-19: Prisons and human rights in the time of COVID-19, University of Western Australia, 14 May https://www.news.uwa.edu.au/archive/2020051412082/uwa-public-policy-institute/covid-19-prisons-and-human-rights-time-covid-19/

Communicable Diseases Network Australia (2020): *CDNA national guidelines for the prevention, control and public health management of COVID-19 outbreaks in correctional and detention facilities in Australia* (3rd ed).

Corrections Victoria (2020): *Our response to coronavirus (COVID-19)*, viewed 17 November, https://www.corrections.vic.gov.au/covid19.

Corrective Services NSW (2020): *Corrective services*, viewed 17 November, https://www.coronavirus.dcj.nsw.gov.au/services/corrective-services.

Farquhar, L., and Scully, A. (2020): Coronavirus restrictions spark unrest in prisons as cell fires confirmed in NSW. *ABC News*, 3 April, https://www.abc.net.au/news/2020-04-03/coronavirus-restrictions-spark-inmate-unrest-in-nsw-jails/12113820.

Federation of Community Legal Centres Victoria and Law Institute Victoria (2020): *Pathways to decarceration: A justice system response to COVID-19*, 26 April, https://d3n8a8pro7vhmx.cloudfront.net/fclc/pages/715/attachments/original/1598396294/FCLC_DecarcerationStrategy_WebSinglePgs%2824aug2020%29.pdf?1598396294

First Nations families (2020): *Open letter: Urgent action from Australian governments needed to prevent COVID-19 Black deaths in custody*, 29 April, https://www.alsnswact.org.au/open_letter_from_families_clean_out_prisons.

Flynn, C. et al. (2020): *Maintaining family contact during COVID-19: Describing the experiences and needs of children with a family member in prison.* Report prepared for SHINE for Kids. https://shineforkids.org.au/wp-content/uploads/COVID-19_PrisonVisiting_October2020.pdf.

Gerry, F., Anthony, T., and Bartels, L. (2020): *Second national open letter to Australian governments on COVID-19 and prisons and youth detention centres*, https://www.greenslist.com.au/assets/papers/Second%20open%20letter%20to%20Australian%20governments%20re%20prisons%20and%20COVID-19%20-%20with%20signatures.pdf.

Goldsworthy, T., and Lincoln, R. (2020): Explainer: why police will be crucial players in the battle against coronavirus. *The Conversation*, 27 March, https://theconversation.com/explainer-why-police-will-be-crucial-players-in-the-battle-against-coronavirus-134392.

Gramenz, E., McKenna, K. & Paula Doneman, P. (2022, January 2): Queensland mask rules toughened as COVID-19 spreads in vulnerable youth detention centres, Torres Strait communities. ABC News Online.https://www.abc.net.au/news/2022-01-02/qld-coronavirus-covid-torres-strait-detention-masks-outbreaks/100732906

Hepatitis Australia (2017): *Responding to blood-borne viruses in Australian prisons.*

Hurley, M. (2020): Children should never be subjected to solitary confinement. *Brisbane Times*, 17 September, https://www.brisbanetimes.com.au/national/queensland/children-should-never-be-subjected-to-solitary-confinement-20200911-p55uvs.html.

Institute for Crime and Justice Policy Research (2020): *World prison brief – Australia*, viewed 17 November, https://www.prisonstudies.org/country/australia.

Jervis-Brady, D. (2020): Coronavirus fines an "absolute last resort", ACT police chief says. *Canberra Times*, 1 April, https://www.canberratimes.com.au/story/6707692/fines-for-coronavirus-gathering-breaches-an-absolute-last-resort/.

Justice Action (2012): *Policy proposal: Computers in cells*, https://www.justiceaction.org.au/computers-in-cells/policy-proposal

Justice Action (2017): *Rapid build prison dormitories.* Media release, 16 November, https://www.justiceaction.org.au/prisons/prison-issues/conditions/920-rapid-build-prison-dormitories.

Mills, T. (2021): Prisoner quarantine based on 'alarming absence' of health advice. The Age, 30 March, https://www.theage.com.au/national/victoria/prisoner-quarantine-basedon-alarming-absence-of-health-advice-20210329-p57evu.html.

National Aboriginal and Torres Strait Islander Legal Services (2020a): *Legal sector sign on to open letter calling for urgent release of people from adult and youth prisons as COVID-19 spreads rapidly in prisons.* Media release, 13 August.

National Aboriginal and Torres Strait Islander Legal Services (2020b): *Victorian government risks COVID-19 prison outbreak and must urgently release people from prison to prevent COVID-19 black deaths in custody.* Media release, 21 July.

National Aboriginal and Torres Strait Islander Legal Services, Anthony, T., and Gerry, F. (2020): *Open letter calling for safe release of adults and children from prisons and youth detention centres and protection of their rights and health in the COVID-19 pandemic*, August 2020, https://www.natsils.org.au/open-letter-calling-for-safe-release-of-adults-and-children-from-prisons-and-youth-detention-centres-and-protection-of-their-rights-and-health-in-the-covid-19-pandemic-august-2020/.

National Aboriginal and Torres Strait Islander Legal Services, Danila Dilba Health Service, Aboriginal Peak Organisations of the Northern Territory and Andreea Lachsz (2020): *Joint submission for the report of the Special Rapporteur on the rights of Indigenous peoples to the General Assembly – Impact of COVID-19 on Indigenous peoples*, http://www.amsant.org.au/apont/wp-content/uploads/2020/06/Joint-submission-to-Special-Rapporteur-on-rights-of-Indigenous-peoples-Impact-of-COVID-19-19-June-2020-FINAL.pdf.

NSW Bureau of Crime Statistics and Research (2020): *NSW custody statistics: Quarterly update September 2020.*

NSW Inspector of Custodial Services (2021, 29 October): Review of COVID Response, https://www.inspectorcustodial.nsw.gov.au/inspector-of-custodial-services/current-inspections/adult-inspections/review-o-covid-19-response-.html (accessed 13 December 2020).

NSW Ombudsman (2021): 2020 hindsight: The first 12 months of the COVID-19 pandemic. https://www.ombo.nsw.gov.au/__data/assets/pdf_file/0017/115073/2020-hindsight_the-first-12-months-of-the-COVID-19_pandemic-Special-Report.pdf.

Office of the Children's Commissioner of the Northern Territory (2020): *Don Dale youth detention and Alice Springs youth detention monitoring reports.* Media release. 24 June.

Office of the Inspector of Custodial Services Western Australia (2020): *Our response to COVID-19*, https://www.oics.wa.gov.au/about-oics/our-response-to-covid-19/?doing_wp_cron=1605596808.9813969135284423828125.

Penal Reform International (2016): *Contact with the outside world*, https://cdn.penalreform.org/wp-content/uploads/2016/10/Chapter-3-Contact-with-the-outside-world-final.pdf.

Productivity Commission (2020): *Report on government services, 2020: Corrective services.*

Public Defenders NSW (2020): *COVID-19 resources for criminal lawyers*, https://www.publicdefenders.nsw.gov.au/Pages/c19resources.aspx.

Public Health Association of Australia (2017): *Prisoner health background paper*, https://www.phaa.net.au/documents/item/2579.

Queensland Corrective Services (2020): *QCS announces new isolation procedures for prisoners*. Media release, 8 April, viewed 17 September, https://corrections.qld.gov.au/qcs-announces-new-isolation-procedures-for-prisoners.

Rapisarda, S., and Byrne, J. (2020): An examination of COVID-19 outbreaks in prisons and jails in Oceania. *Victims & Offenders*, DOI: 10.1080/15564886.2020.1835767

Richardson, H. (2020): Fire at Borallon prison, west of Brisbane, the second Queensland prison blaze since coronavirus lockdown was enforced. *ABC News* (online), 3 September, https://www.abc.net.au/news/2020-09-03/queensland-prison-riot-fire-covid-coronavirus-lockdown/12623858.

Sarre, R., Bartels, L., and Makkai, T. (2020): We need to consider granting bail to unsentenced prisoners to stop the spread of coronavirus. *The Conversation*, 26 March.

Smee, B: (2020a): Queensland urged to appoint independent justice inspector after minors locked down. *The Guardian*, 8 September, https://www.theguardian.com/australia-news/2020/sep/08/queensland-urged-to-appoint-independent-justice-inspector-after-minors-locked-down.

Smee, B. (2020b): Some prisoners spending 22 hours a day in solitary confinement due to Queensland Covid lockdown. *The Guardian*, 16 September, https://www.theguardian.com/australia-news/2020/sep/16/vulnerable-prisoners-sent-to-solitary-confinement-during-queenslands-covid-lockdown-lawyers-say.

UN Committee on Economic, Social and Cultural Rights (2000): *General Comment No. 14: The right to the highest attainable standard of health (Art. 12 of the Covenant)*, 11 August 2000, E/C.12/2000/4.

UN Human Rights Committee (HRC) (2001): *CCPR General Comment No. 29: Article 4: Derogations during a state of emergency*, 31 August 2001, CCPR/C/21/Rev.1/Add.11.

UN Subcommittee on Prevention of Torture and other Cruel, Inhuman or Degrading Treatment or Punishment (2020): *Advice of the subcommittee on prevention of torture to states parties and national preventive mechanisms relating to the coronavirus pandemic* (adopted on 25 March 2020).

Victorian Aboriginal Legal Service (2020a): *The COVID-19 outbreak should be undertaken by professional cleaning staff, who have access to PPE*. Media release, 11 August, https://www.vals.org.au/the-covid-19-outbreak-should-be-undertaken-by-professional-cleaning-staff-who-have-access-to-ppe/.

Victorian Aboriginal Legal Service (2020b): *Public accounts and estimates committee COVID-19 submission*, September, https://www.parliament.vic.gov.au/images/stories/committees/paec/COVID-19_Inquiry/Submissions/87._Victorian_Aboriginal_Legal_Service.pdf.

Victorian Department of justice and Community Safety (2020): *Youth justice coronavirus (COVID-19) update - fact sheet for stakeholders*, 2, https://www.liv.asn.au/getattachment/Professional-Practice/Supporting-You/COVID-19-Hub/Information-from-Profession/Fact-sheet-for-stakeholders---Roadmap-for-YJ-custodial-facilities---December-2020.pdf.aspx.

Victorian Ombudsman (2019): *"Unlawful and wrong" - solitary confinement and isolation of young people in Victorian prison and youth justice centres*. Media release, 5 September.

World Health Organization (2020a): *Frequently asked questions about prevention and control of COVID-19 in prisons and other places of detention.*

World Health Organization (2020b): *Preparedness, prevention and control of COVID-19 in prisons and other places of detention: Interim guidance.*

Worldometer (2022): *Coronavirus cases*, viewed 10 January, https://www.worldometers.info/coronavirus/.

World Health Organization Regional Office for Europe (2020): *Preparedness, prevention and control of COVID-19 in prisons and other places of detention interim guidance*, 15 March.

3 Austria

Karin Bruckmüller, Walter Hammerschick and Lukas Linser

1 Introduction – general situation of the prison system

In the early days of the pandemic, only minor changes were observed with respect to the numbers of prisoners in Austrian prisons; however, subsequently the numbers dropped quite significantly. In 2019, an average of 9,329 persons were imprisoned. By 1 May 2020, the numbers had decreased to 8,674 and by January 2021, they had declined further to 8,488 inmates (Figure 3.1).

According to the Austrian Ministry of Justice and representatives of the prison system,[1] there have not been any large outbreaks of COVID-19 in the prisons for almost a year since the outbreak of the pandemic. Some prisoners entering the facilities as well as prison staff were reported to have

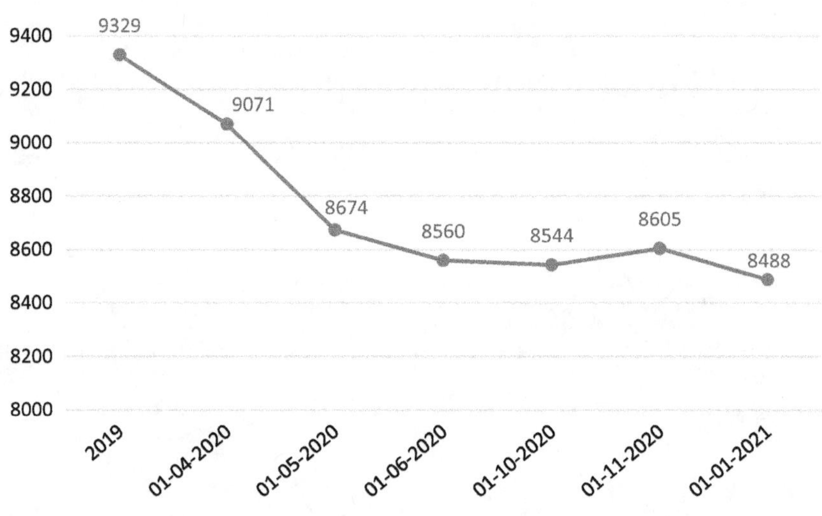

Figure 3.1 Recent developments of the total numbers of prisoners.[2, 3]
Source: Annual security report (Sicherheitsbericht) of the Austrian Ministry of Justice 2019[4] and monthly publications of basic data on prisoners by the Ministry.[5]

DOI: 10.4324/9781003169178-3

been infected. However, the virus was successfully kept out of prisons. This was achieved by the prison staff taking care to maintain the highest safety and hygiene standards inside the facilities,[6] as well as by promptly adopting measures when it was suspected that staff members might be infected.

When the rate of infection was high, prisoners had to quarantine for 14 days on admission to prison. This was especially difficult for juveniles coming into prison; no distinction was made between adults and young offenders in this regard. In times of low infection, new prisoners were housed in separate cells for ten days and required to wear a face mask whenever they left their cells. Prison staff were also required to wear mouth and nose coverings at all times.

Social distancing was required at all times, and surfaces were disinfected frequently. All persons entering prisons had to undergo a risk assessment and have their temperature taken. Prison staff were assigned to phase two of the Austrian vaccination plan. Phase two was characterised by an improved availability of vaccines and by vaccinations no longer restricted to the highest risk groups according to age- and health-related risks. Phase two aimed to reach people between 65 and 79, younger ones with specific health-related risks and certain professional groups like teachers and police officers. For prisoners, the same rules applied as for the general public, with access to vaccines according to age and health conditions, but – according to the national vaccination plan – in any case all people in "Community Accommodations" (as in prisons) have to be vaccinated in phase 3[7] (Scherndl, 2020; Bundesministerium für Soziales und Gesundheit – Federal Ministry of Social Affairs and Health, 2021).

According to prison representatives, promptly granting extensive leave of absence for staff members reporting suspicious symptoms was an important preventive measure. While this strategy was sensitive to the spread of the virus, it caused severe problems for the running of prisons, work with the prisoners, preparation of prisoners for release, and, in the end, for the overall conditions of imprisonment. Prison officers in Austria already had very high rates of sick leave before the pandemic[8] (Rechnungshof Austria, 2020). The lack of available staff was a factor contributing to a situation in which prisoners were largely restricted to their cells.

For shift work, prison staff in each prison were organised into groups. The groups did not have any direct physical contact with each other, in order to ensure at least a basic functioning of the system if members of one group tested positive for the virus. While there is no doubt that the pandemic made the work situation extremely stressful for prison staff, many of the measures introduced also infringed the rights of prisoners severely.

The prison system appears to have reacted quickly with respect to security, hygiene, and protective measures. Extensive measures were already introduced in late February 2020, by a decree (*Erlass*) of the Austrian Ministry of Justice,[9] when general figures on the spread of the pandemic were still low in Austria. The decree was expanded further when the situation called for it.

At an early stage, the decision makers at the prisons still had some agency, but later the guidelines from the Ministry became much stricter.

The protection of health is a distinct priority of the prison system, to which measures to ease the current difficult living conditions in prison have clearly been subordinated. Thus far, the handling of the COVID-19 crisis in the Austrian prison system has been characterised by extensive measures to reduce the risk of "importing" the virus and spreading it in the prisons. The main strategy was and is to reduce new admissions, to keep all contact with the outside world to a minimum, and, finally, to reduce activities in the prison to a minimum. Of course, this has extensive and very painful consequences for the organisation and in shaping prison life, not least for the preparation of prisoners for release and the life outside. While there were already shortcomings in this respect, mainly due to the high numbers of prisoners and a lack of resources (both personnel and material) in many prisons, the situation was severely exacerbated by the pandemic. It must be highlighted that no sanctioning rules were changed or adapted to reduce the number of new entries into prison. Only entry by certain groups was postponed.

Given the structural conditions and considering the risks that the pandemic posed for prisoners, the prisoner numbers still appeared rather high. The current stricter rules because of the pandemic may lead to concern that the current Austrian prison regime may not meet generally acknowledged and required standards of imprisonment. Unfortunately, there is no indication that measures will be introduced to reduce the numbers of prisoners by means of an exit strategy. This means that the fastest and most effective way of reducing the number of prisoners considerably appears to have been ignored. Most of the procedures for doing so would require legal changes. For instance, thus far no initiatives have been taken to change or adapt any rules to suspend already enforced sentences, particularly for high-risk groups like the elderly; similarly, rules relating to early release have remained unchanged. During the first lockdown, the numbers of prisoners decreased only slightly. Most prisons were still overfull or at least close to their regular capacity (9,071 prisoners on 1 April, see Figure 3.1). Only after some months did the number of prisoners decline more substantially (8,560 prisoners on 1 June). Apparently, there is not sufficient (political) will to introduce more substantial changes. From the point of view of the health situation in prison, this could be risky. If the virus were to find its way into the prison system, the prisons close to capacity and those that remain partially overcrowded would provide favourable conditions for the virus to spread swiftly. Even strict measures concerning hygiene, health protection, and separation from the outside world cannot guarantee that the virus will be kept out of the prison system. Unfortunately, this was proven true when a cluster of infected inmates was reported from an Austrian prison in early February 2021. By the time of the completion of this chapter, no detailed information was available, neither on the reasons for the virus intrusion into this facility, nor the effects of the measures to prevent it from spreading further.

Even though reports from the prison system claim that the atmosphere in prison appears to be good, as the prisoners are cooperative and understanding, there are also reports about frightened prisoners and prisoners suffering due to harsh restrictions imposed on them (see especially Section 4 – not being able to see their family in person, concern for relatives, or a lack of frequent and varied activities). With the restrictions continuing for a longer period, the reports stressed that it might become more difficult to maintain order.

While restrictions are ubiquitous in all Austrian prisons, the situation differs considerably among the different prisons – with respect to the numbers of prisoners, the room/space situation, and the extent to which prison life is closed down, among other factors. As mentioned before, prison activities have been reduced to a minimum in many prisons. However, some prisons have reported that they have managed to maintain a prison regime in which prison conditions are quite close to what they normally are. The differences are often due to existing conditions and structures, but they also depend on the creativity with which staff members attempt to overcome the crisis, and the related restrictions (Birklbauer, 2020a, 2020b).

2 Prison and penal policy concerning the execution of prison sentences during the COVID-19 crisis

2.1 Sentenced prisoners and sentences

The main strategy to reduce the number of prisoners is based on a decree ordering a reprieve. The execution of sentences of up to three years must be postponed, excluding those sentences imposed for certain violent and sexual offences.[10] At first, the operation of this regulation was limited until the end of April 2020, but it was prolonged by a new decree.[11] There have been no reports of any intention to change or adapt any sanctioning rules (e.g. changing short sentences into community service or substituting imprisonment for failure to pay a fine with community service). Time limits for the payment of fines as well as for any sentences offenders are obliged to carry out have been extended.[12]

It has to be assumed that the reprieved sentences will lead to new and possibly even more severe overcrowding as soon as the restrictions are lifted. The option of an amnesty has been discussed, but so far there are no indications that this course will be adopted.

2.2 Pre-trial detention

A decree of 7 April 2020 by the Ministry of Justice[13] stressed that the grounds for detention and the principle of proportionality had to be re-evaluated by taking into consideration the current situation and developments with respect to the pandemic. This might justify not detaining someone or releasing them from detention. Measures restricting the freedom of movement taken because of the pandemic might, for instance, make detention unnecessary. However, prosecutors (reportedly especially those in Vienna) do not seem to be changing their practices, and were reported to be ordering pre-trial detention as usual. More flexibility in decision making (as proposed in the decree) was reported to be hardly observed.

Nevertheless, practitioners reported having fewer pre-trial detainees entering prison since the outbreak of the pandemic. This, however, could be due to fewer reports to the courts from the police (and possibly also fewer reports to the police from the public). It will be interesting to study the developments with respect to the numbers of offences reported during the pandemic. Criminal lawyers noted above all an improvement in the likelihood of getting their clients out of detention (e.g. usually a suspect without a job has little chance of being released, while recently not being employed has been reported to appear of little relevance). This is ironic, since one would assume that pre-trial detention should be avoided in the first place, in an effort to keep suspects suitable for release or for alternatives out of the system and to avoid unnecessary detention. Still, the number of pre-trial detainees has dropped from an average of 1,756 in 2019 to 1,529 on 1 January 2021.

It should be mentioned that about 70% of all pre-trial detainees in Austria are foreign nationals (Bundesministerium für Justiz, 2019). One can certainly question detention practices with respect to suspects who are foreign nationals, but it is also a fact that in their case it is more difficult to substitute pre-trial detention with alternatives that will ensure that they stand trial.

2.3 House arrest with electronic monitoring (EM) – front and back door

In Austria, house arrest with EM is not a sanction in itself, but it is a way of executing prison sentences.[14] During the first months of the pandemic, the numbers of prisoners subject to this regime had decreased overall. While the average number of EM-prisoners in 2019 was 348, only 245 prisoners were electronically monitored in May and June of 2020, resulting in a decrease of 29.6%. By November 2020, the numbers of prisoners in EM had again risen to 356 (4.1% of all prisoners; Figure 3.2).

Front door clients of the electronically monitored house arrest regime serve all of their sentences at home. During the early phases of the pandemic, new entrances of front door clients into house arrest were postponed, presumably to save the staff resources.

However, it can also be assumed that potential candidates for EM may have lost their jobs because of the pandemic. Usually, a job is a prerequisite for the acceptance of sentenced offenders for the house arrest regime, but not during the pandemic.

Back door (BD) entrances into electronically monitored house arrests (after having served parts of the sentence in prison) were also suspended during the first phase of the pandemic. This appears a little strange because such

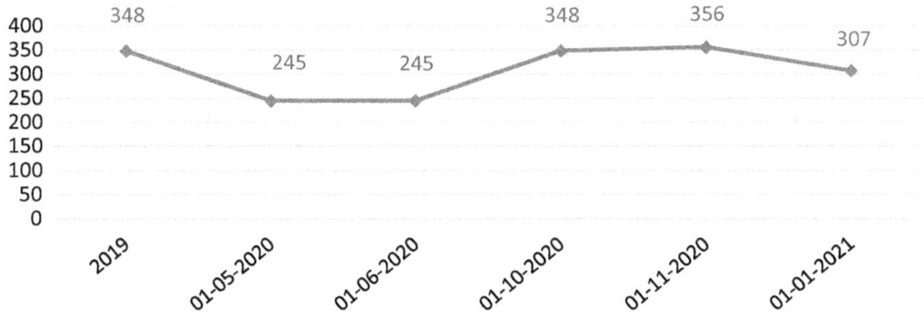

Figure 3.2 Recent developments of the numbers of prisoners in House Arrest with EM.

Source: Annual security report (Sicherheitsbericht) of the Austrian Ministry of Justice 2019[15] and monthly publications of basic data on prisoners of the Ministry.[16]

EM provides a legal option for reducing the number of people in prison. While the pandemic made it even more difficult for potential EM-clients to find a job, it remained a promising option. By the autumn of 2020, access to BD EM was back to normal (given that requirements were fulfilled, see Bruckmüller, 2019: 23–24; Hammerschick, 2017: 403–404). Usually, house arrest prisoners are granted two weeks to find a new job, if they have lost their previous job. During the pandemic, it was reported that prison administrations granted more time before house arrest prisoners had to continue their sentence in prison.

2.4 *Early release*

As already mentioned, there is no intention so far to legally extend the possibilities of early release. Practitioners who were interviewed also did not observe that early (conditional) release of prisoners had been extended in practice. On the contrary, there are concerns that conditional release could be allowed less frequently because of reduced activities of the courts, with many judges mainly working from home. It seems that this option for reducing the numbers of inmates, to lessen the burden imposed on the penal system by the threat of possible infections, will remain largely unused in Austria.

3 Restrictions of contact with the outside world

During the period when the rate of infection was high, all direct, personal contact of prisoners with the outside world was suspended:

- At first, visits of defence lawyers were reported to have been restricted to urgent cases. Video conferencing was arranged with lawyers. There were some complaints about restricted communication with clients. With the decrease of the infection numbers, lawyers were allowed to speak to clients in person, a practice continued later on despite higher infection numbers. At the time of low rates of infection, lawyers were obliged to have their temperatures taken, wear mouth and nose protection, and were only allowed to talk to prisoners with a glass screen separating them.

- Questioning and hearings by the courts were also largely carried out via video connections.
- As with lawyers, probation officers' contacts with their clients in prison were reportedly also restricted at first. Contacts often took place via telephone, and sometimes via video conferencing. Like lawyers, probation officers were subsequently also allowed to see their clients in prison; this continued, despite higher infection numbers, with the same rules and requirements applying. Probation officers were also asked to announce visits ahead of time. In the expert interviews, representatives of probation work surprisingly reported good experiences with probation work conducted at a distance.
- At first, most therapy sessions were cancelled. Such sessions were later held but in compliance with strict safe distance rules, the therapists being obliged to have their temperature taken when entering the prison. With respect to therapy, however, there were and are differences among prisons. There are still major restrictions in some prisons, while in others, therapy sessions are largely available, in part using video conferencing.
- To protect inmates, no daytime leave for work or education, furlough, or other forms of prison leave were allowed.

During the times when infection rates were low:

- Prisoners were granted leave for important personal matters, such as funerals of relatives. Daytime leave for work or education might be allowed in compliance with strict hygiene measures.
- Prisons were opened for visitors as well, but only under strict conditions: the visits had to be booked ahead of time and take place behind glass panes, allowing no direct contact, and only single visitors. Furthermore, visitors were obliged to wear a face mask covering mouth and nose. As of 26 December, all visits were prohibited again as COVID-19 numbers were increasing rapidly.

4 Restrictions inside prisons

All activities in prison were reduced to avoid the risks of infection and spread of the virus in prison, but also to manage the demand with respect to the staff needed. Apart from the shortages of staff, additional protection and security measures reduced the staff available for other activities.

There are, however, considerable differences among prisons. While most workshops were closed and only essential work needed to run the system was carried out in most prisons at the beginning of the pandemic, they were reopened under the condition that inmates and prison staff maintain a safe distance from each other. Hence, the work process was partially changed and the size of the groups reduced in some prisons.

Some Austrian prisons started to produce face masks, primarily for internal use, and to a lesser extent for external use. In one of the prisons contacted, the production of face masks was introduced for prisoners who used to leave the prison on a daily basis for work.

Opportunities for unemployed prisoners to leave the cells were extended by introducing measures of hygiene, but the time spent outside of cells remained much too short in many prisons. It remains to be seen whether crime rates in prisons will rise and lead to an increase in the number of victims (particularly for bodily injury and coercion). However, we have to be aware that many assaults in prisons remain unreported.

The differences among the prisons are also true with respect to leisure activities, with many prisons largely suspending most or even all such activities, while some others carry on with a few. In some prisons, schooling for young inmates continued, albeit on a restricted basis.

In most prisons, active preparations for release were reduced considerably during the early phases of the pandemic. Due to the importance of these measures for the prevention of recidivism, these activities have been increased again in close cooperation with the probation services.

5 Compensatory measures

Overall, it has to be stressed that during the time with high rates of infection, indirect contact was unable to substitute for the personal and immediate contact with family and friends. Therefore, it is of utmost importance to allow personal visits in prisons as soon as infection rates and protective measures allow.

In practice, opportunities to engage in video conferencing with family and others were gradually extended in order to broaden the offers of this kind of contact with the outside world in all prisons. These developments have been promoted during the coronavirus crisis. In Vienna, video conferencing is also used for the so-called social net conferences, with juveniles using a software application originally introduced to support interpreters. In these (few) conferences, families and other important social net actors are included to establish conditions for young offenders that might allow their release from pre-trial detention. The young offender is in prison at this point, accompanied by court assistance staff, while family and others are at the premises of the Verein NEUSTART, the main organisation in Austria working with (ex)offenders. The conferences are guided by NEUSTART staff.

Access to and permission for phone calls were also extended. In general, there is a telephone accessible to inmates in each division. Mobile phones are largely forbidden in prisons. This did not change during the COVID-19 crisis. However, prisoners detained in some open sections of prisons were allowed to carry mobile phones. In new prisons, there are also cells in open sections equipped with prepaid telephones, which can be used with permission. Such telephones allow access to specific telephone numbers that are not blacklisted. Allegedly, easy access to telephones has led to a considerable decline in the illegal possession of mobile phones.

In addition, an expert has reported improvements in the degree of trust between prison staff and prisoners during the pandemic crisis. Prisoners address their concerns more freely and, in turn, the prison staff are able to respond more readily. This allows the staff to deal with potentially critical developments more easily.

In some expert talks, it was regretted, that e-learning opportunities are still very limited in Austrian prisons. These possibilities would pay off in times of crises like the COVID-19 pandemic.

6 Legal basis for restrictions and relaxations of the prison regime

Austrian legislation on measures to avoid the spread of the COVID-19 virus has been convoluted. There are different "levels" of regulations for all Austria, namely decrees (*Erlässe*), enactments (*Verordnungen*), and statutes (*Bundesgesetze*). This approach enables continuous and fast reactions by the legislator and/or administration in times of higher and lower infection figures. Different levels of legal intervention are also necessary to meet the requirements of the Austrian constitution (but also carry the risk of causing confusion). The measures introduced by the different regulatory instruments have been mentioned in the corresponding sections above.

On the one hand, rules have been introduced regulating the situation in prisons, in particular introduced by

- *Statute: Bundesgesetz betreffend Begleitmaßnahmen zu COVID-19 in der Justiz (1. COVID-19-Justiz-Begleitgesetz – 1. COVID-19-JuBG)* which came into effect on 23 March 2020[17] and has been modified twice already. It has been modified by the 2. COVID-19-Law on 21 March 2020 and the 3. COVID-19-Law on 4 April 2020.[18]

Based on the statute law

- enactments have been published: *Verordnungen der Bundesministerin für Justiz, mit der zur Verhinderung der Verbreitung von COVID-19 besondere Vorkehrungen in Strafsachen getroffen werden* from 23 March,[19]

24 March, 8 April, 27 April, 29 May, 25 June, 30 September, and 20 November 2020. They were all largely based on the first enactment, with later enactments introducing some modifications depending on the rate of new infections.

Based on the enactments

- decrees were elaborated: *Erlässe zur Änderung der Verordnung über besondere Vorkehrungen im Anwendungsbereich des Strafvollzugsgesetzes zur Verhinderung der Verbreitung von COVID-19* (1st, 2nd, 3rd, 4th, 5th COVID-19-StVG-Erlass) from 27 March,[20] 30 April,[21] 30 June,[22] 30 July,[23] and 31 August[24] 2020 (they were all based on the first one and contained only some modifications depending on the rate of new infections. Additionally, there was a so-called "overview" of the first measures published on 7 April.[25]

On the other hand, there are enactments and statutes of a general nature, which are also applicable to prison regimes. These include general standards of hygiene and distancing to which everyone must adhere.[26]

7 Returning to normal

At the time of completion of this contribution, Austria has not yet succeeded in controlling the pandemic. A second lockdown was decreed and also regional restrictions. Even at the time of the review of the chapter the pandemic was not under control and a third lockdown was an unpleasant reality, of course also affecting the prison system. In the meanwhile, the prisons had gone back to some more normality, with the restrictions however still dominating. Another cluster at a prison once again showed that the virus can find ways into prisons despite all measures in place. The ways to control the difficult situation did not change much.

A main strategy to deal with COVID-19 in the prison system remains a continuation of postponing the implementation of sentences and thereby keeping the numbers of prisoners somewhat lower than before the pandemic. This, however, means that the number of people who have to serve their sentences some time in the future continues to grow. Considering the fact that Austrian prisons were overcrowded before the pandemic, this carries the risk of even worse overcrowding than before. Urgent measures are needed to avoid such developments.

Early release of certain groups of offenders is seemingly not yet planned. The prison system will continue to focus on maintaining high hygienic standards and on strict measures to reduce the risk of infections being transmitted inside prisons. Since this risk can never be fully excluded, the current strategies to control the pandemic in the prison system appear too narrow. The longer the pandemic lasts, the higher the need for the prison system to implement strategies to suitably prepare the inmates for life after imprisonment and for a life hopefully without crime.

Austria's response to the pandemic, as well as reports from other countries on their developments during this crisis indicate that changes in criminal policies, such as avoiding prison sentences more often and alternatives to imprisonment, do not endanger the security of the population. There is no (visible) increase of crime rates. This observation should be considered a good reason for future changes in this direction. Imprisonment is supposed to be an ultima ratio; it is expensive and often it is not what is required to prepare prisoners for a better and more law-abiding life.

The situation in prisons during the pandemic made clear that digital tools for inmates to communicate with the outside world do not necessarily create unmanageable risks and problems of control. The prison system can control these risks very well. They are important tools to facilitate and promote social contacts and to support preparations for release, such as providing occupational perspectives. The prison system should continue to extend these provisions and offers for inmates when the pandemic is under control. Not least, prisons should take advantage of, and continue to extend e-learning possibilities. Considering that about half of all prisoners in Austria are not Austrian nationals and that many of them have no regular place of residence in Austria, one should aim to foster more cross-border cooperation, allowing for better communication between inmates and their families and friends or other relevant contacts in their home countries, while also enabling them to take advantage of e-learning opportunities.

Notes

1 This report reflects the status early in 2021 and is based on talks with representatives of the prison system and with other legal experts in contact with prisoners and prisons, as well as on relevant legal changes and adaptations introduced in connection with the pandemic.

2 https://www.justiz.gv.at/home/justiz/daten-und-fakten/berichte/sicherheitsberichte~2c94848525f84a630132fdbd2cc85c91.de.html (last visit on 7 Dec. 2021)

3 Verteilung des Insassinnen- bzw. Insassenstandes (justiz.gv.at) (last visit on 8 Dec. 2021- website always presents the current month)

4 https://www.justiz.gv.at/home/justiz/daten-und-fakten/berichte/sicherheitsberichte~2c94848525f84a630132fdbd2cc85c91.de.html.

5 https://www.justiz.gv.at/home/strafvollzug/statistik/verteilung-des-insassinnenstandes~2c94848542ec49810144457e2e6f3de9.de.htm.

6 https://www.justiz.gv.at/home/covid-19/haeufige-fragen~7bd.de.html (status of all Justiz.gv.at pages: Dec. 2020).

7 See https://www.sozialministerium.at/Corona-Schutzimpfung/Corona-Schutzimpfung---Fachinformationen.html (last visit on 8 Dec. 2021).

8 In 2018, prison officers were reported to have been on sick leave for 26 days on an average.

9 GZ 2020-0.178.957.

https://www.justiz.gv.at/file/2c94848b6ff7074f0170d4177caf44a8.de.0/erlass.pdf?forcedownload=true

10 Article 3, Verordnung der Bundesministerin für Justiz über besondere Vorkehrungen im Anwendungsbereich des Strafvollzugsgesetzes zur Verhinderung der Verbreitung von COVID-19 BGBl. II Nr. 120/2020. Based on Bundesgesetz betreffend Begleitmaßnahmen zu COVID-19 in der Justiz (1. COVID-19-Justiz-Begleitgesetz – 1. COVID-19-JuBG) BGBl. I Nr. 16/2020.

11 Erlass vom 7. April 2020 über besondere Vorkehrungen in Strafsachen zur Verhinderung der Verbreitung von COVID-19 (Gesamtdarstellung) (30.04.2020) GZ2020-0.220.530, eJABl. Nr. 60/2020.

12 Verordnung der Bundesministerin für Justiz, mit der zur Verhinderung der Verbreitung von COVID-19 besondere Vorkehrungen in Strafsachen getroffen werden BGBl. II Nr. 113/2020.

13 Erlass vom 7. April 2020 über besondere Vorkehrungen in Strafsachen zur Verhinderung der Verbreitung von COVID-19 (Gesamtdarstellung) (30.04.2020) GZ2020-0.220.530, eJABl. Nr. 60/2020.

14 In principle, pre-trial detention can also be served with house arrest and EM. Practically, this option is hardly used.

15 https://www.justiz.gv.at/home/justiz/daten-und-fakten/berichte/sicherheitsberichte~2c94848525f84a630132fdbd2cc85c91.de.html.

16 https://www.justiz.gv.at/home/strafvollzug/statistik/verteilung-des-insassinnen-standes~2c94848542ec4981014 4457e2e6f3de9.de.html.

17 Translation by the authors: Federal law with respect to accompanying issues to COVID-19 for the judiciary BGBl. I Nr. 16/2020.

18 Translation by the authors: Edict of the federal minister for judiciary regarding precautionary measures of COVID-19 in criminal law, It has been modified by the 2nd COVID-19-Law of 21 March 2020 and the 4th COVID-19-Law of 4 April 2020.

19 BGBl. II Nr. 113/2020; the following amendments are published in BGBl. II Nr. 114, 138, 180, 243, 278, 418 and 494/2020.

20 Translation by the authors: Decrees for the amendment of the edict on special precautionary measures in the area of application of the penal system to prevent the spread of COVID-19 GZ2020-0.204.238, eJABl. Nr. 57/2020.

21 GZ2020-0.271.526, eJABl Nr. 63/2020.

22 GZ2020-0.399.485, eJABl Nr. 72/2020.

23 GZ2020-0.485.027, eJABl Nr. 74/2020.

24 GZ 2020-0.551.264, eJABl Nr. 78/2020.

25 Erlass vom 7. April 2020 über besondere Vorkehrungen in Strafsachen zur Verhinderung der Verbreitung von COVID-19 (Gesamtdarstellung) (30.04.2020) GZ2020-0.220.530, eJABl. Nr. 60/2020.

26 Article 1, Bundesgesetz betreffend vorläufige Maßnahmen zur Verhinderung der Verbreitung von COVID-19 (COVID-19-Maßnahmengesetz – COVID-19-MG), Translation by the authors: Federal law regarding precautionary measures to prevent the spread of COVID-19 BGBl. I Nr. 138/2020.

References

Birklbauer, A. (2020a): Chapter 16 – Strafrecht. In: Resch (Eds.): *Corona Handbuch Österreichs Rechtspraxis zur aktuellen Lage*. Wien: Manz, 403–432.

Birklbauer, A. (2020b): Die Verhältnismäßigkeit der Covid-19 Maßnahmen aus strafrechtlicher Sicht. In: Kröll, W., et al. (Eds.): *Die Corona-Pandemie – Strafrecht*. Wien: Nomos, 137–152.

Bruckmüller, K. (2019): Prisoner resettlement in Austria. A supportive Approach. In: Dünkel, F, Pruin, I., Storgaard, A. and Weber, J. (Eds.): *Prisoner Resettlement in Europe*. London, New York: Routledge, 19–36.

Bundesministerium für Justiz (2019): *Sicherheitsbericht 2019 - Bericht über die Tätigkeit der Strafjustiz*, 149.

Bundesministerium für Soziales und Gesundheit (2021): COVID-19-Impfungen: Priorisierung des Nationalen Impfgremiums. https://www.sozialministerium.at/Corona-Schutzimpfung/Corona-Schutzimpfung—Fachinformationen.html.

Hammerschick, W. (2017): Österreich. In: Dünkel, F., Thiele, C., Treig, J. (Eds.): *Elektronische Überwachung von Straffälligen im europäischen Vergleich – Bestandsaufnahme und Perspektiven*. Mönchengladbach: Forum Verlag Godesberg, 401–409.

Rechnungshof Austria (2020): *Bericht des Rechnungshofes – Steuerung und Koordinierung des Straf- und Maßnahmenvollzuges*, 55.

Scherndl, G., Palmai, J., Brickner, I., Mayer, T. and Seidl, C. (2020): *Die wichtigsten Fragen und Antworten zur Corona-Impfung*. Der Standard. https://www.derstandard.at/story/2000122800732/wie-es-nun-mit-den-corona-impfungen-weitergeht.

4 Belgium*

Olivia Nederlandt, An-Sofie Vanhouche and Kristel Beyens

1 Introduction – general situation of the prison system

1.1 Prison population rates – prison overcrowding

The Belgian penal system comprises 32 prisons: 17 in Flanders, 16 in Wallonia and one in Brussels. For several decades, and despite additional capacity, the Belgian prison system has suffered from severe overcrowding, with general overcrowding rates varying between 110 and 120%.

Figure 4.1 shows the development of the prison population before and during the pandemic. After a peak of 11,645 prisoners in 2013, the daily prison population declined in the period before the pandemic and fluctuated between 10,300 and 10,700 prisoners: A detention rate of about 95 prisoners per 100,000 inhabitants. However, the general density rate of approximately 110% in this period underestimates the severe overcrowding in remand prisons, where overcrowding rates varied between 140 and 150% (Beyens and Maes, 2020). The proportion of prisoners in pre-trial detention is high in Belgium, constituting around 35% of its prison population. In addition, even after transferring mentally ill prisoners to forensic detention centres, about 600 (about 5% of the prison population) remain detained in Belgian prisons today. Long-term prisoners with total sentences that exceed three years form the majority of the prison population (accounting for 56% of the total prison population). In addition, a substantial proportion of these serve sentences of between five years and life imprisonment. Such a high proportion of long-term prisoners in prison is explained by the considerable number of persons with sentences of three years or less, who serve their full sentence under electronic monitoring (EM) outside prison. Further, the EM population has constantly risen from 1,338 in 2013 to 1,844 in 2017, an increase in the daily number of persons under EM of 38%.

* This chapter builds on previous publications of the authors on this issue (Beyens, Robberechts and Vanhouche, 2020; Nederlandt, 2020; 2021; Vanhouche and Nederlandt, 2020; 2021; Hachez et al., 2021). See also Fatik, 2020, Special issue about prison and pandemic.

DOI: 10.4324/9781003169178-4

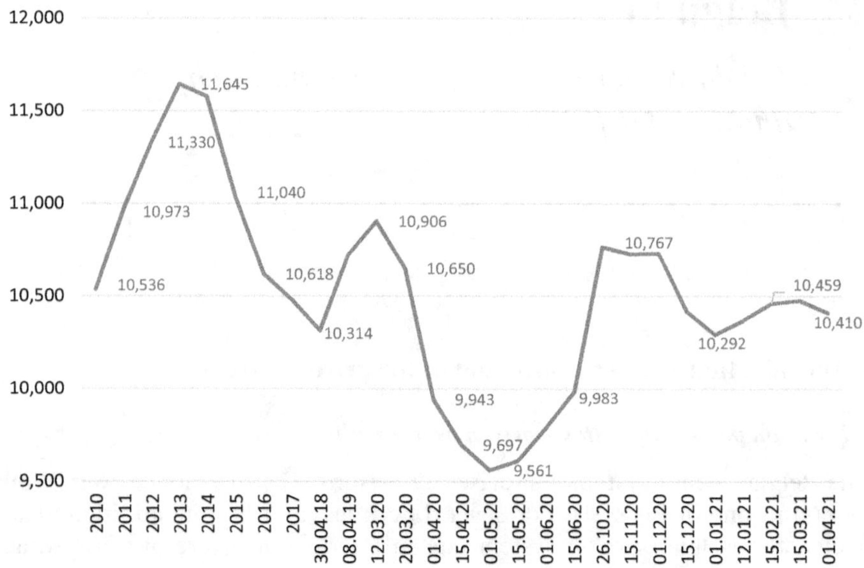

Figure 4.1 Development of the prison population in Belgium between 2010 and 1 April 2021.
Source: Belgian Prison Service.[1]

During the first wave of the pandemic, the prison population decreased rapidly between March and May 2020 (Figure 4.1). This was due to a selection of prisoners being granted provisional release because the implementation of their sentence was interrupted, and by the suspended execution of non-urgent convictions. Due to these measures, 6.6% of the prison population was released between 16 March and 15 September 2020 (Aebi and Tiago, 2020: 25). Despite this, the density rate never went under 100 in Flemish prisons, and only decreased to slightly under 100 in the Brussels and Walloon prisons, which indicates some regional differences in reducing the overcrowding rate (Maes and Nève, 2020: 15).

On 12 March 2020, the day before the COVID-19 measures were issued, 10,906 prisoners were detained in prison. One month later, on 15 April 2020, the numbers had declined by almost 1,000 to 9,686. The lowest number of persons imprisoned was registered on 1 May 2020 (N = 9,561). After the measures were lifted on 16 June 2020, the prison population rapidly increased to the levels prior to the first wave, reaching 10,838 on 23 November 2020. Similarly, the prison density declined from 117.3 on 1 January 2020 to 103.5 on 15 April, only to increase again to 109.5 by 15 September 2020 (Aebi and Tiago, 2020: 24). Although the second COVID-19 wave started in October, anticipatory and temporary releases were only issued by the new Minister of Justice, van

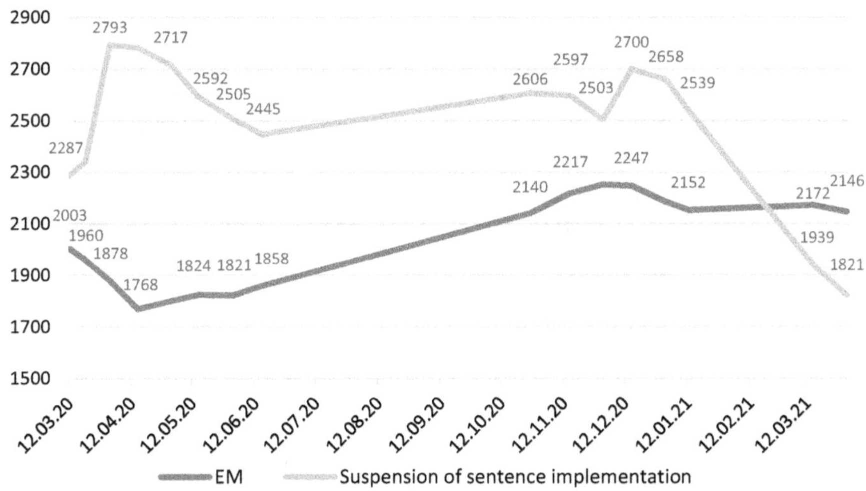

Figure 4.2 Electronic monitoring and suspension of sentence in Belgium between 12 March 2020 and 1 April 2021.

Source: Belgian Prison Service.

Quickenborne, at the end of November/December 2020 (see Section 3). Consequently, the drop in the prison population was less marked than during the first wave. Since then, up to the beginning of April 2021, the prison population has fluctuated between 10,300 and about 10,500, substantially higher than during the first wave, when numbers dipped below 10,000.

As noted above, the last 15 years witnessed a significant expansion in the use of EM as a non-custodial measure to tackle the prison crisis. It will be interesting to explore whether EM was also used as a means to reduce the prison population during the pandemic.

Against all expectations, the daily number of persons under EM dropped during the first wave, indicating that the decline in the prison population cannot be explained, or was not compensated by an increased use of EM. However, during the second wave, the number of persons under EM shows a higher incidence than prior to the pandemic. Moreover, Figure 4.2 shows another remarkable phenomenon: The sharp rise in 'suspensions of sentence implementation' for those awaiting the activation of EM. This sharp rise during the first wave probably compensated for the decline of the number of persons under EM. This had reversed by March 2021. Thereafter, the number of people in EM was higher than those in receipt of 'sentence suspension'. This indicates a degree of adaptation in the processes of EM centres, since greater levels of technical equipment and staff would have been needed to monitor more people.

1.2 COVID-19 infections of prisoners and prison staff members

During the first wave, the number of COVID-19 infections among prisoners was limited. Prisons were largely closed to all except staff, the prison population had dropped significantly and the internal regimes were very strict. On 4 September 2020, only 44 prisoners had tested positive since testing began in March 2020. However, during the second wave, there were steep rises in the number of infections consequent upon outbreaks in some prisons. The number of prisoners testing positive rose rapidly from 199 on 30 October to 803 by 1 April 2021, an increase of just over 303%.

Regarding staff, the only information provided hitherto is the number of staff in quarantine and ill on a daily basis. As the sickness data do not differentiate between COVID and non-COVID-related illness, these data cannot be used as indicators of COVID-infected staff.[2] To get an idea of staff absences due to COVID-19, we looked at the number of staff in quarantine. In January 2021, the number of staff in quarantine fluctuated between 15 and 70, and the number of ill prison officers fluctuated between 706 and 901. On 15 January 2021, the rate of absent prison officers was 14.5% (13.8% due to illness and 0.7% due to quarantine leave). In 2021, the general absence rate of prison officers stayed high and even increased, reaching 16.4% on 1 April 2021. However, five prisons had a much higher absence rate, fluctuating between 21.8 and 35%. This means that some prisons were operating with three quarters or less of the staff required. This would be challenging under normal conditions, but has to be regarded as a significantly greater problem in the taxing circumstances of COVID-19.

2 Prison and penal policy concerning the execution of prison sentences during the COVID-19-induced crisis

There are distinctions among the measures the prison administration adopted in response to the 2020 COVID-19 pandemic. While some were put into practice from the beginning of the pandemic, others were used for a limited period, and within the framework of the first, and then the second and third waves.

On 13 March 2020, the Belgian authorities declared a state of emergency at federal level, and later conferred special powers on the Government by virtue of two laws dated 27 March 2020. On the basis of one of these laws, the Government issued the Royal Decree n°3 on 9 April 2020 that provided for temporary rules relating to criminal proceedings and the implementation of sentences (applied between 9 April and 17 June 2020). During the second wave, a COVID law was adopted on 20 December 2020, applicable until 31 March 2021. At the start of the third wave, a Royal Decree extended the validity of this law until June and July 2021, depending on the measures. While the decree was adopted very quickly after the start of the first wave, the COVID law lagged behind the onset of the second wave. The Royal Decree and the COVID law provided for back-door measures to reduce the prison population and to limit the number of people entering and leaving prison (see Section 4.4). None of these regulated the detention conditions within prisons. As a consequence, the visiting regime and the conditions of detention were only regulated through unofficial (unpublished) 'coronavirus instructions' issued by the prison administration (see Sections 4.4 and 4.5), with no legal basis.[3] In addition to the 'back-door' measures provided for by the Royal Decree and the COVID law, as well as the measures taken by the prison administration, the public prosecutor's office also adopted 'front-door' measures.

2.1 Back-door measures provided by the Royal Decree n°3 and the COVID law

To reduce the prison population by regulating the flow of convicted prisoners, two main measures ('back-door' strategies) have been adopted: (i) the interruption of the execution of the sentence due to COVID-19, and (ii) the anticipatory release due to COVID-19. Only persons already convicted and physically in prison could benefit from these measures. They did not apply to convicted persons serving one or several sentences totalling three years or less, because they already benefited from the special EM regime and provisional release.

Interruption of the execution of the sentence due to COVID-19 (IEP) enables convicted prisoners to temporarily leave prison if they meet several conditions. They must have a fixed address, sufficient means of subsistence and belong to one of the following two categories: (1) they have already spent a prison leave outside with no problems, or are serving their prison sentence under a regime of limited detention[4] with prison leave; (2) they belong to an at-risk group who are vulnerable to the development of severe COVID-19 symptoms.[5] Certain categories of offenders are excluded from these measures, even if they belong to one of the two categories described above: Persons convicted to one or more sentences totalling more than ten years, those convicted of acts of terrorism, sexual offences and similarly serious crimes. In addition to these exclusions, a risk analysis (assessing the risk of removal, risk of re-offending, risk of disturbing the victim(s) or the potential of not complying with health measures) needed to be carried out by the prison governors before this measure could be granted. An IEP meant that those who were convicted were free, since their sentence had been suspended. During the second and third waves, the IEP was reshaped and tightened to include new exclusionary grounds for certain categories of convicted persons. Three periods of prison leave had to be successfully completed rather than one, and the category of vulnerability to COVID-19 was removed – which was, and is, a matter of concern since this group is in particular need of protection. During the first wave, the conditions were applicable from 20 March to 17 June 2020, resulting in 508 IEPs being granted. With the second wave and the arrival of the third wave, the measure was applied from 3 December 2020 to 31 March 2021 and was extended until 15 July 2021.

Anticipatory release due to COVID-19 could be granted by prison governors to convicted prisoners who had access to accommodation and sufficient means of subsistence, if the remaining sentence did not exceed six months. As with the IEP, the same categories of offenders were excluded from the measure. If granted, conditions were imposed (not to commit new offences, not to bother victims and to comply with health measures). This measure was handled far more strictly during the second and third waves, with additional grounds for exclusion added. Between 9 April and 17 June 2020 (first wave), 209 prisoners left prison due to this special form of COVID-19 release. The measure was applied again from 27 November 2020, and has since been extended until 31 March, and then again to 30 June 2021 consistent with the arrival of the second and third waves. The number of released prisoners during the second and third waves is unknown at the time of writing.

Three conclusions can be drawn about these back-door measures.

First, prison governors have a decisive role, not only in granting or rejecting both measures, but also in revoking these measures in specific circumstances. Their decisions cannot be appealed. This fits the general policy trajectory in Belgium, where prison governors possess considerable powers and responsibility in the decision-making process over provisional release.

Second, with prisoners sharing small cells, and the attendant poor hygiene, measures should have been taken to reduce the overcrowding pressure in the most congested prisons (remand prisons), but the measures taken only had an impact on the prisons for convicted prisoners. More generally, the impact of these measures can be questioned, as we observed an increase in the prison population long before the effects of the measures should have ceased.

Third, it is very hard to understand why eligibility for the measures was tightened during the second and third waves, given that few, if any, revocations took place during the first wave and the number of prisoners who tested positive for COVID-19 was much higher during the second and third waves. To explicitly exclude convicted prisoners who are vulnerable to COVID-19 from the IEP seems disproportionate and has a negative effect on detained persons' right to health (especially in a context of poor health care in prisons: KCE, 2017). More generally, excluding convicted persons with higher COVID-19 risks on the basis of their sentence length, or the type of offence committed, appears to be egregious, particularly since risk assessments were carried out prior to release.

2.2 Front-door measure of the college of public prosecutors (appeal courts)

Neither governmental measures, nor laws have provided for front-door measures. However, the college of public prosecutors at the level of appeal courts has adopted two circulars allowing for the postponement of the implementation of new prison sentences under certain conditions. The first applied between 26 March and 26 June 2020, and the second from 5 November

2020 and is still in force. The suspension does not apply to those with sentences over five years, nor to persons under arrest or detained on different charges. Further grounds for refusing suspension include the dangerousness of individuals concerned, and the nature of the offence (for example, those offences involving the use of violence, or terrorist offences). During the first wave, the execution of 2,500 sentences was postponed.

3 Restrictions of contact with the outside world

3.1 The prison administration's instructions regarding visits and compensatory measures

All prison visits, except for those by lawyers, were cancelled from 13 March 2020. In general, this hard lockdown narrowed the already limited social contacts of prisoners even more. As one prisoner explained: "We could not receive visits from our loved ones, family and friends. For me this was the hardest part because my girlfriend usually visits. On March 13, it felt like I lost something. I felt empty. We make phone calls on a daily basis but that is not the same. I can't feel her" (De Bolle et al., 2020: 22, our translation).

As compensation, prisoners were granted financial support for phone calls and in addition, from May 2020, video calls of 20 minutes a week were allowed with the use of the Webex system. A prisoner reported on his experiences with these calls:

> I had three video calls now, but only two worked. There was a problem, and my visitors weren't on time. I was frustrated but heard others had a similar problem. It's new, and we need to be patient. But my call itself was nice...It's less heavy for them and less expensive. But an additional question is: who do you call first? One call a week gives you limited opportunities. What do you do when your children live at different places?
> (De Bolle et al., 2020: 22–23, our translation)

As this prisoner explained, despite limitations, the experiences with video calls were also positive. Video calls are less burdensome and involve no travel costs for visitors. They also offer the possibility to 'see' family members who are not able to travel to the prison because of a disability or the travelling distance. Moreover, the possibility to see the interior of the family house, or to enable children to talk to their parent in an environment that is less harsh than the prison, is regarded as a plus.

At the end of May 2020, the prohibition on physically meeting visitors was gradually abolished. However, physical contact with visitors and conjugal visits became the central point of dispute with the prison officers in September 2020, when the central prison administration finally allowed prisoners to receive conjugal visits after approximately six months. The consequence of this was that prison staff unions initiated several strike actions. Not long thereafter, in October 2020, the second COVID-19 wave hit Belgium hard, resulting in the abolition of all visits between 2 November and 7 December. Since December 2020, visits have resumed, but in a considerably more limited manner with regard to the number of visits, visitors and modalities. Prisoners are only permitted to see their relatives, which for the moment includes only one person through acrylic glass and physical contact is forbidden (which, regarding children and their detained parents, can be regarded as inhumane). Quarantine as a consequence of physical contact during visits has been denounced as a "disguised sanction" by the Central Monitoring Board (Advice of 24 December 2020).

3.2 Prison leave

All forms of sentence implementation that involved entering and leaving the prison were suspended. With the exception of leave for humanitarian reasons, this included short leave (16 hours), prison leave (36 hours) and limited detention (day outside, night in prison). During the second and third waves, a second exception was provided: The director could not suspend these leaves if 'such suspension seriously jeopardizes reintegration'. This suspension lasted between 24 March and 17 June 2020 during the first wave. It was reapplied from the end of October with the arrival of the second wave, and, because of the third wave, extended until 30 June 2021.

This suspension of leave is counterproductive with regard to one of the main objectives of the health measures adopted, namely reducing the prison population. By slowing down the release process of convicted prisoners, the opportunity to take steps to prepare a reintegration plan was hampered (Beyens, 2019). The justification of this measure aimed at limiting the number of prisoners going back and forth between prison and the outside world should also be questioned. In fact, prison staff and many other actors, including lawyers, monitoring boards, psychosocial services, chaplains and services offering help for rehabilitation, enter and leave prisons on a daily basis, with no question that this is problematic.

3.3 Impact on court hearings

An additional measure to reduce the number of incoming and outgoing prisoners was a further requirement that convicted persons, internees and victims be represented by a lawyer at hearings of the sentence implementation courts (unless the courts decided otherwise). The decision was also taken to allow these courts not to hold hearings in prison (as they usually do). This measure applied from 9 April until 17 June 2020 during the first wave, and with the arrival of the second and third waves, it applied from 24 December 2020 and has been further extended until 30 June 2021.

4 Restrictions inside prisons

The material conditions in Belgian prisons have long been subject to criticism, and in some (old) Belgian prisons, high levels of overcrowding have led to poor hygiene. In this context, the COVID-19 pandemic placed another formidable burden on several Belgian prisons already facing problems to reach the minimum standards for living conditions.

The conditions of detention in Belgian prisons, the internal regime, the nature of visits and forms of communication with the outside are regulated according to the Belgian Prison Act of 2005. During the pandemic, all measures regarding the conditions of detention were only taken through the 'COVID-19 instructions' of the central prison administration, which were regularly updated and applied continuously from the beginning of the crisis. Derogations to the Act of 2005 were thus adopted through the prison administration outside of any legal basis.

During the first wave, all group activities were cancelled, except for labour and outdoor time on the courtyard. During these activities, prisoners were obliged to keep a distance of 1.5 metres, and were mostly organised in *compartments* ('bubbles') based on the section or wing in which the prisoner was housed. Prisoners could generally still order books from the library (but were not allowed to visit it) and could individually participate in religious services. All collective activities (for example, educational and cultural activities in groups) were cancelled, although some services developed forms of individual support, through free phone calls, for example. With regard to educational provision, efforts were made to provide educators and prisoners access to digital learning platforms, albeit in very few prisons. Moreover, some services developed applications such as *fit@cell workouts* (De Rode Antraciet vzw, 2020) or provided games and newspapers to kill time inside the prison cell.

After the first wave, during July-August 2020, activities gradually started up again, and once more, labour and outdoor time in the courtyard could take place. However, restrictions were reintroduced under the strictures of the second and third waves and collective activities were abolished with limited exceptions, for example, for examinations. This meant that individual offers had to be developed. These intrusive restrictions increasingly led to boredom and isolation, as one prisoner explained: 'It's hard. Even in a world where we are used to being incarcerated, it's incoming prisoners and the medical isolation of prisoners with symptoms.'

It should also be pointed out that despite general instructions, the conditions of detention varied across prisons. There are substantial differences between being confined in a dilapidated prison, in a single cell, or sharing a small cell with one or even two more prisoners with poor hygienic conditions, without an in-cell shower, or even running water, and serving a sentence in a newer, cleaner prison with in-cell showers. It is also different to be detained in a prison where certain activities and/or prison work may or may not have been maintained, in a prison where relations between prisoners and prison staff are generally calm or, conversely, tense, in a prison where the 'open door' regime has been maintained, or not. In short, differences in the prison experience are both manifest and legion.

The measures taken have been, and are, highly prejudicial to the fundamental rights of the persons detained, and, significantly, are not subject to effective remedies. The health crisis has worsened the conditions of detention in Belgian prisons to the extent that many detainees have been, or are, still exposed to treatment that can be described as degrading or even inhumane: Isolation in cells, (almost) no activities, no work and no visits. Furthermore, this has been the case over a long period of time, against a background of anxiety generated by the risk of contracting the virus, and uncertainty about the end of a difficult detention regime. The European Court of Human Rights has qualified a situation as degrading treatment where the conditions of detention were similar (i.e. the period of strikes by prison staff in spring 2016), but less drastic because it was limited to two months and in the absence of the anxiety linked to the health crisis (*Clasens v. Belgium*, 28 May 2019).

5 Compensatory measures

Compensatory measures concerning the restrictions of visits are described under Section 3.1.

6 Legal bases for restrictions and relaxations of the prison regime

This issue is described under Sections 2–4.

7 Returning to normal

It is important to stress the different policies during the first and second/third waves, and to raise the serious question of how one gets used to hard restrictions of prisoners' rights, once the shock effect has worn off. During the first wave, measures were taken quickly, the prison population fell by more than 10% and the pandemic was kept outside prisons. By contrast, during the second and third waves, measures were taken very late, the prison population decreased less and prisons became clusters of infection. In addition to this later and more restricted political response, it would be interesting to know how the reactions to the different waves at the different levels of the penal system manifested themselves. Indeed, the limited quantitative impact of the two back-door measures, compared to the steep decrease of the prison population of about 10% during the first wave, can only be understood taking into account the combined effect of multiple factors, *inter alia*: A decrease in criminal justice activities ultimately leading to fewer convictions, decisions by the judiciary who may have favoured alternatives to prison at the pre-sentence, sentence and post-sentence stages and the potential decrease in offences during the first hard lockdown. However, due to a lack of research and data, it is not known which actors intervened, and for what reasons, during the first and second waves, and how, and for what reasons, they might have reacted differently. The key conclusion is clear: The prison population did not decrease during the second wave as it did during the first. It is also important to mention that Belgium had different Ministers of Justice in the first and second waves, which might also explain the different approaches.

Prisons symbolise the ultimate place of exclusion. The health crisis has further reinforced this characteristic with the abolition of the post-authoritarian permeability of prisons (eliminating the entry of relatives into prison and prison leave of convicted prisoners). The requirements to benefit from the temporary or anticipatory release due to COVID-19 are also a salutary reminder that imprisonment is often used as a last resort for the people 'without': Prisoners 'without' housing, 'without' means of subsistence and/or 'without' a residence permit could not, and cannot, benefit from the COVID-19 measures. The pandemic has shown that imprisonment is used as a last resort for those who fall foul of the lack of social assistance outside. This observation once again calls into question the current repressive policy, which invests massively in the criminal justice system and the construction of new prisons rather than in the social system.

While it is well known that the size of the prison population is only loosely related to the development of crime rates, the COVID-19 crisis vividly confirms the fact: In less than a month, the prison population was reduced by more than 10% with no consequent reduction in public safety (Central Monitoring Board, Advice of 18 June 2020). Once the health crisis is over, one wonders whether this observation will catalyse the will to fight against the extensive use of imprisonment. Despite their necessity, the measures to reduce the prison population were adopted less quickly, and to a lesser extent, in the second wave. Alongside the repressive policy trajectory, the new Government and new Minister of Justice have recently announced that for the next few years, they find little optimism about the future. However, we hope that the COVID-19 crisis might at least become the catalyst to finally transfer prison health care from the Federal Public Service Justice to the Federal Public Service Public Health, which would, in our view, significantly improve health services in prison.

Notes

1 The state of emergency was officially declared at the federal level on 13 March 2020.

2 Figure 4.1 is based on data published by the Prison Service in their yearly reports between 2010 and 2017 and (from 30 April 2018 onwards) on non-published data the authors received from the Prison Service.

3 We know that also before the pandemic the absence rate due to illness was significant in the Belgian prisons.
4 Some of these instructions can be found on https://www.europris.org/COVID-19-prevention-measures-in-european-prisons/.
5 Limited detention means that prisoners are allowed to leave the prison during the day to go to work.
6 Convicted persons who have reached the age of 65, those with serious chronic illnesses (diabetes, heart and lung or kidney disease) and those with a weakened immune system.

References

Aebi, M. F., and Tiago, M. K. (2020): *Prisons and prisoners in Europe in pandemic times: An evaluation of the medium-term impact of the COVID-19 on prison populations.* Council of Europe, Unil, Ecole des sciences criminelles, https://wp.unil.ch/space/files/2020/11/Prisons-and-the-COVID-19_2nd-Publication_201109.pdf.

Beyens, K. (2019): Belgian release policies, rationales and practices. *European Journal of Probation, 11*(3), 169–187, https://doi.org/10.1177/2066220319895776

Beyens, K., and Maes, E. (2020): Het lappendeken van tien jaar strafuitvoering in België. *Panopticon, 41*(1), 10–41.

Beyens, K., Robberechts, J., and Vanhouche, A.-S. (2020): De coronacrisis als momentum voor het gevangeniswezen? *Panopticon, 41*(3), 365–372.

Central Monitoring Board (2020): Advice of 18 June 2020 and 24 December 2020, https://ccsp.belgium.be/.

Centre fédéral d'Expertise des Soins de santé (KCE) (2017): *Soins de santé dans les prisons belges: situation actuelle et scénarios pour le futur*, 18 octobre 2017, Synthèse en français. https://kce.fgov.be/sites/default/files/atoms/files/KCE_293Bs_Soins_de_sante_prisons_belge_Synthese.pdf.

De Bolle, E., Edame, E., Janssens, G., Vissers, I., and Vanhouche, A.-S. (2020): De klok is geen vriend. Persoonlijke ervaringen met de coronamaatregelen in de gevangenis van Beveren. *Fatik – Tijdschrift voor Strafbeleid en Gevangeniswezen, 166*, 19–24.

De Rode Antraciet vzw (2020): Fit @ cell. https://www.youtube.com/playlist?list=PLqVgIsaI4D5TgJ6p_WvpVq7ZNaE6Nih8U

Fatik – Tijdschrift voor Strafbeleid en Gevangeniswezen, 2020/166: Special Issue Sentence Implementation in Times of Corona.

Hachez, I., Hardt, M., Losseau, L., Nederlandt, O., Sarolea, S., Triaille, L. (2021): Des personnes vulnérables aux situations de vulnérabilité : à quoi sert le droit en temps de Covid ? », *Revue trimestrielle des droits de l'homme, 128*, 929–990.

Maes, E., and Nève, J. (2020): Detentie in tijden van Corona. Impact van COVID-19-maatregelen inzake strafuitvoering op de omvang van de gevangenisbevolking. *Fatik, 166*, 12–18.

Nederlandt, O. (2020): *Actualités en droit de l'exécution des peines privatives de liberté: Un état de crise permanent?* In: Kuty, F. and Guillain, C. (Eds.): *Actualités en droit pénal et exécution des peines.* Bruxelles: Larcier, 223–243.

Nederlandt, O. (2021): Droit pénitentiaire et pandémie: quand la crise ordinaire se double d'une crise sanitaire. *E-legal, Revue de droit et de criminologie de l'ULB*, Dossier spécial covid-19, http://e-legal.ulb.be/special-covid19/

dossier-special-covid19/droits-des-personnes-incarcerees-durant-la-pandemie-quand-la-crise-ordinaire-se-double-d-une-crise-sanitaire.

Vanhouche, A.-S., and Nederlandt, O. (2020): Een bespreking van het koninklijk besluit over de strafprocedure en de uitvoering van straffen en maatregelen in het kader van de strijd tegen de verspreiding van het coronavirus COVID-19. *Fatik – Tijdschrift voor Strafbeleid en Gevangeniswezen, 166*, 4–11.

Vanhouche, A.-S., and Nederlandt, O. (2021): De tweede golf van het coronavirus: Een overzicht van nieuwe maatregelen voor gedetineerden en gevangenissen. *Fatik – Tijdschrift voor Strafbeleid en Gevangeniswezen, 169*, 23–28.

5 Brazil

Ellen Rodrigues and Eduardo Khoury

1 Introduction

Brazil is the largest country in South and Latin America and has more than 210 million inhabitants. The 1988 Federal Constitution defines Brazil as a presidential federal republic comprised of 26 states plus the Federal District of Brasília.

According to the National Justice Council (CNJ),[1] in July 2019, the prison population in Brazil numbered 812,564. After a COVID-19-induced decline by about 6% (see section 2 below), the prison population increased to 885,071 in December 2020 and to 901,945 in March 2021 (+19% since July 2020). This was a rate of approximately 424 per 100,000 of the national population (Instituto Brasileiro de Geografia e Estatística, 2020).[2] In July 2019, 41.5% of the prison population consisted of pre-trial detainees. In December 2020, this proportion went up to 44.7% of the prison population and in March 2021 the proportion was 45.2%. Considering that another 22% could still appeal their sentences, in March 2021, only about a third of inmates were serving a final sentence.

The pattern of social and racial inequality in Brazil is reflected in the profile of its prisoners: 95% are male, 64% are black and 55% are between 18 and 29 years old; 50% of the females incarcerated in the country are between 18 and 29 years old, 62% are black and 74% have children.[3] These patterns can also be observed in the juvenile socio-educational facilities, in which most inmates are males (96%), 59% are black and 57% are between 16 and 17 years old. There are currently about 28,000 juveniles subject to measures of restriction or deprivation of liberty in Brazil (115 per 100,000 of the juvenile population).

Social inequality, highly uneven wealth distribution and high rates of poverty among the most vulnerable social groups have been constant throughout Brazilian history. The COVID-19 pandemic has exacerbated these inequalities and especially the effects of extreme poverty, since for inhabitants of *favelas,* as well as the inmates of Brazilian prison facilities, it

DOI: 10.4324/9781003169178-5

is practically impossible to maintain social distancing or adequate hygiene practices (Garófalo et al., 2020; Lofgren et al., 2020).[4]

The first confirmed case of a person infected by COVID-19 in the country occurred on 23 January 2020, and the first registered death on 17 March 2020. The number of infected persons continued growing, increasing to 6.88 million on 13 December 2020, when 181,686 deaths had been reported throughout the country (Conselho Nacional de Justiça, 2020).

The first occurrence of COVID-19 in a prison facility confirmed by a laboratory test happened on 8 April 2020. According to the CNJ, on 7 December 2020, there were 52,937 confirmed cases of the new coronavirus in the Brazilian prison system: 40,479 prisoners and 12,458 workers in the prison system. 216 deaths due to COVID-19 had been registered, 126 of them among prisoners and detainees and 90 among staff in prison facilities. By 30 November 2020, 162,358 prisoners had been tested for the virus, while 55,052 tests had been done on the staff of prison and criminal justice facilities (Conselho Nacional de Justiça, 2020a).[5] This means that about every fourth prisoner tested had been infected by COVID-19, and about 30% of the prison staff. Both numbers reveal a horrific scenario of prisons being one of the most dangerous places in Brazil, both for prisoners and for staff.

Numbers of prisoners tested positive further increased to 48,143 cases and 147 deaths by 8 March 2021 (see Figure 5.1).

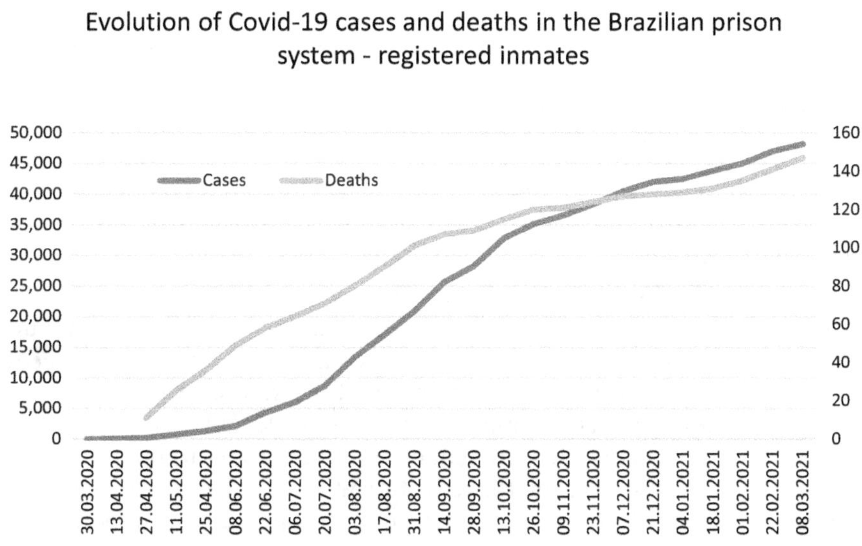

Figure 5.1 Evolution of COVID-19 infections in the Brazilian prison population.
Source: Conselho Nacional de Justiça.

2 Prison and penal policy concerning the execution of prison sentences during the COVID-19-induced crisis

At the start of the pandemic and the reporting of the first COVID-19-related death in Brazil, the CNJ, which is an autonomous administrative public entity responsible for the inspection and regulation of the judiciary, enacted Recommendation n° 62 on 17 March 2020 (Conselho Nacional de Justiça, 2020d),[6] establishing an emergency criminal policy aimed at avoiding the spreading of COVID-19 within both the adult prison system and juvenile socio-educational system. The Recommendation was originally enacted to be in force for 90 days, but on 17 June 2020[7] its effectiveness was extended for 90 days and on 15 September 2020[8] it was extended for a further 180 days, i.e. 360 days from its original enactment. The maintenance of its ruling should be reassessed in March 2021.

Although the sets of measures enacted and enforced varied greatly across criminal justice facilities of the different Brazilian states and even within them, this Recommendation was the basis for most federal and state actions regarding the pandemic in the criminal justice system and the prisons. It also served as a yardstick for the later assessment by the CNJ of the policy's efficacy.

In enacting the Recommendation, the CNJ took into consideration the increased risk of COVID-19 contagion in prisons, explicitly acknowledging

> factors such as the agglomeration of people, the insalubrity of these units, the difficulties in ensuring compliance with minimum procedures of hygiene and rapid isolation of symptomatic individuals, insufficient health teams, among others, characteristics inherent to the 'unconstitutional state of affairs' of the Brazilian prison system as recognized by the Supreme Court in the Claim of non-compliance with a fundamental precept n° 347.
>
> (Ibid.)

The CNJ recommended that courts and judges should initiate preventive measures against COVID-19 in the facilities of the prison system and of the socio-educational system. The purpose was protecting the lives of inmates and workers; diminishing the propagation of the virus by adopting necessary measures; and ensuring the continuity of judicial services in conformity with individual rights and guarantees, and due legal process. The main recommendations concerned the reduction of admission to both the adult and youth prison systems, and the reduction in the number of inmates in the institutions, especially the elderly and those suffering from pre-existing conditions. The means of achieving this reduction included detention at home or electronic monitoring; precautionary measures for hearings in court buildings; the replacement of hearings aimed at the confirmation of arrests *in flagrante delicto* by videoconferencing. Contingency plans were drafted in collaboration with local authorities. Visits to inmates were suspended, except for those by lawyers in urgent cases. Work by inmates outside prison was also suspended. In addition to restricting the entry to prison facilities, protocols for testing for the virus were introduced.

In order to implement these recommendations, the National Penitentiary Department (Depen) asked health managers of the states' prison systems for information on the health supplies necessary to avoid the spreading of COVID-19. Information on preventive and cautionary measures in prison routines was conveyed by videoconferencing.[9] From March 2020, a new default set of measures of containment and prevention of the virus was implemented in the federal prison system in accordance with the health authorities' recommendations,[10] as well as in the prison and socio-educational systems in most states.[11]

The CNJ has produced a report about the measures adopted within the criminal justice system to monitor COVID-19 infections and avoid its spreading (Conselho Nacional de Justiça, 2020b).[12] It deals mostly with the measures enacted by means of Recommendation 62/2020/CNJ. The data were obtained by several Regional Coordinators of the CNJ, the so-called "Programa Justiça Presente", directly from the officers responsible for each prison or socio-educational facility, from 13 to 20 April 2020 and from 19 to 29 May 2020. Only for the State of Paraiba were no data obtained. No further assessment of such measures has taken place by March 2021.

According to the report, by May 2020, 35,000 releases from prison had occurred due to the COVID-19 pandemic, 8,194 of which were pre-trial detainees. This corresponds to a decrease of about 6%. No further reliable data on release from prison since then have been made available. As shown above, the number of prisoners increased since July 2020 by 19%, which makes clear that there were no crime policy efforts of the government to reduce the prison population and risks of infections of prisoners.

The report also presents information, although no absolute figures, on transfers to different prison regimes; suspension of therapeutic meetings for offenders subject to security measures; suspension of hearings and obligations to present oneself periodically to court; changes in the functioning of facilities related to the application of penal alternatives, electronic monitoring and attendance of persons recently released from the prison system. It has also assessed changes related to the suspension of visits and permission for relatives to have food delivered to prisoners.

Twenty-two of 26 Brazilian states have reported numbers related to the release of persons in pre-trial detention aimed at reducing the prison population in order to mitigate the risk of COVID-19 infections. Six of them reported that they released no provisional detainees due to measures related to the pandemic, while the other 16 states reported having released a total of 3,466 pre-trial detainees, 35% of whom belonged to the category of people at risk from COVID-19.[13]

Thirteen states reported some change in the prison regime of individuals serving their sentence in a closed regime, seven reported having made no changes to the closed regime due to the pandemic, and for six states no data were made available. Most of these reported changes (85%) corresponded to conversion from closed regime to home detention, with or without the use of electronic monitoring.

Twenty-four of 26 states have reported changing their regime for persons serving their sentence in a semi-open regime. The obligations on offenders to present themselves periodically to court have been suspended in 16 states; 15 states have converted the semi-open regime into house detention and nine have suspended external work for offenders. In half of the states (13), conversions into house detention were to take place in conjunction with electronic monitoring, while in 12 its use was not mandated, and for one state no information on this topic was made available.

In 23 of the 26 states, changes were made to individuals serving a sentence in an open regime. 73% of the states reported having suspended offenders' obligation to present themselves periodically to court; 8% made transfers to home detention with electronic monitoring; 8% transfers to home detention without information related to the use of electronic monitoring.

The CNJ also compiled information about the implementation or suspension of certain steps in the criminal procedure and execution of sentences, which were deemed critical to controlling the pandemic in prisons and the socio-educational system.

The legal obligation for persons under pre-trial release to present themselves periodically to court was suspended in 21 states. In one state, the obligation was maintained, and for four states data were not available.

The obligation for persons on parole to present themselves to court was suspended in 16 states (62%) for those serving a semi-open regime and in 19 states (73%) for those under an open regime.

The postponement of hearings in cases in which the defendant was in liberty has occurred in 16 (62%) states. Hearings via electronic means (videoconferencing) in cases in which the defendant was imprisoned were adopted by 11 states (42%) during the findings of fact, and by 10 states (38%) during the imposition of sentence.

3 Restrictions of contact with the outside world

In order to restrict inmates' contact with the outside world, some states also made changes in rules related to temporary prison leave, which, in accordance with the law, is ordinarily granted to those serving a sentence in a semi-open regime. Eight states reported having extended the duration of those temporary leaves, whereas a further eight states reported having suspended the granting of such leaves.

In accordance with the CNJ's Recommendation 62/2020 and the WHO's directives regarding the COVID-19 pandemic, on 17 March 2020, the

National Penitentiary Department (in Portuguese, *Departamento Penitenciário Nacional*, Depen) suspended visits to inmates and the visits by lawyers, save in cases of emergency, in all federal prisons (Ministério da Justiça e Segurança Pública/Departamento Penitenciário Nacional, 2020).[14] In August 2020, visits by lawyers and videoconferencing with relatives were authorised, and in November 2020 visits to inmates by relatives and friends were authorised with restrictions. In state prisons, visits were also suspended from March 2020. This followed provisions enacted by each state in accordance with Recommendation 62/2020/CNJ (Ministério da Justiça e Segurança Pública/Departamento Penitenciário Nacional, 2020a).[15] Delivery of food to inmates by relatives was completely suspended in nine states, whereas in another nine, they were maintained, but with restrictions. In six states, no modification of such rules was reported and for two no data were available.

Regarding rules for visits in the socio-educational system, all 26 states reported changes due to the pandemic. Twenty-four of them have suspended the visits completely, while two have reported still allowing visits but with restrictions to the number of visitors allowed at a time.[16]

4 Restrictions inside prisons

In relation to internal work inside prison facilities, in eight states (31%), there was no suspension of such activities, and for five no data were available. In 13 (50%) states, measures were taken to suspend internal work within prison facilities. In nine (35%), work in workshops, maintenance and kitchens was suspended, and in another four (15%), only work in workshops was suspended (Ministério da Justiça e Segurança Pública/Departamento Penitenciário Nacional, 2020c).

Regarding support services ordinarily available to inmates, only two states reported no modifications and four have reported no data. 23 states reported suspension of educational activities, 21 reported suspension of religious attendance and in six, legal assistance was suspended. In facilities or those serving an open regime, educational activities were suspended in 14 states, religious assistance in 13 states and legal assistance in four states, whereas six states reported no changes in such services.

The CNJ also assessed the implementation of activities to prevent and treat COVID-19 in prison and socio-educational facilities. Two states have reported no data on this and one state that no such activity had taken place. In facilities of 22 out of 26 states, the recommended hygiene procedures and educative actions aimed at avoiding the spreading of the coronavirus within the prison system were implemented. In 19 states, hygiene kits were distributed to inmates. The treatment of COVID-19 patients from prisons in the general health care system rather than inside prison facilities and provision for adequate isolation areas for symptomatic inmates in prisons were reported by 20 states. Eleven states reported that they had provided for permanent access to water for prisoners.

In facilities for persons serving their sentence in an open regime, adoption of specific hygiene procedures was reported by 12 states, the same number of states that reported having provided for isolation spaces destined to symptomatic individuals.

Eleven states reported the adoption of measures to treat suspected or confirmed cases in the general health care system, and 10 reported educational measures and distribution of hygiene kits. Nine states reported that no such activities had taken place. Eight states reported providing permanent access to water within its open regime facilities as a pandemic preventive measure.

5 Compensatory measures

Nearly all prison and socio-educational facilities have at some point completely restricted visits to inmates due to the pandemic. Many of them have adopted compensatory measures aimed at allowing inmates to communicate with their relatives, despite the restrictions of contact with the outside world. The adoption of such compensatory measures varied greatly across penal facilities in different Brazilian states (Ministério da Justiça e Segurança Pública/Departamento Penitenciário Nacional, 2020b).[17] Several states have designed measures to allow for videoconferencing to take place between inmates and persons who would regularly visit them. In December 2020, such measures had been adopted by the states of Amazonas, Pará, Rondônia, Maranhão, Paraíba, Piauí, Sergipe, Rio Grande do Sul and Santa Catarina (nine states). In federal prisons and in those of most states, however, such compensatory measures were not adopted during the first months of the restriction, and only physical or electronic mail addresses were provided to allow for written communication between prisoners and relatives. Alternatively, other channels of communication between inmates' relatives and prison facilities' social assistants have been made available to allow for the exchange of information. The State of Maranhão also implemented videoconferencing for lawyers.

The suspension of external work for persons serving sentences in semi-open regimes potentially disadvantaged such individuals, as, according to Brazilian criminal law, such work usually results in some partial remission of the punishment. In one third of the states where such work was suspended, this benefit was maintained as a compensatory measure regardless of the work suspension. However, in other states, the suspension of external work implied, at least until further deliberation, that the individuals affected were not able to obtain the legal benefits they were ordinarily entitled to due to external adverse factors.

In April 2020, Anjos da Liberdade Institute (IAL) petitioned the Supreme Court (STF) complaining that Portaria DISPF nº 5/2020,[18] which suspended visits, educational and religious services, attendance of lawyers and other activities for 30 days in all federal prisons, should be ruled unconstitutional for violating STF's binding judicial precedents n° 14 and 53 and prisoners' human rights as set out in the Brazilian Federal Constitution and in the American Convention on Human Rights. The motions for a preliminary injunction and for reconsideration of the first decision were denied on the basis that the norm in question was exceptional, proportional, temporary and therefore did not require urgent resolution according to the Supreme Court Justice Rosa Weber (Supremo Tribunal Federal, 2020a).[19] In February 2021, the motion became moot as Portaria DISPF nº 5/2020 was revoked.[20] It was replaced by Portaria DISPF 35/2020,[21] which authorised the attendance of lawyers in federal prisons provided that COVID-19-related precautionary measures were adopted, and the arrangement of virtual visits to inmates. In September 2020, Portaria DISPF 39[22] authorised the gradual resumption of visits to inmates, although the suspension of educational and religious services remained.

6 Legal basis for restrictions and relaxations of the prison regime

In 2018, the Brazilian Supreme Court accepted the possibility of a so-called collective *habeas corpus*, by means of which it became possible to ask for the recognition of illegal imprisonment and consequent granting of release orders for a number of prisoners. They were all subject to the same illegal deprivation of liberty. It occurred in HC 143641, in which it was determined that pregnant women or women who had children up to 12 years old or with disabilities,[23] excluding some exceptions, should be transferred from pre-trial detention in a prison to home detention. After the initial COVID-19 outbreak, several parties who were already involved in HC 143641 brought motions for the release from prison of all pregnant women and those with children up to 12 years or with disabilities, without regard to other conditions, because of the pandemic. The motion was denied by Justice Lewandowsky on the basis that such a debate should take place in Parliament.[24]

Several public and private institutions have petitioned state, federal and higher courts, by means of the collective *habeas corpus*, for the release of prisoners due to the increased risk posed by confinement in unhealthy facilities in the midst of a pandemic,[25] and taking into account the widely acknowledged, unconstitutional situation in Brazilian prisons and the disregard of the human rights recognised by the Brazilian state. Nationwide, no such release order was granted, although in some states and for some specific groups such orders have been granted, as well as in individual HCs, on the basis of the illegality of the deprivation of liberty due to the situation created by the pandemic and based on the CNJ's Recommendation 62/2020.

The Superior Court of Justice (STJ) on 24 April 2020 granted an injunction after a motion by the State of Minas Gerais Public Defender's Office to transfer to home detention individuals serving their sentences in a semi-open regime in two penitentiaries in the city of Uberlandia, arguing that the conditions of their regime had unduly worsened due to the restrictive measures imposed because of the pandemic.[26] On 3 April 2020, however, the STJ had denied an injunction in a collective *habeas corpus* action by the Federal Public Defender's Office, which aimed at obtaining an order from the court to release from prison all individuals who were in the risk group for a COVID-19 infection, and to avoid such risk groups being sent to prison while the pandemic lasted.[27] In June, the STJ denied an injunction in a similar case. The Federal Public Defender's Office was also unsuccessful with a motion before the Supreme Court in a collective *habeas corpus* legal action, aiming at the release from prison or transfer to home detention of the whole COVID-19 risk group that had committed minor offences and were in custody in overcrowded facilities.

On 16 March 2020, the Marcio Thomaz Bastos Institute of the Right to Defence (IDDD) brought a motion to the Supreme Court, within ADPF 347 (Supremo Tribunal Federal, 2020),[28] requesting that a judicial order be issued for the nationwide release of prisoners in the COVID-19 risk group. The motion for a preliminary injunction was denied by the justice in charge, Marco Aurélio Mello, mainly on formal legal grounds. However, in the same decision, Mello made an appeal, with an unclear legal effect, for judges in charge of the execution of criminal sentences across the country to follow a set of 14 recommendations, which he elaborated, aimed at the reduction of the number of persons in prison as a means of protecting public and individual health, taking into consideration the unconstitutional state of affairs in the Brazilian prison system, as proclaimed by the Supreme Court in 2015 in this same judicial procedure, ADPF 347. Justice Mello subsequently brought the matter to further deliberation by the court, which ruled on 18 March 2020 against the IDDD's motion and also against Mello's decision regarding the enactment of such recommendations. The prevailing rationale was that in providing the motion, the court would be accepting an unlawful extension of the original subject matter of ADPF 347. Gilmar Mendes was the only judge to agree with Mello in confirming the thematic pertinence of IDDD's request and of Mellos's recommendations in relation to the original subject matter of ADPF 347. Mendes also confirmed his understanding that Mello's set of recommendations was constitutionally appropriate from a formal perspective, comparing it to an appellate decision by the German Federal Constitutional Court.[29]

It seems clear that the Brazilian legal system could ensure the observance of human rights standards within its prison system, including the immediate release of prisoners under situations of illegal deprivation of their liberty, while the Brazilian 1988 Federal Constitution is comprehensive in its recognition of human rights. This means that there is a sufficient legal basis to properly establish a rationale that leaves little room for doubt concerning the situation of illegality and disregard of human rights standards in the majority of Brazilian prisons.

7 Returning to normal

In its reports on the effects of the pandemic in the prison system, the CNJ confirmed that, due to the unconstitutional state of affairs of the prison system as diagnosed by the Supreme Court in ADPF 347, the only reasonable solution to the threats posed by the pandemic in the Brazilian prison system would be to implement a policy of a mass release from prison. In spite of that, the Supreme Court ruled that the motion that aimed at the release or transfer to home detention of prisoners at risk during the pandemic was not thematically pertinent to the subject matter of ADPF 347. Recommendation 62/2020, despite the CNJ's importance to the constitutional order, possessed no legal force in itself. Only by means of individual actions and some collective actions aimed at very specific groups, some persons could be released from prison on the basis of Recommendation 62/2020/CNJ, since no nationally enforceable policy had been enacted nor had any judicial order been granted for general collective actions.

In analysing data on the Brazilian prison population, it is noticeable that there has been an increase in the number of individuals deprived of liberty (812,564 against 901,945) and an increase of circa 3.5% in the proportion of pre-trial detainees (41.5% against 45.2%) in relation to the general prison population when comparing data from July 2019 to March 2021. Therefore, one can summarise that the pandemic has had no effect on the release of prisoners or on prison and criminal policy in general. On the contrary, one can state that the government neglected the critical situation for prisoners and prison staff members, also during the second wave of the pandemic.

However, the report by the CNJ and Depen on the assessment of measures related to Recommendation 62/2020/CNJ contains some insightful data regarding criminal policy matters that might be relevant to future decarceration policies.

In assessing data related to the release of individuals under pre-trial detention in response to the emergency criminal policy during the pandemic, it is noticeable that, in spite of the WHO's recommendation to prioritise the release of prisoners who are part of the risk group for COVID-19, only 35% of the pre-trial detainees that received a grant of leave under this policy were released from prison due to being in the risk group, whereas 15% were freed because of being incarcerated in facilities which were overcrowded or that for some other reason were deemed unhealthy, 12% due to being still in prison although their prison terms had already expired, and 23% had committed minor or non-violent offences. Those figures might inform future measures aimed at reducing the prison population in general and the population of provisional detainees in particular.

The report also contains important information regarding the electronic monitoring of offenders. According to the report, in half of the Brazilian states (13), there has been a depressed demand for devices for the electronic monitoring of offenders. According to the same report, such demand is most directly related to early release from closed regimes (ten states), early release from semi-open regimes (eight states), substitution or accompaniment of provisional measures (eight states), protective measures (six states) and early release from open regimes (five states). It is noteworthy, however, that although EM might be a promising alternative to imprisonment, in Brazil, its use in more than 80% of cases has been a means for more intensive control of individuals serving alternative sentences or already serving their sentences in open, semi-open or house detention regimes, apparently causing a kind of net-widening effect (see Rodrigues et al., 2020).

The fact that such generalised inhumane and unlawful conditions in the criminal justice system have been known for quite some time and thus gradually regarded as normal by the authorities and citizens leaves little room for rational hope that the threats posed by the pandemic will lead to a change in this attitude and give rise to release policies. However, the pandemic has definitely been a driver for debates surrounding this possibility.

Notes

1 See https://portalbnmp.cnj.jus.br/#/estatisticas. Last accessed on 11 December 2020.
2 Taking into consideration IBGE's official population projection on 13 March 2021. See https://www.ibge.gov.br/apps/populacao/projecao/.
3 More information available at http://depen.gov.br/DEPEN/depen/sisdepen/infopen-mulheres/infopenmulheres_arte_07-03-18.pdf. Last accessed on 22 April 2020.
4 V. Lofgren et al. The Epidemiological Implications of Incarceration Dynamics in Jails for Community, Corrections Officer, and Incarcerated Population Risks from COVID-19. Preprint. See https://www.medrxiv.org/content/10.1101/2020.04.08.20058842v2.article-info. Last accessed on 11 December 2020.
5 See https://www.cnj.jus.br/sistema-carcerario/COVID-19/. Last accessed on 13 March 2021.
6 English version available at https://www.cnj.jus.br/wp-content/uploads/2020/06/Recommendation-CNJ-n.-62-2020-English-translation-1-1.pdf. Last accessed on 11 December 2020.
7 Recomendação N° 68 de 17/06/2020/CNJ. Available at https://atos.cnj.jus.br/atos/detalhar/3364. Last accessed on 13 March 2021.
8 Recomendação N° 78 de 15/09/2020/CNJ. See https://atos.cnj.jus.br/atos/detalhar/3480. Last accessed on 13 March 2021.
9 More information available at http://depen.gov.br/DEPEN/prevencao-do-coronavirus-no-sistema-prisional/plano_de_contingencia_coronavirus_Fiocruz_20200313.pdf. Last accessed on 22 April 2020.
10 More information available at http://depen.gov.br/DEPEN/POPCoronaVirus2REVISO2303202.pdf and http://depen.gov.br/DEPEN/Nota_Informativa_8___Coronavirus_APS_Prisional.pdf. Last accessed on 22 April 2020.
11 More information available at https://app.powerbi.com/view?r=eyJrIjoiYThhMjk5YjgtZWQwYS00ODlkLTg4NDgtZTFhMTgzYmQ2MGVlIiwidCI6ImViMDkwNDIwLTQ0NGMtNDNmNy05MWYyLTRiOGRhNmJmZThlMSJ9. Last accessed on 11 December 2020.
12 See https://www.cnj.jus.br/wp-content/uploads/2020/07/Relat_Form_Monitoramento_Rec62_1307.pdf. Last accessed on 11 December 2020.
13 Considering the about 900,000 inmates in Brazil, two thirds of them pre-trial detainees (see above), the reduction of the prison population during the pandemic remained almost negligible.

14 See https://www.in.gov.br/en/web/dou/-/portaria-n-4-de-15-de-marco-de-2020-248327975. Last accessed on 11 December 2020.
15 Depen keeps a website with quasi-live data regarding the pandemic in the prison system. See https://app.powerbi.com/view?r=eyJrIjoiYThhMjk5YjgtZWQwYS00ODlkLTg4NDgtZTFhMTgzYmQ2MGVlIiwidCI6ImViMDkwNDI-wLTQ0NGMtNDNmNy05MWYyLTRiOGRhNmJmZThlMSJ9. Last accessed on 11 December 2020.
16 See https://www.cnj.jus.br/wp-content/uploads/2020/07/Relat_Form_Monitoramento_Rec62_1307.pdf. Last accessed on 11 December 2020.
17 See https://www.gov.br/depen/pt-br/assuntos/acoes-contra-pandemia/prevencao-ao-COVID-19-no-sistema-prisional/medidas-concessivas. Last accessed on 11 December 2020.
18 See https://www.in.gov.br/en/web/dou/-/portaria-n-5-de-16-de-marco-de-2020-249490711. Last accessed on 13 March 2020.
19 Ruling available at http://portal.stf.jus.br/processos/downloadPeca.asp?id=15342813880&ext=.pdf. Last accessed on 11 December 2020.
20 See http://portal.stf.jus.br/processos/detalhe.asp?incidente=5880097. Last accessed on 13 March 2021.
21 http://sintse.tse.jus.br/documentos/2020/Ago/14/saude/portaria-no-35-de-12-de-agosto-de-2020-autoriza-a-realizacao-de-visitas-virtuais-por-intermedio-da-d. Last accessed on 13 March 2021.
22 Available at https://www.gov.br/depen/pt-br/assuntos/acoes-contra-pandemia/prevencao-ao-COVID-19-no-sistema-prisional/PORTARIA_DISPF_N__39__DE_5_DE_NOVEMBRO_DE_2020_DOU_Imprensa_Nacional.pdf. Last accessed on 13 March 2021.
23 More information available at http://www.stf.jus.br/portal/cms/verNoticiaDetalhe.asp?idConteudo=370152. Last accessed on 11 December 2020.
24 More information available at http://www.stf.jus.br/portal/cms/verNoticiaDetalhe.asp?idConteudo=439958. Last accessed on 11 December 2020.
25 More information available at https://www.jota.info/stf/do-supremo/stf-nega-81-dos-hcs-baseados-na-recomendacao-62-do-cnj-sobre-a-COVID-19-07082020. Last accessed on 11 December 2020.
26 More information available at https://anadep.org.br/wtk/pagina/materia?id=43948. Last accessed on 11 December 2020.
27 More information available at https://www.stj.jus.br/sites/portalp/Paginas/Comunicacao/Noticias/Negado-pedido-de-habeas-corpus-coletivo-para-todos-os-presos-em-grupos-de-risco-do-coronavirus.aspx. Last accessed on 11 December 2020.
28 In ADPF 347, the Supreme Court ruled in affirmance of the configuration of an "unconstitutional state of affairs" regarding the Brazilian prison system, although no concrete measures in order to address this issue were determined. More information available at http://portal.stf.jus.br/processos/detalhe.asp?incidente=4783560. Last accessed on 11 December 2020.
29 The Justices' manifestations and the Court ruling are available at http://portal.stf.jus.br/processos/downloadPeca.asp?id=15343623422&ext=.pdf. Last accessed on 11 December 2020.

References

Conselho Nacional de Justiça (2020): Boletim Semanal sobre Contágios e Óbitos no Sistema Prisional. https://www.cnj.jus.br/sistema-carcerario/COVID-19/registros-de-contagios-obitos/.

Conselho Nacional de Justiça (2020a): Monitoramento das Ações de Enfrentamento à COVID-19 em Espaços de Privação de Liberdade. https://www.cnj.jus.br/sistema-carcerario/COVID-19/monitoramento-gmfs-tribunais/.

Conselho Nacional de Justiça (2020b): Monitoramento CNJ Recomendação 62/2020. Available at: https://www.cnj.jus.br/sistema-carcerario/COVID-19/monitoramento-cnj/.

Conselho Nacional de Justiça (2020c): Estatísticas do Banco Nacional de Monitoramento de Prisões. https://portalbnmp.cnj.jus.br/#/estatisticas.

Conselho Nacional de Justiça. (2020d). Recommendation N° 62, 17 March 2020. Available at: https://www.cnj.jus.br/wp-content/uploads/2020/06/Recommendation-CNJ-n.-62-2020-English-translation-1-1.pdf.

Conselho Nacional do Ministério Público (2020): Nota Técnica n° 2/2020 – CSP. Estudo e roteiro sugestivo de providências no sistema prisional. https://www.cnmp.mp.br/portal/images/Notas_T%C3%A9cnicas/CNMP-CSP-ROTEIRO-COVID-19.pdf.

Garófalo, S., Santos, A., and Santos, I. (2020): A pandemia no cárcere: intervenções no superisolamento. *Ciênc. saúde coletiva* 25 (9) 28 Ago 2020Set 2020. https://doi.org/10.1590/1413-81232020259.15682020.

Instituto Brasileiro de Geografia e Estatística (2020): Projeção da população do Brasil e das Unidades da Federação. Available at: https://www.ibge.gov.br/apps/populacao/projecao/.

Lofgren et al. (2020): The epidemiological implications of incarceration dynamics in jails for community, corrections officer, and incarcerated population risks from COVID-19. Preprint. https://www.medrxiv.org/content/10.1101/2020.04.08.20058842v2.article-info.

Ministério da Justiça e Segurança Pública/Departamento Penitenciário Nacional (2020): Portaria n° 4, de 15 de março de 2020. Available at: https://www.in.gov.br/en/web/dou/-/portaria-n-4-de-15-de-marco-de-2020-248327975.

Ministério da Justiça e Segurança Pública/Departamento Penitenciário Nacional (2020a): Medidas de Combate ao COVID-19 – Paineis de Monitoramento. Available at: https://app.powerbi.com/view?r=eyJrIjoiYThhMjk5YjgtZWQwYS00ODlkLTg4NDgtZTFhMTgzYmQ2MGVlIiwidCI6ImViMDkwNDIwLTQ0NGMtNDNmNy05MWYyLTRiOGRhNmJmZThlMSJ9.

Ministério da Justiça e Segurança Pública/Departamento Penitenciário Nacional (2020b): Medidas Concessivas Adotadas Pelas Unidades Federativas A Familiares/Visitantes e Presos. https://www.gov.br/depen/pt-br/assuntos/acoes-contra-pandemia/prevencao-ao-COVID-19-no-sistema-prisional/copy_of_TABELAUNIDADESFEDERATIVASMEDIDASCONCESSIVASAFAMILIARES-VISITANTESEPRESOS17.04.2022H1.pdf.

Ministério da Justiça e Segurança Pública/Departamento Penitenciário Nacional (2020c): Recomendações para prevenção e cuidado da COVID-19 no sistema prisional brasileiro. 1ª edição, abril 2020. https://www.gov.br/depen/pt-br/Manual-COVID19DEPEN1edicao.pdf.

Pompeu, A. (2020): STF nega 81% dos HCs baseados na Recomendação 62, do CNJ, sobre a COVID-19. Jota.info. 7 de agosto de 2020. Available at: https://www.jota.info/stf/do-supremo/stf-nega-81-dos-hcs-baseados-na-recomendacao-62-do-cnj-sobre-a-COVID-19-07082020.

Rodrigues, E., Khoury, E., Padua, M., and Lacerda, O. (2020): Elektronische Überwachung in Brasilien im Licht der Kriminologie. In: Drenkhahn, K. et al. (Eds.): Kriminologie und Kriminalpolitik im Dienste der Menschenwürde. Festschrift für Frieder Dünkel zum 70. Geburtstag. Mönchengladbach: Forum Verlag Godesberg, 249–264.

Supremo Tribunal Federal (2020): ADPF 347. http://portal.stf.jus.br/processos/detalhe.asp?incidente=4783560.

Supremo Tribunal Federal (2020a): Reclamação 39.756 Distrito Federal. http://portal.stf.jus.br/processos/detalhe.asp?incidente=5880097.

6 Canada

Sandra Bucerius, Rosemary Ricciardelli and Luca Berardi

1 Introduction

Our chapter provides an overview of how Canadian correctional systems have responded to, and have been affected by, COVID-19, and how the pandemic has sparked public discussions about prison reform in Canada. The chapter is primarily based on secondary sources; however, Section 4.1 provides some supplementary insights gained from a longitudinal project with 39 loved ones of people housed in prisons across the country. In bi-weekly interviews with participants beginning in April 2020, we gained valuable insights into what their incarcerated loved ones reported about incarceration during the COVID-19 pandemic.

1.1 General situation of the prison system in Canada

Prior to COVID-19, approximately 40,000 adult men and women were housed in a correctional institution on any given day in Canada. These numbers represent a national incarceration rate of 139 per 100,000 individuals for the year 2015/2016.[1] According to World Prison Brief, Canada had 38,570 prisoners on 31 March 2019, representing a prison population rate of 104 with an occupancy rate of 99.5%.[2]

Depending on the seriousness of their crimes, individuals are either held in Canada's federal correctional system (governed by Correctional Services Canada (CSC)) or provincial correctional system (composed of 13 provincial/territorial correctional departments).

The federal system arguably houses, sentenced individuals convicted of arguably more serious offences – i.e. those sentenced to a period of incarceration of two years or more. People housed in federal institutions account for a smaller number of incarcerated persons in comparison to those housed in the provincial and territorial systems. On a "typical day" in 2017–2018, 14,015 individuals were housed in one of 43 federal penitentiaries (Correctional Service Canada, 2019). About 8% of federally incarcerated individuals are held in women's prisons (traditionally reserved for those who identify as women, including transgender women). More than half of federally

DOI: 10.4324/9781003169178-6

sentenced people serve sentences of less than five years, while about one quarter are serving life sentences (Public Safety Canada, 2019). Federal facilities can be found throughout the country, and have different security designations (minimum, medium, maximum, and one super-maximum "special handling unit" in the province of Quebec), as well as more specialised facilities, including four "healing lodges" for Indigenous individuals. Generally, federally incarcerated individuals are eligible for parole after serving one-third of their sentence – or for statutory release after serving two-thirds.

The 13 provincial or territorial correctional systems house individuals sentenced to a maximum of two years less a day and those awaiting their trial or sentencing (i.e. remand prisoners). Provincial and territorial prisons could be either designated for sentenced people only, for remanded people only, or mixed facilities holding both sentenced and remanded prisoners. There are 177 provincial and territorial institutions across the country housing approximately 24,000 prisoners. These facilities, like those in the federal system, have security classifications ranging from minimum (e.g. no secure parameter) to maximum (e.g. very secure parameter).

Remand prisoners, though legally presumed innocent, are held in custody rather than released into the community (i.e. they are not eligible for bail due to being considered flight risks or threats to the public). Remand prisoners include individuals arrested for comparatively minor offences, such as minor theft or impaired driving, as well as those accused of serious and high-profile crimes, including murder or terrorist activities. Consequently, all remand facilities are maximum security institutions. Depending on the outcome of their sentencing, remanded prisoners may be transferred to a federal or provincial/territorial institution, be released for "time served," or be released after being found not guilty. Since 2005, remanded people have constituted the majority of the provincial and territorial custodial population (Manitoba Government and General Employees' Union, 9 February 2012; Porter and Calverley, 2011; Statistics Canada, 2017). For example, on an "average day" in 2014–2015, more adults were housed in prison awaiting trial than convicted individuals serving a sentence in custody. In the provincial and territorial systems, for instance, 13,650 of the 24,014 incarcerated adults per day (on average), constituting 57% of the prison population, were incarcerated pre-trial (Statistics Canada, 2017).

The overwhelming majority of Canadians whom the courts sentence to prison are vulnerable in some way. Incarcerated individuals typically have low baseline physical and mental health (Fazel and Baillargeon, 2011; Stewart et al., 2014) and are disadvantaged when it comes to educational attainment. Upwards of 20% of new federal prisoner admissions have less than a grade eight education (Boe, 2005). Many incarcerated people have also experienced homelessness and unstable caregiver situations while growing up (Bucerius, 2020; Schultz, Bucerius, and Haggerty, 2021), with the vast majority being physically and sexually abused as children (Bucerius,

Haggerty, and Dunford, 2021). Their marginalisation is also strongly conditioned by systemic racism related to Canada's colonial history and legacy. A 2013 report from the Office of the Correctional Investigator found that from 2003 to 2013, the incarceration rates for people of colour rose by 75%, with Canada's Indigenous peoples continuing to be grossly overrepresented (Owusu-Bempah and Wortley, 2014; Zinger, 2020).

1.2 COVID-19 pandemic in Canadian correctional institutions and Canadian society

The World Health Organization declared COVID-19 a pandemic on 12 March 2020. Recognising closed-custody correctional facilities (including prisons), correctional centres, and jails, as a high risk for the transmission of COVID-19, lockdown measures were put in place by these institutions. On 12 March 2020, the Union of Canadian Correctional Officers (UCCO-SACC-CSN), representing federal correctional officers employed by CSC, also requested support from CSC to help ensure the health and safety of their members during the pandemic (UCCO-SACC-CSN, 12 March 2020).

As of 1 February 2021, 5,282 COVID-19 cases have been linked to Canadian correctional institutions, consisting of 4,125 prisoners, 1,154 staff, and 3 contractors being infected since the beginning of the pandemic. Of these cases, 1,241 prisoners and 296 staff were infected in the federal system, while the remaining cases were spread across the provincial systems of Alberta, British Columbia, Ontario, Quebec, Manitoba, Nova Scotia, and Saskatchewan (the other provincial and territorial systems have yet to report a case thus far) (http://tpcp-canada.blogspot.com/). During the same period, the Government of Canada has reported a total case count of 789,651 COVID-19 infections in the general population (https://www.canada.ca/en/public-health/services/diseases/2019-novel-coronavirus-infection.html).

In spring 2020, during the first wave of the pandemic, CSC reported several in-prison outbreaks of COVID-19 that affected both those housed and working in some of its facilities (e.g. Mission Institution in British Columbia and the Multi-level Federal Training Centre in Quebec). The majority of CSC and provincial/territorial prisons, however, did not report any outbreaks during the first wave of the pandemic. Canada's correctional systems were more acutely affected during the second wave of the pandemic, which began in October 2020 and peaked on 9 January 2021, with 9,214 reported cases among the general population (https://graphics.reuters.com/world-coronavirus-tracker-and-maps/countries-and-territories/Canada/). We recognise that the increased numbers during the second wave were partially due to rapid testing, a practice not yet possible during wave one of the pandemic. Yet, Canada was also harder hit during the second wave, thus resulting in more frequent in-prison outbreaks than during the first wave. For example, as of 31 October 2020, 104 of the 161 incarcerated people in the Calgary Correctional Centre had tested positive for COVID-19, comprising 65% of the institution's prison population, as well as 20 staff and officers (Bruch, 2020, 31 October). In Manitoba, at Headingley Correction Centre, 86 incarcerated persons and 24 staff and correctional officers had tested positive as of 3 November 2020 (Unger, 2020, 3 November). Administrators, advocates, and journalists continue to report outbreaks across the country, including at institutions such as the Saskatoon Correctional Centre and Grand Valley Institution (CBC News, 29 November 2020; Ghonaim, 4 December 2020).

As of 4 February 2021, COVID-19 has killed 20,235 Canadians (https://graphics.reuters.com/world-coronavirus-tracker-and-maps/countries-and-territories/canada/). The reported number of deaths in custody has been comparably low, with five incarcerated people and one correctional officer dying from the virus (Correctional Service Canada, 2020).

1.3 COVID-19-related reductions in the prison *population*

Governments across Canada took steps to reduce the prison population during the first few months of the pandemic, which resulted in 7,000 fewer people being in custody in May 2020 in comparison to February 2020 – representing a 19% reduction in the overall prison population across Canada (Statistics Canada, 2020). When looking at the numbers, there were, on average, 37,976 adults in federal and provincial/territorial custody on any given day in February 2020, whereas the average count was down to 30,795 adults in May 2020. Such a stark decrease is unprecedented in the Canadian context, where the average population count is typically stable over time (with minor fluctuations of around 1%). The custodial population remained steady between May and June 2020 (Statistics Canada, 2020), as safety measures increased and correctional facilities established more effective ways of containing the virus within prisons, received personal protective equipment (PPE) for staff, and introduced rapid testing in some institutions.

While the federal system enacted measures to reduce the prison population, it was much less fruitful in this endeavour than the provincial and territorial systems. The overall decline in the federal prison population was approximately 2% each month between March and May (for an overall decrease of 6%). The decline was starker at the provincial and territorial levels, where the average count of adults in provincial/territorial custody fell by 28% from 24,085 to 17,320 adults between February and May 2020. The decrease occurred in both the remand (minus 28%) and the sentenced (minus 27%) populations. The largest decrease occurred at the beginning of the pandemic, with a 21% reduction from March to April. From May to June, the average population count for the remand population increased by 3%, whereas the average case count for the sentenced custody population continued to decrease by 4% (https://www150.statcan.gc.ca/n1/daily-quotidien/200812/dq200812a-eng.htm).

The decline in the provincial and territorial systems was particularly dramatic for female prisoners in provincial and territorial custody. Here, the female prison population declined by 43% between February and May 2020, whereas the male population only declined by 27% during that same period. In June 2020, the prison population increased again in seven territories and provinces, with the female population increasing at a faster rate than the male population in New Brunswick, Ontario, Manitoba, and Saskatchewan, while the male population increased at a faster pace than the female population in Prince Edward Island. In two provincial systems, Nova Scotia and Nunavut, the female population continued to decrease in June while the male population increased. Alberta showed minimal changes in June for both male and female populations. During the same month, the custodial populations continued to decline in the remaining five provinces and territories. While the female custodial population declined at a faster rate than the male population in Newfoundland and Labrador, Quebec, and British Columbia, the reverse was true for the Northwest Territories. The Yukon saw no change for the male custodial population, whereas the female population continued to decline (https://www150.statcan.gc.ca/n1/daily-quotidien/200812/dq200812a-eng.htm).[3] At the time of writing, we do not yet have access to official data beyond June 2020.

2 Prison and penal policy concerning the execution of prison sentences during the Covid-19-induced crisis

The correctional ministries in Canada recognised that holding people in closed custodial settings increases the risk of spreading the contagion. As we outlined elsewhere (Ricciardelli and Bucerius, 2020), the close-proximity living conditions in prisons and the lack of physical distancing options make correctional facilities particularly vulnerable to the spread of COVID-19, especially given concerns about aerosol transmission (Miller, 4 November 2020). As a preventative measure, Canadian courts and correctional systems have tried to reduce the size of custodial populations since the beginning of the pandemic. These measures have included the temporary or early release of those considered as posing a low risk of reoffending, the extension of parole appeal deadlines, and access to medical leave privileges, as well as alternatives to remand custody while awaiting trial, sentencing, and bail hearings. Unfortunately, exact numbers for individuals who were released under the circumstances above are not yet publicly available in Canada.

3 Restrictions of contact with the outside world

During the first wave of the COVID-19 pandemic, in-person visits were cancelled to contain the spread of the virus and inter-regional and international transfers of persons in custody were suspended (Statistics Canada, 2020). In addition, prisons greatly reduced the number of people eligible to enter their institutions, with programming also ceasing with the restriction or banning of volunteers within federal, provincial, and territorial facilities. Although less publicly documented, additional measures also included a reduction in temporary absences from prison, work leaves, and other opportunities for sentenced individuals to have contact with the free world – undertaken to reduce prisoners' likelihood of contracting COVID-19 and bringing it back into the institution upon re-entry.

During summer 2020, i.e. between waves one and two, visits were temporarily reinstated; however, this was short-lived, as the second wave resulted in the cancellation of visits once again. During the period when visits were occurring, prisoners and their loved ones had to comply with general public healthcare measures surrounding COVID-19, such as mask wearing and physical distancing. In practice, this meant that loved ones and prisoners were unable to touch, had to sit six feet apart, and were not allowed to share food. Once visits ceased, other avenues for experiencing and connecting with the outside world were reinstated (e.g. video calls).

The transfer of prisoners between federal institutions did not cease during the second wave of COVID-19; instead, CSC incorporated the use of rapid testing to identify asymptomatic carriers and attempted to contain the spread across institutions by introducing measures such as mandatory quarantine for transferees. For example, after an outbreak at Joyceville Institution in December 2020 (https://www.ctvnews.ca/health/coronavirus/inmates-fear-leaving-in-a-body-bag-as-covid-19-outbreaks-in-prisons-worsen-1.5253369), a number of incarcerated men who tested positive for COVID-19 were transferred to Warkworth and Collin's Bay institutions (https://globalnews.ca/news/7529816/inmates-test-positive-warkworth-institution-coronavirus/). These individuals underwent mandatory quarantine in their receiving institutions and the spread of COVID-19 was mitigated, despite the public outcry that followed the transfer.

4 Restrictions inside prisons

As noted, in an effort to curb the spread of COVID-19 inside prisons, CSC and provincial and territorial correctional systems suspended programming to decrease the number of people frequenting correctional institutions. Although perhaps a controversial decision, the practice was consistent with the suspension of recreational programming and schooling in free society. Correctional Services also imposed additional lockdown measures and a cohort[4] design in order to reduce contact between incarcerated persons and staff across units – with the goal of preventing outbreaks from spreading within institutions. These measures, among others, for instance, successfully contained a December 2020 outbreak at Joyceville Institution to specific units, preventing the spread of COVID-19 across the entire facility.

Additional restrictions have included moving prisoners between several institutions in order to create "quarantine units" and ensuring that all newly admitted prisoners (including institutional transfers) undergo 14 days of quarantine upon arrival to a correctional facility. Further, CSC and other correctional institutions are distributing PPE to correctional staff, while introducing additional measures for containing, testing, and detecting COVID-19 (Statistics Canada, 2020). During the second wave, CSC introduced rapid testing for prisoners and correctional staff. In the federal system, CSC has also started to distribute vaccinations to immunocompromised and elderly incarcerated individuals thought to be acutely at-risk of adverse effects from the virus – another measure that has been quite controversial among members of the public who do not believe that prisoners should be prioritised for vaccinations. The question of when to vaccinate prisoners has also caused some debate within the Conservative party of Canada. In Alberta, for example, the Conservative premier of the province directly opposed the federal Conservative party leader who had publicly stated that all healthcare and frontline workers should be vaccinated before elderly prisoners (https://www.cbc.ca/news/canada/calgary/kenney-otoole-vaccines-covid-inmates-1.5871622).

Even though correctional officers can be exposed to COVID-19 in free society and bring the virus into their institutions, they have yet to be vaccinated. Despite advocacy for staff vaccination, this responsibility lies with the provincial governments in which the staff member resides – even if the correctional officer is working for the federal system. Thus, CSC is unable to vaccinate their employees in the same manner that they are able to vaccinate prisoners. While CSC has encouraged (and made accessible) the use of leave for staff who feel unsafe working in prisons due to COVID-19, correctional officers in some provincial jurisdictions (particularly those where extreme cases of outbreaks have occurred) were asked to continue coming in to work and to isolate when not working (Herring, 2020).

4.1 Insights from the interviews with prisoner loved ones

This section is supplemented by insights from an ongoing longitudinal research project on carceral relations during the COVID-19 pandemic. Two of the authors, Bucerius and Berardi, and their team have been conducting bi-weekly interviews with 39 loved ones of prisoners since April 2020. All interview participants have an incarcerated loved one in Canada – be it a spouse, child, parent, sibling, or close friend. Approximately half of the participants have a loved one in the federal system, while half have a loved one in the provincial or territorial systems. These interviews not only shed light on the many challenges experienced by the loved ones of incarcerated people, but also on the ever-changing conditions in Canadian prisons during a global pandemic – and the impact these changes are having on the health and well-being of people housed in prison. Preliminary findings touch on how the pandemic has affected, among other things, in-person prison visits, prison programming and services, the flow of information between institutions and loved ones, staff compliance with safety guidelines and regulations, and the mental and physical health of incarcerated people.

While acknowledging the importance of suspending in-person visits to manage the spread of disease, the majority of participants described various ways that this measure has negatively affected them, their incarcerated loved one, and their relationship. Not surprisingly, it has increased feelings of isolation among loved ones and their incarcerated kin, especially for those (in both groups) at the greatest risk of contracting COVID-19 and experiencing serious health outcomes. This includes the elderly and immunocompromised, many of whom have been limiting physical interactions with others throughout the pandemic to ensure access to prison visits if and when they resume. Uncertainty around this issue of "if and when" in-person visits might resume (and for how long) has, in its own right, become a major source of stress and anxiety for incarcerated people and their kin.

At the time of writing, in-person visits are taking place at a limited number of federal institutions in Nova Scotia (2 of 2 prisons), Alberta (2 of 8), Saskatchewan (3 of 6), and British Columbia (1 of 11), with all federal institutions in Manitoba, Ontario, Quebec, and New Brunswick closed to visitors (https://www.csc-scc.gc.ca/family/003004-0006-en.shtml). In addition to normal security measures, those visiting incarcerated kin during the pandemic will also be asked COVID-19 screening questions, must have their temperature taken, must wash their hands before entering the institution, and are required to wear a mask throughout their visit. Vending machines have been shut off to discourage the sharing of food and drink, play areas have been closed and children's toys removed, and no physical contact is permitted between visitors and prisoners, with the physical distancing rule of "two meters apart" applying at all times.

Some of our study participants with loved ones in the federal system reported having the opportunity to utilise video visits several times a week; however, this experience required advance registration and was often plagued by sudden cancellations due to lockdowns, schedule changes, and other unforeseen circumstances. A number of participants also expressed frustration that correctional staff were clearly monitoring private video calls between them (and their children) and their incarcerated loved one.

At the beginning of the pandemic, many of our participants expressed frustration that the correctional system was not providing clear, coherent, or timely information about the status of visits, under what circumstances they might occur, or practical guidance on how they might unfold at a given facility – a frustration that has generally subsided over time, as institutions have gained more of a handle on the pandemic. This lack of official information from some correctional systems, however, has extended to other areas as well, with many participants noting that they have been largely left in the dark about the health and safety of their incarcerated kin, the status of the prison and its units (i.e. whether particular units are on lockdown, why, and for how long), and what safety measures are being implemented to prevent and reduce the spread of COVID-19. In most cases, incarcerated individuals have equally limited access to this official information, despite having to negotiate the outcomes of these institutional-level decisions and mandates on a daily basis.

Participants have also expressed serious concerns about COVID-19-related suspension of prison programming, services, and job opportunities (both inside and outside of the prison) on the mental and physical health of their loved ones. Similar concerns have also been raised about the closure of key areas of the prison that, under normal circumstances, facilitate social interaction and increase the overall well-being of prisoners (e.g. gymnasiums, weight rooms, cafeterias, chapels, and visiting centres). While reducing the risk of COVID-19 transmission, the cumulative effect of these suspensions and closures has been the shrinkage of the already limited social and physical worlds of prisoners, resulting in a myriad of potential health concerns.

Finally, our participants reported that prison officials in some institutions were not complying with government-issued health and safety guidelines. Participants noted that their loved ones often commented that only some staff on their living units wore face masks or shields, while others did not (or did not do so consistently or correctly). Some commented that the institution and staff had not provided their loved ones with cleaning supplies or sufficient PPE, including masks, gloves, or disinfectants. Other participants reported that, although some institutions had distributed masks to prisoners, there were no formal rules in place to ensure (or enforce) mask-wearing behaviour in a space where social distancing was impossible.

5 Compensatory measures

Canada's correctional systems have responded to the COVID-19 pandemic by providing and adopting protective measures to reduce the potential for transmission – for instance, introducing cohorts to mitigate potential spread. In addition to PPE for staff (e.g. masks, gloves, gowns, eye protection), Statistics Canada (2020) also states that persons housed in prison and correctional staff have both received, and have been given increased access to, hygiene and cleaning supplies, which offers individuals some control over the cleanliness of their personal space – thereby reducing contamination risk. The introduction of personal hygiene and cleaning supplies is supplemented at CSC institutions by frequent cleaning and disinfecting (https://www.csc-scc.gc.ca/001/006/001006-1102-en.shtml). Correctional Services have also introduced physical health screening protocols upon intake into the systems and for daily symptom checks. These are administered to both prisoners and staff to assist with early identification of COVID-19, thus maximising opportunities to contain the spread (Statistics Canada, 2020). According to Statistics Canada, physical distancing and hand hygiene are also active compensatory measures, along with increased use of laundry bleach. CSC is currently working to increase the hot water capacity and reviewing their ventilation and air filtration technologies within institutions.

To compensate for the ceasing of in-person visits, CSC has increased the use of technology to allow people housed in prison to have video visits with their loved ones. Mobile phones and access to the internet are not provided to incarcerated persons in Canada.

For staff or incarcerated persons who test positive for COVID-19, the standard practice is imposed medical isolation for prisoners and self-isolation for employees (https://www.csc-scc.gc.ca/001/006/001006-1102-en.shtml). According to Statistics Canada, the identification of any positive COVID-19 case results in contact tracing, with over 250 CSC employees currently trained to conduct this analysis. CSC also uses the Integrated Risk Management Framework (IRMF) to inform their operational decisions, which outlines risk levels ranging from Low Risk (Green) to Moderate Risk (Yellow) to Moderate High Risk (Orange) to High Risk (Red), and includes both community and institutional COVID-19 risk assessments. For example, in institutions deemed Moderate-High Risk (Orange) of COVID-19, the infection is located in an identified zone and measures include reduced access to the site, while in a High Risk (Red) assessed prison, which occurs when there is an unidentified source of transmission, the measures imposed include full institutional lockdown.

6 Legal basis for restrictions and relaxations of the prison regime

Arguably, the most controversial practice associated with COVID-19 is the mandatory quarantine period of 14 days for incarcerated individuals. In Canada, such practices are viewed as particularly egregious, given that the segregation of any incarcerated person for more than 14 days in isolation is considered a violation of an individual right, guaranteed by the Canadian Charter of Rights, according to recent legislation opposing administrative (or disciplinary) segregation (http://www.thecourt.ca/scc-to-determine-constitutionality-of-administrative-segregation/). Prisoners' rights advocates, including the Officer of the Correctional Investigator and the Canadian Civil Liberties Association, argue for decarceration and reduced lockdowns rather than quarantines (https://policyoptions.irpp.org/magazines/february-2021/covids-uneven-spread-in-the-federal-penitentiary-system-has-one-solution/; https://www.oci-bec.gc.ca/index-eng.aspx). The recommendations for managing the spread of COVID-19 as put forth by the Chief Public Health Officer of Canada, Dr. Theresa Tam, as well as the Public Health Agency of Canada (PHAC), are therefore in direct opposition to the legislation governing the use of isolation in prisons.

7 Returning to normal

In Canada, the COVID-19 pandemic has sparked public discourse about how Canadian correctional systems are in crisis and require reform. For example, Dr. Theresa Tam, Canada's Chief Health Officer, invited two of the authors, Bucerius and Ricciardelli, to speak about the impact of COVID-19 on correctional populations (both prisoners and staff), to put forth evidence-based policy recommendations to address the spread of COVID-19 in prisons, and to introduce tangible changes for those living and working in prisons (both immediate and beyond the pandemic).

Together with Justin Tetrault, David Pyrooz, and Ben Crewe, Ricciardelli and Bucerius also authored a policy brief for the Royal Society of Canada where they introduced 41 recommendations for correctional systems in Canada (Ricciardelli et al., 2021). In the brief, they acknowledge that the pandemic provides opportunities to re-think various aspects of criminal justice practice, and make recommendations aimed at how Canadian correctional systems should manage COVID-19 – while also addressing what elements of these systems should persist after the pandemic. While the brief focused on ways to reduce the incarcerated population, suggesting processes for reconsidering who can be safely housed in the community, recommendations were also made for managing those who will remain in prison during COVID-19 and beyond.

Although decarceration is an effective means for curbing the spread of the virus by reducing the number of people in closed-custody living conditions, we are also using this moment to draw particular attention to how incarceration is "an expensive and often ineffective means of dealing with crime and public safety" (Ricciardelli et al., 2021: 15). Incarceration has severe consequences on the well-being and life chances of incarcerated people, but also collateral consequences for the loved ones of prisoners, including their children (Murray and Farrington, 2008; Turney and Wildeman, 2013; Wakefield and Wildeman, 2013). We advocate for structured decarceration that balances the individual needs of the prisoner with public safety, ensuring that people being released from custody are provided with the necessary community supports and services that will allow them to re-enter the community in a safe and humane way (e.g. ensuring that individuals have access to safe housing options, and crisis counselling).

Notes

1 See https://www150.statcan.gc.ca/n1/pub/85-002-x/2017001/article/14700-eng.htm (last access 20 April 2021). The prison population rate has been declining since 2011/2012.

2 See https://www.prisonstudies.org/country/Canada; last accessed on 20 April 2021). In 2017, the number of prisoners was 40,770 with a calculated prison population rate of 112. The occupancy level was 102.2% for 2015 (99% in institutions and 104% in provincial/territorial institutions); see World Prison Brief, ibid.

3 Yukon introduced decarceration prior to the COVID-19 pandemic taking hold in Canada, a factor beyond the scope of the current chapter. Thus, their numbers were already reduced and have stayed relatively low throughout the pandemic.

4 Dividing units up into several cohorts, or understanding a living unit as a cohort.

References

Boe, R. (2005): Unemployment risk trends and the implications for Canadian federal offenders. *Forum on Corrections Research 17*(1): 3–5.

Bruch, T. (2020, 31 October): 'Everybody is sick': Those inside the massive Calgary prison outbreak look to the province for help. *CTV News*. Retrieved from https://calgary.ctvnews.ca/everybody-is-sick-those-inside-the-massive-calgary-prison-outbreak-look-to-the-province-for-help-1.5169560.

Bucerius, S. (2020): Prison as a temporary refuge. *TEDx UAlberta*.

Bucerius, S., Haggerty, K. D., and Dunford, D. T. (2021): Prison as temporary refuge: Amplifying the voices of women detained in prison. *The British Journal of Criminology*. doi: 10.1093/bjc/azaa073.

CBC News (9 April 2020): "More than 2,000 inmates released, 6 COVID-19 cases confirmed insider". *CBC News*. Retrieved from https://www.cbc.ca/news/canada/toronto/ontario-jails-coronavirus-1.5527677.

CBC News (29 November 2020): COVID-19 cases at Saskatoon Correctional Centre climb to 128. *CBC News*. Retrieved from https://www.cbc.ca/news/canada/saskatoon/spcc-cases-surpass-100-1.5821298.

Correctional Service Canada (2019): CSC statistics – key facts and figures. *Quick Facts*. Retrieved from https://www.csc-scc.gc.ca/publications/005007-3024-en.shtml.

Correctional Service Canada (2020): Testing of inmates in federal correctional institutions for COVID-19. Retrieved from https://www.csc-scc.gc.ca/001/006/001006-1014-en.shtml

Fazel, S., and Baillargeon, J. (2011): The health of prisoners. *The Lancet, 377*(9769), 956–965.

Ghonaim, H. (4 December 2020): Pandemic management questioned as Grand Valley Institution sees new COVID-19 cases. *CBC News*. Retrieved from https://www.cbc.ca/news/canada/kitchener-waterloo/pandemic-management-grand-valley-kitchener-1.5826858.

Herring, J. (2020, 31 October). Infected inmates allowed to mingle, spreading virus throughout Calgary jail: union. *Calgary Herald*. Retrieved from https://calgaryherald.com/news/local-news/inmates-with-covid-19-symptoms-in-calgary-jail-allowed

Manitoba Government and General Employees' Union (9 February 2012): MGEU President Wales' presentation underscores the overcrowding crisis in Manitoba jails. Retrieved from http://nupge.ca/content/4806/mgeu-president-wales-presentation-underscores-overcrowding-crisis-manitoba-jails.

Miller, A. (2020, 4 November): Canada quietly updates COVID-19 guidelines on risk of airborne spread: Public Health Agency of Canada previously made no mention of aerosol transmission in federal recommendations. *CSC News*. Retrieved from https://www.cbc.ca/news/health/coronavirus-canada-aerosol-transmission-covid-19-1.5789906.

Murray, J., and Farrington, D. P. (2008): The effects of parental imprisonment on children. *Crime and Justice*, 37(1), 133–206.

Owusu-Bempah, A., and Wortley, S. (2014): Race, crime, and criminal justice in Canada. In: Bucerius, S. and Tonry, M. (Eds.): *The Oxford handbook of ethnicity, crime, and immigration*. New York: Oxford University Press, 281–320.

Porter, L., and Calverley, D. (2011): *Trends in the use of remand in Canada* (85-002-X). Ottawa: Government of Canada. Retrieved from https://www150.statcan.gc.ca/n1/en/pub/85-002-x/2011001/article/11440-eng.pdf?st=FXNRC6QK.

Public Safety Canada (2019): *Correctional and conditional release: Statistical overview.* Ottawa: Public Works and Government Services Canada.

Ricciardelli, R., and Bucerius, S. (2020): Canadian prisons in the time of COVID-19: Recommendations for the pandemic and beyond. *Globe and Mail.* Retrieved from https://www.theglobeandmail.com/opinion/article-canadian-prisons-in-the-time-of-covid-19-recommendations-for-the/.

Ricciardelli, R., Bucerius, S., Tetrault, J., Crewe, B., and Pyrooz, D. (2021, January): *Policy brief: Correctional services during and beyond COVID-19.* Policy Brief, Royal Society of Canada, Ottawa, ON, 41 pages.

Schultz, W., Bucerius, S., and Haggerty, K. (2021): "I have to be a man for my son": The narrative uses of fatherhood in prison. *Punishment & Society.* doi: 10.1177/14624745211018760.

Statistics Canada (2017): *Trends in the use of remand in Canada, 2004/2005 to 2014/2015.* (85-002-X). Ottawa: Government of Canada. Retrieved from https://www150.statcan.gc.ca/n1/pub/85-002-x/2017001/article/14691-eng.htm.

Statistics Canada (2020): Changes in federal, provincial and territorial custodial populations during the COVID-19 pandemic. Retrieved from https://www150.statcan.gc.ca/n1/daily-quotidien/200812/dq200812a-eng.htm.

Stewart, L. A., Sapers, J., Nolan, A., and Power J. (2014): *Self-reported physical health status of newly admitted federally-sentenced men offenders.* Research Branch, Correctional Service Canada.

Turney, K., and Wildeman, C. (2013). Redefining relationships: Explaining the countervailing consequences of paternal incarceration for parenting. *American Sociological Review, 78*(6), 949–979.

Unger, D. (2020, 3 November): COVID-19 cases rise within Manitoba's largest jail outbreak. *CTV News.* Retrieved from https://winnipeg.ctvnews.ca/covid-19-cases-more-than-double-within-manitoba-s-largest-jail-outbreak-1.5173047.

Wakefield, S., and Wildeman, C. (2013): *Children of the prison boom: Mass incarceration and the future of American inequality.* New York: Oxford University Press.

Zinger, I. (2020): *Indigenous people in federal custody surpasses 30%.* Ottawa: Office of the Correctional Investigator.

Websites

http://tpcp-canada.blogspot.com/

https://www.canada.ca/en/public-health/services/diseases/2019-novel-coronavirus-infection.htm

https://www.csc-scc.gc.ca/001/006/001006-1102-en.shtml

https://graphics.reuters.com/world-coronavirus-tracker-and-maps/countries-and-territories/canada/

https://www150.statcan.gc.ca/n1/daily-quotidien/200812/dq200812a-eng.htm

7 Chile

Álvaro Castro-Morales, Julio Cortés-Olmedo, Violeta Purán-Rosas and Guillermo E. Sanhueza

1 Introduction

The first case of COVID-19 in Chile was identified and made known on 3 March 2020. As a result, increased sanitary measures of prevention and restriction were applied as of 16 March.

At the end of February 2020, the Chilean prison population was a total of 42,202 (38,674 men and 3,528 women). This number includes both those serving a sentence as a result of a judicial procedure and those in pre-trial detention (which currently represents about a third of the entire prison population). The body in charge of the administration and surveillance of prisons, whether public or private, is *Gendarmería de Chile* (GENCHI).

A characteristic of the Chilean penal system is that penal sanctions may be executed under different regimes. About half of those serving a sentence do so through a substitute sentence, according to the requirements in Law No. 20,603 (BCN, 2012). There is a division between closed, semi-closed and open systems. Those in the closed system (the 42,202 persons mentioned above) are most at risk from the pandemic and the health measures of prevention and protection were mainly directed at them.

In terms of infections, the statistics provided by GENCHI indicate that until 12 March 2021, 2,995 individuals deprived of liberty had been infected as well as 2,258 infections of prison officers, guards and staff members. In addition, 18 inmates and 4 GENCHI personnel had died. The vaccination campaign against respiratory diseases characteristic of the winter season also meant vaccinating 25,851 persons deprived of liberty and 13,496 officials.

The COVID-19 vaccination campaign began in 2021 and, by 12 March 2021, this process has resulted in the vaccination of 1,977 inmates with their first dose and 371 with the required two doses. GENCHI staff have vaccinated 5,078 inmates with their first dose and 1,276 with the two doses. In both cases, this is still a small percentage of the total population. The prison population is not considered a priority group for vaccination, despite the higher risk of infection. Those who have been able to be vaccinated meet the age range or other reasons for vaccination, such as chronic diseases.

DOI: 10.4324/9781003169178-7

However, GENCHI personnel were considered a priority vaccination group in the vaccination schedule as of the seventh week after the start of the campaign.

The infrastructure of Chilean prisons at the time of the health emergency, and the conditions to which the prison population is subject, such as food, hygiene, aggression and violence inside the prisons, access to workshops and activities, have many shortcomings that were criticised by academics and civil society organisations (Alcaíno, 2019; Contesse y Contreras, 2019; INDH, 2020a).[1] In addition, the country's criminal policy in recent years has shown a trend towards an increase in prison sentences, a rise in criminalised conduct and an excessive use of pre-trial detention, which has resulted in a sustained increase in the prison population. In view of their precarious situation with premises where there was neither the infrastructure nor adequate personnel for prevention and protection against the pandemic, the prison population also protested to draw attention to their situation. As a consequence of these demonstrations, there were attempts to escape, protests and riots in some of the riskiest areas such as "Santiago 1 Detention Centre", "Puente Alto Prison", "Colina 1 Prison" and in the "Prison Complex of Rancagua" (Cerna, 2020; Diario Uchile, 2020; Guerra, 2020, Nazif-Muñoz, 2020; Vilches, 2020).

According to data provided by GENCHI, the planning for the management of Chilean prisons in the face of the pandemic began more or less in parallel with the preparation undertaken by the health authorities of the country. Thus, at the time that first infections were identified in Chile, the prison management plan was already in place. This plan envisaged five phases where each considered the joint work of GENCHI with both health and judicial authorities and where, according to the progress of the phases, more restrictive measures could be adopted taking into account both the safety of inmates and the protection of public health, by identifying the population at greatest risk.

The plan, called the COVID-19 Comprehensive Contingency Action Plan (*Plan de Acción Integral por Contingencia COVID-19*, in Spanish) (GENCHI, 2020a), included five stages: (1) a planning stage, developed before the arrival of the virus in the country; (2) the implementation stage, activated when cases of COVID-19 were confirmed in the country; (3) control level 1 stage, initiated when the infection of an official was confirmed; (4) control level 2 stage, initiated when infection of the prison population was confirmed; and (5) control level 3 stage, which would be applied if the previous stages were insufficient and the national health system did not protect the prison population. Throughout this chapter, more aspects of these stages and the measures that each required are discussed.

In addition to this plan, GENCHI developed a set of directions that established protective measures for its employees (2020b), enabling remote working (where possible) and additional measures for those at greatest risk (older adults and people with chronic illnesses), establishing protective mechanisms, training for the staff in charge, protocols for the care and transfer of inmates and the possibility of hiring additional staff to deal with the COVID-19 crisis (2020c).

2 Prison and penal policy concerning the serving of prison sentences during the COVID-19-induced crisis

At the level of prison policy, the admission of individuals into prison facilities was restricted. From March 2020, Law No. 21,226 ordered the suspension of pending judicial proceedings. Their reopening was scheduled for the end of the state of constitutional emergency.[2] Despite this measure, which meant a reduction in the number of sentenced inmates entering prisons, some individuals continued to be admitted to prison facilities for pre-trial detention. In order to reduce the prison population, the Executive Branch enacted a law that, from 17 April (BCN, 2020), allowed for the pardon of 1,860 inmates (1,633 men and 227 women). The law benefited the following groups of people convicted of certain crimes:[3]

- Men and women over 75, commuting the balance of their prison sentences;
- Women over 55 and under 75 and men over 60 and under 75, commuting the balance of their prison sentences if they had served half their sentence and had less than 36 months of sentence remaining;
- Women who were pregnant or had children under the age of two, if such children lived with them in prison;[4]
- Persons serving partial imprisonment or night detention if they had served one-third of their sentence with less than 36 months remaining; and
- Convicted persons who had already served half of their sentence, had less than 36 months of sentence pending and had been granted a controlled release permit.

To this number must be added those who were able to obtain the benefit of parole and those who had been able to opt for a change in their cautionary measure. Probation was granted to 1,591 people and another 250 obtained a change in their precautionary measures (from, for example, pre-trial detention to home detention or to another less restrictive measure).

In total, according to the data provided by GENCHI, adding the pardons of Law No. 21,228, the conditional release and the changes of precautionary measures, the decongestion of the criminal system reached 3,701 persons, representing 9% of the total number deprived of liberty. To these must also be added the figures provided by the Public Defender's Office regarding the suspension of pre-trial detention, which from March to the present benefited 7,909 adults and 470 youths.

However, the same Public Defender's Office indicated that from March 2020 to the time of writing, 11,587 people (10,666 men and 921 women) were subject to pre-trial detention or provisional internment. The national press also reported that between January and June 2020, 33,133 people were admitted to prison (Rivera, 2020), including those serving pre-trial detention. Compared to previous years, there was a considerable drop in prison admissions, which cannot be directly attributed to a policy of reducing the prison population, but rather to the decrease in crime during the periods of quarantine and curfew and the suspension of the hearing of cases. According to these figures, the strategy adopted failed to significantly reduce the prison population or to provide effective mechanisms for suspending admission to prisons.

3 Restrictions of contacts with the outside world

The document prepared by GENCHI that regulated the different phases of management of the pandemic in its first phase restricted the number of visits. The possibility of two visits per week was reduced to having only one and the maximum number of hours of a visit was reduced. At the same time, it prohibited the entry into prison facilities of persons with a higher risk of the disease (older adults, pregnant women) and established a mandatory control at the entrance to prison facilities, to take the temperature of those who entered.

After infection was detected among GENCHI officers, the so-called Control 1 phase started. As a result, visits to prisons were prohibited and protocols were established for the reception of packages. In terms of prison transfers, although there was no transfer planning in the health strategy, there were cases of inmate transfers after the occurrence of some prison riots (in large facilities in Santiago, especially). In addition, the Action Plan prepared by GENCHI envisaged in the Level 3 Control stage the transfer of inmates for medical attention, with the Concepción prison designated as an emergency hospital. This stage was not reached.

4/5 Restrictions inside prisons and compensatory measures

The same document prepared by GENCHI provided that, in the second stage of control, recreational activities inside prison facilities should be restricted. One of the first measures was to establish differentiated schedules in the courtyard for the prison population. This was intended to reduce physical contact between inmates. Another measure was to establish zones of preventive isolation. According to the GENCHI control measures report, from September 2020, 1,749 intra-prison isolation places had been provided in the event of an outbreak of the pandemic. However, the latter actions were not as successful as expected, since they did not prevent the increase in infection among inmates. This can be explained by the conditions of incarceration in Chile, in which there are limitations to physical distancing required to maintain health (ILANUD, 2020).

The use of cell phones inside prisons is allowed for virtual visits. A procedure was established for their use: It ranged from the request for the device, the regulation of the hours (on average two), the days when it could be used (from two to three days) and the prohibitions of its use in cells. Other reasons for using cell phones could apply but needed to be requested and justified to the prison administration personnel in advance (Matus, 2020).

6 Legal basis for restrictions and relaxations of the prison regime

As mentioned above, the main regulations that have emerged under the pandemic are regulatory standards, aimed at improving hygiene, preventing contact both between prisoners and visitors and, ultimately, preventing any form of spread of the virus. In addition to these restrictions, a degree of flexibility also emerged in the prison regime, thanks to the pardon regulations that were developed. However, in the judicial sphere, practices that avoid imprisonment were also implemented. These were mainly aimed at reducing the use of pre-trial detention and granting more benefits such as parole.

Nevertheless, the procedures adopted were also criticised, mainly because they were insufficient and because, given the overcrowding of Chilean prisons, they were difficult to implement. The main organisations that have criticised these irregularities were both government institutions and civil society organisations.

In this regard, we have found opinions and analyses of the prison situation during the pandemic made by two institutions that inspect prisons facilities in Chile, namely the Judicial Prosecutor's Office[5] and the National Institute of Human Rights. The Judicial Prosecutor's Office, in its report issued on 24 April (Fiscalía Judicial, 2020), described the national and international norms relevant to the issue, analysing in particular the procedures adopted by GENCHI. In this regard, the Prosecutor's Office concluded that, given overcrowding levels, the implementation of measures became more complex. It also indicated that it was the responsibility of the Chilean State to ensure both the personal safety of prisoners and the guarantee of their fundamental rights, so that any policy must aim in both directions. It added that the protocols implemented by GENCHI had not been constant or uniform, which led to irregular application of the measures and also indicated that there were not enough materials to ensure hygiene in the premises.

Similarly, the National Institute of Human Rights, through the Report issued on 6 April (INDH, 2020b) and the opinions expressed by its director Sergio Micco, indicated that the prison context was critical even before the pandemic, so that the circumstances of the virus further worsened the situation of prisoners. There were many reasons for this, such as problems with overcrowding and occupancy levels, living conditions, hygiene and sanitation, access to hygienic services—in particular to water 24 hours a day—access to health care, communication with the outside world and adequate food. The same report added that it was the duty of the State to guarantee minimum rights to prisoners because of their particularly vulnerable condition.

Finally, this report criticised the use of pre-trial detention, especially in the context of a pandemic, where confinement in overpopulated rooms—with few hygienic measures—facilitated the spread of the virus. It should also be added that the Institute of Human Rights was an active agent in requesting legislative and regulatory policies to improve the situation of inmates; inspecting prisons (INDH, 2020c); encouraging GENCHI to take control measures (INDH, 2020d) and reporting instances of non-compliance, which was the case with prisons allocated to private companies that did not fully comply with delivering personal protective equipment to prevent COVID-19 infections (INDH, 2020e).

Another relevant institution was the Medical College of Chile, which is a guild institution that aims to promote the improvement, protection, development and rationalisation of the medical profession. It has an important role in the promotion of public health policies. The Medical College also participated in the proposal, analysis and criticism of the measures taken by the government during the pandemic, at a national level and with respect to prisons. For example, at the beginning of the pandemic, the Medical College raised concerns about the situation of the incarcerated, through both a document on health recommendations for the management of the COVID-19 Pandemic in persons deprived of liberty (COLMED, 2020a) and visits made to different prison facilities in the country.

The report of one of the visits made to the Puente Alto Prison Centre was noteworthy, as the context of the visit is described, preventive hygiene measures are analysed, such as those related to water supply, cleaning supplies, contact between prisoners and habitability. It also describes the management of suspected cases, noting several structural deficiencies, referring to overcrowding, poor supply of, and access to, hygienic resources, the lack of an epidemiological approach to face the pandemic, the poor training of GENCHI staff and, ultimately, the insanitary facilities. From this report and others, the Medical College concluded that contagion risk in prison was six times higher than in other spaces (Miranda, 2020), which left inmates in a situation of extreme vulnerability and at a high risk of virus infection. For this reason, the Medical Association sought to promote regulatory measures to help reduce the risk and improve the implementation of these policies, with a primarily medical focus, but also based on respect for the fundamental rights of prisoners (COLMED, 2020b).

Regarding the participation of civil society organisations, the NGO Leasur stands out, raising important points about the transformation of the criminal justice system and the need to respect individuals deprived of liberty and to ensure that they are detained in conditions that meet the standards of human dignity. From the beginning of the pandemic, this organisation was an active agent, not only denouncing poor prison conditions

(Ojeda, 2020), but also promoting public policies to improve the conditions of the inmates and prevent the spread of the contagion. Likewise, Leasur has gathered information, based on documents that contain, on a monthly basis, accounts of what had happened every day in the prison system, all linked to the pandemic (Leasur, 2020a; 2020b; 2020c; 2020d).

It is important to mention that, currently, our prison system is regulated by no specific primary legislation but, rather, by a series of fragmented precepts of a regulatory nature. This has evoked criticism, mainly because such an important matter as that of the restriction of an individual's freedom—which is a fundamental right—should be regulated by a specific law that should be clear and precise. The current system does not protect the dignity of inmates and all the other rights derived from their worth as persons (Carnevali and Maldonado, 2013; Stippel, 2013). In this sense, it is possible to point out that already, in pre-pandemic circumstances, prisoners were extremely vulnerable, so that the virus came to increase even more the precariousness of the life of the prisoners and the persistent anomie in the enjoyment of their basic guarantees.

7 Returning to normal

The impact of the pandemic on Chilean prisons has undoubtedly been significant, not only because of the immediate consequences, but also because it accentuated the poor infrastructure of the facilities, which had been continually denounced by many organisations. For this reason, we consider that the return to normality may not lead to an improvement in prison conditions, but simply a return to a life without the virus. In such a situation, prison life will still be precarious due to overcrowding, poor hygiene conditions, few opportunities for recreation and little access to education and health, to mention just a few aspects (Horvitz, 2018; INDH).[6]

Along with this, merely thinking about a return to a life in prison without COVID-19 is complex, since, in the past, the eradication of other diseases has been complex. Consider, for example, the case of tuberculosis, an infection that was eliminated from the cities decades ago, but that is still present in some prisons and even causes the death of inmates, due to the complications generated by the lack of sanitary conditions in many prison facilities.

However, post-pandemic prison life could bring with it certain undesirable practices, such as the continued use of solitary confinement cells. While, arguably, the use of solitary confinement is justified in the context of a pandemic, as it seeks to prevent the spread of the virus, the use of solitary confinement under normal circumstances may be harmful. It has been a struggle for years to eradicate this practice, so to reapply it would be a major setback.

Along with this, although the use of technology to regulate the form of visits has allowed prisoners to contact family and friends, it should be noted that it does not fully replace face-to-face visits. For the same reason, it is important that after the pandemic, along with virtual visits, face-to-face visits and conjugal visits[7] are also allowed again, so that there is no unnecessary distancing of prisoners from their families and friends.

Nevertheless, there have also been positive aspects of the pandemic in Chilean prisons, such as the use of technology, for example, that has allowed new forms of contact, such as virtual visits. Although they are not equal to the face-to-face interactions, in the context of the pandemic, they were tremendously useful to link inmates and their relatives and promote social and family ties. Likewise, increased access to the internet is a feature that we consider positive, as it allows a fundamental form of interaction. Similarly, we consider that the relaxation of incarceration measures, such as pre-trial detention, and the greater provision of prison benefits, such as parole and the enactment of the Pardon Law, have been necessary measures that should prevail after the pandemic, mainly because prison life in Chile is experienced under a troubled system, leaving prisoners in a condition of extreme vulnerability and precariousness. Imprisonment should only be used exceptionally and then as a last resort.

Finally, another positive aspect of the pandemic, although paradoxical, was to show the extreme vulnerability in which people find themselves inside prison, which makes clear how urgent it is to reconceptualise prison as an institution of punishment, not only from a material point of view, but also from an ethical, political and legal standpoint. This would facilitate the understanding of prisons as places and institutions that should only deprive individuals of their freedom of movement, but not of their personal dignity (as they deserve similar respect and recognition to any other person), status as citizens or membership of the community.

Notes

1 The National Institute of Human Rights (INDH) generates reports with the data gathered during its visits to prisons together with other bodies such as the Judicial Prosecutor's Office (dependent on the various Courts of Appeal (INDH, 2020a).

2 Despite the fact that this state of emergency continues, the hearings and proceedings have been resumed through video conferences. The Public Defender's Office has criticised the use of videoconferences for the conduct of trials in view of the violation of minimum guarantees of due process and the difficulty that it entails, for example, for the assessment of evidence and the presentation of witnesses and experts. This has been pointed out in interviews by their regional authorities (Gálvez, 2020; Moraga, 2020). This has also been pointed out by the press (Ayala, 2020).

3 Those convicted of crimes such as kidnapping (with homicide or rape), abduction of a minor, illicit association, rape, sexual abuse, parricide, femicide, homicide, infanticide and crimes against humanity, among others, are excluded from the benefit.

4 In women's prisons, there were also protests against the uncertainty of health measures and the situation of mothers with children under two years of age. Press coverage can be seen at Diez (2020) and Morales (2020). Regarding the

conditions in which women are deprived of their liberty in Chile and the effects that the pandemic has caused, see Aedo and Romero, 2020.

5 The Judicial Prosecutor's Office is a Chilean institution that belongs to the judicial branch and works in the cases established by law, in defence of the public interest and, according to the nature of the matter, acts as a main, third or auxiliary part of the superior courts of justice. This institution differs from the Public Prosecutor's Office (which in Chile is called Public Ministry), inasmuch as the latter is an autonomous body that does not form part of any of the three branches of government, whose function is to direct the investigation of crimes, bring the accused to court, if appropriate, and provide protection to victims and witnesses.

6 See also the Studies on Prison Conditions in Chile by the INDH, all up to 2018, https://bibliotecadigital.indh.cl/discover?scope=%2F&query=estudio+de+las+condiciones+carcelarias&submit=Ir.

7 Marital visits, which is called in Chile "*venusterio*", is a right of the inmates, regulated in the Regulations of penitentiary establishments. It is regarded as a special type of visit, of an intimate nature, for the purpose of enabling prisoners to have sexual relations with their partners. This right is granted to the extent that the prison premises have facilities for this purpose.

References

Aedo, M., and Romero, L. (2020): Cárcel, pandemia y mujeres privadas de libertad: algunas reflexiones desde la experiencia en Chile. In: I. Rivera (Ed.): *Pandemia, derechos humanos, sistema penal y control social*. Valencia: Tirant Lo Blanch, 295–312.

Alcaíno, E. (2019): Las personas privadas de libertad y el acceso a prestaciones de salud en las cárceles chilenas. In: Centro de Derechos Humanos, Facultad de Derecho Universidad Diego Portales (Ed.): *Informe Anual sobre Derechos Humanos en Chile 2019* [online]. Santiago: Ediciones Universidad Diego Portales, 447–489. [Viewed 12 March 2021] https://derechoshumanos.udp.cl/cms/wp-content/uploads/2020/12/10_Las_personas_privadas_de_libertad_y_el_acceso_a_prestaciones_de_salud_en_las_ca%CC%81rceles_chilenas.pdf.

Ayala, L. (2020): Se corta la señal, su señoría: las quejas por los juicios virtuales. *La Tercera* [online]. Updated 13 June 2020. [Viewed 12 March 2021]. https://www.latercera.com/la-tercera-domingo/noticia/se-corta-la-senal-su-senoria-las-quejas-por-los-juicios-virtuales/5A3H5KAHH5BRPL5CCPL3A5KB4Y/.

BCN (Biblioteca del Congreso Nacional) (2012): Ley 20,603. Modifica la Ley N°18,216 que establece medidas alternativas a las penas privativas o restrictivas de libertad. [Viewed 12 March 2021]. https://www.bcn.cl/leychile/navegar/imprimir?idNorma=1040510.

BCN (2020): Ley 21,228. Concede indulto general conmutativo a causa de la enfermedad COVID-19 en Chile. [Viewed 12 March 2021]. https://www.bcn.cl/leychile/navegar/imprimir?idNorma=1144400

Carnevali, R., and Maldonado, F. (2013): El tratamiento penitenciario en Chile. Especial atención a problemas de constitucionalidad. *Ius et Praxis* [online], 19(2), 385–418. [Viewed 12 March 2021]. http://www.revistaiepraxis.cl/index.php/iepraxis/article/view/35/30.

Cerna, T. (2020): Internos realizan desórdenes en cárcel de Rancagua: gendarmes aseguran que hubo 12 heridos. *Emol* [online]. Updated 15 April 2020 [Viewed 12 March 2021]. https://www.emol.com/noticias/Nacional/2020/04/15/983180/Desordenes-carcel-Rancagua-coronavirus.html.

COLMED (Colegio Médico de Chile) (2020a): Recomendaciones de salud para enfrentar la pandemia de COVID-19 en la población privada de libertad de Chile en el marco de los Derechos Humanos [Viewed 12 March 2021]. http://www.colegiomedico.cl/wp-content/uploads/2020/04/covid_ddhh-3.pdf.

COLMED (Colegio Médico de Chile) (2020b): Comunicado Departamento Nacional de Derechos Humanos [Viewed 12 March 2021]. https://media.elmostrador.cl/2020/06/COMUNICADO-DEPTO-de-DDHH-COLMED-COVID19-y-CARCELES.pdf.

Contesse, J., and Contreras L. (coords.) (2019): *La Insostenible Situación de las Cárceles en Chile: debate sobre la prisión y los derechos humanos*. Santiago: Editorial Jurídica de Chile.

Diario Uchile (2020): Incidentes en Colina 1 terminan con 4 gendarmes y 2 internos heridos. *Diario Uchile* [online]. Updated 14 May 2020 [Viewed 12 March 2021]. https://radio.uchile.cl/2020/05/14/incidentes-en-colina-1-terminan-con-4-gendarmes-y-2-internos-heridos/.

Diez, P. (2020): La realidad de las mujeres privadas de libertad y la importancia de la perspectiva de género en el proyecto de indulto general conmutativo. *El Mostrador* [online] 2 April. [Viewed 12 March 2021]. https://www.elmostrador.cl/braga/2020/04/02/la-realidad-de-las-mujeres-privadas-de-libertad-y-la-importancia-de-la-perspectiva-de-genero-en-el-proyecto-de-indulto-general-conmutativo/.

Fiscalía Judicial (2020): *Situación Recintos Penitenciarios en Pandemia COVID-19* [Viewed 12. March 2021]. https://www.pjud.cl/documents/396588/0/informe+final+carceles+por+pandemia.pdf/9efcd620-b1af-4e82-8e15-5624354e2cad.

Gálvez, C. (2020): ¿Juicios orales por videoconferencia? *DPP* [online] Updated 18 May 2020 [Viewed 12 March 2021]. http://www.dpp.cl/sala_prensa/noticias_detalle/10402/juicios-orales-por-videoconferencia.

GENCHI (2020a): Plan de acción integral por contingencia COVID-19 [Viewed 12 March 2021]. https://html.gendarmeria.gob.cl/doc/141_plan_accion_coronavirus.pdf.

GENCHI (2020b): Complementa y dispone medidas de gestion interna en Gendarmería de Chile, que deben cumplir sus funcionarios y servidores públicos para hacer frente a la situación sanitaria atendido el brote de coronavirus (COVID-19) [Viewed 12 March 2021]. https://html.gendarmeria.gob.cl/doc/RES_EX2253_23_03_2020.pdf.

GENCHI (2020c): Plan de acción en Pandemia Coronavirus (COVID-19) destinado a población adulto mayor y enfermos crónicos recluida en Unidades Penales de Gendarmería de Chile [Viewed 12 March 2021]. https://html.gendarmeria.gob.cl/doc/CIRCULAR_160_02042020.PDF.

Guerra, I. (2020): Gendarmería afirma que 25 reos y 12 funcionarios resultaron lesionados en intento de fuga en Santiago 1. *Emol* [online] Updated 20 March 2020 [Viewed 12 March 2021]. https://www.emol.com/noticias/Nacional/2020/03/20/980441/25-reos-lesionados-fuga-Santiago1.html.

Horvitz, M. I. (2018): La insostenible situación de la ejecución de las penas privativas de libertad: ¿vigencia del Estado de derecho o estado de naturaleza? *Política Criminal* [online] 13(26), 904–951 [Viewed 12 March 2021]. http://politcrim.com/wp-content/uploads/2019/04/Vol13N26A7.pdf

ILANUD (2020): El sistema penitenciario ante la encrucijada producto de la crisis provocada por el COVID-19 [Viewed 12 March 2021]. http://fileserver.idpc.net/library/ILANUD-COVID-19.pdf.

INDH (2020a): *Estudio de las Condiciones Carcelarias en Chile 2018: Diagnóstico del Cumplimiento de los Estándares Internacionales de Derechos Humanos en la Privación de Libertad* [Viewed 12 March 2021]. https://bibliotecadigital.indh.cl/handle/123456789/1704.

INDH (2020b): Informe sobre Estándares de Derechos Humanos en materia de personas privadas de libertad, en relación a aquellas sujetas a la medida cautelar de prisión preventiva y crisis sanitaria por COVID-19. [Viewed 12 March 2021]. https://bibliotecadigital.indh.cl/bitstream/handle/123456789/1713/informe-privados-libertad-covid19.pdf?sequence=1&isAllowed=y.

INDH (2020c): En visita a cárcel de Puente Alto INDH constata que 149 internos y funcionarios están contagiados por COVID-19. *INDH* [Viewed 12 March 2021]. https://www.indh.cl/en-visita-a-carcel-de-puente-alto-indh-constata-que-149-internos-y-funcionarios-estan-contagiados-por-COVID-19/.

INDH (2020d): INDH oficia a Gendarmería para conocer avance del coronavirus en cárceles. *INDH* [Viewed 12 March 2021]. https://www.indh.cl/indh-oficia-a-gendarmeria-para-conocer-avance-del-coronavirus-en-carceles/.

INDH (2020e): INDH advierte que concesionarias no están cumpliendo contratos poniendo en riesgo a reclusos y gendarmes ante el COVID-19. *INDH* [Viewed 12 March 2021]. https://www.indh.cl/indh-advierte-que-empresas-concesionarias-no-estan-cumpliendo-contratos-poniendo-en-riesgo-a-reclusos-y-gendarmes-ante-el-COVID-19/.

Leasur (2020a): Cárcel y COVID-19 en Chile, Marzo 2020 [Viewed 12 March 2021]. https://leasur.cl/wp-content/uploads/2020/04/C%C3%A1rcel-y-COVID-19-S%C3%ADntesis-Marzo.pdf.

Leasur (2020b): Cárcel y COVID-19 en Chile, Abril 2020 [Viewed 12 March 2021]. https://leasur.cl/wp-content/uploads/2020/06/C%C3%A1rcel-y-Covid-Abril-2020-2.pdf.

Leasur (2020c): Cárcel y COVID-19 en Chile, Mayo 2020 [Viewed 12 March 2021]. https://leasur.cl/wp-content/uploads/2020/06/C%C3%A1rcel-y-Covid-Mayo-2020.pdf.

Leasur (2020d): Cárcel y COVID-19 en Chile, Junio 2020 [Viewed 12 March 2021]. https://leasur.cl/wp-content/uploads/2020/07/C%C3%A1rcel-y-Covid-Junio-2020.pdf.

Matus, J., (2020): Gendarmería ha autorizado el ingreso de 1.983 celulares a cárceles. *La Tercera* [online]. Updated 15 June 2020 [Viewed 12 March 2021]. https://www.latercera.com/nacional/noticia/gendarmeria-ha-autorizado-el-ingreso-de-1983-celulares-a-carceles/Q6CDUBLWARC63PZVTBY66MGT3E/.

Miranda, C. (2020): La pandemia en las cárceles: riesgo de contagio de la población penal es 6 veces más alto. *El Mostrador* [online]. Updated 20 May 2020 [Viewed 12 March 2021]. https://www.elmostrador.cl/destacado/2020/05/20/la-pandemia-en-las-carceles-riesgo-de-contagio-de-la-poblacion-penal-es-6-veces-mas-alto/.

Moraga, J. (2020): "Un juicio oral de menor calidad perjudica a todos los que intervienen en él". *DPP* [online]. Updated 14 June 2020. [Viewed 12 March 2021]. http://www.dpp.cl/sala_prensa/noticias_detalle/10558/un-juicio-oral-de-menor-calidad-perjudica-a-todos-los-que-intervienen-en-el.

Morales, P. (2020): Cuarentena: cómo viven la maternidad las mujeres privadas de libertad. *La Tercera* [online] 18 May. [Viewed 12 March 2021]. https://www.latercera.com/paula/noticia/cuarentena-como-viven-la-maternidad-las-mujeres-privadas-de-libertad/5CAKQ57KBVHMHKE3EHDVJN3PD4/.

Nazif-Muñoz, J. (2020): Motines y aumento del contagio. Buscando caminos para evitar ambos problemas en las cárceles chilenas. *Ciper Chile* [online]. Updated 20 May 2020 [Viewed 12 March 2021]. https://www.ciperchile.cl/2020/05/20/motines-y-aumento-del-contagio-buscando-caminos-para-evitar-ambos-problemas-en-las-carceles-chilenas/

Ojeda, J. (2020): Leasur llama a considerar a personas privadas de libertad como población de riesgo frente al COVID-19. *Radio JGM* [online]. Updated 20 March 2020 [Viewed 12 March 2021]. https://radiojgm.uchile.cl/leasur-llama-a-considerar-a-personas-privadas-de-libertad-como-poblacion-de-riesgo-frente-al-COVID-19/.

Rivera, V. (2020): Gendarmería: ingreso de presos a las cárceles desciende en un 44%. *La Tercera* [online]. Updated 9 July 2020. [Viewed 12 March 2021]. https://www.latercera.com/nacional/noticia/gendarmeria-ingreso-de-presos-a-las-carceles-desciende-en-un-44/NPOPFMRXEVAMPHD3TJJBFZDYWY/.

Stippel, J. (2013). *Cárcel, Derecho y Política*. Santiago: LOM.

Vilches, J. (2020): Reportan nuevo amago de incendio en la cárcel de Puente Alto al interior de un dormitorio. *Emol* [online]. Updated 04 April 2020 [Viewed 12 March 2021]. https://www.emol.com/noticias/Nacional/2020/04/04/982088/Amago-incendio.html.

8 China

Spencer D. Li

1 Introduction – general situation of the prison system

China has one of the largest incarcerated populations in the world. According to World Prison Brief, the rate of incarceration in China was 119 per 100,000 of the national population by mid-2014. The most recent data available show that there are 1,657,812 sentenced prisoners in the Ministry of Justice prisons, excluding individuals held in detention centres, which are reported to be more than 650,000. The incarceration rate would increase to 166 per 100,000 if pre-trial detention and other forms of detention were counted (Li and Liu, 2020; Walmsley, 2020).

In China, there are two types of penal systems. The first is an administrative detention system managed by the police departments. The second is a judicial incarceration system managed by the prison administration of local departments of justice. The word "prison" usually refers to the latter, that is, the correctional facilities run by local prison administration under the supervision of the Bureau of Prison Administration of the Ministry of Justice in accordance with the Prison Law. Prisons are generally larger than detention centres. According to official statistics, there were 681 prisons housing 1,640,000 prisoners in China in 2012 (National People's Congress, 2012). On average, each prison housed about 2,000 inmates although very large prisons might hold as many as 7,000 prisoners (Wu, 2003).

Detention centres and prisons are designed to incarcerate different groups of persons, determined by sentence length. According to the Criminal Procedures Law of China (1997), offenders who are sentenced to one year or less should serve their time in detention centres managed by public security agencies; those who serve a sentence longer than one year should be handed over by public security to a prison to serve out their punishment.

Unlike Western prisons where inmates are typically housed in single or double cells, Chinese prisoners usually stay in larger dormitories with other inmates. The average living space is about five square metres per person. Only selected facilities have single or double cells, for instance, facilities that house foreign or violent prisoners (Wu, 2003). Dormitory-type living

DOI: 10.4324/9781003169178-8

arrangement increases interpersonal contact and interaction, making it difficult to contain the spread of infectious viruses such as SARS-CoV-2.

China has no private prisons. The operation of the prisons relies on funding from the central and local governments. As the costs of prison management continue to rise, most prisons are underfunded. This is especially true for those facilities located in economically underdeveloped areas. To compensate for the lack of government funding, prisons generate income by putting inmates to work in businesses that they own and operate inside their facilities. It is not uncommon for prisoners to work long hours daily in crowded workshops or assembly lines in the factories operated by the prisons. Without sufficient protective measures, the work environment inside the prisons may pose additional risks for prisoners to be infected by COVID-19.

2 Prison and penal policy concerning the execution of prison sentences during the COVID-19-induced crisis

Large outbreaks of COVID-19 infections occurred in several prisons in China at the beginning of 2020. By 25 February 2020, the number of confirmed cases rose to 555 in five prisons, including 271 cases in Hubei province, where the COVID-19 pandemic started, and 284 cases outside the province (Z. Li, Qing, Ni, Wei and Liu, 2020). The confirmed cases in the Chinese prison system continued to rise in the next several days. In Wuhan city's prisons alone, the total number of infected prisoners increased to 806 on 29 February 2020 (Z. Yang, 2020). The outbreaks took place at a time when China started bringing the pandemic under control. They raised a serious concern that the increases in the prison system might derail the effort. To prevent this, the central government took swift actions to introduce a series of measures to stop the spread of COVID-19 in all prisons under the supervision of the Ministry of Justice.

To some extent, the Chinese experience has been unique. Worldwide, one of the major strategies taken by correctional institutions to reduce COVID-19 infections in jails and prisons is to release prisoners with relatively lower risks early and place them in community supervision (Rapisarda and Byrne, 2020). This is a strategy promoted by the United Nations, human rights advocates, and many professionals working in criminal justice (Human Rights Watch, 2020). While many countries have adopted this approach (Rapisarda, Byrne and Marmolejo, 2020), China has not shown much interest in early release as a means to control the spread of COVID-19 in prisons. To date, there has been no report of early or temporary release of prisoners to prevent COVID-19 infections in Chinese prisons or detention centres. The decision not to adopt early release could be due to the authorities' confidence in containing the spread of the virus in the correctional system using its highly centralised system and its ability to mobilise organisations and individuals across a wide spectrum of the society to fight the pandemic.

Taking advantage of the top-down organisational structure of the system, the authorities promoted a systematic approach to tackle the public health emergency. The Chinese prison system is a centralised system (Li and Liu, 2019). The Ministry of Justice sets policies and guidelines for the structure and operation of all prisons. It also supervises the performance of all types of prisons and has ultimate control over personnel management in those facilities. Making use of this structure, the Ministry of Justice developed a systematic response to the challenges created by COVID-19. The ministry enacted rules and regulations based on public health guidelines developed by health experts commissioned by the Ministry of Health. Prison management at the local level followed the orders and set up procedures to prevent and control COVID-19 infections in their own facilities. Through this top-down approach, the Ministry of Justice was able to enforce the rules and regulations in the entire system across the country with "wartime efficiency". To ensure compliance, the Chinese Communist Party (CCP) installed emergency party branches to coordinate the efforts at the country/city levels. The party branches regularly inspected work performed by prison staff in response to COVID-19 (C. T. Yang, 2020b). The Ministry of Justice also set up a formal reporting system that prison management could use to track staff performance. Frontline officers were responsible for gathering unit-specific information related to the pandemic work and reporting it to their supervisors, who, in turn, were required to submit regular reports to higher-ranking authorities. The information collected was used to enforce accountability (Zhu, 2020b). Administrators and staff who were found neglecting their responsibilities would face disciplinary actions, including dismissal. For example, several provincial level administrators in Shandong Province, including the Director of the Department of Justice, lost their jobs because of a surge of confirmed infections in a prison under their supervision. Similarly, the government dismissed the warden of a women's prison in Hubei province for the large number of confirmed infections discovered in that facility (Li et al., 2020). There were also many success stories. For example, Guangdong Province in south China, the most populated province with 25 prisons, has reported no COVID-19 infections in its correctional facilities. The authorities attributed their successes to the strong leadership provided by the central government and the "wartime" approach to strengthening individual and collective commitment, solidarity, and actions throughout the correctional system (C. T. Yang, 2020c: 1).

COVID-19 is a pervasive problem that has affected every segment of society. To achieve a high level of success, prisons needed to work with other social institutions that are directly or indirectly related to correctional supervision and treatment. As part of the systematic approach to combat COVID-19, correctional institutions joined other social institutions to form society-wide efforts to contain the spread of SARS-CoV-2. Under this arrangement, the prisons served as a grid in a comprehensive approach to manage the public health crisis affecting society as a whole. For example, prisons collaborated with local governments to ensure that their needs for medical supplies and other critical recourses were met (C. T. Yang, 2020a). Prisons also stepped up their collaboration with community correctional agencies by promoting "seamless connection" (Luo, 2020: 1). In these joint operations, the prisons were responsible for administering a 14-day quarantine of all inmates who were transitioning to community supervision from their facilities. Once the inmates were released to the community, they would continue to be supervised by the community correctional agencies to monitor their health and their risks of being infected and infecting others in the community (C. T. Yang, 2020c).

3 Restrictions of contact with the outside world

Through contact tracing, it was determined that the rapid rise in confirmed COVID-19 cases in the affected prisons was primarily caused by infected prison staff importing the virus into the facilities. To address the problem, the authorities developed a series of measures to block this route of infection. All prisons were required to develop a plan on suspending shift work and quarantining prison staff. For example, in some provinces, such as Guangdong, prison staff were not allowed to leave and re-enter the prisons until the pandemic was judged to be under control. Prison staff on duty stopped working in alternative shifts. Instead, they had to stay on their jobs until the restriction was lifted. In some prisons, staff worked 14 days consecutively and then took 14 days off. Before returning to work, they had to be quarantined for 14 days and test negative for COVID-19. Many prisons adopted similar approaches when scheduling work assignments (G. Li, 2020).

Furthermore, the departments of justice on the provincial level suspended all in-person family visits during the COVID-19 pandemic in order to prevent the transmission of the virus from community to prison. To help prisoners stay connected with their loved ones, prisons provided alternative ways for inmates to communicate with their families. For example, some prisons in Jiangsu province arranged the visits of inmates' families by professional staff for the purpose of making family videos to share with the inmates. Moreover, many prisons provided online meetings via the Internet for the inmates to see and talk to their loved ones (Zhu, 2020c).

4 Restrictions inside prisons

To prevent COVID-19 from spreading in correctional facilities, the prison system accelerated the deployment of grid management with particular emphasis on risk assessment and control. Since 2015, the central government of China has promoted grid management in the correctional system (General Office of the CPC Central Committee of the People's Republic of China, 2015; Li and Liu, 2020). In this type of approach, the management divided the facility into segments, which were further divided into grid cells.

Prison staff collected inmates' information, such as crime history, conviction and sentence records, potential harms to the community, in-facility performance, and personality traits through test, interview, survey, and observation. Based on the information obtained, they classified inmates into different risk levels and assigned them the grid cells suitable for their levels of supervision (Beijing Bureau of Prisons, 2016; Pang, 2016; Wang and Xu, 2019). In consistency with these management principles, the Chinese Centre for Disease Control and Prevention (CHINACDC) officially issued "The Technological Plan of Novel Coronavirus Prevention and Control in Prisons" in March 2020 (CHINACDC, 2020). The guidelines stipulated that when applicable, all correctional facilities should categorise inmates into several groups based on their exposure to COVID-19, including seriously ill inmates, normally ill inmates with COVID-19, slightly ill inmates with COVID-19, suspected cases, inmates with close contact to a positive COVID-19 case, and healthy inmates. Depending on the distribution of inmates in those groups, they should designate sections of the prisons as patient zone, quarantine zone, isolated observation zone, and/or normal zone. Specifically, inmates who tested positive for COVID-19 should stay in the patient zone. Prisoners showing minor symptoms of infection should be quarantined; persons who had been in close contact with confirmed cases should be observed in an isolated observation zone. Only healthy inmates who had been tested negative at the end of the quarantine period should be assigned to the normal zone. Prisons that were unable to meet these guidelines were required to transfer confirmed and suspect cases to local hospitals. Chinese prisons rarely release detailed management data to the public, as the information is generally considered politically sensitive. However, there are some concrete examples. For instance, in the early days of the pandemic control, Qianchuan Prison in Anhui Province relocated all 700 inmates admitted to the facility before the Chinese New Year, which fell on 25 January 2020, to cellblocks deemed appropriate for them. The management then placed all 1,320 inmates admitted after the New Year under isolated observation. They tested the body temperature of the inmates at least once a day and immediately isolated those who showed any sign of potential infection. They then followed it up with nucleic acid testing to determine the needs to quarantine any of the individuals (G. Li, 2020). In April, Zhejiang Province and the city of Wuhan, the epicentre of the COVID-19 pandemic, tested all prison inmates to identify infected cases and assigned them to grid cells appropriate to their health status (Guo and Dai, 2020; Zhou, 2020).

Correctional institutions also developed and implemented good hygiene protocols to address various risks presented by different environmental conditions inside the prisons. For example, staff cleaned and disinfected hard surfaces daily. They opened windows multiple times a day at regular intervals to maintain good indoor ventilation. Staff and prisoners were required to wear face masks when they were in close contact (Zhu, 2020b).

5 Compensatory measures

Prisons invested more resources and efforts in improving healthcare, especially mental health services. After the outbreak of the pandemic, many prisons reoriented their treatment curriculum by focusing on physical and mental health promotion. While face-to-face instructions were cancelled, treatment staff made greater use of videos and online materials to teach prisoners how to improve individual cardiopulmonary function, strengthen their immune system, combat sleep disorder, and relieve mental illness symptoms. The prisons continued to provide treatment to inmates with serious medical conditions in their own hospitals and clinics, and in community hospitals through referrals.

All of the changes in prisons and the reduced contact with the outside world created considerable psychological stress among inmates, exacerbating mental health problems that had already been prevalent in the prison population (Duan and Zhu, 2020). To address this problem, many prisons expanded their mental health services, providing opportunities for inmates to talk to mental health professionals in person or online through remote access. Some prisons set up a 24-hour hotline that inmates with urgent mental health issues could use to seek psychological counselling (Zhu, 2020a, 2020c). These services played a critical role in preventing accidents or disruptive behaviour caused by severe mental health disorders during the pandemic. As mentioned previously, to reduce stress and loneliness, some prisons produced videos of the inmates' families and shared them with the inmates in an effort to connect them with their loved ones.

6 Legal basis for restrictions of the prison regime

The measures described above to prevent infections of prisoners and staff members were instructions issued by the central and regional political government organisations. They are not legislation in the conventional sense of the term, and it is therefore difficult to speak of a legal basis or the rule of law in this regard.

7 Returning to normal – outcome, challenges, and future directions

Judged by the result, the efforts of the Chinese correctional system to control COVID-19 in prisons and prevent the spreading of the disease have been successful. Since the end of 2020, there has been no report of new COVID-19 outbreaks in Chinese prisons. It is possible that some cases were confirmed but were not reported to the public. However, more likely, the lack of new cases reflects the country's overall success in stopping the spread of COVID-19. Since the beginning of March 2020, the daily count of newly confirmed COVID-19 cases throughout China, including Hong Kong, has been trending towards zero, until a recent outbreak in Hong Kong in late July 2020 that pushed the total number of new cases to the 100–200 range on some days (Baidu, 2021). Throughout February 2020, there had been a real concern that prisons might become a major source of infections that would lead to a significant increase in the number of confirmed COVID-19 cases in China. That fear appears to have been overcome.

After some initial missteps, the Chinese prison system has been able to keep COVID-19 under control. Despite the progress, major challenges remain. First, the practice that holds the top management of the prison system responsible for COVID-19-related problems in the facilities under their supervision regardless of the actual circumstances may discourage case reporting. For fear of disciplinary actions, such as demotion or job loss, a prison administration may hide the information of confirmed cases in order to avoid negative attention. To facilitate interagency communication, the central government implemented a "wartime" command system, mandating regular and accurate reporting of COVID-19 cases to the top authority. The system, however, can only be effective if the local administrators working on the "frontline" fully cooperate with the mandate. If the local administrators decided to withhold the information for whatever reasons, the system would break down. Lack of transparency with regard to the number of confirmed cases in the facilities and steps taken to prevent the spread of the virus could then lead to wrong decision-making because the central authority might operate with a false sense of security or success and fail to recognise the real problems and make efforts to address them.

Another challenge is to serve the physical and mental health needs of vulnerable individuals incarcerated in the correctional facilities during the pandemic, including the elderly and prisoners with a chronic health condition, such as high blood pressure, diabetes, liver diseases, and depression. Because of budget constraints and a shortage of qualified physicians and medical equipment, providing adequate medical care has been a difficult task for almost all prisons, especially those in the economically underdeveloped regions (Cheng, 2020). Prisons across the country have been experimenting with various ways to solve the problem, for example, by collaborating with local hospitals to outsource some of the care and working with health service organisations around the country to provide online diagnostics and treatment. Despite these efforts, physical and mental health services for prison inmates remain a major challenge. Its solution requires a greater level of funding and a more coordinated approach among governmental and non-governmental organisations than currently available (Liebrenz et al., 2020).

Third, from the management perspective, it is difficult to sustain all-inclusive control in all prisons for a long period. Social distancing is difficult to implement in Chinese prisons that typically house hundreds and sometime thousands of inmates (Liebrenz et al., 2020). In addition, prisons tend to have a fast and unpredictable population turnover. Newly admitted prisoners and those released continue to move in and out of the facilities as long as the courts continue to process cases. To reduce overcrowding, cut cost, and contain the spread of COVID-19, the authority should seriously consider using early release of selected prisoners as an option to alleviate the heavy burden imposed by the pandemic (Human Rights Watch, 2020). Of course, this option would require a robust system of community corrections, which is still in an early stage of development in China. The Chinese government should invest more resources in building community corrections to serve the future needs of diverting prisoners to community supervision, providing for more options to deal with public health crises such as the COVID-19 pandemic.

Fourth, maintaining family contact and social support became more difficult than ever during the lockdown. Family and social support is important for prisoners' rehabilitation because it keeps them connected with the outside world and lets them feel valued by others. During the pandemic, prisons suspended family visit programmes. The absence of family visits and reduced contact with loved ones may lead to mental distress, maladaptive behaviour, and disruptive conduct. The virtual meetings promoted by the prison system have their limits. For example, some families did not have access to the information technology or did not know how to use it. Likewise, correctional facilities might not have the resources to provide this type of service (G. Li, 2020). Governments should do more to strengthen prisoners' social bond during the public health crisis.

Another challenge is to safeguard the physical health and psychological well-being of the prison staff. In many prisons, staff had to forgo shift work and stayed in the facilities for an extensive period. Long working hours and separation from their family members during the pandemic had a negative impact on their physical and mental health, job performance, and family relationships. Due to prison overcrowding, it was very difficult to practise social distancing. As a result, prison officers were at a heightened risk of being infected once the virus entered the facility (Liebrenz et al., 2020). In China, prison officers have relatively higher social status than prison guards working in Western prisons, which contribute to lower turnover and higher morale. However, undue work pressure could lead to stress and eventually burnout, which can severely affect job commitment and performance. Therefore, prison management should make stronger efforts to ensure a healthy and motivated workforce ready to take on the extraordinarily difficult and unpredictable problems that the pandemic has generated.

In conclusion, the Chinese government has made an enormous effort to prevent and control COVID-19 infections in its prisons. Unlike many other countries that used early release of selected prisoners to reduce prison infections, China relied on facility-based programmes focusing on risk detection and management in its prison system. Similarly, there have been no reports of early release of detainees from jails or other detention facilities (serving shorter sentences than in prisons). The correctional system, especially the prisons, classified inmates based on their health conditions and risks of infection, and used public health protocols, including social distancing, testing, wearing personal protective equipment, and medical isolation, to reduce the risk of infections among the incarcerated population. The system also made great efforts to serve the healthcare needs of the staff and prisoners, especially the rising demand for mental health services during the pandemic. By facilitating multiagency collaboration, the system deployed a highly coordinated and systematic approach to combat the public health emergency while ensuring the secure supervision of the prisoners. Considering that no further cluster infection has been reported since March of 2020. it seems that the preventive and control measures developed and implemented by the Chinese prison system have been effective in containing the spread of COVID-19. The initial aim of the "warlike" operations was to stop the spread of the virus. The measures taken by the system, however, have provided an impetus for more innovations in prison management and stronger humanitarian responses to the needs of the prisoners. Inspired by the successes, many advocates have already called for a more efficient prison system with more attention to the rights of the prisoners (Cheng, 2020; J. Li, 2020; Zhai, 2020). Hence, the emergency measures taken during the pandemic may help spur meaningful reforms in the prison system in the end.

References

Baidu. (2021): Realtime big data report of coronavirus pandemic. Retrieved from https://voice.baidu.com/act/newpneumonia/newpneumonia/?from=osari_pc_3.

Beijing Bureau of Prisons. (2016): Changing concept and operating mechanism in grid management in prisons. Retrieved from http://jyj.beijing.gov.cn/lldt/201912/t20191211_1068260.html.

Cheng, K. (2020): Construction of medical security system for prison inmates. *South Forum*, 2020(4), 62–67.

CHINACDC. (2020): The technological plans of novel coronavirus prevention and control in prisons. Retrieved from http://www.chinacdc.cn/jkzt/crb/zl/szkb_11803/jszl_2275/202003/t20200310_214270.html.

Duan, L., and Zhu, G. (2020): Psychological interventions for people affected by the COVID-19 epidemic. *The Lancet Psychiatry, 7*(4), 300–302.

General Office of the CPC Central Committee of the People's Republic of China (2015): The opinions on strengthening social public security prevention and control system. Retrieved from http://www.gov.cn/xinwen/2015-04/13/content_2846013.htm.

Guo, Y., and Dai, Q. (2020): To consolidate the outcomes of pandemic prevention and control, Zhejiang expanded orderly nucleic acid and antibody testing in orderly. Retrieved from http://zj.people.com.cn/BIG5/n2/2020/0427/c228592-33980454.html.

Human Rights Watch. (2020): Asia: Reduce prison populations facing COVID-19 overcrowding, unsanitary conditions threaten catastrophe. Retrieved from https://www.hrw.org/news/2020/04/06/asia-reduce-prison-populations-facing-covid-19.

Li, G. (2020, February 15, 2020): Keeping Covid-19 out of the prison gate. *Legal Daily.* Retrieved from http://www.legaldaily.com.cn/zt/content/2020-02/15/content_8118023.htm.

Li, J. (2020): A study on the criminal assessment mechanism in China. *Legality Vision, 2020*(7), 15–18.

Li, S. D., and Liu, T. (2019): Problem-solving courts in China: Background, development and current status. *Victims & Offenders: An International Journal of Evidence-based Research, Policy, and Practice, 14*(3), 360–374. DOI: 10.1080/15564886.2019.1595246.

Li, S. D., and Liu, T. (2020): Correctional system's response to the coronavirus pandemic and its implications for prison reform in China. *Victims & Offenders: An International Journal of Evidence-based Research, Policy, and Practice.* DOI: 10.1080/15564886.2020.1824159.

Li, Z., Qing, M., Ni, H., Wei, H., and Liu, Y. (2020, February 22, 2020): Holes exposed in the prevention and control of coronavirus in prison. *Global Times.* Retrieved from http://m.fx361.com/news/2020/0222/6384129.html.

Liebrenz, M., Bhugra, D., Buadze, A., and Schleifer, R. (2020): Caring for persons in detention suffering with mental illness during the Covid-19 outbreak. *Forensic Science International: Mind and Law, 100013,* 1–2.

Luo, X. (2020). Keeping Covid-19 out of the prison gate: COVID-19 prevention and treatment practices in Hunan prions. *Legal Weekly.* Retrieved from https://xw.qq.com/amphtml/20200411A0B4KO00.

National People's Congress. (2012): China had 681 prisons and 1.64 million inmates. Retrieved from http://www.npc.gov.cn/zgrdw/huiyi/cwh/1126/2012-04/25/content_1719250.htm.

Pang, Y. (2016): Promotion of innovative supervision models and grid management in prisons in Sichuan Province. Retrieved from http://scnews.newssc.org/system/20160109/000638053.html.

Rapisarda, S., and Byrne, J. (2020): An examination of COVID-19 outbreaks in prisons and jails throughout Asia. *Victims & Offenders: An International Journal of Evidence-based Research, Policy, and Practice.* DOI: 10.1080/15564886.2020.1835770.

Rapisarda, S., Byrne, J., and Marmolejo, L. (2020): An examination of covid-19 outbreaks in prisons and jails in North America, Central America, and the Caribbean. *Victims & Offenders: An International Journal of Evidence-based Research, Policy, and Practice.* DOI: 10.1080/15564886.2020.1835766.

Walmsley, R. (2020): World prison population list, eleventh edition. Retrieved from https://www.prisonstudies.org/sites/default/files/resources/downloads/world_prison_population_list_11th_edition_0.pdf.

Wang, J., and Xu, M. (2019, July 3, 2019): Using smart applications to improve job performance in Beijing women's prison. *Legal Daily.* Retrieved from http://www.legaldaily.com.cn/zt/content/2019-07/03/content_7924528.htm.

Wu, Z. (2003): Western prisons and Chinese prisons: Focusing on differences. *European Journal of Crime, Criminal Law and Criminal Justice*, 11, 95–113.

Yang, C. T. (2020a): Liaoning prison administration is determined to defeat the coronavirus epidemic with the highest standards, strongest measures, and biggest resolution. Retrieved from http://www.moj.gov.cn/subject/content/2020-03/12/1457_3243845.html.

Yang, C. T. (2020b): The no. 2 prison in Yunnan Province adheres to seven "battle plans" and constructs seven "defense lines". Retrieved from http://www.moj.gov.cn/Department/content/2020-03/30/606_3245159.html.

Yang, C. T. (2020c): Guangdong prisons achieved notable results in big recognization prompted by COVID-19 prevention and control. Retrieved from http://www.moj.gov.cn/subject/content/2020-04/24/1457_3246846.html

Yang, Z. (2020): Cracks in the system: COVID-19 in Chinese prisons. *The Diplomat*. Retrieved from: https://thediplomat.com/2020/03/cracks-in-the-system-covid-19-in-chinese-prisons/.

Zhai, Z. (2020): On the construction of criminal risk assessment and control system. *Justice of China*, 2020(5), 78–83.

Zhou, F. (2020): Wuhan is expanding nucleic acid testing, covering all individuals in several categories. Retrieved from https://www.yicai.com/news/100588214.html.

Zhu, J. (2020a): The Chang Tai prison in Tianjin implemented "four battles" plans to improve inmate psychological treatment programs. Retrieved from http://www.moj.gov.cn/Department/content/2020-03/13/606_3243912.html.

Zhu, J. (2020b): Ding Shan Prison in Jiangsu Province takes strong hold of the management of inmate emotional problems. Retrieved from http://www.moj.gov.cn/Department/content/2020-05/14/606_3248573.html.

Zhu, J. (2020c): The remote video interviewing project in Anhui prisons shows strong effectiveness. Retrieved from http://www.moj.gov.cn/Department/content/2020-05/14/606_3248572.html.

9 Latin American prisons during the COVID-19 pandemic

The cases of Colombia, Bolivia, Perú and Argentina

Juan Sebastián Hernández and César Valderrama

1 Introduction: a constant crisis, criminal policy excesses, and lack of political will

In Latin America, many countries had to face the COVID-19 pandemic's impacts, while their prison systems were already in a general human rights crisis. Overcrowding, deficiencies in infrastructure, the lack of control and proper sanctions for cases of torture and other prohibited practices, rotting food and appalling health services contributed for decades to a chronic human rights crisis in Latin American prisons. In such precarious circumstances, the 2020 pandemic has dragged the prison population to a breaking point: The SARS-Cov-2 virus has not only become an immediate threat to prisoners' health and survival, but it has also found prisons to be the perfect incubator through which it can spread to society in general.

In Colombia, for example, the Villavicencio prison quickly presented a case of mass infection due to overcrowding, swiftly spreading the disease throughout the Department of Meta and prompting the Constitutional Court to issue special orders.[1] Meanwhile, in late August, Peru confirmed that 12,294 of its prison population had COVID-19, as 44% of the tests administered by officials confirmed positive cases.[2] In Bolivia, which has a prison population of 18,000, 40 inmates died as a result of COVID-19, and another 159 were confirmed to have the virus amidst severe overcrowding conditions.[3] In Argentina, the National Committee for the Prevention of Torture reported that, as of late November 2020, the prison system had a total of 1,629 confirmed cases, and another 388 cases were reported in police stations, while the mortality rate of the virus in prisons doubled that of the general population.[4]

In this context, governments in the region had to face the structural problems that caused the prison crises in the first place, which developed mainly from the strategy for dealing with criminal behaviour: Excessive punitive criminal policies made the prisons unmanageable. As a result, the COVID-19 pandemic presented a double challenge: Dealing with the health crisis posed by the virus and, at the same time, facing the structural problems prisons in the region have had for years. This chapter deals with the

DOI: 10.4324/9781003169178-9

responses to the pandemic taken by Colombia, Bolivia, Peru and Argentina, focusing primarily on the (unsuccessful) measures implemented by these governments to protect prisons from the virus. Nevertheless, since the general quarantines limited access to information concerning the evolution of the crisis throughout 2020, this chapter focuses mainly on the Colombian case, where the most information was available, while also presenting some information on Peru, Bolivia, and Argentina.

1.1 The constant crisis: Excessive use of incarceration as a criminal policy problem in Latin America

Before the pandemic reached Latin America and the Caribbean, the general prison crisis in the region and commonplace violations of human rights made Latin American prisons, as described by the *Seattle Times,* an "inhuman hell on earth".[5] To make matters worse, the unlawful practice of torture and other cruel or inhumane treatment by prison guards were also commonplace. However, although varied, most of the human rights violations could be traced back to the excessive use of incarceration, which pushed to the limits the resources of prisons in the region.

According to data from the World Prison Brief,[6] 11 out of 22 countries in the Caribbean have some level of overcrowding, with Haiti (354.4% overcrowding rate), Grenada (133.8%), Antigua and Barbuda (91.3%), and the Dominican Republic (83.2%) as most severe cases.[7] In the case of Central America, six of the eight countries also face high overcrowding rates, with Guatemala (272.0%), El Salvador (115.2%) and Honduras (104.0%) the top four in this respect.[8] Similarly, 9 of the 13 South American countries also face high overcrowding rates, with Bolivia (263.9%), Peru (140.3%) and Brazil (70.7%) the most severe cases.[9]

Although some aspects of the crisis can be attributed to a lack of resources or proper management (e.g. insufficient budget, the number of prison guards is below international guidelines and prison guards often lack proper human rights training), most experts agree that the main cause is of governments to use incarceration beyond the available capacity in their prison systems.[10] As such, the state of crisis must be understood as a result of a general failure of criminal policy design by States, not only as isolated management problems. Simply put, Latin American countries incarcerate more people than they can sustain in humane conditions, usually adopting criminal reforms without considering their effects on prison life. As a result, they have generated a situation of vulnerability which not only affects prison living conditions, but also promotes corruption as a means to gain access to limited resources, violence as a means to survive and the routine use of unlawful practices (such as torture or excessive use of force).

In Colombia, this understanding of the crisis was adopted by the Constitutional Court in its 2013 and 2015 rulings.[11] Earlier, in 1998, the Court had characterised the "unconstitutional state of affairs"[12] of prisons as produced by the Government's neglect of the system (as overcrowding and unconstitutional practices were thought to be caused by lack of investment in infrastructure and proper oversight from state officials). In 2013, however, the Court recognised that the excessive use of incarceration by Congress, the General Prosecutor's Office and reforms promoted by the Executive had become the main cause of unconstitutionality of the prison system, for, even after the Colombian Government invested in a massive expansion of prisons, incarceration increased significantly throughout the 2000s. The prison population almost tripled (from a population of 44,398 in 1998 to 120,032 in 2013), mainly because of legal reforms that increased prison sentences, the number of crimes legally providing prison sentences and the use of pre-trial detention.[13] In its 2013 analysis, the Court concluded that the Colombian criminal policy violated the Constitution of 1991 due to its constant subordination of constitutional rights to public safety and security policy, its lack of a proper empirical and rational basis, its abandonment of the constitutional aim of prison sentences (rehabilitation) and its irrational increase of incarceration – that is, its disregard for the consequences of longer sentences for the living conditions of prisons, for the sustainability of the system and for criminal law principles such as proportionality and *ultima ratio.*[14]

The situation in the region is not very different. As Dammert and Salazar (2009) explain, the political debate in Latin America has been dominated for decades by punitive and security-centred discourses that propose a "strong-hand" approach to criminal policy. These discourses and the fragile security situation of the region (such as the proliferation of drug-trafficking, organised and even street-level crime)[15] have been a fertile ground for "tough-on-crime" policies that, not unlike those of the United States or other Global North countries,[16] have created an ever-increasing prison population that prisons have been unable to manage.

According to the data of World Prison Brief, from 2000 to 2018, the average global increase in the prison population was around 24.0%, but in the case of the Americas, the increase was of 40.8%. However, when measured without the United States,[17] the increase is far more dramatic: In the Americas, without the USA, the total incarcerated population increased 121.2%, from a population of 752,818 in 2000 to 1,665,459 in mid-2018, making it the region with the greatest increase in incarceration on the globe.[18] Several studies have also shown the relation between this phenomenon and the increases in prison sentences for drug offences,[19] for low-level offences and for crimes in general,[20] which have not only increased the prison population in general, but in particular that of the poor, and specifically poor women.[21]

Even if such an accelerated increase has not been unprecedented in other countries that espoused similar punitive policies (such as the USA and the UK), for Latin America, this meant the collapse of their prison systems. Contrary to these Global North examples, Latin American countries lacked both the resources to expand and sustain an ever-growing prison system and the political will to reduce the use of incarceration in the penal system. Prisons in the region consequently became trapped between the demand for harsher sentences fed by political discourses and the increasing demands on their stretched resources – a situation that can only be described as a constant state of crisis. Moreover, as the shift to a punitive and security-based policy has been deepened by right and far-right governments in the region (such as the "tough on crime" stances of the Colombian President, Ivan Duque, Jair Bolsonaro in Brazil and others), there is no solution in sight for the near future: Governments not only lack the resources to properly reform and improve their prisons, but also the political will to reduce incarceration and the human rights violations it currently produces.

2 Failed strategies to face overcrowding and structural problems of the prison system

In this context, the situation prior to the pandemic of the Colombian, Peruvian, Bolivian and Argentinian prisons, although presenting different dynamics particular to each country, is closer to the rule than the exception. This has meant that these countries presented serious deficiencies as COVID-19 reached the region: Severe overcrowding, lack of proper health services or access to water and other factors foreboded mass infection.

2.1 The situation of Colombia, Peru, Bolivia and Argentina before the pandemic

In the case of *Colombia*, incarceration had been kept relatively stable since the declaration of the prison crisis in 2013. According to the official data of the INPEC (The National Prison and Jail Institute of Colombia), since 2013, the prison population on the national prison system varied slightly, ranging from approximately 110,000 to 120,000, registering a total population of 122,079 prisoners in March 2020, a global capacity of 80,763 and an overcrowding rate of 51.2% – that is, an overpopulation of 41,316 inmates (see INPEC, 2020: 29). Of these, 69.7% were sentenced prisoners (over 79,528 male and 5,522 female), while 30.4% were in pre-trial detention (34,027 male and 3,002 female) (INPEC, 2020: 36).

However, even if its average overcrowding rates do not rank among the highest in the region, several Colombian prisons and jails presented individually extremely high rates. Of the 132 national prisons (for both pre-trial and sentenced inmates), 80 had a rate higher than the average, with 27 having a rate higher than 100%, and of those, seven were over 200% overcrowded. Even then, three centres had an overcrowding rate over 300%: Riohacha (343.0%), Santa Marta (326.0%) and Andes (305.4%) (INPEC, 2020: 32-33). In total, Colombia in March 2020 had a total incarceration rate of 376 per 100,000 inhabitants, one that has been, since 2015, between 351 (2015) and 387 (2019) (INPEC, 2020: 17).

It must also be noted that, within each centre, the population was not distributed evenly. This meant that, even in centres with a low overcrowding rate, certain blocks had extremely overcrowded conditions: As the Civil Society's Monitoring Commission pointed out, in some detention centres, some blocks had an overcrowding of up to 718.2%, having a capacity for 22 inmates but housing 180.[22] Additionally, the INPEC does not report data of the whole incarcerated population in Colombia, as some centres lie outside the national system – such as military and juvenile detention centres, municipal jails, police stations and others. Although the INPEC reports the total population of some of these centres (which is significantly smaller),[23] there are no regular public reports that detail their occupancy levels or other data.

A further development was that, as Colombia refused to correct the deficiencies of its criminal policy, the influx of prisoners to the system exceeded the capacity of prisons and jails, so some prisons were unable to receive more inmates. Due to this, police stations and URIs (cells under the General Prosecutor's Office) began to retain this influx, which meant that these centres, which lie outside the penitentiary system, began to execute pre-trial detention and even prison sentences without the legal competence for doing so. They had even greater overcrowding and human rights violations than jails and prisons, as their infrastructure, resources and officials – police officers that do not have prison guard training – were not prepared to guarantee long-term incarceration in humane conditions.[24]

Peru has one of the higher incarceration rates in the region, second only to Bolivia. According to the INPE's (the National Penitentiary Institute of Peru) 2019 statistical report, the national penitentiary system had a total population of 126,064 (of whom 95,548 are in prisons, while 30,516 are in "half-open" centres (in post-penitentiary assistance, alternative measures to prison, etc.). However, the INPE reported that the whole prison system had a total capacity of 40,137, which elevates its overcrowding/occupancy rate to 314% (INPE, 2019: 6). Of the total prison population, 90,392 were males and 5,156 females, while 34,879 were in pre-trial detention (36.5%; INPE, 2019: 25).

As is the case of Colombian prisons, overcrowding in Peruvian prisons varies widely. While some centres are not overcrowded at all, some are severely overcrowded, well beyond the national average. For example, the E.P. of Jaen had an overcrowding rate of 514%, the E.P. of Callao 463% and the E.P. of Chanchamayo 538%. Thus, of the 68 prison centres under the INPE, 14 had overcrowding over 300% (INPE, 2019: 11–14). In the face of such conditions, the Peruvian Government issued a National Criminal Policy Plan to reduce incarceration in 2016,[25] but even after the Peruvian Ministry of Justice recognised the need to reduce overcrowding,[26] the excesses of the Peruvian criminal policy were not properly addressed by the authorities.

Bolivia, while having one of the smaller prison populations, faces the worst overcrowding rate of the countries studied. According to a 2016 public accountability report of the General Direction of the Penitentiary Regime, the Bolivian prison system had a total capacity of 5,013, but housed a total population of 15,831, a global overcrowding rate of 216%.[27] However, the World Prison Brief reports that in 2018, the prison population had risen to over 19,161, which increased the global overcrowding rate to 263%.[28] Moreover, Bolivia had one of the highest pre-trial detention populations in the region, second only to Paraguay: 67.2% were pre-trial detainees. Unfortunately, Bolivia lacks published annual reports concerning prisons; this prevents developing an adequate statistical review of incarceration after 2018.

Argentina has the least severe situation of these countries, as it has a relatively low overcrowding rate and the least inhumane prisons. According to the 2019 Annual Report of the SNEEP (the National Statistic System of Execution of Sanctions), Argentina had a total of 109,405 prisoners in the country – 100,634 in the prison system (95.5% male, 4.4% female) and 8,771 in police stations or other police detention centres (SNEEP, 2019: 6). More than half of the prison population are pre-trial detainees, as, of the 100,634 prisoners, only 56,270 have been sentenced (55.9%). On the matter of overcrowding, Argentina has a rate of 22.9%, as the prison system has a total capacity of 81,904 and houses 100,634 inmates, for an overpopulation of 18,730. However, as in other countries, overcrowding rates vary, depending on the prison: While many of these do not stray too far from the national average, some have high overcrowding rates, such as the SPF centre of Mendoza (with a 189.0% overcrowding rate) as do many others in the provincial prison system. Nonetheless, few prisons have overcrowding rates of over 100% (SNEEP, 2019: 60–65).

2.2 The failed strategy: Insufficient measures to reduce overcrowding

The COVID-19 pandemic reached Latin America during March 2020. International organisations and NGOs, such as the UN, the Inter-American Human Rights Commission and the World Health Organization, warned that the virus posed a serious threat to prison populations on the continent, mainly due to the fact that overcrowding and unsanitary conditions were conducive to mass infection. In most countries, action was consequently taken to mitigate the impact of the pandemic, although in many cases without proper planning or conviction, as most politicians resisted the idea of reducing overcrowding through mass early release policies.

In *Colombia*, the first confirmed case of COVID-19 was detected on 6 March 2020, and the INPEC adopted certain measures (such as the suspension of visits from family members or defence attorneys or the supply of masks and other preventive material) on 12 March. However, on the matter of overcrowding, the Government delayed any measure until 14 April, when, using exceptional powers, President Ivan Duque issued the Legislative Decree 546 of 2020.[29] This Decree created a transitory home detention benefit which allowed judges to give home detention to prisoners under certain circumstances: (1) when the prisoner was 60 years or older; (2) for incarcerated mothers with children under three years; (3) individuals with comorbidities; (4) individuals with movement disabilities; (5) pre-trail detainees for involuntary crimes[30]; (6) individuals with prison sentences under five years and (7) individuals who had served 40% of their sentence. The benefit would only be valid for six months after release.

Early drafts of the decree faced harsh criticism from criminal lawyers, university professors and NGOs, mainly for its insufficient impact on overcrowding due to the severe limitations related to which crimes could receive the benefit.[31] The Government originally aimed to release 10,000 prisoners, but after the General Prosecutor objected to the draft, arguing, without a proper empirical or legal basis, that releasing prisoners was unnecessary and presented a major risk for security during the pandemic,[32] the Decree was issued with a wider prohibition for certain crimes, which included low-level offences (such as drug-related crimes, theft and others) and excluded most of the prison population. The Decree's aim was thus reduced to the release of 4,000 inmates, which would only represent a 5.1% reduction of the system's overcrowding rate and represented less than 10% of the overpopulation as of March 2020. As generally expected, the Decree not only failed to reduce overcrowding effectively but was even unable to reach its aim: According to the 9th Government Monitoring Report concerning the prison crisis, only 815 inmates received transitory home detention in terms of the Decree, between 14 April and November 2020.[33]

Throughout 2020, the Colombian prison system reported a significant decrease in overcrowding, despite the failure of the Decree. According to INPEC reports, the prison population decreased from 122,079 in March to 98,172 at the end of October, registering an overcrowding rate of 21.7% (INPEC, 2020: 27). However, this reduction was caused by multiple factors. First, as the general quarantine lasted for almost four months in Colombia, a substantial reduction of crimes and arrests meant a smaller influx of prisoners. However, more importantly, the Legislative Decree also suspended transfers of inmates from local jails and police stations to the national prisons, which meant that, throughout the pandemic, the Government displaced responsibility for the influx of new inmates to local authorities. Police stations thus faced a dramatic increase in overcrowding: In May 2020, police stations had a capacity of 4,869, but housed a population of 10,343 (an overcrowding of 112%), but in January 2021, it had risen to 19,343, reaching an overcrowding rate of 297.3%.[34]

During this time, COVID-19 cases were on the rise within the Colombian prison system. According to the INPEC's latest report (of 2 December), a substantial portion of the prison population has been infected with COVID-19, even if the total number of current cases was lower: Although in early December there were only 741 active cases in 48 detention centres, there were a total of 19,314 confirmed cases throughout 2020 (17,957 inmates, 1,160 guards, 111 administrative officials, 233 auxiliary guard officials).[35] As these reports show, more than 15% of the prison population were infected by the virus, with several cases of avoidable deaths occurring because of the health services' deficiencies.[36] Moreover, prisoners complained that the authorities at some centres stopped testing for COVID-19 to hide the true scope of infection, as in some prisons, most tests were confirming positive cases.[37] Prisoners also reported that many individuals with symptoms of COVID-19 were not being tested nor treated, as symptoms were dismissed by prison officials as flu or as lies.[38] Thus, although these reports have not been confirmed, they suggest that the scope of infection may be significantly higher.

In the other countries studied, the situation was not substantially different.

In the case of *Peru*, for example, the Government issued the Supreme Decree No 0006-2020-JUS in May, which created a humanitarian pardon. This pardon applies to several groups, such as pregnant women, mothers incarcerated with their children, juvenile prisoners under 16 years old, prisoners over 70 years old and prisoners whose sentence would finish within six months.[39] According to the Government estimate, this sought to reduce the prison population by 3,000.[40] However, this measure was clearly insufficient, even after the Peruvian Constitutional Tribunal declared overcrowding unconstitutional and ordered the Ministry of Justice to take urgent action.[41] As of June, only 1,502 inmates had received pardons,[42] while, as mentioned above, the Peruvian prison system only has a capacity of 40,137, but housed 95,548 prisoners at the start of 2020, an overpopulation of approximately 55,411.[43] Therefore, even if it achieved its aim of releasing 3,000 prisoners, the Decree would have reduced the overcrowding rate only by 7.5%, from 138.0% to 130.5%.

In *Bolivia*, the Government's strategy was similar. On 4 May, it issued Presidential Decree No. 4226, through which it offered humanitarian amnesties and pardons to prisoners over 58 years old, with disabilities or comorbidities and pregnant women, among others.[44] According to the Vice-Minister of the Interior and Police Regime,[45] the Decree would benefit at least 320 prisoners in the Bolivian system, although academic analysts and journalists estimated that it could benefit up to 5,000 prisoners.[46] Taking into account these estimates, the Bolivian Decree, although being insufficient to eliminate overcrowding, would be one of the ambitions in these countries: As the overall overpopulation of Bolivian prisons was of 14,148 (in 2018), it could reduce the overcrowding rate from 263% to 182.5%. However, the Decree's real effects have been underwhelming, as by 9 July, it had led to the release of only 300 prisoners.[47]

In the case of *Argentina*, although it boasts the lowest overcrowding rate of the studied countries, there has been no governmental strategy to release prisoners. On the contrary, in the first days of the pandemic, the main policy issued by the Argentinian Federal Tribunal ordered judges to grant early release for individuals with prison sentences for lesser offences, for those with comorbidities of COVID-19, pregnant women, among others (mainly through home detention, parole and other benefits).[48] This decision would have allowed the early release through various mechanisms of almost 1,900 inmates – that is, nearly 10% of the overpopulation reported in 2019. However, the Argentinian President and several protesters opposed what was viewed as a mass release of "dangerous criminals".[49] As a result, on 5 May, the Argentinian Supreme Court suspended the decision, ending the judicial strategy to reduce overcrowding.[50] While the Argentinian prison system showed a low rate of infection, according to the National Committee for the Prevention of Torture, the prison system showed a higher mortality rate than that in the general population: While the latter presents a mortality rate of 2.1%, in prisons this rate rises to 4.4% – data that show the precariousness of health services in prisons as well as their particular vulnerability during the pandemic.

3 Hidden from the public eye: The general lockdown of prisons, insufficient compensatory measures and lack of accountability

The Latin American countries described above were unable and/or unwilling to reduce overcrowding and mitigate the risks posed by the COVID-19 pandemic. But, most importantly, they also disregarded the negative effects their countermeasures had on the human rights of prisoners. They ignored the recurring demands of the inmates, brutally repressed protests within prisons and were unwilling to publish regular reports on the situation. The main strategy put forward by many governments in the region was the implementation of general lockdowns of prisons – simply put, a "throw away the key" strategy centred on supplying hygiene products and establishing sanitary protocols. Transparency and access to information were disregarded, as many of the governments do not publish clear reports, exaggerate the effects of their actions and even omit the negative effects that their tactics had on the living conditions of prisoners.

The main strategy used by governments in the region was decreeing a general lockdown of prisons, preventing not only access to family members and visits, but also barring defence attorneys, human rights organisations and non-penitentiary personnel from entering. In Colombia, for example, on 11 March 2020, the INPEC issued Directive 004,[51] through which it implemented several preventive measures, such as the obligatory use of masks, the regular washing of hands and the isolation of individuals who developed COVID-19 symptoms. However, on 12 March, the INPEC issued an annexure to Directive 001 of 2020,[52] suspending access to prison from everyone other than prison guards. This included barring not only family visits, but also meetings with defence attorneys and visits from ombudspersons.

Similarly, the Government in Peru issued a general suspension of all visits in the prison system through the Supreme Decree No. 044-2020-PCM,[53] which the INPE argued created a "sanitary security ring" around prison facilities.[54] The same measure was adopted by the Bolivian Government, which implemented a general lockdown of prisons and suspended all visits.[55] In the Argentinian case, due to the federal structure of its prison system, suspension of visits was adopted at different times in penitentiary subsystems, although the press presented most suspensions as a demand from prisoners themselves in face of the pandemic.[56] In Argentina, the suspension in the federal penitentiary system was finally lifted in October, after which several federal prisons allowed family visits with sanitary controls and protocols.[57]

As a rule, the general lockdown of prisons issued by authorities reduced the ability of NGOs, defence attorneys and other actors (such as ombudsperson institutions) to properly survey the situation inside prisons. This meant that, during the pandemic, the human rights of prisoners were severely limited. There were restrictions on the rights to visits (although some prison authorities allowed virtual visits, as is the case in Colombia, but the technological devices required were insufficient to guarantee visits for all prisoners),[58] and the prisoners' ability to denounce abuses, as their access to justice through their attorneys had been barred. Moreover, the lack of resources, such as soap and masks in prisons, forced families to supply their relatives with what they needed – a supply that was obstructed by the general lockdown. Although there are no public data that allow a proper quantitative evaluation of the problem, the general lockdown created a lack of accountability and a heightened vulnerability to abuses and the violation of human rights.

One example is the excesses of Government officials in controlling prisoner protests. Throughout the region, as the pandemic arrived, inmates from many prisons organised protests to denounce their lack of protection from COVID-19, and as the inmates were under quarantine and most lockdowns had already been enforced, only official sources reported what had happened. For example, in Colombia, there were peaceful and violent protests in more than 10 prisons on 21 March, in which inmates demanded proper protection against the pandemic, proper health services and the right to visits. Of these, the most violent took place in "La Modelo" jail in Bogotá, which had a final toll of 24 dead prisoners (most by gunshot) and more than 80 injured.[59] The following day, President Ivan Duque and his Ministry of Justice and Law announced that the incident had been a massive escape plan of the ELN and dissident groups of FARC,[60] although they offered little evidence for such claims.[61] In this vein, the General Prosecutor announced investigations concerning the "escape plan" and the possession of cell phones by prisoners (with which many recorded the protest and abuses of force by prison guards, including the use of tear gas in closed spaces).[62] However, months later, in May, Revista Semana[63] and CeroSetenta[64] published details of the autopsy reports, which showed that 23 of the 24 deceased prisoners had been shot at medium range, in the back or in the head – details that suggest that most were killed while running from guards, being unarmed or defenceless. Moreover, in November 2020, Human Rights

Watch reported that the investigations of these deaths showed severe flaws: Not only did many of the 24 autopsy reports lack evidence such as photographs of the scene or the position of the body, but some even lacked the signature of the forensic officials or were marked as "drafts".[65] As the NGO concluded, most of the evidence suggests that the deaths were intentional (only one showed signs of a struggle with a guard), which not only could be classified as an abuse of force by prison officials, but even as extrajudicial executions.

In Peru, Bolivia and Argentina, prison protests were carried out with similar results, and all demanded an effective protection against COVID-19: From a proper supply of masks and hygiene products to effective solutions to overcrowding. Most prison protests were motivated by the perceived negligence of guard officials and governments alike.

In Peru, for example, there have been several protests in detention centres after inmates died of COVID-19: In the Castro prison, in Lima, one such protest resulted in nine deaths (with gunshot wounds) and 67 prisoners injured on 28 April,[66] while on 18 April, protests in Chicalayo prison (Lima) also resulted in two deaths and one injured.[67] In Lurigancho, the biggest prison in Lima, prisoners themselves instituted security protocols as 30 inmates had died of COVID-19.[68] Even so, on 8 May, the Inter-American Commission of Human Rights condemned the violence with which the Peruvian Government repressed the prison protests and called for a proper protection during the pandemic.[69]

Bolivia has also faced different prison protests. On 3 July, prisoners rose in protest due to fear of the pandemic at the San Antonio prison, which has a capacity of 150, housed 500 inmates.[70] On 28 July, in the San Sebastián prison in Cochabamba, prisoners also protested, as they demanded medical assistance, fast tests for COVID-19 infection and medicine for ordinary diseases.[71] Although there are no reports of prisoners killed during the protest, most of the protests were preceded by the death of several inmates due to COVID-19.[72]

Argentina has faced many protests in several prisons and detention centres: On 25 March, as prisoners protested and demanded access to soap, water, medical attention and measures to reduce overcrowding, five prisoners died during clashes with prison officials.[73] On 21 April, a violent protest took place in the Florencio Varela prison, which resulted in one dead and 40 injured prisoners. As the death was confirmed as caused by unlawful actions of prison guards, the director of the prison and others were fired. However, in some instances, Argentinian prison officials opened negotiations with prisoner organisations: In the Villa Devoto prison, officials signed an agreement with the prisoners after a protest, promising to take action to reduce overcrowding and increase early release measures.[74]

As these cases illustrate, the lack of access to official information has meant that prisoners themselves and the news media became the main source of data concerning thee pandemic within prisons. Although there are not sufficient data to determine the magnitude of the effects of the pandemic on several aspects of prison life – a reliable count of cases of infection, the adequate supply of hygiene and protective materials, most protests and their news coverage show that governments in the region were mostly ineffective: Their solutions to the problem of overcrowding were often negligent and inadequate. Prisoners denounce a lack of proper testing and medical treatment; a lack of access to water, soap and other hygiene supplies. As protests developed, governments abused their power to suppress protestors and discontent. Thus, as many predicted, the structural deficiencies of the Latin American prison systems led, amidst the pandemic, to their natural conclusion: A humanitarian crisis which "tough-on-crime" governments, and the societies they represent, were unable and unwilling to prevent.

4 No way forward: Indifference and lack of plans to tackle the prison crisis

Although many hoped that the pandemic would force Latin American governments to face the shortcomings in their criminal policy and tackle the human rights violations in prisons, COVID-19 and the half-measures taken showed that they are both indifferent to the deteriorating living conditions in prisons and unwilling to solve the structural problems that caused them. Even amidst an unprecedented health crisis, the shift to far-right governments indicates that the constant prison crisis of the region will only deepen as the virus continues to spread – a situation that the lack of transparency and external oversight will only worsen.

Particularly in Colombia, after more than five years since the declaration of the unconstitutional state of affairs, there seems to be no way out of the prison crisis. Even after announcing to the Constitutional Court plans to solve the prison crisis as early as 2018 – plans that recognise that the excessive use of incarceration has overwhelmed the capacities of the system, its health and food services, among others[75] – the Colombian Government has taken little action to implement them and to guarantee humane living conditions in prisons. As the Civil Society Monitoring Commission pointed out in several reports to the Court, even if the Government has recognised the problem, its plans lack detail of the measures to be taken (such as the penal reforms to be adopted) besides expanding infrastructure – a tried and failed strategy. Meanwhile, the Government routinely supports increases in sentences, a constitutional reform to allow life sentences and other negative legislation that only deepens the flaws of its criminal policy.[76]

Moreover, several actors in the public sector have become a serious obstacle for any meaningful reform in criminal policy. For example, the previous General Prosecutor, Nestor Humberto Martinez, regularly opposed, without basis, reforms to reduce the use and length of pre-trial detention.[77] The succeeding General Prosecutor, Francisco Barbosa, followed the steps of his predecessor: Using fallacious arguments to oppose any transitory early release, he argued, without evidence, that there is no link between overcrowding and COVID-19 infections, that any release would be a grievous danger for public safety and that the ordinary alternatives of the penal legislation – the same legislation that allowed overcrowding to appear in the first place – were sufficient to protect prisoners' health.[78]

Due to the fact that the Government quickly caved in to the General Prosecutor's objections, even disregarding the wide array of evidence and diagnosis of the overcrowding problem and the recommendations made by academics, civil society and international organisations (see e.g. Hernández, 2020), it seems highly dubious that the current administration has the will to tackle the causes of the prison crisis, as its solution – the reduction of the use of incarceration – contradicts directly their "tough-on-crime" discourse and their public safety priorities.

Unless the region's governments and legislative officials muster the political will necessary to dismantle decades of prison-centred criminal policy and start to take seriously the human rights violations that became commonplace in prisons, it seems that the constant crisis of Latin American prisons can only deepen the "inhuman hell on earth" that prison have become. As indifference and half-measures continue to be the evading tactics of governments, the judiciary is the only hope for real progress to solve the crisis. In late November, the Colombian Council of State issued a ruling that declared the overcrowded conditions in a Meta prison and the State's negligence to solve it as a cruel and inhuman treatment of women incarcerated there between 2012 and 2014, thus condemning the state to pay 16 billion pesos (around 4 million USD) compensation.[79] The Argentinian Federal Tribunal led the efforts to reduce incarceration, even as the Argentinian Government opposed any protection of inmates that could be seen as a "risk" to public safety, and the Peruvian Constitutional Tribunal has also taken steps to guarantee human rights amidst the pandemic. It remains to be seen if the judiciary will be able to do what not even the pandemic could: Force governments to guarantee human rights in their prisons.

Notes

1 See https://www.eltiempo.com/salud/coronavirus-que-paso-con-el-brote-en-la-carcel-de-villavicencio-498070. For the Constitutional Court decision, see https://www.corteconstitucional.gov.co/noticia.php?Corte-Constitucional-ordena-medidas-urgentes-para-proteger-derechos-fundamentales-de-la-poblaci%C3%B3n-privada-de-la-libertad-en-la-C%C3%A1rcel-de-Villavicencio-8895.

2 See https://www.infobae.com/america/agencias/2020/08/22/peru-registra-mas-de-12000-casos-de-la-covid-19-en-carceles/.

3 See https://www.abc.es/internacional/abci-motin-carcel-cochabamba-bolivia-falta-asistencia-medica-plena-pandemia-covid-19-202007280636_video.html?ref=https:%2F%2Fwww.google.com.co%2F.

4 See https://cnpt.gob.ar/wp-content/uploads/2020/11/Reporte-Estado-de-Situacion-PPL-Covid-al-24-11-2-1.pdf.

5 See https://archive.seattletimes.com/archive/?date=19970217&slug=2524460.
6 The data of the World Prison Brief are the product of a collection of information from official sources from different countries by the Institute for Crime and Justice Policy Research and the Birkbeck University of London. For this reason, the data reported are not for the same period for all countries. They may not reflect the situation during the 2020 pandemic and often does not include all incarcerated population, as it often does not include data of prisoners in police stations, military detention centres and other institutions.
7 See https://prisonstudies.org/highest-to-lowest/occupancy-level?field_region_taxonomy_tid=17. The occupancy level data for Haiti are until December 2015, Grenada until August 2019, Antigua and Barbuda until October 2019 and the Dominican Republic until March 2019.
8 See https://prisonstudies.org/highest-to-lowest/occupancy-level?field_region_taxonomy_tid=18. The occupancy level data for Guatemala are until October 2019, El Salvador until June 2018 and Honduras until September 2019.
9 See https://prisonstudies.org/highest-to-lowest/occupancy-level?field_region_taxonomy_tid=24. The occupancy level data for Bolivia are until June 2018, Peru until April 2020 and Brazil until December 2019.
10 Although there is ample literature concerning the relation between criminal policy excesses and the deterioration of prison conditions (such as the work of Lucía Dammert), in the Latin American region, there are several examples. In the case of Colombia, not only has the Constitutional Court adopted this view, but also the National Planning Department, the Advisory Commission on Criminal Policy and several academics. See DNP CONPES Document 3828 of 2015 (http://www.politicacriminal.gov.co/Portals/0/documento/CONPES%20Pol%C3%ADtica%20penitenciaria%20y%20carcelaria%202015.pdf), the Advisory Commission on Criminal Policy Final Report (http://www.politicacriminal.gov.co/Portals/0/documento/Informe%20de%20la%20Comisi%C3%B3n%20Asesora%20de%20Pol%C3%ADtica%20Criminal.pdf), and Dejusticia's own work on drug policy and overcrowding (https://www.dejusticia.org/publication/delitos-de-drogas-y-sobredosis-carcelaria-en-colombia/). In the case of Peru, the work of Solis (2008) points in the same direction – see https://departamento.pucp.edu.pe/derecho/wp-content/uploads/2019/05/politica-penal.pdf.
11 Colombian Constitutional Court. Sentences T-388 of 2013, MP. María Victoria Calle; and T-762 of 2015, MP. Gloria Stella Ortiz.
12 In Colombia, an "unconstitutional state of affairs" is a type of ruling used by the Constitutional Court when it finds a massive and generalised violation of fundamental rights of a certain group, usually as a result of a systemic or structural failure of a public policy. This type of decision allows the Court to issue general orders to public institutions beyond the scope of the individual lawsuits, and usually adopt monitoring mechanisms that involve civil society and NGOs. See Constitutional Court. Sentence T-025 of 2004, MP. Manuel José Cepeda Espinosa.
13 The National Jail and Prison Institute of Colombia – INPEC – published a study that analysed the impact of the penal legislation reforms in the size of prison population. See https://grupodeprisiones.uniandes.edu.co/images/stories/relatorias/PRISIONES-OCT2011/BOLETINES_ESTADISTICOS/MOMENTOS_HISTORICOS_INPEC_2015-1.pdf.
14 In the sentence T-762 of 2015, the Constitutional Court developed the constitutional guidelines that the Colombian criminal policy should follow and whose infringements have caused the prison crisis. For the Court, these guidelines establish that criminal policy must (i) be preventive and not reactive; (ii) offer a strict and reinforced protection of liberty, which means that it must promote alternatives to incarceration and restrict penal sanctions, specially incarceration,

as the *ultima ratio* or "last measure"; (iii) have as its primordial aim the rehabilitation of the prisoner; (iv) limit pre-trial detention as an exceptional measure; (v) be coherent (e.g. establish sanctions proportionally to the seriousness of the offence); (vi) be grounded on empirical evidence; (vii) be sustainable in terms of economic and rights costs; and (viii) must guarantee the human rights of prisoners. See https://www.corteconstitucional.gov.co/relatoria/2015/t-762-15.htm.

15 According to the UNODC, Latin America displaced in 2013 Africa as the most violent continent worldwide, mainly due to the rise of homicide violence related to drug-trafficking cartels, organised crime and ordinary violence. See https://www.unodc.org/documents/gsh/pdfs/2014_GLOBAL_HOMICIDE_BOOK_web.pdf.

16 Garland (2001) argues that, during the late 1970s and 1980s in the US and the UK, the rise of neoconservatism and neoliberalism began a shift in public penal discourse from a rehabilitation and welfare criminal policy towards a mass incarceration, personal responsibility and exclusion policy that generated a significant rise in incarceration rates. According to Iturralde (2010), this shift was also reflected in Latin America, although it focused, particularly on Colombia, on the repression of communism and insurgence in the 1970s, on drug-trafficking in the 1980s and 1990s, and finally on terrorism and street-level crime in the early 2000s.

17 The prison population of the U.S.A., even if it is the largest worldwide, has remained relatively stagnant throughout the 2000s.

18 See https://prisonstudies.org/sites/default/files/resources/downloads/wppl_12.pdf.

19 Dejusticia has several publications concerning the relation between drug-crime policies and the increase in incarceration. For one of the recent studies,seehttps://www.dejusticia.org/publication/delitos-de-drogas-y-sobredosis-carcelaria-en-colombia/.

20 Dejusticia recently published a study concerning the increases in penal sanctions and the general reduction of alternatives to incarceration for many crimes that impact citizen's security perception, including ordinary and street-level crime. See https://www.dejusticia.org/publication/la-paradoja-punitiva/.

21 Dejusticia and other organisations have pointed out in several publications the particular effects that drug-crime policies have had on the incarceration of women, especially those who are socially and economically vulnerable. See https://www.dejusticia.org/publication/mujeres-politicas-de-drogas-y-encarcelamiento-una-guia-para-la-reforma-de-politicas-en-colombia/.

22 See https://www.humanas.org.co/alfa/dat_particular/ar/arc_11644_q_Tercer_Informe_de_Seguimiento.pdf.

23 According to INPEC, 2020: 16, municipal jails housed 2,834 inmates and the military detention centres a total of 664.

24 In 2018, the Civil Society Monitoring Commission reported to the Constitutional Court an analysis of overcrowding and other human rights violations in police stations and URIs – called "transitory detention centres". See https://www.dejusticia.org/comision-de-seguimiento-a-la-sentencia-t-388-de-2013-responde-a-la-corte-constitucional-sobre-hacinamiento-en-estaciones-de-policia-y-uris/.

25 See https://www.minjus.gob.pe/wp-content/uploads/2016/10/Pol%C3%ADtica-Nacional-Penitenciaria_2016_2020.pdf.

26 See https://www.inei.gob.pe/media/criminalidad/Exposiciones/Gustavo_Adolfo.pdf.

27 See http://www.mingobierno.gob.bo/documentos/rpc/c-regimenpenitenciario.pdf.

28 See https://prisonstudies.org/country/Bolivia.

29 See https://dapre.presidencia.gov.co/normativa/normativa/DECRETO%20546%20DEL%2014%20DE%20ABRIL%20DE%202020.pdf.

30 In the Romano-German penal law tradition, some involuntary crimes can be punishable when they reflect a level of negligence, such as some types of involuntary manslaughter or other negligence-based crimes in common law criminal systems.

31 See https://www.eltiempo.com/justicia/delitos/decreto-de-excarcelacion-por-coronavirus-genera-controversia-por-pocos-beneficiarios-485000 and https://www.semana.com/semana-tv/semana-noticias/articulo/abogados-penalistas-aseguran-que-decreto-de-excarcelacion-no-es-suficiente/663616/.

32 See https://www.dejusticia.org/objeciones-del-fiscal-ponen-en-riesgo-a-la-poblacion-reclusa/.

33 See https://www.minjusticia.gov.co/Portals/0/PublicacionesPC/IX%20INFORME%20SEMESTRAL.pdf and https://www.semana.com/semana-tv/semana-noticias/articulo/cerca-de-4000-presos-saldran-de-las-carceles-para-prevenir-covid-19/663585/.

34 The data of May 2020 were reported in the Legislative Decree 804 of 2020. The data of January 2020 were reported by the Ministry of Justice and Law; see https://www.minjusticia.gov.co/Noticias/ArtMID/5552/ArticleID/198/Min-Justicia-contin250a-liderando-estrategia-para-reducir-hacinamiento-en-centros-de-detenci243n-transitoria.

35 As the data in the INPEC webpage is updated daily, it must be noted that the data reported corresponds to the report of 2 December 2020. See https://www.inpec.gov.co/covid-19-establecimientos-inpec.

36 In July, the women prison "El Buen Pastor" in Bogota registered its first death to COVID-19 after a 63-year-old woman presented severe symptoms, but officials did not transfer her to a health facility. According to the news report of El Espectador, the woman was only transferred to a hospital when her daughter paid for the ambulance. See https://www.elespectador.com/noticias/judicial/carcel-del-buen-pastor-reporta-su-primera-muerte-por-covid-19/.

37 See https://cuestionpublica.com/los-pacientes-covid-19-que-no-importan-en-colombia/.

38 See https://www.dejusticia.org/solicitamos-medidas-inmediatas-para-evitar-un-contagio-masivo-en-las-carceles/.

39 See https://busquedas.elperuano.pe/normaslegales/decreto-supremo-que-establece-criterios-y-procedimiento-espe-decreto-supremo-no-006-2020-jus-1865974-2/.

40 See https://larepublica.pe/politica/2020/04/22/coronavirus-martin-vizcarra-aprueba-liberar-a-3000-presos-por-riesgo-de-covid-19/.

41 See https://semanariouniversidad.com/pais/sala-iv-exige-a-ministerio-de-justicia-plan-para-atender-carceles-en-eventual-brote-de-covid-19/?fbclid=IwAR20E0afi2UfpJ_HBMfwiMfj8xQW0BLm7a8TbHRZFD_Ti5OCbxoQVNTSWrM.

42 See https://www.semana.com/mundo/articulo/peru-libero-1500-presos-por-pandemia-para-aliviar-superpobladas-carceles/679702/.

43 It must be noted that these data correspond to the 2019 INPE's report, as it is the most recent population data available.

44 See https://www.lexivox.org/norms/BO-DP-N4226.xhtml.

45 See https://www1.abi.bo/abi_/?i=448325.

46 See https://www.la-razon.com/nacional/2020/05/18/dos-condenados-por-narcotrafico-los-primeros-en-beneficiarse-con-el-indulto-en-bolivia/.

47 See https://www.lavanguardia.com/vida/20200709/482203093362/el-miedo-a-la-covid-19-acelera-las-medidas-preventivas-en-carceles-bolivianas.html.

48 See https://www.pagina12.com.ar/255619-coronavirus-casacion-penal-pide-que-los-jueces-resuelvan-rap.
49 See https://www.bbc.com/mundo/noticias-america-latina-52496655.
50 See https://www.lavanguardia.com/vida/20200505/48996975142/corte-suspende-fallo-de-excarcelacion-de-presos-en-buenos-aires-por-covid-19.html.
51 See https://coronaviruscolombia.gov.co/Covid19/docs/decretos/INPEC/Directiva_000004_de_2020.pdf.
52 See http://www.politicacriminal.gov.co/Portals/0/autos/Respuesta%20Auto%2024%20de%20marzo%20de%202020/3.1%20Anexo%20Directiva%20004%20-%2011%20Marzo%202020.pdf.
53 See https://www.gob.pe/institucion/inpe/noticias/189626-comunicado-09-2020-inpe and https://www.gob.pe/institucion/pcm/normas-legales/460472-044-2020-pcm.
54 See https://www.inpe.gob.pe/prensa/noticias/item/4154-inpe-establece-anillo-de-seguridad-sanitaria-en-penales-como-medida-de-prevenci%C3%B3n-frente-al-coronavirus.html.
55 See https://www.lostiempos.com/actualidad/pais/20201001/restringen-visitas-carceles-evitar-rebrote-covid-19
56 See https://www.clarin.com/policiales/coronavirus-36-mil-presos-renunciaron-visitas-penales-bonaerenses_0_pMFPgMvv.html.
57 See https://www.ambito.com/informacion-general/ciudad/tras-seis-meses-se-reanudan-las-visitas-familiares-las-carceles-n5141864.
58 According to public announcements by the INPEC, in Colombia, up to 23 June 2020, up to 85,000 virtual visits had taken place in the national prison system since March. This has meant that, considering the total prison population of Colombia between March and June, the INPEC allowed less than one visit per inmate. See https://www.eltiempo.com/justicia/servicios/coronavirus-mas-de-85-mil-visitas-virtuales-a-presos-en-colombia-510182.
59 See https://www.dw.com/es/motines-en-c%C3%A1rceles-de-colombia-por-temor-a-covid-19/a-52877668.
60 The Ejercito de Liberación Nacional (ELN) and the dissident groups of the Fuerzas Armadas Revolucionarias de Colombia (FARC) are left-leaning guerrilla-armed groups involved in the Colombian Armed Conflict.
61 See https://www.eltiempo.com/justicia/investigacion/heridos-y-fallecidos-tras-amotinamiento-en-carceles-del-pais-475872.
62 See https://www.rcnradio.com/judicial/fiscalia-abrio-investigacion-por-amotinamientos-en-la-carcel-modelo.
63 See https://www.semana.com/nacion/articulo/en-exclusiva-masacre-carcel-la-modelo-pruebas-del-amotinamiento-carcelario/677853/.
64 See https://cerosetenta.uniandes.edu.co/siete-horas-de-angustia-en-la-modelo/ and https://cerosetenta.uniandes.edu.co/el-silencio-del-inpec-sobre-el-motin-de-la-modelo/.
65 See https://www.hrw.org/es/news/2020/11/24/colombia-muertes-de-detenidos-habrian-sido-intencionales.
66 See https://www.dw.com/es/suben-a-nueve-los-muertos-en-mot%C3%ADn-carcelario-en-per%C3%BA/a-53275144.
67 See https://www.jornada.com.mx/ultimas/mundo/2020/04/18/motin-en-carcel-de-peru-por-temor-a-covid-19-deja-dos-muertos-2669.html.
68 See https://www.france24.com/es/20200623-carceles-covid19-peru-coronavirus-contencion-hacinamiento.
69 See https://www.oas.org/es/cidh/prensa/comunicados/2020/107.asp.
70 See https://www.infobae.com/america/agencias/2020/07/03/protestas-en-dos-carceles-de-bolivia-en-una-por-temor-al-coronavirus/.

71 See https://es.euronews.com/2020/07/27/decenas-de-presos-se-amotinan-en-cochabamba-para-reclamar-medidas-contra-el-coronavirus.
72 See https://www.semana.com/mundo/articulo/siete-muertos-en-carcel-de-bolivia-por-presuntos-contagio-de-covid-19-mundo-hoy/685027/, https://www.elcomercio.com/actualidad/motin-carcel-bolivia-reos-coronavirus.html and https://es.euronews.com/2020/07/27/decenas-de-presos-se-amotinan-en-cochabamba-para-reclamar-medidas-contra-el-coronavirus.
73 See https://elpais.com/sociedad/2020-03-25/cinco-muertos-en-motines-en-carceles-argentinas-durante-la-cuarentena-por-el-coronavirus.html.
74 See https://www.elespectador.com/noticias/el-mundo/motines-y-protestas-la-pandemia-agudiza-la-crisis-en-carceles-de-argentina-articulo-916552/.
75 See https://www.minjusticia.gov.co/Portals/0/Documentos2019/Plan_Carcelario/Plan_de_Transformacion_y_Humanizacion_del_Sistema_Carcelario_en_Colombia_Resumen_Ejecutivo.pdf.
76 The Civil Society's Commission has reported as such in several reports in the VI, VII and VIIIth. See https://www.humanas.org.co/alfa/61__Comision-de-seguimiento-a-la-T-388-13.html;.see also Hernández (2020).
77 See https://www.eltiempo.com/justicia/delitos/fiscal-nestor-humberto-martinez-critica-ley-de-excarcelacion-masiva-117836, https://www.eltiempo.com/justicia/delitos/fiscal-advierte-sobre-excarcelacion-masiva-por-reforma-la-justicia-287264 and https://razonpublica.com/excarcelacion-masiva-de-delincuentes/.
78 See https://www.eltiempo.com/justicia/investigacion/las-observaciones-del-fiscal-general-al-decreto-sobre-excarcelacion-masiva-de-presos-por-covid-19-481532 and https://www.dejusticia.org/objeciones-del-fiscal-ponen-en-riesgo-a-la-poblacion-reclusa/.
79 See https://www.eltiempo.com/justicia/cortes/hacinamiento-carcelario-colombia-nuevas-demandas-tras-millonaria-condena-contra-el-estado-551888.

References

Dammer, L., and Salazar, F. (2009): *¿Duros con el delito? Populismo e inseguridad en América Latina*. Santiago: FLASCO.

Garland, D. (2001): *The Culture of Control*. Chicago: Chicago University Press.

Hernández, J. (2020): *La paradoja punitiva: las medidas alternativas al encarcelamiento y la política criminal inflacionaria en Colombia*. Bogotá: Editorial Dejusticia.

Iturralde, M. (2010): *Castigo, liberalismo autoritario y justicia penal de excepción*. Bogotá: Siglo del Hombre.

National Jail and Prison Institute of Colombia – INPEC (2020): *Statistical Report – March 2020*. https://www.inpec.gov.co/web/guest/estadisticas/-/document_library/TWBuJQCWH6KV/view_file/1001266?_com_liferay_document_library_web_portlet_DLPortlet_INSTANCE_TWBuJQCWH6KV_redirect=https%3A%2F%2Fwww.inpec.gov.co%2Fweb%2Fguest%2Festadisticas%2F-%2Fdocument_library%2FTWBuJQCWH6KV%2Fview%2F965447%3F_com_liferay_document_library_web_portlet_DLPortlet_INSTANCE_TWBuJQCWH6KV_redirect%3Dhttps%253A%252F%252Fwww.inpec.gov.co%252Fweb%252Fguest%252Festadisticas%252F-%252Fdocument_library%252FTWBuJQCWH6KV%252Fview%252F49294.

National Jail and Prison Institute of Colombia – INPEC (2020): *Statistical Report – October 2020*. https://www.inpec.gov.co/web/guest/estadisticas/-/document_library/TWBuJQCWH6KV/view_file/1175692?_com_liferay_document_library_web_portlet_DLPortlet_INSTANCE_TWBuJQCWH6KV_redirect=https%3A%2F%2Fwww.inpec.gov.co%2Fweb%2Fguest%2Festadisticas%2F-%2Fdocument_library%2FTWBuJQCWH6KV%2Fview%2F965447%3F_com_liferay_document_library_web_portlet_DLPortlet_INSTANCE_TWBuJQCWH6KV_redirect%3Dhttps%253A%252F%252Fwww.inpec.gov.co%252Fweb%252Fguest%252Festadisticas%252F-%252Fdocument_library%252FTWBuJQCWH6KV%252Fview%252F49294.

National Penitentiary Institute of Peru – INPE (2019: *Statistical 2019 Report*. https://www.inpe.gob.pe/normatividad/documentos/4295-informe-estadistico-diciembre-2019/file.html.

National Statistic System of Execution of Sanctions – SNEEP (2019): *Statistical 2019 Report*. https://www.argentina.gob.ar/sites/default/files/informe_sneep_argentina_2019.pdf.

Solís, A. (2008): *Política penal y política penitenciaria*. Lima: Departamento Académico de Derecho de la Pontificia Universidad Católica del Perú.

10 Costa Rica

Carlos Tiffer Sotomayor and Paola Tiffer Hangen

1 Introduction: general situation of the penitentiary system

Costa Rica is a small country in Central America with a population of approximately 5 million. In 2018, 21.40% of the population were between 0 and 14 years old; 68.85% were between 15 and 64 years of age and 9.8% were older than 64 years. Approximately 40% of the population live in rural areas and 60% in urban areas (National Institute of Statistics and Censuses, INEC, 2020c). According to the Human Development Index Report of 2019 prepared by the United Nations Development Program (UNDP) to measure the progress of a country and which shows the standard of living of its inhabitants, Costa Rica was in 68th place worldwide in 2018 (United Nations Development Program, UNDP, 2019).

Since the end of the last century, Costa Rica has faced serious problems with ensuring the safety of its citizens, and there have been social and political concerns about violence and crime. The latter has mainly been reflected in a steep increase in homicides per 100,000 inhabitants. In 1994, a major legal reform took place that increased imprisonment penalties for various crimes; for simple homicide, a prison sentence of 12–18 years was established, and for aggravated homicide the penalty was increased from 20 to 35 years. In addition, the maximum penalty of imprisonment to be imposed in Costa Rica was increased to 50 years, replacing the penalty of 25 years imprisonment in force since 1970. However, this reform did not produce the desired effect. On the contrary, there was an increase in homicide rates, observable in Figure 10.1.

This increase in homicides and in penalties of imprisonment is one of the reasons for the prison overcrowding that Costa Rica has suffered for approximately 20 years. Prison overcrowding has been characterised by an overpopulation of prisons, lack of infrastructure and poor conditions for the enforcement of sentences, leading to a critical overcrowding surpassing the maximum capacity of 120% allowed by the standards set in the United Nations Standard Minimum Rules for the Treatment of Prisoners and the recommendations of the European Committee on Criminal Problems.[1] At

DOI: 10.4324/9781003169178-10

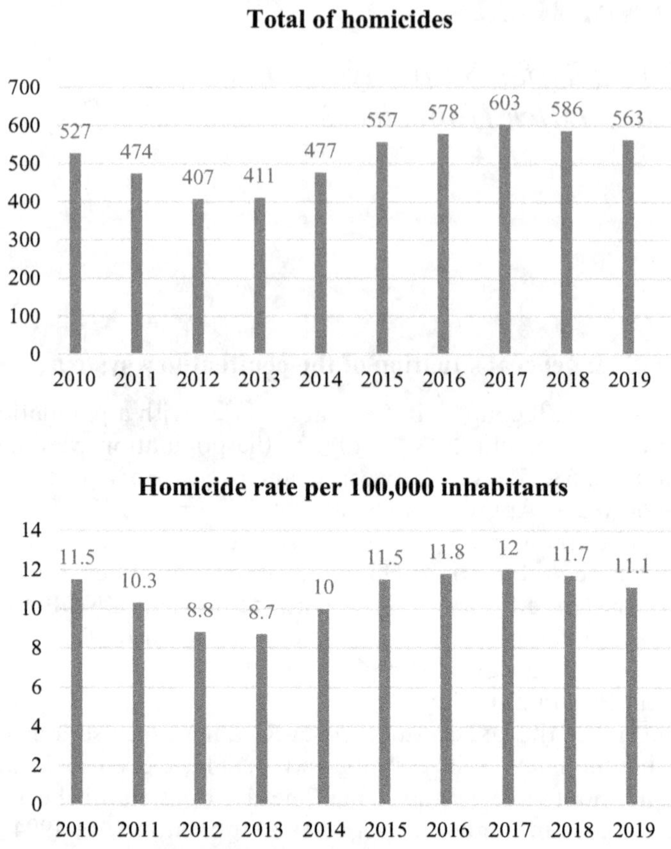

Figure 10.1 Homicide rates in Costa Rica.
Sources: Police Statistics of the Judicial Investigation Agency and Planning Department of the Judicial Branch Statistics Section and population estimates, INEC.

the beginning of 2020, according to the Ministry of Justice, the overcrowding reached approximately 130%.

In normal times, overcrowding results not only in overpopulation, but in conditions where hygiene cannot be maintained. Good hygiene is critical. Especially in the time of a pandemic, there should be adequate physical space for the prevention of infections, as well as for the treatment of infected prisoners. The development of prison overpopulation and overcrowding in Costa Rica can be seen in the following graph (Figure 10.2).

The prison system in Costa Rica is administered by the General Directorate of Social Adaptation, an institution belonging to the Ministry of Justice and Peace. It is responsible, as laid down in the law that established it and other legal provisions,[2] for the custody, location and technical assistance of

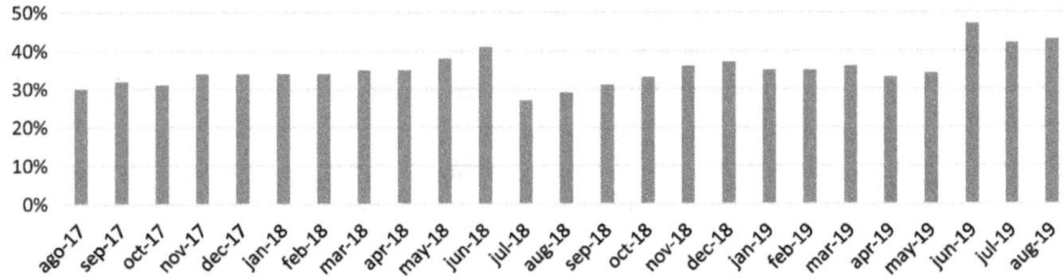

Figure 10.2 Prison overcrowding in Costa Rica.
Source: State of the Nation Program, 2020, with data from the Ministry of Justice and Peace.

people subject to penalties and custodial measures. Likewise, it is in charge of the care of those who benefit from alternative measures to replace imprisonment penalties, imposed by the National Institute of Criminology and by the judicial authorities.

According to official data from the Ministry of Justice, of which the latest is from 2017, the total population in prisons and under provisional judicial control was 36,173 persons, with a distribution of 33,491 men and 2,682 women.[3] The number of minors (under 18 years old) as of 29 October 2020 was 90 minors, 80 men and 10 women. For young adults, for the same date, 631 (46 women and 585 men) were subject to penalties of imprisonment.[4] The following chart demonstrates the historical development since 2007 of the adult population under judicial control, divided between men and women (Table 10.1).

Further relevant data that characterise the Costa Rican prison system is the prison population rate per 100,000 inhabitants, which has been increasing since 1979, as illustrated in Figure 10.3, where it is indicated that this rate for 2017 reached 395 prisoners per 100,000 inhabitants. This increase has not led to new facilities or an increase in the capacity of penal centres.

Sentenced persons are dealt with by four large programmes: An institutional programme, a semi-institutional programme, a community

Table 10.1 Distribution of the population in prisons and under other forms of judicial of control, according to sex, by years 2010–2017[5]

Gender	*2010*	*2012*	*2014*	*2016*	*2017*
Male	17,628	25,746	30,752	33,369	33,491
Female	1,315	1,909	2,330	2,552	2,682
Yearly Average	18,943	27,655	33,082	35,921	36,173

Source: Ministry of Justice and Peace, "Statistical Yearbook 2017", 2018: 38.

programme and a system for the juvenile prison population. The focus of attention, according to the Ministry of Justice and Peace, is oriented towards respect for human rights, as set out by the United Nations Standard Minimum Rules for the Treatment of Prisoners (the Nelson Mandela Rules, 2015). The priority areas that need to be addressed to alleviate the problems of the prison population are violence, drug addiction, community relations, legal matters, coexistence, health, training, work and education.[6]

The institutional capacity throughout the country to care for this population is made up of 12 institutional care centres, 11 semi-institutional care centres and 14 technical offices for the community programme. Specifically, for the care of the juvenile penal population, there are three centres: The Zurquí Formation Centre for minors (mixed boys and girls), the Specialized Young Adult Care Centre (for young persons who have reached the age of majority but who were sentenced in terms of the Juvenile Criminal Justice Law) and the Youth Opportunity Centre, in addition to the Alternative Sanctions Programme (non-custodial sanctions, for example, probation and community service).

2 Prison and penal policy concerning the execution of prison sentences during the COVID-19-induced crisis

The first case of the SARS-CoV-2 virus and the COVID-19 disease appeared in Costa Rica on 6 March 2020. Nine months passed in a period of pandemic that had grave consequences, not only in the field of health, but also in the economic and social spheres.[7] By 14 December, there were a total of 153,169 confirmed cases, 32,722 active cases, 237 in intensive care and 1,936 deaths related to the coronavirus, of which 1,208 were men and 728 women.[8]

The pandemic affects all levels and social strata, also prisons. The first cases of inmates infected with COVID-19 emerged in April 2020. Likewise, on that date, as will be detailed below, the first reactions emerged from the country's courts, which ordered important and urgent measures to ensure the health and safety of the entire prison population, due to the high risk that the pandemic posed in penal centres.

The judges ordered the Ministry of Justice and Peace to make extraordinary assessments of all prisoners who had risk factors for COVID-19. These were inmates with severe and acute health complications, as well as adults over 65 years of age and pregnant women or women with children in prison. On 17 April 2021, there were a total of 66 active cases in 19 prisons throughout the country. These active cases comprised 57 prisoners and nine officials. 19 prisoners had died and 3,539 had recovered. In the Zurqui Training Centre for minors, 20 inmates and one official had been infected by November 2020; none of them had died.

The Ministry of Justice and Peace had no explicit policy to systematically reduce the prison population and infection risks by releasing prisoners or not executing certain prison sentences. In Costa Rica, there is a lack of data on the number of prisoners released due to COVID-19, which must be very few. Therefore, there is no evidence of a decrease in prisoners in the penitentiary system since the pandemic first appeared in Costa Rica in March 2020. The same can be said of a reduction in the use of provisional imprisonment for these reasons. Since December 2020, prisons throughout the country have been gradually opened to family visits, complying with strict protocols, which are detailed below.

3 Restrictions of contact with the outside world

The main and first consequence of the pandemic for Costa Rica's prisons was to restrict contact with the outside world, particularly regarding visits. From 20 March 2020, four types of visits that are routinely used in all prisons in Costa Rica were restricted. *General visits*, which consist of a visit from family or friends, and which normally take place on Saturdays or Sundays; *special visits*, that is, permits granted to relatives or people who find it difficult or impossible to make a general weekend visit; *intimate or conjugal visits*, which offer the possibility to the inmate of contact between the prisoner and his or her partner; and *volunteer visits*, which are normally made by students, researchers, members of NGOs and churches, among other entities or groups. In addition, there was a prohibition on inter-prison visits, that is, visits that in some cases can be authorised between those prisoners (generally family members), who are in different penal centres.

A relevant restriction that was a result of the pandemic in prisons is the suspension of special exit permits. These permits create possibilities for inmates to participate in different activities outside the centre. Transfers to hospitals or medical centres were suspended, as a general rule, and medical complications had to be managed by the health resources of institutions. The latter was problematic, since these resources are limited, and some prisons do not even have medical staff (Chaves, 2020). Transfers to hospitals or medical centres were authorised exclusively in emergency cases, to reduce the chances of infection for prison staff and inmates.

One of the important restrictions on contact with the outside world was the suspension of most of the hearings or trials of a face-to-face nature, so that transfers or departures to the judicial authorities, courts, were also reduced. As a consequence, the Judiciary established a virtual hearing procedure from May.[9] In summary, the restrictions on contacts of those deprived of liberty with the outside world, during the pandemic and since 20 March 2020, were the following (Table 10.2):

Table 10.2 Suspensions of contact with the outside world (since 20 March 2020)

Penitentiary visit	*Special exit permits*	*Transfers to hospitals*	*Court hearings*
General, special, intimate, voluntary, intra-prison.	Extraordinary events or activities.	Except in emergency cases.	Preference for virtual hearings.

4 Restrictions inside prisons

All prisons in the country were affected by the pandemic. In practice from 20 March 2020, when the restriction on visits started, most of the prisons changed their rules of daily life and preventive measures were taken in order to reduce the chances of infection in prisons. The role of the Ministry of Health was also important, since in some cases it decreed quarantines for penal centres. This was either because of suspected or confirmed cases in the national prison system.

These changes in the routine in prisons were influenced by the overcrowded conditions suffered by most institutions. Overcrowding is exacerbated by the lack of infrastructure, and material and human resources to enable preventive measures to be put into practice to avoid infection. An example of inadequate infrastructure is that overcrowding makes it impossible to comply with a recommendation of physical distance between persons.

In Costa Rica, prisoners are not housed in single cells (except in cases of isolation), but in what is known as modules or collective spaces, where 20, 30, 50 or more people are accommodated. Prisoners who are in individual cells, are there for reasons of isolation or punishment, because of problems in their behaviour or because they pose a danger.

A number of complaints have pointed to the lack of adequate areas for the care of sick prisoners within prisons or even areas where such prisoners can be isolated to avoid future infections. Infrastructure deficiencies have forced the prison system to reorganise the limited physical space for either the care or isolation of prisoners with COVID-19. For example, classrooms have been set up as spaces for suspected cases of COVID-19. Spaces normally used for conjugal visits were also used for inmates with suspected or confirmed cases of COVID-19. An important effect of the pandemic, which resulted in significant restrictions for inmates, was the reduction of prison staff, whether due to being infected or suspected of being infected.

There have been restrictions regarding not only infrastructure or material resources, but also the lack of medical care in the prisons themselves. Not all penitentiary centres have health areas, nor do they have 24-hour medical facilities. Some prisons do not even have a health area or a doctor available 24 hours a day. The national media have criticised this situation and have confirmed that the Ministry of Justice and Peace has

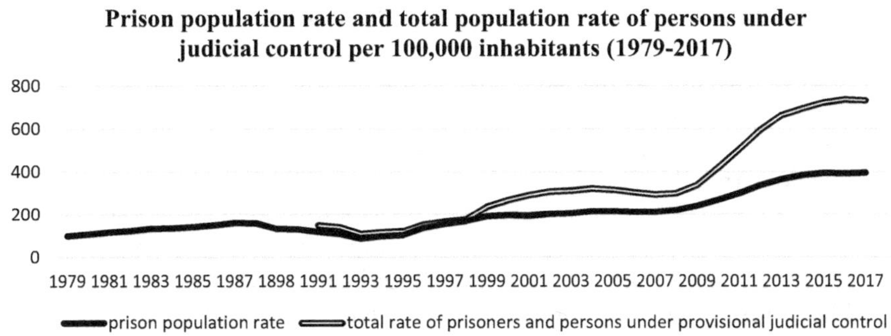

Figure 10.3 Prison population rate and the rate of persons under judicial control in Costa Rica.

Source: Ministry of Justice and Peace, Statistical Yearbook 2017, 2018: 27–29.[10]

only 24 doctors to attend to a population of approximately 16,000 inmates (Chaves, 2020).

All these deficiencies have forced the inmates themselves to create prevention committees, even to do cleaning and maintenance tasks, as well as to make their own masks. Recreational activities, cultural activities or activities with the participation of large groups in penal centres have also been restricted.

5 Compensatory measures

Some compensatory measures have also been applied in penal centres by the Ministry of Justice and Peace (Ministry of Health and Ministry of Justice and Peace, 2020). The first and most important was the installation of more public telephones in conjunction with more time for inmates to communicate with their families. Likewise, access to information and communication technologies was expanded. For example, in penal centres that house juveniles, video links or calls via the WhatsApp application were enabled.

In some prisons, some types of recreational activities among the same groups of inmates were encouraged during the week. Sinks equipped with soap and water were placed out of doors and instructive posters on the prevention and symptoms of COVID-19 were put up.

Another compensatory measure of great relevance for prisons in Costa Rica was that since 1 June, the hours for the reception of parcels[11] or provisions supplied by relatives or friends to prisoners were extended. This is very important, given the lack of supplies that inmates have, especially in this time of pandemic.

After the compensatory measures were adopted in penal centres in Costa Rica, there were changes regarding new conditions and requirements for visits.[12] Furthermore, there is a provision in the case of an increase in COVID-19 cases or the appearance of infections in centres that were previously virus-free; for the authorities to temporarily suspend visits. There are now a set of requirements and conditions, as described below:

- Only one visitor is allowed for each prisoner.
- The visitor must be between 18 and 64 years of age.
- The visit will have a maximum duration of one hour.
- People with babies or children in their arms will not be allowed to enter.
- Visits by people with risk factors or pregnant women are not allowed.
- The entry of people with visible respiratory conditions or with a temperature higher than 38 degrees will not be allowed.
- The admission protocols established by each penal centre must be complied with.

For prisoners who want to receive visitors, the new conditions are:

- The visitors cannot be people suspected of infection with COVID-19 or have been confirmed as positive cases (by a test) or be in a module with a health order or in isolation.
- The prisoner who has received a visit must bath when returning to their respective modules and wash the clothes that they used during the visit.

For both visitors and prisoners who want to receive visits, there are the following requirements:

- Not having restrictive health orders issued by the Ministry of Health.
- Respecting the physical distance of 1.8 meters at all times and in all spaces.
- Mandatory use of a mask throughout the visit, covering the nose and mouth without exception.
- Not consuming food during the time of the visit, or performing any action that requires removing the mask for other purposes.

6 Legal basis for restrictions and relaxations of the prison regime

Unfortunately, in Costa Rica, there is no specific penitentiary law that regulates all relationships between inmates and the administration; nor is it regulated by a special law for the rights and obligations of prisoners. The latter has been a constant source of legal conflicts, which are resolved through the Law on the Creation of the General Directorate of Social Adaptation (Law No. 4762, 1971). Conflicts are resolved by application of the norms of the Criminal Procedure Code of 1996 and the Penal Code of 1970.

It is important to note that for the resolution of conflicts related to the COVID-19 pandemic, selected judicial bodies[13] have played a fundamental role, issuing judgements, both for the restriction and for the validity of rights of those deprived of liberty. Likewise, the same Ministry of Justice and Peace, in charge of enforcement, issued relevant instruments. It also issued guidelines and was forced by the Constitutional Chamber to promulgate a Protocol of Care and Action for the COVID-19 pandemic.

In Costa Rica, as in many other countries, the enforcement of penalties is regulated by enforcement judges, where procedures are established for the resolution of conflicts within the prison environment. Since April 2020, different enforcement courts in different areas of the country have ordered the Ministry of Justice and Peace to carry out extraordinary assessments of all inmates who had risk factors for COVID-19. The enforcement courts ordered that all those inmates with severe complications be evaluated: Chronic kidney failure, heart disease, autoimmune disease, multiple sclerosis, immunosuppressed patients (HIV), prisoners with lung diseases, with cancer, hypertension, diabetes or morbid obesity.

It also ordered the evaluation of all adults over 65 years of age, pregnant women or women with children in the maternal-infant modules. This evaluation had to be done by the Ministry of Justice and Peace to consider transferring those who presented these complications because of their vulnerability to infection. However, the Ministry warned that not only health would be evaluated, but also other factors, such as good behaviour, not representing a risk to society, readiness to serve their sentence, having a short sentence and not awaiting judgement, and having family support (Loaiza, 2020). By 19 August 2020, 300 applications had been submitted from people with risk factors; of these, 180 prisoners were placed in institutional centres (Chaves, 2020).

Another of the judicial bodies that has been relevant in the pandemic has been the Constitutional Chamber.[14] Probably, its most important decision in this regard was issued on 29 May 2020, Decision No. 09738-2020 in which the Ministry of Justice and Peace was ordered to issue a protocol for COVID-19 care within the prison system, in accordance with the provisions of the World Health Organization guidelines for prisoners and detention centres (Table 10.3).

Table 10.3 COVID-19 care protocol in criminal centres. Minimum content (According to Decision No. 09738-2020)

Attention	Sufficient spaces in clinics and penal centres for the care of prisoners.
Beds	Sufficient number of beds to attend to suspects or infected persons.
Infrastructure	Implementation of field hospitals or other structures necessary for the isolation and treatment of suspected or positively tested prisoners.
Supplies	Supplies Protection and disinfection materials, for example: Masks, gloves, respirators, medicines, nursing staff and medical staff.

Note: This protocol corresponds to the General Guidelines for the management of COVID-19 in Penitentiary Centres within the framework of the Coronavirus health alert, prepared by the Ministry of Health in conjunction with the Ministry of Justice and Peace on 30 September 2020.

The Ministry of Justice and Peace also issued important instruments, guidelines and protocols to respond to the crisis generated by COVID-19 in the prison system. Examples of the above are the following:

- COVID-19 contingency plan dated 10 March 2020, which regulates the entry, location and restructuring of spaces for suspected cases of infected persons.
- Guidelines on the emergency situation facing the country due to COVID-19, dated 17 March 2020.
- General guidelines for the management of COVID-19 in Penitentiary Centres within the framework of the Coronavirus health alert, dated 30 September 2020.

7 Returning to normal

The return to normality, even at the national level, is not something that is clear to date, nor in prisons. The effects of the pandemic in Costa Rica have been very serious as regards the economic, social and educational spheres. According to the Continuous Employment Survey for the third quarter of 2020, the unemployment rate was 22.0%, an increase of 10.6% compared to the third quarter of 2019 (National Institute of Statistics and Censuses INEC, 2020a).

From the economic point of view, the pandemic also produced severe effects, according to the Monthly Economic Activity Index, national production in September 2020 fell by 7.1% (Central Bank of Costa Rica, 2020). The latter is reflected in thousands of closed commercial establishments, a serious decrease in consumption, a drop in exports, all of which has affected all the productive sectors of the country, especially the tourism sector with hotel closures and cancellation of reservations (Salas and Fernando, 2020).

In the educational field, the crisis of the pandemic forced the Ministry of Public Education (MEP) to suspend face-to-face classes and online lessons in schools. This measure taken by the Ministry came into effect on 17 March and schools would then resume after the half-year vacation period, which runs from 29 June to 10 July. However, the return to face-to-face teaching was not possible due to the increase in infections by COVID-19. After multiple postponements, the MEP announced on Thursday, 27 August 2020 that face-to-face classes would not resume until 2021. According to the MEP, as of July 2020, 57.8% of students have connections for online lessons in their homes (Ministry of Public Education, 2020).

In November 2020, Costa Rica was in one of the most complex phases of the pandemic, with a significant increase in cases every day, reaching thousands of daily infections, exceeding 120,000 cases in total and more than 1,500 deaths related to this virus.

The penitentiary system was practically isolated and the elaboration of protocols for a reopening, particularly of general visits, was hardly mentioned. Unfortunately, the situation in prisons has not been a priority and the penitentiary situation in Costa Rica has worsened with the pandemic.

Without a doubt, the pandemic has complicated and aggravated the difficult conditions in which those deprived of liberty find themselves in Costa Rica, both the elderly and minors. Unfortunately, there has not been a substitution, for example, of custodial sanctions by other sanctions, nor have anticipated lengths of sentences been decreased. Remedial or compensatory plans have been extremely weak. Only 180 prisoners out of 300 who made requests were transferred to semi-institutional centres. The response to this pandemic had to be focused mainly on guaranteeing the health and life of inmates and with a human development perspective. This was due to the decisive intervention of the Executive Power, the Legislative Power and the Judicial Power.

Notes

1 The Constitutional Chamber of the Supreme Court of Justice, in repeated votes, has recognised these conditions of overcrowding, including critical overcrowding. For example, in the recent vote of 25 August 2020, Vote No. 15892-2020.

2 Law N° 4762, 1971.

3 For the year 2020, specifically in the month of April, the population in the country's penitentiary centres reached about 16,353 prisoners. However, we have presented the official data found on the website of the Ministry of Justice and Peace, which are from the year 2017.

4 Ministry of Justice and Peace, 2020.

5 These data come from the latest official statistics of the Ministry of Justice of Costa Rica for the year 2017, published on the official site http://mjp.go.cr/Documento/Catalogo_DOCU/64 Table No 24 of the Department of Research and Statistics. These data differ from those published by the World Prison Brief where, for example, for the years 2010 and 2017 the number of prisoners was 12,110 and 19,226, respectively.

6 See the official website under www.mjp.go.cr.

7 According to data from the last National Household Survey (July 2020), carried out by the National Institute of Statistics and Censuses, in 2020 there are 1,529,255 poor inhabitants in the country, 321,874 more than in 2019. Poverty reached 26.2% and extreme poverty 7% (1.2 percentage points more than in 2019), see National Institute of Statistics and Censuses (INEC) (2020b).).

8 Ministry of Health, "National Situation Covid-19", data gathered from the official site https://www.ministeriodesalud.go.cr/index.php/centro-de-prensa/noticias/741-noticias-2020/1725-situacion-nacional-covid-19 on 2020.

9 Corte Plena in Session No. 27-2020, held on 18 May 2020, Article VII, approved the Protocol for the holding of oral hearings by technological means in criminal, misconduct, enforcement of sentence and juvenile criminal matters. Effective as of 21 May 2020, with its publication in Circular No. 102-2020.

10 According to the 2017 Annual Statistical Report of the Ministry of Justice and Peace of Costa Rica, this graph shows the entire population within said Ministry's programmes ("attended population") and the population in prison. The "entire population" category includes, in addition to the convicted and under-trial population, who are detained, the population that complies with alternative measures, suspension of the trial procedure and alimony debtors who have defaulted on the payment of an alimony according to Family Law. By 2017, the annual average of the "entire population under judicial control" was 36,173 people, which is broken down as follows: Convicted population (16,735), prosecuted (2,822), alimony debtors (297), population with suspension of the trial procedure (15,580) and population subject to alternative measures (740). See Table no. 8 in page 15 of the referred Annual Statistical Report, which sets out the breakdown of the entire population under judicial control in the programmes run by the Ministry of Justice and Peace.

11 In the Costa Rican penal system, it is very common for relatives to send prisoners hygiene, clothing and food items, which are called "encomiendas" (parcels).

12 Fiorella Salazar Rojas, Ministry of Justice and Peace, Interview on 15 December 2020.

13 The role of the Ombudsman's Office should also be mentioned in the area of reporting the conditions of those deprived of their liberty and requesting preventive measures to avoid COVID-19 infections.

14 Among other judgements, the following of the Constitutional Chamber that attend issues related to COVID-19 in prisons, referring to the conditions, visitation regime, hearings and the location of those deprived of their liberty can be pointed out: Judgement No. 14824-2020, No. 15892-2020, No. 07550-2020, No. 10755-2020, No. 20872-2020 and No 11603-2020; see the details in the reference list.

References

Central Bank of Costa Rica (BCCR) (2020): Monthly Index of Economic Activity. Department of Macroeconomic Statistics. Available at: https://gee.bccr.fi.cr/indicadoreseconomicos/.

Chaves, K. (2020): Justice has 24 doctors to treat 16,000 inmates. La Nación, 10 May 2020.

Loaiza, V. (2020). Inmates with risk factors for Coronavirus may be released from prison. La Nación, 22 April 2020.

Ministry of Health (2020): "National Situation Covid-19", data gathered from the official site https://www.ministeriodesalud.go.cr/index.php/centro-de-prensa/noticias/741-noticias-2020/1725-situacion-nacional-covid-19 on 2020.

Ministry of Health and Ministry of Justice and Peace (2020): LS-SI-006 General guidelines for the management of COVID-19 in Penitentiary Centers within the framework of the Coronavirus health alert, Fifth edition. September 30, 2020. https://www.ministeriodesalud.go.cr/sobre_ministerio/prensa/docs/ls_si_006_lineamientos_generales_manejo_COVID19_centros_penitenciarios_06092021.pdfMinistry of Justice and Peace (2020): Justice and Peace refines protocol that would open the general visit to prisons in December. Available at: https://www.mjp.go.cr/Comunicacion/Nota?nom=Justicia-y-Paz-afina-protocolo- that-would-open-the-general-visit-to-the-penal-centers-in-December.

Ministry of Public Education (2020): MEP announces no return to face-to-face classes during2020,27August2020.https://www.mep.go.cr/noticias/mep-anuncia-no-retorno-clases-presenciales-durante-2020.

National Institute of Statistics and Censuses (INEC) (2020a): Unemployment rate reached 22%. 5 November 2020. Available at: https://www.inec.go.cr/noticia/tasa-de-desempleo-llego-al-22.

National Institute of Statistics and Censuses (INEC) (2020b): National Household Survey July 2020. October 2020. Available at: https://www.inec.cr/sites/default/files/documetos-biblioteca-virtual/renaho2020.pdf

National Institute of Statistics and Censuses (INEC) (2020c): Demographic indicators 2018. November 2019. Available at: https://www.inec.cr/sites/default/files/documetos-biblioteca-virtual/repoblacevbid2018.pdf.

Salas, L. and Fernando, J. (2020): Tourists cancel reservations for 8,000 hotel nights in Costa Rica due to new coronavirus. La Nación [digital], 12 March, 2020. Available at: https://www.nacion.com/el-pais/salud/coronavirus-ocasiona-ya-mas-de-8000-cancelaciones/HAPRHEQBTZA4PHARIZTIUEXL7Y/story/.

United Nations Development Program (UNDP) (2019): Overview. Human Development Report 2019, 26.

Judicial resolutions

Constitutional Chamber of the Supreme Court of Justice. Vote No. 20872-2020 on 30 October 2020. Available at: https://nexuspj.poder-judicial.go.cr/document/sen-1-0007-1000813.

Constitutional Chamber of the Supreme Court of Justice. Vote No. 14824-2020 on 7 August 2020. Available at: https://nexuspj.poder-judicial.go.cr/document/sen-1-0007-988301.

Constitutional Chamber of the Supreme Court of Justice. Vote No. 15892-2020 on 25 August 2020. Available at: https://nexuspj.poder-judicial.go.cr/document/sen-1-0007-991571.

Constitutional Chamber of the Supreme Court of Justice. Vote No. 11603-2020 on 23 June 2020. Available at: https://nexuspj.poder-judicial.go.cr/document/sen-1-0007-981232.

Constitutional Chamber of the Supreme Court of Justice. Vote No. 10755-2020 on 12 June 2020. Available at: https://nexuspj.poder-judicial.go.cr/document/sen-1-0007-979411.

Constitutional Chamber of the Supreme Court of Justice. Vote No. 09738-2020 on 29 May 2020. Available at: https://nexuspj.poder-judicial.go.cr/document/sen-1-0007-977081.

Constitutional Chamber of the Supreme Court of Justice. Vote No. 07550-2020 on 17 April 2020. Available at: https://nexuspj.poder-judicial.go.cr/document/sen-1-0007-980911.

11 Croatia

Maja Munivrana and Elizabeta Ivičvić Karas

1 Introduction: general situation of the prison system

In Croatia, prison sentences are executed in penitentiaries and prisons, which are, along with juvenile correctional institutions and a Diagnostics Centre in Zagreb, organised within the Directorate for the Prison System and Probation, an administrative unit of the Ministry of Justice and Administration (Ministry of Justice) (Munivrana Vajda and Ivičević Karas, 2016, 209). Until 2014, overcrowding in the prison system was a major problem in Croatia, which was confirmed by several judgments of the European Court of Human Rights (ECtHR) finding violations of Article 3 of the European Convention of Human Rights (ECHR) due to inadequate living conditions (Cenbauer, 2006; Štitić, 2006; Longin, 2012, Lonić 2014; Muršić, 2016).[1] After 2014, however, the situation improved significantly. It is arguable that this was, at least in part, the result of penal policy efforts to strengthen the use of alternatives to imprisonment – suspended sentences and community service, as set out in the new Criminal Code of 2011 (CC), which entered into force on 1 January 2013. The reduction of overcrowding in prisons was also noted by the European Committee for the Prevention of Torture in its latest report from October 2018 (CPT Report, 2018, 20). Yet, according to the latest Government Report, in the period from 2015 to 2019, there was again a slight increase in the number of inmates during 2018 and 2019 as the result of the increase in the number of pre-trial prisoners, mainly in cases of illegal immigrants (Government Report, 2020, 9). Even though the current total number of inmates in the prison system is less than the existing accommodation capacity, there is a need for additional accommodation in high-security conditions (Government Report, 2020, 9). As the Ombudswoman pointed out, high-security penitentiaries, or some high-security units within prisons and penitentiaries, are occasionally still overcrowded by up to 175% of capacity (Ombudswoman's Report, 2020, 143).

At the beginning of the COVID-19 crisis in March 2020, the general situation in the prison system was relatively good, in that it did not suffer from overcrowding or any other major deficiency. In spite of that, the rapid development of events during the first wave of the pandemic was a shock to the

DOI: 10.4324/9781003169178-11

system. The first case of infection in the Republic of Croatia was recorded on 25 February 2020, and the Prime Minister announced the establishment of a National Civil Protection Headquarters (NCPH) headed by the Minister of Interior. As early as 19 March, the first lockdown was undertaken, but the gradual easing of restrictions began again on 27 April and had gone through several phases by the end of May 2020.

From June 2020 onwards, the Directorate occasionally reported some cases of infection with the COVID-19 virus among inmates, but until 10 December 2020, there were no reported deaths from the disease among inmates. Yet, the situation in the prison system, as well as in society as a whole, was much more difficult during the second wave of the pandemic, which began by the end of the summer of 2020. From the end of November 2020, it led to new measures of gradual and partial lockdown. There was a gradual slight easing of measures in early February, and a further easing from 1 March 2021, due to a smaller number of new infections on a daily basis. However, since mid-March 2021, the number of newly infected people has been growing again, leading to speculation about the beginning of the third wave of the pandemic, and consequently the third lockdown.

As regards the current situation in the prison system, according to the official data that the authors of this chapter obtained from the Directorate for the Prison System and Probation, on 12 March 2021, a total of 3,624 persons deprived of their liberty were accommodated in the prison system, of whom 34 were positive for COVID-19. Since the beginning of the SARS-CoV-2 disease, a total of 373 inmates were infected with COVID-19; 5,296 had been tested. On the same day, 95 inmates were isolated, in total 7,585 since the beginning of the pandemic, either because they had been in contact with an infected person or had just been admitted. Finally, the number of infected judicial police officers since the beginning of the pandemic was 321.

2 Prison and penal policy concerning the execution of prison sentences during the COVID-19-induced crisis

In April 2020, the Ministry of Justice, Directorate for Prison System and Probation informed Europris that it had regularly monitored the epidemiological situation and the risk of new coronavirus disease (SARS-CoV-2) since the beginning of February (Croatian Report to Europris, 2020). According to the Ministry, already then, even before the first known case of coronavirus infection was reported in Croatia, measures and activities aiming to protect the health of all persons deprived of their liberty and of prison staff had been taken, as recommended by the Croatian Institute of Public Health (CIPH) and the NCPH. These measures and activities included enhanced monitoring of the health of inmates, enhanced hygiene of persons and premises, additional provision of protective equipment to the health departments and the issuing of internal instructions for handling suspected coronavirus infection. The recommendations issued by the CIPH and the

NCPH in February and early March did not concern the prison system explicitly. The first and so far the only specific CIPH instructions regarding the prevention of the epidemic of coronavirus in the prison system were issued on 12 March 2020 and amended on 26 March 2020 (CIPH, 2020). Based on these instructions, as of 14 March 2020, the Directorate for the Prison System and Probation introduced and implemented in all correctional institutions a number of measures described in detail below (Croatian Judicial Police Syndicate, 2020). At the beginning of May, gradual easing of COVID-19 restrictive measures in different sectors of society took place. In the prison system, however, relaxation of measures started only at the end of May, when prison visits were reintroduced under certain strict conditions.[2] Whether other restrictions inside prisons were subsequently relaxed as well is not publicly known. In any case, prison visits were again generally prohibited on 21 October 2020 by Decision of the Minister of Justice, following a major increase of the registered cases of infection in Croatia during the second wave of the pandemic. Bearing in mind the rather exponential rise in the number of cases, it can only be assumed that the other restrictions regulating conduct in prison were also put in place, if they had ever been relaxed.

In addition to restricting a number of rights and benefits of inmates, the Ministry of Justice sought to adjust other prison and penal policies in order to reduce the number of inmates and consequently to avoid overcrowding. Already during the first wave, in March or in early April 2020, it recommended to the county, municipal and misdemeanour courts to extend the date for referring offenders for the enforcement of their prison sentences and for approving offenders' requests for postponement as well as inmates' requests for the suspension of the enforcement of their prison sentences, whenever possible (Croatian Report to Europris, 2020). According to the latest Ombudswoman's report, from the beginning of the application of the measures until 15 May 2020, 75 motions to suspend a sentence for the reason of COVID-19 were filed at the courts, of which only 12 were approved (Ombudswoman's report, 2021, 168). The same recommendation was issued again in late November 2020.[3]

During the first wave of the pandemic, the Assistant Minister of Justice also used her legal right to submit to the courts a request for suspension of the prison sentence for around 60 inmates (Croatian Report to Europris, 2020). As explained by the State Secretary of the Ministry of Justice, suspension was granted in cases of shorter, less severe prison sentences, wherever it was possible without jeopardising the security of others.[4] Finally, courts were instructed not to extend the measure of investigative imprisonment and to rely, as far as possible, on other precautionary measures. All these steps, according to the Assistant Minister of Justice in charge of the prison system, led to a significant reduction in the number of inmates – already on 25 March this number was reduced by 150, and on 17 April there were 370 fewer inmates in the system.[5] Interestingly, however, according to the SPACE 1 report, which analysed trends in European prison populations during the first nine months of 2020, the prison population in Croatia remained stable during the first wave of the pandemic without a significant decrease, with only 120 inmates fewer on 15 April (Aebi and Tiago, 2020, 23).[6]

The legal base of these measures was, however, questionable. The Execution of Prison Sentence Act from 1999, which was in force until mid-February 2021, that is both during the first and the second waves of the pandemic (EPSA,1999), enumerated the reasons justifying extension of enforcement of prison sentences (Articles 54(3) and 55 EPSA, 1999), and the Minister's recommendation was not grounded in one of them. Neither was the Assistant Minister's request for suspending the serving of a prison sentence (Article 155 EPSA, 1999). Furthermore, the Minister of Justice was not entitled by the EPSA, to request an extension of enforcement in the first place. Hence, it is not surprising that his recommendation to extend the date of referring offenders to the enforcement of the prison sentence caused confusion and was criticised by some judges as tampering with their judicial independence.[7] On 20 February 2021, an entirely new Execution of Prison Sentence Act (EPSA, 2021) entered into force, which introduced certain novelties into regulation of suspension of the prison sentence. According to the new law, the Director General (Assistant Minister of Justice) in charge of the prison system can request suspending the serving of the prison sentence because of a large-scale epidemic (Article 164(1) EPSA, 2021). Furthermore, the new law generally entitles the Minister of Justice to take other measures, not explicitly regulated by the law in extraordinary circumstances, such as a large-scale epidemic. These measures include, but are not limited to, changes in the organisation and manner of execution of a prison sentence (Article 21(5) EPSA, 2021).

Finally, what is striking about Croatian penal policies in the time of COVID-19 is the lack of any publicly available discourse or strategy on the use of alternative sanctions and of the probation service as a whole. Even if measures were taken to alleviate the impact of the COVID-19-induced crisis on probation services, this has not been communicated to the public. This is in stark contrast to the Council of Europe recommendation to "provid[e] transparent and regularly updated information to offenders and their families on the crisis situation, including explaining what steps are being taken and the reasons behind them" (Council of Europe, 2020).

3 Restrictions of contact with the outside world

Contacts with the outside world, in the form of receiving visits, are regulated on two levels: As a right of each inmate and as a benefit of more frequent contact that a prison governor may grant to an inmate, based on his or her success in an individual prison programme. In addition, the prison governor may grant an inmate an extraordinary (one-off) release for any of the reasons specified in the EPSA. Since the beginning of the COVID-19-induced crisis, all the use of all these forms of intervention has been significantly reduced. Rights to visits were first severely restricted from 14 March until 26 May,[8] and then again from 23 October 2020 onwards. While these restrictions were in force, a visit was granted only exceptionally, with the special permission of the prison governor, in situations such as the death of a family member or when the presence of a visitor was essential to protect the well-being of the inmate (e.g. to protect the rights of the prisoners in court proceedings or in other urgent and unforeseen cases). Furthermore, with respect to the first category, on 14 March, all activities of civil society organisations in correctional institutions were suspended (Croatian Report to Europris, 2020) and there is no information about whether these activities were resumed at any point, after the first lockdown, or not. Defence counsel could still visit pre-trial detainees, while maintaining physical distance.

Regarding the benefits of more frequent contacts with the outside world, from 14 March onwards, inmates were no longer granted the benefits of going out (prison leave) nor were they referred to work outside the correctional institutions. They were no longer taken to the courts, but video links were used instead in some cases, for example, at court hearings to decide on the abolition or extension of pre-trial detention (Croatian Report to Europris, 2020). Finally, special protocols were put in place for the receipt of packages for inmates.[9] Unfortunately, no information is publicly available as to whether these measures were formally abolished or adjusted between the first and the second waves of the pandemic and then reintroduced, or not.

4 Restrictions inside prisons

According to CIPH instructions from March 2020, group activities inside prisons had either to be cancelled or to be organised in a way that respected the rules of social distancing, so that there were no more than five persons in a group. Group activities should be held in the open whenever possible and otherwise in larger rooms that would allow a distance of two metres between people. Other daily activities had also to be organised in a manner that secured social distancing, e.g. only a maximum of five inmates should go outdoors at the same time (CIPH, 2020). There is no reliable information on how these instructions were implemented in practice and what the effect of the pandemic was on daily prison routines. Recently, a letter by an inmate was published, describing the situation in one of the major prisons in the country as chaotic. The inmate claimed, *inter alia*, that up to 50 inmates were allowed to go outdoors at the same time without wearing protective masks.[10] While in the spring already all prison staff were required to wear a protective mask and gloves,[11] it is not known when or whether inmates had to wear masks during their daily activities, since the general Decision on the obligatory use of protective masks did not apply to them. Yet, inmates were obliged to take all measures to prevent the spread of infectious diseases and to protect their health (Article 103(3) EPSA, 1999 and Article 110(6) EPSA, 2021) and failure to wear protective masks when necessary could result in disciplinary proceedings, since endangering somebody else's health deliberately or by gross negligence as well as resisting measures for the prevention of contagious diseases were and still are serious disciplinary offences (Article 145(3)(9) and (19) EPSA, 1999 and Article 153(3)(12) and (22) EPSA, 2021).

One important restriction inside prisons concerns newly admitted inmates. To ensure that they were not infected and contagious, all newly admitted inmates were housed in separate rooms of the correctional institutions, initially for at least 14 days; later, the duration of isolation in general was shortened to 10 days.[12] Breaching self-isolation is difficult to imagine within the prison system, but it is generally regulated by the Protection of the Population from the Infectious Disease Act (PPIDA) and punishable by a fine of approximately 1,000–2,000 euros (Article 76a PPIDA). In certain cases, it may even amount to the criminal offence of spreading a contagious disease (Article 180 CC), punishable by imprisonment. In September 2020, investigative imprisonment was ordered against one person, who, despite being infected, repeatedly breached the measure of self-isolation, thereby endangering others (Article 180 CC). He was placed in a special COVID-19 section of the Prison Hospital in Zagreb.[13]

5 Compensatory measures

In order to compensate for the restrictions described above and mitigate the negative psychological effects of these restrictions, inmates "were offered more frequent and longer telephone calls, and with the support of UNICEF, video visits were expanded and gradually made available to all prisoners" (convicted and on remand) (Croatian Report to Europris, 2020).

EPSA, 1999 provided for (audio) video conferencing exclusively in the context of judicial proceedings in which decisions on conditional release were made (Article 159 EPSA, 1999). Yet, reliance on video conferencing was already broadened in practice pre-pandemic, through the project "Unbroken Ties", carried out by UNICEF, the Ministry of Justice and a civil society organisation, STORK – Parents in Action in 2018 and 2019. This project enabled children not only to physically visit their incarcerated parents in a family-friendly setting, but, through the supply of necessary equipment and training of prison staff, also to have video contacts with incarcerated parents.[14] This possibility has now been extended to all inmates and other family members, first through CIPH recommendations,[15] and later by an explicit provision of the new law (Article 124(3) EPSA, 2021).[16] The number of video visits increased significantly in 2020, whereas in 2019 there were 300 video visits, organised in cooperation with UNICEF; during the first eight months of 2020, 2,663 video calls took place (Lukovečki, 2020). However, according to information received through informal conversations with judges of execution of prison sentences, some prisons lack the necessary equipment to provide effective alternatives to physical visits. Family members may visit an inmate twice a month and on holidays, for at least one hour, while minor children may visit their parent every week and on holidays (Article 117(1) and (2) EPSA, 1999, Article 124(1) and (2) EPSA2021).[17] Furthermore, according to Articles 124(1) and 125(1), (4) EPSA1999/Articles 131(1) and 132(1), (7) EPSA2021, inmates have the right to unrestricted correspondence by mail and phone calls in compliance with the rules of internal order, at their own expense. The fairness of charging inmates for the calls under these circumstances, when the calls serve *de facto* as the only compensatory measures, can be questioned.

6 Legal basis for restrictions and relaxations of the prison regime

The legal basis for restrictions and relaxation of the prison regime may be found in the general provisions of the EPSA1999 and the EPSA2021, which express the constitutional principle of proportionality (Ivičević Karas, 2016, 60–61). Thus, the rights of an inmate, prescribed by the EPSA, "may be restricted only exceptionally and if this is absolutely necessary in order to protect the order and security of the penitentiary or prison and the inmates themselves" (Article 3(3) EPSA1999/Article 4(3) EPSA2021). Any restriction of the fundamental rights of an inmate must be proportionate to the reasons for which it is applied (Article 3(4) EPSA1999/Article 4(4) EPSA2021). The power to make decisions on the restriction of certain rights of inmates is divided between the prison governor and the judge of the execution of sentences. Thus, for example, the governor may deny the inmate a visit or correspondence, but only for security reasons (Article 118(1) and 124(3) EPSA1999/Article 125(1) and 131(3) EPSA2021). Otherwise, an inmate may file a request for judicial protection with the judge of the execution of sentences against any action or decision by which an inmate is unlawfully deprived or restricted in a right prescribed by the EPSA (Article 17(1) EPSA1999/Article 19(1) EPSA2021). Although the described mechanism works well in principle, the problem is that it is intended for individual decisions in relation to individual inmates, and not for situations in which one decision, made for epidemiological reasons, would limit the rights of all prisoners in a particular institution. Moreover, EPSA1999 and EPSA2021 do not include epidemiological reasons among those for restricting certain rights of inmates.

From the beginning of the pandemic, restrictive measures were taken primarily under the PPIDA in relation to the general population, as well as for the prison system. Yet, given the specific and closed nature of the prison system, and the particular vulnerability of the prison population when it comes to possible risks of fundamental human rights violations, it would be more appropriate for the grounds for additional restrictions on prisoners' rights to be laid down in a basic legal act – EPSA.

The situation is even less clear when it comes to benefits, such as the benefit of more frequent and longer visits from family members, or the benefit of more frequently going out into the local community or to one's place of residence or domicile. These benefits were suspended from March 2020. The decision on benefits is made by the prison governor based on the assessment of the success of a particular inmate in the individual prison programme, and the denial of benefits is related only to disciplinary punishment of inmates, but not to security reasons or the need to protect inmates in case of epidemics. Since benefits are conceived as incentive measures and not as an inmate's right (Ivičević Karas, 2016, 46–48), no judicial control mechanism is envisaged. Therefore, the deprivation or limitation of benefits due to the COVID-19 pandemic has been in a legislative grey zone ever since March 2020.

In addition to judicial supervision, the execution of a prison sentence in the Croatian prison system is also subject to administrative supervision. Administrative supervision *stricto sensu*, as well as inspection as a form of supervision, is carried out by the Ministry of Justice. During the pandemic, and especially during the second wave, the Ministry only occasionally and partially published information on the situation in the prison system. There was an obvious and constant lack of complete and systematic informing of the public.

Finally, in Croatia, Parliamentary supervision is carried out by the Ombudswoman, who also serves in the National Preventive Mechanism for the Prevention of Torture. During the first wave of the pandemic, the Ombudswoman announced that she had "requested information from the Ministry of Justice on measures to protect persons deprived of their liberty and employees in the prison system from infection, and was collecting information from the criminal authorities on whether they had difficulties in implementing these measures" (Osigurati mjere prevencije, 2020). The Ombudswoman also supported replacing visits to inmates by using audio-visual devices (Trajno uvesti video posjete, 2020). However, especially during the second wave of the pandemic, the Ombudswoman was not visibly engaged in strengthening transparency by taking measures to protect everyone in the prison system, especially prisoners as a particularly vulnerable group.

7 Returning to normal

This analysis has shown that the Croatian prison system responded relatively successfully to the challenges of the first wave of the pandemic. This conclusion is supported by the fact that, on the one hand, the prison population was largely preserved from infection and there were no serious health consequences for inmates, while, on the other hand, relatively appropriate compensatory mechanisms were quickly established. However, although the reaction of the Ministry was not entirely systematic and transparent during the first wave either, these shortcomings came to the fore during the second wave of the pandemic that hit Croatia much harder at the end of the summer and persisted for months.

One of the main problems is the lack of an appropriate legal basis for taking measures that in various ways restrict or even deny different rights of prisoners, but also the benefits that prisoners earned. The lack of an appropriate legal basis also proved problematic when it came to measures aimed at reducing the number of pre-trial detention measures imposed, and those enabling the postponement or cessation of imprisonment during the pandemic, all in order to reduce the prison population and thus the risk of spreading the disease in the prison system. These issues are otherwise regulated in detail by the EPSA 1999 and the Criminal Procedure Act, in accordance with the fundamental constitutional principles of legality and proportionality. These two Acts, however, have not been subject to any legislative amendment since the beginning of the pandemic and they did not offer solutions to specific questions and needs that arose during the pandemic. Only recently, in February 2021, the Croatian Parliament adopted the new EPSA 2021, but the legislation now in force still does not address most of the highlighted problems related to the pandemic. The first step in creating a legacy for the future, in the event of possible future pandemics, would certainly be to create an appropriate legal basis for measures to combat the spread of infection in the prison system, which is in many ways specific and particularly risky.

Notes

1 In *Testa v. Croatia*, 2007 (see ECtHR, *Testa v. Croatia*, 20877/04, 12 July 2007), the ECtHR found a violation of Article 3 ECHR due to inadequate prison conditions in connection with the lack of necessary medical care and assistance; see in detail also the cases of the ECtHR of *Cenbauer v. Croatia*, 73786/01, 9 March 2006, *Štitić v. Croatia*, 29660/03, 8 November 2006, *Longin v. Croatia*, 49268/10, 6 November 2012, *Lonić v. Croatia*, 8067/12, 4 December 2014, *Lonić v. Croatia*, 8067/12, 4 December 2014, and *Muršić v. Croatia*, Grand Chamber, 7334/13, 20 October 2016.

2 The first phase of relaxation in the prison system was announced in news section of the official website of the Ministry of Justice on 23 May 2020, https://pravosudje.gov.hr/vijesti/prva-faza-ublazavanja-mjera-u-zatvorskom-sustavu/21970 (10 December 2020).

3 The information became known only through the media and is not available on the website of the Ministry of Justice; see e.g. Jutarnji list, Preporuka Ministra, 27 November 2020, https://www.jutarnji.hr/vijesti/hrvatska/ako-bas-ne-morate-ne-saljite-osudenike-u-zatvor-sucima-iz-ministarstva-stigao-neobican-dopis-15010076 (10 December 2020).

4 The statement was made on the occasion of presenting the draft of the new Execution of Prison Sentence Act to the members of the Parliament on 25 March 2020, https://pravosudje.gov.hr/vijesti/prijedlog-novog-zakona-o-izvrsavanju-kazne-zatvora-i-stanje-glede-covid-19-u-zatvorima-pred-saborom/21723 (10 May 2020).

5 *Ibid.*

6 On 27 November 2020, Croatian media reported that the number of inmates grew again and reached 3,586, https://www.rtl.hr/vijesti-hr/novosti/hrvatska/3934534/rtl-otkriva-ministar-pravosudja-poslao-sucima-preporuku-da-ako-bas-ne-moraju-ne-salju-osudjenike-u-zatvor/ (10 December 2020).

7 Some judges denied its legal relevance while at the same time, based on the Minister's recommendation one prison refused to accept one convicted person who initiated enforcement of his prison sentence, https://www.jutarnji.hr/vijesti/hrvatska/ako-bas-ne-morate-ne-saljite-osudenike-u-zatvor-sucima-iz-ministarstva-stigao-neobican-dopis-15010076 (10 December 2020).

8 In-between visits were generally allowed, but certain limitations in terms of maximum number of visitors, strict disinfection and prohibition of physical contact remained in place.
9 The Croatian Report to Europris does not specify the content of these protocols.
10 Jutarnji list, Pismo iz Remetinca, 11 November 2020, https://www.jutarnji.hr/vijesti/crna-kronika/uprava-krije-kakva-je-situacija-s-koronom-policajci-su-na-rubu-snaga-nema-lijekova-15002228 (10 December 2020).
11 Linen masks have been sewed by female inmates in Požega and distributed not just to prison staff, but to inmates as well, The interview with Assistant Minister of Justice, 17 April 2020, https://pravosudje.gov.hr/vijesti/pomocnica-spero-za-rtl-danas-o-stanju-u-zatvorima-glede-covid-19/21815 (10 May 2020).
12 CIPH revised the recommendations on 27 October 2020, https://dnevnik.hr/vijesti/koronavirus/hzjz-revidirao-preporuke-samoizolacija-skracena-s-14-na-deset-dana---625694.html (10 December 2020).
13 See the official website of the Ministry of Justice, news of 18 September 2020, https://pravosudje.gov.hr/vijesti/u-istrazni-zatvor-zaprimljena-prva-covid-19-pozitivna-osoba/24180 (10 December 2020).
14 For more information about this project, visit https://www.unicef.org/croatia/mediji/videopozivi-i-prostori-za-posjete-u-zatvorima-prilago%C4%91eni-djeci (10 May 2020).
15 CIPH instructions explicitly named "persons of priority" – spouse/partners, parents and family members.
16 EPSA2021 further extended the possibility of audio-video conferencing to all communication with judicial and administrative bodies (Article 188 EPSA2021).
17 Ordinarily, other persons may also visit inmates, but only upon the authorisation of the prison governor. For security reasons, the prison governor may deny a visit, and the visit can be monitored, with exception of the attorney's visit (Munivrana Vajda, Ivičević Karas, 2016, 211).

References

Aebi, M.F. and Tiago, M. (2020): *Prisons and Prisoners in Europe in Pandemic Times: An Evaluation of the Medium-Term Impact of the COVID-19 on Prison Populations*, https://wp.unil.ch/space/files/2020/11/Prisons-and-the-COVID-19_2nd-Publication_201109.pdf (10 December 2020).

Council of Europe (2018): Report to the Croatian Government on the Visit to Croatia Carried Out by the European Committee for the Prevention of Torture and Inhuman or Degrading Treatment or Punishment (CPT) from 14 to 22 March 2017 - CPT Report 2018, 2 October 2018, https://rm.coe.int/16808e2a0e (21 May 2020). Strasbourg: Council of Europe.

Council of Europe (2020): *Follow-up Covid-19 Related Statement by the Council for Penological Co-Operation Working Group (PC-CP WG)*, 14 October 2020, https://rm.coe.int/pc-cp-2020-10-e-rev-follow-up-to-pc-cp-wg-statement-covid-19/16809ff484 (10 December 2020).

Croatian Judicial Police Syndicate (2020): *News of 13 March 2020*, https://www.spph.hr/privremenu-zabranu-pogodnosti-izlaska-i-posjeta-zatvorenicima/ (20 May 2020).

Croatian Report, *Measures and Activities in a Prison System aimed at the Prevention of Spread Of Coronavirus* (Croatian Report to Europris), last updated on 22 April 2020, https://www.europris.org/wp-content/uploads/2020/04/Covid-19-measures-and-activities-Croatia.pdf (20 May 2020).

Execution of Prison Sentence Act (EPSA1999). Official Gazette 128/99, 55/00, 59/00, 129/00, 59/01, 67/01, 11/02, 190/03, 76/07, 27/08, 83/09, 18/11, 48/11,125/11, 56/13, 150/13, 98/19.

Execution of Prison Sentence Act (EPSA, 2021): Official Gazette 14/21.

Hrvatski zavod za javno zdravstvo, Postupnik /upute za sprječavanje i suzbijanje epidemije korona virusom (covid-19) u tijelima zatvorskog sustava (kaznionice, zatvori, odgojni zavodi, centri), Zagreb, 26 March 2020, (CIPH, 2020).

Ivičević Karas, E. (2016): *Penitencijarno pravo*. Zagreb: Narodne novine.

Izvješće o stanju i radu kaznionica, zatvora i odgojnih zavoda za 2019. godinu, Vlada Republike Hrvatske, Zagreb, rujan 2020 (Government Report, 2020), https://mpu.gov.hr/pristup-informacijama-6341/izvjesca-24343/izvjesca-ministarstva-pravosudja/24355 (17 March 2021).

Lukovečki, M. (2020): *Impact of COVID-19 on the Use of Technology During and After the Crisis*, https://www.europris.org/wp-content/uploads/2020/10/Impact-of-Covid-19-on-ICT-2020-Marjan-Lukaveci-23092020.pdf (15 December 2020).

Munivrana Vajda, M. and Ivičević Karas, E. (2016): *International Encyclopaedia of Laws, Criminal Law – Suppl. 57, Croatia*. Wolters Kluwer.

Ombudswoman's Report (2020): Report 2019. Zagreb, https://www.ombudsman.hr/wp-content/uploads/2020/03/Izvje%C5%A1%C4%87e-pu%C4%8Dke-pravobraniteljice-za-2019.pdf (21 May 2020).

Ombudswoman's Report (2021): Report 2020. Zagreb, https://www.ombudsman.hr/hr/download/izvjesce-pucke-pravobraniteljice-za-2020-godinu/?wpdmdl=10845&refresh=6051fe745ccad1615986292 (17 March 2021).

Osigurati mjere prevencije i u zatvorskom sustavu (2020): Official website of the Ombudsman, https://www.ombudsman.hr/hr/osigurati-mjere-prevencije-sirenja-epidemije-i-unutar-zatvorskog-sustava/ (21 May 2020).

Protection of the Population from the Infectious Disease Act (2020): Official Gazette 79/07, 113/08, 43/09, 130/17, 114/18, 47/20, 134/20.

Trajno uvesti video posjete za sve zatvorenike, official website of the Ombudsman, https://www.ombudsman.hr/hr/trajno-uvesti-video-posjete-za-sve-zatvorenike/ (12 December 2020).

12 Czech Republic

Helena Válková and Jana Hulmáková

1 Introduction – general situation of the prison system in the Czech Republic

One of the basic and long-term problems of Czech criminal and sanctions policy even before the COVID-19 pandemic was the large prison population of the Czech Republic. According to the World Prison Brief database,[1] the Czech prison population rates ranked in the top ten in Europe, both before the pandemic and at the end of 2020. After 2009, high per-capita numbers of prisoners in the Czech Republic persisted, with the exception of a significant decline in 2013 which was mainly related to the presidential amnesty. After that, the prisons filled up again relatively quickly. Since 2017, a gradual but not very significant decrease in prisoners occurred, which can be attributed to a general decrease in the number of convicted persons in 2017–2018, in the context of a decrease in registered crime in the Czech Republic (Diblíková et al., 2019). At the end of 2020, i.e. during the second wave of the pandemic, a more significant decline in the prison population is evident, both in absolute numbers and in terms of population (see Figure 12.1).

The problem is mainly the number of persons serving prison terms, as the numbers of persons in custody are not very high and have been declining since 2014. In 2019, the share of persons in custody out of the total number of persons in prisons was less than 9%. Although the number of people in

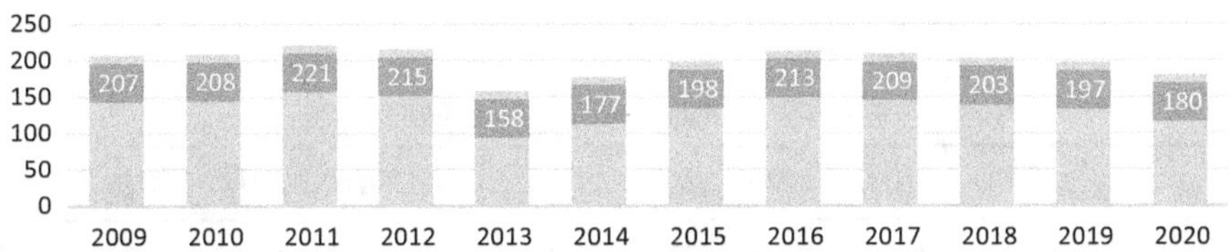

Figure 12.1 Number of prisoners in the Czech Republic per 100,000 of the national population[2] by 31 December of the respective year.

Source: Statistical Yearbooks of the Prison Service of the Czech Republic, The Prison Service of the Czech Republic, available at: https://www.vscr.cz/sekce/statisticke-rocenky-vezenske-sluzby Population per age categories, The Czech Statistical Office.

DOI: 10.4324/9781003169178-12

preventive detention is gradually increasing, it still forms a small share of the prison population: e.g. in 2019, it was only 0.4% (Hulmáková, 2020).

Court statistics[3] suggest that the primary problem is not that courts increasingly impose sentences of unconditional imprisonment. The share of unconditional imprisonment as the main sanction[4] has been between 15 and 16% since 2015. The imposition of unconditional punishments is strongly influenced by the almost two-thirds share of recidivists in the total number of convicted persons (for more details, see Hulmáková, 2020).

The main reasons for the high number of prisoners include the imposition of long prison sentences, the repeated imposition of alternative sentences, especially conditional sentences of imprisonment, and their subsequent conversion, and the execution of such aggregated unconditional suspended sentences (Supreme Public Prosecutor's Office, Institute of State and Law of the Academy of Sciences of the Czech Republic, 2019). The limited use of conditional release is another reason. Its use is limited by relatively strict legal conditions for its application, and probably also because judicial practice often looks at conditional release as a "reward" for low- and medium-risk offenders. Unfortunately, it is not perceived by a criminal practice as an instrument that should be used routinely as a means of treating prisoners serving a sentence and helping their reintegration, i.e. wherever the release of a prisoner is not associated with a significant risk to society.

Between 2009 and 2012, the share of conditional releases in the total number of processed applications ranged from 39 to 42%. In 2013, there was again a significant decrease due to an amnesty. In the years 2013–2019, this share ranged between 25 and 31%. Possible reasons for that include both direct and indirect effects of the amnesty,[5] which show up over a longer time span (Vicherek, 2018). The situation did not change significantly even in 2019, when the share of released prisoners was 31.4% of the total number of the processed applications, although the absolute numbers of conditional releases increased.

The large numbers of the prison population thus significantly affect the conditions of imprisonment (Wooldredge and Smith, 2019). One such indicator is the overcrowding of prisons (van Zyl Smit and Snacken, 2011). As can be seen from Table 12.1, for most of the period under review, except for the short post-amnesty period in 2013, it was impossible to ensure that every

Table 12.1 Average occupancy of prison and jail capacity

Year	*2010*	*2011*	*2012*	*2013*	*2014*	*2015*	*2016*	*2017*	*2018*	*2019*
Occupancy %	111.1	114.3	111.6	77.7	86.6	97.9	106.3	108.3	104.2	103.4

Source: Statistical Yearbooks of the Prison Service of the Czech Republic, Prison Service of the Czech Republic, available at: https://www.vscr.cz/sekce/statisticke-rocenky-vezenske-sluzby.

prisoner had at least 4 m^2 of living space (§17 para. 6 of Decree No. 345/1999 Coll. of Laws, Rules of Execution of Sentences of Imprisonment), which is in conflict with Articles 18 (3) and 18 (4) of the European Prison Rules.[6] At present, the situation has improved: On 31 December 2020, 96.7% of the total prison and jail capacity was being used (82.1% in pre-trial jails and 98.3% in prisons). However, there are also prisons with an occupancy rate of between 108 and 114%, and, in one case, even 121.9%.[7]

The high numbers of prisoners and other issues of sanction policy in the Czech Republic, such as the low effectiveness of criminal sanctions, especially sentences of unconditional imprisonment, or problems with the availability of adequate post-penitentiary care, even in pre-pandemic times, have led to attempts to change this situation, be it by setting new priorities for application practice or by legislative changes (Válková, 2020).

The initiative for a more pronounced change in sanction policy manifested itself during the recodification of substantive criminal law, which culminated in the adoption of the new Criminal Code (CC) in 2010, effective from 1 January 2010, in particular the introduction of house arrest.[8] Unfortunately, the desired change did not occur. On the contrary, both the number of unconditional sentences and their share of all sanctions increased, while, at the same time, the share of unconditional sentences of one to five years increased, too (Scheinost et al., 2015). In 2013, there was a reduction in the number and share of unconditional sentences, both in connection with the amnesty and due to the easing of punishment for some frequently occurring offences – a result of the amended CC. Then again, there was an increase in the number of unconditional sentences, which, however, has stabilised since 2015.

The year 2019 was special in that it was the first full year in which the electronic monitoring system (EMS) was applied nationwide to enforce home detention. Until then, this system was employed rather rarely (its share of all main sanctions was only 0.2%). Even in 2019 their numbers remained very low and its share of the sanctions imposed as the main punishments remained unchanged. This situation was also caused by problems faced by the EMS supplier (Bíba, 2020). Unfortunately, problems with the producer of EMDs may hamper its more frequent application in the future.

In the few years up to the pandemic, efforts were made by the professional community to change the current situation, resulting in amendments to the CC, e.g. mitigation of certain sentences in the field of property and economic crime and the easing of the terms for conditional release, in effect since 1 October 2020. At the same time, even before the pandemic, since 2017 the Supreme Public Prosecutor's Office and the Supreme Court of the Czech Republic stepped up efforts to provide methodological training to lower-level public prosecutor's offices and courts, with the emphasis on the wider application of fines, for instance, accompanied by certain changes to the relevant legislation in Hulmáková (2020).

2 Prison and penal policy on the execution of prison sentences during the COVID-19-induced crisis

Taking a closer look at the changes in the numbers of prisoners before the first wave of the pandemic, i.e. at the beginning of 2020 and onwards, it should be noted that, compared with the previous year, there was a relatively significant reduction in the prison population (see Figure 12.2), both in jail (pre-trial detention cases) and in prison (unconditional sentences of imprisonment). While in 2019 the number dropped by 575 prisoners, in 2020 the number dropped by 1,835. At the same time, compared to 2019, there was a significant year-on-year decrease in the number of both persons in pre-trial detention and of those serving unconditional prison sentences.

Figures available from the Prison Service indicate that the courts are ordering the execution of unconditional sentences less frequently than in the same period of the previous year, because the number of people beginning their prison terms has gone down: In April 2020 (first wave), there were a total of 592 people, while in April 2019 there were 919. Similarly, at the peak of the second wave of the pandemic in the Czech Republic in November 2020, a total of 694 people entered prisons, while in the same period in 2019 there were 959.[9]

Here, informal management tools proved to be very effective, such as briefings for the presidents of regional courts organised by the Ministry of Justice, methodological seminars and internal recommendations of the Supreme Public Prosecutor's Office to lower-level public prosecutors, and the Supreme Court's recommendation for courts to consider carefully before ordering the execution of unconditional sentences of imprisonment. Also, the need for conditional release to be applied in appropriate cases was emphasised at all levels.

Although the available court statistics show an increase in the number of conditional releases, the overall increase, compared with the year before, is not very significant (see Table 12.2). However, the overall lower number of prisoners in 2020 needs to be taken into account.

The system of so-called "early conditional release"[10] also saw a wider application in 2020. The Government Commissioner for Human Rights, in her turn, used the authority of her office to address the General Director

	at 31. 1.	at 28.2. (29.1.)	at 31. 3.	at 30. 4.	at 31. 5.	at 30.6	at 31.7.	at 31.8.	at 30. 9.	at 31.10.	at 30.11.	at 31.12
2019	21,623	21,638	21,685	21,666	21,672	21,601	21,428	21,350	21,227	21,207	21,232	21048
2020	21,121	21,192	21,062	20,770	20,320	20,212	20,133	19,992	19,859	19,763	19,557	19286

Figure 12.2 Prisoners in absolute numbers by month in the years 2019 and 2020.
Source: Monthly Statistical Reports, The Prison Service of the Czech Republic.

Table 12.2 Quarterly comparison of conditional releases in 2019 vs. 2020

2019				
	Qr. I	Qr. II	Qr. III	Qr. IV
Conditional releases in abs. numbers	707	752	784	774
Approved applications in %	32.1	30.8	30.4	31.9
2020				
Conditional releases in abs. numbers	666	893	726	893
Approved applications in %	31.2	32.6	30.9	36

Source: Courts Statistics, CSLAV database, Ministry of Justice.

of the Czech Prison Service in a letter of April 2020 with a request to encourage prison directors to endorse, where reasonable and appropriate inmates' requests for conditional release, or even come up with conditional release applications on their own initiative. The Prison Service responded with a seminar at which prison directors were lectured on the procedures of "premature" conditional release application and its submission. An internal memorandum of the Prison Service says that, while previously this instrument was used very rarely, in the period between 1 April 2020 and 31 December 2020 alone, prison directors produced 230 requests for "premature conditional release", something that may mean a new lease of life for this exceptional instrument. Statistical data on premature conditional release requests from inmates endorsed by prison directors are not yet available.

It should be noted, however, that pandemic-related restrictions on the movement of persons and their contacts, i.e. measures not directly related to changes in criminal and sanction policy, must have been a factor. According to the Czech Police, there was a significant decrease in registered crimes in 2020, compared to 2019,[11] and according to statistics from public prosecutors and courts,[12] there was also a considerable decrease in convictions as well as in the number of unconditional sentences – by 934. However, their share of all main sanctions has not changed, as is the case with home detention. In the last quarter of 2020, the changes in the CC, effective from 1 October 2020, consisting in decriminalisation of property crimes and which facilitated the release of low-risk convicts, may to some extent have projected themselves in this development too. However, neither statistics on this, nor any specification of the released persons, is available.

Other members of the Czech legal community, too, raised the issue of the high risk of prisons being vulnerable to the widespread of the coronavirus. As early as 27 March 2020, Petr Toman, lawyer and member of the presidium of the Czech Union of Barristers, sent a petition to the President of the Czech Republic. He appealed for the president to declare an amnesty[13] and pardon prisoners serving short sentences, which would be both a show of presidential mercy and a contribution to the country's anti-pandemic effort.

However, the president did not declare any amnesty and a number of experts, including some lawyers, agreed, as they drew attention to the risks associated with the release of people who often have neither accommodation nor jobs. This would increase the number of homeless or people in other types of social facilities (hostels, etc.), which could paradoxically have the opposite effect, i.e. the further spread of the COVID-19 infection outside prisons.

The Association of Organisations in the Field of Prisons also voiced its serious concern about the situation in prisons. In Spring 2020, the Association, an umbrella body of 17 Czech non-profit non-governmental bodies facilitating the resocialisation of former prisoners, raised an appeal on 2 April 2020, calling on the prime minister and his government to pay greater attention to the overcrowded prisons: At the time, there were some 21,000 persons in prisons, almost 1,000 of them were over 60; cells were accommodating 10 persons per cell, a number of prisoners were suffering from chronic illnesses making them extremely vulnerable to the infection.

As for the tightening up of punishments for offences committed during the state of emergency, it is possible – because of the aggravating circumstances of a crisis – to impose stiffer and longer punishments, and to bring criminal charges against a person violating quarantine restrictions in a manner which can cause the introduction and/or spread of COVID-19. This ensues from the government decree on the updated list of contagious human diseases, in effect since 13 March 2020. No further criminalising of breaches of valid restrictions has happened so far; less serious offences of this nature are mostly punished by sanctions under administrative law.

3–5 The situation and conditions in Czech prisons after the outbreak of the pandemic – restrictions of contact with the outside world, inside prisons, and compensatory measures

The first cases of the COVID-19 infection were detected in the Czech Republic (population 10,721,000) at the turn of February and March 2020. The first lockdown was approved by the Czech Parliament on 12 March 2020 and lasted until 17 May 2020. The country's response to the first wave of the pandemic was consistent and allowed the government to keep the spread of the disease under control through to early summer 2020. After June 2020, all restrictions were gradually lifted (such as wearing compulsory face coverings in public places, in shops and other closed spaces, restrictions on the attendance of public gatherings, sports, and cultural events). Note that the first case of an infected prisoner was not officially recorded until the end of August 2020 and was officially confirmed on 2 September 2020. Until then, the Prison Service had repeatedly stated that there were no COVID-19 cases in its prisons.[14]

Then, during September 2020, the situation in the country deteriorated severely. The number of infections soared dramatically and escalated at the end of 2020. This trend remained unchanged in the first two months of 2021 (e.g. 23 December 2020 recorded a daily increase of 14,054 cases; by 30 December, there were as many as 16,939 cases per day, while in January and February 2021, the number of cases rose to as many as 12,000 daily). At the beginning of 2021, the Czech Republic thus found itself among the worst affected in Europe with the worst COVID-19 balance of patients and victims.

Of course, prisons could not escape. In November 2020, the infection spread quite widely among inmates in some prisons (e.g. in Ostrava-Heřmanice and Valdice). This development broke into the public domain and was covered extensively by Czech Radio, Czech TV, and online (iDnes.cz, novinky.cz, seznam, cz, blesk.cz).

The Prison Service failed to acknowledge publicly the spread of infection in its correctional facilities, and did not request nationwide COVID-19 tests or the vaccination of prisoners. The prisoners themselves raised the issue by sending written appeals, making phone calls, seeking help from some non-governmental non-profit organisations, addressing MP's and the government's Human Rights Commissioner with warnings not to underestimate the situation and to take action.

However, it should be noted that, as far back as spring 2020, the Prison Service introduced, and later improved and tightened up, a whole system of hygienic preventive measures and procedures[15] aimed to avert the spread of COVID-19 in prisons. Among the toughest was, with respect to the actual epidemiological situation, a ban on inmate visits, which then was gradually eased in the summer months and later reintroduced in autumn. The ban on visits by close relatives was offset by the possibility of communication via Skype and by the introduction of pilot projects of "electronic implementation of convicts' rights".[16]

During the second wave of the pandemic, some prisons temporarily suspended one-hour daily exercise for prisoners outside their cells, something which violates the law on the execution of sentences of the deprivation of liberty. Those prisons were duly notified about the violations by the Prison Service of the Czech Republic and by the Human Rights Commissioner.

By 14 December 2020, the official number of inmates with COVID-19 stood at 560, while 819 had recovered by the same date.[17] Some prisons were hit even harder, e.g. Mirov, a maximum security facility for those serving long-term sentences, 20–30 years, up to life, that is, a facility with the highest degree of isolation.[18] In January 2021, the media reported a similar problem in the prison in the city of Pardubice, where the number of cases among inmates was estimated at 200. In February 2021, the highest numbers of the infected were recorded in the prisons in Horní Slavkov, Stráž pod Ralskem, and Odolov.

There are certain irregularities in statistics on the infected prisoners.[19] For instance, on 15 December 2020, there allegedly were 560 infected inmates in the Czech prisons; by 3 February 2021, the number was cited as 1,214. However, within the next 13 days, i.e. on 16 February 2021, that number is reported to have dropped to a "mere" 446. Such fluctuations are a bit too marked to be called a mishap or a statistical error.

However, politically sensitive this matter can be, despite the current dearth of the vaccine even for the most vulnerable segments of the population, the Ministry of Justice ought to exert maximum efforts to prepare for a situation when inmates, like people in social care institutions (e.g. those for seniors), will have to be given vaccines as a matter of high priority. This is necessary because those afflicted prisons are already overpopulated. Unfortunately, neither the Ministry of Justice nor the Prison Service has yet displayed any noticeable activity in this direction.

As for the health system in prisons, the Ministry of Justice did not make enough improvements to face the second wave of the pandemic, especially as regards the lingering problem of insufficient medical staff. Two prisons operate their own COVID-19 centres: one in Prague, the other in Brno; neither though has lung ventilators. Serious cases therefore have to be taken to the Military Hospitals in Prague or in Brno.

The prison food has not been enriched with the required vitamin supplements. Given their meagre budget (some three Euros per prisoner per day), catering facilities, though improved to an extent, could hardly do much in terms of ensuring food with a higher nutritious value at the time of the pandemic.

Likewise, the conversion of unconditional prison sentences to home detention is still held back by the lack of devices and because of a dispute with the supplier of EMDs. In addition, the legal framework of electronic monitoring, especially with a view to home detention, is not optimal and needs to be better adapted to actual practice.

6 Legal basis for restrictions and relaxations of the prison regime

The basic rights and obligations of prisoners in the Czech Republic are codified primarily in Act No. 169/1999 Coll. on the Execution of Sentences of the Deprivation of Liberty. These rights may be restricted only exceptionally, e.g. upon the imposition of a state of emergency declared in accordance with the Constitutional Law on the Security of the Czech Republic. The first state of emergency due to the COVID-19 pandemic in the Czech Republic was declared for the period March to May 2020 and then for the period October 2020 to February 2021. The Prison Service of the Czech Republic adopted a number of restrictive measures tailored to the specific conditions of the prison environment. Their framework is set out in internal Regulation No. 4/2020 on procedures in case of increased incidence of infectious diseases in the Prison Service of the Czech Republic (hereinafter the Regulation), which was adopted on 19 March 2020, i.e. at the beginning of the first wave. It is still in force.

In the course of 2020, the Prison Service adopted 63 internal measures specifically regulating individual restrictions, such as a ban and/or restrictions on visits and outside exercise, the disinfection of prison premises, and the use of Skype.[20]

Checks of compliance with restrictive measures in prisons are carried out by the MoJ Inspectorate. Between November 2020 and January 2021, during the second wave of the pandemic, nine such checks took place, focusing mainly on the availability of protective equipment, the possibility of purchasing vitamin supplements in prisons, regular disinfection of premises and payphones, temperature measurement at prison entrances, and the availability of medical care. According to the Ministry of Justice, no serious failings were found. However, it has now been confirmed that the capacity of prison doctors and paramedics is almost exhausted and that in the event of further proliferation of the infection among prisoners, their placement in civilian hospitals could be necessary.[21]

The Ministry of Justice is also continuously examining prisoners' complaints of restrictions worsening their current conditions in prison and, if these complaints are justified, takes remedial actions.[22] There are, however, no possibilities for prisoners to complain to courts, nor is there jurisprudence on that issue.

Despite the shortcomings and errors described above, which occurred during the COVID-19 pandemic in Czech prisons over the last year, namely between March 2020 and March 2021, the overall balance is relatively good: A total of "only" eight prisoners died of COVID-19, of whom only one in prison, the others in civilian hospitals, to which they were transported from prison. Data on persons who are currently (as of 15 April 2021) seriously ill are not available; however, according to the Prison Service, care for such persons is well provided in civilian or military hospitals and their number has been low in the past. At present, no one's life is allegedly endangered in Czech prisons in connection with the COVID-19 infection.

As far as vaccination is concerned, unfortunately, prisoners have not been categorised as particularly vulnerable persons and are therefore not vaccinated as a matter of priority. By 15 April 2021, only 143 people over the age of 70 had been vaccinated. Prison workers, however, were classified as particularly vulnerable, following the intervention of the Minister of Justice, and those of them who come into direct contact with prisoners have already received the vaccine. Gradually, other prison staff are being vaccinated. Although the Minister of Justice has repeatedly requested the allocation of vaccines to cover the vaccination needs of prisoners, which could take place in health centres in prisons, her request has not yet been heard in view of the general lack of vaccines in the Czech Republic.

Overall, it can be stated that the initially tragic-looking scenario of the spread of the COVID-19 infection among prisoners in the Czech Republic did not occur; even in overcrowded prisons, its proliferation was kept under control. However, the future will show whether this is the end result of the fight against the pandemic.[23]

Whether the above information is comprehensive and sufficiently objective cannot be verified at a time when access to prisons is strictly prohibited. Thus, only defence attorneys of accused and sentenced prisoners and public prosecutors, who in this country supervise the execution of custodial sentences, are allowed into the prisons. The Ombudsman, who oversees the observance of prisoners' fundamental rights, also limited his prison visits during the second wave of the pandemic. Even the Petitions Committee of the Chamber of Deputies now does not have access to prisons due to epidemiological measures.

7 Returning to normal

It is obvious that the lingering problem of the Czech criminal and sanctions policy – namely, overcrowding of prisons, becomes even more salient at the time of the pandemic, and adds decrease of prisoners in 2020. One of the reasons may be the above-mentioned general decline in registered crime in 2020 and the consequential decrease in prisoner numbers in the criminal justice system. In this regard, alongside restrictions on the movement of persons during the pandemic, the decriminalisation introduced by the amendment to the CC, in effect since 1 October 2020, which also mitigated punishments for property crimes, could be a factor. Another effect is the drop in unconditional sentences; yet, their share of all main sanctions has not changed.

Tailored solutions, dictated by the pandemic, were largely limited to informal communication with courts, focused on non-ordering of the execution of unconditional prison sentences; prison directors were encouraged to endorse or initiate, where possible, more conditional release proposals. This, of course, is not to say that this practice will continue indefinitely. Clearly, deferring the start of incarceration terms is only a temporary solution.

Significant improvements *de lege ferenda* will be needed to improve the current situation as a whole, both in terms of punishing recidivism and in terms of (partial) decriminalisation of the crime of neglecting to pay maintenance (Scheinost et al., 2015). The same applies to the necessary changes to the terms of conditional release, including a review of related legal provisions. Attention also needs to be paid to the aggregation of the terms of execution of converted conditional sentences of imprisonment[24] (Drápal, 2020). Last but not least, international experiences in prison practice during the pandemic are valuable sources of inspiration and ideas; their careful evaluation may lead to practical application even without changes in national legislation.

Notes

1 Highest to Lowest – Prison Population Rate. In: World Prison Brief [online database]. Institute for Crime & Justice Policy Research. [2021-01-18]. See https://prisonstudies.org/highest-to-lowest/prison_population_rate?field_region_taxonomy_tid=14.

2 Since up-to-date data from the Czech Statistical Office were unavailable, calculations were done using census figures at 30 September 2020; prison population data come from the Monthly Statistical Report of the Prison Service, dated 31 December 2020. According to the Statistical Yearbook of the Prison Service 2020, the average occupancy was at 101.5% of the prison capacity in 2000.

3 Hereinafter quoted numbers of persons being prosecuted, those indicted, sentenced, and conditionally released, are taken from the statistics and database of CSLAV of the Czech Ministry of Justice.

4 Main sanctions here mean individual types of punishments as main sanctions, as well as alternatives to punishments – i.e. individual types of alternatives to punishment. Not included here are dropped cases of aggregated punishment or cases of guilty verdicts without sentences.

5 The indirect consequences here include the fact that after the amnesty, when some criminal records were obliterated, incarcerated offenders were perpetrators of serious crimes, or recidivists who, as a rule, did not meet the terms of conditional release.

6 Recommendation of the Committee of Ministers to member States on the European Prison Rules (Adopted on 11 January 2006, and revised and amended on 1 July 2020), Rec (2006)2-rev 2020.

7 The source is the Monthly Statistical Report of December 2020 of the Prison Service of the Czech Republic. Available at: https://old.vscr.cz/wp-content/uploads/2021/01/MSH12-2020.pdf

8 New alternative punishments were introduced, e.g. house arrest, designed to cut the use of unconditional prison sentences. It was hamstrung by the lack of electronic monitoring. In addition, practicalities got in its way, such as offenders' inconsistent work times, or absence of permanent home addresses (Scheinost et al., 2014).

9 See in detail Monthly Statistical Reports of the Prison Service of the Czech Republic. Available at: https://old.vscr.cz/informacni-servis/statistiky/mesicni-statisticke-hlaseni/

10 Premature conditional release as codified in § 88 p. 2 of the Criminal Code. It gives the court a possibility to free a wrongdoer on conditional release, if he/she has a proven record of good behaviour and honest fulfilment of obligations, otherwise required for conditional release, making the completion of the imprisonment term unnecessary (i.e. premature conditional release). Another prerequisite for getting court approval is endorsement of the request by the prison director, or a proposal presented by the director of the prison in which the applicant is held, or the inmate's request endorsed by the prison director. The court will not grant premature conditional release if it is evident that the applicant is unable to lead the life of a law-abiding person.

11 In 2020, there were 165,525 registered criminal acts; out of them, 77,786 were closed. In 2019, there were 199,221 registered criminal acts, and 93,202 were closed. Statistical overviews of crime, Police of the Czech Republic. Available at: https://www.policie.cz/statistiky-kriminalita.aspx

12 In 2020, there were 67,775 prosecuted persons, including shortened preparatory proceedings; 62,121 were indicted, including cases with pending sentences and agreements on guilt and punishment; 48,558 persons were sentenced. In 2019, the respective statistics were 77,237, 70,739, and 55,594 persons. The 2020 data come from the CSLAV database.

13 The letter of Petr Toman of 3 March 2020, addressed to the Czech President, is in the public domain and can be accessed at the website of the law firm Toman, Devátý & partners: https:// iustitia.cz/ blog/clanky/koronavirus/petr-toman-navrhuje-prezidentovi-vyhlaseni-amnestie.html.

14 Internal information of Prison Service of the Czech Republic of September 2020.

15 Concrete procedures and preventive measures are formulated in the Directive of the General Director of the Czech Prison Service no.4/2020, effective from 30 March 2020; they outline actions in the case of an increased rate of infection.
16 Reports of the Prison Service of the Czech Republic presented once or twice a month to the Government Commissioner for Human Rights at the request of the Commissioner's Office, and to the Petition Committee of the lower chamber of the Czech Parliament on the state of human rights of inmates during the pandemic from March 2020 to date.
17 See above Footnote 16.
18 This prison has some 435 convicts, 6 of them are "lifers", and 23 serve exceptional punishments of 20–30 years; it is a graphic example of how it works or does not work in the Czech Republic. On Saturday, 31 October 2020, the parents of one of the inmates in Mirov made a phone call to the Human Rights Commissioner complaining that their son was sharing a cell with another 12 inmates and he was showing signs of COVID-19 infection, and that some other cellmates did not seem to be feeling well, either. This information was immediately forwarded to the General Director of the Prison Service, followed up by an official letter on 2 November 2020 asking for an update on the number of infected persons and on measures taken. On 4 November 2020, a response from the General Director arrived saying that the situation in Mirov was under control and was taken care of by the Prison Service from 31 October and by the Regional Hygiene Service in Olomouc from 3 November. The number of infected persons then stood at 60. However, another report of the Prison Service, dated 4 November, said that the total number of COVID patients in all prisons was 36. About a month later, on 12 December, another official report put the number at 1,379 (out of whom 809 had already "recovered"). These data are, however, hard to verify. One can only hope that the real number of the infected is not higher than officially reported. Definitely though, the situation merits the attention of the Ministry of Justice which governs the Prison Service. The next report on the condition of the infected was to be delivered to MP's and the Government HR Commissioner at the end of January 2021.
19 The official data which was debated by MPs at their session on 16 February 2021 and provided by the Prison Service itself.
20 These measures being internal are not available in the public domain for security reasons.
21 The MoJ report at the meeting of the Petitions Committee of the Chamber of Deputies on 16 February 2021.
22 See above Footnote 21.
23 The information was provided by the Minister of Justice in a letter of 16 April 2021 to the Government Commissioner for Human Rights.
24 The issue of aggregate terms of incarceration of converted alternative punishments, which in total are not commensurate with the gravity of the committed crimes, was raised by the Constitutional Court in its Finding II. ÚS 4022/18 of 30 July 2019.

References

Bíba, L. (2020): Firma SuperCom nedodala 120 elektronických náramků pro odsouzené. Hrozí omezení monitoringu. Hospodářské noviny (*SuperCom failed to supply 120 electronic bracelets. E-monitoring is uncertain)*. Hospodářské noviny. [online] [2020-09-06] https://domaci.ihned.cz/c1-66705720-firma-supercom-nedodala-120-elektronickych-naramku-pro-odsouzene-hrozi-prechodne-omezeni-monitoringu.

Diblíková, S., Cejp, M., Hulmáková, J., et al. (2019): *Analýza trendů kriminality v České republice v roce 2018. (An Analysis of Trends in Criminality in the Czech Republic in 2018).* [online]. Praha: The Institute of Criminology and Social Prevention, [2021-01-13]. ISBN 978–80–7338-179-0.

Drápal, J. (2020): Ukládání trestů v případě jejich kumulace: Jak trestat pachatele, kteří spáchali další trestný čin předtím, než vykonali dříve uložené tresty (*Crminal punishments and their aggregation: How to punish criminals for new crimes before they have completed previous prison terms*). *Jurisprudence*, no. 2, 1–17.

Hulmáková, J. (2020): Trestní a sankční politika v České republice v letech 2009 až 2019 (*Criminal and Sanction Policy in the Czech Republic from 2009 until 2019).* In: Diblíková, S., et al. [online]: *Analýza trendů kriminality v České republice v roce v roce 2019.* Praha: The Institute of Criminology and Social Prevention, 32–49, ISBN 978-80-7338-187-5.

Scheinost, M. et al. (2014): *Sankční politika pohledem praxe* (*Sanctions Policy and Practice).* Praha: The Institute of Criminology and Social Prevention, ISBN 978-80-7338-144-8.

Scheinost, M. et al. (2015): *Teoretické a trestněpolitické aspekty reformy trestního práva v oblasti trestních sankcí IV. Sankční politika a její uplatňování* (*Theoretical and Criminal Policy Aspects of Reform of Criminal Law in the Area of Penal Sanctions IV. Sanctions Policy and its Application*). Praha: The Institute of Criminology and Social Prevention, ISBN 978-80-7338-154-7.

The Supreme Public Prosecutor's Office, the Institute of State and Law of the Academy of Sciences (2019): *Zvláštní zpráva "Věznice"* (*Special Report "Prisons").* [online]. 21. 9. 2019, [2021-01-16]. https://verejnazaloba.cz/wp-content/uploads/2020/01/zvl_zprava_ veznice25_09_ 2019.pdf

Válková, H. (2020): Reform des Strafvollzugs – Chronische Probleme und Hindernisse auf dem Weg zu einem effizienteren Vollzug der Freiheitsstrafe in Tschechien. In: Drenkhahn, K. et al. (Eds.): *Kriminologie und Kriminalpolitik im Dienste der Menschenwürde. Festschrift für Frieder Dünkel zum 70.Geburtstag.* Mönchengladbach: Forum Verlag Godesberg, 955–964.

van Zyl Smit, D., and Snacken, S. (2011): *Principles of European Prison Law and Policy. Penology and Human Rights.* Oxford: Oxford University Press.

Vicherek, R. (2018): *Současné trendy vývoje podmíněného propuštění* (*Present-day Trends in the Practice of Conditional Release*). *Trestněprávní revue*, 1, 6–11.

Wooldredge, J., and Smith, P. (2019) (Eds.): *The Oxford Handbook of Prisons and Imprisonment.* Oxford: Oxford University Press.

13 Denmark

Anette Storgaard and Linda Kjær Minke

1 Introduction: General situation of the prison system

Denmark is a small and relatively wealthy country, belonging to the well-known group of Scandinavian welfare states. While privatisation is broadly implemented in the health sector, the police, courts, and the Prison and Probation Service are run by the state. Employees in the police and justice sector are civil servants. According to section 1 of the Law on the Execution of Punishment, the Prison and Probation Service is an integral state authority organised as a national unit, the Department of Prisons and Probation, and has four regional offices. Even though the justice sector in Greenland is a formal part of the Danish justice sector, Greenland is not part of this report. The Department of Prison and Probation Service is subordinate to the Ministry of Justice.

During recent years, criminal justice statistics reveal a decrease in the number of criminally convicted persons. The average length of unconditional prison sentences was 10.2 months in 2019, which was 0.2 months longer than the year before (Statistics Denmark, 2019: 31). In 2018, the incarceration rate was 63 inmates per 100,000 population (Danish Prison and Probation Service, 2019b: 8), which is low, compared to most other countries, but average compared to the other Scandinavian states. Denmark has a prison capacity of 3,940 places. Of these, 1,802 places are in remand houses (pre-trial), 1,012 places are in mainly closed prisons and 1,127 places are in prisons that are mainly open. "Mainly" means that most prisons have both closed and open places, but with different priorities. The remand houses are organised with a high level of security, meaning that only few inmates may socialise during work- or leisure hours. The closed prisons are organised with a high level of security, too, but prisoners can normally work and cook together and socialise during the daytime. The open prisons have no perimeter walls or fences. The inmates are not allowed to leave the prison site unless they have permission, and they can socialise more freely during the hours when they are not locked up in the cells. Due to shortage of staff, the number of hours during which the prisoners in both open and closed prisons are locked up in the cells for the night has been gradually increasing. In general, convicted

DOI: 10.4324/9781003169178-13

inmates are now locked up in the cells for 12 hours at night and pre-trial detainees are often confined to their cells for up to 23 hours a day.

In 2019, the average daily occupancy rate (for all facilities) was 100.9% (Danish Prison and Probation Service, 2019a: 19). In combination with a decline in staff by 500 employees from 2,700 to 2,200 since 2010, the atmosphere in the prisons was influenced by stress and absence due to sickness among staff even before the pandemic (The Trade Union for Prison Officers, 2019).

Compared to many countries, Danish prisons are small. The largest closed prison has 312 places, of which 92 places are foreseen for pre-trial detainees and the largest open prison has a capacity of 255 places.

Conditional early release has become more and more exceptional. Since an amendment to section 38 of the Criminal Code in 2014, individuals defined as gang-members cannot be subject to conditional early release (Storgaard, 2020). In 2013, the rejection rate for conditional release was 17%, whereas it amounted to 38% in 2019 (Danish Prison and Probation Service, 2019a: 55). This increase in the rejection rate may very well be related to a number of newly implemented changes in the Law on the Execution of Punishment and changes in further laws, regulations and practices, which have a legal basis in this Law, such as the Smoking Ban Law, "zero tolerance" for rude behaviour, and an increase of the number and severity of disciplinary penalties for breaches of regulations for the communication with the outside world, mainly possession of mobile phones. Since 2015, numerous detailed changes have led to a dramatic increase of disciplinary penalties – especially the use of solitary confinement – within the prison system. Rejections of conditional release and prison leave are not considered disciplinary penalties, but prisoners' chances of obtaining permission for these status improvements, and the risks of revocation of such permission are negatively influenced by a disciplinary penalty (Kessing, 2019; Minke, 2019; Minke and Næsborg-Andersen, 2020; Storgaard, 2020).

On 11 March 2020, a massive lockdown of Danish society was initiated by the government due to the international COVID-19 pandemic. Within very few days, a large number of executive orders were confirmed by the parliament. Two executive orders were directed at the prison system, no. 202 of 13 March 2020 and no. 221 of 17 March 2020. Initially, there was a historical political consensus among the members of parliament about this fast and firm action. Later, the government has been criticised for acting too precipitately. An expert committee has been established to analyse the whole process.

Unlike in most other countries, the current Danish government does not control the majority of the votes in the parliament. Also, unlike some other countries, for instance, the neighbouring country Sweden, the power to declare a lockdown for the whole society or for special sectors was in the hands of the political decision-makers from the beginning of the pandemic; it was not within the competence of the health-care system to make such decisions.

After a period of revocation of the lockdown for three to four months, since September 2020, a gradual lockdown has been implemented in the society again. But from March 2021, the lockdown has gradually been relaxed. For example, schools have been re-opened. Restrictions in the prisons are still in effect at the time of writing. Prison leave, for example, is not yet possible, except for serious illness or death of prisoners' close relatives. There are still strict limitations on the number of visits and visitors, and isolation is an immediate response to any "suspicious" symptom. A stepwise revocation of the restrictions is planned from April 2021. In the prisons, as in society, the revocation of restrictions depends to a large degree on the development of infection rates, and also relies on the use of masks and testing for SARS-CoV-2. Prisoners, who tested negative or can prove an earlier COVID-19 infection from which they have recovered, are subject to fewer restrictions.

2 Prison and penal policy concerning the execution of prison sentences during the COVID-19-induced crisis

The interchange between lockdown and a more or less normal life in society has been mirrored in the prisons.

The Danish Prison and Probation Service issued its first emergency plan for prisons, remand houses and halfway houses before the national lockdown of society on 4 March 2020. The purpose of the plan was to reduce the spread of COVID-19 among inmates and employees, mainly by ensuring that prisoners with symptoms of the virus were isolated.[1] Soon after, on 12 March 2020, summons to serve their sentence in prison were stopped for those persons who were not imprisoned immediately after their conviction in court. This summons stop did not include persons convicted for gang-related offences or for assault, i.e. individuals seen as dangerous to society. With the high occupancy rate in mind, this summons stop has, of course, postponed the scheduled execution of a number of sentences, especially for those persons who were not considered to be dangerous to society. The aim was to reduce the risk of COVID-19 being brought into the prisons by newly admitted prisoners. Especially regarding convicted persons not considered dangerous, the same aim might have been reached in other ways, e.g. by extended use of electronic monitoring, which is an option already available to the Prison and Probation Service.

A few days later, on 20 March, media reported that up to 25 prisoners had symptoms of COVID-19 (Jyske Vestkysten, 2020). A further week later (on 28 March), up to 50 staff members were off work sick with symptoms of COVID-19 and the first prisoner was tested positive for COVID-19, while already in quarantine (Danish Prison and Probation Service, 2020a). From 26 March 2020 onwards, inmates showing symptoms of COVID-19 could be tested by the prison health staff and from 31 March 2020 on staff members with mild symptoms could also be tested.[2] In January 2021, the trade union for prison and probation officers announced that they recommended that prison staff members be tested, but testing was not obligatory (The Trade Union for Prison Officers, 2021a).

During 2020, the intensity of COVID-19-related restrictions in the Danish prisons was adjusted over time, similarly to the general situation in society. In the summer of 2020, most restrictions were revoked, but beginning in early October, restrictions were gradually re-introduced. In January 2021, some restrictions were tightened simultaneously with a partial relaxation of the summons stop. As described above, the restrictions are expected to be slowly and gradually revoked from April 2021 onwards.

By the end of October 2020, the Danish Prison and Probation Service reported to the Danish Ombudsman that a total of 238 COVID-19 tests among inmates had been carried out and five of those were COVID-19 positive. According to the report, the rate of COVID-19 positive persons was markedly higher among foreigners who had served a prison sentence and were incarcerated in deportation centres. In this group, 73 tests had been carried out and 18 were positive. The report to the Danish Ombudsman contains no information about the number of tests among staff members, but it reveals that 20 staff members had been tested positive for COVID-19 until the date of the report (Danish Prison and Probation Service, 2020).

The most recent information about the spread of the infection in prisons is from April 2021. The magazine for prison staff reported that in total, 82 prisoners and 207 employees were infected with COVID-19 in the period March 2020–March 2021 (The Trade Union for Prison Staff, 2021b).

In a newsletter of 3 July 2020, the Ombudsman communicated to the Danish Prison and Probation Service that inmates who were isolated due to COVID-19 symptoms, had reported that contact with staff members took place via an intercom system (Danish Ombudsman, 2020b).

To conclude, the summons stop, the isolation of inmates with symptoms, the lack of physical contact between staff and isolated prisoners and the number of infected inmates compared to the number of infected staff members do not indicate that prison staff have been largely exposed to infection in their work. Up until April 2021, there had been no reports published on COVID-19-related deaths of prisoners or prison staff members.

3 Restrictions of contact with the outside world

3.1 Visits

Visits are one of the most popular ways to keep contact with the outside world while serving a prison sentence. The Law on the Execution of Punishment states that every prisoner has the right to receive at least a minimum of a one-hour visit per week. Usually, prison visits will be extended in time, not least when the visitors come from far away. And normally, more than one visitor can be present at the same time.

In order to reduce the risk of visitors bringing COVID-19 into prisons, on 10 March 2020, the possibilities for inmates to receive visitors were curtailed to the legal minimum, meaning one visit per week from close relatives plus a possibility to meet one's lawyer and a representative from a religious community in private. Foreigners also retained the right to see a diplomatic or consular representative from their home country.

Eight days later, on 18 March 2020, the opportunity of receiving private visits was completely cut off, cf. sections 16–17 of Executive order no. 221. At the same time, compensation for the missing visits, in the form of extended telephone conversations especially with the next of kin, was introduced. It was still possible to receive visits from lawyers and representatives of religious communities. Likewise, foreign prisoners still had the possibility to meet with diplomatic or consular representatives. However, as far as possible, such visits were replaced by telephone conversations.

The Danish Ombudsman communicated in a newsletter of 21 March 2020 that a large number of spontaneous complaints from inmates and their relatives were received about these restrictions to visits. It was specifically pointed out that the letters demanded that this restriction be terminated (Danish Ombudsman, 2020a). However, such a decision is not in the power of the Ombudsman; hence, the requests were referred to the Danish Prison and Probation Service.

From 18 May 2020 to 1 October 2020, possibilities of visits were reinstated to a limited extent and under strict hygiene requirements.

On 1 October 2020, the Prison and Probation Service re-introduced several restrictions to reduce the risk of COVID-19 infections in prisons and remand houses. Inter alia, all visitors had to wear face masks while on prison grounds. Only in the visiting room, where the visitor(s) and the prisoners are on their own, could the masks be taken off. Restrictions were also introduced concerning those allowed to visit – close relatives, lawyers and representatives from religious communities. These restrictions had not been revoked by 18 October 2020, as was initially announced (Danish Prison and Probation Service, 2020c). On the contrary, they were tightened in January 2021. Since then, visits are only allowed from three named close relatives, and only once every two weeks (Danish Prison and Probation Service, 2021a). In addition, all visits that due to prison regulations need to be supervised by staff have been replaced by telephone conversations. Initially, the replacement of visits with phone calls was supposed to be reconsidered and revoked after one month, but it was prolonged. Based on Executive order no. 538 of 26 March 2021, this restriction will be upheld until the middle of April 2021.

Based on the experience gained in 2020, there is reason to expect the restrictions in prisons to continue to mirror the restrictions in society at large. At the time of writing, many experts expect them to be prolonged up until summer 2021. In the political debates, the milestone for a general opening of societal activities is the point at which all citizens aged 50 or older have been offered a vaccination.

3.2 Prison leave

On the basis of Executive order no. 202, which is an amendment of an already existing order on prison leave (Executive order no. 182), permission for prison leave could be refused and permits that had already been issued could be revoked, if this could prevent or curb the spread of COVID-19 within prisons. This meant that each individual prison was given the power to revoke permits for prison leave with immediate effect. Procedures were also put in place to admit inmates returning from prison leave.

Just a few days later, on 17 March 2020, all kinds of prison leave were called off at a national level. Exceptions were only made under special circumstances, such as urgent needs for health care, short visits to close relatives who were seriously ill or funerals of close relatives. At the time of writing, the restrictions have been prolonged until the end of April 2021 (Executive order no. 538).

A possibility of "saving" up to four regular periods of prison leave[3] until they are allowed again is foreseen as a kind of compensation. It will be interesting to see how many inmates will benefit from this "compensation", bearing in mind that the average length of sentence is 10.2 months and more than half of all unconditional sentences have a length of up to four months. Recently, admitted prisoners serving long sentences may, however, at some time during their imprisonment profit from their "saved" periods of leave.

4 Restrictions inside prisons

Not only was the contact between inmates and the outside world severely restricted from the very beginning of the COVID-19 pandemic, restrictions were also imposed on daily life behind prison walls. Very early already, on 13 March 2020, the use of fitness rooms, sports and other recreational activities were suspended. Beginning on 18 March 2020, each prison was given the competence to interrupt work and education for the prisoners, if this was necessary to prevent COVID-19 from spreading. Continuing work activities was considered less important. In such cases, the inmates were still entitled to the ordinary payment for work (approximately two Euros per hour). Power to restrict the right to spend one hour outside daily in the courtyard, the right to socialise with other prisoners in small groups, the right to drug treatment and the right to attend religious service was handed over to each prison. At the same time, it was clarified that activities could not be reduced to such a degree that necessary catering and welfare could not be ensured.

After a period of minor relaxations of the restrictions in prisons, which were decided locally, national restrictions on work were re-introduced in December 2020. Drug treatment, therapeutic programmes, like anger management courses, and schooling, which are all important elements in daily prison life, were completely terminated until February 2021 (Danish Prison and Probation Service, 2021a). Since then, the work restrictions are again administered based on local ad hoc risk evaluations (see Executive order no. 538).

All these nationwide restrictions, and the powers granted to prison administrations to implement further constraints on prisoners' rights during the pandemic have always been temporary or at least combined with a fixed date for mandatory reconsideration. However, the time limits have been adjusted and extended several times.

The restrictions in prisons to a large degree mirror restrictions in society. There has been political criticism of the societal restrictions as too tough, mainly because the service sector came under financial pressure. Despite criticism, the majority of the population holds the opinion that Denmark in general has managed the COVID-19 crisis pretty well.

The prison situation has not at all gained the same public attention. Even if the restrictions can be said to mirror the restrictions in society, their extent may be questioned, as the Ombudsman expressed in the title of a newsletter: "Might a future epidemic be dealt with less restrictively in penal institutions?" (Danish Ombudsman, 2020b).

5 Compensatory measures

In order to compensate for the limited opportunities for visits and prison leave, and for other restrictions, the prisons are encouraged by the national Prison and Probation Service to support the following measures on a local basis:

1 Telephone access should be extended as much as possible, e.g. in open prisons, mobile phones may be allowed to be used for video calls. The use of mobile phones is a sensitive issue in Danish prisons. Prisoners are never allowed to possess private mobile phones. In open prisons, there are mobile phones in the cell, which are fixed to the wall by a wire, but their function is limited compared to smartphones. In order to mitigate the consequences of the lack of visits and prison leave, from 1 April 2020, inmates in open prisons have been permitted to use their private smartphones for video calls to close relatives in a room outside their wing and selected by the prison administration. After use, the phone must be handed over to the prison staff, who keep it in a locker.
2 Increased access should be allowed to self-study courses as alternatives for either school in prison or prison leave for education, which are legally foreseen possibilities, but rarely used in practice.
3 There should be increased possibilities for exercising in the prison yard instead of the gym with a maximum of ten inmates participating at a time.
4 Special attention should be paid to keeping up contact between parents in prison and their children. The Danish prison system has a so-called

child-responsible scheme, which obliges each prison to dedicate an officer to pay special attention to the contact between children and their imprisoned parents (Smith, 2014: 16). Among other things, these officers have to ensure child-friendly facilities for visits. Supposedly, this scheme is mentioned in the list of compensatory measures to encourage these specific officers to be aware of alternative methods to keep the contact. One alternative might be the use of video calls.

In addition, local efforts should be made to organise other activities for the prisoners, such as facilitating hobbies that can be practised in the cells and telephone calls with therapists. Finally, game consoles have been purchased for inmates in closed prisons and detention centres (Danish Prison and Probation Service, 2021b).

As already mentioned above (under Section 3.2), those prisoners who qualify for prison leave may "save" up to four periods prisons leave until they can be taken again.

6 Legal basis for restrictions and relaxations of the prison regime

The legal basis for the implementation of restrictions (in prisons and society) had to be established ad hoc. The restrictions mainly involve divergence from legal regulations, supplementary regulations in the form of executive orders or simply changes of practice. The relaxation of these restrictions would in principle mean a return to normal.

In most cases, the restrictive interventions related to the COVID-19 pandemic are legalised through executive orders decided by the government and published by the Ministry of Justice. Among the large number of topical executive orders, no. 202 of 13 March 2020 and no. 221 of 17 March 2020 were explicitly directed at the prison sector. They were both based on the Law on Epidemic Diseases and at the time of their expiry their contents were repeated in Executive order no. 538 of 26 March 2021 with a sunset clause set for 28 April 2021.

The latter order, no. 221, contains many restrictions of different existing regulations in laws and permanent executive orders. The main restrictions included in Executive order no. 221 are presented above under Sections 3.1 and 4. Executive order no. 221 explicitly requires all measures to be proportionate, i.e. measures must not exceed what is necessary to reach the goal, and among a number of equally effective measures, the minimum intervention needs to be chosen. The implementation of the measures may also explicitly not infringe the international duties of Denmark.

The power to implement restrictions has been granted to the institutions. Currently, there is only little chance to evaluate whether the proportionality principle has been fully acted upon. To assess this, one relevant source is the Newsletters of the Ombudsman, which have been mentioned above briefly. A main point of attention by the Ombudsman is contact with the outside world for convicted prisoners and pre-trial detainees, but also the restrictions of contact between the inmates and lack of in-person contact for isolated prisoners. The Ombudsman points to the fact that at least up until July 2020, the restrictions did not seem to have caused more conflicts and disciplinary penalties than "usual". The Ombudsman considers this as positive. Contrary to that optimistic view, the magazine for nurses published an interview with a prisoner in May 2020. In this interview, the prisoner described the atmosphere in his prison as coming towards "boiling point" (Toft, 2020: 14).

Whether the restrictions violate international duties is debateable. The Danish Law on the Execution of Punishment is, with few exceptions, in accordance with the Nelson Mandela Rules and the European Prison Rules, which Denmark has ratified, but a large part of the restrictions introduced in the number of executive orders diverge from the Law and are also not in line with these two international sets of rules and the principle of normalisation in general. This is especially true for the restrictions on contact with the outside world and on activities in prison such as work, school and treatment. That this has not been mentioned at all in any official authoritative source may be explained by the fact that even if the Prison and Probation Service officially wishes to meet the two international sets of regulation that are mentioned here, compliance is not considered as a binding duty. In addition, on the European and international level, regulations and guidelines on the defeat of the COVID-19 pandemic can also override prison regulations. However, this has not been debated, either.

The balancing of prisoners' rights and the necessity of defeating a pandemic has been a new challenge in all public and private sectors. Several evaluations of how the pandemic was managed in Denmark have already been initiated. These should also include the prisons.

7 Returning to normal and what could be learnt for the future

As of April 2021, the COVID-19 pandemic is not yet under control. Restrictions are being relaxed but not removed in penal facilities as well as in society. Hopefully, vaccinations will guide our way out of this situation. In Denmark, a huge vaccination programme is being conducted. The forecasts about the speed of vaccinations have been revised several times. The aim is to offer all citizens a vaccination by late summer of 2021.

All citizens have experienced restrictions of some of their liberties during the pandemic crisis. However, the deprivation of essential rights such as the right to visit or be visited by one's partner and family, to have access to work and at least minimal social contact *while in prison* is of course much more serious and not in accordance with the overall aim of preparing each individual prisoner for a crime-free life in the future.

Notes

1 Questions of the Judicial Committee for the Danish Minister of Justice about COVID-19 initiatives in prisons, 6 April 2020.
2 Questions of the Judicial Committee for the Danish Minister of Justice about COVID-19 initiatives in prisons, 6 April 2020.
3 See detailed information about different types of prison leave in Danish prisons in Storgaard, 2020.

References

Danish Ombudsman (2020a): *Nyhedsbrev af 21 marts, 2020.* Stort antal indsatte klager over coronatiltag [Newsletter 21 March 2020. A huge number of prisoners complain over corona restrictions]. https://www.ombudsmanden.dk/find/nyheder/alle/klager_over_coronatiltag/#cp-title/ (Accessed 18 January 2021).

Danish Ombudsman (2020b): *Nyhedsbrev af 3 juli, 2020.* Kan en fremtidig epidemi håndteres mindre restriktivt i kriminalforsorgens institutioner? [Newsletter 3 July 2020. Can a future epidemic be dealt less restrictive in penal institutions?] https://www.ombudsmanden.dk/find/nyheder/alle/haandtering_af_fremtidig_epidemi/haandtering_af_epidemi (Accessed 18 January 2021).

Danish Prison and Probation Service (2019a): *Statistic 2019.* Copenhagen: Danish Prison and Probation Service. https://www.kriminalforsorgen.dk/wp-content/uploads/2020/08/kriminalforsorgens-statistik-2019.pdf (Accessed 18 January 2021).

Danish Prison and Probation Service (2019b): *Numbers from Danish Prison and Probation Service, August 2019.* Copenhagen: Danish Prison and Probation Service. https://www.kriminalforsorgen.dk/wp-content/uploads/2019/08/tal-fra-kriminalforsorgen-august-2019.pdf (Accessed 18 January 2021).

Danish Prison and Probation Service (2020): *Intern dokument over COVID-19 opgørelse.* [Internal (not official) document about numbers of COVID-19], 26 October 2020.

Danish Prison and Probation Service (2020a): *Nyhedsbrev af 28 marts 2020.* Første indsatte med Covid-19 konstateret [Newsletter 28 March 2020. The first inmate with Covid-19 is identified]. https://www.kriminalforsorgen.dk/om-os/nyt-og-presse/nyheder/foerste-indsatte-med-covid-19-konstateret/ (Accessed 14 December 2020).

Danish Prison and Probation Service (2020b): *Nyhedsbrev af 5 maj 2020.* Kriminalforsorgen åbner op for de første besøg [Newsletter, 5 May 2020. The prison and probation service opens up for visits]. https://www.kriminalforsorgen.dk/om-os/nyt-og-presse/nyheder/kriminalforsorgen-aabner-for-de-foerste-besoeg/ (Accessed 18 January 2021).

Danish Prison and Probation Service (2020c): *Nyhedsbrev af 10 December 2020.* Kriminalforsorgen iværksætter nye tiltag mod smittespredning [Newsletter 10 December 2020. The Danish prison and probation service implements new steps to reduce the spread of infectious disease]. https://www.kriminalforsorgen.dk/om-os/nyt-og-presse/nyheder/kriminalforsorgen-ivaerksaetter-nye-tiltag-mod-smittespredning/ (Accessed 18 January 2021).

Danish Prison and Probation Service (2021a): *Nyhedsbrev af 11 januar 2021.* Kriminalforsorgen skærper COVID-19-restriktioner og indkalder igen til afsoning [Press Release, 11 January 2021.The prison and probation service increases COVID-19 restrictions and summon to enforce sentences]. https://www.kriminalforsorgen.

dk/om-os/nyt-og-presse/nyheder/kriminalforsorgen-skaerper-COVID-19-restriktioner-og-indkalder-igen-til-afsoning/ (Accessed 18 January 2021).

Danish Prison and Probation Service (2021b): Information on covid-19 [Information about Covid-19]. https://www.kriminalforsorgen.dk/corona/ (Accessed 18 January 2021).

Jyske Vestkysten (2020): 50 fængselsbetjente er sygemeldte med tegn på corona. [50 prison officers are absent because of COVID-19 symptoms].

Kessing, V. P. (2019): Strafcelle - isolation af indsatte i danske fængsler [Penalty cell – isolation of prisoners in Danish Prisons]. *Juristen, 2,* 51–61.

Minke, L. K. (2019): *Evaluering af lov nr. 641 af 8. juni 2016: Styrket indsats mod mobiltelefoner i fængsler m.v.* [Evaluation of Law nr. 641 by 8 June 2016: strengthened efforts for mobile phones in Danish prisons]. Justitsministeriets forskningskontor, rapporter vedrørende forskningspuljen. https://www.justitsministeriet.dk/wp-content/uploads/2020/09/evaluering_lov_om_mobiltelefoner-FINAL-a.pdf.

Minke, L. K., and Næsborg-Andersen, A. (2020): De kan hverken ryge eller rejse – Rygeforbuddet i danske fængsler [They cannot smoke nor leave – the smoking ban in Danish prisons]. *Nordisk Tidsskrift for Kriminalvidenskab* 2020(1), 3–23.

Smith, P. S. (2014): *When the Innocent are Punished. The Children of Imprisoned Parents.* Palgrave Studies in Prisons and Penology, UK.

Statistics Denmark (2019): *Kriminalitet 2018* [Crime 2018]. Statistic Denmark. Copenhagen. https://www.dst.dk/Site/Dst/Udgivelser/GetPubFile.aspx?id=29814&sid=krim2018.

Storgaard, A. (2020): Prison leave in Denmark: How a tradition of combining rehabilitation with discipline developed into putting access to justice at risk. *European Journal on Criminal Policy and Research* 26, 213–229. https://doi.org/10.1007/s10610-020-09436-5.

Toft, N. (2020): Vi nærmer os kogepunktet [We are close to the boiling point]. *Danish Journal of Nursing, No. 6, 2020,* p.14.

The Trade Union for Prison Officers (2019): *Fængselsfunktionæren, nr. 3.* [Danish magazine for Prison Staff, 2019, 3] https://faengselsforbundet.dk/download-document/?filename=2019/06/FF_juni_2019_opslag_02.pdf/ Accessed on 18 January, 2021.

The Trade Union for Prison Officers (2021a): *Nyhedsbrev af 16. januar 2021.* Opdatering: To test om ugen er ikke et krav men en opfordring [Newsletter 16 January 2021. Up-date: Two tests per week are not required, but recommended] https://faengselsforbundet.dk/to-test-om-ugen-er-ikke-et-krav-men-en-opfordring/ (Accessed 31 March 2021).

The Trade Union for Prison Officers (2021b): *Nyhedsbrev af 8 april 2021.* Hvor mange har været smittet? [Newsletter 8 April 2021. How many have been infected by Covid-19?] https://faengselsforbundet.dk/fagbladet-net/hvor-mange-har-vaeret-smittet/ (Accessed 14 April 2021).

14 England and Wales

Catherine Heard and Nicola Padfield

1 Introduction – general situation of the prison system

By comparison with our Western European neighbours, the prison population rate in England and Wales has been very high for some years.[1] The small decrease in the size of the prison population in 2020 (see Table 14.1) reflects more the fact that courts closed, than any significant change in early release provisions: we have seen a decrease on the supply side, not the exit side.

First, a brief comment on the prison population of England and Wales. This quadrupled in size between 1900 and 2019, going from just over 17,400 to around 82,900. It doubled between 1994 and 2010. Since 2010, it has remained relatively stable. The number of women in prison has not increased as sharply as that of men: in 2019, 4% of the total prison population was female, down from 17% in 1900. In terms of ethnicity, in 2019, 27% of the prison population identified as belonging to an ethnic minority, compared with 13% of the general population. There is also a large number of foreign nationals – at the end of March 2020, there were just over 9,000 (from 163 different countries) in the prison population.[2]

Table 14.1 Prison population total England & Wales, January 2020 to January 2021

Date	*Prison population*
31 January 2020	83,329
28 February 2020	83,868
27 March 2020	83,189
24 April 2020	81,124
29 May 2020	80,032
26 June 2020	79,453
31 July 2020	79,643
28 August 2020	79,433
25 September 2020	79,263
30 October 2020	79,083
27 November 2020	78,832
18 December 2020	78,700
29 January 2021	78,065

All figures are taken from the Ministry of Justice Prison Population Statistics weekly data at the latest date each month, https://www.gov.uk/government/collections/prison-population-statistics.

DOI: 10.4324/9781003169178-14

As well as size, another characteristic of the English prison system is the poor material conditions of many prisons. In May 2020, 49% of prisons were overcrowded.[3] There has been under-investment for many years, especially given the increasing prison population. Many prisons are very old. Even before the lockdown, many prisoners have been forced to share a small cell, often designed for only one person.[4] Chronic under-investment has resulted not just in poor conditions, but also in low numbers of staff. Recently, as staff recruitment has started to increase, there has been concern about numbers of young and inexperienced staff. There has been regular criticism not only from NGOs (such as the Howard League for Penal Reform and the Prison Reform Trust) but also from "official" inspectors and monitors (such as the National Audit Office (NAO), Her Majesty's Prison and Probation Service (HMPPS) and the Prison and Probation Ombudsman (PPO). By way of example, the NAO (2020) identified leaking roofs, pest control problems, failed heating and plumbing systems, outdated electrical wiring and broken cell windows. The Chief Inspector of Prisons has for many years identified high levels of violence and self-harm in prisons, and declining standards of safety. The poor and outdated infrastructure blighting many prisons extends to under-provision of IT (information technology), telephones, computer terminals and internet connectivity.

1.1 COVID-19 infections and deaths of prisoners and prison staff members

It was therefore not surprising that at the outset of the crisis, there was real concern about how the virus would take off in prisons and there were fears of many deaths.[5] The first case was identified in early March at HMP Manchester. By 12 May, 404 cases had been confirmed amongst prisoners, and 21 prisoners and 7 members of prison staff had died.[6] Regular data have been published since then, showing that, by 31 August 2020[7]:

- There had been 44 deaths since the start of the pandemic among HMPPS service users where COVID-19 was the suspected cause, of whom 23 were prisoners and 21 were probation service users.
- 560 people in custody had tested positive for COVID-19 since the start of the pandemic, across 87 establishments, almost all of whom were adults.
- 315 prisoners had been released under COVID-19 temporary release schemes, 53 on compassionate grounds.

By 31 October 2020[8]:

- 55 prisoners, children in custody and probation service users had died having tested positive for COVID-19 or where a clinical assessment showed that COVID-19 was a contributory factor in their deaths. Of these, 32 were prisoners and 23 were probation service users. Five deaths of prisoners occurred in October 2020, the first deaths of service users since June 2020.
- Of the 55 deaths, 50 were suspected or confirmed to be caused by COVID-19, 28 were prisoners and 22 probation service users.
- 1,529 prisoners or children had tested positive for COVID-19 since the start of the pandemic, across 99 establishments, almost all of whom were adults. The number of new monthly confirmed cases had increased by 883 since September 2020. 45 establishments had prisoners or children testing positive in October 2020.

By 31 December 2020[9]:

- 99 prisoners, children in custody and probation service users had died having tested positive for COVID-19 or where there was a clinical assessment that COVID-19 was a contributory factor in their deaths. Of these, 71 were prisoners and 28 were probation service users.
- Of the 99 deaths, 77 were suspected or confirmed to be caused by COVID-19. 51 were prisoners and 26 probation service users.
- 6,007 prisoners or children had tested positive for COVID-19 since the start of the pandemic, across 116 establishments, almost all of whom were adults.
- The number of new confirmed cases increased by 2,357 since November 2020.
- 91 establishments had prisoners or children testing positive in December 2020.

Data on prison staff[10]:

- Between March 2020 and the end of January 2021, 36 HMPPS staff died having tested positive for COVID-19 or where there was a clinical assessment that COVID-19 was a contributory factor in their deaths.
- This includes 16 directly employed staff and 20 non-directly employed staff. Of the directly employed staff, 12 of these were staff from Prisons and Youth Custody Service. 4 were members of the National Probation Service.
- Over this same period, 12,184 staff tested positive for COVID-19. Of these positive test results, 2,332 were for non-directly employed staff and 9,852 were directly employed.

- In the month of January 2021 alone, there were 4,549 new confirmed cases.
- Staff absent due to COVID-19 sickness rose sharply during the months of December 2020 and January 2021, from 978 at the end of November 2020 to 1,961 at the end of January 2021.

2 Prison and penal policy concerning the execution of prison sentences during the COVID-19 crisis

Prison sentences continue to be served immediately, with no formal expansion of community sentences. However, judges and magistrates were advised by the Court of Appeal in *R v Manning* [2020] EWCA Crim 592 that in the exceptional circumstances of the pandemic, it was appropriate to take account of the conditions in which prisoners were being held in fixing sentences. *Manning* was a prosecution appeal against an allegedly unduly lenient sentence (an Attorney General's reference to the Court of Appeal) where the Court of Appeal's decision not to increase the sentence was informed by the pandemic. Following this, in *R v Jones* [2020] EWCA Crim 764, the Court of Appeal held that in the exceptional circumstances of the pandemic, it was appropriate to take account of the custodial conditions under which an offender was to be held when considering his appeal against sentence. A sentence of eight months' imprisonment was quashed and replaced with a sentence of six months. It is very difficult, if not impossible, to know at this time the number of people who have received community sentences who would in "normal" circumstances have received custodial sentences, or the extent to which sentence lengths may have decreased in the pandemic.

A number of schemes were introduced at the beginning of the pandemic to allow for the release of prisoners, but they have not been used very much. A new End of Custody Temporary Release (ECTR) scheme providing for the early release of some low-risk prisoners who were within two months of their normal release date was introduced, but very few were released under this scheme, and it was ended on 27 August 2020.

Existing rules allow the Secretary of State for Justice (the Minister of Justice) to release prisoners in exceptional compassionate circumstances.[11] Compassionate release under these rules is rare because it is a permanent release, normally given to those who are terminally ill and close to death. The Government decided that it was inappropriate in the context of COVID and that, instead, prisoners should have to apply for Release on Temporary Licence (ROTL) by way of Special Purpose Licence (SPL), whereby release on compassionate grounds for vulnerability reasons is only for the duration of the pandemic. Under ROTL, prisoners can be returned to prison once the justification for temporary compassionate release ends, if they are still serving the custodial element of their sentence at that point. This scheme has been restricted to:

- Pregnant women;
- Prisoners with their babies in custody and
- Those defined by National Health Service guidelines as "extremely vulnerable" to COVID-19.

There have been only 66 releases under this scheme, despite the Minister stating in March that there were about 1,800 prisoners who would have been classified as particularly vulnerable if they were in the community.[12] The ordinary ROTL rules, whereby prisoners work outside prison or might be allowed to attend e.g. a family member's funeral, have been very seriously curtailed. At the end of March 2020, it was announced that all ROTL had been suspended – except in cases of prisoners working as "key workers" or temporary release on compassionate grounds. As a result of these operational changes, there were only 12,643 incidences of ROTL during the quarter ending June 2020, which represents an 88% decrease compared to the same quarter in 2019. More than 80% of the ROTL incidences in the latest quarter were for "Work Related" reasons.

The Government says that it has been working in three other areas to try to create more space in the prison estate: to expedite hearings of remand prisoners (the detention in prison of those awaiting trial), to accelerate the Home Detention Curfew (HDC) process (a standard release scheme which allows fixed term prisoners serving less than four years up to 135 days early release on an electronic "tag") and to expand the prison estate.[13] Let us look briefly at each of these. First, the pre-existing problems relating to remand have been greatly exacerbated by delays in court hearings. The Government responded to the backlog of cases awaiting trial by extending custody time limits (the maximum period someone can be held pre-trial) from 6 to 8 months. The most recent figures show that the remand population has *increased* by 28% over the past year (to 12,274) and by the end of June was at the highest level for around six years.[14] Second, concerning release on HDC, the number of early releases has not increased. 2,825 offenders were released on HDC during the latest quarter for which the statistics are available – this represents a fall of 13% compared to the same quarter in 2019.[15] This fall in the number released on HDC reflects the reduction in the size of the pool of offenders eligible for HDC (also 13% lower than the same period in 2019). In relation to expanding the prison estate, over 300 "temporary cells" were delivered to prisons, and a secure training centre for children (which had recently been closed because of a damning inspection report) re-opened as a prison for adults.

Non-compliance with lockdown restrictions result in Fixed Penalty Notices (FPNs), which are issued by the police.[16] Between 27 March and 19 November, 24,933 FPNs were issued (of which 14,738 were handed out in the first 7 weeks). These now start at £200 (for a first notice), rising to £6,400 (for a sixth and subsequent FPN).[17] Large parties can be shut down by the police – with fines on organisers of up to £10,000. Fewer than 1,000 FPNs have been issued for breaches of international quarantine rules and of face covering regulations.[18] We have found no information on the enforcement of the regulations within prisons.

3 Restrictions on contact with the outside world

There have been huge restrictions on visits, prison leave and transfers. On 23 March 2020, a new instruction stopped all prison visits, all education, training and employment activities (except for essential work like cleaning), all access to gyms, religious association and general association. Limits were placed on numbers of people unlocked or in exercise yards at any one time, and social distancing of two metres for staff and prisoners was to be enforced wherever possible. Intra-prison movement of prisoners was strongly discouraged; and for areas with especially vulnerable prisoners, avoiding staff cross-deployment was advised where possible. Another order on 31 March introduced the policy of "compartmentalisation", reducing more stringently transfers within and between prisons. New cohorting strategies came in, which included establishing:

- Protective Isolation Units (PIUs): to accommodate known or probable COVID-19 cases, "ideally" in single-cell accommodation;
- Shielding Units (SUs): to protect the most vulnerable, with enhanced levels of bio-security, including dedicated staff; and
- Reverse Cohorting Units (RCUs): to accommodate new receptions or transfers in for a period of 14 days to detect any emergent infectious cases before prisoners entered the general population.

On 2 June, the Ministry of Justice published a national framework for prison regimes and services, which was seen as a "conditional roadmap" for the easing of restrictions.[19] Some prisons resumed visits in July, and by mid-August, many prisons were offering limited visits for family and friends. As of 20 September, only one prison, Leicester, was still closed for all social visits.[20] However, in November, all visits stopped again. Since December 2020, individual prisons have made their own decisions as to whether to allow visits.

The significant reduction in the transfer of prisoners between prisons has also made it difficult for prisoners to progress.[21] We should also note the hugely important impact of the stopping of prisoner transfers between courts and prisons. Whilst some court hearings continued by video link or even by telephone, jury trials were suspended on 23 March, and the resulting increase in the backlog of cases has been dramatic.[22] There has also been substantial disruption to the work of the Parole Board, which decides whether indeterminate or recalled prisoners should be released. Oral hearings were for a time stopped completely, and remain severely curtailed.

Many cases have been heard by video or telephone links, and others have been deferred.

4 Restrictions inside prisons

During the pandemic, many prisoners have been spending 23 hours a day in their cells. The Chief Inspector of Prisons wrote in April: "The vast majority [of prisoners] were locked up for nearly the whole day with usually no more than half an hour out of their cells. We found some examples of even greater restrictions. In one prison, a small number of symptomatic prisoners had been isolated in their cells without any opportunity to come out for a shower or exercise for up to 14 days".[23] This has clearly continued, as we see in later reports. For example, a recent report on HMP Pentonville (a large London prison) reports that in October, time out of cell for many prisoners was restricted to about 45 minutes a day, showers and outdoor exercise were offered to these prisoners on alternate days except Saturdays which meant that they were not able to shower and go outside each day, evening meals were served from 3.30 pm and many prisoners were reporting victimisation by staff. Work and education provision became minimal, as those who provided work or education withdrew from prisons.

5 Compensatory measures

On 24 March, the Ministry of Justice announced: "Secure phone handsets will be given to prisoners at 55 jails. This will enable the approved use of 900 locked SIM card handsets, allowing risk-assessed prisoners to speak to a small number of pre-authorised contacts. The phones will not have internet access".[24] On 11 May, the Justice Secretary confirmed that these had been rolled out and that on 3 April the cost of calls was reduced across the prison estate.

Guidance issued by the Ministry of Justice on 27 May, updated on 10 July, stated that "secure video calls" were available to prisoners in 27 prisons, with more prisons being added. The guidance explained that video calls would last 30 minutes and each prisoner could have up to 4 visitors on the call. Secure video calls were free of charge during the pandemic and would be provided through the Purple Visits app.[25] In evidence to the Justice Committee on 8 June, the Prisons Minister said that Purple Visits would be available in all 12 women's prisons by the end of June, but an Inside Time report of 13 July noted that two prisons still did not have the facility.[26] A Government update on 6 November stated: "Prisoners will still be able to see friends and family via secure video calls, with this game-changing technology now in place at over 100 jails. Staff are also helping offenders to keep in touch through phone calls, with more than 1,200 mobile handsets distributed as well as extra phone credit".[27] Prisoners can also continue using the Prison Voicemail service and the Email a Prisoner service, which were in place before the pandemic.

It is difficult to know how effective these measures have been. As the PRT stated, "With up to 40,000 prisoners given very little time out of cell, the demand for 900 mobile phones spread over 55 prisons was certain to overwhelm the supply. The additional phone time these provided could never offset the profound impact of cutting off family contact".[28]

There has been grave concern about the impact of the lockdown on prisoners' mental health. The further loss of liberty and the damage caused by "the extremes of lockdown" were identified in the two 2020 reports of the Independent Advisory Panel on Deaths in Custody (Independent Advisory Panel, 2020a, 2020b). The extreme challenge of prolonged isolation may be particularly harmful for young offenders.

6 Legal basis for restrictions and relaxations of the prison regime

In England and Wales, the Secretary of State (Minister of Justice) has wide powers under the Prison Act 1952 to make rules for the running of prisons. It was therefore easy for new rules to be introduced. There is no formal judicial involvement in the execution of sentences.

On 12 March 2020, the first guidance was provided online.[29] The penal system was put in "command mode", and an "exceptional delivery model" was imposed. These first changes were implemented without changing the Prison Rules. There have since been the Prison and Young Offender Institution (Coronavirus) (Amendment) Rules 2020 (SI 2020 No. 400), which came into force on 6 April; and the Prison and Young Offender Institution (Coronavirus) (Amendment) (No. 2) Rules 2020, which came into force on 15 May 2020. These Rules grant the Secretary of State a discretion to release prisoners temporarily "for the purpose of preventing, protecting against, delaying or otherwise controlling the incidence or transmission of coronavirus".

Whilst the UK grants wide powers to the prison and executive authorities, it also has a complex network of bodies which seek to monitor and hold prisons to account. One of the most important, in England and Wales, is Her Majesty's Inspectorate of Prisons (HMIP). On 17 March 2020, the Chief Inspector of Prisons announced that all of the scheduled inspection work involving visits to prisons or other places of detention had been suspended up to the end of May 2020. This affected inspections, independent reviews of progress and visits as part of thematic inspection work. From April to July 2020, they carried out short scrutiny visits, which involved a small team of inspectors visiting prisons for just one day, focusing on core issues only. These short scrutiny visits were replaced in August 2020 by scrutiny visits.

The PPO and Independent Monitoring Boards (IMBs) continued to carry out their work – but often remotely. New ways of working included telephone updates, emails and virtual visits.[30]

7 Returning to normal and what could be learnt for the future

It is very difficult to predict what the "new normal" will be in prisons, and indeed when it will arrive. There could be beneficial outcomes – more access to the internet, more audio-visual contacts, more in-cell telephones, for example. One time Chief Inspector of Prisons and former Chairman of the Parole Board, Nick Hardwick (2020) provides a positive account of what went right in the pandemic and explores the lessons to be learnt. First, he points out (writing in early November 2020) that the lockdown should be tightened if the epidemic is continuing to spread. The prison service is very good in a crisis. Lockdowns save lives. The primary duty of the state is to keep prisoners safe.

Hardwick's second lesson to be learnt is that quality of time in and out of cell is more important than its quantity. The absence, or slow pace, of purposeful activity has been a key issue in English prisons for decades. One of the big unknowns as yet is the impact of the lockdown on prisoner mental health. Despite the fear of negative effects, there is some evidence that self-harm rates and assaults may have reduced. Why? Hewson et al. (2020) discuss the possible explanations for a fall in the number of cases of self-harm. Perhaps any downturn in recorded cases is due to failures of staff to recognise the problems. But more likely there may be an increase in prisoners' sense of safety and security. Fewer conflicts with other prisoners on the wings, reduced drug use, more pro-active staff support and fewer feelings of injustice could all have played a part. And prisoners at the greatest risk of suicide and self-harm, and those with serious mental health problems, may be more alienated from external support networks and therefore less likely to suffer from the absence of visits. The pandemic could teach us lessons on giving prisoners more individual attention and support.

Hardwick's third lesson is that we should maintain prison population reductions. The prison population of England and Wales is notoriously high, and has risen extraordinarily fast in recent decades. The small decrease during the pandemic has been due largely to court closures, and Hardwick is not alone in worrying about the likely surge in admissions to prison as the backlog of court cases is reduced. He argues that the need to find a mechanism to limit the growth in the prison population is "simply unavoidable".

Hardwick's fourth and final lesson involves recognising that a centrally imposed "circuit-breaker" of restrictive measures in prisons proved important in reducing infections and allowing time for longer-term measures to be put in place. Hardwick suggests that the performance of the prison system compares favourably with that of other institutions in the UK and of other prisons internationally. But he is not naïve or complacent. It will not be easy to reduce the prison population or the amount of violence and self-harm which has been such a shocking part of our prison system in recent years. Will the authorities invest in more purposeful activities? What is needed is a vision for a "new normal" which focuses on prisons as engines of change and social justice (for victims and offenders and society), and not simply as penal warehouses.

It is not clear when or if this "new normal" will start to appear. We have so far had two periods of national lockdown for the country as a whole. Tight national restrictions were again imposed from 5 November until 2 December 2020. From 2 December, local restrictions according to "tiers" have been re-introduced.[31] Despite the hopes for widespread vaccination in the early months of 2021, it is difficult to predict with any confidence when we will return to "normal".

Notes

1 In England and Wales, the rate of prisoners per 100,000 of the population was 130 at the end of January 2021.

2 See Offender Management Statistics. Data in this paragraph are from Sturge, 2020.

3 Ministry of Justice, Population bulletin, monthly May 2020.

4 See Prison Reform Trust & Prison Policy Network, 2020a; 2020b HM Chief Inspector of Prisons, 2019, and House of Commons' Health and Social Care Committee, 2018, all cited in Brennan, 2020.

5 At the end of April 2020, a reasonable "worst-case scenario" prepared for the prison service by Public Health England suggested that 77,800 prisoners could become infected, 4,500 hospitalised and 2,700 die if no action was taken: see O'Moore, 2020.

6 The death of Mr Edwin Hillier, a prisoner at HMP Littlehey, was the subject of an investigation and report by the independent Prisons and Probation Ombudsman which investigates complaints and deaths in custody. The report can be found here: https://s3-eu-west-2.amazonaws.com/ppo-prod-storage-1g9rkhjhk-jmgw/uploads/2021/01/F4175-20-Death-of-Mr-Edwin-Hillier-in-hospital-Littlehey-22-03-2020-NC-60-84.pdf.

7 https://assets.publishing.service.gov.uk/government/uploads/system/uploads/attachment_data/file/919130/HMPPS_COVID19_AUG20_Pub_Doc.pdf.

8 https://assets.publishing.service.gov.uk/government/uploads/system/uploads/attachment_data/file/935053/HMPPS_COVID19_Oct20_Pub_Final.pdf

9 https://assets.publishing.service.gov.uk/government/uploads/system/uploads/attachment_data/file/952359/HMPPS_COVID19_DEC20_Pub_Doc.pdf

10 https://www.gov.uk/government/statistics/her-majestys-prison-and-probation-service-workforce-quarterly-december-2020/hmpps-covid-19-experimental-statistics-annex-31-january-2021#deaths.

11 Under s. 248 of the Criminal Justice Act 2003 in respect of fixed term prisoners, and s.30 of the Crime (Sentences) Act 1997 for indeterminate sentenced prisoners. The policy and guidance on the application of those powers is contained, respectively, in Prison Service Order (PSO) 6000 for determinate sentence prisoners and in PSO 4700 for indeterminate sentence prisoners.

12 House of Commons Justice Committee, 2020 (see Oral Evidence, The Work of the Lord Chancellor, HC 225, 24 March 2020).

13 See, for example, the Secretary of State's letter published at http://www.prisonreformtrust.org.uk/Portals/0/Documents/Letters/2020.11.11%20Robert%20Buckland%20to%20PRT%20and%20HL.pdf.

14 See Offender Management Statistics Quarterly: April to June 2020 (published 29 October 2020: https://www.gov.uk/government/publications/offender-management-statistics-quarterly-april-to-june-2020/offender-management-statistics-quarterly-april-to-june-2020.
15 See footnote 12.
16 The Health Protection (Coronavirus, Restrictions) (England) Regulations 2020, which came into force on 26 March 2020.
17 The Health Protection (Coronavirus, Restrictions) (No. 2) (England) Regulations 2020, which came into force on 24 September 2020.
18 Face coverings have been required on public transport since June and in shops since July.
19 https://assets.publishing.service.gov.uk/government/uploads/system/uploads/attachment_data/file/889689/prisons-national-framework.pdf.
20 https://insidetime.org/three-prisons-still-closed-for-social-visits/
21 In the English system, prisoners often move prisons frequently: perhaps because of the availability of courses or as they progress through the security classifications.
22 As at 5 August, the combined backlog of outstanding cases in the magistrates and Crown courts stood at over half a million.
https://houseofcommons.shorthandstories.com/justice-coronavirus-impact-on-probation-prisons-courts-legal-professions/index.html.
23 HM Inspectorate of Prisons, Report on short scrutiny visits to Local Prisons, April 2020: 7.
24 https://www.gov.uk/government/news/prison-visits-cancelled.
25 https://www.gov.uk/guidance/visit-a-prisoner-using-a-video-call
26 https://insidetime.org/women-still-waiting-for-video-visits/
27 https://www.gov.uk/government/news/coronavirus-preparedness-in-prisons.
28 The Prison Reform Trust & The Prison Policy Network 2020a: 6
29 The website's content changes regularly. See https://www.gov.uk/guidance/coronavirus-covid-19-and-prisons.
30 Independent Monitoring Boards, 2020. The national IMB Annual Report 2019/20 contains references to the impacts of COVID restrictions.
31 We repeat that we are discussing only England and Wales.

References

Beard, J. (2020): *Coronavirus (prisons): England and Wales* (Briefing Paper, Number 8892, May 2020). House of Commons. https://commonslibrary.parliament.uk/research-briefings/cbp-8892/

Brennan, P. K. (2020): 'Responses Taken to Mitigate COVID-19 in Prisons in England and Wales', *Victims & Offenders*, DOI: 10.1080/15564886.2020.1832027

Brown, J. (2020): *Coronavirus: Enforcing Restrictions* (House of Commons Library Briefing Paper No 9024, Dec 2020)

Coker, R. (March 2020): *Expert Report: Covid-19 and Prisons in England and Wales*. Howard League for Penal Reform and the Prison Reform Trust, http://prisonreformtrust.org.uk/portals/0/documents/COKER_Report_HL_PRT.pdf.

Hardwick, N. (2020): *Prisons and Covid-19: What Went Right?* (Crest Advisory). https://www.crestadvisory.com/post/prisons-and-covid-19-what-went-right

Hewson, T. et al. (2020): 'The Effects of COVID-19 on Self-harm in UK Prisons', 16 *Brit J of Psych. Bulletin* 1–3. https://www.ncbi.nlm.nih.gov/pmc/articles/PMC7411440/

HM Chief Inspector of Prisons (2019): *Annual Report 2018–19*, London: HM Stationery Office

House of Commons' Health and Social Care Committee (2018): *Annex 1: Visit to Greenwich Cluster.* https://publications.parliament.uk/pa/cm201719/cmselect/cmhealth/963/96302.htm.

House of Commons' Justice Committee (2020): *Coronavirus (Covid-19): The Impact on Prisons.* https://publications.parliament.uk/pa/cm5801/cmselect/cmjust/299/29902.htm.

Independent Advisory Panel on Deaths in Custody (2020a): *"Keep talking, stay safe": A Rapid Review of Prisoners' Experiences under Covid-19.*

Independent Advisory Panel on Deaths in Custody (2020b): *'Just one thing' Prison Safety and Covid-19.*

Independent Monitoring Boards (2020): *National Annual Report 2019–20.* https://www.imb.org.uk/report/10718/

National Audit Office (2020): *Improving the Prison Estate (Session 2019–20, HC 41).* https://www.nao.org.uk/wp-content/uploads/2020/02/Improving-the-prison-estate.pdf.

O'Moore, E. (2020): *Briefing Paper-Interim Assessment of Impact of Various Population Management Strategies in Prisons in Response to COVID-19 Pandemic in England (Ministry of Justice/Public Health England, HMPPS).* https://assets.publishing.service.gov.uk/government/uploads/system/uploads/attachment_data/file/882622/covid-19-p opulation-management-strategy-prisons.pdf.

Prison Reform Trust & Prisoner Policy Network (2020a): *How Prisons Are Responding to Covid-19: Briefing 1, Families and Communications.* http://www.prisonreformtrust.org.uk/PressPolicy/News/Coronavirus.

Prison Reform Trust & Prisoner Policy Network (2020b): *How Prisons Are Responding to Covid-19: Briefing 2, Regimes, Reactions to the Pandemic, and Progression.* http://www.prisonreformtrust.org.uk/PressPolicy/News/Coronavirus.

Sturge, G. (2020): *UK Prison Population Statistics (House of Commons Briefing Paper Number CBP-04334).* https://commonslibrary.parliament.uk/research-briefings/sn04334/.

15 Estonia

Anneli Soo and Priit Kama

1 Introduction – general situation of the prison system

The present Estonian prison system dates back to the1920s when the Estonian penal law was modernised and democratised, i.e. social class distinctions were abolished and the conditional custodial penalty was introduced in the new Penal Code that was adopted by the parliament in 1929 and entered into force in 1935. In 1940, the Soviet occupation of Estonia started and swiftly implemented its own laws that were in many aspects regressive, undemocratic, and inhumane, designed to serve the needs of a totalitarian regime (Luts-Sootak and Siimets-Gross, 2019: 50–56, 88–94).

The end of the Soviet occupation in 1991 led to significant changes in the system of criminal sanctions. In 1992, the amendments to the Criminal Code abolished Soviet punishments, such as non-custodial correctional work, parole combined with compulsory employment, banishment, and placement in a correctional labour institution. Instead, the Code provided for two main penalties: pecuniary punishment (in the daily rate system) and imprisonment with the possibility of parole (Sootak and Pikamäe, 2001: 42). In 1993, labour colonies were replaced with open, semi-closed, and closed prisons (Ministry of Justice, 2006: 8).

Ultimately, there were nine prisons in Estonia in 2002, a number that was reduced to three by 2020: Tartu Prison, which was opened in 2002, Viru Prison, which was opened in 2008, and Tallinn Prison, which was opened in 2018 (Ministry of Justice, 2018: 9). The Estonian Prison Service currently employs 1,481 people, of whom 883 serve as prison guards (Justiitsministeerium, 2020). All three remaining prisons are chamber system prisons (as opposed to dormitory system prisons), which serves to lessen interaction and spreading of criminal knowledge (the so-called prison culture) among prisoners. Whenever possible, prisoners are placed in the prison closest to their home in order to maintain their social ties and family connections; this aims to facilitate rehabilitation and resocialisation (Ministry of Justice, 2020).

By the end of the 1990s, the prison population in Estonia had increased to almost 5,000 (the general population is about 1.4 million people). Subsequently, this number has steadily declined: 4,352 in 2003; 3,456 in 2008; 3,285

DOI: 10.4324/9781003169178-15

in 2013; and 2,525 in 2018. On 9 November 2020, three Estonian prisons hold in total 2,405 prisoners, of whom 1,901 are sentenced prisoners and 504 are held in pre-trial detention. The majority of prisoners serve sentences of up to four years, and 39 prisoners currently serve a life sentence (Justiitsministeerium, 2020a; Ministry of Justice, 2018: 43).

Although prison rates have steadily declined, the general population has also decreased, compared to the 2000s, by approx. 100,000 people. Today, Estonia finds itself in a situation of its imprisonment rate being significantly higher than the European Union average. With an estimated imprisonment rate of 181 per 100,000 inhabitants in 2020, Estonia ranks tenth among the European countries with the highest imprisonment rate.[1] This correlates with a constantly decreasing but still high level of serious crime, as Estonia has the third highest rate of intentional homicide in Europe (following only Latvia and Lithuania).[2]

Although the general agreement between different state authorities seems to be that imprisonment should be a measure of last resort, targeted to those who endanger other members of society, there is no common understanding who in fact those people are. Despite frequent political discussions about the need for tougher punishments for certain types of offences, it has had little effect on the penal legislation, and the Estonian prison population continues to decline. Estonia's criminal policies cannot be considered tough. A high prisoner number could indicate tough criminal policies if the majority of prisoners were convicted for property crimes, and not for violent crimes (see below). No changes can be detected in the general penal climate during the COVID-19 crisis.

Although the most common type of reported crime in Estonia is crimes against property, those who end up in prison are mainly convicted for violent crime. In 2018, of the 2,134 convicted offenders in total, there were 962 convicted for violent crimes, followed by 585 for drug-related crimes, 284 for crimes against property, and 187 for traffic crimes (Ministry of Justice, 2018: 42). The decline in the number of registered crimes that started in 2009 stopped in 2017, and in the last three years, the number of reported crimes has remained practically at the same level. Although the greatest number of crimes are those against property, their number has been steadily declining. Since 2018, the registration of violent crimes of lesser severity has increased significantly. This can be attributed to greater public awareness of domestic violence and the increased attention of the police to this previously hidden problem. At the same time, the number of the most serious violent crimes has continued to decline (Justiitsministeerium, 2019).

The most recent study on recidivism in Estonia, conducted by the Ministry of Justice, indicated that while the general rate of recidivism[3] within two years after conviction in Estonia is around 17%, it is 32% among those who were released from prison after serving their prison sentence. Recidivism was highest among those who had been convicted for a crime against property, and they were most likely to re-commit the same type of crime. Among those who had been convicted for a serious crime against another person, recidivism has been relatively low (Justiitsministeerium, 2019).

Inasmuch as Estonia's recidivism rate has been studied comparatively with other states, it shows only modest differences. In 2019, a study using methodologically comparable statistics was conducted by a joint venture of the Ministry of Justice of Estonia and the Finnish Criminal Sanctions Agency, which compared recidivism rates in Estonia and Finland. It showed that two-year recidivism rates of offenders released from prison were 34% in Estonia and 35% in Finland (Ministry of Justice, 2019). Nevertheless, Estonia's imprisonment rate is high. Further research is therefore needed to explore the causes of the high rate of first-time entrants, including the topic of intergenerational transmission of crime in Estonia.

The Imprisonment Act[4] provides the procedure for and organisation of execution of imprisonment, detention for misdemeanours (up to 30 days) and pre-trial detention, and the definition and conditions of prison service and service as a prison officer. It follows the principles of the modern Estonian Penal Code,[5] according to which the main purpose of imprisonment is a proper reaction to the committed crime, not changing or improving the convicted offender (Sootak and Pikamäe, 2001: 46).

This, however, does not mean that the goals of rehabilitation and resocialisation have been neglected. The Imprisonment Act § 6 (1) states that the objective of execution of imprisonment is to help prisoners lead a law-abiding life and to defend public order. Here, the return of a prisoner to society may be categorised in three stages: the admission stage, the basic stage, and the release stage.

In the admission stage at the beginning of serving a prison sentence, emphasis is placed on family safety, the ways in which a job could be maintained, and the need to secure one's property. Prisoners' alcohol and drug-related problems are identified, as well as their professional skills, work experience, and the desire to acquire education in prison. In the basic stage, the prisoner is given legal assistance with social problems, support in maintaining and restoring relations with family members, assistance in establishing or maintaining contact with employers, and support in coping with learning difficulties. In the release stage, prisoners are assisted in solving problems caused by reduced contacts outside prison. Preparing for the release, the prison provides assistance in obtaining relevant documents, finding a job and a place to stay, and applying for support from the general welfare services (Ministry of Justice, 2020a).

When it comes to human rights in prison, three main issues have risen in Estonia. First, after the European Court of Human Rights (ECtHR) found a violation of Article 3 of the European Convention of Human Rights (ECHR) due to overcrowding in Italian prisons[6] and consequently gave its pilot judgement in 2013, a similar judgement was given against Estonia.[7] As of 2018, this problem has been solved in Estonia by opening new and modern prisons. Second, although already on 6 October 2005 the ECtHR ruled that the UK's blanket (legislative) ban on convicted prisoners voting breached Article 3 of Protocol 1 to the ECHR,[8] Estonia still has the same general ban in its law. This problem has not reached the ECtHR yet, and therefore is unresolved. Third, the Estonian Imprisonment Act allows inmates to be sentenced to isolation for up to 45 consecutive days, which is not in accordance with the general guidelines given in the UN Mandela Rules, recommending no disciplinary solitary confinement sentence to last over 14 consecutive days. In addition, the Imprisonment Act allows prisoners to be sentenced for multiple offences consecutively, further lengthening the number of consecutive days of the sentence. Like the right to vote, this problem has not reached the ECtHR.

As a result, some prisoners have been sentenced to months of solitary confinement. A 236-day long sentence was overturned by the Supreme Court of Estonia, which decided that a sentence exceeding 120 days of consecutive confinement may not be allowed, as it is damaging to the prisoner's health and well-being (RKHKm 3–15–2943). The Estonian Prison Service has addressed aspects of solitary confinement that scientific researchers have assessed as possible health hazards: the architecture and lightning of any type of solitary confinement (administrative, disciplinary, or protective) does not differ from an ordinary cell. During segregation, prisoners have continuous access to reading materials, mail correspondence, phone calls, and daily newspapers; starting from the 11th day of segregation, the prisoner is offered a Communication Programme that includes regular conversations with different specialists and social workers who are not prison officers, and access to different cognitively stimulating activities (learning materials, Sudoku, puzzles, etc.).

The emergence of COVID-19 brought the following numbers in the society and in prisons as at 15 December 2020. In the society, 18,682 members tested positive for COVID-19, and 157 of them died (The Health Board of Estonia, 2020). In spring 2020, there were no positive tests among prisoners, but the situation changed in October 2020, and the total cumulative number of Corona positive prisoners during the epidemic was 226, all of whom recovered by the end of December 2020. There has been no further wave of infections in 2021 in Estonian prisons. Some prisoners in open prisons who go out to work have been infected. In addition, some newcomers to closed prisons had been infected outside, but only few prisoners in closed prisons were infected during imprisonment.

2 Prison and penal policy concerning the execution of prison sentences during the COVID-induced crisis

Estonia changed neither its penal law, nor its judicial practice, nor its policy of execution of prison sentences during the COVID-19 crisis. Although the execution of prison sentences did not cease during the state of emergency and was not altered by early releases during the first wave in spring, all transfers of prisoners between prisons were suspended. Transfers between police detention centres and prisons were allowed under special circumstances, and after individual case agreements between the police and the prison service. New prisoners were admitted after they were checked with a no-touch thermometer in the transfer bus prior to arriving in prison. In cases of suspected infection, the prison's medical department was notified immediately, and the bus disinfected after the transfer. For all prisoners with clinical signs of infection, there is a quarantine unit, where they have to be housed for 14 days or until the infection risk has passed. Restrictions on the prisoners held in the quarantine unit and other people entering the quarantine unit are set by the medical department. As overcrowding is not a problem in the Estonian prison system, there was also no practical need to consider halting the execution of prison sentences. In 2019, the Estonian prison capacity density per 100 places was 77.5 (based on double occupancy cells).[9]

The Estonian Government declared a state of emergency on 12 March 2020 due to the COVID-19 crisis. The state of emergency lasted until 17 May 2020. Until then, non-compliance with COVID-19-induced restrictions was sanctioned by the Emergency Act.[10] Non-compliance with any such restrictions was punishable by an administrative sanction, namely a penalty of up to 2,000 Euros. After the termination of the state of emergency, the COVID-19 crisis was regulated by the Communicable Diseases Prevention and Control Act[11] and the 31 October 2003 regulation No. 123 of the Minister of Social Affairs "Requirements for Control of Communicable Diseases".[12] Non-compliance with any restrictions prescribed by these acts may be punished by a penalty (i.e. an administrative sanction) of up to 9,600 Euros or a fine for a misdemeanour of up to 800 Euros. No criminal punishments are prescribed for non-compliance with COVID-19 contact restrictions inside and outside of prisons.

3 Restrictions of contact with the outside world

Restrictions of contacts with the outside world and inside prisons differed substantially during the first and second waves of COVID-19, as did the scientific findings and knowledge of COVID-19 at the time. During the first wave of COVID-19, scientific knowledge did not exclude hepatitis C and HIV from the list of high-risk underlying medical conditions (Wei-jie et al., 2020). As around 1,000 (i.e. over 40%) of prisoners in Estonia have these underlying conditions, strict preventive measures were taken to protect the health of prisoners. By the second wave, there was comprehensive scientific knowledge that people with hepatitis C or HIV on effective treatment are not expected to be at a higher risk of becoming seriously ill with COVID-19, and the preventive measures of the second wave were relaxed correspondingly.

During the state of emergency that lasted until 17 May 2020, all visits to prisoners were suspended, except visits by criminal defence lawyers and representatives, who are advocates, ministers of religion, notaries, and consular officers of the country of origin of foreign prisoners. All people entering a prison were checked with a no-touch thermometer. Court hearings were and still are mostly held via video conference. All prison visit tours and similar activities that are not necessary for the everyday functions of prisons were cancelled.

During the second wave, from October 2020, long-term family visits were cancelled. Short visits in secured individual rooms, where visitors and detainees are separated by glass, continued as normal, with the exception of Viru Prison where the number of infected prisoners surpassed 200 and consequently, all visits were suspended. Everyone entering a prison was checked with a no-touch thermometer and in case of flu-like symptoms denied entry. These restrictions did not apply to visits by criminal defence lawyers and the other representatives mentioned above. However, depending on the situation, it could be compulsory for the allowed visitors to use protective masks.

Transfers of prisoners between different prisons were suspended in all prisons during the first wave and only in Viru Prison during the second wave. Admission of new prisoners continued as normal during both waves. Inmates of open prisons were not allowed to leave the premises during the first wave from 17 March to 25 May. During the second wave, movements of prisoners in open prisons were not restricted.

4 Restrictions inside prisons

Work outside prisons was suspended only during the first wave. Group recreational activities were suspended in all prisons during the first wave and only in Viru and Tallinn Prisons during the second wave. Prisoners were allowed to engage in programmes and activities that could be performed individually. During the first wave, prison workshops were closed, except a workshop for female prisoners that manufactured face masks, but as the availability of personal protective equipment improved, that was shut down as well. The laundry unit of the Estonian Prison Industry continued working during the first wave. During the second wave, only Viru Prison workshops were closed. Tartu prison workshops continued to operate as normal and Tallinn Prison workshops worked with a reduced number of prisoners.

During the first wave from 16 March to 25 May, daily one-hour outdoor exercise was cancelled and prisoners were locked in their cells, with the exception of the mother-child unit, where the daily fresh air walk was never restricted. During the second wave, daily one-hour outdoor exercise was organised in small groups and following social distancing measures. The only group of prisoners whose daily outdoor exercise was restricted were COVID-19 close contacts – as assessed according to the State Health Board guidelines. For all prisoners with clinical signs of infection, a quarantine unit had been organised, where they were housed for 14 days or until the infection risk had passed. The original cell of the infected (suspected infected) prisoner who has been transferred to the quarantine unit was disinfected.

All prisons were provided with an adequate amount of disinfection products and medical personal protective equipment: respirators, protective gloves, protective eyewear, and no-touch thermometers. Prison medical departments provided prison officials with protective equipment together with instructions and hygiene requirements for their use. In listed situations, prison officials, prisoners, and allowed visitors had to wear protective masks. All pregnant prison officers and workers were ordered to stay at home and work from there.

5 Compensatory measures

No significant innovative compensatory measures were introduced. Prison stores suspended their activity only during the first wave and prisoners were provided with hygiene products and stationary appliances. No new communication equipment for prisoners was introduced during the COVID-19 crisis. During the first wave, prisoners were granted one private phone call per week, and during the second wave as many as possible but no less than two private phone calls per week. Throughout the crisis, the prison service loaded extra time onto the phone cards of prisoners who did not have sufficient funds to do it themselves.

In order to compensate for the strict preventive measures, all prisoners were provided with cognitively stimulating activities: crosswords, sudokus, books, magazines, additional TV-channels, and newspapers. Prisoners were also provided with simple instructions for yoga and physical exercises to compensate for the restricted movement within the prison.

Most court proceedings in which prisoners were involved were held online. The Estonian legislator made additional amendments to the Code of Criminal Procedure and to the Code of Misdemeanour Procedure concerning the use of technical solutions to make participation in different procedural activities more easily available.

6 Legal basis for restrictions and relaxations of the prison regime

The Estonian prisons are operated according to the Imprisonment Act, which regulates the execution of imprisonment, detention, and pre-trial detention, and the definition and conditions of the prison service and service as a prison officer (§ 1). The Imprisonment Act is the main legal basis for prison operations. Orders and regulations of the Government of the Republic, the Minister of Justice, and the Minister of Social Affairs also regulate how the prisons operate and give further clarification on day-to-day life in prisons. Most of the restrictions imposed on prisoners are described in the Imprisonment Act.

If the law does not provide a specific legal basis for the concrete restriction in a particular situation, the general clause for application of restrictions is the Imprisonment Act § 4^1 (2), which states that,

> Liberties of prisoners, detained persons or persons in pre-trial detention shall be subject to the restrictions provided by law. Unless the law

> provides a specific restriction, a prison, the Ministry of Justice or a house of detention may apply only such restrictions, which are necessary for reasons of security of the prison or house of detention. The restrictions shall comply with their objective of application and the principles of human dignity and may not distort the nature of the other rights and liberties provided by law.

The first section of this paragraph defines the general conditions for deprivation of liberty, providing that:

> Prisoners, detained persons or persons in pre-trial detention are treated in a manner that respects their human dignity and ensures that their serving of the sentence or being held in pre-trial detention does not cause them more suffering or inconvenience than that inevitable in association with detention in prisons or houses of detention.

Prisoners may file a complaint against any restriction applied on them to the administrative courts.

During a state of emergency, the Government of the Republic may impose restrictions on freedom of movement, including for prisoners, under the Emergency Act. For example, in spring 2020, the long-term and short-term visits of prisoners were prohibited by the order of the Government of the Republic. During the COVID-19 crisis, other restrictions on prisoners were imposed by the prison authorities, based on the abovementioned legal provision of the Imprisonment Act. All these restrictions are subject to supervision by administrative courts.

During the COVID-19 crisis, prisoners exercised their right to file a complaint against restrictions, most notably against the cancellation of one hour of outdoor exercise. Prisoners and detainees have complained that the restrictions applied to them were too strict, unnecessary, and detrimental to their mental health. Similar points were made by the Ombudswoman of Estonia. During the first wave, the Ombudswoman noted in a letter to the Estonian prisons and to the Ministry of Justice that outdoor exercise should still be provided, albeit in smaller groups, and more frequent personal phone calls should serve as a compensatory measure.[13]

In its response to the Ombudswoman, the prison service stated that many prisoners belonged to risk groups due the fact that they are HIV or hepatitis C carriers, and therefore measures were needed to protect their lives and health. Although general restrictions applied, there were exceptions. For instance, the Tartu Administrative Court allowed a detainee to exercise outdoors (in a ruling of 8 April 2020, No. 3–20–528), pointing out that at that time the infection rate in Tartu County was low and approximately two weeks had passed since the prison officer who had tested positive had been at work. The court noted that although some prisoners belong to a risk group, there is no reason to apply such strict restrictions to all prisoners.

So far, Estonia's administrative courts have received a relatively low number of complaints concerning COVID-19-related restrictions (around 15%

of all the complaints) during the first wave of the pandemic, with some of them turning out to be successful. As the restrictions ended, the cases did not reach the Court of Appeal or the Supreme Court, and correspondingly there is no case law settled on this matter in Estonia.

7 Returning back to normal

After the first wave of the COVID-19 crisis, the Estonian Prison Service had a 5-step plan to abolish the crisis-related regime changes step-by-step, until the normal daily functioning of prisons had been restored. To date, this plan has not materialised as the crisis continues, and unlike in spring 2020, this time, prisoners have also been infected. Yet, there are a few intermediate notes to be made.

On the one hand, taking into account CPT guidelines for the treatment of persons deprived of their liberty in the context of the pandemic, the crisis has shown that the Estonian prison system has room for improvement, especially when it comes to investing more resources in increased access to alternative means of communication to enable prisoners to manage their daily administrative matters and to engage in resocialisation activities remotely. The crisis has demonstrated how important it is to have sound and timely scientific knowledge to implement proportionate preventive restrictions, while also taking into consideration the capability and resources of the state to handle a possible escalation of the health crisis in the country. As the crisis proceeded in two waves, it gave the Estonian Prison Service a possibility to replay the situation and adjust the preventive restrictions according to the best scientific knowledge at hand.

On the other hand, Estonia's digital capability made it possible to take court and parole proceedings into the online environment, and to continue such procedural activities without interruption.

Another important point about the restrictions of the COVID-19 pandemic concerns single occupancy cells: around two thirds of prisoners and detainees in Estonia do not have a private cell but have to live in two-person cells. That has led to a number of complaints throughout the pandemic, with prisoners claiming that they are at an increased risk of infection. The target for housing an increasing number of prisoners in single occupancy cells is stated in a development programme of the Ministry of Justice. As the number of prisoners in Estonia is continuously decreasing, the relative number of prisoners held in single occupancy cells is growing.

Notes

1 World Prison Brief. Highest to Lowest – Prison Population Rate (Europe). https://www.prisonstudies.org/highest-to-lowest/prison_population_rate?field_region_taxonomy_tid=14.

2 Eurostat Crime statistics, Intentional homicide relative to the population size (police-recorded offences per hundred thousand inhabitants).Available: https://ec.europa.eu/eurostat/statistics-explained/index.php?title=Crime_statistics#assaults_in_the_EU-27_in_2018.

3 That is, among those against whom criminal proceedings were terminated based on the opportunity principle (diversion), who were sentenced with fines, released on parole, or who were released from prison after serving a prison sentence.

4 Passed 14 June 2000, RT I 2000, 58, 376, entry into force 1 December 2000; last amended 07.05.2020. Available: https://www.riigiteataja.ee/en/eli/513052020005/consolide.

5 Passed 6 June 2001, RT I 2001, 61, 364, entry into force 1 September 2002; last amended 20 July 2020. https://www.riigiteataja.ee/en/eli/515072020011/consolide.

6 ECtHR, *Torreggiani and Others v. Italy* – 43517/09, 46882/09, 55400/09 et al., Judgment of 8 January 2013.

7 ECtHR 19 September 2013, *Tunis v. Estonia*, Appl. No. 429/12.

8 ECtHR 6 October 2005, *Hirst v. the UK*, Appl. No. 74025/01.

9 Council of Europe Annual Penal Statistics – SPACE I 2019, Table 16. Prison capacity and prison density on 31 January 2019. See https://wp.unil.ch/space/space-i/annual-reports/.

10 Passed on 8 February 2017, RT I, 3 March 2017, 1, entry into force 1 July 2017; last amended 18 May 2020. See https://www.riigiteataja.ee/akt/117052020003.

11 Passed on 12 February 2003, RT I 2003: 26, 160, entry into force in accordance with § 54; last amended 18 May 2020. See https://www.riigiteataja.ee/en/eli/518052020002/consolide.

12 Passed on 31 October 2003, RTL 2003: 116, 1853, entry into force 17 November 2003; last amended 18 May 2020. See https://www.riigiteataja.ee/akt/115052020021?dbNotReadOnly=true.

13 "Õiguskantsler taunib mõningaid vanglate kriisimeetmeid" ERR (ERR, April 9, 2020). See: https://www.err.ee/1074608/oiguskantsler-taunib-moningaid-vanglate-kriisimeetmeid.

References

Justiitsministeerium (2019): *Kuritegevus Eestis 2019*. https://www.kriminaalpoliitika.ee/kuritegevuse-statistika/.

Justiitsministeerium (2020): *Vanglateenistuse koosseisuliste ametikohtade arv*. https://www.vangla.ee/et/uudised-ja-arvud/vanglateenistuse-koosseisuliste-ametikohtade-arv.

Justiitsministeerium (2020a): Uudised ja arvud. https://www.vangla.ee/et/uudised-ja-arvud/vangide-ja-kriminaalhooldusaluste-arv.

Luts-Sootak, M., and Siimets-Gross, H. (2019): *Eesti õiguse 100 aastat*. Tallinn: Post Factum.

Ministry of Justice (2006): *Estonian Prison System and Probation Supervision Yearbook*. Tallinn. http://www.vangla.ee/sites/www.vangla.ee/files/elfinder/dokumendid/aastaraamat_2006_kodulehele.pdf.

Ministry of Justice (2018): *Yearbook MMXVIII. Estonian Prison Service 2018*. https://www.vangla.ee/sites/www.vangla.ee/files/elfinder/dokumendid/vanglateenistuse_aastaraamat_2018.pdf.

Ministry of Justice (2019): *Vanglast vabanenute retsidiivsus Eestis ja Soomes*. https://www.kriminaalpoliitika.ee/sites/krimipoliitika/files/elfinder/dokumendid/vanglast_vabanenute_retsidiivsus_eestis_ja_soomes.pdf.

Ministry of Justice (2020): *Serving of Sentence*. https://www.vangla.ee/en/serving-sentence.

Ministry of Justice (2020a): *Returning Prisoners to Society*. https://www.vangla.ee/en/serving-sentence/returning-prisoners-society.

Sootak, J., and Pikamäe. P. (2001): *Kriminaaltäitevõigus.* Tallinn: Ilo.

The Health Board of Estonia (2020): *Statistics of Covid-19.* https://www.terviseamet.ee/et/koroonaviirus/koroonakaart.

Wei-jie, G. et al. (2020): *Comorbidity and Its Impact on 1,590 Patients with COVID-19 in China: A Nationwide Analysis.* Internet-publication. https://doi.org/10.1101/2020.02.25.20027664.

16 Finland

Tapio Lappi-Seppälä and Sasu Tyni

1 Introduction

1.1 COVID-19 in Finland

Currently (by 18 February 2021), the Finnish Institute for Health and Welfare reports 52,209 (930 per 100,000 inhabitants) confirmed cases of COVID-19 of whom 725 (13 per 100,000) have died (https://thl.fi/en/web/thlfi-en). These are comparatively very low figures in the European context.[1] In all, 3,131,000 tests have been conducted by 18 February 2021.[2]

The first coronavirus infection among prisoners in Finnish prisons was diagnosed on 6 November 2020. By 22 February 2021, there are below 10 detected transmissions among the prisoners and 16 among the staff (of which over half among administrators not working in prisons). None of the prisoners needed hospital treatment and there are no known cases of hospitalisation among the staff. The transmission rate among prisoners corresponds to 0.2% of annually admitted prisoners. Ten transmissions between March 2020 and February 2021 are 0.8 transmissions per month. There have been no COVID-19-related deaths among prisoners, nor among the staff.

Based on these numbers, Finland and the Finnish prison service have managed comparatively well in this difficult situation. Low infection rates in prisons are partly due to overall low contagion rates in Finland, but also due to effective countermeasures taken by the Finnish prison and probation service.

1.2 National restrictions

In March 2020, emergency legislation was put in force for the period of 17 March–15 June 2020. The restrictions included the following: distance teaching only was allowed in schools and universities; it was strongly recommended that everyone should work from home as far as possible; restrictions on public gatherings (max 10 persons); bars, restaurants, museums, theatres, libraries and sports events were closed down; visits to care homes were banned; people over the age of 70 were obliged to avoid contacts with

DOI: 10.4324/9781003169178-16

other people; travel and movement in the southern part of Finland were restricted by closing the border between the province of Uusimaa and the rest of the country for two weeks; and flights to and from the country were stopped or severely restricted. As the situation started to improve, the government announced a hybrid strategy that combined case-by-case restrictions with gradual dismantling of restrictive measures.[3]

By July, the daily infection rates had declined to the level of 50 and the number of patients in need of hospital treatment was below 10. The second wave took off in October and accelerated in November and December. The government announced new, mostly voluntary restrictive measures without using emergency legislation.[4]

In February 2021, rising transmission rates due to the emergence of new mutations brought Finland to the third wave of the pandemic. On 26 February 2021, the government announced a lockdown to start on 1 March 2021 (this was the first time the term "lockdown" was used by the government). The lockdown covers public events, sports activities and any gatherings with more than 10 people, as well as the closing of restaurants and bars. On 10 March 2021, parts of the Emergency Act were put in force and restaurants were closed. Still, by March 2021, no general curfews have been announced.

2 Enforcement ban and prison populations

2.1 Preparations and actions taken by the prison service

2.1.1 Pandemic disease plan and prison-specific contingency plans

The Prison and Probation Service ("Criminal Sanctions Agency") is the Finnish government agency responsible for all correctional operations in the country. The service was established on 3 March 2020 as a team in response to the global COVID-19 pandemic. The tasks of the team were to monitor the COVID-19 situation in prisons and probation services, to prepare and coordinate the necessary actions and countermeasures, including the drafting of a pandemic disease contingency plan, to provide instructions for the operation of the units during the pandemic and measures to minimise contamination, and to plan and secure proper communication.[5]

The team enacted guidelines for further actions and instructions for the enforcement and administration. All administrative personnel of the Prison and Probation Service started work from home (distance working was already widely used in the agency before the pandemic). All prisons and community sanctions offices were obliged to draft their own contingency plans and keep them updated. Work was led by a board in weekly meetings chaired by the General Director. Statistical follow-up was conducted daily and reported weekly.

2.1.2 The 2020 enforcement ban

In order to prevent the spread of COVID-19 and to maintain the operation of prisons, the Ministry of Justice issued a decree on 19 March 2020 under which the enforcement of new default penalties for fines and new prison sentences with a maximum of six months was suspended until 19 June 2020. An act of parliament on 7 April 2020 extended this ban to cover all new prison sentences until 31 July 2020. Remand prisoners sentenced to imprisonment, however, were not within the scope of application of the Act.

From August 2020 onwards, enforcement practices normalised for a short period. However, as a result of the second wave of COVID-19, on 4 December 2020, the Ministry of Justice issued a new decree on postponing the enforcement of prison sentences with a maximum of six months and conversion sentences for unpaid fines until 3 March 2021. The Probation Service, however, had already adopted these restrictions on 27 November 2020 in line with the "Hybrid Strategy" of the government.[6]

2.1.3 Effects on community sanctions

Changes also took place in the enforcement of community sanctions. Probation offices started to work from home from 17 March 2020 onwards. Workplaces responsible for organising and offering community service were either closed or refused to receive clients. Sentences were temporarily interrupted, or work-programmes were replaced by at-distance organised activities and work. This brought a rapid short-term decline in the number of activities in community service in April and May (see Figure 16.1).

By June, the enforcement volume had returned to the pre-pandemic level. In addition, the enforcement of post-release electronic supervision was

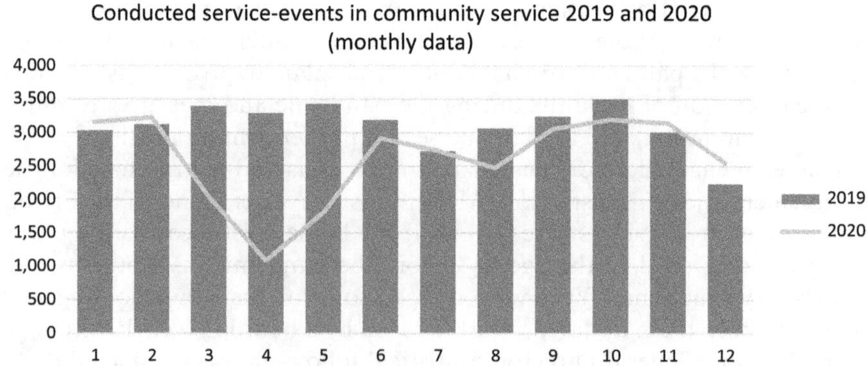

Figure 16.1 Enforcement of community service during the pandemic restrictions. Source: Prison and Probation Service.

partially modified, but this did not affect the number of inmates entering under the programme (which increased slightly in 2020).

While the effects of the pandemic and the related restrictions remained marginal in community sanctions, changes in sentence enforcement were more substantial. The rest of this chapter focuses on prisons and the prison environment.

2.2 Long-term trends of the prison population rates

Overall sentencing and enforcement practices have remained relatively stable during the last 30 years. Incarceration rates are among the lowest in Europe and they have varied around 50–60 prisoners per 100,000 inhabitants (Figure 16.2).

The decline in the number of entries in the early 1990s was a result of the adoption of community service, which replaced the use of short-term prison sentences. A short-term increase in 1998–2005 reflects increases in drug-offences and increased penalties for violent and sexual offences. The last 15 years reveal a smooth downward trend (a drop from 4,000 prisoners in 2005 to 2,600 in 2021), mostly effected by the extension of early release through post-release electronic monitoring, the reduction of the use of fine default imprisonment and generally the declining crime rate.[7]

2.3 The impact of the 2020 enforcement ban on prison entries (flow)

Entry-rates are dominated by short-term sentences, including conversion penalties for default imprisonment. Thus, one may assume that the 2020 enforcement ban also made a visible impact on these figures. Figure 16.3

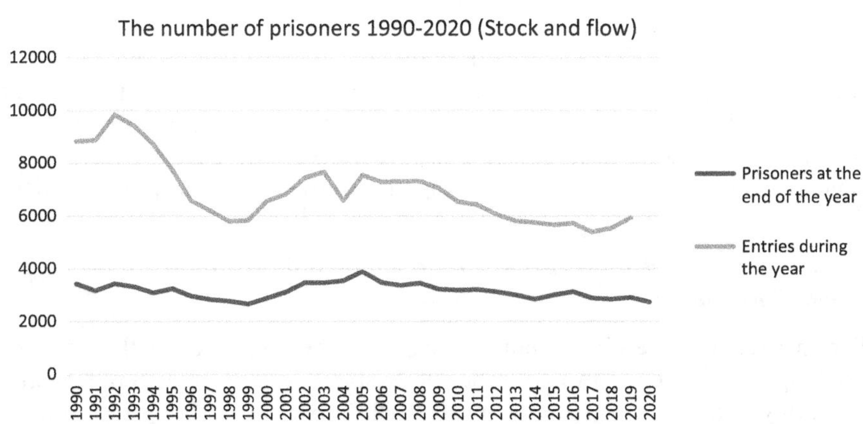

Figure 16.2 Prison population trends in Finland, 1990–2020.
Source: Prison and Probation Service.

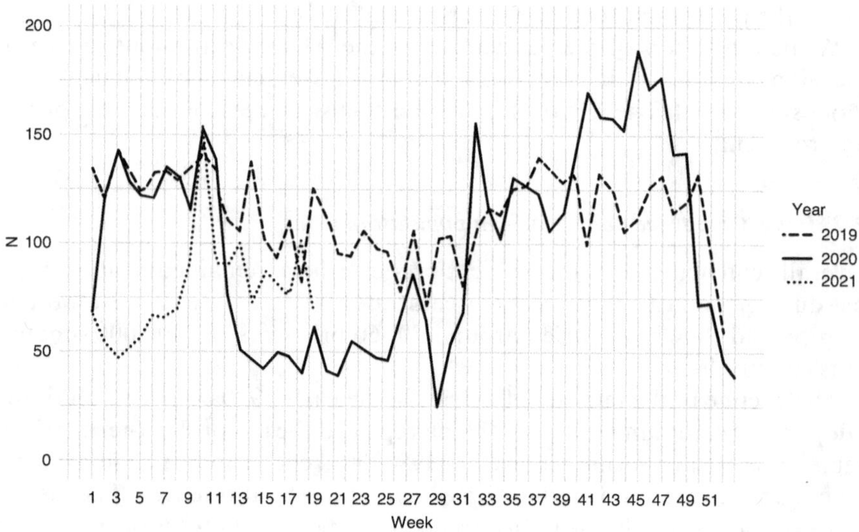

Figure 16.3 Entries to prisons 2019–2020 (flow, weekly data). Enforcement restrictions during weeks 12–31.
Source: Prison and Probation Service.

displays the total number of prisoners entering to penal institutions in 2019 and 2020 (weekly rates).

The 2020 enforcement ban brought an immediate drop in the number of prison entries from week 11 onwards. In March–July, the total number of incoming inmates almost halved. The rates returned to the same level in week 30 (August) and reached their peak in November, only to drop from week 47 onwards. Comparisons between 2019 and 2020 display an overall decrease of around 20% in entries in prisoners serving a sentence as well as in fine defaulters. The number of incoming remand prisoners increased by 5%, but in 2018–2019 their numbers increased by 14%. In addition to the enforcement ban, these changes were also affected by the difficulties created by the pandemic for processing cases in the courts. Verdicts and decisions were suspended in the courts and the processing of criminal cases was partly stalled.

2.4 The impact of the 2020 enforcement ban on daily prison populations (stock)

The impact of the enforcement ban can also be analysed on the basis of stock-figures (indicating the number of prisoners present/registered on any given day). Table 16.1 displays overall stock-figures of both registered prisoners and prisoners present (these figures exclude prisoners in post-release

Table 16.1 Daily prison population. Registered prisoners and present prisoners

	1/20	*3/20*	*7/20*	*11/20*	*2/21*
Registered prisoners	2,950	3,050	2,500	2,950	2,600
Present prisoners	2,650	2,750	2,200	2,600	2,400

Source: Prison and Probation Service.

Table 16.2 Daily prison populations in 2020 by prisoner groups

	25 March 2020	*4 May 2020*	*15 June 2020*	*27 July 2020*	*21 Sept. 2020*	*30 Nov. 2020*	*28 Dec. 2020*	*17 Febr. 2021*
Sentenced prisoners	1,850	1,600	1,400	1,500	1,500	1,650	1,785	1,675
Fine defaulters	50	7	5	5	60	165	40	5
Remand prisoners	650	600	550	550	575	585	525	500

Source: Prison and Probation Service.

EM, absconded prisoners and those placed in outside institutions) in January 2020 until mid-February 2021.

In spring 2020, there was a drop of little over 500 prisoners (18%). By November/December, the rates had returned almost to the same level, but then dropped by around 350–400 prisoners. Daily stock-figures for different groups of prisoners in 2020 are visible in Table 16.2.

By mid-June 2020, the daily number of prisoners serving a sentence had fallen by 25% (from 1,850 to 1,400). The figures remained stable until September. After that followed an increase to almost the original level (1,785) by December, after which a new declining trend took off.

Default imprisonment for unpaid fines reveals a similar profile, with sharper changes. First, the number of default prisoners fell from 50 to well below ten. When the ban was repealed in August, the numbers increased first to 100, and after a short break to over 150. A new enforcement ban in December reduced the numbers again to around five.

Remand prisoners seem to be unaffected by the enforcement ban. The slight decrease in December 2020 may be attributed to new travel restrictions, visible in the declining number of foreigners in pre-trial detention (a decrease by 34%; Table 16.3).

The total number of prisoners in February 2021 is 13% lower than just before the pandemic. About half of this drop is attributable to prisoners serving a sentence (reduction of 9% in the group), around 30% results from the decline of (foreign) remand prisoners and 20% due to the decline of fine defaulters.

Table 16.3 Summaries of the overall change in different prisoner groups over a period of one year

	16 February 2020	*16 February 2021*	*Change*
	N	N	%
All	3,018	2,617	−13,3
Serving a sentence	2,246	2,052	−8,6
Fine default	88	6	−93,2
Pre-trial	684	559	−18,3
Supervision (EM)	241	210	−12,9

Source: Prison and Probation Service.

3 Restrictions of contact with the outside world: visits and prison leave

3.1 Visits

All family and regular visits were shut down in March 2020 (excluding meetings with defence counsel and officials). In addition, the educational staff, co-operation partners and the NGO's were not allowed to enter the prison premises. Compensatory means of contact were offered by Skype calls and by expanding the rights to normal telephone communication (more frequent calls and more time for offenders to speak on the phone). These restrictions

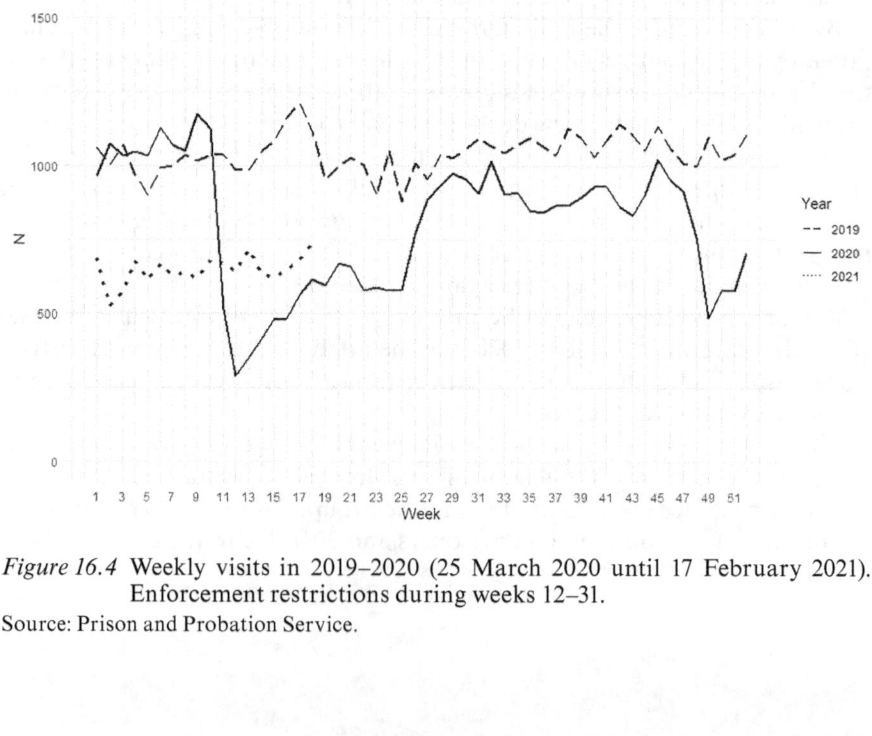

Figure 16.4 Weekly visits in 2019–2020 (25 March 2020 until 17 February 2021). Enforcement restrictions during weeks 12–31.

Source: Prison and Probation Service.

were relaxed on 1 August 2020, but brought back into force on 27 November 2020. However, this time, the officials adopted a more flexible approach, which gave more room for case-by-case considerations. Figure 16.4 displays the number of weekly visits and contacts in 2019 and 2020.

The number of weekly visits fell from 1,400 to below 300 in March. Restrictions were terminated in late June, as is also visible in the graph. A second drop in the visits followed in December 2020 after new restrictions due to the second wave.

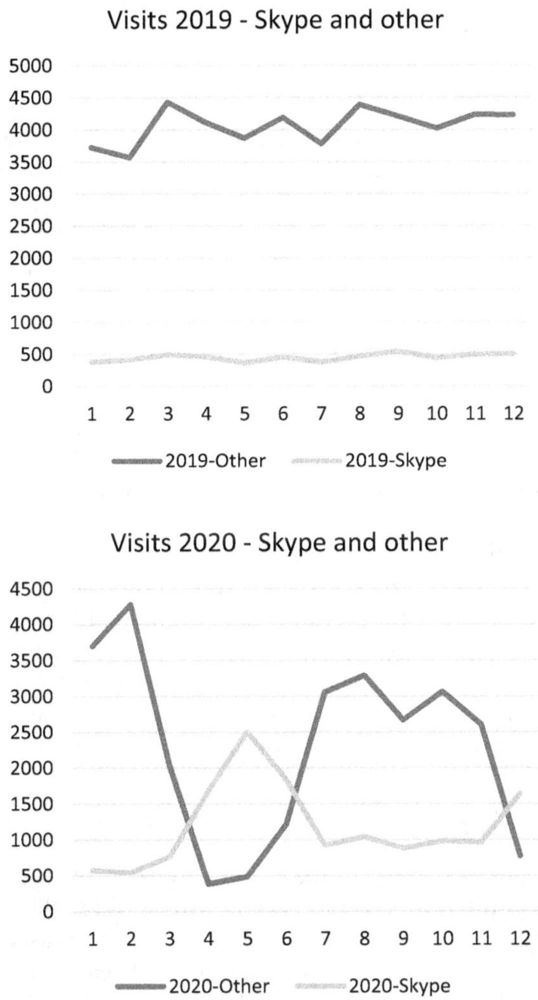

Figure 16.5 Skype meetings in 2019–2020 and other (non-Skype) visits (monthly data).

Source: Prison and Probation Service.

Table 16.4 The effect of restrictions to different types of visits in April–July 2019 and 2020

Visit type	*2019*	*2020*	*%-change*
Counsellor	224	285	+27
Children	165	0	−100
Family	1,778	483	−73
Supervised	9,656	832	−91
Strictly supervised	218	27	−88
Other	126	444	+252
Skype	1,267	6,016	+375
All	13,434	8,087	−40

Source: Prison and Probation Service.

Compensatory means for visits included Skype meetings. Figure 16.5 displays monthly numbers of Skype visits and other (non-Skype) visits in 2019–2020.

The use of Skype meetings increased in spring 2020 from a stable level of 500 to 2,500. This extended use of Skype meetings was also partly due to the recommendation of the CPT. In May 2020, over 80% of meetings took place through Skype. After the restrictions were called off, the number of Skype meetings fell to 1,000, which is still twice the number of calls prior to the restrictions.

Table 16.4 displays information on changes in different visit categories. The main categories are visits with counsellors, with children and with family, supervised and strictly supervised visits, visits through Skype and "other visits".

Visits with children were banned altogether. Other visit types were reduced by 70–90%. However, there are three exceptions. Visits with counsellors increased by 27%. In addition, the numbers of "other visits" almost tripled. This implies that the group also covers some other compensatory devices/means. However, no exact data are available. Skype meetings increased by almost 400%, making this form of contact the most important during restrictions in April–July (75% of all visits/contacts).

3.2 Prison leave and furloughs

Prison leave is a widely used standard practice in Finnish prisons. The annual number of granted prison leaves ranges around 13,000 cases. The share of different sorts of breaches (usually late return) decreased in 1990–2020 from around 10% to 3.5%. The preconditions of leave are defined in the law. COVID-19 added new elements to the criteria to be taken into account when granting leave. As formulated in the pandemic guidelines: "When making decisions on prison leave, consideration should also be given to the circumstances prevailing in society and the risk of spreading the disease

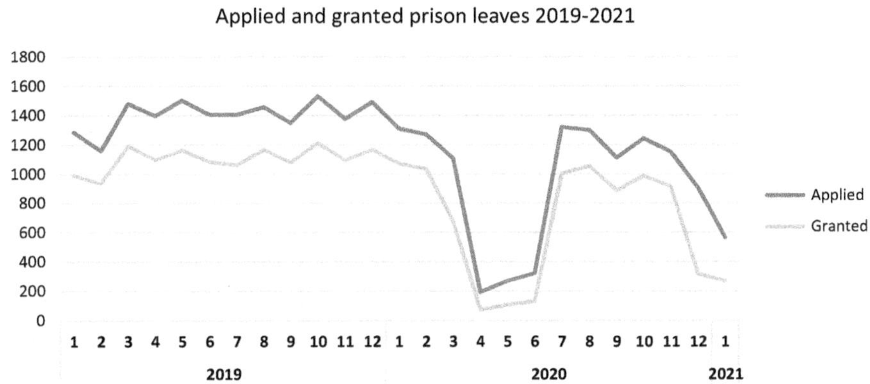

Figure 16.6 Prison leave 2020 (monthly data).
Source: Prison and Probation Service.

by the prisoner returning from leave to prison, in particular with regard to leave granted on the basis of the length of the sentence period and specified important reasons. If necessary, permission already granted may be withdrawn on the grounds laid down in the Imprisonment Act. If permission has been applied for to participate in some event, it may be considered to enable participation via Skype".

This meant that the practice became much more restricted. Both the number of applications and the share of leave granted decreased. The number of applications fell from 1,100 in March 2020 to 200 in April 2020. In addition, the share of granted applications fell from 60% to below 40%. In July, the restrictions were called off, as is also visible in the graph. Not only the number of applications increased, but the share of accepted applications also increased by 35% (Figure 16.6).

There were also some changes in prison escapes. In 2020, the number of "unlawful leaves" (referring usually to absconding from open prison) had increased by 50% (from 45 to 81, the number of actual escapes from closed prisons remained on the level of below 10). This may be attributable to the fact that the restrictions on visits and prison leave had led to increased tensions and dissatisfaction among the prisoners (see also Section 4.1).

4 Restrictions inside prison – work and activities

The guidelines stressed that activities in prison should be organised "as usual". If necessary, changes were to be made; they must be "suitable for the sentence plan", which forms the basis of sentence enforcement in Finland.[8] Changing the activity obligation may mean, for example, moving from one job to another. Substitute activities may also include self-study, distance learning, learning e-services, going through the implementation of the sentence plan, planning continuity more thoroughly than usual, or providing guidance for library services. If necessary, the activities may be arranged in a cell. The assessment of the *opening of cell doors* is based on situation-specific consideration during the restrictions. While prisoner's access to library services was secured, also during the restrictions, only ten persons could be in the library at a time. Books could also be ordered to cells. *Leisure activities* that increased the risk of infection were to be replaced by some other low-risk activities. Substituting leisure activities might include, for example, a gym session, ball games and additional or extended outdoor activities.

Work activities were revoked in open prisons in March. For open prisons, where work activities have a more central role and often take place outside the prison facilities, COVID-19 restrictions forced changes in the everyday routines. Consequently, the operation of open prisons became more restricted. Restrictions on the movement of groups of prisoners to work outside the prison had to be considered on a case-by-case basis. However, allowances and the salary paid in open prisons (which is higher than in closed prisons) were paid to prisoners even if the activity was suspended because of the pandemic. Restrictions do not seem to have had any impact on *programme work*. The number of programmes initiated in 2020 is on the same level (or slightly higher) than in 2019.

Statistics on overall activity rates (counted as percentage of prisoners involved in any sort of activity measured on each Wednesday) in closed and open prisons reveal no changes due to the implementation (or removal) of restriction.

4.1 Accommodation, prison order and security issues under the pandemic

4.1.1 Accommodation in single cells

According to the pandemic guidelines, "prisoners must, as far as possible, be placed in one-person cells". In Finland, prisoners in closed prisons are placed pre-dominantly, but not exclusively, in single cells. The decrease in the number of prisoners enabled the prison authorities further to reduce the use of double bunking.

4.1.2 The use of open enforcement

Enforcement takes place in Finland either in closed or in open prisons: prisoners who participate in work or rehabilitative activities, those who are assessed to be able to adapt to less restrictions and those who, it is assumed, would not leave the open institution premises without permission are allocated to open institutions. The regime in open institutions is more relaxed

Table 16.5 Prisoners serving a sentence[a] in closed and open prisons in February 2020 and 2021

	16 February 2020		*16 February 2021*		*Change %*
Closed prisons	1,079	51.6%	876	47.5%	−18.8%
Open prisons	1,011	48.4%	968	52.5%	+4.2%
All serving a sentence	2,090	100.0%	1,844	100.0%	−11.8%

Source: Prison and Probation Service.
a Remand prisoners excluded.

than in closed institutions (see the sources in note 7). Open prisons are in practice "prisons without walls": the prisoner is obliged to stay in the prison area, but there are no guards or fences.

Open prisons can be deemed to be less risky environments from the epidemiological point of view due to better possibilities for maintaining safe distances. Therefore, it would be in line with the pandemic plan to favour placement in open prison during the pandemic. Table 16.5 displays the allocation of prisoners in closed and open prisons in February 2020 and 2021.

There has been a significant shift from closed to open prisons during the pandemic-year. The share of open enforcement has increased from 48.4 to 52.5%. The number of prisoners in closed prisons decreased by 19% in contrast to the 4% increase in open prisons. These changes are in line with the general policy of the Finnish prison administration to increase the use of open enforcement. It also appears that the circumstances created by the pandemic provided an "extra booster" towards this end. However, according to the information of the prison authorities, there were no extra guidelines towards this end.

4.1.3 Drug-tests

COVID-19 restrictions changed enforcement practices, reduced both contacts to the outside world and prisoners' ability to move, especially in open prisons. This was also reflected in the level of drug-control in terms of reduced drug-tests. Statistics for 2016–2020 are displayed in Figure 16.7.

The number of drug-tests fell in closed prisons from 15,000 to 10,000 and in open prisons from 30,000 to 20,000. The share of positive findings remained in both cases roughly at the same level in 2019–2020 (0.12% in closed prisons and 0.04% in open prisons, but after having fallen from 2018 to 2019). The higher number of tests and the smaller rate of positive tests in open prisons are explainable by the fact that all open institutions are drug-free, meaning that the inmates are required to make a controlled commitment not to use any intoxicants.

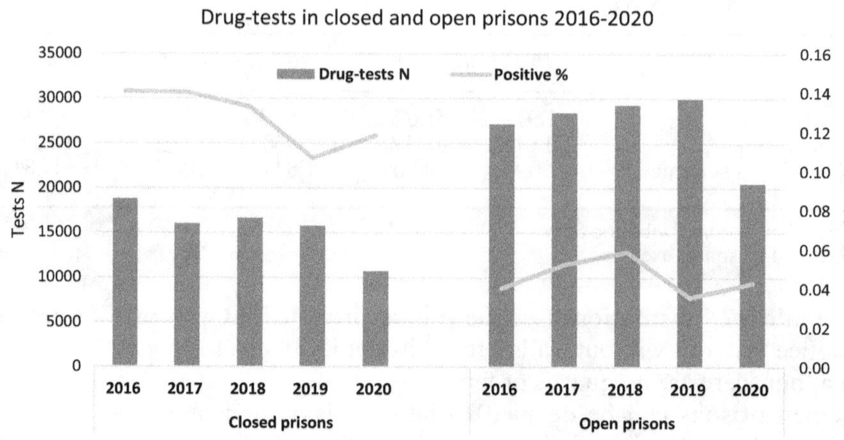

Figure 16.7 Drug-tests 2016–2020.

4.1.4 Prison order and security

One could assume that additional restrictions imposed for prisoners would increase tensions and unrest. Statistics of prison order and of recorded breaches provide partial support for this hypothesis (see Table 16.6).

Breaches against officials and other prisoners increased in 2020 by 20–25%. This can be read as evidence of increased tensions due to restrictions. However, on top of that, this may also reflect increased gang violence in Finnish prisons.

However, the total number of disciplinary infractions has remained on the same level. This can be explained by decreases in breaches related to drugs and alcohol, possession rules and breaches against general prison order. The first two categories may well be due to the reduced number of visits during 2020, as the decline of visits has also reduced the flow of drugs and

Table 16.6 Breaches against prison order

Breaches…	*2019*	*2020*	*Change 2019-2020*	*Change-%*
Against officials	168	211	38	22,6
Against other prisoners	139	165	35	25,2
Against property	60	60	2	3,3
Drugs & alcohol	803	702	−41	−5,1
About possession	180	153	−11	−6,1
Prison order	480	447	−20	−4,2
Permission breaches (incl. escapes)	392	328	−18	−4,6
Refusal of activity	17	13	2	11,8
Other	25	14	−7	−28,0
All	2,264	2,093	−20	−0,9

Source: Prison and Probation Service.

Table 16.7 The use of disciplinary sanctions in 2019 and 2020

Type of disciplinary penalty		*2019*	*2020*	*Change*	*Change-%*
Warning		399	384	−15	−3,8
Loss of rights	Conditional	3	1	−2	−66,7
	Unconditional	44	42	−2	−4,5
	Total	47	43	−4	−8,5
Isolation max seven days	Conditional	169	208	39	23,1
	Unconditional	830	684	−146	−17,6
	Total	999	892	−107	−10,7
Isolation over seven days	Conditional	0	0	0	0,0
	Unconditional	4	3	−1	−25,0
	Total	4	3	−1	−25,0
All penalties	Conditional	172	209	37	21,5
	Unconditional	1,277	1,113	−164	−12,8
	Total	1,449	1,322	−127	−8,8
Crime-reports to the police		234	289	55	23,5

Source: Prison and Probation Service.

forbidden items into prison facilities. While the prison authorities (unofficially) report increased events of "moonshining" in prisons, as a reaction to the diminished supply of drugs due to the ban on visits, these events are not reflected in the overall statistics.

Data on the use of disciplinary sanctions in 2019 and 2020 are presented in Table 16.7.

There has been a general decrease (−9%) in the use of different disciplinary penalties in 2020. The figures are dominated by short-term isolation (max seven days), which covers almost 70% of all sanctions. It is noteworthy that in this category the use of conditional (suspended) isolation has increased by 23%, while the use of unconditional isolation has decreased by 18%. There is no evidence that the prison authorities would have intensified their control and discipline during the restrictions. The reduced number of unconditional sanctions rather indicates the contrary. However, while the use of disciplinary sanctions has decreased, the number of crimes reported to the police has increased by almost a quarter.

5 Compensatory measures

Compensatory measures such as Skype and other video-based communication and additional phone calls have been dealt with under Section 3.1.

6 Legal basis for restrictions of the prison regime – contagions, quarantine and isolation

The legal basis for restrictions of visits and prison leave is in line with the general standards of the prison law, either based on the discretionary power of prison authorities to grant short-term prison leave or based on the exceptional power to restrict prisoners' rights (for receiving visits) by general security clauses of the Prison Act (see also Section 7).

Testing of prisoners for COVID-19 is carried out both by the public health care system and by the prison health services. Prisoners have been transported to the testing point by the staff with a prison car. At times, the public health services have moved to the prison premises.

While there has been only a very limited number of infections detected (in all ten cases among prisoners since the beginning of the pandemic), the prison authorities imposed quarantine and isolation orders in all 32 units. The decisions have been taken by the prison health care unit according to the Infectious Diseases Act.

Quarantine orders were targeted individually (they always concern individual persons). However, at times whole units have been placed in quarantine based on the infection risk. Yet, the general guidelines formulated by the prison service require that the rights of prisoners shall not be restricted beyond what is necessarily caused by quarantine or isolation.

7 Return to normal and conclusions for the post-pandemic time

Up until now (February 2021), the prison service has survived the pandemic without major problems. The number of infections has remained remarkably low among both the prisoners and the staff. So far, 1% of the general Finnish population has tested positive. Among prisoners, the figure is 0.02% (counted relative to the number of all prisoners entering prisons during a year). None of the prisoners (nor the staff) has needed treatment in hospital and no deaths have been reported.

Most substantive changes in daily practices deal with the suspension of the enforcement of short-term sentences and default imprisonment for unpaid fines. As a result of the enforcement ban, the number of incoming prisoners was halved for a short period of time. While the figures afterwards returned to normal levels, still, one year after the pandemic broke out, the number of prisoners remained 13% lower than prior to the pandemic. It is unclear whether this reflects an actual decrease in the use of imprisonment or just the fact that the pandemic has also stalled the handling of the cases through the justice system. Thus, there may be queues in the courts that may affect the future number of prisoners. However, there is no actual enforcement-queue. All incoming sentences are enforced without noteworthy delays. As regards fine defaulters, the case-log resulting from the enforcement ban was resolved in a month or two.

As regards prison conditions, COVID-19 restrictions have affected the daily prison-life in several ways. During the restrictions, visits were largely banned, with the exception of meetings with counsellors. Compensatory remedies were provided mostly by extensive use of Skype calls and increased access to normal telephone calls. Positive experiences with Skype indicate lasting effects on the present – and probably also on the future – enforcement practices.

All actions taken by the prison authorities during the pandemic were in line with the general standards of the prison law. They also fell under the discretionary powers that the law grants to officials. The system of prison leave is based on discretion, not on a prisoner's absolute right to the leave.[9] The Prison and Probation Service concluded that when using this discretionary power, the service can take into account the general societal situation, including health conditions. The regulation on visits, however, is based on the prisoner's right to receive visitors. [10] The additional restrictions imposed on visits during the pandemic required, therefore, a separate justification. That was based on the general clause in Prison Law Ch. 13:1§ (see note 9). As it was argued, the spreading of the disease in the prison environment would endanger "the order and functions of the prison" to such a degree that it provided the authorities with a lawful right to restrict regular visits with relatives and families. There hardly exists disagreement on the fact that a pandemic inside a prison endangers the functions of the system. Having said this, it is clear that a specific regulation on how to take into account the pandemic-type of epidemiological risk factors should be incorporated in substantive prison law. This applies not only to the regulation about visits and prison leave, but also to the use of quarantine-measures and isolation.

Notes

1 Corresponding rates by February 2021 for selected European countries (in the order of death rates) are as follows: Belgium 6,400/188, Italy 4,500/156, Spain 6,400/141, France 5,300/126, Sweden 6,200/124, Germany 2,800/79, Denmark 3,500/40, Finland 930/13 and Norway 1,250/11. See https://covid19.who.int.

2 See for data https://thl.fi/documents/533963/5860112/COVID-19-epidemian+hybridistrategian+seuranta+%E2%80%93+tilannearvioraportti+17.2.2021.pdf/87e97d80-85a3-248b-70c3-19fb025ba5ef?t=1613634831517.

3 *Government Resolution on a plan for a hybrid strategy to manage the COVID-19 crisis.* The Government Resolution specifies the guidelines adopted by the Government on Sunday and Monday for continuing restrictive measures to curb the coronavirus epidemic, and the controlled and gradual dismantling of restrictive measures. See https://valtioneuvosto.fi/en/-/10616/valtioneuvoston-periaatepaatos-suunnitelmasta-koronakriisin-hallinnan-hybridistrategiaksi.

4 See https://minedu.fi/en/-/10616/government-decides-to-supplement-action-plan-for-covid-19-hybrid-strategy.

5 The Agency has published a FAQ-part in the organisations' public website. The website serves prisoners, their families and the staff; see https://www.rikosseuraamus.fi/en/index/topical/corona.html. The Agency has added information and instructions regarding coronavirus in several languages to the prisoners' intranet. General recommendations are given regularly by the staff concerning hygiene (hand washing, sneezing, etc.) and distancing from others.

6 Information provided by the Finnish Prison and Probation Service.

7 Explanations for these different periods are discussed in more detail in Lappi-Seppälä, 2009 and 2020. The sharp decline in the number of incoming

prisoners in 2005 was a result of a computer failure, which prevented the enforcement of the default imprisonment for unpaid fines for that year (something that very few noticed, when it happened).

8 On sentence enforcement and principles of prison law in Finland, see in more detail Lappi-Seppälä 2009 and 2019.

9 See Prison Law Ch. 14:1 § "the prisoner *may be granted* a permission to leave the prison premises for a short period", under the conditions defined in more detail in the other paragraphs of Chapter 14.

10 See Prison Law Ch 13:1 §: "the prisoner *has a right* to receive visitors under necessary supervision … as often as this can be arranged without disturbing the order and functions of the prison", under the conditions defined in more detail in the other paragraphs of Chapter 13.

References

Lappi-Seppälä, T. (2009): Imprisonment and penal policy in Finland. *Scandinavian Studies in Law* 54, 333–379.

Lappi-Seppälä, T. (2019): Prisoner resettlement in Finland. In: Dünkel, F., Pruin, I., Storgaard, A., and Weber, J. (Eds.): *Prisoner resettlement in Europe*. London, New York: Routledge, 104–127.

Lappi-Seppälä, T. (2020): Regulating prison populations: Exploring Nordic experiences with Frieder Dünkel and his comparative project. In: Drenkhahn, K. et al. (Eds.): *Kriminologie und Kriminalpolitik im Dienste der Menschenwürde. Festschrift für Frieder Dünkel zum 70. Geburtstag*. Mönchengladbach: Forum Verlag Godesberg, 161–184.

17 France

Martine Herzog-Evans

1 Introduction

Prisons have historically been places where contagious diseases (in particular, gaol fever [typhus], cholera and dysentery) spread rapidly. A literature review pertaining to the impact of influenza in small, closed settings, such as prisons, uncovered a paradox: germs do penetrate in spite of the closed nature of prisons; they also thrive because of the specific vulnerabilities within prisons (Finnie, Hall, and Leach, 2012). Prison staff and other personnel enter and exit these closed settings on a daily basis, and once germs are in, they prosper, thanks to, inter alia, the absence of fresh air circulation; the close proximity of detainees, particularly if their prison is overcrowded and they have to share their cells; the impossibility to create any form of social distancing; the general lack of hygiene caused by insufficient budgets and the sheer difficulty of daily movement of detainees to showers or water points; the inability of prisoners to make informed decisions as they entirely depend on the institution (United Nations, 2020) and, lastly, the slower access to healthcare, which is also generally of significantly inferior quality (Weston, 2019).

The Spanish flu of 1918 perfectly illustrates these points. Rather similar to COVID-19, it was of pandemic proportion, respiratory in nature, highly contagious and deadly. Overall, the Spanish flu affected roughly a quarter of all prisoners, a prevalence that was much higher than in the general population (Finnie, Copley, Hall, and Leach, 2014). Prisons that organised a form of lockdown were successful in containing the pandemic and had fewer deaths; those that were not had alarming rates of infection and an extremely high number of deaths (Finnie et al., 2012). The lesson learnt from this previous respiratory pandemic is thus that isolating infected prisoners and suspending collective activities are key. However, extreme crises tend to make humans and institutions revert to their main default setting, one that is often flawed. Prisons are total institutions (Goffman, 1961), in which the default setting has historically been to be closed to the outside world, based on total control (Foucault, 1975) and based on keeping people locked inside.

DOI: 10.4324/9781003169178-17

At the time this chapter was drafted, little comparative work on COVID-19 had been done. However, on this scant basis, two major approaches seem to have been proposed: (further) locking prisons down but releasing a lot of prisoners (as in Germany: Dünkel, 2020); or locking prisons down but testing prisoners (as in Italy: Cingolani, Caraceni, Cannovo, and Fedeli, 2020). Unsurprisingly, France has chosen the first approach, given its disciplinary governance since 2002, along with its highly sophisticated legal system pertaining to prisoner release (Herzog-Evans, 2021) and the existence of a desistance-friendly re-entry judge, the *juge de l'application des peines* (JAP; Herzog-Evans, 2014). Like Germany, but to a much smaller degree, it has also used technology to reduce the inevitable tensions that ensue from the extreme lockdown imposed on prisoners.

French prisons have undoubtedly closed in on themselves, going far beyond what health necessities would have required. Like Russian dolls, they have atavistically created multiple layers of deprivation of liberty. If prisoners were certainly not a priority for the French public or the media, it quickly became apparent that prison clusters would cause serious health hazards for the wider community. Thus, paradoxically, a historic opportunity for the mass release of prisoners ensued. France has undisputedly been a leading jurisdiction in this respect. The French COVID-19 situation has, therefore, been contrasted with, on the one hand, a drastic closing down and, on the other hand, a similar drastic opening up.

1.1 French prisons: open to the world, chronically overcrowded and governed by strict discipline

Two months after the lockdown was eased on 11 May 2020, there were 58,695 incarcerated people in French prisons. Compared to July 2019, this statistic represented an 18.1% drop, with 13,015 fewer inmates. However, since then, the number of incarcerations has started to increase again. From June to July, the prison density jumped from 95 to 97%. This has essentially been due to courts opening their doors and resuming their activities. It would, therefore, be presumptuous to expect that the very favourable parentheses which presented itself from March to May 2020 will have a lasting impact on the chronic overcrowding that has been a French characteristic for many decades, to the point that it has been subjected to a quasi pilot judgement of the European Court of Human Rights, *J.M.B. and others v. France* (ECtHR, 30 January 2020).

To be exact, the French prison landscape is rather contradictory. Since the 1980s, it has been very open to the outside world and to community agencies. For example, France was among the first countries in Europe to offer prisoners the same standards of treatment as the general population (Bienvenu, 2006). However, it has not been able to reduce its extreme overcrowding rates. The consequence of this overpopulation, particularly in local prisons, has been the persistent inability to prepare prisoners for their re-entry and to simply deal with the basic needs of prisoners or probationers. From a human rights standpoint, the conditions that prisoners have to endure are nothing short of shocking, as the prison ombudsman has repeatedly documented (and recently: CGLPL, 2018). The overcrowding issue has never been resolved in spite of a great number of law reforms. France has indeed tested numerous technical solutions to put an end to the overcrowding crisis (Synergia, 2016). It has significantly reduced pre-trial detention, and has tried to convince judges not to pronounce custodial sentences and, in particular, short sentences, by creating alternative community sentences and measures.

Perhaps the most innovative of all the techniques utilised in France has been the so-called 'article 723-15' of the PCC. 'Article 723-15' is a procedure whereby custodial sentences of up to one year are not executed in prison but are referred to the JAP who, collaboratively with the offender, his/her lawyer and the prosecutor, and following a report issued by the SPIP, elaborate a supervision plan. This allows the further tailoring to the offender's needs of the sentences that are generally mass-produced by felony courts in an industrial fashion. Crucially, before a law that entered into force in 2020 reduced the threshold down from two years to one year, article 723-15 prevented roughly 20,000 to 30,000 incarcerations each year (Delbos, 2017). French JAPs can choose from a diverse assortment of early release measures. However, the sheer lack of re-entry preparation (probation services do not have the resources to contribute to this efficiently) leads to only roughly 30% of prisoners benefiting from early release (Delbos, 2017).

Notwithstanding all these efforts, France has never been able to overcome its overcrowding crisis as it has consistently tried to solve this multicausal issue by way of legal and technical reforms as opposed to addressing its systemic causes. However, just before COVID-19 hit, a law that had been enacted in March 2019 that actually purported to go further, although in a very contradictory way, was about to enter into force in March 2020. As mentioned above, it reduced article 723-15's scope, thereby taking the risk of increasing the number of people entering prison. More positively, however, the 2019 Act created a complex system, which aims at drastically reducing the number of short sentences that are mostly responsible for prison overcrowding.

As regards prison governance, the situation has deteriorated since the Sarkozy era (Chantraine, 2010) and following 09/11. After having been open to the world, French prisons started closing in on themselves, and a disciplinary form of governance, largely inspired by the United States model, was put in place. Two examples will suffice: the creation of specialised SWAT teams, trained to crush prisoner riots; and the multiple attacks by way of internal regulations against the previously much improved disciplinary procedures (Herzog-Evans, 2019). With the new terrorist wave starting in 2015 and, in particular, since it became evident that prisons themselves were a great source of radicalisation (Khosrokhavar, 2016), and even more so when terrorist attacks started targeting prison officers (Vincent and Jacquin, 2019), the prison regime was drastically hardened (Herzog-Evans, 2019).

When COVID-19 hit French prisons in March 2020, French prisons had thus been both relatively open to the outside world, while being overcrowded and adopting an American style of disciplinary governance. These key components largely explain how they reacted to the pandemic.

2 Prison and penal policy concerning the execution of prison sentences during the COVID-19-induced crisis

2.1 The temporary suspension of incarceration

The reduction of overcrowding rates was essentially caused by the closing of the vast majority of courts, except for a handful dealing with emergencies and serious cases. In addition, the French Ministry of Justice issued internal circulars telling prosecutors to greatly reduce the cases in which they asked judges to incarcerate offenders and to only process those in which public safety was at serious risk (Directorate of Criminal Affairs and Pardons (DACG), Circular, 14 March 2020).

Arguably, another factor was that the courts had been reassured that, while people were on lockdown, it would be possible to detect whether probationers were up to no good, thanks to the police patrolling the streets. When the courts reopened, the number of people processed by French courts increased. Prosecutors immediately started to deal with the backlog that had been created. Additionally, a number of people who had violated the lockdown rules and, later on, people who refused to comply with social distancing and the wearing of masks, started clogging the criminal justice factory all over again. Since then, France has no longer been in total lockdown, and has merely adopted curfew rules. Thus, the courts have returned to their original pace. More positively, a great number of prisoners were released into the community during the lockdown.

2.2 A success story: mass prisoner release

When the lockdown was put in place on 16 March 2020, prisoners were not a priority. Because of my own vulnerabilities, I had put myself on lockdown a few days earlier and was able to start drawing attention to this issue. As we were all forced to stay at home, I used Twitter and received a great number of emails and phone calls from JAPs and prosecutors. I replied by posting on my website (Herzog-Evans, March 2020) a list of all the legal possibilities allowing for the quick release of prisoners.

Initially, the Ministry of Justice declared that using these legal tools was out of the question (Vantighem, 2020). JAPs and prosecutors nonetheless started releasing large numbers of prisoners within the existing legal framework. The Ministry of Justice must be praised for rapidly changing its position. The French government issued an ordinance (ordinance n° 2020–303 of 25 March 2020), which very creatively found ways of adding to the already very generous release system. Among the technical solutions which were created and put in place until the lockdown was eased were:

- two months remission for every single prisoner, which led to the release of a significant number of prisoners, given the fact that the vast majority serve short sentences; and
- a new measure labelled 'home detention', which resembled French citizens' lockdown conditions in their own home without the usually added elements of electronic monitoring (hereafter EM).

Nonetheless, a series of prisoners were excluded from these release measures: prisoners deemed dangerous (e.g. terrorists); domestic violence offenders, given the fact that they would be on lockdown, and it was impossible to control whether they would go back to their spouses or partners; sexual offenders; and also, but probably less justifiably, prisoners who had committed offences while in prison or participated in the riots mentioned below.

2.3 The temporary loosening of release measure net widening

In the French legal system, a great number of measures can be used to release prisoners early. Remission exists in different forms, which sometimes comes with a short period of supervision in the community: semi-freedom and placement in the community, two measures executed under the supervision of the prison services, with, respectively, the night spent either in a prison or in approved premises; EM; sentence suspension on medical grounds and parole. In many cases, there is a combination or a succession of these measures. The easing of the conditions or the added component of furlough can contribute to the continuous adaptation of the early release measure to the offender's needs, circumstances and changing levels of risk. During the lockdown, these measures were fully embraced by JAPs and prosecutors.

Parole is not very restrictive compared to other measures. The excessive use of EM, under the strong pressure of the French prison services, has led to net widening within sentence implementation itself. Indeed, EM is both a form of detention and an alternative measure (Daems, 2020), which, over the years, has gradually marginalised other measures such as parole, placement in the community and semi-freedom. During the lockdown, however, semi-freedom units were largely depopulated in order to create medical wings for COVID-19 patients. As regards EM, it became 'measure non grata', since it involved contact between the prison officer who installed the device and the prisoner. JAPs and prosecutors who had forgotten that parole could also be granted to short and medium sentences, thus rediscovered it and, during this short period of time, disregarded EM.

2.4 Remote released prisoner supervision

Inevitably, the speed with which prisoners were released meant that they were given very little preparation, if at all. Most prisoners were released virtually overnight without a release plan, financial means or continuity of healthcare. What, then, would 'COVID probation' look like?

Very little research has addressed probation in times of acute crisis. Nicola Carr (2012) focused on probation during the troubles in Northern Ireland, but she essentially concentrated on how probation services have negotiated their activity without having to choose sides. In France, Frenkiel-Pelletier (2021), studying WW II has focused on how the rule of law was a prerequisite for the development of probation. As of COVID-19, if there have been serious concerns regarding the regression of human rights and particularly due process (Dervieux, 2020), this has not dramatically impacted probation.

I thus decided to launch an ad hoc study from my own locked-down home and to interview a number of probation officers and their managers during this time. Overall, using a semi-structured grid, I interviewed 22 probation officers and seven managers. With their consent, they were recorded and every interview was transcribed. Many complained that they had to blindly call their probationers since they had not been allowed to take the paper files home or did not have the technology to connect from home to the professional data bank. More so than ever, offender supervision did not include active desistance support, nor did it include any form of treatment or public protection measure. To make matters worse, every single one of their partner agencies was closed. Many probation officers were reduced to hoping for the best. All they could do was to offer psychological support and a friendly voice over the phone. On a more positive note, many probation officers reported that the relationship with offenders became more genuine and more equal since everyone was in the same boat. Since the first lockdown, however, the prison services have opened up to parttime remote probation work and equipped a great number of its staff with laptops and intranet access.

3 Restrictions of contact with the outside world: from locked up to locked down

When the first contagious case appeared in a prison, the recommended approach to prevent an epidemic was to isolate the infected inmates in their cells (Awofeso, 2004). However, once the germs started spreading beyond this initial small cluster, the entire prison organisation had to be reordered.

Other than isolation, the general approach was to drastically reduce or to altogether remove all activities as well as visits, in order to stop people coming into the prisons. Typically, prisons protect themselves from the outside world, traditionally perceived as dangerous. When this is done, it reduces contamination (Finnie et al., 2012; Quinton, 1890). However, the core activity of the prison then becomes warehousing and guarding.

Indeed, the prison default setting is very tightly locking people up and ensuring that they do not go out. With COVID-19, this atavism went a step further. The first decision that the French prison headquarters (*Direction de l'Administration Pénitentiaire*, hereafter DAP) made on 13 March was to reduce the movement of prisoners, that is, the circulation of inmates from their cell to the gym, to the workshops, to the showers or to other activities (DAP, Internal Circular, 13 March 2020). It was followed by another internal circular on 15 March and then again by another which repealed the latter, this on 16 March (DAP, 16 March 2020). The internal circulars now requested that prisons focus on essential activities or duties with, at the top of the list, security and safety, followed by meals, showers and emergency health treatment. Other than these, every single activity taking place in the prison was suspended. Visits were reduced and pregnant women, people with underlying conditions or elderly individuals over the age of 70 were banned from entering prisons. Outdoor exercise was maintained but sessions were reduced in number and length so that a smaller number of prisoners would be in the courtyard. The very next day, as the French president put the entire country on lockdown, yet another circular was issued by the prison headquarters (DAP, 17 March 2020). This time around and initially for a period of 15 days, all activities, including family visits, were suspended. The same day, another circular indicated that probation officers working in prison settings would no longer have contact visits with prisoners but would have to write them letters. The only exception pertained to potentially dangerous or potentially vulnerable (notably suicidal) offenders (DAP, 17 March 2020-Bis). Following this initial two-week lockdown phase, a law passed on 23 March put the country on lockdown for two additional months, and the prison services reacted with their own circular (DAP, 30 March 2020), whereby they simply prolonged the decisions made on 17 March.

One day later, yet another circular tried to distinguish the staff who were more frequently in contact with prisoners and needed to wear masks and those who were not and could do without (DAP 31 March 2020). By then, it was no longer illegal to wear protective gear and the prison services had managed to acquire a number of masks.

However, the pandemic reached an alarming level, fear became the dominant emotion among prisoners and, predictably, a number of riots erupted (Gaubert, 2020; Valdenaire and Roussel, 2020). If arguably every single French citizen was technically locked up at the time as well, prisoner experiences were by far more extreme. The French prison ombudsman published a report whereby she deplored that one of the main victims of COVID-19 had been human rights (CGLPL, 2 July 2020).

4 Restrictions inside prisons: from locked down to locked in

4.1 Restricted access to masks

The COVID-19 pandemic was rapidly perceived, and rightly so, as being a particularly dangerous threat for prisons, their staff and prisoners. Prisons are by nature closed settings and French prisons are quite dramatically overcrowded, with little air circulation and extreme social overcrowding. Yet for many weeks, if not months, France was unable to produce the masks that would have protected the population, including medical staff. The government decided to lie to its citizens and to state that masks were not necessary. The handful of masks that were available (Lepage et al., 2020) – very often ineffective and even mouldy masks going back to the H1N1 pandemic – were immediately rerouted to hospitals. Thus, police (Giuliano, 2020) and prison officers (Radenovic, 2020) were strictly forbidden by their hierarchy, following orders from Paris, from obtaining and wearing masks on their own accord. This created panic among prisoners who saw prison officers as potential carriers of the virus.

Once masks became available, although they were still rare and costly, they were initially allocated to staff and not to prisoners – in September 2020, this was still the case. Some prisoners did challenge this in court. However, the administrative courts (*tribunaux administratifs*, hereafter TAs) generally rejected their claims. During the lockdown and in line with their historical function of defending public services against lawsuits issued by service users, TAs generally responded by accepting the statements made by the prison services that everything was done according to recommendations, rather than by investigating whether this was the case. For instance, the Nice TA rejected the application of an inmate who was asking for hand gel and masks to be distributed to the penal population, arguing that the prison services stated that they had put everything in place and the applicant was unable to prove otherwise. In essence, the TA was asking a prisoner to prove a negative against a total institution, this during a pandemic! The TA also replied that the fact that guards were equipped with masks provided prisoners with sufficient protection (TA Nice, 6 April 2020). The Nice ruling was later confirmed by the highest administrative court, the Council of State (21 April 2020), which further rejected the additional request to test the prison population for COVID-19 (also see Council of State, 8 Oct. 2020). The majority of TAs came to the same conclusion, even when the applicant was a vulnerable inmate with pre-existing medical conditions (TA Lille, 23 April 2020). The Lyon TA was more honest than its counterparts when it bluntly stated: 'it is not seriously disputed that France is currently going through a shortage of tests and masks, which requires that they be primarily allocated to health care personnel' and vulnerable people (TA Lyon, 22 April 2020). As of the second part of 2020, however, prisoners have gradually been equipped with two washable masks.

Perhaps more logically, the Council of State also rejected the coordinated application made by the bars of Paris and Marseille to provide lawyers entering prison premises with masks and hand gel at a time when these items were virtually unavailable in France (Council of State, 20 April 2020). Conversely, the Guadalupe TA courageously granted part of the requests made by the bar of Guadalupe and a number of prisoners. In particular, it ordered the prison services to distribute hand gel and masks to the prisoners in charge of distributing meals; and to test anyone who had been in contact with an infected individual (TA Guadeloupe, 4 April 2020).

4.2 Restricted prisoner circulation

As was mentioned before, inmate movement was reduced to a bare minimum during the lockdown. Most prisoners thus spent 22 to 23 out of 24 hours of every day in their cells. Apart from limited opportunities for outdoor exercise, essential medical treatment and intake appointments, they had nothing to do and nowhere to go. Regarding the outdoor exercise, the Council of State ruled on 8 April that it was the responsibility of prison governors to ensure that each inmate could at least go into the courtyard once a day, providing that the inmates were in small groups comprising the same people in order to limit the risks of contamination (Council of State, 8 April 2020). Regarding access to activities, they were completely banned during the first lockdown, and have remained largely closed since then, but for prisoners' professional activities (DAP 9 Feb. 2021). This mirrors the French government's obsessive focus on the economy. French citizens have complained that all they are allowed to do now is to work, eat and go to bed.

4.3 Limited body searches

Perhaps more positively, body searches were limited in number because of the contact they involved between prison officers and prisoners. They were nonetheless maintained whenever it was deemed necessary; prison officers were simply told to wear masks and gloves.

Following the riots and the rapid degradation of prisoners' mental health as a result of the extreme French lockdown, the prison services focused most of its efforts on trying to keep the prison population disciplined. It did so both by repeatedly reminding prisoners of the rationale for the government's decision and by reinforcing surveillance, monitoring and the use of prison classification systems.

5 Compensatory measures: from locked in to tuned in

According to Article 8.2 of the European Convention on Human Rights, restrictions to private life and family contacts can be deemed legitimate on health and security grounds. Even under normal circumstances, prison services are required by the European court to contribute actively to the maintenance of family ties (ECtHR, *Messina v. Italy*, 2000). In the context of COVID-19, the penological committee of the Council of Europe, the PC-CP, issued a statement whereby it declared that 'Prison authorities shall assist inmates in maintaining adequate contact with the outside world and provide them with the appropriate welfare support to do so' (PC-CP, 2020). In other words, it called for authorities to create compensatory measures for the restrictions inflicted upon families during the lockdown.

In France, several measures have been taken. Measures first consisted of allowing the handful of inmates still present in the semi-freedom wings to keep their mobile phones with them. These mobile phones were not only useful to keep in touch with their families, but they also allowed prisoners to communicate directly with their probation officers, who had been told not to see prisoners except upon admission.

A second and more generalised measure, which was put in place by the Ministry of Justice on 16 March 2020, was the allocation to each inmate of 20 Euros' worth of phone cards (subsequently increased to 40 Euros). An e-mail system was also created, allowing family members to send messages to prisoners, including attached files which were then printed and given to the latter. However, prisoners could not reply in the same way.

Other than these measures, prisoners have not been allowed to use a mobile phone or to access the internet; nor has France created a video conferencing system linking them to their loved ones. Unsurprisingly, the prison ombudsman has concluded that, despite these efforts, 'the benefits that society as a whole has been able to derive from digital technology, whether as a distraction, as a service tool or as a means of communication, have often stopped at the prison gates' (CGLPL, 2 July 2020, p. 75).

6 Legal basis for restrictions and relaxations of the prison regime

In the face of the pandemic, France has reacted according to its bureaucratic-normative tradition by producing a series of circulars, decrees and ordinances, sometimes in a frantic manner in a matter of days, as if the law could be an effective shield against a virus.

The legal justifications for decisions made during the lockdown were derived from either internal circulars or governmental ordinances. Both sources raise serious questions about the separation of powers. Internal circulars originate from subdivisions of various ministries. According to legal theory, they are not binding, and, in particular, cannot have legal consequences for individuals, including for inmates or their families. Conversely, public services staff must comply with them. Nonetheless, historically, the prison services have overused this normative source as it has allowed it to self-regulate without any external control (Herzog-Evans, 2019). Ordinances raise similar issues, except that they do not emanate from legislators but from the executive. They are also strongly criticised inasmuch as they bypass the legislature, intervening in domains which would normally be the prerogative of the legislature. President Mitterrand actually called the 1958 constitution, which allows for these shocking violations of the principle of separation of powers, a permanent 'coup d'Etat' (Mitterrand, 1964).

Another contentious trait of the French legal system resides in the existence of administrative courts. These administrative courts (TA) were created by Napoleon to limit drastically the likelihood that individuals could win legal actions against the state or public institutions. Those who rule in TAs are, in actual fact, not members of the judiciary and are not judges in the real sense of the term. Furthermore, they are not independent from the state. Quite the opposite, they are high-ranking public officials who, during their careers, alternate between working as judges in TAs and holding senior positions in government departments. Additionally, these TAs implement a fully distinct set of legal norms called 'public law', which refers to the regulation of public services, administrations and governmental bodies with the identical goal of restraining the rights of individuals. It is therefore not surprising that, as was detailed above, TAs have rejected virtually every single application made by prisoners, their family members and NGOs regarding the human rights restrictions which were imposed during the lockdown. Most of their decisions have in essence stated that: 'the Minister of Justice says X; therefore, X is true; thus, the case is dismissed'.

As for the judiciary, the picture is more positive since, in contrast with their traditionally very punitive stance, prosecutors have had to comply with the orders issued from Paris –French prosecutors are not independent from the executive – and have supported prisoners' early release. Regarding judges themselves, COVID-19 has provided an experimental opportunity to test our earlier findings which show that JAPs have a desistance supportive culture (Herzog-Evans, 2014). Our earlier results were indeed confirmed, with no fewer than 15,000 prisoners receiving early release from these re-entry judges.

In spite of these positive aspects, however, the main casualty of COVID-19 has been due process. Nearly every single prisoner who was released during this period did not have direct access to a judge, since all hearings were suspended and judges ruled in their offices based on a file. The vast majority of prisoners also did not have access to a lawyer. Lawyers who wanted to visit their clients were even required by the prison services to declare in writing that they were not infectious. Thankfully, this was deemed illegal (TA Toulouse, 29 April 2020). Since masks became available in France during the second half of 2020, lawyers' visits have resumed fairly normally.

7 Returning to normal

By way of a decision made by the President of the Republic, the lockdown ended on 11 May 2020. A decree of 11 May (n°2020–548) organised how the lockdown was going to be eased on French territory. The prison services had pre-empted this by issuing their own circular on 6 May, whereby it was made clear that prisons would not return to their previous situation. Many restrictions still applied, in particular regarding visits. Only one person at a time could visit prisoners, who were only allowed one visit per week as opposed to the three previously allowed. Some prisons pushed the precautionary measures a little too far. For instance, the prison in Caen decided that each visit would take place behind a plexiglass screen. A hard-of-hearing prisoner challenged this regulation as it prevented him from hearing his spouse. Exceptionally, the tribunal considered that this measure was excessive, particularly in view of the fact that the prison in question had had no COVID-19 cases and that the region was in a 'Green Zone' with only a few cases (TA Caen, 26 May 2020).

Since the easing of the March 2020 lockdown, with France now rejecting any full confinement, the prison services have required that all visits should now become non-contact (DAP 9 Feb. 2021) – plexiglass being installed in each prison. This represents a dramatic setback for families who had been able to benefit from contact visits since 1983. Additionally, as mentioned above, prisoners are now essentially deprived of activities, but for work. In many respects, COVID-19 has reverted French prisons back to the beginning of the 20th century.

7.1 Conclusion

The lockdown has created an experimental situation which has allowed academics to test a number of hypotheses. One striking point has been that prison overcrowding is not inevitable. It can be reduced once the will is present and, notably in the French context, when prosecutors are firmly told to comply. Another hypothesis which has been experimentally tested pertains to the fact that when society shuts down and a very serious crisis hits, institutions revert to their default setting; it thus reveals their very core.

What is left of prisons once they have been stripped of their modern human rights features is essentially barricaded warehouses. As for probation, it is about being a friendly voice and, at best, a psychological support system, in line with the English historical mantra of 'advise, assist and befriend' – with the important exception of 'assist'. French re-entry judges, the JAPs, are still desistance-friendly courts ready to release as many prisoners as they possibly can, given the right circumstances and, in particular, when there is no opposition on the part of prosecutors. As for administrative courts, they have unfortunately lived up to what is expected of them, which has always historically been to protect the French state from its own citizens.

Consequently, rather than a window of opportunity, the pandemic has revealed the shortcomings of each institution in charge of prisoners. It has quickly become clear that there will be no Utopian 'day after'. Indeed, no reform is currently being planned to try and draw upon the potentially positive dimensions of the crisis or to learn from the mistakes which have been made. As a second, and then a third wave has hit France, and restrictions have been prolonged, 'back to normal' may very well mean the removal of many of the gains made in the recent decades in terms of due process, the opening of prisons to the world and the substantial rights of detainees.

References

Awofeso, N. (2004): Prisons show prophylaxis for close contacts may indeed help in next flu pandemic. *British Medical Journal* 329(7458), 173.

Bienvenu, N. (2006): *Le médecin en milieu carcéral. Étude comparative France/Angleterre et pays de Galles.* Paris: L'Harmattan.

Carr, N. (2012): Legitimacy through neutrality: Probation and conflict in Northern Ireland. *The Howard Journal of Criminal Justice* 51(5), 474–487.

CGLPL (2018): *Les droits fondamentaux à l'épreuve de la surpopulation carcérale.* Paris: Dalloz.

CGLPL (2020): *Les droits fondamentaux des personnes privées de liberté à l'épreuve de la crise sanitaire.* CGLPL. 2 July.

Chantraine, G. (2010): French prisons of yesterday and today: Two conflicting modernities—a socio-historical view. *Punishment and Society* 12(1), 27–46.

Cingolani, M., Caraceni, L., Cannovo, N., and Fedeli, P. (2020): The COVID-19 epidemic and the prison system in Italy. *Journal of Correctional Health Care.* July. doi:10.1177/1078345820929733

Daems, T. (2020): *Electronic monitoring. Tagging offenders in a culture of surveillance.* Cham: Palgrave Macmillan.

Delbos, V. (2017): *Rapport sur la mise en œuvre de la loi du 15 août 2014 relative à l'individualisation des peines et renforçant l'efficacité des sanctions pénales.* Report to the Ministry of Justice, October 21.

Dervieux, V.-O. (2020): Justice pénale de l'essentiel. L'ordonnance n° 2020–303 du 25 mars 2020 et la procédure pénale. *Actualité Juridique Pénale*, n° 4, 179–186.

Dünkel, F. (2020): The impact of Covid-19 on prisons and penal policy in Germany. *Victims & Offenders* 15(7–8), 1113–1123. DOI: 10.1080/15564886.2020.1813230.

Finnie, T. J. R., Copley, V., Hall, I. M., and Leach, S. (2014): An analysis of influenza outbreaks in institutions and enclosed societies. *Epidemiology and Infection* 142(1), 107–113.

Finnie, T. J. R., Hall, I. M., and Leach, S. (2012): Behaviour and control of influenza in institutions and small societies. *Journal of the Royal Society of Medicine* 105(2), 66–73.

Foucault, M. (1975): *Surveiller et punir.* Paris: Gallimard.

Frenkiel-Pelletier, E. (2021): *Histoire de la probation durant la deuxième guerre mondiale, période d'exception, et sa refondation jusqu'aux années soixante-dix France, Angleterre, Pays de Galles, Israël, PhD,* Université de Reims.

Gaubert (2020): Coronavirus: Inmates in France hit out over prison hygiene amid COVID-19 fears. *Euronews*, 26 March. https://www.euronews.com/2020/03/26/coronavirus-inmates-in-france-hit-out-over-prison-hygiene-amid-covid-19-fears.

Giuliano, C. (2020): Coronavirus: Les masques disponibles dans la police donnés aux soignants? Les syndicats de policiers fulminant. *20 Minutes*, 25 March. https://www.20minutes.fr/faits_divers/2748163-20200325-coronavirus-masques-disponibles-police-donnes-soignants-syndicats-policiers-fulminent.

Goffman, E. (1961): *Asylums: Essays on the social situation of mental patients and other inmates.* New York: Anchor Books.

Herzog-Evans, M. (2014): *French reentry courts and rehabilitation: Mister Jourdain of desistance.* Paris: L'Harmattan.

Herzog-Evans, M. (2019): *Droit pénitentiaire* (3rd ed.). Paris: Dalloz.

Herzog-Evans, M. (2020): Coronavirus: Que faire concernant les détenus? 16 March, http://herzog-evans.com/coronavirus-que-faire-concernant-les-detenus/.

Herzog-Evans, M. (2021): *Droit de l'exécution des peines* (6th ed.). Paris: Dalloz.

Khosrokhavar, F. (2016): *Prisons de France. Violence, radicalisation, déshumanisation: Surveillants et détenus parlent.* Paris: Robert Laffont.

Lepage, E., Guichou, M., Cielenski, C., and Bui, D. (2020): Où sont les masques? Le scandale d'une pénurie. *Le Nouvel Observateur*, 26 March. https://www.nouvelobs.com/coronavirus-de-wuhan/20200326.OBS26599/ou-sont-les-masques-le-scandale-d-une-penurie.html.

Mitterrand, F. (1964): *Le coup d'Etat permanent*. Paris: Plon.

PC-CP WG (Council for Penological Co-operation Working Group). (2020): *COVID-19 related statement by the members of the Council for Penological Co-operation Working Group* (PC-CP [2020] 5). Strasbourg: Council of Europe.

Quinton, R. F. (1890): An epidemic of influenza in a prison. *British Medical Journal* 22, 417–418.

Radenovic, P. (2020): Un surveillant de prison face au coronavirus: 'J'espère qu'après tout ça, la mentalité des gens changera'. *Le Journal du Dimanche*, 23 March 2020. https://www.lejdd.fr/Societe/la-vie-dun-surveillant-de-prison-ici-on-na-pas-de-masque-pas-de-gel-hydroalcoolique-3957262.

Synergia, Italy (2016): *Reducing prison population: Advanced tools of justice in Europe*. Report coordinated by the Comunita' Papa Giovanni XXIII, Rimini. Grant: JUST/2013/JPEN/AG/4489.

United Nations Special Rapporteur on Extrajudicial, Summary or Arbitrary Killings (2020): *COVID-19 and protection of right to life in places of detention* (COVID-19 Human Rights Dispatch No. 2). New York: United Nations.

Valdenaire, L., and Roussel, M. (2020): Incendie et début de mutinerie à la prison d'Ecrouves, près de Toul. *France Bleu*, 17 April. https://www.francebleu.fr/infos/faits-divers-justice/incendie-et-debut-de-mutinerie-a-la-prison-decrouves-pres-de-toul-1587145848.

Vantighem, V. (2020): Coronavirus: 'Nous allons distribuer 100.000 masques en prison', annonce Nicole Belloubet. *20 Minutes*, 17 March. https://www.20minutes.fr/justice/2742191-20200317-coronavirus-allons-distribuer-100000-masques-prison-annonce-nicole-belloubet.

Vincent, E., and Jacquin, J. P. (2019): Prison de Condé-sur-Sarthe: le détenu qui a blessé deux surveillants maîtrisé par le RAID, sa femme tuée. *Le Monde*, 5 March.

Weston, J. (2019): Sites of sickness, sites of rights? HIV/AIDS and the limits of human rights in British prisons. *Cultural and Social History* 16(2), 225–240.

Legal norms and circulars

Law n° 2019–222 of 23 March 2019.

Law n° 2020–290 of 23 March 2020.

Ordinance n° 2020–303 of 25 March 2020.

DAP (2020). Internal Circular. 13 March 2020.

DAP (2020). Internal Circular. 15 March 2020.

DAP (2020). Internal Circular. 16 March 2020.

DAP (2020). Internal Circular. 17 March 2020.

DAP (2020). Internal Circular-Bis. 17 March 2020.

DAP (2020). Internal Circular 23 March 2020.

DAP (2020). Internal Circular 30 March 2020.

DAP (2020). Internal Circular 31 March 2020.

DACG (2020). Internal Circular. 14 March 2020.

Court cases

ECtHR, *J.M.B. and others v. France*, 30 Jan 2020, applic. n° 9671/15 and 31 others).
EHRCtHR, *Messina v. Italy*, 28 Sept. 2000, applic. n° 25498/94.
Council of State, Relief Chamber, 8 April 2020, n° 439821.
Council of State, Relief Chamber, 21 April 2020, n° 440007.
Council of State, Relief Chamber, 20 April 2020, n° 439983, 440008.
Council of State, Relief Chamber, 8 October 2020, n° 444741
TA Guadeloupe, Relief Chamber, 4 April 2020, n° 200200.
TA Nice, Relief Chamber, 6 April 2020, n° 2001637.
TA Lyon, Relief Chamber, 22 April 2020, n° 2002758.
TA Lille, Relief Chamber, 23 April 2020., n° 2003089.
TA Toulouse, Relief Chamber, 29 April 2020, n° 2001989.
TA Caen, Relief Chamber, 26 May 2020, n° 2000922.

18 Germany

Frieder Dünkel and Christine Morgenstern

1 Introduction: the general situation of the German prison system

Germany has been a Federal Republic since 1949, comprising, since 1990, 16 federal states. The legislative competence for criminal law, criminal procedural law and penitentiary law initially lay at the federal level.[1] In 2006, however, a reform of the Constitution (*Grundgesetz,* Basic Law) shifted legislative competencies for penitentiary law to the federal state level. Therefore, between 2007 and 2015, the 16 federal states (*Länder*) all passed their own Prison Acts. While the legislative differences are not very pronounced, the traditional disparities resulting from distinct traditions and regional practices remain considerable.

The general sentencing pattern in Germany has remained largely unchanged for many years and is fairly moderate with a stable distribution of sanctions: about 82% of all sentences for adults over 18 are fines (based on the so-called day-fine system), 12% suspended sentences (without or with conditions such as probation) and 6% are unconditional prison sentences. The average length of unconditional prison sentences is about two years. There is no evidence of a punitive turn in sentencing, even if the legally provided penalties for violent and sexual crimes have been increased slightly (Dünkel, 2019).

1.1 Developments during the first wave of the pandemic (March to June 2020)

Germany in February 2020 had an average daily prison population of 63,852 inmates, 13,137 in pre-trial detention (29.8%).[2] 45,062 served a prison sentence in prisons for adults. Of the latter, 4,773 (= 9.4%) were fine defaulters, serving a substitute prison sentence for not having paid their fine. According to the data collected by the International Centre for Prison Studies in London (ICPS, Birkbeck University)[3] for September 2019, the prison population rate per 100,000 inhabitants was 77, the same as at the end of February 2020. The prison population rate since 2004 (96 per 100,000) had declined already

DOI: 10.4324/9781003169178-18

before the emergence of the pandemic by about 20% and had been roughly stable since 2013. Fears that the large influx of refugees in 2015 and 2016 would result in a growing prison population did not prove true. In March 2020, according to the ICPS data, the prison population rate had already dropped to 71. The absolute numbers of prisoners declined further to 55,525 by the end of June 2020, equating to a prison population rate of 67, which – internationally compared – is exceptionally low (Dünkel, 2017). Despite considerable regional disparities, the downward trend is more or less uniform for all 16 federal states[4] (Figure 18.1).

In 2019, the general occupancy level was 90%; only in one federal state (Baden-Württemberg), it was over 100%. The occupancy at the end of February 2020 remained at that level, which means that overcrowding (apart from a few closed prisons) was not a problem in Germany. The situation has improved further due to the release of prisoners and the cancellation of short-term prison sentences from March 2020, when the occupancy level fell to 83.3%. At the end of June 2020, the occupancy rate was only 76.0%. This means that overcrowding – even in the regions that had difficulties before the outbreak of the pandemic – is not a problem anywhere in Germany.

Infection risk may derive from accommodating too many prisoners in small and unhygienic cells. In principle, prisoners in Germany have a right to be accommodated in a single cell at night. This legal requirement is not met everywhere. At the end of February 2020, 75% of all prisoners (pre-trial

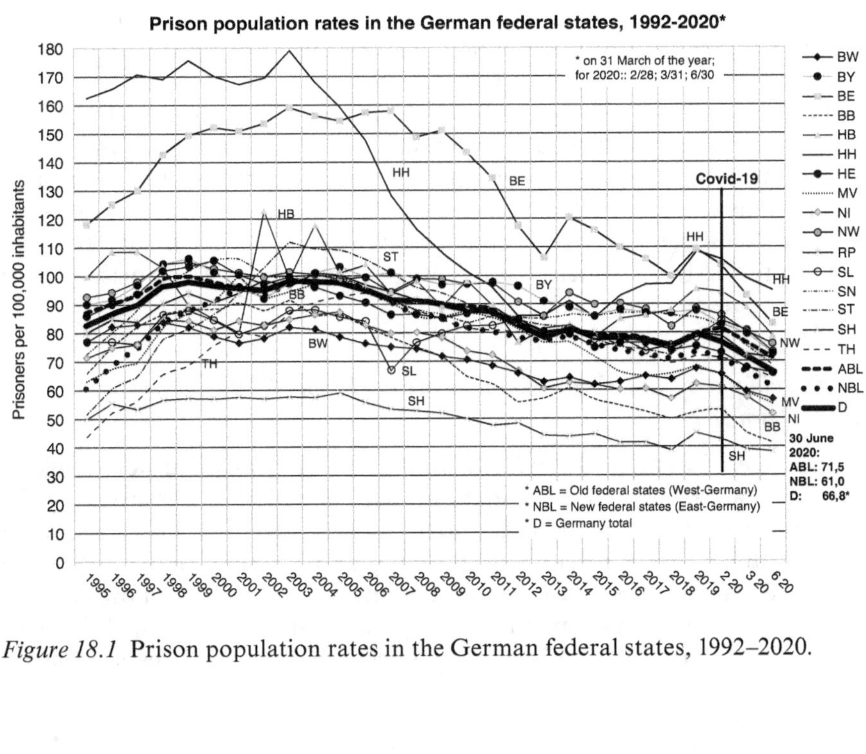

Figure 18.1 Prison population rates in the German federal states, 1992–2020.

and sentenced) were accommodated in single cells (47,855 out of 63,851), and 25% in communal cells, usually with only one more inmate. Again, large regional differences exist. One month later, the prison population had decreased by 4,364 prisoners, which resulted from releases or non-execution of short-term prison sentences because of the COVID-19 pandemic (see below under 2.). The proportion of prisoners accommodated in single cells therefore increased from 75% to 77.5% at the end of March 2020.

The German prison system (as well as the system of community sanctions) is based on the rehabilitative ideal and the principle of social reintegration (*Resozialisierung*). Based on the prisoners' right to human dignity (Art. 1 Basic Law) and the principles of the social welfare state (Art. 20 Basic Law, see Morgenstern, 2016; Pruin, 2019: 150 f.), it is protected by the Constitution and enshrined in substantive penal and penitentiary law. This concept requires a system of graduated relaxation of the prison regime, including regular prison leave and transfers to open prisons at least in the final stage of executing prison sentences (Dünkel and Rössner, 2001: 327 ff.; Dünkel, 2018: 428 ff.). Because of this orientation to re-entry into society, several thousand sentenced prisoners are on temporary leave daily (at the end of February 2020: 2,847, i.e. 5.6% of the population of 50,675 sentenced prisoners). The proportion of temporarily absent prisoners dropped at the end of March 2020 to 3.7% and stood at 4.0% at the end of June 2020. The statistical data therefore clearly show the impact of the pandemic regarding restricted possibilities of prison leave.

Another pillar of the orientation to social reintegration is the transfer to open prisons, which are defined as facilities without physical hindrances to prevent escape (i.e. there are neither perimeter walls nor grilled windows). The principle of a graduated opening of prisons is based on trusting prisoners, who are selected according to their dangerousness and the risk of escape they pose.[5] At the end of February 2020, 15.0% of the 45,062 prisoners serving their sentences in adult prisons were accommodated in an open facility. This share was 8.8% of the 3,557 14- to 24-year-old inmates serving youth prison sentences. By the end of March 2020, not much had changed: 14.9% of the 42,177 prisoners in adult prisons and 8.6% in youth prisons were accommodated in open facilities.[6]

1.2 Developments during the second wave of the pandemic (from October 2020)

At the time of writing, the Federal Bureau of Statistics had not provided further data on the prison population after June 2020. After stopping the execution of short-term sentences and fine default detention in March, some states resumed executing them in the summer. Prisoner numbers therefore may have started to increase again; it is unclear, however, in how far a simultaneous decline in crime may have influenced the situation. After October, a further decline can be expected because of renewed restrictions on executing certain prison sentences, such as imprisonment for fine defaults, and the continuing decline of street and other crime (burglary, etc.) due to the several lockdowns in the general society until May 2021 (see also under 2. below).

1.3 COVID-19 infections and deaths (prisoners and staff members)

From March to the end of July 2020, the numbers of prisoners and staff members who were infected remained low. Infected prisoners were immediately separated in quarantine. No prisoner died because of COVID-19 infection during this period. Although complete data for all federal states are missing, the largest federal state, North Rhine-Westphalia, reported that until mid-July 2020, only 11 prisoners had been infected, and that all of them recovered. With regard to a total prison population of 15,307 in March 2020, this meant a percentage of 0.07%. For the same period, 35 infections of staff members were registered. In the second wave of the pandemic, North Rhine-Westphalia reported 18 prisoners and 46 staff members in October, and in November another 11 prisoners and 16 staff members, again only a small and declining proportion.

As far as data were available for the first wave, most other federal states registered fewer than 10 infections of prisoners. In Bavaria, 13 prisoners and 28 staff members were infected by mid-May (average prison population in March 2020: 11,416, i.e. the infection rate was about 0.1%). In Berlin only two prisoners and in several other states (e.g. Mecklenburg-Western Pomerania, Saarland) none. The general policy was not to isolate the whole group of inmates, but only those who tested positive for the virus.

During the second wave of the pandemic, the situation regarding infections did not change dramatically. The numbers reported by the Ministries of Justice in our survey remained low; the few cases could be handled in the quarantine departments. More infections, but still in the range of less than 5%, were reported for staff members. In December 2020, Saxony – the federal state whose general population was worst affected at that time – reported infections of 42 staff members and 49 prisoners (about 1.7% of the total prison population). In February 2021, the number declined to two prisoners (= 0.07%) and 10 staff members. In Lower Saxony, 15 prisoners and 27 staff members were infected, i.e. 0.4% of the prison population. The enquiry of Schaerff (2021: 35) revealed infection rates for November/December between zero in six federal states (BB, MV, RP, SL, SH, ST) and 4.9 (BE), 6.3 (HE) and 9.1 (HH) per 1,000 prisoners.

In general, one can say that the prison administrations of the German *Länder* were successful in keeping COVID-19 out of prisons. A call by different prisoner rights groups to prioritise prisoners and staff in the eligibility for vaccinations – that referred to the often-problematic health care conditions in German prisons – has not been successful.[7] However, from March 2021, prison administrations of the *Länder* decided to vaccinate prison staff members as they put them on par with teachers, police and other groups that were prioritised (Sillies, 2021: 84). An important reason was that during the second wave of the pandemic, staff members posed a significant risk of infection to the prison population as a whole. Prisoners were put on a par with other citizens outside prisons and vaccinated by prioritising the most vulnerable groups (over 80-, then 70- and 60-years-old, considering also prior health problems).

2 Sentencing and execution of sentences – policies before and after the pandemic and the impact on prison population rates

The following findings about changes in the execution of prison sentences and in prison policies in response to the COVID-19 pandemic are based on two enquiries undertaken by the authors of this paper with the Ministries of Justice of the Federal states in March and November 2020. As mentioned before, Germany is a federal state, and the states (*Länder*) all have their individual prison legislation, policy and practice. The sentencing practice of the courts is based on the (uniform) Federal Criminal Code; nevertheless, there are regional disparities in sentencing practices. During the pandemic, the criminal courts were limited in their work and had to prioritise cases of pre-trial detainees. Nevertheless, there were delays even in these cases, as first court decisions in which the defendants successfully appealed orders of prolonged pre-trial detention show.[8]

Most defendants in Germany remained at large during their trial and often saw their cases postponed. No data are available, but we can assume that a significant backlog of cases was created.[9] The influx of new admissions to prisons was reduced, partly because of the fewer convictions during March to June 2020. Exact numbers are not yet available, but the prison statistics about admissions give some indication of the dimension: in February 2020, 7,799 new arrivals (*Erstaufnahmen im Strafvollzug*) were registered, whereas in March 2020, there were only 5,470, and in June 4,216 (45.9% lower). The police also report a decline of certain crimes, such as burglary, pickpocketing and other street crimes (robbery, assault, etc.), as more people stayed at home or had fewer opportunities to commit crimes. An enquiry conducted by the Ministries of Interior of the federal states revealed a reduction of between 25 and 50% of burglaries during the pandemic.[10] Therefore, the decline of new admissions to prisons can also be attributed to the drop in certain crimes.

Clearly, a significant reduction of prison admissions stems from the non-execution of imprisonment for fine defaults. All federal states indicated that shortly after the beginning of the pandemic in March 2020 they had stopped summoning offenders to serve their fine default sentences and most states released prisoners that already had started serving them. The reduction of the daily prison population serving prison sentences for fine defaults is therefore clearly visible from March 2020 onwards. The absolute numbers dropped by 72% between February and June 2020. This means that the proportion of fine defaulters as a proportion of the overall adult prison population fell from 10.6% to 5.8% at the end of March (see Table 18.1) and further to 3.5% in June (67% lower).

Nevertheless, differences between the federal states are visible, as the declared policy until the end of March was implemented rather reluctantly in Bavaria, Lower Saxony and Saxony-Anhalt. In North Rhine-Westphalia, the decrease was below the average as well. In contrast, in Baden-Württemberg, Berlin, Hamburg and Mecklenburg-Western Pomerania, the fine default population dropped by 75% or more (see Table 18.2).

When the general lockdown was ended in May 2020, some prison administrations gradually sought to get back to normal. Only a few federal states had not only postponed the execution of fine default sentences, but also granted an amnesty concerning the fines imposed originally (see e.g. Berlin, to a lesser extent also Hamburg). However, with the exception of Bavaria, all federal states kept their policy of not executing these short terms of imprisonment during the second wave of the pandemic from October 2020 onwards (see Table 18.3). In both waves of the pandemic, only those fine defaulters who in addition had to serve another prison sentence stayed in prison. For the time period from July 2020 to June 2021 statistical data are available only for 15 of the 16 federal states. Unfortunately the largest state of North Rhine-Westphalia did not report data to the Federal Bureau of Statistics (*Statistisches Bundesamt*, see www.destatis.de). Table 18.2 reveals that the daily prison population of fine defaulters remained clearly below the pre-pandemic level, even after the third wave of the pandemic ended in around May 2021. In particular, the city states of Bremen and Berlin maintained their restrictive policy of executing fine default imprisonment. The

Table 18.1 Fine defaulters in the adult prison system in Germany (absolute numbers at the end of the month)

2019	*Prisoners serving a prison sentence in prisons for adults*	*Of these: fine default sentences*	*Of these: percentage of prisoners in adult prisons*
March	46,477	4,861	10.5
June	45,687	4,482	9.8
September	45,244	4,616	10.2
Average 2019	45,417.75	4,569.5	10.1
2020			
February	45,062	4,773	10.6
March	42,177	2,447	5.8
April	39,528	1,553	3.9
May	38,595	1,312	3.4
June	38,154	1,333	3.5

Table 18.2 Fine defaulters in prisons for adults of the 16 German Länder before and during the COVID-19 pandemic (absolute numbers at the end of the month)

Federal state	*2/28 2020*	*3/31 2020*	*6/30 2020*	*9/30 2020*	*11/30 2020*	*3/31 2021*	*6/30 2021*	*Rate of change February to June 2020 (Index 2/2020=100)*	*Rate of change February 2020 to June 2021 (Index 2/2020=100)*
Baden-Württemberg	543	128	125	290	305	336	336	23.0	61.9
Bavaria	650	555	248	376	422	476	746	38.2	114.8
Berlin	325	87	29	216	212	113	102	8.9	31.4
Brandenburg	175	22	23	73	125	83	83	13,1	47.4
Bremen	53	28	13	38	32	9	12	24,5	22.6
Hamburg	118	29	43	152	94	47	55	36,4	46.6
Hesse	391	166	92	361	290	165	163	23,5	41.7
Mecklenburg-Western Pomerania	78	17	13	106	64	25	63	16,7	80.8
Lower Saxony	358	289	125	363	260	283	278	34,9	77.7
North Rhine-Westphalia	1,089	688	378	n.a.	n.a.	n.a.	n.a.	34.6	n.a.
Rhineland-Palatinate	206	91	44	98	152	143	135	21.4	65.5
Saarland	35	19	13	18	20	19	25	37.1	71.4
Saxony	336	105	71	263	255	211	163	21.1	48.5
Saxony-Anhalt	205	154	60	69	139	142	123	29.3	60.0
Schleswig-Holstein	78	24	19	42	40	49	53	24.4	68.0
Thuringia	133	45	37	55	145	105	86	27.8	64.7
Germany (total)	4,773	2,447	1,333	n.a.	n.a.	n.a.	n.a.	29.0	n.a.

Table 18.3 Measures taken by the Ministries of Justice of the Federal States to reduce the prison population and the risk of infection during the first and second wave of the pandemic

Federal State	*Measures taken March to May/June 2020 (first wave)*	*Measures taken since October 2020 (second wave)*
Baden-Württemberg	No prison sentences of less than 6 months and of fine default imprisonment	All prison sentences are served, in principle also fine default imprisonment, however, fine defaulters only exceptionally are admitted to closed prison facilities "if public security requires so".
Bavaria	No prison sentences of less than 6 months and of fine default imprisonment	No restrictions in serving sentences
Berlin	No execution of prison sentences of less than three years and of fine default imprisonment; interruption of sentences and immediate release	No execution of fine default imprisonment
Brandenburg	No execution of fine default imprisonment	No execution of fine default imprisonment
Bremen	No execution of prison sentences of up to 18 months and of fine default imprisonment	No execution of fine default imprisonment (until 28 February 2021)
Hamburg	No execution of prison sentences of up to three years and of fine default imprisonment; interruption of executing prison sentences with a remainder of less than 18 months	No execution of fine default imprisonment
Hesse	No execution of prison sentences (up to two years), which would have been served in open prisons, and no execution of fine default imprisonment	No execution of fine default imprisonment
Mecklenburg-Western Pomerania	No execution of prison sentences of up to three years and of fine default imprisonment	No execution of fine default imprisonment (until 31 May 2021)
Lower Saxony	No execution of prison sentences of up to 12 months and of fine default imprisonment[a]	No execution of fine default imprisonment
North Rhine-Westphalia	No execution of prison sentences of up to 12 months and of fine default imprisonment; interruption of execution of prison sentences of up to 18 months, if release was planned until July 2020[a]	All sentences are executed, fine default imprisonment only in individual cases

(*Continued*)

Federal State	*Measures taken March to May/ June 2020 (first wave)*	*Measures taken since October 2020 (second wave)*
Rhineland-Palatinate	No execution of fine default imprisonment	No execution of fine default imprisonment for women, for men only of fines less than 90 day-fine units
Schleswig-Holstein	Since March no execution of fine default imprisonment and sentences of up to 6 months, since June short-term sentences executed, but with few exceptions no fine default imprisonment[13]	No fine default imprisonment
Saarland	No execution of prison sentences of up to 18 months and of a remainder of prison sentences of up to 12 months, no execution of fine default imprisonment[a]	No execution of prison sentences of three to 18 months; execution of fine default imprisonment only in exceptional cases
Saxony	No execution of prison sentences for adults and youth prison sentences of up to three years, no execution of fine default imprisonment[a]	No execution of prison sentences for adults and youth prison sentences of up to three years, no execution of fine default imprisonment[a]
Saxony-Anhalt	No execution of fine default imprisonment	No execution of fine default imprisonment for fines of less than 90 day-fine units
Thuringia	No execution of prison sentences of up to 18 months and of fine default imprisonment	No execution of fine default imprisonment for fines of up to 90 day-fine units

Sources: Ministerial responses to our survey; press releases and online information on the ministerial and prison administration websites; see also Schaerff (2021: 32 f).
Exceptions are sometimes made for dangerous sexual and/or violent offenders.

only exception is the state of Bavaria (governed by a conservative political party), where the numbers on 30 June 2021 even exceeded the pre-pandemic level.

Some federal states went further and interrupted executing regular prison sentences up to a certain length by releasing prisoners temporarily.[11] This was the case for sentences of up to six months (Baden-Württemberg, Bavaria), 12 months (Lower Saxony, North Rhine-Westphalia) or even up to three years (Berlin, Hamburg, Saxony).[12] Hamburg did not summon those sentenced to imprisonment to start serving their sentences of up to three years and interrupted the execution of sentences of up to 18 months. In some federal states, however, policy remained unclear, but, apparently, some states did not decide to release short-term prisoners other than fine defaulters. Different occupancy rates and problems of overcrowding cannot explain the differences between e.g. Berlin and Bavaria. The explanation rather lies in regional differences regarding the punitive climate in penal and prison policy, which traditionally is more severe in Bavaria and more relaxed in Berlin.

After considerable fear that prisons could become COVID-19 hotspots before and during the first wave, after the summer, prison administrations seemed to be more confident of managing the crisis: most of them now disposed of enough empty cells to isolate prisoners on admission, and enough tests and hygienic masks were available. This may explain why, during the second wave of the pandemic, since October 2020, most federal states renewed the measures of not executing imprisonment for fine defaults. However, in most states, other prison sentences, even short-term sentences, were and are still executed. There are a few exceptions: Bavaria executed fine default sentences, i.e. there was no restriction of executions during the second wave, whereas Saxony and Saarland renewed all restrictions from the first wave; thus, prison sentences of up to three years and 18 months, respectively, were not executed.

While the courts[14] are responsible for the decision on early release, prisons do exert a certain influence with their statement on the prisoner's development that often forms the decisive basis for the court's decision. Nevertheless, there was no clear indication that the statements of the prison administration concerning the decision of an early release changed in favour of granting more such releases during March 2020 and the following months.

The 16 Ministries of Justice unanimously reported that they had not interfered in favour of more early releases and that only in a few cases an application for a pardon due to a risk of infection (e.g. from specific vulnerable prisoners) was submitted. The outcome of these individual cases is unknown.

3 Restrictions of contact with the outside world

The first direct consequence of the pandemic in all federal states was the restriction, mostly the suspension, of all visits which included personal contact. The regular monthly visits have a duration of between two and four hours in all, with additional visits possible for family members and children (Dünkel, 2021a). Some prisons already had visitors' facilities with glass partitions; other prisons introduced such facilities. Lawyers' visits, particularly in facilities for pre-trial detention, were and are not restricted, but usually also took place with screens. After the first wave of the pandemic, visits were reintroduced reluctantly and the duration and the number of visitors allowed remained drastically restricted. For example, since June 2020, prisoners in North Rhine-Westphalia have been allowed to receive visits from one relative, in addition to their children. There are similar regulations and relaxation of the lockdown measures in other federal states. However, using screen partitioning still seems to be the norm, so that most prisoners have not touched their loved ones for almost a year now.[15] Since the beginning of the pandemic, no long-term visits have been allowed (see for the High Court of Berlin jurisprudence in that respect below under 6.).

During the second wave of the pandemic from October 2020, the restrictions of visits were less severe (Sillies, 2021: 83). The prison administrations applied earlier good practice by using masks and distancing and, if necessary, also visits with Plexiglas. Visitors' rooms were restructured according to hygienic requirements and since March/April 2021 visits can be facilitated by presenting a negative COVID-19 test.

In many regards, prisoners suffered from additional restrictions of their liberty. In closed prisons, prison leave (day leave of several hours and long-term leave of several days) has been stopped. Equally, in open prison regimes, day leave, usually the most common form, was not allowed any longer. We found indications, however, that more often than expected, long-term leave of two weeks or more (in some states long leave of up to six months is possible) was granted in order to prepare for release. In some open prisons, a large part of the prisoners are on long-term prison leave. For example, in one of the largest open prisons (Berlin with a capacity of more than 600 in different units) since the beginning of the pandemic, about 40–60% of prisoners were on long-term leave. This means that they were living at home with their families or in their own apartments (Micheli and Luxa, 2021: 94). This is similar to the practice of home detention in other European countries, in so far as prisoners serve a longer part of their sentence at home. The difference is that the restrictions of daily activities are not comparable, as prisoners on long-term leave can regularly move about freely and go to work, have outside leisure time, etc. In contrast to other European countries, in Germany, electronic monitoring is not used for prisoners on leave as it is seen as disproportionate in cases of offenders with low or medium risks of reoffending (Dünkel, Thiele and Treig, 2017).

4 Restrictions inside prisons: the impact of COVID-19 in daily prison life: activities (work, re-entry programmes, sports, etc.)

All 16 prison administrations of the federal states in March 2020 took immediate action to protect inmates as well as staff members in prisons. In the beginning, there was a shortage of masks and hygiene materials, but by about mid-April, this problem was resolved. Due to the further reduction of the numbers of prisoners and of admissions to prison, all prisons had the capacity to establish quarantine areas and to accommodate new prisoners in these areas for up to two weeks.[16] The quarantine was practised in different forms: in some states, an isolation in single cells with no physical contacts also during day-time was used; in other states, small groups of incoming prisoners were set up, who could share some leisure time or even work activities (e.g. in Hamburg). The German UN National Preventive Mechanism criticised this form of single isolation,[17] although most federal states using it reported that they had provided compensatory leisure time and learning activities, including video- and mobile phone communication. In addition, in some states, special staff members were assigned to take care of prisoners in isolation.

Some common activities (work, recreational activities) have been partly reduced. In particular in pre-trial detention, the situation was and is difficult. It can mean that prisoners are locked up for up to 23 hours per day in their cells. In prisons for sentenced offenders, joint activities with fellow inmates were reduced, in particular team sports such as soccer. However, other sports were expanded (jogging, small group activities, etc.). Some prison administrations reported that they bought additional board and card games and other material for leisure activities, and tried to find a balance between necessary restrictions and calming down prisoners' anxieties and potential anger at staff by providing compensatory activities (see below 5).

Regarding the very low infection rates, after June/July 2020, prison work activities mostly resumed its regular form, while implementing protective measures such as wearing masks and keeping a safe distance. During the second wave of the pandemic, since October 2020, many prisons tried to keep workshops open, albeit with limited capacity, to enable prisoners to continue working there or in other "system relevant" jobs, such as cleaning.

5 Compensatory measures

In recent years, German prisons have seen some significant improvements with regard to the duration and frequency of visits, which have now been put on hold. All federal states aimed at providing compensatory measures to alleviate the impact of the prohibition or drastic reductions of visits mentioned above. Most introduced additional possibilities for telephone calls or video-telephony. In some states, for example, Hamburg, North-Rhine Westphalia and Lower Saxony, even mobile phones were handed out, in particular in open prisons – a measure which was unthinkable before the pandemic. The practice and scope of these additional options, however, depended on infrastructure and the availability of staff. While there is little information on how far prisoners were able to profit from these new options, it nevertheless seems that this form of compensation was more than just symbolic.[18] Whether it was a common practice is difficult to tell from the available information – some of the Ministries of Justice were vague or did not know how far prisons had implemented such schemes. Sometimes, they spoke of "pilot schemes" for video calls and promised to install more telephones soon. Even before the outbreak of the pandemic, Lower Saxony had already introduced telephones in all prison cells in closed prisons. This allowed regular phone calls, through the central prison exchange, with family members and friends. In open prisons, mobile phones were allowed. Other federal states, such as Hamburg, plan to install phones in prison cells as well. All this may have a positive impact on new infrastructure and its regular use, which could benefit all, especially foreign prisoners. Some of these possibilities such as the use of mobile phones, however, were retracted as soon as the pandemic situation allowed for more visits and prison leave.[19]

Problematic was the patchy information handed out by prisons and Ministries at least at the beginning of the pandemic. Prison websites to date often offer no more than basic information about prohibition or restriction of visits, so that relatives or friends of visitors were and are left to information they receive from the prisoners themselves.[20] Even when we consider that the situation was very difficult for staff and prison administrations, the lack of information, and even empathy, in a situation when many prisoners and their relatives were particularly anxious about their loved ones is regrettable. Information in languages other than German was rarely provided.

6 Legal basis and monitoring of pandemic-related measures

The Prison Acts of all federal states allow for the restriction of basic rights of prisoners for specific security reasons and in emergency situations, and generally refer to the Infection Protection Act (*Infektionsschutzgesetz*), according to which communicable and infectious diseases have to be reported immediately to the public health administration. Unless and until this body becomes active, the medical service of the prison is responsible for isolating and treating the prisoner that has been infected or is possibly infected. Plans to deal with outbreaks of diseases had been prepared before the COVID-19 crisis. The measures taken were mostly accepted by prisoners who often have health problems and were fearful of being infected in prison.[21] No riots or other serious cases of disorder have been reported during the pandemic so far. While it is possible and even probable that the numbers of incidents of self-harm or attempted or even committed suicides have risen,[22] no official data exist and our respondents in the Ministries of Justice have not mentioned such cases.

Despite the far-reaching and long-lasting restrictions the pandemic brought for prisoners, and despite the "ample opportunity to make requests or complaints" (Rule 70.1 of the EPR 2020) that exists in Germany,[23] so far only a few prisoner complaints have reached the courts. As mentioned above, some related to the length of proceedings, others to the withdrawal of compensatory measures such as the use of private mobile phones, and yet others to the use of a video hearing instead of a personal one for the release decision due to the pandemic.[24] This is surprising as speedy procedures for urgent problems exist in the legal framework for prisoner complaints and some prisoners know how to make use of them. It is unclear whether courts just have been debilitated by the pandemic and many complaints are queuing up, or whether prisoners simply accepted the measures taken.

In May 2021, an important decision was taken by the High Court of the Federal State of Berlin on long-term visits, that is, unsupervised visits for up to eight hours. A prisoner had applied for such a visit of his wife and the three children, which he had been granted in the past. The Prison Act of Berlin provides for such visits, but gives the prison administration some discretionary power to decide whether to grant them. The *Kammergericht* (KG) Berlin decided that in this instance, the denial of the long-term visit in November 2020 had violated the prisoner's constitutional right protecting marriage and family (Article 6 of the German Constitution). Even in times of the pandemic, the prison administration should allow such visits if they would otherwise be acceptable, in particular if specific measures to ameliorate the risks posed by the virus, such as the quarantine, which the prisoner would have accepted to undergo after the visit, were possible. Organisational problems of the prison authorities to administer such visits were not sufficient grounds for not allowing the visit (see KG Berlin 5 Ws 64/21 Vollz – 594 StVK 220/20 Vollz of 31 May 2021).

The National Preventive Mechanism in Germany has conducted six prison visits since the start of the pandemic and published reports that included information on how prisons dealt with the situation. All of them acknowledged the efforts made by prison staff and administration and even reported favourable developments that should remain in place in the future.[25]

7 Return to normal? The positive side of the pandemic crisis: what could be kept for improving prison conditions and reforming penal law?

The pandemic did not only have a negative impact on prison regimes and daily life in prison. Some of the new forms of internet communication could be managed without increased security problems. Such forms of communication have also been used for court hearings on pre-trial detention or early release. These forms of communication should also be used in future. Allowing prisoners access to Skype or similar communication programmes is in line with the aim of protecting family life and intensifying relations with partners, children and friends. It is particularly beneficial for foreign prisoners and their families. We can conclude that these generally positive experiences make a good case for their regular use, and boost existing efforts by prisons to create the necessary infrastructure. Some Ministries of Justice (e.g. North-Rhine Westphalia) declared that also after the pandemic mobile phones will be accepted in open prisons and video calls will generally become standard in closed prisons.

As to working conditions for staff members, another good experience was allowing them to work from home, at least for some administrative work.

The pandemic has resulted in an interruption of the execution of short-term imprisonment, which – because of its detrimental effects on social reintegration (see Dünkel, 2021) and its negative impact on the prison management (with high numbers of incoming and released prisoners) – is in principle a desirable development. In Germany, we should, however, not revert to the situation before the pandemic after the lockdown comes to an end, but think of replacing short-term imprisonment by alternative modes of executing prison sentences. In countries such as Finland, Austria, the Netherlands, Spain or Switzerland, short prison terms or a short remainder of long-term sentences can be served under probationary supervision, by doing work in the community or by serving a specific term under electronic home detention (Dünkel and Weber, 2019: 408 ff.; for more details, see Chapters 49 and 50 in this volume).[26] For the moment, an amnesty for offenders, whose execution of a short-term prison sentence was interrupted, would be a feasible solution (see for a positive example the practice in Berlin and Hamburg mentioned above; see also Feest, 2020: 120 f.), as it is a particular heavy burden to serve a short prison term perhaps after a year, when the offender has shown his or her social integration into work and family life.

The general penal policy question raised (mainly) by academics and prisoner rights activists is: Should we not use the pandemic as a reminder that we incarcerate people who should not be in prison and instead could be sanctioned in the community? In Germany, the large number of fine defaulters is certainly a concern already picked up by some political parties and initiatives. The German debate refers to other European countries, where fine default imprisonment is widely avoided by alternative forms of executing fines and replacing them by community service or by completely abolishing fine default imprisonment by transferring the execution to civil law agencies (see Dünkel, 2019 with further references; Radtke, 2018; Schaerff, 2021: 37 ff.). The numbers of fine defaulters in Germany could be reduced by half or even two thirds if one day of fine default imprisonment would not only count for one day-fine unit, but – as e.g. in Austria, Poland or Spain for two, or as in Finland and Estonia for three day-fine units (see Drápal, 2018: 470 ff.).

Already in June 2019, a working group of the Federal Ministry of Justice and the Ministries of Justice of the 16 federal states delivered a report proposing changes to fine default imprisonment. The working group recommended a change of the conversion rates and for further prioritising community service instead of fine default imprisonment. The pandemic has contributed to increase the pressure on the legislator. Draft legislation can be expected from the Federal Ministry of Justice for early 2022.

Many academics are also taking the opportunity to recommend the decriminalisation of cannabis and of minor drug offences in general as well as of petty property offences or fare-dodging, which for recidivists may result in prison sentences (Dünkel, 2019; 2021; Harrendorf, 2020; Mohr, 2020). Germany has the largest proportion of short-term prisoners in Europe (see Dünkel, 2017: 642 f.), mainly because of the fine default problem, but also because of many short prison sentences (although a law reform initiative in 1969 had sought to ban them, see Dünkel, 2019). Therefore, the need for further reform of the criminal law and the criminal sanctions system is evident (Mohr, 2020) and could be one of the lessons learned from the COVID-19 crisis (see Bals, Cornel, Dünkel, et al. 2021). The new federal government elected in September 2021, a coalition of Social Democrats, the Greens and the Liberals, has included a number of reform proposals in its programme: Imprisonment for failing to pay day fines will be reduced by changing the conversion rate from one day of default imprisonment for one day-fine unit to one day for two or three units. This should reduce the fine default prison population at least by half. Further reduction of the prison population may be expected from the decriminalisation of cannabis, which is also part of the penal policy of the new government.

Notes

1 See for the development of the German prison system Dünkel and Rössner (2001), Dünkel (2018).

2 The statistical data on the prison are taken from Statistisches Bundesamt (Ed.): Rechtspflege. Bestand der Gefangenen und Verwahrten in den deutschen Justizvollzugsanstalten nach ihrer Unterbringung auf Haftplätzen des geschlossenen und offenen Vollzugs (monthly statistics on prisoners in closed and open prison facilities), https://www.destatis.de.

3 See world prison brief: https://www.prisonstudies.org/country/Germany; the data published by ICPS for June 2020 (69 per 100,000) are not correct as the German Federal Ministry of Justice in the case of the largest federal state North-Rhine Westphalia reported data of 2019, which were considerably higher than in 2020 (last access: 16 February 2021).

4 Abbreviations of the federal states: BB = Brandenburg; BE = Berlin; BW = Baden-Württemberg; BY = Bavaria; HB = Bremen; HE = Hesse; HH = Hamburg; MV = Mecklenburg-Western Pomerania; NI = Lower Saxony; NW = North Rhine-Westphalia; RP = Rhineland-Palatinate; SH = Schleswig-Holstein; SL = Saarland; SN = Saxony; ST = Saxony-Anhalt; TH = Thuringia.

5 It does not mean that only low-risk offenders are allowed to serve their sentence in open prisons. Also medium- and high-risk offenders – at least in the very last stages of the execution of prison sentences – should have the right to be transferred to open prisons in order to alleviate the transition process from closed prisons to an open environment and the after-care situation: Dünkel in Dünkel et al. (2016: 91 ff).

6 At the end of June 2020, the proportion of prisoners accommodated in open prisons for adults was 14.1% and in youth prisons 8.2%, which underlines the proposition that the pandemic had no visible impact on the strategy of furthering the re-entry of prisoners by a graduated release and the transfer to open prisons. However, further statistical analysis is needed to establish which offender groups were selected and whether, as a result, there were differential effects.

7 https://www.grundrechtekomitee.de/details/gemeinsame-forderung-nach-priorisierung-von-gefangenen-bei-der-corona-impfung (last access: 21 February 2021). The reason was that the risk of being infected in prisons appeared to be lower than outside prisons and therefore there was no evidence for prioritising prisoners.

8 See OLG Braunschweig (1. Strafsenat), Beschluss vom 25.03.2020 – 1 Ws 47/20; OLG Stuttgart (4. Strafsenat), Beschluss vom 06.04.2020 – H 4 Ws 71/20.

9 For first impressions from a defence lawyer's point of view, see Fromm (2020: 251).

10 See https://www.sicherheit.info/kriminalitaetsentwicklung-in-zeiten-von-corona-atempause (last access: 21 February 2021). However, (internet) fraud and domestic violence presumably have increased, but there is no detailed research on that.

11 Usually, exceptions applied regarding some offences such as sex offences and partly violent offences. These exceptions were rare as these offences often carry heavier penalties.

12 North Rhine-Westphalia in the response to a Parliamentary Enquiry declared that prisoners who served a fine default or prison sentence of up to 18 months that ended between 20 March and 31 July 2020 had been released by interrupting the execution of the sentence according to sec. 455a Criminal Procedure Act (for organisational reasons). In total, 1,051 prisoners were released, which corresponds to 9.7% of the North Rhine-Westphalian prison population in March 2020; see Parliamentary printed matter, *Landtags-Drucksache* 17/3468 of 8 June 2020.

13 https://www.schleswig-holstein.de/DE/Landesregierung/II/Presse/PI/2020/Justiz/200326_Corona.html; https://schleswig-holstein.de/DE/Schwerpunkte/Coronavirus/FAQ/faq_coronavirus_node.html (last access 21 February 2021).

14 According to sec. 57, 57a Penal Code, sec. 88, 89 Juvenile Justice Act, the Courts for the Execution of Sentences decide upon early condition release after two thirds or, in special cases, after half of the sentence. See for the legal requirements in Germany and in comparison to other European jurisdictions Dünkel (2015); Dünkel and Weber (2019).

15 One notable exception was reported for a women's prison in Berlin where personal contact with children is allowed, but the prisoner then is isolated for seven days and only released from the isolation after a negative test.

16 The practice differed, however, in comparison of the federal states: while in Bavaria all incoming prisoners had to stay in quarantine for 14 days and two more days after testing, other states shortened the period to five days and transferred prisoners after a negative test result to the regular prison departments; see Nationale Stelle zur Verhütung von Folter (2021: 39 f).

17 See Nationale Stelle zur Verhütung von Folter (2021: 40), referring to a decision of the German Federal Constitutional Court (BVerfG, 24 July 2018, Az: 2 BvR 309/15, Rn. 80), which stated that strict isolation without sufficient surveillance by prison staff is comparable to physical fixing and implies the risk of serious health damages.

18 Critical for the early stage of the pandemic Feest (2020) and in an interview Graebsch (https://www.vice.com/de/article/7kzy39/gefangnis-coronavirus-inhaftierte-freilassen_21 February 2021); positive examples can be found in reports by the National Mechanism for the Prevention of Torture, https://www.nationale-stelle.de/besuche/laenderkommission/2020.html and Nationale Stelle zur Verhütung von Folter (2021).

19 A prisoner who wanted to keep his mobile phone he had been allowed to use in an open prison in Hamburg temporarily lost his case before court, LG Hamburg (5. Strafvollstreckungskammer), Beschluss vom 21.10.2020 – 605 Vollz 385/20.

20 For more details, see Dünkel and Morgenstern (2020).

21 Although there is no legal base for the practice of preventive isolation of incoming prisoners for up to 14 days (see Nationale Stelle zur Verhütung von Folter, 2021: 39), there were no complaints about that measure by prisoners in general, but the UN National Preventive Mechanism criticised the strict single isolation practised in some federal states; see above under 4.

22 According to a press release by police, already in March 2020, a foreign prisoner killed himself shortly after he learnt that his wife was not allowed to visit him and all visits were prohibited, www.presseportal.de/blaulicht/pm/110972/4550849 (21 February 2021).

23 All prisoners have the right to a judicial complaint that is decided by the Court for the Execution of Prison Sentences (sec. 109 ff. Prison Law 1977, 92 Juvenile Justice Act; see for more details Dünkel and Morgenstern, 2018). A large body of jurisprudence exists.

24 OLG Karlsruhe (2. Strafsenat), Beschluss vom 05.05.2020 – 2 Ws 84/20 (10 StVK 20/20).

25 https://www.nationale-stelle.de/besuche/laenderkommission/2020.html and Nationale Stelle zur Verhütung von Folter (2021).

26 However, as mentioned above, electronic monitoring (EM) is not an option for Germany, where it is used only for a few (less than 100 in total) released high-risk or "dangerous" offenders under probationary supervision and not for regular prisoners on leave. The principle of proportionality is taken very seriously in Germany excluding EM for low-risk offenders (Dünkel, Thiele and Treig, 2017).

References

Bals, N., Cornel, H., Dünkel, F., et al. (2021): Für eine rationale Kriminalpolitik – Vorschläge des Ziethener Kreises für die Legislaturperiode 2021-2025. *Neue Kriminalpolitik* 33, 383–391.

Drápal, J. (2018): Day fines: A European comparison and Czech malpractice. *European Journal of Criminology* 15, 461–480.

Dünkel, F. (2015): Mandatory release versus discretionary release – a comparative approach. In: Herzog-Evans, M. (Ed.). *Offender-release and supervision: The role of Courts and the use of discretion.* AH Oisterwijk: Wolf Legal Publishers, 167–192.

Dünkel, F. (2017): European penology: The rise and fall of prison population rates in Europe in times of migrant crises and terrorism. *European Journal of Criminology* 14, 629–653.

Dünkel, F. (2018): Strafvollzug. In: Hermann, D., Pöge, A. (Eds.). *Kriminalsoziologie. Handbuch für Wissenschaft und Praxis.* Baden-Baden: Nomos Verlag, 399–438.

Dünkel, F. (2019): Reforms of the criminal sanctions system in Germany – achievements and unresolved problems. *Juridica International* (Estonia) 28, 37–48 (Internet: https://doi.org/10.12697/JI.2019.28.05).

Dünkel, F. (2021): Short-term imprisonment and the 'reductionist' approach. In: Beyens, K. et al. (Eds.): Sonja Snacken: an inspiring humanist. Brussels: VUBPRESS Brussels University Press, 39–54.

Dünkel, F. (2021a): Ehe- und familienfreundliche Gestaltung des Strafvollzugs – Rechtliche und rechtstatsächliche Entwicklungen in Deutschland. In: Ruch, A., Singelnstein, T. (Eds.): *Auf neuen Wegen – Kriminologie, Kriminalpolitik und Polizeiwissenschaft aus interdisziplinärer Perspektive. Festschrift für Thomas Feltes zum 70. Geburtstag.* Berlin: Duncker & Humblot, 545–559.

Dünkel, F. et al. (2016) (Eds.): *European Treatment, Transition Management, and Re-Integration of High-Risk Offenders.* Mönchengladbach: Forum Verlag Godesberg.

Dünkel, F., and Morgenstern, C. (2018): The monitoring of prisons in German law and practice. *Crime, Law and Social Change* 70, 93–112. (https://link.springer.com/article/10.1007%2Fs10611-017-9721-3).

Dünkel, F., and Morgenstern, C. (2020): Der Einfluss von COVID-19 auf den Strafvollzug und die Strafvollzugspolitik in Deutschland. *Neue Kriminalpolitik* 32, 432–457.

Dünkel, F., and Rössner, D. (2001): Germany. In: van Zyl Smit, D., Dünkel, F. (Eds.). *Imprisonment today and tomorrow – International perspectives on prisoners' rights and prison conditions.* 2nd ed., Deventer, Boston: Kluwer, 288–350.

Dünkel, F., Thiele, C., and Treig, J. (2017): "You'll never stand-alone": Electronic monitoring in Germany. *European Journal of Probation* 9, 28–45 (http://journals.sagepub.com/eprint/kpuVBex3FqFAuF2yZkSm/full).

Dünkel, F., and Weber, J. (2019): (Early) release, probation and collateral consequences (directives) after release. Legal conditions and practice. In: Dünkel, F. et al. (Eds.). *Prisoner Resettlement in Europe.* London, New York: Routledge, 403–434.

Feest, J. (2020): Corona und Knast – ein Zwischenbericht. *Neue Kriminalpolitik* 32, 113–122.

Fromm, I. (2020): Über die Auswirkungen der COVID-19-Pandemie auf Straf- und Bußgeldsachen. *Deutsches Autorecht* 90, 251–254.

Harrendorf, S. (2020): Plädoyer für eine umfassende Entkriminalisierung des Umgangs mit Betäubungsmitteln zum Eigenkonsum. In: Drenkhahn, K. et al. (Eds.). *Kriminologie und Kriminalpolitik im Dienste der Menschenwürde. Festschrift für Frieder Dünkel zum 70. Geburtstag.* Mönchengladbach: Forum Verlag Godesberg, 351–379.

Micheli, M., and Luxa, T. (2021): Neue Wege der Gewährung von Vollzugslockerungen. *Forum Strafvollzug* 70, 93–95.

Mohr, N. (2020): *Die Entwicklung des Sanktionenrechts im deutschen Strafrecht – Bestandsaufnahme und Reformvorschläge.* Mönchengladbach: Forum Verlag Godesberg.

Morgenstern, C. (2016): "Der Resozialisierungsgrundsatz". Social reintegration as the dominant narrative for community punishment in Germany? In: Robinson, G. and McNeill, F. (Eds.): *Community Punishment. European Perspectives.* Oxon, New York: Routledge, 72–94.

Nationale Stelle zur Verhütung von Folter (2021): *Jahresbericht 2020.* Wiesbaden. https//www.nationale-stelle.de/Publikationen.

Pruin, I. (2019): Prisoner Resettlement in Germany. In: Dünkel, F. et al. (Eds.). *Prisoner Resettlement in Europe.* London, New York: Routledge, 150–166.

Radtke, H. (2018): Ersatzfreiheitsstrafe abschaffen? *Zeitschrift für Rechtspolitik* 51, 58.

Schaerff, M. (2021): Auswirkungen der COVID-19-Pandemie auf den Justizvollzug – Einstieg in den Ausstieg aus der Ersatzfreiheitsstrafe? *Monatsschrift für Kriminologie und Strafrechtsreform* 104 (1), 27–45.

Sillies, L. (2021): Justizvollzug in Zeiten der Corona-Pandemie. *Forum Strafvollzug* 70, 83–86.

19 Greece

Maria Anagnostaki

1 Introduction

1.1 COVID-19 in the community

In Greece, the COVID-19 pandemic is at its third wave peak at the time of writing (March 2021).[1] During the first wave (February 2020 to June 2020), infection levels remained low, due mainly to early decisions for the implementation of serious restrictions for the general population and an overall consent of the public to abide by the measures and the official guidelines. Some relaxations to the restrictions followed, but in mid-August 2020, the second wave of COVID-19 hit the country with upward trends of the infection rates and deaths, while the National Health System was heavily pressured. Strict restrictions on movement for the general population and on the operation of the economy were re-introduced on 7 November and since then a lockdown has been imposed, which has not been lifted but is expected to be gradually relaxed by the end of April 2021.

1.2 Correctional policy and prison conditions

Greece is one of the countries that have a systemic problem of prison overcrowding and of bad prison conditions that goes back to the 1990s. Additional and interrelated persistent deficiencies include poor hygiene and inadequate health care, low staffing levels, lack of meaningful activities, a poor regime and inter-prisoner violence (Cheliotis, 2012; CPT, 2020b). These enduring problems remained unattended for more than two decades:[2] emergency legislative measures for the decongestion of the prison population were the main tools used to relieve pressure from the system and keep it going (Anagnostaki, 2013; Tzannetaki, 2006; 2016). Meanwhile, there has been an official denial of the problems and lack of long-term planning for a sustainable solution that would result in acceptable prison conditions as well as an integrated policy with clear goals for the social reintegration of inmates. In 2015, the left-wing government (SYRIZA/ANEL) initiated a change of correctional policy, bringing the issue of protecting prisoners' human rights

DOI: 10.4324/9781003169178-19

and improving prison conditions to the fore. The old strategy of emergency decongestion measures was again used as a rapid solution, which reduced the prison population by nearly 18% (see Figure 19.1). This relief for the system was coupled with systematic attempts to draw up long-term plans and create a strategy that would reform the prison system. These efforts were actively supported by the Council of Europe and the CPT. A strategic plan was drafted with the participation of Council of Europe experts (Koulouris et al., 2018: 8; MoJ, 2018), and a report on the reasons that led to prison overcrowding was prepared and made public on March 2019 (Palma et al., 2019). During the period 2015–2019, new initiatives were piloted and preparatory steps were taken for a number of reform actions: recruiting a large number of prison staff, introducing more specialists (social workers, psychologists, etc.) in the system, levelling up health services, introducing telemedicine in cooperation with the Ministry of Health and integrating Korydalos Prison Hospital into the National Health System, extending educational activities to all prisons in cooperation with the Ministry of Education, piloting internet (Skype) communication, creating special visiting spaces for prisoners to meet their children and for long-term family visits, prison staff training and preparation for the creation of a permanent training structure (Prison Academy) (MoJ, 2017, 2018), etc. Nevertheless, these initiatives could not compensate for the imminent and urgent problems that prison administration was very often confronted with, especially issues of inter-prisoner violence and poor health services (CPT, 2020b; Cheliotis and Xenakis, 2021). More time and continuous efforts are needed for reforms to come to fruition.

The July 2019 elections were won by the right-wing party (ND), based to a large extent on a law-and-order rhetoric and a strong adherence to punitive agendas, not only for prisoners, but also for migrants and refugees, local political groups, squatters, etc., in the name of 'security'. This new policy was reflected in the transfer of the responsibility for the prison system from the Ministry of Justice to the Ministry of Citizen Protection, which is the Ministry responsible for the police. This was the first time the General Secretariat for Crime Policy, the central administration branch of government for the implementation of correctional policy and the running of prisons, was transferred to a Ministry with a clear security agenda. This strategic change, and the punitive ideology it implies, has been widely criticised by academics, legal experts, human rights organisations, centre and left-wing opposition parties, as well as the federation of prison staff. The new punitiveness is also reflected in the reluctance of the competent Ministry of Citizen Protection to take any legislative measures to relieve overcrowding during the COVID-19 crisis (see more below). On the contrary, in December 2020, Parliament adopted new legislation, which seriously restricts the use of two reintegrative measures to which prisoners were entitled: regular prison leave and transfers to semi-open farm prisons, thus putting at risk prisoners' rehabilitation and the smooth operation of the prison system.[3]

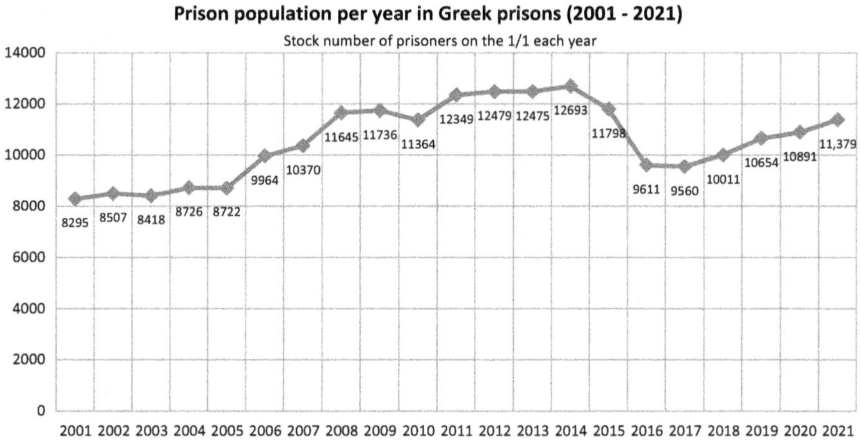

Figure 19.1 Prison population per year in Greek prisons (2001–2020).[4]

The prison population on 1 January 2021 amounted to 11,379 (see Figure 19.1), while the capacity of Greek prisons, according to the most recent measurement adopted by the Ministry of Justice in 2018, is 10,175 prisoners. Even so, this number does not reflect the density of overcrowding in all prisons, since there are facilities which traditionally do not reach their full capacity (like the women's prison, the centre for drug-addicted prisoners and semi-open farm prisons). This means that in closed male prisons, the population is way over their maximum capacity (Koulouris, 2020). In fact, at the beginning of 2020, in 23 out of 34 prison establishments, overcrowding exceeded capacity in percentages that range from 102% to 253%.[5] Official data from last year show that the prison population rose during the COVID pandemic, from 10,891 prisoners in January 2020, to 11,379 in January 2021 (see Figure 19.1), a significant 5% increase (488 prisoners). Due to recent legislation mentioned above, it is expected that the prison population in closed male prisons will increase further. Figure 19.1 shows the levels of the prison population in the last 20 years.

1.3 COVID-19 infections in prisons

During the first wave of the pandemic, there were no COVID-19 infections among prisoners, and only one staff member countrywide (out of about 4,150) was infected. The situation in prisons matched the pandemic situation in the general population (see Section 1.1). The General Secretariat for Crime Policy, following cooperation with the competent authorities, issued and distributed quickly (on 13 March 2020) to prison governors specific instructions on the preventive and restrictive measures to be taken as an immediate response to the crisis. Subsequently, the National Public Health

Organisation issued a detailed protocol for prisons and other places of detention, including preparatory actions, preventive measures, measures for managing suspected cases and infections, and guidelines for staff management (NPHO, 2020).

Since the second wave started (from mid-August 2020 onwards), COVID-19 infections spread among prisons and prisoners, following the course of the pandemic in the community. According to data presented by the Deputy Minister of Citizen Protection in Parliament in March 2021, until 15 February 2021, 426 prisoners and 140 members of prison staff were confirmed cases of COVID-19 infections countrywide. Moreover, 17,780 SARS-CoV-2 tests of prisoners and 9,146 tests of prison staff were administered. The Deputy Minister also reported that by the end of February 2021, 358 prisoners and 134 prison staff, including 32 medical staff, had been vaccinated.[6] Until 15 February 2021, when the latest official data were released, nine prisons (out of 34 prisons in total) had zero infections both among prisoners and staff, eight prisons had zero infections among prisoners and a small number of staff infected, and two prisons had infections among prison staff but not among prisoners. The heavy burden of infections fell mainly on the prisons in the north of the country (Thessaloniki, Larissa, Grevena prisons), analogous to the spread of the COVID-19 virus in the general population. However, the Ministry has not provided data for deaths or for the status of the infection levels in the biggest prison (Korydallos I prison in Attika). Concerns have been expressed that there might be a dark number of cases (Pischoina, 2020), which are not diagnosed because continuous tests are not available in all prisons. The national health authorities are not providing for systematic testing of prisoners and staff. In fact, in Thessaloniki prison, it was the prosecutor who ordered that ill prisoners should be transferred to the local hospital for COVID-19 testing, and the first positive case was found on 28 October 2020. Similarly, in Larissa prison, situated in a town with a high infection rate, once systematic testing started, 200 infected persons were detected. Both prisons face acute overcrowding problems with Thessaloniki prison accommodating 530 inmates (capacity 358) and Larissa prison 729 (capacity 552). According to media reports, an emergency situation appeared in Patra Prison, a prison situated in an area with a high infection load, in February 2021, with 40 prisoners and nine members of staff found positive and testing still in progress.

According to the NPHO protocol for prisons, prison administrations should take necessary measures in several fields. It is most plausible that these measures are followed to a different extent in different prisons, depending, *inter alia*, on the local prison conditions (infrastructure, available space and population density), the staff ratio (level of staff shortage and availability of medical staff), proximity to health services and hospitals and, especially, prison administration and management. However, lack of available space and overcrowding and acute shortage of medical personnel, as well as lack of prison staff in most establishments, make it very difficult to manage the main preventive measures of distancing, personal hygiene and isolation of suspected cases, infections and newly admitted prisoners.

2 Prison and penal policy concerning the execution of prison sentences during the COVID-19-induced crisis

The Greek penal system is under transition as new codes, the Penal Code and the Code of Penal Procedure, came into force very recently (July 2019). Both codes introduced major changes and were finally adopted by Parliament after many years of deliberations by different legislative committees. Nevertheless, there was no political consensus and political objections are still raised on some sensitive issues, including the lowering of maximum penalties for serious crimes. Most importantly, the Penal Code introduced a new system of penalties, which adopts a moderate model of distributing punishment, with an emphasis on aligning sentences imposed by the courts with sentences served in prison. However, necessary administrative provisions and structures for the implementation of the new architecture of the system are still pending.[7] Similarly, the Code of Penal Procedure introduced a new paradigm in penal procedure, importing novel diversion measures and procedures to relieve not only the prison system, but also the judiciary and courts from case overload. However, it will take a long time to absorb these changes.

In relation to COVID-19 infections, as already mentioned, no measures have been taken so far regarding the execution of sentences for any group of prisoners, including vulnerable groups (elderly inmates or those with serious medical conditions). At the beginning of the first wave, the government announced the passing of legislation regarding the release of certain categories of offenders, mainly prisoners serving short sentences or those close to early release. Considerable public pressure was put on the government to use this legislative initiative to reduce overcrowding as a central tool for preventing medical emergencies and the spreading of COVID-19 in prisons. Academics, the Hellenic Bar Association, the Ombudsman, the Hellenic Criminal Bar Association, the Hellenic Federation of Prison Staff, political parties, prison school staff and prisoners' support organisations argued in favour of decongestion and the protection especially of vulnerable prisoners. Prisoners themselves were protesting, claiming mainly the reduction of overcrowding and a more thorough implementation of protective measures.

However, the competent Ministry has refrained from introducing any relevant provisions, mainly based on the punitive agenda and the alleged cost of appearing 'soft on crime'. On the contrary, as mentioned above, during the second wave of the pandemic, the government introduced more severe measures for the execution of prison sentences (more restrictions on prison leave and transfers to semi-open farm prisons). Protests and calls for decongestion measures re-appeared again; in December 2020, a protest letter by female prisoners was sent to the competent authorities and political leadership[8] and in February 2021 an announcement was issued by a prisoners' solidarity organisation (the Initiative for Prisoners' Rights) asking the Ministry to provide accurate official information on the situation of COVID-19 infections in prisons and urging for the reduction of overcrowding and the vaccination of prisoners.[9]

Meanwhile, all courts (including penal courts) have temporarily suspended their operation both during the first and the second wave of the pandemic (from 13 March to 31 May 2020 and from 7 November 2020 to 1 February 2021) following governmental decisions. According to the relevant provisions, the only cases penal courts are handling during the suspension are misdemeanours caught red-handed and felonies in cases where the suspect is remanded in custody and the upper limit of pre-trial detention (18 months) is due to expire. Pre-trial detention continued to be imposed for serious crimes. This has led to a relatively low number of newly admitted prisoners during the pandemic. However, suspension of the operation of criminal courts also means that hearings for prisoners entitled to early release, appeal trials and decisions for the suspension of the execution of sentences until the appeal trial are postponed, so actual releases from prisons are reduced. As the lockdown continues, the number of prisoners of all categories will keep increasing and pressure on the prison system will build up.

From February 2021 onwards, judicial districts are separated according to the infection danger level, ranged from 'increased danger' (e.g. Attika district) to 'monitoring' (all areas that are not marked as 'increased danger' level). Judicial areas designated as 'increased danger' are following the restrictions mentioned above, while the rest of the districts mainly follow distancing measures.

3/4 Restrictions of contact with the outside world and inside prisons

Restrictive measures regarding the prison regime and the execution of prison sentences were enforced from an early stage (March 2020) in all prisons. They include (a) suspension of regular home leave, (b) prohibition of bringing food and clothing to the establishment by visitors, (c) prohibition of open (family and children) visits and gradual prohibition of closed visits (the latter take place by telephone in a cubicle with a separating screen: Koulouris and Aloskofis, 2013), (d) suspension of the operation of educational and leisure time activities and (e) suspension of drug treatment programmes.

Schools in prisons are probably the most important activity, having a considerable impact on prisoners. Schooling is provided by the Ministry of Education and educational personnel usually organise multiple activities and programmes in addition to the curriculum, offering valuable educational experiences to participants. Prison schools issue regular school diplomas with no reference that education was provided in prison.[10] Schools in prisons have not officially closed; their operation is following the policy for the general student population and is regulated by the Ministry of Education. Soon after the beginning of the pandemic, schools were included in the areas of activity that gradually ceased their physical operation (since February 2020) and continued only through distance learning at all educational levels. After a short interval at the beginning of the school year 2020–2021, when schools were re-opened, their operation switched to distance learning again, from 15 November 2020. Schools in prisons have followed the above policy and are open only for online courses. However, their operation is practically impaired, since computers are only available in the school premises for common use. Personal computers are not allowed in cells or dormitories according to prison regulations. School staff in some cases make considerable efforts to keep contact with their students, using photocopies and similar educational material, but delivering such material can also be a challenge.[11] Similarly, participation of prisoners in tertiary education was officially not interrupted; all university departments in the country operate by distance learning. Nevertheless, since inmates do not have access to computers with internet connection, class attendance and participation in the exams are practically impossible.

Equally important for prisoners' mental and physical well-being is communication with the outside world, and especially with their families and children. According to the Correctional Code and prison regulations, each prisoner has the right to receive at least one social visit per week. Remand prisoners can receive two social visits weekly (minimum). By law, each visit should last at least half an hour, but in practice, in overcrowded prisons, it is limited to 15–20 minutes. Visits from non-relatives are allowed with special permission granted by the Ministry of Citizens Protection. Open visits are allowed on a small scale, following permission, between husbands and wives with children. In recent years, special visiting spaces for children to meet with their parent were created in some prisons. A conjugal visit scheme was also developed on a pilot basis in one prison (MoJ, 2017; 2018). However, during the pandemic, all visits were gradually prohibited. This serious deprivation of face-to-face contact also has adverse effects on children who are not allowed to see their parent for very long periods of time. Children of incarcerated parents are victims of imprisonment, too, and should not be overlooked. Severe restrictions on visiting rights and communication with the outside world should be tested against the principle of proportionality because of the serious adverse consequences that they may have; flexibility of implementation according to the guidelines of European and global organisations should be a priority for any prison administration (CPT, 2020a; PC-CP, 2020; UNODC, 2020; WHO, 2020).

Prisoner transfers were reduced to a minimum: only transfers to judicial authorities were executed; transfers to semi-open farm prisons were suspended and transfers to external hospitals and doctors were and are only permitted in emergency cases.

Finally, there are no specific instructions by prison authorities to all prisons concerning lock-up times in cells and isolation, apart from the medical protocol that demands physical distancing, quarantine spaces and isolation procedures for suspected cases and infections. It is most probable that prison governors exercise their authority in different ways to keep the balance between implementing the guidelines and protecting the health of staff and prisoners (see also ENA, 2020).

5 Compensatory measures

As regards compensatory measures, the use of internet communication is worth mentioning. The operation of Skype communication between prisoners and their families was available on a pilot basis before the pandemic in a number of prisons (MoJ, 2017, 2018). Now the measure has been extended and is expected to become operative in all prisons. Distribution of phone cards and increased access to phones was also provided so that prisoners are less isolated from family and friends.

6 Legal basis for restrictions and relaxations of the prison regime

The execution of prison sentences in Greece is regulated in the Correctional Code and in the Regulations for the operation of prisons and young offender institutions. All rights, privileges and obligations are mentioned in detail, for example, visits and communication, regular and educational prison leave, transfer to other facilities, items prohibited and allowed in the cells, time spent out of cells, participation in education, and work and recreational activities. Each prison is supervised by a prosecutor allocated by the competent court, which is the court next to the prison premises. In big prisons, this is a full-time position for a specified period.

Restrictive measures for all fields of public life were introduced by legislative acts of the government, which drew on the general emergency health situation and the prevention of a health crisis.[12] No further legislative measures were issued for prisons to specify the restrictions to be imposed, their duration and the way of their implementation to balance the difficult situation for inmates in a closed institution. Such measures are specified in orders issued by the General Secretary for Crime Policy. The legality of these orders is disputed by the Federation of Prison Staff and some legal experts (Antoniou, 2020), especially because of the duration and the severity of the restrictions.

As regards the role of the Ombudsman in its double status as Ombudsman and as the National Preventive Mechanism against torture and ill-treatment, it seems that, from the beginning of the COVID-19 crisis, on-site visits and investigations were suspended. Alternative ways of communication (phone, surveys, etc.) compensate to a degree for the lack of physical presence and inspection in the prison establishments.

The overall measures have been justified as being in line with the restrictions of movement applicable to the general population and the need for even stricter quarantine rules for the populations in detention, as a preventive measure against possible outbreaks of the virus (European NPM Newsletter, 2020: 40). This issue has not been brought to court and there is no relevant case law. 25 prisoners from Kerkyra prison have addressed a report to the Prosecutor of the Supreme Court commenting on bad prison conditions and asking for the initiation of criminal charges against everyone responsible for the spread of COVID-19 in prison. However, there is no precedent for holding the prison administration responsible for endangering the right to health or life of prisoners due to bad prison conditions, through actions or omissions.

7 Returning to normal

The COVID-19 pandemic has caused a crisis in the prisons, which is forcing prison authorities and politicians to confront the systemic deficiencies of the prison system: overcrowding, shortage of prison staff, poor health services and absence of medical personnel are the most important problems and they are emerging as priorities during the pandemic. There are no easy solutions, but emergency actions are required in several fields so that prisons are not turned into COVID-19 hotspots.

According to the Report of the Council of Europe experts, the root of prison overcrowding is that 'Greece has the highest percentage of long and very long prison sentences in Europe, while its crime rates are lower or equal to the European median. A more moderate penal policy is possible without affecting the protection of society against crime' (Palma, et al., 2019: 4). The experts suggested that addressing prison overcrowding 'would require inter alia reforms of the penal legislation (Penal Code and Code of Criminal Procedure) and practices' (Palma et al., 2019: 3–4). Moreover, the report makes specific recommendations for alternative measures and the organisational and operational reform of the probation service to supervise their implementation (Palma et al., 2019: 31–37).

One of the most important recommendations of the experts committee has already been implemented: the entering into force of the new Penal Code and Code of Penal Procedure, with provisions aimed at reducing both the use and the length of imprisonment. The challenge now for any administration is to ensure that these new provisions become operational and are used in practice. To this end, the committee suggested that academics and the judiciary be involved in this reform, which includes interventions at all stages of the criminal justice system.

However, as mentioned above, there is no consensus on the idea that a moderate policy would not only improve prison conditions and preserve prisoners' dignity and health, but would also render the penal justice system more effective and hence make society safer. This reductionist perspective is still very far from being accepted, as the governing party adopts authoritarian, punitive practices and regards prisoners as undeserving of decent treatment. This approach, cultivating the fear of crime, also ignores the fact that fair and humane treatment in prison leads to better chances for reintegration and reduction of recidivism for the benefit of society.

Notes

1 Although there is no clear passage from the 'second' wave to the 'third', health authorities mark the start of the 'third wave' at the end of January 2021.
2 Twenty-seven years ago, CPT reported following its first periodic visit to Greek prisons that prison establishments 'were grossly overcrowded', 'seriously under resourced from the point of view of staff' and strongly pointed at the low level of health care services provided in prisons (CPT, 1994: 86).
3 For more on these two institutions and their operation in the prison system, see Anagnostaki, 2019; Cheliotis, 2006; Koulouris and Aloskofis, 2013.
4 Stock data, absolute numbers. Source: General Secretariat for Crime Policy, Ministry of Citizen Protection, published online, http://www.minocp.gov.gr/index.php?option=ozo_content&perform=view&id=7055&Itemid=696&lang=GR (last accessed 12 April 2021).
5 This estimate is included in a letter sent to the relevant Ministries in late March by the Greek Ombudsman, in his capacity as NPM, addressed with a list of guidelines and specific recommendations for each category of detention facility, including prisons, https://www.synigoros.gr/?i=kdet.el.news.643469 (accessed 10 December 2020) [in Greek].
6 See the response dated 2 March 2021 of the Deputy Minister with accompanying tables, https://www.hellenicparliament.gr/Koinovouleftikos-Elenchos/Mesa-Koinovouleutikou-Elegxou?pcm_id=12f01615-a41f-4bcb-b76e-accc00db1501&fbclid=IwAR04JBf33kXCqVSZjzO-tsRMd48_pQ3OvQoScEUehp1DidQh0z0JsHqjSPI.
7 For example, instead of extending the implementation of the measure of community sentences already in place (to match the demands of the new Penal Code which upgraded the measure considerably), community sentences were suspended altogether in September 2019 by the new political leadership and have not been brought back into operation.
8 Like the protest letter written and signed by 301 female prisoners at Eleona Women Prison on December 2020, which was sent to the Ministries of Citizen Protection, Health and Justice and the President of the Republic. Prisoners ask for the release of inmates who belong to vulnerable groups, of mothers with children in prison and of those who have only a short remaining time to serve.
9 On 6 February 2021, the Initiative launched a campaign for the collection of solidarity signatures by members of the public in favour of prisoners' rights. For all announcements and the campaign of the Initiative, see http://www.tokeli.gr/.
10 Today, there are ten Second Chance Schools operating in adult prison facilities, offering a two-year course leading to diploma of compulsory education. In juvenile and young adult prisons, regular elementary and high schools are operating (Koulouris and Aloskofis, 2013; Anagnostaki, 2019).
11 An innovative initiative was announced in January 2021 by the School Director at the Young Offender Institution of Avlona. A team of teachers created a TV channel, which will transmit educational material recorded by the school personnel 24 hours a day for students to watch in their cells. Although this is a

one-way communication, it is effective to maintain contact with students during the COVID-19 crisis, since all cells have TV sets.

12 According to the Constitution (art. 44 para. 1 Greek Constitution), the Cabinet may issue acts with legislative content, provided that these acts are ratified by law within 40 days of entering into force.

References

Anagnostaki, M. (2013): Alternative sanctions and measures in Greece under comparative prism. In: University of Athens, Laboratory of Penal and Criminological Research (Ed.): *Essays in Memory of Professor Christos Dedes*. Athens-Komotini: Ant. Sakkoulas [in Greek], 1–26.

Anagnostaki, M. (2019): Resettlement theory and practice in Greece: Advancement and stasis. In: Pruin, I., Dünkel, F., Storgaard A., and Weber, J. (Eds.): *Prisoner Resettlement in Europe*. London: Routledge, 167–184.

Antoniou, C. (2020): Vassilis Dimakis: The story of an outlaw against legality? *Newspaper Avgi*, 1 June 2020, https://www.avgi.gr/entheta/enthemata/355962_basilis-dimakis-i-istoria-enos-paranomoy-apenanti-sti-nomimotita (accessed 10 December 2020) [in Greek].

Cheliotis, L. (2006): Demystifying risk management: A process evaluation of the prisoners' home leave scheme in Greece. *Criminology and Criminal Justice* 6 (2), 163–195.

Cheliotis, L. (2012): Suffering at the hands of the state: Conditions of imprisonment and prisoner health in contemporary Greece. *European Journal of Criminology* 9 (1), 3–22.

Cheliotis, L., and Xenakis, S. (2021): Political orientation, economic conditions, and incarceration in Greece under Syriza-led government. *European Journal of Criminology* (in print).

CPT, Committee for the Prevention of Torture and Inhuman or Degrading Treatment of Punishment (1994): *Report to the Greek government on the visit to Greece from 14 to 26 March 1993*, https://www.coe.int/en/web/cpt/greece (accessed 10 December 2020).

CPT, Committee for the Prevention of Torture and Inhuman or Degrading Treatment or Punishment (2020a): *Statement of principles relating to the treatment of persons deprived of their liberty in the context of the coronavirus disease (COVID-19) pandemic*, 20 March 2020, https://rm.coe.int/16809cfa4b, (accessed 10 December 2020).

CPT, Committee for the Prevention of Torture and Inhuman or Degrading Treatment or Punishment (2020b): *Report to the Greek Government on the visit to Greece from 28 March to 9 April 2019*, https://www.coe.int/en/web/cpt/greece (accessed 10 December 2020).

ENA, Institute for Alternative Policies (2020): *Public health, prohibition of assemblies and the limit of democracy*, https://www.enainstitute.org/publication/ (accessed 10 December 2020) [in Greek].

European NPM Newsletter, New series issue no. 6, March – April 2020: *Greek NPM*, https://www.avokatipopullit.gov.al/media/manager/website/media/European%20NPM%20Newsletter_new%20series%20issue%20no.%206.pdf (accessed 10 December 2020).

Koulouris, N. (2020): Prison overcrowding: The unequal distribution of a tidal phenomenon, *The Art of Crime*, 8, (accessed 10 December 2020) [in Greek].

Koulouris, N., and Aloskofis, W. (2013): Prison conditions in Greece. European Observatory. Detention conditions in the European Union, http://www.prisonobservatory.org/upload/PrisonconditionsGreece.pdf (accessed 10 December 2020).

Koulouris, N., Pantelidou, T., and Spyrea, S. (2018): Quality employment and quality public services. Quality of employment in prisons. Country report: Greece. Belgium: European Public Service Union, Katholieke Universiteit Leuven, Hiva Research Institute for work and society, https://www.epsu.org/sites/default/files/article/files/Country%20report%20Greece%20prisons.pdf (accessed 10 December 2020).

Ministry of Justice, Transparency and Human Rights (MoJ), General Secretariat for Crime Policy (2017): *Penal policy: Present and future.* Athens: National Printing House, http://www.justice.gr/site/LinkClick.aspx?fileticket=7GKtmRR-HUw%3D&tabid=577, (accessed 10 December 2020) [in Greek].

Ministry of Justice, Transparency and Human Rights (MoJ), General Secretariat for Crime Policy (2018): *Strategic plan for the correctional system 2018–2020,* Athens: National Printing House, http://www.justice.gr/ (accessed 10 December 2020) [in Greek].

National Public Health Organisation (2020): Coronavirus SARS-CoV-2 (COVID-19) disease. Guidelines for detention establishments, 7 May 2020, https://eody.gov.gr/wp-content/uploads/2020/05/covid-19-katastimata-kratisis.pdf (accessed 10 December 2020) [in Greek].

Palma, M., Snacken, S., Theis, V., and Carbunaru, L. (2019): Reducing prison overcrowding in Greece. Report of the Directorate General of Human Rights and Rule of Law, Action against Crime Department, Criminal Law Co-operation Unit, Council of Europe, https://theartofcrime.gr/wp-content/uploads/2019/05/REDUCING-PRISON-OVERCROWDING-IN-GREECE.pdf (accessed 10 December 2020).

PC-CP WG, Council for Penological Co-operation Working Group (2020): *Follow-up COVID-19 related statement by the council for Penological co-operation working group*, 14 October 2020 revised, https://rm.coe.int/pc-cp-2020-10-e-rev-follow-up-to-pc-cp-wg-statement-covid-19/16809ff484 (accessed 10 December 2020).

Pischoina, A. (2020): The transmission of coronavirus in prisons and measures to address it, *The Art of Crime*, 8, available at ht (accessed 10 December) 2020) [in Greek].

Tzannetaki, T. (2006): Pathology of the present system of sanctions of the Penal Code. Thoughts and suggestions on a thorough reform in the context of the bill of the new Penal Code. *Poinika Chronika* (7), 590–603[in Greek].

Tzannetaki, T. (2016): The strategy of indirect decrease of sentences: The exhaustion of its limits and the need for paradigm change, *The Art of Crime* 1, https://theartofcrime.gr/november-2016/ (accessed 10 December 2020) [in Greek].

UNODC, United Nations Office on Drugs and Crime (2020): *Position Paper COVID-19 preparedness and responses in prisons*, 31 March 2020, https://www.unodc.org/documents/hiv-aids/publications/UNODC_position_paper_COVID-19_in_prisons_-_FINAL.pdf (accessed 10 December 2020).

WHO, World Health Organisation (2020): *Preparedness, prevention and control of COVID-19 in prisons and other places of detention,* 15 March 2020, Copenhagen: WHO Regional Office Europe.

20 Hungary

Zsuzsanna Juhász

1 Introduction: the general situation of the Hungarian prison system

In Hungary, the Prison Service as a law enforcement agency carries out custodial penalties and measures, pre-trial detention and executes confinements as an administrative sanction (detention for misdemeanours). The Hungarian Prison Service is subordinated to the Ministry of Interior. The Prison Service supervises and operates 30 prison establishments and 12 limited companies aiming the compulsory employment of inmates. Currently, these companies are operated by the Prison Service and carry out mainly agricultural and light-industrial activities. Besides the prison establishments, the Prison Service also involves institutions that are responsible for the training and recreation of the prison staff and the health care of the inmates as well.

An important feature of the Hungarian prison system is that the penitentiary institutions are not only part of national and regional law enforcement mechanisms, but also part of county law enforcement mechanisms. While the main task of the national and regional law enforcement institutions is to execute prison sentences, county institutions primarily carry out pre-trial detention. Currently, tasks relating to incarceration are performed by 15 national or regional law enforcement institutions and 15 county law enforcement institutions. Within the prison system, there are special institutions for females and juveniles.

In Hungary, there are three subtypes of national penitentiary institutions, which are differentiated based on their enforcement severity: maximum security prisons with a strict regime (*fegyház*), medium security prisons with a medium regime (*börtön*) and minimum security prisons with a so-called light regime (*fogház*).[1] Placing detainees in open penitentiary institutions (i.e. in minimum security prisons) is rarely possible in Hungary. There are too many offenders, who committed serious criminal offences and thus have to serve long sentences. The ratio of detainees who serve their sentences in high security prisons is relatively high, and those serving their sentences in medium security prisons can be placed only in closed penitentiary institutions,

DOI: 10.4324/9781003169178-20

that is, in high or medium security prisons. According to the latest data (December 2019) provided by the Prison Service (Hungarian Prison Service 2019: 7), the majority of the prisoners were held in medium security prisons (55%), 39% of the prisoners belonged to the strictest category (high security prison) and the number of those who were under the medium security regime represented the smallest proportion (5.8%).

When reviewing the evaluation of the prison population, it is remarkable that the number of prisoners decreased before the pandemic to 16,334 on 31 December 2019 (Hungarian Prison Service 2019: 4). As of 15 April 2020, 16,551, and as of 31 December 16,752 individuals were held in various institutions of the Hungarian prison system, which means that there was no pandemic-induced further reduction of the prison population (see also Section 2).[2]

The prison population rate per 100,000 of population has decreased in the last years: it was 180 in 2016, and 173 in 2018. It has to be noted that despite the decrease in the prison population rate, we still have a particularly high incarceration rate: in terms of this indicator, Hungary may be classified among the countries with exceptionally high rates, since the number of detainees per 100,000 was over 160 in April 2020, and 171 at the end of December 2020.[3] It is no surprise that the high prison population rate is reflected in overcrowding in the majority of the countries, which is the case in Hungary as well. Because of the prison overcrowding, the majority of prisoners are held in communal cells with the occupancy of 2–10 prisoners, and single cells are relatively rare. They actually exist only for disciplinary, security and solitary confinement purposes.

Another important factor is that due to the capacity expansion project, the number of places to accommodate detainees has increased in the last years. While in 2014, the Hungarian prison system was capable of accommodating only 12,869 detainees in total, according to data for December 2019, the official capacity has increased to 14,829. As a consequence of the decreasing number of prisoners and the increasing capacity of prisons, the occupancy rate decreased in Hungary: the average occupancy rate was 143% in 2014, 113% in 2018 (Hungarian Prison Service 2019: 9), 112% in 2019 and 96% on 31 December 2020.[4] On the one hand, it is important to highlight that the latter indicators show the average occupancy of Hungarian institutions, while there were institutions where overcrowding exceeded 112%. The average occupancy rate in the last years was always above 100% in Hungary. Consequently, prison overcrowding is a long-term, acute problem in Hungary. The current state of Hungarian prisons could be best characterised by the huge number of the prison population and persistent problems with overcrowding.

Given the abovementioned negative indicators, it is not surprising that the European Court of Human Rights (ECtHR) ordered Hungary in its decision published on 10 March 2015 (Varga and others vs. Hungary)[5] to eliminate the structural problems in its law enforcement system. The case law of the

ECtHR finds that detainees in Hungary are often placed in overcrowded penitentiary institutions, which does not comply with the requirement of dignified, healthy detention conditions. At that time, there were approximately 450 requests before the ECtHR that were filed from Hungary and objected to the conditions of detention. Therefore, the Strasbourg Court concluded that due to overcrowding, violations of rights occur in the country on a systemic level.

The Court reiterated that the inadequate conditions of detention originated in a widespread problem within the Hungarian prison system, justifying a pilot judgement procedure because of the recurrent and persistent nature of the problem identified. According to the judgement, the solution would be the reduction of the number of prisoners by more frequent use of non-custodial measures and minimising the use of pre-trial detention. The Court pointed to the recommendations of the Committee of Ministers to encourage prosecutors and judges to use alternatives to detention and redirect their criminal policy towards the reduced use of detention.

It is important to point out that the principal objective of the Hungarian government is the construction of new penitentiary institutions, and the reactivation of institutions that had been closed earlier, thus increasing the number of places. The programme for increasing the number of places started in 2010. New prison quarters were opened in the Budapest maximum and medium security prison, similarly in Martonvásár, Állampuszta, Pálhalma, Sopronkőhida, Szeged, Tököl, Baracska, Veszprém, Tiszalök, Miskolc, and in 2019 the construction process continued with a new building in Kiskunhalas. As a result, the official capacity of the prison system has increased by 2,750 new places and, as noted earlier, the occupancy level dropped to 112% by 2020.

As to the inmate structure of the prison population, it should be emphasised that, despite the general decrease in the number of prisoners, in view of the sentences imposed a sharp increase of long prison sentences (both of five to ten years, and more than ten years) can be observed. While in 2010 631 prisoners (i.e. 3.9% of the total prison population) were serving prison sentences of more than ten years, in 2019, this number climbed to 1,768 (i.e. 13.2% of the total prison population)! The number and percentages of the sentences up to ten years showed a similar trend. The number of persons serving life imprisonment has increased significantly. The number of persons sentenced to life imprisonment at the end of 2020 was 62 (i.e. 0.4% of the total prison population) sentenced to whole life imprisonment as the most severe legal consequence of the Hungarian Criminal Code.[6] The term "whole life imprisonment" means that the Court does not see any possibility of parole, or the exclusion of parole is stipulated by law. Such imprisonment may actually last until the end of the offender's life. Long-term prisoners, particularly life and whole life prisoners, are a constant challenge in terms of placement, security and reintegrative activities. Their detention carries a high risk, and their placement requires great care.

In addition to long-term imprisonment, the proportion of senior detainees (the age group over 60 years) in the entire prison population has been continuously increasing during the last years. The ageing of the prison population is one of the possible effects of the increased application of life imprisonment without parole, life imprisonment and other long sentences. In addition to the general ageing of society, these elements of a punitive criminal policy can significantly influence the number of detainees who spend their later lives in prison. Although currently the number of detainees over 60 years of age is still insignificant compared to the entire prison population (4.0% of all inmates in 2018, Hungarian Prison Service 2019: 5), senior detainees are already challenging the prison system with special tasks. In this regard, health issues enjoy priority, but institutions are often poorly suited for intensive care of older prisoners. Prisons try to place older prisoners in cells with fewer inmates if possible, specifically on lower bunks. In addition, they pay attention to placing detainees of similar age together.

To summarise the present situation, overcrowding and inadequate prison conditions remain a problem in Hungary. Combatting overcrowding in prisons demands a comprehensive strategy. The first step should be an analysis of the reasons for overcrowding. Because in Hungary the key factor contributing to prison overcrowding is the punitive criminal law and penal climate, we have, inter alia, to review and revise our criminal justice legislation and practice. In my opinion, until the capacity building projects are accompanied by a comprehensive legal reform, the extensive prison construction will simply increase the prison population further, and not solve the systematic problem of overcrowding.

In the context of COVID-19 in the wider community in Hungary as of 16 March 2021, there have 529,122 confirmed cases of COVID-19, including 17,226 deaths, reported to the WHO.[7] The mortality rate among people diagnosed with COVID-19 in Hungary amounts to 1,807 cases per 1 million of the country's population.[8] Penitentiary employees and prisoners can be classified as a vulnerable group for whom the risk of contracting COVID-19 is high. According to the information provided by the prison authorities, in prison settings until October 2020, there have been 125 reported cases of COVID-19 among prisoners and 145 among staff members.[9] The Hungarian Prison Service has reported no cases of death from COVID-19 among prisoners and its employees.

In order to prevent the spread of the Coronavirus in prisons during the COVID-19 pandemic, a number of special preventive and restrictive measures have been taken. Thus, on admission, inmates must undergo a medical check-up, which includes a public health examination, as well as an epidemiological enquiry. Without these, new inmates cannot be placed in the community inside prison, i.e. they are totally isolated during this admission period. These examinations involve body temperature checking and also answering a background questionnaire, which contains questions about previous trips and experiences that might be related to COVID-19 infection.

In case of suspicion of infection, the new inmate will be isolated immediately until the laboratory test confirms or excludes the infection. Those who test positive will be taken to the hospital for isolation. After admission, new inmates are placed in isolation for 14 days, irrespective of the regime in which they will serve their sentence. The admission procedure can be continued only if their epidemiological isolation is definitely not necessary. Otherwise, the prison needs to arrange for the inmate to be transported to the nearest epidemiological institution. Testing of the incarcerated population and penitentiary employees was not occurring at the time of our data collection.

As part of the epidemiological protocol, all prisons designated certain areas that were constantly sanitised. Personal protective equipment and digital thermometers were distributed for the medical staff. Handwashing and sanitising possibilities are provided for the inmates several times a day, while the inmates are constantly reminded to follow the hygiene rules. The Hungarian Prison Service produced educational videos containing useful and important information regarding the prevention of the pandemic. These short videos are screened for the inmates several times a day through a closed-circuit television system in all prisons throughout the country. For personal protection, washable masks were distributed for the inmates. Sometime after, a mask regime has been introduced in penitentiary institutions: prisoners, employees and visitors are required to comply with it.

The prison system employed inmates to control the pandemic. On the one hand, they started the production of medical protective masks and equipment and, on the other hand, started to make quarantine leaflets to be displayed on staircases and doors and transit leaflets and signs to inform transit throughout the country. In addition, in April 2020, a mobile epidemiological container hospital with a capacity of 150 people was provided by the Prison Service. This hospital is located within the territory of the National Law Enforcement Institute of Kiskunhalas, but is separated from the prison.

2 Prison and penal policy concerning the execution of prison sentences during the COVID-19-induced crisis

Hungary is one of the countries that has not taken steps to release prisoners earlier in connection with the pandemic. Accordingly, inmates at particular risk of the infection, such as the elderly or those with chronic illnesses or other health problems, have not been released. However, it should be noted that the regulations for postponing the prison sentence and confinement for the period of the emergency, until 31 December 2020, have changed. Thus, the postponement of the execution of prison sentences can now be granted not only on the basis of the convicted person's personal and family circumstances, but also for other reasons related to epidemiological measures or health crises. Up to six months instead of the initial period of three months can be postponed. The duration of a postponement has also changed. It is now possible to grant a postponement of the execution of prison sentences for up to two years.

In addition, in view of the pandemic, Act C of 2012 of the Criminal Code and Act II of 2012 on infringements and infringement procedures (in the following: the Infringement Act) were amended. In the Criminal Code, the range of crimes against public safety was expanded with a new offence, namely the obstruction of epidemic prevention (322/A. §) and the crime of fearmongering was also amended by introducing a qualified case, when it is committed during the period of a special legal order. With regard to the Infringement Act, new infringements have also been introduced, which are mainly related to the violation of the rules on curfew hours, quarantine, the obligation of wearing masks and the limited opening hours of the shops. At the same time, these infringements made it possible to impose higher infringement fines (HUF 5,000–500,000).

In addition to the provisions pointing in the direction of tightening, it is worth mentioning the reclassification of the epidemic violation (361. § of the Criminal Code) as an infringement. However, that conduct constitutes an infringement only if it is committed in connection with the highlighted epidemiological measures ordered with regard to the COVID-19 infection. Thus, the infringement differs from the crime of epidemic violation only in the nature of the infectious disease. Therefore, if one of the four epidemiological measures named in the Criminal Code has been ordered against someone due to an illness other than a COVID-19 infection, their violation is a criminal offence. The explanation of the reclassification as an infringement is presumably to be found in the more rapid enforcement of the infringement procedure. It is also significant that, while the criminal offence shall be punished by confinement based on the Criminal Code, the infringement is punishable with an administrative fine up to 500,000 HUF (about 1,350 Euro) based on the Infringement Act. The amount of this fine is generally higher than the amount that usually governs infringements, so it is a so-called priority infringement, which means that the seriousness of this conduct exceeds the level of seriousness normally found for infringements.

3 Restrictions of contact with the outside world

At the beginning of the outbreak of the pandemic, it was still possible to receive visitors in prisons, but the Hungarian Prison Service had already asked the inmates and their relatives to postpone face-to-face meetings. Prisons informed the inmates through the reintegration officers about the purpose of this measure in small group sessions and, at the same time, they encouraged the contact maintenance via Skype and telephone. As a preventive measure in connection with the reception of visitors, the duration and the number of the visitors were reduced, and physical contact was prohibited during visits. The latter meant that the inmates and their visitors could meet in a reception room equipped with a plexiglass screen. Under the preventive measures, inmates were able to receive visitors once a month from 30 to 60 minutes maximum, and the number of the visitors was also limited to the maximum of two, instead of the original four. Accordingly, family visits have been temporarily suspended and the Prison Service has also advised the inmates not to invite children, those above 60 and relatives who are chronically or currently ill to visit them. In order to maintain personal contact, prisons provided the possibility of extended contact by telephone and Skype. A Skype user guide was prepared for the relatives of the inmates in order to help with using Skype. However, when the pandemic intensified, a temporary Act entered into force in spring 2020, which until 31 December 2020, with respect to the emergency situation, referred the restriction of the inmates' contact to the Prison Director. Following the Prison Director's decision, a ban on visitors to all prisons was in force from 8 March 2020. The ban is still in force (December 2020) as the Hungarian Prison Service Headquarters regard the opening of prisons to relatives would be too risky considering the new wave of the pandemic.

In March 2020, the granting of temporary leave to inmates was also suspended by the Prison Service, including leave that had been granted but had not yet been taken. The goal of this measure was to prevent the possible entry of the virus caused by persons returning from temporary leave. Temporary leave could not take place at the time, nor can it take place at present even in cases of death or serious illnesses of relatives outside the prison. The Prison Service has emphasised that applications that had already be granted will be executed later, if they continue to be justified.

The range of persons entering the prisons was also restricted. Members of churches and civilians who offer pastoral care and services for inmates, as well as the teachers responsible for education were temporarily suspended from their work in prisons. However, in view of the right to defence, the visits of lawyers and legal representatives were not restricted. However, they had to maintain strict hygienic measures (masks, plexiglass screens) in order to prevent infection. The inmates, their relatives and contacts were informed about these preventive measures in line with the epidemiological situation.

4 Restrictions inside prisons

Depending on the epidemiological measures or other reasons related to the health crisis, the Head of the Prison Service had been legally authorised to restrict the forms of contact until 31 December 2020. This included the contacts associated with granting rewards and exceptional leave from prison, employment and education outside prisons. It also made it possible to suspend the employment and aftercare of inmates. Among the inmate's rights, the restriction could also be applied to the right to be in the open air, to participate in cultural and sport activities in prisons, in rehabilitative and/or reintegrative activities, and to express an opinion in inmates' forums.

On this basis, the system of employment of prisoners has been revised with regard to the necessity of work being carried out: in some employment facilities, the processes must be kept going continuously, but in several areas work can be reduced or possibly suspended. The mental care, education and vocational training of prisoners are carried out within the prisons but without the presence of external civilians. Practical training is suspended; education is conducted with the use of written materials, DVD recordings and sound recordings. Programmes involving larger groups of prisoners, such as access to open-air spaces, and employment, are carried out in smaller groups.

National transportation of prisoners is carried out only on the basis of a specific provision, with a smaller number of prisoners and transport vehicles. Instead of transporting prisoners, the public authorities have adapted to remote hearings.

The Prison Service has established epidemiological call centres for all prisons in order to further the rapid dissemination of reliable information. The main objective of these information centres is to provide dial-up information to inmates' relatives about the restrictive preventive measures arising from the epidemiological situation.

5 Compensatory measures

The Prison Service endeavours to provide personal contacts via telecommunications: detainees are allowed to Skype with their relatives; 15 minutes per week are allowed. Moreover, the duration of telephone calls can be increased by 15 minutes per week, but detainees have to pay for the extra time (75 Ft/minute). Prisoners who do not have an in-prison mobile phone may request alternative access to telephones. The Hungarian Prison Service assesses such requests and, if granted, pays the costs of phone calls for a period of 3 × 5 minutes per month.

As an additional compensatory measure, contact persons are authorised to order one extra package per month from the prisons' webshop page for inmates. On individual request of the detainee, the use of the gym is provided free of charge.

With regard to these compensatory measures, it could be a problem in practice that the access to smart devices and internet is not provided for all relatives. Another problem is that more frequent telephone calls are provided in theory, but in practice the high costs must be borne by the inmates.

6 Legal basis for restrictions and relaxations of the prison regime

The provisions related to the epidemiological measures discussed were established by a governmental decree relating to the emergency situation (the so-called emergency decree). Its regulations were also upheld by a Transitional

Act. The latter emphasised that the prosecutor's office supervising the legality of the restrictions must be notified immediately in all cases, which relate to restrictions of the inmates' rights in connection with the pandemic.

In Hungary, as of 1 January 2015, the Commissioner for Fundamental Rights acts as a national preventive mechanism, who regularly examines the treatment of persons deprived of liberty, even in the absence of a complaint and an actual fundamental right's violation. Since the newly introduced epidemiological measures affected, inter alia, the inmates' right to respect their private and family life, the Commissioner for Fundamental Rights carried out a comprehensive ex officio investigation in six prisons. The purpose of the Commissioner's visits was to verify the measures taken to prevent and to avert the consequences of the pandemic and to examine how the daily lives of the inmates were affected by the restrictions imposed. This examination revealed, inter alia, that the lack of face-to-face classes limited the inmates' right to education. However, this measure was proportionate to the aim pursued, mainly because of the possibility of digital learning and written tasks and assignments. According to the investigation, the ban on visits also restricted the exercise of the inmates' right to private and family life, but it was counteracted by the extended duration of telephone calls and the possible use of internet communication channels; thus, according to the Commissioner's statement, there was no breach of fundamental rights.

7 Returning to normal

The penitentiary experiences during the COVID-19 pandemic have so far been very mixed. It is welcome, on the one hand, that despite the prison overcrowding, the number of infections is relatively low, but, on the other hand, it cannot be ignored, that in the absence of symptoms, neither the prison staff nor the inmates are tested. In the longer term, the travel ban could also be of concern. It inevitably raises the question of how the prison administration can fulfil its obligations arising from Article 8 of the European Convention on Human Rights, namely, to allow and support the contact of inmates with their close relatives. It is gratifying that, in order to avoid the disproportionate restriction of rights, the Hungarian Prison Service has extended the duration of telephone calls and provided contact on Skype. However, it needs to be emphasised that the costs of more frequent telephone calls have to be borne by the inmates, and not all relatives can use Skype as they do not have internet access. Nevertheless, we believe that the positive benefit of the pandemic is the extension of contacts via Skype, with the qualification that, in our opinion, maintaining this form of contact in the future should be used as a supplementary option to traditional visits, not as an alternative to it. The pandemic also proved that, despite the acknowledgement of the possible negatives, the Court hearings of prisoners by the judicial and law enforcement authorities can be conducted via online channels without prisoners leaving the prisons.

Notes

1 The types among others differ by the degree of the severity of prison regime and control (supervision); segregation from the outside world; movement within the premises of the prison; life regime, amount of money allotted for personal needs; rewards and disciplinary sanctions, participation in the prison activities, reintegration programmes. The strictest rules are applied in maximum security prisons and the most lenient rules in minimum security prisons. For example, in maximum security prisons, the prisoners may move within the prison only under supervision of prison officers, in medium security prisons, they may move freely in determined areas of the prison and in minimum security facilities, inmates may move freely within the whole prison.
2 See http://www.prisonstudies.org/country/hungary (accessed 1 December 2020 and 28 May 2021).
3 See http://www.prisonstudies.org/country/hungary (accessed 1 December 2020 and 28 May 2021).
4 See http://www.prisonstudies.org/country/hungary (accessed 1 December 2020 and 28 May 2021).
5 Application nos. 14097/12, 45135/12, 73712/12, 34001/13, 44055/13, and 64586/13, judgement of 10 March 2015
6 According to the information provided by the Hungarian Prison Service.
7 World Health Organization (2021): WHO coronavirus disease (COVID-19) dashboard. http://covid19.who.int
8 Worldometer (2021): Reported cases and deaths by Country, territory, or conveyance. http://www.worldometers.info/coronavirus/#countries.
9 No further data are available.

Reference

Hungarian Prison Service (2019): *Review of Hungarian Prison Statistics*. Budapest.

21 India

Madhurima Dhanuka

1 Introduction – general situation of the prison system

As the world witnessed the unfolding of the unprecedented COVID-19 crisis in 2020, a silver lining emerged, with the COVID-19 pandemic also bringing the spotlight on places of detention. Issues that had long plagued prison systems worldwide – overcrowding, inadequate healthcare, resource insufficiency, staff vacancies – suddenly gained the attention of governments, media, academics and researchers. In March 2020, as nations scrambled to reduce prison populations, amid calls from international organisations, local groups, experts and human rights defenders[1] – to suspend arrests, reduce the use of pre-trial detention and decongest prisons – the Supreme Court of India took immediate cognisance, passing a slew of directions[2] to ensure that Indian prisons responded effectively to the crisis. Subsequently, in May 2021, as India witnessed another, much deadlier, wave of infections, the Supreme Court once again reaffirmed its previous directives, and sought the initiation of measures to decongest prisons and protect those who remained inside.

In India, prisons continue to be governed by state laws,[3] framed under a colonial era law – the Prisons Act 1894. Since Independence, very few states have adopted a new prisons act. The existing system has often been criticised as lacking a rights-based approach vis-à-vis prisoners (CHRI Rights Behind Bars, 2020). In 2017, the Supreme Court had aptly remarked that "what is practised in our prisons is the theory of retribution and deterrence and the ground situation emphasises this while our criminal justice system believes in reformation and rehabilitation".[4] While the principles of rehabilitation and reformation have long been recognised as cornerstones for the penal system,[5] "the shift toward a safe, sanitary, rehabilitative environment remains distant" in the Indian context (Tata Trusts, India Justice Report, 2019: 42).

1.1 Prison statistics and trends

In terms of prison population, India with a prisoner population of nearly 0.5 million ranks 5th highest in the world, and forms 4.2% of the world's

DOI: 10.4324/9781003169178-21

total population even though the incarceration rate of 35 prisoners per 100,000 prisoners is low as compared to other countries (World Prison Brief). Interestingly, "India's prison population, from 2000 to 2018 has increased by a staggering 71% against an estimated increase of 28.5% in the country's general population" (Lamba and Dhanuka, 2020). These figures are much higher than the almost 20% increase in the world's prison population since 2000 (Penal Reform International, 2018). Moreover, the average occupancy rate of 118.5% in its 1,350 prisons is an "underestimation of the chronic overcrowding in Indian prisons" (CHRI Newsletter, 2019) with more than a quarter of states and union territories having occupancy rates higher than 150%.

At the end of 2019, 69% of prisoners were unsentenced, and 13.2% prisoners were aged 50 years and above (National Crime Records Bureau, 2019). Further, women prisoners comprised 4.2% of the total prison population, among whom 1,543 women prisoners were held in prison with their 1,779 children.[6] On average, the expenses per prisoner per day in 2019 were Rs 118 (approx. 1.36 Euro), which includes expenditure on food, clothing, medical, recreational activities, etc. These figures and an analysis of trends and patterns provide some insight into the challenges faced by Indian prisons in responding to the pandemic.

Data published in the Prison Statistics India revealed for 2019 a 243:1 prisoner per medical staff ratio; and a prison staff vacancy rate of over 30%. These figures highlighted "several major areas of deep concern about the poor state of Indian prisons and their inability to mitigate the threat of the pandemic" (CHRI Newsletter, 2019).

As feared, between April and December 2020, more than 18,000 prisoners and prison staff were reported[7] to have tested positive for the coronavirus in India. By April 2021, these numbers were again on the rise, with nearly 4,000 infections reported in prisons. In the absence of any official data, these figures are likely to have been far higher and warrant an enquiry into the various measures undertaken by governments and prison authorities to respond to the crisis. Were prison populations reduced? Were admissions suspended? Was there adequate testing? How were prisoners treated? What precautions were followed?

This chapter answers these questions by providing pertinent information on arrests and detention amid the pandemic, vital data on Indian prisons and the response by prisons to mitigate the spread of the coronavirus. This includes a discussion on restrictions placed on prisoners as a response to the pandemic. The chapter also explores the existing mechanisms that are mandated to hold prisons accountable, and their emerging role in mitigating the immediate and long-term impacts of COVID-19. The chapter ends with suggestions on areas of engagement that must be prioritised by policy makers and prison functionaries as we hope to return to normal or rather the "old" normal.

2 Prison and penal policy concerning the execution of prison sentences during the COVID-19-induced crisis

With only four hours' notice, the Government of India imposed a nationwide lockdown to combat the coronavirus on 24 March 2020. Only essential services, including food, medical supplies and municipal cleaning, were permitted to continue operations, while inter-state and district borders were sealed. All persons, barring those engaged in essential services, were to remain indoors and observe physical distancing. States employed measures to test, quarantine and contact trace to detect and prevent further transmission of the virus. To enforce lockdown measures, regulations were issued under the Epidemic Diseases Act 1897 and any breach of orders was criminally punishable. Powers were also invoked under the Disaster Management Act 2005 or under Section 144 of the Code of Criminal Procedure 1973.

The early days of the pandemic witnessed a surge in arrests accompanied by "large-scale suffering, compounded by an insensitive and often brutal response by state authorities" (CHRI Guidelines, 2020). It has also been alleged that the pandemic was used to detain government critics and stifle activists with court closures, struggles in filing for bail and lack of visits in prisons having effectively blocked pathways to justice (Yasir and Schultz, 2020). Additionally, the spreading of fake information related to the pandemic was criminalised, with a large number of arrests nationwide for such violations (Dore, 2020).

While internationally calls were made to suspend arrest and pre-trial detention of persons accused of low-level offences, and for increased use of non-custodial measures (Jayaraman, 2020), in India no such calls were made, or decisions taken. The only directive issued was by the Supreme Court to ensure compliance with arrest safeguards and procedures to curb unnecessary arrests.[8]

Astonishingly, the nationwide figures for arrest (National Crimes Records Bureau, 2020) indicate a rise of nearly 0.9 million arrests in 2020. Possibly a large number of these arrests could have been linked to violations of lockdown measures. For instance, a study (CPAP, 2020: 1) conducted in one state, Madhya Pradesh,[9] found that 68.9% first information reports in urban areas were related to the lockdown, against 32.6% in semi-urban and rural areas. It also found that most reports were filed against people on the streets – pedestrians and persons on two wheelers, whereas shopkeepers and street vendors accounted for every fifth person, against whom a report was filed. It further affirmed that on account of these arrests, efforts to reduce prison populations were rendered futile in the state, with prisons admitting about as many people as it released (CPAP, 2020: 65). Another study analysed the admission data on prisons for six states between 1 April and 30 June 2020, revealing that admissions (38,475) were much lower than in an average quarter in 2019 (72,699). It speculated as to the nature of offences for which the detentions would have been made amid the lockdown restrictions (CHRI Responding to the Pandemic, 2020: 38).

With the onset of the pandemic, the world's attention was drawn to the heightened vulnerability of persons in custody, and governments were urged to find ways to release prisoners, especially those vulnerable to COVID-19, and to take all appropriate public health measures in prisons.[10] A study released in December 2020 on Indian prisons suggests that the impending crisis "made the system spring into action at all levels, from a prison in the remotest area of the country to the highest court of law" (CHRI Responding to the Pandemic, 2020: 23). The next section seeks to understand the contours of this response.

2.1 Initiation of precautionary measures

The inability of India's overcrowded prisons to implement physical distancing was first acknowledged by the Supreme Court of India in March 2020. The court on its own motion issued notices to all states and union territories, in response to which states informed the court of various measures initiated to respond to the pandemic. "Creation of isolation wards, quarantine of new prisoners, including prisoners of foreign nationality, for a specific period, preliminary examination of prisoners for COVID-19, ensuring availability of medical assistance, entry points scanning of staff and other service providers, sanitisation and cleanliness exercises of prison campus and wards, supply of masks, barring or limiting of personal visits of prisoners, suspension of cultural and other group activities, awareness and training with regard to stoppage of transmission of COVID-19 and court hearings through video conferencing"[11] – were listed by the court as some of these measures.

In addition to the directives of the Supreme Court, the Ministry of Home Affairs (MHA), in the Government of India issued an advisory in May titled "Management of COVID-19 in Indian Prisons – Guidelines and Protocols which may be followed while dealing with persons arrested, detained and those in Prisons and Correctional Homes". This advisory was circulated to chief secretaries, the director and inspector general of police and prisons of all states and union territories. It included guidelines on disinfection of common public places; guidelines on rational use of Personal Protective Equipment; Standard Operating Procedures (SOP) for Handling Arrested Persons, Detainees and Inmates during the Pandemic; and Guidelines for use and disposal of protective gear. The SOP included guidance on hand hygiene and respiratory etiquette, social distancing, segregation, security of inmates, health monitoring, minimum movement, tracking and tracing of contacts and remote meetings.

The second wave of infections once again prompted the Supreme Court to issue directions to limit arrests and release prisoners, whereby it reaffirmed that "from limiting arrests to taking care of COVID-19 patients, there is a requirement for effective management of pandemic from within the prison walls so as to defeat this deadly virus".[12] The MHA also issued an advisory – "Prevention and Control of Covid-19 in Prisons and Correctional Homes" in continuation of its previous advisory. Reiterating the preventive and precautionary measures, it inter alia stressed on "test-track-treat protocol, which includes aggressive testing for early detection of Covid-19 positive cases, timely isolation and treatment". The year 2021 also saw the initiation of vaccination drives for prisoners, though the extent has varied across states.[13]

2.2 Measures to reduce the prison population

In its directives of 2020, the court, because of the insufficiency of precautionary measures in controlling the spread of the virus and upholding the right to life and liberty of prisoners as enshrined in Article 21 of the Indian Constitution, directed states to undertake definitive measures to decongest prisons. In order to facilitate this, the court directed the setting up of state level committees, termed High Powered Committees (HPCs). The committee was to comprise a representative from the higher judiciary, the state government and the head of the prison department. The committee was mandated to determine the categories of prisoners to be considered for release on parole or interim bail. The court further directed the weekly functioning of the Under Trial Review Committees (UTRCs) to review cases of prisoners eligible for release. UTRCs are district-level committees constituted as per the directive of the Supreme Court,[14] and mandated to periodically review cases of unsentenced prisoners, in order to effectively check on the unnecessary and prolonged detention of prisoners.

In addition to the Supreme Court directives and the MHA advisory, certain High Courts, too, took *suo moto* cognisance of the situation and issued directives that included release of prisoners on personal bond,[15] automatic extension of bail periods,[16] furnishing details on testing and positive cases among prisoners and prison staff,[17] the introduction of emergency paroles and special furloughs,[18] and effective implementation of precautionary measures within prisons.[19]

According to an interim report released in June 2020 by the National Legal Services Authority India, 42,529 unsentenced and 16,391 sentenced prisoners had been temporarily released across the country in pursuance of the HPCs' recommendations (NALSA, 2020). However, no information was shared on the number of new admissions during this period, making any assessment regarding decrease in occupancy rates difficult. A study, which analysed the prison population of 22 states/union territories, indicated an average decline in prison population by 10.4% between 1 April and 30 June 2020 (CHRI Responding to the Pandemic, 2020: 15). It further indicated that in the 22 states/union territories, the occupancy rate had come down from 107.8% to 93% between 31 December 2019 and 30 June 2020 (CHRI Responding to the Pandemic, 2020: 15). Yet, 27% of prisons in these states remained overcrowded.

While these figures seem encouraging, an important aspect to note here is that the releases were temporary in nature. As a result, from December 2020, directions were issued by various courts directing the surrender of prisoners. This led to the return of almost 90% of prisoners temporarily released,[20] which presumably undid efforts that led to the reduction in prison population and decrease in prison occupancies.

3 Restrictions of contact with the outside world

3.1 Communication with family and lawyers

An analysis of the minutes of the HPCs constituted according to the directives of the Supreme Court indicates that in six states/union territories, prisoners were permitted to speak to their family/relatives on landline phones,[21] whereas mobile communication was permitted in two states[22] and in five states communication via video conferencing was permitted.[23] Some prisons had reportedly also procured mobile phones and permitted video communication using WhatsApp video calls.[24]

To further understand the real situation, the author circulated questionnaires to five prison officers from different regions of India.[25] Three responses were received representing prisons situated in Madhya Pradesh (Central), Punjab (North) and Mizoram (North-east). The responses indicate that in a prison in Madhya Pradesh, physical visits were not allowed from 24 March to 30 October 2020; however, family members were permitted to send only essential clothes and slippers. Further, as an incoming telephone facility was available, prisoners could communicate via telephone free-of-cost. During this period, visits by lawyers, including legal aid lawyers, were also not permitted, although they were permitted to communicate via telephone and video conferencing. Slightly different from this was the situation in Punjab, where physical visits were not permitted, and there were curbs on sending of items. Calls were allowed through the "prison inmate calling system" and WhatsApp calling was also permitted. Lawyers, including legal aid lawyers, were not permitted to visit, but could communicate using telephones or video conferencing. Further, for any signatures required by lawyers in court documents, they could be handed over to the prison representative on the prison main gate, who would have them processed in both these prisons. For Mizoram, physical visits were not allowed; however, sending of money and other items was permitted; all these items were isolated for four days in the prison office. Telephone calls were permitted at own expense thrice a week, whereas censored letters were allowed to be sent to families. The facility of video conferencing was not available. Interestingly, visits by lawyers were permitted to prisons, provided they could produce a COVID-free certificate and communication was also possible by telephone. Amid the second wave, restrictions on visits have been reapplied, leaving prisoners isolated from the outside world, yet again.[26]

4 / 5 Restrictions on essential rights and compensatory measures

In March, the Supreme Court had ruled that "taking into consideration the possibility of outside transmission, we direct that the physical presence of all the under-trial prisoners before the Courts must be stopped forthwith and recourse to video conferencing must be taken for all purposes".[27] Thus, restrictions were placed on the movement of prisoners from the prisons to the courtrooms for court hearings. Further, in its advisory, the MHA too suggested certain restrictions. These included the strict implementation of decisions to limit or restrict visits to prisons; isolation of suspected cases in single accommodation; limiting the mobility of persons within the prisons and/or limiting access of non-essential staff and visitors to prisons. In the SOP annexed to the advisory, among other precautions, it was suggested that visits to prisons by family members should be stopped until the pandemic was controlled and that prisoners should be provided with access to virtual/telephone visit options. It further suggested that non-essential group activities should be stopped, and that consideration be given to reducing the number of prisoners gathering in groups and to reducing the movement of prisoners. Finally, it proposed that prison labour should be used to produce masks and hand sanitisers.

The restrictions of personal visits as described under Section 3.1 were compensated to some extent by permitting video calls and other forms of telecommunication (see also above under Section 3.1).

4. I 5.1 Curbs on recreational activities

An analysis of the minutes of the HPCs indicates that in five states, awareness programmes were conducted regularly to sensitise prisoners regarding the coronavirus, precautions and self-hygiene measures. The responses of the prison officers in Mizoram indicate that all educational, vocational and religious activities and functions continued as usual but without any outside visitors' presence. No initiatives were undertaken to conduct them virtually. In Punjab, prisoners continued to engage in yoga and spiritual sessions, while adhering to physical distancing norms. Prisoners were also motivated to prepare masks in tailoring units. Spiritual music was played using the public announcement systems installed inside prisons. Efforts were also made to screen videos containing educational and vocational material. In Madhya Pradesh, the recreational activities were reduced considerably and only prison radio was transmitted. The prison factory remained functional with prisoners engaged in making masks in large quantities.

4. I 5.2 Changes in day-to-day routine of prisoners

The responses of prison officers in Madhya Pradesh indicate that several changes were introduced by the jail administration whereby ward opening timings were staggered. All newly admitted prisoners were to spend seven days in a quarantine ward, which was separated from other barracks. However, in Punjab, the usual ward opening and closing times were followed, as was the case in Mizoram.

These varied restrictions, while appearing reasonable or aligned with advisories and guidelines issued, may have resulted in the infringement of prisoners' rights. The ban on family visits also triggered violent clashes inside prisons, resulting in loss of life and property in some states. The negative impact on prisoners' rights was acknowledged in an advisory issued by the National Human Rights Commission of India in October 2020, which stated that "the pandemic led to severe curbs on rights of prisoners, particularly their communication with family and lawyers, access to courts, access to medical care, access to rehabilitation and vocational facilities etc." (NHRC, 2020). This begs the question of prison accountability and oversight, which is dealt with in the next section.

6 Legal basis for restrictions and accountability of prisons through monitoring

The preceding sections indicate that the response by prisons in India seemingly centred around the implementation of precautionary measures within prisons, the constitution of committees to oversee decongestion efforts in prisons and the issuing of guidelines and protocols by various bodies, including the central government and human rights commission. However, while it was necessary to take all adequate steps to limit infection, it was important to uphold human rights principles and ensure that prisoners did not suffer undue hardships in the garb of precautionary measures. The response of the prison systems should have adhered to the basic principles as laid down under the 2015 UN Standard Minimum Rules for Treatment of Prisoners (the Nelson Mandela Rules), including the assurance of the safety and security of prisoners, staff, service providers and visitors at all times; non-discrimination; treatment of prisoners with respect due to their inherent dignity and value as human beings; and the need to take into account the individual needs of prisoners.

Thus, it was necessary that "central and state governments adhered to national protocols and international standards in ensuring that rights of prisoners are upheld and not compromised during the pandemic" (CHRI Statement, 2020). To this end, it was vital that prisons and all places of detention continued to be monitored through both internal and external inspections as mandated under Rule 83 of the Nelson Mandela Rules. Among other aspects, it was vital, that prison monitors ensured that healthcare services provided inside prisons were non-discriminatory; prisoners were kept in isolation only for medical purposes and on the recommendation of medical experts; basic human rights standards were ensured within prisons; prisoners and staff had access to all relevant information regarding the coronavirus; and special needs of vulnerable prisoners, such as women, transgender persons, the differently abled and foreign nationals, were adequately addressed.

The existing monitoring mechanisms for Indian prisons comprise both internal inspections by senior prison officers and external inspections by judicial officers, human rights commissions or the board of visitors[28]. In 2019, a total of 51,255 prison inspections were reported which is an average of three inspections per prison per month (National Crime Records Bureau, 2019). However, 12.3% of these inspections were by the executive and 31.6% by the judiciary.

In a bid to facilitate both internal and external monitoring during the pandemic, checklists were also prepared,[29] which were subsequently adopted by a few states,[30] and directives issued for conducting periodic visits by senior prison officers and judicial officers.

Monitoring teams were also directed by the Supreme Court to ensure that all directives issued were complied with scrupulously.[31] However, no further information or guidelines were provided as to the constitution or function of the monitoring teams. The NHRC advisory also emphasised the role of the prison administration in ensuring that fundamental rights of prisoners were not violated. It set forth the need to create reporting mechanisms to ensure daily keeping of records pertaining to sanitisation, health and hygiene, including the inspection and sanitation of prison premises.

Monitoring places of deprivation of liberty is considered a fundamental safeguard against ill-treatment. Even though mechanisms exist in statutory provisions in India, implementation during normal' times has been slack,[32] thus raising concerns about the effectiveness of prison monitoring during the pandemic.

7 Return to normal – prisons in the post-pandemic world

The pandemic has led to increased inequalities and vulnerabilities, and highlighted the need for coordinated efforts by all criminal justice actors. The extensive curbs on prisoner movement and rights have resulted in "an increased burden on the already under-resourced prison system" (NHRC, 2020). The pandemic has laid bare the fault lines within the system, in terms of both the negative impact of overcrowding in disaster situations and the impact of insufficient human resources on prison administration. Prisons in the post-pandemic world will face multiple challenges. These include, but will certainly not be limited to, (a) reduction in budgets – as non-prison-related activities may take priority in state budgets; (b) increases in prison population on account of court closures and increased backlogs of cases; (c) prolonged detention periods due to the inability in securing an effective defence as a result of reduced economic means and (d) continued shortages of staff due to delays in recruitment processes and training.

Yet, the year 2020, while being very challenging, also offered several lessons. These must inform future policy making and COVID-recovery plans, and be treated as an opportunity to ameliorate prisons and cure their maladies. The first lesson is that decongestion of prisons is possible. Overcrowding has been considered a perennial problem; yet in times of crisis, amid scores of restrictions, courts managed to reduce prison populations substantively. The pitfalls of overcrowding have once again been felt with the onset of a deadlier second wave of infections across the country. This has had the judiciary and prisons scrambling to re-initiate decongestion measures. Thus, the future must include implementing regular decongestion measures by courts.

The second lesson pertains to reducing admissions to prisons, through effective pre-trial decision-making. Ensuring appropriate safeguards at arrest and quality pre-trial decision-making at remand hearings can be an effective check on arbitrary arrests and detentions. The third lesson pertains to the exploration of alternatives to imprisonment and non-custodial measures. At present, probation is the only legally available alternative for adult offenders in India[33] and that too is not used effectively.

The fourth lesson is for the judiciary to develop recovery plans to address the backlog of cases. The fifth lesson is that legal services institutions must strengthen service delivery in prisons to ensure that prisoners, unable to afford legal representation, are provided prompt, effective and quality legal representation by the state.[34] One must remember, however, that upholding the right to life and dignity of prisoners must always be at the heart of all future policies and initiatives.

Notes

1 Calls were made by the United Nations (https://news.un.org/en/story/2020/03/1060252), World Health Organization, UNODC, OHCHR and UNAIDS (https://www.who.int/news-room/detail/13-05-2020-unodc-who-unaids-and-ohchr-joint-statement-on-covid-19-in-prisons-and-other-closed-settings), Penal Reform International's Briefing Note on 'Coronavirus: Healthcare and human rights of people in prison', Commonwealth Human Rights Initiative's (CHRI) Guidance document, COVID-19 and Prisons: Ensuring an Effective Response and Covid-19 and Prisons in The Commonwealth: "Ensuring an Effective Response".

2 *In Re: Contagion of Covid 19 Virus in Prisons*, Supreme Court of India, Suo Motu Writ Petition (C) No. 1/2020, order dtd. 16 March 2020.

3 The Indian constitution empowers states to frame rules in regard to prisons. See the State List, Seventh Schedule, Constitution of India 1950.

4 *In Re-inhuman Conditions in 1382 Prisons v. State of Assam and Ors.*, WP(C) 406/2013. Order dtd 15 September 2017.

5 The emphasis on moving towards rehabilitation and reformation was first made by the Indian Jail Committee (1919–1920) in its "Report of the Indian Jail Committee 1919–20"; the Supreme Court too has emphasised on these principles first in 1977 in *Mohammad Giasuddin v. State of Andhra Pradesh*, AIR 1977 SC 1926; see also *Sunil Batra v Delhi Administration & ors* AIR 1978 SC 1675, *Ramamurthy v State of Karnataka AIR 1997* SC 1739, *Re Inhuman Conditions in 1382 Prisons* (2013) WP(c) 406/2013.

6 In India, children can accompany their mothers until the age of six years.

7 CHRI's website tracker on the Number of COVID-19 positive cases and death of prisoners and prison staff.

8 *In Re: Contagion of Covid 19 Virus in Prisons*, Supreme Court of India, Suo Motu Writ Petition (C) No. 1/2020, order dtd. 23 March 2020.
9 Madhya Pradesh is the second largest state in terms of area, and the fifth in terms of population.
10 https://www.who.int/news-room/detail/13-05-2020-unodc-who-unaids-and-ohchr-joint-statement-on-covid-19-in-prisons-and-other-closed-settings and https://news.un.org/en/story/2020/03/1060252.
11 *In Re: Contagion of Covid 19 Virus in Prisons*, Supreme Court of India, Suo Motu Writ Petition (C) No. 1/2020, order dtd. 23 March 2020.
12 *In Re: Contagion of Covid 19 Virus in Prisons*, Supreme Court of India, Suo Motu Writ Petition (C) No. 1/2020, order dtd 7 May 2021.
13 https://www.freepressjournal.in/india/uttar-pradesh-over-116-lakh-jail-inmates-to-get-covid-19-vaccines-on-priority; https://timesofindia.indiatimes.com/city/bhubaneswar/odisha-prisoners-to-get-covid-vaccine-inside-jails/articleshow/81352121.cms?utm_source=contentofinterest&amp&amp&utm_medium=text&utm_campaign=cppst.
14 *Re Inhuman Conditions in 1382 Prisons* (2016) 3 SCC 700.
15 Such directives were issued for Uttar Pradesh [*In Re Respondent: State of U.P. Public Interest Litigation* (Pil) No. - 564 of 2020]; Delhi [*Court of its Own Motion v. State of Delhi*]; Punjab, Haryana and Chandigarh [*Ishu Grover @Ishu @Golu v. U.T., Chandigarh and another*].
16 Andhra Pradesh [*In Re. Corona Virus- COVID-19 Pandemic v. State of Andhra Pradesh and Ors.*]; Maharashtra [*Faruk Khan and ors. V. State of Maharashtra and Ors.*]; Chhattisgarh [*Suo Moto v. State of Chhattisgarh and Ors.*]; Gujarat [*Suo Motu v. State of Gujarat and 2 others*].
17 Maharashtra [*People's Union Civil Liberties and Ors. V. State of Maharashtra and Ors.*].
18 Delhi [*Shobha Gupta and Ors. v. Union of India Ors.*].
19 West Bengal Assam [*Guwahati v. The State of Assam and Ors.* PIL(Suo Moto) 4/2020].
20 *In re: contagion of covid 19 virus in prisons*, Supreme Court of India, Suo Motu Writ Petition (C) No. 1/2020, order dtd 7 May 2021.
21 Karnataka, Haryana, Manipur, Mizoram, Odisha and Chandigarh.
22 Manipur and Mizoram.
23 Haryana, Mizoram, Odisha, Punjab and Chandigarh.
24 Punjab and Tamil Nadu.
25 Please note that the questionnaires were circulated merely to understand ground reality. The responses could not be corroborated through conversations with prisoners due to access restrictions. Therefore, the information may be used in a limited manner.
26 https://www.hindustantimes.com/india-news/delhi-prisons-to-suspend-family-meetings-for-inmates-from-april-5-amid-surge-in-covid-cases-101617366279738.html; https://timesofindia.indiatimes.com/city/madurai/covid-19-madurai-jail-bans-prisoners-from-meeting-kin/articleshow/82294661.cms
27 *In re: contagion of covid 19 virus in prisons*, Supreme Court of India, Suo Motu Writ Petition (C) No. 1/2020, order dtd. 23 March 2020.
28 A board of visitor (BOV) is a district-level body comprising official and non-official visitors mandated to inspect prisons periodically. To read more on BOVs, see CHRI, Monitoring Prisons: A Visitor's Guide, 2017 and CHRI, Looking into the Haze: National Report on Prison Monitoring in India, 2016 and 2019.
29 CHRI prepared two checklists for internal and external monitoring of prisons during the pandemic. Internal checklist [https://www.humanrightsinitiative.org/download/1592228558CHRI_COVID-19_Checklist%20for%20Prisons%20based%20on%20MHA%20SOP.pdf] and external checklist [https://drive.google.com/file/d/1ZxKN8-8zNvkFDinI572aI-ZV0Ssywm-O/view].

30 Haryana Prison Department circulated the internal checklist to all prisons seeking periodic reports; Madhya Pradesh High Court circulated the external checklist to all district judges of each district seeking periodic reports.
31 *In re: contagion of covid 19 virus in prisons*, Supreme Court of India, Suo Motu Writ Petition (C) No. 1/2020, order dtd. 23 March 2020.
32 See CHRI, 'Looking into the Haze: Second National Report on Prison Monitoring in India', 2019. The findings reveal that of the 491 prisons for which data was analysed, only 24% of prisons had a Board of Visitors, which held only 20% of its total mandated meetings.
33 See the Probation of Offender's Act 1958.
34 Article 39A of the Constitution of India mandates the state to ensure access to legal aid for all persons. See also Legal Services Authorities Act 1987.

References

Bhavya Dore (2020): *Fake News, Real Arrests*, 17 April 2020, The Foreign Policy https://foreignpolicy.com/2020/04/17/fake-news-real-arrests/.

CHRI (2016): *Looking into the Haze: National Report on Prison Monitoring in India* https://www.humanrightsinitiative.org/download/Looking into the Haze Report-2016.pdf.

CHRI (2017): *Monitoring Prisons: A Visitor's Guide* https://www.humanrightsinitiative.org/download/1463122956monitoring_prisons_visitor's_guide.pdf.

CHRI (2019): *Looking into the Haze: Second National Report on Prison Monitoring in India* https://www.humanrightsinitiative.org/publication/looking-into-the-haze-2019-second-national-report-on-prison-monitoring-in-india.

CHRI (2020): *Respecting Human Rights while Enforcing the Lockdown: Guidelines for Police* https://www.humanrightsinitiative.org/download/1586324699CHRI%20Guidelines%20to%20the%20Police_Lockdown.pdf.

CHRI (2020): *Responding to the Pandemic: Prisons and Overcrowding*, Vol I https://www.humanrightsinitiative.org/publication/responding-to-the-pandemic-prisons-and-overcrowding-2020.

CHRI (2020): Rights Behind Bars – Landmark Judicial Pronouncements 2010–2019, *CHRI's Website Tracker on the Number of COVID-19 Positive Cases and Death of Prisoners and Prison Staff.*

CHRI Statement (23 July 2020): *Don't Compromise Prisoners' Rights – Prioritise Healthcare* https://www.humanrightsinitiative.org/press-releases/dont-compromise-prisoners-rights-prioritise-healthcare-chri.

Commonwealth Human Rights Initiative's (CHRI) (21 October 2019): Newsletter Jail Mail - *Were Indian Prisons Equipped to Respond to the Pandemic? - CHRI's Analysis of Prison Statistics India 2019* https://www.humanrightsinitiative.org/publication/jail-mail-were-indian-prisons-equipped-to-respond-to-the-pandemic-chris-analysis-of-prison-statistics-india-2019.

Commonwealth Human Rights Initiative's (CHRI) Guidance Document (2020): *COVID-19 and Prisons: Ensuring an Effective Response and Covid-19 and Prisons in the Commonwealth: Ensuring an Effective Response.*

Criminal Justice & Police Accountability Project (2020): *Countermapping Pandemic Policing: A Study of Sanctioned Violence in Madhya Pradesh* https://www.indiaspend.com/wp-content/uploads/2020/11/Countermapping-Pandemic-Policing-CPAProject.pdf.

Global Prison Trends (2018): *Penal Reform International* https://www.penalreform.org/resource/global-prison-trends-2018/.

Lamba, S., and Dhanuka, M. (2020): Data Analysis: Indian Prison Statistics v. Global Prison Trends. *International Legal Aid Group Newsletter, Issue #47,* Spring 2020.

Mythri Jayaraman (2020): *International Legal Foundation's International Fellows Advisory Council Member* https://www.theilf.org/post/coronavirus-prisoners-and-public-defenders.

National Crimes Record Bureau (2020): *Report, Crime in India.* New Delhi.

National Human Rights Commission, India (2020): *Impact of COVID-19 on Human Rights & Future Response: Advisory on the Rights of the Prisoners*, 5 October 2020.

National Legal Services Authority (2020): *Interim Report on Legal Aid during the Pandemic*, June 2020.

Penal Reform International (2020): *Penal Reform International's Briefing Note on Coronavirus: Healthcare and Human Rights of People in Prison.*

Prison Statistics India (2019): *Report, National Crime Records Bureau* https://ncrb.gov.in/sites/default/files/PSI-2019-27-08-2020.pdf.

Tata Trusts (2019): *India Justice Report 2019* https://www.tatatrusts.org/upload/pdf/overall-report-single.pdf.

World Prison Brief Data https://www.prisonstudies.org/highest-to-lowest/prison-population-total.

Yasir, S., and Schultz, K. (2020): India Rounds Up Critics under Shadow of Virus Crisis, Activists Say, *New York Times*, 19 July 2020 https://www.nytimes.com/2020/07/19/world/asia/india-activists-arrests-riots-coronavirus.html.

22 Ireland North and South

Ciara O'Connell, Mary Rogan, Michelle Martyn and Shadd Maruna[*]

1 General introduction

Though their administrative and governance structures diverged after the partition of the island of Ireland[1] and the establishment of the jurisdiction of Northern Ireland in 1921, both prison systems are currently in the lower end of the European average in terms of prison population rates. At 80 per 100,000 of the national population, the rate of imprisonment in Northern Ireland is closer to that of Ireland (74 per 100,000) than that of England and Wales (133 per 100,000). The official occupancy level for the Northern Ireland Prison Service (NIPS) is lower than that of the Irish Prison Service (IPS) (World Prison Brief, 2021). There are 12 prisons, two of which are for women, under the direction of the IPS, while there are three under the NIPS.

Though an island, both jurisdictions took different approaches to managing the SARS-CoV-2 pandemic. There were critical differences in the early stages, with the Republic taking a more stringent approach to restrictions on activities and more expansive testing. The death rate in the south was lower than that of the north (Tomlinson, 2020). Both jurisdictions experienced significant increases in cases towards the end of 2020, and in March 2021 had a comparable daily rate of cases, though with more progress made on vaccinations in the north (Department of Health, Northern Irish Executive, 2021). This chapter examines the situation regarding COVID-19[2] in the prisons across the island of Ireland, with two distinctive approaches evident. While both prison services have used restrictive measures to contain the virus, the approach of the north has been more grounded in regulation.

* The authors would like to acknowledge the COVID-19 Law and Human Rights Observatory at Trinity College Dublin, and also the Director General of the Northern Ireland Prison Service, Ronnie Armour, the Irish Prison Service Press Office, as well asDoireann O'Brien for research assistance provided in developing this chapter.

DOI: 10.4324/9781003169178-22

2 The Republic of Ireland

2.1 Introduction – general situation of the prison system

The pre-pandemic situation of prisons in the Republic of Ireland was one of overcrowding and prison population growth, with the population of prisoners increasing from 3,818 on 12 March 2018 to 4,214 prisoners in custody on 12 March 2020 (Irish Prison Service, 2020). In response to COVID-19, the prison population was reduced through the temporary release[3] of prisoners. On 29 June, following the end of the jurisdiction's first lockdown, the prison population was 3,715, which increased slightly to 3,764 by 30 October 2020, and 3,753 on 30 March 2021 (Irish Prison Service, 2021). The demographics of the prison population include a disproportionate number of elderly prisoners,[4] many of whom are considered vulnerable to the impact of COVID-19 but have been deemed ineligible for temporary release based on the nature of their crime. Both before and during the COVID-19 pandemic, prison healthcare services have been overburdened and unable to provide adequate healthcare to the prisoner population, an issue highlighted by both the European Committee for the Prevention of Torture (2015) and the Office of Inspector of Prisons in Ireland (Reilly, 2016). Further, the IPS has long faced criticism for its poor sanitation practices, whereby a small number of prisoners do not have in-cell sanitation facilities, being required to "slop out" (European Committee for the Prevention of Torture, 2015: 20–21).

The IPS approach to managing the response to COVID-19 has been heralded as "best practice" (Conneely, 2020), and is inclusive of a contact tracing model commended by the World Health Organization (Clarke et al., 2020). The prison service's proactive efforts to prevent transmission of COVID-19 into the prisoner population have resulted in a relatively low number of COVID-19 cases in its prisons. No cases were reported until August 2020, though, betwen then and June 2021, there were 97 confirmed cases among the prisoner population and 312 reported cases among prison staff (House of Oireachtas, 2021a; O'Keefe, 2020). Prior to publication (December 2021) of this chapter, the total number of COVID-19 cases among the prisoner population in 2020 was 23 and 254 in 2021, with two recorded hospitalisations and one death; these hospitalisations and deaths all took place in November 2021 (*Dáil Debates, Parliamentary Questions, Question no 463, 56911/21)*. Vaccination rates are very high amongst the general population in the south, with 93.1% of adults over the age of 18 having been fully vaccinated by December 2021 (information obtained from https://vaccinetracker.ecdc.europa.eu/public/extensions/COVID-19/vaccine-tracker.html#national-ref-tab, last accessed on 6 December 2021). 85% of the prison population has been fully vaccinated (leaving aside booster injections) (*Dáil Debates,* 24 November 2021, written answer to question 141).

Restrictions on contact with the outside world, "cocooning" (Department of Justice and Equality, 2020) of especially vulnerable prisoners and adoption of preventive measures that mirror those implemented across the country, such as social distancing, screening and testing, and mandatory quarantine periods, have proven effective in managing the spread of the virus (McCaffrey, 2020).

The IPS's previous experience responding to an outbreak of tuberculosis in 2017 (Irish Red Cross, 2020) served as the foundation for its successful preventive response to COVID-19. However, as prevalence of the virus in the state ebbs and flows, the prison response continues to seek to strike a balance between the need for protective restrictions and compensatory measures to mitigate the adverse impact of prevention and protection. For much of 2020, the incidence of COVID-19 in the Republic of Ireland generally was the lowest in the EU (European Centre for Disease Prevention and Control, 2020). However, a very considerable rise in cases occurred in late 2020, reversing this position entirely, with its rate being the highest in the world at one point (O'Riordan, 2021).

2.2 Prison and penal policy concerning the execution of prison sentences during the COVID-19-induced crisis

At the beginning of the pandemic, the Minister for Justice approved actions to reduce the prison population (Department of Justice and Equality, 2020). Within one month of the pandemic declaration, the prison population was reduced by 9% from 4,214 on 12 March 2020 to 3,833 on 7 April 2020 (Irish Prison Service, 2021).[5] A significant action was the temporary release of an increased number of prisoners described as "low risk" and assessed for release on a case-by-case basis (Department of Justice and Equality, 2020). There were two categories of prisoners targeted for release: prisoners serving sentences of less than 12 months for non-violent offences and prisoners with less than six months to serve on their sentence (Houses of the Oireachtas, 2020a). Additional Resettlement Coordinators were employed by the state to support structured releases (Ní Chinnéide, 2020).

The Irish Penal Reform Trust (IPRT), a leading non-governmental organisation in penal reform, called for the release of certain cohorts of prisoners during the pandemic, such as the elderly and those with underlying medical conditions (Irish Penal Reform Trust, 2020). However, these groups were not targeted for release. Additional measures were introduced by the IPS to protect vulnerable populations, including the practice of "cocooning". "Cocooning" prisoners did not mix with the rest of the prison population or other prison staff. Those "cocooning" included prisoners aged 70+ and prisoners with medical conditions (e.g. cancer, severe respiratory disease, rare diseases, and pregnant women with cardiovascular disease).

The number of women in prison decreased by nearly one-third during the initial period of COVID-19 restrictions. On 13 March 2020, there were 178 women in prison, compared to 126 on 15 May 2020 (Irish Prison Service, 2021). The highest number of cocooned prisoners due to health reasons, rather than age, was in the main women's prison, Dóchas Centre (Irish Prison Service, 2020, personal communication with Irish Penal Reform Trust, 7 August). At one stage, 52% of the population in Dóchas were cocooned (Irish Prison Service, 2020, personal communication with Irish Penal Reform Trust, 7 August), reflecting the high level of healthcare needs among this population.

During the COVID-19 pandemic, the Probation Service targeted support at the most at-risk offenders in the community (Department of Justice and Equality, 2020). Telephone contact was the primary method used to supervise offenders. The COVID-19 pandemic impacted the number of Community Service Orders. In March 2020, 2,376 people were on a Community Service Order (The Probation Service, 2020a). In July 2020, there was a 26% decrease in the number of people on Community Service Orders at 1,747 (The Probation Service, 2020b). Over the same period, there was an 18% increase in Community Return; 79 people were on Community Return in March 2020 (The Probation Service, 2020a) with numbers reaching 97 in July 2020 (The Probation Service, 2020b).[6]

Ireland entered its second national lockdown on 21 October 2020 (Devane, 2020). On 25 October 2020, legislation that created fines for non-compliance with public health guidelines was introduced (O'Halloran, 2020). In December 2020, restrictions were eased, though an enormous spike in cases precipitated another lockdown, which, by March 2021, remained largely in place (Department of the Taoiseach, 2021).

2.3 Restrictions of contact with the outside world

Although the government initiated its first lockdown on 27 March 2020, the IPS had already implemented restrictions on prisoner contact with the outside world. On 24 March, the prison service limited prisoners to one 15-minute visit per week, with a maximum of two adults and no persons under the age of 18. The following day, this was reduced to one adult per visit. On 27 March, in line with restrictions imposed across the country, all physical friend and family visits to prisons in Ireland were suspended and replaced with video link calls (Irish Prison Service, 2020a). As country restrictions eased along a phased basis, the IPS reinstated in-person visits in late July 2020 (Irish Prison Service, 2020e), but at certain points was required to again suspend visits to prisons in locations placed under increased government restrictions.

As restrictions in the community increased again in the last quarter of 2020, the IPS ceased in-person visits, and informed family members that they could no longer deposit prisoner property. Restrictions imposed by the IPS on contact with the outside world align with restrictions imposed on the general public, with "Level 3" of the *Plan for Living with COVID-19* (Government of Ireland, 2020) resulting in the suspension of family and friend visits. Visits were initially suspended in March 2020, resumed briefly from July 2020 but were again suspended in October 2020 (Pollak, 2020). In March 2021, visits remained suspended (Houses of the Oireachtas, 2021b). While people in prison and prison staff have been instrumental to the prevention of transmission of COVID-19 behind the prison walls, restrictions on contact with the outside world are contentious (*Hannaway v. The Irish Prison Service*, 2020).

2.4 Restrictions inside prisons

To enable social distancing and minimise prisoner and staff contact, prisons in Ireland have ceased in-person work and education, with an exception being made for those working in essential services. Restrictions have resulted in limited numbers of people allowed to attend workshops, and where social distancing is not possible, workshops have been cancelled. Prisoners are encouraged to exercise, but again, access is restricted and usage reduced to enable social distancing (Irish Prison Service, 2020e).

A primary concern of the impact of COVID-19-related restrictions is the increased amount of time that prisoners are required to remain in their cells. Regardless of transmission status, prisoners are experiencing 22 or more hours of lock-up each day.

> Usually we're out of the cells three times a day: morning, afternoon, tea. But you're getting out for two hours a day now because the staff have to [accommodate prisoners] from all the landings going to the yard and going to the gym separately.
>
> (Lally, 2020)

All newly admitted prisoners to the prison system must undergo a 14-day quarantine period, as must all prisoners who present with symptoms of COVID-19 while they are awaiting results (Gallagher, 2020). Prisoners who are "cocooning" (132 in June 2020 and six in November 2020 (MacNamee, 2020)) experience isolation and negative impacts on their mental health and well-being, as evidenced by the Irish Inspector of Prisons' examination of the lived experience of "cocooning" for prisoners (Gilheaney et al., 2020). The Inspector found that people required to "cocoon" in prison expressed feelings of being punished for being vulnerable (older or sick), and anxiety at the prospect of transitioning out of "cocooning". The practice was required for all those over 70 or with specific conditions. The requirement to cocoon ended on 29 June 2020, but those who were cocooning could remain in a restricted regime if they wished (Houses of the Oireachtas, 2020c).

2.5 Compensatory measures

The IPS implemented targeted initiatives to improve contact with the outside world, mitigate the impact of limited access to work and education, and ensure prisoners and staff remain informed.

Prisoners were offered video calls and increased length of phone calls. The prison service also extended video link and phone calls to prison medical and rehabilitative services and to attend court (McCaffrey, 2020). Prisoners under quarantine or "cocooning" restrictions were provided with in-cell phone services since May 2020, where they are allowed to contact support services (Baker, 2020). The IPS also collaborated with the national postal service in order to permit lodging of monies into prisoner accounts from local post offices; prior to this, families would lodge money while visiting the prison (Irish Prison Service 2020f).

In the absence of in-person education, IPS teachers continued to provide educational service to students, and with the assistance of Irish Red Cross volunteers (Irish Ref Cross, n.d.), students were supplied with educational materials such as books, arts supplies, and handouts. Students enrolled in Open University classes were provided with in-cell laptops to complete their assignments, approved by the governor. The prison service provided an extra TV channel that allowed for Netflix shows to be screened on a scheduled basis (Irish Prison Service, 2020e: 17). All prison schools were closed from March 2020, but due to reopen for face-to-face teaching in April 2021 (Irish Legal News, 2021).

The IPS employed new strategies to share details about restrictions and safety and health initiatives. For prisoners, these included the dissemination of information, education, and support services through an in-cell TV channel. The IPS increased communications to ensure that National Public Health Emergency Team (NPHET) guidance was condensed and accessible. It remained unclear, however, if prison service staff would be prioritised for vaccination, an issue that resulted in disruptive action in the prisons in mid-April 2021 (Reynolds, 2021).

The IPS indicated that initiatives designed to compensate for COVID-19-related restrictions, such as the addition of an in-cell TV channel, in-cell learning, and prisoner newsletters, would be retained on a permanent basis (European Committee for the Prevention of Torture, 2020: 52). The IPS also committed to continued use of video links for court attendance and "virtual" visits.

There have been no widespread reductions or commutations of sentences, nor the use of monetary compensation.

2.6 Legal basis for restrictions and relaxations of the prison regime

Some limited amendments to legislation were made to regulate changes in regimes by the IPS. While restrictions on regimes were put in place from the earliest days of the outbreak, it was not until 21 July 2020 that a statutory instrument was signed into law to provide a clear legal basis for limitations on exercise and visits. Under the Prison (Amendment) Rules 2020 (S.I. 250 of 2020), the Director General of the IPS was given the power to direct a prison governor to suspend, restrict, or modify prisoners' entitlements to physical recreation, exercise, or training for a specified period or periods. This direction could be given having regard to advice from health authorities. A prison governor could also make this direction. The Director General or governor must be of the opinion that the restriction was necessary to prevent or limit the spread of an infectious disease, which includes, but is not limited to, COVID-19. Under the original Prison Rules 2007 (S.I. No. 252 of 2007), prisoners are entitled to at least one hour out of cell time each day, and under the Prison (Amendment) Rules 2017, they are, with exceptions, entitled to a minimum of two hours out of cell for meaningful human contact. This 2020 amendment also gave a legal basis for the suspension or restriction of the entitlement to visits (Prison (Amendment) Rules 2020, section 4). It is not clear for what specific period the direction to restrict entitlements on visits and exercise has been made.

While these amendments to the Prison Rules provide for restrictions on visits and exercise, it appears that no amendment has been introduced to provide a specific basis for isolation or separation on the grounds of a need for quarantine, or indeed as a preventive measure in the case of especially vulnerable people. Under Rule 11 of the 2007 Rules, a prisoner is examined by a doctor on admission for, among other things, their isolation on medical grounds where the prisoner is suspected of having a contagious condition. Interestingly, the IPS describes isolation under Rule 103, as the basis for the separation of people related to COVID-19 (Irish Prison Service, 2020d; Irish Prison Service, 2020, personal communication with Mary Rogan, 15 December). However, under Rule 103, a prison governor may not refuse to implement a direction that a prisoner who is suffering from, or suspected of suffering from, a contagious or infectious disease or condition that threatens the health or well-being of others be segregated in order to prevent the spread of the disease or condition. While this rule forbids prison governors from disobeying a doctor's recommendations in such circumstances, it seems a stretch to describe it as a legal basis for isolation itself. Those cocooning were considered to be separated under Rule 63 (Irish Prison Service, 2020, personal communication with Mary Rogan, 15 December), which permits a governor to separate a prisoner from those who "are reasonably likely to cause significant harm to him or her". This form of separation may also be at the prisoner's request. Rule 63 has been typically used in situations where there is a threat of violence, but here we see "harm" being interpreted as harm from COVID-19.

Temporary release was used more frequently and for longer periods to reduce the prison population during the pandemic. Temporary release is provided for under the Criminal Justice (Temporary Release) Act 1960, as amended by the Criminal Justice (Temporary Release of Prisoners) Act 2003. No changes have been made to this legislation arising out of the pandemic. There is no reference in this legislation to considerations of public health, and no reference to the use of temporary release as a means to contain infectious diseases within prisons. However, release can be made on the grounds of a person's individual health needs (section 2(1) (b)(i)). There is, however, a broader ground that release may be "necessary or expedient in order to ensure the good government of the prison" (section 2(1)(c)(i)). Temporary release for other reasons, e.g. compassionate grounds, was not suspended during periods of lesser restrictions nationally (Irish Prison Service, 2020, personal communication with Mary Rogan, 15 December).

The oversight of prisons during the pandemic was carried out in large part by the Office of the Inspector of Prisons (OIP). The Inspectorate carried out visits to all prisons over the course of the pandemic (Gilheaney, 2020).

It is difficult to estimate the precise impact of international human rights standards on decisions made by the prison authorities during this period, but human rights were at the forefront of the Director General's public comments on the IPS's response, noting a "legal duty of care" on the state to safeguard rights of those in prison (McCaffrey, 2020).

There have been some instances where prisoners sought judicial review of decisions to isolate them or restrict their activities. One prisoner sought a declaration that he was entitled to one hour out of his cell per day, and that this was being denied to him after he showed a symptom of COVID-19. Even though the entitlement to one hour's exercise is stated as being conditional only on the weather, the court held that the temporary measure to restrict exercise was not disproportionate or unreasonable and there was no absolute right to the hour, with the emergency circumstances likely to have heavily influenced this position (O'Faolain and Managh, 2020).

2.7 Returning to normal: what can be learned?

The COVID-19 pandemic presents an opportunity to bring about positive change in penal systems globally. The IPS was successful in keeping COVID-19 out of its prisoner population up until the end of August 2020, with some cases occurring in more recent months (Irish Examiner, 2020). However, the COVID-19 pandemic has not been without cost to prisoners and their families. Several lessons are described below, which would have made the crisis safer for prisoners, staff, management, and the wider community, and that should inform future penal policy.

2.7.1 Prison as a last resort

The COVID-19 pandemic demonstrated that decarceration is achievable with policymakers' determination. The release of a substantial number of prisoners during the pandemic did not pose a risk to public safety. Under national legislation, the Criminal Justice (Community Service) Amendment Act 2011 (section 3 (a)(1)(b)) states that:

> Where a court, by or before which an offender stands convicted, is of the opinion that the appropriate sentence in respect of the offence of which the offender is convicted would, but for this Act, be one of imprisonment for a period of more than 12 months and, it is satisfied, in relation to the offender, that the provisions of section 4 have been complied with, the court may make a community service order in accordance with this section.

Short sentences exceeded the number of community sanctions before the pandemic. The release of prisoners serving short sentences during the pandemic should act as an impetus for the full implementation of this law.

2.7.2 Provision of single-cell accommodation

Generally, a reduction in prison population numbers leads to better prison conditions. The COVID-19 pandemic led to a decrease in cell-sharing across the prison estate, from 1,892 people sharing cells with at least one other person in January 2020 to 1,746 in April 2020 to 1,804 in October 2020 (Irish Prison Service, 2020g). If single-cell accommodation had been available throughout the prison estate before the pandemic, it would have meant safer conditions for prisoners. Social distancing, for example, would have been easier to manage.

2.7.3 Address overcrowding

Overcrowding poses a threat to the health and safety of the prison population at all times. During the pandemic, prison authorities were aware of the significant risk posed by overcrowding. By the week of 2 March 2020, 75 people across the prison estate were sleeping on mattresses on floors. By the week of 11 May 2020, two people were reportedly sleeping on mattresses on floors (Irish Prison Service, 2020, personal communication with Irish Penal Reform Trust, 7 August). To achieve a sustained reduction in prison crowding in the long-term, the judiciary, the Probation Service, and legislators play a vital role in tandem with prison authorities.

2.7.4 Publish timely inspection reports to increase oversight and monitoring

One of the key criticisms during the COVID-19 pandemic has been the absence of any published inspection reports by the Office of Inspector of Prisons (Office of the Inspector of Prisons, n.d.). Ireland is one of the last three EU countries yet to ratify OPCAT (Aizpurua and Rogan, 2020). In the absence of published inspection reports, it is difficult to ascertain whether the state upheld prisoners' rights during the pandemic. Out-of-cell time for prisoners during the pandemic is a key concern. In some prisons, the general prison population was locked up for more than 19 hours a day (Houses of the Oireachtas, 2020b). There has also been very little attention to the impact on prisoners' mental health during the lockdown in which one prisoner described the experience of "cocooning" as akin to solitary confinement (Gilheaney et al., 2020: 4). Principles of proportionality and necessity are essential to avoid any breach of human rights (e.g. the right to family life under the Irish Constitution and the European Convention on Human Rights). The COVID-19 pandemic cannot be used to undermine rights, nor should it result in long-term regress in penal policy. Therefore, the publication of timely prison inspections reports is vital. As of March 2021, the OIP began conducting COVID-19 thematic inspections across prisons in Ireland (Houses of the Oireachtas, 2021c). All 12 prisons in the Republic of Ireland were inspected between March and September 2021, with eight inspection reports published by December 2021.

2.7.5 Prison health is public health

A significant outcome of the pandemic has been the recognition of the continuum between prison health and public health. The IPS Executive Clinical Lead was appointed to the NPHET Team Vulnerable Persons Subgroup (Department of Health, Government of Ireland, 2020), and prisons were included in national health guidance. This has played an important role in recognising that prisoners are part of the wider community. This approach should continue beyond the COVID-19 pandemic.

Many lessons can be learned to enhance future penal policy from the experience of the COVID-19 pandemic. The onus is on the state to reflect, implement, and sustain positive measures to protect the prison population both now and in the future, ensuring their right to enjoy the highest attainable standard of physical and mental health (International Covenant on Economic Social and Cultural Rights, 1966, art. 12(1)).

3 Northern Ireland

Northern Ireland (consisting of six counties in the northeast of the island of Ireland) remains part of the United Kingdom. The NIPS is an agency within the devolved Department of Justice Northern Ireland consisting of three prisons, one of which houses women in one unit and young adult men (18–21 years old) in a separate unit. During 2019/20, the average daily population in the NIPS stood at 1,516, around one-third of which (469 men and 33 women) were remanded in custody and still awaiting trial. Despite increasing cooperation in recent years, NIPS is not formally connected with the IPS in any way. That said, there are similarities between the two, relatively small prison systems.

Like in the south, prisons in the north have been successful in preventing a widespread outbreak of COVID-19. As of 18 January 2021, 94 NIPS staff had tested positive for the disease, but only three prisoners in the general population and seven new committals (Northern Ireland Assembly, 2021).

Unlike the south, the NIPS published a specific policy on the temporary release of sentenced prisoners during the pandemic. A total of 220 prisoners were granted temporary early release from 31 March up until the scheme was paused in August. The early release scheme was re-started at the beginning of November 2020 with a further 54 released as of 18 November 2020.

In general, temporary release can be granted under Rule 27 of the Prison and Young Offenders Centre Rules (Northern Ireland) 1995. Rule 27 provides for release "for any special purpose", which is sufficiently wide to cover release on the grounds of public health. As in the south, the power to release is discretionary. The new policy detailed specific categories of sentences which would exclude a person from being released under the policy. These include prisoners serving life sentences that require notification under sexual offences legislation; and prisoners serving sentences for offences involving murder, manslaughter, or attempted murder; offences related to terrorism; offences involving domestic violence; or prisoners recalled from any prior period of temporary release. Any prisoner released under this policy must have immediate access to accommodation in the community. The NIPS must be satisfied that there are no reasonable grounds to believe that the person will be homeless, present a risk to their own well-being, or breach any other aspect of Public Health Agency guidance during the period of release. Those released are required, among other things, to abide by a curfew, to not consume alcohol or drugs, and to abide by public health advice (Department of Justice, Northern Irish Executive, 2020).

The NIPS has sought throughout the crisis to maintain the essence of the "core day", including rates of time out of cell and outdoor exercise in line with the pre-COVID-19 prison regimes. At the same time, there have been considerable changes of course. Visitation and temporary release practices were temporarily suspended on 23 March 2020 but resumed in a more limited capacity by summer 2020 with occasional interruptions in line with changes in risk levels in the wider population. Likewise, access to the prison's "working out unit" resulted in the closure of Learning and Skills and many other activities. These services have been moved to a landing- or house-based regime to limit movement within prisons.

According to the NIPS Director General (2020, personal communication with Shadd Maruna, November), "In essence, prisons were placed in bubbles. This does not mean that prisoners are locked, this is simply a move to reduce movement around each of our prisons and to reduce the potential spread of the virus". Rather than "locking down" prisoners, as is the practice elsewhere, NIPS has sought to implement social distancing measures. In addition, beginning in early April 2020, NIPS was able to implement technology to facilitate "virtual" visits, learning, legal consultations, and court appearances. As of November, over 15,000 virtual visits have taken place across all three prison establishments. The NIPS also began to provide access to telephones in prisoner cells. Additionally, the prison service increased the available weekly phone credit for all prisoners to assist them in maintaining contact by phone and adjusted phone credit limits appropriately. Prison visits were suspended for periods during the pandemic. The Prison and Young Offenders Centre Rules (Northern Ireland) 1995 provide a prison governor with very wide discretion to suspend all or any visits "at any time", for a period which may be approved by the Minister (Rule 67).

The various precautions taken by the NIPS include regular testing of staff and prisoner temperatures, the issuing of face coverings for situations in which social distancing is not possible, and the shielding of older and vulnerable prisoners. Each prison has a dedicated unit to manage individuals who are either symptomatic, or who are newly committed, separate from the rest of the prison population. Perhaps most importantly, the reduction in the prison population resulting from the early release scheme and other factors has meant that all prisons in Northern Ireland now have single-cell accommodation only, with no "doubling up" or cell-sharing. The NIPS has a five-stage operational recovery plan, through which the above adjustments can be relaxed incrementally in line with changes in the rest of society and medical advice.

4 Conclusion

The prison systems on the island of Ireland have done comparatively well in largely keeping COVID-19 out of the prison systems. This position should not be taken for granted and both prison administrations deserve credit for this achievement in such difficult circumstances. Both systems have done this through making difficult choices around isolation, visits, and regimes, though while making efforts to mitigate the worst effects of the changes involved, including through the rapid deployment of technology, which, until now, seemed almost impossible to implement. A key contrast between the jurisdictions concerns the clarity of the position in the north regarding who was not to be permitted release because of COVID-19. Another point of difference was that the south's pre-existing legislation, despite being drafted quite broadly, still did not permit some of the changes necessitated by the pandemic. It is to be hoped that the technological innovations occasioned by COVID-19 will be retained when the restrictions have been lifted. It is also our contention that there is a good deal of room for cross-border cooperation and sharing of learning as a result of these unusual circumstances.

Notes

1 In this chapter, the terms "Republic of Ireland" and "Northern Ireland" are used to distinguish between the two administrations on the island of Ireland. We also use the terms "south" and "north" to describe these jurisdictions. The

Irish Prison Service (IPS) is responsible for the prison system in the Republic of Ireland, and the Northern Ireland Prison Service (NIPS) for Northern Ireland. Each jurisdiction followed different public health guidance generally, with some, but limited, cross-border efforts to contain the virus.

2 From the period of 12 March 2020 up until the end of March 2021.

3 Temporary release is a conditional form of release, where if prisoners breach conditions, they can be returned to prison *(Criminal Justice (Temporary Release of Prisoners) Act 2003)*.

4 In March 2020, 15% of the prison population were over the age of 50 (Irish Prison Service, 2020b).

5 In 2013, the daily average number of prisoners in custody was 4,158. This compares with 3,971 in 2019, a 4% decrease (Irish Prison Service, 2020c; Irish Prison Service 2021). This swift reduction in prison numbers contrasts starkly with the slow implementation of longer-term policy reforms in this area. Despite repeated recommendations made by experts since 2013 to reduce prisoner numbers, there has been little success (Joint Committee on Justice, Defence and Equality, 2013).

6 Community Return is a structured early release programme for qualifying prisoners. For more information, see The Probation Service (n.d.).

References

Aizpurua, E. and Rogan, M. (2020): Understanding New Actors in European Arrest Warrant Cases concerning Detention Conditions: The Role, Powers and Functions of Prison Inspection and Monitoring Bodies. *New Journal of European Criminal Law*, 11 (2), 204–226.

Baker, N. (2020): Coronavirus: Phones in Cells for Affected Inmates from Tuesday, Irish Prison Service Confirm. *Irish Examiner* [Online]. 1 May. www.irishexaminer.com/news/arid-30997184.html [Accessed: 6 November 2020].

Clarke, M., Devlin, J., Conroy, E., Kelly E. and Sturup-Toft, S. (2020): Establishing Prison-Led Contact Tracing to Prevent Outbreaks of COVID-19 in Prisons in Ireland. *Journal of Public Health*, 42 (3), 519–524.

Conneely, A. (2020): Prison Service Submits Best Practice Paper to WHO After No Inmate Tests Covid-19 Positive. *RTE*. [Online]. 10 June. www.rte.ie/news/coronavirus/2020/0610/1146481-covid19-coronavirus-prisons/ [Accessed: 30 October 2020].

Department of Health, Government of Ireland (2020): *National Public Health Emergency Team (NPHET) Covid-19 Subgroup: Vulnerable People*. [Online]. www.gov.ie/en/collection/301f5e-the-national-public-health-emergency-team-nphet-subgroup-vulnerable-/ [Accessed: 15 April 2021].

Department of Health, Northern Irish Executive (2021): *COVID-19 in Northern Ireland: Daily Dashboard Charts & Graphs: 31st of March 2021*. [Online]. https://www.health-ni.gov.uk/sites/default/files/publications/health/doh-db-310321.pdf [Accessed: 14 April 2021].

Department of Justice and Equality (2020): *COVID-19: Information Regarding the Justice Sector COVID-19 Plans*. [Online]. www.justice.ie/en/JELR/Pages/Information_regarding_the_Justice_Sector_COVID-19_plans [Accessed: 5 October 2020].

Department of Justice, Northern Irish Executive (2020): *NIPS Policy on Temporary Release during the Coronavirus (Covid 19) Public Health Emergency Policy*. [Online]. www.justice-ni.gov.uk/sites/default/files/publications/justice/nips-temp-release-29.pdf [Accessed: 3 December 2020].

Department of the Taoiseach (2021): *Extension of Level 5 Restrictions and Introduction of Measures for International Travel.* [Online]. https://www.gov.ie/en/press-release/e2374-extension-of-level-5-restrictions-and-introduction-of-measures-for-international-travel/ [Accessed: 15 April 2021].

Devane, M. (2020): Ireland's Second Nationwide Lockdown Comes into Force. *Irish Independent.* [Online]. 21 October. www.independent.ie/breaking-news/irish-news/irelands-second-nationwide-lockdown-comes-into-force-39653744.html [Accessed: 12 November 2020].

European Centre for Disease Prevention and Control (2020): *Download Historical Data (to 14 December 2020) on the Daily Number of New Reported COVID-19 Cases and Deaths Worldwide.* [Online]. https://www.ecdc.europa.eu/en/publications-data/download-todaysdata-geographic-distribution-covid-19-cases-worldwide [Accessed: 14 April 2021].

European Committee for the Prevention of Torture and Inhuman or Degrading Treatment or Punishment (2015): *Report to the Government of Ireland on the visit to Ireland carried out by the European Committee for the Prevention of Torture and Inhuman or Degrading Treatment or Punishment (CPT) from 16 to 26 September 2014.* [Online]. https://rm.coe.int/pdf%20/1680727e23 [Accessed: 14 April 2021].

European Committee for the Prevention of Torture and Inhuman or Degrading Treatment or Punishment (2020): *Response of the Government of Ireland to the Report of the European Committee for the Prevention of Torture and Inhuman or Degrading Treatment or Punishment (CPT) on its Visit to Ireland from 23 September to 4 October 2019.* [Online]. https://rm.coe.int/1680a078d1 [Accessed: 15 April 2021].

Gallagher, C. (2020): Inmates With Covid-19 Symptoms Kept In 24-Hour Lock-Up. *The Irish Times.* [Online]. 24 April. www.irishtimes.com/news/crime-and-law/inmates-with-covid-19-symptoms-kept-in-24-hour-lock-up-1.4236286 [Accessed: 4 November 2020].

Gilheaney, P. (2020): Ask an Expert: Monitoring of Prisons during the Covid-19 Pandemic [Blog]. *PRILA Ask an Expert Blog Series*, 10 June. https://prilatcd.wordpress.com/2020/06/10/ask-an-expert-monitoring-of-prisons-during-the-covid-19-pandemic-with-patricia-gilheaney-inspector-of-prisons-ireland/ [Accessed: 13 December 2020].

Gilheaney, P., Garrihy, J. and Marder, I. (2020): *Ameliorating the Impact of Cocooning on People in Custody – a Briefing.* [Online]. Nenagh: Office of the Inspector of Prisons. https://www.oip.ie/wp-content/uploads/2020/07/Ameliorating-the-impact-of-cocooning-on-people-in-custody-a-briefing.pdf [Accessed: 16 April 2021].

Government of Ireland (2020): *Resilience and Recovery 2020–2021: Plan for Living with COVID-19.* [Online]. www.gov.ie/en/campaigns/resilience-recovery-2020-2021-plan-for-living-with-covid-19/ [Accessed: 2 November 2020].

Hannaway v. The Irish Prison Service (2020): 2020/651 JR.

Houses of the Oireachtas (2020a): *Prisoner Releases: Dáil Éireann Debate, Tuesday – 23 June 2020, Questions 317, 318, 319, and 320.* [Online]. <www.oireachtas.ie/en/debates/question/2020-06-23/317/?highlight%5B0%5D=thomas&highlight%5B1%5D=pringle&highlight%5B2%5D=release&highlight%5B3%5D=release> [Accessed: 15 April 2021].

Houses of the Oireachtas (2020b): *Prisoner Data: Dáil Éireann Debate, Tuesday – 14 July 2020, Question 946.* [Online]. https://www.oireachtas.ie/en/debates/question/2020-07-14/946/#pq_946 [Accessed: 12 November 2020].

Houses of the Oireachtas (2020c): *Prisoner Welfare: Dáil Éireann Debate, Tuesday – 3 November 2020, Question 1071.* [Online]. https://www.oireachtas.ie/en/debates/question/2020-11-03/1071/. [Accessed: 15 April 2021].

Houses of the Oireachtas (2021a): *COVID-19 Pandemic: Dáil Éireann Debate, Wednesday -3 March 2021, Question 669.* [Online]. https://www.oireachtas.ie/en/debates/question/2021-03-03/669/#pq_669 [Accessed: 8 April 2021].

Houses of the Oireachtas (2021b): *Prison Visiting Regulations: Dáil Éireann Debate, Wednesday -10 March 2021, Question 718.* [Online]. https://www.oireachtas.ie/en/debates/question/2021-03-10/718/#pq_718 [Accessed: 10 April 2021].

Houses of the Oireachtas (2021c): *Prison Inspections: Dáil Éireann Debate, Wednesday -10 March 2021, Question 711.* [Online]. https://www.oireachtas.ie/en/debates/question/2021-03-10/711/ [Accessed 18 April 2021].

Irish Examiner (2020): Prison System Has Its First Ever Case of Covid-19. *Irish Examiner.* [Online]. 22 August. www.irishexaminer.com/news/courtandcrime/arid-40036202.html [Accessed: 6 December 2020].

Irish Legal News (2021): *Prison Schools to Reopen Next Week.* [Online]. 12 April. https://www.irishlegal.com/article/prison-schools-to-reopen-next-week [Accessed: 15 April 2021].

Irish Penal Reform Trust (2020): *Irish Prisons and Covid-19: Proposed Measures (Revised 30 April 2020)* [Online]. www.iprt.ie/site/assets/files/6681/iprt_irish_prisons_and_covid-19_proposed_measures_revised_30_april_2020_final.pdf [Accessed: 15 April 2021].

Irish Prison Service (2020a): *Request Video Call.* [Online]. www.irishprisons.ie/receive-family-video-visit/ [Accessed: 3 November 2020].

Irish Prison Service (2020b): *Monthly Information Note – March 2020.* [Online]. https://www.irishprisons.ie/wp-content/uploads/documents_pdf/MARCH-2020.pdf [Accessed: 14 April 2021].

Irish Prison Service (2020c): *Annual Reports.* [Online]. https://www.irishprisons.ie/information-centre/publications/annual-reports/ [Accessed: 16 April 2021].

Irish Prison Service (2020d): *Census of Restricted Regime Prisoners July 2020.* [Online]. http://www.irishprisons.ie/wp-content/uploads/documents_pdf/July-2020-Restriction.pdf [Accessed: 9 December 2020].

Irish Prison Service (2020e): *Family Information Booklet for People in Our Custody.* [Online]. www.irishprisons.ie/wp-content/uploads/documents_pdf/Family-Information-Booklet-September-2020.pdf [Accessed: 3 November 2020].

Irish Prison Service (2020f): *Lodging Money to Prisoner Account.* [Online]. www.irishprisons.ie/lodging-money-prisoner-account/ [Accessed: 15 April 2021].

Irish Prison Service (2020g): *Prison Population Census Reports 2020.* [Online]. www.irishprisons.ie/information-centre/statistics-information/census-reports/ [Accessed: 12 November 2020].

Irish Prison Service (2021): *Daily Prisoner Population.* [Online]. http://www.irishprisons.ie/information-centre/statistics-information/2015-daily-prisoner-population/ [Accessed: 14 April 2021].

Irish Red Cross (2020): *Irish Prisons Model Best Practice on Handling COVID-19.* [Online]. www.redcross.ie/national-news/irish-prisons-model-best-practice-on-handling-covid-19/ [Accessed: 30 October 2020].

Irish Red Cross (n.d.): *Prison Programme - Community Based Health & First Aid.* [Online]. www.redcross.ie/programmes-and-services-in-ireland/prison-programme-community-based-health-first-aid/ [Accessed: 6 November 2020].

Joint Committee on Justice, Defence and Equality, Houses of the Oireachtas (2013): *Report on Penal Reform.* [Online]. https://webarchive.oireachtas.ie/parliament/media/penal-reform-report-13-march-2013-final.pdf [Accessed: 16 April 2021].

Lally, C. (2020): Locked up in Lockdown: How Prisons Are Coping with Covid-19. *The Irish Times.* [Online]. 1 June. www.irishtimes.com/news/crime-and-law/locked-up-in-lockdown-how-prisons-are-coping-with-covid-19-1.4267071 [Accessed: 4 November 2020].

MacNamee, D. (2020): Just Six Inmates Cocooning in Ireland's Prisons in Massive Drop since June. *Irish Mirror.* [Online]. 2 November. www.irishmirror.ie/news/irish-news/just-six-inmates-cocooning-irelands-22945855 [Accessed: 5 November 2020].

McCaffrey, C. (2020): Managing Prisons during the COVID-19 Pandemic. [Blog]. *PRILA Ask an Expert Blog Series*, 7 July. https://prilatcd.wordpress.com/2020/07/07/ask-an-expert-managing-prisons-during-the-covid-19-pandemic-special-guest-blog-with-caron-mccaffrey-director-general-of-the-irish-prison-service/ [Accessed: 16 October 2020].

NíChinnéide, F. (2020): *In the Matter of the Third Party Intervention of Open Society Justice Initiative, Conectas, and Elas Existem, Affadavit of Fiona NíChinnéide* [Online]. www.justiceinitiative.org/uploads/43205b7b-61a1-4b49-b863-d1fe99f51245/irish-penal-reform-trust-statement_morelos-prison-amparo-lawsuit-en.pdf [Accessed: 15 April 2021].

Northern Ireland Assembly (2021): *Prisons: Positive COVID-19 Tests. Oral Answers to Questions,* 18 January. [Online]. https://www.theyworkforyou.com/ni/?id=2021-01-18.7.1.

O'Faolain, A. and Managh, R. (2020): Prisoner Loses Action Prisoner Over Being Put Into Isolation Due to Covid-19 Fears in Prison. *The Irish Times.* [Online]. 14 April. www.irishtimes.com/news/crime-and-law/courts/high-court/prisoner-loses-action-over-being-put-into-isolation-due-to-covid-19-fears-in-prison-1.4228945 [Accessed: 6 December 2020].

Office of the Inspector of Prisons (n.d.): *What We Do.* [Online]. https://www.oip.ie/what-we-do/ [Accessed: 12 November 2020].

O'Halloran, M. (2020): Bill Allows for Fines for Breaching Covid-19 Rules become Law, *The Irish Times.* [Online].25 October. www.irishtimes.com/news/crime-and-law/bill-allowing-for-fines-for-breaching-covid-19-rules-becomes-law-1.4390974 [Accessed: 12 November 2020]

O'Keefe, C. (2020): At Least 11 Staff at Midlands Prison Test Positive for Covid-19, *Irish Examiner.* [Online]. 3 November. www.irishexaminer.com/news/arid-40075532.html [Accessed: 4 November 2020].

O'Riordan, E. (2021): Ireland Had World's Highest Covid-19 Infection Rate Last Week. *The Irish Times.* [Online]. 11 January. https://www.irishtimes.com/news/health/ireland-had-world-s-highest-covid-19-infection-rate-last-week-1.4455609 [Accessed: 14 April 2021]

Pollak, S. (2020): All In-Person Visits to Prisons After Christmas Eve Cancelled. *The Irish Times.* [Online]. 22 December. https://www.irishtimes.com/news/crime-and-law/all-in-person-visits-to-prisons-after-christmas-eve-cancelled-1.4444201 [Accessed: 16 April 2021].

Prison Amendment Rules 2020, S.I. No. 250 of 2020. Dublin: Stationery Office. http://www.irishstatutebook.ie/eli/2020/si/250/made/en/print [Accessed: 16 April 2021].

Prison (Amendment) Rules 2017, S.I. No. 276 of 2017. Dublin: Stationery Office. http://www.irishstatutebook.ie/eli/2017/si/276/made/en/print [Accessed: 16 April 2021].

Prison and Young Offenders Centre Rules (Northern Ireland) 1995. https://www.justice-ni.gov.uk/publications/northern-ireland-prison-service-prison-rules [Accessed: 16 April 2021].

Prison Rules 2007, S.I. No. 252 of 2007. Dublin: Stationery Office. http://www.irishstatutebook.ie/eli/2007/si/252/made/en/print [Accessed: 16 April 2021].

Reilly, M. (2016): *Healthcare in Irish Prisons.* [Online]. Nenagh: Office of the Inspector of Prisons. https://www.oip.ie/wp-content/uploads/2020/04/Healthcare-in-Irish-Prisons.pdf [Accessed: 14 April 2021].

Reynolds, P. (2021): Withdrawal of Goodwill by Prison Officers over Vaccine. *RTE News.* [Online]. 16 April. https://www.rte.ie/news/2021/0416/1210255-prison-officers-covid-vaccines/ [Accessed 16 April 2021].

The Probation Service (2020a): *Point in Time Statistical Update 1 March 2020* [Online]. http://www.probation.ie/EN/PB/0/5D0D6E3DAA34481280258542003008E5/$File/Web%20Report%20Caseload%20End%20February%202020.pdf [Accessed: 12 November 2020].

The Probation Service (2020b): *Point in Time Statistical Update 1 July 2020* [Online]. http://www.probation.ie/EN/PB/0/43FEEC3A4AA1E2F9802585A0002E5DAD/$File/Web%20Report%20Caseload%20End%20June%202020.pdf [Accessed: 12 November 2020].

The Probation Service (n.d.): *Community Return.* [Online]. http://www.justice.ie/EN/PB/WebPages/WP16000037 [Accessed: 16 April 2021].

Tomlinson, M. (2020): Coronavirus: Ireland Is One Island with Two Very Different Death Rates. *The Irish Times.* [Online]. 22 April. https://www.irishtimes.com/opinion/coronavirus-ireland-is-one-island-with-two-very-different-death-rates-1.4234353 [Accessed: 14 April 2021].

World Prison Brief (2021): *Highest to Lower – Occupancy Level (based on Official Capacity).* [Online]. https://www.prisonstudies.org/highest-to-lowest/occupancy-level?field_region_taxonomy_tid=14 [Accessed: 14 April 2021].

23 Italy

Lorenzo Picotti[1] *and Luisa Ravagnani*

1 Introduction – general situation of the prison system

The Italian prison system is characterised by permanent overcrowding (Pugiotto, 2016: 1204–1229). This has been perceived as inevitable, as numbers continue to rise. Even if it is illegal, it is considered normal.

The important reform of the Italian penitentiary system of 1975 (Law n. 354/1975) was long awaited to finally realise the humanisation of prisons and to give concrete content to the re-educational purpose of sentencing, as required by article 27 of the Italian Constitution (which came into force in 1948, after the experience of the fascist dictatorship: Bricola, 1977). The adoption of the 1975 Law, however, coincided with the period of political terrorism and of a strong resurgence of organised and violent crimes.

The possibilities for the increased use of alternative sanctions and the opening of the prison regime were therefore restricted, until the famous Gozzini Law n. 633/1986, which gave new impetus to the reform process. The Italian prison context seemed to be strongly transformed. Individual treatment and cooperation between inmates and staff aiming at the application of alternative measures were promoted and facilitated through this new legal scheme, developed after the collective claims against institutions (Mosconi and Pavarini, 1993: 149–190; Quadrelli, 2005).

Given this improved legal framework, initiatives at different levels and different political approaches tried to deal with what seemed to be the remaining problem of the Italian prison system: the overcrowding. However, the State finally became used to prison overcrowding, as it proved impossible to enact courageous corrective amendments to the penal law system that would have brought prison into line with the requirements of the Italian Constitution. In the new millennium, there has been a progressive increase in the prison population due to the subsequent introduction of penal policies aimed at maximum social security, motivated by the search for electoral consent. These policies even provoked fear and hatred towards immigrants and marginalised people. This was also the attitude towards prisoners.

DOI: 10.4324/9781003169178-23

Called upon to rule on the Italian prison system, the European Court of Human Rights, on more than one occasion, stated that the situation in Italian prisons is not consistent with human rights. In its well-known pilot judgement (ECtHR, 2013), the Court asked for the immediate application of specific measures to resolve the situation of permanent overcrowding. Unfortunately, the good and positive outcomes immediately reached through the application of the *ad hoc* measures have been jeopardised by their being in effect only temporarily. At the end of January 2020, when the Italian Government declared a state of emergency due to the COVID-19 virus, the Italian prison population was 60,971 inmates against a regular capacity of 50,692.

The pandemic therefore entered Italian prisons while it was still struggling to deal with overcrowding.

The COVID-19 pandemic became one of the most feared threats faced in the modern world. In the last days of February 2020, as soon as the number of infected people in northern Italy became alarming, prisons were immediately identified as places of high risk.

The prison health care system, without the capacity for intensive care, was not equipped to deal with such a serious emergency. In the old and overcrowded Italian facilities, even the identification of adequate spaces for the preventive isolation or for the isolation of COVID-19-infected prisoners was an insoluble problem in some cases.

In summarising the number of COVID-19 cases in prisons, it is reported that during the first outbreak, the inmates who tested positive were about 160 with four deaths; during the second outbreak, there were more than a thousand positive prisoners with seven deaths (Antigone, 2020b). According to the latest update (Antigone, 2021), 18 prisoners have died during the COVID-19 pandemic.

2 Prison and penal policy concerning the execution of prison sentences during the COVID-19 crisis

The circular of 22 February 2020, signed by the Head of the Italian Department of Corrections, was just the first of a long list of measures intended to build a wall of isolation from the outside, with the apparent purpose of preventing the possible spread of the virus among prisoners. The term “apparent” indicates the lack of clarity and the vagueness, and occasional insistencies of some of the contents of the measures and of the relevant new law enacted (Buffa, 2020).

As COVID-19 continued to spread, further legislative initiatives were enacted to limit diffusion of the virus among inmates and to flatten the curve. Law Decree n. 18/2020 (known as *Decreto Cura Italia*) might be considered the first relevant step meant to reduce overcrowding: measures other than imprisonment should be preferred and new admissions to prison avoided as far as possible because it was impossible to guarantee proper social distancing among inmates (Dolcini and Gatta, 2020; Martin, 2020; Minnella, 2020b; Murone, 2020).

Under article 123, eligible inmates who had 18 months or less left to serve would be released to home detention or to private health care facilities until 30 June 2020. Those with more than 6 months to serve in home confinement would be subject to electronic monitoring.

With the same aim, article 124 stated that leave for good conduct for inmates with day release schemes would be extended until 30 June 2020, notwithstanding the normal upper limit of 45 days per year.

It is worth noting that no specific mention was made of inmates in pre-trial detention: it is reported that a third of the prison population falls within this category (Daraio, 2020: 933–956). Despite several calls for changes aimed at having a larger impact on overcrowding, the Decree was converted into Law n. 27/2020.

Following the first months of the COVID-19 crisis that severely affected prisons, more concrete and effective measures were not enacted (Minnella, 2020c). Nevertheless, after the summer season, the Italian prison system had to face a second COVID-19 outbreak (Antigone, 2020c). Since the situation was pretty similar to the one that had occurred in spring, and the risk of riots and outbreaks was extremely high, Law Decree n. 137/2020 (known as *Decreto Ristori*) was enacted. Article 29 stated that additional leave would be granted, notwithstanding the upper limits fixed *ex* article 30 *ter* of Italian Penitentiary Law (Law n. 354/1975), to inmates who had already benefited from the measure and who were involved in some kind of work. For the rest, the Decree basically reiterated what had been enacted through the previous *Cura Italia* Decree (Gianfilippi, 2020). For the sake of completeness, the latest Law Decree n. 7/2021 provides an extension of the measures of article 29 of *Decreto Ristori* until 30 April 2021.

3 Restrictions of contact with the outside world

From the very beginning of March 2020, with the intention of keeping the virus out of the Italian facilities, normal prison routine was completely changed. The most invasive changes involved the temporary suspension of any kind of contact visits and the interruption of all educational activities requiring the presence of people from the outside.

Apart from 20% of the facilities able to grant some form of remote educational support, the abrupt suspension of the school programmes made it impossible for inmates to complete their school year (National Guarantor for the Rights of Persons Detained or Deprived of Liberty, Bulletin 34, 2020).

These limitations were perceived as a suppression of the residual freedom and as elimination of the few remaining ways to stay in touch with the outside world (De Vito, 2020b). Moreover, it is worth noting that the *de facto* elimination of any contact with the outside world strongly affected the already weak possibility of external society checking the legality of the prison system (Lorenzetti, 2020).

Inmates had daily contacts only with prison staff necessarily present inside the facilities. In the first convulsive phase of the emergency, the shortage of personal protective devices put everyone's health at serious risk. At the same time, the chronic shortage of personnel for the medical and nursing care within prison and their uneven distribution at regional and national levels immediately laid bare the difficulties in managing the pandemic in the prison context. Starting from this unexpected and fragmented situation, different policies were applied around the country. Some prisons organised health care in complete autonomy (such as in Lombardy); others (such as in Piemonte) chose external management of the COVID-19 cases (Miravalle, 2020: 110). This was possible because the Italian prison health service, unlike in many other countries, falls under the authority of the Ministry of Health rather than the Ministry of Justice. Each region is therefore responsible for the health care of prisoners held in its area. This is why only one general guideline was released by the central Department of Corrections, applicable in the whole country, stating that new inmates coming from the outside must undergo a quarantine regime. The organisation of all the other relevant procedures was divided according to the autonomy of the different regions and their health centres. This approach gave birth to very different solutions.

It is clear that other factors also played a relevant role in the choice of the applicable strategies. Subjective views (the personal views of the management and their ability to develop a strong network of medical support around the prison) and objective aspects (specific structure of each prison) were crucial too. Despite this apparent lack of a coordinated approach, a balance was found to the extent that the experience of Italian health professionals was taken into account as a good practice for the drafting of the WHO guidance on preparedness, prevention and control of COVID-19 in prisons and other places of detention (WHO, 2020).

4 Restrictions inside prisons

Given the complex and strict rules (Buffa, 2020; De Vito, 2020; Gatta, 2020), it is understandable that all the measures aimed at isolating and putting prisons on lockdown increased concerns and worries among inmates, fearful of catching the virus. At a time when the only way to protect inmates appeared to be the application of specific hygienic guidelines, the use of personal protective equipment and the maintenance of interpersonal distances, inmates were instead forced to live crammed into overcrowded cells. And, even if, after the ECHR pilot judgement these cells were renamed "rooms" in the general attempt to improve prison conditions, they were still narrow and unhealthy places in which the shower, the toilet bowl, the sink and the pantry were together in dangerous proximity (Manconi, 2020). In addition, the prison population consisted of people susceptible to catching the virus, such as the homeless, immigrants, drug users and elderly people with precarious health conditions. The provisions in the enlightened laws on release could not be granted to most of those inmates because of a lack of the required conditions (i.e. home, work, family): these objective limits represent a clear form of discrimination (Lorenzetti, 2020) based on economic resources and social inclusion (Durnescu, Montero Perez de Tudela, Ravagnani, 2017: 450–467).

The fact that prisoners feared for their health was of course a trigger element for dissatisfaction. On 8 and 9 March 2020, protests broke out in several prisons (Aliprandi, 2020; Rizzo, 2020) throughout Italy, causing the death of 13 inmates and injuries to 59 guards. Moreover, 72 inmates broke out of jail in Foggia and entire sections of the facilities were destroyed (Miravalle, 2020) causing the need to move prisoners to another institution at a time when any transfer was avoided (if not strictly necessary) to reduce the risk of contagion.

Other serious episodes of violence among inmates occurred on 7 and 8 April 2020 in the prison of Santa Maria Capua Venere (Caserta, Campania), when it was reported that an inmate with a high fever had been infected with COVID-19, which led to the development of a protest about the lack of protective equipment and adequate health safety measures. Consequently, hundreds of riot police officers intervened to put an end to the protest (Antigone, update 20 April 2020).

These events show a worrying fragility of the Italian prison system and the absence of security and order inside its facilities. Given this framework of fear, concerns and worries among the prisoners, it is noteworthy that violence as a form of protest was used only by a relatively small number of prisoners, as pointed out by Lazzaroni and De Rosa, presidents of the Surveillance Court of Brescia and Milan (De Rosa and Lazzaroni, 2020; Ravagnani et al., 2020).

5 Compensatory measures

Before the COVID-19 pandemic, few Italian prisons were allowed Skype calls. This service was usually reserved for foreign prisoners without contact visits or for Italians held far from their family. However, in attempting not to deprive prisoners of their right to stay in touch with families during the pandemic, the Department of Corrections allowed a widespread use of video calls in each institution. The Head of the Department of Corrections, in the circular about the replacement of contact visits with virtual ones, used the term "can" instead of "must" while discussing the possibility of increasing the number of remote meetings, in order to mitigate the negative effects of the new rules on inmates. The vagueness of the law caused different practices in the country. Since the specific instruction of the central authority was referred to each local prison management and to the guidelines of the regional offices of the department of correction, there were inconsistencies in the application of the provision among different prisons.

6 Legal basis for restrictions and relaxations of the prison regime

Given this legal framework, surveillance judges had a crucial role in managing the spread of the virus (Della Bella, 2020b; Manca, 2020: 1–9). To relieve overcrowding, these judges wanted measures other than imprisonment applied to the greatest extent possible. In April 2020, thanks to the application of the new emergency measures, the prison population decreased to 53,904 inmates.

The judges granted temporary non-custodial measures to inmates who had other serious pre-existing diseases which made them more vulnerable to COVID-19. According to article 47 *ter*, paragraph 1 *ter* Law n. 354/1975 and article 147 Italian Criminal Code, temporary non-custodial measures would be applied when dealing with serious physical conditions. According to the judges, the risk of catching the virus in prison constituted an infirmity. The aim of these provisions was to protect the constitutional rights to health and to prevent inhuman and degrading treatment under article 27 of the Italian Constitution and article 3 of ECHR. Bearing in mind these fundamental human rights, judges granted temporary release from custody to inmates detained for mafia-related crimes under the high security regime *ex* article 41*bis* Law n. 354/1975: in all these cases, the fundamental right to health was considered paramount. As highlighted in the reasoning in several judgements, judges stated that keeping these inmates in prison might be considered an inhuman and degrading treatment in breach of article 27 of the Italian Constitution (Sassari Surveillance Court, 2020).

These decisions had a consistent impact on public opinion (Della Bella, 2020). Fundamental principles, such as the rule of law and the certainty of sentence and punishment, seemed to be undermined (Fiandaca, 2020; Pulitanò, 2020: 1–8). The Minister of Justice therefore proposed a Law Decree adopted by the Ministerial Council as n. 28/2020 (known as *Decreto Bonafede or Decreto Anti-scarcerazioni*,[2] converted into Law n. 70/2020), which provided a periodic reassessment of health factors underlying the benefits granted to inmates convicted for specific crimes, such as mafia-related ones (Daraio, 2020: 949–956; Gianfilippi, 2020b).

Given the controversial scope and aim of this Decree, adopted to reassure public opinion about safety, several surveillance judges raised the question of its constitutional legitimacy (Stella, 2020). Their main concerns were the violation of the principle of separation of powers and the principle of equality *ex* article 3 of the Italian Constitution.

Called upon to rule on these cases, the Italian Constitutional Court issued judgement n. 245 on 24 November 2020 (Aprile, 2021: 537–548). The Court rejected the appeals and clearly stated that the fundamental right to health must be balanced with public safety (Corbetta, 2020). Consequently, a constant and periodic reassessment of grounds and premises of the benefits was a requirement. Finally, as the Court observed, the sphere of autonomy and independence of the Judiciary was not undermined.

In conclusion, it is worth noticing that the Italian Court of Cassation was called upon to rule on cases in which temporary non-custodial measures had been granted to inmates who had other serious pre-existing diseases that made them more vulnerable to COVID-19. Through these new judgements, the Court stated that concrete incompatibility with the status of detention was required, in addition to a real and severe health risk. According to the Court, the assessment should not be based on mere probabilities or theoretical assumptions (Court of Cassation, n. 27197/2020; Court of Cassation, n. 36300/2020; Court of Cassation, n. 35012/2020; Court of Cassation, n. 165/2021; Court of Cassation, n. 7178/2021).

On this issue of right to health in prison, it is worth noting that a call has been made to give first access to COVID-19 vaccines to inmates (Minnella, 2020b); inmates should be considered a vulnerable group of society and they should therefore have a priority access to vaccine. The call was accepted, and it is reported (Antigone, 2021) that, since the beginning of March 2021, prisoners and prison staff have started to be vaccinated (Miella, 2021; Pleuteri, 2021).

7 Returning to normal

What clearly emerges is that the Italian response to the COVID-19 crisis in prisons was mainly aimed at disconnecting and isolating prisons from the community (Giostra, 2020), without any consistent preventive scheme. Scholars, academics and experts hoped for and suggested the application of some structural measures to deal better with overcrowding and related problems in the long term. Such issues and problems are certainly not new (Giostra, 2019), but there is hope that the emergency affecting several sectors, including criminal law, justice and prisons, might represent a starting point to reflect on the system overall (Bozzi, 2020; Eusebi, 2021; Saviano, 2020): the impact of COVID-19 on prisons shows why it is necessary to rethink and reshape the system. (For the sake of completeness, it is worth noting that a call has been made to give first access to COVID-19 vaccines to inmates (Minnella, 2020).)

For reasserting fundamental constitutional values and rights, article 27 of the Italian Constitution suggests the road to be taken (Pugiotto, 2014). Even when dealing with tough and serious crimes, the proper and true role of punishment lies in the re-education of offenders. Human dignity is the focal and ultimate value to be kept in mind, even in the time of COVID-19.

Notes

1 Thanks to Sophie Charlotte Monachini (PhD Student, University of Verona) for the assistance and for the support, even in the translation of the present paper.

2 For the sake of completeness, it is worth to point out that two Law Decrees were adopted: the first one n. 29/2020 was not converted into law, but all the provisions have been included in the conversion law n. 70/2020.

References

Aliprandi, D. (2020): Rivolta nelle carceri: morti, incendi e fughe di massa. *Il Dubbio*, March 9th 2020, https://www.ildubbio.news/2020/03/09/morti-proteste-e-fughe-il-giorno-piu-lungo-delle-carceri.

Antigone (2020): Il carcere nell'Italia ai tempi del Coronavirus (with update), www.antigone.it.

Antigone (2020b): Si chiude il 2020, un anno segnato dalla pandemia anche negli istituti di pena. 31 December 2020, https://www.antigone.it/news/antigone-news/3343-si-chiude-il-2020-un-anno-segnato-dalla-pandemia-anche-negli-istituti-di-pena.

Antigone (2020c): Salute, tecnologie, spazi, vita interna. Il carcere alla prova della fase 2. 10 August 2020.

Antigone (2021): Oltre il virus - XVII Rapporto di Antigone sulle condizioni di detenzione. March 2021, https://www.rapportoantigone.it/diciassettesimo-rapporto-sulle-condizioni-di-detenzione/.

Aprile, E. (2021): Per la Corte Costituzionale non viola il diritto alla salute del detenuto la disciplina contenuta nel "Decreto antiscarcerazioni" adottato durante l'emergenza sanitaria dovuta al virus Covid-19. *Cassazione Penale*, n. 2, 2021, 537–548.

Bozzi, I. (2020): Carceri, cresce la mobilitazione. *Corriere della Sera*, 1 December 2020, http://www.ristretti.org/index.php?option=com_content&view=article&id=95684:carceri-cresce-la-mobilitazione&catid=220:le-notizie-di-ristretti&Itemid=1.

Bricola, F. (1977): *Il carcere "riformato"*. Bologna.

Buffa, P. (2020): Carcere e pandemia. Tra la ricerca di responsabilità e l'urgente necessità di apprendere. *Diritto penale e uomo*, n. 7/8, 1–13.

Corbetta, S. (2020): Costituzionalmente legittima la disciplina del "decreto antiscarcerazioni" come modificato dalla L. 70/2020. *Il Quotidiano Giuridico*, 27 November 2020, https://www.quotidianogiuridico.it/documents/2020/11/27/costituzionalmente-legittima-la-disciplina-del-decreto-antiscarcerazioni-come-modificato-dalla-l-70-2020.

Daraio, G. (2020): Emergenza epidemiologica da COVID-19 e sistema penitenziario. *Diritto penale e processo*, n. 7, 933–956.

De Rosa, G., and Lazzaroni, M. (2020): Lettera al Ministro della Giustizia, On.le Alfoso Bonafede. 15 March 2020, https://www.giurisprudenzapenale.com/wp-content/uploads/2020/03/Trib.-Sorveglianza-Milano-e-Brescia-segnalazione-al-Ministro-della-Giustizia.pdf.

De Vito, R. (2020): Camere senza vista: il carcere e l'emergenza sanitaria. *Questione giustizia*, n. 2, 124–132.

De Vito, R. (2020b): Il vecchio carcere ai tempi del nuovo colera. *Questione giustizia*, 11 March 2020, https://www.questionegiustizia.it/articolo/il-vecchio-carcere-ai-tempi-del-nuovo-colera_11-03-2020.php.

Della Bella, A. (2020): Emergenza COVID e 41bis: tra tutela dei diritti fondamentali, esigenze di prevenzione e responsabilità politiche. *Sistema Penale*, 1 May 2020, https://www.sistemapenale.it/it/opinioni/scarcerazioni-boss-41-bis-milano-sassari-emergenza-covid-decreto-legge-28-del-2020-della-bella.

Della Bella, A. (2020b): La magistratura di sorveglianza di fronte al COVID: una rassegna dei provvedimenti adottati per la gestione dell'emergenza sanitaria. *Sistema Penale*, 29 April 2020, https://www.sistemapenale.it/it/scheda/rassegna-provvedimenti-sorveglianza-emergenza-covid-della-bella#_ftn2.

Dolcini,E.,andGatta,G.L.(2020):Carcere,coronavirus,decreto'curaItalia':amaliestremi,timidirimedi.*SistemaPenale*,20March2020,https://www.sistemapenale.it/it/opinioni/carcere-coronavirus-decreto-cura-italia-a-mali-estremi-timidi-rimedi.

Durnescu, I., Montero Perez de Tudela, E., and Ravagnani, L. (2017): Prisoner transfer and the importance of the 'release effect'. *Criminology & Criminal Justice* 17 (4), 450–467.

European Court of Human Rights (ECtHR) (2013): *Torreggiani and Others v. Italy - 43517/09, 46882/09, 55400/09 et al.* Pilot Judgment of 8 January 2013, https://hudoc/ecthr/coe.int.

Eusebi, L. (2021): Covid-19 ed esigenze di rifondazione della giustizia penale. *Sistema Penale*, 13 January 2021, https://www.sistemapenale.it/it/articolo/eusebi-covid-rifondazione-giustizia-penale.

Fiandaca, G. (2020): Scarcerazioni per motivi di salute, lotta alla mafia e opinione pubblica. *Sistema Penale*, 19 May 2020.

Gatta, G. L. (2020): Carcere e coronavirus: che fare? Considerazioni a margine delle (e oltre) le rivolte. *Sistema Penale*, 12 March 2020, https://www.sistemapenale.it/it/opinioni/carcere-e-coronavirus.

Gianfilippi, F. (2020): Il Decreto legge Ristori, le disposizioni emergenziali per contenere il rischio di diffusione dell'epidemia nel contesto penitenziario. *Giustizia insieme*, 1 November 2020 (https://www.giustiziainsieme.it/it/diritto-dell-emergenza-COVID-19/1371-decreto-legge-28-ottobre-2020-n-137-le-disposizioni-emergenziali-per-contenere-il-rischio-di-diffusione-dell-epidemia-nel-contesto-penitenziario).

Gianfilippi, F. (2020b): La rivalutazione delle detenzioni domiciliari per gli appartenenti alla criminalità organizzata, la magistratura di sorveglianza e il corpo dei condannati nel D.L. 10 maggio 2020 n. 29. *Giustizia Insieme*, 12 May 2020, https://www.giustiziainsieme.it/it/diritto-dell-emergenza-COVID-19/1086-d-l-10-maggio-2020-n-29-rivalutazione-delle-detenzioni-domiciliari.

Giostra, G. (2019): Nuove carceri non creano più sicurezza. *La Repubblica*, 21 January 2019.

Giostra, G. (2020): L'emergenza carceraria non è un incendio al di là del fiume. *Diritto di Difesa*, 28 March 2020, https://dirittodidifesa.eu/lemergenza-carceraria-non-e-un-incendio-al-di-la-del-fiume-di-glauco-giostra/.

Lorenzetti, A. (2020): Il carcere ai tempi dell'emergenza COVID-19. *Osservatorio Costituzionale*, n. 3, https://www.osservatorioaic.it/images/rivista/pdf/2020_3_03_Lorenzetti.pdf.

Manca, V. (2020): Ostatività, emergenza sanitaria e COVID-19: le prime applicazioni pratiche. *Giurisprudenza Penale Web*, n. 4, 1–9.

Manconi, L. (2020): I centimetri del carcere. *La Repubblica*, 9 March 2020, https://rep.repubblica.it/pwa/commento/2020/03/09/news/i_centimetri_del_carcere-250790025/.

Martin, F. (2020): Brevi spunti di riflessione sul c.d. decreto "Cura Italia". *Diritto penale e uomo*, 8 April 2020, https://dirittopenaleuomo.org/wp-content/uploads/2020/04/Martin_Cura-Italia-def.pdf.

Miella, L. (2021): Vaccinare i detenuti rispetta la Costituzione. Ma politici e tecnici si dividono sui tempi. *La Repubblica*, 3 January 2021, https://www.repubblica.it/politica/2021/01/03/news/carceri_appello-280983017/.

Minnella, C. (2020): Dal decreto-legge 'sicurezza-bis' a quello 'ristori': errare humanum est, perseverare autem diabolicum. *Diritto di Difesa*, 8 November 2020, https://dirittodidifesa.eu/dal-decreto-legge-sicurezza-bis-a-quello-ristori-errare-humanum-est-perseverare-autem-diabolicum-di-carmelo-minnella/.

Minnella, C. (2020b): Coronavirus ed emergenza carceri. *Diritto penale e uomo*, 29 April 2020, https://dirittopenaleuomo.org/wp-content/uploads/2020/04/minnella-DEF.pdf.

Minnella, C. (2020c): Evoluzioni giurisprudenziali sulle misure svuota carceri adottate dalla magistratura di sorveglianza. *Diritto e Giustizia*, http://www.ristretti.it/commenti/2020/aprile/pdf11/articolo_minnella.pdf.

Miravalle, M. (2020): Le iniziative dell'Amministrazione penitenziaria. In: Antigone: *Il carcere al tempo del coronavirus - XVI Rapporto di Antigone sulle condizioni di detenzione*, 110, https://www.antigone.it/upload/ANTIGONE_2020_XVIRAPPORTO%202.pdf.

Mosconi, G., and Pavarini, M. (1993): Discrezionalità e sentencing giudiziario in Italia. La flessibilità della pena in fase esecutiva nell'attività dei Tribunali di Sorveglianza. *Dei delitti e delle Pene*, n. 3, 149–190.

Murone, G. (2020): Osservazioni a prima lettura in tema di decreto "cura Italia" e nuova detenzione domiciliare. *Giurisprudenza penale*, 27 March 2020, https://www.giurisprudenzapenale.com/2020/03/27/osservazioni-a-prima-lettura-in-tema-di-decreto-cura-italia-e-nuova-detenzione-domiciliare/.

Pleuteri, L. (2021): Carcere e Covid: ecco qual è la situazione nei penitenziari italiani. *Osservatorio diritti*, 16 March 2021, http://www.ristretti.org/index.php?option=com_content&view=article&id=98618:carcere-e-covid-ecco-qual-e-la-situazione-nei-penitenziari-italiani&catid=220:le-notizie-di-ristretti&Itemid=1.

Pugiotto, A. (2014): Il volto costituzionale della pena (e i suoi sfregi). *Associazione Italiana dei Costituzionalisti*, n. 2, 1–18.

Pugiotto, A. (2016): La parabola del sovraffollamento carcerario e i suoi insegnamenti costituzionalistici. *Rivista italiana di diritto e procedura penale*, n. 3, 1204–1229.

Pulitanò, D. (2020): Pena e carcere alla prova dell'emergenza. *Diritto di Difesa*, 13 May 2020.

Quadrelli, E. (2005): *Gabbie metropolitane: modelli disciplinari e strategie di resistenza*. Roma: DeriveApprodi.

Ravagnani, L. et al. (2020): Le pandemie prigioni – pandemia e carcere. *Rassegna italiana di Criminologia*, n. 4.

Rizzo, G. (2020): Le rivolte nelle carceri sono il frutto di crisi vecchie e nuove. *Internazionale*, 11 March 2020, https://www.internazionale.it/notizie/giuseppe-rizzo/2020/03/11/rivolte-carcere-coronavirus.

Saviano, R. (2020): La certezza dell'umanità. *La Repubblica*, 28 November 2020, https://www.repubblica.it/commenti/2020/11/28/news/la_certezzza_dell_umanita_-276094951/.

Stella, A. (2020): Il DL “anti-scarcerazioni” di Bonafede domani il giudizio alla consulta. *Il Riformista*, 3 November 2020, http://www.ristretti.org/index.php?option=com_content&view=article&id=94811:il-dl-qanti-scarcerazioniq-di-bonafede-domani-il-giudizio-alla-consulta&catid=220:le-notizie-di-ristretti&Itemid=1.

WHO (2020): *Experience of Health Professionals, Police Staff and Prisoners in Italy Informs WHO COVID-19 Guidelines for Prisons*, 28 May 2020, https://www.euro.who.int/en/countries/italy/news/news/2020/5/experience-of-health-professionals,-police-staff-and-prisoners-in-italy-informs-who-COVID-19-guidelines-for-prisons.

24 Japan

Kenji Takeuchi and Akinori Otani

1 Introduction – general state of the prison system

1.1 Problem with COVID-19 in Japan

Japan was hit by the first wave of a rapid spread of infection from the end of March to May 2020, and it was on 7 April that the Japanese government issued a "declaration of a state of emergency in response to the novel coronavirus infection." At first, it covered seven controlled areas that had a large number of infected persons (Tokyo, Kanagawa Prefecture, Saitama Prefecture, Chiba Prefecture, Osaka Prefecture, Hyogo Prefecture, and Fukuoka Prefecture). On 16 April, the geographical range was enlarged to cover the whole country. It was on 25 May that the Japanese government declared an end to the state of emergency. At the time of writing, the Japanese government had not issued any declarations of a state of emergency since then, including the period from the end of July to late August when the second wave of rapid infection spread. As of the end of October 2020, Japan has had a cumulative total of more than 100,000 infected persons and 1,761 deaths.

The legal basis for declaring a state of emergency is the "Act on Special Measures for Pandemic Influenza and New Infectious Diseases Preparedness and Response." This Act authorises the governors of affected prefectures to take measures involving requests for self-restraint on going outside, suspension of access to certain facilities, and other restrictions on personal rights. However, the Act does not provide penalties for violating measures that restrict rights. Essentially, the restrictions on rights are "self-restraint"; in other words, it was no more than the government's request that citizens should refrain voluntarily from exercising their rights, including going outside. This control was informal in nature. Furthermore, Japan has not been thorough in conducting PCR tests and isolating suspected carriers. The number of infected persons nevertheless decreased, and one reason for this is the traditionally strong peer pressure in Japanese society, which leads many people to share the idea that they should not cause inconvenience to others and which has encouraged them to transform their lifestyles (Hamai, 2020: 187).

DOI: 10.4324/9781003169178-24

1.2 Japan's prison system

Rights, obligations, and treatment of inmates in prisons are specified in the "Act on Penal Detention Facilities and the Treatment of Inmates and Detainees" (APDFTID) enacted in 2006.[1] This Act is an amended version of the Prison Act that took effect in 1908. The former Act of 1908 was based on the idea of retribution and emphasised, from the viewpoint of prison managers, systems for carrying out imprisonment as punishment smoothly without accidents and violations. The present Act is different from the former in that it has many provisions regarding the rights and obligations of inmates. However, the basic idea remains unchanged in essence: it is the structure in which prison governors have considerable discretion even regarding matters involving restrictions on rights, and factory personnel in charge of penal labour treat inmates through pseudo-family relationships with them. The way inmates are treated in prison, which is not based on legal rights and obligations, but on emotional relationships, has been called "Japanese-style prison administration." The term "Japanese-style" implies a negative evaluation, i.e. it being different from international standards.[2] However, what this "Japanese-style prison administration" emphasises is not formal control by law but informal control based on emotions.

1.3 Trends in crime and the prison population

In the 2000s, Japan was plagued by the problem of overcrowding in prisons, i.e. prisons detaining inmates in larger numbers than the designated limits. Factors behind the rising prison population were a growing concern among the public about crime, the strict approach taken by the police, public prosecutors, and other criminal justice authorities towards crimes and criminals, and the resulting increases in newly admitted inmates and in the prison detention period (see Hamai, 2011). The overcrowding situation began in 2000, with the total number of inmates peaking at 70,496 in 2006. Thereafter, the number of persons detained in prisons continued to decline, with the total number in 2019 standing at 41,867.[3] The prison population rate (inmates per 100,000 inhabitants) in that year was 34[4] (see Figures 24.1 and 24.2).

However, recent years have seen problematic changes in the nature of inmates. While the total number of inmates has been constantly decreasing since 2006, the percentage of persons aged 60 years and over is on the rise. According to the 2019 statistics, persons aged 60 and over comprised 20.2% (8,470 persons) (see Figures 24.3 and 24.4). The growing percentage of elderly inmates in prisons has given rise to several issues, such as their having difficulty participating in penal labour and treatment programmes or needing nursing care of a welfare nature inside the prisons. In addition, several inmates have some kind of disease or disability. Thus, the primary focus in Japan during the stated period was "border control" to prevent the

Figure 24.1 Number of inmates and prison population rate (per 100,000 of national population).

Source: The Justice Ministry statistics (correction statistics) and Vital statistics (population).

Note: "Number of Prisoners" refers to the number of inmates as of 31 December of the respective year.

Figure 24.2 Occupancy level in prisons (not including pre-trial detainees/remand prisoners).

Source: Ministry of Justice, White Paper on Crime.

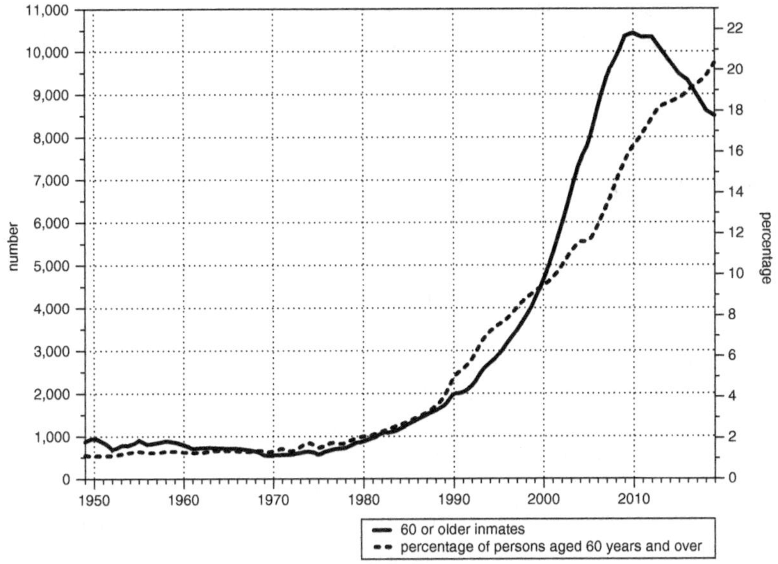

Figure 24.3 Actual number of 60-year-old or older inmates in prison.
Source: The Justice Ministry statistics (correction statistics).
Note: Number refers to the number of inmates as of 31 December of the respective year.

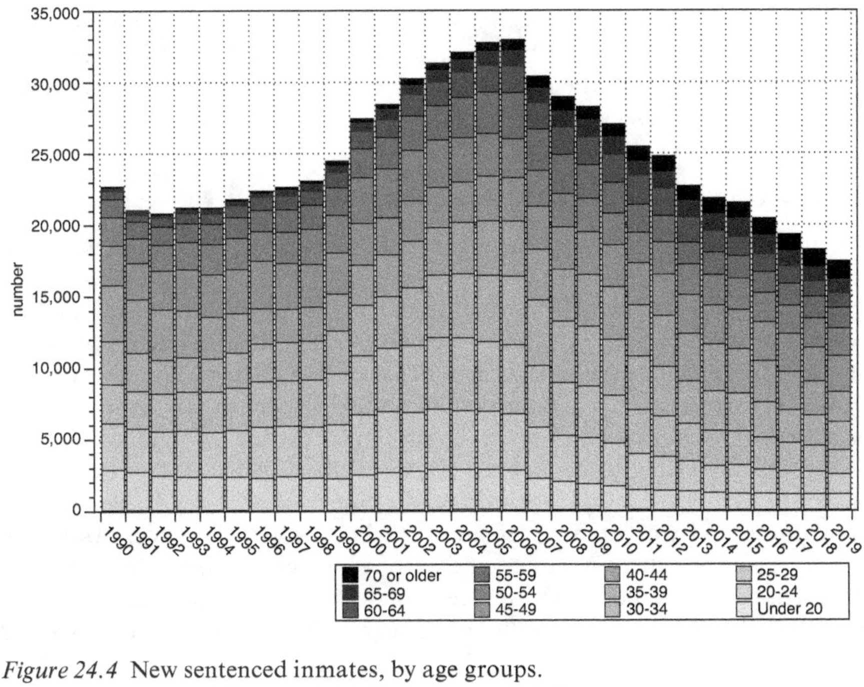

Figure 24.4 New sentenced inmates, by age groups.
Source: The Justice Ministry statistics (correction statistics).

coronavirus from entering prisons and infecting vulnerable prisoners. This means further separation of prisons from society.

To date, seven inmates in Japan have been reported infected with the virus. There has also been a public announcement that the virus infected several prison officers working in prisons and detention facilities.

2 Prison and penal policy concerning the execution of prison sentences during the COVID-19-induced crisis

To date, no substitutes for imprisonment have been applied and no inmates have been released early on the grounds of the COVID-19 pandemic. Japan's penal institutions are not overcrowded at present, and the total number of inmates is on the decrease. As at the end of 2018, the detention ratio, which is the percentage of the actual number of inmates to the designated maximum number, was 63.3% for prisons as facilities for sentenced inmates.[5] This is one of the factors behind the decision that neither substitutes for imprisonment nor early release was necessary.[6]

Since the primary focus is "border control" to prevent the virus from entering prisons, the Ministry of Justice organised a task force of experts in April and prepared a set of guidelines on novel coronavirus infection control measures based on the characteristics of prisons.[7] What the guidelines recommend is to detain newly admitted inmates at correctional institutions in separate single rooms; check their temperatures and health conditions every morning and evening for 14 days, which is the maximum latent period of the novel coronavirus; continue checking the inmates' health after the 14-day period expires if necessary in light of conditions at the facility; and carefully monitor the health of inmates about to be released for a period of two weeks or so before the release, in principle, by means such as checking their temperature every day.

3 Restrictions on contact with the outside world

The present Act is based on the idea that receiving visitors and exchanging correspondence are rights of inmates.

Based on the declaration of a state of emergency, the Ministry of Justice announced that at 38 penal institutions (prisons and detention facilities) located in the seven prefectures (Tokyo, Kanagawa, Saitama, Chiba, Osaka, Hyogo, and Fukuoka) targeted in the declaration, no visitors would be accepted while it was in force, in principle, except for defence counsel or persons intending to be defence counsel. On 20 April, the scope of this measure was expanded to encompass facilities located in 13 special-alert prefectures and was maintained until 25 May, when the declaration was lifted. Of course, there were specific cases in which visitors other than defence counsel were permitted to see inmates. In addition, a decision was made to exclude the number of items of correspondence sent to confirm the safety of inmates and their relatives from the legal number (Hosokawa and Nishioka, 2020: 37).

Contact with the outside by sending and receiving correspondence was restricted in practice partly because of the circumstances of the postal service. Post offices that had confirmed one or more of their staff members were infected with COVID-19 temporarily stopped or scaled down their postal services, which consequently disrupted communication via correspondence at some prisons.[8]

In Japan, a special fixed-amount benefit of 100,000 yen per person was provided as an emergency economic measure in response to the pandemic. Eligible recipients were those registered on the basic resident registers as of the reference date. Inmates were also able to receive the benefit by sending an application and using registered mail. They were not treated inequitably in this respect.

4 Restrictions inside prisons

What should be mentioned first as a problematic restriction inside prisons is related to labour and vocational training. At prisons in the 13 special-alert prefectures designated under the declaration of a state of emergency, penal labour was suspended, in principle, except to the minimum extent necessary to operate the facilities, such as cooking (Hosokawa and Nishioka 2020: 36). In Japan, punishment by imprisonment includes penal labour (Article 12, paragraph 2 of the Penal Code), and is a duty of inmates. Many inmates gather in work areas as a result, and this increases the risk of infection. However, there was a concern that the prolonged suspension of labour might damage relationships with contracted companies or increase stress on inmates, leading to trouble among them. Thus, the Ministry of Justice issued a notice on 7 May that penal labour and vocational training would be conducted at penal institutions located in the special-alert prefectures, too, with certain measures in place to control infection.

It should be noted that the production of isolation gowns, which were in seriously short supply, was conducted in prisons for "social contribution" purposes at the request of the Ministry of Economy, Trade and Industry and the National Security Agency of the Cabinet Secretariat to the Ministry of Justice. This was continued until the end of October 2020, and 1.2 million isolation gowns were manufactured in 42 different prisons (Hosokawa and Nishioka, 2020: 40–42). Prisons with sewing factories prioritised this labour for social contribution over normal labour done under contracts with private-sector companies. Inmates were not given special payment for this work.[9]

Prisons located in the special-alert prefectures cancelled activities, such as guidance sessions, exhortations, and club activities led by outside instructors, but they were resumed simultaneously with the recommencement of penal labour with certain infection control measures in place.

The second issue is whether inmates should wear facemasks or not. Japan is different from Western regions in that it is a common practice to wear facemasks as protection against polio and influenza infection. As to whether inmates in penal institutions should be permitted to wear facemasks or not, however, different institutions have made different decisions. The reason for disapproval is said to be that for security reasons, it is preferable for inmates not to conceal their facial expressions with facemasks.

5 Compensatory measures

As discussed above, as a compensatory measure for inmates' limited visit opportunities, a decision was made to exclude the number of items of correspondence sent to confirm the safety of inmates and their relatives from the legal number.

There is a legal provision in Japan that permits the use of telephones in order to facilitate re-integration into society (Art. 146 APDFTID). However, the use of telephones was not encouraged during the pandemic. In addition, Japanese prisons do not permit inmates to access the internet, and no one makes contact with the outside world by this method.

The present Act includes a provision regarding the authority to let inmates out of penal institutions or release them when an earthquake or fire happens (Art. 215 APDFTID). However, this is not designed for infectious diseases, and this system is not used because COVID-19 is not spreading inside prisons.

One exceptional treatment relates to the "local settlement promotion project," which is intended to provide elderly inmates and those with disabilities with welfare support at the time of their discharge from prison. This project operates under the jurisdiction of the Ministry of Health, Labour and Welfare, not the Ministry of Justice. An administrative circular from the Ministry of Health, Labour and Welfare to the relevant prefectural government sections in charge recommends that, regarding interviews with supported persons in correctional institutions, the sections in charge should consider using non-face-to-face methods such as video conferencing and communication by telephone, when providing support. However, the extent to which this is practised is currently unclear.

6 Legal basis for restrictions and relaxation of the prison regime

The legal basis for visit restrictions during the period when a declaration of a state of emergency applies is not clear, as laws do not provide for visit restrictions in order to control infections. The Ministry of Justice explains that visit restrictions are based on the National Government Asset Act, which requires proper facility management. Furthermore, the suspension of penal labour and remedial guidance has no legal basis. Penal labour is an integral part of imprisonment, and failure to do penal labour amounts to not completing a sentence.

Under the present Act, communication by telephone is permitted only for some inmates, such as those who are treated in open facilities. However, the requirements for permitting communication by telephone are too rigid in the first place, making this system difficult for inmates to access.

7 Returning to normal

The COVID-19 pandemic has highlighted problems with prisons in Japan that have existed up to the present. That is, maintaining discipline and order in prisons and the interests of society at large are put ahead of inmates' human rights, and their rights are restricted not by law but by informal measures.

Inmates are physically isolated from society. Given such a special situation, their opportunities to keep contact with the outside world must be guaranteed in one way or another, even as COVID-19 runs rampant. In Japan, however, inmates' visits were restricted without a clear legal basis and without substitutes provided. Furthermore, for security reasons, Japan did not systematically permit all inmates to wear facemasks. This shows a negative side of "Japanese-style prison administration", in which inmates are regarded as the subjects of control. The questions raised here have been how sincerely Japan would try to meet the requirement under international human rights laws that inmates must be guaranteed human rights, that restrictions on these rights must have a legal basis and be limited to the minimum necessary, and that the standard of living inside prisons must be the same as in society at large.

Issues stemming from the pandemic have spurred the development of communication technologies for connecting people in physically isolated conditions, and such technological advancements present opportunities for solving problems with Japanese prisons.

Japanese prisons have a serious shortage of full-time physicians, but online medical services spreading throughout society at large could serve as major solutions for in-prison medical service problems. Also, as Japanese prisons generally do not accept visit appointments, families coming for visits from remote places experience inconvenience, and visitors have to wait inside prisons for a long time. However, issues uncovered during the COVID-19 pandemic may prompt the introduction of systems for online visit appointments, if not online visit themselves. Supporting the search for employment using online systems from inside prison will also be a major challenge in future.

Addendum

After this paper was submitted, the third wave of the spread of COVID-19 arrived around November 2020, and Japan is still in the middle of it. In response to the third wave, which was larger than the first and second waves, the Japanese government again declared a state of emergency in four prefectures (Tokyo, Kanagawa, Saitama, and Chiba) on 7 January 2021. As of 14 February 2021, the total number of infected people in Japan has exceeded 410,000, with 6,950 deaths.

During this period, there have been clusters of COVID-19 outbreaks within several penal institutions: between 12 and 27 January, inmates and staff were found to be infected in Yokohama Prison (Kanagawa Prefecture), Chiba Prison (Chiba Prefecture), and Hakodate Juvenile Prison (Hokkaido), all of which were identified as clusters. According to data published by the Ministry of Justice, the number of infected persons in penal institutions during the period from 4 January to 14 February 2021 was 175 inmates and 13 staff members in Yokohama Prison, 84 inmates and 9 staff members in Chiba Prison, and 15 inmates and 11 staff members in Hakodate Juvenile Prison. So far, there have been no deaths or serious cases among inmates.

It is thought that the use of common rooms where several inmates sleep and eat together spread the infection. For this reason, the Yokohama and Chiba prisons temporarily transferred about 200 uninfected inmates to outside penal institutions in order to house them in single rooms where the risk of infection was lower. Apart from this transfer measure, the basic measures in Japanese prisons have not changed significantly in nature since the first wave.

Notes

1 An English translation of this Act is available at: http://www.japaneselawtranslation.go.jp/law/detail/?id=2796&vm=04&re=01&new=1.
2 This is the same as the idea of dynamic security in that emphasis is placed on trusting relationships with persons detained in prisons. This, however, is based on vertical, layered relationships, rather than horizontal ones like dynamic security.
3 The figures are based on the Justice Ministry statistics (correction statistics).
4 Calculated from Japan's total population in 2019 of 123,730,000.
5 2019 White Paper on Crime (Japanese). The English version of the paper 2000 to 2018 is available online: http://hakusyo1.moj.go.jp/en/nendo_nfm.html.
6 However, the Center for Prisoners' Rights announced a statement that it would petition the Ministry of Justice, etc., to release inmates earlier on parole because lowering population densities inside the facilities is effective in preventing the spread of infection in the prisons; see Center for Prisoners' Rights Newsletter No. 102 (2020) (Japanese).
7 For details on the activities of the task force for preventing infection in correctional institutions, see Hosokawa and Nishioka (2020: 27–30).
8 Center for Prisoners' Rights Newsletter No. 102 (2020).
9 In Japan, persons who did penal labour receive "work incentives." These work incentives are different from wages and remuneration in that they are not compensation for the labour done, but are intended as commendations for doing the labour. In the fiscal year of 2018, the budget for the work incentive per head per month was 4,360 yen on average.

References

Hamai, K. (2011): *Commentary on Empirical Criminal Policies.* Iwanami Shoten. (Japanese).

Hamai, K. (2020): The Novel Coronavirus Pandemic as Seen from the Perspective of a Criminologist (1st Volume). *Quarterly Keiji-Bengo* (Criminal Defense) No. 103, 180–187. (Japanese).

Hosokawa, T., and Nishioka, S. (2020): Regarding Novel Coronavirus Disease Control Measures at the Correction Bureau. *Keisei*, 131 (10), 27–42 (Japanese).

This work was supported by JSPS KAKENHI Grant Number 20H01433, 20J00787.

25 Kenya

Mercy Deche, Sarah Kinyanjui and Conrad Bosire

1 Introduction: general situation of the prison system

The criminal justice system in Kenya was modelled on the colonial justice system and grounded in retributive philosophy. Historically, this underlying philosophy informed the overreliance on imprisonment as the predominant response to offending (Kinyanjui, 2008: 2; Legal Resources Foundation, 2005: 9; Muhoro, 2000: 325; Wanjala and Mpaka, 1997: 136). In spite of a wide range of penal sanctions provided in statutes such as the Penal Code, the Probation of Offenders Act and the Community Service Orders Act, incarceration remained the leading sentence imposed on offenders (Sentencing Policy Guidelines, para 7.6). This approach resulted in perpetual overcrowding of prisons. The Sentencing Policy Guidelines pointed out that prisoners convicted of misdemeanours, currently attracting imprisonment for a maximum of three years, could be given non-custodial sentences. However, in practice, they were still serving prison terms (para 7.6). While there may be individual circumstances warranting imprisonment, the overreliance on imprisonment for cases, for which non-custodial measures were an option, largely reflected the underlying penal expansionist philosophy. The four-month custodial term at the Kamiti Youth Corrective and Training Centre (KYCTC), designed to provide short, sharp and shock treatment for youth offenders below the age of 21 years, aptly exemplifies penal expansionism (Mukula, 2016: 49).

There has been a gradual paradigm shift, however, towards penal reductionism in the last decade. While still in its nascent stages of implementation, the newly predominant discourse signals this shift. Having conducted research on sentencing trends and practices, with the involvement of criminal justice agencies, the Judiciary developed Sentencing Policy Guidelines in 2016. Paragraph 7.18 of the Sentencing Policy Guidelines expressly guides courts to reserve custodial sentences for those cases in which non-custodial sentences would not serve the underlying sentencing objectives. Further, echoing Article 53(1)(f) of the Constitution, paragraph 7.19 of the Guidelines requires courts to only impose custodial orders for children as a last resort. Similarly, courts are requested to take into account pregnancy,

DOI: 10.4324/9781003169178-25

breastfeeding and caretaking obligations as factors that favour the use of non-custodial sentences (Sentencing Policy Guidelines, paragraph 20.41). This resonates with Article 49(1)(h) and (2) of the Constitution, which guarantees bail as a matter of course, unless there are cogent reasons in favour of detention pending trial.

While there is indeed an increase in non-custodial orders facilitated by statutory framework, the imposition of non-custodial sentences in suitable cases is still not optimal (Penal Reform International, 2016; Kinyanjui and Migai, 2016). The normative reductionism is impacting practice but is yet to be fully realised.

One of the practices that has been linked to penal reductionism is decongestion of prisons undertaken by the Judiciary, which involves the review of prison terms and their substitution with non-custodial sentences. While reductionist in the sense that an expansion of prisons to cater for the population is not at the forefront of the policy, the decongestion process is reactive as opposed to a deliberate reductionist strategy. Aligning judicial practice with the reductionist discourse requires robust strategies for the implementation of the Sentencing Policy Guidelines. Nevertheless, the decongestion of prison processes remains an important tool in addressing the overcrowding of prisons (Deche and Bosire, 2020). It is against this background that the Kenya Prison Service (KPS) was operating before the COVID-19 pandemic.

The KPS was established in the early days of British rule. The enactment of the East Africa Prison Regulations of 1902, when the current Kenyan territory was identified as the East Africa British Protectorate, marks the formal beginnings of penal institutions. The Prisons Department was established as an autonomous public institution in 1911. At independence, in 1963, two laws, the Kenya Prisons Act and the Borstal Institutions Act, were passed to regulate the operations of the KPS. These laws have largely remained in force with minimal change. In terms of administration, the KPS is under the department of Correctional Services, which falls under the national Ministry of Interior and Coordination of Government.

Currently, there are 129 prisons in the country that are managed by the KPS and the Department of Correctional Services; there are no privately run prisons. There are three main types or categories of prisons in the country: Maximum Security Prisons, Main Prisons and Open Prisons. Maximum Security Prisons, nine in number, have enhanced security arrangements and systems and are generally meant to hold prisoners considered to pose a high security risk or persons who have committed serious offences, that is, persons sentenced to 10 years or above or life imprisonment. Forty-six prison facilities are classified as Main Prisons, and these can take both "high-risk" prisoners and general prisoners. The other 70 facilities do not have high security features and only take "low risk" prisoners, who are classified as those serving a maximum of five years. Apart from the general prisons, the KPS also runs and manages three borstal facilities, where child offenders are committed, and one youth corrective training centre (YCTC).

Kenya's prison population has remained between 40,000 and 53,000 over the last 20 years. In the year 2000, the total prison population was 40,100, and this rose to 53,348 at the end of 2019. However, with the acceleration of prison decongestion measures mainly due to COVID-19, the prison population fell sharply in 2020. Statistics as at November 2020 show that as many as 12,000 persons who had been held in prison were released. The prison population fell by 23% to 41,448 (Deche and Bosire, 2020; SOJAR, 2020; UNODC, 2021, 3), although the number is again rising gradually, with a total population of 47,137 in April 2021 (total decline from the end of 2019 until April 2021 is 12%).

The latest official statistics (October 2020) from the KPS indicate that there are a total of 1,700 positive cases of COVID-19 in prison facilities (Julius Otieno, 2020). However, according to the prison authorities, all these cases are limited to regional isolation facilities where new admissions are held before joining the main prison population. No case has been reported in the main prison population. Two employees of the KPS have succumbed to COVID-19: one civilian member of staff and one uniformed officer. Three prisoners, all in the regional isolation facilities, have succumbed to COVID-19.

2 Prison and penal policy concerning the execution of prison sentences during the COVID-19-induced crisis

Kenya's prison facilities have not grown despite a rising number of prisoners over the years. At its peak, the KPS has hosted over 55,000 prisoners against a capacity of 14,000 prisoners (UNODC, 2011; the occupancy rate was 381% at the end of 2019). Thus, when the first case of COVID-19 was reported in Kenya in March 2020, the immediate concern was the vulnerable prison population. In the first instance, the KPS stopped all new admissions to all facilities across the country (NCAJ, 2020). However, this proved unsustainable in the long run.

The police stations, which routinely hold newly arrested suspects, could not cope with the numbers. Police stations are not equipped to hold large numbers of suspects, especially high-risk suspects. The KPS was thus forced to take measures that would allow new admissions, while ensuring minimal risk to its population. The KPS established 59 isolation facilities, arranged according to regions, to ensure that new admissions are held in quarantine for a period of 14 days before being released to the general prison population.

While Kenya has always had legal and policy arrangements to assist in prison decongestion, these regulations were not effectively implemented in the past. The onset of the COVID-19 pandemic provided an opportunity for the resuscitation and active utilisation of these measures. The KPS had, before March 2020, submitted 19,000 files for review to the courts. These files are usually those of prisoners who have either been committed to serve a short sentence (six months) or have served long sentences and have 6 months or less remaining to serve. The National Council made a request to the Judiciary to review these files.

Second, as noted, the law in Kenya provides the option of non-custodial sentences such as community service orders under the Community Service Orders Act (1998) (CSOs) or probation under the Probation of Offenders Act. A list of 7,459 cases was submitted for review in order to provide community service as opposed to physical custody. Statistics up to July 2020 indicate that 4,313 prisoners were released from prisons and instead placed under community service. As the COVID-19 cases rose in the country, the numbers of those recommended to CSOs more than doubled to 15,379 and almost all of them (except 983) were placed on CSOs.

Finally, the NCAJ requested the courts and the Judiciary to review bail and bond terms for those who are remanded in custody. This was done to ensure that bail and bond conditions are revised so as to enable those in physical custody to be released and to facilitate the appropriate decongestion of prisons. As a result, there was a drastic reduction of numbers of those awaiting trial (Deche and Bosire, 2020).

3/4 Restrictions within and outside prisons

At the start of the pandemic, the KPS suspended all physical visits to prisons in order to curb the spread of COVID-19 (Kenya Prisons Service, 2020). Visits to prisons remained suspended and this may have contributed to the minimal cases in the quarantine facilities, and zero infections among the serving inmates. The KPS Guidelines also require all members of staff who are on leave or off duty to stay away from prison facilities. Family members of staff are barred from visiting the prison facilities at any time. All forms of gathering at the Prison Staff quarters are also barred by the regulations. There are regulations, also issued by the KPS, that guide the operation of the regional isolation centres that were discussed earlier. The KPS regulations require officers deployed to isolation centres to be stationed there (without moving) until the end of the pandemic in order to minimise movement of the staff who have interacted with freshly admitted prisoners. Furthermore, in the selection of prison warders and other officers who are to work at the regional isolation centres, officers who do not stay with families should be given priority. Prison transfers are also prohibited during the period, unless for movement into regional isolation facilities.

5 Compensatory measures

The KPS Draft Policy made provision for calls to family members, which are to be offered free of charge (Ministry of Interior and Coordination of National Government, 2020). Each prison facility was required to designate a mobile phone for the purpose of maintaining family contact and the phone is to be used exclusively for that purpose. This was in furtherance of a "remote parenting" policy, which existed prior to the pandemic and enabled inmates to reach their family members. The suspension of all visits to inmates meant that the KPS stepped up the frequency of contact with the family. All the details of the call (name and gender of the caller, duration, date and time of the call, location of the caller, etc.) should be recorded. The policy also referred to "other security measures" that are applicable to such calls. The KPS noted that all prison facilities should embrace virtual courts for all those remanded in custody or inmates whose appeals were ongoing at the courts.

6 Legal basis for restrictions and relaxations of the prison regime

Since COVID-19 descended on the globe without warning or notice, most states, including Kenya, were caught legally unprepared, without legislation tailormade to specifically address a pandemic of that magnitude. All interventions, including restrictions, were therefore made within the pre-existing legal and Constitutional framework and standards. The term restriction is incompatible with the language of human rights, which is a dominant theme in the post-2010 Constitutional dispensation in Kenya. The Constitution of 2010 has a robust bill of rights in respect of which the Kenyan courts have made numerous pronouncements. The courts have in particular reiterated that human rights are "not granted, nor are they grantable, by the State. They attach to persons, all persons, by virtue of their being human and respecting rights is not a favour done by the state or those in authority. They merely follow a constitutional command to obey" (*Attorney General v Kituo Cha Sheria & 7 others* [2017] eKLR). These rights are available to all, including persons in lawful detention to the extent that the rights are not incompatible with the fact that they are detained.

In addition to the Constitution, Kenya is bound by international standards relating to prisons. Under Article 2 of the Constitution, international law and standards form part of the law in Kenya. Those that are specific to the rights of prisoners include the United Nations Basic Principles for the Treatment of Prisoners, 1990, Basic Principles for the Treatment of Prisoners, Body of Principles for the Protection of All Persons under Any Form of Detention or Imprisonment, Standard Minimum Rules for the Treatment of Prisoners, Convention Against Torture and Other Cruel, Inhuman or Degrading Treatment or Punishment, United Nations Rules for the Treatment of Female Prisoners and Non-Custodial Measures for Women Offenders (the Bangkok Rules).

At the domestic level, the rights of prisoners are expressly recognised. Article 51 of the Constitution guarantees the enjoyment of human rights by prisoners except those that are not compatible with the reality of imprisonment. Further, the Constitution required the enactment of legislation for those rights to be realised and in particular for the relevant international legal instruments to be incorporated. In compliance with the Constitution, the Persons Deprived of Liberty Act (2014) was passed. Section 24 of the Act guarantees a person held in lawful custody or detained in prison the right to receive at least one visitor once every seven days. Those detained in prison in execution of a lawful sentence are entitled to be visited at least once every 14 days. Visits by legal counsel or other representatives pursuant to the exercise of the detainee's right of access to justice are unlimited. Section 25 further grants a prisoner the right to designated family days, during which they may be visited and interact with their family members at least once every three months. These rights are similar to those set out in the Borstal Institutions Act that relate to borstal institutions which serve child offenders aged 16 years and above.

The restrictions introduced in prison during COVID-19 curtailed the rights stated above, including accessing justice through physical court appearances. While Article 24 expressly requires the limitation of rights to be effected solely through law, the onset of the pandemic was deemed an unforeseen emergency and the limitation would be reasonable and justifiable in an open and democratic society. In the circumstances, courts adopted innovations to assist them to dispense justice. For instance, one essential category is that the restrictions excluded from prison were probation officers whose social enquiry reports are critical in informing a court's decision on bail and sentencing. The courts opted to proceed notwithstanding the absence of probation officers' social enquiry reports. In lieu of these reports, courts innovated by accepting reports from the officers in charge of prisons regarding the prisoner's personal character, discipline and conduct. This was the case in *Victor Obonto Okello & 2 others v Republic* [2020] eKLR.

The greater challenge posed by restrictions was with regard to the right of access to medical expertise not available in the prison hospital, as access to outside consultants was discontinued with the onset of COVID-19. This issue has been the subject of determination by a court in several instances. In *Republic v Francis Maina Wairimu* [2020] eKLR, the issue was the failure to take the prisoner to a referral hospital for specialised treatment for injuries inflicted during his arrest. In *SMM & another v Officer in Charge Kamiti Maximum Prison & another* [2020] eKLR, the applicants, who were convicted of serious transnational, terror-related charges, approached the court for leave to receive specialised treatment in a private hospital during COVID-19 restrictions. In both cases, the courts were reluctant to bend the restrictions in favour of the inmates. They held that it was incumbent on the inmate to prove that the intervention needed outside the prison was unavailable in the prison hospital. However, in *Lincoln Kivuti Njeru v DPP* [2021] eKLR, the court ruled in favour of the offender and substituted imprisonment with a probation order owing to the offender's acute asthmatic condition, which placed him in a precarious position during the COVID-19 pandemic.

Related to access to health services is the capacity to manage infectious diseases within prisons. The Prisons Act, which was enacted in 1963, envisaged such an occurrence and set out protocols in section 41, relating to isolation of offenders with leprosy. While the treatment of individuals with leprosy may be outdated, this reiterates the need for robust protocols in prisons for dealing with infectious diseases. The COVID-19 pandemic necessitated the development of health protocols for prevention against infection and treatment of individuals infected with COVID-19. The KPS, as well as the Department of Children Services and the Kenya Probation and After Care Service, developed emergency COVID-19 protocols. While these were expeditiously developed, the need for robust standard protocols for infectious diseases and disasters which would form a basis of custom-made protocols for unique occurrences is evident.

Apart from the role played by the court in ensuring accountability of the prison authorities in implementing the restrictions, the other organ that is critical in facilitating accountability in the implementation of the restrictions is the National Council on the Administration of Justice (NCAJ, 2020). The NCAJ is a high-level, policy-making organ that brings together critical state and non-state actors in the justice sector in order to ensure coordination, coherence and harmony in the administration of justice. It is established under national legislation (Judicial Service Act, 2011) and has representation from the Judiciary (with the Chief Justice and the Chief Registrar of the Judiciary as the chair and secretary, respectively), Director of Public Prosecutions, Police Service, Prisons Service, Probation and Aftercare Services, Department of Children Services, the Kenyan Bar, the Executive and Non-Governmental Organisations. Section 35 of the Judicial Service Act outlines the core responsibilities of the NCAJ to include the formulation and development of policies and strategy for the administration of justice, and the mobilisation of resources to assist in the administration of justice.

The NCAJ is devolved to the smallest unit at the court station level as Court User Committees (CUCs). The CUCs are typically composed of justice sector agencies at the court level who assist in decentralised decision-making in the administration of justice. CUCs have been established at each of the 128 court stations in the country, and are headed by the head of the court station. At the county level, the CUCs are headed by the Presiding Judge in the county. A CUCs manager, appointed by the Judicial Service Commission and based at the Secretariat of the NCAJ, assists in coordinating the major activities of the CUCs and compiles quarterly reports of activities undertaken by CUCs. The quarterly reports assist the NCAJ to distil and understand specific issues in the administration of justice for purposes of crafting appropriate policy responses to ensure effectiveness and efficiency (Deche and Bosire, 2020). Monitoring implementation of the restrictions at the CUC level has proved effective. The CUCs have also been used to trace inmates' relatives in case of emergencies.

While access to courts curtailed during the COVID-19 pandemic has been remedied through virtual sessions and other innovations discussed above, remedial measures addressing the prohibition on prison visits by relatives and legal representatives are yet to be provided. Courts are yet to make a pronouncement on the issue. A possible explanation is that prison restriction is not an isolated event. It cannot be interrogated outside the context of simultaneous events that were unfolding outside the prison gates as restrictions were not unique to the prison. The general population has also been under varying degrees of lockdown. It started with a dusk to dawn curfew, restriction of movement between counties, lockdown in certain areas (Cabinet Secretary for Interior, 2020). These were thereafter escalated to a total ban on social, religious, cultural, economic, sporting, entertainment, political, academic, fundraising or similar activities: social institutions like golf clubs, night clubs, bars, casinos, barber shops, massage parlours, beauty salons, gymnasiums, spas, theatres and cinemas, Dine-in restaurants and food courts were also shut down. The cabinet was given powers to shut down any other place or premises it deemed fit (Cabinet Secretary Health, 2020). With this scenario, the focus was not so much on prisons as the situation outside the prison gates was no better. The restrictions in prisons may have been relegated to the back burner and not robustly interrogated, hence the scarce jurisprudence.

7 Returning to normal

Amidst the challenges posed by COVID-19 for prisons, there have been positive outcomes. One of the most significant has been enhanced access to justice through virtual court proceedings. Pursuant to section 205 of the Criminal Procedure Code, courts require accused persons to appear before them in between hearings, a practice referred to as “mentions”. During the COVID-19 pandemic, mentions have been effectively carried out virtually, a practice that is cost effective and time saving. Another gain has been the deliberate imposition of non-custodial sentences in suitable cases. As noted above, the short moratorium on admission of offenders to prison led the Judiciary to proactively impose non-custodial sentences in suitable cases, thus implementing the normatively supported reductionist penal philosophy. Third, and linked to sentencing, is the revitalisation of the prisons’ decongestion initiative, which is anchored in law but had not been routinely undertaken. Fourth is the entrenchment of the critical role played by the NCAJ. The demands of COVID-19 required the engagement of all criminal justice agencies, which was effectively done under the framework of the NCAJ.

Also illuminated by the COVID-19 pandemic are issues of concern that have been the subject of perennial discussions in Kenya. First, the overcrowding of prisons undermines the realisation of basic human rights as well as those specifically related to prisoners. The required standards of sanitation and accommodation cannot be attained when prisons are overcrowded.

Second, and linked to overcrowding, is the failure to meet the required standards envisaged by the right to health. With overcrowding and poor sanitation, the containment of contagious diseases and pandemics such as COVID-19 is compromised. Further, with inadequate access to health services, sick prisoners fail to get the required treatment.

Third, the immediate need for decongestion of prisons reflected the need for courts to routinely impose non-custodial sentences in suitable cases as envisaged by the Sentencing Policy Guidelines. As contextual realities are exacerbated during pandemics, the COVID-19 period has made addressing these perennial shortcomings urgent.

Fourth, the pandemic revealed the need for robust protocols for infectious diseases and disasters which would provide a starting point for custom-made protocols for unique occurrences such as the COVID-19 pandemic.

8 Conclusion

The COVID-19 pandemic provided the much-needed impetus for embracing penal reductionism, which was already supported by the legal and policy frameworks. It is strategic to maintain the momentum and especially peg it on the implementation of the Sentencing Policy Guidelines. Further, the gains made in entrenching digitisation of the Judiciary as well as the KPS to facilitate virtual hearings should be sustained post-COVID. Since the effectiveness of the criminal justice system is dependent on the performance of all its agencies, digitisation of the other agencies should also be pursued. For instance, the Probation and After Care Service, whose services are critical in the promotion and implementation of non-custodial sentences, requires digital capacity to support the digitisation of the court processes.

Under the auspices of the NCAJ, criminal justice agencies cohesively adapted to the COVID-19 disruptions. In the same vein, the realisation of optimal use of non-custodial sentences in suitable cases requires collective resolve, implementation and support by all the criminal justice agencies. This endeavour should be spearheaded under the NCAJ which occupies a strategic coordinating position. With specific reference to the Judiciary, the Sentencing Policy Guidelines require deliberate dissemination and engagement with judicial officers.

While the ongoing prison reforms in Kenya are acknowledged, prison conditions remain below standard. The COVID-19 experience presents an opportunity for appraisal and appreciation of the urgency in the improvement of prison conditions. Strategically, this experience should foster momentum in advocating for prison reforms.

References

Cabinet Secretary Health (2020): The Public Health (Covid-19 Restriction of Movement of Persons and Related Measures Variation) Rules, 2020. http://kenyalaw.org/kl/fileadmin/pdfdownloads/LegalNotices/2020/LN56_2020.pdf accessed 16 January 2020.

Cabinet Secretary Interior (2020): The Public Order (State Curfew) Order, 2020. http://kenyalaw.org/kl/fileadmin/pdfdownloads/LegalNotices/2020/LN36_2020.pdf accessed 16 January 2020.

Deche M., and Bosire, C. (2020): The Silver Lining in the Covid-19 Cloud: An Appraisal of Accelerated Prison Decongestion in Kenya. *Victims & Offenders*, 15 (7–8), 921–932. DOI: 10.1080/15564886.2020.1827470.

Julius, Otieno (2020): Three Prisoners Dead, 1700 Infected with COVID-19. *The Star* 24 October 2020.

Kenya Prisons Service (2020): Protocol for Kenya Prisons Service during COVID-19 Lockdown. Nairobi: Kenya Prison Service.

Kinyanjui, S. (2008): *A Genealogical Analysis of the Criminal Justice System in Kenya: Rebirth of Restorative Justice for Juveniles?* Leicester: University of Leicester.

Kinyanjui, S., and Migai, A. (2016): Towards Structure Sentencing in Kenya: A Case for Reform. *African Journal of Criminology and Justice Studies* 9(1), 266–278.

Legal Resources Foundation (LRF) (2005): *Non-Custodial Sentencing in Kenya: Research Report*. Nairobi: LRF.

Ministry of Interior and Coordination of National Government (State Department for Correctional Services) (2020): Kenya Prisons Service COVID-19 Policy Framework (Draft).

Muhoro, P. (2000): *Crime Prevention: Current Issues in Correctional Treatment and Effective Countermeasures*. Tokyo: UNAFEI.

Mukula, M. (2016): *Control and Training of Youthful Offenders in Kenya: The Case of Kamiti Youth Correction Training Centre, 1990-2017*. Nairobi: University of Nairobi.

NCAJ (2020): *Statement on the Administrative and Contingency Management Plan to Mitigate COVID-19 in Kenya's Justice Sector of 15th March 2020*. National Council on Administration of Justice: Nairobi.

Penal Reform International (2016): *A Study on Community Service and Probation for Women in Kenya: Towards Gender-Sensitive Alternatives to Imprisonment*, London: Penal Reform International. <https://www.penalreform.org/resource/community-service-and-probation-for-women-a-study/> [accessed 10 November 2020].

State of the Judiciary and the Administration of Justice (SOJAR) (2020): *Annual report 2019/2020*. Nairobi: The Judiciary of Kenya.

United Nations Office for Drugs and Crime (UNODC) (2021): *Covid-19 guidance note. Emergency release mechanisms for detainees and prisoners during COVID-19: findings and recommendations*, https:// www.unodc.org/res/justice-and-prison-reform/nelsonmandelarules/Guidance_Note_ER.pdf.

Wanjala S., and Mpaka, C. (1997): Penal Law and Procedure in Kenya: Some Suggestions for Reform. In: Wanjala, S., and Kibwana, K. (Eds.): *Democratization and Law Reform in Kenya*. Nairobi: Claripress.

26 Latvia

Ilona Kronberga

1 Introduction: the overall situation in the prison system

The correctional system in Latvia has undergone several historical changes, as it developed in step with the state. Before Latvia gained independence on 18 November 1918, its prison system evolved under the influence of both the German and the Russian empires. At the beginning of the Second World War, Latvia first found itself under Soviet occupation, then – under the Nazis, and, as the war came to its end – once again under Soviet rule. It was not until 4 May 1990 that Latvia could reassert itself as a sovereign state. Beyond doubt, the dynamic historical development has had an impact also on the prison system that Latvia inherited after regaining independence.

In 1990, Latvia had 15 prisons in total with 10,000 inmates. The prison reform commenced in 1993, and its principal objective was to move from the former Soviet prison camp system to a civilised, contemporary correctional procedure. The Soviet Union characteristically had large prison camps with huge premises and a high number of inmates, who were accommodated in communal dormitories.[1] The prison terms were long, whereas the principal objective in executing criminal sentences was the economic benefit gained from prisoner labour force that worked for free.

Despite the considerable amendments and the introduction of the principle of progression in the Sentence Execution Code of Latvia[2] in 1994, there were still problems relating to provision of effective prison workplaces in line with European standards, due to the unsuitable premises in the prison buildings. In 2005, a prison development strategy[3] was developed for addressing the problem through a plan of constructing new prison buildings to replace outdated and unsuitable premises. However, due to the financial crisis, the strategy was not implemented. The 2014 Guidelines for Prisoner Re-socialisation 2015–2020, apart from planning for new prison buildings, set the scene for the development of a resocialisation system for prison inmates. There were now two parallel development focuses: refurbishment of the prison buildings and also a focus on fighting recidivism and thus reducing prisoner numbers.

DOI: 10.4324/9781003169178-26

Currently, because of a focused correctional system reform over a number of years, Latvia has eight prisons and one juvenile correctional facility populated by 3,230 inmates, including 264 women and 27 persons in the juvenile correctional facility.[4] Latvia has managed to limit and, indeed, eradicate overcrowding in prisons; in fact, the Latvian prison system is operating at just 68% of its capacity.[5] The aim of the Latvian prison system is enshrined in Section 35 Paragraph 2 of the Criminal Law and it states that the purpose of punishment is to protect public safety and resocialise convicted offenders.[6] A considerable reduction of the prison population has been achieved, leading to the closure of four prisons, namely, Parlielupe Prison in 2008, Skirotava Prison in 2014, Vecumnieki Prison in 2017, and Brasa Prison in Riga: the latter was closed on 1 April 2019.

On 4 June 2020, the Government of Latvia gave their support to the Ministry of Justice's initiative of launching a new prison building project as early as in 2021, so that the remaining old prisons might be closed. The initiative was also justified in the context of COVID-19: it was important from the perspective of the justice sector, as well as the national economy to work both on boosting economic activity and speeding up the reform in the prisons and in the broader correctional system, so that there would be less risk of repeated crime and any additional burden on the law enforcement system would be reduced.

Due to consistency in policies and planning, COVID-19 did not take the Latvian prison system by surprise or find it unprepared. In the spring of 2020, during the first wave of the COVID-19 outbreak, extensive testing was carried out in the Latvian prisons with no subjects testing positive. The first COVID-19 case was identified on 1 October 2020. From 1 October to 1 December, only 83 prisoners tested positive, of whom 13 have now fully recovered and four have been released on completing their sentence.

2 Prisons and correctional policies during the COVID-19-induced crisis

The Latvian journey through the COVID-19 pandemic can provisionally be divided into three periods according to the decisions taken by the national government:

1. The first state of emergency was declared on 13 March 2020 and lasted until 9 June 2020.
2. The state of emergency was discontinued on 10 June 2020, as the epidemiological situation began to improve rapidly, although a number of restrictions were maintained with regard to how many people were allowed to meet and how the work of public administration and local authorities was to be managed.

3 The second state of emergency was imposed on 9 November 2020 and was scheduled to last until 11 January 2021. However, only on 7 April 2021, the emergency situation was cancelled, although some restrictions remained in force.

In all three periods, the COVID-19 restrictions relating to the correctional system were governed by legislation targeted to limit the spread of the pandemic[7] and mitigate its consequences,[8] rather than through the instruments of national correctional policies. Such an approach was established to maintain progress towards the initial developmental goals of prisons and probation, as well as to keep the focus of overall correctional policies in line with the goals of punitive justice as part of the Criminal Law. At the same time, the approach allowed for sufficient flexibility to make timely changes in the execution of individual sentences and other court-imposed sanctions in the whole justice sector. Among other things, it was possible to impose certain restrictions, which could later be lifted.

In the spring of 2020, the Cabinet issued an Order declaring a state of emergency and setting out the procedure for containing the spread of COVID-19. The Order stated that the management of all types of crisis situations in prisons was the responsibility of the Head of the Prison Administration or his or her authorised representative; similar authority was delegated to the Head of the Probation Service. For example, the Order contained provisions to the effect that:

a The Head of the Prison Administration had the right to take decisions restricting the legal rights of prisoners. Such rights of the Administration included the right to order an early release procedure implemented by the Prison or the State Probation Service or extend the custodial part of the sentence.
b Commencement of short-term custodial sentences would be postponed, and the detention and transfer of persons sentenced to short custodial terms or custodial terms in replacement of fines or community service would be suspended. Short-term deprivation of liberty in Latvia is a criminal sanction from 15 days to three months. Persons who had already started serving this sentence at the beginning of the pandemic were not released from prison until the end of their sentence. A second group were offenders sentenced to short-term imprisonment, which had not yet been implemented. For this group, the commencement of the sentence was postponed until the end of the emergency. In practice, for the execution of a short-term sentence, persons are invited to appear at the place of execution by an official letter. This means that these persons received official letters after the end of the emergency, that is, after 7 April 2021 and in the order of the queue.
c Transporting of prisoners, including to court hearings, would cease, compensated as far as possible by holding court hearings by video conferencing.

d Transfer of prisoners between prisons would be suspended, except for the transfer of prisoners to the Latvian Prison Hospital in Olaine Prison and for the commencement of serving their custodial sentence.
e Detention for administrative violations[9] would be postponed regardless of the limitation period. In addition, it was stated that administrative arrest, that had not been executed by reason of the state of emergency and was time-barred, would no longer be enforceable after the state of emergency had been lifted.
f Transfer and acceptance of persons convicted and arrested abroad for continuation of their custodial term or detention in the territory of the Republic of Latvia would be postponed.

Such restrictions represented a significant deviation from the usual procedure in the Latvian correctional legislation. Nevertheless, adopted in a state of emergency, they had the required result. No prisoners became ill during the first emergency in the spring of 2020. In addition, the principle of proportionality was respected: as soon as the need for the restrictions was no longer present, they were lifted within a relatively short time, by 9 April 2020. At the same time, the postponement of short custodial terms (between 15 days and three months) led to a situation when sentenced individuals were placed on a waiting list for a summons to report to the prison for serving their term. Return to normality was facilitated by a number of conditions. First, the state of emergency was lifted on 9 June 2020 and the correctional authorities began to return to their daily routine. Second, the number of persons sentenced to short terms of imprisonment was not considerable and did not exceed 1,000. Thus, there is a reason to believe that the state of emergency implemented in spring 2020 did not have a significant impact on the Latvian correctional system or on overall correctional policies.

As the state of emergency was lifted, on 10 June 2020, a number of legal provisions entered into force restoring the standard procedures after the state of emergency and providing for an appropriate set of measures to ensure the rights and obligations for individuals in proportion with public health and safety interests. In recognition of the probability that COVID-19 is hardly likely to disappear in the near future and that morbidity rates may once again surge, a special section has been included in the Law on the Management of the Spread of COVID-19 Infection[10] to set out specific procedures for correctional institutions under COVID-19.

3/4 Restrictions of contact with the outside world and inside prisons

In summer 2020, an instruction was issued giving the Head of the Prison Administration the authority, for reasons of ensuring epidemiological safety, to introduce temporary restrictions with regard to visitors to prisons and the legal rights of prisoners. Additionally, the Head of the State Probation Service could order temporary restrictions with regard to the legal rights of probation clients, including the right to leave the country. Certain functions of the State Probation Service could also be suspended or reduced within a certain area or nationally.

When admitting a prisoner from abroad to a correctional institution, he or she first must spend time in a quarantine cell for a period of up to 14 days. During that time, such a prisoner is subject to the same rules as individuals:

1 who are COVID contacts;
2 who have been diagnosed with COVID-19 infection; and
3 who are suspected of being COVID positive.

The prisoners stay in quarantine under the supervision of medical staff. They are not taken to court hearings; they do not take part in any resocialisation activities in the prison; they are not entitled to brief or lengthier meetings; they do not have the right to receive guests telephone calls or video communications; and they lose the right to temporary respite periods or registration of marriage. Therefore, one can state that during the quarantine, the minimum of "meaningful contacts" with the outside world as required by the UN Mandela Rules was not guaranteed. It should, however, be emphasised that such quarantine provisions are of a temporary nature of no longer than 14 days and apply only to the categories of persons mentioned above. The necessity for these restrictions was explained to prisoners, and – as far as can be seen – nobody complained about it to the national courts or even the ECtHR. The reason might be that, in practice, these restrictions only lasted until the prisoner underwent a COVID-19 test, which took a few days. If the test was negative, the prisoner was granted all rights without any restrictions.

If the prisoner has been banned from receiving visitors due to quarantine, illness, or isolation, he or she is provided with the opportunity of having brief and longer meetings with relatives and other persons after the restriction period and with regard to the date when their application was submitted. The prisoners who have been under restrictions due to the state of emergency are given priority for receiving visitors, which can be seen as a kind of compensatory measure.

Transfer of a prisoner to a medical facility outside the prison for health care services, including for pre-arranged consultations with medical professionals, diagnostic examinations, and inpatient treatment, takes place in the order the appointments were requested after the medical facility has approved the relevant service to the prisoner.

If quarantine is declared in any of the prisons or the prison system at large, the restrictions regarding contacts initially refer to all prison inmates. The Prison Management is responsible for reviewing the quarantine regulations on a regular basis and for lifting restrictions that have become obsolete.

For example, on 5 November 2020, one of the regional prisons outside the Latvian capital was placed under quarantine. This led to a Prison Administration Management Order establishing a commission of experienced professionals from both the prison and the health care systems who not only followed the implementation of the restrictions in the particular prison, but also monitored development to identify restrictions that remained relevant and suggest any changes in the list. Among the restrictions imposed in this case were the suspension of:

a brief meetings of prisoners with any third parties;
b on-site visits by representatives of national and local government institutions, sworn notaries, lawyers;
c resocialisation and education programme activities;
d employment measures for prisoners;
e marriage registration;
f operation of the prison (risk and needs) evaluation commission;
g transfer of prisoners between prisons across the country; and
h taking them to the courts.

At the same time, it was stipulated that inmates who had previously been allowed freedom of movement within a certain area of the prison should now stay in their accommodation, and that, subject to national restrictions with regard to distancing (the distance requirement being two metres between any two individuals), the inmates who were not ill or had not tested positive could still exercise out of doors for at least one hour a day and that food, books from the library, and goods from the prison outlet should be delivered to their accommodation.

Prisoners who were unwell with COVID-19 were conditionally divided into three groups: (1) those with a severe illness who were in the care of the prison hospital and fully separated from the other prison inmates; (2) the more moderate cases with lung lesions and signs of pneumonia who were placed separately from the first category in the prison hospital; (3) the mild or asymptomatic cases who were treated in a separate unit in the prison where they were serving their court-imposed sentence. Those prisoners in the third category who developed symptoms (for example, fever and shortness of breath) were transferred to the prison hospital for further treatment.

On 27 November 2020, the quarantine in the abovementioned prison was lifted, and the prison gradually returned to standard procedures, as the quarantine restrictions became inapplicable. Accordingly, the first steps were to remove the restrictions inside the prison and to provide for the usual prison routines and daily life of the inmates, their resocialisation, employment, education, and only then going on to re-establish contacts with third parties, including relatives, legal aid providers, and other persons.

5 Compensatory measures

The need for additional restrictions affected the entire society in Latvia, and prisoners as part of it. Undoubtedly, the imposition of additional restrictions on prisoners is closely linked to their legal status and should be considered in the context of restricting rights in a correctional setting with regard to the type of custodial control.

There are three essential points:

1. From a public perspective, as well as the perspective of the individuals in custody, it is of paramount importance to clarify in simple language the nature of the restrictions, what exactly they require from individuals, and the reason why they have been introduced. A clear signal should be sent that these restrictions are of a limited duration, that the imposition of the restrictions and their implementation is monitored, and that they will be lifted as soon as they become obsolete. It is further important that these restrictions are in fact lifted (rather than just stating this on paper as a promise), even if there is a risk that they may need to be reintroduced in the future. Such practice has been implemented in Latvia with a positive result.
2. The system of restrictions must be designed to be sufficiently flexible; in other words, it needs intrinsic mechanisms for responding to a dynamically changing situation. For this reason, the Latvian approach was to impose part of the restrictions on the correctional system at large (these were the restrictions for the general public, but in the context of the correctional system), whereas the other part related to the individual prisons. In practice, this means that it is possible to place individual prisons in quarantine without applying it to the whole prison system. One of the system's advantages is that every prison under quarantine and stronger restrictions can apply a set of restrictions that have been developed for that prison in particular. The approach makes the correctional institution open to the specific needs of a range of inmate groups: juveniles, seniors, women, prisoners with specific health problems, and individuals sentenced to life imprisonment.
3. As restrictions are imposed, there must be awareness of the mechanisms in place for lifting them. These include phasing out rules and deciding which of the restrictions will be relinquished first.

This approach, apart from ensuring full clarity, also provides for predictable change management and returning to routine. Moreover, there is no need for special compensatory mechanisms since individuals understood the need for the restrictions and saw them as short-term difficulties.

Given the changes in the treatment of individuals in custody that took place long before COVID-19, there was little need to introduce new measures for remote communication. Remote court hearings with the help of video conferencing were used before. The parties involved in this process were thus familiar with them. In addition, remote communication platforms, such as Skype, had been used before for enabling inmates to communicate with their relatives or other persons. Therefore, as the COVID-19 situation evolved, these approaches were simply used more actively and for a wider range of prisoners.

For most prisoners, except for those at mid-stage and the start of serving their custodial sentence in a closed prison, restrictions on the number of phone calls had already been lifted. Now, under COVID-19, these two categories of prisoners were also allowed to have additional communication with relatives *via* the prison phone. The use of individual smartphones is prohibited in Latvian prisons, except in open prisons, where inmates are allowed to use personal computer equipment with Internet access and a personal mobile phone which is registered in accordance with the procedures specified by the head of the custodial institution.[11]

6 Legal basis for restrictions and relaxations of the prison regime

In Latvia, legal order is established, first, by the Constitution of the Republic of Latvia[12] (Satversme), and, second, by the legislative acts (laws) issued by the Parliament (Saeima) and the Cabinet Regulations deriving from them.

The management of the prison system has been delegated by law to the Ministry of Justice and is supervised by its subordinate institution, the Prison Administration.[13] The prison system is guided by the recommendations of the CPT[14] and other international organisations in developing methods and approaches for managing the prison system in the context of COVID-19, including during periods of emergency.

Thus, the restrictions and relaxations of the prison regime in Latvia are based on the rules and regulations issued by the United Nations, the European Union, the Latvian Parliament, and the government. The national regulatory framework under COVID-19, in turn, includes (a) general legislation issued for the mitigation and prevention of the pandemic (that applies to all citizens) and (b) legislation that applies to separate groups with a special legal status. Such special legal status may relate to the performance of professional duties (for example: doctors and teachers) or some other special status described in the rules and regulations (including convicted persons deprived of their liberty).

It should be noted in this context that as the first state of emergency was implemented across the country on an operational basis (in spring, starting from 13 March), not all the laws referred to in the present chapter (drafted during the second state of emergency – in autumn, starting from 9 November) were yet in place. Thus, the state of emergency in spring was declared on the basis of the Law on Emergency Situation and State of Exception.[15]

This law was enacted to establish a procedure for declaring and revoking a special legal regime, i.e. an emergency situation or a state of exception, and the related rights, restrictions in rights, and special duties of national and local government institutions and natural and legal persons, and also for ensuring the rule of law during such a regime. According to Latvian law, a state of emergency is a special legal regime, during which the government has the right to restrict the rights and freedoms of state administration and local government authorities, natural persons, and legal persons, as well as to impose additional duties on them according to and to the extent prescribed by law.

The law on states of emergency sets out the types and extent of restrictions of personal rights, stipulating also that during a state of emergency all natural and legal persons should comply with the legal requirements issued by the state administration and local government institutions, as well as their officials. It is important to emphasise that according to the law, any measures introduced for coping with an emergency situation may not conflict with international regulations on human rights, which are binding on the Republic of Latvia. On the basis of this law, the government decided on declaring a state of emergency[16] and it was the government's decision that provided a framework for the restrictions imposed on the individuals sentenced to deprivation of liberty, whereas the Ministry of Justice in collaboration with the Prison Administration were charged with the task of developing the implementation procedure for the restrictions, including compensatory measures.

In the period from 10 June to 8 November 2020, when the state of emergency was lifted, the Latvian Government and Parliament adopted the full regulatory package for COVID-19 pandemic management, containment, and risk management. It included the Law on the Suppression of Consequences of the Spread of COVID-19 Infection, Law on the Management of the Spread of COVID-19 Infection, Epidemiological Safety Measures for the Containment of the Spread of COVID-19 Infection, and a number of other measures.[17]

Thus, when a second state of emergency was declared, Latvia had a comprehensive regulatory framework in place for the operation of public administration, local governments, and the law enforcement system. Under these conditions, the Prison Administration decides on restrictions and relaxations for prisoners regarding the situation in the prisons. Prevention is planned along the same lines to ensure that infection does not spread in prisons and is contained, if detected.

7 Returning to normal

At the time of this publication, Latvia is still under the state of emergency declared on 6 November.[18] Given the instability of the situation, there have been six amendments to the Cabinet Decision. To ensure proportionality and compliance with the epidemiological situation, the Prison Administration has issued 23 Orders on changes in the execution of custodial sentences since 1 October 2020, providing for more relaxed or more stringent conditions depending on the epidemiological situation. In addition, the Parliament is preparing to review amendments to the Law on the Management of the Spread of COVID-19 Infection. For the justice and correctional systems, it means maximising the use of remote communications.[19]

Given that all the resources are focused on risk mitigation and stabilisation of the epidemiological situation, the possible impact of COVID-19 and the related state of emergency on the justice and correctional systems are difficult to assess. The need to focus on the current priorities has hindered a broader discussion on how to return to normal. However, the implementation of the principle of proportionality provides correctional institutions with an opportunity to test situations that might tentatively be defined as "return to normal". For example, in those prisons where the epidemiological system is becoming more stable, the restrictions are lifted with an immediate effect. In fact, these situations are periodically posing a test for "returning to normal". We also see that some penal sanctions, for example, short-term detention for up to three months, have become difficult to implement in these conditions.[20] Notably, a few years ago, the legislator was not prepared to waive this type of sanction, although many penal justice professionals pointed out that it did not provide for resocialisation and, thus, could not achieve the aim of punishment enshrined in Section 35 of the Criminal Law.

In conclusion, we would like to note the growing role of remote technologies in correctional procedures. Apart from remotely organised court hearings (also before COVID-19), technology is likely to be used more widely in prisoner education and resocialisation, communication with relatives and service provision. Technological innovation, in turn, will lead to developing a broader circle of professionals and better accessibility of services in prisons, and enable specialists to work on a remote basis.

Notes

1 Zahars, V. (2000): *Par reformu, ko prasa Eiropa un cilvēcība [The Reform Stipulated by Europe and on Humanitarian Grounds].* Latvijas Vēstnesis, 18 January 2000, No. 13, https://www.vestnesis.lv/ta/id/323 [last visited 12 November 2020]

2 *The Sentence Execution Code of Latvia.* Entry into force: 1 April 1971, https://likumi.lv/ta/en/en/id/90218 [last visited 12 December 2020]

3 *Par Ieslodzījuma vietu attīstības koncepciju [On the Development Strategy for Prisons].* Cabinet Regulation No. 280, adopted on 2 May 2005.

4 Author's remark: The statistics is based on the data of the Latvian Prison Administration as of 1 December 2020.

5 World Prison Brief data, https://www.prisonstudies.org/country/latvia [last visited 12 November 2020].

6 *The Criminal Law.* Entry into force: 1 April 1999, see https://likumi.lv/ta/en/en/id/88966 [last visited 12 December 2020].

7 *Par ārkārtējās situācijas izsludināšanu [Regarding Declaration of the Emergency Situation].* Cabinet Order No. 103 of 12 March 2020, https://likumi.lv/ta/id/313191-par-arkartejas-situacijas-izsludinasanu [last visited 12 November 2020].

8 *Law on the Suppression of Consequences of the Spread of COVID-19 Infection.* Entry into force: 5 June 2020, https://likumi.lv/ta/id/315287 [last visited 11 November 2020].

9 Administrative detention is a type of administrative sanction that was applied in Latvia until 1 July 2020. With the entry into force of the new Administrative Violations Law, it has been repealed. This sanction was mainly imposed for driving under the influence of alcohol and other addictive substances.

10 *Law on the Suppression of Consequences of the Spread of COVID-19 Infection.* Entry into force: 10 June 2020, https://likumi.lv/ta/en/en/id/315278-law-on-the-management-of-the-spread-of-covid-19-infection [last visited 23 November 2020].

11 *The Sentence Execution Code of Latvia.* Entry into force: 1 April 1971. Section 50.6, part 4.2, https://likumi.lv/ta/en/en/id/90218 [last visited 12 December 2020].

12 *The Constitution of the Republic of Latvia.* Entry into force: 7 November 1922, https://likumi.lv/ta/en/en/id/57980-the-constitution-of-the-republic-of-latvia [last visited 12 November 2020].

13 Latvian Prison Administration, see https://www.europris.org/agency/latvian-prison-administration-lvl/?tab=epis [11 November 2020].

14 Statement of principles relating to the treatment of persons deprived of their liberty in the context of the coronavirus disease (COVID-19) pandemic (2020). European Committee for the Prevention of Torture and Inhuman or Degrading Treatment or Punishment, https://rm.coe.int/16809cfa4b [last visited 10 November 2020].

15 On Emergency Situation and State of Exception. Entry into force: 10 April 2013, https://likumi.lv/ta/en/en/id/255713-on-emergency-situation-and-state-of-exception [last visited 23 November 2020].

16 *Par ārkārtējās situācijas izsludināšanu [Regarding Declaration of the Emergency Situation].* Cabinet Order No. 103 of 12 March 2020, https://likumi.lv/ta/id/313191-par-arkartejas-situacijas-izsludinasanu [last visited 12 November 2020].

17 COVID-19 laws, see https://likumi.lv/ta/tema/covid-19 [last visited 20 October 2020].

18 Regarding Declaration of the Emergency Situation. Cabinet Order No. 655. Adopted 6 November 2020, see https://likumi.lv/ta/en/en/id/318517-regarding-declaration-of-the-emergency-situation [last visited 12 December 2020].

19 Amendments to the Law on the Management of the Spread of COVID-19 Infection, https://titania.saeima.lv/LIVS13/SaeimaLIVS13.nsf/0/74C10BD43ADA54C5C2258625003C9731?OpenDocument#B [last visited 12 December 2020].

20 This special, "short-sharp-shock" sanction of deprivation of liberty is provided for offences, which otherwise could be sentenced with up to five years of imprisonment. It is determined by Section 38, Paragraph 2.1 of the Criminal Law. See *The Criminal Law.* Entry into force: 1 April 1999, https://likumi.lv/ta/en/en/id/88966 [last visited 12 April 2021].

27 Lithuania

Gintautas Sakalauskas

1 Introduction – general situation in the Lithuanian prison system

The most recent report of the European Committee for the Prevention of Torture and Inhuman or Degrading Treatment or Punishment (CPT), issued on 25 June 2019 after its visit on 20–27 April 2018, revealed that the Lithuanian prison system has the same problems as those identified by the CPT in its previous reports (2011, 2014, and 2018). According to the CPT, no substantial changes have been made, particularly regarding the living space of prisoners, violence from other prisoners and officials, and health care. The CPT will return to Lithuania again in 2021.

All prisons of Lithuania were built before the Second World War or immediately after it and no longer meet current needs and human rights standards (Sakalauskas, 2019b, 2020c). Unfortunately, the situation in Lithuanian correctional facilities is one of the worst in the European Union. As a result of a lack of political focus and managerial competence during the last 30 years, the culture of punishment in the Lithuanian prison system, formed during many years of the totalitarian system, has not been brought closer to the standards applicable in Western Europe. To make it more similar to the latter rather than to the prison system of the former Soviet Union, it was and is necessary to introduce major reforms (see further Sakalauskas, 2015, 2020a).

The problems in Lithuanian prisons are systemic and cannot be resolved without a fundamental overhaul of not only the entire prison infrastructure, but also staff training and professional development, thus fundamentally changing the management culture and the quality of relations between staff and prisoners (Sakalauskas, 2020a). There is no doubt, that in the time of the COVID-19 crisis, these difficulties further stimulated tension and confrontation, leading to even greater shortcomings, despite the declining number of prisoners.

At the beginning of 2021, Lithuania again had the highest prison population rate (prisoners per 100,000 residents) in the European Union (Aebi and Tiago, 2020: 6) – 190, despite a remarkable decrease in the last ten years (from 330 prisoners per 100,000 residents at the end of 2011) (see Figure 27.1).

DOI: 10.4324/9781003169178-27

Figure 27.1 shows the stabilisation of numbers of imprisoned persons per 100,000 in Lithuania from 2003 to 2007 (237–245), but the prison population started growing again in 2008–2009. Since 2012, we can see a consistent decrease of the prison population in Lithuania. However, the image of positive trends is deceptive. The dynamic from 2012 to 2018 can be described as the way to normalisation (we can see almost the same prison population in 2003 and 2018). The increase in 2008–2011 was caused by the financial crisis and growing punitiveness. The question of what the main reasons are for trends since 2019 and how long it will continue is very difficult to answer. In 2018, the number of new entries into prison following an arrest or a custodial sentence[1] has once again increased by 27%, compared to 2017 (Figure 27.2). However, in 2019, this number decreased by 25%, reaching the lowest point over the entire period of Lithuania's independence (4,484; the lowest previous number recorded in 2015 was 4,618). In 2020, this number decreased again by 23% (to 3,454), but it is remarkable that almost 300 persons sentenced to an arrest sentence are waiting to serve this sentence and are not included in this total number of entries. Nevertheless, the average length of fixed-term custodial sentences that prisoners have to serve has increased in every year since 2016. At the end of 2020, it was 87 months in comparison to 58 months in 2006 (see further Sakalauskas, 2014, 2019a).

Moderate penal policies have their roots in a consensual and corporatist political culture, in a high level of social trust and political legitimacy, and in a strong welfare state (Lappi-Seppälä, 2011). The high prisoner rate in Lithuania is caused by the frequent imposition of custodial sentences

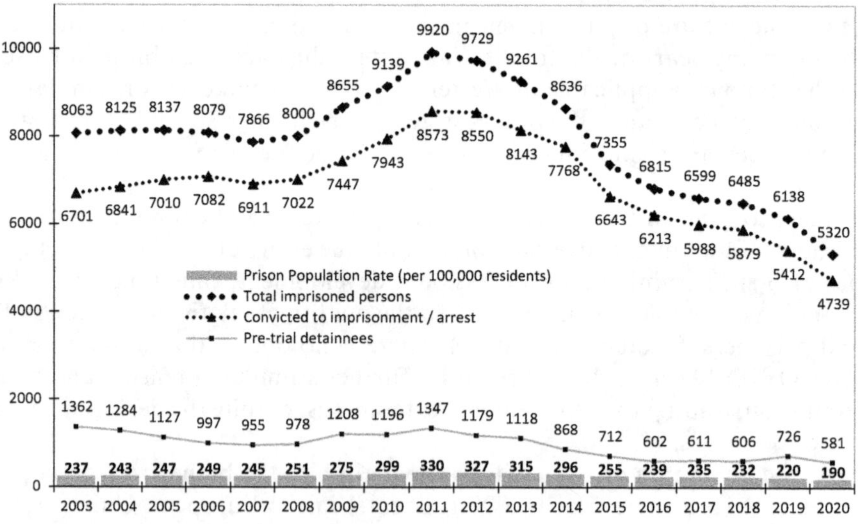

Figure 27.1 Imprisoned persons in Lithuania, 2003–2020 (one-day snapshots at the end of every year).

and further by very long terms of imprisonment (Sakalauskas and Dünkel, 2017). It has proved difficult to change some views about the role and (in-)effectiveness of custodial sentences in the contemporary penal system. A lack of political interest, caused by the expectation of a negative reaction in society, and general indifference to the problems of social integration of prisoners create an unfavourable atmosphere for changes in the penal climate. The large number of prisoners not only shows a highly repressive culture of punishment compared to other EU countries, but also makes it more difficult to ensure human rights and implement the necessary reforms in the prison system.

The former Lithuanian Government (2016–2020) did take some steps towards reform of the prison system and the reduction of the use of imprisonment. On 1 July 2019, the most famous prison in Lithuania, the Lukiškės Prison in the centre of Vilnius (built in 1903), was closed, following national courts and the European Court for Human Rights ordering that prisoners should be paid substantial compensation for poor prison conditions. Almost 600 prisoners have been transferred to other correctional facilities from this prison since January 2019.

On the one hand, depriving this building of its function as a prison was a positive decision, but its immediate closure has caused other problems. After the closure of Lukiškės Prison, the number of prisons in Lithuania decreased by 10%, leading inevitably to shortages of places for prisoners in other prisons. The transfer of prisoners from the Lukiškės Prison was carried out very hastily, without concern for the preparation of the displaced prisoners, as well as the adaptation in the new prisons, which added to

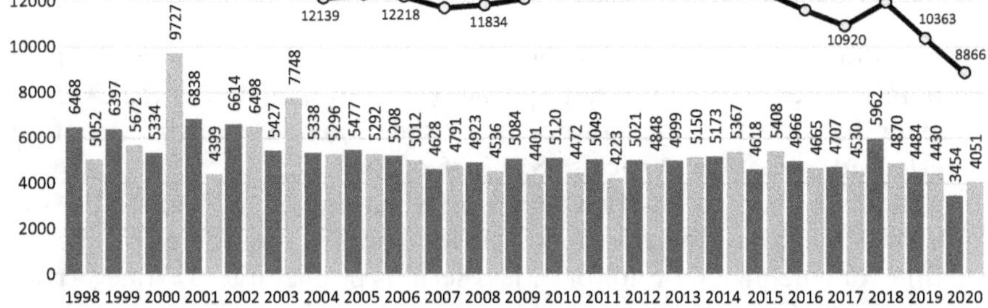

Figure 27.2 Imprisoned persons for a custodial sentence or an arrest sentence in Lithuania 1998–2020 (flow, new entrances and release).

tensions and complaints. The human rights of prisoners were violated during their transfer from Lukiškes Prison, the latest report by the ombudsman of the Lithuanian Parliament concludes. It states that

> most of them were informed about the transfer less than one day before the start of the transfer procedure. There have even been cases when prisoners were not informed about the transfer at all and had only one hour to prepare
>
> (The Baltic Times, 11 November 2019)

The report also draws attention to the fact that the place of residence of the convicted persons or their relatives was not taken into account, potentially hindering possibilities for prisoners to keep in touch with their families. The report also highlights that the prisons that received the transferred prisoners were not prepared to provide them with the opportunity to continue their education or work. In his report, the Parliamentary ombudsman also noted that prisoners were often not provided with an adequate minimum of furniture, as there were cases where not all persons in the cell had enough seats. Moreover, prisoners were forced to wash their clothes in buckets with cold water and dry them in the same cells that also lack proper lighting.

The Parliamentary ombudsman also made recommendations to the Department of Prisons, obliging it to take measures to ensure that prisoners have adequate conditions of detention, hygiene, material and domestic supplies. He also recommended that all transferred prisoners be provided with the opportunity to continue their education and work, thus ensuring appropriate social rehabilitation opportunities for these prisoners. But all these problems remained, in particular with life-sentenced prisoners, who have been distributed to different facilities throughout Lithuania and have to spend their sentences separated from other prisoners.

In 2019–2020, some important changes to the Lithuanian Criminal Code (CC) and the Lithuanian Code of Execution of Penalties (CEP) came into force, prepared by the former Lithuanian Government. One of the main purposes of these changes was to reduce the application of custodial sentences and the prison population. This was done by:

- repealing the possibility to replace an evaded community service sentence or fine sentence with an arrest sentence (Articles 46 and 47 of the CC);
- extension of electronic monitoring by the sentence of restriction of liberty and probation (Articles 48 and 75 of the CC);
- obliging a court to justify its decision when imposing all custodial sentences (including an arrest sentence) for a person prosecuted for the first time for a negligent or minor or less serious premeditated crime (Article 55 of the CC);
- making it possible to suspend an arrest sentence (Article 75 of the CC);

- making it possible to suspend a part of a fixed-term custodial sentence (Article 75 of the CC);
- obliging a court to justify its decision when not suspending custodial sentences, if it was possible to suspend it (Article 75 of the CC);
- making early release possible only on the basis of a decision taken by the commission of release on parole (without necessary approval of a court) for prisoners sentenced for negligent crimes, and for other inmates if the sentence imposed does not exceed four years as well as juveniles after serving one-third of the sentence imposed (Article 157 CEP); and
- providing for automatic early release with obligatory electronic monitoring after serving three-quarters of a sentence imposed, with the exception of high-risk offenders and offenders sentenced for grave and some serious crimes (Article 157 CEP).

It is too early to assess the impact of these innovations. In any case, the two last mentioned reforms have stimulated positive changes: almost 45% of all prisoners released in 2020 (984 of 2,195) were released on parole – the largest number since 2010. The practice of granting conditional release had become even more restrictive after the law reform in 2011, although the opposite was intended. In 2012, 36.5% of all released prisoners were released conditionally, in 2013 only 34.2%, in 2014–2017 only approximately 30%, and in 2018–2019 only approximately 20%, in comparison to 65% in 2003 (see in detail Sakalauskas, 2014: 212–214, 2019a: 246). No doubt, the recent increase in conditional release was the main reason for the decrease in the prison population in 2020. Hopefully, this tendency will be continued in the next years. However, these reforms were not connected with the COVID-19 pandemic; they were just a result of the decisions of the former Government in 2018–2019.

In such a turbulent situation, the Lithuanian prison system met the COVID-19 pandemic with great anxiety about the health of prisoners and staff. The problems of the pandemic had to be faced with old, badly ventilated buildings. Many prisoners were accommodated in large rooms, with dozens of prisoners in one room, creating conditions conducive to the spread of the virus.

2 Prison and penal policy concerning the execution of prison sentences during the COVID-19-induced crisis

The first quarantine to reduce the threat posed by the coronavirus in Lithuania was announced on 16 March 2020. Unfortunately, one of the first steps taken by the Lithuanian Government was to amend the existing law in order to strengthen the criminal and administrative liability for violations of the quarantine regime.

Article 277 of the Lithuanian Criminal Code now defines criminal liability for violation of the regulations governing control of epidemics or contagious diseases. A person who, having been informed by a medical establishment about his illness and warned of the protective measures which he must observe while communicating with people, exposes another person to the danger of becoming infected with a dangerous or an especially contagious disease shall be considered to have committed a crime (previously, a misdemeanour) and shall be punished by a fine or by restriction of liberty or by arrest or by a custodial sentence for a term up to one year (the latter punishment had not been foreseen before). A person who violates the requirements of the legal provisions regulating health care or contagious disease prevention, where this results in the spread of a disease or causes an epidemic, shall be punished by a fine or by a custodial sentence for a term of up to five years, instead of three years as before. By these changes, the sanctions were automatically extended, according to the principle of "more of the same", with a naive hope of making general prevention more effective. In practice, in 2020, just 41 such offences were registered, but nobody was sentenced to imprisonment.

Together with criminal liability also came an increased administrative liability for violation of the quarantine regime. The fines were increased from 250 euros to 1,500 euros for private individuals and from 1,500 to 6,000 euros for heads of legal entities.

In the penal policy concerning the execution of prison sentences, just one exception was introduced – the execution of an arrest sentence was temporarily suspended for three months when the convicted person was not in pre-trial detention and contacted the prison administration in advance requesting that the execution of this sentence be delayed to a later date.

3 Restrictions of contact with the outside world

Quarantine in Lithuanian prisons was ordered on 28 February 2020 by the Director of the Department of Prisons in the Ministry of Justice of the Republic of Lithuania, that is, more than two weeks earlier than in Lithuania as a whole. Almost all contacts with the outside world were prohibited for the next three and a half months (until 17 June 2020). This meant:

- no visits by persons (except meetings with lawyers);
- no mass events inside;
- no prison leave for work, education and rehabilitation, with strict exceptions;
- no short-term prison leave to return home;
- no long-term (day-long) or short-term visits; and
- limited participation in resocialization programs.

The quarantine in Lithuania as a whole was lifted on 16 June 2020, but many restrictions remained in prisons. Only short one-hour visits without contact were allowed, while under normal conditions, visits can continue for up to three hours according to Article 94 CEP. Only after 3 July were four-hour visits allowed and provision was made for one long visit to be replaced by three short visits or five video or telephone calls. Prison leave was only allowed from open prisons and halfway houses. Visits of members of non-governmental organisations and priests were allowed only on an *ad hoc* basis, by permission of a director of the prison. This regulation was in force until 30 October 2020 when the old regulation with total restriction of contacts with the outside world, with the exception of special permission for NGO members and priests, came into force again. The prisoners, who had a right to a short-term visit, could have it replaced by three video or telephone calls.

From 6 March 2021, a short visit of up to one hour has been allowed. However, a prisoner can receive a maximum of two visitors, at least one of whom must be an adult. During the visits, a social distance of at least two meters between persons must be preserved, and all parties must wear respirators or masks that fit snugly and completely cover the nose and mouth. Noteworthy is also that, according to the general requirements of quarantine in Lithuania in force at this time, it is not possible to go to another municipality without justifiable cause: visiting a prisoner is not such a cause. Theoretically therefore, at the time of writing, visits by residents of a municipality other than that where the prison is are still not possible.

4 Restrictions inside prisons

Between 31 July and 30 October 2020, the organisation of sports, cultural events, meetings or other gatherings inside the prison were allowed only if they did not exceed the specified maximum number of participants in the room and/or open space in which they were held.

According to the statistics of the Department of Prisons, during the last 11 months from the beginning of quarantine, 681 prisoners were infected with COVID-19; 613 prisoners recovered fully from COVID-19. Nine infected prisoners were released after serving their sentence, and one infected prisoner died, but this death was not caused by the virus. At the beginning of February 2020, 58 prisoners were ill and 404 were isolated after contacts with ill persons or because they had recently been admitted to prison. There were also 58 staff members who were suffering from COVID-19 and 18 staff members in self-isolation.

A very important question is what kind of processes resulted from the imposition of the quarantine and all these restriction inside the prisons? Over the past 15 years (2004–2019), an average of almost 9 prisoners have committed suicide in Lithuanian prisons each year. This number is 3 times higher than the suicide rate per 100,000 of the general population (25 suicides per 100,000 population), which would be equal to about 80 suicides among a corresponding number of prisoners (Sakalauskas, 2020b: 104). In 2018, this number was half the average of the last 10 years (with four registered prisoner suicides), in 2019 – eight and in 2020 – seven. The number of prisoners with mental disorders due to the use of narcotics or psychotropic substances increased dramatically in 2019 – 1,331, in comparison with 851 in 2018, 791 in 2017, 851 in 2016, 951 in 2015 (one day snapshots at the end of every year). In 2020, this number was 1,035.

The number of crimes registered inside Lithuanian prisons has been increasing dramatically, especially considering the absolute numbers here and the flow of prisoners decreasing until 2018. This number was the highest in 2020. The number of registered crimes inside prison is more than four times higher than in Lithuania in general. In 2020, there were 166 registered crimes per 10,000 residents in the wider population, while in Lithuanian prisons, if one uses the same ratio, there were 671.[2] The majority of registered offences in prison relate to illegal drugs (72.6% in 2020). However, relatively high levels of violence are also recorded. These numbers are known not to represent the real situation due to a high dark figure.

5 Compensatory measures

No measures were introduced to compensate prisoners for the additional restrictions required by the COVID-19 pandemic, except for the possibility of replacing the short visits with video or telephone calls. There is no research about the practice, but probably video calls were mostly impossible because of lack of equipment and the bad internet connection in prisons. There was one report by the Parliamentary ombudsman, where he encouraged the administration of prisons to ensure that prisoners could maintain good contact with their relatives, but the effectiveness of this report is doubtful.

6 Legal basis for restrictions and relaxations of the prison regime

Restrictions and relaxations of the prison regime can only be introduced through orders of the director of the Department of Prisons, who follows the decisions taken by the Lithuanian Government.

7 Returning to normal

The Lithuanian prison system needs strategic decisions and systemic changes that go beyond what is required to deal with the pandemic and its aftermath. It is notable that, for the past 16 years, each new Lithuanian Government adopted several programmes, the implementation of which should have considerably improved the infrastructure of detention facilities and incarceration conditions, but essentially nothing has been changed (Čepas and Sakalauskas, 2010: 206; Sakalauskas, 2020a; 2020b; 2020c).

The new Lithuanian Government (2020–2024) has also indicated a willingness to introduce some key new initiatives. It wants to have “a clear vision of penal institutions”. Together with experts, it will develop a clear vision and a plan for reforming penal institutions. In its words:

> We need to identify what the structure and decisions of our penal institutions should look like in the long run. Making use of best practices and models from other countries, as well as with the help of experts in the field, we will assess not only the current but also the planned need for buildings and officers based on the actual and projected number of persons serving prison sentences, and will develop a plan for reorganisation of penal institutions.
>
> (Programme of the Eighteenth Government of the Republic of Lithuania, 2020: 78)

The Government will expand the network of open and semi-open prisons, review and improve programmes for resocialisation and work with offenders, which will ensure proper preparation for their return to society and help address the problem of reimprisonment. Officials and staff of penal institutions must have methodological support, professional training opportunities, information on risk assessment and management, and opportunities to improve their motivation, develop values and strengthen internal communication. In cooperation with experts in the field, the Government will review the principles and content of management and supervision of penal institutions, and will regulate the status of officials and staff of penal institutions in accordance with the best practices of the Member States of the European Union. According to the new Lithuanian Government:

> in line with the case law of the European Court of Human Rights and the recommendations of the Council of Europe, we will ensure that imprisonment conditions of sentenced persons do not threaten human dignity, and that great attention is paid to a good atmosphere and maintaining of humane interpersonal relations. We will seek increased occupation of persons serving imprisonment sentences, thus preparing them for life after they serve their sentence. We will provide institutions with modern technologies, thus ensuring security and order, and greater efficiency in the work of officials. We will pay special attention to readiness of penal institutions to meet challenges of the pandemic, and will strive to ensure the safety of officials, staff, prisoners, and the public, as well as implementation of the rights of prisoners.
>
> (Programme of the Eighteenth Government of the Republic of Lithuania, 2020: 78)

Lithuania also needs completely new prison buildings; the old ones must be closed. New facilities could help to create a new culture, as they would have the right infrastructure, staff-friendly working conditions. Partial upgrading of certain sectors of old institutions would not address infrastructure issues.

> The reformed system of penal institutions has to ensure that prison conditions meet standards, that the number of complaints from prisoners

is reduced, and that the problem of reimprisonment is addressed. It is important to ensure that the purpose of sentencing is implemented in practice, and not just formally, and to improve the preparation of prisoners to return to society. With a view to balancing the system of sentences, and their criminal and administrative effects, an ex post facto evaluation of the relevant legislation is needed.

At the beginning of 2021, the Department of Prisons in the Ministry of Justice of the Republic of Lithuania presented a Concept for the Reform of Prisoners' Resocialisation. This concept deals with different topics of prisoners' resocialisation, beginning with education and competence of staff, separation and differentiation of prisoners, staff structure, supervision and reflection on professional experience, the role of NGO's and volunteers, education and employment of prisoners, importance of prison leave, and ends with a section about criminological research in the prison system. Hopefully, it can be a document that leads to real transformation and the emergence of a more humane prison system in Lithuania.

Notes

1 According to Article 49 of the Lithuanian Criminal Code, arrest means a short-term jail sentence, imposed for a period of from 15 up to 90 days for a crime and from 10 to 45 days for a misdemeanour, served under strict conditions in cells. A fixed-term custodial sentence may be imposed for a period of from three months up to 20 years, and if a new crime is committed before a sentence for the previous crime has been fully served, a custodial sentence of up to 25 years may be imposed (Article 50 of the CC). Life imprisonment shall be imposed by a court in the cases provided for in the Special Part of the Criminal Code (Article 51 of the CC).

2 Calculating for 8,866 inmates (flow) in 2020 (see Figure 27.1).

References

Aebi, M. F., and Tiago, M. M. (2020): *Prisons and Prisoners in Europe in Pandemic Times: An Evaluation of the Medium-term Impact of the COVID-19 on Prison Populations*. Strasbourg: Council of Europe.

Čepas, A., and Sakalauskas, G. (2010): Lithuania. In: Newman, R. G., Aebi, M. F., and Jaquier, V. (Eds.): *Crime and Punishment around the World. Europe*. Vol. 4. Santa Barbara: ABC-CLIO, 197–207.

Lappi-Seppälä, T. (2011): Explaining Imprisonment in Europe. *European Journal of Criminology* 8(4), 303–328.

Programme of the Eighteenth Government of the Republic of Lithuania. Approved by Resolution No XIV-72 of the Seimas of the Republic of Lithuania of 11 December 2020. https://lrv.lt/uploads/main/documents/files/PROGRAMME%20OF%20THE%20EIGHTEENTH%20GOVERNMENT%20OF%20THE%20REPUBLIC%20OF%20LITHUANIA.pdf

Sakalauskas, G. (2014): Lithuania. In: Drenkhahn, K., Dudeck, M., and Dünkel, F. (Eds.): *Long-Term Imprisonment*. London and New York: Routledge, 198–217.

Sakalauskas, G. (2015): Strafvollzug in Litauen: Blick zurück oder nach vorne? *Neue Kriminalpolitik* 27, 190–201.

Sakalauskas, G., and Dünkel, F. (2017): Kriminalpolitik und Sanktionspraxis in Litauen im europäischen Vergleich. *Monatsschrift für Kriminologie und Strafrechtsreform* 100, 103–122.

Sakalauskas, G. (2019a): Criminal policy and imprisonment. The case of Lithuania: open prisons, prison leave and release on parole. In: van Kempen, P. H. P., and Jendly, M. M. (Eds.): *Overuse in the Criminal Justice System*. Cambridge, Antwerp, Chicago: Intersentia, 229–249.

Sakalauskas, G. (2019b): Prisoner resettlement in Lithuania – Between Soviet tradition and challenges of modern society. In: Dünkel, F., I. Pruin, I., A. Storgaard, A. and Weber, J. (Eds.): *Prisoner Resettlement in Europe*. Routledge: London, New York, 219–239.

Sakalauskas, G. (2020a): Conditions of imprisonment and premises for social integration of prisoners. Summary. In: Sakalauskas, G., Jarutienė, L., Kalpokas, V. and Vaičiūnienė, R. (Eds.): *Kalinimo sąlygos ir kalinių socialinės prielaidos*. Vilnius: Lietuvos teisės institutas, 434–456.

Sakalauskas, G. (2020b): Prisons. In: *Human Rights in Lithuania 2018–2019*. Vilnius: Human Rights Monitoring Institute, 104–108.

Sakalauskas, G. (2020c): Wie überwindet man den Totalitarismus im Strafvollzug? In: Drenkhahn, K. et al. (Eds.): *Kriminologie und Kriminalpolitik im Dienste der Menschenwürde. Festschrift für Frieder Dünkel zum 70. Geburtstag*. Mönchengladbach: Forum Verlag Godesberg, 909–926.

The Baltic Times (2019): *Prisoners' Rights Violated during Lukiskes Prison Eviction – Lithuanians Parliamentary Ombudsman*. https://www.baltictimes.com/prisoners__rights_violated_during_lukiskes_prison_eviction___lithuanian_partl_ombudsman/.

28 The Netherlands

Jolande uit Beijerse and Miranda Boone

1 Introduction: the general situation in Dutch prisons

In the Netherlands, approximately 11,000 offenders and suspects are held in closed institutions: 9,100 persons in 28 prisons, 1,330 persons in nine forensic psychiatric centres and 450 young and young adult persons in 6 juvenile detention centres. In addition, 825 young people are held in closed youth-care facilities as a measure of protection, and 400 people without a legal permit to remain in the Netherlands in centres for immigration detention.[1] In this chapter, we restrict ourselves to the first three forms of deprivation of liberty, which are related to a criminal sanction.

While, from a historical point of view, the Netherlands was well known for its very low prison population (Downes, 1988), the size of the prison population in the Netherlands has fluctuated significantly in recent decades. Between 1990 and 2005, the prison population rate doubled from 46 prisoners per 100,000 inhabitants to 94 per 100,000 in 2005. From 2005 to 2016, the number decreased again to 52, a reduction of 46%, although since 2016, the number of prisoners has again grown slightly. Boone et al. point out that the decrease to 2016 cannot be attributed to one single factor. While the decline in the number of crimes seems to be an important factor, it is clear that the sentencing decisions of the courts cannot be overlooked: the number of prison sentences has decreased, but the average prison sentence length has been reduced too. In how far these tendencies can be explained by the fact that fewer serious crimes were committed, or the courts became less punitive, or because less serious crimes were brought before the court, is, as yet, unclear (Boone, Pakes and van Wingerden, 2020).

It is clear, however, that the reduction of the prison population did not go hand in hand with a milder penal climate. The decline went together with the increase of the maximum term of determinate prison sentences from 20 to 30 years; the increase of maximum terms for many offences, the introduction of very intrusive anti-terrorism laws and the continuation of a policy towards inmates serving life sentences that is uniquely harsh in Europe (Boone and van Swaaningen, 2013).

DOI: 10.4324/9781003169178-28

2 Prison and penal policy concerning the execution of prison sentences during the COVID-19-induced crisis

After the emergence of COVID-19, the Dutch policy was characterised by a series of consecutive measures that remained in force for short periods. The measures, specifically aimed at prisons, forensic psychiatric centres and juvenile detention centres, were announced in a series of "policy letters" (notices) of the Minister for Legal Protection to the Prison Service. The Minister for Legal Protection is a new function since 2017. It is a minister without a portfolio, who operates next to the Minister of Justice and Security and the State Secretary of Justice and Security under the Ministry of Justice and Security.

On 13 March 2020, measures effective until 30 March were announced.[2] On 2 April 2020, the measures were extended until 28 April 2020.[3] A further policy letter of 14 April 2020 was a response to an anonymous letter sent to the Minister for Legal Protection by a number of concerned prison officers.[4] On 29 May 2020, a relaxation of the measures was announced,[5] with a further extension announced on 15 June[6] and an update of the situation given on 26 June.[7] On 6 October, a tightening of the measures was announced.[8] In addition, the Minister of Justice and Security, the Minister for Legal Protection and the State Secretary of Justice and Security sent more general letters in which the consequences of the measures for inmates were mentioned. The letter of 15 March 2020 noted that despite the fact that the courts were closed, cases in which the judge had to decide on the extension of pre-trial detention were still being heard.[9] A letter of 23 April 2020 proposed that the transport of detainees to the courts should be restricted as much as possible in order to prevent the risk of infection.[10] The letters of 25 June[11] and 18 September[12] dealt specifically with the backlog caused by the measures.

On 13 March 2020, the Minister for Legal Protection announced that, in order to avoid infection and deal with bottlenecks in staffing, the new intake of two groups of prisoners had been stopped:

1. those guilty of minor offences and with short sentences who were waiting for the execution of their sentence, and
2. persons serving default detention because of not having paid a fine or not having finished community service.

The execution of these sentences was postponed. However, from July, the first group began to be called to report to prison so that their sentences could be executed. With regard to the second group, it was revealed that due to miscommunication within the police, many fine defaulters were still being brought to prison. Because the group consists mainly of homeless people, people with mental disorders who do not always adhere to hygiene rules, the risk of infection from this group is high (De Korte, 2020). Although not explicitly related to the pandemic, it is interesting that a motion was accepted recently by the Lower House of Parliament to research the possibility of creating a legal basis to replace fine default detention with community punishment.[13]

The Minister for Legal Protection also announced the suspension of the execution of the prison sentences of the restricted group of inmates who, during the last phase of their prison sentence, stay in prisons with very limited security, while working outside and spending weekend nights at home. The rationale for that was to restrict the daily movements from and to prison as much as possible. These inmates were granted a longer period of leave combined with electronic monitoring. By 2 April 2020, the number of prisoners with electronic monitoring had increased from 700 to 900. On 14 April 2020, the Minister for Legal Protection announced that, as a result of these measures, the capacity utilised in the prisons had decreased from over 98% to 85%, which allowed more prisoners to be held in single cells. By 22 June 2020, the percentage of prisoners, staying in double cells, had been reduced from 30 to 12%. Due to the various measures to reduce the prison population, the overall imprisonment rate dropped from 57.3 on 31 March 2020 to 52.3 per 100,000 on 15 September 2020, a decline of 8.8% (see Aebi and Tiago, 2020: 7).

3 Restrictions of contacts with the outside world

The Dutch prison system is based on the rehabilitative ideal. The principle of social reintegration is enshrined in substantive penal and penitentiary laws. This principle requires a system of a graduated relaxation of the prison regime, including regular prison leave and the transfer to more open prisons, at least in the last stage of executing prison sentences (Boone and uit Beijerse, 2019). A drastic measure was that from 14 March 2020 all outstanding options for leave as well as visits were suspended, except for visits of parents and legal aid providers to juveniles and visits necessary in order to advance the criminal procedure (De Korte, 2020). Transport to the court was restricted to cases in which the judge decided that the defendant should be present, or the defendant wanted to be present. For pre-trial detainees, hearings in open court were mostly replaced by video-hearings, a change that needed a significant extension of the infrastructure in prisons. From 2 April 2020, visits of parents and legal aid providers to juveniles were also suspended, except for very special cases for which the director could give permission under specific conditions. This was necessary because when walking to and from the visiting areas, it often proved impossible to maintain a distance of 1.5 metres.

On 2 June 2020, visits and leave were restarted in forensic psychiatric centres and juvenile detention centres. Forensic psychiatric detainees could receive one visitor for one hour per week and juvenile detainees could receive a maximum of two parents or legal guardians for one hour per week. The Minister for Legal Protection emphasised the pedagogical importance of contact with the parents or legal aid providers and the limited risk of infection for juveniles. Plexiglas separated detainees and their visitors and visitors had to complete a questionnaire before the visit to test for signs that could indicate that they might be infected by the coronavirus. Receiving visitors behind Plexiglas appears to have been particularly frustrating for fathers due to the lack of physical contact with their children (Verhagen, Janssen and Claes, 2020).

Detainees in forensic psychiatric centres and juvenile detention centres were also allowed a maximum of two hours of supervised leave once a week as a part of their supervision plan, if this was in the interest of their reintegration. The supervising staff member had to identify whether and how the offender was adhering to the guidelines. If necessary, they could be quarantined if they had not complied with the guidelines. Prison visits were only restarted on a trial basis in three pilot prisons for one hour per week to examine how visits could be conducted in an orderly and safe manner with a distance of 1.5 metres. Here, too, visitors were separated by Plexiglas and had to fill in a questionnaire. Prisoners could only obtain an incidental leave in exceptional situations, such as attending a funeral of a family member. The Minister for Legal Protection justified the broader arrangement for detainees in forensic psychiatric centres and juvenile detention facilities on the basis that for these detainees, visits and leave are part of their treatment and thus contribute to a safe and controlled return to society. In contrast, in prisons, the essence of the punishment is the deprivation of liberty, not the treatment. Another argument was that prisons are bigger and have a larger population with more incoming and outgoing movements that required more preparation to ensure protection against infection.

From 15 June 2020, detainees in the forensic psychiatric centres and juvenile detention centres could receive visitors for two hours a week and juvenile detainees could also receive visitors other than parents or legal guardians. An exception was made for one specific youth institution due to infections among employees.

Because the first experiences in the three pilot prisons were positive, the Minister for Legal Protection announced that from 15 June 2020 all prisoners could receive one visitor for one hour per week who could bring one child up to four years old, if the child sat on the visitor's lap. Incidental leave was no longer limited to funerals, but was also possible for examination or study purposes. On 26 June 2020, the Minister reported that 19 of the 27 prisons met the conditions for safe visits. From 30 June, both the duration of visits and the duration of unaccompanied leave were extended again in forensic psychiatric centres and juvenile detention centres, while more targeted activities could be undertaken during these leaves, such as shopping or visiting the municipal social service in preparation for release. From 1 August 2020, children of all ages could visit their incarcerated parent.

From 6 October 2020, visitors were urged to wear a facial mask and the options for unaccompanied leave were restricted again. Only targeted unaccompanied leave for purposes of rehabilitation (such as work and education) continued and unaccompanied leave not directly aimed at rehabilitation was suspended.

4 Restrictions inside prisons

Apart from restrictions regarding contacts with the outside world, incoming detainees were screened for symptoms of COVID-19 and tested if the Health Service saw reason to do so. This admission process, in terms of which prisoners were put in quarantine for 14 days after arrival, in a section, which was equipped to deal with COVID infections, was considered one of the most important measures in the fight against the coronavirus. From August, the period of quarantine changed from 14 days to 8 days. The Council for Criminal Law Enforcement and Youth Protection (CCY) criticised this measure and pointed out that if new detainees were tested upon admission, they could participate in the day programme earlier and avoid unnecessary isolation (RSJ. 2020).

During these eight days as well as afterwards, new inmates were continuously monitored for COVID-19-related symptoms. In accordance with the policy of the Health Service, detainees with COVID-19-related symptoms were isolated in their own cells. After some weeks, it was reported that inmates were refusing to mention health problems because they were afraid of being isolated in their own cells. Because the staff must be able to identify inmates and assess their state of mind based on their facial expressions, detainees were not obliged to wear a mask. The director of a penitentiary could, however, exceptionally advise, order or forbid detainees to wear a face mask. Employees use them in specific situations, for instance, when a room is searched, or when coming into contact with an inmate with a suspected infection.

Despite the high risk of mutual infection, the double person cells were still used in order to create room to place detainees in a one-person cell in case of a suspected infection. According to the Minister for Legal Protection, the maximum was done to follow the guideline of keeping a distance of 1.5 metres inside the prisons and even in double cells, although this seemed to be quite a challenge in practice. A director of a penitentiary noted, based on personal experience, that it is not easy to maintain hygiene measures in a community where many inmates show behavioural problems, are addicted or have mild intellectual disabilities (Molleman, 2020). The CCY commented in its Advice that the use of double cells is irresponsible at the time of the pandemic, as it is logically impossible to keep a distance of 1.5 metres in a double cell (RS, 2020).

From 2 April, the Minister for Legal Protection emphasised that the most fundamental rights, such as the right to food, to medication and to spend 30 minutes in the open air twice daily, would not be affected, but that, if necessary, the detainees' daily programme could be curtailed. Because activities were offered in smaller groups, in some penitentiaries, the right to sport was reduced to once, instead of twice, 45 minutes per week and the duration of the weekly visit to the library was halved (De Korte, 2020). In June 2020, the director of a penitentiary noted mounting frustration. There were more confrontations and more kicking against cell doors and tapping on radiators. In addition to boredom and frustration with the more limited programme, a probable explanation is that because of limited visits the availability of drugs was diminished, which put extra pressure on the relationships between prisoners (Molleman, 2020).

With respect to that issue, concerned prison officers sent an anonymous letter to the Minister for Legal Protection in which they suggested, among others, providing inmates with soft drugs to keep them calm. Especially in the period that visits and leave were cancelled, drugs were needed more than ever, but could not be smuggled in anymore. On 13 April 2020, there was an uprising in the penitentiary of Lelystad: as a protest against restrictions in the day programme, 36 detainees barricaded themselves in the kitchen. After two hours of negotiation, the internal assistance team forced the entrance door, used pepper spray and took each of the 36 inmates in handcuffs to their cells. Six of them, who were considered the instigators, received a disciplinary sentence of 14-day solitary confinement in another penitentiary.[14] On 14 April 2020, the Minister downgraded this to "an incident that involved six inmates". According to him, it had to be judged in the light of the big impact of the measures and the reduction of the daily programme as a result of the high absenteeism rate among employees. In reaction to the anonymous letter of the prison staff, he simply stated that drugs were not allowed inside, ignoring the implicit signal of the prison staff that under normal circumstances inmates get their drugs from visitors and that it is a means to stay calm.

5 Compensatory measures

The restrictions in visits and prison leave were compensated by wider possibilities for contact by telephone and, where possible, by communications software on a secure computer tablet. A prison director noted that this possibility would not have arisen, had there not been a pandemic, and that it could well be that this means of communication continues to be used after the coronavirus crisis. Better security was needed to prevent abuse or continuation of criminal acts (De Korte, 2020). Within a week, 400 tablets were available. At the end of June, there were 850 tablets for 8,500 detainees. However, research in six penitentiaries showed that digital communication got off to a very slow start and that in mid-April, there were still few or no opportunities for contact between imprisoned fathers and their children. There were tablets, but it took time to arrange the logistics and to make safety decisions. In the Vught penitentiary, it took three months to do so. In various penitentiaries, there were also too few tablets to meet the demand, which meant that the duration of calls had to be limited (Verhagen, Janssen and Claes, 2020).

To compensate for the restrictions surrounding visits, on 2 April, the Minister for Legal Protection granted extra call credit to allow detainees to phone for longer than guaranteed by the penitentiary legislation. To compensate for the limitations of visiting through Plexiglas, various penitentiaries purchased toys that a child who had visited their father could take home afterwards. Some penitentiaries also asked mothers to film activities of their children and e-mail them to the penitentiary, so that fathers could remain involved with their children. This had a side-effect that beautiful conversations originated about parenting. When the facilities for video calling are working, it is commonly experienced as a valuable addition to the opportunities for personal contact with friends or family, even while they are abroad. For example, some fathers could see their children's rooms for the first time and so got a better picture of their child's life, which increased their involvement (Verhagen, Janssen and Claes, 2020). On 15 June, the Minister concluded that the possibilities that had been created for digital visits turned out to be so satisfying that they remained available in addition to regular visits.

Furthermore, the Minister for Legal Protection encouraged initiatives at a local level to keep the situation manageable and safe. In practice, inmates were offered extra time outside the cells to cook. In many penitentiaries, staff brought games, puzzles, DVDs and magazines to keep the prisoners busy. Inmates sent postcards to nursing homes to express their sympathy and made face masks in the workrooms. To send a tangible signal home, inmates could have a Polaroid photo made of themselves with a written message (Molleman, 2020). The newspapers reported that inmates of the penitentiary of Leeuwarden were making "thank you"-cards to send to homes for elderly people, the fire department and the police department, and also published pictures of a big banner that inmates in the Zaanstad penitentiary had made. The banner was displayed outside the penitentiary where it could be seen by the public and carried the words "Wij blijven binnen, u ook?", which can be translated as "We stay inside, you too?".

Inmates could participate in court hearings through a video connection, between the penitentiary and the court, if such equipment was available. Several penitentiaries, however, lacked such facilities, especially juvenile detention centres. Normally, juvenile defendants are obliged to be present at a court session. On 23 April 2020, the Minister for Legal Protection reported that for each penitentiary, at least one tele-hearing room had been set up, or a video conference facility was made available. In the short term, additional equipment would be placed at the locations with the biggest need. A director of a penitentiary said that in his institution, this facility had been available for four years already, but the courts were never really interested in using it. However, since the pandemic the courts were lining up to use it and he expected that this form of hearing would continue to be used after the coronavirus pandemic (De Korte, 2020).

On 23 April 2020, the Minister for Legal Protection announced that for the longer term, organisations like the Probation Service would be connected to correctional institutions by expanding their technical facilities. On 6 October, the Minister stated that visits to the Probation Service, psychologists and psychiatrists who have to report on a suspect, also had to take place digitally as much as possible. He also preferred contact with defence lawyers to be digital, unless the lawyer or inmate insisted on face-to-face contact. According to a director of a penitentiary, defence lawyers increasingly used the telephone instead of paying visits to their clients (De Korte, 2020). A defence lawyer reported in the newspapers that the rules leave room for different interpretations, and every prison director deals differently with the extent to which they allow defence lawyers to enter the prison.[15]

6 Legal basis for restrictions and relaxations of the prison regime

The measures that have been taken have major consequences for the detainees and entail a restriction of the Penitentiary Principles Act. The Minister for Legal Protection thought that this was justified in view of the need for protection because COVID-19 can have major consequences for staff and detainees due to the closed nature of a judicial institution.

The Penitentiary Principles Act provides several ways for prisoners to have a say in the affairs of the penitentiary where they are held or to complain about the decisions made against them. The law prescribes that the director must ensure regular consultation with detainees on matters that directly affect their detention. Normally, the director has monthly meetings with a designated inmate committee, but during the pandemic, some directors chose to contact the inmates at least twice a week. One director reported that he chose to consult the inmates who work as cleaners, because these inmates usually have a lot of influence on the wing and move across the entire institution. This significantly improved information exchange. He stated that this new form of communication would probably be continued after the pandemic (De Korte, 2020).

Dutch penitentiary law also offers the right to complain to an independent complaint committee of the supervisory committee of the prison, forensic psychiatric centre or juvenile detention centre, as well as a right to appeal to a national committee of appeal of the CCY. The supervisory committees have an advisory as well as a judicial function in mediating and handling complaints. In the first months of the coronavirus pandemic, the number of complaints fell. A director of a prison believed that this was due to the general understanding of the necessity of the measures (De Korte, 2020). This decline can, however, also be the result of the fact that the members of this supervisory committee no longer physically entered the penitentiaries. Face-to-face meetings of the committee with the director were replaced by more frequent contact by telephone between the chairperson of the committee and the director. The personal visits of the monthly delegate of the supervisory committee to the penitentiaries, aiming to mediate between the prison director and complaining prisoners, were also replaced by contact by (video)phone. In addition, there was a stricter assessment of the necessity of handling the complaints via a hearing, while the hearing itself was conducted digitally.[16] The CCY in its Advice strongly recommended the renewal of the face-to-face contacts with the members of the supervisory committees as soon as possible, because of its importance for the legal protection of detainees. However, the Council supported the further development of the use of digital means to hear those involved (RSJ, 2020).

In addition, to complaining at the supervisory board of the prison, both the prisoner and the prison director can appeal against the decision of a supervisory board at the Appeal Board of the CCY. The board made some important mitigations to the general policy described above. Against the general policy to suspend all prison leave, incidental leave and temporarily interruptions of prison sentences due to personal circumstances that require the prisoner's leave, the board ruled that such leave always remained possible. In particular, requests for leave to say farewell to a terminally ill family member, were granted several times, even when the pandemic was at its peak (RSJ 1 May 2020, R-20/6593/GV; RSJ 2 June 2020, R-20/7049/GV). Even an appeal against a decision to deny a general leave was considered to be well founded, because the applicant had had a personal reason for his request and would not return to the institution after his leave, since the sentence would be further executed in an extra-mural penitentiary programme (RSJ 17 July 2020, S-20/3996/SGA). Requests of prisoners for temporary interruption of their sentence because of their vulnerable health were seriously considered, although no such request has yet been granted (RSJ 22 May 2020, R-20/6826/GV; RSJ 2 June 2020, R-20/6865/GV). The Appeal Board seems to be less principled with regard to the use of double cells. Although the Board strongly rejected the use of double cells during the pandemic in its first decisions (RSJ 29 April 2020, S-20/3503/SGA), it became more flexible at a later stage. As long as the additional health risks were limited or the situation made these risks acceptable (no infections in the prison, for example, or no signs of infection of the roommate), using double cells was considered to be acceptable (RSJ, 18 May 2020, S-20/3627/SGA; RSJ 14 May 2020, S-20/3576/SGA). Therefore, although the use of double cells is irresponsible according to the Advisory Division of the CCY, the Appeal Board found it acceptable under certain conditions.

7 Returning to normal

Six months after the start of the crisis, the CCY concluded that despite the understanding and acceptance of restrictive measures directly after the outbreak, the measures also led to unrest, dissatisfaction and feelings of insecurity among inmates and staff. Another consequence of the measures was that detainees became more isolated than usual by the temporary suspension of visits and leave, the limitation of mutual contact in the institution or clinic and the limitation or exclusion of lawyers from the institution or clinic. According to the Council, the measures that were – and for some still are – in force are sometimes at odds with the legal framework and individual interests of detainees (RSJ, 2020).

The Health and Youth Inspectorate concluded that the number of COVID-19 infections among inmates had remained relatively low. From March to early September 2020, 14 prison inmates, six people in forensic psychiatric centres and three inmates in juvenile detention centres were infected. The general conclusion is that the measures within the institutions have proved effective, although in January 2021 the numbers were rising rapidly in at least some prisons.

The most pressing danger is that some measures may be maintained after the pandemic. We observed a similar response after an earlier crisis (Boone, 2006). From the perspective of efficiency and order, limiting the contact with the outside world can be very appealing to prison directors and policy makers. The strong legal position and scale of the right to complaint of prisoners in the Netherlands has often been criticised as well. However, two independent studies showed that it was not possible to restrict the right to complaint without hollowing out the whole system (van Goudoever-Herbschleb, 1994; Bleichrodt, 2012). We fear that the relatively smooth cooperation of detainees with the restrictive measures and the lack of visible drawbacks will be used as an argument to further restrict detainees in the future.

However, the crisis offers opportunities as well. Verhagen, Janssen and Claes express the wish to address the COVID-19 crisis, in accordance with the original Latin meaning of the word crisis, as a turning point in implementing the Council of Europe recommendation concerning children with imprisoned parents[17] and putting children's interests first, for example, by expanding the possibilities for video calling (Verhagen, Janssen and Claes, 2020).

Notes

1 Website DJI, infographic Dit is DJI, juli 2020: 70558-Infographic_DitIsDJI_HR.
2 Minister for Legal Protection 13/3/2020, *Kamerstukken II*, 2019/20, 24587/25295, nr.763.
3 Minister for Legal Protection 2/4/2020, *Kamerstukken II*, 2019/20, 24587/25295, nr.765.
4 Minister for Legal Protection 14/4/2020, *Kamerstukken II*, 2019/20, 24587/25295, nr.767.
5 Minister for Legal Protection 29/5/2020, *Kamerstukken II*, 2019/20, 24587/25295, nr.768.
6 Minister for Legal Protection 15/6/2020, *Kamerstukken II*, 2019/20, 24587/25295, nr.771.
7 Minister for Legal Protection 26/6/ 2020, Verzoek update situatie gevangeniswezen tijdens corona.
8 Minister for Legal Protection 6/10/2020, *Kamerstukken II*, 2019/20, 24587/25295, nr.784.

9 Minister of Justice and Security, Minister for Legal Protection and the State Secretary of Justice and Security 15/3/2020, *Kamerstukken II*, 2019/20, 25295, nr.114.
10 Minister of Justice and Security, Minister for Legal Protection and the State Secretary of Justice and Security 23/4/2020, *Kamerstukken II*, 2019/20, 25295, nr.126.
11 Minister of Justice and Security and Minister for Legal Protection 25/6/2020, *Kamerstukken II*, 2019/20, 29297, nr.601.
12 Minister of Justice and Security and Minister for Legal Protection 18/9/2020, *Kamerstukken II*, 2019/20, 29297, nr.614.
13 *Kamerstukken II*, 2029-2020, 24587, nr. 779.
14 website DJI, voorvallen DJI april 2020: https://www.dji.nl/themas-cijfers-en-publicaties/voorvallen-dji/voorvallen-dji.aspx?select=2&q=&df=01-01-0001&dt=31-12-9999&dctermsType=&kw=&dl=False&SortBy=Datum.
15 Volkskrant 13 mei 2020 Oud-gevangenisdirecteur: 'Coronamisstanden in gevangenissen, gedetineerden worden monddood gemaakt' (*Corona-abuses in prisons: detainees are silenced*).
16 Handreiking KBG CvT's in coronatijdperk (commissievantoezicht.nl).
17 Council of Europe, Recommendation CM/Rec(2018)5 of the Committee of Ministers to Member States concerning children with imprisoned parents (Adopted by the Committee of Ministers on 4 April 2018).

References

Aebi, M. F. and Tiago, M. M. (2020): *Prisons and Prisoners in Europe in Pandemic Times: An Evaluation of the Medium-term Impact of the COVID-19 on Prison Populations*. Strasbourg: Council of Europe.

Bleichrodt, F. W. (2012): *Toenemend appel. Een verkennend onderzoek naar de toename van het aantal beroepszaken ex. Artikel 69 van de Penitentiaire beginselenwet (Growing appeals. An exploratory study of the growth in the number of appeal cases ex. Art. 69 of the Penitentiary Principles Act)*. Rotterdam: Erasmus School of Law.

Boone, M. (2006): De noodwet drugskoeriers als proeftuin voor een grootschalige versobering van het gevangeniswezen (The Emergency Act Drugs Couriers as a testing ground for large-scale austerity in the prison system). *PROCES* 4, 140–153.

Boone, M., Pakes, F., and van Wingerden, S. (2020): Explaining the collapse of the prison population in the Netherlands: Testing the theories. *European Journal of Criminology* 17, 1–18.

Boone, M. and uit Beijerse, J. (2019): Prisoner resettlement in the Netherlands: Great initiatives for too few people. In: Dünkel, F. et al. (Eds.): *Prisoner Resettlement in Europe*. Oxon: Routledge, 240–251.

Boone, M. M. and van Swaaningen, R. (2013): Regression to the mean: Punishment in the Netherlands. In: Ruggiero, V., and Ryan, M. (Eds.): *Punishment in Europe. A Critical Anatomy of Penal Systems*. Basingstoke: Palgrave Macmillan, 9–32.

De Korte, A.J. (2020): De coronacrisis in het gevangeniswezen (The coronacrisis in prison). *Sancties* 31, 176–178.

Downes, D. (1988): *Contrasts in Tolerance*. Oxford: Clarendon Press.

Molleman, T. (2020): De gevangenis in tijden van een pandemie (Prison in times of a pandemic). *Sancties* 32, 179–182.

RSJ (2020): *Advies coronamaatregelen* (Advice corona measures). Den Haag: DJI.

Van Goudoever-Herbschleb, M. (1994): Zij mogen niet klagen (They are not allowed to complain). *Delikt en Delinkwent* 25(3), 233–243.

Verhagen, A. C. J., Janssen, J. H. L. J., and Claes, B. (2020): Herstel de relatie tussen gedetineerde ouder en kind – juist in tijden van COVID-19 (Restore the relation of the detained parent and child-in particular in times of COVID-19). *Sancties* 77, 344–351.

29 New Zealand*

Alice Mills

1 Introduction – general situation of the prison system

New Zealand is well known to be a punitive jurisdiction and has the seventh highest rate of incarceration in the OECD at 188 per 100,000 population (World Prison Brief, 2020). In June 2020, the prison population stood at 9,469, of which 6.6% were women and almost 6% were over 60 years old. All but one of the 18 prisons in New Zealand are run by the Department of Corrections (hereafter known as "Corrections"), three are designated for women and one is maximum security (Corrections, 2020a). Māori, the indigenous population of New Zealand, are drastically over-represented in prisons, comprising 52.3% of the prison population but just 16.5% of the general population (Corrections, 2020a; Stats NZ, 2020). Māori continue to suffer ongoing trauma from the effects of colonisation, including land theft, socioeconomic deprivation, cultural subjugation and loss of political power, in addition to systemic and institutional racism (Jackson, 1988: McIntosh and Workman, 2017).

For the last 30 or so years, the New Zealand prison population has experienced continued growth, largely driven by "penal populism" whereby successive governments have introduced "tough on crime" policies in response to media and public debates (Gluckman and Lambie, 2018). However, in December 2017, the then Minister of Justice, Andrew Little, announced the intention to reduce the prison population by 30% in the next 15 years (see New Zealand Herald, 2 December 2017). Since March 2018, the number of people in prison has been slowly decreasing, although this decline is threatened by the rapid increase in the remand population as a result of changes to bail and people spending longer on remand (Ministry of Justice, 2020).

Various pieces of domestic legislation and standards, notably the Corrections Act 2004 and the Prison Operational Manual (Corrections, 2005), set out a range of minimum entitlements for prisoners. In practice, however, prison conditions can vary substantially. Section 29 of the Crimes of Torture

* The author would like to thank Amnesty International New Zealand for their assistance in finding resources to prepare this chapter.

DOI: 10.4324/9781003169178-29

Act 1989 gives the Ombudsman the authority to conduct unscheduled, unrestricted inspections of places of detention to assess compliance with the United Nations Optional Protocol to the Convention against Torture. Such inspections have found that prisons are often unclean, unhygienic and unsafe (No Pride in Prisons, 2016). At Northland Regional Correctional Facility restricted access to toilets and fresh water was deemed to be degrading treatment and therefore a breach of Article 16 of the United Nations Convention Against Torture (Boshier, 2019). In 2017, the prison network had a capacity gap of over 1,700, leading to a high amount of double-bunking[1] (Corrections, 2017); yet, many double cells do not meet international standards for the minimum size of a two-person cell (No Pride in Prisons, 2016).

Prisoners in New Zealand are entitled to a standard of healthcare that is "reasonably equivalent" to that offered to the general public (Corrections Act 2004, section 75 (2)). However, several concerns have been raised about the quality of healthcare in New Zealand prisons (No Pride in Prisons, 2016). For example, an internal review of Auckland Region Women's Correctional Facility found that women's healthcare needs went unmet due to a punitive culture and a lack of healthcare staff, despite a disproportionately large demand for health services (Corrections, 2020b).

Prisoners in New Zealand also suffer from poor health outcomes. The prevalence of mental disorders and addictions is substantially higher amongst prisoners than in the general population (Indig et al., 2016), but they also experience higher rates of chronic and communicable diseases (National Health Committee, 2010). Additionally, Māori and Pacific people in general have a lower life expectancy, higher rates of co-morbidities, smoking, obesity and persisting health inequities (Parr-Brownlie et al., 2020). They are likely to experience the age-related risk of COVID-19 earlier as they suffer chronic health conditions at an earlier age (Ministry of Health, 2020); yet, healthcare services do not recognise or provide appropriate services for Māori (Waitangi Tribunal, 2019).

At the time of writing in March 2021, prisons in New Zealand have been relatively COVID-free, with just one confirmed case which involved a woman who arrived from overseas and refused to be tested. Consequently, she was jailed for ten days under section 70 of the Health Act 1956 and tested positive for COVID-19 with the results becoming known just after her release.[2] The lack of COVID-19 in prisons is reflective of the low number of cases in the community due to New Zealand's "go hard, go early" approach which prioritised public health and developed national unity to combat the virus (Jamieson, 2020). The approach consists of four alert levels:

- Level 4: Lockdown
- Level 3: Restrict
- Level 2: Reduce
- Level 1: Prepare

On 23 March 2020, New Zealand entered Level 3 for 48 hours before moving to Level 4 on 25 March for four and a half weeks, and Level 3 for a further two and half weeks until 14 May, before another three and a half weeks at Level 2 (Jamieson, 2020). At Level 4, people were instructed to stay at home other than for essential personal movement, travel was severely limited and schools, universities and businesses were closed apart from essential services. At Level 3, restrictions were lifted slightly, allowing some businesses to open without physical interaction with customers (Jamieson, 2020).[3] Auckland was also placed in further Level 3 lockdowns for two and half weeks in August 2020, three days in February 2021 and one week in March 2021, whilst the rest of the country was placed in Level 2 during these times. By March 2021, New Zealand has had 2,501 cases of COVID-19, with 26 deaths (New Zealand Government, 2020a). All persons now entering New Zealand are required to stay in managed isolation facilities for at least 14 days and to test negative for COVID-19 before they can leave (New Zealand Government, 2020b).

Despite the apparent success of the New Zealand approach, it has come at the expense of various liberties, particularly in prisons, some of which could be said to breach international human rights standards on the prevention of torture. This chapter will now briefly review penal policy during the COVID-19-induced crisis, before discussing the restrictions faced by those incarcerated in New Zealand and the challenges to such measures. It will then examine the implications of the COVID-19 crisis for future penal policy.

2 Prison and penal policy during the COVID-19-induced crisis

New Zealand has not enacted any sentencing and penal policies, such as early release measures, as a result of COVID-19. The Levels 4 and 3 lockdowns did, however, have substantial effects on court services. Criminal court proceedings were limited to urgent, time-sensitive matters concerning the liberty of the individual or their personal safety and well-being, and jury trials were suspended until the end of July (Winkelmann, 2020). Prior to the pandemic, the average wait for a jury trial in Auckland was already 436 days (Lynch and Tinsley, 2020), and further delays will lengthen the amount of time spent on remand and may breach individual rights to be tried without undue delay (Lynch and Tinsley, 2020). Reports to establish suitability for electronic monitoring were also delayed due to pressures on Corrections staff (Morris, 2020), as were home detention address checks (Block, 2020).

During Levels 4, 3 and 2, the police laid 989 criminal charges over breaches of the COVID-19 restrictions, most of which fell under the Health Act 1956, further adding to the backlog in the District Court[4] (Smith, 2020). Additionally, several people have been found guilty of failing to comply with the COVID-19 Public Health Response Act 2020[5] by escaping managed isolation facilities. The case of a mother who was jailed for 14 days after absconding to ensure her children could attend their father's tangi[6] has raised accusations of institutional racism when compared with the case of a man who escaped to buy alcohol but was sentenced to just 40 hours community work (Dillane, 2020).

Rather than reducing the prison population, during Level 4, measures were proposed to potentially increase it by keeping people with suspected or confirmed COVID-19 in prison to reduce the risk to the general public. In a memo to Crown solicitors and public prosecutors in April 2020, the Solicitor-General proposed that formal orders under the Health Act 1956 could be used to keep those applying for bail with confirmed or suspected COVID-19 in prison (Espiner, 2020a). More strikingly, the memo also recommended that bail be declined for those in the community who tested positive for COVID-19 or were awaiting a test (Espiner, 2020a), potentially inviting COVID-19 into prisons (Espiner, 2020b). Unsurprisingly, these proposals faced considerable opposition from defence lawyers who argued that suspicion of having COVID-19 is an invalid reason to refuse bail. Such proposals also raised substantial questions about the erosion of individual rights in the name of public health at a time when heightened respect for human rights is needed, as one barrister noted, "to make sure that what we are doing is both sensible and lawful" (Douglas Ewen cited in Espiner, 2020b). Although these provisions do not appear to have been enacted, parole was revoked or delayed for prisoners if their planned accommodation was no longer available due to the lockdown. For example, Mr Hapuku was due to be released on 30 March. His parole was revoked on 26 March for this reason, and he was not released until 29 July 2020 (New Zealand Parole Board, 2020).

3 Restrictions of contact with the outside world

During the Levels 4 and 3 lockdowns, New Zealand prisons heavily restricted face-to-face contact with community members to reduce the spread of COVID-19. All private visits and non-essential movements, including visits from family, friends and volunteers, were suspended (Corrections, 2020c). This move was criticised by the Chief Human Rights Commissioner, Paul Hunt, who noted that a ban on visitors risked exposing vulnerable people to panic, despair and worsening mental and physical health (Human Rights Commissioner, 2020). Prisoners were largely able to keep in contact with family and friends through telephone and mail, although mail was quarantined for 48 hours to reduce the risk of COVID-19 transmission and in one prison, prisoners were unable to receive parcels from family and friends (Espiner, 2020c). Prisoners' families have complained of receiving little information from Corrections about the new procedures (Espiner, 2020d). At Level 2, visits were allowed, with visitors required to comply with various requirements, including temperature checks and physical distancing (Corrections, 2020e).

Release to work, community work and other reintegration activities, including temporary releases, were halted during Levels 4 and 3, which may have had an effect on parole eligibility (Block, 2020). Transfers between prisons continued but prisoners who had visited anywhere in between, such as court or hospital, were placed into isolation for 14 days (Espiner, 2020c).

4 Restrictions inside prisons

Prisoners in New Zealand have faced significant and controversial restrictions as a result of measures introduced to keep COVID-19 out of prisons. Under Levels 4 and 3, all incoming prisoners were placed into a cohort or "bubble" based on their arrival date and kept separate from other prisoners for 14 days. For those already in prison, each unit operated as its own "bubble", with physical distancing maintained between "bubbles". Prisoners considered to be particularly vulnerable to COVID-19, such as those with chronic health conditions, were placed in "medical isolation" and kept in dedicated units. Any prisoner suspected of having COVID-19 was tested and placed into medical isolation until they received a negative test result (Boshier, 2020).

During this time, most employment and recreational activities were suspended, along with most rehabilitation programmes, despite the potential implications of this for parole eligibility (JustSpeak, 2020a). Most prisons provided various in-cell activities, such as activity books, educational tasks and work-out programmes. Healthcare continued to be provided, although in some prisons this was done through phone consultations (Boshier, 2020).

The amount of time New Zealand prisoners spent locked up in their cells and their lack of access to physical exercise in fresh air during Levels 4 and 3 have been the subject of considerable criticism from human rights and other organisations. Research by an investigative journalist found that some prisoners were locked up for 23 or more hours a day even when in minimum security (Espiner, 2020d). The prison reform group, People Against Prisons Aotearoa, have argued that this meets the definition of solitary confinement under Rule 44 of the United Nations Standard Minimum Rules for the Treatment of Prisoners (the Nelson Mandela Rules), which stipulates that anything longer than 22 hours in a cell without meaningful human contact is considered solitary confinement and should only be used as a last resort. Corrections' National Commissioner, Rachel Leota, denied that any prison had a 23-hour lock-up policy, but confirmed lock-up hours varied according to different sites and "operational requirements" (Espiner, 2020c).

Under section 70 of the Corrections Act 2004, all prisoners are entitled to take at least one hour of physical exercise daily, which may be taken in the open air if the weather permits. During Level 3, inspections by the Ombudsman found that prisoners in four prisons were not receiving this, and those isolated for COVID-19-related reasons were less likely to have access to at least one hour of fresh air every day (Boshier, 2020). The Ombudsman interpreted this as a breach of Rule 23(1) of the Nelson Mandela Rules which provides for this as a minimum standard. In one unit, prisoners only had access to an hour of fresh air every other day, whilst another could only provide 20 minutes daily (Boshier, 2020).

One of the key challenges for agencies monitoring human rights in New Zealand is the lack of publicly accessible, comprehensive and accurate information about policies and practices in prisons. The majority of the Ombudsman's inspection reports on individual prisons are not publicly released (No Pride in Prisons, 2016), and much information is only accessible through formal requests under the Official Information Act 1982. State agencies will often resist such requests, at least initially. In mid-April 2020, Amnesty International requested nationwide data on the numbers of hours prisoners have spent locked up in their cells, noting that "some rights, including the right to be free from torture and other forms of ill-treatment can never be risked, especially during a time of crisis" (Amnesty International, 2020). Initially, the Minister of Corrections, Kelvin Davis, maintained that Corrections did not have such data. However, information subsequently released to an RNZ journalist revealed a Corrections review of prison lock-up periods for a one-week period in April 2020, which found that on average 96% of prisoners received their minimum entitlement of at least one hour of physical exercise outside their cells daily, but 10% of prisoners in mid-North Island prisons did not receive this (de Ronde, 2020). At the Auckland Region Women's Corrections Facility, CCTV footage had to be reviewed to calculate the time out of cell due to the lack of written records. This review found that women were locked up for longer than 23 hours on 16 out of 30 occasions and on 2 April, one group of women were let out of their cells for just 14 minutes (Espiner, 2020e).

5 Compensatory measures

To keep in contact with the outside world, all prisoners in New Zealand are entitled to at least one 30-minute visit a week (Corrections, 2021a) and can buy phone cards (or have them posted to them) for use in phones placed in common areas throughout prisons (Corrections, 2021b). They can also write up to three free letters a week and receive emails. Recognising that the suspension of private visits during Levels 3 and 4 was likely to increase the risk of tension in prisons, Corrections provided all prisoners with a $5 phone card each week (Corrections, 2020c) and more than 200 new phones were installed (Block, 2020). In some prisons, in-cell telephones, or access to unlimited calls for a set cost were provided or prisoners could use Audio-Visual Links (AVL) to maintain family contact (Boshier, 2020), a method of contact not usually offered. Weekly phone usage data from the Auckland Region Women's Corrections Facility showed that calls reached a peak of over 8,000 in the week of 18–24 March, and between 6,700 and 7,350 calls were made weekly during Levels 4 and 3, suggesting that women were "able to access phones during the lock down period without issue" (Corrections, 2020b: 5). Increased use was also made of incoming prisoner email (Corrections, 2020c). The Ombudsman has praised Corrections' efforts to support prisoners in maintaining contact with the outside world, stating that prisoners spoke of feeling supported, safe and well-informed (Boshier, 2020).

During Levels 4 and 3, legal visits, court hearings, parole hearings, cultural interviews and meetings with psychological and psychiatric professionals were conducted virtually using AVL facilities or telephone calls (Boshier, 2020; Corrections, 2020b). Prisons increased the number of AVL booths and implemented a secure system to allow lawyers to talk privately with prisoners. However, arranging legal representation and other forms of support via these methods could be challenging. Khylee Quince, who writes pre-sentence cultural reports, complained of poor technical capabilities in prisons, making it difficult to receive instructions from clients (cited in Block, 2020). Those with intellectual disabilities may be unable to give instructions to lawyers if they cannot talk face-to-face with them, and court-ordered psychiatric assessments conducted by phone could be hindered by the inability to judge body language (Morris, 2020).

6 Legal basis for the restrictions of the prison regime and associated challenges

The measures and restrictions introduced into New Zealand prisons appear to have largely been enacted using existing legislation. Section 69(2) of the Corrections Act 2004, for example, allows minimum entitlements, such as access to physical exercise, to be suspended if there is an emergency in the prison or the security of the prison or the health and safety of any person is threatened. The Minister for Corrections justified the use of restrictive measures such as reduced time out of cell on public health grounds, arguing that "If COVID-19 gets into our prisons then we will have people complaining that we didn't do enough" (cited in Espiner, 2020d).

Nevertheless, academics and organisations which monitor human rights in New Zealand have raised substantial concerns about Corrections' handling of the pandemic and the need for balance between public health, the interest of prisoners and their access to justice, due process and human rights (Block, 2020), particularly as the usual systems of accountability and monitoring were also affected by prison lockdown measures. The ban on outside visits included Visiting Justices (Human Rights Commissioner, 2020), who under section 19(4) of the Corrections Act 2004 have powers to visit and inspect prisons, examine the treatment and conduct of prisoners, enquire into alleged abuses and deal with offences against prison discipline, although arrangements were made for them to conduct hearings and appeals by AVL or teleconference (Corrections, 2020d). Similar visits by the Office of the Inspectorate, which under section 28 of Corrections Act 2004 is required to ensure that all prisoners are treated in a way that is fair, safe, secure and humane (Office of the Inspectorate, 2020), were also suspended under Level 4 but resumed in Level 3 (Adair, 2020).

As the country moved to Level 4, Corrections initially attempted to suspend inspection visits from the Ombudsman. However, the Ombudsman argued that the use of extraordinary public health measures did not override his statutory duty to inspect places of detention, noting that such measures "must not have unnecessary or disproportionate impact on people's rights" (Boshier, 2020: 7). A compromise was reached whereby announced visits by the Ombudsman could take place, although this prevented surprise checks, an important part of any effective monitoring system (Amnesty International New Zealand, personal communication). The Ombudsman's teams inspected nine prisons when New Zealand was at Level 3 and concluded that New Zealand prisons responded to the COVID-19 pandemic in a "well-resourced, balanced, and efficient manner" (Boshier, 2020: 7). However, this had come at the expense of some prisoners' rights particularly in relation to access to fresh air, and most of the complaints received by the Ombudsman from prisoners related to extended lockdown hours (Espiner, 2020f).

7 Returning to normal

New Zealand has been relatively successful at controlling COVID-19 and ensuring that it did not spread into penal establishments. However, this success has come at a substantial price for those incarcerated and the response to the pandemic has not adequately balanced public health considerations with the human rights of prisoners. The COVID-19-induced crisis now presents New Zealand with a unique opportunity to rethink its approach to the use of imprisonment and consider changes that "support communities to flourish" after this pandemic (JustSpeak, 2020a). Such changes should involve a concerted effort to further reduce the number of people in prison to ensure that in future the spread of disease such as COVID-19 can be managed or prevented in a safe and humane manner, and to uphold prisoners' human rights and protect New Zealand's vulnerable communities. This could be done by various means, including reducing the remand population by ensuring that bail decisions consider the public health implications of detaining more people in prisons (JustSpeak, 2020b).

A reduction in the prison population is particularly important for Māori who are not only vastly over-represented in prisons and have poorer health outcomes but have also been "failed over and over again by deeply biased health care and justice systems" (JustSpeak, 2020b). Corrections' Hōkai Rangi strategy introduced in 2019 aimed to reduce the over-representation of Māori in the criminal justice system through working in genuine partnership with Māori and humanising the treatment of those in prison by ensuring that they are treated with dignity and respect (Corrections, 2019). However, the length of time prisoners were confined to their cells during the pandemic and recent disturbing reports of inhuman and degrading treatment at the Auckland Region Women's Corrections Facility and Auckland prison, including the use of pepper spray to remove prisoners from cells, have undermined this strategy (Johnsen, 2020) and highlighted the urgency of such a reduction. In the words of JustSpeak (2020a), a New Zealand penal reform organisation, decreasing the prison population will have "long-term positive impacts which will help us build the better and more just society we've been given the chance to reinvent".

Notes

1 Accommodating two people in one cell.
2 See RNZ, 11 May 2020, https://www.rnz.co.nz/news/national/416366/covid-positive-traveller-jailed-after-refusing-medical-examination.
3 The legality of the Levels 4 and 3 lockdown was challenged in the High Court, which ruled that it was lawful (LawTalk, 2020).
4 The lower level of criminal court.
5 See http://www.legislation.govt.nz/act/public/2020/0012/latest/LMS344134.html.
6 Māori cultural ceremony marking the death of a member of the community.

References

Adair, J. (2020, April 24): *Covid-19 Update from the Chief Inspector.* https://inspectorate.corrections.govt.nz/news/news_items/covid-19_update_from_chief_inspector.

Amnesty International (2020, 16 April): *Call for Transparency from Corrections on Prisoner Lockdown Hours.*

Block, G. (2020): Coronavirus: Prison 'timebomb' fears as frustration and boredom build. *Stuff,* 8 May, https://www.stuff.co.nz/national/300007046/coronavirus-prison-timebomb-fears-as-frustration-and-boredom-build.

Boshier, P. (2019): *OPCAT Report: Report on an Unannounced Inspection of Northland Regional Corrections Facility under the Crimes of Torture Act 1989.* Office of the Ombudsman. https://www.ombudsman.parliament.nz/sites/default/files/2019-09/final_opcat_report_2019_-_nrcf_-_pdf_.pdf

Boshier, P. (2020): *OPCAT Covid-19 Report: Report on Inspections of Prisons under the Crimes of Torture Act 1989.* Office of the Ombudsman. https://www.ombudsman.parliament.nz/sites/default/files/2020-06/Report_on_inspections_of_prisons_under_the_Crimes_of_Torture_Act_1989_062020.pdf.

Corrections (2005): *Prison Operations Manual.* https://www.corrections.govt.nz/resources/policy_and_legislation/Prison-Operations-Manual.

Corrections (2017): *Making the Prison Network More Safe, Humane and Effective: Paper 1: Avoiding Severe Prison Capacity Shortages.* https://www.corrections.govt.nz/__data/assets/pdf_file/0015/33414/Cabinet_Paper_-_Making_the_Prison_Network_More_Safe_Humane_and_Effective....pdf.

Corrections (2019): *Hōkai Rangi: Ara Poutama Aotearoa Strategy 2019–2024.* https://www.corrections.govt.nz/__data/assets/pdf_file/0003/38244/Hokai_Rangi_Strategy.pdf.

Corrections (2020a): *Prison Facts and Statistics – June 2020.*

Corrections (2020b): *Focus on Various Areas of Custodial Practice across Auckland Region Women's Correctional Facility over a Four-month Period (January–April 2020).*

Corrections (2020c, March 23): *Ministerial Briefing: Measures to Mitigate the Risks Posed by Covid-19.*

Corrections (2020d, April 6): *Ministerial Briefing: Proposed Legislative Amendment to Section 139 of the Corrections Act 2004.*

Corrections (2020e): *Visiting Prison under Covid-19.*

Corrections (2021a): *Visits.* https://www.corrections.govt.nz/working_with_offenders/prison_sentences/staying_connected_with_friends_and_family/visits.

Corrections (2021b): *Phone Calls.* https://www.corrections.govt.nz/working_with_offenders/prison_sentences/staying_connected_with_friends_and_family/phone_calls.

de Ronde, M. (2020): Time for PM to step in over minister's handling of prison concerns. *RNZ*, 10 September, https://www.rnz.co.nz/news/on-the-inside/425725/time-for-pm-to-step-in-over-minister-s-handling-of-prison-concerns.

Dillane, T. (2020): Booze run vs father's funeral: Questions of systemic racism over quarantine escapees' contrasting sentences. *New Zealand Herald,* 29 August, https://www.nzherald.co.nz/nz/booze-run-vs-fathers-funeral-questions-of-systemic-racism-over-quarantine-escapees-contrasting-sentences/FLG5GV3EXGPNU4HY35KWTBU23A/.

Espiner, G. (2020a): Recommendations to push back release of virus-risk prisoners condemned. *RNZ*, 16 April, https://www.rnz.co.nz/news/national/414370/recommendations-to-push-back-release-of-virus-risk-prisoners-condemned.

Espiner, G. (2020b): Concerns prisons will turn into Covid-19 "quarantine facilities". *RNZ*, 22 April, https://www.rnz.co.nz/news/in-depth/414834/concerns-prisons-will-turn-into-covid-19-quarantine-facilities.

Espiner, G. (2020c): Covid-19: Prisoners in cells up to 23 hours a day. *RNZ*, 6 April, https://www.rnz.co.nz/news/in-depth/413538/covid-19-prisoners-in-cells-up-to-23-hours-a-day-guards.

Espiner, G. (2020d): NZ prisoners kept in solitary during Covid-19 outbreak, says prison reform group. *RNZ*, 8 April, https://www.rnz.co.nz/news/covid-19/413728/nz-prisoners-kept-in-solitary-during-covid-19-outbreak-says-prison-reform-group.

Espiner, G. (2020e): Inmates at New Zealand's largest women's prison neglected due to 'punitive culture', lack of staff, review finds. *RNZ*, 7 September, https://www.newshub.co.nz/home/new-zealand/2020/09/inmates-at-new-zealand-s-largest-women-s-prison-neglected-due-to-punitive-culture-lack-of-staff-review-finds.html.

Espiner, G. (2020f): Ombudsman 'discouraged' from accessing prisons amidst Covid-19 lockdown concerns. *RNZ*, 24 April, https://www.rnz.co.nz/news/in-depth/415026/ombudsman-discouraged-from-accessing-prisons-amidst-covid-19-lockdown-concerns.

Gluckman, P., and Lambie, I. (2018): *Using Evidence to Build a Better Justice System: The Challenge of Rising Prison Costs.* Office of the Prime Minister's Chief Science Advisor.

Human Rights Commissioner (2020): Prison lockout for coronavirus lockdown goes too far. *Stuff*, 17 April, https://www.stuff.co.nz/national/crime/121089746/prison-lockout-for-coronavirus-lockdown-goes-too-far-human-rights-commissioner.

Indig, D., Gear. C., and Wilhelm, K. (2016): *Co-morbid Substance Use Disorders and Mental Health Disorders among New Zealand Prisoners.* Department of Corrections.

Jackson, M. (1988): *The Māori and the Criminal Justice System: A New Perspective: he whaipaangahou.* Department of Justice.

Jamieson, T. (2020): "Go hard, go early": Preliminary lessons from New Zealand's response to Covid-19. *American Review of Public Administration* 50(6–7), 598–605. Doi: 10.177/0275074020941721.

Johnsen, M. (2020): Prison report shows failure to implement Hōkai Rangi strategy – advocate. *RNZ*, 15 December, https://www.rnz.co.nz/news/te-manu-korihi/432917/prison-report-shows-failure-to-implement-hokai-rangi-strategy-advocate.

JustSpeak (2020a, 17 April): *Justice Leaders Must Take Urgent Action to Protect People in Prison form Covid-19.* https://www.justspeak.org.nz/ourwork/justice-leaders-must-take-urgent-action-to-protect-people-in-prison-from-covid-19.

JustSpeak (2020b, 24 April): *People in Prisons Are at Risk and Here's How We Can Protect them.* https://www.justspeak.org.nz/ourwork/people-in-prisons-are-at-risk-and-heres-how-we-can-protect-them-op-ed.

LawTalk (2020): High court releases judgement on the legality of the 'lockdown'. *LawTalk*, 943, 29–30.

Lynch, N., and Tinsley, Y. (2020): Court adjourned: How the pandemic is delaying justice in criminal cases. *The Spinoff*, 12 May. https://thespinoff.co.nz/society/12-05-2020/court-adjourned-how-the-pandemic-is-delaying-justice-in-criminal-cases/.

McIntosh, T., and Workman, K. (2017): Māori and prison. In: Deckert, A., and Sarre, R. (Eds.): *The Palgrave Handbook of Australian and New Zealand Criminology, Crime and Justice.* Palgrave Macmillan, 725–735.

Ministry of Health (2020): *Covid-19: Border Controls.* https://www.health.govt.nz/our-work/diseases-and-conditions/covid-19-novel-coronavirus/covid-19-response-planning/covid-19-border-controls.

Ministry of Justice (2020): *Justice Sector Prison Population Projects 2019–2029.* Ministry of Justice.

Morris. D. (2020): Mentally disabled prisoner disadvantaged by being unable to talk face-to-face with lawyer. *Stuff*, 3 April, https://www.stuff.co.nz/national/crime/120789671/mentally-disabled-prisoner-disadvantaged-by-being-unable-to-talk-facetoface-with-lawyer.

National Health Committee (2010): *Health in Justice: Improving the Health of Prisoners and their Families and Whānau.* Ministry of Health.

New Zealand Government (2020a): *Covid-19: Current Cases.* https://www.health.govt.nz/our-work/diseases-and-conditions/covid-19-novel-coronavirus/covid-19-data-and-statistics/covid-19-current-cases.

New Zealand Government (2020b): *Managed Isolation and Quarantine.* https://covid19.govt.nz/travel-and-the-border/travel-to-new-zealand/managed-isolation-and-quarantine/.

New Zealand Parole Board (2020): *Trent Owen N. Hapuku 13/7/2020.* https://www.paroleboard.govt.nz/decisions/2020/trent_owen_n._hapuku.

No Pride in Prisons (2016): *Torture in New Zealand Prisons.* https://papa-site-assets.ams3.cdn.digitaloceanspaces.com/publications/torture-in-new-zealand-prisons.pdf.

Office of the Inspectorate (2020): *About Us.* https://inspectorate.corrections.govt.nz/about_us.

Parr-Brownlie, L. C., Water, D. L., Neville, S., Neha, T. and Muramatsu, N. (2020): Ageing in New Zealand: Ka haere kit e ao pakeketanga. *The Gerontologist*, 60(5), 812–820. Doi: 10.1093/geront/gnaa032.

Smith, A. (2020): Defence lawyers call for urgent review of Covid-19 prosecutions. *RNZ*, 22 July, https://www.rnz.co.nz/news/national/421714/defence-lawyers-call-for-urgent-review-of-covid-19-prosecutions.

Stats NZ (2020): *New Zealand's Population Reflects Growing Diversity*. https://www.stats.govt.nz/news/new-zealands-population-reflects-growing-diversity.

Waitangi Tribunal (2019): *Hauora: Report on Stage One of the Health Services and Outcomes Kaupapa Inquiry, Wai 2575*. https://forms.justice.govt.nz/search/Documents/WT/wt_DOC_152801817/Hauora%20W.pdf.

Winkelmann, H. (2020, 8 April): *Operation of the Courts under Covid-19 Alert Levels, Supreme Court of New Zealand*. https://www.courtsofnz.govt.nz/assets/20-04-08-CJ-to-profession_A.pdf.

World Prison Brief (2020): *Prison Population Rate*. https://www.prisonstudies.org/highest-to-lowest/prison_population_rate?field_region_taxonomy_tid=All.

30 North Macedonia

Gordana Lažetić and Elena Mujoska Trpevska

1 Introduction

1.1 General background

The Republic of North Macedonia (hereinafter: RNM) is a small country in the Balkans that received its independence from the former Yugoslavia in 1991. Based on an agreement with Greece adopted in June 2018, the country, previously known as the Former Yugoslav Republic of Macedonia,[1] was renamed the Republic of North Macedonia in February 2019.

1.2 Basic characteristics of the Macedonian system of sanctions

The system of sanctions provided in the Criminal Code of the RNM (hereinafter CCRNM)[2] comprises punishments, alternative measures, safety measures and educational measures, which is a well-integrated, pluralistic system of sanctions, concentrating on penalty as the primary sanction. Imprisonment and its alternatives are the only sanctions for adult, accountable and guilty perpetrators, except for security measures which can be imposed on persons who are not mentally competent or have diminished mental competence, as well as drug and alcohol addicts.

Great progress has been made in criminal justice reform by creating a juvenile justice system, separate from the Criminal Code. The main reason for this partition was the need to improve both the legal framework and the mechanisms for its implementation in order to comply with international norms and standards. The new Law on Child Justice (Official Gazette-148/13, 152/2019; 275/2019) promotes the idea of restorative justice, giving priority to diversion, mediation, alternative measures and application of institutional, educational measures or punishment only as a last resort.[3]

Since 2004, amendments to the CCRNM have introduced a flexible new system of sanctions. There are now two main punishments, i.e. imprisonment and fines, and four secondary prohibitions: prohibitions on practising a profession, on performing an activity or duty, on operating a motor vehicle and on attending sports competitions, as well as expulsion of a foreigner from the country (Article 33 CCRNM).

DOI: 10.4324/9781003169178-30

Prison law has undergone two reform phases. The first phase began with the adoption in 2004 of the Law on Execution of Sanctions, which remained in force until 29 May 2019, when a new Law on Execution of Sanctions was adopted (Official Gazette-99/2019, 220/2019, hereinafter: LES) and the second phase of reforms of the penal system started. The latest Law regulates the execution of sanctions imposed for crimes and misdemeanours following the Nelson Mandela Rules and the recommendations of the European Committee for the Prevention of Torture (CPT hereinafter). The adoption of this legislation was necessary to comply with the guidelines of the National Strategy for Development of the Penitentiary System (2015–2019).[4] Thus, solutions were offered for improving the situation in prisons by simultaneous harmonisation with the new Law on Probation (Official Gazette-226/2015).[5] The purpose of the new LES is to regulate the overall system while reaching precise hierarchical arrangements between the Directorate for Execution of Sanctions and the penitentiary and correctional-educational institutions. The new LES completely redefines the provisions regarding the prison police as the unit providing security (prison guards), which simplifies the procedure for employment, promotion, mobility and evaluation of its members.

The Law on the Execution of Sanctions is in line with international standards and best practice in the field of execution of sanctions, with particular emphasis on the 2015 UN Standard Minimum Rules for the Treatment of Prisoners (the Nelson Mandela Rules), and the European Prison Rules of the Council of Europe.[6] However, in practice, there are problems regarding its implementation, which are elaborated below.

1.3 The Macedonian prison system, penal policy and conditions in penal institutions

The CCRNM distinguishes between time-limited and life imprisonment. The legal minimum of the determinate imprisonment is 30 days; the general legal maximum is 20 years. For offences punishable by life imprisonment, a sentence of up to 40 years in prison may be imposed. The Law explicitly excludes the imposition of this punishment for an offender who at the time the crime was committed has not turned 21 (Article 35 CCRM).

There are two types of prisons in the country: penitentiary institutions and correctional-educational institutions. Children (from 16 to 18 years of age) are sentenced to youth imprisonment to serve their sentence in special youth prisons. There are 11 penitentiary institutions[7] in the RNM (hereinafter: prisons) and one correctional-educational facility (hereinafter: CEF) in Volkovija, Tetovo. The new CEF offers much better conditions for the implementation of the correctional-educational process than the facility in the former Ohrid Prison, and there are possibilities for respecting children's rights.[8]

According to the level of security, the level of restriction of freedom of movement and the types of treatment applied to sentenced persons, prisons are divided into institutions of closed (there is physical and material security), semi-open (there are prison police (prison guards) to provide discipline and to control the movement of prisoners) and open types (there is no physical and material security).

The main problems of the prison system, which complicates the rehabilitative process as prerequisite for successful re-integration into society, are corruption, inadequate prison conditions and overcrowding. The CPT has described the appalling conditions, especially in Idrizovo Prison, in each of its six visit reports since September 2006. After the 2010 and 2011 visits, some modest efforts were made to clean Wings 5 and 2, respectively. However, at the time of the 2016 visit, severely overcrowded living conditions as well as an unsafe and unhygienic environment prevailed in many of the living quarters. Two days of intense cleaning before the delegation's visit made little difference. The conditions in prisons have developed continuously since 2017. The latest reports from the 2019 and 2020 CPT visits have not yet been published.[9]

To get a clear picture of Macedonian prisons today, we will refer to the latest EC progress report by European Commission for 2020.[10] While construction and refurbishment in the prison system continue, conditions in the closed section and "ambulance" of the Idrizovo Penitentiary remain inhumane. The authorities should urgently transfer prisoners out of the most derelict buildings and accelerate the rehabilitation of unsuitable facilities.

Despite implementing the 2017 corruption mitigation plan, regular supervision is essential to curb persistent corruption in prisons. The report specifies, among other things, that the authorities are aware that corruption exists within Idrizovo Prison:

> seven officers have been dismissed and 16 disciplined in the past two years, and a recent case of a prison officer selling drugs to inmates made national news. However, there does not appear to be a realisation that the problem is endemic.[11]

The report reveals that virtually every aspect of prison life is up for sale. The violence in Idrizovo Prison is integrally linked to the endemic corruption that has pervaded the whole prison and implicates prison officers of all grades, up to the most senior officers and educators. There is a need to put in place a robust strategy that diminishes the opportunities for corruption, for example, by reducing the overcrowding and improving the living conditions so that prisoners do not have to buy a place in a better cell.

Healthcare services must also be reinforced. The payment of health insurance for convicted people to the Health Insurance Fund started in June 2019. However, healthcare in prisons remains a serious concern, including for juveniles and the treatment of drug addicts.

From 2010 to 2017, the RNM faced continuous overcrowding of the prisons, which additionally caused other problems for prisoners in terms of accommodation, nutrition, general and personal hygiene, and insufficient and inadequate healthcare, poor sanitation and frequent conflicts between the prisoners. In its annual reports, the Ombudsman noted appeals regarding cases of non-compliance with the domestic and international standards for the accommodation of persons deprived of liberty.[12] The frequent imposition of imprisonment, followed by overcrowded prison facilities, has led to exceptional demands, such as the adoption of amnesty laws. In 2018, after the adoption of the Law on Amnesty (Official Gazette-11/2018), the number of sentenced persons in certain prisons had significantly decreased. Nevertheless, the lack of sufficient space in prisons continued in 2019 and 2020. In general, the overall picture of the prison system began to improve markedly with the change of Government in 2017, and the transformation of authorities in the Directorate for Execution of Sanctions. The emphasis should remain on developing alternatives to detention to avoid overcrowding and improve rehabilitative measures to prevent re-offending.

The total capacity of the prison system is 2,256. According to the latest data obtained for this research (November 2020), the total number of persons in prisons was 2,106 (occupancy rate: 93.4%), of whom 1,845 (87.6%) are convicted and 261 (12.4%) are on remand.

1.4 Developments after the emergence of COVID-19

In February 2020, a crisis group for all activities in the RNM related to COVID-19 was established, after which the Government and the Ministry of Health adopted recommendations for measures and actions to prevent the spread of the virus. On 18 March 2020, the President of the RNM declared a state of emergency.

2. Prison and penal policy during COVID-19

2.1 Penal policy to reduce the prison population and infections inside prison

As mentioned above, a decrease of the prison population started already in 2018 under the new Government and the penal policy described under Section 1.3. In addition, a Decree was passed after the state of emergency was declared in order to further reduce prison overcrowding and the risk of COVID-19 infections. Only one Decree with legal force that affected the application of the LES was adopted and published on 8 April 2020. This Decree was adopted in order to prevent or reduce the admission of new prisoners, and thus to neutralise the risk of spreading COVID-19. It provides the following:

- Judges appointed for the execution of sanctions will not issue referral acts for the execution of prison sentences of up to three years until 1

September 2020, except in cases where there is a risk for the expiration of the statute of limitations regarding the execution of the sentence;

- If a referral act has already been submitted, its execution shall be postponed until 1 September 2020, except for referral acts for which international arrest warrants have already been issued; and
- Detained persons shall be immediately referred to serve their prison sentence after the verdict becomes final.

Regarding the work of the courts across the RNM, on 17 March 2020, the Judicial Council of RNM adopted a decision on the operation of the courts under increased threat from COVID-19.[13] In addition to the preventive measures, the courts were obliged to act only in essential matters, such as the trials of criminal cases where defendants were in custody, house arrest or other measures imposed for ensuring their presence during the procedure; criminal cases where the parties did not have a place of residence or stay in the RNM; criminal cases for which there was a risk of the expiration of the statute of limitations; urgent misdemeanour cases and cases that were in the adjudication phase, as well as those for which there was a risk of violation of the principle of trial within a reasonable time and which by virtue of the Law were urgent.

As a result, the influx of admissions to prisons was further reduced. On 30 March 2020, the Government adopted a Legal Decree,[14] which postponed the issuing of referral acts for imprisonment of up to three years until 1 September 2020, except for cases where the execution of the sentence became time barred.

2.2 Covid-19 infections and deaths in prisons

In the beginning, the preventive measures taken showed great efficacy. During the period until 31 March 2020, there were no cases of infected prisoners, detainees or employees.

When the so-called "second wave" of the virus gained momentum, the number of infected prisoners and prison staff rose. As of 27 November 2020, a total of 14 infected prisoners and 23 prison staff members were registered. 60 prisoners and 21 staff members have undergone self-isolation.

According to the data provided by the DES, there was one case of the death of a prisoner registered in early December 2020. In April 2021, five prisoners in the prison in Štip and one in Idrizovo were infected with COVID-19, as well as six of the employees in the prisons – three in the prison in Štip and three prison guards in Idrizovo.[15]

As for the prison staff, the occurrence of COVID-19 infections was more common than among prisoners, because the staff have to remain in contact with their families and the wider outside world. However, during the whole pandemic, the prison staff worked exclusively with masks and gloves provided by the institutions, and they regularly had access to disinfectants during the work process.

3 Restrictions of contact with the outside world

Following the declaration of a state of emergency, the country sought to alleviate the challenges faced by sentenced persons and detainees, as well as employees in those institutions. On 10 March 2020, the DES within the Ministry of Justice issued an order requiring action in all prisons in the country.[16] Consequently, each institution issued additional internal orders with more precise rules of conduct.

By 31 March 2020, each prison and correctional-educational institution had implemented special preventive measures. All contacts of the prisoners with the outside world were banned by prohibiting home leave, annual leave with their family, visits by family members and work outside the institutions. Hygiene and disinfection of the premises were raised to the highest level and have continued with the same intensity throughout the duration of the pandemic until today (March 2021). Each newly admitted prisoner spends the first 14 days in isolation. He/she cannot interact with others until it is checked whether he/she shows any symptoms of the disease. In any case, when a sentenced person has fever, all prisoners with whom he/she communicated are immediately placed in isolation to exclude risks of spreading the infection. Due to these measures, the infection rate in the Macedonian prisons has been very low, and there have been no cases of internal transmission of the virus at all.

During the summer of 2020, the DES relaxed the restrictions in prisons. However, the prisoners remained obliged to meet the recommendations and measures for protection and prevention of COVID-19 during any form of prison leave. From June, prisoners were allowed such leave, i.e. use of benefits (except for vacation – starting from 16 July 2020), termination of punishment or another type of leave determined by law. The directors of prisons were obliged to implement all precautionary measures recommended by the Commission for Infectious Diseases within the Ministry of Health and to inform the DES about all the implemented measures on a weekly basis.

On 18 November 2020, in response to changes in the situation and the sharp increase in the number of infected persons, the director of the DES issued a new order to limit prisoners' contacts with the outside world, except for visits by family members, which had not been limited but had been conducted under measures for keeping distance and without personal contact. The new order introduced additional bans on:

- the use of specific benefits for prisoners that consist of more frequent contacts with the outside world, such as a visit by a spouse or other partner in a separate room without supervision,
- visits outside of the institution's premises,
- short-term leave for up to seven hours,
- home leave,
- annual leave outside the institution and
- work engagement outside the institution.

The measures were in force for 30 days (18 November 2020 to 18 December 2020). On 17 December 2020, the Director of DES issued a further administrative notification (no. 08-1664/2) informing the prison employees that the previous administrative order would remain in force until the country reached an improvement of the epidemiological situation. With notification (no. 02-171/1) from 20 January 2021, the order from December 2020 was repealed, so from 21 January 2021, the prisoners could again use the benefits, i.e. more frequent contacts with the outside world as well as to be employed outside the institution. These orders do not prohibit visits by the families of prisoners.

As already mentioned, each prison adopted internal regulations for dealing with COVID-19. Prisons across the country proved that catastrophic prison situations could be avoided with good organisation and coordination, under the constant supervision of the DES. A positive example is the adoption of a Protocol for exercising the right to visit inmates in the Ohrid Prison, regarding convicted juveniles and detainees from the Ohrid area. According to the Protocol:

- The right to visit the sentenced persons will be exercised by limiting the number of visitors, to not more than three close family members or a person who has previously obtained consent from the director of the institution.
- Visitors must wear masks and gloves and keep a distance of two metres when contacting a prisoner or member of the prison staff.
- Upon checking-in to the prison, those who have been granted a visit have their temperature measured, and they must immediately disinfect.
- Visitors shall answer whether they have been in contact with another infected person; in case of giving a false statement, the person will be held criminally liable.
- Visits take place in precisely marked areas.
- Close contact (hugging, handshakes or any other physical contact) is strictly prohibited.
- For any failure to comply with the instructions given in the Protocol, the prison police are obliged to intervene.

Another encouraging example is Bitola Prison. As early as March 2020, a prevention strategy was developed in the institution. On 10 March 2020, the Director and the Management Team of the Bitola Prison published written guidelines, which were displayed in prominent places in the premises. On the same day, several members of the medical personnel from the Bitola Clinical Hospital were appointed to be contact points for any necessary urgent professional assistance, and two telephone numbers were given to the Head of the prison police, as emergency contacts, available 24/7. Subsequently:

- An order was issued for solar heating as an additional opportunity for maintaining personal hygiene.
- The first protective masks, gloves and disinfectants were supplied according to the number of sentenced persons and cells, and divided among prisoners and staff according to the needs.
- Increased control by the prison police was introduced regarding the visits, the receipt of packages and the prevention of possible prohibited contacts of the prisoners.
- The written notification was explained on a general and individual level, as needed. Due to the reduced personal contacts with their families, prisoners were allowed access to mobile telephone communication with their families, which has been a practice to this day.
- The engagement of a larger group of prisoners in the open air (in the fresh air) every day, with their consent, was supported.
- At the same time, staff worked very carefully to maintain hygiene and protect the health of the prisoners and their personal health.
- As part of their treatment, prisoners' needs were met through group and individual conversations. They were given additional educational advice, instructions, guidelines for prevention, i.e. raising awareness regarding the consequences, prevention and protection against COVID-19, which was implemented at least once a month, and more often, if necessary.
- Three-month action plans were made, and prisoners who met the conditions in the specified period were prepared for release.

The pandemic has a psychological aspect for prisoners, i.e. their emotional state and how they experience the pandemic. Therefore, each prisoner is allowed to contact a psychologist to seek professional help. Moreover, in the Bitola Prison, as well as in all other prisons, there is one disinfected closed room where infected persons can be quarantined. In the larger prisons, such as the Shtip Penitentiary Facility, there are 11 quarantine rooms. Additionally, a larger quantity of food products is kept in stock for a longer period. Every morning at 07.30 and in the evening at 19.30, one person from the prison police is responsible for measuring the body temperature of the staff on duty and the prisoners, and this is recorded daily in a special list.

By respecting all the above-mentioned preventive measures, the Bitola Prison has not registered a single case of an infected prisoner. There is no infected prisoner in the Struga Prison either, which is very interesting because it is an open-type prison.

In March 2020, in several prisons, expert talks on preventive measures were conducted with prisoners and staff members. At the beginning of November 2020, each prisoner in the Prilep Prison was given a package of vitamin therapy (vitamin C, zinc and vitamin D) to prevent the spread of the virus.

4 Restrictions inside prisons

With regard to restrictions inside prisons, contacts were further limited by reducing the time prisoners could share (apart from being locked up in communal cells).

As a rule, prisoners' work is performed in the institutions. The Law on the Execution of Sanctions allows the convicted persons in open prisons also to work outside the institution. Convicted persons with treatment in a semi-open prison may occasionally also work under the supervision of other legal entities and other institutions, if the conditions for the execution of the prison sentence determined by this Law are met and if appropriate working conditions are provided. Prisoners who have started using facilities outside the institution may be employed in jobs that are outside the circle of the institution. According to the Law, work outside prison can be either employment by contractors in the free society or in places which are part of the institution itself (Article 165). However, from March 2020 to January 2021, the prisoners were not allowed to work outside prison.

Regarding the possibility for outdoor and sport activities, according to Article 180 of the Law, the prisoners were not denied the right to spend at least two hours a day outside the closed part of the institution. However, up to mid-March 2021, they were not allowed to do any free or sport activities outside prisons. As stated in the 2020 EC Report, cooperation between the public and private sectors and civil society exists and it should be further developed. There has been progress in interagency cooperation. However, the level of purposeful activities (educational, recreational and vocational) on offer is insufficient for sentenced and non-existent for remand prisoners. Educational and resocialisation services, as well as treatment programmes, should be reinforced in all penitentiary facilities and especially in educational-correctional facilities.

5 Compensatory measures

The Law on Execution of Sanctions permits regular and frequent access to telephones in prisons. Every prison has a public pay phone and, in the past, prisoners were given telephone cards so they could use them for a longer period of time. That is no longer the case. The public telephones, especially in bigger prisons, are out of order and the prisoners are using mobile phones. During the COVD-19 crisis, telephone conversations were permitted more frequently than before. In addition, the Law allows a telephone conversation at the request of the family if it is necessary for the convicted person to be informed of something urgent that cannot be delayed. The Law stipulates that the authorities may require that a telephone conversation in a closed institution must be held in the presence of an official and this rule is often applied.

On 31 August 2020, the German organisation Help (*Hilfe zur Selbsthilfe*),[17] with the support of the German Government, donated assistance as a COVID-19 response to the DES. The cooperation between the organisation Help, DES and the Macedonian Society of Penology[18] was established in June 2020 as part of the Programme "Support for socio-economic stability in the western Balkans region 2019-2020" in particular about the project component "Improvement of treatment programmes in correctional institutions". The donation covered 4,126 FFP2 masks for protection and 30 devices to the DES for the needs of the Directorate and Idrizovo Prison, Ohrid Prison for juveniles, ECI Tetovo and Shtip Prison. The aim was to support institutions to implement COVID-19 protection measures through the delivery of communication devices, tablets and internet connections as an alternative communication channel, enabling family visits at times visits are prohibited, as emergencies and similar situations as well as through the delivery of protective masks for prisons.[19]

6 Legal basis for restrictions and relaxations of the prison regime

The legal basis for restrictions can be found in the decision to declare the state of emergency published in the Official Gazette no. 68/2020, and the Decree that affected the application of the LES, adopted on 8 April 2020 mentioned above.

Several other decrees are related to the prison police. Members of the prison police shall be exempt from statutory decrees pertaining to public sector employees, limiting some of their rights (for example, the payment of salary supplements and the freedom to use annual leave).

The Ombudsman is a special body for the protection of the rights of prisoners. The Ombudsman, representing the National Preventive Mechanism (hereinafter: NPM), regularly examines the treatment of prisoners in order to strengthen the protection against torture and other cruel, inhuman or degrading treatment or punishment. The impact of COVID-19 has increased the risk of ill-treatment of prisoners and posed new challenges to the actions of the NPM. Thus, on 26 March 2020, the Ombudsman published recommendations in order to indicate that

> The measures and activities taken to protect and deal with the consequences of the pandemic must not result in any inhuman or degrading treatment of persons deprived of their liberty and recommended for the authorities to consider the above principles of the CPT when dealing with such persons.[20]

Furthermore, the latest data obtained for this research indicated that the new situation imposed the need to adjust and harmonise the monitoring process. Considering the fundamental principles in conducting preventive visits, primarily the principle of "do no harm", visits to prisons were suspended until October 2020.

At the same time, after the entry into force of the Government Decree, all legal and preclusive deadlines were suspended, which significantly restricted access to justice. According to Petkoska, in situations when the courts operated with a minimum capacity and worked only in emergency cases, many urgent court hearings were postponed due to mandatory isolation. The result has been that the fair trial principle has been seriously jeopardised.[21]

7 Returning to normal

In the recent past, the competent authorities in the RNM were faced with real challenges. The pressure to deal with the consequences of COVID-19 is even more significant when it comes to prisons. However, all measures taken were and are aimed at keeping the infection rate of prisoners as low as possible. No case of violation of orders and protocols has been reported. This indicates that the prisoners have accepted the "new normal" behaviour in prisons.

Furthermore, the prisons were under constant inspection by the NPM. Despite the restrictions, the complaint mechanisms are continuously available to prisoners. Thus, even in an emergency, prisoners have the opportunity to file complaints of violation of their rights, and have the possibility to contact the Ombudsman by phone. In October 2020, after the initial suspension of visits, the team of the NPM continued to carry out preventive visits to prisons and places with persons deprived of liberty, following the established safeguards for the prevention of the spread of the virus in planning, organising and conducting preventive visits. From 2 to 7 November 2020, nine prisons as well as other places of deprivation of liberty were visited.

Directors, however, are obliged to continue to apply the measures for protection against COVID-19 following the recommendations of the Commission for Infectious Diseases within the Ministry of Health and to notify the DES of each new case of infected prisoners or staff members.

Although there are no measures that restrict the admission of new prisoners, the management of the prisons are applying health protection measures following the recommendations of the Commission for contagious diseases within the Ministry of Health.

8 Concluding remarks

All measures related to the prisons during the COVID-19 pandemic could be assessed as necessary and proportionate. This is in line with the European Commission's recommendations that emergency measures taken in the context of the COVID-19 pandemic should be proportionate, restricted to what is necessary and limited in time, so that the rule of law and human rights standards are respected.

The measures for protection from the COVID-19 pandemic were twofold: restrictions on entry of new prisoners sentenced to imprisonment up to three years, and measures inside prisons regarding restrictions of weekends and holidays with the family, visits by family members as well as work engagement outside prisons. Those measures were effective until the beginning of summer 2020. They were back into force by mid-March 2021, since with new cases of COVID-19 the situation in the country has become extremely serious. However, there have been only a few COVID-19 positive inmates and prison staff members with only one case of a prisoner who died from COVID-19.

Notes

1 Often referred to as FYR of Macedonia; the previous name will still be found in earlier papers and reports.
2 Criminal Code of the Republic of North Macedonia, Official Gazette, No. 37/1996; 80/1999; with 36 further amendments between 2001 and 2018; https://pretsedatel.mk/wp-content/uploads/2020/03/Krivicen-zakonik.pdf.
3 The main idea for the system of measures, as well as the procedure against children, where the judge for children has the central position, is the idea of protecting and assisting the child. However, youth imprisonment as a last resort is provided for at least 16-year-old juveniles and for the most serious offences (punishable with a minimum sentence of five years according to the general Penal Code), if educational or alternative measures cannot be applied.
4 National Strategy for Development of the Penitentiary System 2015–2019, https://www.pravda.gov.mk/Upload/Documents/Nacionalna_strategijaMK_12_2014.pdf.
5 Law on Probation, http://www.slvesnik.com.mk/Issues/eeb157f5bde94f0d918a4ccc23a3c092.pdf#page=8.
6 The Law was enacted before adoption of the revised Recommendation Rec (2006)2-rev in July 2020.
7 Penitentiary institutions are the following: Penitentiary facility Idrizovo with an open ward in Veles, Penitentiary facility Shtip, Penitentiary facility Prilep, the open-type Penitentiary facility Struga, Bitola Prison, Gevgelija Prison, Kumanovo Prison with an open ward in Kriva Palanka, Ohrid Prison, Skopje Prison, Strumica Prison, and Tetovo Prison.
8 The construction of a new correctional facility was expected for more than 19 years and is a permanent solution to the long-term problem of accommodation of sentenced juveniles. See more at www.msp.org.mk.
9 Periodic visit 2 December 2019–12 December 2020, Report not yet published. Ad hoc visit and high-level talks 7–9 December 2020, Report under preparation.
10 Commission staff working document, North Macedonia 2020 Report Accompanying the Communication from the Commission to the European Parliament, the Council, the European Economic and Social Committee and the Committee of the Regions, Brussels, 6 October 2020.
11 Ibid.
12 Annual reports on the work of the Ombudsman, http://ombudsman.mk/mk/godishni_izveshtai.aspx.
13 Judicial Council of RSM, Decision on the action of the Courts in the Republic of North Macedonia in conditions of increased danger from the COVID-19 from 17 March 2020, www.sud.mk.
14 The Decree was published in the Official Gazette of RNM, No. 84/2020.
15 Statement of the Director of the Director for Execution of Sanction, 8 April 2021, https://p.dw.com/p/3riLx..

16 Initially, these measures were planned to last 14 days from 11 March 2020 to 24 March 2020, and then it was extended until the state of emergency imposed in connection with the pandemic is lifted.
17 See https://www.help-ev.de/en.
18 The authors of this chapters are co-founders of the Macedonian Society of Penology. Visit: www.msp.mk.
19 Source: https://msp.mk/en_US/2020/08/31/help-and-german-embassy-donated-equipment-to-macedonian-prisons/.
20 Source: http://ombudsman.mk/mk/novosti_i_nastani/241625/preporaki_za_postapuvanje_so_licata_lisheni_od_sloboda_vo_uslovi_na_pandemija_od_virusot_kovid-19.aspx.
21 See Forsina Petkovska, Fair and Equal Trial in pandemic: https://all4fairtrials.org.mk/?p=3250&lang=mk.

31 Norway

Berit Johnsen

1 Introduction – general situation of the prison system

Norway closed down on 12 March 2020 to curb the spreading of SARS-CoV-2. On this day, there were 3,189 prisoners in Norwegian prisons, who occupied 91% of the available prison capacity.[1] To minimise the risk of infection, the prison administration started to reduce the number of prisoners the next day, in line with the recommendations of the European Committee for the Prevention of Torture and Inhuman or Degrading Treatment or Punishment (CTP) (2020) and Subcommittee on Prevention of Torture and Other Cruel, Inhuman or Degrading Treatment or Punishment (STP) (2020). During a period of almost two months, until 5 May 2020, the prison population was reduced to 2,591, a reduction of 19%, and the prisons were running at 75% capacity (Norwegian Ministry of Justice, 2020). This made it easier to maintain physical distancing and to safeguard standards of hygiene (see also Nilsen and Schlanbusch, 2020).

On 5 May 2020, all prisoners were serving their sentence in single cells (Norwegian Ministry of Justice, 2020). Before starting to reduce the capacity, about 200 prisoners served their sentence in communal cells, the great majority in open prisons. On 18 May, the prisons had available single-cell capacity and could start receiving prisoners again, but only if they were able to manage the risk of infection. However, this did not apply to fine defaulters, who anyhow have the opportunity to "pay" their fine by community service.

During the whole period of the first wave of the COVID-19 virus, from 12 March until 22 June, when the prisons as far as possible went back to normal operation again (Directorate of the Correctional Service [DCS], 2020a), the prisons had to admit remand prisoners. Partly due to lower rates of registered crime during the lockdown period (until late April/beginning of May),[2] the demand for remand prison places was quite low.

An important incentive to start admitting prisoners again was the growing number of persons waiting to serve their sentence. In Norway, prisons are usually not overcrowded. Persons sentenced to imprisonment should

DOI: 10.4324/9781003169178-31

start serving the sentence within 60 days after receiving a sentence that is legally enforceable. For humanitarian reasons, a person should have some time to arrange their life before going to prison. The "prison queue" has been understood as a sign of humanism (Pratt, 2008; Pratt and Eriksson, 2013), but Laursen et al. (2019) have documented the pains of waiting to serve a prison sentence. In general, persons sentenced to imprisonment have priority over fine defaulters. Since the queue was quite long in 2020, fine defaulters were seldom admitted to prison in 2020.

During the first wave of COVID-19, altogether 6 prisoners, 3 probationers and 11 staff members[3] were infected. The six prisoners were imprisoned at Bastøy prison, which is an open prison (low security). That open prisons would be more vulnerable to the virus than closed prisons (high security) was expected, as these prisons had not been under a strict lockdown. Later, there were serious outbreaks in closed prisons as well, for example, in Oslo prison with 13 infected prisoners in December 2020 and Ullersmo prison with 26 infected prisoners in March 2021. As the situation in the first months of the pandemic was unpredictable, Agder, a prison with 300 beds that had not yet opened, was held in a state of readiness in case the pandemic situation in the prisons worsened. Fortunately, this extra capacity was not needed.

As the first wave of infections was over in June, the total number of infected persons in the Correctional Service stayed quite low in the period July to September (altogether one probationer and seven staff members). However, the number of infected people started to rise quite dramatically in October 2020, both in the general population and among people in the Correctional Service. In this month, five prisoners, two probationers and 18 staff members were infected. At the peak of the second wave, in November and December 2020, 18 prisoners, six probationers and 46 staff members were infected. The numbers of infected persons dropped in the general population and in the Correctional Service in January and February 2021 (altogether six probationers and 22 staff members), but in March 2021, the third wave of infections commenced in Norway. In this month, 83 prisoners, 6 probationers and 38 staff members were infected. By 7 April 2021, a total of 137 prisoners and probationers plus 147 staff members were infected. So far, no staff, prisoners or probationers have died of the infection.[4]

The lockdown in spring 2020 was implemented not long after the one-week winter holiday in Norway, and staff who had been abroad, either for work or a holiday, had to be in quarantine for 10–14 days before they could go back to work in prisons. The staff situation was therefore somewhat critical at the beginning of the epidemic, but was soon stabilised. After this initial phase, the prison administration did not experience staff shortages (Parliamentary Ombudsman [PO], 2020). However, during the second and third waves, some prisons needed extra staff to uphold the staffing level.

2 Prison and penal policy concerning the execution of prison sentences during the COVID-19-induced crisis

The decrease of 598 prisoners in the period 12 March to 5 May 2020 was due to early releases, increased use of electronic monitoring (EM) and temporary suspensions of the execution of sentences. Concerning early release, an advanced early release regime was introduced: prisoners serving sentences shorter than 90 days could be conditionally released 10 days earlier than they would have been in an ordinary situation, prisoners with sentences between 90 days and 6 months 20 days earlier, and those having sentences for 6 months or more 30 days (DCS, 2020b).

There were no exceptions to this early release regime concerning types of crime, but there were restrictions concerning groups of prisoners. Foreign prisoners, for example, could not be included in the early release regime without this being coordinated with the police concerning deportation out of the country. However, the Correctional Service could not prohibit foreign prisoners from being released on ordinary conditions, e.g. when they had served their full sentence, because deportation could not be arranged by the police. The pandemic has also put a stop to the transfer of prisoners to other countries.

Several prisoners were granted temporary suspension of the execution of their sentence, but it was reported that some prisoners did not approve of this.[5] During the suspension period, the prisoners were subjected to stringent restrictions, such as having to reside at home, to only leave the house to do necessary errands and to stay at home between 8 p.m. and 6 a.m. In spite of these restrictions of liberty, this period did not count as serving a sentence, and prisoners experienced the suspension as a prolongation of their sentence.

In December 2019, the Parliament passed an Act to extend the period for serving sentences by EM from four to six months – front-door as well as back-door.[6] The Act also extended the target group of offenders that could be granted EM by including certain types of violent offences – sexual offenders are still not in the target group. The Act was not yet applicable at the first outbreak of the pandemic, but was put into force by a change in the regulations on 27 March 2020,[7] based on the "Corona Enactment"[8] (see below). The extension of EM served two purposes; first, to reduce the mounting number of persons waiting to serve their sentences, i.e. an increase of the prison queue (see above), and, second, to reduce the number of prisoners. The extended opportunity for back-door EM was especially relevant for prisoners in open prisons or halfway houses who were granted daily leave for going to work or school; this was mostly suspended during the lockdown phase. Serving at home made it possible for them to uphold their daily activities. However, as persons serving their sentence by EM are probationers, the workload of the probation service did not decrease because of the COVID-19 situation.

On 16 March 2020, the Director General of Public Prosecution (DGPP) published regulations on how offences against the Act Relating to Control of Communicable Diseases[9] and regulations concerning the COVID-19 pandemic situation[10] should be sanctioned. The DGPP stated that the purpose of the restrictions was to reduce the risk of infection by strengthening general deterrence. The regulations gave the police authority to sanction violations of national as well as local rules set by the different municipalities, such as quarantine rules, by fines. During the second and third waves, there were mostly local rules to curb outbreaks within certain areas. A lockdown of a municipality close to the Swedish border in August 2020 due to a rapid increase of infections affected the prison in this community, Eidsberg prison, too, and prisoners could not receive visits in this period. The lawfulness of national and local restrictions, such as quarantine regulations and fines, has been disputed with the objection that the restrictions put on citizens were too severe. During the first wave, the police were quite reluctant to enforce the rules, but during the second and third waves, the rules were enforced more actively.

3 Restrictions of contact with the outside world

Due to the lockdown of society in March 2020, the Correctional Service introduced heavy restrictions on prisoners' contacts with the outside world to curb the spreading of the virus inside prisons. Prison leave was reduced to a minimum. Prisoners in Norway are not entitled to such leave, but prison administrations merely have discretion to grant this in accordance with the Execution of Sentences Act (ESA) paras. 33 and 35.[11] There were, according to the Directorate of the Correctional Service (DCS or the Directorate) (2020c, 2020d), no legal obstacles to such a reduction. These restrictions were relaxed on 18 May 2020, and all restrictions were revoked on 22 June.

According to the ESA para. 31, prisoners have a right to receive visits, but on 17 March 2020, the Directorate ordered that prisoners could not receive visits from family and friends (DCS, 2020e; PO, 2020). Exceptions could be made if necessary, but lawyers should have contact with their clients via telephone or video link, alternatively consult their clients in the prisons separated by a glass screen. The abolition of visits was criticised by the National Preventive Mechanism (NPM)[12] represented by the PO (see PO, 2020), assessing this as unlawful. The Directorate, however, held that the suspension of visits could be based on the principle of necessity to prevent an outbreak of the pandemic in prisons (ibid.). The prohibition of visits was later based on the "Corona Enactment" (see below) and a temporary change to the ESA, which allowed the Correctional Service to prohibit visits in case of special risks of infection, or if the number of staff would make it disproportionately demanding to arrange visits.[13]

On 22 June 2020, when prisons went back to almost normal operation again, they also opened for visits. Yet, all visitors had to be tested for

COVID-19 infection prior to their visit. In addition, the prison facilities for family visits over the weekends remained closed. On 1 November 2020, the temporary change in the ESA to prohibit visits was repealed, but at this time the infection rates were steadily increasing, and the government initiated a new proposal to change the law to curb infections in prisons (DCS, 2020d).[14] These changes were adopted, took effect on 18 December 2020 and will last until 1 June 2021.

Another element of the Correctional Service management of the first wave of the pandemic was to limit the transfer of inmates between prison facilities (DCS, 2020f). The transfer of prisoners from closed to open facilities is considered a central step in the prisoners' rehabilitation process. Therefore, the Directorate stressed that transfer to less strict prison regimes for the purpose of rehabilitation was considered as a right according to ESA para. 15, which states that prisoners should not be subjected to stricter conditions than necessary. Closed prisons were used as quarantine units for newly admitted prisoners who later were transferred to open prisons, as quarantine arrangements were difficult to manage in open prisons.

4 Restrictions inside prisons

During the first wave of the pandemic in spring 2020, newly admitted prisoners had to spend 14 days in quarantine irrespective of whether they had symptoms of COVID-19 or not (DCS, 2020g). In practice, this meant solitary confinement (being locked up in single cells for 22 hours or more a day). The reasons for isolating newly arriving prisoners as a standard procedure were the lack of testing capacities for COVID-19, worries about a possible shortage of health personnel inside prisons and the protection of vulnerable prisoners who were at risk (PO, 2020). The isolation of prisoners is a controversial matter in Norway, and the practice of solitary confinement has been criticised by CPT for years (see e.g. CTP, 2019). The NPM therefore paid special attention to the practice of solitary confinement. In investigating how the effort to curb COVID-19 influenced prisoners, the NPM criticised the Correctional Service for using solitary confinement as a standard procedure for newly admitted prisoners although Health Authorities advised against this practice (PO, 2020). While the NPM did not find this standard procedure necessary and proportionate when evaluating it according to human rights standards (Nilsen and Schlanbusch, 2020; PO, 2020; see also CPT, 2020; SPT, 2020; NOU, 2021: 6), the Courts of Appeal rejected an appeal from a remand prisoner, who argued that this standard procedure to which he was subjected was too comprehensive and that the procedure could not be considered to accord with the principle of necessity in an emergency situation.[15] However, the Courts of Appeal stated that after the initial emergency phase of the pandemics was over, the legal basis for the practice should be clarified, and persons should be assessed individually to decide whether it was necessary for them to spend time in quarantine (see also NOU, 2021: 6). On 18 May 2020, the practice of quarantine for 14 days as a standard procedure was terminated and individual checks were introduced (DCS, 2020f).

The same precautions that took effect outside prisons were applied inside prisons: keeping distance (minimum one meter), washing hands often and thoroughly, and wearing masks. In general, good hygiene became important, and prisoners entering the prison were as far as possible located to prisons with high hygienic standards.

As the educational departments and most of the workshops also closed down on 13 March 2020, the daily activities for the prisoners were reduced to a minimum. The juvenile prisons, however, used distance teaching during the first lockdown period (first wave), and later adapted the teaching to local community rules. According to the NPM, the reduction of daytime activities was more noticeable in open prisons than in the closed prisons (PO, 2020). In addition, other social activities were reduced, such as sharing meals, and the opportunity to use the gym, but how much these restrictions influenced prison life varied from prison to prison. Even if the prisoners' social activities were reduced, prison administrations reported that prisoners were not necessarily more isolated during the lockdown in the first wave than before. As staff learned to handle the necessary measures to prevent infections better, later lockdowns were less strict.

5 Compensatory measures

In the revised national budget, passed in spring 2020, 7 million NOK were granted to buy 700 iPads and to extend the telephone time for prisoners (free calls) in order to provide for prisoners' contact with families and friends (Government press release, 12 May 2020). The Directorate reported to the NPM that more than 10,000 calls were made by iPad until mid-May 2020 (PO, 2020). Even if 30% of the prisoners reported to the NPM that they had not used an iPad, other prisoners had more time for contact with relatives and friends by the use of extended phone time and iPads than before the lockdown (ibid.). The iPads were also used for distance learning for imprisoned pupils and students.

According to the NPM, the prisons had introduced several measures to compensate for the reduction of daytime activities (PO, 2020). For example, prisoners in Bergen prison started to sew personal protective equipment for staff working at local health facilities.[16] More prisoners than usual were involved in cleaning, as it was important to uphold good hygienic standards. Different spare time activities were also introduced, and outdoor exercise for small groups of prisoners were arranged. DVDs and videos with exercise programmes and yoga activities were also distributed to prisoners. Some prisons extended the subscription of television channels, and some prisons managed to uphold the library services. Some prisons also extended their food budget as they experienced that making good food was a compensation that prisoners appreciated. As staff learned how to handle the restrictions, several prisons expanded their offer of activities (PO, 2020).

A critical issue at the beginning of the lockdown period in the first wave was to inform prisoners about the restrictions in place, and why these restrictions were introduced. The Correctional Service therefore distributed information pamphlets about the COVID-19 situation in prisons. They were first released in Norwegian, English and Russian on 17 April 2020, and later on in seven other languages. The Correctional Service also cooperated with the prisoners' radio programme to spread information. A telephone line for family and friends was opened on 15 April 2020, where they could receive general information about COVID-19 restrictions in prisons. In April 2021, the line was still operating.

6 Legal basis for restrictions and relaxations of the prison regime

The powers given to the Correctional Service by the ESA, which regulates the serving of sentences in prison as well as in the community, are quite wide. Release from an ordinary unconditional prison sentence or grants of prison leave, for example, are decided by the Correctional Service with no involvement from the courts. Besides, EM in Norway is a way of serving an unconditional prison sentence, and is based on an administrative decision by the Correctional Service after a court issues an unconditional sentence (Øster and Rokkan, 2018). A general principle in Norwegian public administration is that decisions should be made at the lowest level possible, but with opportunities for the citizens to appeal or complain to a higher authority. Decisions on early release of prisoners at the beginning of the pandemic, or on transfer of prisoners to serve their sentence on EM, have therefore been made by the prisons (local level), with some exceptions for the longest sentences (more than ten years), which have been decided at the regional level. The main rule of local decision-making keeps the system operational, but it also makes it vulnerable regarding the flow of information. Information needs to be communicated from the central level (Ministry and Directorate) to the regional and local levels in order to coordinate the practice, and the number of circulars and letters with directives from the Directorate to the regions and prisons has been extensive.

In this text, I have referred several times to the NPM's investigation concerning torture and inhuman treatment of prisoners during the lockdown period, published in the Parliamentary Ombudsman's report (2020). The NPM's critique of the Correctional Service in this situation is primarily based on the lack of legal authority to introduce measures that limit the fundamental rights of prisoners. By passing the "Corona Enactment" on 24 March 2020, the Parliament gave the government authority to make changes to 62 laws, among them the ESA, without consulting the Parliament. As we have seen, changes were made on the basis of this Enactment to prohibit visits, but no changes were made concerning the legal basis for the general use of a 14-day quarantine for newly admitted prisoners even after the Courts of Appeal emphasised that this should be clarified. The "Corona Enactment" was repealed on 27 May 2020, but on 18 May 2020, the Parliament passed a temporary change to the ESA.[17] Yet, the opportunity to clarify the legal basis for the use of a general period of quarantine was not taken, although the use of solitary confinement is controversial in Norway. This may be due to the termination of the general use of 14-day quarantine on the same day (18 May 2020). The temporary changes in the act were repealed on 1 November 2020, but new temporary changes concerning visits, solitary confinement, EM, temporary suspension of the execution of the sentence and leave took effect on 18 December 2020 (see above; ESA Chapter 3A).

7 Returning to normal

The policy of local rules to fight outbreaks of COVID-19 within certain areas, including the prisons in these areas, has continued in the third wave of the pandemic. The prisons have created preparedness plans in line with local health regulations to handle COVID-19 outbreaks in prisons, in which the cooperation with the local health service has been crucial. To increase readiness to react in critical situations both at a central level and at a local level has been a priority in Norwegian society since the assessment of the terror attacks of 22 July 2011 (NOU 2012: 14), and the COVID-19 situation has increased a general understanding of the value of preparedness and cooperation.

Without the COVID-19 pandemic, a "digital revolution" – as the Governor at Oslo Prison characterised it – would most likely not have happened in prisons. The introduction of iPads has expanded the prisoners' possibilities for contact with the outside world, and such technological solutions will most likely be permanent. The COVID-19 situation has proved it possible to find "unimaginable" solutions in a very short period, and this shows a great potential for further development of digital solutions in prisons as well as in probation, as the supervision of probationers was digitalised in this period as well.

The restrictions imposed on prisoners (and staff) have been successful in stopping the virus from entering and being spread in prisons (see also NOU, 2021: 6). However, the restrictions have had severe implications for the prisoners, and the laws regulating imprisonment and prison life in Norway have proven to be insufficient in such an acute and critical situation. The legal protection of prisoners, also in relation to international human rights standards, must be secured in such situations, and this issue needs to be addressed immediately, as we are not over this critical situation yet and we never know when new critical situations will arise.

Postscript: 3 December 2021

From October 2021 onwards, prisons in Norway began operating on a normal basis again. Outbreaks of the COVID-19 virus, as well as single incidents, were handled in accordance with temporary changes in the ESA. However, these provisions were repealed on 1 December 2021, in a period with increased infection rates in the society, including the spread of the new omicron variant. While the enforcement of new provisions in the ESA were awaited, an appeal was made to prisons to continue to isolate prisoners if an emergency arose and to deny visits in order to fight renewed outbreaks of the virus. By 3 December 2021, visits conducted via video links had become the new norm.

Notes

1 According to Aebi and Tiago (2020), there were 3,026 prisoners in Norway on 1 January 2020, which equals a prison population rate of 56.4 per 100,000 inhabitants.
2 See e.g. https://www.politiet.no/globalassets/04-aktuelt-tall-og-fakta/strasak/2020/Anmeldt-kriminalitet-Strasak-forste-tertial-2020. (Accessed 7 August 2020). Even if the number of registered crimes was low, there was a general concern about unregistered crime, especially regarding domestic violence and domestic sexual crimes.
3 Includes prison as well as probation staff.
4 Source: the Directorate of the Correctional Service.
5 See e.g. https://www.tv2.no/a/11307543/ (Accessed 8 August 2020).
6 LOV-2019-12-20-105 Lov om endringer i straffegjennomføringsloven mv. (gjennomføringstiden for straffegjennomføring med elektronisk kontroll mv.).
7 FOR-2020-03-27-461 Midlertidig forskrift om straffegjennomføring for å avhjelpe konsekvenser av utbrudd av Covid-19.
8 Prop. 56 L (2019-2020) Midlertidig lov om forskriftshjemmel for å avhjelpe konsekvenser av utbrudd av Covid-19 mv. (koronaloven).
9 LOV-1994-08-05-55 Act Relating to Control of Communicable Diseases.
10 FOR-2020-03-12-270 Vedtak etter lov om vern mot smittsomme sykdommer § 4-1 andre ledd om møteforbud og stenging av virksomhet.
11 LOV-2001-05-18-21 Act relating to the execution of sentences, etc. (The Execution of Sentences Act – ESA).
12 When Norway assigned the Optional Protocol to the Convention against Torture (OPCAT) in 2013, the Parliamentary Ombudsman was assigned the task of exercising the mandate by establishing a National Preventive Mechanism.
13 LOV-2020-05-26-49 Midlertidig lov om endringer i straffegjennomføringsloven (tiltak for å avhjelpe negative konsekvenser av covid-19).
14 Prop.36 L (2020-2021) Midlertidig lov om endringer i straffegjennomføringsloven (tiltak for å avhjelpe negative konsekvenser av covid-19).
15 Borgarting Courts of Appeal, Sentence 3 April 2020 (LB-2020-50640).
16 https://www.bt.no/nyheter/lokalt/i/Ady2zz/innsatte-sydde-smittevernutstyr-til-sykehjemmet. (Accessed 30 November 2020).
17 LOV-2020-05-26-49.

References

Aebi, M. F., and Tiago, M. M. (2020): *Prisons and Prisoners in Europe in Pandemic Times: An Evaluation of the Medium-Term Impact of the COVID-19 on Prison Population*. Strasbourg: Council of Europe.

Director General of Public Prosecution (DGPP) (2020): *Koronavirus (COVID-19) – Riksadvokatens Retningslinjer og direktiver.* Letter, 16 March 16. www.riksadvokaten.no/wp-content/uploads/2020/03/Retningslinjer-smittevern-160320.pdf. (Accessed 6 April 2021).

Directorate of the Correctional Service (DCS) (2020a): *Oppheving av iverksatte tiltak i forbindelse med COVID-19.* Letter to regional administrations and KRUS, 19 June.

Directorate of the Correctional Service (2020b): *Rundskriv om fremskutt løslatelse i medhold av straffegjennomføringsloven § 42 fjerde ledd – grunnet utbrudd av koronavirus.* Circular Letter 4/2020, 15 March.

Directorate of the Correctional Service (2020c): *Konsekvensene av COVID-19 utbruddet – tiltak for å redusere og forsinke smittespredning i fengslene.* Letter to regional administrations, 13 March.

Directorate of the Correctional Service (2020d): *Oppdaterte føringer pr. 6. november for håndtering av COVID-19 i kriminalomsorgen.* Letter to regional administrations, 6 November.

Directorate of the Correctional Service (2020e): *Midlertidig opphevelse av innsattes rett til besøk.* Letter to regional administrations and KRUS, 17 March.

Directorate of the Correctional Service (2020f): *Lemping av iverksatte tiltak for å redusere smittefaren og forsinke smittespredning i fengsel.* Letter to regional administrations and KRUS, 8 May.

Directorate of the Correctional Service (2020g): *Rundskriv KDI 6/2020 – gjennomføring av karantene og isolasjon i forbindelse med Coronavirus i kriminalomsorgen – gjeldende pr. 01.04.2020.* Circular Letter 6/2020, 3 April.

European Committee for the Prevention of Torture and Inhuman or Degrading Treatment or Punishment (CTP) (2019): *Report to the Norwegian Government on the visit to Norway carried out by the European Committee for the Prevention of Torture and Inhuman or Degrading Treatment or Punishment (CPT) from 28 May to 5 June 2018.* Strasbourg, 17 January 2019. https://rm.coe.int/1680909713. (Accessed 7 December 2020).

European Committee for the Prevention of Torture and Inhuman or Degrading Treatment or Punishment (CTP) (2020): *Statement of Principles Relating to the Treatment of Persons Deprived of their Liberty in the Context of the Coronavirus Disease (COVID-19) Pandemic*, CPT/Inf(2020)13, 20 March. https://rm.coe.int/16809cfa4b. (Accessed 7 December 2020).

Government Press Release, 12 May 2020. https://www.regjeringen.no/no/aktuelt/ikt-utstyr-til-kriminalomsorga/id2701915/?epsremainingpath=id2701915. (Accessed 30 November 2020).

Laursen, J., Mjåland, K., and Crewe, B. (2019): 'It's like a sentence before the sentence' - exploring the pains and possibilities of waiting for imprisonment. *British Journal of Criminology*, 60(2): 363–381. https://doi.org/10.1093/bjc/azz042. (Accessed 8 August 2020).

Nilsen, J. F., and Schlanbusch, M. D. (2020): Use of solitary confinement to prevent the spread of COVID-19 in Norwegian prisons. *Adapting to COVID-19: Medical*

Isolation and Quarantine in Prison during a Pandemic. Special issue 7 October. https://icpa.org/wp-content/uploads/2020/10/Expert-Network-Newsletter-_Special-Issue-6-CORRECTED.pdf. (Accessed 30 November 2020).

Norwegian Ministry of Justice (2020): *Informasjon vedrørende konsekvenser av COVID-19 for mennesker som er frihetsberøvet*. Letter to the Parliamentary Ombudsman, May. https://www.sivilombudsmannen.no/wp-content/uploads/2020/07/Svar-fra-JD-vedr.-Sivilombudsmannens-henvendelse.pdf. (Accessed 1 December 2020).

NOU 2012:14 *Rapport fra 22. Juli-kommisjonen*. Oslo: Departementenes servicesenter, Informasjonsforvaltning. https://www.regjeringen.no/contentassets/bb3dc76229c64735b4f6eb4dbfcdbfe8/no/pdfs/nou201220120014000dddpdfs.pdf (Accessed 1 December 2020).

NOU 2021: *6 Myndighetenes håndtering av koronaepidemien*. Oslo: Departementenes sikkerhets- og serviceorganisasjon, Teknisk redaksjon. https://www.koronakommisjonen.no/files/2021/04/Koronakommisjonens_rapport_NOU.pdf (Accessed 19 April 2021).

Øster, M. K., and Rokkan T. (2018): The Norwegian Approach to Electronic Monitoring: Changing the System and Making a Difference. *Federal Sentencing Reporter* 31(1), 75–84.

Paliamentary Ombudsman (PO) (2020): *Ivaretakelse av innsatte i fengsel under covid-19 pandemien*, June. https://www.sivilombudsmannen.no/wp-content/uploads/2020/06/Innsattes-forhold-i-fengsel-under-covid-19.pdf. (Accessed 8 August 2020).

Pratt, J. (2008): Scandinavian Exceptionalism in an Era of Penal Excess. Part I: The Nature and Roots of Scandinavian Exceptionalism. *British Journal of Criminology* 48(2), 119–37.

Pratt, J., and Ericsson, A. (2013): *Contrast in Punishment. An Explanation of Anglophone Excess and Nordic Exceptionalism*. New York: Routledge.

Subcommittee on Prevention of Torture and Other Cruel, Inhuman or Degrading Treatment or Punishment (SPT) (2020): *Advice of the Subcommittee to States Parties and National Preventive Mechanisms Relating to the Coronavirus Disease (COVID-19) Pandemic (adopted on March 25th, 2020)*, CAT/OP/10, 7 April. https://undocs.org/CAT/OP/10. (Accessed 7 December 2020).

32 Poland

Barbara Stańdo-Kawecka

1 The penal climate and current state of the prison system

Before 1989, criminal policy in Poland, like in other countries of Central and Eastern Europe, was characterised by a high level of punitiveness and a large prison population as compared to Western Europe. The reforms of the criminal justice system carried out in the 1990s aimed mainly at adjusting the criminal law to international standards and making it more humane, liberal and rational (Stańdo-Kawecka, 2020: 944 f.). In 1997, the Code of the Execution of Penalties (CEP), the Penal Code (PC) and the Code of Criminal Procedure (CCP) were passed by the parliament. The work on the draft of the penal codification from 1997 happened in a period that was characterised by a broad political and social consensus on the need for liberalisation of the repressive criminal policy implemented by the authoritarian state in the post-war period. However, shortly after the adoption of the 1997 Codes, the penal climate began to change. As a result, the 1997 PC was subject to various criticisms, and since its adoption, it has been amended several dozen times.

An extensive criminal law reform was implemented in 2015. Its primary goal was to change the structure of sentences imposed by criminal courts in previous years because of the overuse of suspended prison sentences. In the period preceding the 2015 reform, the latter sentences amounted to over 60% of the total number of adjudged penalties. For some critics, such a widespread use of suspended imprisonment was unacceptable because it seemed to be 'too soft on crime'. Others raised the issue of the frequent revocation of the suspension of imprisonment in cases in which an offender committed a new offence or violated conditions or obligations attached to his sentence. A large number of suspended and then revoked prison sentences contributed to an increase in the size of the prison population (Krajewski, 2014: 108).

Generally, the 2015 criminal law reform reduced the application of suspended prison sentences in favour of fines and the penalty of restrictions of liberty in the community. The latter is executed in the community and includes the offender's obligation to perform unpaid work for public purposes. Exceptionally, if offenders have permanent employment, certain

DOI: 10.4324/9781003169178-32

deductions (10–25%) from their remuneration are possible instead of or in addition to unpaid work (Art. 34 and 35 of the 1997 PC). This sentence is a mixture of a fine and community service in other countries. Additionally, in 2015, the legislator introduced a 'split sentence' previously unknown in the Polish criminal law. This sentence combines short-term imprisonment of up to three, or in some cases up to six months, and the penalty of restrictions of liberty in the community up to two years (Muszyńska, 2020: 194). The rationale for the change was the idea of a 'short shock therapy' in a prison followed by the execution of the community sanction.

The 2015 criminal law reform resulted in significant changes in the structure of imposed penalties. The proportion of fines and penalties of restrictions of liberty in the community in the total number of penalties were increasing. The 'split sentence' was imposed very rarely. Also rare were penal measures (similar to additional penalties in other countries such as deprivation of public rights, interdiction of driving vehicles and forfeiture; see Art. 39 of the 1997 PC) adjudicated as the only penal reaction. At the same time, there was a marked decline in the share of suspended imprisonment. In the years 2001–2014, the percentage of the latter sentence fluctuated between 54 and 60% while in the years following the 2015 reform, it was constantly dropping, to 20% in 2018. The legislator therefore managed to achieve the goal of reducing the use of suspended sentences. However, statistical data indicate a side effect of this reform, which is an increase in the share of immediate imprisonment (Ministry of Justice, 2019). Ultimately, the reform did not bring the expected fall in the number of prisoners.

The total prison population in Poland consists of three categories of inmates: pre-trial detainees, offenders serving their prison sentence (in case also after a recall of a suspended sentence or parole) and persons jailed for a petty crime.

Pre-trial detainees are accommodated in remand prisons. The specific short-term detention penalty (for minor offences) lasts up to 30 days. The prison sentence for an offence is imposed for the period of one month to 15 years and exceptionally to 20 years. Additionally, the 1997 PC provides for two separate prison sentences of 25 years and life imprisonment. The vast majority of persons deprived of their liberty in prisons are perpetrators sentenced for offences; the percentage of those jailed for petty offences in the prison population is very small. The overall number of prisoners started growing soon after the enactment of the 1997 PC, which entered into force in September 1998. In 1999, the prison population rate in Poland was 147 per 100,000. In the next decade, it generally exceeded 200, and in the peak year 2006, it even amounted to 232 (Nawój-Śleszyński, 2013: 213). The current prison population rate in Poland (over 180) exceeds not only the corresponding rates in Western European countries but also in several countries of Central and Eastern Europe (Aebi and Tiago, 2020: 7).

The rapid increase in the number of prisoners after the law reform of 1997 mentioned above resulted in serious prison overcrowding. In the first decade of this century, the total number of prisoners, including remand prisoners, significantly exceeded the official capacity of institutions despite the fact that the latter is defined according to one of the lowest norms in European countries; this is three m^2 minimum space per one prisoner. In 2009, the prison overcrowding in Poland was recognised by the ECtHR as a structural problem (*Orchowski v. Poland*, 22 October 2009, application no. 17885/04; *Norbert Sikorski v. Poland*, 22 October 2009, application no. 17599/05). At the same time, domestic judicial decisions urged the Polish authorities to intensify their efforts aiming at solving that problem (see also Stańdo-Kawecka, 2014: 231f.). In recent years, the prison population density was less than 100%. On 4 December 2020, it amounted to 85% (Central Administration of the Prison Service, 2020). However, the official minimum standard of three m^2 of living space per prisoner has not changed since the enactment of the 1997 CEP, despite repeated recommendations of the European Committee for the Prevention of Torture (European Committee for the Prevention of Torture, 2018: 5) and the National Mechanism for the Prevention of Torture (Rzecznik Praw Obywatelskich, 2020a: 79).

The small living space per prisoner is not the only problem regarding the living conditions in penitentiary institutions. Another issue of special importance in the time of the COVID-19 pandemic relates to multi-person prison cells. Already in 2018, the Ombudsman drew the attention of the Central Administration of the Prison Service to the problem of prison cells for too many inmates. He asked the Director General of the Prison Service to prepare a plan concerning the removal of all prison cells designated for more than 10 inmates (Rzecznik Praw Obywatelskich, 2018). The latest report on safety of prisoners, published by the Supreme Audit Office in 2020, reveals that there still were numerous prison cells housing more than 10 inmates. As of 28 October 2019, there were 85 cells with a capacity of more than 10 persons in closed prisons (Najwyższa Izba Kontroli, 2020: 36).

1.1 The spread of the COVID-19 epidemic in the country, including prisons

The outbreak of the COVID-19 pandemic happened in Poland later than in Western Europe. The first case was diagnosed on 4 March 2020. For several weeks prior to this, the mass media had reported the dramatic course of the epidemic in other countries, in particular Italy and Spain. It was obvious that if the epidemic were to spread rapidly in Poland, the underfunded healthcare system would collapse completely. Therefore, it can be assumed that it was the fear of the collapse of the health service that prompted the government to announce the state of an epidemic threat shortly after the first cases of COVID-19 were confirmed. Educational institutions were closed on 12 March 2020. One week later, an ordinance announcing the state of epidemic was issued.[1] On the basis of this, shopping centres, restaurants, cinemas, theatres and some other places frequented by the public were closed. An amendment to the ordinance, issued four days later,[2] also introduced severe restrictions on citizens' movement.

Undoubtedly, the early lockdown combined with a high level of social discipline caused by the fear of COVID-19 contributed to the restriction of the epidemic. In March and April 2020, the daily numbers of confirmed infections with SARS-CoV-2 in Poland, which has 38 million inhabitants, were around 300. In May 2020, certain restrictions were gradually loosened. The state of epidemic was not cancelled, and some restrictions also applied in the summer. However, they were not observed by citizens during their holidays as carefully as before. Additionally, in Poland in June and July 2020, two rounds of the presidential election took place. The campaign preceding the election also had an impact on reducing political and public support for the imposed restrictions. After children returned to school in September and students started their university courses in October, a rapid increase in the daily number of COVID-19 cases was recorded. The spread of the pandemic resulted in the government restoring several restrictions in October and November 2020. Shopping centres, cultural institutions, restaurants, swimming pools and fitness clubs were closed again, children and young people returned to E-learning instead of attending schools and universities, and wearing masks became obligatory in all public places. Since the beginning of December 2020, a significant decrease in the number of reported cases of COVID-19 has been observed. However, fear of another wave of COVID-19 led to many of the restrictions being kept in place, and only some of them were gradually cancelled in January and February 2021. In February 2021, the daily numbers of COVID-19 cases began to grow again and in March they exceeded 35,000 (COVID-19 w Polsce, 2021). As a result, the policy of tightening restrictions was reimplemented.

As far as problems caused by the spread of COVID-19 in prisons are concerned, there is little reliable information on this subject in Poland. In May 2020, Ewa Siedlecka, a journalist from the weekly, *Polityka*, wrote an article with the meaningful title 'Strange oases of health, or a virus in Polish prisons' (*Dziwne oazy zdrowia, czyli wirus w polskich więzieniach*). As she noted ironically, it seemed that Poland was a world leader in the fight against the pandemic in prisons, because prisoners sewed masks, were hardly ill and did not protest. In her article, she recalled the statistical data presented by the spokeswoman of the Central Administration of the Prison Service, according to which, at the beginning of May 2020, there were 16 persons suffering from COVID-19, including 11 prison officers and five prisoners. The latter were not infected inside prisons, but before their admission to the institution (Siedlecka, 2020).

On 12 November 2020, the Ombudsman unsuccessfully asked the Minister of Justice, Zbigniew Ziobro, for information on the number of COVID-19 cases reported among prisoners and prison staff members (Rzecznik Praw Obywatelskich, 2020b). According to data obtained by the Helsinki Foundation for Human Rights from the Central Administration of the Prison

Service, 400 prisoners and 3,119 staff members had tested positive for SARS-CoV-2 by 3 December 2020 (Helsińska Fundacja Praw Człowieka, 2021). In early March 2021, the journalist Marcin Terlik (2021) referred to data provided by the Prison Service and wrote that about 1,053 prisoners and 4,598 staff members had been infected with SARS-CoV-2 since the beginning of the pandemic.

2 The penal policy concerning the execution of prison sentences during the COVID-19 pandemic

Thus far, the COVID-19 pandemic has not resulted in extensive legal changes in the execution of prison sentences. However, two new institutions were introduced by the Act of 31 March 2020.[3] The new institutions concerned a special type of break in the enforcement of prison sentences and serving prison sentences under electronic monitoring. The Act of 31 March 2020 added an additional reason (apart from the existing reasons of mental illness or serious illness) to Art. 153 CEP: a break in the enforcement of prison sentences may be granted by the penitentiary court at the request of the prison director during the period of the COVID-19 epidemic, if it may contribute to the reduction or elimination of the epidemic. This special kind of a break may last no longer than until the end of the announced state of the COVID-19 epidemic or epidemic threat. It applies to perpetrators of non-serious crimes and requires a positive criminological prognosis. This special break was conceived as a safety valve enabling a temporary reduction in the number of prisoners during the epidemic. However, restrictive premises severely limited its possible application. In January 2021, the Director General of the Prison Service stated that no prisoner had benefited from such a break because of the stable situation in prisons (Aby wróciła normalność, 2021: 5).

The possibility of serving a short prison sentence outside a prison under electronic monitoring was provided for in Polish criminal law before the outbreak of the pandemic (see Stańdo-Kawecka and Grzywa-Holten, 2015: 162). Since 2016, electronic monitoring may be applied as a way of enforcement of prison sentences outside prisons. Furthermore, it can be used as a safety measure (including post-penal measure) against perpetrators posing a threat to the public, as well as in conjunction with such penal measures as a ban on entering a mass event or approaching the victim. In practice, it has been mainly used as an alternative way of serving prison sentences. Before changes introduced by the Act of 31 March 2020, the possibility of serving a prison term under electronic monitoring was limited to sentences not exceeding, in total one year (Stańdo-Kawecka and Grzywa-Holten, 2017: 412f.). Under the amended regulations of the CEP, it was extended to sentences up to one year and six months. As previously, offenders may apply for such permission before entering the prison (front door) or after being

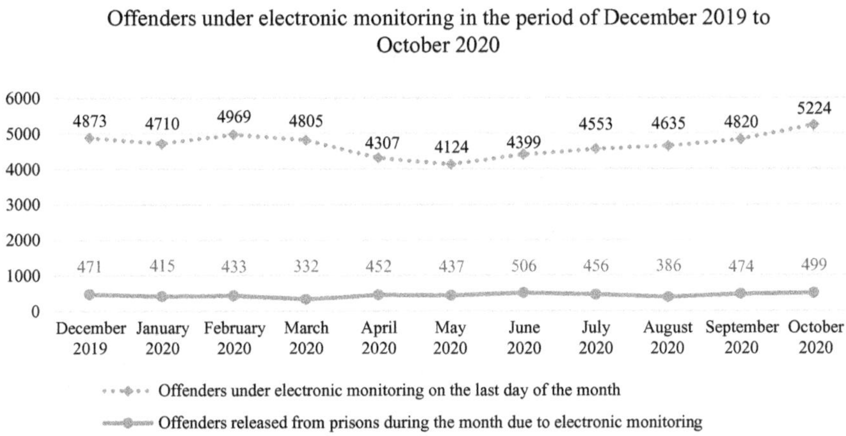

Figure 32.1 The number of offenders under electronic monitoring and released from prisons due to electronic monitoring (from December 2019 to October 2020).

Source: Central Administration of the Prison Service (2019–2020a).

admitted to it (back door). In the light of statistical data, the extension has not had a significant impact on the prison population. Figure 32.1 shows the number of prisoners released from prison as a result of the penitentiary court permission for serving the remainder of their sentence under electronic monitoring. After a certain decline in March 2020, in the following months, the number of such prisoners stabilised at a level similar to that before the outbreak of the pandemic. Since May 2020, the total number of offenders under electronic monitoring has showed an upward trend. However, in October 2020, it did not differ significantly from that before the pandemic.

The total number of prisoners in the period of the pandemic, that is between 29 February and 31 October 2020, decreased by 9.4%. As can be seen from Figure 32.2, at the end of February, the prison population amounted to nearly 76,000, while at the end of October, it dropped to around 68,500. The decline occurred among prisoners sentenced for offences (11.6%) and jailed for petty crimes (17.4%). The number of detainees in remand prisons in the same period rose by 7.8%.

The decrease in the number of prisoners sentenced for offences and punished for petty crimes resulted mainly, as Figure 32.3 reveals, from the lower number of admissions to prisons, which was clearly visible in the period from March to May 2020. Undoubtedly, it was related to the temporary suspension of court activities in criminal cases, with the exception of cases determined by law as urgent.

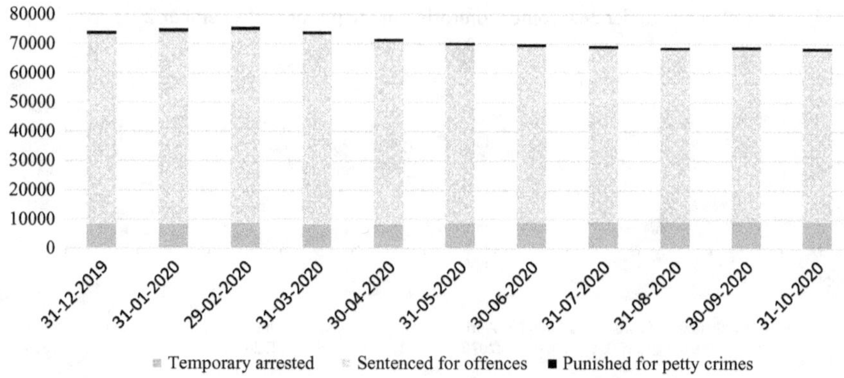

Figure 32.2 The number of prisoners according to their legal status (from 31 December 2019 to 31 October 2020).
Source: Central Administration of the Prison Service 2019–2020a.

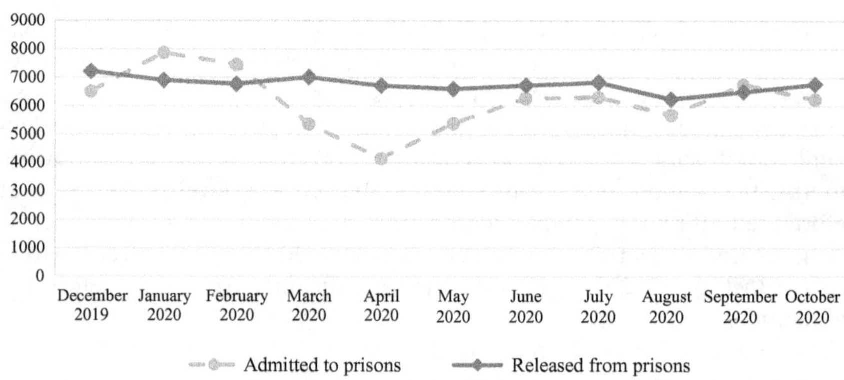

Figure 32.3 The number of prisoners admitted to and released from prisons (from December 2019 to October 2020).
Source: Central Administration of the Prison Service, 2019–2020a.

The Act of 31 March 2020 contained numerous provisions aimed at tightening criminal liability for the crime of direct exposure of another person to infection with a serious incurable or life-threatening disease, as well as provisions concerning administrative fines for breaking certain restrictions imposed in order to prevent and combat the epidemic. Statistical data on their implementation are not yet available.

3 Restrictions of contact with the outside world

According to the 1997 CEP, prisons for sentenced offenders, including offenders punished for petty crimes, are organised by differentiating closed, semi-open or open regimes. Remand prisons are closed institutions. Semi-open and open prisons have fewer security arrangements and are characterised by a lower degree of isolation of the inmates. In closed prisons, the cells are locked at night and, as a rule, they are closed during the day as well. Education, training, cultural and sports activities are organised within the prison. The same applies to prison labour; inmates in closed prisons are allowed to work outside the institution only exceptionally. In prisons with a semi-open and open regime, the cells are unlocked during the day and even at night. Educational, cultural, sports and therapeutic activities may be organised outside the prison. The prisoners can be employed outside the establishment, not only without a guard, but also in single workplaces.

The authors of the 1997 CEP adopted the principle of normalisation as one of its basic principles and provided sentenced prisoners with an opportunity to obtain different types of leave. Home leave for up to 14 days, but not exceeding 28 days per year could be granted as a reward after at least half of the term required for conditional release had been served. Short leave of up to 30 hours is also specified among such rewards. The total number of the latter is limited to 28 per year. Additionally, inmates serving their terms in semi-open prisons may be granted prison leave for up to 14 days, while inmates placed in open prisons may be given up to 28 days per year. These periods of leave are granted by the prison governor irrespective of prison leave granted as a reward. A new form of prison leave for up to 14 days may be granted to prisoners in the six months before release in order to enable them to look for work or for accommodation. Furthermore, prisoners could be granted home leave for up to five days for important personal or family reasons; if necessary, they are escorted by guards.

Statistical data clearly indicate that all types of prison leave have been significantly reduced because of the pandemic. In the last quarter of 2019, over 4,000 prisoners obtained over 10,000 prison leaves in order to take part in educational, therapeutic and recreational activities. In the first quarter of 2020, both of these numbers almost halved. In two consecutive quarters, such leave was granted exceptionally, while several other types of leave were abandoned (Central Administration of the Prison Service, 2019–2020b).

Article 105 of the CEP stipulates that sentenced prisoners should be allowed to maintain ties primarily with their families and other relatives through visits, correspondence, phone calls, parcels and money orders. In justified cases, and with the consent of the prison director, they should also be allowed to maintain these ties through other means of communication. The number of visits depends on the type of prisons. In closed prisons, they are entitled to receive two, in semi-open prisons three visits a month, and in open prisons, an unlimited number of visits are allowed. The situation of detainees on remand is less favourable. They are entitled to receive at least one visit a month; however, they need the consent of the public prosecutor or the court.

Due to the epidemic threat in mid-March 2020, family visits in prisons were suspended. They became possible again in August 2020, but to a limited extent. Only one adult family member was allowed to visit a prisoner, while children could not attend such visits. The lack of direct contact with children due to the suspension of visits and prison leave created the risk of weakening family ties and caused a lot of suffering for many prisoners and their families. For this reason, the Ombudsman requested the Minister of Justice to consider granting prisoners visits with children while maintaining sanitary standards (Rzecznik Praw Obywatelskich, 2020c). However, since mid-October 2020, all family visits in prisons have been suspended again. Therefore, many prisoners have not met their children since March 2020.

4 Restrictions inside prisons

Basic information concerning the situation inside prisons shortly after the outbreak of the pandemic is included in the letter of the Ministry of Justice of 1 April 2020 sent to the Ombudsman in response to his questions. Measures aimed at preventing the spread of COVID-19 were introduced in prisons in consultation with sanitary and epidemiological services. All persons entering prisons were subjected to mandatory temperature measurement. The possibility of non-staff members, including clergy of various denominations and probation officers, entering prisons was strictly limited. All newly admitted prisoners were quarantined for a period of 14 days. At the same time, transfers of persons deprived of their liberty between different penitentiary institutions were limited, as was the number of prisoners working outside prisons. A special prison hospital was established for inmates with COVID-19 (Ministry of Justice, 2020). The restrictions on entering prisons in some cases were so far-reaching that even defence lawyers encountered serious difficulties in meeting their clients, which resulted in the Ombudsman's intervention (Rzecznik Praw Obywatelskich, 2020d).

According to available data, at the very beginning of the pandemic, the number of prisoners employed outside prisons was strictly limited. On 2 April 2020, the employment of prisoners was also suspended inside prisons for health and safety reasons (Krawczyńska, 2020a). The gradual return of prisoners to work started in July 2020, but a few months later (in October) certain restrictions were reintroduced. Data collected by the National Mechanism for the Prevention of Torture indicate that at least in some prisons the movement of inmates within the institution was strictly limited. The number of inmates in groups taking prison walks was reduced. Prison cells in open and semi-open prisons were locked, although, according to the 1997 CEP, they should be unlocked at least during the day (Krajowy Mechanizm Prewencji Tortur, 2020). Inmates attending prison schools could continue their education by means of materials delivered to their cells (Łupińska, 2020). A certain number of prisoners in various penitentiary institutions performed unpaid work consisting of sewing masks and producing other protective equipment for medical facilities or care institutions (Pietrasik, 2020; Pytel, 2020). Without appropriate research, however, it is impossible to characterise the scale of restrictions on group activities in particular prisons.

5 Compensatory measures

Undoubtedly, the basic way of compensating for the prohibition of direct contacts between prisoners and their relatives was extending permission to make calls by telephone or on Skype. Under Article 105 of the CEP, sentenced prisoners have the right to use a telephone installed in the prison ward at their own expense or at the expense of the caller. According to the ordinance of the Minister of Justice, sentenced offenders serving their terms in closed prisons may use a telephone once a day. The prison director may allow them to make an additional phone call. In semi-open or open prisons, phone calls may be allowed more often. Generally, a telephone call may not exceed five minutes at any one time. During the pandemic, the prisoners' access to a telephone was broadened. However, changes to the rules governing the use of a telephone by sentenced prisoners have not been determined by law. They have been left to the decision of the prison director.

As was mentioned above, sentenced prisoners should be allowed to maintain ties with their families and other relatives through means of communication other than visits, correspondence, phone calls or parcels. Before the outbreak of the COVID-19 pandemic, they were allowed to use 'other means of communication' in the form of calls on Skype relatively rarely and mainly in cases of foreigners whose families lived far away. During the pandemic, Skype calls between inmates and their families became more popular. However, the greater access to telephone and Skype calls did not apply to persons detained on remand. The provisions of the 1997 CEP on the enforcement of the temporary arrest state that such detainees may use a telephone only with the consent of the public prosecutor or the court. Unlike for sentenced prisoners, the relevant CEP provisions do not provide expressly for the possibility of maintaining family ties by persons temporarily arrested through 'other means of communication'. During the pandemic, the Ombudsman received numerous complaints from this group of prisoners. They alleged that they were deprived of contacts with their relatives, as they had not obtained consent to contact their families by phone. At the same time, they were denied connections via Skype due to the lack of clear legal regulations. In October 2020, the Ombudsman asked the Minister of Justice for changes to legal provisions in order to provide temporary arrested persons with a real possibility of contacts with their families (Rzecznik Praw Obywatelskich, 2020e).

Apart from the wider use of a telephone and internet communication via Skype in some prisons, other measures were used to compensate for the prohibition of direct contacts between prisoners and their families. Inmates participated in cultural and educational activities, which allowed them to write, read, illustrate and record fairy tales for their children, as well as to record songs for them. The printed or recorded materials were sent to the children (Goss and Kamińska, 2020; Krawczyńska, 2020b). It seems that restrictions introduced in prisons due to the pandemic contributed to the development of various compensatory activities.

6 Legal basis for restrictions and relaxations of the prison regime

The authors of the 1997 CEP attached great importance to the clear legal status of persons deprived of their liberty and tried to determine prisoners' rights and obligations as precisely as possible. Additionally, they anticipated that in certain situations, it might be necessary to limit some of the prisoners' rights temporarily and created the suitable legal basis for such restrictions. According to Article 247 of the Code, in cases justified by special hygiene or health reasons or a serious threat to security, the prison director may temporarily suspend or limit the employment of inmates as well as prison visits and walks, collective educational, cultural or sports activities and religious services. The prison director is also entitled to introduce other restrictions regarding prisoners' contacts with the outside world and inside the institution.

All restrictions may be introduced by the prison director for a period of up to seven days and they are immediately notified to the penitentiary judge. The CEP allows for the extension of the duration of the restrictions with the consent of the same judge. After the outbreak of the COVID-19 pandemic, prison directors referred to these provisions when they issued or prolonged orders to suspend visits and employment outside the facility or the performance of religious services. The pandemic highlighted the need for appropriate legal regulations relating to prisoners' contacts with the outside world via the internet. Currently, in cases concerning persons detained on remand, there is no clear legal basis permitting such contacts. When it comes to sentenced prisoners, such contacts depend on a discretionary decision by the prison director.

7 Returning to normal

Unfortunately, issues concerning the enforcement of prison sentences during the COVID-19 pandemic are not a priority for the Ministry of Justice. For several years, the Minister of Justice and Prosecutor General, Zbigniew Ziobro, has been involved in 'judicial reform' which in fact means the subordination of the Constitutional Court to the ruling party, the reduction of the independence of other courts and the total politicisation of the prosecution service. In recent months, he has been mainly concerned with the fight against the rule of law mechanism in the European Union (Tatała, Rutynowska and Wachowiec, 2020: 4f.). Currently, long-term changes in criminal policy due to the pandemic experience are not being discussed. The information gathered by the (still) independent Ombudsman and the National Mechanism for the Prevention of Torture operating in his office as well as articles published by the Prison Service magazine show that, in practice, numerous programmes have been implemented in prisons in order to compensate for the introduced restrictions. Among such programmes, the production of masks and other protective equipment for local health or childcare facilities, the communication of prisoners with their families via Skype, writing and recording fairy tales or recording Christmas carols for children may be mentioned. The lockdown prompted the use of the videoconferencing system by courts, including cases concerning early conditional release (Krawczyńska, 2020c). Undoubtedly, good practices developed during the pandemic should be the subject of further research aimed at their identification and dissemination.

Notes

1 Rozporządzenie Ministra Zdrowia z dnia 20 marca 2020 r. w sprawie ogłoszenia na obszarze Rzeczypospolitej Polskiej stanu epidemii, Dz. U. 2020, poz. 491.
2 Rozporządzenie Ministra Zdrowia z dnia 24 marca 2020 r. zmieniające rozporządzenie w sprawie ogłoszenia na obszarze Rzeczypospolitej Polskiej stanu epidemii, Dz. U. 2020, poz. 522.
3 Ustawa z dnia 31 marca 2020 r. o zmianie ustawy o szczególnych rozwiązaniach związanych z zapobieganiem, przeciwdziałaniem i zwalczaniem COVID-19, innych chorób zakaźnych oraz wywołanych nimi sytuacji kryzysowych oraz niektórych innych ustaw, Dz. U. 2020, poz. 568.

References

Aby wróciła normalność (2021): *Forum Służby Więziennej* 1, 4–5. Online, https://www.sw.gov.pl/assets/07/56/35/cba6a426ee7412135b82b2b744e8d5a63c9bdcf5.pdf [accessed: 7 March 2021].

Aebi, M. F., and Tiago, M. M. (2020): *Prisons and Prisoners in Europe in Pandemic Times: An evaluation of the medium-term impact of the COVID-19 on prison populations*, Council of Europe, Strasbourg and Lausanne. Online, https://wp.unil.ch/space/publications/2199-2/ [accessed: 10.12.2020].

Central Administration of the Prison Service (2019–2020a): *Miesięczna informacja statystyczna* (*Monthly Statistical Information*). Online, https://www.sw.gov.pl/dzial/statystyka [accessed: 20 December 2020].

Central Administration of the Prison Service (2019–2020b): *Kwartalna informacja statystyczna* (*Quarterly Statistical Information*). Online, https://www.sw.gov.pl/dzial/statystyka [accessed: 20 December 2020].

Central Administration of the Prison Service (2020): *Komunikat o zaludnieniu aresztów śledczych i zakładów karnych*, Online, https://www.sw.gov.pl/strona/statystyka--komunikat [accessed: 20 December 2020].

COVID-19 w Polsce: liczba zakażeń koronawirusem i zgonów [AKTUALIZACJA] (2021): Online. https://pulsmedycyny.pl/covid-19-w-polsce-liczba-zakazen-koronawirusem-i-zgonow-aktualizacja-984368 [accessed: 29 April 2021].

European Committee for the Prevention of Torture (2018): *Report to the Polish Government on the visit to Poland carried out by the European Committee for the Prevention of Torture and Inhuman or Degrading Treatment or Punishment (CPT) from 11 to 22 May 2017.* Strasbourg: Council of Europe.

Goss, K., and Kamińska, E. (2020): Święta na odległość. *Forum Służby Więziennej* 12, 19. Online, https://www.sw.gov.pl/assets/85/76/14/348b7efa06cf5c0dfc3315a1a2bee4830d18f79f.pdf [accessed: 20 December 2020].

Helsińska Fundacja Praw Człowieka (2021): Wystąpienie HFPC do Ministra Sprawiedliwości, 29 stycznia 2021. Online, https://www.hfhr.pl/wp-content/uploads/2021/01/wystapienie-HFPC_pandemia-jednostki-penitencjarne_fin.pdf [accessed: 7 March 2021].

Krajewski, K. (2014): Different penal climates in Europe. *Kriminologijos Studijos* 10, 86–111. Doi: 10.15388/CrimLithuan.2014.1.3678.

Krajowy Mechanizm Prewencji Tortur (2020): *Koronawirus. Zakażenia w zakładach karnych w Iławie i Opolu Lubelskim.* Online, https://www.rpo.gov.pl/pl/content/koronawirus-zakazenia-w-zakladach-karnych-ilawa-opole-lubelskie 2020-12-03 [accessed: 20 December 2020].

Krawczyńska, A. (2020a): Praca wraca. *Forum Służby Więziennej* 8, 8–11. Online, https://www.sw.gov.pl/assets/52/77/66/a39da14ee006dae6474f314d1c7cc3cdda70a57c.pdf [accessed: 20 December 2020].

Krawczyńska, A. (2020b): Zjednoczyć rodziny. *Forum Służby Więziennej* 12, 20–21. Online, https://www.sw.gov.pl/assets/85/76/14/348b7efa06cf5c0dfc3315a1a2bee4830d18f79f.pdf [accessed: 20 December 2020].

Krawczyńska, A. (2020c): E-spotkania. *Forum Służby Więziennej* 12, 8–11. Online, https://www.sw.gov.pl/assets/85/76/14/348b7efa06cf5c0dfc3315a1a2bee4830d18f79f.pdf [accessed: 20 December 2020].

Łupińska, A. (2020): Nauka i praca. *Forum Służby Więziennej* 5, 8. Online, https://www.sw.gov.pl/assets/08/73/37/321b9adbd293e7b8efaeda63ec5efbe35fd648f1.pdf [accessed: 20 December 2020].

Ministry of Justice (2019): *Prawomocne skazania i warunkowe umorzenia osób dorosłych w latach 2001–2018 – czyn główny*, Wydział Statystycznej Informacji Zarządczej Departament Strategii i Funduszy Europejskich Ministerstwa Sprawiedliwości. Online, https://www.sw.gov.pl/dzial/statystyka [accessed: 20 December 2020].

Ministry of Justice (2020): *Odpowiedź z dnia 1.04.2020 na pismo Rzecznika Praw Obywatelskich.* Online, https://www.rpo.gov.pl/sites/default/files/Odpowied%C5%BA%20MS%2C%201.04.2020.pdf [accessed: 20 December 2020].

Muszyńska, A. (2020): Uwagi na temat kierunku zmian prawa karnego materialnego w latach 2015–2019. *Acta Universitatis Wratislaviensis No. 3978. Przegląd Prawa i Administracji*, CXX/2: 191–202. Doi:10.19195/0137–1134.120.62.

Najwyższa Izba Kontroli (2020): *Bezpieczeństwo osadzonych.* Online, https://www.nik.gov.pl/plik/id, 22869,vp, 25572.pdf [accessed: 20 December 2020].

Nawój-Śleszyński, A. (2013): *Przeludnienie więzień w Polsce – przyczyny, następstwa i możliwości przeciwdziałania*, Wydawnictwo Uniwersytetu Łódzkiego, Łódź.

Pietrasik, M. (2020): Z aresztu do dzieci. *Forum Służby Więziennej* 8, 17. Online, https://www.sw.gov.pl/assets/52/77/66/a39da14ee006dae6474f314d1c7cc3cd-da70a57c.pdf [accessed: 20 December 2020].

Pytel, M. (2020): Co odsłoniła maska. *Forum Służby Więziennej* 5, 9. Online, https://www.sw.gov.pl/assets/08/73/37/321b9adbd293e7b8efaeda63ec5efbe35fd648f1.pdf [accessed: 20 December 2020].

Rzecznik Praw Obywatelskich (2018): *Wystąpienie do Dyrektora Generalnego Służby Więziennej w sprawie warunków bytowych osadzonych w wieloosobowych celach mieszkalnych z dnia 2018-11-22.* Online, https://www.rpo.gov.pl/sprawy-generalne/index.php?sprawa=11656 [accessed: 20 December 2020]

Rzecznik Praw Obywatelskich (2020a): Raport Rzecznika Praw Obywatelskich z działalności Krajowego Mechanizmu Prewencji Tortur w 2019 r. *Biuletyn Rzecznika Praw Obywatelskich. Źródła*, 3. Online, https://www.rpo.gov.pl/sites/default/files/Raport_RPO_z_dzialalnosci_KMPT_2019.pdf [accessed: 20 December 2020].

Rzecznik Praw Obywatelskich (2020b): *Koronawirus. RPO pyta o zakażenia w więzieniach, aresztach, zakładach poprawczych.* Online, https://www.rpo.gov.pl/pl/content/koronawrius-rpo-pyta-o-zakazenia-wiezieniach-aresztach-zakladach-poprawczych [accessed: 20 December 2020].

Rzecznik Praw Obywatelskich (2020c): *Pismo do Służby Więziennej w sprawie widzeń podczas pandemii, 9.9.2020.* Online, https://www.rpo.gov.pl/sites/default/files/Pismo%20do%20S%C5%82u%C5%BCby%20Wi%C4%99ziennej%20ws.%20widze%C5%84%20podczas%20pandemii%2C%209.9.2020.pdf [accessed: 20 December 2020].

Rzecznik Praw Obywatelskich (2020d): *Wystąpienie do Dyrektora Generalnego Służby Więziennej w sprawie wniosków osób pozbawionych wolności z dnia 7.05.2020.* Online, https://www.rpo.gov.pl/sites/default/files/WG%20do%20DGSW%20ws.%20wniosk%C3%B3w%20os%C3%B3b%20pozbawionych%20wolno%C5%9Bci%2C%207.05.2020.pdf [accessed: 20 December 2020].

Rzecznik Praw Obywatelskich (2020e): *Wystąpienie z dnia 19.10.2020 do Ministra Sprawiedliwości w sprawie rozmów przez Skype osób aresztowanych.* Online, Wystąpienie do MS ws. rozmów przez Skype osób aresztowanych, 19.10.2020.pdf [accessed: 20 December 2020].

Siedlecka, E. (2020): Dziwne oazy zdrowia, czyli wirus w polskich więzieniach. *Polityka*, 23 May. Online, https://www.polityka.pl/tygodnikpolityka/spoleczenstwo/1957646,1,dziwne-oazy-zdrowia-czyli-wirus-w-polskich-wiezieniach.read [accessed: 20 December 2020].

Stańdo-Kawecka, B. (2014): Poland. In: Drenkhahn, K., Dudeck M., and Dünkel, F. (Eds.): *Long-term imprisonment and human rights.* Routledge: London-New York, 218–235.

Stańdo-Kawecka, B. (2020): Execution of prison sentences in Poland – 20 years of application of the 1997 Code of the Execution of Penalties. In: Drenkhahn K. et al. (Eds.): *Kriminologie und Kriminalpolitik im Dienste der Menschenwürde. Festschrift für Frieder Dünkel zum 70. Geburtstag.* Forum Verlag Godesberg: Mönchengladbach, 941–953.

Stańdo-Kawecka, B., and Grzywa-Holten, J. (2015): Offender electronic monitoring in Poland: Expectations and results. *Neue Kriminalpolitik* 27, 158–170.

Stańdo-Kawecka, B., and Grzywa-Holten, J. (2017): Polen. In: Dünkel, F., Thiele, C., and Treig, J. (Eds.): *Elektronische Überwachung von Straffälligen im europäischen Vergleich – Bestandsaufnahme und Perspektiven*. Forum Verlag Godesberg, Mönchengladbach, 411–424.

Tatała, M., Rutynowska, E., and Wachowiec, P. (2020): *Rule of Law in Poland 2020: A Diagnosis of the Deterioration of the Rule of Law from a Comparative Perspective*. Civil Development Forum (FOR)/ Forum Obywatelskiego Rozwoju. Online, https://for.org.pl/en/publications/for-reports/rule-of-law-in-poland-2020-a-diagnosis-of-the-deterioration-of-the-rule-of-law-from-a-comparative-perspective [accessed: 20 December 2020].

Terlik, M. (2021): Wirus za kratami. Czy w polskich więzieniach ukrywa się zakażenia? *Onet. pl*, 9 March. Online, https://wiadomosci.onet.pl/tylko-w-onecie/koronawirus-w-polsce-czy-w-wiezieniach-ukrywa-sie-zakazenia/yt0trqd [accessed: 29 April 2021].

33 Portugal

Anabela Miranda Rodrigues and Inês Horta Pinto

1 General situation of the prison system

1.1 Penal policy and prison conditions

Portugal's criminal law and jurisprudence are based on a humanistic tradition. In Portugal, there is no life imprisonment, and the most severe sentence is imprisonment of up to 25 years. Imprisonment is considered a punishment that should be used only as a last resort, and the Penal Code provides for a wide range of alternative sanctions. Portugal has a tradition of progressive penitentiary laws, based on rehabilitation as the main goal of imprisonment. Portuguese penal law is generally in line with the European human rights standards and with the European penal policy principles. Insofar it has resisted penal populism.

However, *law in action* often does not fully meet the standards of *law in books*. Despite the *ultima ratio* approach, and even though Portugal is among the safest countries in the world, with low crime rates, the prison population rate is relatively high (124 per 100,000, as of 31 December 2019),[1] and the average term of imprisonment is relatively long, compared to other European countries. Even though the prison system, when considered as a whole, is not overcrowded (the occupancy rate at the end of 2019 was 97.7%), many prisons remain overcrowded, as highlighted by the European Committee for the Prevention of Torture and Inhuman or Degrading Treatment or Punishment (hereinafter the CPT) in its last report.[2] Detention conditions are also a problem in some prisons, with old facilities and a lack of human and financial resources hampering opportunities for effective rehabilitation.[3]

1.2 Prison population before and after the pandemic

In April 2020, before the law providing for exceptional measures aimed at preventing the spread of the coronavirus in the prison system came into force, the Portuguese prison population totalled 12,553 inmates, 800 of whom were over 60 years old (including 24 people over 80 and one person over 90), for a total of 49 prisons.[4]

DOI: 10.4324/9781003169178-33

Under the new law, between April and May 2020, 2,035 inmates were released (either temporarily or permanently) from the prison system.[5] The prison population decreased from 12,553 (as of 1 April) to 10,997 inmates (as of 15 May), which means a drop of the occupancy rate from 97.7% to 85% (as of 15 May 2020). In the following months, the population rose again to 11,315 (1 December 2020).[6]

1.3 COVID-19 infections in prisons

There were no records of COVID-19 infection in Portuguese prisons until late March.[7] Initially, after that, all infections were of inmates who were entering the system from the community and were detected at the time of entry. These people were immediately isolated and treated without having had contact with other prisoners. This is how it was possible to avoid the spread of the virus within the prison system during the "first wave" of the pandemic.

Only during the "second wave" did a first outbreak occur in a prison. In November 2020, in the women's prison of Tires (Lisbon area), 127 inmates were diagnosed with COVID-19, as well as two children living in the prison with their mothers and some prison staff. The inmates were separated from the rest of the prison population and placed in isolation, where they were monitored by clinical staff from the Prison Hospital. Visits, as well as work and educational activities, were suspended, meals were taken inside the cells instead of being served in the common dining hall and time spent outdoors was limited to two hours a day, in shifts to allow for social distancing. All the inmates recovered. Outbreaks in five other prisons followed in the same month. Similar preventive measures were adopted. In no case was the legal right to spend at least one hour a day in the open air withdrawn.

As of 14 December 2020, there were 97 active infections in the prison system (34 of which were inmates). 681 cases have recovered (461 of which are inmates and two children). So far, infected inmates have shown mild symptoms only or have been asymptomatic. There have been no deaths reported.[8] In the general population, on the same date a total of 350,938 cases (=34,463 cases/1,000,000 population) and 5,649 deaths from COVID were registered in Portugal.[9]

2 Prison and penal policy regarding the execution of prison sentences during the pandemic

In the context of the state of emergency declared in March 2020 and reinstated in November due to the aggravation of the pandemic, many extraordinary measures were adopted, affecting almost all sectors of Portuguese society. Prisons were no exception.

2.1 Legislative measures

Following recommendations from international bodies (in particular, the World Health Organisation and the CPT) and from the Portuguese Ombudswoman (who also acts as the National Preventive Mechanism (NPM)), the Government proposed a law, passed by Parliament without delay, adopting exceptional measures concerning the implementation of prison sentences. Law No. 9/2020 of 10 April 2020[10] allowed for the immediate release – either permanent or temporary – of inmates, by means of:

1 A *collective pardon* for sentences of up to two years and for the remainder of up to two years of longer sentences provided that the prisoner had served at least half of the sentence and was already serving the last two years. It did not apply to those convicted of certain crimes, such as murder, domestic violence, sexual offences, corruption, crimes against police or prison officers, crimes committed by politicians, public office-holders or police or prison officers, among many other serious offences.
2 An exceptional *individual pardon* by the President of the Republic, to be decided on a case-by-case basis, following a recommendation from the Minister of Justice. This measure applied to inmates who were 65 years old or over and suffered from poor health. The same exclusions regarding certain categories of offences applied.
3 Special *prison leave*, granted by the Director General of the Prison Service, of 45 days, renewable for new periods of up to 45 days, depending on the person's conduct and the evolution of the pandemic. This leave could only be granted if all general conditions for granting prison leave had been met, and with the additional condition that the inmate had previously benefited from judicial prison leave. Unlike regular prison leave, this special leave entailed the obligation for the inmate to remain at home, under the supervision of the Probation Service and/or the police.
4 For persons granted special leave, the court responsible for the execution of sentences might decide on *early release* (in the form of granting parole up to six months before the date when the inmate would normally be eligible for it). That "bonus period" was to be served in home confinement, under supervision of the Probation Service and/or the police.

The measures described above only applied to persons already serving their sentences.

The law did not include rules regarding the execution of prison sentences which, at the time of its entering into force, had already been imposed but not yet implemented. According to an Opinion by the Consultative Council of the Attorney General's Office, the issuance and execution of arrest warrants were also suspended.[11] Although the Opinion was not binding on courts, it was likely to influence the decisions on whether to issue or execute arrest warrants during this period. As a result, this was likely to cause, on the one hand, a reduction of new entries in prison during this period and, on the other hand, a significant flow of new entries afterwards (Brandão, 2020a).

5 Regarding *remand prisoners*, courts were mandated to review pre-trial detention orders in order to decide on the possibility of replacing them by non-custodial alternatives. The law also stated that pre-trial detention would only be imposed if all other measures of restraint were manifestly insufficient.

Should offenders be recalled to prison (namely if the pardon, leave and early parole were revoked due to non-compliance with the conditions), they would be subject to a 14-day quarantine period when admitted.

The *goals of the law*, according to the Government's proposal, were to minimise the risks stemming from the concentration of people in prison facilities; to make social distancing possible inside prisons and to ensure the social reintegration of convicted persons without harming the social order and the safety of the community. At the parliamentary hearing to discuss the draft law, the Minister of Justice stressed that the proposal was exclusively inspired by humanitarian goals, rebutting accusations by some parliamentarians that the pandemic was being used as an excuse to reduce the prison population and thus solve overcrowding problems.

In application of the law, 1,415 inmates benefited from the collective pardon, 726 were granted special prison leave, 14 inmates aged 65 or over and suffering from poor health were granted individual pardons by the President and four remand prisoners had their pre-trial detention converted to home detention with electronic monitoring.[12]

The collective pardon resulted in a sudden release of many prisoners, without proper preparation. Despite the efforts of the Prison Service to make arrangements with social security services, charities and municipalities in order to find accommodation for persons eligible for pardon but who were homeless, there were reports in the media of released prisoners who had nowhere to go and were sleeping on the streets.[13]

As special prison leave implied an obligation of home confinement, it was not granted to persons who lacked a place to live. The monitoring and support for inmates on special prison leave was partly provided by the Probation Service by means of telephone calls and e-mail, and occasionally by home visits from probation staff and/or the police. However, the frequency of those contacts was limited due to social distancing rules and to the increased workload of both the probation staff and the police.

Only 70 of the inmates released had their pardons revoked due to reoffending. Regarding inmates granted special prison leave, 84 were recalled to prison due to the breach of conditions and 14 did not have their licence renewed after the 45-day period. It is interesting to notice that 33 chose to withdraw their consent and voluntarily returned to prison. In addition, 281 of the inmates on special prison leave were granted parole or early release and 26 were released because they had reached the end of their sentence.[14]

According to the Prison Service, the release of prisoners under the exceptional measures made available much-needed space inside prison facilities, which was crucial to allow for the separation of vulnerable inmates and the isolation and clinical monitoring of infected inmates or suspected cases.

In our opinion, the combination of collective pardons, presidential pardons and prison leave adopted by the new law was not the most appropriate solution from both a penal policy point of view and the point of view of coherence with the legal system. Besides the unnecessary complexity (which forced courts, the President of the Republic and the prison administration to select eligible inmates in a short period of time and distinguish those who were eligible for each of the three types of measures), the pardon raises doubts about the fulfilment of the purposes of punishment and about the compliance with the principle of equality. Special prison leave, however, also appears problematic, not only because of its inconsistency with the aim of prison leaves (which, according to the Code, is "intended to maintain and promote family and social ties and to prepare for life in freedom", not for public health purposes), but also because it was granted by the prison administration, rather than by the judge. This raises constitutional problems, given the fact that the extended duration of leave (for several months) turns it into a substantial modification of the sentence that ought to be decided by a judge.

Imperfect as the solution may appear from a doctrinal perspective, it has to be understood in the context of the urgency of taking action to avoid a spread of the virus inside the prison system, which did not allow for a broad debate. In addition, at that early stage of the pandemic, it was probably not expected that it would last so long and that prison leave would have to be renewed repeatedly.

However, in our view, the Portuguese law already contained a mechanism which, with minor adaptations, could have offered a more appropriate and simple solution. The "modification of the execution of the prison sentence", provided for in the Code on the Implementation of Prison Sentences (Articles 118–122), allows inmates with a serious and irreversible disease, with a serious and permanent disability or of advanced age to request the judge to serve the rest of their sentence at home or at a health or social facility, with or without electronic surveillance. This alternative would have the advantages of making use of an already existing mechanism which serves a similar purpose; being decided by a judge; not generating impunity, since the sentence would still be served; and as a single measure for all eligible inmates, reducing complexity. This hypothesis was discussed during the parliamentary debate on the law, but the Minister of Justice justified its rejection on the grounds that there were not enough human resources and electronic surveillance equipment. This reasoning, however, is unconvincing, since the "modification of the execution of the prison sentence" does not imply mandatory electronic surveillance and does not seem to require more human resources than the prison leave with an obligation to remain at home created by the new law.

2.2 *Criminalisation of non-compliance*

The Penal Code provides for the crime of "spreading of contagious disease" (Article 283). However, it is hard to prove all the elements of the crime – the contagion and the causation of a specific danger to the life or body of others (Lamas Leite, 2020: 186; Oliveira e Silva, 2020). Of course, the crime of bodily injury could also apply. However, in order to ensure compliance with the restrictive measures adopted in the course of the state of emergency, the Portuguese Government chose to criminalise the refusal by infected persons or persons required to self-isolate by health authorities to comply with the duty of isolation, as well as non-compliance with the duty to close businesses.[15] Questions were raised by legal scholars regarding the constitutionality of the provision, with some authors claiming that it violated the legality principle.[16] The Constitutional Court has not yet ruled on the matter.

In addition, fines were applicable to businesses not complying with the rules on occupancy and distancing between clients, as administrative offences.[17] From October 2020, wearing a mask on the street became mandatory, non-compliance being an administrative offence subject to a fine.[18]

3 Restrictions of contact with the outside world

In February 2020, the Prison Service adopted a contingency plan,[19] which included, among others, the following measures: temporary suspension of visits in all prisons; temporary suspension of open regimes involving working outside the prison (only in those parts of the country more affected by the pandemic); temporary suspension of administrative prison leave and temporary restrictions on clothes and food coming in from the outside.

However, the law adopting exceptional measures regarding court proceedings during the pandemic stated that all remand prisoners must be ensured conditions to meet with their lawyers in person to prepare their defence.[20] Even during the state of emergency and the general lockdown, it was determined that some offices of the Ministry of Justice, including Prison and Probation Services, should remain open to the public.[21]

The above restrictions were progressively withdrawn, as procedures were adopted in coordination with health authorities, aimed at minimising the risks. Visits, which were suspended in March 2020, resumed in June, after a refurbishment of the visiting areas to ensure social distancing (visiting booths and/or glass partitions). Prison leave was resumed, with the return of inmates from leave to designated facilities, being subject to a 14-day isolation period.

However, the aggravation of the pandemic during the second wave and the subsequent renewal of the state of emergency in the country required prison authorities to reinstate many of the previous restrictions. In November 2020, visits at weekends were suspended, and, in higher risk regions, also work outside the prisons and work for external companies (with some exceptions, when it was possible to carry on working without contact between inmates and external staff), as well as educational, recreational and religious activities (except when they could take place outdoors, with social distancing, or, in the case of school, through e-learning tools). In prisons with ongoing outbreaks, collective activities and visits were completely suspended.[22]

Regarding prison leave that is traditionally granted during the Christmas season (about 1,500 cases foreseen), prison wardens were instructed to subject their granting to the capacity of the prison to guarantee the 14-day isolation period for every returning inmate. If this was not possible, the inmates would still be entitled to leave, but it would have to be postponed to a later date.[23]

4 Restrictions inside prisons

The contingency plan of the Prison Service included, among others, the following measures:

4.1 Activities

- Temporary suspension of transfers of inmates between prisons;
- Temporary suspension of educational and occupational activities involving staff coming from the outside.
- Schooling, training and work were progressively resumed.

4.2 Facilities

- Admission of new inmates in designated facilities only and subject to prophylactic isolation in the first 14 days of admittance;
- Separation of inmates who, due to age or health conditions, need special protection (by the means of separate accommodation and different schedules for their daily activities);
- Meals staggered, in order to avoid large gatherings;
- Designation of sections in each prison to serve as quarantine areas if necessary; and
- Telework and shift work implemented for some staff to allow for social distancing.

4.3 Clinical services

- Preparedness of backup infirmaries in some prisons, as well as field hospitals provided by the Army, for the event of an outbreak;
- Intensification of cleaning and hygiene procedures in prison facilities, complying with the guidelines of the health authorities;
- Distribution of personal protective equipment to the clinical service of every prison in case of infection;
- Systematic testing of prison staff;
- Mandatory use of masks for prison staff, as well as for inmates when leaving the accommodation area (i.e. when they attend work, vocational training, school, administrative offices, clinical services or meetings with their attorneys);
- Temperature of all inmates taken once a day;
- Following a pre-existing agreement with the Ministry of Health, electronic prescription of medication and access to medical appointments through video conferences;
- Conclusion of an agreement with public health institutes to ensure testing of both inmates and staff (9,500 tests done as of 14 December 2020); and
- Creation of a crisis management office within the Prison Service.

5 Compensatory measures

The Prison Service invested 3.5 million euros in combatting the pandemic (including personal protective equipment, additional hiring of clinical staff and renovation work to adapt prison facilities to social distancing rules).[24] To make up for the suspension of visits, the number of telephone calls permitted per day was increased from 1 to 3.

It is worth mentioning the beginning of two pilot projects to set up landline telephones in cells. This was a project of the Directorate-General for Prison Services, which had already been planned before the pandemic, with the aims of allowing greater contact with families and of relieving the tension arising from rigid schedules, strict time limits and queues for the use of telephones in common areas. The two pilot projects (one in a male prison and the other in a female prison) started in September 2020 and enabled these inmates to strengthen contact with their families during the pandemic.[25]

Reference should also be made to the possibility of making video calls. This system has been available in every prison since December 2019. It is installed in a private room and its use is allowed on a weekly basis, with a 20-minute duration. It also allows for the communication between inmates from the same family living in different prisons.[26]

During the periods when school was suspended, the Prison Service, in cooperation with the Ministry of Education, sought to ensure distance learning in prisons equipped with the necessary technology.[27] However, we were not able to confirm whether this alternative was in fact available to a significant number of inmates.

Also meant to make up for the restrictions during the pandemic, an arrangement between the Ministry of Justice and the Ministry of Culture allowed for the availability of 70 movies to be shown in prisons during this period.

6 Legal basis for restrictions and relaxations of the prison regime

According to Article 30 § 5 of the Portuguese Constitution, those serving a prison sentence "retain their fundamental rights, subject to the limitations inherent to the court's decision and the requirements of the implementation of the sentence". This means that only those restrictions on the fundamental rights of prisoners that result from the judicial decision itself or are necessary to ensure order and security in the prison are constitutional.

The implementation of the prison sentence is based on the legality principle and is governed by the Code of Execution of Prison Sentences of 2009.[28] The Code establishes the rights and duties of prisoners and rules on the various aspects of execution, such as the different regimes (ordinary, open and security regimes), health, hygiene, clothing, food, social support, freedom of religion, education, training, work, rehabilitation programmes and activities, contacts with the outside world, relations with the media, disciplinary regime, means of order and security, and the right to judicial review. The Code generally conforms to the European Prison Rules.

In Portugal, there are specialised courts – the courts for the execution of sentences – that are competent to decide on matters such as conditional release and to review certain decisions taken by the prison administration, such as disciplinary sanctions and restrictions on contacts with the outside world. There are also non-judicial mechanisms that monitor the activity of the prison administration at different levels: from the hierarchical structure itself (Directorate-General of Re-integration and Prison Services and Minister of Justice), through the administrative control mechanisms (such as the Inspectorate-General of the Justice Services), to independent constitutional bodies, such as the Ombudsman (who also acts as the NPM).

A relevant role is also played by international bodies such as the CPT, within the framework of the Council of Europe, and the Subcommittee for the Prevention of Torture and Other Cruel, Inhuman or Degrading Treatment or Punishment of the Committee against Torture, within the framework of the United Nations.

The Portuguese NPM, after an initial period of suspension of face-to-face activity, in line with the guidelines of the health authorities and with the option of other NPMs, gradually resumed monitoring visits, making use of videoconferencing where possible and carrying out face-to-face visits in compliance with the required safety measures aimed at preventing the contagion. As of October 2020, the NPM had already carried out in-person visits in six prisons.[29]

7 Returning to normal – the long-term effects of the pandemic and lessons learnt for the future of prisons

The restrictions on interactions with the outside world, as well as the suspension of educational activities and other programmes, together with the reduction to the strictly necessary face-to-face contacts with probation officers and other professionals, are likely to have a strong impact on inmates and their families and on the work towards offenders' rehabilitation. Besides the psychological distress, delays in the reintegration process and releases without proper preparation are probable consequences. Depending on how long the restrictions caused by the pandemic will last in the end, it might be necessary to think about ways to make up for the time lost.

The pandemic also had negative impacts on non-custodial sanctions. In Portugal, the procedures adopted by the Probation Service during the state of emergency included a reduction of in-person meetings and the suspension of group rehabilitation activities for persons serving community sentences or sentences with electronic monitoring.

If the issue of prison reductionism and enhancing the alternatives to prison was already on the agenda due to the problem of overcrowding (and all the problems that come with it, as the jurisprudence of the ECtHR on Article 3 of the European Convention on Human Rights continuously highlights), this pandemic, and the risk of similar events in the future, makes the need to take the principle of *ultima ratio* of deprivation of liberty seriously even more pressing. The model of mass imprisonment and overcrowded prison systems that has prevailed until now must definitely be overcome.

The fact that the vast majority of people released from prison under the exceptional measures did not pose a risk to society or cause a public outcry supports the claim that imprisonment is unnecessary in many cases. Non-custodial alternatives should be designed to be meaningful, supportive and truly rehabilitating, tackling the individual criminogenic needs of the offenders – not measures of pure control.

The pandemic also showed how overcrowded facilities with poor living conditions and lack of hygiene and ventilation pose a risk to public health. A significant reduction of imprisonment would allow for individual accommodation, sufficient personal space per inmate and more decent detention conditions in general. The importance of robust healthcare within the prison system was something else highlighted by the pandemic.

Technology should also play an important role in the future of the prison. It should serve the purpose of keeping contact with families and meaningful social relations, reinforcing the ties with the outside world and preparing reintegration into society. It can be particularly useful to communicate with families when they live far from the prison or abroad and, therefore, cannot visit regularly. It also provides more opportunities for rehabilitation, such as distance learning when courses are not available nearby or when the prison regime of the inmate does not allow for activities outside the prison. Videoconferencing may also cater for the participation in programmes or activities that, for any reason, cannot be attended in person. In addition, communication technologies could be used to provide a closer and more regular support by the Probation Service in the case of non-custodial sanctions. It seems important, however, that the availability of technology does not become an excuse to close the prison to the outside world. Technology should be used to supplement, not replace, human contact.

Notes

1 Sources: Prison Service (prison population of 12,793) and National Statistics Institute (resident population in Portugal of 10,295,909); also, the CPT report on its visit to Portugal in December 2019, CPT (2020), § 44.
2 See the CPT report on its visit to Portugal in December 2019, CPT (2020), § 44.
3 See, e.g., the CPT report on its visit to Portugal in December 2019, CPT (2020), §§ 56 ff.
4 Sources: Prison Service Statistics (https://dgrsp.justica.gov.pt); Tayumi Ishiy (2020); figures regarding the age of prisoners were provided by the Minister of Justice to the Parliament at the hearing regarding the draft law, on 8 April 2020.
5 See detailed figures below.
6 Source: Prison Service Statistics (https://dgrsp.justica.gov.pt).
7 The first case among staff members was confirmed on 27 March (a prison guard). On 28 March, a detainee (infected prior to her detention) was tested positive and remained in isolation in the Prison Hospital. The first infections of inmates were confirmed in early May 2020 (two inmates who were in quarantine following their return from prison leave).
8 Source: Prison Service (reply to Authors' questionnaire, 14 December 2020). The Authors would like to thank the Portuguese Prison Service for the information provided.
9 Source: Ministry of Health (https://covid19.min-saude.pt/).
10 Law available at https://data.dre.pt/eli/lei/9/2020/p/cons/20200529/pt/html. For an overview and analysis of these legal measures, see Brandão (2020).
11 Opinion No. 10/2020, available at http://www.ministeriopublico.pt/sites/default/files/documentos/pdf/parecer_10-20.pdf.
12 Sources: Prison Service (collective pardons, prison leaves); Official Journal (https://data.dre.pt/eli/diario/1/82/2020/1/pt/html, presidential pardons); High Council of the Judiciary (remand prisoners).
13 Não quero esta liberdade. Os reclusos que a covid tirou das prisões, *Expresso* online, 16 November 2020, https://multimedia.expresso.pt/reclusoscovid19. Allegedly, some inmates have falsely informed that they had a place to go, since they feared that they would not be released if they admitted they had not.
14 Source: Prison Service (reply to Authors' questionnaire, 14 December 2020).
15 Article 3 of Decrees No. 2-A/2020, of March 20, No. 2-B/2020, of April 2, and No. 2-C/2020, of April 17, declaring the state of emergency.
16 For the discussion, see Brandão, 2020b; Aires de Sousa, 2020: 159; Lamas Leite, 2020: 191.

17 Law Decree No. 87-A/2020, of October 15, modifying Law Decree No. 28-B/2020, of June 26, available at https://data.dre.pt/eli/dec-lei/87-A/2020/10/15/p/dre.
18 Law No. 62-A/2020 of October 27, available at https://data.dre.pt/eli/lei/62-A/2020/10/27/p/dre.
19 Regularly updated. A synopsis of the plan was provided by the Prison Service.
20 Article 2 of Law No. 16/2020, of May 29, modifying Law No. 1-A/2020, of March 19, available at https://data.dre.pt/eli/lei/16/2020/05/29/p/dre.
21 Order No. 3614-C, of March 23, available at https://dre.pt/home/-/dre/130600788/details/maximized.
22 Internal Order No. 17/GDG/2020, of 24.11.2020 (provided to the Authors by the Prison Service).
23 Internal Order No. 16/GDG/2020, of 10.11.2020 (provided to the Authors by the Prison Service).
24 Interview to the Director-General of the Prison Service, *Expresso* newspaper, 20 November 2020: 28.
25 See Response of the Portuguese Government to the report of the CPT on its visit to Portugal from 3 to 12 December 2019, CPT/Inf (2020) 34, § 82.
26 See Response of the Portuguese Government to the report of the CPT on its visit to Portugal from 3 to 12 December 2019, CPT/Inf (2020) 34, § 82.
27 According to Internal Order No. 17/GDG/2020, of 24 November 2020.
28 *Código da Execução das Penas e Medidas Privativas da Liberdade*, enacted by Law No. 115/2009, of 12 October, available at https://data.dre.pt/eli/lei/115/2009/p/cons/20190328/pt/html.
29 Covid-19. MNP retoma atividade de monitorização de locais onde se encontram pessoas privadas de liberdade, Statement by the Ombudsman Office, 23 October 2020, available at http://www.provedor-jus.pt/?idc=35&idi=18342.

References

Aires de Sousa, S. (2020): Sobre a protecção penal da saúde pública em tempos de pandemia: "isto já não é o que nunca foi". *Revista do Ministério Público*, special issue on the covid-19 pandemic, June 2020, 159 ff.

Brandão, N. (2020): A libertação de reclusos em tempos de COVID-19. Um primeiro olhar sobre a Lei n.º 9/2020, de 10/4. *Julgar Online*, April 2020 (http://julgar.pt/a-libertacao-de-reclusos-em-tempos-de-covid-19-um-primeiro-olhar-sobre-a-lei-n-o-92020-de-104/).

Brandão, N. (2020a): Prazos e perdão de penas: Parecer n.º 10/2020 do Conselho Consultivo da PGR. Internet-publication, https://itercriminis.blog/2020/05/02/prazos-e-perdao-de-penas-parecer-n-o-10-2020-do-conselho-consultivo-da-pgr, 2 May 2020.

Brandão, N. (2020b): Um "take" sobre a desobediência no estado de emergência. Internet-publication, https://itercriminis.blog/2020/05/08/um-take-sobre-a-desobediencia-no-estado-de-emergencia, 8 May 2020.

CPT (2020): Report to the Portuguese Government on the visit to Portugal European Committee for the Prevention of Torture and Inhuman or Degrading Treatment or Punishment (CPT) from 3 to 12 December 2019, CPT/Inf (2020) 33, https://rm.coe.int/1680a05953.

Lamas Leite, A. (2020): "Desobediência em tempos de cólera": a configuração deste crime em estado de emergência e em situação de calamidade. *Julgar Online*, April 2020, 186 ff, http://julgar.pt/a-libertacao-de-reclusos-em-tempos-de-covid-19-um-primeiro-olhar-sobre-a-lei-n-o-92020-de-104/.

Oliveira e Silva, S. (2020): Entre a desobediência e a propagação de doença: como se punem as condutas "irresponsáveis" de contágio? *Revista do Ministério Público*, special issue on the covid-19 pandemic, June 2020, 193 ff.

Tayumi Ishiy, K. (2020): Relatório sobre a população reclusa em Portugal de 2019 (e os primeiros impactos da Lei n.º 9/2020 no sistema prisional). *Revista Portuguesa de Ciência Criminal* 1/2020, 169 ff.

34 Romania

Ioan Durnescu and Ioana Mihaela Morar

1 Introduction – general situation of the prison system

Romania is a former Communist country in Eastern Europe with 19.41 million inhabitants.[1] Up until 2014, the penal policy was driven mainly by the Penal Code adopted in 1968, with some minor reforms in 1990, 1992 and 1996. Due to this tradition, the high number of prisoners was always a public and a human rights concern in the post-Revolution Romania.

Prison overcrowding continues to be an issue but its magnitude is much lower nowadays with a prison occupancy rate of around 110%[2] (21,456 prisoners in October 2020). At the beginning of 2020, prisoners were accommodated in 34 penitentiaries (one for women), two education centres, two pre-trial detention centres and six hospitals.

To prepare the implementation of the new Penal Code, a new law on the enforcement of prison sentences was adopted in 2013 – Law no. 254/2013. Mirroring trends in penal policy, this law is considered to be modern and in line with the European standards.

In spite of the significant steps forward, in the last 30 years the Romanian penitentiary system was subject to international criticism mainly related to prison overcrowding and its associated negative consequences, such as poor living conditions, sub-standard medical care, a limited number of reintegration activities, physical ill-treatment and inter-prisoner violence. These problems were highlighted in the last reports published by the Committee for Prevention of Torture (CPT reports, hereinafter) in 2018 and 2019,[3] and also in several decisions of the European Court of Human Rights (ECtHR, hereinafter), culminating with the adoption of the pilot judgement *Rezmives and other v. Romania,*[4] on 25 April 2017. In brief, this pilot decision called on the Romanian authorities to reduce overcrowding, improve material conditions of detention and consolidate the preventive and compensatory remedies for prisoners who had had their rights violated. The response of the Romanian Government had three aims: to enlarge the prison capacity, to reform the Penal Code in order to promote more alternatives to imprisonment and to introduce a new scheme for compensatory remedies.

DOI: 10.4324/9781003169178-34

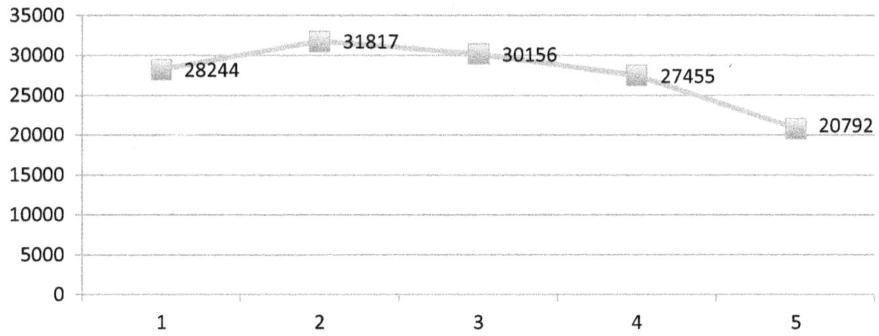

Figure 34.1 Prison population 2012–2019.
Source: World Prison Brief (https://www.prisonstudies.org/country/romania).

In order to expand the prison capacity, the Romanian authorities created 672 new detention places in 2016 and 170 in 2017. Important steps were taken towards building two new prisons – P47 Berceni and P48 Unguriu.

In order to promote more alternatives to detention, the Romanian Parliament adopted a new Penal Code in 2009 (Law no. 286/2009 on the new Penal Code), which entered into force in February 2014. Apart from including more alternatives to imprisonment, the new Penal Code changed the minimum and the maximum limits of sentences and replaced the sanctioning system for juveniles with educative measures. All these reforms aimed at decreasing the prison population, which was confirmed after 2014.

The Romanian Parliament also adopted Law no. 169/2017 on compensatory remedies, which provided that for every 30 days served in sub-standard conditions, prisoners are entitled to a discount of 6 days. In other words, for 30 days served in bad prison conditions, prisoners were considered as if they have served 36 days of their initial sentence. This legislative measure was not an innovation in Europe. The Italian Parliament had adopted a similar measure a few years before, responding to the judgement in *Torreggiani and others v. Italy* in 2013 (Favuzza, 2017). Although there are no rigorous studies on this matter, some estimates state that between 12,000 to 21,000 inmates were released earlier due to this new law[5] between 2017 and 2019. This was not the intention of the law – to release prisoners early – but this was one of the main effects that prisoners and the public will remember (Figure 34.1).

The Penal Code reform together with the law on compensatory remedies speeded up the exit process of prisoners from the prison system, leading to a relief of prison overcrowding from an occupancy level of 140% in 2010 to 107% in 2018.

Following some tragic events after some ex-inmates released earlier on the compensatory remedy law committed horrific crimes,[6] the Romanian

Parliament adopted a cancellation law – Law no. 240/2019 on the abrogation of the compensatory remedy law. The pressure from the public was so strong that public protests were organised.

At the beginning of 2020, the Romanian prison population was stabilising around 20,000 inmates, which amounts to about 110 prisoners per 100 prison places. Although this is still considered a highly overcrowded system (Aebi and Tiago, 2020), the radicalised public and cautious authorities have made it impossible to even consider early release as a preventive measure related to the pandemic, as in other jurisdictions.

1.1 Romania during the COVID-19 crisis

The first case of COVID-19 in Romania was detected on 26 February 2020. According to the Minister of Health, 80% of the first 277 cases in Romania came from abroad.[7] Due to the quick development of the crisis, the president declared a state of emergency for 30 days on 16 March 2020. This was prolonged for another 30 days. Due to a slight decrease in the number of new cases, the state of emergency was replaced with a less strict regime. The first wave of COVID-19 was relatively well managed due to early measures, but the second wave, which started in August/September 2020, was more aggressive. For many days, the number of new cases detected was higher than 10,000 which influenced the government to impose restrictions such as closing the schools, restricting access to some localities, online work and so on. Up until the end of October 2020, there were 241,339 cases registered.[8] The end of November 2020 was marked by a medical crisis due to the pressure on the intensive care units in the COVID-19 hospitals.

2 Prison and penal policy concerning the execution of prison sentences during the COVID-19 crisis

From the beginning of the COVID-19 crisis, the first priority of the National Administration of Penitentiaries was the protection of the right to life, physical integrity and the health of the persons in custody.

As mentioned above, the penal and political climate did not favour a penal policy of further reducing the prison population by not executing certain prison sentences or expanding earlier release of prisoners, as was the case in many European countries. As a consequence, recent prison population data from World Prison Brief show an increase of the prison population rate from 107 in 2018 to 115 on 28 February 2021 (see https://www.prisonstudies.org/country/Romania, accessed on 11 March 2021).

The Romanian administration's approach was to focus on reducing human interactions as far as possible, while preparing the health system to detect and intervene in case of COVID-19 infections. In this respect, one can define the Romanian approach to the pandemic crisis as an administrative-medical one as opposed to the penal one embraced by many other EU countries, which released significant proportions of inmates before their term.

The administrative-medical approach embraced by the Romanian prison authorities was based on the adoption of complex measures in order to provide the necessary conditions for safe interactions between staff and inmates, and between inmates, while also limiting the contact between inmates and the outside world. An important advantage for the Romanian prison system in this respect was that a dedicated medical directorate located within the prison system offers the medical services for prisoners. The medical service is thus placed under the penitentiary administration, which made it possible for the prison authorities to coordinate all medical and administrative measures swiftly. From the perspective of managing the condition of the inmates in the epidemiological context, the ten principles promoted by the European Committee for the Prevention of Torture and Inhuman or Degrading Treatment or Punishment (CPT, 2020a; 2020b) were disseminated to all prisons. The measures deriving from this document were implemented by and large in all Romanian prisons.

One of the first measures for protecting inmates' health was to limit the contact of the prison population with possible sources of infection, by suspending some of the activities taking place outside the prison units. For the accommodation and medical monitoring of the inmates extradited to Romania by other states, at the prison system level certain penitentiary units were specially designated for implementing quarantine. In addition, measures were taken to carefully monitor the health condition of all inmates who had returned from a prison leave or furlough, by imposing quarantine for 14 days.

Another important measure consisted in the identification of new spaces for quarantine, monitoring and isolation for the inmates who, after an epidemiological screening, had symptoms of the new coronavirus infection. Thus, the administration established, within the penitentiary system settings, dedicated areas, for inmates considered as suspects or suffering from COVID-19, in 5 units: Penitentiary Hospital of Bucharest – Jilava, Penitentiary of Aiud, Penitentiary Hospital of Constanţa – Poarta Albă, Penitentiary of Drobeta Turnu Severin, and Penitentiary of Baia Mare. Through the Order of the Minister of Health no. 489 from 23 March 2020, the Hospital Penitentiary of Bucharest – Jilava was designated as the medical unit to carry out testing and intervention in COVID-19 cases.

Medical assistance for inmates considered suffering from COVID-19, or suspected of being infected, was ensured by specialised medical staff. Moreover, all such cases were to be reported to the county public health departments and, depending on the situation, the National Single Service for Emergency Calls was to be contacted by calling 112, and medical care was ensured through the public medical network. This protocol was established for severe cases.

The medical staff were given specific training. Moreover, written guidelines were issued to complement the instructions of the Minister of Health and of the National Committee for Special Emergency Situations regarding the use of the protective equipment and increasing efficiency of using this equipment. Video materials regarding the health and hygiene measures and instructions for putting on/removing the protective equipment were also disseminated to all penitentiary units and to all staff categories.

Special attention was given to providing information to the inmates in order to explain the preventive measures, and how and why they were necessary. For this purpose, information campaigns for inmates were carried out in all prisons, with distribution of information materials (e.g. flyers, posters), and periodically producing and broadcasting announcements regarding SARS-CoV-2 through the system's closed circuit radio and TV. Individual counselling (educational, social and psychological) was ensured, in order to raise awareness and acceptance of strict hygiene measures. The accommodation and other spaces were sanitised and disinfected.

3 Restrictions of contact with the outside world

The biggest challenge, caused by the preventive measures implemented after the start of the pandemic, was to restrict the physical contact of prisoners with their family members and their loved ones during the 60 days of the state of emergency.

With the declaration of the state of emergency in Romania, a plan was established for the entire penitentiary system. Instructions were provided for the implementation of several necessary measures, including social distancing, limitation of contact between prison officers and inmates, and extending online communications.

In line with the provisions of Article 47 of the Presidential Decree no. 195/16.03.2020 declaring the state of emergency in Romania, those serving prison sentences and measures involving deprivation of liberty had these rights suspended: the right to receive visits, the right to receive conjugal visits and the right to receive goods through the visiting sector, as well as rewards consisting of prison leave (furloughs).

When the visit programme restarted and the state of emergency state was replaced by the state of alert, the families of inmates were requested to come to the prison wearing personal protection, including masks and gloves. Presidential Decree no. 240 issued on 14 April 2020 ordering the extension of the state of emergency in Romania stipulated that all transfers between penitentiary units must be performed with the approval of the Medical Supervisory Directorate within the National Administration of Penitentiaries. Subsequently, even after the state of emergency ended, during the state of alert, the monitoring and approval of transfers between the penitentiary units continued in order to prevent the effects of the COVID-19 pandemic in the prison system.

4 Restrictions inside prisons

In the context of the legal framework, and according to the preventive measures adopted by the Romanian prison administration during the pandemic, all activities involving inmates were reassessed, so that they were performed in small groups, by using different rooms for the same activity at the same time. For the same purpose, interaction with inmates was limited, and access to the prison wings was granted only to the staff designated for activities such as surveillance, management or special interventions.

For social reintegration, the radio and television studios were used to broadcast relevant preventive information for inmates. To comply with the right of the inmates to be informed, prisons tried to ensure good reception of public television programmes and to produce and broadcast their own shows through their radio-TV studio, for information, educational, moral and religious purposes. Group activities were suspended and carried out individually. Professional training activities, volunteering and inter-penitentiary activities, which involved interaction with persons from outside the penitentiary, were interrupted.

5 Compensatory measures

In order to maintain contact with their support system, the duration and the number of telephone conversations for the inmates within the maximum security regime were increased to a maximum of 45 minutes per day, while for the inmates in the closed, semi-open, open and temporary regimes, or for those who had not yet been classified, the number and duration of conversations were increased to a maximum of 75 minutes per day. The right of the inmates to have online conversations, regardless of their disciplinary status and periods of contact with their family, was supplemented according to the number of visits to which they were entitled.

For inmates included in the maximum security regime, the number of phone conversations was increased from three to five calls per day, with a total maximum duration of 45 minutes/day. Following the requests of the prison authorities, both telephone service providers approved lower charges for phone conversations of inmates.

During the state of emergency, there was an increase of almost 100% in telephone calls compared to the similar period in 2019 (from the perspective of the number of phone call minutes spent by the persons in custody; from 6.1 million in 2019 to 11.7 million minutes in 2020). Online communications of inmates increased by 98% between 16 March and 15 May 2020, compared to the same period of 2019.

Moreover, during detention, inmates had the possibility to communicate with the prison administration daily, in order to inform them about any aspect related to a possible breach of their rights or any abuses, or to contact the judge supervising the deprivation of liberty or the prison director, or the persons appointed by the latter.

A significant factor in maintaining a good atmosphere and discipline inside the prison during this period was the extension of access to video communications between inmates and their families via the internet. Thus, the right of the inmates to have online conversations, regardless of their disciplinary status and the periods of online contact with their family, was supplemented according to the number of visits to which they were entitled, based on their execution regime (NAP, 2020d).

Prisoners' families were informed by the prison staff about the measures taken to reduce the direct contact of the inmates with the outside world. Internet and phone conversations were the main tools to facilitate inmates keeping contact with their families or relatives. Lower fees for telephone conversations were negotiated with the main telephone providers in prison. As illustrated above, that led to a significant increase in the number of minutes spent on telephone calls. More individual psychological and counselling sessions were offered to inmates while observing the health instructions.

As the restrictions diminished after the state of emergency, more activities were resumed, but only within the conditions imposed by the medical requirements. For example, group activities were allowed but only with inmates who lived together in the same cell.[9] Contact between inmates from different cells or prison wings was strictly forbidden. Overall, the crucial compensating measure for the inmates was most probably better communication and awareness of why these measures were necessary and of genuine interest in compensating the restrictions with the enhancement of remote communication.

6 Legal basis for restrictions and relaxations of the prison regime

The primary or secondary legislation of Penal and Penitentiary Law did not undergo any changes from the beginning of the pandemic to the present. However, the two presidential decrees, namely Decree No. 195/2020 on the establishment of the emergency state on the Romanian territory (issued on 16 March 2020) and Decree No. 240/2020 on the extension of the emergency state (issued on 14 April 2020) and Law no. 55/2020 on certain measures to prevent and fight the effects of the COVID-19 pandemic, included certain legislative provisions to be applied to the prison system.

Overall, these provisions stipulated the possibility for persons deprived of liberty of exercising certain rights in an atypical manner or, where appropriate, the suspension of some of the rights for a limited time, while compensating with other rights (e.g. increasing the duration and number of telephone calls, supplementing the granting of the right to online communications) in order to maintain a reasonable balance.

The restrictions on receiving visits and goods from visitors as well as being granted prison leave were based on Decree no. 240/2020. The compensatory measures of increased phone calls and internet-communication were based on Article 47, paragraph 2 of Decree no. 195/2020 and Article 70, paragraph 2 of Decree no. 240/2020.

During the 60 days of the state of emergency, persons deprived of liberty who did not have financial resources were allowed to use 10% share of the income recorded in their name[10] for the purchase of goods and for making telephone calls, according to Law no. 254/2013, in order to substitute the constraints arising from the temporary suspension of the right to receive goods through the visiting sector and those caused by the objective impossibility of performing remunerated work.

From the beginning of the pandemic, the prison administration's campaign against the spread of COVID-19 was implemented through the decisions of the Director General of the National Administration of Penitentiaries, both during the state of emergency and during the period of alert (see National Administration of Penitentiaries, 2020a, 2020b, 2020c, 2020e).

General measures and measures for the safety of places of detention were taken in order to protect the life, integrity and the health of the persons deprived of their liberty, staff and any other persons, according to the plans approved by decisions of the Director General of the National Administration of Penitentiaries (e.g. Decision No. 446/14.05.2020, that has been amended, complemented and permanently updated in accordance with the evolution of the epidemiological context and Decision No. 10/07.01.2021). The action plans were updated or amended whenever the situation changed and they were in line with the national legislation.

7 Returning to normal

Since the risk of spreading COVID-19 has the potential to impact on all activities of both the prison population and the prison staff, one of the conclusions highlighted by the experience of this period was the need to adapt the measures applied to the general population to the peculiarities/specificities of the prison system. Undoubtedly, monitoring the application of the measures in all detention units and intensifying the collaboration with the public health directorates were absolutely necessary.

Ever since the outbreak of the pandemic, the spread of the virus within the prison system was limited to sporadic cases of infection among the staff; thus, continuity in specific activities could be ensured. From the beginning of the pandemic up to the end of September 2020, for approximately seven months, there were no confirmed cases of COVID-19 among inmates (except for seven imported cases, brought in from the Pre-Trial Arrest and Detention Centres of the Ministry of Home Affairs, already confirmed with COVID-19 before entering București-Jilava Prison Hospital).

From the end of September, at the time of the dramatic increase of COVID-19 cases at the national level, the first confirmed COVID-19 cases were registered among inmates, which created a challenge to the entire prison staff. Many cases were registered in some prison units such as Timisoara, Craiova, Galați, Bacau, Ploiesti and Targsorul Nou. Thus, one important lesson learned is that anticipation of the epidemiological evolution is crucial in order to establish suitable (next) measures.

Among the most useful lessons of the pandemic is the importance of extending of online communication and technical support for online school and other social reintegration activities, in order to ensure a broader range of occupations for inmates. Most probably, online communication will continue to play an important role in prison life also after the pandemic, not only for enhancing contacts with families but also for delivering education or other rehabilitative programmes.

In the context of the restrictive medical-administrative measures taken, it may be useful to further explore the psychological and experiential costs of those measures, for the inmates and their families, during the state of emergency, in order to develop new strategies for the future.

The experience with the pandemic had no impact on penal and prison policies towards reducing the prison population and the still serious problem of overcrowding. Due to the recent experience with the compensatory remedies in law and other political adventures (e.g. the recent attempt of the former government to push through a pardon law to save corrupt politicians), public attitudes seem to be quite punitive. In this sort of climate, debates about replacing short-term imprisonment with alternatives to imprisonment or improving the conditional release prospects for inmates seem quite unrealistic. Current debates around introducing electronic monitoring technologies in the supervision practice may change public attitudes. However, it is too soon to tell.

Acknowledgement

The authors are grateful for the support provided by the Romanian Administration of Penitentiaries.

Notes

1 Source: Eurostat–https://ec.europa.eu/eurostat/en/web/population-demography-migration-projections/statistics-illustrated.
2 Source: https://www.prisonstudies.org/country/romania.
3 CPT reports available here: https://www.coe.int/en/web/cpt/Romania.
4 EHCR pilot decision available at http://hudoc.echr.coe.int/eng?i=001- 173351.
5 See, for instance, this article: https://romania.europalibera.org/a/legea-recursului-compensatoriu-care-a-scos-peste-21-000-de-de%C8%9Binu%C8%9Bi-%C3%AEnainte-de-termen-a-fost-abrogat%C4%83-merge-la-promulgare/30307121.html.

6 See,forinstance,thissummary:https://www.nineoclock.ro/2019/01/16/compensatory-remedy-law-and-its-effects-theme-of-tough-debate-in-society-president-demands-from-govt-in-depth-analysis-solutions-jusmin-toader-we-are-analyzing-the-consequences-of-deeds-committ/.
7 Source: *Ministrul Sănătății: Toate vârstele, afectate de coronavirus, nu este cineva la adăpost. Vârful epidemiei, aflat peste 10 zile.* Realitatea, 19 March 2020.
8 Source: *„Coronavirus România, INFORMAȚII OFICIALE'. Digi24.*
9 The Romanian prison system allows the accommodation of more than one prisoner in a cell. Most prisoners are accommodated in communal cells with more than two prisoners.
10 By law, 10% of the prisoner's income has to be preserved for the moment of release.

References

Aebi, M.F. and Tiago, M.M. (2020): *Prisons and Prisoners in Europe in Pandemic Times: An Evaluation of the Medium-Term Impact of the COVID-19 on Prison Populations*. Strasbourg: Council of Europe.

CPT (2020a): *Statement of Principles Relating to the Treatment of Persons Deprived of their Liberty in the Context of the Coronavirus Disease (COVID-19) Pandemic*, https://rm.coe.int/16809cfa4b.

CPT (2020b): *Follow-up Statement Regarding the Situation of Persons Deprived of their Liberty in the Context of the Ongoing COVID-19 Pandemic*, https://rm.coe.int/16809ef566.

Decree no. 195 of 16 March 2020 on the Establishment of the State of Emergency in the Territory of Romania, Published in the Official Gazette no. 212 of 16 March 2020.

Decree no. 240/2020 on the Extension of the State of Emergency in the Territory of Romania, Published in the Official Gazette, Part I no. 311 of 14 April 2020.

Favuzza, F. (2017): Torreggiani and Prison Overcrowding in Italy. *Human Rights Law Review* 17(1): 153–173.

LAW no 55/15 May 2020 on Certain Measures to Prevent and Combat the Effects of the COVID-19 Pandemic Published in the Official Gazette of Romania no. 396 on the 15 May 2020.

National Administration of Penitentiaries (2020a): *The Decision of the General Director of the National Administration of Penitentiaries No. 381/16.03.2020 for the Approval of the Plan of Measures for the Penitentiary System, at the Establishment of the State of Emergency in the Territory of Romania* (Internal document).

National Administration of Penitentiaries (2020b): *The Decision of the General Director of the National Administration of Penitentiaries No. 419/15 April 2020 for the Approval of the Plan of Measures for the Penitentiary System, upon the Extension of the State of Emergency in the Territory of Romania* (Internal document).

National Administration of Penitentiaries (2020c): *The Decision of the General Director of the National Administration of Penitentiaries No. 446/14 May 2020* (Internal document).

National Administration of Penitentiaries (2020d): *The Decision of the General Director of the National Administration of Penitentiaries No. 450/18 May 2020* (Internal document).

National Administration of Penitentiaries (2020e): *The Decision of the General Director of the National Administration of Penitentiaries No. 633/12 October 2020* (Internal document).

35 Russia

Sergei Ovchinnikov

1 Introduction – general situation of the Russian prison system

The current situation in the world associated with the spread of a new coronavirus, COVID-19, provides an opportunity to look afresh at current social, economic, political, cultural, and other processes. Changes have affected not only the global economic and political components, but also our daily life in general. The measures taken by the authorities to ensure social distance among the population have a synergistic effect. The famous French writer Albert Camus in his novel "The Plague" noted that "All that a person is able to win in the game with the plague and with life is knowledge and memory". This conclusion directs our research to questions about the influence of the policy of imposing restrictions on current processes and whether the measures that have been taken will persist.

Data from the World Health Organization shows that Russia with 4,409,438 positive cases, as of 16 March 2021, has the highest number of such cases in Europe. However, the mortality rate among people diagnosed with COVID-19 in Russia amounts to 637 cases per 1 million of the country's population, which is much lower than in several other European countries (Worldometer, 2021). As in much of Europe, there have been two "waves" of COVID-19 infections in Russia.

In order to understand the context of this research, a few words should be said about the structure and current state of the Russian prison system. In accordance with Article 16 of the Code on the Execution of Criminal Sanctions of the Russian Federation, the structure of the penal system includes inspectorates that enforce criminal sanctions (prison sentences as well as community sanctions and measures such as house arrest, suspended sentences, compulsory labour, correctional labour, and restriction of freedom). Currently, there are 81 inspectorates of the execution of criminal sanctions and 1,348 branches in the prison system of Russia, accounting for 452,747 people sentenced to community sanctions and 7,921 people suspected and (or) accused of having committed crimes under house arrest (Federal Penitentiary Service of Russia, 2021a).

DOI: 10.4324/9781003169178-35

The sentence of forced labour is carried out by correctional centres. As of 1 February 2021, there are 26 correctional centres and 82 isolation sections, functioning as correctional centres, in which 6,282 inmates sentenced to forced labour were registered (Federal Penitentiary Service of Russia, 2021). Punishments, in the form of imprisonment for a specified period and life imprisonment, are enforced by correctional institutions. According to paragraph 9 of Article 6 of the Code on the Execution of Criminal Sanctions, deprivation of liberty is executed by correctional institutions such as colony-settlements, educational colonies for minors, medical correctional institutions, correctional colonies of general, strict, or special regimes, or prisons.[1]

As of 1 February 2021, 478,714 inmates were held in various institutions of the Russian prison system, including:

373,917 people serving sentences in 670 correctional colonies, including:

- 106 colony-settlements with 29,427 inmates serving their sentences;
- 7 correctional colonies for those sentenced to life imprisonment and persons for whom the death penalty by way of pardon was replaced by imprisonment with 1,980 inmates serving their sentences;
- 8 (maximum-security) prisons with 1,276 inmates serving their sentences; and
- 18 educational colonies for minors, with 946 inmates.

Currently, 39,100 women are held in correctional facilities, including:

29,974 individuals in correctional colonies, medical correctional institutions, medical institutions, and 9,126 in pre-trial detention centres. The women's colonies have 13 nurseries with 330 children.

Those accused of committing criminal offences, who have been selected to serve a form of detention as a preventative measure, are held in pre-trial detention centres. At present, 105,000 inmates are held in 209 pre-trial detention centres and 92 facilities functioning as pre-trial detention centres in colonies.

- As to the dynamics of the number of sentenced persons and persons in remand custody, it should be noted that, compared with the data as of 1 January 2020, there is a decrease. For example, the number of sentenced persons held in correctional facilities decreased from the beginning of 2020 to 1 February 2021 by 43,445 (−8,3%) inmates, sentenced women by 2,281 (−6,2%), and minors by 203 (−17,9%). This decline in the number of inmates held in correctional institutions is a continuation of a long-term trend in Russia for more than ten years (see Dünkel, 2017; World Prison Brief, 2021). On the one hand, this trend is due to a decrease in the number of registered crimes. Thus, in the period from 2008 to 2019, the number of registered crimes decreased by more than a third (37.7%)

(Judicial Department at the Supreme Court of the Russian Federation, 2020). This affected the decrease in the number of sentenced persons, including persons sentenced to imprisonment. Over the past decade, the largest decline has been observed among sentenced minors. If in 2008 there were 73,333, in 2019, there were only 16,858, that is, an overall decrease for this period by 77.0%. At the same time, the decrease in the number of women sentenced during the period under review was 40.2%.

An analysis of the judicial statistics for 2008–2019 indicates a long-term trend towards a reduction in the number of prison sentences. During this period, their number decreased by almost half (43.9%) from 312,137 to 175,122. At the same time, this indicator for minors decreased almost six times from 16,520 in 2008 to 2,755 in 2019.

2 Prison and penal policy concerning the execution of prison sentences during the COVID-19-induced crisis

To what extent has the situation related to the spread of the new coronavirus infection influenced these long-term trends? We can see this from the analysis of judicial statistics for the first half of 2020 in comparison with data for the first half of 2019.

First, there is a slight decrease in the number of crimes by 0.1%. In this case, the expected decrease in the number of crimes committed in public places is 10.6%. Street robberies decreased by 23.6%, robberies by 20.7%, thefts by 19.6%, and theft of vehicles by 28.7%. Along with this, the number of IT-crimes continued to grow, including fraud using information technology. In the first half of 2020, such an increase was 91.7% compared to the second half of 2019, and the share of these illegal acts in the overall structure of crime reached 22.3% (Ministry of Internal Affairs of the Russian Federation, 2020).

Second, the number of criminal cases submitted to the court decreased by 8.1%. At the same time, the courts began to use pre-trial detention less often. Thus, the number of occasions on which the courts acceded to requests for the imposition of pre-trial detention fell by 11.2%. Despite this, the number of people in pre-trial detention centres increased in 2020. As of 1 October 2020, their number increased by 7,219 compared to 1 January 2020. This is partly due to the duration of pre-trial detention. For example, in the first half of 2020, the number of criminal cases reviewed within 1.5 months to 3 months increased by 28.1%, and the number of criminal cases reviewed from 3 months to 1 year increased by 38.3%. And this trend is noted despite the fact that the number of court sessions held using video conferencing has increased by almost a quarter (22.6%), when suspects or accused can participate remotely, which significantly reduces the risk of contracting a coronavirus infection during transportation.

Another trend that should be noted is a decrease of 19.7% in the number of convictions in criminal cases. The number of convicted women and minors in the first half of 2020 compared to the first half of 2019 decreased by 20.4% and 23.2%, respectively. There was a decrease in the number of people sentenced to imprisonment by almost a quarter (24.6%), of which women by 24.8% and minors by 26.2%. Also in 2020, there was a decrease in the number of persons on whom community sanctions were imposed. The overall decline here was 18.2%, while the number of women sentenced to alternatives to imprisonment decreased by 19.7%, and of minors by 23.6%.

These statistics explain the decrease in the number of prisoners held in correctional institutions in 2020. That means that the Russian criminal justice system has reduced the number of suspects, accused and sentenced persons entering correctional institutions.

Judicial statistics recorded in the first half of 2020, compared to the first half of 2019, a decrease in the number of persons released on parole. Thus, the number of applications for parole, granted by the court, decreased by 14.7%. It should be noted that this downward trend has been observed for more than ten years. For example, for the period from 2008 to 2019, this indicator decreased by almost two thirds from 124,718 to 45,387.

3 Restrictions of contact with the outside world

As shown above, changes in the judicial practice in 2020 impacted on the dynamics of the number of persons held in prison facilities. The measures taken in the Russian prison system during the pandemic were aimed at changing the procedures for the operation of correctional institutions. This was due to the need to prevent the spread of COVID-19 among suspects, accused and sentenced persons, as well as among employees of correctional institutions.

The employees of the prison system and persons held in correctional institutions are especially vulnerable to the risk of infection. 49 laboratories are currently engaged in tests to identify infections in the prison system. As of 1 October 2020, 263,790 such laboratory tests had been carried out. The volume of testing of inmates and employees of the prison system amounted to 33,421.73 per 100,000 people, which is 6.8% more than the national average of 31,292.52 per 100,000 of the general population (Rossiyskaya gazeta, 2020).

Over the entire period of the pandemic, 1,591 laboratory-confirmed cases of a coronavirus infection were detected among inmates throughout the country, including 590 cases in pre-trial detention centres. One prisoner who fell ill with COVID-19 died. As of 22 October 2020, 1,452 people, or 91.2%, have recovered of those who were diagnosed with a coronavirus infection (Federal Penitentiary Service of Russia, 2020a).

The largest number of identified cases among inmates in the Central Federal District was 233. In the Ural Federal District, there were 111 confirmed cases. At the same time, in 28 regions, there were no cases among inmates (Federal Penitentiary Service of Russia, 2020b). Among employees, the picture is different. Only three regions reported no cases of COVID-19 among employees. This confirms the general European trend noted above. In European countries, the number of COVID-19 cases was also higher among prison staff than among inmates.

Undoubtedly, the main threat that still remains is the introduction of the virus into correctional institutions from the outside. Therefore, when employees enter, they must undergo a medical examination and temperature check. Since the beginning of the epidemic, a number of restrictions have been introduced, including shift duty for staff in some regions. Employees go on duty for 14 days without the opportunity to leave the institution during this entire period in order to exclude any contacts from outside. For those newly admitted to prison facilities, the quarantine period was extended to 20 days, since the disease cannot be detected in its first phase. All vehicles entering the premises of prisons are sanitised with disinfectants at specially equipped areas.

Another potential source of infection is the transport of prisoners to courts. While it may be possible to ensure the separation of inmates in pre-trial detention centres, this is likely not the case in court rooms. Therefore, a number of regions began to use video conferencing for court hearings. In the first half of 2020, compared to the first half of 2019, the number of court hearings held using videoconferencing increased by almost a quarter (22.6%).

In addition, control over the receiving of parcels was strengthened. Currently, employees handle parcels while using personal protective equipment. Premises for receiving parcels are equipped with bactericidal irradiators. Employees disinfect packages and the air in the room as well as the parcels with open-type bactericidal irradiators.

Hand sanitisers have been installed in the reception rooms of prisons. Wet cleaning of premises (using detergents and disinfectants) is carried out at least twice a day.

Further restrictive measures was the suspension of visits. From 16 March 2020 and until further instruction, long- and short-term visits were suspended in some regions. From mid-August, depending on the epidemiological situation in these regions, restrictive measures were gradually lifted. Some institutions allowed short-term and long-term visits. Short-term visits with relatives and other persons were conducted through glass screens in compliance with the requirements of individual protection.

It also became necessary to introduce measures to limit visits to correctional institutions by representatives of public organisations. Lawyers were admitted if they used personal protective equipment and with negotiations through protective glass screens. In addition, despite the implementation of complex sanitary and anti-epidemic measures, including restrictive measures, from 16 March 2020, members of public monitoring commissions visited the institutions of the Russian prison system 202 times. Remote consideration of appeals by email from inmates and their relatives was organised. Monitors found excessive restrictions on, and violations of, the rights of inmates such as the right to daily exercise and to receiving parcels from relatives (Russia Today, 2020).

However, due to the deterioration of the sanitary and epidemiological situation in certain regions, the previously cancelled restrictions on short-term and long-term visits of prisoners with their relatives were reintroduced, and continue up to the present in some regions.

4 Restrictions inside prisons

In order to prevent the spread of COVID-19 in certain regions of Russia, special restrictive measures were taken. Thus, a regime of special conditions was introduced in pre-trial detention centres in 15 regions.[2] In addition, quarantines were announced in individual correctional institutions in 48 regions. In regions where the situation stabilised, quarantine measures in institutions were relaxed. As of 4 August 2020, the quarantine regime was maintained in individual prisons in 29 regions. However, because of the worsening of the sanitary and epidemiological situation in some regions and prisons, restrictive measures were introduced again. Restrictive measures (quarantine) were introduced in a number of institutions of 53 territorial bodies of the penal system. To date (March 2021), restrictive measures are in force in 45 regions, including 41 pre-trial detention centres in 20 regions (Federal Penitentiary Service of Russia, 2020b).

Along with the adoption of quarantine measures, the regional authorities made extensive use of preventive sanitary and anti-epidemic measures. For example, a mask regime was introduced in correctional institutions. Employees and visitors are required to comply with it. When visiting prisoners, visitors undergo temperature checks. At all facilities, disinfection measures are carried out daily with the use of disinfectants and bactericidal irradiators. In addition, a sanitation day is held in all prisons once a week.

The existing bacteriological and immunological laboratories were also redesigned to detect diseases such as tuberculosis and HIV infections, and to work to identify the COVID-19 virus, where diagnostics and testing of persons with symptoms of coronavirus is carried out. Patients with clinical symptoms are immediately isolated in medical institutions and medical-sanitary units.

Currently, the vaccination of staff and inmates has begun. Thus, in the institutions of St. Petersburg, sentenced and remand prisoners undergo voluntary vaccination (Federal Penitentiary Service of Russia, 2021b). Based on the sanitary and epidemiological situation, restrictions on the movement of prisoners outside the institution were issued and the quarantine period on admission was increased. In addition, in some institutions, training was done remotely.

5 Compensatory measures

During the period of restrictions, compensatory measures were provided to ensure communication with relatives and close friends. Thus, in accordance with current legislation, inmates can communicate with their relatives by telephone and use video communication without restrictions. Currently, there are about 8,500 telephones in the Russian prison system, through which inmates make more than 8 million calls annually, as well as 514 video terminals, supporting more than 45,000 video calls a year.

Measures were also taken to compensate the employees of correctional institutions. First, there are incentives for those staff members who work with inmates who have COVID-19. According to the order No. 1230-r, of the Government of the Russian Federation, dated 8 May 2020, 230.1 million roubles from the reserve fund of the Government of the Russian Federation were allocated to provide additional monetary incentives for employees of correctional institutions working with people with a coronavirus infection. These funds were used to pay appropriate compensation to 8,500 employees of the Federal Penitentiary Service of Russia (Government of the Russian Federation, 2020).

Attempts were also made to decongest prisons to reduce contacts between inmates. In order to reduce the number of persons held in pre-trial detention centres, the leaders of the Federal Penitentiary Service of Russia appealed to the Supreme Court of the Russian Federation not to order pre-trial detention for those suspected or accused of having committed crimes of low to medium severity, but rather, to apply alternative measures in the community (Rosbusinessconsulting, 2020).

90 people have been transferred through land checkpoints to foreign states (in fulfilment by the Russian Federation of international legal obligations on extradition), and 31 people have been admitted to Russia. The extradition of persons on the international wanted list took place with eight states, such as the Republic of Belarus, Kazakhstan, Ukraine, Azerbaijan, Georgia, Poland, South Ossetia, and China. All extradited persons were examined for the presence of COVID-19 before being sent from Russia (Federal Penitentiary Service of Russia, 2020b).

6 Legal basis of restrictions and relaxations of the prison regime

The restrictions imposed in correctional institutions are based on the requirements of penal legislation. As already noted, in accordance with Article 85 of the Code on the Execution of Criminal Sanctions of the Russian Federation, in cases of a natural disaster, the imposition of a state of emergency or martial law in correctional institutions, and during mass riots or group disobedience by prisoners, a regime of special conditions may be introduced. During the special regime, the exercise of some of the rights of sentenced persons provided for in Articles 88–97 (the right to receive parcels, meetings with relatives, telephone conversations, exercise, etc.) may be suspended, an enhanced version of protection and supervision may be introduced, a special procedure adopted for admitting parcels or other goods, the daily routine may be changed, and the activities of production, utilities, cultural and educational and other services, with the exception of medical and sanitary services, may be limited. Regional authorities also enacted laws, according to which restrictions and prohibitions were established to ensure compliance with the rules of conduct in the pandemic.

7 Returning to normal

Summing up, it should be noted that the spread of the new coronavirus infection has undoubtedly influenced the established rules of ensuring law and order. On the one hand, long-term tendencies in the reduction of crime have continued and, consequently, a reduction in the number of offenders sentenced to imprisonment and to alternative types of punishment could be observed. On the other hand, an increase in the number of crimes committed with the use of information technology and the internet was not unexpected. There has also been an increase in the use of information technology in the administration of criminal justice. How long-term these trends will be and whether the experience of working during a pandemic will lead to any structural changes in the field of the execution of criminal sanctions largely depend on the persistence of the threat of the spread of the COVID-19 or other coronavirus infections.

Notes

1 According to Article 58 of the Criminal Code of the Russian Federation, depending on the severity of the crime committed and other circumstances, sentenced persons may be assigned to serve imprisonment in correctional colonies of general, strict, or special regime.

   a In *colony-settlements*, offenders are serving their sentences to imprisonment for crimes committed through negligence, intentional crimes of average gravity, as well as prisoners transferred from correctional colonies of the general and strict regime on the basis and in the order of encouragement.
   b In the *general regime* of correctional colonies, convicted men serve their sentences, with the exception of those who are serving sentences in correctional institutions of other types, as well as convicted women.
   c Men who are sentenced to imprisonment for the first time for the commission of especially grave crimes are serving their sentences in penal colonies with a *strict regime*; the same applies in case of recurrence of crimes and the so-called dangerous recidivists, if the convicted person has previously served imprisonment.
   d In correctional colonies of a special regime, convicted men serve their sentences with a special danger of reoffending with serious crimes, sentenced to life imprisonment, as well as offenders for whom the death penalty by way of pardon has been replaced to imprisonment for a certain period or life imprisonment.
   e Persons sentenced to imprisonment for a term of more than five years for committing especially grave crimes, sentenced to imprisonment for committing crimes provided for in Articles 205-205.5, 206, 208, 211, 220, 221, 277–279, 281, 317, 360, 361 of the Criminal Code of the Russian Federation, sentenced as especially dangerous recidivists, as well as sentenced persons who are malicious violators of the established procedure for

serving sentences, transferred from correctional colonies serve their sentence in the so-called prisons, which represent cell-based accommodation under maximum-security conditions.

f Juveniles sentenced to imprisonment serve their sentences in educational colonies until they reach the age of 19.

2 In accordance with Article 85 of the Criminal Executive Code of the Russian Federation, in cases of natural disaster, the imposition of a state of emergency or martial law in the area where a correctional facility is located, and in other emergency circumstances, a regime of special conditions may be introduced in prisons. During the period of the special conditions regime, the exercise of certain rights of sentenced persons may be suspended.

References

Dünkel, F. (2017): European penology: The rise and fall of prison population rates in Europe in times of migrant crises and terrorism. *European Journal of Criminology* 14, 629–653.

Federal Penitentiary Service of Russia (2020a): *Interview of the Deputy Director of the FPS of Russia Alexander Khabarov to the Information Agency TASS.* http://fsin.gov.ru/news/index.php?ELEMENT_ID=512204.

Federal Penitentiary Service of Russia (2020b): *Interview of the Deputy Director of the FPS of Russia Valery Boyarinev to the Information Agency TASS.* http://fsin.gov.ru/news/index.php?ELEMENT_ID=528506.

Federal Penitentiary Service of Russia (2021a): *Brief Characteristic of the Criminal Executive System.* http://fsin.gov.ru/structure/inspector/iao/statistika/.

Federal Penitentiary Service of Russia (2021b): *In the FPS of Russia in St. Petersburg and Leningrad Region a Vaccination Campaign Was Started.* https://fsin.gov.ru/news/index.php?ELEMENT_ID=547956.

Government of the Russian Federation (2020): *Order of the Government of the Russian Federation dated 05/08/2020 No. 1230-r.* http://publication.pravo.gov.ru/Document/View/0001202005100003.

Judicial Department at the Supreme Court of the Russian Federation (2020): *Judicial Statistics Data.* http://www.cdep.ru/index.php?id=79.

Ministry of Internal Affairs of the Russian Federation (2020): *Brief Description of the State of Crime in the Russian Federation in January–June 2020.* https://*мвд.рф*/reports/item/20597695/.

Rosbusinessconsulting (2020, 19 April): FSIN asked not to arrest for minor crimes because of the virus. http://www.rbc.ru/society/18/04/2020/ 5e9ae92c9a79477104514365.

Rossiyskaya gazeta (2020, 1 October): Freedom from the virus. https://rg.ru/2020/10/01/bolee-13-tysiachi-rossijskih-zakliuchennyh-vylechi lis-ot-covid-19.html.

Russia Today (2020, 14 May): The public monitoring commission of Moscow reported on the reduction in the number of walks in a number of pre-trial detention centres. http://russian.rt.com/russia/news/746528-sizo-moskvy-progulki-sokraschenie-onk.

World Health Organization (2021): *WHO Coronavirus Disease (COVID-19) Dashboard.* http://covid19.who.int.

Worldometer (2021): *Reported Cases and Deaths by Country, Territory, or Conveyance.* http://www.worldometers.info/coronavirus/#countries.

World Prison Brief (2021): *World Prison Brief data.* https://www.prisonstudies.org/country/russian-federation.

36 Scotland

Katrina Morrison and Hannah Graham

1 Introduction – general situation of the prison system

1.1 The Scottish penal policy context

Scottish penality is beset with contradictions. Despite some penal practices which could be said to be based in welfarism and parsimony (see McAra, 2005; Scottish Government, 2019), Scotland has an astonishing appetite for punishment. Scotland had the highest rate of imprisonment in all of Western Europe (McCallum, 2019), and within this overall figure, the highest rate of life sentences in all of Europe (van Zyl Smit and Morrison, 2020). Scotland also has very high rates of community punishment, the highest in all of Europe, behind only Lithuania, Georgia and Turkey (Aebi and Hashimoto, 2019). Taking imprisonment and community rates together, it has been argued that Scotland has one of the highest *correctional rates* in all of Europe (Graham and McNeill, 2019). Towards the end of 2019, Scottish prisons were operating at 9% over their maximum operational capacity (SPS, 2021a). While many in Scotland believe our approach to punishment to be progressive (certainly in comparison with England and Wales), it has recently been argued that reforms of imprisonment over recent decades have merely civilised punishment, rather making it humanitarian by reducing the penal power exercised by the state (Brangan, 2019).

While there have been moments of political courage with penal reform over recent decades (Graham, 2020a), within the bigger picture, these appear tokenistic or preliminary. Nonetheless, the Scottish Government (led by the Scottish National Party (SNP) for the past 14 years) has long spoken about the need to reduce the prison population (McCallum, 2019), but measures to achieve this have been limited. The prison population fluctuated in 2020, for reasons which are identified in this chapter. On 13 March 2020, at the very beginning of the pandemic, the prison population was 8,094 people; then, it decreased to 6,869 on 29 May 2020, and increased gradually to 7,176 on 16 April 2021 (Scottish Prison Service, 2020a, 2021b).

DOI: 10.4324/9781003169178-36

1.2 The prison system

There are 15 prisons in Scotland, 13 public and 2 private, though there has recently been a commitment to take the private prisons back into public ownership at the end of their contracts. Scotland's prisons are located primarily in and around the "central belt" (the more densely populated region encompassing the cities of Glasgow, Edinburgh and Stirling), with some outliers including two prisons in the Highlands. Prisons vary in size from a capacity of just under 1,000 to just over 100, though recent available data indicates that 9 out of 15 prisons held more than their maximum capacity (Scottish Parliament, 2020).

Prior to the pandemic, prisons in Scotland were not in a good position to safely respond to this public health emergency. Prisons were overcrowded with many cells designed for single prisoners holding two or more people. Parts of the prison estate had already been judged "not fit for service", particularly for the growing numbers of older prisoners and prisoners with disabilities and health conditions (HMIPS, 2020). Healthcare in prisons (offered by the public National Health Service (NHS) and local health boards) has been subject to criticism for years and these concerns have not yet been substantively addressed.

2 Prison and penal policy concerning the execution of prison sentences

The rest of this chapter focuses on the impact of and responses to the COVID-19 pandemic in 2020 and early 2021. In the Scottish Parliament, the Coronavirus (Scotland) Act 2020[1] was introduced, debated and passed in a matter of days, with cross-party consensus, from 1 April 2020. It included emergency powers enabling the Scottish Government to change the Prison Rules and to authorise early release of prisoners during the COVID-19 pandemic. These reforms were administered using secondary legislation under the auspices of the Act: the Prison and Young Offenders Institutions (Scotland) Amended Rules 2020,[2] Prison and Young Offenders Institutions (Scotland) Amended Rules 2021,[3] and the Release of Prisoners (Coronavirus) (Scotland) Regulations 2020.[4] A bounded overview of the implementation and impact of these regulations is discussed in the following sections.

Early release of prisoners was considered by the Scottish Government in the early part of the pandemic and then approved by Scottish Parliament with the passing of the Release of Prisoners (Coronavirus) (Scotland) Regulations 2020 on 4 May 2020. The policy note accompanying these regulations justifies early release on the policy grounds of "a necessary and proportionate response to the effects coronavirus is having, and is likely to have, on prisons generally, for the purpose of protecting (a) the security and good order of prisons; and (b) the health, safety and welfare of prisoners and those working in prisons" (Scottish Government, 2020a: 1). It also emphasises increasing single-cell occupancy rates and cites issues of prison workforce capacity.

In waiting for news of the executive early release scheme, families wrote to Scottish Government Ministers and MSPs "begging" for information, help and the early release of loved ones, expressing feelings of anguish and "constantly worrying", "not being told enough", being "in limbo", raising concerns over prison conditions and difficulties with physical distancing, making impassioned pleas that "everyone has the right to live", and stories of separation (in Scottish Government, 2020b: 17, 23, 46).

After being discussed for weeks, the early release scheme was implemented wholly in May 2020. People serving a short sentence of less than 18 months, who had three months (90 days) or less until their release date, were eligible for early release. There were exclusions from eligibility for people who had committed certain offences (sexual, terrorism, COVID-19-related, domestic abuse) or were subject to a non-harassment order. Notably absent from policy rationalisations of release eligibility was any consideration of the health vulnerabilities of each individual or if they were a child.

Those approved for this scheme were released from prison unconditionally (not out on licence), without an electronic monitoring tag. Release was risk assessed and fell within the victim notification scheme. Charities and social enterprises in justice, health and welfare collaborated with justice social work and community justice (i.e. probation) agencies to support the liberation and resettlement of those released.

According to the Scottish Prison Service, of the 445 people who met the eligibility criteria, a total of 348 people were released from prison early during May 2020. That is 314 men and 34 women, the vast majority of whom were under 47 years old. A discretionary veto by prison governors prevented the early release of 63 people. Of those released through this scheme, the types of crimes for which they had been sentenced and imprisoned were varied. These included shoplifting, housebreaking and other thefts, drugs, breach of the peace (a low-level public order offence), common assault, dangerous and careless driving, handling offensive weapons, attempted murder and serious assault (Scottish Government, 2020c). Importantly, around 10% of all of those who were released were immediately rearrested by Police Scotland on outstanding warrants pre-dating their imprisonment, suggesting that a "joined up" approach across the justice system was found wanting. This was the only executive release of prisoners in Scotland in 2020 and early 2021.

Concurrent to the early release scheme, normal liberations continued with an estimated 100–150 people released per week (Graham, 2020c). Critical analysis of the Scottish prison population over the course of 2020 indicates that the "front door" and decision-making of the courts and Crown Office and Procurator Fiscal Service (COPFS, the Scottish prosecution service) have much more influence on prison populations than "back door" measures such as this early release scheme (Graham, 2020c).

3/4 Restrictions of contact with the outside world and inside prisons

The Prison and Young Offenders Institutions (Scotland) Amended Rules 2020 (which were further extended until September 2021 in the Prison and Young Offenders Institutions (Scotland) Amended Rules 2021) changed the Prison Rules, enabling far greater discretion for each prison governor to take decisions to keep prisoners safe from the virus and to manage staffing issues (e.g. workforce absence). In May to June 2020, reports from two prisons stated that prisoners were kept locked in cells for 23 hours a day, with 30 minutes for outdoor exercise and 30 minutes to shower and use the phone. Furthermore, those held in isolation because they were suspected to be symptomatic were not, at this stage, getting access to either fresh air or phones. Other prisons managed 22 hours or more a day inside cells, with 30 to 45 minutes outside. Furthermore, if two people are sharing a cell and one becomes symptomatic, then they must both be held in isolation for 14 days (SPS, 2020b).

Efforts were made to occupy prisoners when locked in cells for so long, including fitness and mental health mindfulness courses on cell TVs, expanded television and gaming options, and the education provider, Fife College, provided in-cell education packs for prisoners. HMP Perth was commended by the Inspectorate for efforts to promote prisoner voice and participation with the "quality and regular occurrence of Prisoner Information Action Committees" (HMIPS, 2020b: 2).

As the pandemic progressed, prisons had learned how to manage infections and regimes differently than in the early days, by, for example, organising prisoners into larger groups of "households", enabling a greater number to be able to take exercise outside or engage in purposeful activity, at any one time. By late 2020/early 2021, most prisoners were able to take one hour of exercise a day, as well as restricted activities in education, gym and recreation (Scottish Parliament, 2020).

Family visits were halted for the first time from 23 March 2020, and there was a significant delay before alternatives were made available (see further, below, in Section 5). Family visits were re-introduced again (albeit with mask wearing and social distancing measures in place) on 3 August 2020, in line with an easing in restrictions in the community round the same time. Visits were halted on Christmas Day 2020, and commenced again on 26 April 2021. Although in-person visits with lawyers were still possible throughout the whole pandemic, most took advantage of video-conferencing facilities made available by the Legal Aid Board Scotland.

The Scottish Human Rights Commission (2020) raised substantive concerns with the Scottish Government about prisoners being kept in isolation tantamount to solitary confinement for extended periods during the earlier part of the pandemic, concerns which the Scottish Parliament Justice Committee (2021) further scrutinised in their questions and correspondence with the Scottish Prison Service.

Throughout the pandemic, reports on the numbers of prisoners in self-isolation fluctuated considerably on a week-by-week basis, though these statistics were only published after a degree of public pressure following stories in the press. In March 2020, 125 people were self-isolating, this reduced to 7 at one point in June, and was as high as 1,285 people self-isolating in February 2021 (SPS, 2021b). Clear figures of numbers of confirmed infections have been difficult to ascertain but, at one point in February 2021, there were outbreaks in some prisons, including one in which 230 people had tested positive – just under half of the entire population in that prison (STV, 2021). Prison staff were affected too: in April 2020, the Prison Officers' Association said that a quarter of the 4,000+ prison workforce were reported to be absent from work, and staffing shift changes had to be rapidly implemented to help cope with absences (Fairlie in BBC News, 2020).

Finally, the Scottish Prison Service has given different figures for deaths, stating, in different forums, that either five or six deaths of people in prison have been COVID-related, alongside the death of one prison officer. Tragically, there have been a series of other non-COVID-related deaths in custody while prisons have been in lockdown or restricted regime during 2020, all men, mostly aged in their 20s–40s, including self-inflicted deaths.

One of the pronounced consequences of the pandemic and prison regime changes has been the effect on access to purposeful activity (broadly, relating to employability, skills acquisition, education, rehabilitation programmes and well-being). These group-based activities were significantly affected during prison lockdown, with the number of hours spent in them reducing from half to a third across the prison estate. The cessation of regular human engagement and the opportunity to "improve themselves" through these activities would have implications not only for prisoners' mental health and well-being, but it would also have important and negative consequences for prisoners' ability to progress through their sentence, either to the "top end" (open conditions), or to gain parole. This is particularly true for access to programmes, the prescribed rehabilitation and offending behaviour risk reduction programmes which may significantly influence how a prisoner's application for release on parole is perceived. In November 2020, it was revealed that it could take over *five years* to clear the backlog on some key programmes (SPS, 2020c). This has clear implications for those individuals who would otherwise be eligible to progress or to be released on parole. Following sustained pressure from penal reform organisations and from the Parliamentary Justice Committee, the Scottish Prison Service advised that it was working to ensure that progression and parole would not be adversely affected by the pandemic (Scottish Parliament Justice Committee, 2021).

Across the estate, prisoner accounts of lockdown and restricted regimes brim with human concerns: feelings of boredom and emptiness, anger and frustration, loneliness and longing for human connection, worry about hygiene and prison conditions, fears for loved ones and an uncertain future, and clapping and cheers of thanks for the NHS and key workers during the first lockdown. An interdisciplinary team of researchers from the University of Glasgow investigated the impact of lockdown in Scotland through a mixed methods study, including people with convictions and their family members, and practitioners involved in the Scottish Justice system (see Armstrong and Pickering, 2020; Gormley et al., 2020). Their qualitative and quantitative findings offer salient insights:

> We are forgotten people of the COVID-19 pandemic [...] there has been no compassion shown to us human beings. We are locked up 23 hours a day. How is this good for anyone's mental health, on top of that we are stressed out to the max worrying about our families, praying our loved ones manage to get through this.
>
> (prisoner quoted in Gormley et al., 2020: 58)

> Locked down 23 ½ hours a day, put weight on, feel depressed, don't get gym enough… prison cells are really bad for cleanliness, all this puts people into a bad state and depressions. This prison is not fit and lockdown has made it 100% worse.
>
> (prisoner quoted in Gormley et al., 2020: 58)

The researchers found a common thread of participants with convictions "being in limbo", affecting access to services, frustrating opportunities for progression and significantly affecting the severity, intensity and time/prolongation of punishment (Gormley et al., 2020).

The effects of the pandemic have exacerbated existing problems within the Scottish Justice system, one of which is the high numbers of people held in pre-trial, or pre-sentencing detention. Prior to the pandemic, the remand population was around 20% of the overall prison population, a figure which had been the focus of political attention in the preceding years (Scottish Parliament Justice Committee, 2018). Courts continued to operate during the pandemic, processing "essential and critical business", including making decisions around remand and bail for certain cases. Crucially, however, jury trials were halted between March and June 2020, and when they did resume, had to do so at a reduced capacity. The effects on the remand population have been dramatic, and by April 2021, 27% of the overall prison population (n = 1,995) were on remand (Scottish Prison Service, 2021). Of the 1,995 people on remand, 1,783 were untried, and 212 were convicted, awaiting sentence. In an interview about prisons during the COVID-19 pandemic, the Cabinet Secretary for Justice, Humza Yousaf, spoke of the "punitiveness" of the Scottish judiciary, saying "there are far too many people spending time on remand", and he also spoke of efforts underway to introduce electronic monitoring tagging with bail to try to help reduce remand numbers (in Leapman, 2021).

Perhaps most concerning out of the small number of 16- and 17-year-olds in custody by April 2021 (n = 17), 16 (94%) of them were on remand, all of them had yet to appear in court for trial. Out of the 184 18- and 19-year-olds in custody, 89 (48%) of them had yet to stand trial or receive sentence (SPS, 2021a). Equivalent figures from previous recent years are around 35% under 21 on remand. Despite the plea from the UNCRC to release children in all forms of detention, whenever possible throughout the pandemic, it is clear that this has not occurred in Scotland (Lightowler and Adamson, 2020). In November 2020, the Children and Young People's Commissioner and the Children and Young People's Centre for Justice sharply criticised authorities for this neglect and called for urgent action to meet human rights obligations to avoid young people being in extended periods of isolation, emulating that of solitary confinement (Lightowler and Adamson, 2020; Nolan, 2020).

The lengthy time spent on remand for adults during conditions of prison lockdown was tested in the Appeal Court in *HM Advocate v JD and BK* [2020] HCJAC 15 (HCJAC, 2020). Despite finding against the appeal, the court also concluded that "the length of time during which a person is likely to remain on remand is a factor in deciding whether to grant bail. This factor must be given greater weight than hitherto". One way of reducing the numbers on remand in custody is the imminent implementation of secondary legislation, passed by Scottish Parliament in late 2020, enabling the introduction of electronic monitoring tagging to be used with bail.

Despite prevention and de-escalation efforts, some critical incidents have occurred in Scottish prisons. Being locked in cells approximately 23 hours a day and being unable to have in-person family visits over a period of months have been reported as influential factors (Gillies, 2020). In March 2020, in HMP Addiewell, several male prisoners destroyed property, injured two prison officers and lit fires in disturbances attributed to COVID-19-related tensions (McGivern, 2020). In November 2020, a violent incident occurred in Polmont, a young offenders' institution (for ages 16–20 years), when a football match intended to ease tension and boost morale instead ended in fighting, with prison officers among the injured (Hind, 2020).

Despite calls from penal reform and prisoner advocacy organisation during 2021 that prisoners be prioritised for vaccine due to the very adverse effects of prison lockdown, people in custody have instead been vaccinated in line with the age profile of the general population. There have been COVID-19 outbreaks across the prison estate during this time, but there is no further indication of any further plans for executive release.

5 Compensatory measures

The Scottish Prison Service announced the suspension of all family visits for the first time on 23 March 2020, with immediate effect. On 24 March, the Government announced that they were looking into alternative means of visiting, and in mid-April, they announced in Parliament that all prisoners[5] would be provided with a security-restricted mobile phone to facilitate family contact, in lieu of visits. It later emerged that the funds to do this had already been earmarked for the provision of landline phones in cells at the Young Offenders Institution Polmont, following an enquiry into mental health support for young people in custody. However, the roll-out of mobiles was significantly delayed with the first mobiles only being provided to prisoners on 15 June 2020, nine weeks after they had been announced, and 12 weeks after visits had been suspended. This delay was due to technical difficulties both with the handsets and with existing phone-blocking technology in some prisons which had to be dismantled for the mobiles to work.

Between 24 March and 17 June 2020, there were only two other means of contact between prisoners and their families. First, there was the pre-existing email-a-prisoner scheme, whereby messages can be emailed to the prison and printed out for the prisoner to read. Second, from 20 May 2020, voicemails could be retrieved by prisoners through the communal phone in prisons alongside the provision of £ 2.50 (€ 2.80) free credit to access them. However, there have been reports of prisoners being reluctant to use these communal phones during this time out of fear of infection in light of inadequate cleaning provision in between users (Maycock and Dixon, 2021). In any case, on 16 June 2020, a day before the first mobiles were introduced to prisons, virtual visits (similar to a video-conferencing call) also began to be rolled out across prisons, although they were limited with the ability to book only one 30-minute "visit" per month. Both mobile phones and virtual visits remain in place at the time of writing (April 2021).

In total, around 7,500 mobiles were distributed to prisoners across Scotland. These are "dumb", (i.e. not internet enabled smart phones) Nokia handsets, which had been programmed to only allow calls to pre-agreed, and pre-vetted, numbers, as well as the Independent Prison Monitors (part of the national prisons inspectorate), and Samaritans (a mental health and suicide prevention charity). According to the Scottish Government, prisoners called the Samaritans approximately 5,284 times using these mobiles in the second half of 2020. These restrictions are equivalent to those in place for phones on the prison landings. No incoming calls are allowed, and usage is restricted to 300 minutes per month.

Despite some criticisms of the cost of these phones from those on the political right in Scotland (Musson, 2020), the introduction of mobiles has also been praised by the prisons inspectorate, saying "this is a step forward in Scotland's enlightened approach to penology and will be welcome even after the current crisis" (HMIPS, 2020: 35).

6 Legal basis for restrictions of the prison regime

As pointed out under Sections 2–4, measures taken during the pandemic were based on substantive legislation, with prison-related regulations enabled by underpinning legislation, the Coronavirus (Scotland) Act 2020, and the Coronavirus (Scotland) Act 2021.

7 Returning to normal

In considering Scotland's future after the COVID-19 crisis, journalist and lawyer Michael Gray (2020: 88, 93) contends that real progress can be made in the midst of adversity and uncertainty; yet, whether progress *will* be realised is far from given: "in times of crisis, all kinds of change seem possible... [this] experience demonstrates that we can rapidly change the priorities of our democracy with intense political will. All engaged in this type of work understand that it can be frustratingly incremental". While some of the measures which were taken are temporary or unlikely to be repeated, other measures look as though they are here to stay (such as mobile phones for prisoners). There may be some reasons for cautious hope; some measures (such as using electronic monitoring to try to reduce use of remand) have the potential for enduring and positive effects, added to which the Scottish Government are on record as saying "[w]e certainly cannot go back to [prison population] levels where we were pre-pandemic" (McQuillan, 2020). However, Scottish penal history is replete with such good intentions, with little, or no, longer-term decarceration effect.

The account we offer in this chapter is not entirely dispassionate. In 2020, a constellation of voices, including our own, have called for Scottish justice to change, centring on diversion, decarceration and social justice (Graham, 2020a; 2020b; Howard League Scotland, 2020; Lightowler and Adamson, 2020; Scottish Human Rights Commission, 2020; Scottish Prisoner Advocacy and Research Collective (SPARC); 2020). Realising such change will take some consensus and cooperation as well as courage, from politicians, to practitioners and the judiciary, through to civic society, local communities and citizens. The impact of the COVID-19 pandemic in exacerbating existing problems should not be under-estimated. Its legacy will be apparent for some time to come. What could not be more apparent is that the status quo is no longer sustainable and, in seeking change, we need more deeds, not just words.

Notes

1 https://www.legislation.gov.uk/asp/2020/7/contents.
2 https://www.legislation.gov.uk/ssi/2020/122/contents/made.
3 https://www.legislation.gov.uk/ssi/2021/80/contents/made.
4 https://www.legislation.gov.uk/ssi/2020/138/contents/made.
5 This is with the exception of one of the private prisons, HMP Kilmarnock, where hard-wired in-cell telephone services were introduced, not mobile phones.

References

Aebi, M., and Hashimoto, Y. (2019): *Persons under the Supervision of Probation Agencies - Space II Council of Europe Annual Penal Statistics*. https://wp.unil.ch/space/files/2020/06/SPACE-II_Final_report_2019_200610.pdf, accessed December 2020.

Armstrong, S., and Pickering, L. (2020) (Eds.): *Left Out and Locked Down: Impact of COVID-19 Pandemic for Marginalised Groups in Scotland.* Glasgow: University of Glasgow.

BBC News (2020): Coronavirus: Almost a quarter of Scottish prison staff absent from work, 2 April 2020, https://www.bbc.co.uk/news/uk-scotland-52133835, accessed December 2020.

Brangan, L., (2019): Civilizing imprisonment: The limits of Scottish penal exceptionalism. *British Journal of Criminology* 59(4), 780–799.

Gillies, C. (2020): Coronavirus: Ex-Inmate Warning Over Barlinnie 'tensions'. *BBC Scotland News,* 4 May 2020, https://www.bbc.co.uk/news/uk-scotland-glasgow-west-52539415.

Gormley, C., Schinkel, M., Barkas, B., Casey, R., Cornish, N., and McNeill, F. (2020): Criminal justice involved. In: Armstrong, S., and Pickering, L. (Eds.): *Left Out and Locked Down: Impact of COVID-19 Pandemic for Marginalised Groups in Scotland.* Glasgow: University of Glasgow (Chapter 5).

Graham, H. (2020a): *Courage of Convictions: Progressive Visions and Allies in Uncertain Times,* Apex Scotland Annual Lecture 2020, 1 September 2020. https://www.apexscotland.org.uk/resources/publications/annual-lecture-2020/.

Graham, H. (2020b): Changing Scottish justice will take courage and cooperation. In: Hassan, G., and Barrow, S. (Eds.): *Scotland after the Virus,* Edinburgh: Luath Press, 188–194.

Graham, H. (2020c): Pressured times call for emergency measures in Scotland's prisons. Centre for Crime and Justice Studies blog, 10 June 2020, https://www.crimeandjustice.org.uk/resources/pressured-times-call-emergency-measures-scotlands-prisons, accessed December 2020.

Graham, H., and McNeill, F. (2019): Submission to the Scottish Parliament Justice Committee on the Presumption against Short Sentences Bill. https://www.parliament.scot/S5_JusticeCommittee/Inquiries/PASS-GrahamMcNeill.pdf, accessed December 2020.

Gray, M. (2020): People and Politics: Reshaping how we debate, discuss and listen. In: Hassan, G., and Barrow, S. (Eds.): *Scotland after the Virus.* Edinburgh: Luath Press, 88–94.

High Court of Justiciary (HCJAC) (2020): HM Advocate v JD and BK [2020] HCJAC 15 judgement of the court. https://www.scotcourts.gov.uk/docs/default-source/cos-general-docs/pdf-docs-for-opinions/2020hcjac15.pdf?sfvrsn=0, accessed January 2020.

Hind, S. (2020): Violent chaos at Polmont as riot kicks off after Glasgow v Edinburgh football match. *The Daily Record,* 19 November 2020.

HM Inspectorate for Prisons Scotland (HMIPS) (2020): *Annual Report 2019/20.* https://www.prisonsinspectoratescotland.gov.uk/publications/hm-chief-inspector-prisons-scotland-annual-report-2019-20, accessed December 2020.

HM Inspectorate for Prisons Scotland (HMIPS) (2020b): *COVID-19 Pandemic Emergency Liaison Visits - Report on a Liaison Visit to HMP Perth, 16–17 September, 2020,* Edinburgh: HMIPS.

Howard League Scotland (2020): Three keys to unlocking the problem of prisons in a pandemic, 25 June 2020, http://howardleague.scot/news/2020/june/three-keys-unlocking-problem-prisons-pandemic.

Leapman, B. (2021): Too many in prison, for too long. *InsideTime UK,* 3 January 2021. https://insidetime.org/too-many-in-prison-for-too-long/, accessed 3 January 2021.

Lightowler, C., and Adamson, B. (2020): "Not cut out for prison": Depriving children of their childhood. Children and Young People's Centre for Justice blog, 20 November 2020, https://www.cycj.org.uk/not-cut-out-for-prison-depriving-children-of-their-childhood/, accessed December 2020.

Maycock, M., and Dickson, G. (2021): Analysing the views of people in custody about the management of the COVID-19 pandemic in the Scottish prison estate. *International Journal of Prisoner Health,* [advance access online].

McAra, L. (2005): Modelling penal transformation. *Punishment & Society* 7(3), 277–302.

McCallum, F. (2019): Twenty Years of Imprisonment. *The Scottish Parliament Information Centre.* https://spice-spotlight.scot/2019/11/04/twenty-years-of-imprisonment/, accessed 3 December 2021.

McGivern, M. (2020): Addiewell jail riot during coronavirus tensions leaves two officers injured. *The Daily Record*, 25 March 2020.

McQuillan, R. (2020): Justice Secretary talks of 'worrying rise' in prison population during pandemic. *Holyrood Magazine*, 18 August 2020.

Musson, C. (2020): Pay as you go: Prison bosses spend £2.7million on mobile phones for every inmate in Scotland. *The Scottish Sun*, 15 November 2020. https://www.thescottishsun.co.uk/news/scottish-news/6286332/scottish-prison-mobile-phones-covid/, accessed December 2020.

Nolan, D. (2020): *"Spend time with me": Children and Young People's Experiences of COVID-19 and the Justice System [June 2020].* Glasgow: Children and Young People's Centre for Justice, University of Strathclyde.

Scottish Government (2019): News: presumption against short sentences extended. https://www.gov.scot/news/presumption-against-short-sentences-extended/, accessed January 2020.

Scottish Government (2020a): *Policy Note - for the Coronavirus (Scotland) Act 2020 (Release of Prisoners Regulations 2020) SSI 2020/138.* Edinburgh: Scottish Government.

Scottish Government (2020b): Prisoners released early under COVID-19 regulations: FOI release, 17 September 2020. Edinburgh: Scottish Government Justice Directorate.

Scottish Government (2020c): Early prisoner release: FOI release, 26 June 2020. Edinburgh: Scottish Government Justice Directorate.

Scottish Human Rights Commission (2020): Commission writes to Cabinet Secretary for Justice on prison conditions during COVID-19, 23 June 2020. https://www.scottishhumanrights.com/news/commission-writes-to-cabinet-secretary-for-justice-on-prison-conditions-during-covid-19/, accessed 1 March 2021.

Scottish Parliament (2020): Written questions from Liam McArthur (S5W-31783). https://www.parliament.scot/S5ChamberOffice/WA20200928.pdf, accessed January 2020.

Scottish Parliament Justice Committee (2018): Inquiry into the use of remand in Scotland. https://www.parliament.scot/parliamentarybusiness/CurrentCommittees/107390.aspx, accessed December 2020.

Scottish Parliament Justice Committee (2021): COVID-19-related scrutiny and correspondence. https://www.parliament.scot/parliamentarybusiness/CurrentCommittees/114916.aspx, accessed April 2021.

Scottish Prisoner Advocacy and Research Collective (SPARC) (2020): Scottish Prisoner Advocacy and Research Collective (SPARC) submission to the Scottish Parliament Equalities and Human Rights Committee. https://scottishprisoneradvocacy.com/category/covid-19/, accessed December 2020.

Scottish Prison Service (SPS) (2020a): Prison population. https://www.sps.gov.uk/Corporate/Information/SPSPopulation.aspx, accessed April, June, 2020.

Scottish Prison Service (SPS) (2020b): Covid 19 regime for those in isolation. https://insidetime.org/download/Information/coronavirus/SPS-Regime-for-those-in-isolation_28_April_2020.pdf, accessed January 2021.

Scottish Prison Service (SPS) (2020c) FOI request – ref: HQ200164. https://www.whatdotheyknow.com/request/702498/response/1667944/attach/4/HQ200164%20response.pdf?cookie_passthrough=1, accessed January, 2021.

Scottish Prison Service (SPS) (2021a) Covid-19 information hub. https://www.sps.gov.uk/Corporate/Information/covid19/covid-19-information-hub.aspx, accessed February 2021.

Scottish Prison Service (SPS) (2021b): Prison population. https://www.sps.gov.uk/Corporate/Information/SPSPopulation.aspx, accessed April 2021.

STV (2021): Hundreds catch Coronavirus in major prison outbreak. https://news.stv.tv/west-central/hundreds-catch-coronavirus-in-major-prison-outbreak?top, accessed April 2021.

van Zyl Smit, D., and Morrison, K. (2020): The paradox of Scottish life imprisonment. *European Journal of Crime, Criminal Law and Criminal Justice* 28(1), 76–102.

37 Serbia

Milan Škulić

1 Introduction – general situation of the prison system

The first case of the coronavirus (COVID-19) infection in Serbia was officially recorded on 6 March 2020, and on 10 March 2020, the Government of the Republic of Serbia proclaimed COVID-19 an infectious disease emergency caused by the SARS-CoV-2 virus. Due to the pandemic of this infectious disease, on 15 March 2020, the President of the Republic, the President of the National Assembly, and the Prime Minister issued a decision proclaiming a state of emergency (*Official Gazette of the RoS,* Nr. 29/20).[1] The state of emergency lasted until 6 May 2020 when the National Assembly adopted a decision on its termination.[2] During the state of emergency, a number of restrictive measures were imposed, such as the prohibition on gatherings in public spaces and indoors, restrictions and prohibitions of free movement during certain hours, special restrictions, and prohibitions on the free movement of senior citizens. Some of these measures also had implications for the deprivation of liberty.

The total number of persons deprived of their liberty in Serbia on 1 October 2020 was 10,600,[3] which included persons sentenced to prison or juvenile prison (7,376), as well as prisoners awaiting trial, including the persons in detention during their trial (2,002), while the remaining 1,222 persons deprived of their liberty fell under the following categories: (1) persons sanctioned for misdemeanours; (2) persons subjected to mandatory psychiatric treatment and custody in a medical institution; and (3) juveniles subjected to the educational measure of remand to a correctional institution.

Since, according to official population estimates, Serbia currently has 6,945,235 inhabitants,[4] it follows that there are 152 persons deprived of their liberty per 100,000 inhabitants. This is a large number compared to the average number of persons deprived of liberty in Europe, which contradicts the official targets of the Government of Serbia, formulated in current national strategies for achieving a greater reduction in the prison population. This is particularly striking as, prior to the pandemic (when there were around 11,500 persons deprived of their liberty), the number of persons deprived of liberty was 165 per 100,000 inhabitants.

DOI: 10.4324/9781003169178-37

For the purpose of reducing the number of those in prisons and other facilities for the enforcement of criminal sanctions, in May 2017, the Government of the Republic of Serbia adopted a Strategy for reducing the number of those confined to facilities for the enforcement of criminal sanctions in the Republic of Serbia by 2020.[5] The Strategy stipulated measures and actions that would contribute to solving the issue of prison overcrowding and improving the conditions of accommodation in correctional facilities. Solving the issue of prison overcrowding during the pandemic, in addition to the construction of new accommodation, was achieved by increasing the number of releases on parole, imposing alternative sanctions, and reducing the number of sentenced prisoners. This was accomplished within the existing legal framework, i.e. without enacting new regulations.

In accordance with the recommendations in the Statement of principles relating to the treatment of persons deprived of their liberty in the context of the COVID-19 pandemic issued by the Council of Europe on 20 March 2020, mechanisms for early release from prison and termination of detention were applied, and whenever the requirements prescribed by the law were fulfilled, detention was substituted by other measures. By applying release on parole, early release, termination of detention, and its replacement by other measures, and by restricting the admission of new inmates to prisons, in the period from 15 March until 10 May 2020, the overall number of persons deprived of their liberty was reduced by 979. As of 1 October 2020, the overall number of persons deprived of their liberty was reduced by 900, that is, by 7.8%, in comparison to the period immediately prior to the epidemic outbreak.

The conditions in Serbian correctional facilities could be regarded, in principle, as conforming to the European standards, as regards the rights and status of persons deprived of their liberty. Based on the Strategy for the development of the system of enforcement of criminal sanctions until 2020,[6] as well as the Strategy for the reduction of prison overcrowding by 2020,[7] many facilities have been modernised and many new facilities were constructed too.

During the COVID-19 pandemic in Serbia, there were a number of infected persons in the facilities for the enforcement of criminal sanctions. There were slightly more cases of infected persons among the staff in the facilities (which includes both the guards and other employees) than among persons deprived of their liberty. There were no fatalities due to the COVID-19 infection, neither among persons deprived of their liberty nor among the staff of the correctional facilities.

In the period from 15 March to 10 October 2020, there were 91 persons deprived of their liberty (and 103 staff members) in Serbia who tested positive for the COVID-19 virus. Consequently, on 1 October 2020, 0.9% of persons deprived of their liberty were infected by the COVID-19 virus out of the total number (10,600) of persons deprived of their liberty. If compared to the number of persons deprived of their liberty at the outbreak of the pandemic

(11,500), the calculation shows that 0.8% of persons deprived of their liberty were infected with the COVID-19 virus. This is a relatively small number, particularly bearing in mind that infections are always more intense among clusters of people, i.e. in collective environments. For example, Serbia had a far greater rate of infection in nursing homes. What is particularly important is that during the observed period, there were no fatalities among the persons deprived of their liberty as a result of infection with the COVID-19 virus. The data on the number of the infected among the persons deprived of their liberty and the absence of fatalities in the correctional facilities in the period from 15 March until 1 October 2020 are particularly encouraging when one takes into account that in that period there were 33,662 cases of the COVID-19 virus in Serbia, and that 750 people died as a result of these infections.[8]

Release on parole is generally an excellent way of reducing numbers in prison. All the strategies mentioned also stipulate the increased rate of release on parole as one of their targets. Several decades ago, this rate used to be constantly above 50%, but it faced a crisis after that, followed by a recovery in the rate of release on parole in recent years. From 2012 until today, release on parole has generally been on the rise. The percentage of persons released from prisons on parole, in comparison to the overall percentage of sentenced prisoners varied from the very low 8% in 2012 up to 26.9% in 2016. The release on parole rate in 2013 was 16.25%; in 2014 20.6%; in 2015 26.4%; in 2016 26.9%; in 2017 26.7%; and in 2018 26.1%.[9] In 2019, there was a slight drop in the number of persons released on probation (24.5%), while final data for 2020 are not available yet.

2 Prison and penal policy concerning the execution of prison sentences during the COVID-19-induced crisis

Penal policy in Serbia, if by this term criminal justice norms that have a direct impact on penal practice are meant, has been mainly characterised as "penal populism". This characterization of the Serbian penal policy has to be differentiated as diverging orientations can be seen: In recent years, among the academic community in Serbia, but also among the representatives of the relevant authorities, there has been a strong emphasis on the further development of the system of alternative criminal sanctions. In May 2019, this development culminated in amendments to the Criminal Code of Serbia.[10] However, these legal changes have also created the normative requirements for a significantly, and unfortunately far-reaching, more severe penal policy. This is reflected especially in five areas of criminal justice legislation: (1) a prohibition on mitigating the penalty for certain types of criminal offences; (2) a mechanism for more severe punishments for multiple recidivism; (3) significant limitation on possibilities of suspended sentencing; (4) the introduction of life imprisonment; and (5) a legal prohibition on release on parole for certain categories of offenders sentenced to life imprisonment.

For certain criminal offences, an absolute prohibition on the mitigation of the penalty was introduced in 2009. This meant that under no circumstances could the penalty be below the statutory minimum, which for some of these criminal offences already seemed high. It included a number of criminal offences selected seemingly arbitrarily, which "cannot be defended by criminal policy arguments" (Stojanović, 2019: 289).

Under the provisions of Article 55a of the Criminal Code of Serbia, more severe punishment for multiple repeat offenders was introduced. For a premeditated criminal offence punishable with imprisonment, the court must impose punishment above the middle range of statutory penalties under the following conditions: (1) if the offender had already been sentenced twice or more often to imprisonment of at least one year for premeditated criminal offences; and (2) if less than five years had elapsed from the day the offender had been released from serving the punishment before a new criminal offence was committed.

Certainly, the most radical contribution to the risk of future prison overcrowding was the unnecessary limitation of the option of a suspended sentence, which is now impossible in criminal offences for which a sentence of eight years' imprisonment or a more may be imposed. Prior to the amendments to the Criminal Code of May 2019 this limit had been ten years. Although in practice, until the present, a suspended sentence would often be pronounced for some criminal offences for which the special maximum was a sentence of eight years imprisonment, it would be realistic to expect that in future this might lead to significant lengthening of prison sentences.

According to the amendments to the Criminal Code of May 2019, the sentence of 30–40 years of imprisonment was substituted by a sentence of life imprisonment. Severe criticism should be directed at the legislator's unnecessary introduction of an absolute prohibition on the release on parole of those sentenced to life imprisonment for some of the gravest sexual offences. This seems to represent a surrender to the influence of a "moral panic" (Škulić, 2019: 54–55).

During the pandemic caused by COVID-19, no new regulations were introduced in Serbia that would lift or suspend the enforcement of certain criminal sanctions, like short-term imprisonment. Still, short-term imprisonment, like other sentences of imprisonment based on pre-existing regulations, was not enforced to the full extent throughout the pandemic. There was a significant reduction in enforcing sentences of imprisonment. The widely used and already existing mechanisms (primarily stipulated in the Law on Execution of Criminal Sanctions) allowed for early release of offenders from prisons, and more extensive use of the practice of release on parole and early release from prison, in addition to the option of postponing the sending of offenders to serve their sentences of imprisonment. As a result, the population of prison offenders during the pandemic was reduced by around 900, when compared to the period prior to the pandemic.

During the pandemic, there were no special regulations introduced that would concern women who were subject to the enforcement of criminal sanctions. This is a result of the fact that in Serbia, there are only a few women deprived of their liberty, compared to the overall population of persons deprived of their liberty. At this moment, there are 273 women serving time, 94 women pre-trial detainees, including the women in detention during their trial and 13 female juveniles remanded to a correctional institution.[11] Thus, there are 380 women deprived of their liberty in total, which represents only 3.6% of the total number of persons deprived of their liberty in Serbia.

Throughout the pandemic, no new special regulations were introduced to enable more extensive use of alternative criminal sanctions, or regulations that would prevent or limit replacing fines with imprisonment. Incidentally, such a practice is very rare in Serbia, if one speaks about fines as a criminal sanction. Fines are neither a frequent punishment in Serbian criminal law, nor do they have much significance in practice, which is not justified in terms of criminal policy. This might explain why no special regulations were introduced that would preclude or limit such a replacement of sentence. Fines, after all, are a sanction for minor misdemeanours. In practice, fines are rarely replaced by prison sentences.

During the state of emergency in Serbia, which was proclaimed for the purpose of protection against the pandemic induced by COVID-19, several thousand citizens were fined by Misdemeanour Courts for violations of the prohibition on free movement or for quarantine violations.[12] A far smaller number were prosecuted for the criminal offence of failure to act pursuant to health regulations during the epidemic. The Government Decree that enabled derogations from the *ne bis in idem* principle, as regards certain misdemeanours and the criminal offence of failure to act pursuant to health regulations during an epidemic, the main characteristics of which are in fact identical, was pronounced unconstitutional by the Constitutional Court.[13]

The issue, in practice, especially during the first weeks of the state of emergency, was that citizens, who violated health regulations during the pandemic and were consequently prosecuted (which was far less common than being subjected to the provisions of the Misdemeanour Law) were sometimes, seemingly unnecessarily, detained,[14] which was not rational since the very decision entailed a risk of being infected while in detention.

3 Restrictions of contact with the outside world

During the COVID-19 pandemic, some measures were taken in Serbia that led to necessary restrictions of contact by prisoners and other detainees with the outside world. These were provisional restrictions and suspensions of visits to sentenced persons, prohibition on work outside the correctional facilities, and restrictions on the use of out-of-facility rights and benefits. Such measures were implemented for the protection of prisoners, including a general notion that the level of protection of their rights should not be reduced, except to the extent absolutely necessary for preventing the possible spreading of the COVID-19 virus inside the prisons. Such necessary restrictions were to some extent compensated with other rights.

Starting from 30 March 2020, by order of the Director of the Administration for the Enforcement of Criminal Sanctions, all visits to prisoners were prohibited. The rights of defence counsels to visit detained defendants were subject to the application of a range of protective measures, including glass or other transparent protective barriers, as well as the mandatory use of protective masks and protective gloves.

The restrictive measures in prisons were revisited at regular intervals, in accordance with the recommendations issued by the competent authorities and based on the current situation of the pandemic in the country. From 12 May 2020, visits to prisoners were resumed, but were limited to 15 minutes and only one visitor per prisoner, followed by a series of protective measures against the infection. The measures included (1) mandatory taking of visitors' body temperature; (2) passing of visitors through "disinfectant barriers"; (3) mandatory disinfection of hands, as well as (4) mandatory use of protective masks and protective gloves.

During the visiting times, the wearing of face visors was introduced for persons deprived of their liberty, as well as keeping the necessary physical distance, and disinfection measures once the visits ended. On 3 June 2020, all restrictions related to visits to persons deprived of their liberty were lifted, but observation of all measures for the protection against the infection remained in force.

4 Restrictions inside prisons

During the pandemic, there were no restrictions on transfers to open-type facilities, or changes of the regime of execution of correctional criminal sanctions. Only the necessary changes in the regime and organisation of work in prisons were made. These were reduced to organising prisoners staying outdoors for longer periods of time and excluding work engagements outside the facility, and limiting the use of extended rights and benefits outside the facility.

During the pandemic, there were corresponding minor changes in the regime of using free time and related to sports and recreation activities inside prisons, mainly "group downsizing". Gatherings of persons deprived of their liberty were reduced to smaller groups, without larger gatherings. Physical exercises and sports activities were organised for smaller groups.

During the pandemic, there were no changes in the usual regime of indoor lockdown. Apart from longer hours in the fresh air, there were no major changes in the regime of execution of sanctions, such as isolation of certain prisoners by using additional lockdowns that kept them in their cells. Prison hospital premises were used to isolate only infected prisoners, and this was done in accordance with health protocols.

5 Compensatory measures

During the pandemic, some measures were introduced to compensate for restrictions to prison regimes. Restrictions on visits were compensated by granting more telephone calls to prisoners and to detainees. This was arranged in consultation with trial judges. This was also in accordance with the Statement of principles relating to the treatment of persons deprived of their liberty in the context of the coronavirus disease (COVID-19) pandemic issued by the Council of Europe on 20 March 2020. Depending on organisational and technical capabilities, in some correctional facilities, prisoners were provided with the possibility of communicating online with their families via the Skype and Viber platforms. All categories of persons deprived of their liberty were able to spend more time outdoors in the fresh air.

6 Legal basis for restrictions and relaxations of the prison regime

All restrictions to, and relaxations of the prison regime during the COVID-19 pandemic were implemented on the basis of pre-existing legal enactments concerning the execution of criminal sanctions, including any forms of deprivation of liberty, pre-trial detention, and detention during the trial, but primarily in accordance with the provisions of the Law on the Execution of Criminal Sanctions.

Courts were involved to a considerable extent with restrictive or compensatory measures in the execution of criminal sanctions. Judges for the enforcement of criminal sanctions inspected the measures implemented during the pandemic through regular visits to correctional facilities and through the grievance mechanisms and requests for judicial protection.

The Ombudsman also played an important role regarding the control of the restrictive measures introduced. Through his visits and the grievance mechanism for persons deprived of their liberty, he inspected the measures implemented during the pandemic and launched a 24-hour telephone line for persons deprived of their liberty. In practice, this was an important mechanism of external oversight of the system for the enforcement of criminal sanctions. In addition to the existing grievance mechanisms within the Administration for the Enforcement of Criminal Sanctions, and given the fact that persons deprived of their liberty are entitled to lodge an appeal with a judge for the enforcement of criminal sanctions, this represented an efficient system of protection of the rights of persons deprived of their liberty under these specific circumstances.

The relevant international legal standards in the field of human rights, which are applied directly in the legal system of Serbia, also refer to the system of enforcing criminal sanctions. These standards had an important role during the pandemic regarding the principles of compensatory measures in prisons. Pursuant to Article 18, paragraph 1 of the Constitution of Serbia, human rights guaranteed by the Constitution shall be implemented directly.

The Administration for the Enforcement of Criminal Sanctions distributed a Serbian translation of the Statement of principles relating to the treatment of persons deprived of their liberty in the context of the coronavirus disease (COVID-19) pandemic issued by the Council of Europe to all correctional facilities. Through daily contacts with the correctional facilities and by transmitting orders to the facilities on methods of procedure during the pandemic, the Administration applied national regulations and international standards on the protection of human rights. The text of the World Health Organisation's publication, "Prevention and control of COVID-19 in prisons and other places of detention",[15] was translated into Serbian and distributed to all facilities for the enforcement of criminal sanctions.

7 Returning to normal

During the pandemic, the Administration for the Enforcement of Criminal Sanctions did act and respond adequately and within the existing normative framework, by undertaking necessary and timely measures to reduce the prison population, thus significantly minimising the risk of spreading the infection inside prisons. The return to "normal", however, will be neither quick nor easy and it is very important to learn lessons from the experience gained during the pandemic.

There is a possibility that the COVID-19 pandemic will have long-term effects on the system for the enforcement of criminal sanctions in the Republic of Serbia. This primarily refers to the realisation of how significant prison overcrowding is, and how important it is to have solid mechanisms in place for the prevention of spreading such infections inside prisons. Based on the experiences gained during the pandemic, it would be wise to further develop the probation system, release on parole, the mechanism for suspending the enforcement of prison sentences, and the possibility of early release from prison. From the experience gained during the pandemic, it is clear that in the long run, it would be more important, and more beneficial for society, to create normative and factual prerequisites for reducing the prison population, rather than continuing to construct or extend prison facilities.

Although relatively quickly after the beginning of the pandemic in Serbia, the overcrowding of correctional facilities was reduced significantly by using the existing normative framework, the (too) high number of persons deprived of their liberty, in comparison to the number of inhabitants, indicates that it is time that the "penal populism", which culminated in the amendments to the Criminal Code of May 2019, be abandoned. These amendments directed at drastically harsher penal policy could, unless the damage already done is repaired, quickly lead to further, potentially dangerous, overcrowding of prisons. This is not only in direct contrast to the current state strategies for reducing prison overcrowding, but also in dissonance with the trends in criminality in Serbia, which cannot be considered to be increasing "dramatically" by any objective criteria. Much harsher penal policy risks producing prison overcrowding as a result of specific provisions of the amended Criminal Code. Taking into account the possibility of a new pandemic, this would be very dangerous.

Interestingly, a large number of inmates in Serbian prisons volunteered to take part in the production of protective masks and clothing for preventing the spread COVID-19. The inmates also organised a campaign of offering meals to the economically most vulnerable citizens during the pandemic. One may conclude that in the crisis that affected the whole country, prisoners became actively involved in the fight against the pandemic, motivated by the idea of solidarity and rendering help to others. The impression is that the stigmatisation of this marginalised group might have been slightly mitigated by adequate presentation in the media of these activities of prisoners.

Notes

1 This was done under Article 200 paragraph 5 of the Constitution.

2 *Official Gazette of the RoS*, number 65/20.

3 Data on the number of persons deprived of liberty, as well as other data referring to the system for the enforcement of criminal sanctions in prisons in Serbia (like data on the number of prisoners and staff in prisons infected by COVID-19 virus, etc.) were obtained from daily reports about the number of persons deprived of liberty issued by the Administration for the Enforcement of Criminal Sanctions within the Ministry of Justice of the Republic of Serbia. Such data are not made public, but were obtained directly the competent authorities of the Administration for the Enforcement of Criminal Sanctions within the Ministry of Justice of the Republic of Serbia, specifically from Mrs Aleksandra Stepanović, Head of the Department for the protection and implementation of the rights of persons deprived of their liberty.

4 Data of the Republic Statistical Office based on results of the population census and results of statistical processing of natural and mechanical population changes: https://www.stat.gov.rs/sr-Latn/oblasti/stanovnistvo/procene-stanovnistva. Accessed on 29 November 2020.

5 *Official Gazette of the RoS, number* 43/2017, dated 5 May 2017, Belgrade, 2017: 3–7.

6 *Official Gazette of the RoS, number* 114/2013, Belgrade, 2013: 157–169.

7 *Official Gazette of the RoS, number* 43/2017, Belgrade, 2017: 3–7.

8 Source: https://www.zdravlje.gov.rs/vest/350760/informacija-o-aktuelnoj-epidemioloskoj-situaciji-u-vezi-sa-novim-korona-virusom-u-republici-srbiji-za-01-oktobar-2020-godine-.php. Accessed on 2 December 2020.

9 Data obtained from the Administration for the Enforcement of Criminal Sanctions within the Ministry of Justice of the Republic of Serbia.

10 *Official Gazette of the RoS, number* 35/2019, dated 21 May 2019.

11 Data obtained from the Administration for the Enforcement of Criminal Sanctions within the Ministry of Justice of the Republic of Serbia.

12 No data are available on the number of fines replaced with sentences by imprisonment, but this must be a relatively small number in comparison to the overall number of fines.

13 Decision of the Constitutional Court number IUo-45/2020 dated 17 September 2020.

14 The dominant reason for ordering detention in such situations was assessment by the courts that there was a danger of recidivism within a short time period.

15 Source: https://www.euro.who.int/en/health-topics/health-determinants/prisons-and-health/focus-areas/prevention-and-control-of-covid-19-in-prisons-and-other-places-of-detention. Accessed on 30 November 2020.

References

Stojanović, Z. (2019): *Komentar Krivičnog zakonika* (Commentary of the Criminal Code). 9th Edition, Belgrade: Official Gazette Publishing.

Škulić, M. (2019): *Krivična dela protiv polne slobode* (The Crimes against Sexual Freedom). Belgrade: Official Gazette Publishing.

38 Slovakia[1]

Miroslava Vráblová

1 Introduction – general situation of the Slovak prison system

The Slovak prison system has undergone significant changes over the last 50 years. One of the major milestones in the development of Slovak prison system was reached in 1969. Due to political changes (the transformation of the Czechoslovak Socialist Republic into the Czech and Slovak federation), the prison system underwent organisational changes, systemic changes, and changes in the conditions of serving sentences of imprisonment. The prison system was reorganised. The jurisdiction over it was transferred from the ministry of interior of the unitary state to the ministries of justice of the republics of the federation (Fábry, 2009: 54; Griger and Papáčová, 2019: 35). In 1969, the prisons in Slovakia began to be managed by Slovak bodies – i.e. the Bureau of Corrections (currently, it is the General Directorate of the Corps of Prison and Court Guards).

On 1 January 1993, the independent Slovak Republic was established. Czechoslovak legal stipulations and laws that did not contradict the wording and nature of the new Slovak Constitution were taken over into the new legal framework. The Criminal Code and the Code of Criminal Procedure of 1961 remained in effect. They were amended only in 2005, as the criminal codices were re-codified. The parliament adopted a new Criminal Code, a new Code of Criminal Procedure, and the respective legal regulations of the prison system, laying the foundation for further development of the principles of democratisation and humanisation of the prisons as the executive branch of the prison policy system.

The re-codified Criminal Code focused on the "deterrent" aspect of the sentences and the possibility of long-term exclusion of criminals from society (Samaš, 2017: 733). The main focus of the penal policy in the Slovak Republic is strict penal repression – in the form of higher sentences, stricter regulations for imposing sentences, lowering the age of criminal responsibility from 15 to 14 years of age, the introduction of legal criminal accountability of legal entities, and new criminalisation with the enactment of 40 new offences since 2005 (Vráblová, 2019: 412). There has been a significant shift in sanction policy over the last 15 years – towards a positive penal policy –

DOI: 10.4324/9781003169178-38

by introducing new alternative sentences (mandatory labour, home detention, banishment from public events), implementing elements of restorative justice, out-of-court agreements, and using electronic control systems. However, restorative justice does not entirely balance out the retributive justice now applied in Slovak law (Dianiška and Strémy, 2016: 94).

The punitive aspects of the penal policy are manifested in everyday practice, as well. There is a long-term trend of imposing sentences of imprisonment. In the monitored period from 2006 to 2019, suspended imprisonment sentences were imposed on average in 63.4% of the cases, while sentences of imprisonment with immediate effect were imposed in 18.5% of the cases. In 2019, 60.7% of those convicted received a suspended sentence and 20.1% received a sentence of imprisonment with immediate effect.

This is also reflected in the Slovak prison system. The growing number of inmates contributes to the negative development of the prison population index (see Figure 38.1). The prison population data suggest that there are 2–2.5 times more inmates per 100,000 of the national population than in the Western European countries. The prison population rate (number of inmates per 100,000 inhabitants) for 2019 was 194. In 2020, it was 193.1 (as of 15 April), 193.1 (as of 15 June), 195.3 (as of 15 September), and 195.0 (as of 31 December). We can see that during the COVID-19 outbreak, the prison population remained stable and has not been significantly reduced since.

The prison population consists of pre-trial detainees and sentenced prisoners. In 2019, 85.4% of the prison population were sentenced prisoners and 14.6% were pre-trial detainees. The number of sentenced prisoners has grown since 2005, when the criminal law was re-codified – from 67.4% of the prison population in 2005 to 85.4% in 2019 (see Figure 38.2). The number of sentenced prisoners has not been reduced despite registered crimes dropping over the last years. However, the number of short prison sentences has grown. In 2018, approximately 15% of prisoners served a sentence of up to one year (Griger and Ľorko, 2018: 419; Griger, 2019: 274).

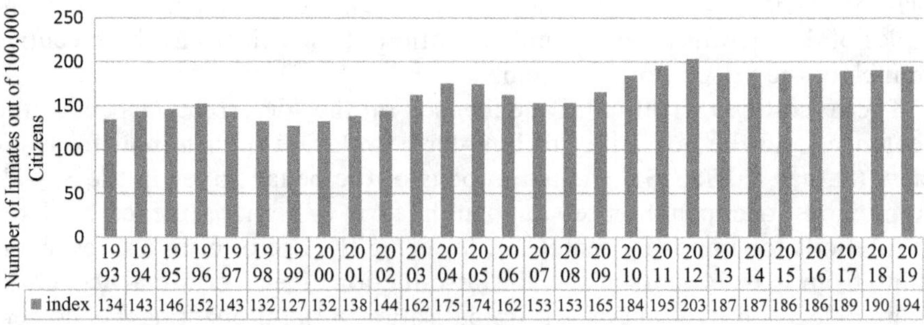

	1993	1994	1995	1996	1997	1998	1999	2000	2001	2002	2003	2004	2005	2006	2007	2008	2009	2010	2011	2012	2013	2014	2015	2016	2017	2018	2019
■ index	134	143	146	152	143	132	127	132	138	144	162	175	174	162	153	153	165	184	195	203	187	187	186	186	189	190	194

Figure 38.1 The prison population rate in the Slovak Republic (1993–2019).
Source: Statistical Data of Corps of Prison and Court Guards.

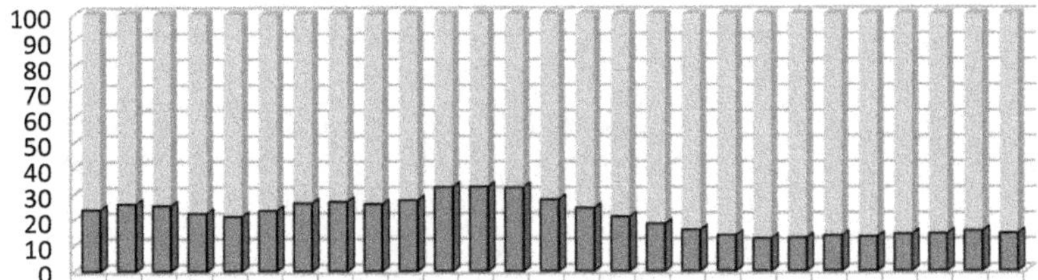

	1993	1994	1995	1996	1997	1998	1999	2000	2001	2002	2003	2004	2005	2006	2007	2008	2009	2010	2011	2012	2013	2014	2015	2016	2017	2018	2019
convicted (%)	76	74	74	78	79	76	73	73	74	72	67	67	67	72	75	79	82	84	86	87	87	86	87	86	86	84	85
detained (%)	24	26	26	22	21	24	27	27	26	28	33	33	33	28	25	21	18	16	14	13	13	14	13	14	14	16	15

Figure 38.2 Prison population in the Slovak republic – sentenced offenders and pre-trial detainees (1993–2019).

Source: Statistical Data of Corps of Prison and Court Guards.

The Slovak prison system comprises 18 custodial facilities for detainees and sentenced prisoners. The growing number of inmates results in prison overcrowding. On 31 December 2019, the indicator of imminent prison overcrowding (defined by the methodology of the European Committee on Crime Problems as the condition when a prison is filled at more than 90% of its capacity) was reached in 11 Slovak prisons. In five of them, they exceeded 100% of their capacity. Prison overcrowding has been a long-term problem of the Slovak prison system (Dianiška, Strémy and Vráblová, 2016: 163). In the last decade (monitored period from 2011 to 2020), the average occupancy of the prisons did not drop below 90%. On 31 March 2020, the Slovak prisons were filled at 91.1% of their capacity, on 30 June, it was 90.2%, and on 23 October, 90.5%.

On 6 March 2020, the first case of COVID-19 infection was confirmed in the Slovak Republic. On that day, there were 10,679 inmates in prisons all over the country (9,082 of them sentenced prisoners and 1,597 of them pre-trial detainees). When the numbers for the time before the COVID-19 outbreak (January and February 2020) and in the time of the pandemic (March to October 2020) are compared, it appears that the numbers did not change significantly (see Table 38.1). In the first months after the COVID-19 outbreak, the number of inmates dropped slightly and then it stabilised at the pre-crisis level in June 2020. In 2019, the average number of inmates was 10,605, while in 2020, it was 10,561.

The stable level of inmates may be related to the overall development of the pandemic in the country. The strict regulations and measurements implemented at the beginning of the pandemic helped keep the number of infections under control in spring and summer. From 6 March to 30 June 2020, only one inmate was infected (0.001% of all the infected in Slovakia at that point). From 1 July to 23 October 2020 – after some of the restrictions had been lifted – more inmates were infected. As many as 85 inmates (0.01%

Table 38.1 Development of inmate numbers from January to October 2020

	31 Jan.	*28 Febr.*	*31 March*	*30 April*	*31 May*	*30 June*	*31 July*	*31 Aug.*	*30 Sept.*	*28 Oct.*
Pre-trial detainees	1,637	1,632	1,598	1,569	1,603	1,638	1,661	1,695	1,652	1,674
Sentenced	8,954	9,060	9,049	8,898	8,865	8,966	8,993	9,009	9,012	8,929
Total	10,591	10,692	10,647	10,467	10,468	10,604	10,654	10,704	10,664	10,603

Source: Statistical Data of Corps of Prison and Court Guards.

of all the infected at that point) and 164 prison staff members (0.02% of all the infected) got COVID-19. In late October 2020, there was blanket testing in Slovakia, with several inmate groups participating – inmates working at external and internal workplaces, inmates in open sections of prisons with minimum security, underage inmates, inmates nearing the end of their detention or sentence, or inmates with surgical procedures scheduled. Inmates with any COVID-19 symptoms were tested as well. The testing identified 78 infected inmates (0.02%) and 43 infected prison staff members (0.01%). In November 2020, the situation started to get significantly worse. Mass testing of the inmates and of prison staff identified many infected. The most critical months were January through March 2021, with 2,131 of inmates and 468 of prison staff infected. Two inmates died of COVID-19. One of the major problems of the prison system, which became manifest during the outbreak, is the overcrowding of the prisons and the current system of lodging the inmates together in large rooms and cells housing from 4 up to 20 sentenced prisoners.

2 Prison and penal policy concerning execution of prison sentences during the COVID-19-induced crisis

In the penal area related to the execution of sentences during the COVID-19 pandemic, no major legislative changes towards the targeted reduction of the prison population were adopted. The Slovak penal law has its legal framework and regulations allowing conditional release from prison, early conditional release from prison with the parolee wearing an electronic tag, transformation of the rest of a prison sentence to home detention, suspension of execution of the prison sentence, or the possibility of imposing alternative sentences. The legal conditions for applying any of them have not changed during the COVID-19 crisis. Nevertheless, there has been a drop of admissions to prisons. The average number of new admissions during the COVID-19 crisis (February to September 2020) was 3.5% lower than the average number of admissions in the months before (July 2019 to January 2020). The declining trend of prison admissions to serve sentences also continued from October 2020 to January 2021. The statistical data of the Ministry of Justice prove that the courts allowed suspension of sentence execution in 7.4% more cases in the first half-year of 2020 than in the preceding half-year of 2019.

Table 38.2 Prison policy before and during the COVID-19 crisis (June 2019 to September 2020)

Before COVID-19: 6/2019-1/2020	*6/ 2019*	*7/ 2019*	*8/ 2019*	*9/ 2019*	*10/ 2019*	*11/ 2019*	*12/ 2019*	*1/ 2020*
Prison intakes	408	421	405	402	457	404	481	462
Conditional release from prison	145	108	129	168	137	139	180	131
Transformation of rest of sentence to house arrest	0	0	2	4	1	1	2	1
During COVID-19: 2/2020-9/2020	2/ 2020	3/ 2020	4/ 2020	5/ 2020	6/ 2020	7/ 2020	8/ 2020	9/ 2020
Prison intakes	469	370	312	398	524	441	386	417
Conditional release from prison	118	89	126	156	131	137	96	146
Transformation of rest of sentence to house arrest	4	2	1	3	0	3	0	3

Source: Statistical Data of Corps of Prison and Court Guards.

By the end of the lockdown, upon the decision of the Minister of Justice, the measure to restore the duty of the custodial facility directors to file proposals for early conditional release from prison with the parolee wearing an electronic tag and the proposals for transformation of the rest of the prison sentence to home detention were implemented, effective as of 2 June 2020. When comparing the average number of cases in which courts decided to allow conditional release from prison during the COVID-19 crisis (February to September 2020) with the period before it (July 2019 to January 2020), it is apparent that this measure was used in 11.9% fewer cases than in the previous year. This is related to the long-term decrease in the number of conditionally released inmates There was no radical change in the number of conditional releases from prison in the following months (from October 2020 to January 2021).

However, from February to September 2020, the measure of the transformation of the remainder of the prison sentence to house arrest was implemented in 45% more cases than in the time before the crisis (see Table 38.2). This rising trend also continued from October 2020 to January 2021. There were no special measures of suspension of short sentences or cases of release of special groups of inmates, such as women and the elderly.

If a person fails to comply when ordered to isolate or to accept increased medical supervision or supervision by a physician or fails to comply when ordered to quarantine, he or she commits an offence against public health.[2] The same applies to the administrative offence of failure to comply with a regulation for personal sanitation, using preventive and other protection equipment, and maintaining the necessary distance from other people. The offence can be sanctioned by up to 1,659 Euros (in ticket proceedings, up to 99 Euros). If such an offence is committed during a crisis (state of emergency), the ticket sanction may increase to 1,000 Euros. The most frequent offences committed were failure to comply when ordered to quarantine, failure to comply with the obligation to wear a face mask, and violations of closure of businesses.

The penal law was not reformed. The current criminal law provides protection from spreading a dangerous, contagious disease.[3] Criminal actions include the deliberate or negligent increasing of the risk of bringing in or spreading dangerous contagious human diseases.[4] In case of deliberate actions, the sentence is one to five years of imprisonment. If the contagious disease is spread during a state of emergency, the sentence is four to ten years of imprisonment. COVID-19 is not defined as a contagious human disease in the Slovak legal framework. Thus, in any criminal proceedings, an evaluation by an expert in public health and pharmacy would be necessary.[5]

3 Restrictions of contact with the outside world

The COVID-19 crisis has affected all areas of society, including the prison system. The rights of detainees and sentenced prisoners have been restricted by the implementation of epidemiological measures. After the first case of COVID-19 had been identified, the country adopted several measures and restrictions to fight the pandemic. Among them was a ban of visits in all prisons.

The implementation of epidemiological measures in the prison system can be divided into three stages. The first covers the period from 6 March to 30 June 2020. During this first wave of the disease, a state of emergency was declared (16 March to 14 June 2020). The second stage was from 1 July to 23 October 2020. The strict measures were relaxed, and the country was getting ready for the second wave of the disease. The third stage started on 24 October 2020 and was characterised by a steep increase of infections all over Slovakia, including among inmates and the prison staff. This stage has seen extensive measures implemented to fight the virus (from regional measures based on pandemic traffic lights to nation-wide measures), as well as increased testing of the prison population.

The measures as regards the inmates (detainees and sentenced prisoners) were divided, based on the pandemic traffic lights. Those monitor and signal how the COVID-19 disease is spreading. The individual levels of spreading were labelled by colours and apply to respective parts of Slovakia (regions or districts). Green signals only basic measures in place – face masks indoors, maintaining a two-metre distance from other people, disinfection of hands. Orange means mild worsening of the epidemic and the implementation of mild protective measures. Red indicates a severe level of spreading of the virus and implements complex measures to fight it. Black signals a critical situation and preparation for lockdown. The measures were divided in accordance with these pandemic traffic lights and the location of the individual prisons. The more cases of infection in the region, the stricter epidemiologic measures were adopted in the prison.

According to the epidemiological situation, the custodial facilities adopted various restrictive measures limiting the contact of inmates with the outside world. During the first and third stages, all physical visits for detainees and sentenced prisoners were cancelled. During the second stage (after the measures were relaxed), it was possible to meet people from the outside world to a limited extent – only contactless meetings, one visit could last only up to one hour, the number of visitors was reduced from five to three people, and the room was sanitised after each visit (germicide irradiation of the room for at least 20 minutes).

Legal aid was not limited in any way. During all the stages, visiting the detained and convicted by their lawyers, attorney, or legal representatives was allowed. They had to wear face masks, use hand sanitisers, and maintain a two-metre distance from others. Persons entering the facility (such as attorneys) had to comply with contactless measurement of their body temperature. If their temperature was higher than 37.5°C, if they had symptoms of COVID-19, or if they refused to have their temperature measured, they were not allowed to enter the facility.

Reward for good discipline is a significant motivational tool to achieve positive results in managing detainees and sentenced prisoners (Tittlová, 2017: 200). During the outbreak, the restrictive measures affected their disciplinary rewards as well. For the duration of the crisis, some systems for rewarding good discipline were suspended (special visits, special passes to spend time outside the facility, receipt of packages allowed). Time spent outside the facility was granted to a limited extent only. While during the first stage, it was possible to get a pass in extraordinary cases, during the third stage, it was impossible to grant such passes (due to the curfew effective for the whole of Slovakia).

Special measures were also implemented for the admission of detainees and sentenced prisoners to the prisons. In all the stages, the detainees and sentenced prisoners had to undergo mandatory quarantine. The prisons implemented mandatory ten-day isolation of new inmates, followed by COVID-19 tests according to the level of infection risk of the inmates. In case of inmates transferring from abroad – risky countries outside the EU – they had to take an RT-PCR test for COVID-19.

The epidemiological measures affected transfers of the inmates as well. In prisons located in regions designated as black by the pandemic traffic lights, movements of inmates between cells, rooms, and blocks were minimised. Transfers between prisons were possible only with court orders. It was forbidden to perform group escorts. In order to minimise escorting inmates to their court hearings, the courts were advised to hold hearings primarily via videoconferences.

4 Restrictions inside prisons

Special epidemiological measures were also implemented inside the custodial facilities. Detainees and sentenced prisoners experienced the restrictions in several areas, with activities either suspended or limited. Assignment of prisoners to work outside prisons was on an individual basis, with the criterion being the intensity of contact with civilians at the workplace and during transport. During the crisis, all activity at workplaces employing prisoners outside the prisons was suspended. The same applied to the workplaces inside prisons, excluding those used for internal operations and for the production of certain goods. Since the COVID-19 outbreak, inmates have participated in producing face masks for their institutions, the courts, the prosecutor's offices, as well as the police and fire departments. Assigning prisoners to work at the internal workplaces was conducted in the standard manner during all the stages – respecting the basic protective measures (face masks, two-metre distance from others, and disinfection of hands).

The placement of inmates in custodial facilities with open sections was conducted in the standard manner during all the stages. With the first case of COVID-19 infection in the custodial facility with an open section in Bratislava, the whole open section was shut down to prevent the spreading of the disease. The other open sections of the prison system were not closed. Only those where inmates or prison staff members were infected were closed.

Education and cultural activities or leisure activities for detainees and prisoners were suspended in the first stage. Later, they were transformed into secluded activities in the individual lodging units (cells, rooms, or blocks). Education was resumed in a distanced format and the admission of third parties for cultural or public education purposes was limited. The holding of religious services was limited, too. Some activities, such as using libraries, reading rooms, fitness centres, or gyms, were suspended entirely (temporarily). Walking for exercise and shopping for personal items were allowed in small groups of inmates from the same cell, room, or block. In prisons in regions with black on the pandemic traffic lights, prisoners were forbidden to use their own clothes due to the risk of infection. Group meals in communal canteens were also forbidden.

5 Compensatory measures

In order to moderate some restrictive measures and maintain social contacts of the inmates with the outside world, several compensatory measures were adopted. The banning of visits was compensated by more frequent and longer phone calls, later amended to video calls. During the first stage, the inmates were granted "calling minutes" worth two Euros (approximately 12 minutes when calling to numbers of the mobile operators in Slovakia). They could also purchase more credit for calling without settling their previous debts. On 15 May 2020, a video-visit project was launched, which allowed adult inmates to make at least one free 20-minute internet video call per month with their approved contact person. Underage inmates were allowed to make such a call once a week. Prisons use Skype for video calls. On 3 September 2020, the video-call project was introduced in the custodial facility in Leopoldov (the plan is to introduce it to other custodial facilities soon). Unlike video-visits, video calls are supplementary to standard phone calls (using the same software), and since they are provided by the phone service provider, they are not free of charge.

6 Legal basis for restrictions and relaxations of the prison regime

The current prison system in Slovakia is based on differentiation between detention and execution of a sentence of imprisonment, in an effort to minimise the negative effects of temporary suspension of rights as regards legal restriction of freedoms, and progressive social re-integration based on the individualisation of sentence execution. The legal basis of the prison system is the Criminal Code, the Code of Criminal Procedure, the Act on Detention, and the Act on Prison Sentence.[5]

Custodial detention is the most severe constitutional intervention with the freedom of individuals who have not yet been lawfully sentenced. The Slovak Constitution stipulates that a person may be detained only on reasonable grounds for the time stipulated by law and upon the decision of a court. The reasons for custody are stipulated by the Code of Criminal Procedure. A judge decides on detention in the preliminary proceedings. The detention can last only for the necessary time. The time is divided based on the category of the offence. For misdemeanours, it cannot exceed 12 months. In case of offences, it cannot exceed 36 months and in case of felonies, it cannot exceed 48 months. The maximum detention period is 60 months. The execution of detention is governed by Act No. 221/2006 Coll. on Detention.

A prison sentence is the strictest form of punishment available. The Criminal Code differentiates between imprisonment for a fixed period and life imprisonment. Special forms of punishment are the suspended imprisonment sentence and conditional release from prison with probation monitoring. The execution of a prison sentence is governed by Act No. 475/2005 Coll. on Prison Sentences. The prison sentence shall be executed in one of the prisons based on the level of security required (minimum, medium, and maximum security). The mode of executing imprisonment was modified by adopting the rules derived from the UN Standard Minimum Rules on the Treatment of Prisoners and the European Prison Rules.

The prosecutor monitors the execution of the sentence, as well as how the legal provisions are being adhered to in the prison. The supervisory bodies of the execution of detention and of the prison sentence are the National Council of the Slovak Republic, the Minister of Justice, the General Director of the Corps of Prison and Court Guards, and legal entities and natural persons, if stipulated by special regulations or international agreements.

During the COVID-19 pandemic, the treatment of inmates was subject to epidemiological measures. The Slovak government adopted many restrictions to fight the virus, based on the recommendations of the Central Crisis Staff of the Slovak Republic. The Ministry of Justice made rules for the courts and the Corps of Prison and Court Guards (the "Corps") to apply.

The prison system was subject to many restrictions inside custodial facilities, as well as in their relations with the outside world. However, there were compensatory measures, as well (see above). At the same time, the Corps had to comply with the measures of the Public Health Authority of the Slovak Republic.

Internal regulations of the Corps[6] established a unified approach when implementing epidemiological measures inside the Corps as regards the second stage of the COVID-19 pandemic, in particular, at the admission of detainees and sentenced prisoners inspection of persons entering the facility, provision of meals to the inmates, measures related to the personnel and social activities department, special regulations at convict workplaces, special regulations of imprisonment, special regulations for detainees and prisoners based on the pandemic traffic lights, as well as a unified approach and rules of testing for COVID-19.

The legal framework for the compensatory measures is Section 102(2) of the Act on Prison Sentences, which allows the Minister of Justice to approve verification of new and different methods of treating the sentenced prisoners, if the application of such methods represents mitigation of the limitation of their civil rights.

7 Returning to normal

The Slovak prison system faced its long-standing problem of prison overcrowding also during the COVID-19-induced crisis. The growing number of inmates was not the result of increased intakes of prisoners. The criminal law and the prison system should be reformed to deal with the issue of overcrowding by reducing the number of prisoners serving short-term sentences and making more use of conditional release from prison.

In order to reduce the number of inmates and increase the efficiency of treating them, there are discussions about implementing a mixed model of conditional release from prison, consisting of, first, a mandatory system of conditional release for sentences of up to one year (approximately 20% of the prisoners); those sentenced for up to one year would be released automatically after half the time served, if they did not get any disciplinary sentence while in prison. The probation period would cover the rest of their sentence.

Second, there should be a mandatory system of conditional release with the inmates complying with electronic monitoring and an individual programme (approximately 25% of prisoners). Prisoners with a sentence of one to three years would be released automatically after half of the time served if they did not get any disciplinary sanction while in prison and if the technical conditions for electronic monitoring were met. The probation period would cover the rest of their sentence (approximately 25% of prisoners).

Third, it is proposed to have a discretionary system of conditional release of prisoners with sentences exceeding three years. These would be subject to the current system and its existing formal, material, and procedural conditions.

In the area of penal policy, no criminalisation of a failure to comply with isolation, a failure to comply with quarantine, or a failure to comply with the measures is being considered, as the administrative legal consequences seem to be sufficient.

The Slovak parliament amended the Criminal Code and removed the disproportionally drastic criminal consequences for offences committed during the state of emergency. According to the criminal law valid until 31 December 2020, offenders who had committed misdemeanours before faced imprisonment for 10–15 years for small crimes, like theft of goods worth a few Euros in a store. The Criminal Code amendment, effective as of 1 January 2021, stipulates that the stricter punishment for an offence committed during a crisis shall not apply unless the offence was committed in relation to a state of emergency or a similar exceptional state.

Minimising the negative consequences of temporary limitation of the rights of inmates as regards the legal limitation of freedoms and restrictive measures implemented remains a challenge of the prison system. It is necessary to use compensatory measures and other measures to fulfil the goal of the prison system – in particular, to create an environment for the correction of inmates, by changing their attitude towards criminal activities and integrating them into society. Further expansion of the compensatory measures (like the possibility to use mobile phones by inmates) is not planned. The right of the inmates to make phone calls (in cells, rooms, during exercise), including the possibility of video calls via Skype, is currently regarded as sufficient. The restrictive measures should be implemented only to the extent necessary to limit the negative impacts of imprisonment from the psychological, social, and economic perspectives.

Notes

1 This work was supported by Slovak Research and Development Agency under Contract No. APVV-16-0106.

2 Act No. 355/2007 Coll. on protection, support and development of public health, and on amendments to certain acts, Section 56.

3 Act No. 300/2005 Coll. (Criminal Code), Sections 163 and 164: Offence of Spreading a Dangerous Contagious Human Disease.

4 Regulation of the General Prosecutor's Office of the Slovak Republic dated 19 March 2020, file No. IV/1 Spr 194/20/1000-1, concerning the unification of approach of prosecutors in criminal proceedings when assessing the legal qualification of suspicious behaviour of natural persons in relation to spreading of COVID-19 virus, who have tested positive or are suspected to have contracted COVID-19.

5 Act No. 300/2005 Coll. (Criminal Code); Act No. 301/2005 Coll. (Code of Criminal Procedure); Act No. 221/2006 Coll. on Detention; Act No. 475/2005 Coll. on Prison Sentences.

6 Order No. 44/2020 of the General Director of the Corps of Prison and Court Guard regulating the approach at epidemiologic measures in the Corps of Prison and Court Guard in relation to the second stage of the COVID-19 disease outbreak; Order No. 54/2020 of the General Director of the Corps of Prison and Court Guard regulating the procedure and testing rules for COVID-19 disease in the Corps of Prison and Court Guard during the COVID-19 pandemic.

References

Dianiška, G., and Strémy, T. (2016): Alternative Sentences Applied in Slovak Republic. *Časopis pro právní vědu a praxi*, 24 (1), 93–101.

Dianiška, G., Strémy, T., Vráblová, M., et al. (2016): *Kriminológia.* 3rd edition. Plzen: Vydavateľstvo Aleš Čeněk.

Fábry, A. (2009): *Penology.* Bratislava: Eurokódex.

Griger, J. (2019): Perspective of Conditional Release from Prison in Face of Current Options of Support of Sentenced Prisoners Transferring to Civilian Life. In: Romža, S. (Ed.): *Košické dni trestného práva 2019, III. ročník – Kriminologické a organizačno-technické aspekty privatizácie trestného práva.* Zborník príspevkov z konferencie. Pavel Jozef Šafárik University, Košice, 273–284.

Griger, J., and Ľorko, J. (2018): Are Court Decisions Solely Responsible for Prison Overcrowding? In: *Míľniky práva v stredoeurópskom priestore 2018*: zborník príspevkov z medzinárodnej vedeckej konferencie, 416–423 (https://www.flaw.uniba.sk/fileadmin/praf/Veda/Konferencie_a_podujatia/milniky_zborniky_2011_2018/Zbornik_Milniky_2018.pdf).

Griger, J., and Papáčová, I. (2019): 1969 from Perspective of Slovak Prisons. *Zvesti*, 51 (1), 35–37.

Samaš, O. (2017): One More Time about the Extraordinary Sentence Reduction. *Justičná revue,* 69 (5), 733–735.

Tittlová, M. (2017): Act on Prison Sentence. Commentary. Bratislava: Wolters Kluwer.

Vráblová, M. (2019): Criminal Code – 13 Years from Re-Codification (Common and Different Trends). In: Jelínek, J. et al. (Eds.): *Deset let od přijetí českého trestního zákonníku.* Prague: Leges, 411–425.

39 Slovenia

Danijela Mrhar Prelić and Robert Friškovec

1 Introduction – general situation of the prison system

The Prison Administration of the Republic of Slovenia was established in 1995 in order to manage six prison facilities operating in fourteen different locations, as well as one correctional home. Prisoners are classified according to gender, age, nature of the sentence, duration of the sentence and the degree of security. Almost half of the prisoners in Slovenia are serving sentences for property crime, followed by those sentenced for crimes against life and limb, and crimes against human health (mostly drug-related offences). The prison system in Slovenia has been faced with an increasing prison population in the years after independence in 1991, which has caused overcrowding in several prisons. Slovenia has been grappling with the problem as the prison population increased by more than 40% from 2005 to 2019. There has been a significant increase in foreigners among inmates as well, with non-Slovenes composing 30% of the entire prison population. Nevertheless, according to the data provided by the Institute of Crime & Justice Policy Research, Birkbeck University of London, the prison population in Slovenia was relatively stable between 2008 (68 per 100,000 of the national population) and 2018 (66 per 100,000). It decreased by 19.7% during the pandemic, to 53 per 100,000 of the national population on 15 April 2020 (see World Prison Brief, https://www.prisonstudies.org/country/Slovenia). Slovenia therefore belongs to the countries with a low rate of incarceration, comparable to the countries characterised by the so-called "Scandinavian exceptionalism" (for explanations, see Dünkel, 2013).

2 Prison and penal policy concerning the execution of prison sentences during the COVID-19-induced crisis

In February 2020, because of predictions that coronavirus SARS-CoV-2 might also occur in Slovenia and because it was aware of the necessity and importance of adequate protection for all persons in prisons and in the correctional home, the Prison Administration of the Republic of Slovenia closely monitored the occurrence of coronavirus and its spread. In taking

DOI: 10.4324/9781003169178-39

action, the Prison Administration primarily followed the recommendations for prevention of infection prepared by the National Institute of Public Health.

The entire situation regarding the COVID-19 epidemic in Slovenia can be divided into two periods or two waves: the spring and the autumn of 2020. Before the official declaration of an epidemic in March 2020, the Director General had presided over two board meetings with all the directors of prison institutions in order to look for solutions to the looming crisis. As the situation changed, so the measures for protection against infection were adapted. Different scenarios were prepared in case of wider infection. First and foremost, the institutions were affiliated with local health bodies and epidemiological services. The focus was on protecting the health and safety of prisoners and employees. The Head Office and all correctional sites kept in daily touch about developments.

Already in March 2020, the Prison Administration had included an international comparison in its initial planning, especially with a focus on most of the neighbouring countries: Italy, Austria, Hungary and Croatia. Subsequently, Slovenia was involved in various channels of communication through EuroPris and other international contacts. On 13 March 2020, the Government of the Republic of Slovenia declared an epidemic.[1] Different preventive measures were taken after the adoption of the Act on Provisional Measures for Judicial, Administrative and Other Public Matters to Cope with the Spread of the Infectious Disease SARS-CoV-2 (COVID-19) on 20 March 2020. The Act, which entered into force on 29 March 2020, included several provisions related to the enforcement of criminal sanctions. According to the Act, summoning persons to prison so that they could begin serving their sentences of imprisonment was halted and new procedures were not to be initiated. In order to prevent the spread of the disease, the Act stopped transfers of inmates to other correctional facilities, allowed suspension of imprisonment for up to one month, with the possibility of extension where no security concerns existed, and early release of prisoners under certain conditions, at least six months before completion of their sentence. In this way, alternatives to the deprivation of liberty, such as early release of prisoners, were included. Courts carried out only urgent hearings and therefore there was a large decline in transfers from the courts to the prisons.

On 18 August 2020,[2] the official mobile application for protection of health and lives of people #OstaniZdrav (#StayHealthy) was presented nationwide. Promotion of application #OstaniZdrav took place also among prison staff.

The Government introduced an Ordinance on temporary measures to reduce the risk of infection and spreading of COVID-19, requiring the use of protective masks or other coverings of the mouth and nose area when it was not possible to ensure a social distance of at least two metres.[3] Prisons were asked to produce protective masks and were successful in providing enough masks.

On 9 October 2020, three cases of infection among prison staff in Maribor Prison were confirmed. Health authorities sent employees who had been in contact with the infected persons to preventive quarantine. In Dob pri Mirni Prison, a contractor was infected as well. There was a rapid increase of cases of infection all over the country. Again, measures were gradually implemented to prevent further infections.

In accordance with instruction from doctors responsible for health in prisons and correctional homes, regular tests were performed on prisoners suspected of having been infected. There was no confirmed infection among prisoners at any prison facility at the start of the second wave. Infections however spread among prison staff.

At the board meeting with the Director General on 14 October 2020, an Action Plan was issued, drawn up in accordance with the plan proposed by the Government. The principle of a "gradual approach" was taken.

The Government again declared a state of epidemic on 19 October 2020.[4] Up until 31 December 2020, the Prison Administration recorded 57 cases of inmates and 115 prison employees who were infected. In contrast, in the first wave, there were only two prisoners (at the largest prison, Dob pri Mirni Prison, both of whom recovered) and no prison employees that were infected. However, in the first wave, there was a case of infection of one employee of an outside company operating in the prison.

Before the official declaration of an epidemic on 1 March 2020, the prison occupancy level was at 110% of capacity, but it declined during the first wave and on 20 April was at 82% as a result of measures such as the suspension and non-execution of short-term prison sentences. During the intermediate period of the summer months, the occupancy level again rose to 101% on 20 August 2020. During the second wave, when these measures were again implemented, the occupancy level dropped to 93% on 10 November 2020.

The Slovenian Probation Administration also introduced temporary measures to prevent the spreading of coronavirus among those on probation and probation staff. In the first period of the epidemic, all direct contacts with probationers were abolished from 14 March 2020 and further communication with probationers was maintained by telephone (and different apps such as Viber and WhatsApp) or e-mail. The probation units operated on a smaller scale; in case of any additional questions, probationers could contact the probation officers' mobile numbers or the official contacts of each unit. In relation to the adopted Act on Provisional Measures for Judicial, Administrative and Other Public Matters to Cope with the Spread of Infectious Disease SARS-CoV-2 (COVID-19), the execution of all newly received probation orders was suspended. In the same framework, the community service deadlines for probationers did not apply, if the court had set a fixed deadline for community. During the spring period, the supervision of house arrest was delivered by only one probation officer, without any direct contact with the probationer or entering their homes. All conversations were held by telephone (and different apps). Instructions for washing hands and proper oral hygiene were displayed at all probation offices and were accessible to all employees and later probationers and visitors. The implementation of the measures was monitored by the Office of the Ombudsman, which offered its assistance whenever necessary.

3 Restrictions of contact with the outside world

All visits were suspended from April 2020 until June 2020. In the second wave, visits were suspended in most prison locations from October 2020 onwards. The Prison Administration was aware that meaningful contact of prisoners with their relatives and friends was much needed, so prisoners were encouraged to make more phone calls to their family members and friends. Visits by lawyers, consular agents and probation officers were carried out behind glass screens. In seeking compensation for the temporary suspension of visits, other options were considered as well, but unfortunately there were legal and technical barriers to their implementation. All physical contacts with external NGOs were also suspended.

4 Restrictions inside prisons

Special working groups, the Crisis Units, were set up at major prisons. The groups consisted of representatives of all departments of the prison services. The special task of the Crisis Unit was to adjust daily all the activities of prisons in order to protect prisoners and employees as best as possible, to maintain health, to perform all necessary duties, while at the same time protecting the health of all prisoners.

Recognising the fact that the responsible behaviour of each individual was crucial in preventing the virus infection and spread, it was important that everyone should take precautionary measures to reduce the chance of infection. In doing so, the following general preventive measures were followed at all locations within the prison system:

- avoidance of close contact with people (safety distance),
- no touching the eyes, nose and mouth,
- compliance with the cough hygiene rule,
- washing hands regularly with soap and water and
- smokers washing or disinfecting their hands before smoking.

Accurate instructions for washing hands and proper cough hygiene in the form of infographics were posted on bulletin boards at all locations and were accessible to all persons. Prisoners were also informed about preventive measures by staff at individual units and encouraged to follow them. From the beginning, it was recognised that the situation was stressful and could cause distress for individuals. Staff were tasked with reducing stress.

An important preventative factor was hand sanitising. All detainees were provided with soap and towels. Sanitisers were available to everyone at different key places in each institution. Disposable gloves were also available. In case of suspected illness, the institution would contact the competent health institution immediately, which would then provide more detailed instructions regarding the action to be taken. Each institution settled for a special protocol of treatment on a course of infection control in collaboration with a health centre that covered individual locations within the public health network.

All employees were briefed on the instructions of the National Institute of Public Health. Prison employees were also supported by psychologists as part of their phone consultation options. Employees throughout the prison system were informed daily about developments on the national level. They were also briefed on international documents that encouraged professionalism and respect for human rights during the coronavirus crisis.

From the outset, special care was taken that all the actions had a legal basis (as presented above). At individual prisons, all newly admitted prisoners had their temperature checked before entering the prison, and if fever was detected, a doctor was notified immediately. The temperature of imprisoned persons was also checked if they showed symptoms of viral illness and, if necessary, the doctor was informed.

Hooks, switches and work surfaces, tables and bathrooms were regularly disinfected (at least 2–3 times a day). All living and working facilities were ventilated several times a day. Employees were also regularly alerted that these actions were needed.

Newly admitted prisoners were placed in living quarters separated from others where possible. Overcrowding is a general problem in Slovenia; prisoners are mostly accommodated in communal cells, in newer institutions also in individual cells, and the occupancy level, for example, on 20 September 2020 was at 105%. Particular emphasis was placed on vulnerable groups, most of whom were included in measures of support under the Act on Provisional Measures for Judicial, Administrative and Other Public Matters to Cope with the Spread of the Infectious Disease SARS-CoV-2. When this could not be done, however, the best possible health care at each location was provided. Due to the epidemic, escorts to health care facilities were not readily available. In most prison locations, the daily meals were served at different times to different groups; sometimes, meals were distributed in the cells. If this was not possible, the meals were organised in small group dining rooms, maintaining the safety distance (minimum 1.5 metres).

The organisation of prison health care in Slovenia is part of the public health network. As clinics in health care centres shifted to a different level of operation due to the epidemic, this also affected the health care inside the prison. Regular check-ups of newly admitted prisoners and emergency medical services still operated.

All prison workshops and outside work of prisoners were stopped. Only urgent work required for the smooth operation of the institution (laundry, kitchen, etc.) was performed.

Institutions received sufficient protective equipment (disinfectants, face masks, gloves, overalls, goggles, etc.). However, in the beginning, it was necessary to cooperate with other institutions. The prison staff wore face masks and gloves for all prison operations. In the second half of April 2020, detainees began to make face masks at individual locations as part of their leisure activities.

Prison staff informed prisoners that the measures taken were carried out solely for the purpose of preserving and protecting their health and the health of their relatives (among prisoners, there are persons with weakened immune systems, the elderly, etc.). Information was also provided to foreign citizens who did not understand the Slovenian language. Prisoners understood and accepted the measures. At the state level, transfer between municipalities was prohibited,[5] and thus the general population was in general not allowed to move from municipality to municipality. Regarding foreigners, especially those who were to be deported, contact was made with the police and their consular missions, when assistance was needed in returning them to their home country in the event of release or early release.

Prisoners were allowed exercise in the fresh air as set by the house rules. Group sports were temporarily restricted.

5 Compensatory measures

Prisoners received information through TV, radio, newspapers, magazines and through contact with prison staff. They were offered more frequent telephone contact and more frequent visits to the library. The prisons also provided additional TV sets to prisoners. Because of the suspension of visits, prisoners twice received free 5 EUR phone cards to enable calls. This was repeated during the second wave. Prisons were equipped with tablet computers, as part of a pilot project for additional communication via Skype with the outside world. This was aimed especially at those who had less opportunity of contact with their families, such as foreigners, because of the closing of the border. This pilot project was very well received among prisoners.

During the second wave, more attention was paid to activities that could be possible under the measures for the protection of health and prevention of the spread of the virus. Various activities were provided such as chess competitions,[6] sports and social games. A series of workshops and lectures on developing life skills during the prison sentence and making social reintegration easier after release (with topics about communication, emotions, accepting past and present, values, setting goals, conflict resolution, and sense of duty and community) was provided by one of the NGOs. In all workshops, tablet computers were used.

At the Head Office, an initiative for literature and painting competitions in prisons entitled "My Corona Period" was proposed. All prisons took part in the competition; the commission to evaluate the results received 32 literary works and 44 drawings to be judged. Prisoners also took part in a short movie entitled "What I am Grateful for".[7] This was to encourage reflection about the positives in every life, no matter the restrictions faced.

6 Legal basis for restrictions and relaxations of the prison regime

In Section 2, we focused on the procedural nature of coping with the advance of the coronavirus COVID-19 in Slovenian prison system, while in this section the legal basis for the procedures is introduced. In connection with the global spreading of COVID-19, the Slovenian Government adopted several laws with the aim of preventing the spread of the virus and eliminating the consequences of the epidemic, among others, the laws also referred to the execution of penal sanctions. One was the Act on Provisional Measures for Judicial, Administrative and Other Public Matters to Cope with the Spread of Infectious Disease SARS-CoV-2 (COVID-19).

The Government found on 21 May 2020 that the grounds for interim measures under the Act of 20 March had ceased; therefore, the measures were repealed with effect from 1 June 2020. On the basis of the national plan for protection and rescue in cases of contagious disease, epidemics released on 23 July[8] and in accordance with the plan of readiness accepted by the Ministry of Justice for the pandemic, an "Action plan of the Prison Administration of the Republic of Slovenia in the epidemic or pandemic of the SARS-CoV-2 virus" was developed. In this document, experiences with dealing with this crisis were summarised and further steps for the restriction of the virus in the second wave were proposed.

Due to the rapid deterioration of the epidemiological situation in Slovenia, the Government declared an epidemic again on 19 October 2020. After the second declaration of epidemic, two additional legal acts entered into force, both included provisions regarding the enforcement of criminal sanctions. On 24 October 2020, the Act Determining Temporary Measures to Mitigate and Remedy the Consequences of COVID-19 came into force. The Act stopped all summons for convicted persons to begin their prison sentences or alternative imprisonment for misdemeanours, while all procedures already started were suspended. Directors of prisons could terminate prison sentences of prisoners for one month if such an action was needed to prevent the spread of the SARS-CoV-2 virus and there were no security impediments. The suspension of the execution of prison sentences could be prolonged if the reasons for a suspension were still in place. The Director of a prison could also approve early release of those prisoners who met all conditions, but no longer than six months before the expiry of their sentence, and if such action was needed for the prevention of the spread of the

SARS-CoV-2 virus. On 31 December 2020, there were 100 prisoners whose sentences were postponed, while 87 prisoners were on early release.

On 26 November 2020, the Act Determining the Intervention Measures to Mitigate the Consequences of the Second Wave of the COVID-19 Epidemic entered into force. The Act stipulated that the time limit for performing community service did not run if a probationer was temporarily unable to perform the imposed number of hours for reasons caused by the COVID-19 epidemic (inability to provide an organisation where community service could be executed, suspension of the organisation's cooperation with the probationer, inability to send a probationer to undergo a medical examination (which is a condition for performing community service) and inability to come to work due to non-operation of public transport (where the person depends on this type of transport, and due to the COVID-19 disease)).

Both Acts regulated measures up to 31 December 2020 but contained a provision that measures might be extended by a Government decision. Since the epidemiological situation did not improve, the Government decided on 23 December 2020 to extend all measures regarding prison sentences until the end of March 2021, and those regarding probation until the end of June 2021.

Before the declaration of the epidemic and during the epidemic itself, the Ministry of Justice adopted several recommendations based on recommendations of the National Institute of Public Health (NIJZ). Both bodies of the Ministry – The Prison Administration and the Slovenian Probation Administration – adopted their own measures, based on recommendations of the Ministry of Justice and the National Institute of Public Health.

7 Returning to normal

By the end of April 2020, some preventive measures in the prison and probation systems began to be relaxed. On 7 May 2020, all bodies of the Ministry of Justice were asked to prepare an exit strategy. On 13 May, the Slovenian Government proclaimed an end to the coronavirus epidemic; the epidemic officially ended on 31 May 2020.[9]

On 30 April, prison directors were called upon to consider which measures in prisons could be relaxed. Gradually, the focus moved to the relaxation of measures, while still abiding by all the existing safety standards and recommendations of the National Institute of Public Health. In the plan for the relaxation of measures by the Prison Administration, the following objectives were stated: in all prisons, the recommendations that all employees and prisoners had already received at the start of epidemic should be followed (namely personal hygiene care, disinfection, ventilation of facilities, keeping an appropriate distance, cough hygiene, etc.).

From 11 May 2020, the transfer of prisoners among prison facilities restarted. From 18 May 2020, the gradual relaxation of measures concerning visits took place. Every prison had to prepare visit protocols and establish measures and possibilities with regard to spatial arrangements and characteristics of the prison population. Visits were initially limited to one person without signs of infection and were limited to one hour. The gradual return of prisoners from the suspension of executing their sentence on the basis of the Intervention Law started from 1 June 2020. First, all prisoners from the open regime (Rogoza, Puščava and Ig prisons) returned, with the exception of those on the so-called "weekend prison" regime. On 1 July 2020, all other prisoners, whose execution of their sentence had been postponed in accordance with the Intervention Law, returned as well and were placed in the closed regime. From 1 June 2020, the professional treatment of prisoners began again in full, while still observing all measures set by the National Institute of Public Health. These were taken into account in individual and group settings (smaller groups, work with smaller groups, etc.). From 1 June 2020, new work contacts were also re-established with Government and non-governmental organisations and religious representatives (delivering group services). The possibility of long-distance collaboration was evaluated and the option of personal relationships while complying with the standards set by the National Institute of Public Health was re-established. All employee training (for instance, of newly appointed prison officers) resumed, and supervision of the less restrictive measures aimed at re-establishing prisoners in society began again.

After the proclaimed end of the (first) coronavirus epidemic, the Prison Administration still constantly examined the epidemic and health situation and epidemic circumstances of prisoners. This was carried out by regional health centres. Even if the situation seemed to improve, there were still challenges in particular prisons, especially with persons who came to the remand prison from regions or States who were declared as red zones by the Government. These prisoners were put into quarantine by the health authorities. The difficulties of foreign prisoners, who could not receive visits because of the closure of the borders, were acknowledged.

In the course of the second wave of the COVID-19 epidemic, at the beginning of 2021, there were no noted cases of infections among inmates. Measures prescribed in legislation are still in place.

The Slovenian Probation Administration similarly prepared an exit strategy in May 2020. The aim of the strategy was to establish direct contacts with probationers in accordance with the measures taken and executing probation tasks. First, direct contacts were made with probationers for the most demanding probation tasks (conditional sentence with probationary supervision and conditional release with supervision), then for those with less demanding tasks and with those who continued performing their probation, despite certain restrictions. Contacts at probation units were carefully planned, in small groups, without prolonging conversations, obligatory masks during the personal contact with probationers and in common areas of the probation unit, sufficient intervals between interviews to allow the premises to be adequately ventilated and the surfaces to be disinfected.

Work with probationers started from 18 May 2020 (the most demanding cases), and probationary duties were fully implemented in June 2020.

In the second period of the epidemic (autumn 2020), direct contacts with probationers were held in accordance with the measures taken, direct personal contacts decreased, but other types of contacts (e.g. telephone and using apps) intensified. Where possible, probation tasks were carried out. House arrest was supervised by two probation officers; interviews with prisoners were held outside of the premises (in special cases inside the premises if there was no doubt about COVID-19) in accordance with all preventive measures.

One of the objectives of getting the probation service involved was to diminish overcrowding in prisons. The Prison and Probation Administration signed a protocol on cooperation in the execution of criminal sanctions with the aim to strengthen the cooperation between the two administrations as well as to strengthen the imposition of conditional release with probationary supervision and house arrest. Directors General of both administrations have also agreed to work together to strengthen the cooperation with all judicial stakeholders, also with an aim to increase the imposition of alternative sanctions.

Notes

1 A Slovenian version of this Act is available: https://www.uradni-list.si/glasilo-uradni-list-rs/vsebina/2020-01-0532/.
2 https://www.gov.si/teme/koronavirus-sars-cov-2/mobilna-aplikacija-ostanizdrav/namestitev-in-delovanje-aplikacije/.
3 A Slovenian version of this Act is available: https://www.uradni-list.si/glasilo-uradni-list-rs/vsebina/2020-01-2178/odlok-o-zacasnih-ukrepih-za-zmanjsanje-tveganja-okuzbe-in-sirjenja-okuzbe-z-virusom-sars-cov-2.
4 Slovenian version of this act is available: https://www.uradni-list.si/glasilo-uradni-list-rs/vsebina/2020-01-2588/odlok-o-razglasitvi-epidemije-nalezljive-bolezni-COVID-19-na-obmocju-republike-slovenije.
5 Slovenian version of this act is available: https://www.uradni-list.si/glasilo-uradni-list-rs/vsebina/2020-01-0688/odlok-o-zacasni-splosni-prepovedi-gibanja-in-zbiranja-ljudi-na-javnih-mestih-in-povrsinah-v-republiki-sloveniji-ter-prepovedi-gibanja-izven-obcin.
6 https://www.gov.si/novice/2020-12-23-sahovski-turnirji-v-zavodih-maribor-in-ljubljana/.
7 https://www.gov.si/novice/2020-12-23-video-natecaj-v-zaporih-in-v-prevzgojnem-domu-za-kaj-sem-hvalezen/.
8 Slovenian version of this act is available: https://www.gov.si/assets/organi-v-sestavi/URSZR/Datoteke/DNZiRpandemija_23_7.pdf.
9 Slovenian version of this act is available: https://www.uradni-list.si/glasilo-uradni-list-rs/vsebina/2020-01-1030/.

Reference

Dünkel, F. (2013): Slovenian Exceptionalism? – Die Entwicklung von Gefangenenraten im internationalen Vergleich. In: Ambrož, U. M., Filipčič, K., Završnik, A. (Eds.): *Essays in Honour of Alenka Šelih. Criminal Law, Criminology, Human Rights*. Ljubljana: Institute of Criminology at the Law Faculty, University of Ljubljana, 61–93.

40 South Africa

Lukas M. Muntingh

1 Introduction

South Africa has one national prison system and all prisons[1] resort under the Department of Correctional Services (DCS), headed by the National Commissioner who reports to the Minister of Justice and Correctional Services (hereafter, the Minister). Following the declaration of a State of Disaster (SoD) on 15 March 2020,[2] South Africa went into a hard lockdown on 27 March 2020, placing severe restrictions on movement and contact between people as well as restricting certain goods.[3] The movement and activities of people and goods were, and continue to be, managed through a series of restriction levels (Table 40.1) governed by regulation and directives issued by line ministers.

On 26 March 2020, the Minister of Justice and Correctional Services issued directions concerning the administration of justice. The directions essentially limited court operations to only urgent and essential matters and furthermore ordered that all matters be postponed to a later date. The postponement could be done in person, or by audio-visual link or *in absentia*.[4] The lockdown brought the criminal justice system to a standstill, even if it was stated that essential court services could continue. The practical situation was extremely challenging, especially when lawyers had matters requiring urgent attention and wished to consult their clients (PMG, 2020a).

Table 40.1 Restriction levels in South African prisons under the COVID-19 pandemic

Restriction level	*From*	*To*	*Duration (days)*
5 (most restrictive)	27 March 2020	30 April 2020	34
4	1 May 2020	31 May 2020	30
3	1 June 2020	17 August 2020	77
2	18 August 2020	20 September 2020	33
1 (least restrictive)	21 September 2020	28 December 2020	98
3	29 December 2020		1+

DOI: 10.4324/9781003169178-40

This applied to both people in and outside of custody, whether awaiting trial or sentenced. The human rights impact on the administration of justice has received scant attention, except when a remission was granted to sentenced prisoners as discussed below.

1.1 General situation of the prison system

The principal legislation governing prisons is the Correctional Services Act, while the Constitution also affords prisoners unusually detailed rights.[5] There is a substantial body of progressive jurisprudence on prisoners' rights relating to the right to life, right to vote, right to health, sentence administration and parole, to name a few.

The transition to democracy was formalised in 1994, but from 1990 onwards, there was a rapid increase in violent crime having significant consequences for the overall approach to crime that would follow. Violent crime remains prevalent and public sentiment is generally not forgiving of offenders.[6] The violent crime wave created public panic and 1998 saw the introduction of mandatory minimum sentences.[7] Mandatory minimum sentences, high levels of violent crime and the abolition of the death penalty[8] saw the record-breaking use of life imprisonment (van Zyl Smit and Appleton, 2019: 98).

South Africa is the African country with the largest prison population, housed in 235 prisons,[9] and has the sixth highest imprisonment rate on the continent at 259/100,000 of the population.[10] Prisons comply with the minimum separation requirements, i.e. gender (male and female), sentence status (sentenced and awaiting trial) and age (adults and children). More nuanced segregation requirements are entirely dependent on available space at a facility. The overwhelming majority of prisoners are accommodated in communal cells with a capacity of 15 to 30 people. In the prison system, there is significant diversity in conditions of detention, access to services, programme availability, age of buildings, technology utilised, architecture, size (ranging from below 100 to 3,000 bedspaces), locality (rural and urban), type of accommodation, security level (minimum to super-maximum) and so forth. Making generalisations is thus difficult.

Table 40.2 presents the overall profile and distribution of the South African prison population as at 31 March 2020.[11] Prisons were occupied at 28% above capacity. However, occupation levels vary greatly from prison to prison. Moreover, the occupation level is calculated at a space norm of 3.344 m^2 per prisoner in a communal cell,[12] which is below what is regarded as acceptable in the international guidelines (European Committee for the Prevention of Torture, 2015).

Oversight is fourfold. First, Parliament oversees the work of the DCS. Second, the designated oversight structure is the Judicial Inspectorate for Correctional Services (JICS) which is headed by a judge of the High Court (the Inspecting Judge – IJ) with the mandate to inspect and report on the treatment and conditions of detention.[13] Third, following OPCAT ratification in 2019,

Table 40.2 South African prison population according to provinces

	Sentenced			*Unsentenced*			
Region	*Male*	*Females*	*Total*	*Male*	*Females*	*Total*	*Total*
Eastern Cape	13,981	238	14,219	6,221	119	6,340	20,559
Gauteng	21,412	661	22,073	13,661	477	14,138	36,211
Free State and Northern Cape	15,382	349	15,731	5,221	91	5,312	21,043
KwaZulu-Natal	17,779	400	18,179	6,784	157	6,941	25,120
Western Cape	14,464	512	14,976	11,394	474	11,868	26,844
Limpopo, Mpumalanga and North West	17,289	374	17,663	6,879	130	7,009	24,672
Total	100,307	2,534	102,841	50,160	1,448	51,608	154,449

the South African Human Rights Commission (SAHRC) was designated as a holding structure of the National Preventive Mechanism (NPM). Together with the JICS, the Military Ombudsman[14] and the Health Ombudsman,[15] they form the NPM. Fourth, Members of Parliament, judges and magistrates are also mandated to visit prisons announced and unannounced.[16]

1.2 COVID-19 infections and deaths of prisoners and prison staff members with reference to the development of the pandemic in the general society

The first COVID-19 case in South Africa was reported on 5 March 2020 and the first prison system case, that of an official, on 6 April 2020 (Muntingh, 2020), followed by a prisoner on 10 April 2020.[17] In overview, it appears that nationally the pandemic was managed reasonably well and that infections reached a peak, resulting in a relaxation of restrictions as reflected in Table 40.1. However, on 9 December 2020, the Minister of Health acknowledged that South Africa was experiencing a second wave and that a second strain of the virus had been detected.[18] On 29 December 2020, the President announced a return to Level 3 restrictions, resulting in the immediate prohibition of visits by members of the public to prisons.[19]

Numerical data on the impact of COVID-19 on the DCS as at 3 February 2021 are presented in Table 40.3, showing nearly 7,000 officials and nearly 3,800 prisoners infected, with 226 deaths ascribed to COVID-19, with the majority of these being officials. Unfortunately, disaggregated data are not available; earlier data showed a concentration in two provinces (Eastern and Western Cape; see PMG, 2020a).

Table 40.3 COVID-19 infections and deaths in South African prisons

Category	*Officials*	*Prisoners*	*Total*
Infections	6,869	3,785	10,564
Deaths	162	64	226

Table 40.4 Accomodation in single and communal cells for quarantine and isolation measures

Type	*Single cells*	*Communal cells*	*Total*
Quarantine	944	3,636	4,580
Isolation	1,212	1,312	2,524
Total	2,156	4,948	7,104

Prison overcrowding is a longstanding problem and government grasped the risk COVID-19 posed to prisoners. It accepted that a reduction in prisoner numbers would assist in reducing the risk of transmission (UN-SPT, 2020; WHO-Europe, 2020). The Minister also made it clear that social distancing is not possible in overcrowded facilities (PMG, 2020a). The first issue is that the overcrowding problem is in the large metropolitan prisons for unsentenced prisoners and not, primarily, in the prisons for sentenced prisoners. Releasing unsentenced prisoners, especially when serious charges are involved, is more difficult than releasing a sentenced prisoner with a release date and a confirmed address. Second, most prisoners are housed in communal cells. The architecture is in general not conducive to social distancing and has been identified as a contributing factor in the transmission of tuberculosis.[20] Under such conditions, social distancing is indeed impossible, raising the question of how many releases are needed to enable social distancing in communal cells?

Apart from releasing prisoners to ease congestion, it was also necessary to prepare for ill prisoners. The DCS reported to Parliament that it had created quarantine and isolation capacity for prisoners as set out in Table 40.4 (see PMG, 2020a).

2 Prison and penal policy concerning the execution of prison sentences during the COVID-19-induced crisis

Since the criminal justice system had come to a halt, it seems that new sentences were not imposed. Available data for the Western Cape province, which at the end of March 2020 held 17.4% of the prison population, shows that (see Figure 40.1), at least in the Western Cape, there was a notable decline in sentenced and awaiting trial prisoners until the end of the Level 3 lockdown. After this, the awaiting trial population continue to decline, but the sentenced population shows an increase. This seems to be largely a proportional redistribution between the two categories, since the total population shows a very slight increase. In short, from Level 4 onwards, courts were again able to try cases and suspects awaiting trial were now being convicted and sentenced. A further observation is then that new cases were still, in the latter half of 2020, not entering the criminal justice system in large numbers in the Western Cape and that awaiting trial prisoners remain below the pre-lockdown level.

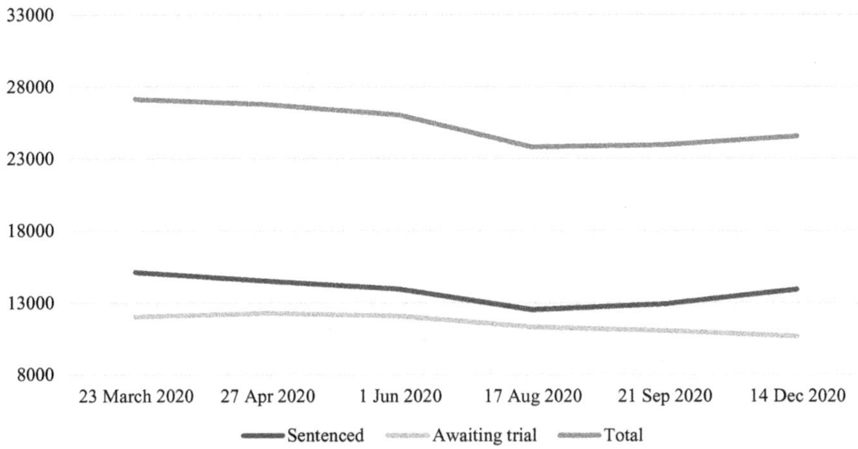

Figure 40.1 The prison population in Western Cape, March–December 2020.

The country's borders were also closed and deportations could not take place. Foreign nationals with expired sentences were transferred to temporary DCS facilities to await deportation.[21] Prior to the lockdown, there were some 16,100 foreign nationals in South African prisons and by June 2020, this had declined to 13,600.[22] The decline can be attributed to a reduction in both sentenced and unsentenced foreign nationals detained, although the bulk can be attributed to a reduction in sentenced foreign nationals. It is very likely that a reduction in all new admissions also affected new foreign national admissions.

2.1 Forward displacement of early release

The Correctional Services Act makes provision for the earlier release of sentenced prisoners and mandates the President to authorise the early release[23] of any sentenced prisoner subject to the conditions laid down by the Correctional Supervision and Parole Board, or Minister, in the case of persons sentenced to life imprisonment.[24] Such a remission of sentence was announced by the President some three months prior to the COVID-19 lockdown on 16 December 2019 resulting in the release of 15,911 low-risk sentenced prisoners.[25] The following prisoners were excluded from the December 2019 remission and the same criteria were applied when the planned release of some 19,000 prisoners was announced in early May 2020 as a result of COVID-19:

- prisoners serving sentences for sexual offences, child abuse, violations under the Domestic Violence Act,[26] murder, attempted murder, armed robbery, sedition, high treason, sabotage and terrorism;

- offenders declared as dangerous by a court[27];
- offenders sentenced to life imprisonment;
- any escaped/absconded inmate who evaded the justice system after being released on bail pending appearance and was still at large on 16 December 2019 and
- those certified as mentally ill and detained accordingly.[28]

In terms of the May 2020 remission, the President authorised the consideration of parole for selected low-risk qualifying sentenced offenders who had or will have reached their minimum non-parole period (generally half of the sentence imposed)[29] within five years. By July 2020 (the latest data), only some 5,500 of the planned 19,000 had been released.[30]

The five-year window period, as provided for in the May 2020 remission, was perhaps not properly thought through as it enabled the release of certain prisoners after serving only a fraction of their sentence: in one case, nine months of a ten-year sentence, and in another, three months of a three-year term.[31] The remission criteria were unsuccessfully challenged in the High Court.[32]

2.2 Release of certain groups of offenders such as the elderly, female prisoners, etc.

In an April 2020 briefing, the Deputy Minister stated:

> that a list of 19,000 inmates who would be suitable for release would be presented to the President and he would make the final decision. Inmates that were vulnerable – those infected with HIV/AIDS and Tuberculosis - were given special attention.
>
> (PMG, 2020a)

The relatively narrow criteria for eligibility under the COVID-19 remission should be seen against the context of violent crime in general, as well as two additional factors. First, over several years, there have been a number of controversial releases on parole and medical parole of high-profile individuals. Even when no wrong-doing had been proven, such releases have not bolstered confidence in the parole system, as they all had the traits of special treatment for politically connected or otherwise influential people. Second, there were also a number of high-profile cases where parolees committed serious crimes. This resulted in a public backlash against the DCS in particular.[33] All indications are therefore that the DCS would not go beyond the criteria set out in December 2019 and predating COVID-19. It is therefore unlikely that elderly or female prisoners would benefit in addition to what is laid down in law. Whether AIDS and tuberculosis patients were indeed given special attention, as raised by the Deputy Minister, is unknown. "Special attention" should also not be read to mean a higher likelihood for release, as the duty still rests with the DCS to ensure that a parolee has a fixed address and access to the necessary health care and support services. In many instances, prisoners lack basic family support structures and a fixed address, and their release on parole would thus be problematic from a duty of care perspective.

2.3 Penal law reforms in this context

The legislation provides for a wide range of non-custodial sentencing options as well as bail provisions.[34] Parole is also a well-established principle and practice and used as the core mechanism to alleviate overcrowding. Although many variations are possible, the rule of thumb after October 2004 has been that a prisoner serving a determinate sentence must serve one quarter if the sentence is 24 months or less, and one half if longer, before being considered for parole.[35] Prisoners serving life and all determinate sentences longer than 25 years must serve 25 years before being considered for parole.

The need to create prison space and thus reduce the risk of infection consequently did not require any law reform, as various forms of mass release are part and parcel of the prison system and have been implemented periodically.[36] The challenge with the COVID-19 pandemic was that the courts had come to a standstill, and, even if the law provided for a range of non-custodial options, the courts were not sitting for trials.

2.4 Reforms to administrative and penal law: criminalisation of non-compliance to COVID-19-induced contact restrictions inside and outside prisons

Regulations issued shortly before the lockdown[37] set the basic framework and prohibited gatherings (at that stage 100 or more people) and a limit of 50 people at places where alcohol was sold or consumed. The regulations furthermore criminalised non-compliance pertaining to the closure of schools and day-care centres, visits to places of detention, restrictions on the sale of alcohol and emergency procurement procedures. All visits by members of the public to prisons, police holding cells, military detention barracks, and holding and accommodation facilities under the Department of Social Development were suspended. The following were criminalised:

- misrepresenting COVID-19 infection status;
- spreading misinformation and
- intentionally exposing another person to COVID-19.

While misrepresentation and deception about COVID-19 could attract a fine and/or imprisonment (up to six months), intentional exposure could result in a charge of assault, attempted murder or murder.

On 25 March 2020, additional regulations restricted the movement of people and goods.[38] These regulations also defined essential goods and services. Two categories are relevant – court officials and law enforcement officials, which included prison officials, but excluded staff of the JICS and the Independent Correctional Centre Visitors (ICCV).[39]

The lockdown created a number of arrestable offences, such as interfering with a police official in enforcing the regulations; holding a gathering or funeral unless in compliance with the regulations and a person leaving his or her house unless for a permitted purpose (e.g. buying groceries). Even if the regulations tried to curtail the powers of arrest, they were still very broad and their enforcement largely left to the discretion of the police.[40] Contraventions of the regulations can attract a fine and/or imprisonment of up to six months.[41] Between March and August 2020, the police arrested nearly 300,000 people for lockdown violations.[42]

The sale of cigarettes was banned under the lockdown regulations from 27 March 2020 to 18 August 2020.[43] Regardless of the merits of smoking, tobacco plays an important role in the prison economy. It is also the case that prisoners share cigarettes and smoking would therefore be a high-risk behaviour in the COVID-19 prison context. The DCS reported to Parliament in late April 2020 that the termination of visits resulted in a reduction in contraband being seized (PMG, 2020a: 9). There are also reports that the DCS used the termination of visits (by family members as well as the JICS) and the absence of effective oversight to intensify searches,[44] but it is unknown whether this was always done in compliance with what the law and human rights standards require. Not only were visits and cigarettes banned, but also prisoners receiving money from outside.[45] The reason for this is not evident. At St Albans Prison in Port Elizabeth (Eastern Cape), the ban on cigarettes and not having access to the courts were cited as the main reasons for a riot there which resulted in the kitchen being set on fire.[46] Prison riots were reported from five localities[47] and it is perhaps surprising that their incidence was so limited in scale and scope.

3 Restrictions of contact with the outside world

The regulations to combat the spread of COVID-19 prohibited visits to all places of detention, including correctional centres and remand detention. The April 2020 Correctional Services Directions contain the following restrictions:

- Day parole approved for sentenced offenders is suspended, unless the parolee is rendering an essential service.[48]
- Prisoner transfer will only be done with Head Office approval.[49] The applicable criteria were not disclosed.
- Sentenced prisoners who are illegal foreign nationals and whose sentences will expire during the lockdown period will be released into and detained at temporary deportation facilities at a current correctional centre (designated by the Department of Home Affairs – DHA) until after the lockdown period.[50] They will be released into DHA-facilities after the lockdown period for further processing.[51]

- Visits by members of the public, including legal representatives, to all places of detention are suspended.[52]
- Prisoners are allowed to consult with their attorneys telephonically with the permission of the Head of Centre.[53] Telephonic consultations will only be allowed for urgent matters resources permitting.

On 4 September 2020, the restrictions were relaxed:

- prisoners could now receive one non-contact visit per month; non-contact consultations with legal practitioners; the transfer of inmates between facilities was permitted; inmates could be referred to external health care service providers;
- parolees and probationers at community corrections offices could be released and community services programmes resumed;
- visits to correctional centres from essential service providers, and external non-essential health care providers, and judicial statutory oversight inspections could resume.[54]

4 Restrictions inside prisons

The overall impression gained is that the generally restrictive regime inside prisons intensified during the lockdown:

- Work activities, rehabilitation and educational programmes were stopped.
- Structured recreational activities did not take place but it seems that the mandatory minimum one hour per day outside of the cells[55] was complied with. However, the cancellation of work, recreation and educational activities resulted in prisoners generally spending more time in the cells than prior to the lockdown.
- Since new admissions had to be isolated for 14 days prior to being mixed with the general prison population, there was an increase in the number of prisoners placed in isolation for medical reasons.[56]

5 Compensatory measures

All indications are that the daily regime in prisons became more restrictive and that access to the few amenities that there are, were largely terminated, save for phone calls. "Amenities" are recreational and other activities, diversions or privileges which are granted to inmates in addition to what they are entitled to as of right and in terms of the Act and includes exercise; contact with the community; reading material; recreation and incentive schemes. Amenities must not be confused with minimum rights. Access to phone calls and visits is determined by a prisoner's security classification, which ranges from Maximum to Minimum, and in each of these, there are a number of sub-categories setting out the respective ranges of access to amenities

(Muntingh, 2006). It can be safely assumed that only essential work performed by prisoners would have continued (e.g. kitchens, food production and cleaning) and that the remainder of prisoners would, save for the one hour per day exercise, be confined to their cells.

JICS reported that prisoners had additional access to the landline phones installed in prisons. However, prisoners are required to pay for these calls and DCS staff were mandated to assist prisoners who could not afford this.

Prisoners are not permitted to have mobile phones, chargers or SIM cards and are dependent on landline pay phones installed in prisons. These require pre-paid phone cards available from prison shops. It is not clear how prisoners were supposed to pay for this as they could not receive money from outside. In emergencies or for official communication (e.g. legal representative), departmental phones may be used. It is at least anecdotally known and observed by the author that the phones installed for prisoner-use are frequently out of order, giving a further impetus for mobile phones in the prison economy. Despite the prohibition of mobile phones, they are commonly found in prisons.

There are at present 46 courts that have facilities for audio-visual links to prisons, which enable them to communicate directly with prisoners in prison (PMG, 2020a). These links can be used to enable postponements or releases on unopposed bail,[57] and are exclusively for these purposes.[58] Audio-visual links prevent the accused from having to be transported to court to appear in person, with all the risks (security and COVID-19 transmission) associated with this. However, the limited number of such links meant that they could be used in only a minority of cases. For all other cases, the police are responsible for the transportation of pre-trial prisoners to and from courts, but under the lockdown police resources were in high demand. The result was an inevitable delay in prisoners getting to the courts, which could order their release.

6 Legal basis for restrictions and relaxations of the prison regime

The overall prison oversight architecture is described above, with four entities being named: Parliament, the JICS, judges and magistrates, and the NPM under OPCAT. It was reported that the IJ was able to visit prisons and on 5 May 2020 he visited Johannesburg Medium A Prison.[59] The extent to which other judges and magistrates, and Members of Parliament were able to visit prisons is unknown, but it is more than likely that such visits did not take place as they were not explicitly provided for in the Regulations.

The core issue during the lockdown was that the JICS Inspectors and the ICCV were not listed as essential services and consequently were prevented in law from visiting prisons. It is in particular the ICCV functioning as a lay visitor scheme at each prison that is critical to transparency.[60] Despite other shortcomings, the almost daily presence of ICCV in prisons ensures that

Table 40.5 Complaints and measures of restraint in prisons during the pandemic

Category	*Jan–March 2020*	*April–June 2020*	*Change %*
Complaint to IJ	120	28	−76.7
Complaint to ICCV	7,189	174	−97.6
Use of segregation	733	1,112	51.7
Use of force	123	237	92.7

external people are in prisons and have access to the expertise of the Inspectorate as well as the IJ in the event of serious transgressions. The exclusion of ICCV from the definition of essential services exacerbated the problem, since there had already been an effective collapse of the mandatory reporting system prior to the lockdown.[61]

The impact of the lockdown on the functioning of the JICS was substantial (PMG, 2020b). Table 40.5 presents performance information from JICS. First, the number of complaints lodged with the IJ and ICCVs plummeted due to the restriction on prison visits. Simultaneously, there were increases in segregation and the use of force, with the latter nearly doubling. Given the inefficiencies in the mandatory reporting system already noted, the near doubling in the instances of the use of force reported is an ominous trend.

It appears that the DCS had developed Standing Operating Procedures (SOP) for dealing with COVID-19 by 16 March 2020, presenting them to Parliament on 28 April 2020 (PMG, 2020a). As commendable as this responsivity may have been, the SOP are entirely focussed on health care concerns, omitting human rights issues that could or had already developed as a result of COVID-19. For example, access to external complaints mechanisms is not dealt with in the SOP.

7 Returning to normal

A return to normal seems unlikely for the foreseeable future. The already closed and centralised institution has become even more closed and centralised. Symptomatic of the state's weakness and history of poor governance over the past decade, it has relied on the criminal justice system to enforce compliance with the lockdown regulations. This has been met with strong criticism from civil society and the private sector in particular. With regard to the prison system, at least four issues stand out as obstacles towards normalisation:

- the closing down of oversight;
- executive overreach into the domain of the judiciary;
- the exclusion of civil society and
- the lack of accurate and disaggregated data.

Closing down of oversight: Since the JICS was excluded from the definition of essential services and no other visits from family and legal representatives were permitted, the prison system returned to a situation not unlike under apartheid – shrouded in utmost secrecy. However, the lockdown did see a number of prison protests, and a return to severe Levels 4 and 5 restrictions may well see a successful challenge to ensure that effective oversight and monitoring are maintained.

The failure of the NPM to get off the ground and enable visits and monitoring of all places of detention must be regarded in a serious light, although the exact reasons seem to be somewhat of a mystery. As custodian entity of the NPM, the SAHRC has remained silent on the issue, increasing the risk of inaction on the part of the NPM.

Executive overreach into the domain of the judiciary: As well-intentioned as the remission of sentences was, it is also evident that the executive interpreted and applied its powers in a manner that severely undermined the intentions of trial courts in some instances where parole was granted. It is not clear how government came to the five-year window period for eligibility, but this seems to have been done without a rational basis. While mass remissions have been a regular feature of the prison system, it seems that the mark was overstepped. It simply does not build trust in the criminal justice system, and specifically the courts, if a prisoner is released (even if on parole) after serving three months of a three-year sentence or nine months of a ten-year sentence. Importantly, this release mechanism was not created by an act of Parliament (such as in the Correctional Services Act), but by ministerial regulation. Therein lies a real risk, but also a situation ripe for a constitutional challenge.

Exclusion of civil society: There is no formal platform for dialogue between the DCS, the JICS and civil society, especially where it concerns governance and human rights issues. During Levels 3–5 of national COVID restrictions, a consortium of civil society organisations under the banner of the *Detention Justice Forum* developed and collected data using a monitoring tool based on the SPT public advice and submitted their findings to the NPM on three occasions, but no reply was ever received.

It is also the case that civil society organisations active in prisons are entirely dependent on the DCS for access. Such access can be revoked at a moment's notice. The situation is not uniquely South African and, as is the case elsewhere, ensures that civil society organisations toe the line. The lockdown restrictions emphasised the ease with which transparency can be removed from the prison system, emphasising the urgent need for formalised and intersectoral monitoring and sharing of information.

Lack of data: Since 2011, quantitative information on prisons has been scarce and erratic, and in many instances only released when an application under the Promotion of Access to Information Act is made. Monitoring the situation in prisons during the lockdown was challenging as information was simply not forthcoming. What was released was often in an aggregated format with virtually no breakdown, making trend analysis over time impossible. The general uncertainty and lack of reliable data created confusion, and a real risk of widespread prison protests. Accurate, accessible and disaggregated data need to be available to ensure that decisions are based on evidence. The COVID-19 experience has shone the light into prisons again. It has stress-tested constitutional protections, revealed shortcomings. Even if the South African prison population and system have emerged seemingly well from the fourth wave of infections, this should not result in complacency but rather create the opportunity for thorough review of remedial measures that could be taken.

Notes

1 Police holding cells resort under the South African Police Service (SAPS) and immigration detention under the Department of Home Affairs. Children may also be detained awaiting trial and sentenced in Child and Youth Care Centres.

2 Declaration of a National State of Disaster, 15 March 2020, *Government Gazette*, No. 43096.

3 Regulations issued in terms of Section 27(2) of the Disaster Management Act, 2002, *Government Gazette*, No. 43107, 18 March 2020.

4 Directions issued in terms of Regulation 10 of the Regulations under the Disaster Management Act (2002), *Government Gazette*, No. 43167 on 26 March 2020. Dir. 2, Directions issued in terms of Regulation 10 of the Regulations under the Disaster Management Act, 2002 published in GN No. 43191 on 31 March 2020. (Hereafter referred to as Court Directions). Below are the Directions concerning criminal matters:

- If accused persons are in custody (i.e. in prison or police holding cell), the court will only hear the case if it is a first appearance, a bail application or a matter where special arrangements have been made with the judicial officer.
- Special arrangements have been made for the continued referral of awaiting trial prisoners to court for the consideration of their length of detention and bail review as per the Directions to reduce the remand population ('Correctional Services Directions').
- All trials enrolled during the lockdown will be postponed to dates after the lockdown, except for trials where the interests of justice dictate otherwise or where special arrangements have been made with the judicial officers involved in the matter.
- All matters where children are detained in Child and Youth Care Centres will be postponed in the absence of the accused.
- Where possible, audio-visual facilities available at correctional centres linked to courts will be used to postpone cases where accused persons are in custody.
- In all criminal cases where the accused is not in custody, the case will be postponed in the absence of the accused and he/she will be summonsed with a date of next appearance (Court Directions Dir 3(a-d and g); Dir. 3, Directions issued in terms of Regulation 10(2) (a) of the Regulations under the Disaster Management Act, 2002 published in GN No. 43225 on 9 April 2020. (Hereafter referred to as 'Correctional Services Directions'); S 191. (1) Children's Amendment Act 41 of 2007).

5 See, for example, section 35(2) of the Constitution:

Everyone who is detained, including every sentenced prisoner, has the right – (a) to be informed promptly of the reason for being detained; (b) to choose, and to consult with, a legal practitioner, and to be informed of this right promptly; (c). to have a legal practitioner assigned to the detained person by the state and at state expense, if substantial injustice would otherwise result, and to be informed of this right promptly; (d) to challenge the lawfulness of the detention in person before a court and, if the detention is unlawful, to be released; (e) to conditions of detention that are consistent with human dignity, including at least exercise and the provision, at state expense, of adequate accommodation, nutrition, reading material and medical treatment; and (f) to communicate with, and be visited by, that person's (1) spouse or partner; (2) next of kin; (3) chosen religious counsellor; and (4) chosen medical practitioner.

6 Indicative of this is the murder rate at an estimated 36/100 000 of the population in 2020 (N = 21,325), which is significantly down from 63/100,000 of the population in 1995 (ISS Crime Hub https://issafrica.org/crimehub/facts-and-figures/national-crime; Macrotrends website https://www.macrotrends.net/countries/ZAF/south-africa/murder-homicide-rate).

7 Criminal Law Amendment Act 105 of 1997. Criminal Law (Sentencing) Amendment Act 38 of 2007.

8 *S v Makwanyane and Another* (CCT3/94) [1995] ZACC 3; 1995 (6) BCLR 665; 1995 (3) SA 391; [1996] 2 CHRLD 164; 1995 (2) SACR 1.

9 DCS (2020) *Annual Report 2019/20*: 84.

10 Rwanda (511/100 000); Seychelles (345/100,000); Cape Verde (Cabo Verde) (296/100,000); Namibia (295/100,000) and Swaziland/eSwatini (278/100,000). *World Prison Brief*, Accessed 16 November 2020.

11 DCS (2020) *Annual Report 2019/20*: 44.

12 DCS B-Orders, Order 2, Chapter 2, Section 2.1.

13 Chapters 9–10, Correctional Services Act 111 of 1998.

14 Military Ombud Act 4 of 2012. The defence force has its own disciplinary code and procedure as is commonly the practice across the world. There are also two military prisons for defence force employees convicted and sentenced accordingly under the Military Discipline Code.

15 National Health Amendment Act 12 of 2013. The Health Ombudsman oversees the public health care system which would include places where people are admitted as involuntary health care system users, such as psychiatric patients, criminal suspects sent for observation to determine if they are fit to stand trial and people admitted to a so-called TB hospital for treatment of MDR-TB and XDR-TB.

16 Section 99 (1–3) Correctional Services Act 111 of 1998.

17 *Presentation: Department of Correctional Services: Standard Operating Procedures for Preparedness, Detection and Response to COVID-19,* see PMG, 2020a.

18 'COVID-19: Health minister announces SA in second wave', *eNCA*, 9 December 2020, https://www.enca.com/news/covid-19-health-minister-announces-sa-second-wave; "Don't blame South Africa for UK second wave, Mkhize warns" *BusinessTech*, 25 December 2020, https://businesstech.co.za/news/trending/458262/dont-blame-south-africa-for-uk-second-wave-mkhize-warns/

19 Regulation 41(a), Directions issued in terms of Regulation 27(2) of the Regulations under the Disaster Management Act (2002), *Government Gazette*, No. 44044 on 29 December 2020.

20 Para 8, *Lee v Minister of Correctional Services* (CCT 20/12) [2012] ZACC 30; 2013 (2) BCLR 129 (CC); 2013 (2) SA 144 (CC); 2013 (1) SACR 213 (CC) (11 December 2012).

21 Correspondence with JICS, 10 December 2020, on file with author.

22 *JICS Quarterly Report 2019/20 Q4 & 2020/21 Q1*; PMG, 2020b.

23 On previous occasions, this has been referred to as an 'amnesty' or 'remission' and has been applied to particular categories of prisoners, such as women and children.

24 S 82(1) Correctional Services Act. With this should be read the power of the President, afforded by the Constitution (s 84(2)(j)), to pardon or reprieve any offender and remitting any fines, penalties or forfeitures.

25 DCS (2020) *Annual Report 2019/20*: 13. Press statement: *Minister Ronald Lamola: Special Coronavirus COVID-19 parole dispensation statement*, 8 May 2020, https://www.gov.za/speeches/minister-ronald-lamola-special-covid19-parole-dispensation-statement-8-may-2020-0000.

26 Domestic Violence Act (116 of 1998).

27 S 286 A of the Criminal Procedure Act (51 of 1977).

28 Mental Health Act (Act 17 of 2002); Press statement: *Minister Ronald Lamola: Special Coronavirus COVID-19 parole dispensation statement*, 8 May 2020, https://www.gov.za/speeches/minister-ronald-lamola-special-covid19-parole-dispensation-statement-8-may-2020-0000.

29 The minimum non-parole period can range from one sixth of the term of imprisonment to 25 years, since all sentenced prisoners must be considered for parole after serving 25 years regardless of the sentence length imposed. As a rule of thumb, for the majority of prisoners, this will be one half of the sentence. There are, however, numerous variations and exceptions.

30 "Outcry over number of prisoners released since parole announcement" *IOL*, 10 Jul 2020, https://www.iol.co.za/mercury/news/outcry-over-number-of-prisoners-released-since-parole-announcement-50801321.

31 "Bedrieër kry 6 maande na vonnis parool," *Die Burger*, 15 August 2020, [Copy on file with author] (Transl. Fraudster gets parole six months after being sentenced] "Andile Lungisa released from prison", *IOL*, 1 December 2020, https://www.iol.co.za/news/andile-lungisa-released-from-prison--53eeac28–6094-4ffd-af9e-1786f449bc6a.

32 "This submission by the applicant is not correct. As mentioned above, the purpose of the proclamation was to reduce the prison population in order to lessen practical difficulties experienced by the DCS in their efforts to prevent, combat and generally manage the Covid-19 disease. The decision to identify sentenced offenders who are low-risk offenders and who have served the bulk of their sentences was, in my view, a reasonable and rational approach, and the manner in which it was done was not arbitrary or irrational." "Prisoner with chronic illnesses loses bid to be released on 'Covid-19 parole'" *TimesLive*, 3 September 2020, https://www.timeslive.co.za/news/south-africa/2020–09-03-prisoner-with-chronic-illnesses-loses-bid-to-be-released-on-covid-19-parole/.

33 "Special justice team to scrutinise system after parolees linked to serious crimes" *IOL* 24 February 2020, https://www.iol.co.za/capetimes/news/special-justice-team-to-scrutinise-system-after-parolees-linked-to-serious-crimes-43347432; MPs raise concerns over parolees who commit serious crimes, *EWN*, 13 March 2020, https://ewn.co.za/2020/03/13/mps-raise-concerns-over-released-prisoners-who-commit-serious-crimes#.

34 S 276-276A Criminal Procedure Act and S 58–70 Criminal Procedure Act (51 of 1977).

35 Most of the deviations from the rule of thumb concern cases sentenced before October 2004 when the new parole regime was promulgated.

36 For example, on 10 December 1990, 30,179 prisoners were released in an amnesty of seasonal goodwill; on 30 April 1991, a six-month amnesty and one-third amnesty for first offenders on 1 July 1991 saw the release of 25,467 and prisoners, respectively [Final Report of the Commission of Inquiry into unrest in prisons (1995) (*Kriegler Commission*: 72].

37 Regulations issued in terms of section 27(2) of the Disaster Management Act, 2002, *Government Gazette*, 18 March 2020, No. 43107.

38 Regulation 11 B, Regulations issued in terms of section 27(2) of the Disaster Management Act, 2002, *Government Gazette*, 25 March 2020, No. 43148.

39 Annexure B, Section B, paras 16 and 18, Regulations issued in terms of section 27(2) of the Disaster Management Act, 2002, *Government Gazette*, 25 March 2020, No. 43148.

40 Regulation 31, Disaster Management Act 2002, Regulations issued in terms of section 27(2) of the Disaster Management Act 2002, *Government Gazette*, 29 April 2020, No, 43258. The police may only arrest persons for violating the following general provisions in the Regulations:

- A person who convenes a gathering, except a funeral in accordance with the Regulations;
- A person who hinders, interferes with or obstructs an enforcement officer in the exercise of his or her powers in terms of the Regulations;
- A person who is not confined to his or her residence, except where a person is performing a permitted service;
- A person who is not confined to his or her residence during 20H00 until 05H00, except where a person has been granted a permit to perform an essential service;
- A person who visits any public place or amenity that is prohibited during the lockdown;
- Any person who violates the Regulations on the sale, dispensing or transportation of liquor;
- Any persons who violate the Regulations on tobacco products, e-cigarettes and related products;
- Any persons who violate the Regulations on the prohibition of evictions;
- Retail stores selling goods not provided for under Table 1 of the Regulations.

41 Regulation 31, Disaster Management Act 2002, Regulations issued in terms of section 27(2) of the Disaster Management Act 2002, *Government Gazette*, 29 April 2020, No, 43258.

42 "To date, 298,252 people have been arrested and charged with contravention of the Disaster Management Act. 181 579 were released on warning to appear before the court. 28 337 of these arrested were found guilty of violations ranging from liquor, gathering, transport business and cross-border related offences. Unfortunately, most of the people arrested will come out with criminal records and it is not our aim to criminalise South Africans." "Almost 300 000 arrested for contravening lockdown regulations: Crime Stats", *SABC News*, 14 August 2020, https://www.sabcnews.com/sabcnews/almost-300-000-arrested-for-contravening-lockdown-regulations-crime-stats/.

43 "South Africa lifts COVID-19 ban on tobacco and alcohol sales" *AfricaNews*, 18 August 2020, https://www.africanews.com/2020/08/18/south-africa-lifts-covid-19-ban-on-tobacco-and-alcohol-sales//.

44 Ellis, E. "Prison riots about cell phones and cigarettes not coronavirus, authorities claim" *Daily Maverick*, 23 April 2020, https://www.dailymaverick.co.za/article/2020–04–23-prison-riots-about-cellphones-and-cigarettes-not-coronavirus-authorities-claim/.

45 Prisons are cashless and prisoners can receive money on their accounts (known as their *Property*) from which they can then transact through the prison shop.

46 "Cigarette ban, court dates behind riot at EC's St Albans prison" *EWN*, 7 May 2020, https://ewn.co.za/2020/05/07/cigarette-ban-court-dates-behind-riot-at-ec-s-st-albans-prison; "'We want cigarettes', say inmates as fire breaks out at St Albans prison", *Sowetan*, 6 May 2020, https://www.sowetanlive.co.za/news/south-africa/2020–05–06-watch-we-want-cigarettes-say-inmates-as-fire-breaks-out-at-st-albans-prison/.

47 These were reported from St Albans, Worcester, Krugersdorp, Leeuwkop and Baviaanspoort.
48 Dir. 2, Directions issued in terms of Regulation 10(2)(a) of the Regulations under the Disaster Management Act (2002), *Government Gazette*, No. 43225.
49 Dir. 3, Directions issued in terms of Regulation 10(2)(a) of the Regulations under the Disaster Management Act (2002), *Government Gazette*, No. 43225.
50 Dir. 1 (a) – (c), Directions issued in terms of Regulation 10(2)(a) of the Regulations under the Disaster Management Act (2002), *Government Gazette*, No. 43225.
51 Dir. 1 (d), Directions issued in terms of Regulation 10(2)(a) of the Regulations under the Disaster Management Act (2002), *Government Gazette*, No. 43225.
52 Regulations 4 (1) and 7 (a) and (b), Disaster Management Act Regulations, 2002, published in GN No. 318 on 18 March 2020, as amended by GN No. 43148 of 25 March 2020, GN No. 43168 of 26 March 2020, GN No. 43199 of 2 April 2020.
53 Dir. 4 (1), Correctional Services Directions.
54 Directions for Alert level 2, issued in terms of regulation 4(2), read with Regulation 58(a) and (b) of the regulations made under the Disaster Management Act, 2002: Measures to address, prevent and combat the spread of COVID-19 in all correctional centres and remand detention facilities in the Republic of South Africa, 4 September 2020, *Government Gazette* No. 43688.
55 S 11 Correctional Services Act.
56 Direction 3(b-c), Department of Correctional Services, Directions issued under Regulation 4(2) of the Regulations under the Disaster Management Act 2002, *Government Gazette*, Vol. 660, 22 June 2020, No. 43463.
S30(1)(c) Correctional Services Act.
57 S 159A(2)(e)(i-ii) Criminal Procedure Act (51 of 1977).
58 Directives issued by the Chief Justice regarding COVID-19 in terms of the Superior Courts Act (2013), General Notice 187 of 2020, Published in *Government Gazette* no. 43117 on 20 March 2020.
59 Cameron, E. "A visit to 'Sun City' prison: Nightmare to manage the virus in confined spaces" *News24*, 14 May 2020, https://www.news24.com/news24/Columnists/GuestColumn/edwin-cameron-a-visit-to-sun-city-prison-nightmare-to-manage-the-virus-in-confined-spaces-20200514.
60 As on 31 March 2020 there were 234 ICCV posts allocated to enable monitoring at the 243 prisons (eights are closed for repairs), and only 21 posts were vacant (Office of the Inspecting Judge (2020) *Annual Report 2019/20*: 74).
61 The DCS is obliged by law to report to the IJ all cases of prisoner deaths, segregation, mechanical restraints and use of force: S 15(2), 30(6), 31(3)(d) and 32(6) Correctional Services Act 111 of 1998; see PMG, 2020.

References

European Committee for the Prevention of Torture (2015): *Living Space per Prisoner in Prison Establishments*. CPT Standards, CPT/Inf (2015). Strasbourg: Council of Europe.

Muntingh, L. (2006, revised 2010, 2017): *A Guide to the Rights of Inmates as Described in the Correctional Services Act and Regulations*. Belville: ACJR Research Report, https://acjr.org.za/resource-centre/prisonersrights_text_jan2018-with-cover.pdf.

Muntingh, L. (2020): Africa, Prisons and COVID-19. *Journal of Human Rights Practice*, huaa031, https://doi.org/10.1093/jhuman/huaa031.

PMG (2020): Report on the Meeting of the Portfolio Committee on Justice and Correctional Services, 28 February 2020, See presentation 'Judicial Inspectorate: Business Operation Model', https://pmg.org.za/committee-meeting/29920/.

PMG (2020a): Report on the Joint Meeting of the Portfolio Committee on Justice and Correctional Services and the Standing Committee on Security and Justice (Measures Taken by Department to Deal with COVID-19), 28 April 2020, https://pmg.org.za/committee-meeting/30118/.

PMG (2020b): Report on the Meeting of the Portfolio Committee on Justice and Correctional Services, *JICS Quarterly Report* 2019/20 Q4 & 2020/21 Q1, 7 October 2020, https://pmg.org.za/committee-meeting/31140/.

UN-SPT (2020): Subcommittee on Prevention of Torture and Other Cruel, Inhuman or Degrading Treatment or Punishment. *Advice of the Subcommittee on Prevention of Torture to States Parties and National Preventive Mechanisms relating to the Coronavirus Pandemic*. CAT/OP/10.

van Zyl Smit, D., and Appleton, C. (2019): *Life Imprisonment – a Global Human Rights Analysis*. Cambridge: Harvard University Press.

WHO-Europe (2020): *Preparedness, Prevention and Control of COVID-19 in Prisons and Other Places of Detention.* https://www.euro.who.int/en/health-topics/health-determinants/prisons-and-health/publications/2020/preparedness,-prevention-and-control-of-covid-19-in-prisons-and-other-places-of-detention,-15-march-2020-

41 Spain[1]

José Cid, Laura Negredo López and Carles Soler

1 Introduction – general situation of the prison system[2]

The evolution of imprisonment in Spain in the democratic period after the Franco regime[3] has been characterised by a progressive adaptation to the three-fold ideal of the European criminal policy: reduction of the use of imprisonment, normalisation of prison life and rehabilitation and reintegration as the main aims of prison sentences (Cid and Andreu, 2017). Regarding the first principle – reduction of the use of imprisonment – Spain has been effective in using imprisonment as a last resort, achieving one of the lowest rates of admission to prison in the EU.[4] However, Spain has not been effective in reducing the duration of imprisonment that is among the highest in the EU[5] and explains the increasing rates of imprisonment until 2010. In the last decade, a combined trend to a reduction of prison admissions with a stabilisation of the length of imprisonment has produced an important decrease of the prison population rates. As shown in Figure 41.1, the rate of imprisonment in 2019 was 125 prisoners per 100,000 inhabitants, a rate moderately high among the EU countries.[6]

Regarding the second principle – normalisation of prison life – the legislation grants inmates a framework of rights and living conditions in line with international conventions. The fulfilment of these standards, according to national and international monitors, in general, is positive. The dialogue between European criminal policy and the Spanish prison administration has been effective in improving of the Spanish penitentiary system (Cid and Andreu, 2017). The latest report of the European Committee for the Prevention of Torture and Inhuman or Degrading Treatment or Punishment (hereafter, CPT) on Spain (CPT, 2020)[7] acknowledges the effort of the Spanish penitentiary administration in meeting their long-standing concerns, such as the reduced number of activities of prisoners in the closed regime, and the careful investigation of accusations of ill-treatment and of the means of physical and chemical containment of inmates who misbehave. The answer of the Spanish Government (2020) shows willingness to follow the recommendations of the CPT. One positive aspect is the high number of inmates in respect or participation units,[8] in which the fulfilment of the principle of

DOI: 10.4324/9781003169178-41

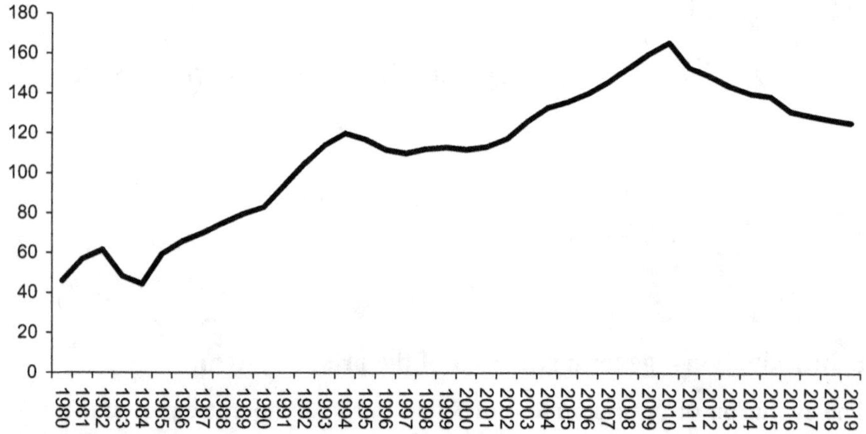

Figure 41.1 Rate of imprisonment in Spain (1980–2019).
Source: Spanish prison administration.

normalisation and the quality of life is higher (Enjuanes, 2020). However, recent research on Catalan prisons reveals that a high number of inmates still assess the prison environment as unsafe (Cid, Pedrosa and Navarro, 2020).

Finally, about the third principle, rehabilitation and reintegration as the aim of prison sentences: the penitentiary system enable prisoners to participate in educational, training, drug-treatment or cognitive-behavioural programmes, such as those for violent or sexual offenders, according to their assessed criminogenic needs (Cid et al., 2020). Moreover, the system provides a resettlement plan to those inmates who progress normally during their prison sentence. The resettlement plan that operates during their period in an open regime or on conditional release provides for a supervision officer who assists prisoners during their transfer to community facilities to deal with rehabilitation or re-entry needs, and to find employment. However, one of the main shortcomings of the Spanish prison system is the high number of inmates released directly from the ordinary regime, without a transitional period in the community (Cid and Ibáñez, 2019). The process of re-entry for these inmates released is harder, as shown by their higher rates of recidivism (Capdevila, 2015).

COVID-19 has had an impact on the application of the three principles in both the two penitentiary administrations in Spain – the Catalan Administration, which deals with the execution of prison sentences in Catalonia, and the General Administration of the State, which deals with the execution of prison sentences in the rest of Spain. As we will see below, the prison population has decreased due to the reduction of prison admissions during the pandemic. The principle of normalisation has suffered due to the restrictions both in the contact of inmates with the outside world and in activities inside prison. The principle of rehabilitation has been restricted to the extent that many rehabilitation activities have been suspended or limited during the most critical moments of the pandemic. Finally, the principle of resettlement has been transformed, replacing open prisons by virtual prisons. However, some measures to moderate the negative impact on the last two principles (normalisation and resettlement) have been adopted by the prison administration.

All the measures adopted by the prison administration were aimed at preventing the spread of the disease among inmates and staff. From a health point of view, the data summarised in Table 41.1 indicate that the policy has been successful and the spread of the virus among the prison population has been contained. The key factor in the success of the Spanish prison administrations was the adoption of measures to contain the spread of the virus from the first day on which the Government declared the state of emergency.[9]

Table 41.1 COVID-19 infections. Prison and community in Spain (2020)

	Catalonia		*General administration of the State*		*Spain*		*General population*
	Inmates	*Staff*	*Inmates*	*Staff*	*Inmates*	*Staff*	
N.	8,049	4,590	48,105	24,354	56,506	28,944	47,329,981
N. infected	362	348	722	912	1,084	1,260	1,650,000
% infected	4.5	7.6	1.5	3.7	1.9	4.4	3.5

Note: Infections from March to November 2020. Sources: Spanish Ministry of Health and Spanish Prison Administrations.

2 Prison and penal policy concerning the execution of prison sentences during the COVID-19-induced crisis

COVID-19 has had four main consequences for the execution of prison sentences. First, a reduction in prison admissions and therefore in imprisonment rates. Second, an increase in the use of the open regime. Third, a transfer of prisoners admitted to the open regime to serve their sentence under a home-detention curfew. Fourth, a redefinition of the way of doing the supervision process, both of convicted offenders with a suspended sentence and of prisoners released early. None of these changes is due to legal reforms in the system of execution of prison sentences, which has remained unmodified, but to changes in the application of the law by the judiciary and the prison administration in order to prevent the spread of the pandemic inside prisons.

The first consequence of COVID-19 has been a reduction in prison entries. Although, as shown in Figure 41.2, there is a long trend of reducing prison admissions during the democratic era, the decrease in 2020 was larger than in previous years (a 13.7% reduction of admissions) and produced a 3.7%

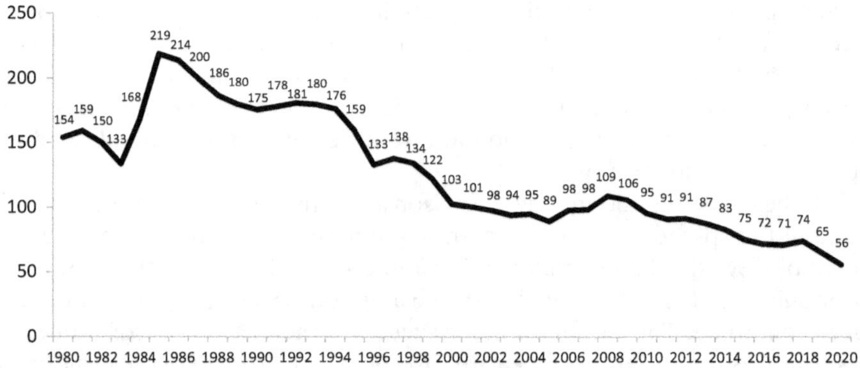

Figure 41.2 Rate of prison admissions in Spain (1980–2020).
Source: Spanish prison administration.

drop of the prison population rate (the average rate of 2020 is 120 prisoners per 100,000 inhabitants). The reasons for this important decrease in prison admissions are two-fold: on the one hand, during the period of restrictions under the state of emergency (March–May 2020), the non-urgent activities of criminal judges and courts were suspended; on the other hand, in 2020, there was a 20% decrease in crime rates.[10] Both factors influenced a reduction of convictions and pre-trial detention during 2020.

The second consequence of COVID-19 has been an increase in the number of prisoners who serve their sentence in the open regime. In Spanish prison law, the open regime is a system of serving a prison sentence granted by the prison administration to sentenced offenders from the start of a prison sentence (as initial classification) or as a progression from the ordinary regime. The open regime is an umbrella concept that includes different modalities of serving a prison sentence. We may distinguish between the institutional modality (in which inmates need to spend the nights of the working days in an open prison or in a communitarian, non-security facility), and the home-detention curfew (in which the inmates need to spend the nights of the working days at home and are electronically or personally monitored). In both modalities, during the day, inmates should be in the community, working or doing other resettlement activities, under the supervision of the prison system. During the weekends, inmates are on leave.[11] Although, as shown in Figure 41.3, there was a moderate tendency to increase the use of the open regime in recent years, the growth in 2020 has been larger (7.7%)[12] and it seems motivated not only by the willingness to reduce the occupancy of ordinary prisons, but also by the belief that some of the prisoners in the ordinary regime had a low risk of reoffending.

The institutional open regime – in which prisoners spend only the night inside the prison – was considered as a risk for spreading the virus, because

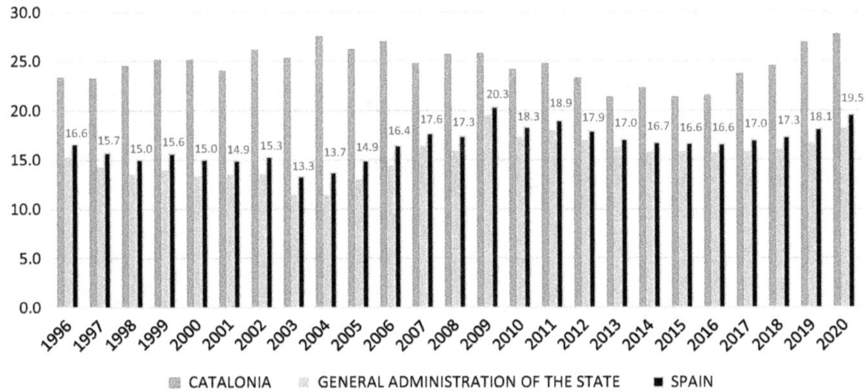

Figure 41.3 Use of open regime in Spain (1996–2020).

Source: Spanish prison administration. Data at 31 December. The percentage is of the sentenced prison population that is classified (91.5% of the total sentenced population, in November 2020).

of the interactions prisoners in open regime may have during the day in the job settlement or in other places. This consideration brought the two prison administrations to develop a third policy consisting of transferring inmates, classified to serve their sentence in an open institution, from institutional facilities to home-detention curfews. As shown in Figures 41.4 and 41.5, this policy was quite radical and made home-detention curfew the usual way in which prisoners admitted to open prisons served their sentences.[13] There was a different policy in the two administrations regarding the supervision of these sentences: in the General Administration of the State, the inmates (97%) were monitored electronically to guarantee that they comply with the home curfew, particularly at night. In Catalonia, electronic monitoring was practically absent (only 6.3% of inmates in home-detention curfew were submitted to EM) and the supervision of the curfew was carried out through different means, such as telephone calls or interviews.

The fourth consequence of COVID-19 in the execution of prison sentences relates to the way in which offenders who are on probation (a suspended prison sentence with probation requirements) or early release (in the open regime or under conditional release) are supervised. The more intense form of supervision was the one given to prisoners released early to the institutional open regime. These inmates should return to the correctional facility every night, when they may have meetings with their supervision officer to assess the progress in their rehabilitation process, but during the day their supervisor may visit them at the location where they should carry out their rehabilitation duties (work or other rehabilitation activities). In the case of conditional release, the supervision was normally less intense, but parolees should visit the parolee centre regularly to have face-to-face meetings with

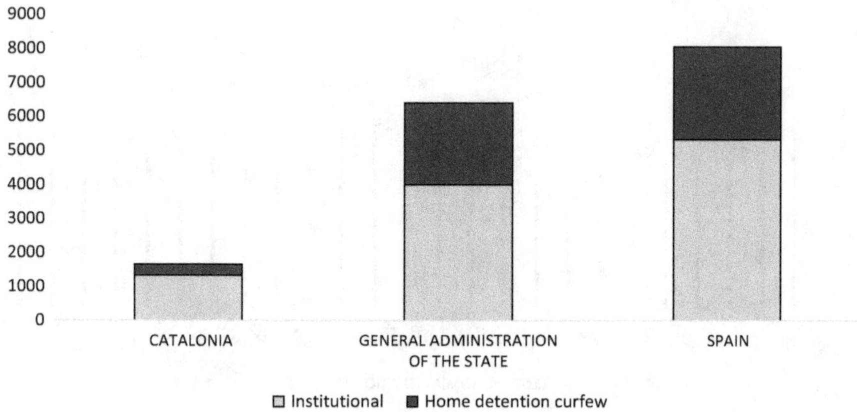

Figure 41.4 Modalities of open regime in Spain (2019).
Source: Spanish prison administration. Data: December 2019.

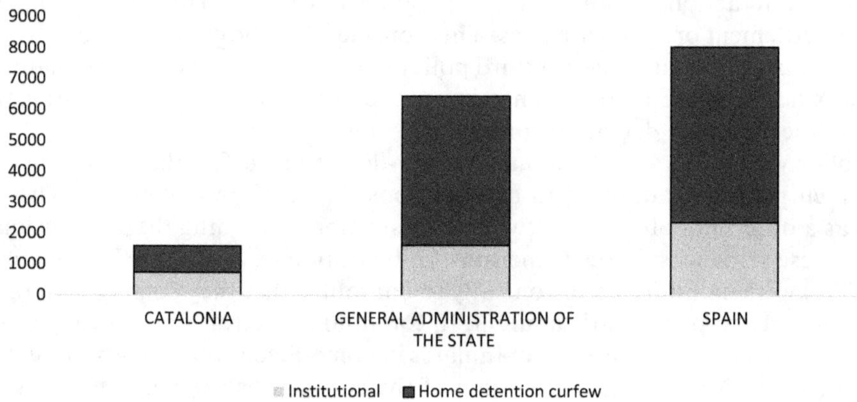

Figure 41.5 Modalities of open regime in Spain (2020).
Source: Spanish prison administration. Data: November 2020 (Catalonia) and October 2020 (General Administration of the State).

their supervision officer. Regarding probation, offenders should normally follow a treatment programme and have face-to-face meetings with their supervision officer. Supervision, in which face-to-face meetings are an essential part, has been completely altered during the pandemic, which has required that people reduce personal interactions. In order to adapt to this situation, two kinds of answers have been given by the prison administrations. On the one hand, face-to-face meetings have been replaced by telephone calls or by videoconferences. On the other hand, in order to replace the treatment programmes, in the General Administration of the State, professionals have been trained to deliver individual or group treatment programmes virtually.

3 Restrictions of contact with the outside world

The pandemic has deeply affected the rights and living conditions of prisoners. The motivation for the restrictions described in this and in the following paragraph has been the prevention of the spread of COVID-19 within correctional facilities. These restrictions have mainly affected the prison population in custodial institutions,[14] which, as shown in Figure 41.6, represents approximately 85% of the imprisoned population.[15]

The two main aspects restricted during the pandemic were visits and leave. Visits and leave are an essential part of the normalisation and humanisation of prison life, but were also considered as a potential risk for spreading the virus inside prisons. As we will see, the restrictions were adopted in accordance with the changes of the evolution of the pandemic and modulated accordingly. Other areas in which there have been restrictions are supervised activities and outdoor work activities.

The Spanish prison law establishes the right of prisoners to receive visits from relatives, friends, volunteers and professionals. The law designs three kinds of visits: normal visits (in which the prisoner and the visitor are separated by a window and they cannot have physical contact); family visits (in which relatives and inmates share a room without the supervision of staff)

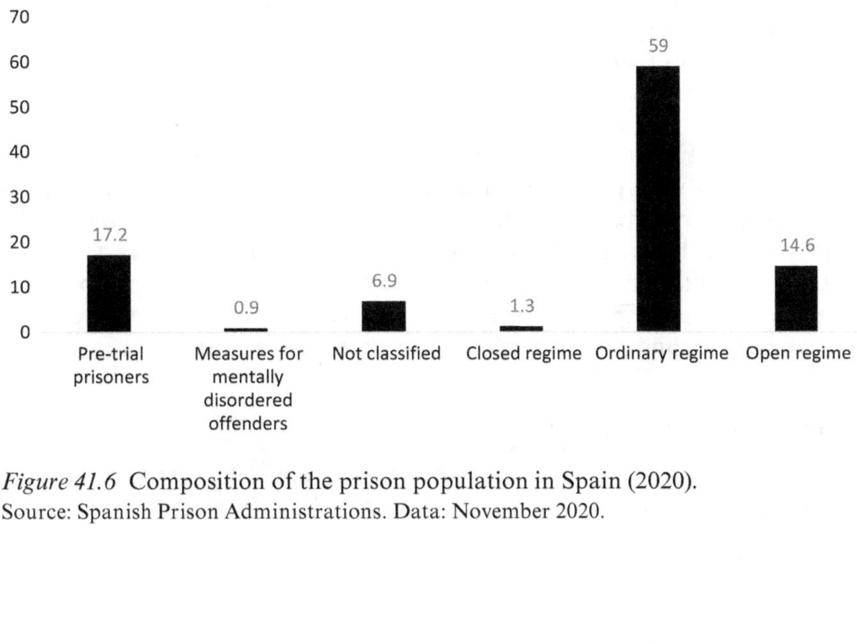

Figure 41.6 Composition of the prison population in Spain (2020).
Source: Spanish Prison Administrations. Data: November 2020.

and conjugal visits (restricted to the partner of the inmate and in which they may have sexual intercourse).

Normal visits have been suspended during the period in which there were general constraints on the Spanish population (between March and May 2020). During this period, only visits of lawyers to pre-trial prisoners were allowed. Once the general constraints ended, normal visits were resumed with limitations in order to reduce the number of visitors in the communication area.

Family and conjugal visits suffered a longer suspension because personal contact between family members and the inmate increases the risk of infection. Only in periods in which the spread of the virus was under control were these visits allowed, however, with reduced numbers and safety measures.

Leave is one of the main elements for the humanisation of imprisonment. In Spanish prison law, there are three types of leave for sentenced prisoners. First, ordinary leave, for prisoners who have served a quarter of their sentence and are not subject to disciplinary sanction. A period of prison leave may last up to seven days with a maximum of 36 days per year for prisoners in the ordinary regime and 42 days for prisoners in the open regime. Second, weekend leave, for prisoners in the open regime. Third, extraordinary leave, for exceptional circumstances such as family deaths and the birth of children. It is controversial whether leave is a prisoner's right or only a benefit in the discretion of the prison administration or the prison judge. The truth probably lies in the middle. Once the prisoner meets the legal conditions and asks for leave, a denial should be based on the risk of further offences or on the risk of absconding (Cid, 1998). In practice, approximately 50% of the prisoners who have served at least a part of their sentence in the ordinary regime benefited from ordinary leave (Cid and Ibañez, 2019).[16] Ordinary leave was also suspended during the period of restrictions (April–May 2020), and after this period were granted or suspended according to the evolution of the pandemic.[17] In the periods where leave was permitted, inmates had to quarantine after the leave.[18] Extraordinary leave and weekend leave for prisoners in the open regime were not changed.

Finally, other measures that allow inmates to have contact with the outside world were also restricted. Supervised exits for rehabilitation, cultural or leisure activities in the community were suspended during the time of restrictions. They were permitted afterwards in the periods in which the pandemic was under control. The same happened with the possibility allowed by the prison law, that prisoners in the ordinary regime may work, or take part in other rehabilitation activities, outside the prison, without supervision. This special regime was suspended during the period of restrictions to avoid contact between inmates and people outside prison, but was permitted afterwards.

4 Restrictions inside prisons

Prison life was also severely affected by the pandemic. The restrictive measures inside prisons had a double aim: to avoid the infection of prisoners by people coming from outside and to prevent infection between inmates and between inmates and prison staff.

One measure adopted from the start of the restrictions was the suspension of the entry into prison of volunteers and members of non-profit organisations. Their cooperation is essential in many leisure and rehabilitation activities in prisons and these were seriously affected. The suspension lasted during the period of restrictions and afterwards was gradually resumed: first for non-profit organisations and later for volunteers. Some limitations due to health reasons, such as a reduced number of groups, remained during the whole period. Moreover, the staff available in prisons was reduced in order to prevent infection, or for COVID-related matters and this affected the development of activities inside prison.[19]

Two main aspects of the prison regime were affected by the pandemic: rehabilitation programmes (education, training, drug-treatment and cognitive-behavioural programmes for different categories of offenders) and prison work programmes. The restrictions impaired the aim of rehabilitation and resettlement, but also the principle of normalisation, because they reduced the social life of the inmates.

Rehabilitation and resettlement are the constitutional aim of prison sentences. Once prisoners acquire the status of sentenced prisoners, they are subject to an assessment by the rehabilitation board of the prison to identify criminogenic needs and social bonds. The reports cover the following main areas: (1) Personal: does the offender present problems of self-control, lack of personal skills and antisocial cognition that may be related to the current offence? (2) Health and addiction: does the offender suffer from mental health problems and/or problems of drug addiction? (3) Family: what is the relationship between the prisoner and their family, in order to check whether the family should be involved in the resettlement process? (4) Education and vocational training: does the offender have deficits in formal education and in vocational training that may be relevant for job settlement? (5) Reparation: does the offender have the obligation to pay compensation to the victim, and what are the possibilities of doing so?

Based on this screening, an "Individualized Treatment Programme" indicates the areas the prisoner should address. For example, if a case of drug dependence is found, it is expected that the person takes part in drug-treatment programmes inside prison (motivation to quit drugs, therapeutic units). In case of personal shortcomings, such us lack of self-control, lack of skill in solving problems or problems in social adjustment, it is expected that the person takes part in specific cognitive-behavioural programmes devoted to increasing self-control, learning social skills and challenging antisocial thinking or antisocial attitudes.[20] In the case of lack of vocational training, the person is expected to take part in a training course to acquire the skills and credentials to facilitate job settlement on re-entry (Cid and Ibáñez, 2019).

The pandemic suspended all group programmes devoted to confronting the criminogenic needs of the offenders. These group programmes were mainly done in closed spaces in the prison and could put inmates and professionals at risk of getting infected by COVID-19. Only after the spread of the pandemic was reduced and prisons were considered safe, were these programmes resumed with a reduced number of inmates. During the period in which the programmes were suspended, the only intervention related to criminogenic needs was individual support or advice by staff members.

Prison labour is an important element of the principle of normalisation. According to the data provided by the prison administration, before COVID-19, 45% of the inmates who served their sentence in an ordinary prison were working. Although the salary received by prisoners is low,[21] it is indisputable that the prison workshops contribute to spending a meaningful time in prison, to provide money for prisoners' expenses and for helping the family.

During the first month of the pandemic, the activity of the workshops in prison was reduced, which had a negative impact on the salaries received by inmates.

5 Compensatory measures

The prison administration has been aware that the restrictions were in conflict with the principle of normalisation and with the aim of promoting the rehabilitation and resettlement of prisoners. Some measures were implemented to moderate the harms produced by these restrictive policies.

All personal contact with families was avoided in the period of restriction. Both administrations made available public mobile phones in order that the inmates could make video calls to the family. However, resources were rather limited and usual phone calls continued to be the normal way of contact with families and friends.[22] The number of phone calls allowed was augmented. Moreover, the Catalan Administration established a telephone number to inform families about the welfare of the inmates and the measures taken during the pandemic.

To help inmates lacking financial means, they were allowed free phone calls and received a modest sum to buy convenience goods (such as tobacco and extra food).

To compensate for the reduction of rehabilitation programmes during the first months of the pandemic (March–May 2020), information was provided to the inmates about the causes of COVID-19 and the prison's policy to prevent the spread of the virus. Individual advice was given to the inmates in order to alleviate their distress.

The restrictions of the contact of inmates with the outside world led to the reduction of the spread of illegal drugs in the ordinary prisons. There was a risk that once contact with the outside word was resumed and illegal drugs were again available in prison, some inmates could overdose. In order to prevent this, the prison administrations developed a prevention programme based on information campaigns and workshops. That seems to have been effective, and cases of overdose were lower than in the previous year.[23] Apart from the data on death by overdose, we considered data on suicide and misbehaviour to assess whether the compensatory measures were effective in order to reduce the distress of the inmates produced by the restrictions in prison life and contact with the external world. Regarding suicide, there was an increase in 2020, comparing with 2019,[24] although it is uncertain whether this is due to the restrictions because the trend towards an increase started already in 2017.[25] Regarding misbehaviour, data from Catalonia show that misbehaviour did not increase in comparison with 2019, although the number of incidents was high if we look at the data of the previous five years.[26] Data on interpersonal violence and violence against staff follow the same pattern.[27] Our conclusion is that, although the restrictions have surely had a negative impact on prisoners' welfare, the compensatory measures have probably prevented a major crisis in the Spanish prison system.

6 Legal basis for the restrictions and relaxations of the prison regime

The restrictions adopted during the pandemic that suspended the main forms of contact between inmates and their families and relatives –visits and leave – were in contradiction with the prison law and required a legal justification. The legal framework for establishing the suspension of these means of contact of prisoners with the external world was the declaration of a state of emergency in Spain on 14 March 2020. A state of emergency is regulated in the Spanish Constitution and allows the temporary suspension of some constitutional rights. In a state of emergency, the constitutional right to free movement on Spanish territory may be suspended. On the basis of the law that declared the state of emergency, the Spanish ministry of the interior suspended visits and leave on 15 March. This suspension was in force until 13 May 2020; then a new decree established that gradually by balancing the protection of public health, ordinary visits and leave could be authorised. The state of emergency ended on 21 June 2020. Afterwards, the restrictions on visits and leave permitted by the prison administration should be based on the protection of health (Law 3/1986, on the protection of public health). On 25 October 2020, a second state of emergency was declared, providing a clearer framework for the restrictions that the prison administration had to adopt.

The policy adopted by the Spanish prison administrations followed the international recommendations on how to deal with the pandemic in the prison system. A first document of the World Health Organization (WHO, 2020) of 15 March 2020 asked governments to implement a policy, by which the protection of the health of the imprisoned population should be balanced with the protection of human rights. The main recommendations of this document were protecting the health of the imprisoned population; reducing the prison population by using alternatives to incarceration and releasing low-risk offenders; and maintaining inmates' contact with the external world. Of course, the balance asked by the WHO was difficult, but we think that the Spanish prison administrations have followed this policy. The restrictions on visits and leave were in operation only in the worst moments of the pandemic, compensatory measures were applied and the prison authorities extended the use of open regime and diverted prisoners from open facilities to home-detention curfew.

During these months of the pandemic, the supervision authorities (prison judges, prison prosecutors, ombudsman) were active and no major issues of violation of human rights due to the pandemic were noted (Defensor del Pueblo, 2020). Neither were incidents of conflict in Spanish prisons observed during 2020.

7 Returning to normal

At the start of this chapter, we noted that the Spanish penitentiary system has progressed during the democratic era by meeting three principles of a humanitarian penal policy: the reduction of the use of imprisonment, the normalisation of prison life and the orientation of prison sentences to rehabilitation and resettlement. COVID-19 had an impact on the three principles. It contributed to a reduction of the use of imprisonment, but it put at stake some aspects of the normalisation principle and changed the way in which rehabilitation officers pursue the aims of rehabilitation and resettlement.

In conclusion, we reflect on the lessons we can extract from the experience of COVID-19 and its impact on the Spanish prison system.

The first lesson regards the impact of COVID-19 on the use of imprisonment. There has been an important reduction in prison admissions (13.7%) but only a 3.7 decrease of the prison population rate. It seems strange that in the context of the pandemic and with the pressure to reduce the prison population, the administration did not foster the use of conditional release. On the contrary, as shown in Figure 41.7, the use of conditional release has continued to decrease, a process that started in 2015.

The reason for this radical reduction in the use of conditional release (50% decrease comparing 2020 with 2014) is due to the penal law reform of 2015 (Law 1/2015), which, instead of limiting the period of conditional release to the remainder of the prison sentence, established a minimum duration of two years under supervision and laid down that, in case of revocation, the time of the sentence on conditional release does not count as time served. This new structure of conditional release has been less attractive for inmates who preferred to end their sentences in the open regime, without being subject to an additional period of at least two years of supervision. The penological consequence has been that the use of early release has been reduced.

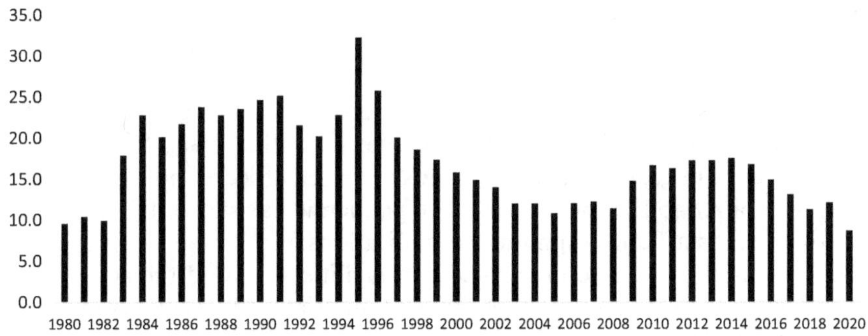

Figure 41.7 Use of conditional release in Spain (1980–2020).

Source. Spanish Prison Administration. Number of conditional releases granted per 100 sentenced prisoners.

From the total population of prisoners and parolees, 28% were in an open regime or on parole in 2015, but only 22.8% in 2020. The lesson is that, if we wish to advance in reducing the use of imprisonment, we need to ease the legal requirements of early release, making it more attractive, in order to motivate inmates to want it.

The second lesson regards the principle of normalisation. One of the measures adopted during the pandemic to compensate for the suspension of visits was the use of video calls. The value of personal visits for the principle of normalisation and for favouring the process of resettlement is clear, but telephone calls have coexisted with personal visits to maintain the social bonds of persons incarcerated. The lesson is that, as video calls that have already been allowed by prison administrations, they and probably other internet services may be incorporated into prison life, thus advancing the achievement of the ideal of normalisation (Redondo et al., 2020).

However, and this is our third lesson, the pandemic has reaffirmed the important role of the way in which prison life was organised before the pandemic. Visits and leave, education, work, training and treatment, and the participation of volunteers and non-profit organisations in prison life, were essential elements for the welfare of inmates. Although the compensatory measures have probably prevented a major crisis, the restrictions have not helped to improve indicators of prison life, such as suicides or misbehaviour. We think that only fully recovering and extending all the traditional elements of the process interrupted by the pandemic will advance the ideal of the normalisation of the prison life.

Our fourth lesson is about the aim of prison sentences to achieve rehabilitation and resettlement. During the pandemic, the open regime changed and prisoners, who before spent the night in institutional facilities, were transferred to their own homes and were subject to home-detention curfews. Of course, we need research to know the effects of this change on recidivism

(Montero, 2020). The question is whether the supervision process needs to be based on spending the nights in the institution or the supervision of prisoners in the open regime may be equally intensive with home-detention curfew.

Our final lesson is about the roles of the personnel in this pandemic. In the culture of prison, we think it is assumed that surveillance and treatment are two different things, the first in the hands of prison officers and the second in the hands of rehabilitation officers. The pandemic has shown the important role treatment staff and community organisations may have in the prevention of conflict and to welfare in correctional facilities. Beyond the activities of prison officers, the involvement of the rehabilitation officers and community actors, in providing information about the disease, giving emotional support, preventing conflict and furthering contacts with families, has probably contributed to preventing a major crisis in Spanish prisons.

Notes

1 José Cid wants to state that his contribution to the research described in this paper has been funded by the Spanish Ministry of Science, Innovation and Universities (Granting reference: DER2017-9052-REDT, Development of an evidence-led criminal policy).
2 Comparisons among EU countries consider only the 24 countries that provided information in Space on rates of imprisonment, prison admissions and length of imprisonment.
3 The Franco regime lasted until 1975. The democratic transition culminated with the new Constitution of 1978.
4 In 2017, the rate of admissions in the EU was 160 admissions per 100,000 inhabitants. The Spanish rate was 71 (Space I, 2018).
5 In 2017, the average duration of imprisonment in the EU was 11.6 months. In Spain, it was 21.7 months (Space I, 2018).
6 In 2019, the rate of imprisonment in the EU was 118 prisoners per 100,000 inhabitants (Space I, 2019). For a detailed analysis of the evolution of the rates of imprisonment in Spain, see Cid (2020).
7 This report was based on a visit to Catalan prisons.
8 Respect units are modules in which inmates are admitted provided they accept the rules of these units. The main rules are the prohibition of violence and the use of drugs. In comparison with ordinary modules, inmates benefit from a higher level of autonomy and more participation in the collective activities within the unit. Participation units are similar, but they do not have strict rules of admission.
9 In order to reflect on the differences between the two administrations, it should be taken into account that in June 2020 the Catalan Administration tested all inmates and staff.
10 Source: Spanish Home Office. Comparison January-September 2020 with the same months of 2019. http://www.interior.gob.es/prensa/balances-e-informes/2020.
11 There is also a restrictive modality of the open regime, in which inmates are accommodated in an ordinary prison or in an open prison and benefit from a weekend leave, but they do not necessarily spend the day in the community or have a more reduced schedule in contact with the community during the working days.

12 3% in Catalonia and 9% in the rest of Spain.
13 In the worst moment of the pandemic (April 2020), the percentage of inmates in open regime that were submitted to home-detention curfew was 88%. In the following months, the use of this regime decreased to a ratio of 53% in November 2020.
14 We use the term "custodial institutions" to include all the imprisoned population – pre-trial prisoners, sentenced prisoners (not classified, closed regime and ordinary regime) and prisoners under preventive measures for mentally disordered offenders – which are accommodated in facilities in which they spend their time and only exceptionally may be in the community (leave and outdoor work).
15 Given the wider use of open regime by the Catalan Administration, the percentage of the population imprisoned in custodial facilities and submitted to the restrictions described in this paragraph is higher in the correctional facilities managed by the General Administration of the State (84.7%) than by the Catalan Administration (80.2%).
16 Cid and Ibañez (2019) provide this data from a research done in Catalan prisons in 2016–2017.
17 During all this time, leaves have continued to be granted, but the execution has been suspended until the moment in which the pandemic evolved positively.
18 In Catalonia this quarantine period has been reduced to three days, doing a PCR test to all inmates that were on leave (this measure was adopted in September 2020).
19 Although the Catalan Penitentiary Administration hired new officers to deal with the problem.
20 Some programmes are classified according the offence and some of the programmes are sex offenders, gender-based violence offenders, hate-crime offenders, white-collar offenders and violent offenders.
21 Sources: 2018 Report of the Prison system, General Administration of the State and 2018 Report of the Ministry of Justice, Catalan Government. According to the latest report, in Catalonia 60% of the prison population in ordinary regimes who are able to work are working (p. 158). According to the same report, the average salary per day is 13 € (prisoners usually work four hours per day).
22 Data of the Catalan Administration record 41,174 video calls between March and June 2020 that correspond approximately to two video calls per month per inmate. Source: Catalan Prison Administration.
23 The number of deaths by overdoses in 2019 were 45 (76.2, per 100,000 inmates) and in 2020 were 33 (58 per 100,000 inmates) (2020 data of the General Administration of the State – 29 deaths by overdoses – is provisional). Source: Spanish Prison Administrations.
24 The number of deaths by suicide in 2109 were 50 (84.7 suicides per 100,000 inmates) and in 2020 have been 61 (107.3 suicides per 100,000 inmates). Data on suicides in 2020 from the General Administration of the State (50 suicides) is provisional. Source: Spanish Prison Administrations.
25 Rates of suicides per 100,000 inmates in the previous years: 2015 (51.3); 2016 (52.6); 2017 (61.7); 2018 (69.1). Source: Spanish Prison Administrations.
26 Cases of misbehaviour submitted to disciplinary procedure in 2020 and in previous years: 2015: 10,408 cases (115 cases per 100 inmates); 2016: 9,704 cases; (111 cases per 100 inmates); 2017: 10,408 cases (121 cases per 100 inmates); 2018: 9,704 cases (115 cases per 100 inmates); 2019: 11,607 cases (137 cases per 100 inmates); 2020: 11,066 cases (138 cases per 100 inmates). Source: Catalan Prison Administration.
27 Number of assaults to staff in 2019 were 225 (2.7 assaults per 100 prisoners) and in 2020 were 218 (2.7 assaults per 100 inmates). Number of assaults to other

inmates in 2019 were 3,182 (35 assaults per 100 prisoners) and in 2020 were 2,884 (35.8 assaults per 100 prisoners). Source: Catalan Prison Administration.

References

Capdevila, M. (coord.) (2015): *Tasa de reincidencia penitenciaria 2014.* Barcelona: Centro de Estudios Jurídicos y Formación Especializada.

Cid, J. (1998). Derecho a la reinserción social (A propósito de la reciente jurisprudencia constitucional en materia de permisos). *Jueces para la democracia* 32, 36–48.

Cid, J. (2020). The future of imprisonment: the Spanish case. In: Drenkhahn, K., et al. (Eds.): *Kriminologie und Kriminalpolitik im Dienste der Menschenwürde: Festschrift für Frieder Dünkel zum 70. Geburtstag.* Mönchengladbach: Forum Verlag Godesberg, 17–38.

Cid, J., and Andreu, A. (2017): European prison policy and Spanish prison Practices: Understanding confluences and gaps. In: Daems T., and Robert, L. (Eds.): *Europe in Prisons.* London: Palgrave-MacMillan, 255–289.

Cid, J., and Ibàñez, A. (2019): Prisoner resettlement in Spain. Good practices for early-released prisoners and prisoners lost in transition that fully serve their sentences. In: Dünkel, F., Pruin, I., Storgaard, A., and Weber, J. (Eds): *Prisoner resettlement in Europe.* London: Routledge, 313–327.

Cid, J., Pedrosa, A., and Navarro, C. (2020): Experiencing imprisonment in Spain. *Criminology-The Online Journal,* 2(2), 139–159. Doi.org10.18716/ojs/krimoj/2020.2.3.

CPT (2020). Report to the Spanish Government on the visit to Spain carried out by the European Committee for the Prevention of Torture and Inhuman or Degrading Treatment or Punishment (CPT) from 6 to 13 September 2018. https://rm.coe.int/16809a5597.

Defensor del pueblo (2020): *Actuaciones ante la pandemia del Covid-19.* https://www.defensordelpueblo.es/wpcontent/uploads/2020/12/Documento_COVID-19.pdf.

Enjuanes, J. (2020): *Hacia la construcción de las bases de un modelo de ejecución penal en base al concepto de ciudadanía activa. Estudio de tres casos en el sistema de ejecución penal español y catalán. (Ph. Dissertation*). https://tesisenred.net/handle/10803/668815#page=1.

Montero, E. (2020): Telematic control and semi-freedom as a response to the pandemic: The Spanish penitentiary system experience. *Victims & Offenders.* DOI: 10.1080/15564886.2020.1819496.

Redondo, S., Gonçalves, R., Nistal, J., Soler, C, Moreira, J., Andrade, J., and Andrés-Pueyo, A. (2020): Corrections and crime in Spain and Portugal during the Covi-19 pandemic: Impact, prevention and lessons for the future. *Victims and Offenders.* DOI: 10.1080/15564886.2020.1827108.

Spanish Government (2020): CPT/Inf (2020) Response of the Spanish Government to the report of the European Committee for the Prevention of Torture and Inhuman or Degrading Treatment or Punishment (CPT)on its visit to Spain from 6 to 13 September 2018. https://rm.coe.int/16809a5253.

World Health Organization (2020): *Preparedness, prevention and control of COVID-19 in prisons and other places of detention. Interim guidance. 15 March 2020.* https://www.euro.who.int/en/health-topics/health-determinants/prisons-and-health/publications/2020/preparedness, -prevention and-control-of-covid-19-in-prisons-and-other-places-of-detention,-15-march-2020-produced-by-whoeurope.

42 Sweden

Lars Håkan Nilsson and Jenny Kärrholm

1 Introduction – general situation of the prison system

The Swedish Prison and Probation Service (SPPS) is the Swedish government agency responsible for all correctional operations in the country, specifically remand prisons, prisons and probation offices. The National Transport Unit is also a part of the agency and responsible for transport within the SPPS and on assignment for other government agencies.

In 2020, on average, almost 7,000 persons were in remand prisons (2,100) or prisons (4,900) on a given day. That is about 68 per 100,000 of the national population. 95% of the prison population is male, but in remand prisons, there is a slightly higher proportion of female inmates. Most of the criminality relates to illegal substances (about 50%) and violent crimes (20%). Violence between rival gangs is on an upward trend, as is illegal possession of weapons. On 21 September 2019, the government introduced 34 new measures to combat gang crime. This resulted in longer prison sentences for certain crimes, which has led to an increasing number of inmates. The SPPS has admitted more than 500 additional prisoners compared to previous years and is therefore facing overcrowding of all prisons.

The Public Health Agency in Sweden has the authority to make recommendations and place restrictions on citizens during a pandemic. They chose an approach to minimising the spread of infection that differs from most other countries. Instead of enforcing strict general lockdowns or quarantines, the Public Health Agency in Sweden provided all Swedish citizens with recommendations to control and minimise the spread of infection, such as proper hand washing procedures, physical distancing, working from home if possible, walking or bicycling to work instead of using public transport, and avoiding crowds. Beyond these recommendations, the Public Health Agency in Sweden put forth measures to facilitate public compliance, including cancelling sporting events, and restricting shows and other gatherings to a limited number of people. Currently, the Public Health Agency in Sweden reports 1,027,934 confirmed cases of COVID-19 (9,900 per 100,000 inhabitants) of which 7,253 have been treated at an intensive care unit and 14,267 (about 140 per 100,000) have died.[1] With the spread of COVID-19

DOI: 10.4324/9781003169178-42

in Sweden, all government agencies prepared for and implemented major changes in day-to-day operations, according to the recommendations of the Public Health Agency in Sweden.[2]

The first case of a COVID-19 infection of a prisoner was confirmed on 30 March 2020. At that time, there was a lack of testing capacity, so no further infection tracing was carried out and other inmates with suspected symptoms could not be tested. To date, the SPPS has had 803 confirmed COVID-19 cases among prisoners and of these 766 have recovered.[3] Fortunately, there have been no deaths among the inmates and only a handful of them were in need of hospital care. The SPPS has no data on the persons on probation because they are covered by the general health care system.

During the spring of 2020, most of the COVID-19 cases were derived from a few local outbreaks in the areas with a high rate of infections in the community. Sick leave among employees at the SPPS spiked quickly at the beginning of the pandemic due to the recommendation that anyone with symptoms of infection should stay at home. The sick leave rate became the highest ever recorded within the SPPS, but in April the rate started to decline. From the beginning of summer, sick leave in the SPPS trended towards the lowest ever (4.2% of the total staff). Currently, 5.9% of all staff are on sick leave.[4] According to national law, government agencies are not allowed to register the health status of their staff. Therefore, the SPPS have no perception about how COVID-19 infections spread among the staff apart from anecdotal reports. However, it is obvious that most of the COVID-19 outbreaks in the SPPS were due to infections spreading among staff. However, COVID-19 infections occurred only in a small number of units, and it was only in a few cases that prisoners were verifiably infected by staff members. The SPPS regards testing of staff as essential for the prevention of infections, but such testing has to be done by either the Regional Infection Control Agency or the Occupational Health Care.

To understand the situation within the SPPS, it is necessary to explain how general health care is organised. In Sweden, there are 21 health-care regions responsible for health care. That means, for instance, both material for testing and laboratory analyses should be provided by those health care regions. During spring 2020, there was a general lack of testing kits, sampling stations and capacity for laboratory analysis in the health care regions. Thus, only patients in need of hospital care were tested initially. Testing patients with COVID-19 suspected symptoms was not possible at that time. The consequence was that the spread of infection escalated without control in certain areas during early spring of 2020. In May 2020, the Public Health Agency in Sweden recommended the testing of prisoners and the regional infection protection units started conducting more general testing of inmates with symptoms at prisons. At this time, the testing capacity increased, but it was in August 2020 that it first reached a level at which it was possible to extend it to the whole Swedish population.

2 Prison and penal policy concerning the execution of prison sentences during the COVID-19-induced crisis

While correctional departments in some countries decided to release some of their prisoners due to the pandemic, Sweden did not take any such measures and the SPPS continues to handle the situation with all inmates serving their sentences as ordered by the courts. The strategy was instead to arrange smaller units for inmates at risk. Prisoners at risk were not brought together at certain prisons due to the danger of fatal consequences if there should be an outbreak of COVID-19 in such an institution. There might have been a slightly more lenient assessment of prisoners at risk, giving them the possibility to complete their sentence by electronic monitoring. In addition, inmates at risk have, for a part of their sentence, been transferred to treatment centres for addiction or other psychiatric disorders before release. However, the Legislator had not made any reforms to administrative and penal laws due to the pandemic in Sweden. The SPPS has managed the situation on its own by making adjustments allowed by the existing legislation.

3 Restrictions of contact with the outside world

Visits to pre-trial detainees and sentenced prisoners were unsupervised before the pandemic. The Director General decided early on in March 2020 to cancel all visits to inmates and leave from pre-trial detention and prison. As knowledge about SARS-CoV-2 increased, the SPPS could grant a few requests for prison leave. However, all leave requires staff monitoring to ensure that the prisoners follow the recommendations of physical distancing.

In April 2020, a parliamentary ombudsman investigated the SPPS actions in response to the COVID-19 outbreak and criticised the SPPS for the tight restrictions placed on inmates through the cancellation of visits and prison leave (Påhlsson, 2020). Before the parliamentary ombudsman finished the report, the SPPS decided on 25 June 2020 to start gradually returning to more standard procedures. Preparations were made to be ready for enforcing or cancelling previous restrictions in order to adjust procedures to the general spreading of COVID-19 infections. A decision was made on 1 July 2020 to allow visits in low security prisons from 1 September 2020. The visits were to take place with a protective acrylic glass pane between the visitor and the inmate to mitigate the risk of contagion. There was a discussion on whether it would be possible to have visits by children without such a screen, to make limited physical contact of prisoners with their children possible. Following recommendations from the Public Health Agency in Sweden, visits without a protective panel were allowed for children under the age of 12. During autumn 2020, visits separated by protective panes were allowed also in medium and maximum security prisons. As the second wave of COVID-19 started, visits of prisoners did not have to be restricted further, thanks to the measures taken to reduce the risk of contagion. This was much appreciated by the prisoners and their relatives. However, local restrictions on visits were introduced according to the local contagion level in each municipality. Inmates who tested positive for COVID-19 and then recovered were given the opportunity of physical contact at visits. They can also be granted unattended prison leave. These relaxations are available to prisoners who have recovered from COVID-19 for at least six months after recovery, which is the time limit for immunity as decided by the Public Health Agency in Sweden.

Many units have had weekly information meetings with inmates, a strategy to keep prisoners informed of the situation in society, but also of the different measures taken by the SPPS to keep them safe. By 1 June 2020, prisoners were also provided with general information about COVID-19 in the four most commonly spoken languages in pre-trial detention and prisons (English, Arabic, Spanish and Russian), in addition to Swedish (see Lindström, Ahlstrand and Kärrholm, 2020).

4 Restrictions inside prisons

As soon as the first cluster of infected inmates was confirmed by 1 April 2020, the prisons acted immediately, following the instructions issued by the SPPS national crisis management team. Infected prisoners were isolated, and staff used proper precautionary actions when in contact with them. As mentioned above, testing was only possible in cooperation with the general health care system and very few inmates were tested in order to trace the infection. It was not until the end of May 2020 that the Public Health Agency in Sweden assessed the SPPS to be comparable to residential homes for the elderly, allowing for more widespread testing.

Most inmates arrive at prison from pre-trial detention, but a few arrive on their own and the police bring in a few more. Knowing about the asymptomatic spread of COVID-19, new inmates were placed in isolation until the prison nurse had made an assessment. The procedure is now to test new inmates and keep them isolated until the test results return negative. The question of isolation is ultimately a matter for the local prison manager. Within the SPPS, standard practice is to provide all prisoners with their own cells. However, because the prison population in relation to the capacity has continuously reached well over 90% and even over 100% at times since 2019, accommodating two persons per cell has become a strategy to handle the increase of the prison population. Currently, and over the past year, the SPPS has placed two prisoners in one-person cells in some prisons due to overcrowding.

At one medium security prison in the Stockholm area, there was an ongoing spread of infections with continuous outbreaks. The regional infection control unit decided to come to the prison with a sampling station bus offering testing of all inmates. Fifty-three out of 56 prisoners accepted testing and 25 of them tested positive for COVID-19, of which only eight showed current symptoms. The prison was then divided into two parts. One part for those infected, who were allowed to move around the ward, but with the staff using protective equipment, and the other part for those who should be protected. If any of the protected prisoners showed symptoms, they were isolated and tested again.

In a Swedish prison, inmates are obliged to take part in some kind of structured activity. It could be either studying at a learning centre, working at the prison workshop or attending treatment programmes. All activities were maintained during the pandemic, but with fewer participants in each session and keeping physical distance. Access to the gym continued, but only for a few prisoners at a time. Outdoor exercise on the prison premises takes place for at least one hour per day in pre-trial detention and prisons. In remand prisons, prisoners are locked in their cells during the rest of the time, normally due to restrictions imposed by the prosecutor. When the restrictions are lifted, they can be transferred to a community ward. If such a ward is not available in a remand prison, prisoners can also be transferred to a remand prison with such a community ward.

5 Compensatory measures

The Director General decided to provide prisoners with no-charge phone calls to compensate them for the restriction of visits and prison leave, and to maintain the treatment plans of many prisoners in need of social contacts as part of their rehabilitation.

The no-charge phone call policy has continually been reviewed each month. At the first review of the decision, the SPPS decided to keep providing no-charge phone calls within Sweden, but to charge all international calls at half the normal rate. This decision was made based on a major increase in the costs incurred for international phone calls. Because prisoners may not leave Sweden while on prison leave, and visits from family and friends from other countries are rare, the reduced charge for international calls serves as a form of compensation for the restrictions in place during the pandemic. To compensate for the lack of visits, prisoners with children were allowed to communicate via Skype on tablets from the end of April 2020; this was very much appreciated.

6 Legal basis for restrictions of the prison regime

According to Section 5 of the Communicable Diseases Act (2004: 168), a person with a generally dangerous disease can be isolated due to a decision made by a physician at an infection control unit. The SPPS also has the option of placing prisoners in isolation for a variety of reasons, one of which is to minimise the risk of spreading a disease (Chapter 6, Section 7, Act on Imprisonment 2010). This regulation allowed the SPPS to develop routines to use isolation as a form of quarantine for newly admitted prisoners, as well as prisoners with suspected or confirmed COVID-19 infections. In the Prison Act, it is also stated that prisoners should have access to treatment recommended by a physician, and at the beginning of the pandemic, this was also used as an argument for keeping infected inmates isolated.

The parliamentary ombudsman criticised the SPPS for placing new inmates in isolation until the prison nurse had made an assessment. Currently, and over the past year, the SPPS in some prisons has placed two prisoners in one-person cells due to overcrowding (see above). The parliamentary ombudsman also criticised this routine and pointed to the impossibility to practise physical distancing and minimise spread of infection. The SPPS has never, and never will, allow a prisoner with a suspected or confirmed infection to share a cell with another prisoner. In addition, in order to reduce overcrowding, the SPPS are already building new prisons.

7 Returning to normal

The SPPS, as well as all other parts of Swedish society, was taken by surprise by the impact of the pandemic. There was a general lack of testing kits, protective equipment and possibilities to trace infections. The roles between different actors were also unclear.

In summary, the SPPS took a structured approach to managing the COVID-19 pandemic. The SPPS acted early, taking measures such as

- rapid formation of a national crisis management team,
- competent and compliant staff who managed to minimise the spread of infection even before they had access to adequate and proper protective gear,
- the swift decision to cancel all prison leave and visits,
- the cancellation of the national correctional officer training programmes and lastly
- continuous communication with units, staff and prisoners.

The SPPS received great support from a national crisis management team to help it to adjust the decision-making process to the situation during the most acute phases. The crisis management team was replaced by a smaller group handling the day-to-day COVID-19-related issues in order to support prison managers with updated advice and guidance for infection protection.

The SPPS met many challenges during the pandemic. It became obvious that society in general lacked understanding of how the SPPS operates and under what conditions. It took several months before the Public Health Agency in Sweden acknowledged the SPPS in its recommendations, just to mention an example.

The investigation by the parliamentary ombudsman showed that central judicial instances were not aware of the actual situation, but also that the SPPS as a government agency must operate according to and in line with current laws and regulations and not only focus on infection control. There is still some uncertainty about how the SPPS should act when there is a need for separation of prisoners.

In addition, the shortage of protective equipment globally required creative solutions, such as temporarily producing protective equipment in the prison workshops. The SPPS prepared for many negative reactions from the prison population, but there were relatively few. The SPPS attributes this beneficial outcome to the hard work of correctional officers and other staff as they managed to keep the prison population calm and informed during these challenging circumstances.

Three different stages of the pandemic in Sweden can be distinguished. The first stage was the first wave of the spread of infection, which mainly affected Stockholm and the southwest region of Sweden (the Gothenburg area). The second stage occurred when the spread of infection decreased during the summer of 2020 and the SPPS prepared for visits and prison leave in autumn. The third stage could be set to October, when there was an increase of infection rates again. This is when the second wave of the infection rolled in, with increasing death rates among the population in general and an increase in demand for intensive care at hospitals. In March 2021, a third wave of COVID-19 infections started, mainly due to a mutated virus variant. It seemed to peak in the middle of May 2021 when the spread of infection decreased in some regions.

The COVID-19 pandemic provided the SPPS with an opportunity to learn and prepare not only for future pandemics, but also for other catastrophic events. As the pandemic is not over yet, it is too early to make an evaluation. Even though handling of the pandemic by the SPPS was not perfect, the government agency can take some pride in that, to date, there has been a limited number of infected prisoners, few cases so severe that they needed hospital care, and, most importantly, no deaths due to COVID-19.

It is also too early to foresee the potential long-term impact of the SPPS COVID-19 strategies, especially since the pandemic is still active. However, the experience of handling COVID-19 has given the SPPS insight into future needs of correctional practices. The most important measures to maintain are to securely organise visits to inmates to keep infections out of prisons and to keep up the structured activities, despite the requirements of physical distancing and other restrictions.

The arrival of new antigen tests with high accuracy has given the SPPS the possibility to acquire better test kits, which help to mitigate the spread of the virus. Another insight is the importance of utilising access to video services for meetings and maintaining relationships between prisoners and their children.

Now, as vaccination is available, the SPPS has developed a vaccination plan. Unfortunately, it is not possible for the SPPS to allocate vaccines on its own. The vaccines have to be distributed through the 21 health care regions, which means that the SPPS needs to sign agreements with each one of them, considering that the agreements will differ in both time of delivery and performance. Thus far, two prisons have vaccinated all their inmates, one (60 inmates) by the prison's own medical staff, but the other (about 250 inmates) by hired nurses.

In conclusion, the SPPS has taken successful measures to mitigate the spread of COVID-19, while at the same time trying to operate with minimal disturbance and without radical changes in the day-to-day routine at all prisons, as well as minimising the negative effects for the inmates the SPPS has the duty to care for.

Notes

1 Public Health Agency in Sweden, figures published 12 May 2021 on website. Statistics Sweden, population registered by 31 December 2020 (10,379,295).
2 See Lindström, Ahlstrand and Kärrholm, 2020. The reference to all facts reported until the summer of 2020 can be found in this chapter.
3 Swedish Prison and Probation Service, figures reported 7 May 2021.
4 Swedish Prison and Probation Service, figures reported 7 May 2021.

References

Lindström, M., Ahlstrand, E., and Kärrholm, J. (2020): Sweden's Response to the COVID-19 Outbreak. *Victims & Offenders* 15 (7–8), 1203–1214.

Påhlsson, K. (2020): *Initiativ angående Kriminalvårdens åtgärder med anledning av covid-19 och konsekvenserna för intagna.* Stockholm: Riksdagens Ombudsmän.

43 Switzerland

Melanie Wegel and Jonas Weber

1 Introduction – general situation of the prison system

Just eight weeks passed between the emergence of the first COVID-19 cases in Wuhan, China, and the first reports of prison revolts in northern Italy against restrictions due to the COVID-19 pandemic. On 11 March 2020, a state of emergency was declared in the Swiss canton of Ticino due to the first COVID-19 deaths, and a closure of the border with Italy was discussed. A state of emergency was announced for the whole of Switzerland on 16 March 2020, resulting in border closures, lockdowns and, above all, social distancing measures. These measures were conceived for society as a whole. Recommendations and assistance on how social distancing should be implemented in closed institutions, this being of particular importance for the penal system, were largely lacking.

In Switzerland, which has a population of around 8.8 million people, the penal and correctional system comprised 102 institutions with 6,906 inmates in April 2020, according to the Federal Statistical Office (BfS) 2020. Of these, 1,902 persons were in pre-trial detention, 267 in administrative detention under the Aliens Act, 980 were serving preliminary sentences[1] and 3,592 were serving sentences following final conviction.[2] In addition, in the case of Switzerland, a linguistic distinction between prisons, correctional centres and therapy facilities is important. The prisons, sometimes also referred to as detention centres or regional prisons, are primarily responsible for pre-trial detention and the execution of short prison sentences (see Article 234 Paragraph 1 of the Swiss Code of Criminal Procedure (CH-StPO)). However, prisons often also serve as entry institutions for the execution of longer prison sentences before a transfer to a correctional centre or a therapy facility.

In view of the fact that 72.1% of adult prisoners do not hold Swiss citizenship, the national heterogeneity of the prison population poses major practical challenges to the penal system (BfS 2021). This is particularly due to the fact that the Swiss prison system as a rule applies a progression system (closed institution, open institution, residential custody, residential and occupational custody, conditional release), which gradually prepares

DOI: 10.4324/9781003169178-43

prisoners for re-entry into Swiss society. Progression levels and relaxation are not granted by the prisons, but by the enforcement authorities. This system hardly works for foreign prisoners, as lack of a permanent residence permit in Switzerland is considered to pose a risk of escape, which conflicts with progressions.

This is despite the fact that the structure of the prison system is uniformly governed by Article 75 Paragraph 1 CH-StGB[3] for all prisoners, irrespective of their nationality and subsequent stay in Switzerland: "The execution of sentences must encourage an improvement in the social behaviour of the prison inmates, and in particular their ability to live their lives without offending again. The conditions under which sentences are executed must correspond as far as possible with those of normal life, guarantee the supervision of the prison inmates, counteract the harmful consequences of the deprivation of liberty and take appropriate account of the need to protect the general public, the institution staff and other inmates".[4].

Due to an often-assumed risk of escape, a considerable number of prisoners in Switzerland, despite the progression system, are released directly from a closed institution or deported to their home country without prior relaxations in enforcement (Patzen et al., 2018). Contrary to this practice, in "regular" cases according to the law, prisoners are conditionally released after two thirds of the prison sentence have been served and are supervised by probation officers during a probationary period.

The cantons have the competence and responsibility for legislation and organisation of the prison system, and must provide the institutions necessary in this context (Articles 372 and 377 CH-StGB). Because the smaller cantons in particular are not (any longer) able to individually run appropriate institutions for the various criminal sanctions, the 26 cantons have organised themselves into three penal "concordats".[5] The three concordats are intended to ensure the availability of a sufficient number of adequately differentiated prisons, as well as a largely similar implementation of the prison system and probation service.

The enforcement system in Switzerland is still shaped by federalism, so that practices in the prison system can vary greatly from canton to canton, due to different structures and local circumstances. Not every canton has all forms of enforcement. The cantons therefore cooperate with other cantons. However, progression within a canton that holds all forms of enforcement available is usually less problematic than cross-cantonal progression. Of significance, accordingly, is the geographic distribution of penal institutions across Switzerland, their respective size and function, and the groups of persons for which they are suitable.

1.1 References to research findings

From today's perspective, it is known that the risk of COVID-19 spreading in imprisonment is especially high when the occupancy rates are high and prison cells contain multiple inmates. Saloner et al. (2020) focused on the inmate death rate due to the COVID-19 pandemic; this rate was 5.5 times higher than the general death rate of the US population. The authors show that COVID-19 death rates in prisons also escalated faster than in the general population, although people aged 65 or older and considered to be particularly vulnerable make up a smaller proportion of the prison population.

Another study from the USA (Akiyama, Spaulding and Rich, 2020) finds that prison overcrowding is a major problem, because rules on social distancing are particularly difficult to implement in prisons. In view of this, the authors recommend releasing all inmates with a low risk of recidivism, as well as elderly and infirm inmates. The authors call on the police and courts to suspend, as far as possible, the arrest and conviction of people for minor crimes and offences. Detainees who are infected should at all costs be isolated and separated from the general prison population. Burki (2020) argues that prisons are generally not equipped to deal with the COVID-19 pandemic, as many prisons are overcrowded and prisoners share toilets, bathrooms, sinks and dining rooms. Burki (2020) and Akiyama et al. (2020) reveal the problems that have led to a drastic spread of COVID-19 in prisons. These findings collected in the USA are not of major relevance to the Swiss prison system, since overcrowding occurs only in a few prisons meant mainly for pre-trial detention and sharing of toilets as well as other sanitary facilities is not the rule.

1.2 Empirical basis of the COVID-19 study in the penal system

In Switzerland, there were a total of 102 custodial institutions in 2020 (BfS, 2020). This number varies annually as smaller institutions close or, less frequently, new, usually specialised, institutions are opened. For a quantitative assessment of implemented preventive measures against COVID-19, an online questionnaire has been developed, which addresses the situation before the first lockdown, the implemented preventive measures, as well as the situation after the first wave of the pandemic. As explained above, the Swiss cantons are grouped into three penal concordats. The larger prisons are operated as the so-called concordat facilities. The survey link was sent to all directors of the German-speaking concordat institutions. A total of 25 institutions are thus represented. Also included was one prison from Latin Switzerland with a German-speaking directorate. The total sample accordingly comprises 26 facilities, which together cover around one third of the inmates incarcerated in Switzerland. The response rate was 100% and the result represents the German-speaking concordats. In addition to the standardised survey, qualitative interviews were conducted with prison directors of three cantons of the German-speaking concordats to assess the extent to which practices of confinement and relaxation have been adapted to the COVID-19 pandemic.

1.3 Occupancy rates

Differentiation between the various parts of Switzerland is necessary with regard to occupancy rates. In the 19 cantons of German-speaking Switzerland, occupancy rates were well below 100%. This does not apply to the French-speaking cantons or Ticino, where the largest penal institution, Champ-Dollon, was documented to have an occupancy rate of 159% on 1 March 2020. However, this rate could subsequently be reduced to 118% at the beginning of June 2020 (Wolf, 2020).

Across Switzerland, the average occupancy rate for 2020 was around 93.5%. Compared to the previous year, the occupancy rate in all of Switzerland decreased by 0.4 percentage points (Statista, 2020). Occupancy rates of less than 80% are known for individual prisons in eastern Switzerland. Regarding risk factors associated with the spread of COVID-19 in prison, it can be established that only a few prisons were affected by overcrowding, their occupancy rate being significantly reduced at the onset of the pandemic. This is particularly important because multiple occupancy of cells is standard in some prisons in French- and Italian-speaking Switzerland, but not in German-speaking Switzerland. Of the 26 prison directors interviewed, only one said that overcrowding at the time of the pandemic was a problem. The basic conditions for combating the pandemic can therefore be established as advantageous, i.e. positive in a global comparison.

2 Prison and penal policy concerning the execution of prison sentences during the COVID-19-induced crisis

In accordance with suggestions also by Dünkel and Morgenstern (2020), who emphasise the significance of occupancy rates in dealing with COVID-19, admissions in Switzerland were reduced, even though capacities in custodial institutions in German-speaking Switzerland were not yet exhausted before COVID-19. According to the prison survey, there were no early releases for members of risk groups. Based on Article 86 Paragraph 4 CH-StGB, this would, in principle, be possible already after half of the sentence has been served, if justified by "exceptional personal circumstances", which might be applied to persons belonging to a risk group in times of a pandemic. It is up to the cantonal enforcement authorities to decide whether to suspend custodial sentences after the execution of two thirds of the sentence. The surveyed prisons could therefore only provide information as to whether they were housing inmates for whom early conditional release had been granted, or at least considered.

The clearest reactions to the COVID-19 pandemic were reported for alternative custodial sentences for fine defaulters, although no uniform approach to implementation could be ascertained here, either. In some cantons, written decrees were issued to the detention authorities[6]:

> From now on and until further notice, no alternative prison sentences for fine defaulters will be executed, irrespective of the length of the sentence or imminent statutory limitation of enforcement; this halt of

> execution does not apply to alternative prison sentences which are to be served together with other prison sentences. Telephone enquiries from convicted persons regarding the execution of alternative prison sentences or 'voluntary' serving of such sentences are answered in the negative ...

In other cantons, suspension of the serving of short and alternative prison sentences was agreed on bilaterally between the cantonal administration and prison directorates, justified by the need to build capacity to establish quarantine stations. In the survey, 16 prison directors stated that serving of short and alternative prison sentences had been suspended altogether. Only one director was aware of early releases before two thirds of the prison sentence had been served.

Another way to reduce occupancy in institutions would be to use community-based forms of serving short prison sentences. For prison sentences with an initial or remaining sentence length of up to six months – after deducting the time spent in pre-trial detention – Switzerland provides the option of serving sentences through community work in accordance with Article 79a CH-StGB. For prison sentences of up to 12 months, electronic monitoring is provided as an enforcement alternative (Article 79b CH-StGB). According to the interviewed prison directors, however, these options were not used much more frequently during the COVID-19 period, since the convicted persons failed to meet general requirements (housing; employment or vocational training; ability to cooperate; compliance with sentence schedule).

3–5 Restrictions of contacts with the outside world, inside prisons and compensatory measures

Already before the first lockdown in March 2020, most institutions had purchased – or increased stockpiles of – food, hygiene products, disinfectants, protective clothing and face masks. Signs instructing compliance with minimum distances were affixed, accompanied by markings on the ground to observe social distancing rules. In addition, dispensers for disinfectants were installed at central locations, and internal procedures were adapted. An important point was informing prisoners about preventive measures, this being implemented by all of the 26 institutions surveyed. This was achieved in a variety of ways. The main method of spreading information was by directors of the institutions directly addressing prisoners.

Quarantine stations were set up at most institutions. In some cantons, a certain prison was designated as an entry institution and/or quarantine station and equipped accordingly. In addition, a disused prison was reopened in the canton of Zurich and utilised as an entry quarantine institution. Another relieving factor was the reopening of a custodial institution in autumn 2019 in the canton of Graubünden. Prison leave was temporarily suspended, and visits from outside were halted, at least for a short period. This was done, first, to limit the overall number of persons in the institutions.

Another reason to suspend the visits from outside was to relieve the staff. A visit to an inmate requires the deployment of personnel. Visitors must be searched and accompanied to the visiting areas. Because prisons often had to work with limited staff numbers during the COVID-19 pandemic, work processes could be made more effective by reducing the visits from outside. This also included pastoral care and visits by lawyers and therapists. Second, in spring 2020, it was not possible to test visitors for a possible COVID-19 infection. At most institutions, work by some external employees was also temporarily suspended. In particular, people who work in the field of leisure activities for inmates; however, access for suppliers and craftspeople was largely stopped, too. To compensate for a lack of visits by family and others, video calls were introduced or expanded at 18 institutions, and telephone times were generally extended.

Work at half of the institutions surveyed was temporarily suspended. This was done because social distancing at workplaces could not be guaranteed, and because a short internal quarantine period was imposed. This was necessary to check whether the pandemic had already spread in the prison. Although inmates in Swiss prisons are usually housed in individual cells, they usually have the option to move freely around the units during certain times. These units operate in different workplaces and might thus allow the spreading of COVID-19 infections in a prison. After the brief internal quarantine period, it became possible to resume work if distancing regulations could be observed on the way to work and at the facilities, or if this could be enabled by installing acrylic glass screens. Prisoners belonging to vulnerable groups were free to choose whether they wanted to work, or rather quarantine themselves. Because suspension of work at the institutions was only partial, the daily schedule could be upheld. Care was taken to ensure that only inmates from the same housing units were together during courtyard hours. In general, the problems of a reduced daily schedule were more likely to occur on weekends, when visits were not possible and daily activities were reduced. In particular, it should be noted that there is a duty to work in Swiss prisons. Prisoners who were unable to work at the related facilities during lockdown continued to receive their remuneration. As a further compensation, inmates at some institutions were able to borrow a tablet to play games. Work at closed correctional facilities was also shut down; here, the inmates themselves created a programme consisting of puzzles, tasks and games to structure their daily routine. In prisons where prisoners took their meals together before the COVID-19 pandemic, these were now either taken in the cell, or the number of persons per table in the dining hall was reduced. This, in turn, meant that the staff had to cope with the extra effort needed to deliver food to the cells (Figure 43.1).

The figure shows that not all institutions have implemented all measures. For example, in some institutions, meals were already taken in the cell before the pandemic, and in a few institutions, the option of video telephony

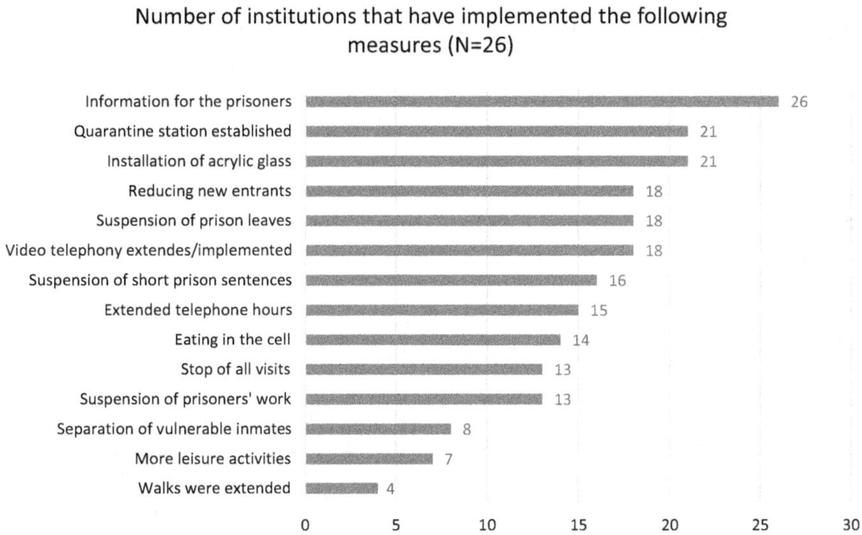

Figure 43.1 Preventive measures implemented by institutions.

was already available before the pandemic. The suspension of work was not necessary everywhere and also lasted for different time spans. Similarly, a quarantine station did not have to be set up in all institutions. For example, in the canton of Bern, one facility was set up as a quarantine station for several prisons, and in the canton of Zurich, a former prison that had been shut down years ago, was put back into operation to function as a quarantine station. The infrastructural conditions posed a special challenge to implementing social distancing measures. At facilities dating back to as far as the 19th century, it was often not possible to enforce distancing regulations, whereas the corridors at more recent facilities were built in a way that a distance of two metres between prisoners could be maintained. 17 of 26 prison directors stated in the survey that infrastructural conditions considerably hampered an implementation of social distancing measures. Hence, the way institutions implemented the preventive measures most significantly depends on the architecture and layout of the different institutions, and on occupancy levels.

Nevertheless, there are no significant negative correlations with the implementation of the measures. This means that despite considerable difficulties, all necessary measures were implemented. Two different strategies became apparent from the survey, however: For some of the directors, it was particularly important to implement all possible measures to pursue a zero-risk strategy. Other directors only implemented the most necessary measures, to allow the inmates' daily schedule to be largely maintained.

6 Legal basis for restrictions and relaxations of the prison regime

The prison system of Switzerland is the responsibility of the cantons. The Swiss penal code contains only a few basic provisions. They include, for example, the general right to contact persons outside institutions, pursuant to Article 84 Paragraph 1 CH-StGB. This provision establishes the right to receive visitors at institutions. In addition, Article 86 Paragraph 6 CH-StGB grants the right to temporary prison leave. These rights are specified in provisions issued by cantons and concordats. Such rights may only be restricted, given a public interest and in line with the principle of proportionality.

A general legal basis for restrictions of prisoners' rights, based on the principle of proportionality, can be found in Article 74 CH-StGB: "Their rights may only be limited to the extent that that is required for the deprivation of their liberty and their co-existence in the penal institution".[7] In addition, various laws allow for restrictions which apply, for example, when the health of the inmates or staff is endangered. The obligation of the prison system to protect prisoners' health is based on the care principle according to Article 75 Paragraph 1 Clause 2 CH-StGB, which requires, inter alia, the implementation of protective measures which could not be taken by prisoners themselves.

A legal basis for restrictions of prisoners' rights in connection with COVID-19 exists in the Swiss Epidemics Act.[8] In view of the spread of the COVID-19 virus, on 28 February 2020, the Swiss Federal Council classified the pandemic situation in Switzerland as special, based on the Epidemics Act. On 13 March 2020, the COVID-19 ordinance 2 entered into force.[9] Article 6 Paragraph 2 provides for the closing of publicly accessible facilities. Article 6 Paragraph 3 regulates exceptions to the closure requirement, among others, for public administration (Article 6 Paragraph 3 lit. j). The explanatory notes[10] on the ordinance state, inter alia, that custodial institutions are covered by this exception.[11] In this context, the adherence to the relevant guidelines of international organisations, i.e. the World Health Organization (WHO) and the Council of Europe, is recommended to reduce the risk of contagion.[12]

The cantons were responsible for implementing COVID-19 ordinance 2. Via their own regulations or simple governmental resolutions, for example, they prohibited visits to prison facilities temporarily until 30 April 2020. This usually did not include visits by lawyers, for example, though these must take place separated by an (acrylic) glass screen. To maintain relations with the outside world, increased access to telephones and the distribution of telephone cards was meant to have a compensatory effect.[13]

Cantonal regulations are implemented by the cantonal agencies of the judiciary who, in turn, delegate certain decisions to individual institutions. The prisons mostly report that inmates supported the COVID-19 restrictions. Those who objected were entitled to request an individual order, against which an objection could be raised with the institution's directorate. This decision can, in turn, be passed via the internal administration to the ministry. Against this decision, an appeal to the administrative court is possible, and finally an appeal in criminal matters to the Swiss Federal Court. An Ombudsman to whom prisoners may turn and who may then seek a compromise with the institution is not yet available in the Swiss prison system.

7 Returning to normal and conclusions

Under the direction of the federal government, social distancing measures for society were relaxed until autumn 2020. From the beginning of the second wave in autumn 2020, the preventive measures, shutdowns and social distancing rules varied from canton to canton. The timing of relaxation measures at institutions, however, turned out to be problematic (Figure 43.2).

Visits were allowed again for most prisons from mid-May 2020; at some institutions, (acrylic) glass screens had already made this possible before that date. Visits making use of such screens turned out to be especially complicated if children visited a detained parent and the social distancing

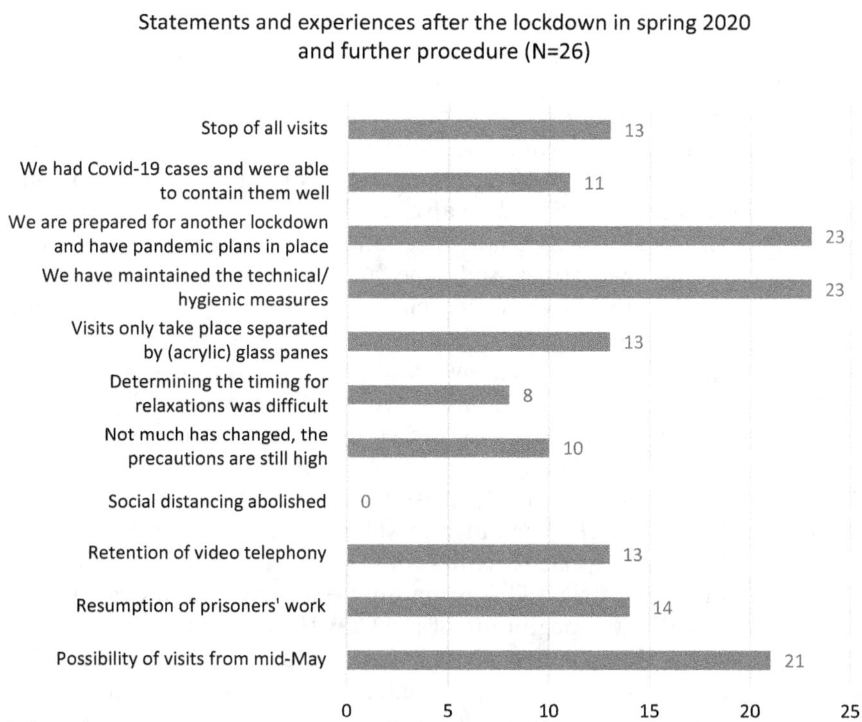

Figure 43.2 Statements and experiences after the lockdown in spring 2020.

regulations still in force could hardly be complied with or were difficult to monitor.

Only some of the institutions still provide the option of video calls. Yet, those institutions which considered video calls as useful also mainly agreed to retain this medium (.667*).[14] The working conditions for prisoners at 14 institutions, from May 2020 onwards, almost corresponded to those before the lockdown. Most importantly, social distancing instructions were maintained at all institutions; furthermore, after the first cases of positively tested COVID-19 inmates after the lockdown in spring 2020, the wearing of face masks was additionally ordered and is still being maintained at most institutions to date (April 2021). There were cases of COVID-19 infections among people at 11 institutions, but they were treated well. In principle, it can be said that the pandemic was properly managed in the spring of 2020, although the lockdown was considered a challenging period due to staff shortages and significant extra work. Most directors answered in the survey that they were confident that they would be able to cope well with a next wave, especially because of their previous experience, pandemic plans and technical equipment for social distancing. For different scenarios of the pandemic, instructions for action and preventive measures were, for example, developed, in the pandemic plans, taking into account staff shortages and longer confinement times due to the pandemic. Innovative measures to compensate for staff shortages turned out to be a special factor for success, e.g. allowing airport police personnel to act as assistants in one canton, or short-term employment of students of social work and also social workers who returned from sabbaticals and journeys to other countries were employed during the first wave of the pandemic in spring 2020 to compensate for prison staff shortfalls. The data also show a perception by the directors that employees were strongly challenged, and inmates became increasingly restless as the lockdown progressed. One factor certainly seen as an advantage during the first lockdown in March 2020 was the expectation of being able to achieve a reduction in infection rates as temperatures increased, thus bringing an end to the lockdown and promising a return to a kind of normality at the beginning of summer. Currently, in April 2021, custodial institutions find themselves in a lockdown again; or in other words, some institutions never turned back to normal after the first wave in spring 2020. Despite this, the institutions of the prison system in Switzerland have been able to handle the COVID-19 pandemic well.

COVID-19 has had less far-reaching consequences in the Swiss prison system than in other countries. This is mainly because only a few institutions were overcrowded at the beginning of the COVID-19 pandemic, and single cells in prisons are the rule. Especially in regional prisons where, in addition to pre-trial detention, short prison sentences are mainly served, occupancy rates had to be reduced. Even at institutions with low occupancy rates, these were further reduced to convert the few cells with double occupancy into single cells, create room for quarantine stations and keep the number of prisoners low. This reduction in occupancy was mainly achieved by a halt to the serving of alternative custodial sentences for fine defaulters.

Within the institutions, COVID-19 had a particular impact on contact with the outside world. Reception of visitors at institutions and prison leave were temporarily suspended. Instead, many prisons established different options for video calls within a very short period of time; these have been used actively by the prisoners. Foreign prisoners who did not receive visits previously, because their relatives live in distant countries and do not have the financial means to travel to Switzerland, could also benefit from this. The measures adopted were well received by the inmates, at least according to the directors. The prisoners were mainly concerned for their families outside prison. One factor influencing acceptance of measures was the media. Reports about non-incarcerated people not adhering to social distancing measures were met with incomprehension by the inmates. At the same time, the need to implement measures against COVID-19 was also made clear via the media.

All in all, Switzerland's prison system has mastered the COVID-19 pandemic well, especially during the lockdown in spring 2020. However, it must be stressed that achieving this placed a considerably higher workload on staff, and some efforts were also required by the inmates themselves. Only a few infections occurred in Swiss prisons. What must be hoped now is that the innovations introduced for contacts with the outside world in view of COVID-19, especially video calls, will outlast the pandemic and become a new standard. The COVID-19 pandemic would thus provide an outcome which has long been desired, especially by foreign prisoners, and which undoubtedly promotes attainment of the aim of resocialisation.

Notes

1 Serving a preliminary sentence is the option of transfer from pre-trial detention to a penal institution before the sentence is final. The preliminary serving of a sentence is ordered by the director of proceedings at the request of the person concerned. The reasons for such a request are usually the 23-hour cell confinement and the lack of work and leisure opportunities in pre-trial detention. Because preliminary sentencing is an alternative to pre-trial detention, it is regulated in the Code of Criminal Procedure (Art. 236 CH-StPO).

2 All key figures are based on data of the Swiss Federal Statistical Office see BSF, 2018a and 2018b. Online at: https://www.bfs.admin.ch/bfs/de/home/statistiken/kriminalitaet-strafrecht/justizvollzug.assetdetail.12667350.html

3 Swiss Penal Code, SR 311.0.

4 Translation taken from https://www.fedlex.admin.ch/eli/cc/54/757_781_799/en (last retrieved on 12 April 2021).

5 Penal concordats of eastern Switzerland, northwestern and central Switzerland, as well as Latin Switzerland.

6 The decree is available to authors, but only reproduced in part without naming the canton for confidentiality reasons.

7 Translation taken from https://www.fedlex.admin.ch/eli/cc/54/757_781_799/en (last retrieved on 12 April 2021).

8 Federal Act dated 28 September 2012 and concerning the control of communicable human diseases (Epidemics Act, EpG), SR 818.101.
9 Ordinance 2 dated 13 March 2020 and concerning measures to control the coronavirus (COVID-19 ordinance 2; SR 818.101.24), replaced in June 2020 with COVID-19 ordinance 3 (SR 818.101.24).
10 Federal Office of Public Health, explanatory notes on ordinance 2 dated 13 March 2020 and concerning the control of coronavirus (COVID-19 ordinance 2), version dated 3 April 2020.
11 Federal Office of Public Health, explanatory notes on COVID-19 ordinance 2, p. 21.
12 Explanations on COVID-19 ordinance 2, p. 23.
13 For instance, decision 300/2020 dated 18th March, 2020 (RRB) by Bern canton council, available at: https://www.rr.be.ch/etc/designs/gr/media.cdwsbinary.RRDOKUMENTE.acq/91583a97545c43cebde2d4a49d9796be-332/6/PDF/2020.SIDGS.253-RRB-D-203508.pdf.
14 Pearson correlation is significant at the 0.01 level (2-sided).

References

Akiyama, M. J., Spaulding, A. C., Rich, J. D. (2020): Flattening the curve for incarcerated populations — Covid-19 in jails and prisons. *The New England Journal of Medicine*. https://www.nejm.org/doi/full/10.1056/NEJMp2005687.

Bundesamt für Statistik (BFS) (2018a): Massnahmenvollzug: Einweisungen nach Art der Massnahme. https://www.bfs.admin.ch/bfs/de/home/statistiken/kriminalitaet-strafrecht/justizvollzug/unterbringung-vollzugsaufenthalt.assetdetail.6686382.html.

Bundesamt für Statistik (BFS) (2018b): Massnahmenvollzug: Mittlerer Insassenbestand nach Art der Massnahme. https://www.bfs.admin.ch/bfs/de/home/statistiken/kataloge-datenbanken/tabellen.assetdetail.6686361.html.

Bundesamt für Statistik (BfS) (2021): Insassenbestand nach Alter, Geschlecht und Nationalität. https://www.bfs.admin.ch/asset/de/je-d-19.04.01.31

Burki, T. (2020): Prisons are "in no way equipped" to deal with Covid-19. https://www.ncbi.nlm.nih.gov/pmc/articles/PMC7252088/.

Dünkel, F., and Morgenstern, C. (2020): Der Einfluss von Covid-19 auf den Strafvollzug und die Strafvollzugspolitik in Deutschland. *Neue Kriminalpolitik* 32, 432–457. DOI: 0934–9200-2020-pp002.

Patzen, H. J., Treuthardt, D., Erismann, M., and Mayer, K. (2018). Die Bewährungshilfe in der Schweiz. *Bewährungshilfe* 65(3), 224–241.

Saloner, B., Parish, K., Ward, J. A., DiLaura, G., and Dolovich, S. (2020): COVID-19 Cases and Deaths in Federal and State Prisons. https://jamanetwork.com/journals/jama/fullarticle/2768249.

Statista (2020): https://de.statista.com/statistik/daten/studie/958268/umfrage/belegungsquote-der-gefaengnisse-in-der-schweiz/#professional.

Wolf, H. (2020): Le Temps March 2020. https://www.letemps.ch/suisse/hans-wolff-faut-prix-empecher-virus-se-propager-champdollon.

44 Turkey

Galma Akdeniz and Idil Aydinoglu

1 Introduction – general situation of the prison system

The prison population of Turkey ballooned from about 50,000[1] in 2000 to about 300,000 before the COVID-19 pandemic.[2] This unprecedented growth resulted in Turkey having one of the highest prison population rates in Europe (Aebi and Tiago, 2019). At the end of 2019, the rate was 351 per 100,000.[3] This dramatic increase in the prison population has been driven by the transformation of the criminal justice approach in Turkey into a neoliberal penal regime that values increased punitiveness (Yıldırım and Kuyucu, 2017: 862) and chooses incarceration as a preferred form of punishment (Korkut et al., 2018). It has been characterised by closures of older and smaller prisons, and construction of large prison complexes in their stead. This trend is continuing at full speed:[4] since 2002, 191 new prisons have opened,[5] and in 2019 alone prisons with space totalling 1.3 million m^2 have been completed (Ministry of Justice, Directorate of Strategy Development, 2020: 44). Finally, the attempted coup in 2016 was followed by a large number of prosecutions and convictions, further contributing to the rise in the prison population, as can be seen in Figure 44.1.

The race to construct, however, has not solved the problem of overcrowding, which is one of the most severe in Europe (Aebi and Tiago, 2020: 9). In January 2019, the prison population in Turkey exceeded the prison capacity by 22% (122 persons per 100 beds). As shown in Figure 44.1, by the end of 2019, excess population reached 33% (133 persons per 100 beds).

In the past, overcrowding in Turkish prisons has usually been dealt with through amnesties and amnesty-like measures (Demirbaş, 2020; Green, 2000). Such stopgap measures usually involve changes in how prison sentences are executed, such as a reduction of the proportion of the sentence that must be served in prison, expansion of the early release options, and introduction of the option to serve a part of the sentence through probation instead of in prison. Historical prison population data suggest that such measures usually provided only temporary relief, and that, in the absence of a more comprehensive penal reform, the prison population always bounced back within just a few years (Akdeniz, Elveriş and Alpan, 2019; Özgenç and

DOI: 10.4324/9781003169178-44

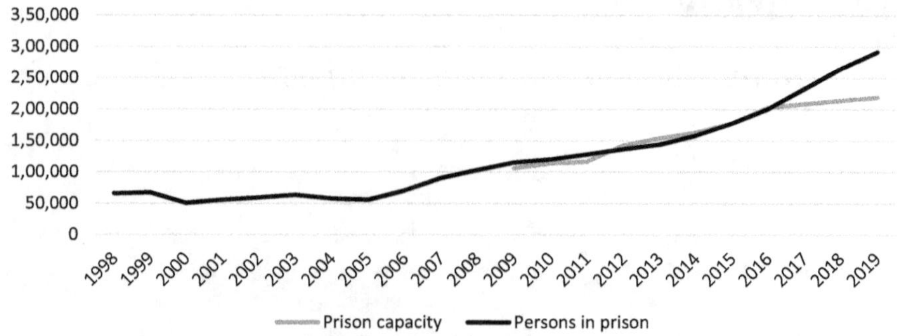

Figure 44.1 Prison population and prison capacity 1998–2019.[6]

Bayraktarlı, 2019). Selective decriminalisation or other types of reform of the Turkish Penal Code by, for example, shortening the prescribed sentence ranges for offences have not been a policy of choice since the current Turkish Penal Code entered into force in 2005. In the absence of a comprehensive approach to the problem of overcrowding, this has and will remain a persistent problem in Turkish prisons.

The majority of the prison population (in 2019, 79%) consists of prisoners serving their sentence.[7] Of 281,605 persons that entered prisons to serve their sentence in 2019, 4% were women and 4.6% were minors (TÜİK, 2020). Fifteen per cent were convicted of theft, 12% of assault, 11% of drug related offences, 5% of robbery, 5% of criminally threatening behaviour, 3.5% of homicide, with those convicted of other offences accounting for smaller percentages (TÜİK, 2020). The Turkish prison population is only slightly younger than the European average, with a median age of 33, and with only 10% above the age of 50 (Aebi and Tiago, 2019).

In Turkey, prisons consist of "cells", which can accommodate different numbers of prisoners (depending on the type of prison, this number can be anywhere from one to 50 persons). While there are large differences in internal architecture, in prisons constructed over the last two decades, each cell is de-facto a complete living space, as each cell has a toilet, a kitchenette area, a sleeping area, and a small walled-in outdoor courtyard. Common areas are limited to workshops, educational spaces, and sport-recreational spaces, and participation in any of the activities that take place in these spaces is not guaranteed to all prisoners.[8] Consequently, many prisoners are spending most, or even all, of their time in their cells with their cellmates in small quarters with limited access to fresh air or exercise. In newly constructed prisons, food provided by the prison administration is brought to each cell by prison staff, and consumed in the cell as well. However, prisoners often resort to purchasing additional food from the prison commissary, due to the insufficient amounts and the low quality of food provided (Ekinci and Eren, 2015/2018).

As a result of overcrowding, most prisons operate at above planned capacity. Inmates sleeping on mattresses on the floor, and even sharing of mattresses have been reported. Insufficient numbers of chairs and tables have also been reported, as well as an insufficient number of toilets (see CPT, 2020).

Basic healthcare is normally provided on site. However, the number of medical staff is often insufficient, and normally medical exams provided upon admission are perfunctory.[9] Access to hot water is problematic, and under normal circumstances inmates are not provided with soap and other hygiene products, but have to purchase them from the prison commissary instead. Many have no access to washing machines for clothes and sheets, and prisoners are allowed limited amounts of clothing (such as only two sets of sleepwear). Cells are meant to be cleaned by inmates themselves, using detergents that they themselves purchase, again from the commissary (Ekinci and Eren, 2015/2018). Maintaining good hygiene and health under these conditions is a challenge even in normal times.

From March 2020 onwards, after the first case of COVID-19 was officially identified in Turkey, prisons had started to provide disinfectant and cleaning supplies in order to improve the hygiene.[10] And from June 2020, the provision, free of charge, of other hygiene products for inmates commenced as well. This practice has not been uniform, as there are reports of such supplies not being offered in some prisons (CISST, 2020a). While the Ministry of Justice claims that prisoners are provided with masks and gloves to be worn when leaving their cells, reports by civil society indicate that this has not always been the case, and that masks in some prisons were not even available for purchase, thus making them completely inaccessible for inmates (CISST, 2020). It should be noted that masks were never made mandatory in the cells for prisoners.[11] Health screenings on admission became more vigilant in March 2020, and starting in May 2020, PCR testing became a part of the prison admission process, with a negative result being a requirement for admission.[12]

The government has not been reporting statistics regularly regarding COVID-19 infections of prisoners and staff members. In April 2020, 120 cases had been reported, in June 2020 72, in November 2020 120, in February 2021 240, and in October 2021 115.[13] Cumulative totals are not available. Reportedly, since be beginning of the pandemic, 18 inmates have died from complications directly related to COVID-19, while 27 inmates died of chronic illnesses.[14] Statistics regarding infections and COVID-19 related deaths among the prison staff were never reported.

The spread of COVID-19 in prisons in Turkey appears to have been held under control. However, the reported statistics should not be taken at face value. It is unclear how accessible testing is to inmates, whether asymptomatic inmates get tested at all, and whether contact tracing is conducted among the inmate population following identification of positive cases. There are reports of inmates who experienced COVID-19 infection-type symptoms having been refused access to testing (CISST, 2020). The Turkish Ministry of Health has been criticised for lack of transparency, as up until November 2020 official COVID-19-related statistics reflected only a number of those diagnosed as "sick" (presumably positive cases with symptoms, but exact criteria have never been made public), rather than all positive cases.[15] Furthermore, other sources of data suggest that all COVID-19-related deaths are not classified as such in Turkey either, and that the number of deaths due to COVID-19 is probably much higher than officially acknowledged (Kisa and Kisa, 2020). As it is unclear what criteria were used in statistics reported by the Ministry of Justice in relation to COVID-19 infections and deaths of inmates, and, given that such statistics are not made public at regular intervals, it is hard to assess their accuracy.

Efforts to prevent, and limit, the spread of coronavirus in prisons in Turkey have focused on two strategies: (a) reduction of prison population, in order to reduce the likelihood of spread of the infection inside the prisons; and (b) limiting contact with the outside world, in order to prevent or delay entry of the virus into the prison population. How those two strategies were implemented is covered in the following pages.

2 Prison and penal policy concerning the execution of prison sentences during the coronavirus crisis

In Turkey, it is difficult to talk about comprehensive penal policy. Rather, since 2005, when the current Turkish Penal Code[16] came into force, the most dramatic penal policy changes consisted of finding ways to shorten the length of the prison sentences, in order to manage the size of the prison population, and the development of diversion mechanisms (such as penal mediation) with the goal of reducing the workload of an overwhelmed court system. In other words, most policy changes have been reactive, rather than proactive, aiming to respond to existing and growing problems in the criminal justice system. As discussed previously, rather than changing the length of the sentences prescribed by the Turkish Penal Code or even decriminalising certain offences, the government has preferred to make changes to how sentences are executed, effectively shortening the portion of sentences that needs to be served in prison and under the supervision of the criminal justice system (Akdeniz, Elveriş and Alpan, 2019). These changes to how sentences are executed have been presented as acts of "compassion", thus allowing the government to continue to claim to be "tough on criminals".

The execution of all types of sentences in Turkey is regulated by the Law on the Execution of Sentences and Penal Sanctions (the Law).[17] This Law regulates how prison sentences are to be executed and administered, including mandatory minimums that need to be served in closed prisons, conditions of transfer from closed to open prisons, conditions of release on probation, and conditional release from probation supervision. The Law specifies how the duration of each of these four steps is calculated, and how transition from one step to another is administered. In effect, the minutiae of this Law determine how much time convicted offenders will spend in a closed prison, in an open prison, under probation, and when eventually they will be conditionally released from supervision.

In 2018, a change to this Law was proposed by the government's alliance partner.[18] The proposal included amendments to reduce the time that needed to be served in prison by five years for a number of offences, which would have resulted in an immediate release of a large proportion of the prison population. However, the threat of a political backlash deterred the government from endorsing the proposal,[19] which halted the political push to pass the legislation at that time. In the fall of 2019, the discussion was revived and a new proposal was to be submitted in early 2020.[20] The COVID-19 pandemic provided a political cloak allowing the government to frame the new proposal to amend the Law as a matter of public health, rather than a matter of penal policy, and it acted quickly. Legislation that would amend the Law on the Execution of Prison Sentences and Penal Sanctions was proposed on 31 March 2020, as "The Law to Amend the Law on the Enforcement of Sentences and Security Measures and Some Other Laws".[21] It was adopted on 14 April, and entered into force one day later. While some of the changes will be applicable to future sentences only, some were intended to produce immediate results.

In order to make it possible to release inmates immediately, a number of changes have been made to how sentences are executed. These changes are applicable to both inmates who were in the process of serving their sentences, as well as to accused persons who were still in the criminal justice process. The process of sentence execution has been altered to make it possible for inmates to move more quickly through the various steps, resulting in immediate release for many, and earlier release for others.

First, the portion of the prison sentence that needs to be served[22] prior to conditional release from probation supervision was decreased from two thirds to half of the sentence imposed by the courts.[23] For repeat offenders, the proportion was decreased from three fourths to two thirds.[24] These changes, however, do not apply to sentences imposed for intentional homicide, aggravated physical injury, torture, sex offences, drug-related offences, offences against state secrecy,[25] as well as offences under the Anti-Terror Law.[26]

Second, the portion of a prison sentence that can be served under probation (instead of in prison) was extended from one to three years for offences committed prior to 30 March 2020, again with the same offences being outside of the scope.[27] For women with young children under six years of age staying with them in prison and for elderly inmates (over the age of 70), the time that could be served under probation instead of in prison was extended from two to four years.[28] For inmates over 65 years of age who could not meet their own needs due to severe health problems, disability, or age, it became possible to serve the full prison sentence under probation. They were also provided with a vaccine against pneumonia as a preventive measure.[29] For minors, how "time served" was calculated was also changed, further shortening the overall time that they needed to spend in prison prior to conditional release.[30]

Further, amendments made it possible for inmates to transfer from closed to open prisons a year earlier than was the case previously, and after serving only a small portion of the sentence in a closed prison.[31] Finally, inmates eligible for such transfers, alongside those already in open prisons as well as those on probation, were released "on leave" until the end of May 2020. Changes in the Law also gave the Ministry of Justice the authority to extend that leave for two months at a time, initially for a total of six more months.[32] Further amendments allowed for the leave to be extended until May 2022, and as of December 2021, the "leave" is still continuing, and will likely continue until the pandemic is declared over.

Consequently, the government made it possible to effectively release a large proportion of prisoners already serving their sentences, but it did so in a rather convoluted way. At the same time, those convicted of the most serious crimes, whose release would lead to a public backlash, and terrorism-related offences, were not affected by the changes made and were not released. However, prisoners continue to be released earlier than they otherwise would have, as they move through the steps of sentence execution and become eligible for transfer to open prison, which effectively means that they get released "on leave".

While changes in the Law that made it possible to release a large portion of the prison population were in fact in the works for more than two years, the pandemic provided a public health justification for what otherwise would have been a politically difficult and unpopular move.

The full impact that these changes have had on the prison population is not completely clear. The General Director of Prisons and Reformation Houses has stated that 90,000 inmates were released from prisons immediately in April, and that an additional 28,000 were released by June 2020.[33] As of October 2021, a total of 88,767 inmates were still reportedly "on leave".[34] Since MOJ stock statistics still count those "on leave" as inside prison (since they have not been officially "released" and their prison sentences are in fact still continuing), it is hard to tell in reality how many persons are physically inside prisons.[35] However, many of those who are currently on leave will never return to prison, since their official serving times will run out before the leave expires. Consequently, the full impact of the legal changes will not be apparent until the end of the COVID-19-related leave.

In February 2021, the Ministry of Justice reported that vaccination against the corona virus had started in prisons on voluntary basis, in line with the National COVID-19 Vaccination Plan.[36] By October 2021, 91,2% of the total prison population had received one vaccine dose, while 80% were vaccinated twice.[37]

3 Restrictions of contact with the outside world

Two days after the first COVID-19 diagnosis was officially announced in Turkey, on 13 March 2020, the Ministry of Justice announced a range of restrictions to be implemented in the prisons, in accord with the recommendations issued by the Coronavirus Scientific Advisory Board and the Ministry of Health,[38] mostly focused on limiting and controlling contact between the inside and outside of prison, in an attempt to prevent contamination from the outside world. Changes were made to the inmate entry process, different types of visits were eliminated or limited, and restrictions on staff were introduced.

3.1 Limits on visits and movement between prisons

Starting in March 2020, all contact between inmates and the outside world was suspended. This included all visits by family[39] as well as lawyers,[40] prison leave (such as in cases of death in close family), non-mandatory transfers of prisoners between prisons, and work outside of the prison. Initial suspension was for two weeks; however, that was later extended. In June, visits by lawyers were allowed again, however, as non-contact visits, and in accordance with the measures set by the Coronavirus Scientific Advisory Board.[41] Starting in June 2020, one non-contact visit a month by one visitor was reinstated and in August this was further increased to two visits per month with two visitors per visit.[42] In September 2020, it became mandatory for all visitors, including foreign nationals,[43] to obtain and submit a tracking code, issued by the Ministry of Health, that allowed for contact tracing in case of an identified infection.[44] No data are available on whether the reinstatement of visits in any way contributed to the spread of infection inside prisons. Additionally, in spring 2020, children staying with their mothers in prisons were removed and placed with their families or close relatives outside.

As of the end of November 2021, one contact visit per month was reinstated, in addition to two non-contact visits per month, each limited to two visitors. Full vaccination, having recovered from COVID-19 within the last three months, or a negative PCR test are mandated for visitors over 6 years of age.[45] Masks are mandatory for all during such visits.

In order to prevent any spread of the virus through infected surfaces, starting in March 2020, all letters, books, and parcels were held for 24 hours before being delivered. Similarly, any personal items brought by visitors were delivered to inmates only after being held for 24 hours.[46]

To reduce the risk posed by crowding in courthouses, all judicial proceedings were suspended in March 2020 by the Council of Judges and Prosecutors.[47] Initially, suspension was until the end of April, but it was extended until the end of June 2020.[48] An exception was made for "urgent and compelling" circumstances, including detention on remand hearings. Such proceedings were to be held via video conferencing to eliminate the need for the transfer of prisoners to court. On 15 June 2020, the suspension ended, and all courts in Turkey opened again to all judicial proceedings. Improved hygiene of vehicles that transfer inmates to and from courts was also among the announced precautionary measures, although it remains unclear whether social distancing rules are being respected during such transfers.[49]

3.2 Entry controls

On March 13, 2020, the Ministry of Justice announced that the prison admission process had been changed in order to prevent entry of potentially positive individuals into prison. At that time, probably due to the lack of availability of tests, the criterion for entry was the absence of symptoms of an infection. Even then, all new inmates were to be held separately from the general prison population for 14 days, to ensure that any asymptomatic or pre-symptomatic cases were also eliminated. Those with symptoms were not allowed entry until after receiving treatment, supposedly in a hospital. How either of those was implemented is not well documented.

Starting in May 2020, PCR tests were introduced into the prison admission process. Inmates receive PCR tests twice: first during the initial admission process, and then again following the 14-day isolation period. During the isolation period, inmates are supposed to be housed in single cells.[50] However, given that many prisons simply do not have sufficient single cells, it is unclear how this is being executed in practice. There have been reports of inmates "quarantining" in 20-person cells, basically eliminating any potential benefit of the quarantine and isolation. Furthermore, in some prisons, inmates transferring from other prisons were held together with newly arrived inmates, thereby combining populations unnecessarily and increasing the risk of potential infection during what should have been an "isolation" period.[51]

3.3 Staff controls

To minimise the risk of spreading infection, starting in April 2020, prison staff began working in shifts, requiring them to isolate for two weeks in arranged accommodation, before coming into contact with the prison population. Following the isolation period, they would work for two weeks, while also staying in provided accommodation without contact with the outside world.[52] In September 2020, however, reports indicated that the procedure had changed, and that staff were requested to isolate at home and get PCR tests 48 hours prior to their working shifts, which were reduced to one week. Further, PPE had become mandatory for the prison staff.[53] In June, pilot tests of digital counting of prisoners via fingerprints were initiated,[54] so that the prison staff no longer needed to enter cells on a daily basis, thereby reducing physical contact between inmates and staff (CISST, 2020a).

4 Restrictions inside prisons

Measures taken inside of prisons were very limited. Starting on 13 March 2020, all activities that require mixing of inmates from different prison blocks, and, as already mentioned, all transfers of inmates between prisons were suspended. Social activities and work in workshops that did not require mixing of inmates from different blocks continued as usual,[55] and in fact prison workshops were used for the production of masks.[56] While the suspension was initially announced for two weeks, it was extended every two weeks until June. In June 2020, mandatory transfers between prisons resumed, however, only for inmates with negative PCR test results.[57]

Use of masks was never made mandatory inside of cells and dormitories, but it was made mandatory in all other areas. No additional information is available on whether any other additional restrictions were introduced inside prisons. However, as social interactions between prisoners are already relatively limited due to the lack of common areas, additional restrictions may have not been seen as necessary.

5 Compensatory measures

Normally inmates have the right to one 10-minute telephone conversation per week, paid for by the inmate. In order to compensate for suspended visits, in March 2020, this was increased to two conversations per week.[58] Towards the end of March, a "Regulation on the Management of Prisons and Execution of Sentences and Penal Measures" was adopted,[59] specifically allowing the Ministry of Justice to increase the number and the length of telephone calls that inmates are allowed during pandemics, allowing further flexibility.

Towards the end of March 2020, the Ministry of Justice announced an initiative to develop infrastructure that would allow for video calls, which was actually being developed as part of the Project of Integration of Smart Technologies in Prisons that was already underway since 2019. Pilot tests of such technology started in October 2020 in two prisons for women.[60]

In June 2020, non-contact visits commenced; however, they were limited to one visit per month with one visitor only, to reduce the crowds. In order to compensate for visits that did not happen over the previous few months, it was announced that additional visits would be allowed. In August 2020, non-contact visits were increased to two visits per month with two visitors per visit.[61] After monthly contact visits were reinstated in November 2021 inmates were given an option of using it instead as an additional non-contact visit.[62]

6 Legal basis for restrictions and relaxations of the prison regime

When it comes to decisions regarding the restrictions (and relaxation) of the prison regime, the authority is fully with the Ministry of Justice, as administratively all prisons are operated by the General Directorate of Prisons and Detention Houses, which is a department within the Ministry of Justice. All rules regarding visits, communication, etc., are regulated through bylaws, which are issued by the Ministry of Justice. In other words, the Ministry of Justice is single-handedly in control of decisions regarding restriction and relaxation of the prison regime.

When decisions regarding the changes in the prison regime were made by the Ministry of Justice during the course of the COVID-19 pandemic, the Ministry announced that they were following the recommendations made by the Coronavirus Scientific Advisory Board (the Board), which was established by the Ministry of Health in January 2020 (Turan and Çelikyay, 2020). The Board is composed of medical professionals and medical scientists. It provides non-binding recommendations, which are then assessed and translated into policy by the relevant Ministries. The status of the Board within the government structure is somewhat unclear. It is not listed among other official boards that operate under the auspices of the Ministry of Health,[63] it does not have a website, nor is it clear who the members are or how they were selected. More troublingly, recommendations made by the Board are not published, nor does the Board issue public statements. In other words, the Board provides recommendations to the Ministries, which then have full discretion to decide if, to what extent, and how to follow and implement those recommendations.

This lack of transparency makes it impossible to assess which of the recommendations of the Board with regard to prisons were adopted, which were ignored, and whether the changes to the regime that have been implemented are in fact those recommended by the Board. In other words, while the Ministry of Justice has full discretion to make changes to the prison regime, it can claim that changes are based on recommendations made by the Board, which is impossible to assess, thereby avoiding any real scrutiny regarding the soundness of the changes proposed or implemented.

As discussed earlier, the reduction of the prison population has been achieved through legislative changes, in particular by amending the Law on the Execution of Sentences and Penal Sanctions. Amendments, on the one hand, shortened the proportion of the sentence that must be served in closed prison by allowing for earlier transfer to open prisons and, on the other hand, allowed for many prisoners to be released "on leave" temporarily.[64] While the length of this leave was initially two months, the Law gives the Ministry of Justice the authority to extend it, based on the recommendation by the Ministry of Health. These two measures combined resulted in a quick and rather drastic reduction in the prison population, and gave the Ministry of Justice the discretion to continue keeping a large proportion of prisoners out.

To summarise, changes made to the prison regime in response to COVID-19 have been channelled either through changes in legislation that shortened sentences to be served in prisons, or through the executive authority that the Ministry of Justice has as the administrator of prisons. Further, legislative changes that were made in the meantime also granted new discretionary powers to the Ministry, such as the authority to extend the duration of "leave" that allowed for the temporary release of some of the prisoners, or the authority to increase the number of telephone calls prisoners were granted to compensate for the lack of visits.

7 Returning to normal

As of early December 2021, in Turkey, about 60% of population (82% of adult population) had received two doses of the vaccine (Ministry of Health, 2021). Given the possibility that the emergence of the Omicron variant will lead to new waves of infections, it is hard to expect that the COVID-19 pandemic will be fully under control any time soon. Hence, we cannot predict what a "return to normal" will look like, when, or even if it will ever take place. Consequently, at this time (December 2021), we have likely not "learned the lessons" yet.

It has become apparent that the COVID-19 pandemic will have a permanent effect on how societies function. In years to come, the COVID-19 pandemic will not be seen as a glitch, but rather as a catalyst and a transformative moment, especially when it comes to the role of technology in the management of everyday lives, from work to education, shopping, and communication. This will likely also translate into prison regimes, as some changes that may have been more difficult to explain and justify under regular circumstances will become more acceptable. This leads us to believe that increased use of technology will become a permanent part of the management of post-pandemic prison life. Such technology will reduce the amount of physical contact between the inmates and the outside world, by making it possible to attend court hearings virtually, conduct "visits" virtually, consult with lawyers virtually, etc. Further, it will also minimise the amount of physical contact between the inmates and the prison staff, by making it possible to count prisoners electronically. It might also create opportunities to deliver better education and training to inmates, through technology-supported learning.

For some prisoners, this may be a positive development, allowing them to communicate more with their families and lawyers, and giving them easier access to medical services and education. Given the size of the country and its prison system, technological solutions could provide some benefits. However, as we have all learned during the pandemic, "virtual" and technology-based solutions are far from perfect replacements of simple live communication and physical contact. There is a danger that once prison administrations become accustomed to technological solutions, managing those activities in real physical mode (rather than virtually) may simply be seen to require too much effort and resources to be justified. Consequently, following the pandemic, we expect prisoners to become even more isolated, with some of physical isolation compensated through technological solutions. Hence, while the COVID-19 pandemic did not trigger the introduction of more technology into prison life, it has demonstrated the need for it. Returning to "normal", however, will not lead to the abandonment of such technologies; rather, it is likely to remain a permanent fixture in Turkish prisons in the future.

It may be argued that the COVID-19 pandemic opened the way to a quick reduction in the prison population in Turkey. As explained earlier, this will be a mischaracterisation of the reality. An existing chronic overcrowding problem demanded that the prison population should somehow be reduced, and preparations were being made for that since 2018. Even without the pandemic, in 2020, the government would have amended the Law on the Execution of Sentences and Penal Sanctions to allow large swathes of the prison population to be released. This was easily foreseen (Akdeniz, Elveriş and Alpan, 2019). However, the way that the Law was amended has cemented the government's ability to amend the Law in the future (if or when the need arises) to again release prisoners. In effect, the Law on the Execution of Sentences and Penal Sanctions has become the law that determines actual sentence lengths, the punitiveness of the criminal justice system, and the extent of the use of probation, thereby replacing the Penal Code as a dominant tool of penal policy. While this development has not been triggered by the pandemic, its effect became clearly visible during the pandemic, but it will likely endure as a policy approach.

Notes

1 The prison population oscillated around 50,000 between the 1970s and 2000.
2 TÜİK, Hükümlü ve tutuklu sayısı (Number of Sentenced and Detained), 1998–2019, https://data.tuik.gov.tr/Kategori/GetKategori?p=adalet-ve-secim-110.
3 TÜİK. (2 November 2020). Ceza İnfaz Kurumu İstatistikleri, 2019. Document no 33625. Ankara: TÜİK. https://data.tuik.gov.tr/Bulten/Index?p=Ceza-Infaz-Kurumu-Istatistikleri-2019-33625#:~:text=Her%20y%C3%BCz%20bin%20ki%C5%9Fiden%20351,2019%20y%C4%B1l%C4%B1nda%20351'e%20ula%C5%9Ft%C4%B1.
4 Between 2000 and 2017, 171 prisons were built, while a large number of small local prisons were closed; see Korkut et al., 2018. In 2016 only, 38 new prisons were put into function, adding a total of 26,572 beds (and averaging 760 per prison); Ministry of Justice, General Directorate of Prisons and Detention Houses (MOJ, GDPDT), 2017. In 2021, the opening of 39 new prisons has been planned (T24, 23.10.2020 https://t24.com.tr/haber/adalet-bakanligi-2021-yilinda-39-yeni-cezaevi-acmayi-planliyor,910866).
5 The Great National Assembly of Turkey, The Plenary of the Assembly Minutes, 27th Legislative term, 3rd Legislative year, 30th session, 11 December 2019 https://www.tbmm.gov.tr/tutanak/donem27/yil3/ham/b03001h.htm.
6 Data in the figure are from the following sources: Persons in prison - TÜİK, Hükümlü ve tutuklu sayısı, 1998–2019, https://data.tuik.gov.tr/Kategori/GetKategori?p=adalet-ve-secim-110; Prison capacity data for 2009–2018 - Eurostat, Prison capacity data for 2019 – Reply from the Ministry of Justice to an inquiry

submitted by Parliament Representative Onursal Adıgüzel https://www.chp.org.tr/haberler/chp-genel-baskan-yardimcisi-adiguzelin-cimer-basvurusuna-yanit-geldi-88-bin-kapasiteli-137-yeni-cezaevi-yolda.

7 Those who have been sentenced and are serving their sentence, even though the appeal process is ongoing, are counted as "sentenced" in Turkish prison statistics. Eurostat, Crime and Criminal Justice Database, Prisoners by legal status of the trial process https://ec.europa.eu/eurostat/web/crime/data/database.

8 Law on the Execution of Sentences and Penal Sanctions (Law No 5275), Art. 87 states that such activities are to be offered to the extent of "means available"; therefore, access to such activities is not designated as a right of an inmate, nor is provision of such access an obligation.

9 One doctor and 5 nurses per more than 2,500 persons have been reported; see CPT, 2020.

10 Ministry of Justice, Office of Press and Public Relations (MOJ, OPPR), Press Statements:18 March 2020; 20 March 2020

11 MOJ, GDPDH, Public Statement: 17 June 2020.

12 MOJ, OPPR, Press Statement: 15 May 2020.

13 MOJ, GDPDH, Public Statements: 28 April 2020; 16 June 2020; 8 November 2020; 18 February 2021; 1 October 2021.

14 MOJ, GDPDH, Public Statement: 1 October 2021.

15 Kozok, F. (1 October 2020): Turkey's Covid Stats Haven't Been Including All Cases For Months. *Bloomberg News*, https://www.bloomberg.com/news/articles/2020-10-01/turkey-s-covid-stats-haven-t-been-including-all-cases-for-months.

16 Türk Ceza Kanunu (Law No: 5237), Adopted on 26/9/2004, Published in Resmi Gazete on 12 October 2004, Vol 25611, https://www.mevzuat.gov.tr/MevzuatMetin/1.5.5237.pdf.

17 Ceza ve Güvenlik Tedbirlerinin İnfazı Hakkında Kanun (Law No 5275) Adopted on 13 December 2004. Published in Resmî Gazete on 29 December 2004, Vol. 25685, https://www.mevzuat.gov.tr/MevzuatMetin/1.5.5275.pdf.

18 Proposed Law on Conditional Reduction of Sentences for Some Offences and Release of the Detained and Prisoners (Bazı Suçlarla İlgili Ceza Sürelerinden Şartlı İndirim ile Tutuklu ve Hükümlülerin Salıverilmesine Dair Kanun Teklifi), 24 September 2018, 2018/2929. https://www.tbmm.gov.tr/develop/owa/tasari_teklif_sd.onerge_bilgileri?kanunlar_sira_no=237862.

19 TGRT Haber (22 October 2018). Cumhurbaşkanı Erdoğan: Cezaevi kapısını rastgele açmayız, https://www.tgrthaber.com.tr/politika/cumhurbaskani-erdogan-cezaevi-kapisini-rastgele-acmayiz-260384.

20 CNN Türk (27 November 2019). Af yasası haberleri. İnfaz rejimi değişikliği Meclis'e ne zaman gelecek? https://www.cnnturk.com/turkiye/af-yasasi-haberleri-infaz-rejimi-degisikligi-meclise-ne-zaman-gelecek.

21 Ceza ve Güvenlik Tedbirlerinin İnfazı Hakkında Kanun ile Bazı Kanunlarda Değişiklik Yapılmasına Dair Kanun (Law No 7242), Adopted on 14 April 2020. Published in Resmî Gazete on 15 April 2020, Vol. 31100. https://www.resmigazete.gov.tr/eskiler/2020/04/20200415-16.htm.

22 "Time served" refers to the total time served in a closed prison, an open prison, and on probation. After the prisoner has completed this part of their sentence, they are released conditionally for the remainder of their sentence. Conditions of release may include different measures and different levels of supervision, as decided by the Sentence Execution Judge, but it may also include no additional supervision. The sentence is considered fully executed and completed only at the end of the conditional release period.

23 Article 48 of the Law No. 7242 amending Article 107 of the Law No. 5275.

24 Article 49 of the Law No. 7242 amending Article 108 of the Law No. 5275.
25 Article 48 of the Law No. 7242 amending Article 107 of the Law No. 5275.
26 Article 65 of the Law No. 7242. Persons convicted by Anti-Terror Law have to serve three quarters of their sentence before being conditionally released.
27 Article 52 of the Law No. 7242 adding the Provisional Clause 6 (1) to the Law No. 5275.
28 Article 52 of the Law No. 7242 adding the Provisional Clause 6 (2) to the Law No. 5275.
29 MOJ, GDPDH, Public Statement: 18 February 2020.
30 Article 52 of the Law No. 7242 adding the Provisional Clause 6 (4) to the Law No. 5275. According to this article, every day spent serving is counted as two days for those aged 15–18, and as three days for those under the age of 15.
31 Article 53 of the Law No. 7242 adding the Provisional Clause 9 (6) to the Law No. 5275.
32 Article 53 of the Law No. 7242 adding the Provisional Clause 9 (5) to the Law No. 5275.
33 The Great National Assembly of Turkey, The Human Rights Inquiry Committee Meeting Minutes, Date: 25 June 2020, 8–9, https://www.tbmm.gov.tr/develop/owa/komisyon_tutanaklari.goruntule?pTutanakId=2555.
34 MOJ, GDPDH, Public Statement: 1 October 2021.
35 Table showing prison population stock statistics published by MOJ (https://cte.adalet.gov.tr/Resimler/Dokuman/istatistik/istatistik-1.pdf) includes a following note "Data above include inmates released on leave due to covid-19 in line with the Law no 7242", which suggest that the reported stock numbers do not reflect physical reality in prisons.
36 MOJ, GDPDH, Public Statement: 18 February 2021.
37 MOJ, GDPDH, Public Statement: 1 October 2021.
38 MOJ, OPPR, Press Statement: 13 March 2020.
39 According to the Bylaw on the Visitation of Convicts and Prisoners on Remand (17 June 2005: https://resmigazete.gov.tr/eskiler/2005/06/20050617-4.htm), under normal circumstances, an inmate serving his sentence has a right to four visits a month, one being vis-a-vis, with up to three visitors, and for a duration of 30–60 minutes each.
40 Non-contact visits and visits by a lawyer continued to be allowed only in compulsory circumstances, and subject to approval by the Public Prosecutor. How "compulsory circumstances" were defined remains unclear.
41 MOJ, GDPDH, Public Statement: 17 June 2020.
42 MOJ, OPPR, Press Statements: 29 May 2020; 11 May 2020.
43 Civil Society in the Penal System Association, "Answer to the Right to Information Request on the right to visit of convicted and on remand prisoners by the Ministry of Justice, 20 November 2020 https://hapisteyabanci.wordpress.com/2020/11/20/tutuklu-ve-hukumlulerin-gorus-haklarina-dair-bilgi-edinme-basvurusu-cevabi/.
44 MOJ, GDPDH, Public Statement: 31 August 2020.
45 MOJ, GDPDH, Public Statement: 29 November 2021.
46 MOJ, OPPR, Press Statements: 16 March 2020; 27 July 2020.
47 Council of Judges and Prosecutors, 30 March 2020 Resolution of General Assembly.
48 Council of Judges and Prosecutors, 30 April 2020 Resolution of General Assembly.
49 MOJ, GDPDH, Public Statement: 27 August 2020.
50 MOJ, OPPR, Press Statement: 15 May 2020.

51 Human Rights Foundation of Turkey. (6 November 2020). Covid-19 Salgınında Mahpusların Tedavi ve Sağlık Hakkı: Ortak Açıklama, https://tihv.org.tr/basin-aciklamalari/covid-19-salgininda-mahpuslarin-tedavi-ve-saglik-hakki/.
52 MOJ, OPPR, Press Statement: 23 April 2020.
53 MOJ, OPPR, Press Statement: 11 September 2020.
54 MOJ, OPPR, Press Statement: 29 May 2020.
55 MOJ, OPPR, Press Statement: 13 March 2020.
56 TRT Haber (24 April 2020). Cezaevlerinde 1 milyonun üzerinde maske üretildi. https://www.trthaber.com/haber/gundem/cezaevlerinde-1-milyonun-uzerinde-maske-uretildi-478861.html.
57 MOJ, GDPDH, Public Statement: 17 June 2020.
58 MOJ, GDPDH, Public Statement: 17 June 2020.
59 Ceza İnfaz Kurumlarının Yönetimi ile Ceza ve Güvenlik Tedbirlerinin İnfazı Hakkında Yönetmelik (Regulation on the Management of Prisons and Execution of Sentences and Penal Measures), Presidential decision date and no: 28 March 2020/2324, Official Gazette 31083, 29 March 2020 Vol. 31083. https://www.mevzuat.gov.tr/MevzuatMetin/21.5.2324.pdf.
60 MOJ, OPPR, Press Statement: 30 March 2020; MOJ, GDPDH, Public Statements: 27 June 2019; 22 October 2029.
61 MOJ, GDPDH, Public Statement: 17 June 2020; MOJ, OPPR, Press Statements: 29 May 2020; 11 May 2020.
62 MOJ, GDPDH, Press Statement: 29 November 2021.
63 Ministry of Health, Boards and Commissions (Sağlık Bakanlığı, Kurul ve Komisyonlar). https://shgm.saglik.gov.tr/TR,46061/kurullar-ve-komisyonlar.html.
64 Law No 5275, Provisional Clause 9/5.

References

Aebi, M. F. and Tiago, M. M. (2019): SPACE I -2019 – Council of Europe Annual Penal Statistics: Prison Populations. Strasbourg: Council of Europe. https://wp.unil.ch/space/files/2020/04/200405_FinalReport_SPACE_I_2019.pdf.

Aebi, M. F. and Tiago, M. M. (2020): Prisons and Prisoners in Europe 2019: Key Findings of the SPACE I report. Strasbourg: Council of Europe. https://wp.unil.ch/space/files/2020/04/Key-Findings-2019_200406.pdf.

Akdeniz, G., Elveriş, İ., and Alpan, A. (2019): Görünen Ceza, Görünmeyen İnfaz: Türkiye'de Ceza ve İnfaz Politikaları Işığında Hükme Riayet. *İstanbul Medipol Üniversitesi Hukuk Fakültesi Dergisi* 6(1), 5–38.

CISST (2020): Hapishanelerden Gelen Koronavirüs (Covid-19) Kaynaklı Şikayetler/ 15–30 Ekim. Istanbul, Turkey: Ceza İnfaz Sisteminde Sivil Toplum Derneği. http://cisst.org.tr/raporlar/hapishanelerden-gelen-koronavirus-covid-19-kaynakli-sikayetler-15-30-ekim/.

CISST (2020a): The Complaints About the Coronavirus (COVID-19) Outbreak Received from Prisons / 15–26 June. Istanbul, Turkey: Ceza İnfaz Sisteminde Sivil Toplum Derneği. http://cisst.org.tr/en/reports/the-complaints-about-the-coronavirus-covid-19-outbreak-received-from-prisons-15-26-june/.

Committee for the Prevention of Torture and Inhuman or Degrading Treatment or Punishment (CPT). (2020): Report to the Turkish Government on the visit to Turkey carried out by the European Committee for the Prevention of Torture and Inhuman or Degrading Treatment or Punishment (CPT) from 6 to 17 May 2019. (CPT/Inf (2020) 24). Council of Europe. https://rm.coe.int/16809f20a1.

Council of Judges and Prosecutors. (2020). Resolutions of General Assembly. https://www.hsk.gov.tr/Arsiv/2020.aspx.

Demirbaş, T. (2020): 7242 Sayılı kanun ve dolaylı af. *Suç ve Ceza* 2, 387–405.

Ekinci, B. and Eren, M. (2015/2018): CİSST Mahpus Hakları El Kitabı. Istanbul, Turkey: Ceza İnfaz Sisteminde Sivil Toplum Derneği. http://cisst.org.tr/wp-content/uploads/2020/07/mahpus_haklari_elkitabi_2018_internet-2.pdf.

Green, P. (2000): Criminal justice and democratisation in Turkey: The paradox of transition (pp. 195–220). In: Grene, P. and Rutherford, A. (Eds.): *Criminal policy in transition.* Hart Publishing (Oñati International Series in Law and Society).

Human Rights Foundation of Turkey (6.11.2020): Covid-19 Salgınında Mahpusların Tedavi ve Sağlık Hakkı. https://tihv.org.tr/basin-aciklamalari/covid-19-salgininda-mahpuslarin-tedavi-ve-saglik-hakki/.

Kisa, S., and Kisa, A. (2020): Under-reporting of COVID-19 cases in Turkey. *The International Journal of Health Planning and Management* 35(5), 1009–1013.

Korkut, B. E., Şekerci, C., Aydınoğlu, İ. Usturumcalı, S. and Engin, Y. (2018): *Prisons of Turkey Report.* European Prison Observatory and Ceza İnfaz Sisteminde Sivil Toplum Derneği. http://cisst.org.tr/wp-content/uploads/2020/07/Prisons-of-Turkey-Report.pdf.

Ministry of Health. (2021). Türkiye Aşı Tablosu. https://covid19asi.saglik.gov.tr/.

Ministry of Justice, Directorate of Strategy Development (2020): *2019 Bakanlık Faaliyet Raporu.* Ankara: Adalet Bakanlığı. https://sgb.adalet.gov.tr/Resimler/Dokuman/16720201409152019%20Y%C4%B1l%C4%B1%20Bakanl%C4%B1k%20Faaliyet%20Raporu.pdf.

Ministry of Justice, General Directorate of Prisons and Detention Houses. (2017): *2016 Yılı Birim Faaliyet Raporu.*

Ministry of Justice, General Directorate of Prisons and Detention Houses. (2020–2021). Public Statements. https://cte.adalet.gov.tr/Home/TumHaberler/1

Ministry of Justice, Office of Press and Public Relations. (2020–2021). Press Statements. https://basin.adalet.gov.tr/Arsiv/manset.

Özgenç, İ, and Bayraktarlı, İ. Y. (2019): İnfaz kurumlardaki hükümlü sayısındaki artış sorunu ve çözüm önerisi. *Ankara Hacı Bayram Veli Üniversitesi Hukuk Fakültesi Dergisi* 23(1), 129–139.

TÜİK (2 November 2020): *Ceza İnfaz Kurumu İstatistikleri, 2019.* Document no 33625. Ankara: TÜİK, https://data.tuik.gov.tr/Bulten/Index?p=Ceza-Infaz-Kurumu-Istatistikleri-2019-33625#:~:text=Her%20y%C3%BCz%20bin%20ki%C5%9Fiden%20351,2019%20y%C4%B1l%C4%B1nda%20351'e%20ula%C5%9Ft%C4%B1.

Turan, A., and Çelikyay, H. H. (2020): Türkiye'de KOVİD-19 ile Mücadele: Politikalar ve Aktörler. *Uluslararası Yönetim Akademisi Dergisi* 3(1), 1–25. https://doi.org/10.33712/mana.733482.

Yıldırım, İ., and Kuyucu, T. (2017): Neoliberal penality and state legitimacy: Politics of amnesty in Turkey during the AKP period. *Law and Society Review* 51(4), 859–894.

45 The US government's response to COVID-19 outbreaks in federal, state, and local corrections

James Byrne, Don Hummer, Sabrina S. Rapisarda, and Kimberly R. Kras

1 Introduction

The United States includes about 5% of the world's population, but as many watchdog groups have pointed out, we house 25% of the world's prison population (Heard, 2020). Unfortunately, we can now add the following grim statistic: the United States has 25% of the world's COVID-19 cases (Nowonty and Piquero, 2020). In the following chapter, we describe the status of federal, state, and local sentencing and corrections just prior to the start of the pandemic, and then provide the statistics on the nature and extent of COVID-19 outbreaks in both institutional and community corrections. We offer our assessment of the root causes of these outbreaks, and then highlight the full range of mitigation strategies employed by federal, state, and local governments to address the problem. We conclude by offering a review of the available evidence on the impact of these mitigation strategies on prisoner and staff health, the size of the US's corrections population, and public safety.

1.1 An overview of sentencing and corrections reforms prior to the start of the pandemic

The United States has the world's largest prison system with over 5,000 adult prisons and jails across the country,[1] housing over 2.1 million inmates in federal prisons, state prisons, and local jails in 2019. These numbers—while staggering—actually represent a decade-long downsizing trend (2009–2019), but the overall prison and jail population totals are still higher than at the start of 2000 (Byrne, Pattavina, and Taxman, 2015; Byrne, 2019). Prior to the start of the pandemic in the United States in early 2020, the country had begun reform efforts designed to reduce prison and jail populations. Reductions in the size of the federal prison population can be linked to the passage of the First Step Act, a major federal reform effort (Byrne, 2019; Hummer, 2020). Reductions in prison populations at the state level can be linked to major sentencing reform efforts that resulted in reduced prison populations in 33 states between 2018 and 2019. According to a recent review by the

DOI: 10.4324/9781003169178-45

Bureau of Justice Statistics, the number of prisoners sentenced to more than one year in a state prison declined in 33 states and the BOP between 2018 and 2019, while 13 states increased their prison populations, and 4 showed no changes (Carson, 2020). Similarly, national jail reform initiatives had significantly reduced the size of local jail populations prior to the start of the pandemic (Zeng, 2020). Between 2008 and mid-year 2018, for example, jail populations declined by 6% (738,400 in 2018 versus 758,500 in 2008).

1.2 The extent of COVID-19 outbreaks in the US prisons and jails

It should come as no surprise that COVID-19 outbreaks are worse in closed prison settings than in the general community. As Nowonty and Piquero (2020: 839) recently observed: "Prisons and jails are designed for security, not public health and health care delivery". According to recent data released by the Marshall Project, as of 4 April 2021, 393,747 inmates in federal and state prisons have tested positive for COVID-19, and 2,655 have died. In addition, 109,308 prison staff have tested positive, and 171 staff members have died. These numbers will continue to rise in the coming months as the virus, in all its variant forms, continues to spread. Overall, one in five inmates has tested positive for COVID-19, compared to one in 20 in the general population of the United States. Even these stark numbers likely undercount the prevalence rates in US prisons, because not all inmates are tested; in fact, state-level variations in the number of tests administered have been documented by the Marshall Project. The death data we report are also underestimates; not all deaths are being attributed to the virus, including deaths that occur after infected inmates are released to the community. In addition, the above state-level testing, infection, and death numbers do not include either the country's jail population,[2] or its community corrections population.

1.2.1 COVID-19 outbreaks in state prisons

Table 45.1 provides a recent snapshot of the extent of COVID-19 outbreaks in state prison systems across the United States (as of 9 April 2021). Significant variation in the number and rate of infections among both inmates and staff is documented here, along with inmate and staff deaths. Among state inmates, the rate of positive tests varied from a low of 680 per 10,000 prisoners in Georgia to a high of 6,425 per 10,000 prisoners in Arkansas. Variation was also documented in the number and rate of death across state prison systems. Not surprisingly, the states with the largest prison systems also had the largest number of inmates and staff members who tested positive for the COVID-19 virus, led by California—the country's largest prison system with 129,920 inmates. In California alone, there have been 49,221 known COVID-19 positive tests among inmates and 16,084 positive tests among staff. However, California was not the state with the highest number

Table 45.1 State-level variation in the extent and impact of COVID-19 outbreaks in US prisons (updated 9 April 2021)[a]

State	*Number of prisoner cases*	*Rate per 10,000 prisoners*	*Number of prisoner deaths*	*Rate per 10,000 prisoners*	*Number of staff cases*	*Number of staff deaths*
Alabama	1,614	1,061	64	30	1,040	3
Alaska*	2,396	5,017	5	10	313	0
Arizona	12,215	2,884	53	13	2,742	1
Arkansas	11,245	6,425	52	30	813	4
California	49,221	4,184	219	19	16,084	26
Colorado	8,820	5,015	29	16	1,639	0
Connecticut*	4,434	3,608	19	15	1,634	0
Delaware*	2,012	3,990	13	26	746	1
Federal	49,324	2,866	243	14	6,773	4
Florida	17,994	1,919	214	23	5,782	7
Georgia	3,739	680	93	17	1,703	4
Hawaii*	1,968	4,069	9	19	225	0
Idaho	4,227	5,408	6	8	472	0
Illinois	10,857	2,940	88	24	4,342	1
Indiana	3,567	1,324	51	19	1,576	4
Iowa	4,839	5, 671	19	22	701	2
Kansas	6,118	6,240	16	16	1,284	6
Kentucky	7,899	6,495	48	39	1,093	5
Louisiana	3,202	2,125	36	24	927	6
Maine	170	786	1	5	59	0
Maryland	4,357	2,145	26	13	2,198	4
Massachusetts	3,095	3,884	21	26	980	0
Michigan	26,156	6,851	140	37	4,039	5
Minnesota	4,072	4,573	12	13	1,826	0
Mississippi	1,464	791	23	13	220	2
Missouri	5,856	2,275	48	19	2,576	6
Montana	1,135	2,518	6	13	282	0
Nebraska	982	1,747	6	11	558	0
Nevada	4,527	3,655	53	43	978	3
New Hampshire	458	1,882	3	12	176	0
New Jersey	4,684	2,540	53	29	2,255	3
New Mexico	2,972	4,511	28	43	951	0
New York	6,404	1,497	35	8	5,029	8
North Carolina	10,007	2,921	53	15	3,812	12
North Dakota	638	4,200	1	67	296	1
Ohio	9,701	1,983	135	28	4,810	10
Oklahoma	7,401	2,966	55	22	1,044	3
Oregon	3,580	2,476	42	29	842	0
Pennsylvania	9,520	2,045	119	26	4,368	6
Rhode Island*	1,202	4,495	2	7	412	1
South Carolina	3,241	1,790	40	22	1,094	2
South Dakota	2,348	6,344	7	19	191	0
Tennessee	6,639	3, 071	42	19	1,501	5
Texas	34,479	2,461	253	18	11,487	45

(Continued)

State	*Number of prisoner cases*	*Rate per 10,000 prisoners*	*Number of prisoner deaths*	*Rate per 10,000 prisoners*	*Number of staff cases*	*Number of staff deaths*
Utah	3,450	5,000	16	23	399	0
Vermont*	457	2,760	–	0	100	0
Virginia	9,028	3,095	56	19	2,511	5
Washington	6,196	3,589	14	8	1,158	2
West Virginia	1,593	2,676	9	15	531	2
Wisconsin	10,931	4,921	26	11	2,519	0
Wyoming	865	3,875	3	13	296	0
TOTAL	**393,747**	–	**2,655**	–	**109,329**	**171**

* An asterisk denotes state counts that include both pre-trial detainees and sentenced prisoners under a unified system of jails and prisons (https://www.themarshallproject.org/2020/07/16/prison-populations-drop-by-100-000-during-pandemic); https://www.prisonpolicy.org/virus/virusresponse.html#state

a The table presents prison data only; no jail information is included. Data within this table compiled from The Marshall Project's "A State-by-State Look at Coronavirus in Prisons" and The COVID Prison Project's "National COVID-19 Statistics" (https://www.themarshallproject.org/2020/05/01/a-state-by-state-look-at-coronavirus-in-prisons & https://covidprisonproject.com/data/national-overview/) as of 4/9/2021

of COVID-19-related inmate deaths; that distinction went to the state of Texas with 253 reported COVID-19-related deaths. Regional variation in rates of infection can be identified, with the Northeastern region of the country reporting the lowest rates of infection nationally; the Southern and Midwestern regions have the highest rates.

1.2.2 COVID-19 outbreaks in the US Bureau of Prisons

The federal US Bureau of Prisons (BOP) houses the largest number of prisoners in the United States with a pre-COVID prison population (as of 1 January 2020) of over 150,000 inmates located in over 120 prisons located across the country (Hummer, 2020). According to the BOP, 49,144 federal inmates have tested positive for COVID-19 and 236 have died from COVID-19 illness as of 23 February 2021. The BOP reported that 6,452 staff members tested positive, with four deaths related to COVID-19, as of 23 February 2021. In the United States, federal prisoners typically transition from prison to the community via residential community corrections centres. The BOP does not run any residential community centres; instead, they contract with a mix of private-for-profit and private non-profit organisations to provide these services. Major service providers include GEO Reentry Services among the private-for-profits, and Dismas Charities and Volunteers of America among the non-profits. There are approximately 170 federal BOP residential centres in operation, with a current population of 6,108 (February 2021).[3] No estimates of the extent of COVID-19 outbreaks in these facilities are available. Similarly, no estimates of the extent of COVID-19 outbreaks among inmates transferred from prison to home confinement are available. The current home confinement population is 7,615 (February 2021). Finally, federal inmates typically transition from prison to residential community centres or home confinement and then to another federal agency, federal probation, which is located administratively in the Administrative Office of the US Courts. The most recent data on the federal probation population is from 2018; in that year, there were 128,200 individuals under federal community supervision (Kaeble and Alper, 2020). We do not know how many individuals currently under federal probation supervision have tested positive for COVID-19, and how many deaths have occurred in this population due to the virus. For this reason, we are certain that the extent of the problem in the federal corrections system is much worse than we report here. How much worse? We simply do not know.

1.2.3 COVID-19 outbreaks in county jails across the United States

The United States has a large jail population. According to the Bureau of Justice Statistics, the mid-year 2018 nationwide jail population was 738,400, with an additional 57,900 persons under jail custody status but placed in programmes in the community, in a variety of programmes, including day reporting centres, drug and alcohol treatment programmes, community work programmes, and home confinement with electronic monitoring. When you factor in turnover and length of stay, the jail population system of the United States cycled through about 11 million admissions and releases in 2018 (Zeng, 2020). Individuals being held in jails across the country include both pre-trial defendants and short-term sentenced offenders. The average length of stay in jail is about three weeks (Zeng, 2020). Unfortunately, there is currently no comprehensive county jail database available to review, so the following estimates on the extent of outbreaks in jails nationally must be viewed as preliminary and incomplete. According to a recent review of a subset of all county jails by Harvey, Taylor and Wang (2020: 5), "Detained populations are thought to have high risk of contracting and spreading COVID-19 due to population density, movement through facilities, and pre-existing health conditions. However, data on the incidence of COVID-19 in jails, and on transmission between jails and communities, are sparse. According to data collected by *The New York Times*, of the nation's 3,162 jails, at least 174, or 5.5%, have experienced COVID-19 clusters of at least 50 cases as of 15 November 2020. Jails with clusters of at least 50 COVID-19 cases are much larger, on average, than the typical jail, with an average facility capacity of 1,151, relative to the average facility capacity of 285. Jails with clusters of at least 50 cases are also located in more urban counties with fewer White, more Black and more Hispanic residents. Beyond this, little is known about COVID-19 incidence in jails".

Both pre-trial detainees and sentenced offenders move into and out of jail at a pace that makes both inmate and staff infections difficult to control

(Collica-Cox and Molina, 2020). Once infected, these same inmates and staff pose a significant risk for spreading the virus, not only in the jail, but also throughout the community upon release/return home. The impact of county jails on the community rates of infection has been documented in recent epidemiological studies (see, for example, Reinhart and Chen's 2020 study of jail releases in Chicago, Illinois).[4]

1.2.4 COVID-19 outbreaks in the US's community corrections system

We need to examine the extent of COVID-19 outbreaks in both crowded and resource-poor prison and jail systems *and* in crowded and resource-poor community corrections systems. Unfortunately, no one currently collects data on the extent of COVID-19 outbreaks in community corrections systems across the United States (Viglione et al., 2020). There are constant reminders in the professional literature and in the media that the United States is a world leader in the rate of incarceration, but there is much less talk about the rate of community correctional control in this country compared to other countries. We know, for example, that the United States has about 5% of the world's population but 25% of the world's prisoners. But what percentage of the global community corrections population is being supervised in the United States? As we have pointed out in a recent review (Byrne et al., 2020), it is currently impossible to answer this question definitively, because no one currently collects data on community corrections populations globally. However, data collected by the newly formed global community corrections initiative (www.globcci.org) suggests that the United States is likely the global leader in this category as well. Focusing on the 50 countries with the largest prison populations, researchers collected data on the size of the community corrections populations in 27 of these 50 countries. They found that over 50% of the known global community corrections population (8 million plus) was in the United States (Byrne et al., 2020). The reason we mention this new statistic here is to make a simple point: we should not be ignoring the extent of the COVID-19 outbreaks in the US's community corrections system, which has a current population of 4.4 million individuals (Kaeble and Alper, 2020). As we discuss later in the chapter, it is assumed by many prison reform advocates that during a pandemic, prisons and jails should utilise community-based alternatives as front-end and back-end mitigation strategies, but how do you justify this strategy without access to basic data on the extent of the outbreak in the community corrections system?

2 The root causes of COVID-19 outbreaks

The authors of this chapter have examined the root causes of COVID-19 outbreaks in corrections systems globally in an earlier review (Byrne et al., 2020). What we identified as the three main causes of these outbreaks globally—overcrowded prisons and jails, inadequate infrastructure, including poor health care systems, and individuals in prisons and jails with pre-existing conditions that made them higher risk for infection, hospitalisation, and death—certainly applies to the US corrections system (Novisky et al., 2020; Nowonty and Piquero, 2020; Rapisarda et al., 2020; Wetzel and Davis, 2020).

2.1 The impact of prison and jail overcrowding on COVID-19 outbreaks

Overcrowded prisons strain correctional resources in ways that are important to understand. First, crowding places a premium on inmate control-based funding (e.g. funding for line staff and technology), which results in less funding available for treatment programming. Second, crowded prisons are more violent prisons, with prison crowding consistently identified as the leading cause of prison violence (Byrne et al., 2008). Third, crowded prisons are—by definition—resource-poor, with major staffing quality and turnover problems, inadequate physical structure, and perhaps most germane to this review, a poorly staffed and funded health care system (Akiyama et al., 2020; Heard, 2020; Nowotny and Piquero, 2020). We view overcrowded prisons as one of the root causes of the higher rate of infection and death in prison than in the general community. We examined the extent of prison crowding in state prison systems across the United States before the start of the pandemic (as of 31 December 2019). Both lowest and highest capacity rankings were examined. Using the lowest capacity criterion, 25 states were at or above 100% capacity before the start of the COVID-19 pandemic in the United States.[5] It is these state corrections systems that likely had the most difficulty responding to outbreaks at the start of the pandemic.

2.2 The impact of inadequate infrastructure and health care systems on COVID-19 outbreaks

In addition to overcrowded facilities, state prison systems across the United States had an inadequate health care infrastructure in place at the start of the pandemic (Heard, 2020; Nowonty and Piquero, 2020). According to a recent review by Kurland (2021), most states operate correctional health care systems that do not meet the accreditation standards established by several organisations, including the American Public Health Association, the National Commission on Correctional Healthcare, and the American Correctional Association. While there is disagreement on what constitutes "adequate" prison health care, it would be difficult to argue that prison health care is comparable in quality to the standard of care found in the community.[6] A variety of problems with prison health care have been documented, including inadequate staffing levels, poor staffing quality, lack of medication, and insufficient bed space (Rich, Allen, and Williams, 2014;

Heard, 2020). It is our view that the problems identified in many of these state systems have likely been exacerbated by the decision to privatise health care services in state prison systems. Unfortunately, we cannot state this definitively, because a detailed comparative assessment of publicly operated versus privately contracted prison heath care systems in the United States has yet to be conducted (Byrne et al., 2019).

2.3 The impact of inmates and detainees with pre-existing conditions on COVID-19 outbreaks

One final "root cause" of the COVID-19 crisis in US prisons is that many of the individuals incarcerated in the United States have significant physical and mental health problems. According to one recent study by Carson (2020), over 800,000 incarcerated people have at least one chronic health problem, which increased their risk of contracting illness while incarcerated (Kurland, 2021). These health problems likely began before they arrived in prison, due to deficits in the health care systems within their home communities.

It is well-documented that non-white (and foreign-born) individuals are overrepresented in corrections systems in the United States, and that these individuals tend to also reside in high crime, high poverty, but resource-poor communities with inadequate health care systems (Heard, 2020). Nowonty and Piquero (2020: 840) report that individuals in prison have been found to be more likely than community residents to have one or more of the following chronic underlying health conditions: "diabetes, heart disease, chronic lung disease, chronic liver disease, and lower immune systems from HIV (Maruschak et al., 2015)". They also report that "In the U.S., it is estimated that up to a quarter of the prison population has been infected with TB (Hammett et al., 2002), with a rate of active TB infection that is 6–10 times higher than the general population (Centers for Disease Control and Prevention, 2006). Thus, it is not surprising that San Quentin prison in California has been an epicentre of three epidemics: 1918 influenza and 2009 swine flu epidemics (Chaddock, 2018), and currently, the COVID-19 pandemic (Egelko, 2020)" (Nowonty and Piquero, 2020: 840).

In addition to their physical health problems, individuals in US prisons and jails have well-documented mental health problems, with one recent study estimating that half the population currently residing in these facilities has a diagnosed mental illness (Al-Rousan et al., 2017). According to a review by Kurland (2021: 6), "More people are confined in prisons and jails than are housed in hospitals, by a factor of 10 in some states (Torrey et al., 2010). In communities with insufficient behavioural and mental health care resources, prisons become de facto- and, in some cases, the only-way that community members can access the behavioural and mental health treatment they need".

Physical and mental health problems exhibited by individuals upon entering prisons and jails are often made worse during their time in prison.[7] The prison experience may also result in *new* physical and mental health problems due to a variety of factors, including "overcrowding, violence, reduced access to medical treatment, availability of drugs, poor diet, limited opportunities for exercise, limited activity and interaction with others, reduced access to natural light and fresh air, lack of contact with family members and support networks, and high levels of boredom, tension and despair" (Heard, 2019: 7). Given this grim profile of what she found in each of the ten countries in her review, it is not surprising that she links these conditions to higher rates of suicide and self-harm in prison than in the community,[8] and to the onset of major psychiatric disorders while in prison.

3 Mitigation strategies: region and state-specific variations across the United States (prison policies to reduce the prison population and restrictions of contact with the outside world and inside prisons)

There are three main types of COVID-19 mitigation strategies that have been employed by corrections managers to respond to COVID-19 outbreaks in prisons and jails—before and after the fact—that can be identified:

1 front-end mitigation strategies designed to limit the movement of the virus into prison,
2 in-prison mitigation strategies designed to limit the spread of the virus among inmates and staff in prison, and
3 back-end mitigation strategies designed to reduce the risk of infection among vulnerable subgroups of both inmates and staff.

In the following section, we document the types of mitigation strategies used, and highlight variation in strategies within and across regions of the United States. Table 45.2 identifies the primary mitigation strategy used in each state at the outset of the pandemic.[9] We found that in 18 states (and the federal prison system), no primary mechanism for population reduction could be identified. We have included details on the impact of these strategies on initial reductions in state prison populations during the first few months of the pandemic (March–June 2020). It is clear to us that some states moved more quickly at the outset of the pandemic than others to reduce their prison populations during these initial months. While these variations can be linked to the uneven spread of the virus across the country, it is also likely that political leaders in these states did not view the prison health crisis as requiring a rapid response, perhaps because they viewed community protection as trumping inmate and staff health concerns.

Table 45.2 State-level variation in the impact and response to the COVID-19 outbreak in US prisons

State	*Reduction in population (%) March–December 2020⁺*	*Primary mechanism for population reduction⁺⁺*
Alabama	16	30-day suspended admission on all inmate intakes; issuance of summons and complaint in lieu of custodial arrests for certain low-level crimes; early release for individuals who have served minimum time for technical parole or probation violations
Alaska*	5	None
Arizona	11	None
Arkansas	15	Early release of non-violent offenders who are due for release in the next six months
California	21	Early release of offenders who have six months or less to serve on their sentences (later expanded to some offenders who have committed violent offences, contingent on "close [community'] supervision" for the rest of their sentence; temporary suspension of intake of all youth offenders
Colorado	22	Temporary suspension of all offenders into custody with a few exceptions; early release for low level offences and close to sentence's end
Connecticut*	26	Early release of low risk offenders, (with stable home plans), those offenders who are at least 60 years old or who have health conditions, and a furlough of up to 45 days for offenders serving sentences of two years or less
Delaware*	17	None
Federal	17	Early release for inmates with medical preconditions and/or low predicted risk of recidivism
Florida	15	None
Georgia	13	Early release of non-violent, low-level offenders with six months or less remaining
Hawaii*	14	Early release for those charged with misdemeanours
Idaho	6	None
Illinois	21	Suspended admission; early release of low- to medium-risk inmates who are within nine months of their release date and are eligible for certain good-time credits medical release

State	*Reduction in population (%) March–December 2020*+	*Primary mechanism for population reduction*++
Indiana	12	None
Iowa	12	Early release
Kansas	13	None
Kentucky	19	Pre-trial release; Early release
Louisiana	6	Early release
Maine	20	Early release
Maryland	9	Early release
Massachusetts	18	Pre-trial release; Early release
Michigan	12	Suspended admissions; Early release
Minnesota	17	None
Mississippi	13	Pre-trial release
Missouri	10	Pre-trial release; Early release
Montana	20	None
Nebraska	6	None
Nevada	10	None
New Hampshire	12	None
New Jersey	31	Medical Release; Early release
New Mexico	11	Early release
New York	19	Early release
North Carolina	14	Early release
North Dakota	20	Early release
Ohio	10	Early release
Oklahoma	13	Early release
Oregon	12	Early release
Pennsylvania	13	Early release
Rhode Island*	22	Early release
South Carolina	13	None
South Dakota	15	None
Tennessee	10	None
Texas	14	None
Utah	21	Early release
Vermont*	22	Early release
Virginia	17	Early release
Washington	14	Early release; commutations
West Virginia	33	Early release
Wisconsin	15	Early release
Wyoming	1	None

\+ Data from The Marshall Project (https://data.world/associatedpress/marshall-project-covid-cases-in-prisons).

++ Suspended admissions refer to allowing no new admissions from jails to prison facilities; Medical release refers to legislation or executive orders releasing individuals with designated medical conditions; Early release refers to legislation or executive orders releasing individuals based on good-time formulas, certain low-level non-violent convictions with a lesser amount of time remaining (such as six months), and early parole granted; Pre-trial release refers to releasing individuals held in prisons for pre-trial; None refers to no action taken to release prisoners or injunctions by the court.

Data from https://www.brennancenter.org/our-work/research-reports/reducing-jail-and-prison-populations-during-covid-19-pandemic.

* Data extracted from The Marshall Project on 15 January 2021. Rates reflect cases per 10,000 inmates.

3.1 Front-end mitigation strategies

A variety of front-end mitigation strategies can be identified for state prisons and county jails. For individuals sentenced to state prison terms at the outset of the pandemic, state courts in four states—Alabama, Colorado, Illinois, and Michigan—suspended all new admissions. Several other states reduced the number of potential new admissions by suspending all court hearings and/or trials during these initial few months of the pandemic, likely out of concern for the health and safety of court personnel. A third front-end mitigation strategy employed by corrections leaders involved either the curtailment of all prisoner transfers within their corrections system, or the testing and quarantining of any new admissions or transfers to a facility (Wetzel and Davis, 2020). Fourth, prison administrators tried to keep the virus out of prison by suspending all visits from families and/or attorneys.[10] And finally, prison administrators in several states decided to adjust the schedules of staff in order to keep them in prison for longer periods (two weeks on site, followed by one week away, and return following positive COVID test results).

County jail administrators in four states—Kentucky, Massachusetts, Mississippi, and Missouri—expanded eligibility for pre-trial release, typically via home confinement. As we noted above, several states simply closed their courts during these early months of the pandemic, thus reducing admissions to county jails for both pre-trial and short-term sentenced offenders.

3.2 In-prison mitigation strategies

Our review of in-prison mitigation strategies reveals significant variations in how quickly state corrections systems moved to detect and to prevent outbreaks in their facilities; and once outbreaks were detected, we have found significant state-level variations in the *types* of mitigation strategies employed, and the *intensity* of these mitigation efforts. In terms of the *types* of in-prison mitigation strategies employed, there were several used by all prison administrators: (1) testing of inmates and staff, (2) suspension of programming,[11] (3) quarantining infected inmates, and (4) the use of lockdowns for most of the prison population. However, there was significant state-level variation in the use of each of these mitigation strategies, in particular in the testing of both inmates and staff.

In the federal BOP, the suspension of most programmes was documented in a report by the Office of the Attorney General (2020), where it was noted that "Despite the BOP's efforts, COVID-19 has had a major impact on programme delivery. BOP's first priority is the safety of its inmates. As a result, some programmes were suspended and capacity in others reduced to allow for social distancing and to prevent spreading of the virus (p. 20)". According to the report, most programmes fell into the high impact designation, which resulted in the suspension of programming:

"Most programs were significantly affected by COVID-19, including some that have been shut down entirely since the outbreak began. Highly impacted programmes often require inmates to interact across housing units, allowing the potential for the pandemic to spread. They also may involve physical activity or the sharing of items (such as tools used in vocational training programs). Even with delivery of programs taking place at facilities with low infection rates, the need for social distancing required a reduction in capacity. In some instances, staff delivering these programmes became unavailable due to illness, deployment to other locations, or a temporary change in responsibilities. Highly impacted programmes include: Anger Management, Assert Yourself, Basic Cognitive Skills, Literacy Program, Cognitive Processing Therapy, Criminal Thinking, Dialectical Behavior Therapy, Emotional Self-Regulation, Foundation, Illness Management & Recovery, National Parenting from Prison, Non-Residential Drug Abuse, Occupational Education, Resolve, Seeking Safety, Seeking Strength, Sex Offender Treatment Program – Non-Residential, Social Skills Training, Threshold, and all [productive activities]PAs" (Office of the Attorney General, 2020, 49).

Unfortunately, since BOP did not systematically track programme participation by inmates prior to the pandemic, pre-post comparisons in reductions in programme participation can be offered for only 3 programmes: "Inmate participation in three BOP programmes (the Bureau Literacy Program, Residential Drug Treatment, and Challenge) was systematically tracked prior to January 2020 when all inmates received their initial post-FSA needs assessments" (Office of the 2020, 46). In these three programmes, significant reductions in programme completion can be identified.

Finally, there is one in-prison mitigation strategy that certainly reflects the view of political leaders towards prisons and staff in the US prisons and jails: vaccination policy. In October 2020, the CDC released the COVID-19 Vaccination Program Interim Playbook for Jurisdiction Operations. Since then, each state has developed a vaccination response plan, which is intended to establish who will receive the vaccination and in what order. To date,[12] 14 states have included incarcerated persons as part of Phase I of vaccine distribution), while 20 states have opted to disseminate vaccinations to inmates in Phase II (COVID Prison Project). Two of the plans—Michigan and Rhode Island's—explicitly differentiate medically vulnerable incarcerated persons from the remainder of this population by limiting Phase I vaccines to the medically vulnerable. Tennessee and Missouri provided vaccinations to inmates during Phase III, while prioritising correctional staff as the highest need (Phase I).

3.3 Back-end mitigation strategies

Several back-end mitigation strategies were used by prison managers across the country, in conjunction with parole authorities. Table 45.2 reveals that early release from prison was the primary prison population reduction strategy utilised in 30 states at the start of the pandemic. The median initial reduction (March–June 2021) in prison population in these states was 7%, with a range from 1% (New Mexico) to 22% (Connecticut). During this initial review period, the BOP reduced their federal prison population by 10%. However, BOP was authorised to reduce their federal prison population with the passage of the CARES Act on 27 March 2021, but the strategies—including early release for medical reasons—did not impact these initial prison population reductions, because they took time to implement (Hummer, 2020). The legal basis for the population reduction strategies employed by the federal BOP can be found by reviewing the legislation authorising the CARES Act.[13]

4 The effectiveness of current mitigation strategies

We have documented the nature and extent of the COVID-19 outbreaks in prisons, and we have also documented how the federal, state, and local government responded to the pandemic, focusing on prison and jail mitigation strategies. Did these strategies work? To answer this question, we examined the available data on (1) impact on inmate and staff health, (2) impact on prison/jail population total, and (3) impact on public safety.

4.1 Impact on prisoner health

Data were available from The Marshall Project reflecting the total numbers of positive COVID-19 cases in the US prisons through early March 2021.[14] The trend lines of positive cases among inmates mirror that of the spikes, or "waves", that affected the nation in general throughout most of 2020 and early 2021. Overall, the number of reported new cases of COVID-19 among US prisoners peaked at over 5,000 cases in the last week of December 2020, with significant declines through March 2021 (under 3,000 new cases). Even with mitigation strategies in place, infection rates peaked during periods of increased community spread, indicating that the efficacy of such efforts is dependent on how well measures to prevent infections are implemented society wide. As of early March 2021, roughly 84% of the 386,765 prisoners infected with COVID-19 have recovered.

4.2 Impact on crowding in prisons and jails

Table 45.3 highlights pre- and post-COVID prison capacity in state and federal prison systems. While the federal prison system[15] and a majority of state prison systems reduced their populations after the onset of the pandemic, 40% continued to have inmate populations over their stated operational capacity. Further, many state systems that did drop below operational capacity were only slightly below—of the roughly 60% operating below operational capacity, 28% of that group had a total population of at least 90%

Table 45.3 Pre- and post-COVID prison occupancy in the US prison system

State	*Pre-COVID operating level based on lowest occupancy rate**	*Post-COVID operating level based on lowest occupancy rate***	*Per cent change*
Alabama	176%	153%	−23%
Alaska	93%	85%	−8%
Arizona	109%	98%	−11%
Arkansas	100%	103%	3%
California	135%	110%	−25%
Colorado	119%	117%	−2%
Connecticut+	–	–	0%
Delaware	124%	125%	1%
Federal Bureau of Prisons	110%	103%	−7%
Florida	94%	106%	12%
Georgia	105%	87%	−18%
Hawaii	102%	120%	18%
Idaho	110%	118%	8%
Illinois	84%	69%	−15%
Indiana	93%	83%	−10%
Iowa	119%	105%	−14%
Kansas	100%	88%	−12%
Kentucky	97%	80%	−17%
Louisiana	92%	92%	0%
Maine	92%	73%	−19%
Maryland	91%	91%	0%
Massachusetts	106%	93%	−13%
Michigan	97%	94%	−3%
Minnesota	96%	78%	−18%
Mississippi	87%	110%	23%
Missouri	88%	85%	−3%
Montana	174%	214%	40%
Nebraska	157%	158%	1%
Nevada	130%	117%	−13%
New Hampshire	136%	117%	−19%
New Jersey	100%	110%	10%
New Mexico	125%	125%	0%
New York	88%	71%	−17%
North Carolina	95%	84%	−11%
North Dakota	100%	97%	−3%
Ohio+	–	–	0%
Oklahoma	107%	87%	−20%
Oregon	98%	95%	−3%
Pennsylvania	97%	85%	−12%
Rhode Island	68%	63%	−5%
South Carolina	84%	73%	−11%
South Dakota	86%	75%	−11%
Tennessee	136%	126%	−10%
Texas	89%	101%	12%
Utah	75%	84%	9%
Vermont	90%	88%	−2%
Virginia	95%	86%	−9%
Washington	105%	95%	−10%
West Virginia	100%	111%	11%

Note: Lowest capacity refers to the highest amount of overcrowding based on operational capacity, or the number of people a facility can hold based on staffing and services.
* Based on Bureau of Justice Statistics population data released December 2019.
* Based on a variety of state data sources in 2020; for detailed data see: https://www.prisonpolicy.org/blog/2020/12/21/overcrowding/#capacity_appendix
+ Connecticut and Ohio do not report operational capacity data.

of capacity. Preliminary evidence suggests that once guidelines for correctional settings are eased, populations rebound quickly. Harvey, Taylor, and Wang's (2020) report on COVID-19 in local jails suggests that institutional populations decreased dramatically in March 2020 after the federal guidelines outlined in "30 Days to Stop the Spread" were implemented in correctional facilities, and subsequently extended until 30 April 2020. After the expiration of the guidelines at the end of April, jail populations grew steadily throughout 2020, but remained well below pre-pandemic levels.[16]

4.3 Impact on public safety

There has been much debate over the impact of various virus mitigation strategies on crime and public safety. Researchers have identified significant increases in homicide, aggravated assaults, gun assaults, and domestic violence (Abrams, 2020; Leslie and Wilson, 2020; Rosenfeld and Lopez, 2020; Piquero et al., 2021), but decreases in both residential burglary (down 20%), and drug offences (down 57%) during the first few months of the pandemic (March–June 2021). However, these data do not tell us anything about the public safety impact of either changes in sentencing practices, or about prison and jail early release policies. To answer this question, we need data on (1) the subsequent criminal behaviour of individuals sentenced via a community sanction during the pandemic and (2) the subsequent criminal behaviour of individuals released early from federal, state, and local facilities due to the pandemic.

The Office of the Attorney General's report (2020) offers a preliminary answer to these questions for those individuals released early from the custody of the federal BOP. The report notes that over 19,000 inmates were released directly from prison to home confinement due to the pandemic and provides recidivism data for about a third of this release cohort, including "7,251 inmates released from federal prison under the FSA through September 26, 2020. This data is based on four non-mutually exclusive groups of inmates released to U.S. communities:

- Inmates released due to retroactive application of the Fair Sentencing Act;
- Inmates who receive a compassionate release, also known as a Reduction in Sentence;
- Inmates who were released because of the expansion of good conduct time (GCT) under the FSA on July 19, 2019, when the new retroactive GCT calculation went into effect; and
- Inmates transferred to community custody under the FSA's reauthorisation of the Elderly Offender pilot program" (Office of the Attorney General, 2020: 22).

Examination of recidivism data for this subgroup of releases revealed an overall recidivism rate of 11.3% with an average follow-up period of ten months in the community post-release. The authors of the report examined these recidivism data—based on a definition of recidivism as any rearrest or technical violation during the follow-up period—by conviction offence type, length of stay, security level, and risk classification. Examination of these data reveals that early release of individuals from federal prison did *not* pose a significant threat to public safety. In fact, it appears that the initial recidivism risk posed by this release cohort was minimal, regardless of conviction offence, but there was significant variation in recidivism by length of stay and institutional security level.[17]

We should also note that while the new risk classification system used by the BOP is based on a prediction of the risk of recidivism during a three-year follow-up period, it is worth considering that the Office of the Attorney General's review found very little variation in recidivism during the first year of release by risk level, with an overall recidivism rate of only 2.1%, and little variation across four risk categories: minimum (0.6%), low (1.8%), medium (3.2%), and high risk (4.5%). These data—while preliminary—suggest that policies designed to exclude medium- and high-risk inmates from early release during a health crisis due to public safety concerns need to be revised, because *predicted* risk does not appear to be even remotely linked to *actual* risk for this group of federal inmates, at least during this initial release period.[18]

While we do not yet have these data for either sentenced offenders receiving non-incarcerative sanctions or early prison releases from state prisons, data are available to assess the impact of *jail* release policies on the rate these individuals are rearrested. According to an examination of rebooking rates across a large national sample of 253 US jails by Harvey, Taylor, and Wang (2020:18), "Relative to the average rebooking rates observed in January 2020, 30-day rebooking rates have decreased by an average of 33%, 60-day rebooking rates have decreased by an average of 30%, 90-day rebooking rates have decreased by an average of 21%, and 180-day-rebooking rates have decreased by an average of 13%; these decreases are all statistically significant at the 95% level. To the extent that rebooking rates measure the average net public safety risks of releasing individuals from jail, the public safety risks of jail releases are lower now than prior to the pandemic". These results suggest that pre-trial jail release options can be expanded across the United States with no increased threat to public safety. We need similar data on state and federal prison releases to assess the public safety impact of early release strategies on these populations.

5 Conclusion (returning to normal and penal policy recommendations)

The pandemic has provided a unique opportunity to conduct a natural experiment on the effects of various prison and jail reforms. In the United States, the federal and state governments have reduced prison and jail populations in the short-term using a variety of front-end and back-end mitigation strategies. The pandemic has also highlighted the lack of basic information currently available on the community corrections systems that have been tasked with managing individuals—placed in probation, parole, or other community corrections programmes due to these crisis-driven reforms—in the community.

For the past few decades, prison reform advocates have made the case that prisons should be viewed as a last resort, and that a prison or jail term should be applied parsimoniously, targeting convicted offenders who commit violent crime and/or pose an immediate threat to public safety. An examination of global prison population trends over the past two decades suggests that reformers have failed to convince governments to change their view on the need for incarceration; this is especially true in the countries with the largest prison populations, including the United States (Byrne et al., 2015). The pandemic has forced the US government to implement some of these recommended reforms on an emergency, short-term basis. Will these reforms take root and serve as harbingers of long-term reforms in sentencing and corrections policies? We suspect that without an aggressive research programme, we will miss a unique opportunity to evaluate the impact of a wide range of major corrections reforms, which will increase the likelihood of governments—absent evidence to the contrary—returning to their old ways. We offer the following three-pronged COVID-19-based research agenda for consideration: (1) research on jail reform during the pandemic, (2) research on prison reform during the pandemic, and (3) research on community corrections reform during the pandemic.

Our review has revealed that it is the pre-trial population that was the initial target of early release strategies devised in the United States. Some policymakers fear that reducing pre-trial populations will come with a cost: more crime in the community due to their resumption of (alleged) criminal activity. However, there is little support for continuing the use of pre-trial detention on the scale being used, based on our review of the research on the criminal behaviour of individuals during pre-trial release. Safe release is not only possible, but it is probable at the pre-trial stage, based on the available data on crime commission during pre-trial release (Harvey, Taylor and Wang, 2020). However, we will need more than these preliminary data to convince policymakers that significant, long-term reductions in pre-trial populations can be achieved without compromising public safety.

A second category of crisis-driven, short-term reforms includes the mitigation strategies designed to reduce the number of people being sent to prison and those reforms designed to let them leave prison early. Early release strategies that target older inmates serving long sentences can certainly be justified, both from a public health *and* from a public safety perspective.[19] Unfortunately, our review could only document *what* is being done in response to COVID-19 outbreaks in prison systems across the United States; we do not yet have access to the data needed to assess the effectiveness of these strategies.

Another prison reform area that needs to be examined involves the impact of in-prison mitigation strategies, particularly those strategies that reduced prison access to programmes designed to address documented deficits in mental health, education/employment, substance abuse, and cognitive development. What impact did a lack of programming during the pandemic have on in-prison and post-release behaviour? These impacts need to be documented. It will be critical to examine the impact of restrictions on visits and the use of lockdowns on in-prison mental and physical health, in-prison behaviour, and on post-release health and behavioural outcomes. Without this research, we will not be able to assess the unintended consequences of these short-term crisis management strategies.

A third component of our proposed research agenda focuses on community corrections. We need to evaluate the impact of strategies used to mitigate the spread of COVID-19 among community corrections personnel and clients across the country. One assumption that many prison reform advocates often make is that "anything" is preferable to a prison or jail sentence, but even a cursory examination of return to prison rates for technical violations of probation or parole conditions underscores an important reality: technical violators make up a significant proportion of new prison admissions each year. In the United States, it is estimated that 25% of the individuals entering the country's prison system have not committed a new crime; instead, they violated the technical conditions of probation or parole supervision (Justice Center, 2020). Viglione et al. (2020) report that technical violators are not being admitted to prison during the first several months of the pandemic; they reported that new prison admissions for technical violations are down 75% since the start of the pandemic. It will be critical to evaluate the impact of this natural reform experiment on public safety, because—if the results are positive—placing a moratorium on the use of incarceration for technical violators would have a major effect on the US's prison population (Byrne et al., 2015).

Notes

1 In the United States, there are 3,134 jails, 1,833 state prisons, 110 federal prisons, and 80 Indian Country jails. In addition, there are 1,772 juvenile facilities across the country. The actual number of facilities is then 6,929. Our focus in this review is on adult corrections facilities.

2 In six states included in The Marshall Project's database, both county and state reports and deaths are combined:

> For six states with unified prison and jail systems—Alaska, Connecticut, Delaware, Hawaii, Rhode Island, Vermont—we count testing and case numbers from both detainees awaiting trial and sentenced prisoners. Similarly, in Maryland, several pre-trial facilities in Baltimore City are included in the figures

https://www.themarshallproject.org/2020/05/01/a-state-by-state-look-at-coronavirus-in-prisons.

3 For details on these contracts, go to https://www.bop.gov/about/facilities/residential_reentry_management_centers.jsp.

4 The following studies on the link between jail and community COVID-19 outbreaks are identified by Harvey, Taylor and Wang (2020, note 1): Jiménez, M. C., et al., Epidemiology of COVID-19 Among Incarcerated Individuals and Staff in Massachusetts Jails and Prisons. *JAMA Network Open*, 3:8, e2018851–e2018851, August 2020; Lofgren, E., et al., The Epidemiological Implications of Incarceration Dynamics in Jails for Community, Corrections Officer, and Incarcerated Population Risks from COVID-19, medRXiv preprint doi 10.1101/2020.04.08.20058842, 4 May 2020; Reinhart, E., and Chen, D. L., Incarceration and Its Disseminations: COVID-19 Pandemic Lessons From Chicago's Cook County Jail. *Health Affairs*, 39:8, 1412–1418, June 4, 2020; Alsan, M., and Yang, C., National Commission on Correctional Health Care COVID-19 Survey of Correctional Facilities, 1 June 2020.

5 If the highest capacity criterion is used, 8 states were at or above 100% of their highest capacity at the start of the pandemic: Colorado, Hawaii, Idaho, Iowa, Nebraska, North Dakota, Washington, and Wisconsin.

6 See the ABA standards for the treatment of prisoners (ABA, 2012); and the Mandela Rules (UNODC, 2016).

7 Heard (2019) has also documented the mental health problems found among the prison populations examined in her 10-country review, which included the United States:

   1 higher prevalence in prison population than in general population of serious mental health conditions ("depression, personality and anxiety disorders, schizophrenia, bipolar disorder and psychosis" (WHO, 2014; Fazel et al., 2016; Heard, 2019: 4);
   2 higher prevalence of intellectual disabilities in prison populations (Fazel et al., 2008), and new evidence of higher prevalence of traumatic brain injury (Williams et al., 2018);
   3 higher prevalence of drug and alcohol disorders, higher rates of comorbidity with substance abuse and mental health (Butler et al., 2011), and higher prevalence of trauma and abuse (Durcan, 2008)

8 Heard (2019) observes that the country-level research on the link between overcrowding and various forms of self-harm, including suicide, is mixed. See, for example, the 24-country comparative review by Fazel et al. (2016).

9 We base this assessment of state-level responses from a variety of data sources, including the Marshal Project database. See notes to Table 45.3 for more details.

10 These restrictions could also be described as in-prison mitigation strategies, but in our view, they take place outside the prison prior to entering a closed prison system rather than in the prison itself.

11 Details on the nature and extent of programme availability are found in the following American Bar Association Report on the implementation of the First Step Act: https://www.americanbar.org/content/dam/aba/publications/criminaljustice/2021/first-step-report.pdf

12 As of 10 April 2021. For more details, see the Marshal Project & COVID Prison Project data: https://www.themarshallproject.org/2020/05/01/a-state-by-state-look-at-coronavirus-in-prisons & https://covidprisonproject.com/data/national-overview/ See also: Source: COVID Prison Project (2020). https://covidprisonproject.com/blog/ (data updated on 9 April 2021)

   Source: Michaud, J., Kates, J., Dolan, R., and Tolbert, J. (2020). States are getting ready to distribute COVID-19 vaccines. What do their plans tell us so far?–State plans. Retrieved from: https://www.kff.org/report-section/states-are-getting-ready-to-distribute-covid-19-vaccines-what-do-their-plans-tell-us-so-far-state-plans/

13 Coronavirus Aid, Relief, and Economic Security Act available at https://www.congress.gov/116/bills/s3548/BILLS-116s3548is.pdf.

14 Source: The Marshall Project, *A State-by-State Look at Coronavirus in Prisons*. https://www.themarshallproject.org/2020/05/01/a-state-by-state-look-at-coronavirus-in-prisons Retrieved 8 March 2021

15 According to a review by the ABA (2021, 20):

> In December 2020, BOP Director Carvajal reported to the House Judiciary Committee that 18,112 individuals had been transferred to home confinement, with an additional 175 individuals already scheduled to be transferred soon after, about a 200% increase. 99 Although this number may seem significant, the BOP has 123,105 individuals in its custody; 100 therefore only about 15% of the inmate population has benefitted from being placed on home confinement

https://www.americanbar.org/content/dam/aba/publications/criminaljustice/2021/first-step-report.pdf

16 Source: Harvey A., Taylor O., and Wang, A. (2020): *COVID-19, Jails, and Public Safety: December 2020 Update*. Washington, DC: Council on Criminal Justice. December, 2020.
https://cdn.ymaws.com/counciloncj.org/resource/resmgr/covid_commission/covid-19,_jails,_and_public_.pdf.

17 See Appendix of the Attorney General's Report (2020: 21–24). Available at https://nij.ojp.gov/first-step-act/the-attorney-generals-first-step-act-section-3634-annual-report-december-2020.pdf.

18 Data were included for only 2,523 federal inmates released through September 2020 for whom risk classification data were available. According to the report, the other inmates included in the recidivism analyses were released prior to the implementation of the new risk classification system.

19 We recognise that critics often conflate risk of recidivism with the stakes involved, if even a single violent crime is committed by a released inmate. Violent criminals (e.g. murderers and individuals who were charged with sexual crime(s)) have the lowest recidivism risk of any release cohort, but it is their conviction offence, not their risk, that leads policymakers to make these groups ineligible for release, even during a pandemic when their age and underlying health problems identify them as "high risk" for infection and death while incarcerated. For many, it is not the *probability* of a new crime by these high stakes inmates that matters, but rather the *possibility*. For further discussion on this topic, see Byrne (2008).

References

Abrams, D. (2020): COVID and crime: An early empirical look. University of Pennsylvania Working Paper, August 2020.

Akiyama, M. J., Spaulding, A. C., and Rich, J. D. (2020): Flattening the curve for incarcerated populations - Covid-19 in jails and prisons. *The New England Journal of Medicine, 382*(22): 2075–2077.

Al-Rousan, T., Rubenstein, L., Sieleni, B., Deol, H., and Wallace, R.B. (2017): Inside the nation's largest mental health institution: A prevalence study in a state prison system. *BMC Public Health, 17*: 342 https://doi.org/10.1186/s12889-017-4257-0.

Alsan, M. and Yang, C. (2020): National Commission on correctional health care COVID-19 survey of correctional facilities, June 1, 2020. https://www.ncchc.org/study-of-covid-19-in-correctional-facilities.

American Bar Association (ABA). (2012): *ABA Standards for Criminal Justice: Treatment of Prisoners*. Chicago: American Bar Association.

American Bar Association (ABA). (2021): *A Report on Behalf of the American Bar Association Criminal Justice Section Task Force on the Implementation of the First Step Act.* Chicago: American Bar Association. https://www.americanbar.org/content/dam/aba/publications/criminaljustice/2021/first-step-report.pdf

Butler, T., Indig, D., Allnutt, S., and Mamoon, H. (2011): Co-occurring mental illness and substance use disorder among Australian prisoners. *Drug and Alcohol Review*, 30(2), 188–194. https://doi.org/10.1111/j.1465-3362.2010.00216.x.

Byrne, J. (2008): Editorial introduction: The social ecology of community corrections: Understanding the link between individual and community change. *Criminology and Public Policy*, 1(2): 1201–1213.

Byrne, J. (2019): The effectiveness of prison programming: A review of the research literature examining the impact of federal, state, and local inmate programming on post-release recidivism. First Step Act Independent Review Committee. https://firststepact-irc.org/wp-content/uploads/ 2019/12/IRC-Effectiveness-of-Prison-Programming.pdf

Byrne, J., Hummer, D., and Stowell, J. (2008): Prison violence, prison culture, and offender change: New directions in theory, research, and policy. In: Byrne, J., Hummer, D, and Taxman, F. (Eds.): *The Culture of Prison Violence.* Boston, MA: Allyn & Bacon, 202–219.

Byrne, J., Kras, K. R., and Marmolejo, L. M. (2019): International perspectives on the privatization of corrections. *Criminology and Public Policy,* 18(2), 477–503. https://doi.org/10.1111/1745-9133.12440.

Byrne, J. M., Pattavina, A., and Taxman, F. S. (2015). International trends in prison upsizing and downsizing: In search of evidence of a global rehabilitation revolution. *Victims & Offenders*, 10(4), 420–451. https://doi.org/10.1080/15564886.2015.1078186.

Byrne, J., Rapisarda, S., Hummer, D., and K. R. Kras (2020): An imperfect storm: Identifying the root causes of COVID-19 outbreaks in the world's largest corrections systems. *Victims & Offenders, 15*(7–8): 862–909.

Carson, E. A. (2020): *Prisoners in 2018.* Washington, DC: U.S. Department of Justice, Office of Justice Programs, Bureau of Justice Statistics.

Centers for Disease Control and Prevention. (2006): *Prevention and Control of Tuberculosis in Correctional and Detention Facilities: Recommendations from CDC.* Atlanta, GA: Department of Health and Human Services, Centers for Disease Control and Prevention. https://www.cdc.gov/mmwr/preview/mmwrhtml/rr5509a1.htm.

Chaddock, D. (2018): *1918 Flu Pandemic Puts Prison Medical Staff to Test.* Sacramento, CA: California Department of Corrections and Rehabilitation. https://www.cdcr.ca.gov/insidecdcr/2018/10/18/1918-flu-pandemic-puts-prison-medical-staff-to-test/.

Collica-Cox, K., and Molina, L. (2020): A case study of the Westchester County New York's Jail. Response to COVID-19: Controlling COVID while balancing service needs for the incarcerated - a national model for jails. *Victims & Offenders,* 15(7–8), 1305–1316.

Durcan, G. (2008): *From the Inside: Experiences of Prison Mental Health Care.* London: Sainsbury Centre for Mental Health.

Egelko, B. (2020): San Quentin must release or transfer half its prisoners because of lack of COVID care, court rules. *San Francisco Chronicle.* https://www.sfchronicle.com/bayarea/article/San-Quentin-must-release-or-transfer-half-its-15662794.php.

Fazel, S., Hayes, A. J., Bartellas, K., Clerici, M., and Trestman, R. (2016): Mental health of prisoners: Prevalence, adverse outcomes, and interventions. *The Lancet Psychiatry*, *3*(9): 871–881. https://doi.org/10.1016/S2215-0366(16)30142-0.

Fazel, S., Xenitidis, K., and Powell, J. (2008): The prevalence of intellectual disabilities among 12 000 prisoners—A systematic review. *International Journal of Law and Psychiatry*, 31(4), 369–373. https://doi.org/10.1016/j.ijlp.2008.06.001.

Hammett, T.M., Harmon, M.P., and Rhoades, W. (2002): The burden of infectious disease among inmates of and releases from US correctional facilities, 1997. *American Journal of Public Health,* 92(11), 1789–1794.

Harvey A., Taylor O., and Wang, A. (2020): *COVID-19, Jails, and Public Safety: December 2020 Update.* Washington, DC: Council on Criminal Justice. December, 2020. (https://cdn.ymaws.com/counciloncj.org/resource/resmgr/covid_commission/covid-19,_jails, _and_public_.pdf).

Heard, C. (2019): *Towards a Health-Informed Approach to Penal Reform? Evidence from Ten Countries.* Birkbeck Institutional Research Online. https://eprints.bbk.ac.uk/id/eprint/27743

Heard, C. (2020): Commentary: Assessing the global impact of the Covid-19 pandemic on prison populations. *Victims & Offenders*, 15(7–8): 848–861.

Hummer, D. (2020): United States Bureau of Prisons' response to the COVID-19 pandemic. *Victims & Offenders,* 15(7–8), 1262–1276.

Jiménez, M., Cowger, T., Simon, L., Behn, M., Cassarino, N., and Bassett, M. (2020): Epidemiology of COVID-19 among incarcerated individuals and staff in Massachusetts Jails and Prisons. *JAMA Network Open*, *3*, 8, e2018851–e2018851, August 2020.

Justice Center. (2020): *Confined and Costly: How Supervision Violations Are Filling Prisons and Burdening Budgets.* New York: Justice Center, the Council of State Governments. https://csgjusticecenter.org/publications/confined-costly/

Kaeble, D., and Alper, M. (2020): *Probation and Parole in the United States, 2017–2018.* Washington, DC: U.S. Department of Justice, Office of Justice Programs, Bureau of Justice Statistics.

Kurland, A. (2021): *Using Research to Improve Health and Health Care in U S Correctional Facilities.* Washington, DC: Urban Institute, Justice policy Center.

Leslie, E., and Wilson, R. (2020): *Sheltering in Place and Domestic Violence.* Washington, DC: Council on Criminal Justice, August 2020.

Lofgren, E., Lum, K., Horowitz, A., Madubuonwu, B., and Fefferman, N. (2020): The Epidemiological implications of incarceration dynamics in jails for community, corrections officer, and incarcerated population risks from COVID-19. medRXiv preprint doi 10.1101/2020.04.08.20058842, May 4, 2020.

Maruschak, L. M., Berzofsky, M., and Unangst, J. (2015): *Medical Problems of State and Federal Prisoners and Jail Inmates, 2011–12.* Washington, DC: U.S. Department of Justice, Office of Justice Programs, Bureau of Justice Statistics.

Novisky, M.A., Narvey, C.S., and Semenza, D.C. (2020): Institutional responses to the COVID-19 pandemic in American prisons. *Victims & Offenders,* 15(7–8), 1244–1261.

Nowonty, K. M., and Piquero, A. R. (2020): The global impact of the pandemic on institutional and community corrections: Assessing short-term crisis management and long-term change strategies. *Victims & Offenders,* 15(7–8), 839–847.

Office of the Attorney General. (2020). *The Attorney General's First Step Act Section 3634 Annual Report.* Washington, DC: United States Department of Justice.

https://nij.ojp.gov/first-step-act/the-attorney-generals-first-step-act-section-3634-annual-report-december-2020.pdf

Piquero, A., Jennings, W., Jemison, E., Kaukinen, C., and Knaul, F. (2021): *Domestic Violence during COVID-19: Evidence from a Systematic Review and Meta-analysis.* Washington, DC: Council on Criminal Justice.

Rapisarda, S. S., Byrne, J., and Marmolejo, L. (2020): An examination of COVID-19 outbreaks in prisons and jails in North America, Central America, and the Caribbean. *Victims and Offenders,* 15(7–8), 1234–1243.

Reinhart, E. and Chen, D. (2020): Incarceration and its disseminations: COVID-19 pandemic lessons from Chicago's Cook County Jail. *Health Affairs,* 39(8), 1412–1418, June 4, 2020.

Rich, J.D., Allen, S.A. and Williams, B.A. (2014): The need for higher standards in correctional healthcare to improve public health. *Journal of General Internal Medicine, 30*(4), 503–07.

Rosenfeld, R., and Lopez, E. (2020): *Pandemic, Social Unrest, and Crime in U.S. Cities. Council on Criminal Justice.* https://cdn.ymaws.com/counciloncj.org/resource/collection/D26974EF-0F75-4BDE-ADE7-86DA0741DC49/Impact_Report_-_Crime.pdf.

Torrey, E.F., Kennard, A.D., Eslinger, D., Lamb, R., and Pavle, J. (2010): *More Mentally Ill Persons Are in Jails and Prisons than Hospitals: A Survey of the States.* Arlington, VA: Treatment Advocacy Center. https://www.treatmentadvocacycenter.org/storage/documents/final_jails_v_hospitals_study.pdf.

United Nations Office on Drugs and Crime (UNODC). (2016): *The United Nations Standard Minimum Rules for the Treatment of Prisoners.* Vienna: United Nations Office on Drugs and Crime.

Viglione, J., Alward, L.M., Lockwood, A., and Bryso, S. (2020): Adaptations to COVID-19 in community corrections agencies across the United States. *Victims & Offenders*, 15(7–8): 1277–1297. https://doi.org/10.1080/15564886.2020.1818153.

Wetzel, J.E., and Davis, J.M. (2020): The response to the COVID19 crisis by the Pennsylvania department of corrections. *Victims & Offenders*, 15(7–8), 1298–1304. https://doi.org/10.1080/15564886.2020.1830324.

Williams, W. H., Chitsabesan, P., Fazel, S., McMillan, T., Hughes, N., Parsonage, M., and Tonks, J. (2018): Traumatic brain injury: A potential cause of violent crime? *The Lancet Psychiatry*, 5(10), 836–844. https://doi.org/10.1016/S2215-0366(18)30062-2.

World Health Organization, Regional Office for Europe. (2014): *Prisons and Health. World Health Organization.* https://www.euro.who.int/en/health-topics/health-determinants/prisons-and-health/publications/2014/prisons-and-health.

Zeng, Z. (2020): *Jail Inmates in 2018.* Washington, DC: U.S. Department of Justice, Office of Justice Programs, Bureau of Justice Statistics.

46 International prisoners and the pandemic – seeking release, improved conditions and family contact before international criminal courts

Róisín Mulgrew

1 Introduction

International prisoners are persons who have been accused or convicted of genocide, crimes against humanity and war crimes by international criminal courts. These courts are directly responsible for the conditions of detention of accused or convicted persons housed in their international detention facilities. The sentences of imprisonment of the majority of convicted persons, however, are enforced in the national prison systems of cooperating states.

Although enforcing states are responsible for the day-to-day imprisonment of convicted persons, the sentencing international court remains responsible for the sentence and the prisoner. Enforcing states cannot unilaterally release international prisoners. During the COVID-19 pandemic, requests have been received by international criminal courts for interim release from pre-trial detention (International Criminal Court (ICC)), provisional or early release from an enforcing state (International Residual Mechanism for the Criminal Tribunals (IRMCT)) and temporary transfer from one enforcing state to another (Residual Special Court for Sierra Leone (RSCSL)). These requests have been based on rights-related grounds: the right to health(care), degrading conditions of detention and reduced contact with the outside world. The resulting decisions have raised the possibility of modifications to conditions of detention and the introduction of alternative means of communication. To date, all release and transfer requests have been unsuccessful. This is due, in part, to the inappropriateness, vagueness and impossibility of the forms of relief sought. Based on recent international jurisprudence, this chapter highlights the reality of international imprisonment during the COVID-19 pandemic, identifies obstacles to granting release for persons accused or convicted of core crimes and reveals gaps in the supervisory powers of the international criminal courts.

2 Right to health and access to healthcare

Prisoners typically have a weaker health profile than the general community (UNODC, 2020: 2) and physical and emotional responses to custody (stress and poor sleep) may weaken their immune systems (Barnert, Ahalt and Williams, 2020: 964). Prisons can be amplifiers of infectious diseases

DOI: 10.4324/9781003169178-46

and epicentres of outbreaks. The reality of carceral environments (confined space, inability to social distance, poor ventilation, shared facilities, the use of metals that COVID-19 can survive on for long periods, physical interactions between staff and prisoners) means a higher risk of exposure, transmission and infection (Barnert, Ahalt and Williams, 2020: 964; De Carvalho, dos Santos and Santos, 2020: 3494; Franco-Paredes et al., 2020; Prost et al., 2020: 2; World Health Organisation, 2020: 1).

2.1 Risk of contracting COVID-19

International prisoners seeking release and transfer have argued that they are not only vulnerable to catching COVID-19 while in custody, but are more at risk of serious or fatal consequences due to their advanced age.[1] Morbidity and advanced age are "known predictors of COVID-19 severity and fatality" (De Carvalho, dos Santos and Santos, 2020: 3496). Factors cited in requests include the number of reported cases within a detention facility, an inability to social distance, reliance on shared facilities, contact with prison staff, overcrowding and insufficient access to hygiene facilities and protective equipment (Semanza Decision at 2). At the RSCSL, however, Taylor failed to provide evidence of the direct impact of the virus prevention regime on his physical or mental health (Taylor Decision, paras. 43, 62). His request for transfer also cited an Inter-American Court on Human Rights case involving serious overcrowding and deplorable conditions, prompting the designated judge to ask "if the Plaintiff seriously intends to convince this court that it is a valid comparator to his present conditions" (Taylor Decision, para. 67). In the end, many of Taylor's submissions in relation to conditions were rejected in light of contradictory reports from the Acting Governor of the UK prison where Taylor is held (Taylor Decision, paras. 28–29, 43, 63, 65, 71). Semanza argued that the pandemic constituted "special circumstances and an acute justification warranting his provisional release related to humane and compassionate considerations" (Semanza Decision at 2). While there were no specific legal grounds for release due to health or age concerns in the IRMCT legal framework, medical factors can be a reason for granting release without or without conditions at this tribunal.[2] As in *Taylor*, however, the Registrar reported that the Beninese prison authorities were taking appropriate measures to manage the pandemic (Semanza Decision at 6).

2.2 Overcrowding

Overcrowding can impact detrimentally on prisoners' health and cause high rates of infectious disease and mortality (Mariner and Schleifer, 2013: 298). Overcrowding can increase the risk of the spread of COVID-19 and act as an obstacle to preventing or responding to outbreaks as it places pressure on capacity, staffing, equipment and the authorities' ability to isolate (suspected) infected persons (Barnert, Ahalt and Williams, 2020: 964; Franco-Paredes et al., 2020: 3; UNODC, 2020: 2; UNODC, WHO, UNAIDS and OHCHR, 2020).

International courts (and prosecutors) have drawn attention to the reality that international prisoners are often held in safe, uncrowded environments, in single cell accommodation with access to medical care. The ICC argued that those held at the ICCDC had a lower risk of contracting the virus than those held in national prisons (Al Hassan Decision, paras. 81, 90). In *Taylor*, the Prosecutor applied this argument to international prisoners serving sentences in enforcing states: as Category A prisoners in the UK enjoyed a privileged regime and were isolated from the wider prison population, they had a lower risk of contracting the virus (Taylor Decision, paras. 12, 14). A UN Special Rapporteur also highlighted that many prisoners serving sentences for the commission of core crimes "usually enjoy conditions of detention ... that avoid mass contact ... placing the prisoner at an advantage in terms of safety and health" (UN SR, 2020). In contrast, Semanza's counsel argued that he was being held in a large overcrowded prison (Porto Novo) in Benin where the risk of contracting the disease was higher than for international prisoners in other enforcing states who were held in separate wings from the general population (Rugiririza, 2020). Following this warning, four ICTR convicted persons serving their sentences in Benin tested positive for COVID-19. Though three prisoners were asymptomatic, one prisoner required treatment in intensive care at a separate location.[3]

2.3 Access to medical treatment

International prisoners also raised concerns about their ability to access appropriate medical treatment. The WHO has emphasised that prisoners should enjoy the same standard of healthcare as those in the community, without discrimination on the grounds of their legal status (2020: 3). The European Committee for Social Rights has stressed that healthcare provided during the pandemic "must be effective" and "that groups at particularly high risk... [including] persons detained in prison... must be adequately protected by the healthcare measures put in place" (2020: 4). Even though human rights law does not typically provide an individual right to health, a failure by authorities to prevent the spread of disease or to provide access to appropriate medical treatment may constitute a violation of the prisoner's right to protection against inhuman and degrading treatment (Rogan, 2017: 5). The decision of authorities to deprive a person of their liberty implies that they take on a duty of care to provide medical treatment and to protect health. Penal Reform International notes that "this duty of care is critical, because prisoners have no alternative but to rely on the authorities to ... protect their health ... and to be able to exercise their right to health" (2020: 4). This positive obligation is broader than simply providing access to healthcare: it includes preventative, supportive and curative care (Mariner and Schleifer, 2013; UNODC, WHO, UNAIDS and OHCHR, 2020).

COVID-19 does, however, create difficulties for medical care provision within prisons. Few prison doctors are specialists in geriatric or palliative care. Older prisoners with underlying health conditions are at a heightened risk of "hospitalisation, intensive care placement and death" (Prost et al., 2020: 1). The restrictions put in place to prevent the spread of the disease may result in immobility, deconditioning and cognitive decline for persons over 55, and it may be difficult to diagnose COVID-19 as it can present differently in older persons (Prost et al., 2020: 2–3). The right to healthcare also includes the provision of specialist treatment in prison or civil hospitals when required (PC-CP WG, 2020). The reality is that respiratory care is usually limited within prison medical services, and in most cases, those requiring emergency or inpatient treatment will need to be transferred to an external medical care facility (Barnert, Ahalt and Williams, 2020: 964; Prost et al., 2020: 2). Transfers of persons infected with COVID-19 to community medical care would occur when the capacity to "handle a large influx of critically ill patients from prisons is limited" (Franco-Paredes et al., 2020). *Taylor* claimed his status as a Category A prisoner in England would obstruct or prevent his transfer to an external hospital if he required intensive respiratory care, as a transfer would "require such heavy security that it may be next to impossible to be provided during the situation of the pandemic" (Taylor Decision, para. 4). The RSCSL decision did not address this specific point directly, but responded that despite this concern, he wanted to be transferred to a prison in another country that would involve logistically difficult international travel that could increase his exposure to and risk of infection.

2.4 Psychological support

The UN Sub-Committee for the Prevention of Torture (SPT) has urged authorities to ensure appropriate psychological support for all detainees affected by regime restrictions and those in quarantine (SPT, 2020). This directive may have particular significance for persons imprisoned following a conflict situation. Al Hassan applied for interim release on the basis that his reduced regime, placement on a wing by himself, the COVID-19 related restrictions and the lack of appropriate treatment would create irreversible mental harm given his status as a torture survivor (Al Hassan Request, paras. 2–4, 17, 35, 43). He had been diagnosed with PTSD with dissociative symptoms and severe depression (Al Hassan Request, paras. 9, 15, 17). An expert advised the ICC that the lack of stimulation and the isolating impact of the current regime would exacerbate his psychological distress and create a risk of serious psychological deterioration (Al Hassan Decision, para. 23). Defence counsel argued that while medical care in Mali was unlikely to be better, being at home would allow for family contact, which is crucial for the rehabilitation of torture survivors (Al Hassan Request, para. 45). The ICC argued, however, that medically necessary treatment remained available to detainees at the ICCDC and his defence and the Registrar could engage on how to improve this, and for these reasons his health did not provide a reason to grant release (Al Hassan Decision, paras. 36–37, 82).

3 Restrictions to regimes and rights

Prisoners are considered to be susceptible to a *dual vulnerability* during the current pandemic: they are prone to both a higher risk of infection from the virus *and* human rights violations (WHO, 2020: 3). All applications for release and transfer referred to the rights implications of the restrictions that had been implemented in the international detention facility (ICC DC) and enforcing states (UK and Benin) to prevent the import and spread of the virus.

3.1 Interim release from the ICC detention centre

At the ICCDC, measures introduced in response to COVID-19 included the suspension of all visits, activities and non-acute medical appointments (Al Hassan Decision, para. 27). Defence counsel applied for interim release on the basis that the radical changes to conditions introduced in light of the pandemic were not compatible with fundamental human rights law and that the *cumulative effect* and *unknown duration* of restrictions amounted to *degrading treatment* that exceeded the level of suffering acceptable in detention (Al Hassan Request, paras. 1, 29, 32, 38). While there was recognition that measures had been implemented on health grounds, it was argued that the prohibition against inhuman and degrading treatment was absolute and applied irrespective of the gravity of the offence (Al Hassan Request, para. 30). The ICC noted that while similar measures were being introduced all around the world due to the exceptional circumstances of the pandemic, it agreed that public health requirements do not detract from the non-derogable duty to "protect detainees from conditions that amount to inhuman or degrading treatment" (Al Hassan Decision, para. 28; CPT, 2020). It recognised further that the impact of restrictive measures may be higher for those in detention and in particular for those under an already restricted regime of detention (Al Hassan Decision, para. 28). Despite finding that the conditions of Al Hassan's detention were "not ideal", the ICC found that the measures were "necessary and proportional in the face of the current situation and did not amount to a situation of inhuman or degrading treatment" (Al Hassan Decision, para. 31). This finding was supported by their temporary nature, the public health protection goal and the fact that mitigating facilities were available (fresh air and sports, books, DVDs) (Al Hassan Decision, paras. 32–33).

3.2 Transfer to a third safe state

Taylor's application before the RSCSL focused on the threat to his health from continued imprisonment in the UK due to the rising rates of infection and fatalities and the inability of the prison to observe public health guidance (Taylor Decision, para. 5). The argument focused on the positive human rights obligation to protect the *life* of detained persons from foreseeable dangers and to prevent prisoners' exposure to undue risk (Taylor Decision, paras. 1, 6, 64). The Judge held that this positive obligation was not absolute and should be applied in a manner that does not impose an *impossible or disproportionate burden* on authorities in light of "the operational choices which must be made in terms of priorities and resources" (Taylor Decision, paras. 18, 73, 75). Further, a positive obligation would only arise if authorities failed to take reasonable measures within the scope of their powers to avoid a foreseeable, real and immediate risk to life (Taylor Decision, paras. 19, 68–69, 72–73). This did not apply to Taylor's situation given the measures that had been implemented to minimise his risk of contracting the virus (Taylor Decision, para. 19). As HMP Frankland had suspended visits and educated inmates about hygiene measures and social distancing in line with public health advice, the judge felt that the prison had "complied as far as they might be expected to avoid any potential risk" (Taylor Decision, para. 74).

4 Contact with the outside world

One of the most significant restrictions imposed in response to COVID-19 has been the suspension of all visits to places of detention, leading to complaints from international prisoners of a situation of virtual isolation (Al Hassan Request, para. 2).

4.1 ICC detention centre

Al Hassan's defence argued that, under human rights law, meaningful contact should be assessed both quantitatively and qualitatively (Al Hassan Request, paras. 34–35). While they acknowledged that the quantitative and qualitative reduction of his interaction fell just under the bar of solitary confinement, they argued this did not lessen the impact of restrictions and that a prolonged, indefinite prohibition on visits could cause suffering exceeding the level inherent in detention (Al Hassan Request, para. 35). This reduction in interaction and reliance on phone calls should be seen in the context of the realities of international detention: Al Hassan had only received one visit from some members of his family in two years and a proposed second visit was postponed due to COVID-19 (Al Hassan Request, para. 14).

Rather than grant release, the ICC felt that measures could be implemented to relieve the impact of conditions of detention: the need for emotional support and contact with family could be addressed by alternate means of communication (Al Hassan Decision, para. 38). Al Hassan's defence had requested private visits with his wife, increased time to speak with family and access to videoconferencing and video messages (Al Hassan Request, para. 10). The ICC rejected the request for visits but granted the right to receive video messages. The ICC noted, however, that videoconferencing was the Registry's responsibility (Al Hassan Request, para. 11). Previous attempts to implement videoconferencing at the ICCDC had been unsuccessful: the Registry had not found "a feasible solution" that enabled monitoring (Al Hassan Request, para. 12). The ICC directed the Registry to explore measures to alleviate the effects of lockdown, make specific arrangements for immediate access to spiritual visits, family videos, communication and to continue to assess the feasibility of videoconferencing (Al Hassan Decision, para. 39).

The Registry decided in December 2020 that while videoconferencing was both logistically and technically feasible, it could only provide a one hour video call with close family members every four months.[4] When this was challenged by other detained persons, the Single Judge felt that given the continued ban on family visits (and likely further extension of this ban), it was necessary to provide more frequent and extensive videoconferencing to render the accused persons' right to family visits effective (Yekatom and Ngaïssona Decision, para. 11). In line with the Detention Centre's policy in relation to family visits, he instructed the Registry to provide each detained person with one videoconferencing session per month of 90 minutes (Yekatom and Ngaïssona Decision, paras. 13, 16).

4.2 IRMCT's detention unit

Karadžić, housed in the same building as Al Hassan (although in the UN Detention Unit), first requested the right to use Skype to contact his family in November 2016. Despite repeated judicial requests for the introduction of videoconferencing, the UNDU Commanding Officer and Registrar repeatedly resisted these requests due to security concerns, referring in particular to monitoring challenges and the risk of livestreaming to social media.[5] In March 2020, the COVID-19 pandemic prompted Karadžić to file a (further) motion requesting the immediate implementation of a videoconferencing system (Karadžić Decision, para. 19). He argued that videoconferencing would reduce the isolation caused by the ban on visits and decrease anxiety about family members (Karadžić Decision, paras. 31, 45). He argued that the lack of videoconferencing (available in many domestic prison systems) violated his right to family life in the context of his lengthy detention and distance from his family (which only allowed for two visits a year) (Karadžić Decision, paras. 23, 28). The Registrar countered that the UNDU rules, based on international standards, provide for regular family visits and other forms of communication, that contemporary standards do not include a right to videoconferencing and the right to family life is not absolute and may be restricted in the interests of security (Karadžić Decision, paras. 24, 37). President Agius was not persuaded by the argument that a lack of access to videoconferencing violated the right to family life or that this right contained a right to videoconference. However, he acknowledged that this form of communication would enhance the ability of detained persons to exercise this right. He also noted that the security risks posed by videoconferencing were also posed by phone calls, and existing rules provided means to mitigate these risks: live-monitoring, limited number and duration of calls, specific times for calls and written guarantees from users with penalties for violations (Karadžić Decision, para. 42). Moreover, he questioned the potential resource constraints given that were only three persons detained at the UNDU. While acknowledging that the solution may be complex, President Agius agreed with his predecessor that the IRMCT should "move on with the times" and "be open to modern technology" (Karadžić Decision, para. 44). He requested that the Registrar make videoconferencing available as soon as practicable, even if on a limited and temporary basis during the pandemic until a more permanent solution could be found (Karadžić Decision, paras. 44, 48–50). Further, given that the ban on visits was likely to be extended, an email system should also be introduced as soon as possible (Karadžić Decision, paras. 26, 46). While it is encouraging that there is an openness among the international judiciary to enhance the enjoyment of the right to family life through the implementation of alternative means of communication, feasibility due to security concerns remains a real obstacle in practice. Further, some of the mitigation measures referred to such as access to the library and sports activities do not involve meaningful social contact.

4.3 A human rights perspective

The application of public health restrictions within a penal setting, while necessary and legitimate, can have the unintended consequence of creating "a superposition of confinement … [or] overisolation" (De Carvalho, dos Santos and Santos, 2020: 3494). The UN High Commissioner for Human Rights has drawn attention to the fact that "suddenly halting contact with the outside world risks aggravating what may be tense, difficult and potentially dangerous situations" (OHCHR, 2020). Detained persons may have a different psychological reaction to the imposition of (further) restrictions than persons in the community (De Carvalho, dos Santos and Santos, 2020: 3496–3497). It is imperative that authorities take steps to ensure that the "disruptive impact of such measures … [is] *actively mitigated*" (UNODC, WHO, UNAIDS and OHCHR, 2020). In relation to contact with the outside world, mitigation strategies have focused on the provision of "increased means and opportunities" (PRI, 2020: 6) through alternative and additional methods of communication, including increased phone calls and access to email, video messages and videoconferencing. The SPT has stressed that such communication should be facilitated, encouraged, frequent and free (SPT, 2020: para. 9(k); see also PC-CP WG, 2020).

While there have been complex feasibility/security issues with the introduction of videoconferencing at international detention facilities, national prison systems have introduced video calls to preserve family ties and reduce isolation during the pandemic. Security measures include time-limited calls, software restrictions and the use of secure laptops in designated rooms (Ministry of Justice (England & Wales), 2020). The CPT has recognised that the pandemic is resulting in national authorities taking "resolute action" on long-standing issues and that "emergency measures put in place temporarily must be made sustainable" (CPT, 2020a). There appears to be ample judicial support at the international level for the roll-out of videoconferencing in international detention facilities to enhance the detained persons' right to family life. It is critical that the introduction of alternate means of communication during the pandemic is compensatory in the short term and complementary in the long term. While videoconferencing brings benefits (seeing the entire family at once, participating in celebrations), this form of communication cannot replace family visits (Europris, 2020: 2); "neither written communication nor telephone calls can replace face to face encounters" (Karadžić Decision, para. 47). Family contact can be restricted in exceptional circumstances for a limited period, but it cannot be prohibited (WHO, 2020: 5; Articles 44(3), 58(1), 106 Nelson Mandela Rules). As Evans points out: "with stricter internal regimes in operation, there should be enhanced, not reduced, external contact" (Evans, 2020: 11). The requirement to lift restrictions as soon as they are no longer necessary is particularly pertinent for limitations on contact with the outside world (CPT, 2020a). Penal Reform International has advocated setting time periods for reviews for lifting restrictions (PRI, 2020: 6). The WHO, UN Office for Drugs and Crime, the SPT, CPT and UN High Commissioner for Human Rights have all stressed the human rights principles that should guide the review of restrictions on prison regimes: restrictions implemented in response to COVID-19 must be necessary, evidence-based, proportionate to the health emergency, non-arbitrary, respectful of human dignity, have a legal basis and be restricted in time (CPT, 2020: para. 4; SPT, 2020; UNODC, WHO, UNAIDS and OHCHR, 2020).

5 Remedial obstacles

Rather than grant temporary or early release or transfer requests, international decisions have highlighted measures that have been or could be adopted to reduce the risk of contracting the disease and to reduce the impact of COVID-19 restrictions by modifying conditions of detention. There have been calls, however, from the Association of Defence Council practising before the International Criminal Courts and Tribunals to grant early release to convicted persons that have served two-thirds of their sentences and to grant provisional release to those who have not yet done so but who are elderly and/or medically vulnerable (Rugiririza, 2020). Gerontologists have also called on authorities to consider granting early release on medical or compassionate grounds to those at high risk of poor health outcomes from either the virus or the restrictive measures put in place to prevent or manage the outbreak (Prost et al., 2020: 3). While human rights law does not recognise a right to release on health grounds, it does acknowledge that the continued detention of a seriously ill person, a person of advanced age or living with a short-term fatal prognosis, can violate the duty to prevent inhuman or degrading treatment (PC-CP WG, 2020; Rogan, 2017: 6).

5.1 Appropriateness of reliefs for international prisoners

Many authorities have adopted release policies to reduce overcrowding and the health implications of possible outbreaks in national prison systems. The challenge for international prisoners lies in the fact that domestic release schemes (compassionate, conditional or early) are not applied simply on account of age and health, but also on the basis of the seriousness (violent or sexual nature) of the crime committed, the length of the sentence imposed, the amount of time remaining to be served and the risk to the public if the applicant was released (Al Hassan Request, para. 90; Taylor Decision, para. 15; UNODC, 2020: 4–5; see also UNODC, WHO, UNAIDS and OHCHR, 2020). Indeed, in *Taylor*, it was noted that he did not meet the COVID-19 domestic criteria for early release (Taylor Decision, para. 33). Further, a UN Special Rapporteur has stated that measures adopted to prevent the spread of COVID-19 in prisons (amnesties, pardons, exemptions from criminal liability and benefits of enforcement of sentences) should not result in *de jure or de facto impunity* for persons convicted of serious violations of human rights and any that do are null and void, i.e. have no legal effect (UN SR, 2020). The only instance, in which a humanitarian pardon would be acceptable, he argues, is cases of terminal illness of imminent resolution. In all other circumstances, prisoners housed in overcrowded conditions should be *relocated* to facilities with safer and healthier conditions rather than be released. It is only if relocation is not possible that *temporary house arrest* can be granted (but only for as long as the emergency situation). These options (relocation and house arrest) pose considerable legal and logistical difficulties for courts responsible for supervising persons accused of or convicted for international crimes.

First, any decision to relocate an international prisoner within a national prison system would ultimately be a decision for domestic prison authorities. Though international courts and national prison authorities have been working closely together to ensure adequate protective measures are in place for international prisoners (Taylor Decision, paras. 25–27, 30) and the international courts have adopted a more proactive approach to oversight (seeking regular information about conditions during the pandemic[6]), ultimately, conditions of detention and allocation decisions are the responsibility of enforcing states (see Article 25 IRMCT Statute; Article 3(2) UN-Benin enforcement agreement).

Second, house arrest is not a viable option for most internationally accused or convicted persons who are detained in countries they are not citizens or legal residents of. In April 2020, former President of Chad, Hissène Habré (convicted of crimes against humanity and sentenced to life imprisonment by an African Union backed trial in Dakar) was granted temporary release (60 days) from a Senegalese prison to be spent in house arrest with his family. It was granted due to his advanced age (78) and high risk of contracting COVID-19 in a prison being used as a quarantine facility for new detainees (Al Jazeera, 2020; Maclean, 2020). Typically, however, house arrest for international prisoners would necessitate international travel to their country of origin or residence (or another state willing to accept them). This raises the issue of flight risk. In his application for interim release from pre-trial detention, *Al Hassan* offered to submit to electronic monitoring, to remain under house arrest and to comply with conditions (Al Hassan Request, paras. 3, 22, 28; Al Hassan Decision, para. 74). The request was refused, inter alia, on the grounds of flight risk. The ICC felt that given his connections with well-resourced armed groups, his previous attempts to evade justice by fleeing to another country and the lack of government control in parts of the requested state, the flight risk was high and it would be very difficult to secure his arrest and transfer if he fled either within or beyond Mali (Al Hassan Decision, paras. 65, 75–76, 78–79). Trotter underlines that although there have been no cases of internationally accused persons absconding while on provisional release, international courts face very real limitations in their ability to rearrest absconders, particularly given the political instability in many of their countries of origin (Trotter, 2016: 37, 40–41).

5.2 Impossibility of relief

Another problem has been the *impossibility* of granting the relief requested due to the lack of a legal basis. In *Semanza*, the IRMCT held that there was no legal basis for ordering the provisional release of a person serving their sentence in an enforcing state. The provision cited (Rule 68(1)) could only be applied to convicted persons who remained in custody under direct authority of the IRMCT in its detention facility pending appeal or transfer (Semanza Decision at 4–5). In other words, this remedy could not be granted to convicted persons with finalised sentences housed in enforcing states. Further, the alternative remedy requested – early release – could only be granted following consultation with other judges, and as a request had already been submitted and was being considered – the current request for early release due to the risks posed by COVID-19 was seen as seeking "to circumvent the existing proceedings" (Semanza Decision at 5–6). This is a questionable conclusion, given that the early release request had been submitted in July 2018 and the decision was not delivered until September 2020. Although *Semanza* had served the requisite two-thirds of his sentence, the application was denied on account of the high gravity of his crimes and a failure to demonstrate sufficient rehabilitation.[7] In September 2020, Semanza's counsel filed a complaint with the UN Office of Internal Oversight Services due to the "serious management deficiencies and negligence" of the IRMCT in dealing with early release requests of ICTR and ICTY convicted persons, referring in particular to the *lengthy delay* in deciding cases. The fact that applications were taking over two years to decide, despite numerous motions seeking remedy, stood in stark contrast to the practice direction, which recommends that decisions be rendered seven days prior to eligibility for release. This complaint illustrates that the cumbersome and lengthy process for considering early release applications is not suitable for release on urgent humanitarian and health grounds, particularly if circumstances have changed significantly since the initial submission.

In *Taylor*, the designated judge held that there was no legal basis to order the temporary transfer of a convicted person serving his sentence in an enforcing state to another country (Taylor Decision, para. 45). The RSCSL legal framework (Statute and enforcement agreement with the UK) only permits the *termination* of the enforcement of sentences to enable transfer to another state and not the *suspension* of enforcement (Article 23(3) RSCSL Statute; Article 3(2) UK enforcement agreement). While Defence counsel argued that the RSCSL had an inherent power to order a temporary transfer (Taylor Decision, paras. 7–8), the Prosecutor countered that the RSCSL could cede more authority to enforcing states on "matters it lacks capacity or technical ability to manage", including conditions during a pandemic (Taylor Decision, para. 16).

5.3 Vagueness and burden of the relief

Requests for release and transfer have also been rejected due to their *vagueness* and the *burden* of securing the relief sought in the current situation.

A major issue has been the *duration* of the relief sought. *Al Hassan* requested interim release for the duration of the pandemic or for such time as the Chamber deemed appropriate (Al Hassan Request, para. 48). The Chamber pointed out that in the two instances where interim release had been granted in exceptional humanitarian circumstances, this had been for a 24-hour period and the released person had remained in custody at all times. This was in stark contrast to a request for release to another country for an unknown period given there were no indications as to when the pandemic would end or whether he would be able to return to The Hague within any established time frame (Al Hassan Decision, paras. 77, 88). At the RSCSL, Taylor's request also set a potentially indefinite limitation for his transfer request, stating he would return to continue serving his sentence when the UK and its prisons were free from the virus (Taylor Decision, para. 9).

What was perhaps more challenging about Taylor's request was that he asked to be temporarily transferred to a prison in a "third and safe country". The vagueness of the request to be transferred to an unnamed "safe" country was condemned by the Prosecutor, who felt the request was "downright unthinkable" and demonstrated a "woeful lack of grasp of reality" of the threat of the pandemic (Taylor Decision, paras. 11, 23). The Registrar's submission also noted the global scale of the pandemic and the reality that the handful of countries that had not declared any cases of COVID-19 (at that time) had not entered into enforcement agreements with the RSCSL (Taylor Decision, paras. 26, 31). The Registrar also commented on the logistical difficulties of transfers given travel restrictions and quarantine requirements (Taylor Decision, para. 32). The designated judge pointed out that the applicant's failure to identify a country offended against the principle that the party seeking relief should give a clear defined statement of the relief sought (Taylor Decision, paras. 44, 50). She felt that the request for a transfer to a third and safe country must be taken to mean to a country with which the RSCSL had an enforcement agreement and which was free from COVID-19 (Taylor Decision, paras. 48–51). All the countries with agreements with the RSCSL had reported cases and as the countries that had not reported cases did not have agreements with the RSCSL, they had no legal obligation to (temporarily) enforce Mr. Taylor's sentence (Taylor Decision, paras. 53–54). On this basis, the RSCSL could not order clear, enforceable or legal relief.[8] The request was therefore essentially asking the RSCSL to identify a safe country and to undertake lengthy and extensive negotiations with this state (which had no legal obligation to receive him) to agree an enforcement agreement to provide temporary relief. The designated judge felt that this would impose an impossible and disproportionate burden on the RSCSL and as such was not required under a rights obligation to protect his life (Taylor Decision, para. 76).

6 Seeking shelter from the pandemic and its impact on prison life

There has been national judicial recognition that the impact of the significant and unforeseen restrictions introduced to prison regimes in response to COVID-19 could result in a reduction of the time to be served on custodial sentences.[9] As the cases outlined above show, international judges have been open to the adoption of mitigating measures within the custodial setting to alleviate the detrimental impact of restrictions for international prisoners. Despite this, the challenges of balancing public health considerations and prisoners' rights within the legal, political and operational constraints of the international penal system have resulted in all requests for release or transfer being denied. The gravity of the offences and the legal and logistical requirements for transfers generally, and for persons accused or convicted of atrocity crimes and during a pandemic in particular, make such requests very difficult to grant. Further, the courts highlighted the lack of any legal basis in their constituent documents to permit the grant of the specific reliefs requested. In this way, the case-law highlights gaps in the international supervisory and legal frameworks in terms of the relief that can be granted in cases of imminent dangers to health.

The global nature of the pandemic also means that more nuanced discussions of relief were not addressed. What if the pandemic had been localised or contained within one region? In other words, if international travel was possible and there was a "safe" country or facility to transfer prisoners to? Temporary transfers have been used to transfer convicted persons to international detention facilities to provide testimony at trials. What if the prisoner was not held in "safer" conditions and was in fact housed in an overcrowded unhygienic facility? Would there be a positive rights obligation to move a prisoner from harm's way in this situation? Can an enforcing state relocate or grant temporary release/house arrest to an international prisoner? The case law and pronouncements of rights bodies and officials seem to suggest that irrespective of any rights-based arguments that could be made for (temporary) release in such circumstances, these should not be applicable to persons accused of or convicted for core international crimes. Finding feasible remedial solutions for persons detained and supervised by international criminal courts is more difficult than for regular prisoners of national prison systems on account of governing legal frameworks, operational dependencies and the public safety significance of such decisions.

Notes

1 Situation in the Republic of Mali, *Prosecutor v Al Hassan Ag Abdoul Aziz Mohamed Ag Mahmoud*, Public redacted version of 'Urgent Defence request for interim release' ICC-01/12-01/18, 23 March 2020, para. 2 (hereafter Al Hassan Request); *Prosecutor v Laurent Semanza*, Decision on Motion for Provisional Release, MICT-13-36-ES.2, 21 April 2020 at 2 (hereafter Semanza Decision);

Decision of the Designated Duty Judge, The Application of Charles G. Taylor to the Temporarily Transferred to a Safe Third Country to Continue his Imprisonment due to the Massive Outbreak of Covid 19 in the UK (RSCSL-03-01-ES-1442) 04.09.20, para. 2 (hereafter Taylor Decision).
2 Situation in the Republic of Mali, *Prosecutor v Al Hassan Ag Abdoul Aziz Ag Mohamed Ag Mahmoud*, Public Redacted version of 'Decision on the Defence request for Interim release' ICC-01/12-01/18, 29 May 2020, para. 80 (hereafter Al Hassan Decision).
3 President of the Mechanism, Third Order to the Registrar related to Laurent Semanza's Urgent Petition for Early Release, MICT-13-36.ES.2, 26 March 2021.
4 *Prosecutor v Alfred Yekatom and Patrice-Edouard Ngaïssona*, Decision on the Non-Privileged Video-Conferencing at the Detention Centre, ICC-01/14-01/18, 03.02.21, para. 3 (hereafter Yekatom and Ngaïssona Decision).
5 See *Prosecutor v Radovan Karadžić*, Decision on request for review of the Registrar's decision on video communications, MICT-13-55-ES, 16 April 2020, paras. 4, 13, 25 (hereafter Karadžić Decision).
6 See President of the IRMCT, Third Order for Covid-19 Updates from Enforcement States, MICT-12-01-ES, 28 August 2020; Semanza Decision at 6.
7 *Prosecutor v Semanza*, Decision on Laurent Semanza's Application for Early Release, MICT-13-36-ES.2, 17 September 2020.
8 Taylor Decision, para. 46. The option of relying on the Convention for the Transfer of Sentenced Persons was explored but ruled out as Taylor did not have the nationality of any member State that not reported COVID-19. However, it is unclear on what basis this Convention could have been relied on given that the RSCSL is not party to the Convention and the case does not discuss asking the UK to request such a transfer (see paras. 55–58).
9 See *R v Manning* [2020] EWCA Crim 592, para. 41; *R v Jones* [2020] EWCA Crim 764, paras 17, 19.

References

Al Jazeera (2020): Chad: Ex-president temporarily released from jail due to COVID-19, 7 April 2020, https://www.aljazeera.com/news/2020/04/07/chad-ex-president-temporarily-released-from-jail-due-to-covid-19/ (accessed 25 September 2020).

Barnert, E., Ahalt, C., and Williams, B. (2020): Prisons: Amplifiers of the Covid-19 pandemic hiding in plain sight. *AJPH* 110(7), 964–966.

CPT (2020): Statement of principles relating to the treatment of persons deprived of their liberty in the context of the coronavirus disease (COVID-19) pandemic. *CPT/Inf* (2020), 13, 20 March 2020.

CPT (2020a): Follow-up statement regarding the situation of persons deprived of their liberty in the context of the ongoing COVID-19 pandemic. *CPT/Inf* (2020), 21.

De Carvalho, S. G., dos Santos, A. B. S. and Santos, I. M. (2020): The pandemic in prison: Interventions and overisolation. *Ciência and Saúde Coletvia* 25(9), 3493–3502.

European Committee of Social Rights (2020): *Statement of interpretation on the right to protection of health in times of pandemic*, 21 April 2020.

Europris (2020): *Overview of European prison services' response to the COVID-19 crisis*, 3rd Edition, 24 July 2020.

Evans, M. (2020): Advice of the SPT to states parties and NPMs relating to the Coronavirus. In: Expert Network on External Prison Oversight and Human Rights and International Corrections and Prisons Association (Ed.): *Adapting to Covid-19: Prison oversight and monitoring during a pandemic*, Special Issue, 20 April 2020.

Franco-Paredes, C., Jankousky, K., Schultz, J., Bernfeld, J., Cullen, K., Quan, N. G., Kon, S., Hotez, P., Henao-Martínez, A.F. and Krsak, M. (2020): Covid-19 in jails and prisons: A neglected infection in a marginalised population. *PLOS* 14(6), e0008409.

Maclean, R. (2020): Chad's ex-president, sentenced to life, given temporary reprieve from prison. *The New York Times*, 6 April 2020, https://www.nytimes.com/2020/04/06/world/africa/Hissene-Habre-chad-senegal.html (accessed 25 September 2020).

Mariner, J., and Schleifer, R. (2013): The right to health in prison. In: Zuniga, J. M., Marks, S. P., and Gostin, L. O. (Eds.): *Advancing the human right to health*. OUP, 298.

Ministry of Justice (England and Wales) Press Release: Secure video calls to help prisoners maintain family ties, Press Release 15 May 2020.

PC-CP (2020): COVID-19 Related Statement by Members of the Council for Penological cooperation Working Group, 17 April 2020.

Penal Reform International (2020), *Coronavirus: Healthcare and human rights of people in prison*, Briefing note, 16 March 2020.

Prost, S. G., Novisky, M., Rorvig, A. L., Zaller, N., and Williams, B. (2020): Prisons and Covid-19: A desperate call for gerontological expertise in correctional health care. *Gerontologist*, July 2020, 1–5.

Rogan, M. (2017): Human rights and correctional health policy: A view from Europe. *International Journal of Prisoner Health* 13(1), 3–9.

Rugiririza, E. (2020): Covid-19: Should we release vulnerable convicts? 16 April 2020, https://www.justiceinfo.net/en/other/44138-covid-19-should-we-release-vulnerable-convicts.html (accessed 25 September 2020).

Special Rapporteur on the promotion of truth, justice, reparation and guarantees of non-repetition (2020): *Information Note: COVID-19, prison overcrowding, and serving sentences for serious human rights violations*, https://www.ohchr.org/EN/Issues/Truth-JusticeReparation/Pages/infonotecovid.aspx (accessed 8 October 2020).

SPT (2020): Advice of the Subcommittee to States parties and national preventive mechanisms relating to the coronavirus disease (COVID-19) pandemic, CAT/OP/10, 7 April 2020.

Trotter, A. (2016): Provisional release form international remand detention. In: Mulgrew, R. and Abels, D. (Eds.): *Research handbook on the international penal system*. Cheltenham: Elgar, 23–53.

UN Office of Drugs and Crime (2020): Position Paper, *Covid-19 preparedness and responses in prison*, 31 March 2020.

UN Office of the High Commissioner for Human Rights (2020): Urgent action needed to prevent COVID-19 "rampaging through places of detention", 25 March 2020.

UN Office of the High Commissioner for Human Rights (2020a): Covid-19 no excuse for impunity for those convicted of crimes against humanity. UN expert on transitional justice, 29 April 2020, https://www.ohchr.org/EN/NewsEvents/Pages/DisplayNews.aspx?NewsID=25840&LangID=E (accessed 8 October 2020).

UNODC, WHO, UNAIDS and OHCHR (2020): Joint statement on COVID-19 in prisons and other closed settings, 13 May 2020, https://www.who.int/news-room/detail/13-05-2020-unodc-who-unaids-and-ohchr-joint-statement-on-covid-19-in-prisons-and-other-closed-settings (accessed 8 October 2020).

World Health Organisation (2020): *Preparedness, prevention and control of COVID-19 in prisons and other places of detention*, Interim Guidance, 15 March 2020.

47 International human rights and COVID-19 in prisons

Medical isolation and independent oversight

Róisín Mulgrew and Dirk van Zyl Smit

1 Introduction

The COVID-19 pandemic has had a material impact on prison conditions worldwide. Not only has it led to greatly increased healthcare demands in prisons, but it has also resulted in large numbers of prisoners being subjected to reduced regimes and forms of isolation. Moreover, "the ability of those responsible for running places of detention is potentially severely comprised" and prisons are now "faced with some of the most challenging situations imaginable" (Evans, 2020: 9). In this new environment, "coronavirus related restrictions … in a detention setting, unless very sensitively managed … can degenerate into inhuman and degrading treatment" (Kelly, 2020: 19). This chapter focuses, from the perspective of international human rights law, on two difficult questions that have emerged in the context of the COVID-19 pandemic. First, how should national authorities be dealing with the additional healthcare demands of the pandemic without infringing international standards that forbid indefinite or prolonged solitary confinement? Second, must independent monitoring continue during a pandemic and if so, how must this be done?

2 Solitary confinement and medical isolation or quarantine during the COVID-19 pandemic

One of the most positive developments in international prison standards has been the recent recognition that indefinite or prolonged solitary confinement is an inhuman or degrading form of treatment and, in its more extreme manifestations, a form of torture. For some time, there had been an indication that this was the case (Shalev, 2014). But the 2015 adoption of the revised UN Standard Minimum Rules for the Treatment of Prisoners (Nelson Mandela Rules) brought clarity at the international level: "[t]he question whether indefinite or prolonged solitary confinement is cruel, inhuman, and degrading treatment or punishment, or torture, has now been settled through [the Nelson Mandela Rules]" (Méndez, 2020: 124). Rule 44 of the Nelson Mandela Rules defines solitary confinement as "the confinement of

DOI: 10.4324/9781003169178-47

prisoners for 22 hours or more a day without meaningful human contact". Prolonged solitary confinement, Rule 44 goes on to say, is "for a time period in excess of 15 consecutive days". The definition of "prolonged solitary confinement" is important because Rule 43 of the Nelson Mandela Rules (2015) makes it clear that neither "restrictions" nor "disciplinary sanctions" may "in any circumstances" amount "to torture or other cruel, inhuman or degrading treatment or punishment". This prohibition is sharpened further by the statement in the same Rule that certain practices shall be prohibited, including "indefinite solitary confinement" and "prolonged solitary confinement".

The definitions and prohibitions in the Nelson Mandela Rules were developed mostly in the context of solitary confinement as a disciplinary sanction. These Rules can, however, clearly be read more widely as limiting forms of isolation other than solitary confinement as a disciplinary sanction. The definition of solitary confinement in Rule 44 is not linked explicitly to prison discipline, while Rule 43 refers to "limitations" as well as "disciplinary sanctions". A further indication that restrictions on solitary confinement may apply also to its use outwith the disciplinary system can be found in Rule 37, which includes "solitary confinement" as a form of involuntary separation from the general prison population that requires authorisation by law or regulation and the promulgation of policies and procedures to govern its use and review.

The newly emergent clarification of what is meant by solitary confinement, also largely adopted in the 2020 amendments to the European Prison Rules (EPR, 2020: Rules 53A and 60), must be seen against the background of the long-standing, but also positively evolving, international standards for healthcare in prison. At its international law core lies Article 12 of the International Covenant of Economic Social and Cultural Rights, which requires states to recognise the right of "everyone to the enjoyment of the highest attainable standard of physical and mental health" and to work towards the implementation of this right. At both the international (NMR, 2015: Rules 24–35. See also Mariner and Schleifer, 2013: 292) and regional (EPR, 2020: Rules 39–48; IACHR, 2008: Principle 10) levels, there have been systematic efforts to ensure that the right to health guarantees prisoners' healthcare needs are met in practice.

Among the many health risks that prisoners have a right to be protected against is the risk of infections. Observers of prisons worldwide, from John Howard (1792) in the 18th century onwards, have recognised this risk. But what if the risk of infection to prisoners is posed by other prisoners? Historically, the response has been to separate prisoners who pose a severe risk of infecting others by keeping them in conditions akin to solitary confinement. Solitary confinement, however, is increasingly recognised as problematic.

Leaving the problematic aspects of solitary confinement aside for a moment, the question arises whether any form of medical isolation, let alone solitary confinement, is required at all to deal with certain infections. In the panic that arose in the 1980s and early 1990s around the risk of HIV transmission in prison, the initial reaction in many countries was to isolate prisoners. However, as knowledge of the pandemic grew, such isolation was widely condemned as being contrary to human rights and international prison standards emerged to indicate this forcefully. Thus, in 1993, the World Health Organization (WHO) explained that "since segregation, isolation and restrictions on occupational activities, sports and recreation are not considered useful or relevant in the case of HIV-infected people in the community, the same attitude should be adopted towards HIV-infected prisoners" (WHO, 1993: Recommendation 27). Further, such prisoners should have equal access to the full range of programmes available to the general prison population (WHO, 1993: Recommendation 27). The non-isolation and the full participation of HIV positive prisoners had become the norm in international standards.[1]

HIV/AIDS is not the only pandemic with which prisons worldwide have had to deal in recent decades. The growing problem of drug-resistant tuberculosis in prisons has been recognised as something that authorities have to address in order to protect other prisoners (Lines, 2006: 271). International standards have cautiously recognised that this can be done by isolating highly infectious prisoners as part of a wider programme of tuberculosis prevention (Dara, Chorgoliani, and de Colombani, 2014). While some of these standards are applicable to COVID-19 in prisons, this is not automatically the case, given the differences in the challenges posed by the diseases and the recently clarified definitions of what amounts to solitary confinement since the TB guidance was issued.

While COVID-19 is highly infectious, the best strategy for dealing with it is not necessarily by putting prisoners in quarantine in single cells normally used for solitary confinement. As medical doctor Cloud and his colleagues explain (Cloud et al., 2020: 2), while infected prisoners can be isolated from uninfected prisoners, they can be housed with other infected prisoners. Individual quarantine that keeps prisoners entirely separate from other prisoners can be limited to those with an unknown infectious status. Such quarantine can be kept short by regular testing: it should never be as long as 15 days (the point at which it would become prolonged solitary confinement). In fact, as we explain below, it should not be solitary confinement at all depending on the way in which it is implemented.

The way of ensuring that quarantine (or isolation) does not become solitary confinement (as defined by the Nelson Mandela Rules) was well summarised and put in a wider context in a UNODC Policy Paper released at an early stage of the COVID-19 pandemic (UNODC, 2020):

> Ensuring the health and well-being of prisoners, prison officers, other prison personnel and visitors must be at the heart of infection prevention and control measures [for COVID-19], while respecting the fundamental safeguards outlined in the … [Nelson Mandela Rules]. Importantly,

> these include the requirements to limit the confinement of prisoners for 22 hours or more a day without meaningful human contact to an exceptional measure, and never beyond a maximum of 15 consecutive days (prolonged solitary confinement); to ensure continued access of external inspection bodies and legal advisers to prisoners; to have clinical decisions taken only by health-care professionals; and to abstain from suspending family contacts altogether. Under no circumstances whatsoever must COVID-19 measures in prisons amount to inhumane or degrading treatment.

The Council of Europe's Council for Penological Cooperation also noted the potentially deleterious effects of isolation to prevent the spread of COVID-19 if it were to result in solitary confinement:

> As solitary confinement and in particular prolonged periods of such confinement, have noteworthy negative impact on the mental and physical health of detainees, as detailed in the recently revised and updated European Prison Rules and in their commentary (Rules 53 and 60.6), any such confinement for sanitary and safety reasons [related to COVID-19] should be coupled with counterbalancing activities, such as an increased number of free-of-charge phone calls, books and other reading material, TV and other media, in-cell educational, training and recreational activities and others. Such periods of solitary confinement should be ended immediately with the end of the reason for their imposition.[2]

Other international and regional bodies have emphasised similar points. Thus, the Sub-committee for the Prevention of Torture (SPT), the United Nations body set up by the Optional Protocol to the Convention Against Torture (OPCAT) to monitor places of detention, has highlighted the importance of "prevent[ing] the use of medical isolation taking the form of disciplinary solitary confinement" (SPT, 2020). It has underlined that "medical isolation must be on the basis of an independent medical evaluation, proportionate, limited in time and subject to procedural safeguards".[3] The European Committee for the Prevention of Torture (CPT) noted that: "In cases of isolation or placement in quarantine of a detained person who is infected or is suspected of being infected by the SARS-CoV-2 virus, the person concerned should be provided with meaningful human contact every day" (CPT, 2020, para. 8). And the European Commissioner for Human Rights also warned that: "The absolute nature of the prohibition of torture and ill-treatment should never be compromised by measures taken in prisons including in the case of isolation for health reasons".[4] These international and regional COVID-19 policy statements do not directly amend any existing standard governing solitary confinement or healthcare in prisons. However, they are likely to have a lasting impact on the implementation of international law in prisons in both areas.

3 Monitoring and oversight during the pandemic

In March 2020, the WHO stated categorically that COVID-19

> must not be used as a justification for objecting to external inspection of prisons and other places of detention by independent international or national bodies whose mandate is to prevent torture and other cruel, inhuman or degrading treatment or punishment,

adding that inspection bodies should continue to have access to all persons deprived of their liberty, including persons in isolation.[5] The CPT communicated directly with states to highlight that "monitoring by independent bodies, remains an essential safeguard against ill-treatment" (CPT, 2020). Under international treaty law, national and international inspection bodies must be granted full access to all places of detention, all persons detained therein and all information requested.[6] OPCAT and the European Convention for the Prevention of Torture do however allow state authorities to prevent visits in a narrowly defined set of exceptional circumstances. Under Article 14(2) OPCAT, states may only object to a visit "on urgent and compelling grounds of national defence, public safety, natural disaster or serious disorder in the place to be visited that temporarily prevent the carrying out of such a visit". Under Article 9(1) ECPT, state authorities, in exceptional circumstances, can "make representations to the Committee against a visit at the time or to the particular place proposed… [but] only on grounds of national defence, public safety, serious disorder…or the medical condition of a person…". The ECPT makes clear that such representations should result in immediate consultations and arrangements to enable the CPT to "exercise its functions expeditiously".[7] Indeed, the CPT issued a Statement of Principles during the pandemic which states that monitoring by independent bodies (NPMs and CPT) "remains an essential safeguard against ill-treatment" and that states should "continue to guarantee access for monitoring bodies to all places of detention, including where persons are kept in quarantine" (CPT, 2020, para. 10).

Similarly, the OPCAT exception only permits a temporary restriction on visits to a particular place and cannot be used to justify a ban on visits completely (Evans, 2020). It has been argued that as the access limitation clause in OPCAT (Article 14(2)) only applies to the SPT: "under no circumstances can detaining authorities prevent National Preventive Mechanisms from having access… to carry out their mandate" (Muralt, 2020: 28). In a contradictory statement, however, the SPT noted that "although not expressly stated, it is implicit from the structure of the Optional Protocol that national preventive visits may, like those of the Subcommittee, be temporarily restricted in accordance with article 14(2) of the Optional Protocol" (SPT, 2020: para. 11). This interpretation means that although a particular visit from an NPM could be objected to on public safety grounds (including medical emergencies necessitating quarantine), access can only be restricted temporarily for strictly defined reasons (SPT, 2020a: paras. 5–6).

International prison monitors, such as the SPT and CPT, were forced to suspend their programme of visits in the earlier stages of the global pandemic. Kelly (2020) laments that the closing of national borders and the cessation of international air travel resulted in the CPT having to suspend its regular visiting programme for the first time in its working history.[8] These practical realities, he argued, meant that the work of national oversight bodies assumed even greater significance. Unfortunately, many NPMs were unable to continue with their regular programme of visits. The South African NPM (Judicial Inspectorate for Correctional Services) could not visit prisons due to national regulations, whereas visits by the Mozambique NPM, although permitted, were not possible due to the suspension of donor funding (Muntingh, 2020). The majority of NPMs, however, felt compelled to suspend their regular programme of visits on the basis of the *do no harm principle*. A lack of PPE, the impossibility of social distancing in overcrowded prisons and the absence of access to hygiene facilities were all relevant considerations (Muralt, 2020).

Rather than suspending visits, the SPT (2020) advocates the continuation of preventive visits with adapted working methods. Visits assumed greater importance given that "the potential exposure to … ill-treatment faced by those in places of detention may be heightened as a consequence of … public health measures". It urged NPMs to continue monitoring visits, while respecting public health limitations on their methods, "to reduce the possibility of detainees suffering forms of inhuman and degrading treatment as a result of the very real pressures that detention systems and those responsible for them now face" (SPT, 2020: para. 7).

3.1 The "Do No Harm" principle

The CPT (2020) highlighted that monitoring bodies must take all precautions to observe the "do no harm" principle, particularly when dealing with older persons and those with pre-existing medical conditions. This principle is now of "cardinal importance" and involves reducing the risk of inspection teams becoming "vectors for COVID-19 infection" (Kelly, 2020: 21). In order to safeguard the monitors, prisoners, prison staff and general public health, inspection bodies should adopt measures to operationalise the "do no harm principle" in the context of prison visits during a public health pandemic. These include precautionary measures prior to visits (seeking professional health advice, medical checks, voluntary participation for monitors) and proactive measures during visits (use of PPE, interviewing individuals with barriers/social distancing) (Muralt, 2020: 29–30).

3.2 Adapted and supplementary working methods

Evans accepts that it is "proper for NPMs to set aside for now some of the standard expectations of preventative visiting and to focus on new approaches to the fulfilment of their mandates" (Evans, 2020: 8). NPMs have adapted their working practices to develop innovative methods for triangulating information (Muralt, 2020: 30), and to minimise social contact while offering effective opportunities for preventative engagement (SPT, 2020: para. 12). New approaches include:

- Reliance on individual complaints
- Direct phone and electronic (email, videoconferencing) communication with prisoners
- Engagement with third parties with access to prisoners (families, lawyers, NGOs) and recently released prisoners
- Use of technology - video footage of detention, remote access to files, virtual visits to prisons

In addition to these alternative means of acquiring the information that would usually be acquired during visits, inspection bodies can also bolster their preventive mandate through:

- online communication and dialogue with state and prison authorities to gain information about measures being imposed,
- scrutiny of local and national legal and policy measures and their human rights implications, and
- provision of guidance and recommendation to prison authorities.

3.3 The resumption of prison visits

According to Rogan (2021), the adoption of OPCAT and the revision of the Nelson Mandela Rules upgraded the principle that prison inspections can promote the protection of prisoners' rights into an effective universal obligation on states to ensure that prisons are subject to independent monitoring. The ability to access prisons and all persons detained within such facilities is "one of the strongest powers" of inspection bodies and "an essential tool" in the protection of prisoners' rights (Muralt, 2020: 9). Indeed, Penal Reform International has warned that "[i]n times of emergency, the ability of independent bodies to monitor developments in detention facilities is essential to prevent excessive use of quarantine, abuse of power, use of torture or ill-treatment" (PRI, 2020: 9). Thankfully, by July 2020, the CPT and many national monitoring bodies had resumed visits to places of deprivation of liberty (CPT, 2020a). However, in recent months, many countries have re-imposed stringent public health measures and even re-entered national lockdowns. It is vitally important that inspection bodies are able to continue their crucial work. It is essential, therefore, that restrictions imposed on independent inspection bodies are no greater than those imposed on other persons working with detained persons (Evans, 2020: 9). Further, the work of NPMs must be categorised "as an essential service to continue during periods of lock-down" (Evans, 2020:10).

4 Conclusion

The worldwide COVID-19 pandemic has raised questions about the sufficiency of international human rights standards relating to the treatment of prisoners under pandemic conditions, and about the efficacy of the international institutions set up to monitor their implementation. Perceived shortcomings in international standards and practices have led to international organisations from both governmental and non-governmental sectors issuing a wide range of exhortations to national authorities responsible in these conditions, while rethinking how monitoring should operate during the pandemic.

As far as *solitary confinement* is concerned, it is clear that international law increasingly frowns on its use. One way of avoiding this problem is to ensure that prisoners who are separated from others for medical (or indeed any other) reasons have at least two hours of "meaningful human contact". However, "meaningful human contact" is itself difficult to define. One widely quoted attempt to do so regards "meaningful human contact" as:

> the amount and quality of social interaction and psychological stimulation which human beings require for their mental health and well-being. Such interaction requires the human contact to be face to face and direct (without physical barriers) and more than fleeting or incidental, enabling empathetic interpersonal communication. Contact must not be limited to those interactions determined by prison routines, the course of (criminal) investigations or medical necessity.[9]

In the time of COVID-19, this understanding is being rethought. Physical interactions without barriers may be impossible and careful attention is being paid to the use of electronic communications in ways that make (family) contact via the internet more fulfilling. It is only a matter of time before courts will be called upon to determine whether such forms of contacts are truly "meaningful". If they pass muster, one may expect them to become a permanent feature of separating prisoners for non-disciplinary reasons other than medical quarantine.

The wider role of healthcare professionals in the implementation of the separation and solitary confinement should also be reconsidered. While healthcare professionals do not want to be involved in the imposition of disciplinary punishment, measures to combat COVID-19 require them to pay attention to the details of how prisoners are isolated from others for health reasons. One may expect that this experience, coupled with growing scientific knowledge of the negative effects of all but the shortest periods of solitary confinement (WMA, 2019), will encourage healthcare professionals to intervene more readily and actively to prevent solitary confinement (and forms of separation that do not meet the definition of solitary confinement) being imposed on prisoners or, where they are imposed, being kept in place for periods that harm the physical and mental health of the prisoners concerned.

The SPT has emphasised that the "prohibition of torture and other cruel, inhuman or degrading treatment or punishment cannot be derogated from, even during exceptional circumstances and emergencies that threaten the life of the nation".[10] This prohibition necessitates the continuing oversight of prisons during a pandemic. It is unclear how the suspension of visits and the adapted work practices adopted by NPMs have impacted on their effectiveness to protect prisoners. Carver and Handley argue that the effectiveness of NPMs can be assessed in light of their processes (ability to conduct its work (inputs) and the actual work it carries out (outputs)) and the short-term and long-term outcomes of these processes (state compliance with recommendations and the prevention of torture and ill-treatment) (Carver and Handley, 2020: 3–4). It cannot be ignored, however, that both an NPM's processes and outcomes are influenced by political, social and legal factors operating in a country-specific context (Carver and Handley, 2020: 6). For the SPT, the "overriding criterion must be that of effectiveness in securing the prevention of ill-treatment of those subject to detaining measures" even if the "parameters of prevention have been widened by the extraordinary measures that States have had to take" (SPT, 2020: para. 14). In the face of the practical and public health challenges faced by prison inspection bodies, it has been argued that states should assume an increased duty of transparency that includes the provision of detailed information on not only COVID-19 outbreaks in prisons but also on the measures that have been adopted in relation to the prison regime and healthcare (De Rue, 2020). In this way, adapted forms of scrutiny can continue irrespective of the situation in particular prisons, regions or countries.

Notes

1 See the 2001 CPT Annual report; UNODC, 2008.

2 *Follow-up Covid-19 Related Statement by the Council for Penological Co-Operation Working Group*, para. 6.

3 Ibid. See also PRI Briefing Note, *Coronavirus: Healthcare and human rights of people in prison* (16.03.20).

4 Commissioner for Human Rights *COVID-19 pandemic: urgent steps are needed to protect the rights of prisoners in Europe* Strasbourg, para. 8.

5 WHO, 2020. The SPT also confirmed that NPMs must be granted access to "any place where a person is held in quarantine and from which they are not free to leave" (CPT, 2020a: para. 3).

6 See Articles 14 and 20 of the Optional Protocol to the Convention Against Torture; Article 8 of the European Convention for the Prevention of Torture.

7 Articles 9(2) 8 of the European Convention for the Prevention of Torture.
8 Visits stopped in March 2020 until their resumption with a visit to France in July 2020.
9 See PRI and Essex Human Rights Centre, 2017, on the initial guidance on the interpretation and implementation of the Nelson Mandela Rules, 88-89. The CPT has applied this definition – see the Report on the UK Visit [CPT/Inf (2019) 29], para. 74 (fn. 55); Report on the Norwegian Visit [CPT/Inf (2019) 1], para. 82 (fn. 2).
10 SPT, 2020: para. 5. See also Art 2(2) of the Convention against Torture; Articles 4 and 7 of the International Covenant on Civil and Political Rights.

References

Carver, R., and Handley, L. (2020): Evaluating national preventive mechanisms: A conceptual model. *Journal of Human Rights Practice* 12, 1–22.

Cloud, D., Augustine, D., Ahalt, C., and Williams, B. (2020): The ethical use of medical isolation – not solitary confinement – to reduce COVID-19 transmission in correctional settings *Amend* 9 April 2020. https://amend.us/wp-content/uploads/2020/04/Medical-Isolation-vs-Solitary_Amend.pdf.

Commissioner for Human Rights (2020): *COVID-19 pandemic: Urgent steps are needed to protect the rights of prisoners in Europe*, 6 April 2020.

Council of Europe, Council for Penological Co-Operation Working Group (2020): *Follow-up Covid-19 Related Statement by the Council for Penological Co-Operation Working Group*, 14 October 2020.

CPT (2020): *Statement of principles relating to the treatment of persons deprived of their liberty in the context of the coronavirus disease (COVID-19) pandemic*, CPT/Inf (2020) 13, 20 March 2020.

CPT (2020a): *Follow-up statement regarding the situation of persons deprived of their liberty in the context of the ongoing COVID-19 pandemic*, CPT/Inf (2020)21, 9 July 2020.

Dara, M., Chorgoliani, D., and de Colombani, P. (2014): TB prevention and control care in prisons. In: Enggist, S. et al. (Eds.): *Prisons and health*. Copenhagen: WHO Regional Office Europe, 55–71.

De Rue, M. (2020): Access to healthcare and social distance during COVID pandemic cannot stop at the prison gate. *Strasbourg Observers Blog*, 18 May 2020.

EPR (2006): *The European Prison Rules* (Adopted by the Committee of Ministers of the Council of Europe on 11 January 2006 and revised and amended by the Committee of Ministers on 1 July 2020.

Evans, M. (2020): Advice of the SPT to States Parties and NPMs relating to the Coronavirus. In: International Corrections and Prisons Association (Ed.): *Adapting to Covid-19: Prison oversight and monitoring during a pandemic*, 20 April 2020. Brussels: ICPA.

Howard, J. (1792) *The state of the prisons in England and Wales*. London: Johnson, Dilly and Cadell.

IACHR (2008): *Principles and best practices on the protection of persons deprived of Liberty in the Americas* (Approved by the Inter-American Commission on Human Rights Commission during its 131st regular period of sessions, held from March 3-14, 2008)

Kelly, M. (2020): Respecting the human rights of detainees during the coronavirus pandemic: A new statement of principles by the CPT. In: International Corrections and Prisons Association (Ed.): *Adapting to Covid-19: Prison oversight and monitoring during a pandemic, 20 April 2020*. Brussels: ICPA.

Lines, R. (2006): From equivalence of standards to equivalence of objectives: The entitlement of prisoners to health care standards higher than those outside prisons. *International Journal of Prisoner Health* 2(4), 269–280.

Mariner, J., and Schleifer, R. (2013): The right to health in prison. In: Zuniga, J. M., Marks, S. P., and Gostin, L. O. (Eds.): *Advancing the human right to health*. Oxford: Oxford University Press, 290–315.

Méndez, J. (2020): Torture, solitary confinement, and international law. In: Lobel, J., and Scharff Smith, P. (Eds.): *Solitary confinement*. Oxford: Oxford University Press, 117–126.

Muntingh, L. (2020): Africa, Prisons and COVID-19. *Journal of Human Rights Practice* 12(2), 284–292.

Muralt, A. (2020): What does prison monitoring and oversight mean in times of COVID-19? In: ICPA (Eds.): *Adapting to Covid-19: Prison oversight and monitoring during a pandemic*, 20 April 2020. Brussels: ICPA.

NMR (2015): United Nations Standard Minimum Rules for the Treatment of Prisoners (the Nelson Mandela Rules). Adopted by the General Assembly on 17 December 2015 (A/RES/70175). New York: United Nations.

PRI (Penal Reform International) (2020): *Coronavirus: Healthcare and human rights of people in prison*, 16 March 2020. London: PRI.

PRI and Essex Human Rights Centre (2017): *Initial guidance on the interpretation and implementation of the Nelson Mandela Rules*. London: PRI.

Rogan, M. (2021): Prison inspection and monitoring: The need to reform European Law and Policy. *European Journal on Criminal Policy and Research*, 27, 285–305.

Shalev, S. (2014): Solitary confinement as a prison health issue. In: Enggist, S., et al. (Eds.): *Prisons and health*. Copenhagen: WHO Regional Office Europe, 27–35.

SPT (2020): Advice of the Subcommittee to States parties and national preventive mechanisms relating to the coronavirus disease (COVID-19) pandemic, CAT/OP/10, 7 April 2020. Geneva: United Nations.

SPT (2020a): Advice provided by the Subcommittee to the National Preventive Mechanism of the United Kingdom of Great Britain and Northern Ireland regarding compulsory quarantine for coronavirus (COVID-19 virus), CAT/OP/9, 31 March 2020. Geneva: United Nations.

UNODC (2008): *HIV and AIDS places of detention: A toolkit for policymakers, programme managers, prison officers and health care providers in prison settings*. Vienna: United Nations.

UNODC (2020): *Position paper: COVID-19 preparedness and responses in prisons*, 31 March 2020. Vienna: United Nations.

WHO (1993): *Guidelines on HIV infection and AIDS in prisons*. WHO/GPA/DIR/93.3. Geneva: United Nations.

WHO (2020): *Preparedness, prevention and control of COVID-19 in prisons and other places of detention*. Interim Guidance, 15 March 2020. Geneva: United Nations, WHO.

WMA (2019): *Statement on solitary confinement*. Tbilisi, October 2019.

48 Prison populations before and during the pandemic

Lessons from COVID-19 about over-incarceration and its consequences for health

Catherine Heard

1 Introduction

Recent decades have seen rapid and sustained growth in the global prison population, with the result that around 11 million people are in prison worldwide. Of these, more than 3 million are held in pre-trial or some other form of remand detention. Some countries and regions have seen extraordinary growth in prisoner numbers in recent years, while others have achieved steady declines.

The causes of prison population growth are complex and highly context-specific (Jacobson et al., 2017), but many of the consequences are clear: they include overcrowded prisons with inhumane and degrading conditions which negatively impact on prisoners' mental and physical health, the safety of prisoners and prison staff, and prisoners' prospects of rehabilitation. When the COVID-19 pandemic emerged, this was the picture in a substantial majority of countries' prison systems. According to their own official measures of capacity, the prison systems of over 60% of countries worldwide were overcrowded at the start of 2020.

The pandemic prompted many countries to implement measures to reduce their prison populations to ease overcrowding where it existed and to ensure the risk of infection spreading within prison was limited. Early indications suggest that prison populations have declined in the course of the pandemic. It is important to note, however, that other factors relating to the pandemic, but unrelated to deliberate population measures, have impacted prison population numbers over the course of the pandemic and will continue to do so.

The pandemic also led to unprecedentedly restrictive and closed regimes being introduced in prisons across the world. These resulted in visits being suspended and in purposeful activity and engagement also being greatly curtailed, leading to prisoners spending lengthy periods locked in their cells or dormitories with little or nothing to do (see Dünkel, Harrendorf and van Zyl Smit, Chapter 49). These further restrictions have taken a particularly heavy toll on prisoners' mental and physical health over the course of 2020 – and continue to do so.

DOI: 10.4324/9781003169178-48

2 World prison populations when COVID-19 emerged

2.1 Overview

Published a year before the first cases of COVID-19 emerged in Wuhan, the twelfth edition of the World Prison Population List (Walmsley, 2018) ("WPPL 12") provides the best available overview of the world's total prison population as at the start of the pandemic; and of prison population trends across countries, regions and continents since 2000 (when the first edition of the List was published).[1] World Prison Population Lists are based on the most accurate available prison population numbers and comprise data for both pre-trial detainees/remand prisoners and prisoners who have been convicted and sentenced. All World Prison Population Lists, from the first to the twelfth edition, have charted steady increases in overall global prisoner populations. The Lists have revealed vast disparities in prison populations and rates around the world, and notable divergences between countries and regions in terms of prison population trends.

WPPL 12 showed that there were well in excess of 11 million prisoners worldwide. This figure was based on prison population data available for 223 countries and territories, which produced a total figure of 10.74 million, increased to include numbers then estimated to be held in pre-trial and administrative detention centres in China and in prisons camps in North Korea.

WPPL 12 revealed very steep increases in prison populations in several regions since 2000. In South America, the total prison population had almost tripled in size (an increase of 175%), while south-eastern Asia's total prison population had more than doubled (increasing by 122%), and Oceania's had almost doubled (an increase of 86%).

WPPL 12 also showed that there had been extraordinary increases in many countries' prison population rates (numbers of prisoners per 100,000 of general population) over the three-year period since the previous edition of the List had been published. Among the countries with the sharpest increases in prison population rates over this brief period were Cambodia (68%), Nicaragua (61%), Egypt (53%), the Philippines (48%) and Indonesia (45%).

During the same three-year period, there were also significant falls in prison population rates in some countries. These included Mexico (−23%), Romania (−22%), Kazakhstan (−21%), Ukraine (−19%), Japan (−15%), Vietnam (−11%) and the Russian Federation (−10%). When WPPL 12 was published in late 2018, there was no recent published figure for the USA's total prisoner population, but data released subsequently reveals a decrease of almost 5% in America's prison population over the same three-year period. The USA remained the country with the largest prison population and the highest prison population rate, with almost 2.1 million people in prison and 639 prisoners per 100,000 of the general population.

2.2 Pre-trial / remand prisoners

The most recent World Pre-trial/Remand Imprisonment List (Walmsley, 2020) reveals far starker increases since 2000 in the pre-trial population of prisoners than the increases in the combined population of sentenced and pre-trial detainees shown in WPPL 12. More than 2.9 million pre-trial detainees are held in 217 countries. Taking account of the more than 200,000 such prisoners believed to be held in China, detainees omitted from national totals in some countries because they are held in police facilities at the pre-court stage and those held in the other eight countries on which official information is not available,[2] the overall total will be well over 3 million. Numbers of pre-trial detainees grew particularly rapidly in the Americas, Asia and Oceania, far outstripping general population growth in these three continents. By contrast, Africa (excluding Rwanda[3]) saw a rise in the pre-trial/remand population which was less than half that of the growth in the continent's general population.

The number of people in pre-trial/remand imprisonment has grown by more than 30% since 2000. This is 5% higher than the growth in the world's general population since that time. The substantial falls since about 2000 in the pre-trial detainee numbers in Rwanda and the Russian Federation have had a large effect on the change in the global pre-trial detention population. If these countries are omitted from the calculation, the pre-trial/remand imprisonment total in the rest of the world grew by 49% in the two decades up to the start of the pandemic.

2.3 Female prisoners

Numbers of women prisoners have also increased at a faster rate than general prison populations. The most recent edition of the World Female Imprisonment List revealed that the global female prison population rose by more than 50% since 2000, whereas male prisoner numbers grew by around 20% in the same period (Walmsley, 2017). Numbers of women prisoners rose in all five continents, but by larger margins in the Americas, Asia and Oceania than in Europe and Africa.

2.4 Older prisoners

The proportion of older people in custody has also been rising steadily. Between 1990 and 2009, the total prison population of America doubled, but the number of prisoners aged 55 or older increased by over 300% (Williams et al., 2012). There are several distinct reasons for this growth. Many countries have increased their use of life or other indeterminate sentences (Heard & Jacobson, 2021; Jacobson et al, 2017; van Zyl Smit & Appleton, 2019); and prisoners serving these sentences often spend more years in prison than previously, staying well into their old age and, in some cases, until their death. Other reasons include longer custodial sentences, mandatory sentencing laws and a greater preponderance of older people being sentenced to custody for serious offences (notably, when "historic" crimes are prosecuted).

2.5 Non-national prisoners

There have also been significant increases in the numbers of foreign and ethnic minority prisoners over recent decades, particularly in western European countries (see, for example, Aebi et al., 2018).[4]

3 Extent of prison overcrowding when pandemic emerged

ICPR's World Prison Brief database contains information on the extent to which the world's prison systems are overcrowded, based on each system's official capacity. World Prison Brief data analysed in 2019 (Heard, 2019) indicate that, of the 205 countries worldwide for which official prison capacity numbers are available, 60% had occupancy rates above 100% when the pandemic emerged.[5] This includes 24 countries with occupancy rates above 200%.

By continent, overcrowding levels are worst in Africa, where 87% of all states in 2019 were operating above official capacity (and 13 had occupancy rates above 200%). In the Americas, 68% of countries were operating above official capacity (of which seven have occupancy rates above 200%). In Asia, 66% of countries were operating above official capacity (and four countries had occupancy rates above 200%). In Europe and Oceania, many countries were operating above official capacity but none had occupancy levels as high as 200%. In late 2019, Europe's highest occupancy rates were to be found in Cyprus (141%) Turkey (131%), Hungary (118%), France (116%) and Italy (114%). In Australia, available data for late 2019 indicate that prisons were operating at 112% of official capacity.[6]

The public health risks presented by this level of overcrowding are serious and will have resulted in unnecessary numbers of COVID-19 cases and deaths (among prisoners, staff, their families and wider communities). Over and above these direct and potentially avoidable harms, overcrowded prisons will also have resulted in undue hardship and adverse mental and physical health impacts by reason of protracted regime restrictions introduced in an effort to control spread of the disease (discussed further in Section 5). Many of the countries with severe overcrowding also have large prison populations, with potentially hundreds of thousands of individuals passing through their prisons each year. Many also have relatively low standards of community public health provision and carry heavier burdens of transmissible diseases, including HIV/AIDS, hepatitis and tuberculosis.

Prison overcrowding is usually a consequence of over-use of imprisonment (including at the pre-trial stage), combined with insufficient investment in prison buildings, staffing and other resources. Tackling overcrowding is a precondition of better prisoner health and mitigating harms resulting from COVID-19 and the restrictive measures designed to limit spread of the disease in prisons (see further under Sections 5 and 6).

3.1 Assessing the severity of overcrowding

The occupancy rate alone cannot be taken as a definitive indicator of the extent of overcrowding or the impact it may have on health, for several reasons. First, there are no fixed rules on how much physical space should be allowed per prisoner, although standards on living space have been issued in Europe (by the Committee for the Prevention of Torture) and minimum space recommendations have been made by the International Committee of the Red Cross (ICRC, 2012). Many countries' prisons provide accommodation that would not come close to meeting either set of standards. In much of the world, the official capacity figures published by national prison administrations are based on cell accommodation that provides so little space per prisoner that anything close to 100% occupancy rates in such a country would amount to serious overcrowding.

It is also important to recognise that occupancy levels fluctuate over a given period, with many more people entering a country's prison system in the course of a year than the "stock" number represented by national prison statistics and shown on the World Prison Brief. Consequently, there may be far greater numbers in custody at certain points over a given year than there are on the date to which the stock figure refers. Prison stock data can also be many years behind the current year because some countries are slow to publish prison statistics. Overcrowding can also exist in some prisons of a country even when its overall occupancy rate is below 100%.

The severity of prison overcrowding and its potential health impact should not be assessed purely by reference to the physical space available to each prisoner. The amount of time prisoners are locked in their cells and whether cells are shared with others will also affect the impact of overcrowding on health. Being locked for up to 23 hours a day in a cell intended for one person but shared by two or three requires cellmates to eat, and to use the toilet, in the same small space. Such conditions may be worse for prisoners' health than sleeping in a crowded communal cell at night and then spending the day outside the cell working and interacting with others. However, if night-time conditions in a dormitory cell make sleeping impossible because of noise, bright lights or lack of personal space, the health impact of overcrowding will be worse.

3.2 Overcrowding and health

It follows that the mental and physical health impacts of overcrowding depend not only on the physical living space provided in the cell, but also on factors such as time locked up in the cell; number of people sharing the cell;

sleeping conditions; opportunities to exercise, work and interact with others; access to light and fresh air; standards of sanitation; access to drinking water; quality and sufficiency of diet; and availability of medical treatment and healthcare. These factors are crucial in preventing disease and limiting risks of disease transmission, but are often compromised when prisons are overcrowded and under-resourced. The health and well-being of prisoners and staff, particularly their vulnerability to contagious diseases such as COVID-19, are at risk as soon as resources come under pressure, as they do in any prison operating above official capacity.

Prison overcrowding is a significant contributor to the damage that imprisonment can cause to the health of both prisoners and prison staff. It is a cause of severe psychological stress, which exacerbates mental health conditions. It is a major factor in the spread of infectious disease and the worsening of chronic conditions. Overcrowding also makes rehabilitation all but impossible, presenting a heightened risk of re-offending after release. Overcrowded prisons mean cramped and unhygienic accommodation; a constant lack of privacy (even when using the toilet); reduced out-of-cell activities (due to pressure on staff and less access to facilities); limited access to treatment and medicine due to overburdened healthcare services; poor conditions for sleeping; unsafe conditions due to weakened prison management; and increased tension and despair among prisoners, which can result in violence, substance misuse, self-harm and suicide.

4 Prisoner health

In developed and less developed countries, prison populations are typically drawn disproportionately from the poorest and most marginalised sections of society, in which mental and physical health problems tend to be more prevalent than in the general population. Certain kinds of mental health conditions can, in themselves, propel people into the criminal justice system and ultimately into custody. Once in prison, individuals' health is at a higher risk of worsening due to the interlinked problems of overcrowding, poor material conditions, social and psychological stresses, availability of illicit substances, and violence and mistreatment among prisoners and staff.

4.1 Health problems with which people enter prison

It is usually possible to identify the marginalised groups in any society by analysing its prison population (Coyle et al., 2016). Health problems seen in marginalised groups in the community will frequently be mirrored in the health of those in prison. Prisons are too frequently used as a place to hold people with problematic drug or alcohol use disorders or mental health conditions who (perhaps as a result) cannot find secure work or accommodation and who live in poverty. Prisons often hold disproportionate numbers of people from racial and other minority backgrounds.

Physical health problems are also more prevalent among those entering custody, some of whom may have untreated (even undiagnosed) conditions. Infectious disease prevalence is higher among people coming into prison than in general populations. Prisoners show higher prevalence for tuberculosis, hepatitis B, hepatitis C and HIV/AIDS and other infections. They may be more susceptible to infection because their general immunity is lower, due to pre-existing health conditions, poverty, substance use, homelessness and previous incarceration. They may have had little or no access to information and treatment.

This greater prevalence of infectious disease among people entering custody has been noted in higher income countries as well as low- and middle-income ones. For example, it has been highlighted as a particular concern in England & Wales (House of Commons Health and Social Care Select Committee, 2018) and in New South Wales, Australia (Butler and Milner, 2003).

People entering custody are also at a higher risk for some of the main non-communicable diseases, including diabetes, cancer, heart disease and respiratory illness. This may be due to prior histories of smoking, alcohol or drug abuse, poor diet and other factors connected with socio-economic deprivation. Numbers of older people in prison, many with chronic physical health problems or mental health impairments, are rising exponentially in many parts of the world (see Sections 2.4 and 4.2.2).

A wide range of mental health conditions are associated with criminal conduct or with behaviour that might be perceived as disruptive or threatening. Many people who enter custody (whether on remand or under sentence) do so on account of behaviours that, to some extent, *reflect* an existing mental health condition. In much of the world, there is a higher prevalence in prison populations than in general populations of mental health conditions such as depression, personality and anxiety disorders, schizophrenia, bipolar disorder and psychosis (Fazel et al., 2016; World Health Organization, 2014). Major depression and psychotic illnesses are estimated to affect one in seven prisoners (Fazel et al., 2016; Fazel and Seewald, 2012). Women and young people in prison have a higher prevalence of mental health conditions than adult males (Borril et al., 2003; Chitsabesan and Hughes, 2016).

A UK study found that life challenges such as trauma and abuse, limited education, poverty, debt, homelessness, unemployment and addiction or problematic substance use are more likely to have been experienced by people entering prison with a mental health problem (Durcan, 2008). Such challenges can easily propel people with underlying mental health problems into (often frequent) contact with the criminal justice system. In lower income countries, there may be more people with severe mental illness in prison than in psychiatric hospitals, because there are fewer resources for community psychiatric care (Fazel et al., 2016). Drug and alcohol use disorders are highly prevalent among people entering custody (Fazel et al., 2006). People entering custody also have high rates of comorbidity for substance misuse and mental illness (for example, Butler et al., 2011). These factors, too, will leave many prisoners who have been in custody during the pandemic at a higher risk of lasting harm as a result of the various additional restrictions imposed on their daily lives in custody.

4.2 Damage to health caused by incarceration

Once in a prison environment, people often experience exacerbation of pre-existing mental and physical health problems. They may also develop new health problems due to the conditions and regime, including lack of access to treatment and a failure to conduct routine screening or to employ harm reduction methods, often simply because there are insufficient staff to provide these measures.

4.2.1 In general

The typical physical conditions and regime of a prison are not conducive to physical or mental well-being either of prisoners or of staff (World Health Organization, 2014). Incarceration in much of the world usually involves reduced access to natural light and fresh air; poor diet; limited opportunities for exercise; reduced access to medical treatment; the availability of illicit drugs and the presence of drug users; lack of contact with family members or other support network; limited activity and interaction with others; the risk of intimidation or violence; and high levels of boredom, tension and despair. These aspects of incarceration heighten the risk of disease, violence and mistreatment and can lead to psychological stress, self-harm and even suicide. They have all increased in the wake of the pandemic, principally as a result of the regime restrictions introduced to curb risk of COVID-19 spreading inside and beyond prison walls, as discussed in Section 5.2.

It has long been recognised that prisons can be fertile breeding grounds for infectious diseases, particularly tuberculosis, hepatitis B and hepatitis C. There tends to be greater prevalence of infections among people entering custody; and infections are more likely to occur in prison due to the characteristics of the environment (World Health Organization, 2014). Intravenous drug use, unprotected sex, raised levels of violence and lack of sanitation and healthcare are all factors increasing the risk of disease transmission.

Many of the world's prisons have a rapid turnover of people entering custody, particularly remand prisons and low- to medium-security establishments. This presents challenges for limiting infection through screening and treatment. The risks of infection are further compounded when prisons are overcrowded or have limited access to clean water, sanitation, healthcare, vaccination programmes and basic harm prevention tools – the case for many countries' prison systems.

Brazil has experienced rapid rises in cases of tuberculosis among its prison population: recent research has concluded that controlling the disease in prisons is critical for reducing its prevalence in the community (Sacchi et al., 2015). Another recent study compared the incidence of tuberculosis among prisoners and in the wider community over several years (Mabud et al., 2019). It found that the prison environment drives the incidence of TB to a greater extent than do characteristics of the prison population itself, despite that population generally having higher risks of infection. This exemplifies the link between prison health and public health, which has come into sharper focus with COVID-19.

Worldwide, numbers of people suffering from heart disease, diabetes, cancer and respiratory illness are on the rise, particularly in lower income countries and in more marginalised communities. Studies have shown that prisons carry a heavier burden of these diseases than wider communities (for example, Herbert et al., 2012) and that their prevalence in prisons is growing. This is, in part, a reflection of their greater preponderance among socially and economically disadvantaged groups in all societies. A further factor is the rapidly rising number of older people in prison in many countries (in particular in the USA, Australia and England & Wales). This, too, has resulted in more prisoners having one or more of these illnesses. The obvious risks faced by this ageing and chronically ill prison population in the context of COVID-19 have led reformers to demand more coherent, inclusive and speedy early and compassionate release schemes to be implemented, with varying results.

It has long been recognised that psychological harm can result from the loss of liberty, separation from family and community, deprivation of autonomy and material deprivation – all factors that characterise imprisonment. The experience of being taken into custody (for the first time, in particular) can exacerbate pre-existing mental illness and can propel people with mental health vulnerability into violence, substance abuse, self-harm and even suicide. People with existing mental health conditions have been found to be more likely to be involved in violence, victimisation and prison rule infractions (Fazel et al., 2016).

In the context of very long or indeterminate sentences, psychological harm may result from specific features of these, for example, when prisoners have no way of knowing how much longer they will be held once the tariff set by the court has been served (Crewe, 2011). Prisoners serving such sentences have complained of the unpredictability and obscurity of the assessment and decision-making processes involved. These aspects of the sentence may have adverse effects on mental health and hinder prisoners' efforts to come to terms with their offence and make sense of the sentence they are serving.

Suicide risk is considerably higher in prisoners than in people in the general population of similar age and gender. The relative risk of death by suicide in male prisoners is three to six times greater than that of the general population; and even higher than this for female prisoners (Fazel et al., 2017). There is evidence that recently released prisoners are at an even greater risk of suicide than serving prisoners, particularly in the year after release, with this risk being higher still in the first four weeks (Pratt et al., 2006; Spittal et al., 2014).

4.2.2 In relation to vulnerable prisoners

Being in prison carries greater health risks for some people due to their specific characteristics or vulnerabilities. When conditions are overcrowded and prisons are under-resourced, the potential impact on their health may be even more serious. Reduced levels of staff monitoring and intervention together with raised levels of tension and violence may leave them more susceptible to abuse and they may find it more difficult to access treatment and support. Several such groups are increasing in number in prison populations across the world, including women prisoners, older prisoners, non-national prisoners and prisoners with physical and mental health problems, as set out in Sections 2 and 4. The mental and physical health impacts of COVID-19 and the associated regime restrictions will be more damaging for people in these groups.

Women in prison have frequently suffered physical, mental or sexual abuse and often have untreated health problems (Moloney et al., 2009). Rates of mental illness are higher in female prisoners than male (Binswanger et al., 2010). Women are likely to have histories of substance misuse and childcare issues and are at a significantly higher risk of self-harm and suicide in prison (Corston, 2007). As most prison systems have been designed to accommodate male prisoners, they are rarely equipped to meet women's specific needs. Health services for women in prison are sometimes minimal. Standards of prison healthcare often fall below those of women's health services in the community (World Health Organization, 2011).

Prisoners tend to experience age-related health problems at a rate equivalent to people a decade older in the community. Accordingly, 50-year-old prisoners show the same signs of age-related infirmity and cognitive decline as 60-year-olds in the general population (Baidawi et al., 2011). This could result from deprivation, stress and the numerous health disadvantages associated with imprisonment. Many of the mental and physical health problems faced by older people are exacerbated by factors typical of prison settings, including smoke-filled environments, lack of exercise, poor diets, higher levels of victimisation, and lack of social interaction and mental stimulation. Most prisons lack any form of geriatric healthcare service and do not cater for the needs of older prisoners with health problems, rendering them more vulnerable in custody (Potter et al., 2007).

Older prisoners typically suffer from chronic (often multiple) physical health problems. They are susceptible to illnesses such as heart disease, diabetes, hypertension, cancer, hearing and vision impairment and a range of physical disabilities, including dental problems and eating difficulties (World Health Organization, 2014). Older prisoners' mental health can be affected by conditions such as dementia, Alzheimer's disease, memory loss, Parkinson's disease, depression and fear of dying – particularly dying in prison.

Some elderly people are imprisoned with a pre-existing (possibly undiagnosed) cognitive impairment or psychiatric disorder. These conditions can be accelerated or worsened by the physical and social conditions in custody. Prisoners are more prone to developing dementia than the general population because of the risk factors associated with incarceration (Christodoulou, 2012). These include inactivity, poor nutrition, smoking and a lack of social interaction. In addition, mental health conditions common among prisoners and associated with dementia (such as depression, traumatic brain injury and attention deficit hyperactivity disorder) might also contribute to higher rates of dementia among prisoners.

Prisoners from minority groups and non-national prisoners may have special healthcare needs as a result of prior socio-economic marginalisation (World Health Organization, 2014). They may have received inadequate medical care prior to imprisonment. They may also be at a higher risk of some conditions. Foreign national prisoners have been found to suffer higher rates of both physical and mental health disorders and to find it more difficult to access healthcare in custody (Till et al., 2019). Prisoners in either group can find it difficult to access treatment in custody due to lack of translated or accessible materials and other support. Separation from family and community can also take a heavier toll on prisoners in these groups (World Health Organization, 2014). For these reasons, it is likely that these prisoners may be more at risk of direct and indirect harmful impacts as a result of COVID-19.

Prisoners with physical disabilities are increasing in number and generally have greater healthcare and rehabilitation needs. An absence of suitably qualified staff and the failure to make necessary adaptations to the physical environment can present risks to their health and well-being. Prisoners with sensory disabilities often become isolated in the prison environment, causing difficulties in accessing care and treatment and potentially leading to mental health problems (World Health Organization, 2014).

People with intellectual disabilities are at a significantly higher risk of experiencing fear and anxiety in the prison environment and of being subjected to bullying, segregation or use of restraint or control techniques (Talbot, 2008). They may incur unwarranted disciplinary sanctions for conduct related to poor judgement or difficulty in complying with rules and instructions.

Prisoners with mental health problems are at a higher risk of self-harm, suicide, substance misuse, sexual victimisation, and of experiencing and committing violence in custody (World Health Organization 2014; Yoon, 2017). They are also more likely to be segregated or placed in solitary confinement, the adverse health consequences of which have been found to be particularly severe for prisoners with mental health problems (for example, Grassian, 2006).

5 How the pandemic has impacted prison populations

When the WHO declared COVID-19 a global pandemic on 11 March 2020, there was immediate concern about the impact this would have on prisoners, due to many of the factors discussed above, including the close proximity in which most inmates are detained, particularly in overcrowded systems; the higher prevalence of underlying mental and physical health conditions, health inequality and specific vulnerabilities; and the porous nature of prison walls and boundaries, meaning that there is a risk of outbreaks spreading to the local communities. These concerns were expressed by Carina Ferreira-Borges, the WHO's coordinator for prison health, in a media interview on 23 March 2020 in which she warned that: "Once Covid-19 gets inside prisons, everyone will be contaminated very quickly. There is a risk of a huge mortality rate and unprecedented burden on the national health systems of countries that are already overstretched".[7]

Prison administrations in much of the world proceeded to take steps to control the risk of outbreaks in prison settings, including direct health interventions in prisons, such as screening and testing, contact tracing, vaccinations or provision of Personal Protective Equipment (which are beyond the scope of this chapter, but see Dünkel, Harrendorf and van Zyl Smit, Chapter 49); measures to manage prison population numbers to reduce prison population size, ease overcrowding and limit "churn"; and restrictions placed on routine interactions among prisoners and between prisoners and those outside prison such as family members, lawyers, prison inspectors, healthcare providers, companies providing work or training, and voluntary organisations involved in prisoner rehabilitation, education, sport, religious and other activities.

5.1 Population control measures

5.1.1 The measures

From the outset of COVID-19 being declared a pandemic, it was recognised that reducing numbers of prisoners would be a key weapon in the fight against COVID-19. The WHO recommended that "enhanced consideration should be given to resorting to non-custodial measures at all stages of the administration of criminal justice, including at the pre-trial, trial and sentencing as well as post-sentencing stages". Similar calls came from other international agencies and from civil society organisations the world over.

On 13 May 2020, the UNODC, WHO, UNAIDS and OHCHR issued a joint statement on COVID-19 in prisons and other closed settings, which "urge[d] political leaders to consider limiting the deprivation of liberty, including pre-trial detention, to a measure of last resort, particularly in the case of overcrowding, and to enhance efforts to resort to non-custodial measures... A swift and firm response aimed at ensuring healthy and safe custody, and reducing overcrowding, is essential to mitigate the risk of COVID-19 entering and spreading in prisons and other places of deprivation of liberty".[8]

In the weeks and months after March 2020, many national governments and justice systems took bold steps to reduce their prison populations, as other chapters in this volume have described (for a summary, see also Dünkel and Snacken, Chapter 50). To varying extents, prison systems sought to address prison overcrowding and mitigate the risk of infection by implementing measures aimed at (a) reducing entry into prisons, whether at the remand/pre-trial stage, at the point of sentence or following violations of parole, licence or other conditions of release; and (b) increasing rates of release from prisons, for example, through early release schemes, amnesties or increased use of compassionate release. International comparative studies analysing the nature and effect of these measures are discussed below, but it should be noted that some notably large-scale measures taken by some countries were of a temporary nature only. For example, Iran approved the temporary release of 85,000 prisoners; and India announced that the largest New Delhi prison complex was releasing over 1,100 prisoners on (temporary) "emergency parole"; over 2,000 under-trial prisoners had been released on bail.[9] A more recent report by the Commonwealth Human Rights Initiative indicates that by 21 April 2021, nearly 70,000 prisoners may have been released in India since the start of the pandemic.[10] As explained in Chapter 21 (Section 2.2) of this volume, the releases were largely temporary in nature and most prisoners will since have been required to return to custody.

5.1.2 Their effects on prisoner numbers

Because of significant time lags in the availability of national prison population data for most countries, as well as the absence of official figures on numbers released under the various schemes announced by national administrations, it is too soon to know what effects the various initiatives states have been taking to reduce prisoner numbers will have had on prison population sizes worldwide. In addition, it will be difficult, perhaps impossible, to distinguish the impacts of these initiatives from those of other factors attributable to the pandemic, including fewer reported crimes, arrests and prosecutions as well as the temporary closure of many courts. In countries, such as Turkey (see Chapter 44) where convicted prisoners were released on house arrest, they may still be recorded as serving prisoners in national statistics, making it impossible to know how fully or permanently release schemes were implemented, or their effect on overcrowding.

Despite these challenges in understanding precisely how prison population reduction policies have impacted prisoner numbers worldwide so far in the pandemic's history, we can obtain insights from prison population data for countries where (a) there was accurate information on the national prison population size as at the start of 2020, and (b) that information has been updated over the course of the pandemic.

Table 48.1 lists the eight countries that had prison populations of at least 50,000 in February 2020 and have published monthly prison population data since then. Significant reductions in the prison populations of all eight countries took place between February 2020 and January 2021. However, this trend largely came to a halt (in some cases reversing) from February 2021. The combined total prison populations of these eight countries decreased by 11% between February 2020 and May 2021, with by far the most significant reductions occurring in the period to January 2021.

There is significant variation across these eight countries in terms of factors that may explain the reductions: further data would be needed to assess the relative effects of targeted decarceration measures, community lockdowns, reduced court activity and fewer reported crimes. With respect to five of the countries listed in the table, other chapters in this volume (7: Chile, 9: Colombia, 14: England & Wales, 23: Italy and 35: Russian Federation) set out the national measures taken to reduce prisoner numbers.

In relation to the other three countries, Nigeria announced the release of almost 8,000 prisoners, including the elderly or sick, and those with six months or less to serve. Indonesia announced that over 39,000 prisoners had been released early or granted parole, with a further 11,000 releases planned. Thailand announced (in April 2020) that the sentences of 8,000

Table 48.1 Prison population changes in eight countries between February 2020 and (a) January 2021; and (b) May 2021[a]

Country	*Prison population February 2020*	*Prison population January 2021*	*% change February 2020–January 2021*	*Prison population May 2021*	*% change January–May 2021*	*% change February 2020–Ma[y] 2021*
Chile	43,110	38,847	−10%	39,395*	1%	−9%
Colombia	122,085	97,303	−20%	97,248	0%	−20%
England & Wales	83,868	78,065	−7%	78,104	0%	−7%
Russian Federation	519,618	482,888	−7%	478,182	−1%	−8%
Nigeria	74,106	65,741	−11%	65,292	−1%	−12%
Indonesia	269,062	251,546	−7%	265,514	6%	−1%
Thailand	371,461	338,806	−9%	310,830	−8%	−16%
Italy	61,230	53,329	−13%	53,660	1%	−12%
				*Figure is for 30 April 2021		Av. decrease, 11%

Note: All percentages rounded to nearest whole number.

a Data are drawn from the World Prison Brief site and reflect the latest available figures as at 8 June 20[21]; see https://www.prisonstudies.org/

prisoners were being suspended to reduce prison overcrowding during the pandemic.[11] In December 2020, a royal decree was issued pardoning at least 30,000 prisoners and reducing the sentences of 200,000 others.[12] (Thailand has for several years used collective pardons as a means of maintaining some degree of control over the extraordinary increases seen in its prison population as a result of highly punitive drug law enforcement policies.)

Aebi and Tiago (2020) analysed prison population rates across the Council of Europe and evaluated changes in rates across 35 countries and territories whose prison administrations provided data as at four key dates in 2020: before the pandemic (1 January), after the first month of lockdowns, where imposed (15 April), when lockdowns had been lifted (15 June) and at the end of summer (15 September). Overall, the study found that over the entire period, the average incarceration rate of the 35 countries fell by 4.6% – from 121.4 to 115.8 inmates per 100,000 of the general population (see also Dünkel and Snacken, Chapter 50). The study found that prison population changes were closely aligned to lockdowns in general populations. Lockdowns resulted both in less opportunity for some types of crime to occur and in less activity in criminal justice systems. When lockdowns were lifted, many countries saw a rise in prisoner numbers. Nevertheless, deliberate measures taken to reduce prison population size were also found to have contributed to reductions. As recorded in this study, some of the most notable overall decreases of prison populations during the first nine months of 2020 occurred in Montenegro (−21.1%), France (−13.4%), Portugal (−12.5%), Bulgaria (−12.7%), Italy (−10.8%) and Lithuania (−10.0%). Countries where prison population rates *increased* over this period included Sweden (+5.8%), Denmark (+5.4%), Greece (+5.2%), Romania (+2.7%), Hungary (+2.5%) and Norway (+1.8%).

Other international studies have analysed potential changes in prison populations in larger groups of countries, focusing specifically on decarceration measures implemented in those countries. A report by DLA Piper (2020) analysed the potential impact of measures adopted in 53 jurisdictions across Asia Pacific, Europe, the Middle East, Africa, North and Central America (of which 15 were American states). It concluded that at least 475,000 prisoners comprising convicted prisoners and pre-trial detainees were likely to have been released across the 53 jurisdictions between March and July 2020 (see also Dünkel and Snacken, Chapter 50).

The NGO Harm Reduction International (HRI, 2020) also monitored decarceration measures adopted worldwide between March and June 2020 and found evidence of such schemes in 109 countries. They concluded that the cumulative effect of such schemes if implemented would have reduced the global prison population by less than 6% as at 24 June 2020.

In view of the findings of the European study, it is possible, even likely, that the declines in prison populations discussed in the DLA Piper and the Harm Reduction International studies may have halted or reversed, once national lockdowns had been lifted and criminal justice systems had resumed activity and begun to deal with backlogs and process new cases. Several of the measures taken at the national level were, in any case, temporary – as explained above – and many who were released could be recalled to prison later (or sentenced to a custodial term, where they had been released on bail).

5.2 Regime restrictions and their impacts: evidence from prisoners in ten countries

In addition to measures taken to reduce prison population size, prison authorities throughout the world introduced restrictive measures to control the risk of the virus spreading within prisons. They included the suspension of visits to prisons by families, lawyers, inspection bodies, NGOs and community organisations providing services in prisons; the restriction of movement by prisoners within prisons; and restrictions on prisoners leaving prisons, for example, on temporary licence to work or visit their families (see in detail Dünkel, Harrendorf, and van Zyl Smit, Chapter 49; and Fair and Jacobson, 2021).

Unsurprisingly, these restrictions and the additional amount of time locked in cells have had profoundly negative effects on prisoners. To obtain evidence of how prisoners' health and well-being were impacted, the prisons research team at ICPR (along with overseas research partners) conducted semi-structured interviews with over 40 people who had been in prison, or had a close family member in prison, at or after March 2020, in a diverse group of countries. The research was conducted as an additional component of an ongoing international comparative research and policy project "Understanding and reducing the use of imprisonment in ten countries", launched in 2017.[13]

Interviews were conducted between August and November 2020, in Kenya, South Africa, Brazil, Thailand, India, Hungary and the Netherlands. In a further three jurisdictions (England & Wales, Australia and the USA), selected material, including formal inspection reports and academic research, was reviewed for first-hand accounts of how prisoners and their families were impacted by restricted regimes. The material gathered complemented primary research we conducted before the pandemic about life in custody, in interviews with over 40 people who were either in custody (the majority of them sentenced prisoners) or had recently been released from prison at the time of the interview. This allowed for a comparison to be made, albeit across a relatively small sample of individuals, between the pre-pandemic and the pandemic eras, across topics relevant to prisoner health and well-being, including family and social visits; daily routines and time out of the cell.

5.2.1 Comparing life in custody before and during the pandemic

5.2.1.1 FAMILY AND SOCIAL VISITS

In interviews with prisoners and ex-prisoners before and during the pandemic, a recurring theme was the importance of regular contact with family members and other loved ones. Visits were described as a source of hope and positivity, something that helped foster future planning focusing on a better life. Prisoners interviewed before the pandemic frequently said that the worst thing about being in prison was being separated from their loved ones. In the wake of the pandemic being declared, family and social visits were completely suspended and several of the prisoners we interviewed had not received a visit for several months. Almost all the interviewees said that they had been adversely affected by the restrictions on visits and in-person contact with others from outside the prison (as further described in Section 5.2.2). (For a detailed account of the impact of restrictions on prisoners' health and well-being, see Heard, 2021.)

The sudden suspension of visits also meant going without essential items like medicines and extra food supplies in some countries. Before the pandemic, in-person visits were an opportunity for prisoners to receive essential goods lacking in custody, including food, medication, clothing, hygiene and sanitary supplies. Interviewees in several countries said that they had to go without essential items during the pandemic due to the lack of visits from family and outside voluntary agencies.

5.2.1.2 DAILY ROUTINES AND TIME OUT OF THE CELL

In the pre-pandemic research interviews, prisoners often described how important it was for them to be able to work or take part in training and education. They said that work and other activities made their prison sentence easier to bear, helping to keep boredom at bay and giving purpose to the day. For some, work had been an important source of income to buy health or sanitary essentials, or pay for phone calls.

Unsurprisingly, the research highlighted wide variation across the ten countries in how much time prisoners would generally spend locked up or engaged in activities before the pandemic; and wide variation within the same country between different prisons. In Kenya, Brazil, India and Thailand, prisoners we interviewed said that, before the pandemic, it was only during night-time hours that they were confined to their cells or rooms (which in these countries were, typically, overcrowded communal cells or dormitories). During the day, they would be out of their sleeping areas for several hours, engaging in activities, taking exercise, receiving training and working in libraries, canteens, factories, workshops or farms within the prison, or as prison cleaners, or (far less frequently) working on day release outside the prison. By contrast, in England & Wales in 2019, most prisons were locking people up for far too long "to the point of solitary confinement for a few" and there were very poor levels of purposeful activity available (HMIP, 2020).

The pandemic severely curtailed out-of-cell activities in the ten countries, including opportunities to associate with other prisoners, spend time in the open air, take part in education, training, religious services, work or sports, access health services, or attend health, dental or eye care appointments outside the prison. The COVID restrictions also brought an abrupt halt to many prisoners' progress with studies or efforts to obtain vocational qualifications. Prisons in several countries missed what was an obvious opportunity to provide learning materials to inmates with so much time on their hands.

For prisoners who had not had regular visits from family members even before the pandemic, visits by voluntary or statutory organisations had been a lifeline, and one that they sorely missed. Organisations that had previously come into prisons to train or supervise prisoners at work largely suspended their prison operations. Prisoners eligible for temporary leave on licence said that these periods of leave and visits were no longer allowed. Even where limited access to work remained available (for example, in England & Wales, the Netherlands and Kenya), social distancing requirements and the need to limit prisoner circulation reduced the time prisoners could spend working or in recreation, and often meant more time locked in the cells. Many prisoners described the negative mental health impacts of these various restrictions (see Section 5.2.2).

5.2.2 Impact of restrictions

In the first months of the pandemic, levels of anxiety – across most sectors of society – were high and many people struggled to adjust to the new realities of a global health emergency. The abrupt imposition of highly restricted regimes with significant reductions on prisoners' activities and interactions would, in any circumstances, have had major consequences. But in the febrile and uncertain weeks after early March 2020, our research in ten countries found that these new restrictions led to protest, disorder and serious violence. As the weeks turned into months, what became a protracted "double lockdown" took a heavy toll on the mental and physical health of those in custody.

5.2.2.1 PROTEST, VIOLENCE AND DISORDER

There were frequent media reports of protest, disorder and conflict in prisons around the world in the initial weeks after prisons closed their doors to visitors.[14]

Many of the individuals we interviewed described similar problems. In South Africa, one prisoner described "awful gang warfare, riots and violent incidents daily", and another spoke of inmates scaling walls and climbing onto the roof, and ferocious attacks on guards and fellow-inmates. Another said that after a violent initial phase involving "huge resistance" to the restrictions, talks were initiated with management. After this, information was provided more transparently, extra supplies of soap and sanitiser were handed out and people began to live with the situation, accepting that the rule changes were for their own protection.

In Brazil, angry protests marked the start of the restrictive regime, with criticism of the government for suspending home leave and visits while allowing annual carnival festivities to proceed. One ex-prisoner described feeling "outrage against the state and the system" for not offering any alternative means to stay in contact with family members. A refusal by prisoners to go back to their cells led to more generalised disorder, which was subdued by a rapid intervention force using rubber bullets. Prisoners who had protested were beaten or placed in solitary confinement.

Riots also occurred at Australian prisons in the initial weeks after lockdown restrictions were imposed. One official described an incident at a New South Wales prison as "one of the worst riots we've had in 20 years" and speculated that the cause was frustration at the supply of drugs being interrupted.[15]

In England & Wales, HM Inspector of Prisons reported that violence, intimidation and bullying had not stopped, but had merely "taken other forms" (HMIP, 2021). Women prisoners said that they were seeing more tension, anger and behavioural problems emerge as restrictions became more prolonged. This points to significant mental health impacts of the deterioration in prisons' social climate due to lengthy periods of isolation, inactivity and boredom.

In the Netherlands, some interviewees reported fights breaking out and aggressive behaviour towards staff. Protest took the forms of hunger strikes and formal complaints to management. Anger at the loss of personal contact with loved ones and a refusal to accept the measures as necessary were seen as the main cause of protest. Insufficient or broken telephones, problems with video calling, the cancellation of activities and the increased number of hours spent locked in cells were further causes of unrest. One interviewee said illicit drug supplies had dried up, leading to increased trade in prescription drugs as well as use of "home-made" drugs created from cleaning liquids and other chemicals.

In India, there were fewer accounts of resistance; and more of resigned cooperation. One Indian prisoner said that all the inmates in the prison had gone on hunger strike in protest at the cancellation of visits and activities; "Then the prison said they'd arrange facilities for us all to make phone calls, so we promised to cooperate and follow the rules". However, one inmate of an overcrowded women's prison said: "There's only abuse and conflict, the women fight, even over minor things". The Kenyan prisoners said that there had been little resistance and much cooperation, largely due to fear of the virus.

5.2.2.2 PHYSICAL HEALTH

Several interviewees expressed concern that their physical health and well-being had been adversely affected by the lockdown and shortcomings in the basic support and services provided to prisoners. In most of the countries, healthcare services were reduced to emergency provision only. Important services like dentists and opticians remained unavailable for months. The sedentary nature of prisoners' lives during the pandemic caused their physical health to deteriorate. Significant weight gain was a common complaint as was pain due to long periods of inactivity locked in small cells with poor quality furniture and bedding. Some prisoners associated the stress from so little time out of the cell with worsening health conditions.

Prisoners in some countries feared that their health would be compromised by the prisons' failure to keep them safe by enforcing mask-wearing or social distancing. Many complained of insufficient supplies of soap, hand sanitisers and masks. The cessation of visits led to a shortage of soap and other basic sanitation products in some countries. Interruptions to medical visits or treatments for existing conditions were also feared to be impacting on prisoners' health and well-being.

The lack of visits from loved ones was felt by some prisoners to have impacted on their physical health because of the sudden break in supply of foods, medicines and other products. To take one example, a Brazilian prisoner had relied on her partner to provide medication because the only medication available in prison was pain relief. This prisoner was one of several in Brazil who mentioned the importance of family visits and parcels to supplement the meagre and poor prison diet. Another Brazilian interviewee said that visits also represented a basic safeguard against mistreatment.

5.2.2.3 MENTAL HEALTH

A near-universal impact emerging from the interviews was that of sadness and depression resulting from lack of contact with family and other loved ones, exacerbated by the cessation of routines and activities, which for many led to increased anxiety. Interviewees described a range of consequences, including not sleeping, using more medication, use of illicit drugs, incidents of self-harm and attempted suicide. There were also descriptions of physical symptoms commensurate with severe anxiety, such as hypertension.

Many prisoners described feelings of loneliness and frustration making their time in custody harder to bear, and increasing their anxiety about their own well-being at this uncertain time. Some interviewees said that the restrictions had left them feeling oppressed and struggling to adjust; others described trying to cope once they had accepted that the restrictions were for their own benefit.

The lack of visits and regular communication led many prisoners to worry about their families and how they might be impacted by the pandemic. Many prisoners said that their depression was made worse not only by the lack of visits and activities to distract them, but also by pervasive anxiety about the risk of becoming infected in prison. Stress and anxiety over case progress was reported by remand prisoners whose hearing dates were cancelled due to court closures, and by prisoners close to their release date. Even in countries where prisoners were able to receive non-contact visits or communicate remotely with their loved ones, or have non-contact visits behind screens, the lack of physical contact with partners and children had negative psychological impacts.

The loss of a daily routine involving work, education and interaction with other people had the effect of increasing a sense of helplessness and anxiety for some. Prisoners expressed the desire to return to purposeful activity saying that they missed routine, work and education, as these made them feel useful and gave them purpose, something to look forward to each day and the chance to socialise with prisoners from other wings.

For prisoners in some countries, there was another adverse consequence of being denied access to activities and programmes. It robbed them of the opportunity to demonstrate good behaviour or rehabilitation and made it harder to prepare for release. Unable to spend time in education, programmes, workshops or a job on the wings, and no longer permitted temporary leave, prisoners had almost no way to demonstrate their progress in custody. Several prisoners feared that this would reduce their prospects of being re-categorised, transferred to an open prison or released on parole, because there would be nothing to inform the relevant risk assessments or recommendations. These factors, too, will have adversely impacted prisoners' mental health and well-being.

5.3 COVID cases and deaths among prisoners globally

Availability of information on the numbers of cases of, and deaths from COVID-19 varies considerably. For some countries, data are published on a weekly or monthly basis, but this is far from universal.

Since the pandemic was declared, the NGO Justice Project Pakistan[16] has been collating information on the number of COVID-19 cases and deaths in prison populations around the world, using data collected from official government figures, leaked reports and media coverage. Their data show that by 10 June 2021, there had been at least 548,489 prisoners who had tested positive for COVID-19 in 122 countries, and at least 3,968 deaths due to COVID-19 in 47 countries.

The true figure will be much higher, for four main reasons. First, there was little or no testing capacity in much of the world, including prisons.

Second, information on COVID in prisons is not available (or published) for many countries. Third, as explained in Section 4, prisoners are more vulnerable to contagious disease; and prison populations contain disproportionate numbers of people who will have raised risk levels to COVID-19. Fourth, as explained in Section 3, prison overcrowding, which blights the prison systems of most countries, many of them with exceptionally large prison populations, represents a particular danger when COVID-19 outbreaks occur in the prison setting. With the pandemic still raging in many countries with very large prison populations (notably Brazil, and India), it is an unfortunate reality that numbers of infections and deaths will continue to rise for some time to come.

6 Concluding points – and lessons for policy reform

In the year 2000, the world's prison population numbered around 8.7 million; when the pandemic struck, it exceeded 11 million. This rapid growth exacerbated prison overcrowding and, coupled with failings to invest in additional staff and infrastructure, created prison conditions of extreme material deprivation in much of the world, with poor standards of sanitation and healthcare, compromising the well-being and safety of prisoners and staff. In the face of a global health emergency, the consequences for health could hardly be more serious. People in prison already carry disproportionately high burdens of ill health; and overcrowded, under-resourced prisons cannot offer healthy environments or adequate care and treatment.

The widely divergent trends in patterns of imprisonment around the world in the period leading up to the pandemic show that there is nothing inevitable about continued prison population growth. Many factors combine to determine the extent to which a country incarcerates its people; but where there is political will to curb the use of imprisonment, this can be achieved. This is evident from the speed with which many countries implemented measures to limit new entries to prison and to release prisoners, to reduce overcrowding and better enable prison administrations to protect inmates and staff from infection. The extent to which reductions in prison populations will be sustained remains to be seen. Just as there is no single explanation for the widely varying trajectories of differing countries' use of imprisonment, there is no single route towards effective reform. But it is clear that certain cross-cutting issues must be addressed if reform efforts are to have any success (see Dünkel and Snacken, Chapter 50).

Over the course of the year since the COVID-19 pandemic was declared, prisoners have had to adjust to highly restrictive regimes. They have experienced severe and prolonged social and material deprivations going well beyond the loss of their liberty. Prisoners have experienced protracted periods of isolation and inactivity. They have seen lengthy disruption of their engagement with education, work, training, and access to legal advice and other key services (which, in much of the world, were minimally or poorly provided even before the pandemic). At a time when greater social isolation has been imposed on most communities, the social deprivations forced on prisoners may well have even more harmful, longer lasting consequences.

It is too early to know whether the gains in terms of infections and deaths prevented will outweigh the adverse consequences to health and well-being, or the loss of progress in education and rehabilitation. However, as the pandemic shows no signs of abating, it is important that lessons are learned from the impacts already evident in order to mitigate further harm from continued infection control measures and ensure that the cure (in terms of prolonged, severe restrictions) is not worse than the disease itself. Key short-term priorities for prison administrations include:

- Restoring a daily routine, with access to work, education and interaction with others, and a full day spent outside the cell.
- Re-instating in-person family visits, in line with public health guidance.
- Supplementing in-person visits with remote contact where feasible.
- Ensuring decent living conditions.
- Improving access to healthcare, screening and treatment and addressing treatment backlogs.
- Promoting prisoners' health and well-being.

It is clear that the health and social impacts of the pandemic and the measures taken to contain it will prove more severe in countries with overcrowded, under-resourced prisons. Limited physical space and infrastructure and inadequate staffing levels will have placed more constraints on (already stretched) provision of rehabilitation, education, work, visits and social interaction than would have been necessary otherwise.

There are indications that in many countries prisoner numbers have decreased as a result of lockdowns, fewer arrests and court hearings, and measures to reduce the size of national prison populations (see also Dünkel and Snacken, Chapter 50). This positive outcome will need to be sustained by means of deliberate longer term decarceration policies. Prison overcrowding is a major and avoidable public health threat in a time of pandemic. Reducing prison populations is the single most effective strategy to contain the public health risks presented by COVID-19 and other contagious diseases, without causing unnecessary collateral damage to the mental and physical health of prisoners, prison staff and their families.

Notes

1 World Prison Population Lists are researched and compiled by Roy Walmsley with assistance from Helen Fair. Together with the World Female Imprisonment List (the fourth edition of which was published in November 2017) and the World Pre-trial/Remand Imprisonment List (fourth edition published in April 2020), they complement data held on the World Prison Brief. This is an online database available at www.prisonstudies.org, and is updated monthly. Since 2014,

the Institute for Crime & Justice Policy Research (ICPR) at Birkbeck, University of London (www.icpr.org.uk), has hosted and maintained the World Prison Brief database and published the Prison Population Lists.

2 These countries are Bhutan, Cuba, Equatorial Guinea, Eritrea, Maldives, North Korea, Northern Mariana Islands and Somalia.

3 The pre-trial/remand total in Rwanda in the year 2000 was exceptionally high because of the large number of persons awaiting trial following the genocide of 1994.

4 The proportion of non-national prisoners for almost all countries can be found in individual country pages on ICPR's World Prison Brief website, using data largely derived from governmental or other official sources. https://www.prisonstudies.org/

5 The countries for which official capacity numbers are not available are Egypt; Central African Republic; Republic of the Congo; Democratic Republic of Congo; Equatorial Guinea; Gabon; South Sudan; Eritrea; Ethiopia; Somalia; Cuba; Oman; Qatar; Saudi Arabia; Yemen; Bhutan; Laos; Vietnam; China; North Korea and Tuvalu.

6 Australia has not published a national official capacity figure since 2013: this was 31,335. We have sourced more recent state/territory capacity figures, to arrive at a current national capacity figure of 36,730, as reflected on the World Prison Brief database.

7 https://www.theguardian.com/global-development/2020/mar/23/everyone-will-be-contaminated-prisons-face-strict-coronavirus- controls.

8 https://www.who.int/news/item/13-05-2020-unodc-who-unaids-and-ohchr-joint-statement-on-covid-19-in-prisons-and-other-closed-settings.

9 https://www.indiatoday.in/cities/delhi/story/delhi-police-tihar-jail-inmates-emergency-parole-decongest-prisons-covid-1791162-2021-04-15

10 https://www.humanrightsinitiative.org/content/stateut-wise-prisons-response-to-covid-19-pandemic-in-india.

11 https://www.bangkokpost.com/thailand/general/1899685/8-000-inmates-released-to-ease-risk.

12 https://www.aljazeera.com/news/2020/12/5/thai-king-to-pardon-cut-jail-sentence-of-tens-of-thousands.

13 The countries under study in the project are Kenya, South Africa, Brazil, the USA, India, Thailand, England & Wales, Hungary, the Netherlands and Australia. More information can be found on the project website: https://www.prisonstudies.org/ten-country-prisons-project.

14 Such countries included Sierra Leone, Lebanon, Jordan, Indonesia, Sri Lanka, El Salvador and Trinidad, in addition to the many countries covered in this volume where riots and disorder were reported. The ICPR prisons research team compiles news stories relating to COVID-19, published on a dedicated page on the World Prison Brief website: https://www.prisonstudies.org/news/international-news-and-guidance-covid-19-and-prisons-1-december-onwards.

15 Riot at Wellington Correctional Centre over Easter weekend, 13 April 2020, Taylor Jurd, Wellington Times, https://www.wellingtontimes.com.au/story/6720458/riot-at-wellington-correctional-centre-over-easter-weekend/.

16 https://www.jpp.org.pk/covid19-prisoners/.

References

Aebi, M. F. and Tiago, M. M. (2020): *Prisons and prisoners in Europe in pandemic times: An evaluation of the medium-term impact of COVID-19 on prison populations*. Strasbourg: Council of Europe.

Aebi M. F. et al. (2018): *Foreign offenders in prison and probation in Europe: Trends from 2005 to 2015 (inmates) and situation in 2015 (inmates and probationers)*. Strasbourg: Council of Europe.

Baidawi, S. et al. (2011): Older Prisoners: A challenge for Australian corrections. *Trends and Issues in Crime and Criminal Justice* 426, 1–8.

Binswanger, I., et al. (2010): Gender differences in chronic medical, psychiatric, and substance-dependence disorders among jail inmates. *American Journal of Public Health* 100, 476–482.

Borrill, J., et al. (2003): *Differential substance misuse treatment needs of women, ethnic minorities and young offenders in prison*. London: Home Office Online Report, 33/03.

Butler, T., and Milner, L. (2003): *The 2001 New South Wales inmate health survey*. Sydney: NSW Corrections Health Service.

Butler, T., et al. (2011): Co-occurring mental illness and substance use disorder among Australian prisoners. *Drug and Alcohol Review* 30, 188–194.

Chitsabesan, P., and Hughes, N. (2016): Mental health needs and neurodevelopmental disorders amongst young offenders: Implications for policy and practice. In: Winstone, J. (Ed.): *Mental health, crime and criminal justice: Responses and reforms*. London: Palgrave Macmillan, 109–130.

Christodolou, M. (2012): Locked up and at risk of dementia. *Lancet Neurology* 11(9), 750–751.

Corston, J. (2007): *The Corston report: A review of women with particular vulnerabilities in the criminal justice system*. London: The Home Office.

Coyle, A., et al. (2016): *Imprisonment worldwide: The Current situation and an alternative future*. Bristol: Policy Press.

Crewe, B. (2011): Depth, weight, tightness: Revisiting the pains of imprisonment. *Punishment & Society* 13(5), 509–529.

DLA Piper (2020): *A global analysis of prisoner releases in response to COVID-19* https://www.dlapiper.com/en/austria/news/2021/03/swift-targeted-action-to-reduce-prison-population-during-covid-19/.

Durcan, G. (2008): *From the inside. Experiences of prison mental health care*. London: Sainsbury Centre for Mental Health.

Fair, H. and Jacobson, J. (2021): *Keeping COVID out of prisons: Approaches in ten countries*. London: ICPR, https://www.prisonstudies.org/sites/default/files/resources/downloads/keeping_covid_out_of_prisons.pdf.

Fazel, S., Bains, P. and Doll, H. (2006): Substance abuse and dependence in prisoners: A systematic review. *Addiction* 101(2), 181–191.

Fazel, S., Ramesh, T. and Hawton, K. (2017): Suicide in prisons: An international study of prevalence and contributory factors. *Lancet Psychiatry* 4(12), 946–952.

Fazel, S. and Seewald, K. (2012): Severe mental illness in 33,588 prisoners worldwide: Systematic review and meta-regression analysis. *British Journal of Psychiatry* 200(5), 364–373.

Fazel, S., et al. (2016): Mental health of prisoners: Prevalence, adverse outcomes, and interventions. *Lancet Psychiatry* 3(9), 871–881.

Grassian, S. (2006): Psychiatric effects of solitary confinement. *Journal of Law and Policy* 22, 325–383.

Harm Reduction International (HRI) (2020): COVID-19, prisons and drug policy: Global scan March–June 2020, https://www.hri.global/covid-19-prison-diversion-measures.

Heard, C. (2019): *Towards a health-informed approach to penal reform: Evidence from ten countries.* London: ICPR, https://www.prisonstudies.org/sites/default/files/resources/downloads/icpr_prison_health_report.pdf.

Heard, C. (2021): *Locked in and locked down – prison life in a pandemic: Evidence from ten countries.* ICPR: London, https://www.prisonstudies.org/sites/default/files/resources/downloads/locked_in_and_locked_down.pdf.

Heard, C. and Jacobson, J. (2021): *Sentencing burglary, drug importation and murder: Evidence from ten countries.* London: ICPR, https://www.prisonstudies.org/sites/default/files/resources/downloads/sentencing_burglary_drug_importation_and_murder_full_report.pdf.

Herbert, K. et al. (2012): Prevalence of risk factors for noncommunicable diseases in prison populations worldwide: A systematic review. *The Lancet*, 379(9830), 1975–1982.

Her Majesty's Prisons Inspectorate (HMIP) (2020): *Annual report 2019–2020,* https://www.justiceinspectorates.gov.uk/hmiprisons/wp-content/uploads/sites/4/2020/10/HMI-Prisons_Annual-Report-and-Accounts-2019-20-WEB.pdf

Her Majesty's Prisons Inspectorate (HMIP) (2021): *What happens to prisoners in a pandemic? A thematic review*: HMIP, https://www.justiceinspectorates.gov.uk/hmiprisons/wp-content/uploads/sites/4/2021/02/What-happens-to-prisoners-in-a-pandemic.pdf.

House of Commons Health and Social Care Select Committee (2018): *Prison health, twelfth report of session 2017–2019,* October 2018. London: House of Commons.

International Committee of the Red Cross (ICRC) (2012): *Water, sanitation, hygiene and habitat in prisons: Supplementary guidance,* Geneva: ICRC.

Jacobson, J., Heard, C., and Fair, H. (2017): *Prison: Evidence of its use and over-use from around the world,* London: Institute for Criminal Policy Research and Fair Trials, https://www.prisonstudies.org/sites/default/files/resources/downloads/global_imprisonment_web2c.pdf.

Mabud, T. S. et al. (2019): Evaluating strategies for control of tuberculosis in prisons and prevention of spillover into communities: An observational and modelling study from Brazil. *PLoSMed* 16(1), 1–16.

Moloney, K. P. et al. (2009): Women in prison: The central issues of gender characteristics and trauma history. *Public Health* 123(6), 426–430.

Potter, E. et al. (2007): The healthcare of older inmates in the correctional setting. *International Journal of Prisoner Health* 3(3), 204–213.

Pratt, D. et al. (2006): Suicide in recently released prisoners: A population-based cohort study. *Lancet* 368, 119–123.

Sacchi, F. P. et al. (2015): Prisons as reservoir for community transmission of tuberculosis, Brazil. *Emerging Infectious Diseases* 21(3), 452–455.

Spittal, M. J. et al. (2014): Suicide in adults released from prison in Queensland, Australia: A cohort study. *Journal of Epidemiology and Community Health* 68, 993–998.

Talbot, J. (2008): *No one knows: Prisoners' voices: Experiences of the criminal justice system by prisoners with learning disabilities and difficulties.* London: Prison Reform Trust.

Till, A. et al. (2019): The mental health of foreign national prisoners. *Journal of Forensic and Legal Medicine* 2(62), 14–18.

van Zyl Smit, D., and Appleton, C. (2019): *Life imprisonment: A global human rights analysis.* Cambridge: Harvard University Press.

Walmsley, R. (2017): *World female imprisonment list*, 4th edition. London: Institute for Criminal Policy Research.
Walmsley, R. (2018): *World prison population list*, 12th edition. London: Institute for Criminal Policy Research.
Walmsley, R. (2020): *World pre-trial/remand imprisonment list*, 4th edition. London: Institute for Criminal Policy Research.
Williams, B. et al. (2012): Addressing the aging crisis in U.S. criminal justice healthcare. *Journal of the American Geriatrics Society*, 60(6), 1150–1156.
World Health Organization (2011): *Imprisonment and women's health: Concerns about gender sensitivity, human rights and public health.* WHO Bulletin, *Bulletin of the World Health Organization* 89(9), 689–694.
World Health Organization (2014) *Prisons and health.* Ed. Enggist, S., Møller, L., Galea, G. and Udesen, C. Copenhagen: World Health Organization Regional Office for Europe.
Yoon, I. A., Slade, K. and Fazel, S. (2017): Outcomes of psychological therapies for prisoners with mental health problems: A systematic review and meta-analysis. *Journal of Consulting and Clinical Psychology* 85(8), 783–802.

49 Summary analysis of the state of prisons and penal policies before, during and after the COVID-19 pandemic

Frieder Dünkel, Stefan Harrendorf and Dirk van Zyl Smit

1 Introduction

The COVID-19 pandemic, which initially emerged in China in November 2019 and spread around the world, presented prison systems everywhere with unique challenges. Part 2 of this chapter brings together in summary form the findings of our contributors on the conditions that pertained in the prisons in the countries and jurisdictions that are described in this book, immediately before they were confronted by the pandemic and then turns to the rates of COVID-19 infections to which both prisoners and prison staff were subject as the pandemic ebbed and flowed throughout 2020 and the first few months of 2021. Although the book largely reflects the situation only until early 2021, after the second and during the third wave of the pandemic, we tried to integrate relevant information until finalising the editing in January 2022 at least for some countries. The results found are highly relevant to the current situation as the problematic situation and living conditions in prisons did not change significantly during the following waves, which showed high infection rates (in particular in the general population), but increased vaccination rates, too. In prisons, problems the pandemic raises have an even greater impact than for the general society. This summary chapter mainly refers to countries which also provided a country report in Chapters 2–44 of this volume. The names of these countries are italicised here. Where appropriate, we have also added information from other sources and for other countries, to give a more complete picture.

Part 3 of this chapter considers the developments at international and national levels of penal policies that were introduced to deal with the COVID-19 pandemic. Further parts consider more specific matters: restrictions of contact with the outside world (Part 4), restrictions inside prisons (Part 5) and the compensatory measures that can be taken to assist prisoners whose pains of imprisonment have been aggravated by the pandemic (Part 6). The legal bases for restrictions and relaxations of the prison regime during the pandemic are summarised in Part 7. Finally, in Part 8, the chapter focuses on what has been learnt during the pandemic that should perhaps be kept in

DOI: 10.4324/9781003169178-49

place after the pandemic has run its course. This summary chapter therefore closely follows the structure of the individual country reports. Sections 2–8 of this summary refer to the results reported in detail in Sections 1–7 of the different country reports.

The methodology used for this comparative study is a classical one, relying on individual country reports on the one hand and overarching, comparative chapters on the other. The core comparative chapter is this one, supported and complemented by other cross-national and cross-sectional chapters (1, 46–48 and 50). This means that the standardisation of country replies has mainly been restricted to providing a common structure (outline) for the national reports (see Chapter 1), and on peer review by the editors, combined with suggestions for improvement of the individual chapters. Such an approach has obvious advantages. Especially, it provides a well-established, easy-to-use methodology for comparative studies, which can be quickly adapted to acute and emerging phenomena like the global COVID-19 pandemic. On the downside, comparability of country results is reduced compared to studies which collect data using a survey method (de Bondt, 2015; Harrendorf, 2018). This is because the legal architecture of criminal justice systems and prison regimes differs significantly across the world. The same is true for statistical recording procedures of prison data in the individual countries as well as for substantive factors like prison subcultures, self-concepts and role models of prison staff and the willingness of the population to reintegrate prisoners. Legal, statistical and substantive factors (and many others) affect the comparability of any kind of criminal justice data (Harrendorf, 2018, 2019; von Hofer, 2000). This needs to be kept in mind for the comparison of country results and successful strategies for dealing with a global pandemic like COVID-19 in prison: What works in one country will not necessarily work everywhere.

For the comparative chapters in this book, however, the impact of this methodological problem can be alleviated by basing comparisons on a fundamentally normative approach, rooted in international human rights and a liberal (reductionist) understanding of criminal law, seeing imprisonment as a last resort. And regarding the empirical side of research, i.e. the question of "what works" in successfully coping with a global pandemic in prison, the comparability issues are also of somewhat reduced importance, since the problems of a global pandemic are also fundamentally dependent on biological and medical factors, such as contagion risks, reproduction numbers and the effects of masks and vaccinations. Such factors can be compared across the world relatively easily, allowing for first impressions, also from an empirical perspective, on best practices for dealing with COVID-19 in prison. It is obvious, however, that the substantive, legal and statistical differences between countries are much too large to consider what we are reporting on here as the results of a kind of natural experiment.

2 General situation of the prison system

2.1 Penal and prison systems and sentencing practices before the pandemic

When the COVID-19 pandemic began, little was initially known about the dangerousness of the new virus and the ways in which it would spread worldwide. However, it was clear from the beginning that prisons posed potential risks as social distancing was difficult or impossible. Many prison systems suffered from overcrowding. Prisons in Asia (*China*, *India* and *Japan* as representative examples in the present book), Latin American and (traditionally) Eastern Europe an prisons are based on the principle of accommodating prisoners in communal cells, which a priori makes it a difficult task to prevent COVID-19 infections.

The emergence of the COVID-19 pandemic impacted on prison systems that found themselves in very different situations: in Europe, prison populations in most countries had been declining since the early 2000s (Dünkel, 2017), in particular in Eastern Europe, whereas Latin America faced exploding prison population rates with strong overcrowding. In Africa, prison population rates were relatively stable.

The situation in these regions can be analysed in more detail. Figure 49.1 gives a useful overview of occupancy rates (prisoners per 100 places) in Europe shortly before the pandemic struck.

Most problematic were the high occupancy rates in Cyprus (141%),[1] *Turkey* (131%), *Belgium* (121%), *France* (116%), *Italy* (114%), *Romania* (113%), *Greece* (111%), *England & Wales* or *Hungary* (each 110%), *Slovenia* (109%), the *Czech Republic* (106%) and *Serbia* (105%). However, all other countries with occupancy rates of 85% and above would also be required to take action in order to be able to separate incoming or infected inmates in quarantine departments.[2] As can be shown by the information given in Table 49.1, only three out of the 11 countries with high overcrowding (occupancy rate of at least 105%) in Europe revealed a strong reductionist policy (*Turkey*, *France*, *Italy*) and another five only moderate reductions (*Belgium*, *Czech Republic*, *England & Wales*, *Serbia*, *Slovenia*), three even small increases of the prison population (*Greece*, *Hungary*, *Romania*). Looking at the ten jurisdictions represented in this volume with occupancy rates between 85% and around 100%, three succeeded in substantially reducing the prison population (*Germany*, *Poland*, *Portugal*), another four showed a moderate reduction (*Austria*, *Lithuania*, *Scotland*, *Switzerland*) and three (*Denmark*, *Ireland* and *Slovakia*) no change or even an increase of the prison population[3] (see for some explanations below under Section 3).

The situation was much worse in Latin American countries which – with the exception of *Chile* and Mexico[4] – suffered from extreme overcrowding of between 124% in *Colombia*,[5] 129% in *Costa Rica*, 154% in Venezuela, 171% in *Brazil*, up to 240% in *Peru* and 364% in *Bolivia*.

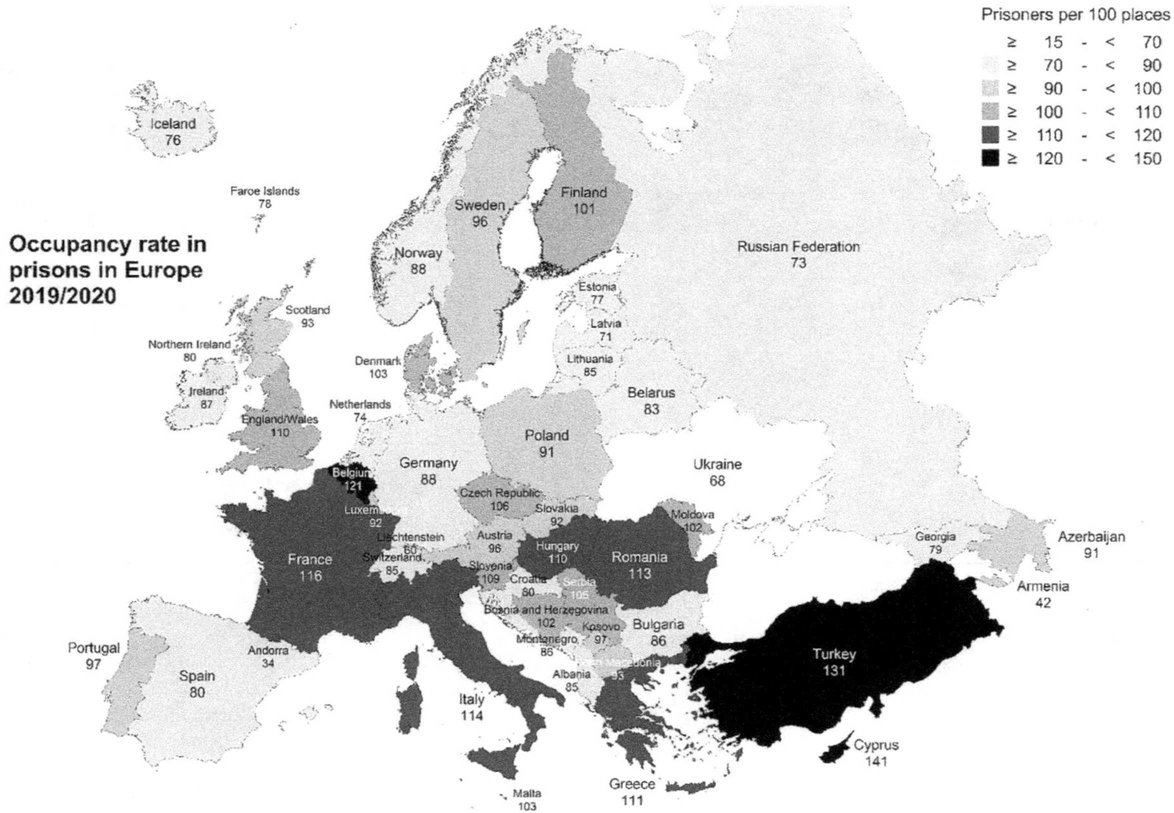

Source: International Center for Prison Studies, World Prison Brief, Internet-Publication, http://www.prisonstudies.org/info/worldbrief (last query 18.05.2020)

Figure 49.1 Occupancy rates in prisons in Europe 2019/early 2020, before the pandemic.

Table 49.1 Situation before and penal policies during the pandemic and their impact on prison population rates in 48 jurisdictions (2020/2021)

Countries / jurisdictions	*Situation before the pandemic*		*Explicit reductionist policy (government)*[a]	*Impact on prison population rates*					*Infection rates prisoners 1st / 2nd wave*	*Remarks*
	Prison pop. trends since 2010:	*Occupancy rate 2019/ early 2020*		*Strong*	*Moderate*	*None*	*Increase of prison population*	*Only temporaril*	*1=very high; 2=high; 3=low; 4=very low*	
Australia	Increase	112%	In some states or territories		X	X			4/4	
Argentina	Stable	123%	No, but early release measures by the judiciary		X				2/2	Early release measures had a higher impact on overcrowding than in BO, CO and PE. Infection rates higher than in the civil society
Austria	Stable	96%	Yes		X				4/4	
Belgium	Incr., from 2014 decrease	121%	Yes		X			X	3/3	
Bolivia	Increase	314%	Yes			X			2/2	Implementation of reductionist attempts failed; infection rates based on grounded estimations
Brazil	Increase	182%	No				X		1/1	
Canada	Stable	100%	No						4/3-2	
Chile	Decrease	100%	Yes		X				3/2	
China	Stable	Unknown	No			X			4/4	Strict isolation and separation of prisoners and staff

Colombia	Increase	151%	Yes			X				2/2	Impact negligible; less than 5% reduction of overcrowding; displacement of overcrowding to police detention
Costa Rica	Increase	129%	No			X				No data	
Croatia	Stable	80%	Yes		X					4/3	Only small impact
Czech Republic	Stable	106%	Not explicit		X					4/2	Sentencing practice: more alternative sanctions, less conv., decrease of crimes
Denmark	Stable	103%	No				X	X		4/4	Small impact, less convictions during first wave
England/ Wales	Stable	110%			X					3/2	Reluctant implementation of reductionist attempts; -4.4% by Sept. 2020, -6.9% by Jan. 2021
Estonia	Decrease	78%	No			X				4/4	No need for reducing prison pop., no overcrowding
Finland	Decrease	101%	Yes	X					4	4/4	
France	Increase/ stable	116%	Yes	X						4/3	
Germany	Decrease	90%	Yes	X						4/4	
Greece	Incr., from 2014 decrease	111%	No			X	X			4/2	During the 2nd wave in some prisons high infection rates
Hungary	Incr., from 2016 decrease	110%	No				X			3/3	
India	Stable	119%	No, but Supreme Court	X				X		2/2	
Ireland	Stable	86%	No		X					4/4	

(*Continued*)

Countries / jurisdictions	*Situation before the pandemic*		*Explicit reductionist policy (government)*[a]	*Impact on prison population rates*					*Infection rates prisoners 1st / 2nd wave*	*Remarks*
	Prison pop. trends since 2010:	*Occupancy rate 2019/ early 2020*		*Strong*	*Moderate*	*None*	*Increase of prison population*	*Only temporarily*	*1=very high; 2=high; 3=low; 4=very low*	
Italy		114%	Yes	X					2/4	As of 14 June 2021: 86.7% of prisoners are vaccinated
Japan	Decrease	57%	No			X			4/4	Reduction not felt necessary, no overcrowding
Kenya	Decrease	381%	Yes	X					4/4	
Latvia	Decrease	71%	No		X				4/4	Only minor efforts to reduce short-term PS (up to 3 months)
Lithuania	Decrease	85%	Yes, but only moderate	X					4/4	Coincidence with law reform 2019/2020 aiming at reducing the prison pop.
Netherlands	Decrease	98%	Yes		X				4/4	
New Zealand	Incr., decrease from 2018	94%	No		X				4/4	Impact from general policy independent from pandemic
Northern Ireland	Incr., from 2014 decrease	80%	No			X			4/4	
North Macedonia	Decrease from 2018	93%	Yes		X				4/4	Reductionist policy since 2017, independent of pandemic
Norway	Stable	91%	Yes	X				X	4/4	-19% reduction of prison pop. until 5 May 2020; all prisoners in single cells; reduction by 7 April 2021: -8.9%

Peru	Increase	238%				X			2/2	Reluctant attempts to reduce prison population failed
Poland	Decrease from 2012	91%	Yes	X					4/4	Strong impact on sentenced, increase of remand prisoners
Portugal	Decrease	97%	Yes	X					4/3	
Romania	Decrease from 2014		No				X		4/4	Penal moderation from 2014 (p.p.: -30%), a reverse populist policy since 2019
Russia	Decrease	73%	Yes		X					Decrease of prison. population from 2000: 54%
Scotland	Stable	93%	Yes		X				4/3	Early release legislation 2020
Serbia	Stable	105%	Yes		X				4/4	Moderate decrease in first wave, counteracted by a penal law reform of May 2019 increasing penalties
Slovakia	Stable	90%	Yes/No			X			4/2	Only moderate attempts to reduce prison population
Slovenia	Stable	110%	Yes	X				(X)	4/4	Reduction of prison pop. by 19.7% until 15 April 2020, and by 15.2% until 31 Dec. 2020
South Africa	Stable	About 130%	No/yes		X			X	3/3	No decisive and coherent reductionist policy
Spain	Decrease	80%	Yes		X				4/4	Infection rate less than in civil society
Sweden	Decrease	96%	No				X		4/4	
Switzerland	Stable	94%	Yes		X				4/4	No uniform reductionist policy, dependent from Cantons (Federal States)
Turkey	Increase	133%	Yes	X					(4/4) statistics problematic	About 30% of the p.p. released to serve the PS under HD (estimated)
USA	Decrease	100%	Yes/in 17 States No	X, some Fed. States	X, some Fed. States	X, some Fed. States			1/1	Strategies vary between Fed. States, in general back-door strategies prevail

a Avoiding pre-trial detention, suspension of executing sentences/increasing alternative sanctions, (forwarded) conditional release, long-term prison leave, etc.

The African prison populations were largely stable when the pandemic began (see e.g. *South Africa*, Togo), and was even declining in some countries (Ghana, *Kenya* and Tanzania). Only a few countries showed a prison population increase at that stage (e.g. Morocco and Nigeria, where occupancy rates reached 137% and 147%, respectively, at the end of 2018).

The situation in *Japan* with an occupancy rate of 63% was comparatively quite relaxed. In contrast, *India* had an occupancy rate of 119%. The Indian imprisonment rate of 35 per 100,000 of the national population was already very low before the pandemic, but with an absolute number of about 466,000 prisoners at the end of 2018, preventing infections in prisons presented a serious challenge.

2.2 The impact of COVID-19 on prisoners and prison staff (infection rates)

2.2.1 Infection rates

Infection rates of prisoners often mirror the situation in the general population. Countries that underestimated or neglected the dangers of COVID-19 had high infection and death rates, both in prisons and in the larger society. Most prominent examples are the *USA* and *Brazil*. Data for the USA are reported by the Marshall Project. As Byrne and colleagues point out in Chapter 45, the situation in the US prisons is even worse than in the general society: one out of five prisoners has tested positive, whereas the ratio in the general society is one out of 20. As of 21 June 2021, the total number of prisoners infected since March 2020 in the USA amounted to almost 400,000.[6]

For *Brazil*, similarly high infection rates are reported. Every fourth prisoner tested by the end of 2020 was positive with regard to the COVID-19 virus, as well as about 30% of staff members tested in the same period. 10,000s of infections and almost 150 deaths of prisoners were registered, with an apparently very high dark figure. These "numbers reveal a horrific scenario of prisons being one of the most dangerous places in Brazil, both for prisoners and staff" (Rodrigues and Khoury in Chapter 4).[7]

Other South American countries presented a mixed picture: countries such as *Argentina* and *Colombia* responded immediately with strict lockdowns also in prisons and were initially able to keep their infection rates low, whereas others that waited longer before reacting faced serious problems.[8]

In Asia, we find that *Japan* and *China* introduced a strict isolation and segregation policy at an early stage, isolating prisoners in quarantine for 14 days after admission and before release, which successfully prevented the spread of the virus inside prisons. Reports on other Asian countries, such as Thailand, Indonesia, the Philippines, Myanmar, Laos, Vietnam and Cambodia, revealed low infection rates during the first wave of the pandemic in the civil societies and in prisons as well, which may be attributed to cultural values of distancing and avoiding physical contacts (Rapisarda and Byrne, 2020: 953). Iran announced a release of 85,000 prisoners (i.e. one third of its prison population) in order to prevent the spreading of the virus. Exact numbers on the effect of this strategy have not been published.[9] The data are somewhat contradictory and unclear, but it can be assumed that strategies of restricting visiting contacts as well as using front-end (decreasing the flow of prisoners into prison) and back-end strategies (increasing the flow of prisoners out of prison) to reduce crowding, and in some cases also authoritarian governmental strategies of strict lockdowns of prisons, were successful in keeping COVID-19 under control in most Asian countries (Rapisarda and Byrne, 2020: 954 ff.).

Australia and *New Zealand* also succeeded in widely preventing infections inside prisons. This was achieved by keeping the infection rates in wider society low with very strict policies limiting entry to their countries and quarantining the few nationals who were allowed to return.

In Europe, experiences have varied among countries and between the first and second waves of the pandemic. *Austria, Denmark, Estonia, Finland, Germany, Ireland, Latvia, Lithuania, The Netherlands, Northern Ireland, North Macedonia, Norway, Poland, Romania, Scotland, Serbia, Sweden, Switzerland* all revealed very low infection rates in both waves of the pandemic (March to June 2020 and from October 2020 to March 2021). *Croatia*, the *Czech Republic, Portugal* and *Slovakia* had no problems during the first wave, but experienced elevated infection rates in the second wave. High infection rates, especially in the second wave, were also seen in *England & Wales* and *Greece*. The opposite development took place in *Italy*, which had large problems during the first wave and almost no infection cases in the second one (see Table 49.1, column 10).

2.2.2 Vaccinations

As to *vaccinations* in the prison context, two different approaches have been adopted worldwide. The dominant strategy is to treat prisoners similarly to the general population and to priority groups that are also recognised outside prisons. Therefore, elderly prisoners and prisoners with specific health problems and risks have been vaccinated early in many countries. As the large majority of prisoners, because of the "lockdown within the lockdown" that has been imposed in most European countries, do not face higher risks of being infected than citizens in the outside society, it may be acceptable not to give them priority. However, one could raise the argument that there is an increased risk of not being able to guarantee social distancing in prison systems where prisoners are predominantly accommodated in communal cells, as is the case in Eastern Europe.

The situation is different in the *USA* or *Brazil* and in other countries with highly overcrowded prison systems and low hygienic standards. There prisoners must be seen as particularly endangered and vulnerable, and therefore should be prioritised with regard to vaccinations. Indeed, some US Federal States, such as New York and Oregon, provided vaccinations for all prisoners as a priority group.[10] The report of Byrne et al. in Chapter 45 reveals that as of 10 April 2021, "14 states had included incarcerated persons as part of Phase I of vaccine distribution …, while 20 states opted to disseminate vaccinations to inmates in Phase II". Two states (Michigan, Rhode Island) "differentiate medically vulnerable incarcerated persons from the remainder of this population by limiting Phase I vaccines to the medically vulnerable". Prison staff members in all the US states are prioritised under Phase I or II. As far as can be seen in other countries, especially in Europe, prison staff have also been given the same priority as teachers and the police. In *South Africa*, "persons who are working or living in detention" (i.e. also prisoners) benefited from outreach vaccination programmes (mobile clinics) during Phase II of the vaccine roll-out plan (United Nations Office on Drugs and Crime, 2021a: 4).

As of 29 June 2021, only a few countries in Europe had implemented a vaccination strategy prioritising prisoners. According to data of EuroPris, 86.7% of the prisoners in *Italy* had received their vaccination by June 2021.[11] In *Estonia*, as of 22 June 2021 all prison staff members and about 50% of prisoners had been vaccinated.[12] In *Australia*, people in prison were a dedicated 1B priority category for vaccination, but by mid-2021 some states had still not commenced vaccination of people detained in prison.[13]

3 Prison and penal policy concerning the execution of prison sentences during the COVID-19 pandemic

From an early stage of the pandemic, several international human rights organisations raised concerns about how COVID-19 would be dealt with in prison and sought to develop policy guidelines on how it could best be done. On 20 March 2020, the European Committee for the Prevention of Torture and Inhuman or Degrading Treatment or Punishment (CPT) had issued a "statement of principles relating to the treatment of persons deprived of their liberty in the context of coronavirus disease" emphasising that "any restrictive measures … should have a legal basis and be proportionate, respectful of human dignity and restricted in time" (see CPT/Inf(2020)13, under Section 4). It also asked for "concerted efforts" to resort to alternatives to deprivation of liberty, which should be "imperative" in particular in situations of overcrowding (demanding greater use of alternatives to pre-trial detention, commutation of sentences, early release and probation, etc. (see CPT/Inf(2020)13, under Section 5). In a further statement, the CPT made clear that the pandemic was resulting in national authorities taking "resolute action" on long-standing issues and that "emergency measures put in place temporarily must be made sustainable" (CPT, Follow-up statement regarding the situation of persons deprived of their liberty in the context of the ongoing COVID-19 pandemic, CPT/Inf (2020)21).

A working group of the Council for Penological Co-operation (PC-CP) of the Council of Europe on 17 April 2020 released a "COVID-19 related statement", which emphasised (apart from providing the necessary health care and preventive measures against SARS-CoV-2 infection) that restrictions of prison life activities and contacts with the outside world must be proportionate and allow an acceptable minimum level of contact. It further recommended considering immediate or early release of certain groups of offenders and preparing them by providing accommodation and guaranteeing medical support. The probation services should be better equipped in order to prevent "probation overcrowding", i.e. "to use effectively meaningful community sanctions and measures and to avoid mass supervision" (see PC-CP (2020) 5: 6). Restrictions concerning visits inside prisons should be compensated by measures such as free-of-charge phone calls or video-calls through the internet and other restrictions of daily prison life (work, recreational activities) should be compensated as well.

The United Nations have also increased their efforts to protect rights in prisons during the pandemic, also as a reaction to growing unrest in prisons worldwide. The UN Human Rights Office (OHCHR) in a message of 5 May 2020 "expressed concern that in the Americas, infections are spreading rapidly amid chronic overcrowding and unhygienic conditions, coupled with the lack of proper access to healthcare" (see https://news.un.org/en/story/2020/05/1063292). According to the same source, such problems were also an issue in countries in which UN Peacekeeping was involved in prison management and administration, like the Democratic Republic of Congo, and had led to the UN Peacekeeping recommendation of early prisoner release particularly in states facing serious overcrowding. Prison riots and COVID-19 outbreaks with deaths of prisoners also occurred in the Central African Republic, Venezuela, Peru and elsewhere (see also Heard in Chapter 48), and in Europe (*Italy, Ireland*), too. Already in March, the UN High Commissioner for Human Rights, Michelle Bachelet, had asked to "examine ways to release those particularly vulnerable to COVID-19, among them older detainees and those who are sick, as well as low-risk offenders" (25 March 2020). In summary, it can be concluded that the Council of Europe (Penological Council and CPT), the UN and several NGOs, such as Penal Reform International, all asked for reductionist intervention (see Heard in Chapter 48; Dünkel and Snacken in Chapter 50).

To achieve the aim of preventing the spread of COVID-19 inside prisons, two primary strategies recommended by international bodies were pursued at the national level: on the one hand, restricting the influx of new prisoners, in particular with short-term sentences; on the other, limiting contacts with the outside world by suspending visits and other activities based on incoming and outgoing persons. Therefore, prison leave for prisoners as well as leisure time activities, sports, etc., with volunteers and other external personnel coming in, were stopped or at least reduced. Prisons had to establish quarantine sections/departments and therefore – even where overcrowding was not an issue – prison administrations were interested in reducing the prison population. This was a real challenge in prison systems where overcrowding and also accommodation in communal cells or dormitories were a part of everyday life

Most prison administrations reacted relatively promptly, but not equally effectively. Many European jurisdictions applied a mix of front-door and back-door strategies (see in detail Chapter 50). A few states claimed to be trying to reduce their prison populations in the face of the pandemic but failed to do so as their governments were not really interested in improving prison conditions. The worst example is certainly *Brazil* where there was no reduction; on the contrary, the prison population increased further. The President of *Brazil*, Jair Bolsonaro, was not the only poor leader in this respect; there are further bad examples in *Colombia*, *Peru* and *Bolivia*, all countries suffering from extremely high overcrowding and demonstrating their incapability or unwillingness to substantially change prison conditions, even in a time of crisis. A strange situation in this respect occurred in *Argentina*, where a judicial intervention of the Federal Tribunal asking for the early release of prisoners with lesser offences and vulnerable offenders (e.g. with comorbidities) was rejected by the Supreme Court, after protests of the Argentinian president and others who made the populist argument that "dangerous prisoners" should not be released (see Valderrama and Hernandez in Chapter 9).

The European reductionist landscape is diverse. While most countries, particularly those facing the additional pressure of serious overcrowding, such as *France* and *Italy*, reduced their prison populations by more than 10%, the developments in *Greece* and *Romania* went in the opposite direction. In both countries, *no explicit governmental strategy* to reduce overcrowding was visible. In *Romania*, the positive development of reducing the prison population before 2019 was stopped because of some serious crimes committed by early released prisoners resulting in a law reform in 2019 demanded by the media and the public. During the pandemic, no reductionist actions were accepted, and the government tried to prevent infections by a purely medical approach of limiting contacts inside prisons. In *Slovakia*, although there were 3.5% fewer admissions to prisons between February and September 2020 and 7.8% more sentences suspended (on probation) than in 2019, the prison population rate remained stable (see Aebi and Tiago, 2020 and Table 50.1 in Chapter 50). In *Serbia*, the attempts to reduce the prison population had only limited effects,[14] possibly as they were counteracted by a populist law reform in May 2019 increasing penalties for recidivist and violent offenders. In *England & Wales*, the attempts to reduce the prison population were implemented rather reluctantly, but finally a decline of 6.9% was attained by January 2021 (see Chapter 14 and Table 1).

The initial situation in *Turkey* was characterised by dramatic overcrowding (occupancy rate of 133%). This was the result of a strong focus "on a neoliberal penal regime that values an increased punitiveness" (Akdeniz and Aydinoglu in Chapter 44). The prison population increased from about 50,000 in 2000 to about 300,000 at the end of 2019. On 14 April 2020, immediately after the pandemic began, a reform law was passed, which lowered the minimum terms to be served before an early release from two thirds to a half, and from three quarters to two thirds for repeat offenders. Probation (conditional suspended sentences) was extended from up to one year to three years for women with children, and from two to four years for offenders over the age of 70. Furthermore, the possibilities for transfers to open facilities were expanded and those eligible for such transfers could be sent on leave serving their sentence in home detention. According to the General Director of Prisons, about 90,000 persons were released on leave in April 2020 and a further 28,000 in June 2020. In February 2021, about 78,500 prisoners were reported to be on leave. The data of World Prison Brief do not reflect this policy as persons on leave are still counted as prisoners (see Chapter 44). Between 78,500 and 90,000, persons serving their sentence in home detention would account for a reduction of about 26–30% and result in an occupancy rate of around 100%.

The Scandinavian countries, well known for having quite uniform, liberal penal policies (see Lappi-Seppälä, 2007, 2020), interestingly followed diverse strategies in response to the pandemic. There was no policy to reduce the prison population in *Denmark* and *Sweden*, compared to a reductionist approach in *Finland* and *Norway*, which to some extent, however, had only a temporary effect. In *Norway*, during the first two months, a reduction of 19% was attained, but after an increase by 7 April 2021, the overall reduction compared to February 2020 was "only" 8.9%.

A radically different policy was implemented in *China*, *Russia* and *Japan*. The Chinese and Russian governments and prison administrations followed a policy of segregation and isolation of prisoners as well as of staff members, who had to remain and live inside the prison facilities for shifts of 14 days. With this lockdown applied also inside prisons, the infection rates were held under control. In *China*, prison governors were personally made responsible if infections were registered and some of them lost their jobs. The strategy in *Japan* was based on a relatively relaxed situation in prisons. Since 2008, the prison population had decreased considerably to one of the lowest in the world: 34 per 100,000 in 2019. The occupancy rate had also fallen from about 115% to 63% at the beginning of the pandemic. Therefore, there was enough space to separate incoming prisoners and accommodate them in single cells. Further actions were not seen as necessary.

The pandemic-induced measures in most countries were temporary – execution of sentences was only postponed. A few countries, however, chose an enduring form of non-execution by granting a collective pardon. This was the case in some *German* Federal States with imprisonment for fine defaulters (in Berlin and in a few instances in Hamburg), but it was far wider reaching in *Portugal*, where prisoners, sentenced to up to two years of imprisonment, and other prisoners, who had served half of their sentences, were all fully pardoned instead of being released conditionally.

Long-lasting effects were also achieved with certain *back-door strategies*. These included bringing forward early (conditional) release (*Turkey*), long-term prison leave (*Germany*) or allowing sentences to be served at home (home detention) (e.g. *France* and *Turkey*), sometimes combined with

Table 49.2 Restrictions of contact with the outside world and inside prisons and compensatory measures during the COVID-19 pandemic

Countries/ jurisdictions	*Restrictions of contact with the outside world*					*Restrictions inside prisons*					*Compensatory measures*			
	Visits (relatives, friends)	*Visits of Lawyers/*	*Prison leave*	*Transfer to open prisons*	*Preparatory measures for release (PO, Aftercare Services)*	*14-days quarantine for incoming / isolation of vulnerable inmates*	*Work (Yes / Temporarily / No)*	*Group leisure time activities (sports)*	*Treatment/ re-entry programmes*	*Moving between prison departments/ unitsa*	*Additional phone calls / mobile phones (MP)*	*Video communication*	*Additional/ adapted learning and leisure activities*	*Long-term leaves (LTL)/ home detention (HD), etc.*
Australia	X	No restr.			X	X	Yes	X	X			X		
Argentina	X		X		X			X	X					
Austria	X	Temp.	X		X		Yes / temp.	X	X	X	X / MP in open prisons	X		HD
Belgium	X	No restr.	X		X		No	X	X		X	X	X/X[c]	HD
Bolivia	X	X	X		X			X	X					
Brazil	X	X (first wave)	X		X		Majority fed. states.: no		X			X, only some fed. states		X (some fed. states)
Canada	X		X		X	X		X	X	X		X		
Chile	X		X		X	X		X	X	X	X	X		
China	X		X		X	X	No		X	1		X	X	
Colombia	X	X	X		X			X	X					
Costa Rica	X	No r.	X		X			X	X		X	X		
Croatia	X	No r.	X		X	X		X	X		X	X		
Czech Republic	X		X		X				X		X	X		
Denmark	X		X		X		X depending on prisons	X	X		X	X	X	
England/ Wales	X		X	X	X	X	X	X	X	X	X	X		
Estonia	X	No restr.	X	X (first wave)	X	X	X (first wave)	X	X		X	X	X	
Finland	X	No restr.	X		X		X in open prisons		No		X	X	X	

France	X	2	X		X	X		X	X		X	No		X
Germany	X[b]	No restr.	X	No restrict.	X	X	Temp.	X	3	No	X / MP in open prisons	X	X	LTL
Greece	X		X	X	X	X		X	X		X	X	X/X[c]	
Hungary	X		X		X		2	X	X	X	X[g]	3	X[c]	
India	X	X, only phone contacts allowed	X	X	X	X		X	X	X	X[d]/3[g]	3		
Ireland	X		X		X	X	X	X	X	X	X	X	X/X[c]	
Italy	X	No r.	X		X	X		X	X	X	X[d]	X[d]		HD
Japan	X	No r.	X		X	X	X	X	X	X	3	3	3	
Kenya	X		X	X	X	X		X	X	X	2	2		
Latvia	X	X	X		X	X	X[d]	X[d]	X[d]	X	X / MPs in open prisons	X		
Lithuania	X		X	X	X	X		X	X	X	2	3		
Netherlands	X	Partial-ly rest.	X			X, later red. to 8 days		X	X		X	2	X	HD
New Zealand	X		X		X	X		X	X	X	X	X	X	
Northern Ireland	X							X		2	X	X	X/X[c]	
North Macedonia	X		X		X	X	Partially restricted	X	X		X/MPs allowed	X	2	
Norway	X	X, only phone/ video contacts	X	Not res-tricted, seen as a right		X (only until 18 May 2020)	2 (with social distancing)	2	2	X	X	X	X	HD + EM
Peru	X	No r.	X		X			X	X		X			
Poland	X	2	X	X	X	X	Partially restr.	X	X	X	X (in principle every day)	X	X	
Portugal	X		X	X	X	X	Temp.	X	X	X	X (from 1 to 3 per day)	X	X (distance learning)	

(*Continued*)

Countries/ jurisdictions	*Restrictions of contact with the outside world*					*Restrictions inside prisons*					*Compensatory measures*			
	Visits (relatives, friends)	*Visits of Lawyers/*	*Prison leave*	*Transfer to open prisons*	*Preparatory measures for release (PO, Aftercare Services)*	*14-days quarantine for incoming / isolation of vulnerable inmates*	*Work (Yes / Temporarily / No)*	*Group leisure time activities (sports)*	*Treatment/ re-entry programmes*	*Moving between prison departments/ unitsa*	*Additional phone calls / mobile phones (MP)*	*Video communication*	*Additional/ adapted learning and leisure activities*	*Long-term leaves (LTL)/ home detention (HD), etc.*
Romania	X		X		X	X		X	X	X	X (+45/75 min. per day)	X	X	
Russia	X		X			X (20 days)		X		X	No inf.	No inf.		
Scotland	X		X		X			X	X	X	X / MPs widely allowed	X (pre-pandemic e-mail schemes)	X	HD + EM
Serbia	X	No r.	X	No r.	X		2	X	2		X	2	X	
Slovakia	X	No r.	X		X	X (10 days)	X	X	X	X	X	3	X	
Slovenia	X	No r.	X		X	X	X	X	X		X	No	X	
South Africa	X	X	X	X	X	X	X	X	X		X / no MPs	No, but audio-visual links to some courts	-	-
Spain	X[e]	No r.	X		X	X	2	X	X		X	2		HD
Sweden	X[f]		X[f]		X	X		X	X		X	X		
Switzerland	X	No r.	X		X	X	X[d]	X	X[d]		X	2	X[d]	HD
Turkey	X	X	X		X	X		X	X	1	3	3 (only 2 pilot proj.)		HD
USA	X		X		X	X		X	X[d]	X	[d]	[d]		HD[d]

a Segregation, apart from quarantine units; restricted out-of-cell activities.
b Jurisprudence intervening during the second wave, emphasising the importance of physical contacts with family members; prison administration must also provide long-term-visits during the pandemic under consideration of hygiene measures, testing and quarantine provisions.
c Digital learning platforms/programmes provided.
d Variations in comparison of Federal States/Cantons/territories/regions.
e "Normal visits", where inmates and visitors are separated by a window, were suspended only for a short period (March to May 2020), family and conjugal visits for longer times.
f Prisoners who tested positive for COVID-19 and then recovered were given the opportunity of physical contact at visits and also to unattended prison leaves.
g Additional phone calls have to be borne by inmates.
X = yes; no = no restriction / expansion; temp. = temporarily restricted; Incr. = increase; PO = Probation Officers; restr., r. = restriction(s).
Differentiation: 1 = strong (restrictions/expansion); 2 = medium size (restrictions/expansion); 3 = weak (restrictions/expansion).

electronic monitoring (e.g. *Austria*, *Poland*, *Switzerland* and *Spain*). And finally, a lower prison population was also based on the reduction of certain (street) crimes, including burglaries, car thefts and assaults. During the pandemic and general lockdowns, the opportunities for committing crimes were significantly reduced. Unfortunately, this did not extend to domestic violence, which increased in many countries.

Table 49.1 summarises the situation before and penal policies during the pandemic and their impact on prison population rates. The impact of measures taken to reduce the prison population was characterised as "strong", if the reduction was 10% or more, as "moderate" if it was between 5% and 10% and as "none" if it was less than 5% (see also further details in Table 49.2, as well as Table 50.1 of Chapter 50 and the comments on it).

4 Restrictions of contact with the outside world

International human rights standards require that all prisoners, including those in solitary confinement or other forms of segregation, must be guaranteed a minimum of meaningful contact with the outside world. Therefore, during the pandemic, international human rights organisations continued to claim that this minimum should be granted.[15] These were mostly realised by alternative ("compensatory") forms of communication via the internet (Skype and other platforms, see Section 6 below). These were also often made available to prisoners subject to special regimes such as solitary confinement (see Section 5 below). In so far as such contact was maintained, Rule 42 of the UN Nelson Mandela Rules was followed.[16] Rule 43.3 emphasises in this context that "... restrictive measures shall not include the prohibition of family contact. The means of family contact may only be restricted for a limited time period and as strictly required for the maintenance of security and order".

Herzog-Evans in Chapter 17 notes that European law requires that such contacts must be maintained:

> Even under normal circumstances, prison services are required by the European court to contribute actively to the maintenance of family ties (ECtHR, Messina v. Italy, 2000). In the context of COVID-19, the penological committee of the Council of Europe (PC-CP), issued a statement whereby it declared that 'Prison authorities shall assist inmates in maintaining adequate contact with the outside world and provide them with the appropriate welfare support to do so' .... In other words, it called for authorities to create compensatory measures for the restrictions inflicted upon families during the lockdown.

4.1 Visits

All jurisdictions, without exception, implemented some *restrictions on contacts with the outside world*, in particular on *visits* of relatives, children and friends. In countries with visiting facilities that allowed the physical separation of visitors and prisoners, by using acrylic glass panes, for example, visits could be organised to a limited extent: such facilities existed before the pandemic, for example, in *Spain*, and for special groups of prisoners in *Germany* (especially terrorists, drug dealers or addicts). During the first wave of the pandemic, some prisons reorganised their larger visiting facilities by providing more spaces for visits separated by glass panes. Nowhere, however, were these facilities available throughout the whole system.

In some regions, visits serve functions beyond just meeting and talking; they are also necessary to support prisoners with additional food or other goods in order to alleviate the harsh conditions of prison life. This is particularly the case in African and Latin American prisons.[17] In some African states, food for prisoners is budgeted on the official capacity. Therefore, overcrowding leads to food shortages and endangered the survival of prisoners already before the pandemic.[18] Although in *India* families were allowed to send cloths and food to their relatives in prisons during the pandemic,[19] the ban of family visits led to violent incidences with deaths of prisoners.

In Europe, complaints by prisoners in *The Netherlands* about the suspension of visits, because the regular smuggling of soft drugs into prison was interrupted, are certainly unique; however, they illustrate the wider function of physical contacts through prison visits! In *Spain* as well, the prison authorities realised that the spread of illegal drugs was reduced because of the restrictions of visits. In order to prevent overdoses and serious health problems after returning to "normal prison life", the prison administration developed information campaigns and workshops on that issue.

A serious human rights problem was the denial of visits not only for relatives and friends but also for lawyers, as was temporarily the case in *Brazil*,[20] *Colombia*, *South Africa* and *Turkey*.[21] This is certainly unacceptable and therefore the practice to use acrylic glass panes and masks (*Russia*, *Serbia*, *Slovenia* and many other jurisdictions) is the only acceptable kind of restriction.

4.2 Monitoring of **prisons** *during the pandemic*

Prison visits of another kind were restricted during the pandemic as well. In some countries, prison *inspectors* and *monitors* were prevented from visiting prisons at the height of the pandemic or their access to prisons was severely restricted. In *Australia*, the activities of inspectors were reduced, while in *England & Wales*, inspections were fully suspended from March to the end of May 2020. In *South Africa*, the official Independent Correctional Centre Visitors were not listed as essential services and consequently were prevented by law from visiting prisons, leading to a reduction in complaints even though prisoners were subject to more segregation and use of force during the pandemic.

Yet, international standards require, and human rights organisations insisted, that monitoring visits should continue during the pandemic (see Muralt in Networks Working Together/International Corrections & Prisons Association, 2020: 27 ff.). The World Health Organization (WHO), for example, has criticised such practices and emphasised that COVID-19 should not be used as a justification to suspend "external inspection of prisons and other places of detention by independent international or national bodies" (see Mulgrew and van Zyl Smit in Chapter 47). There were, however, also instances of good practice. All monitoring systems continued to work in *India*, for example.

4.3 Long-term prison leave, transfers to open prisons and home detention

Other ways of maintaining contact with the outside world were the transfer of prisoners to open facilities or the use of long-term leave (in *Germany* theoretically up to six months, in practice for a few weeks) or of home detention (also see above, under Section 3). Prison leave from closed prisons was generally suspended, but the transfer to open prisons and from there to home detention (see e.g. *Austria* and *Spain*) or long-term prison leave (*Germany, The Netherlands, Portugal*) as a form of executing prison sentences was used to a greater extent than before the pandemic in a number of countries/jurisdictions. In *Austria, Belgium, Canada, England & Wales, Finland, France, Germany, Italy, Lithuania,*[22] *Norway, Poland, Spain, Turkey* and many Federal States in the *USA*, such back-door strategies had a moderate to important impact on the prison population rates (see Table 49.1). However, in 22 of the 48 jurisdictions represented in this volume, no such back-door strategies to reduce the prison population were applied. The primary aim of these mechanisms was not to uphold family and other contacts with the outside world, but to reduce contagion risks by reducing the prison population.

5 Restrictions inside prisons

Restrictions of the daily regimes in prisons concerned the admission period in quarantine facilities, prison work, rehabilitative and other training or re-entry programmes, leisure time activities and the possibilities of associations with other inmates.

5.1 Quarantine facilities and other forms of segragation / isolation

Prison administrations' main concern was to prevent contagion with COVID-19 by incoming prisoners. Therefore, quarantine facilities were established where prisoners had to stay for 14 days (mostly in single accommodation). In the later phases of the pandemic, some states shortened the isolation period to ten or even seven days coupled with testing of the prisoners concerned. Not much information exists about how the quarantine periods were implemented. As mentioned above, even under restrictive measures of segregation in quarantine facilities, a minimum of human contacts must be upheld. It is not clear whether the countries represented in this volume were sensitive to this requirement and could provide technical means of maintaining prisoners' contacts with family members outside.

International human rights standards require that a minimum of two hours per day of out-of-cell activities should be guaranteed to inmates who are segregated (see Mulgrew and van Zyl Smit in Chapter 47). Therefore, the practice of temporarily keeping prisoners in their cells for 24 hours a day observed in *Australia* or in some other cases providing out-of-cell times of less than one hour per day in *England & Wales* or *New Zealand* is not acceptable. In *Latvia*, prisoners in quarantine units were not allowed to receive phone calls or to take part in video communication, which should be seen as a violation of international human rights standards, although it lasted only for a maximum of 14 days (it often concerned prisoners coming from abroad, who were further discriminated against in that way).

Another problem in this context was that inmates of vulnerable groups isolated in special facilities, such as elderly prisoners (over 70), claimed that they were punished for belonging to a risk group (*Ireland*).

From a human rights perspective, the *granting of at least one hour of exercise* in the open air (see Rule 23 of the UN Nelson Mandela Rules) and some more hours out-of-cell is indispensable also in crisis periods.[23] In the light of these requirements, it was totally unacceptable that the one hour of exercise in open air was denied in some prisons in *New Zealand* and during the second wave of the pandemic in some *Czech* prisons. In *Russia*, complaints were raised that the daily exercise times in fresh air were not guaranteed everywhere, either. *Scotland* initially provided only 30 minutes per day for outdoor exercise and 30 minutes for taking showers, which is certainly a problematic minimum standard, but it was subsequently expanded.

While the general approach of many prison administrations was to lock down prisoners as far as possible in order to prevent the spreading of the virus, *Northern Ireland* emphasised social distancing, which was facilitated by the reduced prison population and the possibility of accommodating prisoners in single cells. Similar strategies were adopted in prison systems allowing single accommodation (e.g. *Scandinavian* counties, *Germany* and *The Netherlands*).

5.2 Work

Many countries during the first wave of the pandemic closed prison workshops, but most of them re-opened these facilities fairly soon, as the alternative of locking down prisoners for up the 23 hours per day in their cells created much stress, discontent and was seen as a possible source for riots and other collective actions. Indeed, the unrest observed in many countries (see Heard in Chapter 48) – apart from dissatisfaction concerning the restrictions of contacts with the outside world (family visits) – was often related to restrictions of work with the consequence that prisoners did not earn money, which was needed to buy goods they used daily, such as cigarettes, tobacco, tea and coffee. Some prison administrations granted a kind of substitute pocket money to alleviate prisoners' discontent and possible collective complaints.

5.2.1 Rehabilitative and re-entry programmes

Most rehabilitative or training programmes were suspended during lockdowns because of the pandemic. This was particularly the case for those programmes run by external staff or volunteers (see e.g. *Canada*). A serious problem was to continue preparation for release and re-entry programmes, which are based on regular short-term prison leave, sometimes including daily work outside the prison premises and returning only for spending the night inside. All these transitional activities were suspended in closed prisons, whereas they could be upheld to some extent in open facilities where priority could be given to release to home detention or long-term prison leave (e.g. in *Germany*).

5.2.2 (Group) leisure time activities

Team sports were reduced or totally suspended, but smaller group and individual sports activities were allowed and, in some countries, offered as a kind of compensatory measure. Movements inside prisons between different houses/wings/departments were specifically restricted in some countries (e.g. in *China*). There were also countries in which additional TV-sets were handed out in order to provide more opportunities for in-cell leisure time activities.

6 Compensatory measures

The suspension of visits of relatives was the most common measure for preventing the spreading of the virus in prisons. The contact restrictions were compensated by the wider use of telephone call, either through additional and free ordinary telephone calls or by internet communication through video-calls or, less often, by using mobile phones, usually only in open prisons or for certain low-risk offender groups (e.g. *France* and *Germany*).

In some countries, telephones had already been installed in prison cells before the pandemic, which proved to be of great advantage (some Federal States of *Germany*). In *Ireland*, in-cell telephones were installed in the quarantine or segregation departments in order to compensate the general restrictions of contacts and to provide support. In *Northern Ireland* and *New Zealand*, in-cell telephones were provided. The technology for video communication in some countries existed already before the pandemic and therefore was just used more frequently from March 2020 (e.g. *Latvia*).

However, some countries, such as *Japan*, categorically denied internet communication; also in *China* and *South Africa*, such options were not provided. Often it remains unclear from the national reports if alternative communication forms have been implemented on a nationwide basis, as internet access, for example, was not provided on a larger scale.

From an empirical point of view, we lack information about the extent to which prisoners were profiting from one or another communication system. An exception is the report on *Finland* referring to excellent statistics on phone calls (Skype, etc.) in relation to the number of traditional visits. It can be said that prisoners despite reduced physical contacts through visits had about the same amount of contact by alternative communication forms. Other national reports indicate that the provision of technical devices for internet communication or additional phone sets was often inadequate, for example, in *England & Wales*, *The Netherlands* or *Lithuania*.

7 Legal basis for restrictions and relaxations of the prison regime

The rule of law requires that all aspects of the prison regime that affect the rights of prisoners have a clear legislative basis (van Zyl Smit and Snacken, 2009). Such a legal basis not only protects prisoners against abuse, but also provides an indication of what the prison authorities need to do to ensure that the prison regime does not infringe prisoners' rights. As empirical studies of the pains of imprisonment have become more sophisticated, it has increasingly been recognised that many aspects of the prison regime can affect prisoners' rights and need to be further regulated in binding legislation. Prominent among prisoners' rights are not only very basic rights to food, clothing, accommodation and medical treatment, but also rights to human interaction, be it with other prisoners or with family outside prison. This is of particular significance during a pandemic. A good example is the absolute requirement of the Nelson Mandela Rules that prisoners may not be held in "prolonged solitary confinement", that is, held for more than 15 days in conditions where they do not have "meaningful human contact" for at least two hours every day. "Prolonged solitary confinement" is clearly a cruel inhuman or degrading form of treatment, if not outright torture (Chapter 47, Mulgrew and Van Zyl Smit). It is noteworthy that in *Canada* mandatory quarantine cannot be for longer than 14 days, as such isolation would be regarded as an unconstitutional infringement of a fundamental human right. In *Norway*, the courts appear to have gone further, holding that even quarantine for 14 days should not be applied routinely to all newly admitted prisoners, but that, for reasons of proportionality, the period of quarantine for each case should be assessed on its individual merits.

The introductions to the national reports in this volume reveal that all modern prison systems have legal bases that recognise (with varying degrees of precision and efficacy) the rights of prisoners and impose duties on the prison authorities to provide prison regimes that allow prisoners to live in conditions where these rights are not infringed. The focus in this section is on how the legal bases that recognised prisoners' rights were modified to deal with the COVID-19 pandemic, both by introducing legal restrictions on prisoner's rights and by granting prisoners limited additional rights to relaxation of certain rules in order to compensate for the restrictions imposed.

7.1 Restrictions

How much attention worldwide has been paid to ensuring that restrictions introduced to deal with the pandemic in prisons have a sound legal basis? One legal mechanism that was widely used as a legal basis for additional restrictions was to apply general emergency "health" laws to the prisons. *Switzerland,* for example, simply applied existing laws dealing with pandemics to COVID-19 and introduced supplementary legislation to be interpreted by the cantons, which have primary responsibility for the prison matters. In a formal sense, such laws did provide justifications for restrictions on prisoners' rights, but there was a risk that they would not be sufficiently nuanced to deal with the particular needs of prisoners or prison staff.

This risk was clearly recognised in some countries. In *Austria*, for example, the federal law regarding the precautionary measures to prevent the spread of COVID-19 did not deal specifically with prisons, but it was utilised directly in prisons to provide a basis for standards of hygiene and social distancing to which all persons, including prisoners, were expected to adhere. However, the application of this general "health" law was combined with specific legislation aimed at the judicial system as a whole and at the prisons in particular, in order to create a comprehensive legal basis for restrictions on prisoners' rights necessitated by the COVID-19 pandemic. A similar result was achieved in *Scotland* where general legislation to deal with the pandemic (the Coronavirus Scotland Acts 2020 and 2021) included specific provisions for restrictions in prisons.

Germany is a rare example of a country where the need for a legal basis for dealing with pandemics was anticipated before the system was confronted by COVID-19. Existing prison legislation of the various Federal States already referred specifically to legislation designed to deal with epidemics, and it was simply a matter of invoking it as the basis for restrictions designed to deal with COVID-19.

In countries where the recognition in primary legislation of prisoners' rights is relatively weak, the prison authorities intervened more freely. In *England & Wales*, for example, initial restrictions on the prison regime were made without amending primary or even subordinate legislation. By going into what is known as "command mode" and thus not even amending the Prison Rules, that is, the secondary legislation that spells out much of what the prison service is required to do, the Secretary of State for Justice (the political head of the prison service) could simply order restrictions without spelling out the legal basis for them. *Chile*, too, has a weak legal basis and similar problems.

Similarly, in *Turkey* all decisions on COVID-19-related restrictions (and relaxations) of the prison regime were simply made administratively by the Ministry of Justice and not published. The lack of transparency made it hard to evaluate the sufficiency of their legal basis. In *Denmark,* too, there have been a plethora of regulations rather than primary legislation authorising restrictions in prisons. Although they are not supposed to infringe Denmark's international obligations, there are doubts about whether the imposed restrictions, as they operate during the pandemic, meet the standards set by the Nelson Mandela Rules and other international norms to which Denmark professes to adhere.

The most extreme example of disregard for legal niceties appears to have been the case in *China*, where instructions on the prevention of infection in prisons were simply issued by state authorities, with no attention to their legal basis.

7.2 Relaxations

In contrast to the perceived need in most systems for a clear legal foundation for additional restrictions, direct relaxations of prison regimes were not generally seen to require a specific legal basis. Extra telephone or video calls could simply be allowed by the individual heads of prisons, or they could be instructed to do so by their bureaucratic superiors, without the need for a change in the law.

One indirect way of improving prison regimes during the pandemic was to reduce the number of prisoners held in prison. This did not always require legal change, as in many instances criminal courts were simply not sitting during the pandemic and therefore were sentencing fewer people to imprisonment. In some instances, existing executive powers of pardon or early release provided a legal basis for reducing the number of incarcerated persons of all kinds. However, some means of reducing prison numbers did require a changed legal basis. Several South American countries, including *Bolivia, Columbia* and *Peru,* introduced special legal powers that allowed for the number of prisoners to be reduced by administrative steps (whether they were used sufficiently is a different question).

Some of the failures to implement release policies can be attributed to their inadequate legal basis. A powerful example of this is the failure to release (or grant relaxation of their regimes) to international prisoners because of the limited legal authority of *international courts* to intervene, even in a pandemic (Mulgrew in Chapter 46).

7.3 The role of the courts

As has become apparent, the legal framework for restrictions and relaxations of the prison regime was primarily a matter of statutory law. In a limited number of countries, for example, in *Brazil,* the courts have used fundamental constitutional rights, rather than specific legislation, as the legal basis to intervene directly to order not to keep certain classes of persons in prison during the pandemic.

Courts were often called upon to enforce these laws and sometimes came to different conclusions than the prison officials. Thus, for example, in *Estonia*, the Tartu Administrative Court allowed a detainee to exercise outdoors pointing out that at that time the infection rate in Tartu County was low. In *Germany*, the constitutional right to protection of the marriage and family has also been used by the High Court of Berlin to insist that visits continue to be allowed during the pandemic, even if they are hard to implement organisationally.

Direct challenges to the legislation establishing the legal basis for controlling the COVID-19 pandemic in prisons have been rare. In *Italy*, however, the Constitutional Court has had to deal with challenges to a law restricting the power of judges to release persons convicted of certain crimes, such as those involving the Mafia, by requiring that the health benefits of such release be reassessed from time to time. However, the Italian Constitutional Court upheld this law, finding that reassessing the balance of the right to health against the right to public safety in release decisions was constitutional and did not undermine the authority of surveillance judges.

8 Returning to normal – What should be kept beyond the time of the pandemic?

8.1 Prisons as learning institutions

Overall, prisons in the second wave of the pandemic have learnt to cope with the pandemic in a more proportionate way, relying less on restrictions.[24] One reason certainly was that testing and hygienic devices were becoming a common standard, and that more was known about how the virus was spreading. Therefore, the COVID-19 pandemic proved that *prisons are learning institutions*. This ability of the institutions to learn and improve should be actively fostered.

8.2 Prison overcrowding and the reductionist approach

One effective measure, at least in some countries, has been to reduce the influx into prisons by expanding alternatives to pre-trial detention, by expanding alternative sentences to avoid short-term and middle-term prison sentences (community service, restriction of liberty sentences, etc.) and to increase regular and forwarded early release. The mixture of front- and back-door strategies has contributed to reduce prison population rates in several countries (see for general crime policy considerations in that respect Dünkel and Snacken in Chapter 50), without posing problems for national security or increasing crime rates. Other countries that failed in this respect (e.g. *Brazil* and the *USA*) faced serious problems and many infections and deaths in prison. This shows that opportunities to reduce prison populations can and should be used more frequently than before and that a reductionist approach is feasible. Altogether, one may conclude that the pandemic has paved the way for more rational crime policies aiming at imprisonment only as a last resort (see also Chapters 48 and 50 in this volume).

8.3 Single cell accommodation

The COVID-19 pandemic has shown that countries providing single cell accommodation had an advantage over countries that traditionally house two or more prisoners in one cell, or even use larger dormitories, as social distancing could be implemented much more easily and with less restriction of liberty inside prisons. This advantage in health crises is an additional reason to call for single cell accommodation as a worldwide standard for prisons.

8.4 Modern communication technologies in prison

Before the pandemic, modern communication technologies, such as mobile phones, internet access and video links, were not available in most prisons in most countries. The COVID-19-related restrictions of physical contacts with the outside world then made it necessary to quickly introduce compensatory measures. Hence, in many countries, modern communication technologies were implemented in prisons to keep contact with relatives, friends and the outside world more generally. In addition, they were also actively used to provide educational and other programmes via internet or video links. These technical measures usually turned out to be very successful and were also seen positively by prisoners (e.g. in *Belgium*). Prison administrations worldwide should therefore continue providing access to modern communication technologies for prisoners, as an additional means for education and contact with the outside world. They should also ensure that prisoners can keep up with the technical developments outside, fostering their reintegration after release, especially in the case of long-term imprisonment.

8.5 Legal precautions for possible future pandemics

In times of a pandemic, such as that caused by COVID-19, legal certainty is particularly important. The overall lesson from the examination of the legal bases for restrictions and relaxations of the prison regime during the pandemic is that it is best to have an appropriate legal basis in place, before a pandemic strikes. The law should spell out clearly and in advance what restrictions can be adopted, not only in society, but specifically in prison. Such restrictions should be designed to maintain a minimum level of human contact for all prisoners. Thought should be given in advance to how this can be done even if a long period of lockdown is necessary to prevent the pandemic from spreading. The legislation should give prison authorities an explicit discretion to introduce relaxations of the prison regime. Where a reduction in the number of prisoners is urgently required in order to make the regime tolerable for those that remain, the law must provide emergency powers for doing so by ordering the release of some prisoners or by changing the operation of the courts to ensure that during the pandemic fewer prisoners are admitted to prison in the first place. The law should prescribe a duty to implement such population reduction measures if they are essential to protect the basic rights of prisoners during a pandemic.

Notes

1 Data from other jurisdictions than covered by the national reports in the present volume were obtained from https://www.prisonstudies.org/.

2 In this context, the situation in the following countries/jurisdictions required action: *Denmark* (103%), *Bosnia* and *Herzegovina* (102%), *Portugal* and *Kosovo* (each 97%), *Austria* (96%), *Scotland* (93%), *Poland* (91%), *Germany* (88%), *Ireland* (87%), *Bulgaria, Montenegro* (each 86%), *Lithuania* and *Switzerland* (each 85%).

3 Data refer to the first wave of the pandemic between the end of February and September 2020; see Aebi and Tiago, 2020 and Dünkel and Snacken in Chapter 50.

4 For Mexico, however, the number of prisoners increased during the pandemic from 202,221 in January 2020 to 211,999 in June 2020 (+4.8%), while at the same time monthly average releases declined from about 440 to 80; see https://www.fairtrials.org/news/commentary-covid-19-and-prisons-latin-america (accessed 25 June 2021). Apparently, this was a cynical way of dealing with the most vulnerable and discriminated groups of the society by keeping them locked up under very poor and dangerous conditions, instead of protecting them by releasing larger parts of them.

5 The data for Colombia presented in the World Prison Brief database are an underestimate, as the Colombian government displaced overcrowding to some extent to police detention facilities, which are not counted in prison statistics; see Valderrama and Hernandez in Chapter 8.

6 See for the Marshall Project https://www.themarshallproject.org/2020/05/01/a-state-by-state-look-at-coronavirus-in-prisons (last accessed 1 July 2021). 398,627 prisoners were infected by the end of June 2021 and 2,715 died from COVID-19. But not only prisoners were at a high risk of being infected: 114,237 prison staff members tested positive, and prisons publicly reported 209 deaths among staff.

7 Relating the data for the *USA* and *Brazil* to the estimate of the UN Office on Drugs and Crime, that as of 21 May 2021 "nearly 550,000 prisoners in 122 countries have become infected with COVID-19, with close to 4,000 fatalities in prisons in 47 countries" (United Nations Office on Drugs and Crime, 2021: 1), it becomes clear that these two countries represent the large majority of infections and diseases in prisons worldwide.

8 For example, Mexico with high infection rates and deaths of prisoners; see Rapisarda, Byrne and Marmolejo, 2020: 1011; 2020a: 1239. In contrast, Cuba succeeded in preventing infections, i.e. by releasing more than 10% of the prison population; see Rapisarda, Byrne and Marmolejo, 2020a: 1239.

9 According to World Prison Brief (https://www.prisonstudies.org/), the prison population rate decreased already before the pandemic from 294 in 2018 to 189 per 100,000 inhabitants (= −22%) on 1 January 2020. Further data are not yet available.

10 See New York Supreme Court, *Holden and Frias vs Zucker,* State of New York, 22 March 2021, Index Number: 801592/2021E. On p. 16 of its judgement, the Court refers to a similar decision in Oregon.

11 See EuroPris Feedback collection of 29 June 2021: https://www.europris.org/wp-content/uploads/2021/07/Feedback-collection-June-29.pdf.

12 See https://www.europris.org/wp-content/uploads/2021/07/Feedback-collection-June-29.pdf (on p. 2); see for the numbers of staff members https://www.vangla.ee/en/news-and-numbers/number-full-time-positions-prison-service (last accessed 15 July 2021).

13 See https://www.croakey.org/survey-raises-serious-concerns-about-covid-vaccination-rollout-to-prisons/.

14 Aebi and Tiago (2020) reported a reduction of 4.0% from February to mid-September 2020 (see Table 50.1 in Chapter 50), Škulić of 7.8% until October 2020; see Chapter 37.

15 See the statements of the CPT and PC-CP in Europe and of the UN Human Rights Office cited above under Section 2.

16 Rule 43 stipulates that

> general living conditions addressed in these rules, including those related to light, ventilation, temperature, sanitation, nutrition, drinking water, access to open air and physical exercise, personal hygiene, health care and adequate personal space, shall apply to all prisoners without exception.

17 See for Latin American prisons the report prepared by the Sociedad de Criminologia Latinoamericano and presented by ICPA in June 2020: https://icpa.org/wp-content/uploads/2020/06/The-Effects-of-Coronavirus-in-Latin-America-EN.pdf. Many of the conflicts and riots in that region were based on demands "for greater contact with family members, since in practice these relatives provide many of the goods that the inmates consume (food, clothing, and in some cases, even narcotics)"; see p. 27; Marmolejo et al., 2020: 1072 reported that in an enquiry on prisoners in *Argentina*, "85% of respondents depended on their families to access basic goods such as food and clothes and 35% to have access to medications".

18 In the DR Congo, 60 people died from hunger at the beginning of 2020. In Niger, pre-trial detainees are not provided with any food; see Burki (2020: 1412).

19 In contrast, the prison administration in *Portugal* suspended this kind of support by relatives temporarily; see Chapter 33.

20 In *Brazil*, the suspension of visits of lawyers during 30 days in the first wave was accepted by the Supreme Court, but the legal regulations were changed at the time of the second wave allowing such visits under hygiene measures.

21 In Turkey, visits of lawyers were only exceptionally allowed in "compulsory circumstances" without defining such circumstances; see Akdeniz and Aydinoglu in Chapter 44.

22 Lithuania had already changed its Law on the Execution of Sentences in 2019 and brought forward early release, including home detention with EM; see above under Section 2.

23 Rule 25.2 of the European Prison Rules (EPR) provides that the prison regime "shall allow all prisoners to spend as many hours a day outside their cells as are necessary for an adequate level of human and social interaction"; see Rec (2006)2-revised 2020. The commentary to the EPR in that respect says:

> It is unacceptable to keep prisoners in their cells for 23 hours out of 24, for example. The CPT has emphasised that the aim should be to ensure that all prisoners (untried as well as sentenced) are able to spend a reasonable part of the day (i.e. eight hours or more) outside their cells, engaged in purposeful activity of a varied nature (work, preferably with vocational value, education, sport, recreation and association,
>
> (see 25th General Report of the CPT [CPT/Inf (2016) 10], paragraph 58).

24 The report on *Norway* (Chapter 31) states that even

if the prisoners' social activities were reduced, prison administrations reported that prisoners were not necessarily more isolated during the lockdown in the first wave than before. As staff learned to handle the necessary measures to prevent infections better, later lockdowns were less strict.

References

Aebi, M. F., and Tiago, M. M. (2020): *Prisons and Prisoners in Europe in Pandemic Times: An Evaluation of the Medium-Term Impact of the COVID-19 on Prison Populations*. Strasbourg: Council of Europe.

Burki, T (2020): Prisons are "in no waye quipped" to deal with COVID-19. *The Lancet* 395, 1411–1412.

De Bondt, W. (2015): SPOCs and surveys: A novel way of conducting comparative research into criminal justice systems. *Crime Science* 4 (DOI: 10.1186/s40163-015-0019-4).

Dünkel, F. (2017): European penology: The rise and fall of prison population rates in Europe in times of migrant crises and terrorism. *European Journal of Criminology* 14, 629–653.

Harrendorf, S. (2018): Prospects, problems, and pitfalls in comparative analyses of criminal justice data. *Crime and Justice: A Review of Research* 47, 159–207.

Harrendorf, S. (2019): Criminal justice in international comparison – Principal approaches and endeavors. In: Dessecker, A., Harrendorf, S., and Höffler, K. (Eds.): *Angewandte Kriminologie – Justizbezogene Forschung. 12. Kriminalwissenschaftliches Kolloquium und Symposium zu Ehren von Jörg-Martin Jehle, 22./23. Juni 2018*. Göttingen: Universitätsverlag Göttingen, 323–347.

Lappi-Seppälä, T. (2007): Penal policy in Scandinavia. In M. Tonry (Ed.): *Crime, Punishment, and Politics in Comparative Perspective. Crime and Justice. Vol. 36*. Chicago: University of Chicago Press, 217–295.

Lappi-Seppälä, T. (2020): Regulating prison populations –exploring Nordic experiences with Frieder Dünkel and his comparative project. In: Drenkhahn, K. et al. (Eds.): *Kriminologie und Kriminalpolitik im Dienste der Menschenwürde. Festschrift für Frieder Dünkel zum 70. Geburtstag*. Mönchengladbach: Forum Verlag Godesberg, 161–184.

Marmolejo, L., Barberi, D., Bergman, M., Espinoza, O., and Fondevila G. (2020): Responding to COVID-19 in Latin American Prisons: The cases of Argentina, Chile, Colombia, and Mexico. *Victims & Offenders: An International Journal of Evidence-based Research, Policy, and Practice* 15: 7–8, 1062–1085 (DOI: 10.1080/15564886.2020.1827110).

Networks Working Together and International Corrections & Prisons Association (2020): Adapting to COVID-19. Prison oversight and monitoring during a pandemic. Special Issue, April 2020. https://rm.coe.int/expert-network-newsletter-special-issue-5/16809e416a.

Rapisarda, S., and Byrne, J. (2020): An examination of COVID-19 outbreaks in prisons and jails throughout Asia. *Victims & Offenders* 15: 7–8, 948–958 (DOI: 10.1080/15564886.2020.1835770).

Rapisarda, S., Byrne, J., and Marmolejo, L. (2020): An examination of COVID-19 outbreaks in South American prisons and Jails. *Victims & Offenders* 15: 7–8, 1009–1018 (DOI: 10.1080/15564886.2020.1832028).

Rapisarda, S., Byrne, J., and Marmolejo, L. (2020a): An examination of covid-19 outbreaks in prisons and jails in North America, Central America, and the

Caribbean. *Victims & Offenders: An International Journal of Evidence-based Research, Policy, and Practice.* Victims & Offenders, 15: 7–8, 1234–1243 (DOI: 10.1080/15564886.2020.1835766).

United Nations Office on Drugs and Crime (2021): COVID-19 guidance note. Emergency release mechanisms for detainees and prisoners during COVID-19: Findings and recommendations. https://www.unodc.org/res/justice-and-prison-reform/nelsonmandelarules/Guidance_Note_ER.pdf.

United Nations Office on Drugs and Crime (2021a): COVID-19 guidance note. Mitigating the disruptive impact of infection prevention and control measures in prisons: core principles and recommendations. https://www.unodc.org/res/justice-and-prison-reform/nelsonmandelarules/Guidance_Note_IPC.pdf.

van Zyl Smit, and Snacken, S. (2009): *Principles of European Prison Law and Policy.* Oxford: Oxford University Press.

von Hofer, H. (2000): Crime statistics as constructs. The case of Swedish Rape Statistics. *European Journal on Criminal Policy and Research* 8, 77–89.

50 What could we learn from COVID-19? – A reductionist and penal moderation approach

Frieder Dünkel and Sonja Snacken

1 Reductionist and moderate policies as human rights issues

Individual liberty is a basic human right, recognised by all international human rights treaties and national constitutions. Restrictions imposed on this fundamental right must be necessary to achieve an important societal aim in order to be legitimate (United Nations Office on Drugs and Crime, 2007: 4). Prison research consistently shows that imprisonment has many detrimental psychosocial effects on prisoners and their families, hampers reparation towards victims of crime, and fails to protect society in the long run by hindering desistance from crime (Liebling and Maruna, 2005; McNeill and Weaver, 2010). Despite this evidence, prison population rates have increased in many parts of the world in recent years, leading to prison overcrowding and many other violations of basic human rights. As a result, international prison standards emphasise the importance of using imprisonment only as a measure of last resort and of fostering the application of non-custodial sanctions and measures wherever possible.[1] This principle is expressed in the 1990 United Nations Standard Minimum Rules for Non-custodial Measures (the Tokyo Rules) (Rule 1.5); the 2015 UN Standard Minimum Rules for the Treatment of Prisoners (Nelson Mandela Rules, Preamble, 12); the 2006 European Prison Rules (Preamble); the 2002 Robben Island Guidelines by the African Commission on Human and Peoples Rights; the 1969 American Convention on Human Rights Art.7.2 (as interpreted by the Inter-American Court of Human Rights: Paul, 2017).

Such a reductionist approach (Rutherford, 1984; Snacken, 1986) aims at reducing both the application and the duration of imprisonment. This can be attained through "front door-strategies", limiting the inflow into prison (less remand custody and fewer prison sentences) and "backdoor strategies" fostering forms of early release. While reducing imprisonment has been argued to constitute a human rights issue in itself (Snacken, 2006), this is even more so when prisons face additional human rights violations, such as prison overcrowding, or health crises such as the COVID-19 pandemic.

While reductionist policies refer to quantitative reductions in the number of prisoners, the more recent concept of penal moderation encapsulates

DOI: 10.4324/9781003169178-50

both the scale of imprisonment and the quality of prison regimes. It focuses on conditions based on human dignity, human rights and preparation for reintegration, and is applied in opposition to "punitive" policies (Loader, 2010: 355; Snacken, 2015, 2021). The measures taken following the COVID-19 pandemic should be evaluated from both a quantitative reductionist and a qualitative moderate approach.

In Europe, systemic failures violating prisoners' fundamental rights, such as endemic prison overcrowding or lack of adequate health care, have led to pilot judgements by the European Court of Human Rights, requiring member states of the Council of Europe to alter their prison or penal policies. Following the recommendations on prison overcrowding by the Committee of Ministers of the Council of Europe,[2] national authorities have been invited to decriminalise certain offences (among which drug offences and illegal immigration), foster community sanctions and measures and early release, resort to shorter sentences, and impose shorter periods of, and alternatives to, remand custody (for an overview, see Cliquennois, Snacken and van Zyl Smit, 2021).

The COVID-19 pandemic poses comparable challenges. According to the European Committee for the Prevention of Torture (CPT), similar policies should be developed when tackling the COVID-19 pandemic: national authorities are invited to resort to alternatives to pre-trial detention, commutation of sentences, early release and probation.[3] At the international level, the United Nations have issued similar recommendations. According to the High Commissioner for Human Rights: "States should... urgently explore options for release and alternatives to detention to mitigate the risk of harm within places of detention".[4] The United Nations Subcommittee on the Prevention of Torture (SPT) similarly advises: "The measures include considering reducing prison populations by implementing schemes of early, provisional or temporary release of low-risk offenders, reviewing all cases of pre-trial detention, extending the use of bail for all but the most serious cases".[5]

In the following paragraphs, we concentrate on three groups of offenders, which (should) have been the focus of front-door and/or back-door reductionist strategies during the COVID-19 pandemic.

- *Pre-trial detainees*, who are often kept in the most overcrowded prisons with the least developed prison regimes. Alternatives to remand custody have long been developed in many countries, including bail (front-door strategy) or temporary conditional release (back-door strategy).
- *Short-term prisoners* (up to one year[6]) as representing an equally high risk of spreading the virus inside prisons due to the high influx under unfavourable conditions for social distancing and good hygiene. The detention of this group in particular should be rethought from a reductionist perspective. They mostly are not dangerous or violent, but pose a risk of repetitive reoffending by committing petty or minor crimes.

- The third group to focus on are *long-term prisoners* (serving five years and more), often also elderly, who in a pandemic are a highly vulnerable group with distinctive health problems (drug, alcohol addiction, other illnesses), whose stay in prison could be shortened through early release schemes that provide, if necessary, intensive aftercare and control (back-door strategy).

The proportion of these subgroups in national prison populations varies greatly. As a consequence, the impact of potential reductionist policies will also differ. A reductionist strategy aimed at reducing prison population rates (in general or during a pandemic) must take into account the different inmate structures in the jurisdictions, as front-door strategies are especially effective when applied to pre-trial detention and short-term sentences, including secondary imprisonment, while back-door strategies can also be used for long-term prisoners.

We first look into the penological evidence concerning the specific problems raised by each subgroup. We then turn to the international human rights standards, as these can be seen as a "cultural consciousness" of ethical and political consensus on how certain values of organising prisons and sentencing policies should be established. Finally, we evaluate the measures that have been taken following the COVID-19 pandemic towards these three groups in the countries discussed in this book (see also Chapters 48 and 49).

2 Pre-trial detention

2.1 Penological insights: use and abuse of remand custody; conditions of imprisonment

In most jurisdictions, a judge can remand a person in custody when there is reasonable suspicion that such a person has committed an offence; when there are reasons for believing that, if released, the person would either abscond, or commit a serious offence, or interfere with the course of justice, or pose a serious threat to public order.

Pre-trial detention raises many problems. Around 30% of the prison population worldwide is made up of pre-trial detainees (around 3 million people), and nearly 15 million people pass through pre-trial detention globally over the course of a year.[7] Figures are increasing worldwide, with the exception of Europe. Arrest rates and length of pre-trial detention vary greatly between regions. In 2014, detainees were held on average four months in the 27 Council of Europe countries, compared to a reported average of three years in Nigeria. Even in Europe, the proportion of remand prisoners in the total prison populations ranges from 8% to 70%. Many suspects are detained due to lack of alternatives or because they cannot afford to pay a bail fee. In some countries, remand custody is used to force confessions or as an immediate sanction. Arrest and length of detention can be influenced by a lack of adequate legal assistance, thus undermining the chance of a fair trial. The prevalence of pre-trial detention contributes to prison overcrowding, exacerbates poor prison conditions and heightens the risk of suicide, torture and ill-treatment. Overcrowded remand prisons are usually unsanitary and unhealthy, and the chances of catching COVID-19, TB, hepatitis C and HIV/AIDS are much increased by such detention. Even in countries offering better prison conditions, prison regimes are usually less developed for pre-trial detainees than for sentenced prisoners, often resulting in confinement for 22–23 hours a day and/or de facto isolation from the outside world (CPT 26th General Report CPT/Inf (2017)5; Morgenstern, 2018; Penal Reform International, 2021).

2.2 Human rights standards

Pre-trial detention infringes the right to liberty of a person who still enjoys the presumption of innocence and should hence be the exception rather than the rule. Under international law, it should only be imposed when strictly necessary and as a measure of last resort; detention should be applied for the shortest possible time, as suspects are entitled to a trial within a reasonable time; and it should never be used for punitive reasons. Access to legal representation is of key importance, including to facilitate the use of non-custodial measures (Council of Europe Rec (2006)13, General Principles 3–4; International Covenant on Civil and Political Rights, Article 9.3; UN Tokyo Rules, 6.1–6.2; UN Principles and Guidelines on Access to Legal Aid in Criminal Justice Systems, 2012; see also the case law of the ECtHR: Snacken, 2021). In order to avoid inappropriate use of remand custody, the widest possible range of alternative, less restrictive measures relating to the conduct of a suspected offender, should be available.

Such alternatives may consist of ordering an accused person to do one or more of the following (United Nations Office on Drugs and Crime, 2007: 3.2):

- to appear in court on a specified day or as ordered to by the court in the future;
- to refrain from: interfering with the course of justice; engaging in particular conduct; leaving or going to specified places or districts, or approaching or meeting specified persons;
- to remain at a specific address;
- to report on a daily or periodic basis to a court, the police, or other authority;
- to surrender passports or other identification papers;
- to accept supervision by an agency appointed by the court;
- to submit to electronic monitoring; or
- to pledge financial or other forms of property as security to assure attendance at trial or conduct pending trial.

Many countries have introduced such alternatives, often both as front-door and back-door strategies. Common law countries make widespread use of monetary bail as a precondition for release. Electronic monitoring has gradually become a major tool of technological surveillance in some Western countries, resulting in house arrest or in GPS-tracking (Beyens, 2017; Nellis, Beyens and Kaminski, 2013). Both measures raise particular challenges of social (in)justice, as less affluent suspects may be unable to pay bail or the places where they live may not have the technical links needed to implement electronic monitoring (Dünkel, Thiele and Treig, 2017; United Nations Office on Drugs and Crime, 2007: 3.3). In this context, electronic monitoring is often used disproportionately, for if suspects have a permanent place of residence, they may not pose a risk of absconding and of not standing trial (Dünkel, 2017a).

2.3 COVID-19 policies towards pre-trial detention

Both front-door and back-door strategies concerning remand custody can be adopted in principle by the judiciary and applied on an individual basis. Prison administrations are normally not competent to interfere with these decisions in case of a pandemic. But where detention causes a severe health risk, it could be argued that the grounds for pre-trial detention and the appropriate balance between the risks to society and the risks to the detainee should be re-evaluated. This was certainly advocated by many organisations, including the World Health Organization (2020) and argued by defence lawyers in individual cases.

Reductionist front-door policies were nevertheless developed in several countries. A report commissioned by the Association for the Prevention of Torture, covering 53 jurisdictions across Asia Pacific, Europe, the Middle East, Africa, North and Central America (DLA Piper, 2020), found that half the jurisdictions undertook measures to reduce new prison admissions through policies adopted by police, prosecutors and judges, including the use of "cite and release" notices, ceasing arrests for minor offences, postponing prosecutions, the use of summons to attend court, suspending short-term prison sentences and only imposing pre-trial detention in the most serious of cases.

As far as *back-door strategies* are concerned, the same report found that:

> almost half of the jurisdictions released adult pre-trial detainees (43%) in the wake of COVID-19. Eligibility criteria uniformly included that the person was charged with a minor or non-violent offence and/or fell into a vulnerable category of prisoner due to age or ill health. Releases of pre-trial detainees were effected through a combination of existing provisions (often bail hearings) as well as new release measures which were implemented to speed up the release process and reduce the burden on individual judges.
>
> (DLA Piper, 2020: 5).

No reliable figures are available to assess the real impact of these decisions and measures on decongesting the prisons, due to the lack of publicly available, timely, accurate, disaggregated data provided by governments on prisoners released in response to COVID-19 (DLA Piper, 2020: 10). Strikingly, the eligibility criteria mentioned by the countries refer to characteristics that, according to international human rights standards, should already have led to avoiding remand custody in the first place, independent of the pandemic. More positively, we could conclude that the pandemic has finally convinced some policymakers and practitioners that human rights standards are indeed realistic.

The pandemic also led to an increasing use of remote video technology as a valuable tool for judges in certain jurisdictions (see in more detail, Chapter 49). Concern has been expressed that such technology may hamper proceedings in terms of quality, reliability and engagement of all parties involved, and of defendants more particularly (DLA Piper, 2020; Fair Trials, 2020; International Commission of Jurists, 2020).[8]

3 Short-term imprisonment

3.1 Penological insights: short-term imprisonment as an ambivalent crime policy

Short-term imprisonment has been under critical discussion since the 1870s.[9] In many countries, it was widely used, in particular also in Germany. It was the German penal lawyer and reformer Franz von Liszt who became a forerunner of the fight against short-term imprisonment claiming that the negative effects of short-term prison terms override the possible special preventive effects.[10] Prisons were "schools of crime" that should be used only if longer prison sentences were inevitable. It took almost a century before Germany largely banned short-term imprisonment of under six months (see the reform law of 1969 and § 47 German Criminal Code). However, this reform remained incomplete. Some reforms, such as the increased use of fines, were counterproductive as fine defaults led to incarceration, a particular problem not only in Germany, but also in the Netherlands and Switzerland (see Aebi et al., 2015: 73). In most countries though, short sentences would continue to be applied alongside the alternative sanctions introduced to replace them, such as suspended sentences and probation. With the development of the so-called second generation community sanctions and measures, intermediate sanctions that imply more control and supervision such as electronic monitoring, the heightened risk of revocation in case of non-compliance or just technical violations could lead to even more subsidiary imprisonment (van Zyl Smit, Snacken and Hayes, 2015). In addition, limiting the application of short-term sentences by converting their implementation to fines (e.g. Greece), community service (e.g. Switzerland) or electronic monitoring (e.g. Belgium) would lead judges in some countries to impose longer sentences

(Greece, Belgium) or to the counterproductive use of pre-trial detention as a "quasi-short-term sentence", a "short sharp shock" of a few weeks or months, subsequently followed by a partially suspended sentence or probation (Beyens, Snacken, van Zyl Smit, 2013; Snacken, 2007; Snacken, 1994: 15, 18 f.; Tzannetaki, 2020; for a comparative European perspective, see Morgenstern, 2018). This abuse of pre-trial detention has diminished in some countries following law reforms extending compulsory legal representation in juvenile and adult criminal procedures induced by the EU-directive 2016/1919 of 26 October 2016 on legal aid for suspects and accused persons in criminal proceedings and for requested persons in European arrest warrant proceedings.[11]

Not all European countries followed the German approach of outlawing short-term imprisonment. The Scandinavian and Dutch approach to short-term imprisonment was to prefer short-term to longer-term imprisonment. If imprisonment were unavoidable, the sentence should be as short as possible in order to avert the even more detrimental negative effects of long-term imprisonment. In Switzerland, short-term imprisonment is still a very common sentence. However, it is substituted by community service in more than 50% of the cases, whereas electronic monitoring plays a rather limited role in replacing unconditional prison sentences.[12]

Most European countries, though, combine all these sanctions: short-term prison sentences, alternatives such as fines, community service, mediation, suspended sentences, probation and electronic monitoring, and (very) long-term sentences. International human rights standards therefore focus, on the one hand, on avoiding short sentences through alternatives (front-door) and, on the other, on shortening long sentences through early release (back-door). Hence the status of short sentences is ambivalent, reflecting either more moderate or more punitive policies.

3.2 Human rights standards

The principle of using imprisonment only as a last resort and replacing short-term imprisonment in particular by alternative or community sanctions whenever possible has long been recognised in international human rights standards (see e.g. Council of Europe Recommendation (195) of 1959 of the Parliamentary Assembly[13]; the Preamble of the European Prison Rules[14]; Basic Principle No. 10 of the European Rules for juveniles subject to sanctions or measures[15]; Rule 18 of the CM/Rec (2017)3 on Community Sanctions or Measures[16]; Rule 1.5 of the UN Tokyo Rules[17]).

The problems of implementing short-term prison sentences are evident. Rehabilitative measures and reintegration programmes and even simple preparation for release are often not possible due to the lack of time spent in the institution.[18]

Short-term prisoners often have health problems, including drug and alcohol addictions. They tend to lack stable social bonds and to face social structural disadvantages such as unemployment and homelessness.[19] These factors should be taken into account when replacing or converting short sentences within the framework of COVID-19.

International standards tend to emphasise only the principle of avoiding short-term imprisonment without specifying how it should be done. Future standards should address the problem by spelling out more precisely how best to reduce the use of short-term imprisonment, as the COVID-19 pandemic has made evident the serious dangers for prisoners and staff members through the large influx of short-term prisoners (see Sections 3.3 and 3.4).

3.3 Varying proportions of short-term versus long-term prisoners – the example of Europe

Reductionist strategies must take into account the variations in the legal bases on which prisoners are detained and the length of their stay in prisons, as front-door strategies are especially adequate for pre-trial detention and short-term sentences, including secondary imprisonment, while back-door strategies can also be used for long-term prisoners. To take the example of Europe, data collected by SPACE-I-statistics under the direction of Marcelo Aebi show that the proportion of short-term prisoners (serving a sentence of

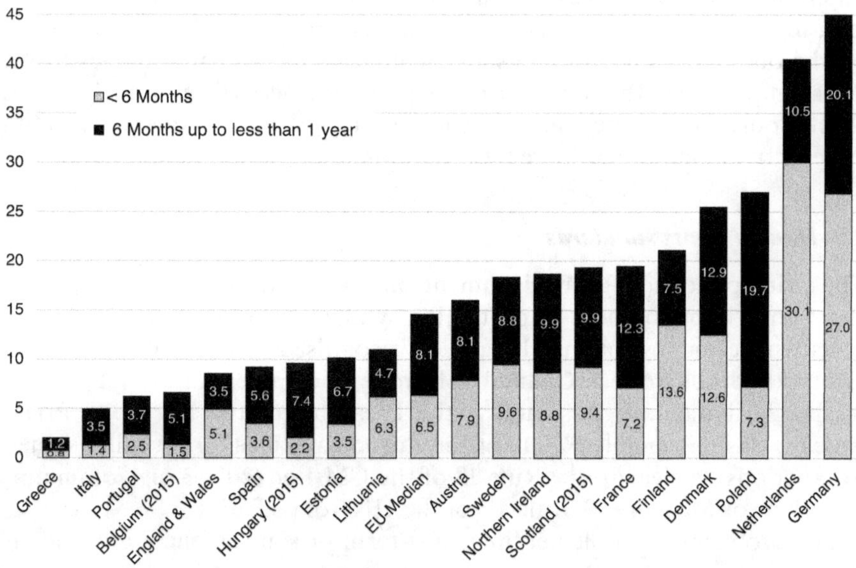

Figure 50.1 Short-term prisoners (Prison sentences of up to 1 year) in a European comparison, on 31 January 2018 (percentages).

Source: Aebi and Tiago (2019), Table 11, p. 48.[20]

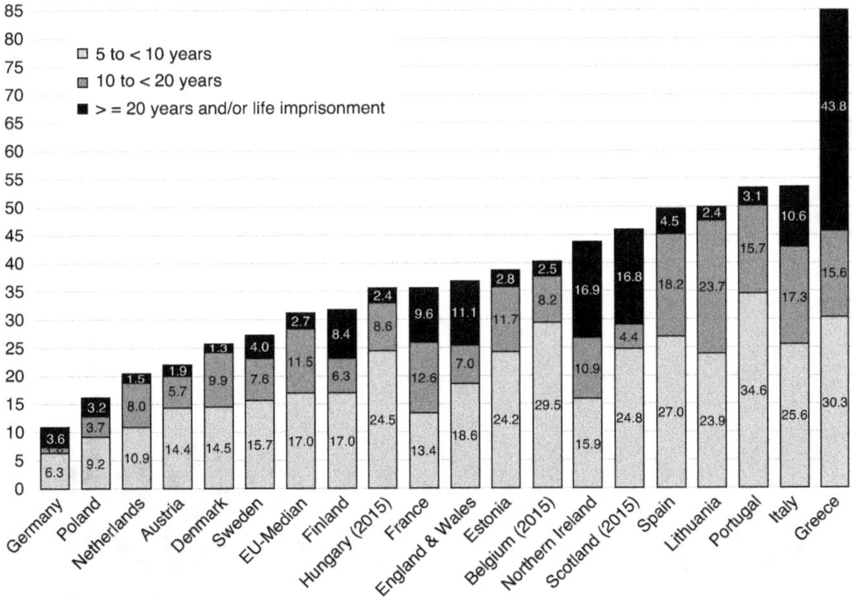

Figure 50.2 Long-term prisoners (sentences of 5 years or more) in a European comparison on 31 January 2018 (percentages).

Source: Aebi and Tiago (2019), Table 7.1, p. 96.

up to one year) on a given day in Europe varies between 2% in Greece and 42% in the Netherlands up to 47% in Germany. Italy, Belgium, Portugal, England & Wales, Spain and Hungary revealed a proportion of less than 10% short-term prisoners per day, whereas France, Finland, Denmark and Poland registered more than 20% to almost 30% short-term prisoners per day (see Figures 50.1 and 50.2).

3.4 The specific problem of secondary short-term imprisonment

Secondary short-term imprisonment refers to detention imposed for fine defaults and for failure to comply with non-custodial dispositions. This raises particular challenges with regard to reductionist strategies following COVID-19, especially where secondary imprisonment sanctions are imposed for a failure to comply with community sanctions that were intended to replace imprisonment. Non-implementation of such secondary imprisonment is often excluded by law. But ideally replacement by a stricter community sanction or postponement of the implementation should still be possible.

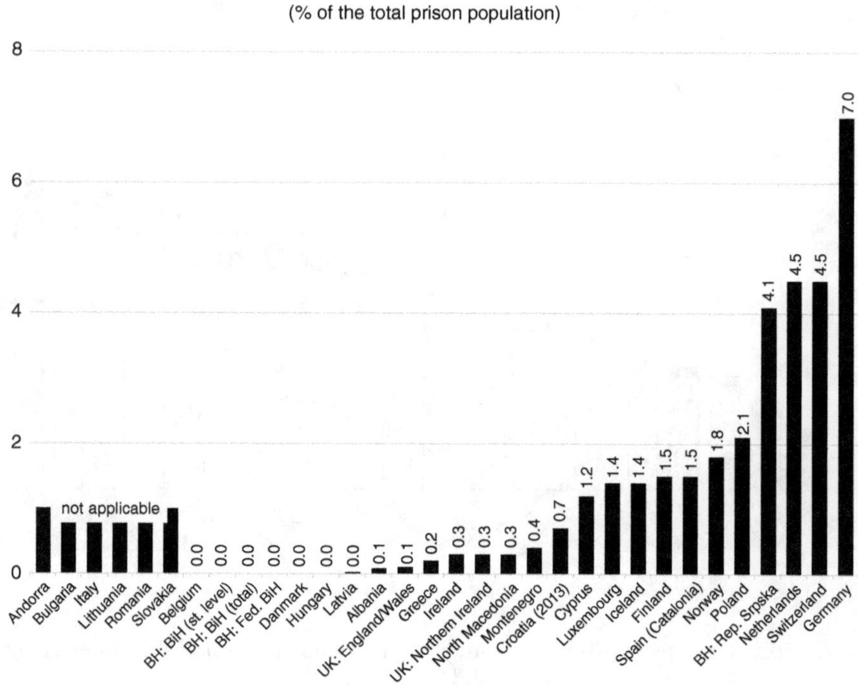

Figure 50.3 Prisoners serving fine default detention in Europe, 1 September 2015.
Source: Aebi et al. (2017), Table 5, p. 73. Note: In Switzerland in 2013 the proportion was 8.6%, in the Netherlands 10.7%.

In Europe, Germany has the highest proportion of fine default detention[21]: on 1 September 2015, 7% of German prisoners were serving a substitute fine default sentence, compared to less than 1% or 2% in almost all other European jurisdictions. Only Switzerland and the Netherlands seem to have similar problems to Germany. If one looks only at the sentenced adult prison population, the German statistics become even less favourable: the proportion was no less than 10.4% on 31 August 2017. From taking this substantial (10%!) inappropriate occupation of prison capacity into consideration, the need for reforms becomes evident (Figure 50.3).

A solution could be to abolish fine default sentences and to enforce fines in a similar way to other legal obligations, e.g. in civil law, as it is the case in Sweden. In Germany, the reform debate has found support from the Green and the Left-wing parties, but "main-stream" opinion does not go that far. Community service has been introduced as a priority substitute sentence, but with limited effects (for a successful model in Mecklenburg Western-Pomerania, see Dünkel and Scheel, 2006).

An effective way to reduce the fine default population in prisons would be to change the conversion rate of a day fine into the substitute prison sentence. In Germany, at present, one day-fine unit corresponds to one day in prison. In future, one day in prison should correspond to at least two day-fine units, as is the case in Austria, Liechtenstein, Poland, Slovenia and Spain. In Finland and Estonia – as mentioned above – one day in prison even counts for three day-fine units (see Drápal, 2018: 470 ff.). The Austrian model would immediately reduce the population of fine defaulters in prison (4,122 on 31 March 2020) by half, the Finnish one by two thirds. A conversion rate of 2 or 3 to 1 is in line with justice considerations "that a day in prison is a much heavier burden than the loss of a day's net income".[22]

3.5 COVID-19 policies towards short-term detention

The present volume has shown that during the COVID-19 pandemic, many states – in particular in Europe – tried to reduce their prison populations in order to prevent infections by limiting the large number of admissions to prisons by short-term prison sentences (see Dünkel et al. in Chapter 49 and Heard in Chapter 48). In Germany at the outbreak of the pandemic, the execution of all substitute prison sentences for fine defaulters was stopped (regularly sentences of up to 90 days)[23] and some states went further, not executing prison sentences of up to one, in some states (Berlin, Hamburg, Saxony) even up to three years (see Dünkel and Morgenstern in Chapter 18). The immediate result between February and June 2020 was a 13.0% decrease of the prison population rate. Also in Finland, conversion (substitute) sentences for unpaid fines or a sentence of imprisonment of six months at most were not executed resulting in a further decline of the prison population rate to 48 (an almost 10%-decline since the end of 2019 and a historical downward trend of 30% since 2003; see Lappi-Seppälä in Chapter 16). Remarkable decreases of prison populations during the pandemic can be seen also in Bulgaria (−12.7%), France (−13.4%), Italy (−10.8%), Lithuania (−10.0%), Montenegro (−21.1%) and Portugal (−12.5%), whereas in other countries no effects and in Denmark, Greece, Slovakia or Sweden even increasing prison populations are visible (see Table 50.1; Aebi and Tiago, 2020b).[24]

An overview of other European and Non-European countries reveals an emerging sensitivity to the problems posed by short-term imprisonment linked to the COVID-19 pandemic, as the large influx of prisoners increases the danger of infection. The traditional negative effects were also aggravated: no meaningful activities in prison, no preparing for reintegration through prison leaves or working programmes outside prison (work release) and no through care and handing-over of clients to the aftercare services, as these services are overburdened ("mass supervision": see McNeill and Beyens, 2013). The DLA Piper Report (2020) found that, despite many jurisdictions in their study having a range of non-custodial sentencing options available, there were limited examples of jurisdictions increasingly using

Table 50.1 The development of prison population rates during the pandemic in European prison systems

	Prison population rates				*Change September–January*
Country	*31 January 2020*	*15 April 2020*	*15 June 2020*	*15 September 2020*	
Belgium	94.2	83.8	86.3	90.5	**−3.9**
Bulgaria	106.0	108.7	106.6	92.5	**−12.7**
Czech Rep.	196.9	195.7	189.4	186.0	**−5.6**
Denmark	67.9	68.1	67.1	71.6	**+5.4**
England/ Wales	140.1	137.7	134.7	133.8	**−4.4**[25]
Estonia	184.4	179.5	176.7	177.4	**−3.8**
Finland	48.3	47.0	41.2	44.6	**−7.6**
France	105.3	93.0	88.5	91.2	**−13.4**
Germany*	77.0		67.0		**−13.0**
Greece	101.7	105.5	106.9	107.0	**+5.2**
Hungary	166.9	169.4	168.8	171.0	**+2.5**
Italy	100.9	91.3	88.9	89.9	**−10.8**
Latvia	179.0	174.0	163.3	166.2	**−7.1**
Lithuania	219.7	215.4	203.1	197.7	**−10.0**
Luxembourg	97.1	83.7	79.4	89.0	**−8.4**
Montenegro	175.9	172.1	150.4	138.8	**−21.1**
Netherlands	57.3	52.3	51.0	52.3	**−8.8**
Northern-Ireland	78.9	73.5	75.2	78.6	**−0.5**
Norway	56.4	49.4	49.1	57.4	**+1.8**[26]
Poland	195.3	189.3	184.1	182.0	**−6.8**
Portugal	122.7	113.4	105.6	107.4	**−12.5**
Romania	106.5	106.1	104.5	109.4	**+2.7**
Scotland	148.0	133.8	125.6	135.2	**−8.7**
Serbia	159.4	157.4	154.7	153.0	**−4.0**[27]
Slovakia	194.7	193.1	193.1	195.3	**+0.3**
Slovenia	69.1	53.5	59.6	66.1	**−4.3**[28]
Spain	123.6	121.9	117.4	117.1	**−5.3**
Sweden	65.1	67.8	69.0	68.8	**+5.8**

Source: Aebi and Tiago (2020b).

such sentences in the wake of COVID-19 to address overcrowding and limit new prison admissions. Some examples of jurisdictions where non-custodial sentences were imposed more frequently after COVID-19 are New South Wales (Australia), France, Italy, Scotland, Germany, Jordan, Nigeria and Honduras.

The crisis, however, could also be seen as an opportunity for revising the policy to impose and execute short-term imprisonment: Why should we not better use other substitute forms of executing fines than fine default detention? Why can we not replace short-term prison sentences more effectively by alternatives such as community service or home detention (without the purely technocratic solution of electronic monitoring)? And last but not least: Why should we not shorten longer- or long-term sentences through reducing or limiting extended minimum sentences or through a wider use of early release schemes? Some answers will be given under Section 5.

4 Long-term imprisonment

4.1 Penological insights: detrimental psychosocial problems

Long terms of imprisonment (five years and more) raise many existential problems of coping for the inmates. Studies of the detrimental effects of long-term imprisonment have a long history in penology, starting with Sykes' (1958) concept of "prisonisation", over the attempts at "psychological survival" described by Cohen and Taylor (1974), the dangers of psychological regression known as "institutionalization" (resulting from the length of continuous detention, the monotony of the regime, the lack of autonomy for the prisoners and their lack of contact with the outside world; see Goethals, 1980), to the current imposition in many countries of "life trashing sentences" – very long sentences imposed on (young) adult offenders, served under strict prison regimes and with no prospect for release in any near future (Simon, 2001) – described as the new forms of inhuman and degrading treatment (Liebling, 2011).

Mental distress and coping mechanisms result from the interaction between personal characteristics of the prisoner, which influence individual attempts at psychological survival, and situational, community and structural variables (personal situation; prison regime; possibilities for autonomy, meaning and agency; family and social support; see Dudeck et al., 2011; Haney, 2005).

Life imprisonment (with or without possibilities of parole) and indefinite preventive sentences that amount to life imprisonment raise even more penological and human rights challenges. With the progressive abolition of the death penalty in many countries over the last 50 years, life imprisonment has become the other "ultimate" penalty – often resulting in very strict and poor prison regimes, sometimes akin to solitary confinement for the first ten years of their sentence, offering no programmes that would enable prisoners to prepare for their reintegration (van Zyl Smit and Appleton, 2019).

4.2 Human rights standards

International human rights standards have only gradually recognised the many detrimental effects of long-term imprisonment. The imposition of lengthy periods of imprisonment is seen as a prerogative of national legislators and courts. The ECtHR, for example, will only exceptionally declare a particular sentence imposed to be disproportionately harsh; this would depend on the sex, age and state of health of the defendant. Moreover, life imprisonment as such is not considered contrary to Article 3 ECHR (Snacken, 2021; van Zyl Smit and Snacken, 2009). Only where the severity of the penal policies leads to prison overcrowding resulting in systemic inhuman and degrading treatment has the Court interfered in domestic sentencing policies (Cliquennois, Snacken and van Zyl Smit, 2021).

The same restriction does not apply though to the European and international standards on prison regimes for life-sentence or long-term prisoners and the possibilities of early release or parole. The ECtHR has declared *life without parole* to violate human dignity protected by the Convention (*Vinter v UK*, 2013). It referred in its reasoning to Recommendation (2003)22 on Conditional Release – parole, which emphasises the need to provide possibilities of parole to all prisoners, including lifers. And to Recommendation (2003)23 on the Management by Prison Administrations of Life-sentence and other Long-term Prisoners, which stresses the need to organise prison regimes for long-term prisoners in accordance with the principles of individualisation, normalisation, responsibility, safety and security, non-segregation and progression. Reintegration has been recognised by the Court, the CPT and the Committee of Ministers as an equally important aim of imprisonment as retribution or deterrence (Cliquennois, Snacken and van Zyl Smit, 2021).

Similar principles are found in the 2015 UN Nelson Mandela Rules: Rule 87 refers to the fact that "before the completion of the sentence, it is desirable that the necessary steps be taken to ensure for the prisoner a gradual return to life in society". Rule 55 emphasises the importance of the "social rehabilitation of the prisoners", Rule 89 1 stresses that "the fulfilment of these principles requires individualisation of treatment" and Rule 93 further elaborates on this classification and individualisation.

4.3 COVID-19 policies towards long-term prisoners

As mentioned, back-door strategies of releasing long-term prisoners earlier than would have been the case without the pandemic are the most realistic for this population. The DLA Piper Report (2020) found that all 53 jurisdictions in their study had existing mechanisms which allowed for the release of convicted prisoners (not only long-term prisoners!), and three quarters of jurisdictions relied on existing laws to release prisoners in response to COVID-19. Despite this, two-thirds of jurisdictions implemented new measures to release prisoners, given the unique risks associated with the COVID-19 infection and transmission in overcrowded facilities. The majority (72%) relied on executive powers to release prisoners via regulations and decrees, while 28% enacted new legislation via parliaments. Release eligibility was however usually restricted to (a combination of) three key criteria: (1) the nature of the offence committed by the prisoner – commonly referring to minor or non-violent crimes and excluding serious violent and sexual offenders (83% of jurisdictions), (2) the nature or status of the prisoner's sentence – requiring the prisoners to have served a minimum period in prison or being within days or months of their release date/completing their total sentence (85% of jurisdictions) and (3) whether the prisoner had particular vulnerabilities (62% of jurisdictions) – most commonly elderly prisoners aged between 50 and 70 (38% of jurisdictions), prisoners with chronic health issues (55% of jurisdictions), female prisoners, pregnant or breastfeeding prisoners, and mothers with children living with them in prisons (25% of jurisdictions). Releases were often conditional on a prisoner complying with one or more terms (75% of jurisdictions), such as good behaviour (42%), supervision by prison or corrections staff (34%), compliance with COVID-19 directions, including quarantining and testing (13%), home detention (13%) and electronic monitoring (21%). Most releases were granted on a permanent basis (83% of jurisdictions). 17% released prisoners only temporarily.

Again, the lack of official data on prisoner releases did not allow to confirm the exact number of prisoners released across the 53 jurisdictions in response to COVID-19, nor whether this related to pre-trial, short-term or long-term prisoners. Nevertheless, using both official and non-official prisoner release data, the report estimates that, between March and July 2020, at least 475,000 prisoners were released across the jurisdictions (DLA Piper, 2021: 46). As 83% of jurisdictions referred to minor or non-violent crimes and excluded serious violent and sexual offenders, we can assume that long-term prisoners will have been marginally – if at all – represented.

The examples mentioned in this book indicate that releases mainly concerned short- and medium-term prison sentences (sometimes up to two or even up to three years), but could also apply to longer sentences when prisoners were relatively close to a (conditional) release or presented special health vulnerabilities (older or ill prisoners; women with small children in prison). Exclusion from release modalities usually referred to the most serious categories of offences. In certain countries, additional conditions relating to accommodation were imposed (e.g. Northern Ireland, Belgium). The most common form of release was the enhanced and forwarded application of early release or parole (Belgium, Czech Republic, France, Norway, Portugal, Lithuania, Scotland, Serbia, Slovenia, Turkey, Canada, South Africa). Some countries imposed electronic monitoring on top of the release (Norway; Poland, Slovakia, Spain, Sweden, Switzerland). More exceptionally was imprisonment replaced by community service (Kenya, Switzerland); special prolonged prison leaves (Germany, the Netherlands, Portugal, India, Turkey) or were prison sentences pardoned (collective or individual pardons leading to remission of several months: Portugal, France).

Countries where release policies were not altered refer mainly to explicit political unwillingness to "soften" crime policies (Europe: Estonia, Greece, Hungary, Romania; Sweden; China; South America, with the exception of Chile and Brazil).

A larger application of releases seems linked to several potential mechanisms. A quantitative analysis of COVID-19 policies in all 47 Council of Europe member states shows that, for the 16 countries who resorted to early release or pardoning of prisoners, the only statistical correlation found with speed of adoption of these measures was the degree of prison overcrowding (Zeveleva and Naziv-Munos, 2021). This also seems valid for Kenya and India (Chapters 21 and 25 in this book). Other more qualitative possible indicators emerging from the national reports in this book seem to be (1) pre-existing more moderate penal policies, resulting in shorter sentences (e.g. Norway, the Netherlands); (2) pre-existing strong traditions of resorting to (different forms of) early releases, applied by specialised judges or by the local prisons (e.g. Belgium, France, Portugal; South Africa); (3) pre-existing attempts at more flexible release policies, that could be pushed through, thanks to the pandemic (e.g. Turkey). What does this tell us about the future of more moderate penal and prison policies as a result of COVID-19?

5 From a "reductionist" approach to "penal moderation"

The COVID-19 crisis exemplifies the distinction made by Loader between a "reductionist" approach, aiming at a quantitative reduction of the number of prisoners, and "penal moderation" as a public philosophy of punishment based on "a convincing rationale for radically reducing the harshness and scale of the present penal system" – both quantitatively and qualitatively (Loader, 2010: 352).

Several successful strategies for a reductionist approach can be identified, which aimed at reducing the prison population rates in – for example – Finland, the Netherlands or Japan. Most important seems to be "a coherent reductionist penal policy", which does lead to a decrease of the average prison population (Snacken, 2006: 144). Finland is certainly one of the best examples for such a coherent reductionist policy by lowering the sentences for non-violent property offences, introducing alternative sanctions with mechanisms to guarantee that they replace custodial sanctions (avoiding net-widening) and increasing early release (see Lappi-Seppälä, 2007, 2010). However, the decrease of prison populations in the last 10–15 years in many European countries was not always the result of such a reductionist strategy, but was related to a sharp downward trend of crime rates, in particular violent crimes (Dünkel, 2017). The continuing (further) decline of prison population rates in Eastern European countries, but also in Germany, Sweden or Spain until 2020 can be seen in Figure 50.4. The latest development in 2020 with a particular decrease during the Corona pandemic was the result of strategies to prevent infections of prisoners and staff members through reducing the high numbers of influx of short-term offenders into prisons (see Aebi and Hashimoto, 2020 and the national chapters in this volume as well as Heard in Chapter 48). Hopefully, such reductionism can foster recognition of the feasibility of more moderate penal policies.

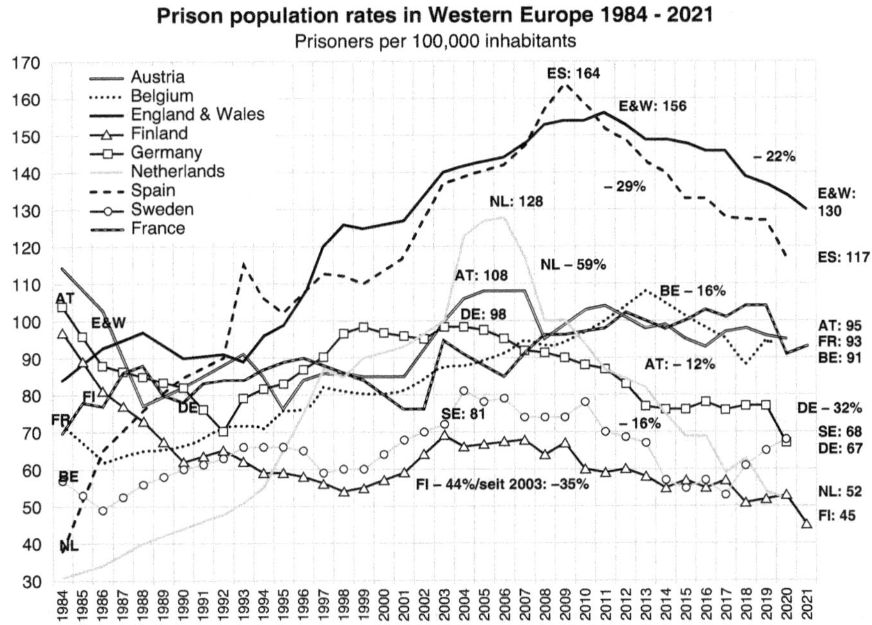

Figure 50.4 Prison population rates in Western Europe 1984–2021.
Source: World prison brief. http://www.prisonstudies.org/info/worldbrief/ (Last access 7 April 2021 for 5 September 2020 see Aebi and Tiago (2020a)).

In some Eastern European countries, a strong downward trend continues (see Figure 50.5), sometimes as a consequence of a declared political will to reduce the prison population (as in Russia or Estonia), and in most countries largely influenced by a decline in (serious) crime rates. Russia thus has cut down its prison population by 51% before the emergence of the pandemic, and further 4% during the pandemic (altogether −54%). Similar reductions took place in Latvia (−57%), Romania (−54%), Estonia (−48%) and Lithuania (−44%). The only countries with – until recently – increasing prison population rates are the Czech Republic, Hungary and Poland (see Figure 50.5). However, the pandemic, at least in the Czech Republic and Poland had some influence, with decreases of 11.3% and 8.2%, respectively. The conservative governments there are not at all "penal moderate" and the political will to counter overcrowding is restricted to "technocratic" reductionist solutions by extending electronic monitoring, with no measurable effects.

Attempts to reduce prison rates that are not based on "penal moderation" often result in "bifurcation" policies (Snacken, 2006: 145 with reference to Bottoms, 1977), characterised by harshening penalties in the area of violent and sex offences and mitigating those for non-violent property offences. As a consequence, the structure of prison populations has changed with higher

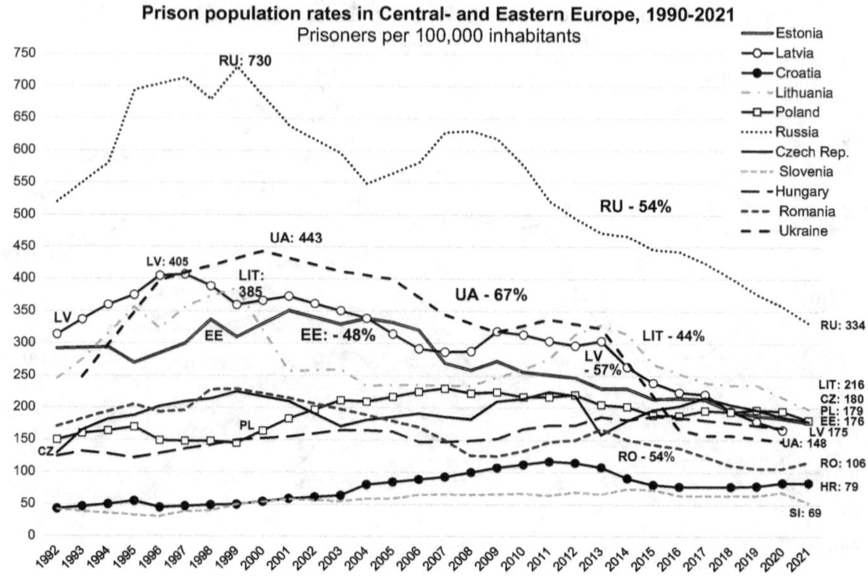

Figure 50.5 Prison population rates in Central- and Eastern Europe, 1999–2021.
Source: World prison brief. http://www.prisonstudies.org/info/worldbrief/ (Last access: 21 February 2021).

proportions of violent instead of (minor) property offenders. This policy is not fully in line with the principle of proportionality, in particular if violent and sex offenders are not only receiving longer sentences, but are discriminated against by having to serve longer parts of their sentences before being granted early release (see Dünkel and Weber, 2019: 403 ff., 410 ff.).

The release of prisoners as part of the COVID-19 policies discussed in this book raises similar questions when approached from the perspective of penal moderation. In some countries, temporary release or suspension of the imprisonment was coupled to supervision by police or probation officers or to electronic monitoring. This was not always counted as serving the prison sentence (e.g. Norway, Chapter 31), which then results in double penalisation raising questions of legality and proportionality (cf. Belgian Supreme Court August 2020: Chapter 4).

Penal moderation also emphasises the need during detention to work towards a successful reintegration of the prisoners. This requires sufficient preparation for release without imposing disproportionate conditions or supervision where these are not necessary (van Zyl Smit, Snacken and Hayes, 2015). The national reports in this book illustrate diverse problems in this regard. In some countries, the COVID-19 measures hampered preparation for parole, e.g. because transfers to open prisons were suspended (e.g. Norway), access to prescribed rehabilitation and risk reduction programmes was hampered (e.g. Scotland), or hearings with decision-making bodies were suspended (e.g. Austria, Greece). Other countries illustrate, however, that a solution could have been reached for each of these problems, for example, by increasing transfer to open prisons to facilitate parole (e.g. Turkey) by emphasising the right of prisoners to such transfers (e.g. Norway), or by videoconferencing with decision-making bodies (e.g. Poland).

In some countries, such as France and Portugal, prisoners were released without any preparation, which may have caused problems for a successful reintegration for those who had no support or place to go to. However, requiring accommodation, means of subsistence and/or a residence permit as a condition for release was criticised as discriminating against the people who cannot meet these conditions (e.g. Belgium, Northern Ireland). Solutions could again be found in examples such as Scotland, where charities and social enterprises in justice, health and welfare collaborated with the probation agencies to support the resettlement of those released; or in Spain, where supervision and programmes turned virtual.

Finally, one should remain cautious about the lasting impact that COVID-19 measures aiming at reducing the prison population may have on future penal and prison policies. In that sense, the future of penal moderation can be compared to the lessons societies and politicians will draw – or not – from the COVID-19 pandemic with regard to mobility, teleworking or climate change. The crisis induced by the pandemic has illustrated that other attitudes, behaviours and policies are possible, but lasting changes require that convictions have fundamentally been altered.

Apart from traditional arguments for more moderate policies – that prison causes pain and empirically is less effective for crime reduction than community sanctions or measures – a human development approach supported by the United Nations is becoming increasingly influential. It is based on economic theories developed by Mahbub Ul Haq and Amartya Sen and – in brief – is "concerned with developing the full potential of people so as to increase their access to opportunity and choice" (Coyle et al., 2016: 129). It is clear that prisons are not the best place for such positive developments (although the Good-lives-approach and other rehabilitative programmes based on humanistic psychology in some reform prisons may go in the same direction). Reducing the recourse to imprisonment and thus lowering imprisonment rates are part of the United Nations' Sustainable Development Goals. Goal 16 is the promotion of "peaceful and inclusive societies" by building "effective, accountable and inclusive institutions at all levels" (Coyle et al., 2016: 130). This is another good argument for using imprisonment only as a very last resort.

The reductionist perspective may inform many legislative and practical innovations[29]:

First: The decriminalisation of certain forms of deviant behaviour, including

- decriminalising cannabis as is the case in more and more states of the USA as well as in Uruguay, Portugal and the Netherlands; further considering, in principle, the decriminalisation of the consumption and possession for consumption of all illegal drugs; and
- decriminalising minor property crimes, such as shoplifting[30] or using public transport without buying a ticket.

Second: Widening the scope of diversionary practices, including in particular restorative justice measures.

Third: Greatly restricting short-term prison sentences at the court level by expanding community alternatives, with legal mechanisms that exclude imposing imprisonment altogether for certain offences, thus limiting net-widening effects, and avoiding mass supervision of offenders in the community by restricting individual conditions to offenders who really need them.[31]

Fourth: Abolishing or strictly reducing secondary imprisonment for non-compliance with community supervision (probation) or non-paying a fine.

Fifth: At the stage of the execution of sentences, authorising the courts or the prison administration to convert short-term imprisonment or the last parts of longer sentences to community service or other community sentences (see the examples of Finland and Switzerland).[32]

Sixth: With regard to longer sentences (which cannot be suspended on probation immediately, normally sentences of more than two years), regularly allowing early release after at most half or two thirds of the sentence.[33] This can be done by using early release as a strategy for better organising the re-entry of prisoners into society with the support and through care of probation and aftercare services (Dünkel et al., 2019).

There are a few positive examples of a direct impact of COVID-19 on penal policy. One is the non-execution of fine default imprisonment in *Germany*, which in most Federal states remains in force (April 2021). A reform commission of the Federal states and the Federal Ministry of Justice is preparing a draft legislation, which will reduce fine default imprisonment by at least 50%.[34] Similarly in the *Netherlands*, a motion in the Lower House of Parliament was accepted to create a legal basis to replace fine default detention with community punishment (see uit Beijerse and Boone in Chapter 28). There is not always a direct relation to the pandemic, but COVID-19 has supported ongoing reductionist policies. A third example of such a coincidence between governmental attempts to reduce the prison population and the emergence of the COVID-19 pandemic can be seen in *Lithuania*, where far-going law reforms were passed in 2019/20 expanding suspended prison sentences (probation) and early release. It was and is the declared will of the new government from 2020 to reduce the prison population and to improve living conditions of prisoners and to provide more effective re-entry programmes (see Sakalauskas in Chapter 27).

The pandemic impacted directly on the law reforms passed in *Scotland* in May 2020 (expanding early release by a forwarded unconditional release of prisoners with prison sentences up to 18 months if less than 90 days had to be served), and of 14 April 2020 in *Turkey*, which lowered the minimum terms to be served before an early release from two thirds to a half, and from three quarters to two thirds for repeat offenders.[35] The possibilities for transfers to open facilities were expanded and those eligible to such transfers could be sent "on leave" serving their sentence in home detention.[36]

It is clear that the reduction of prison population rates that go beyond what was achieved during the COVID-19 pandemic will be possible only if more drastic measures are taken by tackling long-term prison sentences at the sentencing stage (e.g. reducing high minimum sentences), as well as at the early release stage. But if penal policy addresses short-term imprisonment as well, the impact on the number of offenders having the often criminogenic experience of imprisonment is even larger. To cope better with diseases and pandemics in the future, penal policy should carefully evaluate the experiences with reducing the high influx of short-term prisoners, as this has contributed to lowering infection risks considerably. Such a quantitative reductionist policy is an intrinsic part of penal moderation, but it must be accompanied by qualitatively improved prison regimes, including better preparation for release, accompanied by support programmes for those who will be in prisons in the future (Dünkel et al., 2019).

Figure 50.2, which deals with *long-term prisoners*, shows a very different picture: countries such as Greece, Italy, Portugal, Lithuania and Spain are now in the top five leading jurisdictions with the highest proportion of long-term prisoners, Greece with the outstanding proportion of no less than 85% of its prisoners serving long-term prison sentences of at least five years. At the other end of the spectrum, Germany, Poland and the Netherlands recorded only between 11% and 20% long-term prisoners per day in early 2018.

Notes

1 The main examples in this chapter come from Europe, but we think that emphasising reductionist strategies and penal moderation is of global value. The problems of overcrowding and the need for action are particularly urgent in Latin America (Chapters 5, 7, 9 and 10), and in Africa (Chapters 25 and 30). See also the overview by Heard in Chapter 48.

2 The 1999 Recommendation (99) 22, concerning Prison Overcrowding and Prison Population Inflation; the 2016 White Paper on Prison Overcrowding CM (2016)121-add3.

3 Statement of principles relating to the treatment of persons deprived of their liberty in the context of the coronavirus disease (Covid-19) pandemic, 20 March 2020, CPT/Inf(2020)13.

4 Covid19 Guidance: https://www.ohchr.org/_layouts/15/WopiFrame.aspx?sourcedoc=/Documents/COVID-19Guidance.docx&action=default&DefaultItemOpen=1 (assessed 19 March 2021).

5 COVID-19: Measures needed to protect people deprived of liberty: https://www.ohchr.org/EN/NewsEvents/Pages/DisplayNews.aspx?NewsID=25756 (assessed 19 March 2021)

6 Definitions vary from up to six months (traditional international definition: Snacken, 1986) to one year (Howard League for Penal Reform, 2011).
7 See also Heard in Chapter 48 (under Section 2.2) and Coyle et al. (2016).
8 International Commission of Jurists (2020): *Videoconferencing, Courts and COVID-19 – Recommendations Based on International Standards,* November 2020: https://www.unodc.org/res/ji/import/guide/icj_videoconferencing/icj_videoconferencing.pdf; Fair Trials: Dr Thomas Smith, *Commentary: Pre-trial detention decision-making during the COVID-19 crisis: the urgent need for open justice,* 8 April 2020: https://www.fairtrials.org/news/commentary-pre-trial-detention-decision-making-during-covid-19-crisis-urgent-need-open-justice (accessed 22 March 2021).
9 At the first International Penitentiary Congress of 1872 in London, the question of whether short-term imprisonment should not be better replaced by forced labour without deprivation of liberty was discussed: see Snacken (1986: 363).
10 Since then, empirical research revealed the negative effects of short-term imprisonment; see e.g. Snacken (1986); in summary van Zyl Smit and Snacken (2009: 49 f).
11 See e.g. the reform law in Germany: Gesetz zur Neuregelung des Rechts der notwendigen Verteidigung (Law on the reform of compulsory legal representation), BGBl. I: 2128) and Parliamentary Recommendation, BT-Drucksache, 19/15162. The reform extends the requirement of having defence lawyers to all cases where deprivation of liberty is to be expected.
12 See Bundesamt für Statistik 2020, Statistik der Gemeinnützigen Arbeit, Table 19.04.03.11. Bundesamt für Statistik, 2020, Statistik der elektronischen Überwachung, Table 19.04.03.31.
13 "that Member Governments be asked to adopt, as part of their national law, the following principles: a. that a first offender who has committed an offence punishable by imprisonment shall, unless a serious crime is involved, receive a suspended sentence or be placed on probation or accorded some similar treatment".
14 "Reiterating that no one shall be deprived of liberty save as a measure of last resort and in accordance with a procedure prescribed by law".
15 "Deprivation of liberty of a juvenile shall be a measure of last resort and imposed and implemented for the shortest period possible. Special efforts must be undertaken to avoid pre-trial detention". Rule 10 is to be seen together with Rule 9, which the "principle of minimum intervention" laid down in Rule 9. Therefore, deprivation of liberty should be restricted to "exceptional cases (as stipulated also by Rule 17 of the UN Recommendation for the Administration of Juvenile Justice of 1985 (so-called Beijing-Rules) meaning that "normally other less intrusive sanctions should have been tried first", Council of Europe (2009: 38).
16 "National law shall allow for reducing recourse to sentences involving deprivation of liberty by providing for non-custodial sanctions or measures as the appropriate response for certain offences".
17 Resolution 45/110 of the United Nations, Economic and Social Council.
18 Sometimes, prison laws exclude certain preparatory measures such as weekend leave for this group (see e.g. the 16 German Federal prison laws providing long-term leave regularly only for prisoners having served at least six months of their prison sentence).
19 See, for a summary of research on the specific problems of short-term prisoners, Treig and Pruin (2018).
20 These proportions may be the result of short-term prison sentences being imposed more frequently (e.g. the Netherlands and Germany) or from the substitution of short-term sentences by community sanctions at the execution stage (e.g. Belgium and Greece).
21 The high proportion of prisoners serving short prison terms in Germany has been unexpected, as the German law reform of 1969 has tried to make short-term

imprisonment the absolute exception. § 47 Penal Code stipulates that judges should impose sentences of less than six months only if it is deemed to be necessary because alternatives such as a fine or a suspended prison sentence will fail. The aim of the reform was to expand fines and indeed it was a success by increasing the proportion of fines to 84% of all convictions in adult criminal law and decreasing unconditional prison sentences from 23% in 1965 to about 6% in 1975 (and 5% in 2015, see Heinz, 2017, p. 112, Dünkel, 2019). However, fines in Germany in practice cover only sentences of up to 90 day-fine units, i.e. comparable to prison terms of one to three months (only 7% of the fines imposed comprise more than 90 day-fine units; see Heinz 2017, 113). The widespread use of fines (more than 567,000 in 2015) also leads to problems of executing these sentences as they may in practice be imposed on people who lack the ability to pay them. In more than 80% of cases, they are imposed through a summary written procedure (*Strafbefehlsverfahren*), with only an estimate of the economic situation of the offender relevant for a day-fine unit. This is one possible reason for fine default and later secondary detention, if also community service as a substitute to fines has failed; see Dünkel (2019).

22 See the draft bill proposal of the then (2004) German government in Bundestagsdrucksache 15/2725: 19; for a summary of the reform proposals, see Dünkel (2019).

23 The daily prison population of fine defaulters in Germany is one of the highest in Europe; see Figure 3, which in part can be explained by the fact that fines are the principal sentences in Germany covering more than 80% of judicial convictions; see Dünkel and Morgenstern in this volume, Chapter 18.

24 The data are not always exactly corresponding to the evidence in the national reports and Chapter 49, as these also reflect the longer effects during the second and third waves of the pandemic until about April 2021. This does, however, not undermine the result of diverse "reductionist" policies in a European comparative perspective.

25 See Snacken (2006); van Zyl Smit and Snacken (2009: 86 ff).

26 Good examples are Eastern European countries decriminalising property offences of up to 150 € or more, as in Lithuania or Russia, and sanctioning them only as civil law infringements subject to administrative fines, thus avoiding custodial sanctions entirely.

27 A good practice example is the Finnish criminal policy; see Lappi-Seppälä (2007: 2010). See also van Zyl Smit, Snacken and Hayes (2015).

28 We explicitly do not support (and mention) that some countries use electronic monitoring (often as a stand-alone measure) for low-risk offenders. For us, this is a disproportionate sanctioning policy: for a critical European review, see Dünkel (2017a), Dünkel, Thiele and Treig (2017).

29 The European early release systems are either based on a quasi-automatic early release or on individual risk- oriented prognostics. A good solution for regular early release is provided by section 46 of the Austrian Criminal Code, according to which an early release should be the rule, if there is no evidence that serving the full sentence will *better* prevent future recidivism. As release after serving the full sentence in most cases does not imply the support and care by probation and aftercare services, it is unlikely that it will lead to less recidivism than early release; in Austria, the increase in early releases of violent sex offenders has reduced their recidivism rates considerably: see Rettenberger and Eher (2019).

30 If in the future one day of detention counts for two days instead of one day of day fine, this will immediately reduce the fine default population by 50%. Further reforms planned are expanding the prioritisation of community service in fine default cases; see Dünkel and Morgenstern in Chapter 18.

31 Furthermore, probation (conditional suspended sentences) was extended from up to one to three years for women with children, and from two to four years for offenders over the age of 70 years.

32 These measures had a major impact on the prison population in Turkey (about 90,000 cases) reducing overcrowding considerably; see Akdeniz and Aydinoglu in Chapter 44; see also the summary analysis in Chapter 49 under 2.

33 According to Heard and Padfield in Chapter 14 of the present volume, there was a further reduction until January 2021, which amounted to a total of 6.9%.

34 According to Johnsen in Chapter 31 of the present volume, the reduction was 19% until 5 May 2020 and still 8.9% by 7 April 2021; see www.prison.org, World Prison Brief (last access 28 July 2021).

35 According to Škulić in Chapter 37 of the present volume, the reduction was 7.8% until 1 October 2020.

36 According to Mrhar Prelić and Friškovec in Chapter 39 of the present volume, the reduction was 19.7% by 15 April 2020 and still 15.2% by 31 December 2020; see also www.prison.org, World Prison Brief (last access 28 July 2021).

References

Aebi, M. F., and Tiago, M. M. (2020a): *SPACE I -2019 – Council of Europe annual penal statistics: Prison populations.* Strasbourg: Council of Europe.

Aebi, M.F., and Tiago, M.M. (2020b): *Prisons and prisoners in Europe in pandemic times: An evaluation of the medium-term impact of the COVID-19 on prison populations.* Strasbourg: Council of Europe.

Aebi and Tiago (2019). *SPACE I – Council of European, Annual Penal Statistics: Prison populations. Survey 2018.* Strasbourg: Council of Europe

Aebi, M.F., Tiago, M.M., and Burkhardt, C. (2017): *SPACE I – Council of Europe Annual penal statistics: Prison populations. Survey 2015.* Strasbourg: Council of Europe.

Beyens, K. (2017): Electronic monitoring and supervision: A comparative perspective. *European Journal of Probation* 9(1), 3–10.

Beyens, K., Snacken, S., and van Zyl Smit, D. (2013): Truth in (the implementation of) sentencing: Belgium and elsewhere. In: Daems, T., van Zyl Smit, D., and Snacken, S. (Eds.): *European penology?* Oxford: Hart Publishing, 263–282.

Bottoms, A. (1977): Reflections on the renaissance of dangerousness. *Howard Journal of Criminal Justice* 2, 70–96.

Cliquennois, G, Snacken, S., and van Zyl Smit, D. (2021): Can European human rights instruments limit the power of the state to punish? A tale of two Europes, in: Special Issue "Human rights, prisons and penal policies" (Issue editors: G. Cliquennois, S. Snacken, D. van Zyl Smit), *European Journal of Criminology* 18(1), 11–32.

Council of Europe (2006): *Recommendation Rec(2006)13 of the Committee of Ministers to member states on the use of remand in custody, the conditions in which it takes place and the provision of safeguards against abuse.* Strasbourg. https://pjp-eu.coe.int/documents/41781569/42171329/CMRec+%282006%29+13+on+the+use+of+remand+in+custody%2C+the+conditions+in+which+it+takes+place+and+the+provision+of+safeguard+against+abuse.pdf/ccde55db-7aa4-4e11-90ba-38e4467efd7b.

Coyle, A., Fair, H., Jacobson, J., and Walmsley, R. (2016): *Imprisonment Worldwide: The Current Situation and an Alternative Future.* Bristol: Policy Press.

DLA Piper (2020): A global analysis of prisoner releases in response to COVID-19. December 2020, www.dlapiper.com/~/media/files/insights/publications/2021/03/dla-piper-prison-population-during-covid-19.pdf?la=en&hash=F5C1EBBA0D3D86BDDA58FAC87DB9EF3CAE3815DF.

Drápal, J. (2018): Day fines: A European comparison and Czech malpractice. *European Journal of Criminology* 15, 461–480.

Dudeck, M., Drenkhahn, K., Spitzer, C., Barnow, S., Kopp, D., Kuwert, P., Freyberger, H.J., and Dünkel, F. (2011): Traumatization and mental distress in long-term prisoners in Europe. *Punishment & Society* 13(4), 403–423.

Dünkel, F. (2017): European penology: The rise and fall of prison population rates in Europe in times of migrant crises and terrorism. *European Journal of Criminology* 14, 629–653.

Dünkel, F. (2017a): Electronic monitoring – Some critical issues. In: Bijleveld, C. and van der Laan, P. (Eds.): *Liber Amicorum Gerben Bruinsma.* Den Haag: Nederlands Studiecentrum Criminaliteit en Rechtshandhaving (NSCR), 108–117.

Dünkel, F. (2019): Reforms of the criminal sanctions system in Germany – Achievements and unresolved problems. *Juridica International* (Estonia) 28, 37–48, https://doi.org/10.12697/JI.2019.28.05.

Dünkel, F., Pruin, I., Storgaard, A., and Weber, J. (Eds.): (2019): *Prisoner Resettlement in Europe.* Abington, Oxon: Routledge.

Dünkel, F., and Scheel, J. (2006): *Vermeidung von Ersatzfreiheitsstrafen durch gemeinnützige Arbeit: das Projekt "Ausweg" in Mecklenburg-Vorpommern.* Mönchengladbach: Forum Verlag Godesberg.

Dünkel, F., Thiele, C., and Treig, J. (Eds.): (2017): *Elektronische Überwachung von Straffälligen im europäischen Vergleich – Bestandsaufnahme und Perspektiven.* Mönchengladbach: Forum Verlag Godesberg.

Dünkel, F., and Weber, J. (2019): (Early) release, probation and collateral consequences (directives) after release: Legal conditions and practice. In: Dünkel, F. et al. (Eds.): *Prisoner Resettlement in Europe.* Abingdon: Routledge, 403–434.

Goethals, J. (1980): Les effets psycho-sociaux des longues peines d'emprisonnement. Actualités bibliographiques. *Déviance et Société* 1, 81–101.

Haney, C. (2005): The contextual revolution in psychology and the question of prison effects. In: Liebling A., and Maruna, S. (Eds.): *The effects of imprisonment.* Cullompton: Willan, 66–93.

Heinz, W. (2017): *Kriminalität und Kriminalitätskontrolle in Deutschland – Berichtsstand 2015 im Überblick. Stand: Berichtsjahr 2015; Version: 1/2017.* Originalpublikation im Konstanzer Inventar Sanktionsforschung, http://www.ki.uni-konstanz.de/kis/

Howard League for Penal Reform (2011): *No winners. The reality of short term prison sentences.* London: Perennis.

Lappi-Seppälä, T. (2007): Penal policy in Scandinavia. *Crime and Justice* 36, 217–295.

Lappi-Seppälä, T. (2010): Vertrauen, Wohlfahrt und politikwissenschaftliche Aspekte – Vergleichende Perspektiven zur Punitivität. In: Dünkel, F., Lappi-Seppälä, T., Morgenstern, C., and van Zyl Smit, D. (Eds): *Kriminalität, Kriminalpolitik, strafrechtliche Sanktionspraxis und Gefangenenraten im europäischen Vergleich.* Mönchengladbach: Forum Verlag Godesberg, 937–996.

Liebling A. (2011): Moral performance, inhuman and degrading treatment and prison pain. *Punishment & Society* 13(5), 530–550.

Liebling, A., and Maruna, S. (Eds.): (2005): *Effects of imprisonment.* Cullompton: Willan Publishing.

Loader, I. (2010): For penal moderation: Notes towards a public philosophy of punishment. *Theoretical Criminology* 14(3), 349–367.

McNeill, F., and Beyens, K. (Eds.): (2013): *Offender supervision in Europe.* New York: Palgrave, Macmillan.

McNeill F., and Weaver, B. (2010): *Changing lives? Desistance research and offender management*. Glasgow: Scottish Centre for Crime and Justice Research.

Morgenstern, C. (2018): *Die Untersuchungshaft. Eine Untersuchung unter rechtsdogmatischen, kriminologischen, rechtsvergleichenden und europarechtlichen Aspekten*. Baden-Baden: Nomos Verlag.

Nellis, M., Beyens, K., and Kaminski, D. (Eds.): (2013): *Electronically monitored punishment: International and critical perspectives*. London/New York: Routledge.

Paul, A. (2017): The American Convention on Human Rights. Updated by the Inter-American Court. *Juris Dicto* 20, 53–81.

Penal Reform International (2021): *Pretrial justice – key facts*, https://www.penalreform.org/issues/pre-trial-justice/key-facts/ (accessed 22 March 2021).

Rettenberger, M., and Eher, R. (2019): *Mehr Sicherheit durch weniger Haft? Wie in Österreich trotz abnehmender Inhaftierungsquoten die Rückfallraten bei Sexualstraftätern (noch weiter) reduziert werden konnten*. Presentation at the conference of the Kriminologische Gesellschaft (KrimG), Vienna, 6 September 2019.

Rutherford, A. (1984): *Prisons and the process of justice. The reductionist challenge*. London: Heinemann.

Simon, J. (2001): Entitlement to cruelty: The end of welfare and the punitive mentality in the United States. In: Stenson, K., and Sullivan, R.R. (Eds.): *Crime, risk, and justice. The politics of crime control in liberal democracies*. Portland: Willan, 125–143.

Snacken, S. (1986): Les courtes peines de prison. Actualités bibliographiques. *Déviance et Société* 10, 363–387.

Snacken, S. (1994): Belgium. In: Dünkel, F., and Vagg, J. (Eds.): *Waiting for trial. International perspectives on the use of pre-trial detention and the rights and living conditions of prisoners waiting for trial*. Freiburg i.Br.: Max-Planck-Institut für ausländisches und internationales Strafrecht, 1–40.

Snacken, S. (2006): A reductionist penal policy and European human rights standards. *European Journal of Criminology and Policy Research* 12, 143–164. https://doi.org/10.1007/s10610-006-9014-3.

Snacken, S. (2007): Penal policy and practice in Belgium. In: Tonty, M. (Ed.): *Crime, punishment and politics in comparative perspective, crime and justice*, Vol. 36. Chicago: Chicago University Press, 127–216.

Snacken, S. (2015): Punishment, legitimate policies and values: Penal moderation, dignity and human rights, *Punishment & Society*, Special Issue: Punishment, Values, and Local Cultures, 17, 397–423.

Snacken, S. (2021): The European Court of human rights and national penal policies: Fostering quantitative and qualitative penal moderation through Articles 3 and 5 ECHR. In: Cliquennois, G., de Suremain, H. (Eds.): *The evolving protection of prisoners' rights in Europe*. London/New York: Routledge.

Treig, J., and Pruin, I. (2018): Kurze Freiheitsstrafen und Ersatzfreiheitsstrafen als Herausforderung für den Strafvollzug – Möglichkeiten und Grenzen. In: Maelicke, B., and Suhling, S. (Eds.): *Das Gefängnis auf dem Prüfstand*. Wiesbaden: Springer, 313–349.

Tzannetaki T. (2020): Potentially perverse effects of front- and back door penal policies – The Greek example. In: Papacharalampous, C. (Ed.): *The aims of punishment. Theoretical, international and law comparative approaches*. Athens, Thessaloniki: Sakkoulas Publications, 249–275.

United Nations Office on Drugs and Crime (2007): *Handbook of basic principles and promising practices on alternatives to imprisonment.* Criminal Justice Handbook Series. New York: United Nations.

van Zyl Smit, D., and Dünkel, F. (Eds.) (2001): *Imprisonment today and tomorrow – International perspectives on prisoners' rights and prison conditions.* 2nd ed., Deventer, Boston: Kluwer (1st ed. 1991).

van Zyl Smit, D., and Snacken, S. (2009): *Principles of European prison law and policy.* Oxford: Oxford University Press.

van Zyl Smit, D., Snacken, S., and Hayes, D (2015): One cannot legislate kindness: Ambiguities in European legal instruments on non-custodial sanctions. *Punishment & Society* 17(1), 3–26.

van Zyl Smit, D., and Appleton, C. (2019): *Life imprisonment. A global human rights analysis.* Cambridge/London: Harvard University Press.

World Health Organization (2020): *Preparedness, prevention and control of COVID-19 in prisons and other places of detention*, Interim guidance, 15 March 2020.

Zeveleva, O., and Naziv-Munos, J.I. (2021): COVID-19 and European carcerality: Do national prison policies converge when faced with a pandemic? *Punishment & Society,* March 2021 https://doi.org/10.1177/14624745211002011

Index

Note: f = plus the following page, ff = plus the two following pages.

alternative sanctions *see* penal law reforms

Argentina 102–120, 638, 642, 646, 648, 662; compensatory measures (video/internet communication inside prisons etc.) 110ff; COVID-19 infections in prisons 102; general situation of the prison system, prison population rates, penal climate 103ff, 105ff; legal basis for restrictions and relaxations of the prison regime 110ff; penal policy concerning the execution of prison sentences during the COVID-19-induced crisis 107ff; perspectives for future prison and penal policies (possible long-term effects of COVID-19) 113ff; restrictions inside prisons 110ff; restrictions of contact with the outside world 110ff

Australia 7–25, 610, 613, 615, 622, 625, 630, 638, 643f, 648, 652, 654, 676; compensatory measures (video/internet communication inside prisons etc.) 16; COVID-19 infections in prisons 7f; general situation of the prison system, prison population rates, penal climate 7–11; legal basis for restrictions and relaxations of the prison regime 8–11, 17–19; penal policy concerning the execution of prison sentences during the COVID-19-induced crisis 11–14; perspectives for future prison and penal policies (possible long-term effects of COVID-19) 19f; restrictions inside prisons 15f; restrictions of contact with the outside world 14

Austria 26–38, 636, 638, 643, 648, 653, 657, 661, 672f, 675, 681, 683, 687; compensatory measures (video/internet communication inside prisons etc.) 33f; COVID-19 infections in prisons 26ff; general situation of the prison system, prison population rates, penal climate 26–29; legal basis for restrictions and relaxations of the prison regime 34f; penal policy concerning the execution of prison sentences during the COVID-19-induced crisis 29ff; perspectives for future prison and penal policies (possible long-term effects of COVID-19) 35f; restrictions inside prisons 32f; restrictions of contact with the outside world 31f; vaccination of prisoners and staff 27

Belgium 39–51, 636, 638, 648, 653, 660, 670–674, 676, 679–681, 683, 686 ; compensatory measures (video/internet communication inside prisons etc.) 45f; COVID-19 infections in prisons 42; general situation of the prison system, prison population rates, penal climate 39ff; legal basis for restrictions and relaxations of the prison regime 42–48; penal policy concerning the execution of prison sentences during the COVID-19-induced crisis 40f, 42–45; perspectives for future prison and penal policies (possible long-term effects of COVID-19) 47ff; restrictions inside prisons 47f; restrictions of contact with the outside world 45f

Benin 582f, 585
Bolivia 102–120, 636, 638, 646, 648, 658; compensatory measures (video/internet communication inside prisons etc.) 110ff; COVID-19 infections in prisons 102; general situation of the prison system, prison population rates, penal climate 103ff, 105ff; legal basis for restrictions and relaxations of the prison regime 110ff; penal policy concerning the execution of prison sentences during the COVID-19-induced crisis 107ff; perspectives for future prison and penal policies (possible long-term effects of COVID-19) 113ff; restrictions inside prisons 110ff; restrictions of contact with the outside world 110ff
Brazil 52–65, 614, 622f, 625f, 628, 630, 636, 638, 642f, 645, 646, 652, 658f, 661f, 679; compensatory measures (video/internet communication inside prisons etc.) 58f; COVID-19 infections in prisons 53f; COVID-19 infections in the general society 52; general situation of the prison system, prison population rates, penal climate 52, 54ff; legal basis for restrictions and relaxations of the prison regime 59f; penal policy concerning the execution of prison sentences during the COVID-19-induced crisis 54ff; perspectives for future prison and penal policies (possible long-term effects of COVID-19) 60ff; restrictions inside prisons 57f; restrictions of contact with the outside world 56f
Bulgaria 621, 661, 674f, 676

Cambodia 608, 642
Canada 66–78, 638, 648, 653, 655f, 679; compensatory measures (video/internet communication inside prisons etc.) 74f; COVID-19 infections in prisons 68f; general situation of the prison system, prison population rates, penal climate 66ff, 76; legal basis for restrictions and relaxations of the prison regime 75; penal policy concerning the execution of prison sentences during the COVID-19-induced crisis 69f; perspectives for future prison and penal policies (possible long-term effects of COVID-19) 76; restrictions inside prisons 71f; restrictions of contact with the outside world 70f, 72–74; vaccination of prisoners and staff 72
Chile 79–90, 620, 636, 638, 648, 657, 679; compensatory measures (video/internet communication inside prisons etc.) 82f; COVID-19 infections in prisons 79f; general situation of the prison system, prison population rates, penal climate 79f; legal basis for restrictions and relaxations of the prison regime 83–85; penal policy concerning the execution of prison sentences during the COVID-19-induced crisis 81f; perspectives for future prison and penal policies (possible long-term effects of COVID-19) 85f; restrictions inside prisons 82f; restrictions of contact with the outside world 82; vaccination of prisoners and staff 79f
China 91–101, 634–636, 638, 642, 647f, 655, 658, 679; compensatory measures (video/internet communication inside prisons etc.) 96; COVID-19 infections in prisons 92ff; COVID-19 infections in the general society 92ff; general situation of the prison system, prison population rates, penal climate 91f; legal basis for restrictions and relaxations of the prison regime 96; penal policy concerning the execution of prison sentences during the COVID-19-induced crisis 92ff; perspectives for future prison and penal policies (possible long-term effects of COVID-19) 96–99; restrictions inside prisons 94f; restrictions of contact with the outside world 94
Colombia 102–120, 620, 636, 639, 642, 646, 648, 652, 661; compensatory measures (video/internet communication inside prisons etc.) 110ff; COVID-19 infections in prisons 102; general situation of the prison system, prison population rates, penal climate 103ff, 105ff; legal basis for restrictions and relaxations of the prison regime 110ff; penal policy concerning the execution of prison sentences during the COVID-19-induced crisis 107ff; perspectives

for future prison and penal policies (possible long-term effects of COVID-19) 113ff; restrictions inside prisons 110ff; restrictions of contact with the outside world 110ff
compensatory measures *see* prisons, prison regimes and the national chapters
conditional release *see* early release
contact with the outside world *see* prisons, prison regimes and the national chapters
contacts with lawyers, probation officers etc. *see* prisons, prison regimes and restriction of contacts with the outside world
Costa Rica 121–133, 636, 639, 648; compensatory measures (video/internet communication inside prisons etc.) 127f; COVID-19 infections in prisons 124f; general situation of the prison system, prison population rates, penal climate 121–124, 131f; legal basis for restrictions and relaxations of the prison regime 128–130; penal policy concerning the execution of prison sentences during the COVID-19-induced crisis 124f; perspectives for future prison and penal policies (possible long-term effects of COVID-19) 130f; restrictions inside prisons 126f; restrictions of contact with the outside world 125f
COVID-19, comparative aspects 635ff, 642ff; deaths in prison 627, 642, 645, 652, 659, 661; human rights (international human rights) 596ff; infection rates in prisons 638–641, 642f, 647, 659, 661; testing of prisoners 650, 653, 659; vaccination of prisoners 635, 643ff; vaccination of prison staff 643ff
Croatia 134–144, 639, 643, 648, 674, 682; compensatory measures (video/internet communication inside prisons etc.) 139f; COVID-19 infections in prisons 135; general situation of the prison system, prison population rates, penal climate 134f; legal basis for restrictions and relaxations of the prison regime 140f; penal policy concerning the execution of prison sentences during the COVID-19-induced crisis 135–137; perspectives for future prison and penal policies (possible long-term effects of COVID-19) 141f; restrictions inside prisons 138f; restrictions of contact with the outside world 137f
Czech Republic 145–157, 636, 639, 643, 649, 676, 679, 681f; compensatory measures (video/internet communication inside prisons etc.) 151, 153; COVID-19 infections in prisons 150ff; general situation of the prison system, prison population rates, penal climate 145–147; legal basis for restrictions and relaxations of the prison regime 152ff; penal policy concerning the execution of prison sentences during the COVID-19-induced crisis 148–150, 152, 155; perspectives for future prison and penal policies (possible long-term effects of COVID-19) 154f; restrictions inside prisons 151; restrictions of contact with the outside world 151; vaccination of prisoners and staff 151, 153

Denmark 158–168, 636, 639, 643, 647f, 655, 661, 672ff, 675f; compensatory measures (video/internet communication inside prisons etc.) 164f; COVID-19 infections in prisons 160f; general situation of the prison system, prison population rates, penal climate 158–160; legal basis for restrictions and relaxations of the prison regime 165f; penal policy concerning the execution of prison sentences during the COVID-19-induced crisis 160ff; perspectives for future prison and penal policies (possible long-term effects of COVID-19) 166; restrictions inside prisons 163f; restrictions of contact with the outside world 161f, 163; vaccination of prisoners and staff 162, 166

early release 638, 641, 644ff, 658f, 662, 665ff, 671, 677–680, 682, 684f, 687; *see also* penal law reforms and national chapters under penal policy concerning the execution of prison sentences
Egypt 608, 630

elderly prisoners *see* prisoners
electronic monitoring 651, 669f, 671, 677, 679, 681 *see also* national chapters under penal policy concerning the execution of prison sentences
England & Wales 169–180, 584, 588, 613, 615, 620, 622, 624f, 630, 636, 639, 643, 646, 648, 652–657, 672ff, 676, 681; compensatory measures (video/internet communication inside prisons etc.) 175f; COVID-19 infections in prisons 170–172; general situation of the prison system, prison population rates, penal climate 169f; legal basis for restrictions and relaxations of the prison regime 176; penal policy concerning the execution of prison sentences during the COVID-19-induced crisis 172–174; perspectives for future prison and penal policies (possible long-term effects of COVID-19) 177f; restrictions inside prisons 175; restrictions of contact with the outside world 174f
Estonia 181–191, 639, 643f, 648, 659, 672f, 675f, 679, 681f; compensatory measures (video/internet communication inside prisons etc.) 187; COVID-19 infections in prisons 184; COVID-19 infections in the general society 184; general situation of the prison system, prison population rates, penal climate 181–184; legal basis for restrictions and relaxations of the prison regime 187–189; penal policy concerning the execution of prison sentences during the COVID-19-induced crisis 184ff; perspectives for future prison and penal policies (possible long-term effects of COVID-19) 189; restrictions inside prisons 186f; restrictions of contact with the outside world 185f

Finland 192–208, 639, 643, 647f, 653, 656, 672–676, 680f, 684; compensatory measures (video/internet communication inside prisons etc.) 198–200; COVID-19 infections in prisons 192f; COVID-19 infections in the general society 192f; general situation of the prison system, prison population rates, penal climate 195–198; legal basis for restrictions and relaxations of the prison regime 205f; penal policy concerning the execution of prison sentences during the COVID-19-induced crisis 194f; perspectives for future prison and penal policies (possible long-term effects of COVID-19) 206f; restrictions inside prisons 201–205; restrictions of contact with the outside world 198–201
foreigners *see* prisoners, non-national prisoners
France 209–223, 610, 621, 636, 639, 646f, 649, 653, 655, 672f, 675f, 679ff, 683; compensatory measures (video/internet communication inside prisons etc.) 217f; COVID-19 infections in prisons 209; general situation of the prison system, prison population rates, penal climate 209–212; legal basis for restrictions and relaxations of the prison regime 218f; penal policy concerning the execution of prison sentences during the COVID-19-induced crisis 210ff, 212–214; perspectives for future prison and penal policies (possible long-term effects of COVID-19) 219f; restrictions inside prisons 215–217; restrictions of contact with the outside world 214f

Germany 224–242, 636, 639, 643, 647, 649, 652–655, 657, 659, 661, 670, 672–676, 679ff, 684–687; compensatory measures (video/internet communication inside prisons etc.) 235f; COVID-19 infections in prisons 227f; general situation of the prison system, prison population rates, penal climate 224–227; legal basis for restrictions and relaxations of the prison regime 236f; penal policy concerning the execution of prison sentences during the COVID-19-induced crisis 228–233; perspectives for future prison and penal policies (possible long-term effects of COVID-19) 237–239; restrictions inside prisons 234f; restrictions of contact with the outside world 233f; vaccination of prisoners and staff 227f

Ghana 642
Greece 243–254, 620, 636, 639, 643, 646, 649, 670–676, 679, 683, 685; compensatory measures (video/internet communication inside prisons etc.) 250; COVID-19 infections in prisons 245–247; COVID-19 infections in the general society 243; general situation of the prison system, prison population rates, penal climate 243–245; legal basis for restrictions and relaxations of the prison regime 250f; penal policy concerning the execution of prison sentences during the COVID-19-induced crisis 247f; perspectives for future prison and penal policies (possible long-term effects of COVID-19) 251f; restrictions inside prisons 248–250; restrictions of contact with the outside world 248–250; vaccination of prisoners and staff 246, 248

harm reduction 614, 621; *see also* prisons; health problems in prisons
health conditions in prisons, 612–618, 626; *see also* prisons
health problems in prisons 612ff, 616f; *see also* prisons
home detention *see* penal law reforms
Hungary 255–264, 610, 621f, 630, 636, 639, 649, 672ff, 676, 679, 681f; compensatory measures (video/internet communication inside prisons etc.) 262; COVID-19 infections in prisons 263; general situation of the prison system, prison population rates, penal climate 255–259; legal basis for restrictions and relaxations of the prison regime 262f; penal policy concerning the execution of prison sentences during the COVID-19-induced crisis 259f; perspectives for future prison and penal policies (possible long-term effects of COVID-19) 263; restrictions inside prisons 261f; restrictions of contact with the outside world 260f

India 265–277, 619, 622f, 625, 638, 630, 636, 639, 642, 649, 652f, 679f; compensatory measures (video/internet communication inside prisons etc.) 270f; COVID-19 infections in prisons 265f, 268, 274; general situation of the prison system, prison population rates, penal climate 265f; legal basis for restrictions and relaxations of the prison regime 272f; penal policy concerning the execution of prison sentences during the COVID-19-induced crisis 267–269; perspectives for future prison and penal policies (possible long-term effects of COVID-19) 273f; restrictions inside prisons 270ff; restrictions of contact with the outside world 270; vaccination of prisoners and staff 269, 275
Indonesia 620, 630, 642
infection rates, comparative aspects 5, 638ff, 642ff; in prisons 638ff; in the general society 638; *see also* national chapters
inmates *see* prisoners
International prisoners *see* prisoners
Ireland (including Northern Ireland) 278–294, 636, 639f, 643, 645, 649, 654f, 661, 672ff, 676, 679, 683; compensatory measures (video/internet communication inside prisons etc.) 282f; COVID-19 infections in prisons 279f; COVID-19 infections in the general society 280; general situation of the prison system, prison population rates, penal climate 278, 279f; legal basis for restrictions and relaxations of the prison regime 283–285; penal policy concerning the execution of prison sentences during the COVID-19-induced crisis 280f; perspectives for future prison and penal policies (possible long-term effects of COVID-19) 285–287, 289; restrictions inside prisons 282; restrictions of contact with the outside world 281f; vaccination of prisoners and staff 278f, 283
isolation of prisoners *see* prison regimes and the national chapters under restrictions inside prisons
Italy 295–305, 610, 620f, 636, 640, 643–646, 649, 651, 653, 659, 672–676, 685; compensatory measures (video/internet communication inside prisons etc.) 299f; COVID-19 infections in

prisons 296; general situation of the prison system, prison population rates, penal climate 295f; legal basis for restrictions and relaxations of the prison regime 300f; penal policy concerning the execution of prison sentences during the COVID-19-induced crisis 296f; perspectives for future prison and penal policies (possible long-term effects of COVID-19) 301; restrictions inside prisons 298f; restrictions of contact with the outside world 297f; vaccination of prisoners and staff 301

Japan 306–315, 608, 636, 640, 642, 647, 649, 655, 680; compensatory measures (video/internet communication inside prisons etc.) 312; COVID-19 infections in prisons 310, 314; COVID-19 infections in the general society 306, 313f; general situation of the prison system, prison population rates, penal climate 307–310; legal basis for restrictions and relaxations of the prison regime 312f; penal policy concerning the execution of prison sentences during the COVID-19-induced crisis 310, 314; perspectives for future prison and penal policies (possible long-term effects of COVID-19) 313; restrictions inside prisons 311f; restrictions of contact with the outside world 310f

Kazakhstan 440, 608
Kenya 316–325, 622–624, 626, 630, 640, 642, 649, 679f; compensatory measures (video/internet communication inside prisons etc.) 319f; COVID-19 infections in prisons 319; general situation of the prison system, prison population rates, penal climate 316–318; legal basis for restrictions and relaxations of the prison regime 320–323; penal policy concerning the execution of prison sentences during the COVID-19-induced crisis 318f; perspectives for future prison and penal policies (possible long-term effects of COVID-19) 323f, 325; restrictions inside prisons 319; restrictions of contact with the outside world 319

Laos 642
Latvia 326–336, 640, 643, 649, 654f, 674, 676, 681f; compensatory measures (video/internet communication inside prisons etc.) 332f; COVID-19 infections in prisons 327; general situation of the prison system, prison population rates, penal climate 326f; legal basis for restrictions and relaxations of the prison regime 333f; penal policy concerning the execution of prison sentences during the COVID-19-induced crisis 327ff; perspectives for future prison and penal policies (possible long-term effects of COVID-19) 334f; restrictions inside prisons 329ff; restrictions of contact with the outside world 329ff
leaves (prison furloughs, work release) *see* prisons, prison regimes and national chapters under contact with the outside world
legal basis for restrictions and relaxations of the prison regime *see* prisons, prison regimes and national chapters under legal basis for restrictions …
Liechtenstein 675
Lithuania 337–347, 621, 636, 640, 643, 649, 653, 656, 661f, 672–676, 679, 681f, 684f, 687; compensatory measures (video/internet communication inside prisons etc.) 344; COVID-19 infections in prisons 343; general situation of the prison system, prison population rates, penal climate 337–341; legal basis for restrictions and relaxations of the prison regime 344; penal policy concerning the execution of prison sentences during the COVID-19-induced crisis 341f; perspectives for future prison and penal policies (possible long-term effects of COVID-19) 344–346; restrictions inside prisons 343f; restrictions of contact with the outside world 342f
living conditions *see* prisons, prison regimes

Mali 584, 591, 593f
Mexico 608, 636, 661

migrants *see* prisoners
Montenegro 621, 661, 674ff
Myanmar 642

Netherlands 348–359, 622, 624f, 630, 640, 643, 649, 652, 653, 654, 656, 670, 672ff, 676. 679, 680f, 684ff; compensatory measures (video/internet communication inside prisons etc.) 353ff; COVID-19 infections in prisons 357; general situation of the prison system, prison population rates, penal climate 348; legal basis for restrictions and relaxations of the prison regime 355f; penal policy concerning the execution of prison sentences during the COVID-19-induced crisis 349f; perspectives for future prison and penal policies (possible long-term effects of COVID-19) 356f; restrictions inside prisons 352f; restrictions of contact with the outside world 350ff
New Zealand 360–371, 640, 643, 649, 654f; compensatory measures (video/internet communication inside prisons etc.) 365f; COVID-19 infections in prisons 361f; general situation of the prison system, prison population rates, penal climate 360ff; legal basis for restrictions and relaxations of the prison regime 366f; penal policy concerning the execution of prison sentences during the COVID-19-induced crisis 362; perspectives for future prison and penal policies (possible long-term effects of COVID-19) 367f; restrictions inside prisons 364f; restrictions of contact with the outside world 363f
Nicaragua 608
Nigeria 620, 636
Northern Ireland 287–289; *see also* Ireland
North Macedonia 372–384, 640, 643, 649, 674, 685; compensatory measures (video/internet communication inside prisons etc.) 380f; COVID-19 infections in prisons 376, 383; general situation of the prison system, prison population rates, penal climate 372–375; legal basis for restrictions and relaxations of the prison regime 381f; penal policy concerning the execution of prison sentences during the COVID-19-induced crisis 375f, 382f; perspectives for future prison and penal policies (possible long-term effects of COVID-19) 382; restrictions inside prisons 380; restrictions of contact with the outside world 377–379, 382f
Norway 385–395, 621, 640, 643, 647, 649, 653, 656, 662, 674, 676, 679f, 682f; compensatory measures (video/internet communication inside prisons etc.) 390f, 393; COVID-19 infections in prisons 386, 393; general situation of the prison system, prison population rates, penal climate 385f; legal basis for restrictions and relaxations of the prison regime 391f; penal policy concerning the execution of prison sentences during the COVID-19-induced crisis 387f; perspectives for future prison and penal policies (possible long-term effects of COVID-19) 392; restrictions inside prisons 389f; restrictions of contact with the outside world 388f, 393

overcrowding *see* prisons, overcrowding

penal law reforms, comparative aspects: alternative sanctions 666–671, 677, 680, 684, 687; early release 665ff, 671, 677f, 680, 682, 684f, 687; home detention 647–650, 653, 655, 662; long-term imprisonment 677–680; long-term imprisonment, COVID-19 policies 678ff; long-term imprisonment, human rights standards 677f; long-term imprisonment, penological insights: detrimental psychosocial problems 677; penal moderation 5, 641, 665f, 671, 680–685; pre-trial detention 667ff; pre-trial detention, COVID-19 policies 669ff; pre-trial detention, human rights standards 668f; pre-trial detention, penological insights: use and abuse of pre-trial detention 667f; reductionist policies 665ff; short-term imprisonment 670–677; short-term imprisonment, COVID-19 policies 675ff; short-term imprisonment,

human rights standards 671f; short-term imprisonment, proportions of short-term versus long-term prisoners in Europe 672f; short-term imprisonment, secondary short-term imprisonment (fine default imprisonment) 673ff; substitute prison sentences 671, 673–676, 687
Peru 102–120, 636, 641, 645f, 649, 658; compensatory measures (video/internet communication inside prisons etc.) 110ff; COVID-19 infections in prisons 102; general situation of the prison system, prison population rates, penal climate 103ff, 105ff; legal basis for restrictions and relaxations of the prison regime 110ff; penal policy concerning the execution of prison sentences during the COVID-19-induced crisis 107ff; perspectives for future prison and penal policies (possible long-term effects of COVID-19) 113ff; restrictions inside prisons 110ff; restrictions of contact with the outside world 110ff
Philippines 608, 642
Poland 396–410, 636, 641, 643, 649, 651, 653, 661, 672–676, 679, 681ff, 685; compensatory measures (video/internet communication inside prisons etc.) 405f; COVID-19 infections in prisons 398ff, 400; COVID-19 infections in the general society 398ff; general situation of the prison system, prison population rates, penal climate 396–398; legal basis for restrictions and relaxations of the prison regime 406; penal policy concerning the execution of prison sentences during the COVID-19-induced crisis 400–402; perspectives for future prison and penal policies (possible long-term effects of COVID-19) 406f; restrictions inside prisons 404f; restrictions of contact with the outside world 403f
Portugal 411–423, 621, 636, 641, 643, 647, 649, 653, 661f, 672f, 675f, 679f, 683ff; compensatory measures (video/internet communication inside prisons etc.) 418f; COVID-19 infections in prisons 412, 421; general situation of the prison system, prison population rates, penal climate 411f; legal basis for restrictions and relaxations of the prison regime 419f; penal policy concerning the execution of prison sentences during the COVID-19-induced crisis 411f, 412–416; perspectives for future prison and penal policies (possible long-term effects of COVID-19) 420f; restrictions inside prisons 417f; restrictions of contact with the outside world 416f
preparation for release *see* prisons, prison regimes
pre-trial detention, remand custody, comparative aspects 667ff
prisoners: elderly (older) prisoners 616f, 620, 643, 654; female prisoners 609f, 613, 616, 679; foreigners (non-national prisoners) 610, 617; international prisoners 581ff; international prisoners, contact with the outside world 586ff; international prisoners, human rights perspectives 588ff; international prisoners, remedial obstacles 589ff; international prisoners, restrictions to regimes and rights 584ff; international prisoners, right to health and health care 581f; migrants (*see* foreigners, non-national prisoners); pre-trial (remand) prisoners 607, 609, 667–670; sentenced prisoners 608ff, 622, 668, 674; women (*see* female prisoners); young offenders 613
prison overcrowding, comparative aspects *see* prisons, overcrowding
prison population rates, comparative aspects 1, 3–5, 608, 617, 621, 636, 638–641, 647, 653, 659, 665, 667, 676, 680ff, 685
prisons, prison conditions, prison regimes, comparative aspects: compensatory measures (more frequent and longer telephone calls; use of mobile phones; internet communication) 645, 648–651, 655f, 660 (*see also* national chapters under compensatory measures); contact with the outside world 634, 648–654 (*see also* national chapters under contact with the outside world); contacts with lawyers, probation officers etc.

(*see* contact with the outside world); communal cells, dormitories 623, 636, 643, 645; disciplinary punishments 597, 599, 603, 617; disorder 612, 617, 624f, 630, 645, 654, 662 (*see also* protests); health care and overcrowding 582f, 611f; health conditions 612–618, 626; health problems (mental and physical health) 581ff, 612–617; isolation of prisoners (solitary confinement, medical isolation, quarantine) 596–599, 603f, 636, 642, 645, 648ff, 653–656, 668; leaves (prison furloughs, long-term leaves, work release) 624f, 627, 641, 645, 647-650, 653, 655, 675, 679 (*see also* restrictions of contact with the outside world); legal basis for restrictions and relaxations of the prison regime 644, 654–659, 660 (*see also* national chapters under legal basis …); leisure time activities 648ff, 653, 655 (*see also* restrictions inside prisons); living conditions (*see* prisons, restrictions inside prisons); monitoring and oversight during the pandemic 599–603, 652ff; overcrowding 582f, 610ff, 665f, 668, 676, 678, 680f, 685; preparation for release 655, 666, 671, 682f, 685; pre-trial (remand) prisons 607-610, 618f, 621, 644, 666–669, 671f, 679; quarantine (*see* isolation and restrictions inside prisons); re-entry programmes 623f, 645, 648ff, 655, 684 (*see also* restrictions of contact with the outside world); restrictions inside prisons (work, leisure time activities, time spent outside cells, lock-up times in cells) 648ff, 653ff (*see also* national chapters under restrictions inside prisons); single cells 598, 640, 647, 654; solitary confinement (*see* isolation); testing of prisoners, staff members, visitors (*see* national chapters under restrictions inside prisons); time out of cell (*see* restrictions inside prisons); transfers to open prisons 648ff, 653, 655, 682f; vaccination of prisoners and staff 614, 618, 643f (*see also* national chapters under vaccination …); video communication, conferences with family members, relatives, etc. 588f, 602, 648ff, 654f (*see also* national chapters under compensatory measures); video court hearings (*see* national chapters under restrictions of contact with the outside world and compensatory measures); visits, restrictions of visits 600ff, 652 (*see also* national chapters under restrictions of contact with the outside world); work (*see* restrictions inside prisons)

protests (violence, disorder in prisons) 604ff, 625, 645, 654, 662

(Psychological) harm of deprivation of liberty 610ff, 614–617, 621, 626, 629

reductionist policies *see* penal law reforms

restrictions inside prisons *see* prisons, prison regimes and national chapters under restrictions inside prisons

riots in prisons *see* protests

Romania 424–433, 608, 621, 636, 641, 643, 646, 650, 674, 676, 679, 681f; compensatory measures (video/internet communication inside prisons etc.) 429f; COVID-19 infections in prisons 426; general situation of the prison system, prison population rates, penal climate 424–426; legal basis for restrictions and relaxations of the prison regime 430f; penal policy concerning the execution of prison sentences during the COVID-19-induced crisis 426–428; perspectives for future prison and penal policies (possible long-term effects of COVID-19) 431f; restrictions inside prisons 429; restrictions of contact with the outside world 428

Russia 434–442, 608f, 620, 636, 641, 647, 650, 652, 654, 681f, 687; compensatory measures (video/internet communication inside prisons etc.) 439f; COVID-19 infections in prisons 437; COVID-19 infections in the general society 434; general situation of the prison system, prison population rates, penal climate 434ff; legal basis for restrictions and relaxations of the prison regime 440f; penal policy concerning the execution of prison sentences during the COVID-19-induced crisis 436f; perspectives for future prison and penal policies (possible long-term effects of COVID-19) 441; restrictions inside prisons 439f; restrictions of contact with the outside world 437ff; vaccination of prisoners and staff 439

Scotland 443–454, 636, 641, 643, 650, 654, 657, 661, 672f, 676, 679, 683, 685; compensatory measures (video/internet communication inside prisons etc.) 449f; COVID-19 infections in prisons 447; general situation of the prison system, prison population rates, penal climate 443f; legal basis for restrictions and relaxations of the prison regime 450; penal policy concerning the execution of prison sentences during the COVID-19-induced crisis 444f; perspectives for future prison and penal policies (possible long-term effects of COVID-19) 451; restrictions inside prisons 446–449; restrictions of contact with the outside world 446–449; vaccination of prisoners and staff 449

security measures *see* prisons, prison regimes

Serbia 455–464, 636, 641, 643, 646, 650, 652, 676, 679; compensatory measures (video/internet communication inside prisons etc.) 461; COVID-19 infections in prisons 456f; general situation of the prison system, prison population rates, penal climate 455–457; legal basis for restrictions and relaxations of the prison regime 461f; penal policy concerning the execution of prison sentences during the COVID-19-induced crisis 456, 457–459; perspectives for future prison and penal policies (possible long-term effects of COVID-19) 462f; restrictions inside prisons 460; restrictions of contact with the outside world 459f

short-term imprisonment *see* penal law reforms and national chapters under penal policy concerning the execution of prison sentences

Slovakia 465–476, 636, 641, 643, 646, 650, 674ff, 679; compensatory measures (video/internet communication inside prisons etc.) 472f; COVID-19 infections in prisons 467f; general situation of the prison system, prison population rates, penal climate 465–468; legal basis for restrictions and relaxations of the prison regime 473f; penal policy concerning the execution of prison sentences during the COVID-19-induced crisis 468ff; perspectives for future prison and penal policies (possible long-term effects of COVID-19) 474f; restrictions inside prisons 471f; restrictions of contact with the outside world 470f

Slovenia 477–486, 636, 641, 650, 652, 675f, 679, 682; compensatory measures (video/internet communication inside prisons etc.) 482ff; COVID-19 infections in prisons 479f; general situation of the prison system, prison population rates, penal climate 477; legal basis for restrictions and relaxations of the prison regime 483f; penal policy concerning the execution of prison sentences during the COVID-19-induced crisis 477ff; perspectives for future prison and penal policies (possible long-term effects of COVID-19) 484ff; restrictions inside prisons 480ff; restrictions of contact with the outside world 480

South Africa 487–504, 601, 622, 635, 630, 641f, 644, 652, 655, 679f; compensatory measures (video/internet communication inside prisons etc.) 495f; COVID-19 infections in prisons 489f; COVID-19 infections in the general society 489f; general situation of the prison system, prison population rates, penal climate 487, 488ff; legal basis for restrictions and relaxations of the prison regime 496f; penal policy concerning the execution of prison sentences during the COVID-19-induced crisis 490–494; perspectives for future prison and penal policies (possible long-term effects of COVID-19) 497ff; restrictions inside prisons 495; restrictions of contact with the outside world 487, 494f

Spain 505–520, 636, 641, 647, 650–653, 672–675, 679ff, 683, 685;

compensatory measures (video/internet communication inside prisons etc.) 514f; COVID-19 infections in prisons 506f; general situation of the prison system, prison population rates, penal climate 550ff; legal basis for restrictions and relaxations of the prison regime 515f; penal policy concerning the execution of prison sentences during the COVID-19-induced crisis 507–511; perspectives for future prison and penal policies (possible long-term effects of COVID-19) 516ff; restrictions inside prisons 512ff; restrictions of contact with the outside world 511f
staff 607–617, 625, 628ff, 634f, 638, 642ff; risk of infections 607, 610ff, 628f, 642ff, 661; staff training (qualified staff) 617, 628f, 635; working conditions under the pandemic 610ff, 614, 616f, 628f, 638, 647, 655, 657
substitute prison sentences *see* penal law reforms
suicide (risk) in prisons 612, 614–617, 626
Sweden 521–528, 621, 641, 643, 647, 650, 672–676, 679ff; compensatory measures (video/internet communication inside prisons etc.) 525; COVID-19 infections in prisons 522, 524, 526f; general situation of the prison system, prison population rates, penal climate 521f; legal basis for restrictions and relaxations of the prison regime 525f; penal policy concerning the execution of prison sentences during the COVID-19-induced crisis 523; perspectives for future prison and penal policies (possible long-term effects of COVID-19) 526–528; restrictions inside prisons 524f; restrictions of contact with the outside world 523f; vaccination of prisoners and staff 527f
Switzerland 529–540, 636, 641, 643, 650f, 657, 661, 670f, 674, 679, 684; compensatory measures (video/internet communication inside prisons etc.) 534f; COVID-19 infections in prisons 538f; general situation of the prison system, prison population rates, penal climate 529f, 532; legal basis for restrictions and relaxations of the prison regime 536f; penal policy concerning the execution of prison sentences during the COVID-19-induced crisis 532f; perspectives for future prison and penal policies (possible long-term effects of COVID-19) 537–539; restrictions inside prisons 533ff; restrictions of contact with the outside world 533ff

Tanzania 636
Thailand 620–623, 630, 642
transfers to open prisons *see* prisons, prison regimes and national chapters under restrictions of contact with the outside world
Turkey 541–556, 610, 619, 636, 641, 646f, 650, 652f, 657, 662, 679f, 683, 685, 688; compensatory measures (video/internet communication inside prisons etc.) 549; COVID-19 infections in prisons 543f; general situation of the prison system, prison population rates, penal climate 541–544; legal basis for restrictions and relaxations of the prison regime 549ff; penal policy concerning the execution of prison sentences during the COVID-19-induced crisis 544–546; perspectives for future prison and penal policies (possible long-term effects of COVID-19) 551f; restrictions inside prisons 549; restrictions of contact with the outside world 547f; vaccination of prisoners and staff 546f, 551

Ukraine 608, 682
United States of America, USA 557–580, 608, 615, 622, 630, 641–643, 650, 653, 659, 661, 684; COVID-19, impact of induced (early) release programmes on crowding in prisons and jails 570–572; COVID-19 infections in prisons 531, 558–562; COVID-19, root causes of COVID-19 outbreaks 562–565; general situation of the prison system, prison population rates, penal climate 557f; legal basis for restrictions and relaxations of the prison regime 565ff,

568ff; penal policy concerning the execution of prison sentences during the COVID-19-induced crisis 565ff, 569f, 570ff, 575; perspectives for future prison and penal policies (possible long-term effects of COVID-19) 573–575; prisoner health 570; recidivism (public safety) 572f; restrictions inside prisons 568ff; restrictions of contact with the outside world 568, 575; vaccination of prisoners and staff 569

Venezuela 636, 645
video conferences, video court hearings *see* prisons, prison regimes and national chapters under restrictions of contact with the outside world and compensatory mesasures
Vietnam 642
violence *see* protests

women *see* prisoners

young offenders *see* prisoners

For Product Safety Concerns and Information please contact our EU representative GPSR@taylorandfrancis.com
Taylor & Francis Verlag GmbH, Kaufingerstraße 24, 80331 München, Germany

www.ingramcontent.com/pod-product-compliance
Lightning Source LLC
LaVergne TN
LVHW021246011026
849160LV00010BA/739
* 9 7 8 0 3 6 7 7 6 9 7 3 4 *